TABLE OF CONTENTS

OMNIBUS 4

by
OSAMU TEZUKA

Translation
FREDERIK L. SCHODT

Lettering and Retouch
DIGITAL CHAMELEON

DARK HORSE MANGA

President and Publisher **MIKE RICHARDSON**

US Editor **CHRIS WARNER**

Assistant Editor **JEMIAH JEFFERSON**

Consulting Editor **TOREN SMITH**

Collection Designer **JUSTIN COUCH**

Digital Art Technician **CONLEY SMITH**

English-language version produced by
DARK HORSE MANGA

Dark Horse Manga, a division of Dark Horse Comics, Inc.
10956 SE Main Street, Milwaukie, OR 97222
DarkHorse.com

First edition: June 2016 | ISBN 978-1-61655-956-4

1 3 5 7 9 10 8 6 4 2
Printed in the United States of America

To find a comics shop in your area, call the Comic Shop Locator Service toll-free at 1-888-266-4226.

This volume collects stories previously published in *Astro Boy* Volumes 10, 11, 12, and 13,
published by Dark Horse Comics. The artwork of this volume has been produced
as a mirror image of the original Japanese edition.

ASTRO BOY® OMNIBUS VOLUME 4
TETSUWAN ATOM by Osamu Tezuka © 2002, 2003, 2016 by Tezuka Productions. All rights reserved. Originally
published in Japan in 1952. English translation rights arranged with Tezuka Productions. ASTRO BOY is a registered
trademark of K.K. Tezuka Productions, Tokyo, Japan. Unedited translation © 2002, 2003 Frederik L. Schodt. All
other material © 2016 by Dark Horse Comics, Inc. Dark Horse Manga™ and the Dark Horse logo are trademarks of
Dark Horse Comics, Inc. No portion of this publication may be reproduced, in any form or by any means, without
the express written permission of the copyright holders. Names, characters, places, and incidents featured in this
publication either are the product of the author's imagination or are used fictitiously. Any resemblance to actual
persons (living or dead), events, institutions, or locales, without satiric intent, is coincidental.

Neil Hankerson, Executive Vice President; Tom Weddle, Chief Financial Officer; Randy Stradley, Vice President of
Publishing; Michael Martens, Vice President of Book Trade Sales; Matt Parkinson, Vice President of Marketing;
David Scroggy, Vice President of Product Development; Dale LaFountain, Vice President of Information
Technology; Cara Niece, Vice President of Production and Scheduling; Nick McWhorter, Vice President of
Media Licensing; Ken Lizzi, General Counsel; Dave Marshall, Editor in Chief; Davey Estrada, Editorial Director;
Scott Allie, Executive Senior Editor; Chris Warner, Senior Books Editor; Cary Grazzini, Director of Print and
Development; Lia Ribacchi, Art Director; Mark Bernardi, Director of Digital Publishing; Michael Gombos, Director
of International Publishing and Licensing

A NOTE TO READERS

Many non-Japanese, including people from Africa and Southeast Asia, appear in Osamu Tezuka's works. Sometimes these people are depicted very differently from the way they actually are, in a manner that exaggerates a time long past, or shows them to be from extremely undeveloped lands. Some feel that such images contribute to racial discrimination, especially against people of African descent. This was never Osamu Tezuka's intent, but we believe that as long as there are people who feel insulted or demeaned by these drawings, we must not ignore their feelings.

We are against all forms of discrimination and intend to continue to work for its elimination. Nonetheless, we do not believe it would be proper to revise these works. Tezuka is no longer with us, and we cannot erase what he has done, and to alter his work would only violate his rights as a creator. More importantly, stopping publication or changing the content of his work would do little to solve the problems of discrimination that exist in the world.

We are presenting Osamu Tezuka's work as it was originally created, without changes. We do this because we believe it is also important to promote the underlying themes in his work, such as love for mankind and the sacredness of life. We hope that when you, the reader, encounter this work, you will keep in mind the differences in attitudes toward discrimination when the work was created and those of today, and that this will contribute to an even greater awareness of such problems.

— Tezuka Productions and Dark Horse Comics

A S T R O ' S
B E E N
S T O L E N !

First serialized from June to September 1965 in
Tetsuwan Atom Kurabu (Mighty Atom Club).

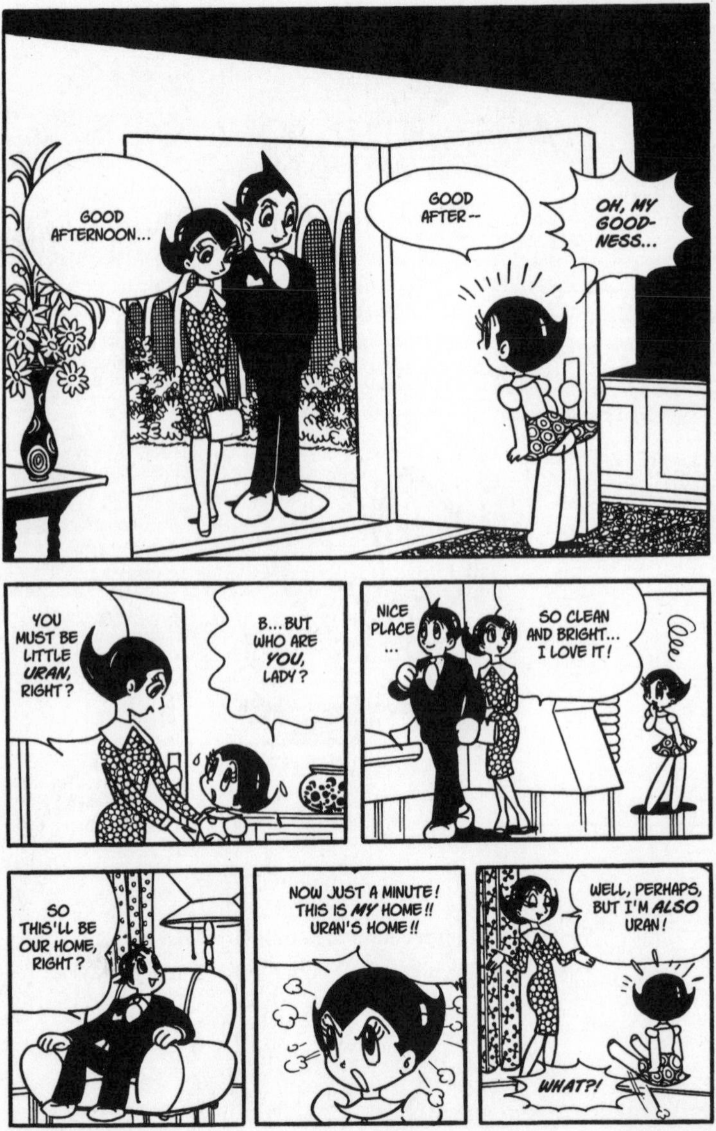
GOOD AFTERNOON...
GOOD AFTER--
OH, MY GOOD-NESS...
YOU MUST BE LITTLE *URAN*, RIGHT?
B... BUT WHO ARE *YOU*, LADY?
NICE PLACE ...
SO CLEAN AND BRIGHT... I LOVE IT!
SO THIS'LL BE OUR HOME, RIGHT?
NOW JUST A MINUTE! THIS IS *MY* HOME!! URAN'S HOME!!
WELL, PERHAPS, BUT I'M *ALSO* URAN!
WHAT?!

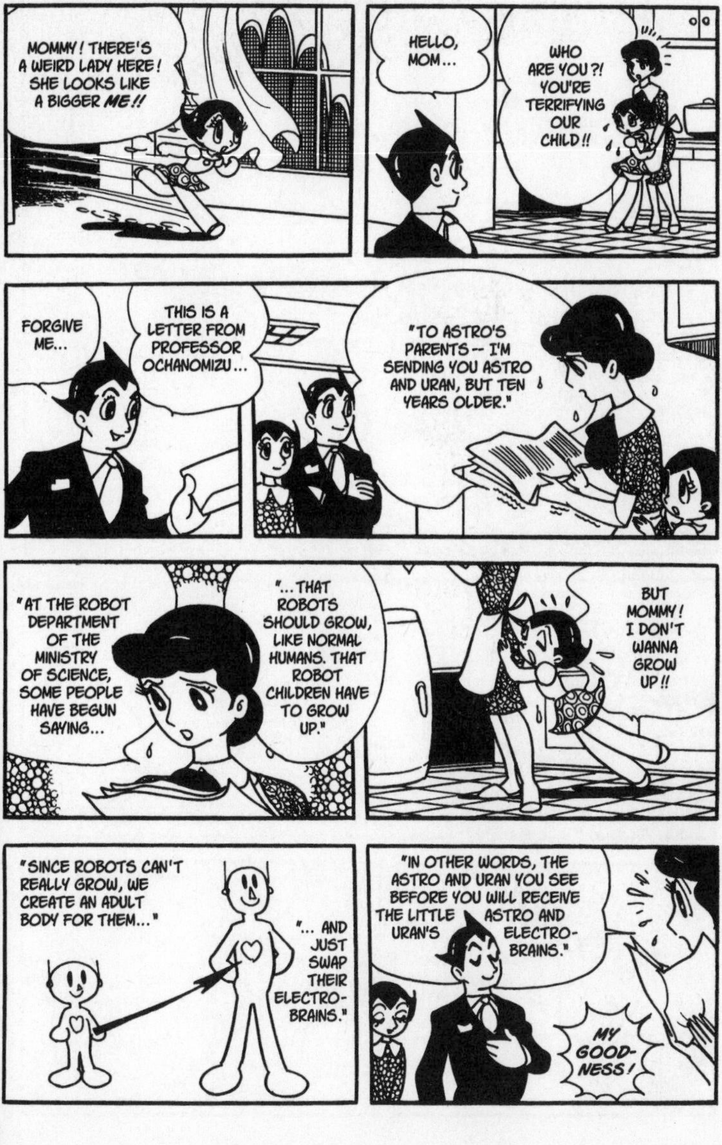

MOMMY! THERE'S A WEIRD LADY HERE! SHE LOOKS LIKE A BIGGER ME!!
HELLO, MOM...
WHO ARE YOU?! YOU'RE TERRIFYING OUR CHILD!!
FORGIVE ME...
THIS IS A LETTER FROM PROFESSOR OCHANOMIZU...
"TO ASTRO'S PARENTS -- I'M SENDING YOU ASTRO AND URAN, BUT TEN YEARS OLDER."
"AT THE ROBOT DEPARTMENT OF THE MINISTRY OF SCIENCE, SOME PEOPLE HAVE BEGUN SAYING...
"...THAT ROBOTS SHOULD GROW, LIKE NORMAL HUMANS. THAT ROBOT CHILDREN HAVE TO GROW UP."
BUT MOMMY! I DON'T WANNA GROW UP!!
"SINCE ROBOTS CAN'T REALLY GROW, WE CREATE AN ADULT BODY FOR THEM..."
"... AND JUST SWAP THEIR ELECTRO-BRAINS."
"IN OTHER WORDS, THE ASTRO AND URAN YOU SEE BEFORE YOU WILL RECEIVE THE LITTLE ASTRO AND URAN'S ELECTRO-BRAINS."
MY GOODNESS!

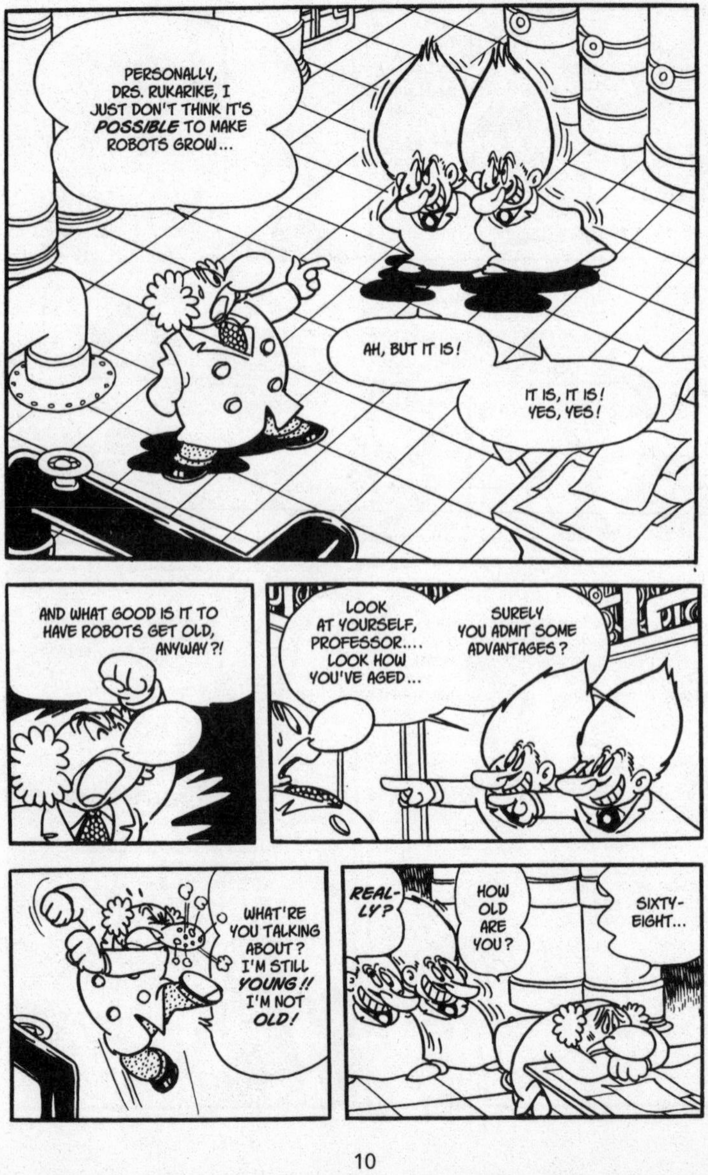
PERSONALLY, DRS. RUKARIKE, I JUST DON'T THINK IT'S *POSSIBLE* TO MAKE ROBOTS GROW...
AH, BUT IT IS!
IT IS, IT IS! YES, YES!
AND WHAT GOOD IS IT TO HAVE ROBOTS GET OLD, ANYWAY?!
LOOK AT YOURSELF, PROFESSOR.... LOOK HOW YOU'VE AGED...
SURELY YOU ADMIT SOME ADVANTAGES?
WHAT'RE YOU TALKING ABOUT? I'M STILL *YOUNG!!* I'M NOT *OLD!*
REAL-LY?
HOW OLD ARE YOU?
SIXTY-EIGHT...

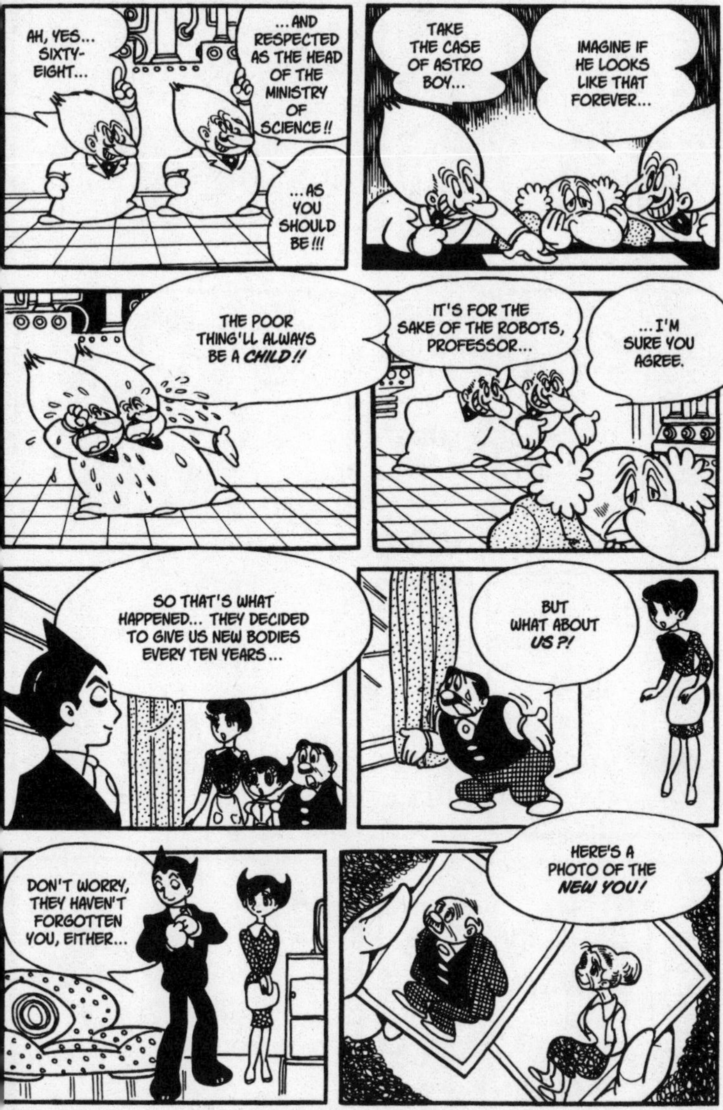
AH, YES... SIXTY-EIGHT...
...AND RESPECTED AS THE HEAD OF THE MINISTRY OF SCIENCE!!
...AS YOU SHOULD BE!!!
TAKE THE CASE OF ASTRO BOY...
IMAGINE IF HE LOOKS LIKE THAT FOREVER...
THE POOR THING'LL ALWAYS BE A *CHILD!!*
IT'S FOR THE SAKE OF THE ROBOTS, PROFESSOR...
...I'M SURE YOU AGREE.
SO THAT'S WHAT HAPPENED... THEY DECIDED TO GIVE US NEW BODIES EVERY TEN YEARS...
BUT WHAT ABOUT *US?!*
DON'T WORRY, THEY HAVEN'T FORGOTTEN YOU, EITHER...
HERE'S A PHOTO OF THE *NEW YOU!*

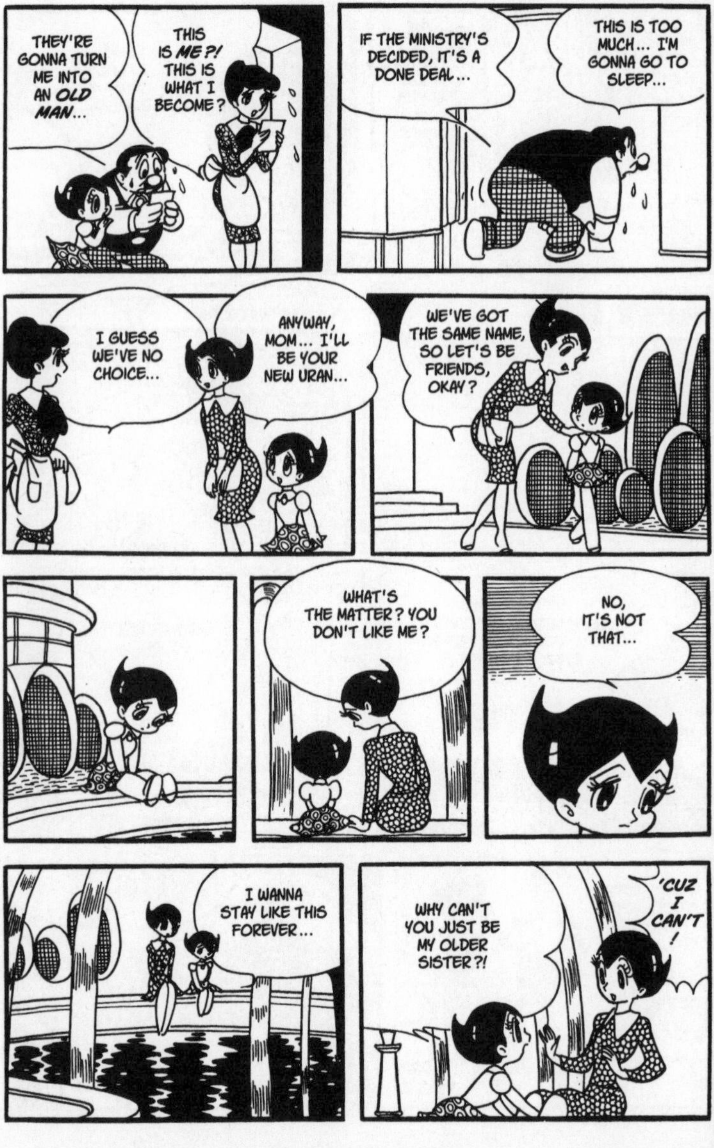
THEY'RE GONNA TURN ME INTO AN *OLD MAN*...
THIS IS *ME?!* THIS IS WHAT I BECOME?
IF THE MINISTRY'S DECIDED, IT'S A DONE DEAL...
THIS IS TOO MUCH... I'M GONNA GO TO SLEEP...
I GUESS WE'VE NO CHOICE...
ANYWAY, MOM... I'LL BE YOUR NEW URAN...
WE'VE GOT THE SAME NAME, SO LET'S BE FRIENDS, OKAY?
WHAT'S THE MATTER? YOU DON'T LIKE ME?
NO, IT'S NOT THAT...
I WANNA STAY LIKE THIS FOREVER...
WHY CAN'T YOU JUST BE MY OLDER SISTER?!
'CUZ I CAN'T!

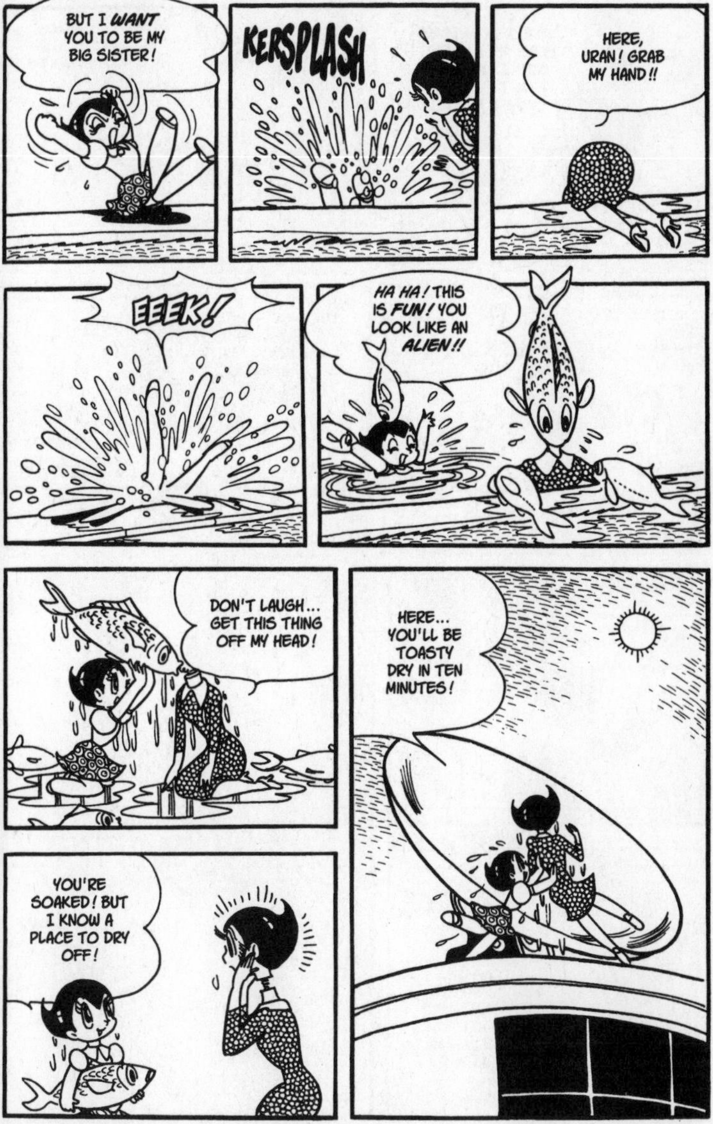
BUT I WANT YOU TO BE MY BIG SISTER!
KERSPLASH
HERE, URAN! GRAB MY HAND!!
EEEK!
HA HA! THIS IS FUN! YOU LOOK LIKE AN ALIEN!!
DON'T LAUGH... GET THIS THING OFF MY HEAD!
HERE... YOU'LL BE TOASTY DRY IN TEN MINUTES!
YOU'RE SOAKED! BUT I KNOW A PLACE TO DRY OFF!

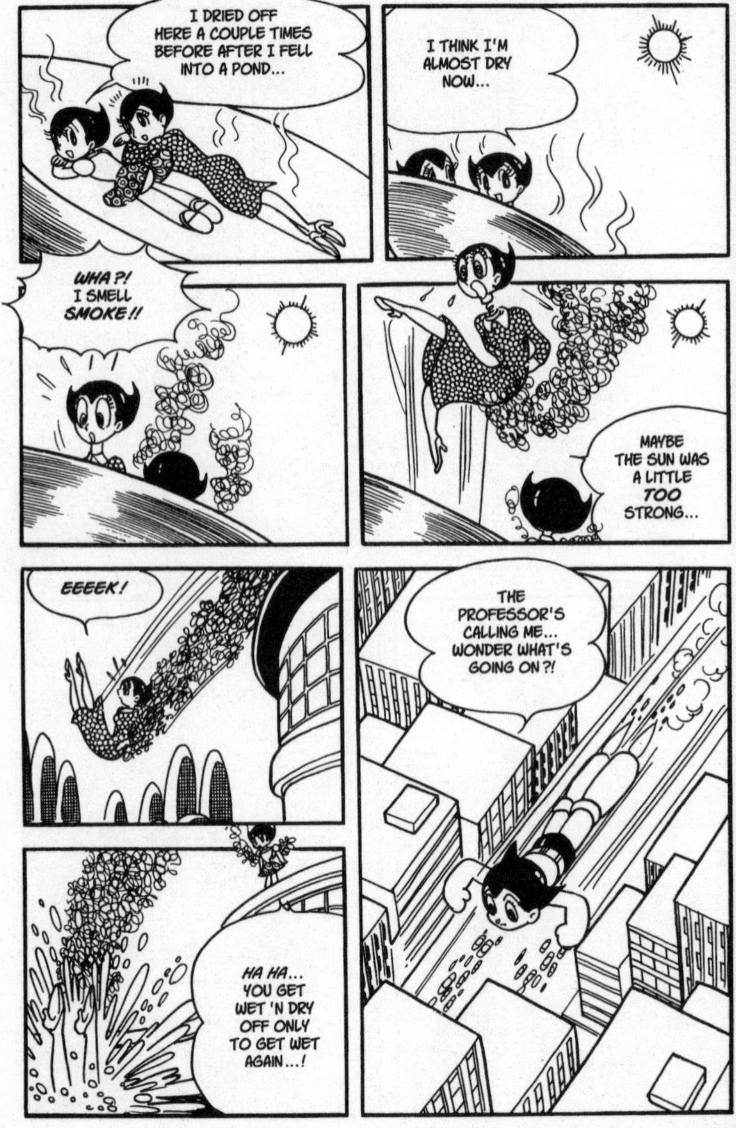
I DRIED OFF HERE A COUPLE TIMES BEFORE AFTER I FELL INTO A POND...
I THINK I'M ALMOST DRY NOW...
WHA?! I SMELL SMOKE!!
MAYBE THE SUN WAS A LITTLE TOO STRONG...
EEEEK!
THE PROFESSOR'S CALLING ME... WONDER WHAT'S GOING ON?!
HA HA... YOU GET WET 'N DRY OFF ONLY TO GET WET AGAIN...!

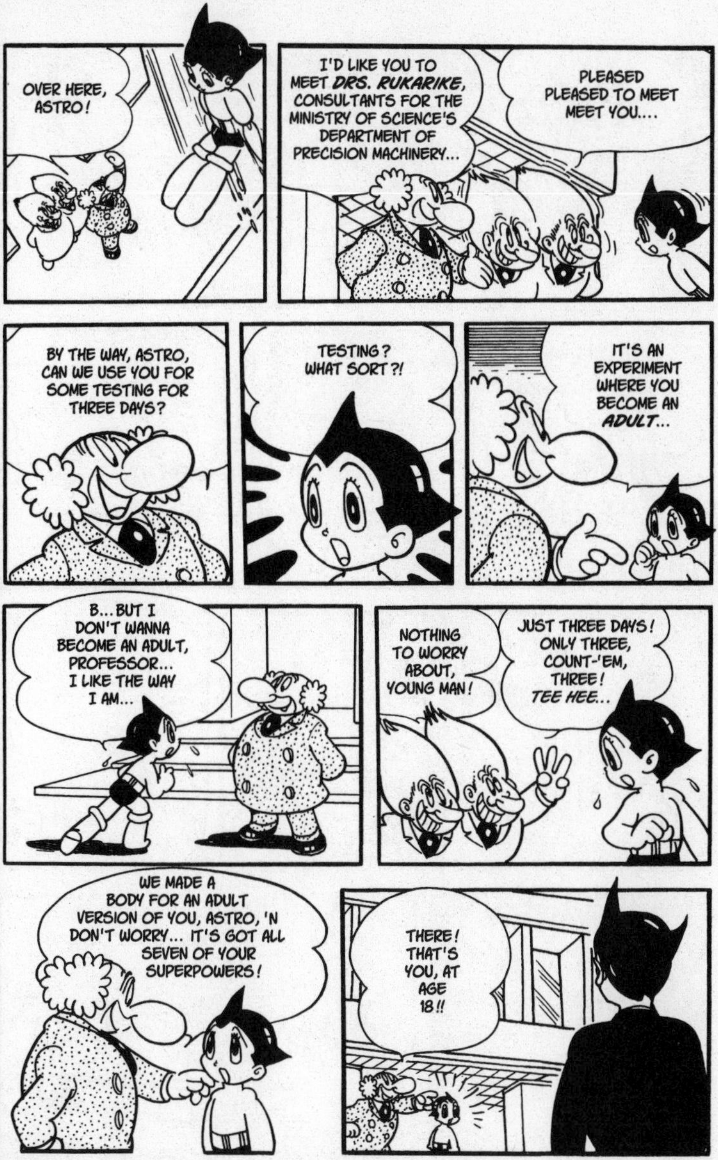
OVER HERE, ASTRO!
I'D LIKE YOU TO MEET DRS. RUKARIKE, CONSULTANTS FOR THE MINISTRY OF SCIENCE'S DEPARTMENT OF PRECISION MACHINERY...
PLEASED PLEASED TO MEET MEET YOU....
BY THE WAY, ASTRO, CAN WE USE YOU FOR SOME TESTING FOR THREE DAYS?
TESTING? WHAT SORT?!
IT'S AN EXPERIMENT WHERE YOU BECOME AN ADULT...
B...BUT I DON'T WANNA BECOME AN ADULT, PROFESSOR... I LIKE THE WAY I AM...
NOTHING TO WORRY ABOUT, YOUNG MAN!
JUST THREE DAYS! ONLY THREE, COUNT-'EM, THREE! TEE HEE...
WE MADE A BODY FOR AN ADULT VERSION OF YOU, ASTRO, 'N DON'T WORRY... IT'S GOT ALL SEVEN OF YOUR SUPERPOWERS!
THERE! THAT'S YOU, AT AGE 18!!

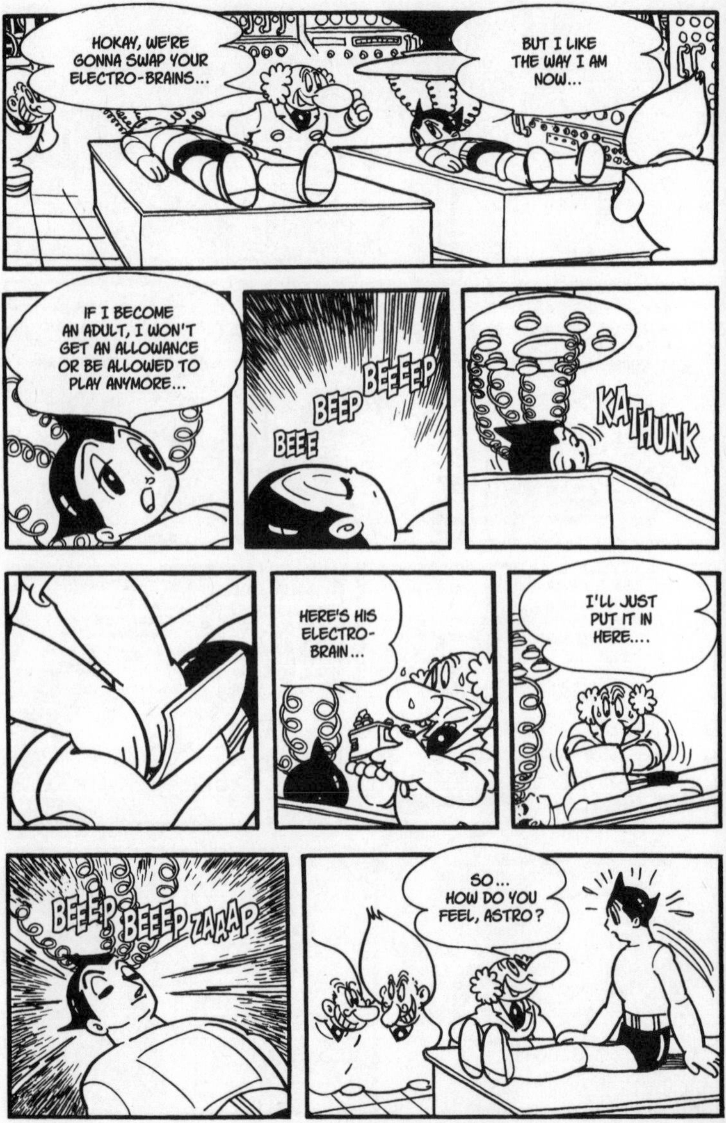
HOKAY, WE'RE GONNA SWAP YOUR ELECTRO-BRAINS...
BUT I LIKE THE WAY I AM NOW...
IF I BECOME AN ADULT, I WON'T GET AN ALLOWANCE OR BE ALLOWED TO PLAY ANYMORE...
BEEEP
BEEP
BEEE
KATHUNK
HERE'S HIS ELECTRO-BRAIN...
I'LL JUST PUT IT IN HERE....
BEEEP BEEEP ZAAAP
SO... HOW DO YOU FEEL, ASTRO?

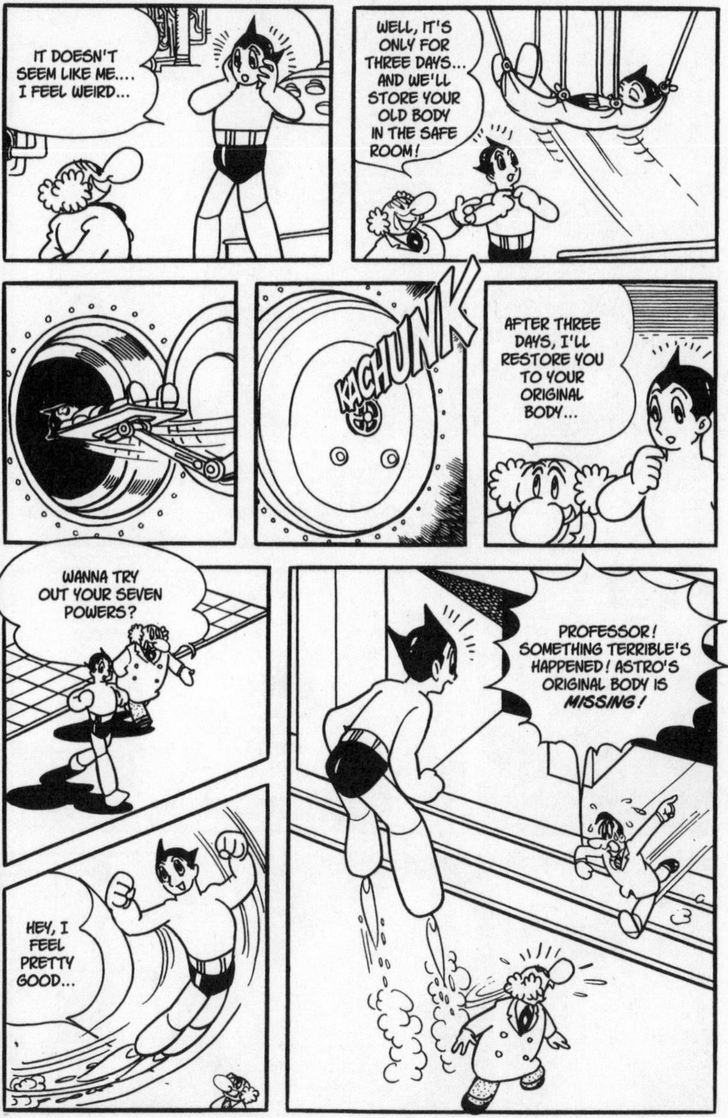
IT DOESN'T SEEM LIKE ME.... I FEEL WEIRD...
WELL, IT'S ONLY FOR THREE DAYS... AND WE'LL STORE YOUR OLD BODY IN THE SAFE ROOM!
KACHUNK
AFTER THREE DAYS, I'LL RESTORE YOU TO YOUR ORIGINAL BODY...
WANNA TRY OUT YOUR SEVEN POWERS?
HEY, I FEEL PRETTY GOOD...
PROFESSOR! SOMETHING TERRIBLE'S HAPPENED! ASTRO'S ORIGINAL BODY IS *MISSING!*

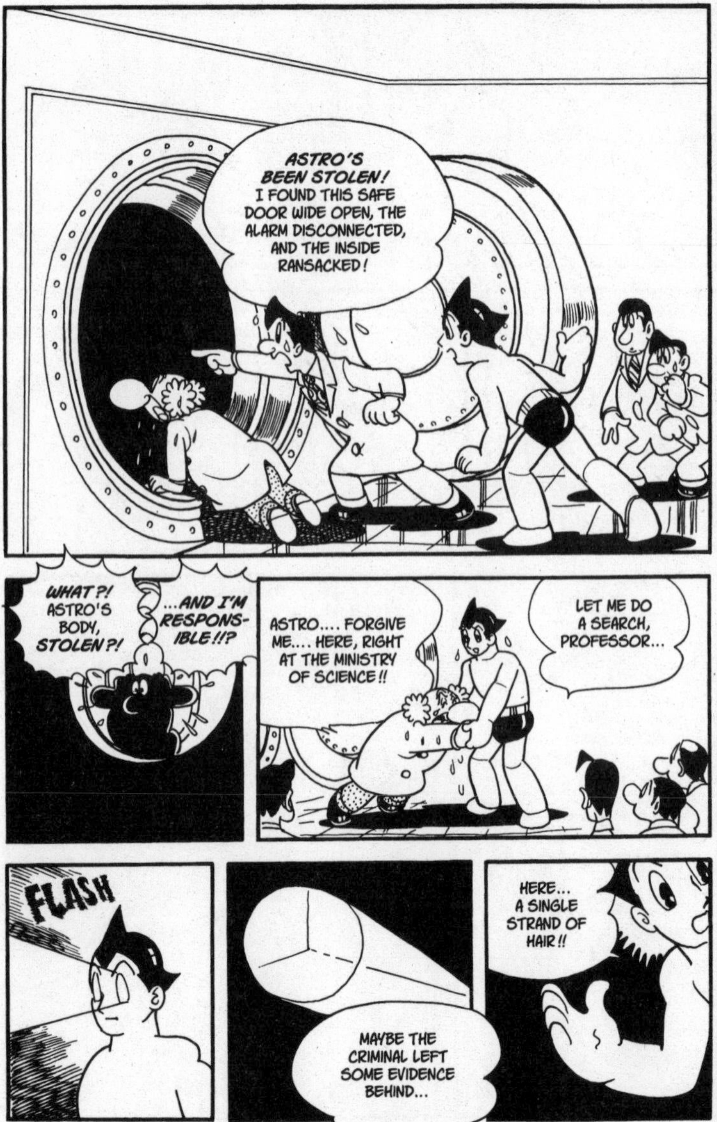
ASTRO'S BEEN STOLEN! I FOUND THIS SAFE DOOR WIDE OPEN, THE ALARM DISCONNECTED, AND THE INSIDE RANSACKED!
WHAT?! ASTRO'S BODY, STOLEN?!
...AND I'M RESPONS-IBLE!!?
ASTRO.... FORGIVE ME.... HERE, RIGHT AT THE MINISTRY OF SCIENCE!!
LET ME DO A SEARCH, PROFESSOR...
FLASH
MAYBE THE CRIMINAL LEFT SOME EVIDENCE BEHIND...
HERE... A SINGLE STRAND OF HAIR!!

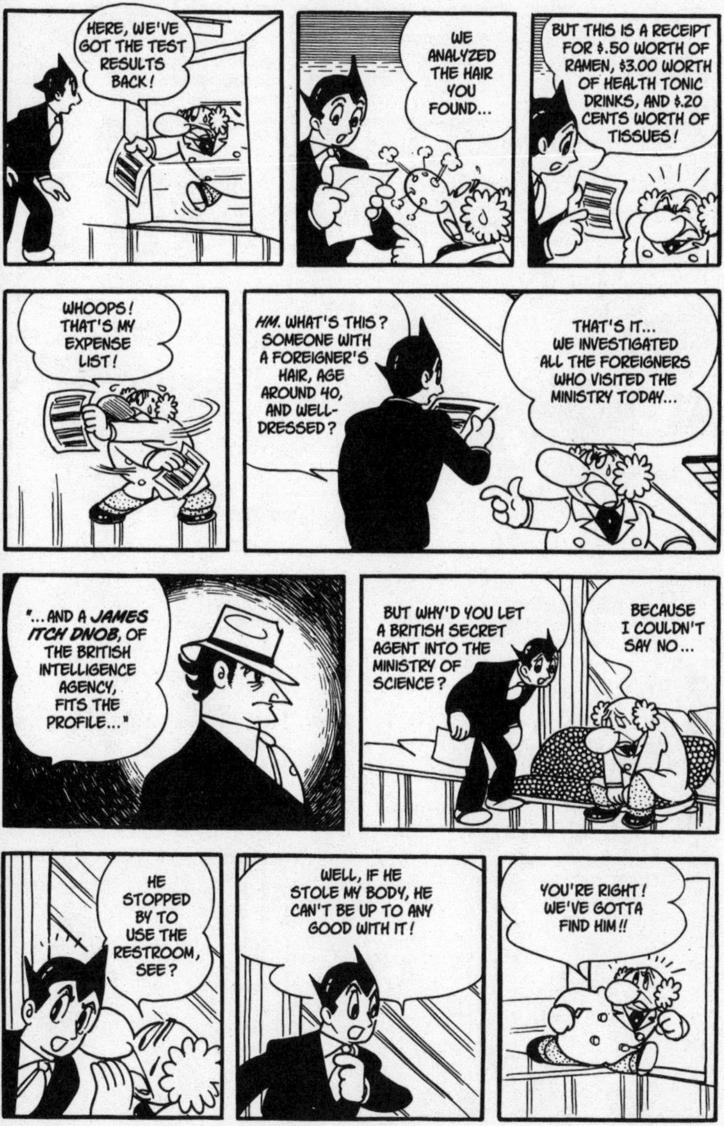
HERE, WE'VE GOT THE TEST RESULTS BACK!
WE ANALYZED THE HAIR YOU FOUND...
BUT THIS IS A RECEIPT FOR $.50 WORTH OF RAMEN, $3.00 WORTH OF HEALTH TONIC DRINKS, AND $.20 CENTS WORTH OF TISSUES!
WHOOPS! THAT'S MY EXPENSE LIST!
HM. WHAT'S THIS? SOMEONE WITH A FOREIGNER'S HAIR, AGE AROUND 40, AND WELL-DRESSED?
THAT'S IT... WE INVESTIGATED ALL THE FOREIGNERS WHO VISITED THE MINISTRY TODAY...
"...AND A JAMES ITCH DNOB, OF THE BRITISH INTELLIGENCE AGENCY, FITS THE PROFILE..."
BUT WHY'D YOU LET A BRITISH SECRET AGENT INTO THE MINISTRY OF SCIENCE?
BECAUSE I COULDN'T SAY NO...
HE STOPPED BY TO USE THE RESTROOM, SEE?
WELL, IF HE STOLE MY BODY, HE CAN'T BE UP TO ANY GOOD WITH IT!
YOU'RE RIGHT! WE'VE GOTTA FIND HIM!!

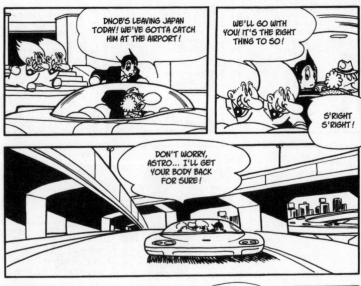

DNOB'S LEAVING JAPAN TODAY! WE'VE GOTTA CATCH HIM AT THE AIRPORT!

WE'LL GO WITH YOU! IT'S THE RIGHT THING TO SO!

S'RIGHT S'RIGHT!

DON'T WORRY, ASTRO... I'LL GET YOUR BODY BACK FOR SURE!

ANYONE ON THE PASSENGER LIST NAMED DNOB?

LESSEE... YESSIR, HERE HE IS...

WE'LL WAIT HERE AND AMBUSH HIM...

WONDER WHAT HE'S PLANNING TO USE MY BODY FOR?

WELL, IF IT ISN'T INSPECTOR TAWASHI...

HOWDY, PROFESSOR...

20

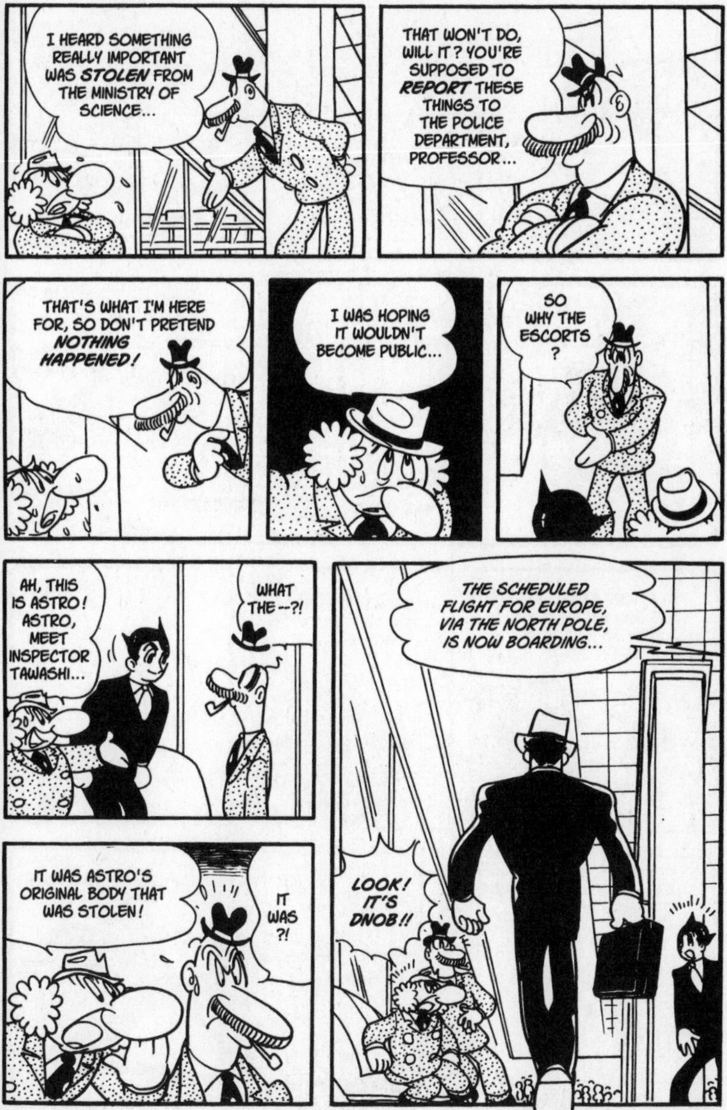
I HEARD SOMETHING REALLY IMPORTANT WAS *STOLEN* FROM THE MINISTRY OF SCIENCE...
THAT WON'T DO, WILL IT? YOU'RE SUPPOSED TO *REPORT* THESE THINGS TO THE POLICE DEPARTMENT, PROFESSOR...
THAT'S WHAT I'M HERE FOR, SO DON'T PRETEND *NOTHING HAPPENED!*
I WAS HOPING IT WOULDN'T BECOME PUBLIC...
SO WHY THE ESCORTS ?
AH, THIS IS ASTRO! ASTRO, MEET INSPECTOR TAWASHI...
WHAT THE--?!
IT WAS ASTRO'S ORIGINAL BODY THAT WAS STOLEN!
IT WAS ?!
THE SCHEDULED FLIGHT FOR EUROPE, VIA THE NORTH POLE, IS NOW BOARDING...
LOOK! IT'S DNOB!!

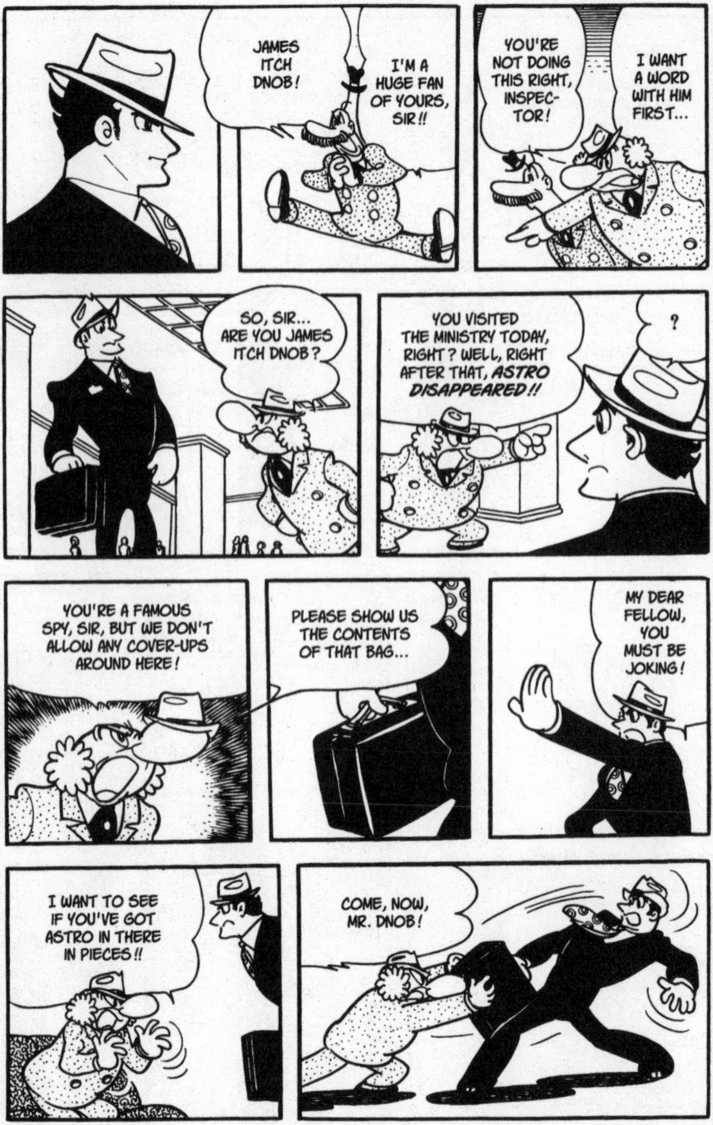
JAMES ITCH DNOB!
I'M A HUGE FAN OF YOURS, SIR!!
YOU'RE NOT DOING THIS RIGHT, INSPECTOR!
I WANT A WORD WITH HIM FIRST...
SO, SIR... ARE YOU JAMES ITCH DNOB?
YOU VISITED THE MINISTRY TODAY, RIGHT? WELL, RIGHT AFTER THAT, ASTRO DISAPPEARED!!
?
YOU'RE A FAMOUS SPY, SIR, BUT WE DON'T ALLOW ANY COVER-UPS AROUND HERE!
PLEASE SHOW US THE CONTENTS OF THAT BAG...
MY DEAR FELLOW, YOU MUST BE JOKING!
I WANT TO SEE IF YOU'VE GOT ASTRO IN THERE IN PIECES!!
COME, NOW, MR. DNOB!

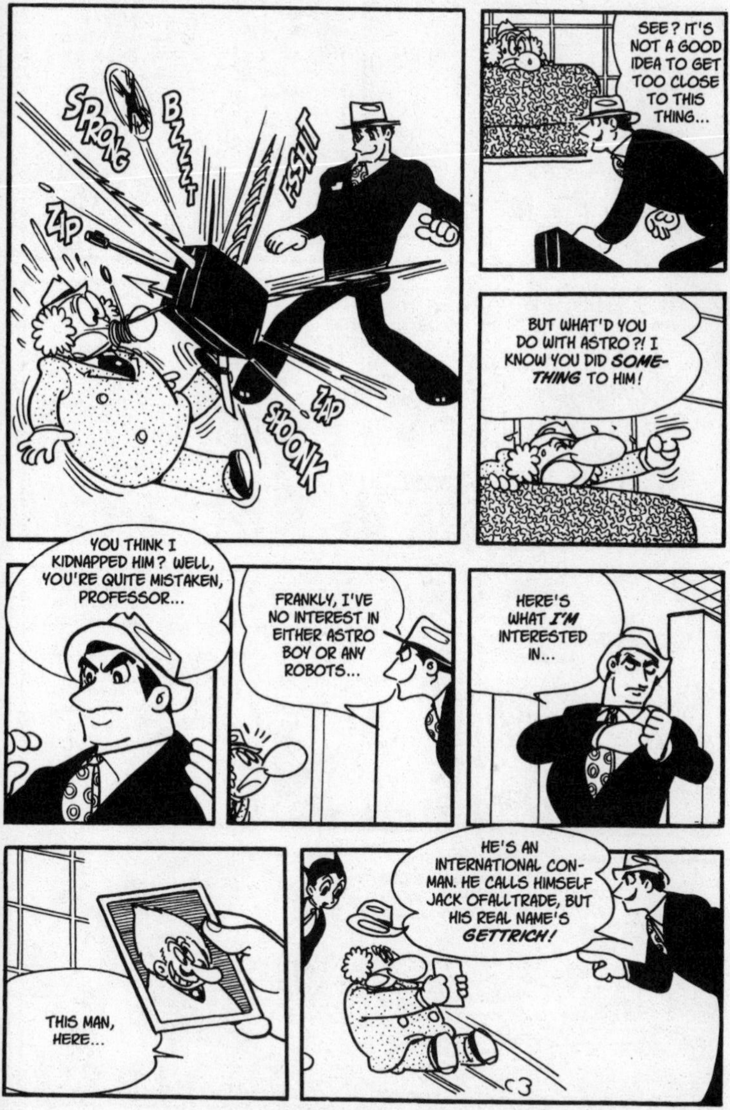
SPRONG
BZZZT
FSHHT
ZAP
ZAP
SHOONK
SEE? IT'S NOT A GOOD IDEA TO GET TOO CLOSE TO THIS THING...
BUT WHAT'D YOU DO WITH ASTRO?! I KNOW YOU DID SOMETHING TO HIM!
YOU THINK I KIDNAPPED HIM? WELL, YOU'RE QUITE MISTAKEN, PROFESSOR...
FRANKLY, I'VE NO INTEREST IN EITHER ASTRO BOY OR ANY ROBOTS...
HERE'S WHAT I'M INTERESTED IN...
THIS MAN, HERE...
HE'S AN INTERNATIONAL CON-MAN. HE CALLS HIMSELF JACK OFALLTRADE, BUT HIS REAL NAME'S GETTRICH!

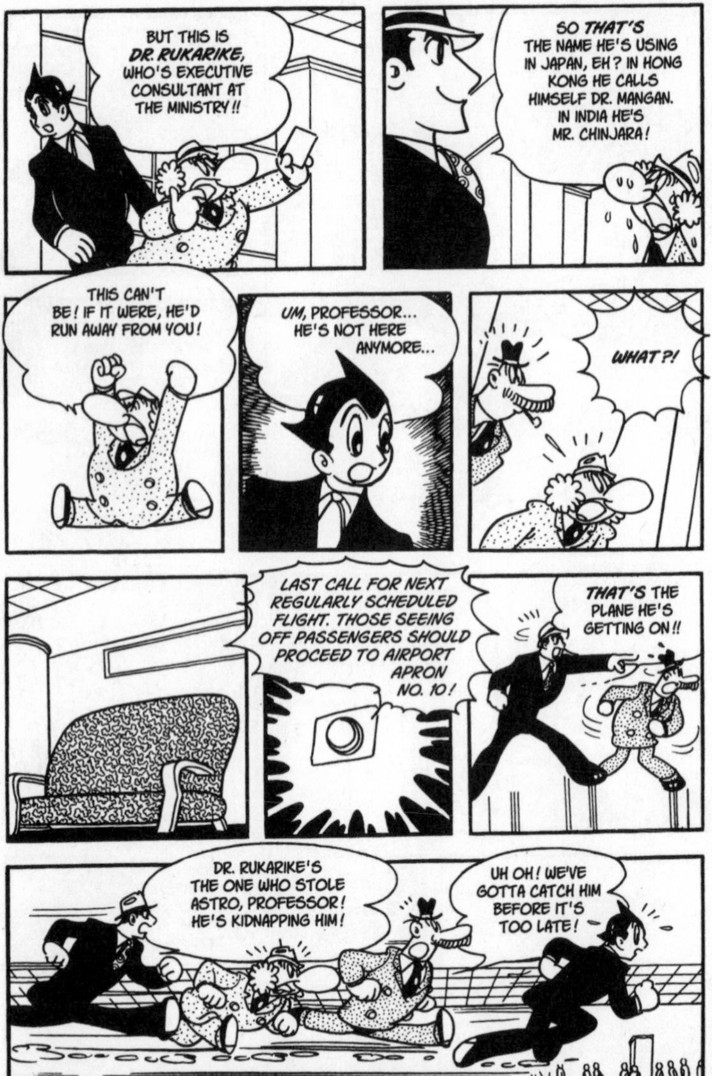
BUT THIS IS DR. RUKARIKE, WHO'S EXECUTIVE CONSULTANT AT THE MINISTRY!!
SO THAT'S THE NAME HE'S USING IN JAPAN, EH? IN HONG KONG HE CALLS HIMSELF DR. MANGAN. IN INDIA HE'S MR. CHINJARA!
THIS CAN'T BE! IF IT WERE, HE'D RUN AWAY FROM YOU!
UM, PROFESSOR... HE'S NOT HERE ANYMORE...
WHAT?!
LAST CALL FOR NEXT REGULARLY SCHEDULED FLIGHT. THOSE SEEING OFF PASSENGERS SHOULD PROCEED TO AIRPORT APRON NO. 10!
THAT'S THE PLANE HE'S GETTING ON!!
DR. RUKARIKE'S THE ONE WHO STOLE ASTRO, PROFESSOR! HE'S KIDNAPPING HIM!
UH OH! WE'VE GOTTA CATCH HIM BEFORE IT'S TOO LATE!

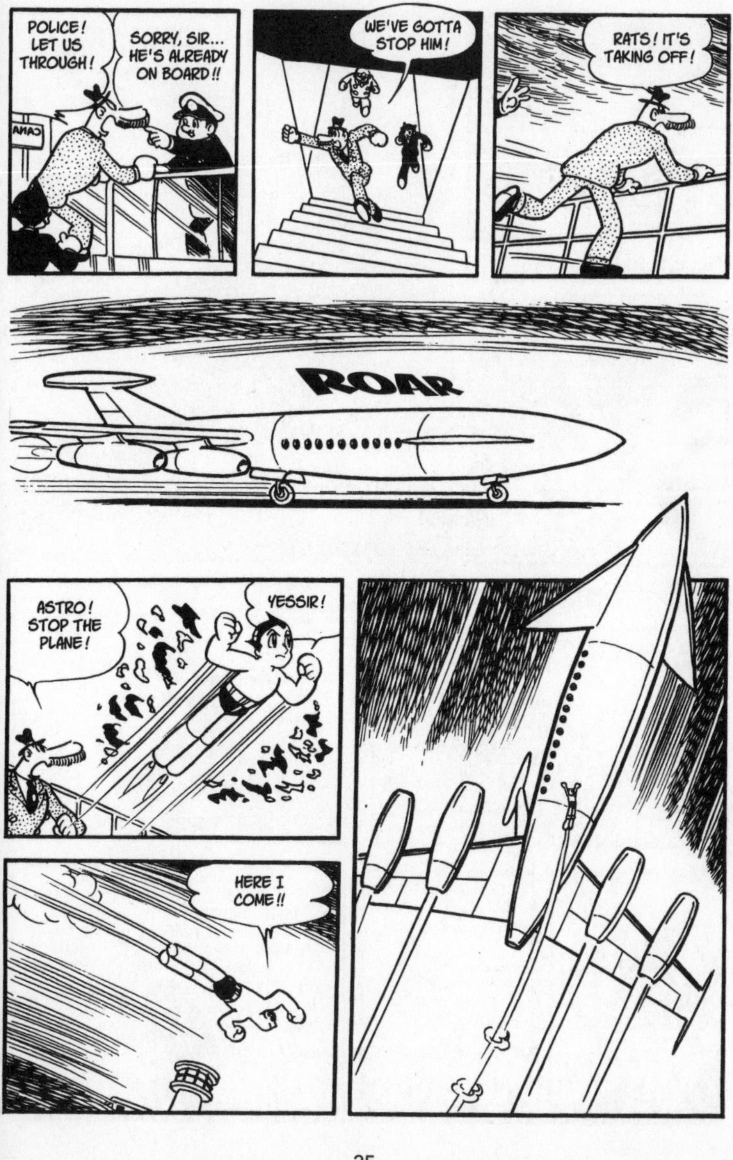
POLICE! LET US THROUGH!
SORRY, SIR... HE'S ALREADY ON BOARD!!
WE'VE GOTTA STOP HIM!
RATS! IT'S TAKING OFF!
ROAR
ASTRO! STOP THE PLANE!
YESSIR!
HERE I COME!!

SORRY, FOLKS...

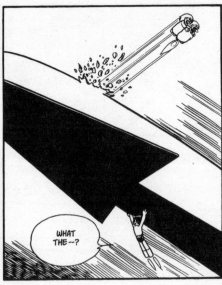

WHAT THE --?

...BUT WE'VE GOTTA LAND AGAIN...

TEE HEE. LAND AGAIN? ARE YOU *KIDDING*?

WE PART WAYS HERE, PAL...

SAYONARA, SAYONARA!

BLAST IT!

BUT WHAT'S GETTRICH DOING WITH A TWIN?

I GET IT! ONE'S A RO-BOT!!

SOMEBODY SAY *"ROBOT"*?!

RIGHT. THERE'S ONLY ONE GETTRICH! HE MUST HAVE MADE A TWIN!!

THE TWIN'S HELPING HIM IN HIS CRIMES!!

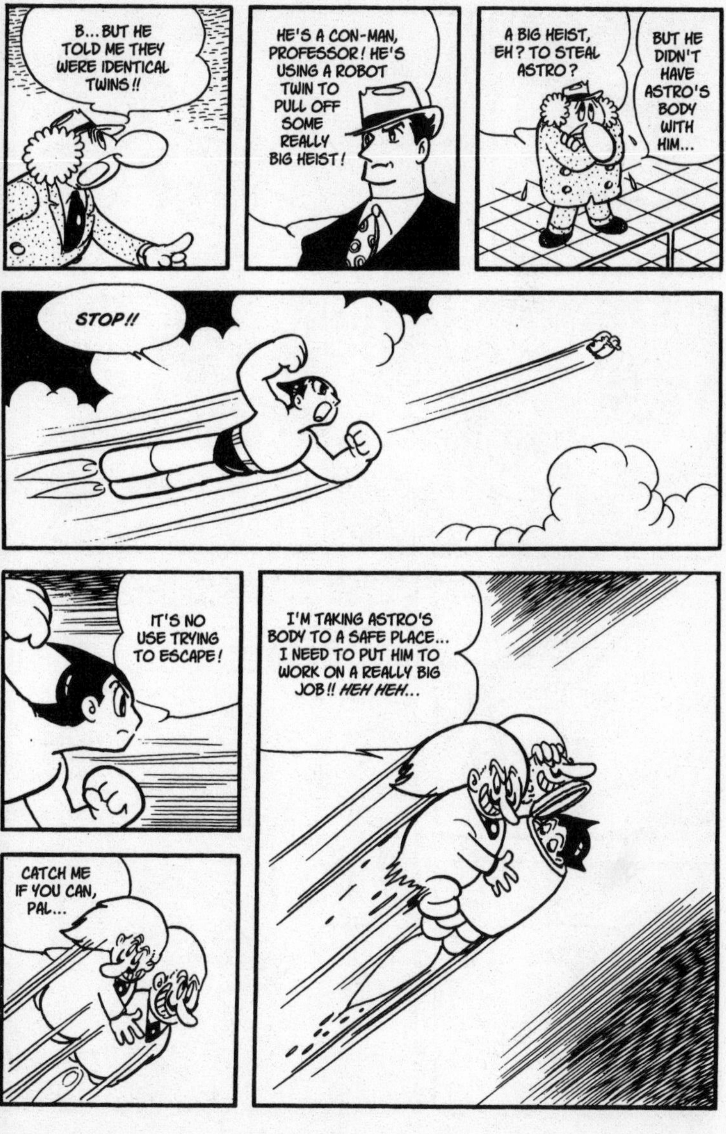
B...BUT HE TOLD ME THEY WERE IDENTICAL TWINS!!
HE'S A CON-MAN, PROFESSOR! HE'S USING A ROBOT TWIN TO PULL OFF SOME REALLY BIG HEIST!
A BIG HEIST, EH? TO STEAL ASTRO?
BUT HE DIDN'T HAVE ASTRO'S BODY WITH HIM...
STOP!!
IT'S NO USE TRYING TO ESCAPE!
CATCH ME IF YOU CAN, PAL...
I'M TAKING ASTRO'S BODY TO A SAFE PLACE... I NEED TO PUT HIM TO WORK ON A REALLY BIG JOB!! HEH HEH...

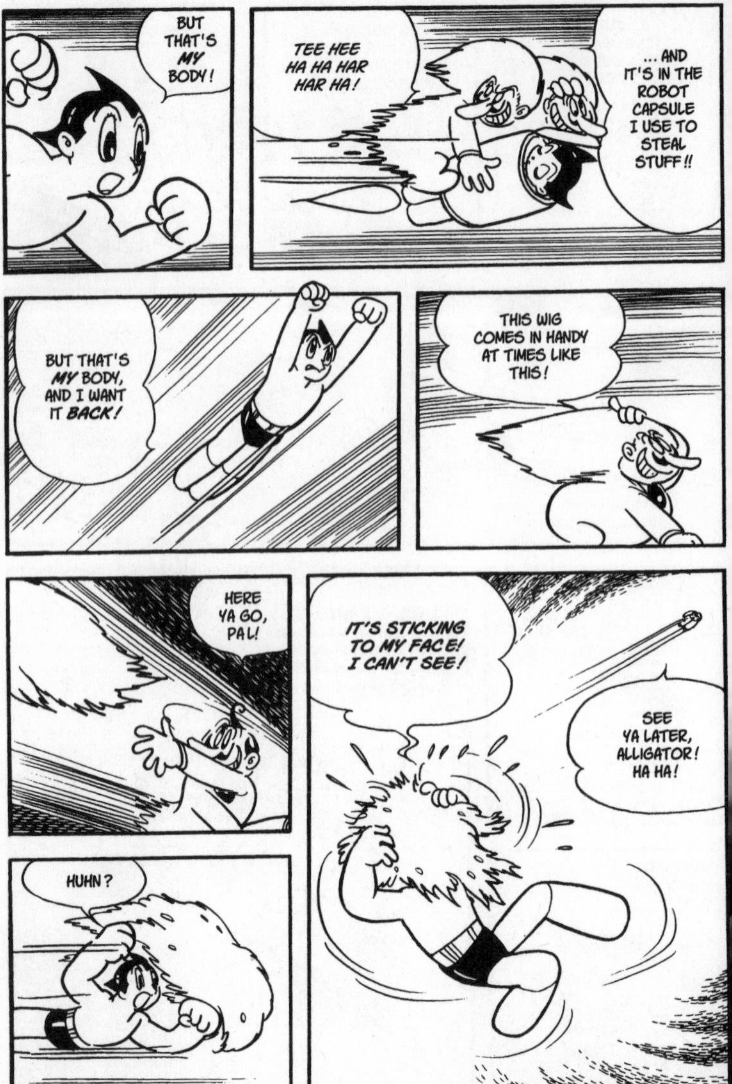

BUT THAT'S MY BODY!
TEE HEE HA HA HAR HAR HA!
... AND IT'S IN THE ROBOT CAPSULE I USE TO STEAL STUFF!!
BUT THAT'S MY BODY, AND I WANT IT BACK!
THIS WIG COMES IN HANDY AT TIMES LIKE THIS!
HERE YA GO, PAL!
HUHN?
IT'S STICKING TO MY FACE! I CAN'T SEE!
SEE YA LATER, ALLIGATOR! HA HA!

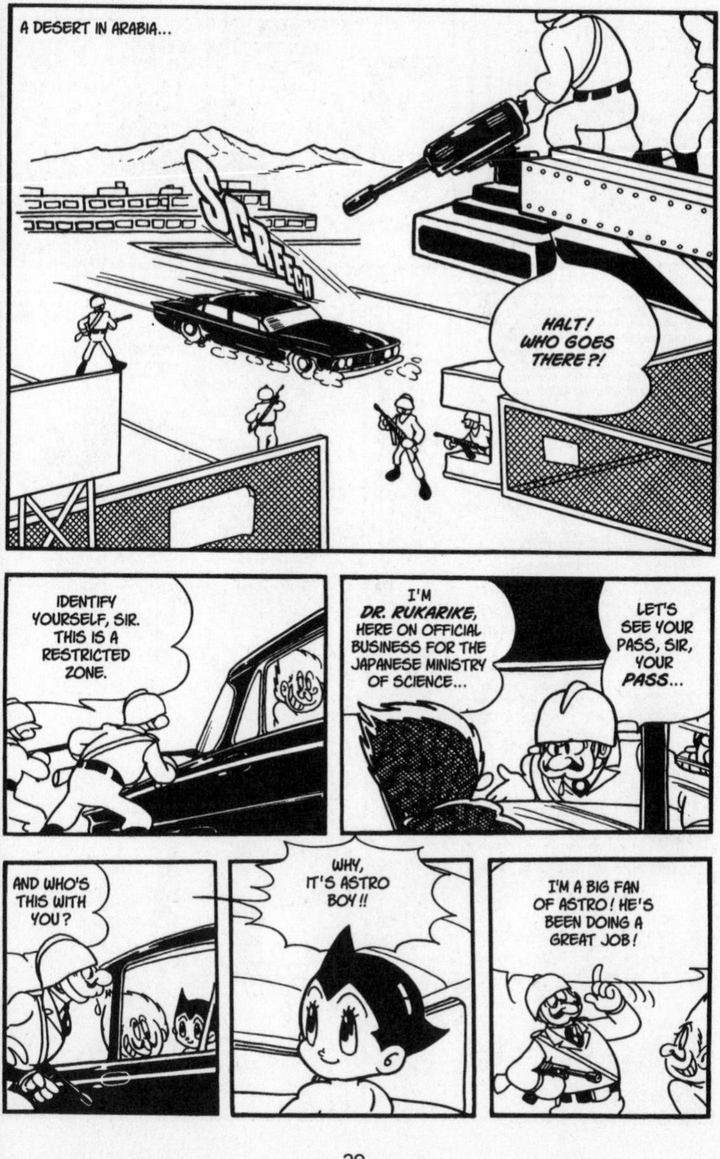
A DESERT IN ARABIA...
SCREECH
HALT! WHO GOES THERE?!
IDENTIFY YOURSELF, SIR. THIS IS A RESTRICTED ZONE.
I'M DR. RUKARIKE, HERE ON OFFICIAL BUSINESS FOR THE JAPANESE MINISTRY OF SCIENCE...
LET'S SEE YOUR PASS, SIR, YOUR PASS...
AND WHO'S THIS WITH YOU?
WHY, IT'S ASTRO BOY!!
I'M A BIG FAN OF ASTRO! HE'S BEEN DOING A GREAT JOB!

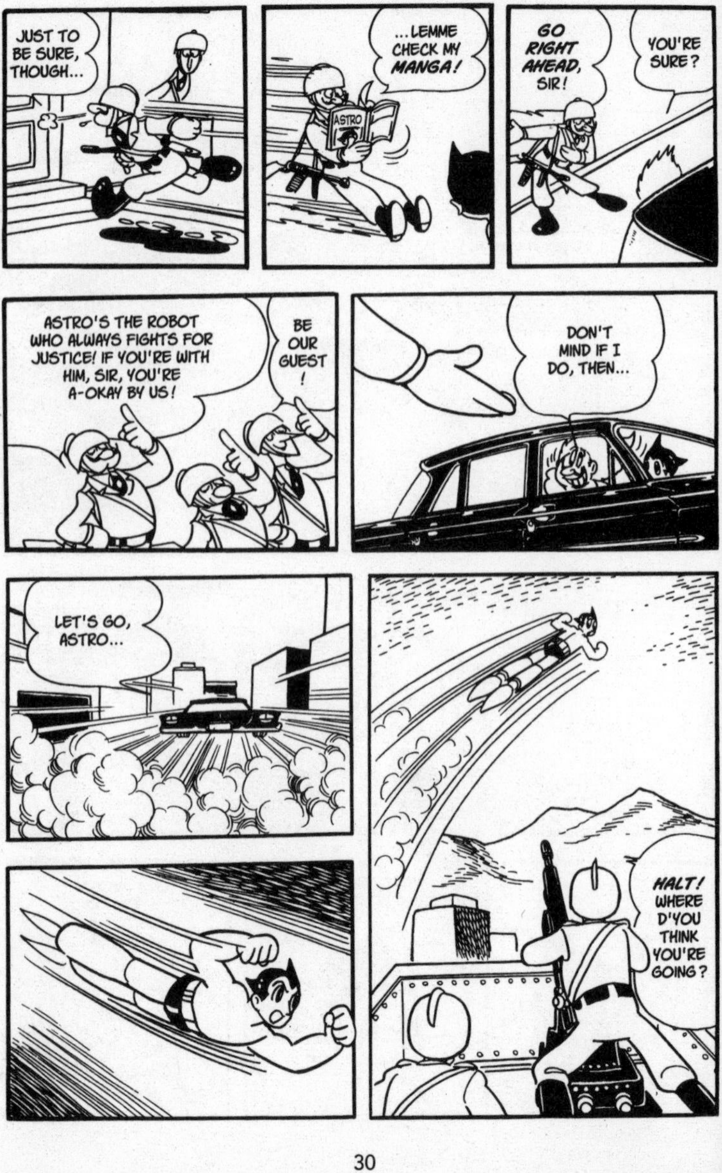
JUST TO BE SURE, THOUGH...
...LEMME CHECK MY MANGA!
ASTRO
GO RIGHT AHEAD, SIR!
YOU'RE SURE?
ASTRO'S THE ROBOT WHO ALWAYS FIGHTS FOR JUSTICE! IF YOU'RE WITH HIM, SIR, YOU'RE A-OKAY BY US!
BE OUR GUEST!
DON'T MIND IF I DO, THEN...
LET'S GO, ASTRO...
HALT! WHERE D'YOU THINK YOU'RE GOING?

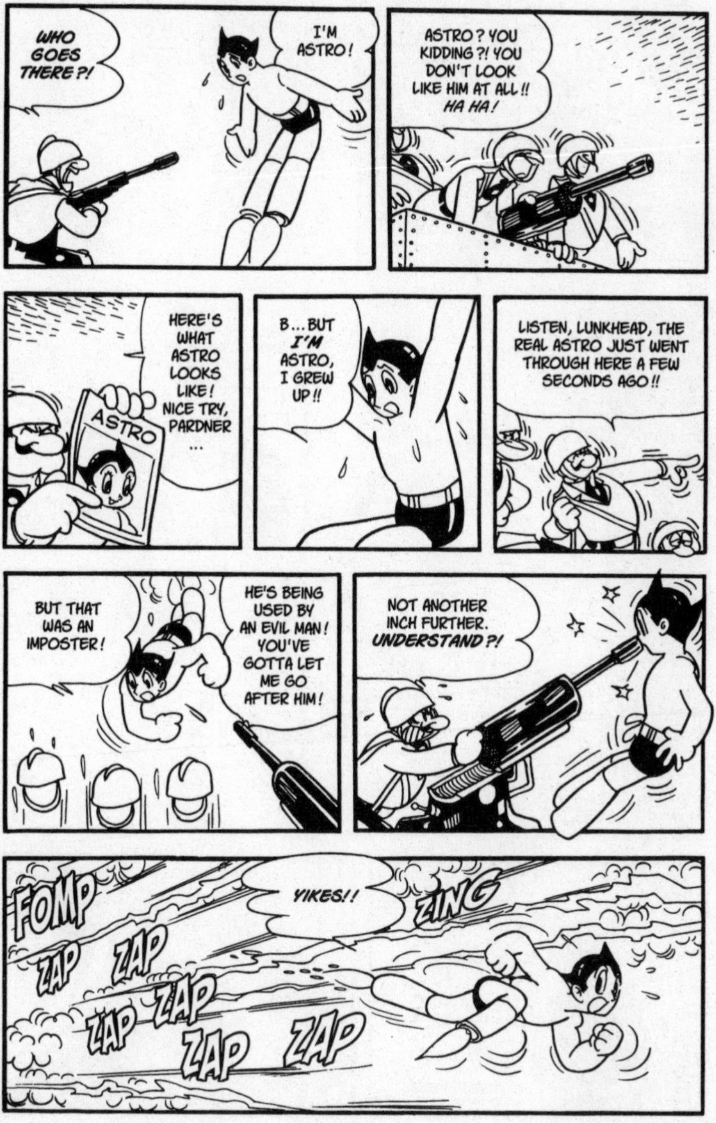
WHO GOES THERE?!
I'M ASTRO!
ASTRO? YOU KIDDING?! YOU DON'T LOOK LIKE HIM AT ALL!! HA HA!
HERE'S WHAT ASTRO LOOKS LIKE! NICE TRY, PARDNER ...
ASTRO
B...BUT I'M ASTRO, I GREW UP!!
LISTEN, LUNKHEAD, THE REAL ASTRO JUST WENT THROUGH HERE A FEW SECONDS AGO!!
BUT THAT WAS AN IMPOSTER!
HE'S BEING USED BY AN EVIL MAN! YOU'VE GOTTA LET ME GO AFTER HIM!
NOT ANOTHER INCH FURTHER. UNDERSTAND?!
FOMP
YIKES!!
ZING
ZAP
ZAP
ZAP
ZAP
ZAP
ZAP

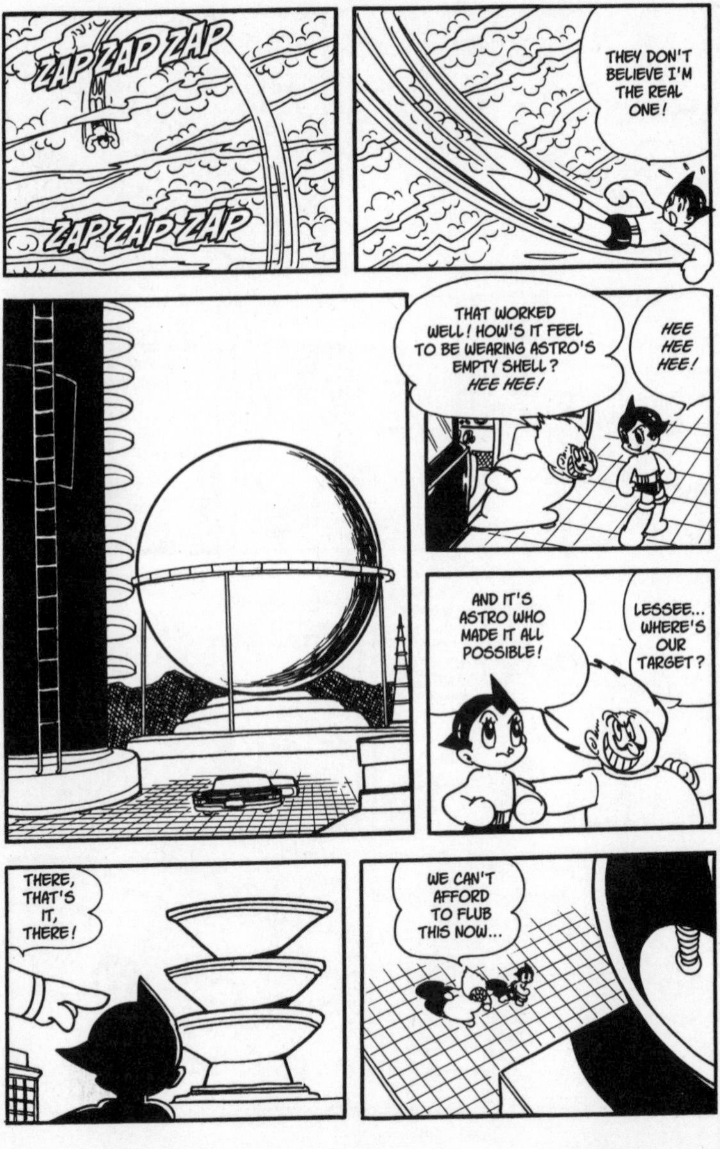
ZAP ZAP ZAP
ZAP ZAP ZAP
THEY DON'T BELIEVE I'M THE REAL ONE!
THAT WORKED WELL! HOW'S IT FEEL TO BE WEARING ASTRO'S EMPTY SHELL? *HEE HEE!*
HEE HEE HEE!
AND IT'S ASTRO WHO MADE IT ALL POSSIBLE!
LESSEE... WHERE'S OUR TARGET?
THERE, THAT'S IT, THERE!
WE CAN'T AFFORD TO FLUB THIS NOW...

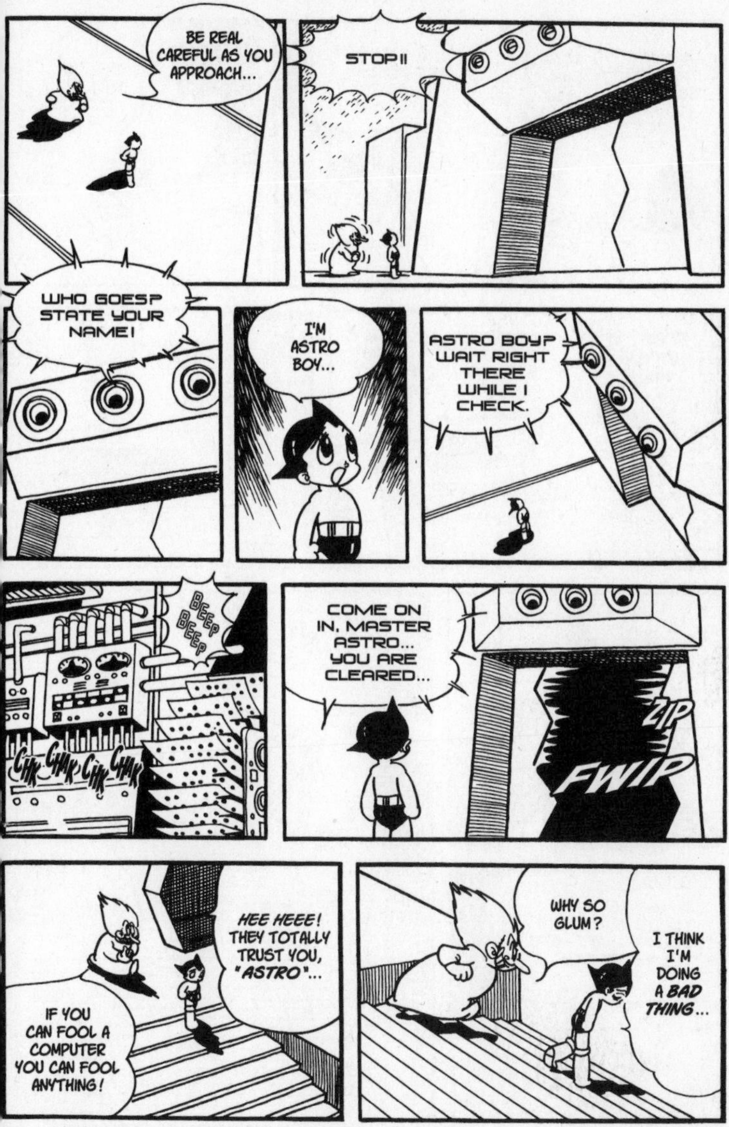

BE REAL CAREFUL AS YOU APPROACH...
STOP!!
WHO GOES? STATE YOUR NAME!
I'M ASTRO BOY...
ASTRO BOY? WAIT RIGHT THERE WHILE I CHECK.
BEEP BEEP
CHK CHAK CHK CHAK
COME ON IN, MASTER ASTRO... YOU ARE CLEARED...
ZIP
FWIP
HEE HEEE! THEY TOTALLY TRUST YOU, "ASTRO"...
IF YOU CAN FOOL A COMPUTER YOU CAN FOOL ANYTHING!
WHY SO GLUM?
I THINK I'M DOING A BAD THING...

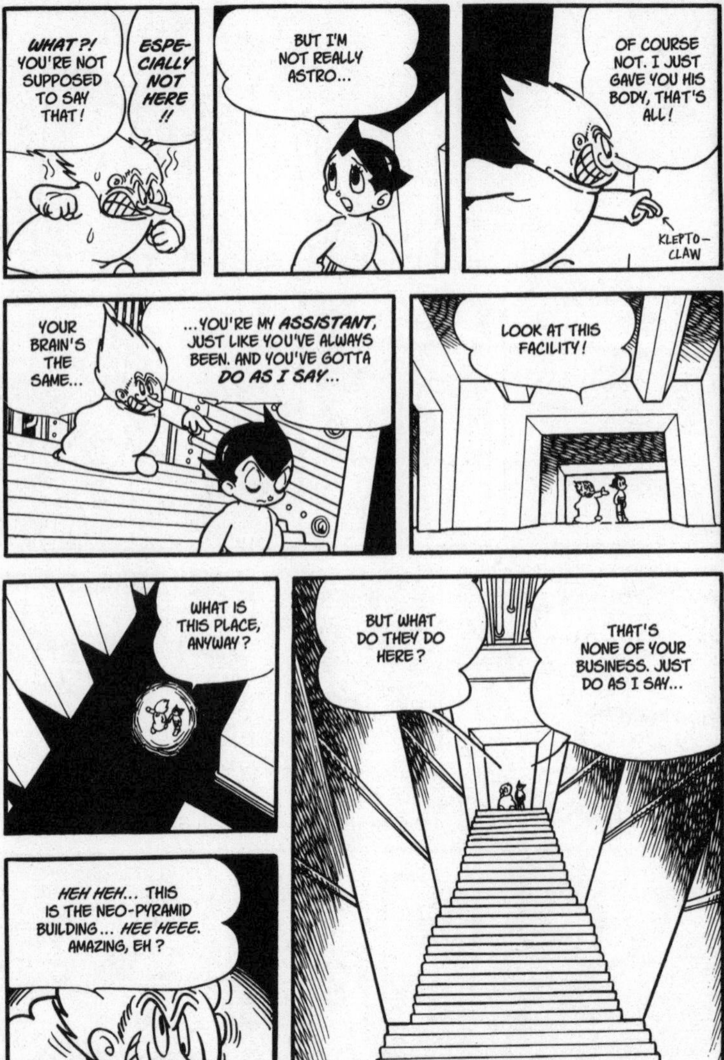
WHAT?! YOU'RE NOT SUPPOSED TO SAY THAT!
ESPECIALLY NOT HERE!!
BUT I'M NOT REALLY ASTRO...
OF COURSE NOT. I JUST GAVE YOU HIS BODY, THAT'S ALL!
KLEPTO-CLAW
YOUR BRAIN'S THE SAME...
...YOU'RE MY ASSISTANT, JUST LIKE YOU'VE ALWAYS BEEN. AND YOU'VE GOTTA DO AS I SAY...
LOOK AT THIS FACILITY!
WHAT IS THIS PLACE, ANYWAY?
HEH HEH... THIS IS THE NEO-PYRAMID BUILDING... HEE HEEE. AMAZING, EH?
BUT WHAT DO THEY DO HERE?
THAT'S NONE OF YOUR BUSINESS. JUST DO AS I SAY...

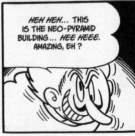

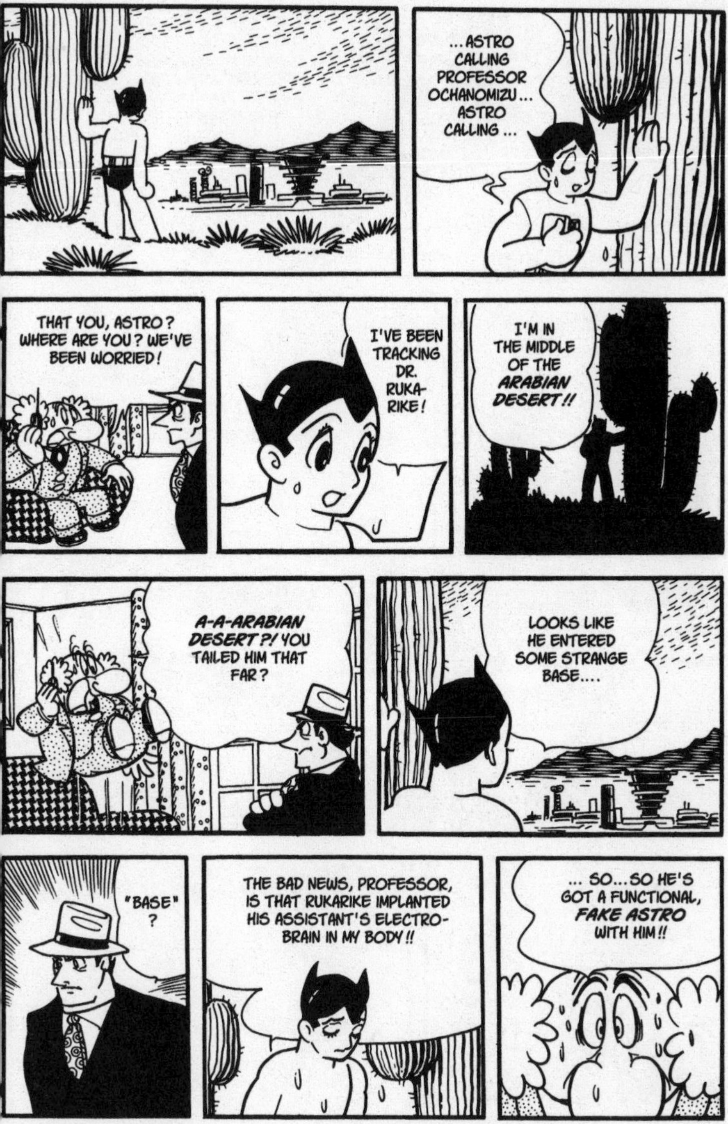
...ASTRO CALLING PROFESSOR OCHANOMIZU... ASTRO CALLING ...
THAT YOU, ASTRO? WHERE ARE YOU? WE'VE BEEN WORRIED!
I'VE BEEN TRACKING DR. RUKA-RIKE!
I'M IN THE MIDDLE OF THE ARABIAN DESERT!!
A-A-ARABIAN DESERT?! YOU TAILED HIM THAT FAR?
LOOKS LIKE HE ENTERED SOME STRANGE BASE....
"BASE" ?
THE BAD NEWS, PROFESSOR, IS THAT RUKARIKE IMPLANTED HIS ASSISTANT'S ELECTRO-BRAIN IN MY BODY!!
... SO...SO HE'S GOT A FUNCTIONAL, FAKE ASTRO WITH HIM!!

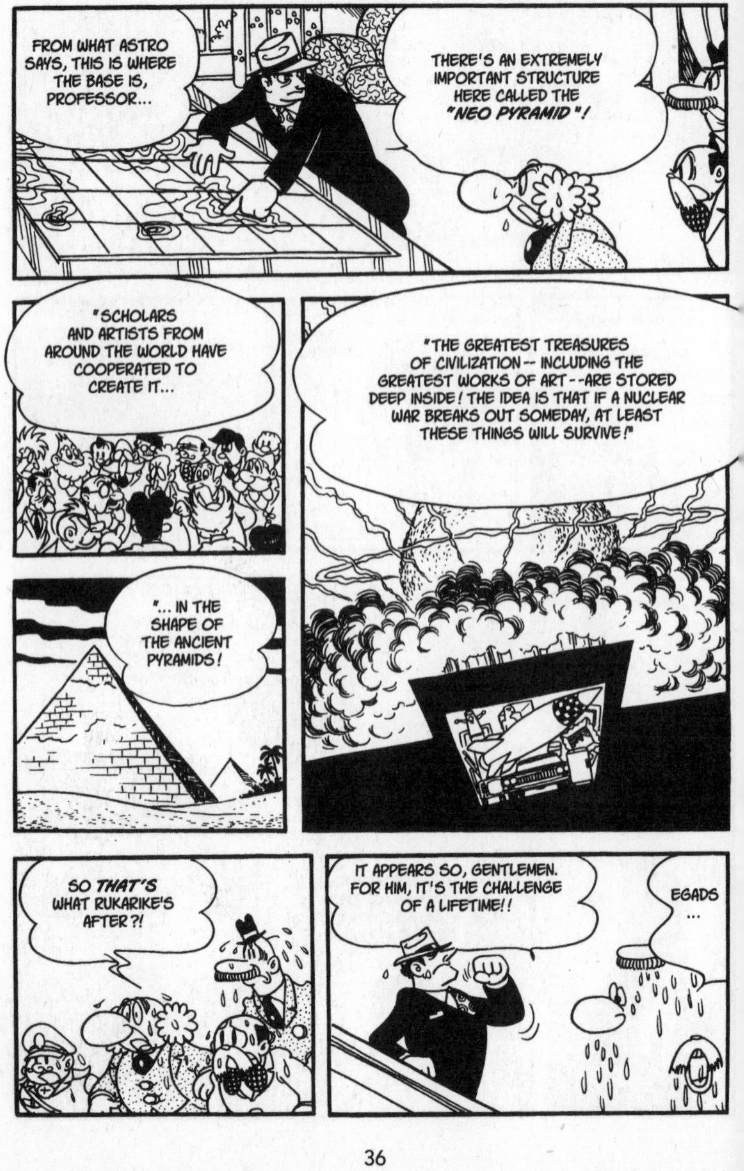
FROM WHAT ASTRO SAYS, THIS IS WHERE THE BASE IS, PROFESSOR...
THERE'S AN EXTREMELY IMPORTANT STRUCTURE HERE CALLED THE "NEO PYRAMID"!
"SCHOLARS AND ARTISTS FROM AROUND THE WORLD HAVE COOPERATED TO CREATE IT...
"... IN THE SHAPE OF THE ANCIENT PYRAMIDS!
"THE GREATEST TREASURES OF CIVILIZATION-- INCLUDING THE GREATEST WORKS OF ART--ARE STORED DEEP INSIDE! THE IDEA IS THAT IF A NUCLEAR WAR BREAKS OUT SOMEDAY, AT LEAST THESE THINGS WILL SURVIVE!"
SO THAT'S WHAT RUKARIKE'S AFTER?!
IT APPEARS SO, GENTLEMEN. FOR HIM, IT'S THE CHALLENGE OF A LIFETIME!!
EGADS ...

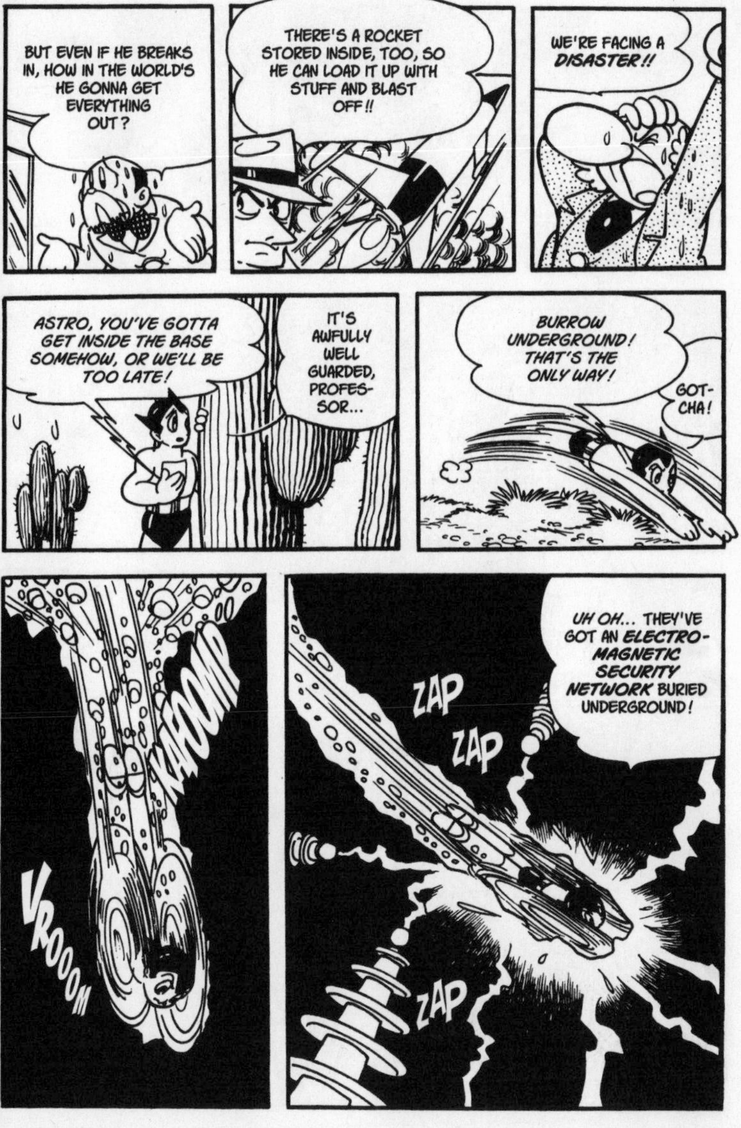

BUT EVEN IF HE BREAKS IN, HOW IN THE WORLD'S HE GONNA GET EVERYTHING OUT?
THERE'S A ROCKET STORED INSIDE, TOO, SO HE CAN LOAD IT UP WITH STUFF AND BLAST OFF!!
WE'RE FACING A DISASTER!!
ASTRO, YOU'VE GOTTA GET INSIDE THE BASE SOMEHOW, OR WE'LL BE TOO LATE!
IT'S AWFULLY WELL GUARDED, PROFES-SOR...
BURROW UNDERGROUND! THAT'S THE ONLY WAY!
GOT-CHA!
KAPOOMP
VROOOM
UH OH... THEY'VE GOT AN ELECTRO-MAGNETIC SECURITY NETWORK BURIED UNDERGROUND!
ZAP
ZAP
ZAP

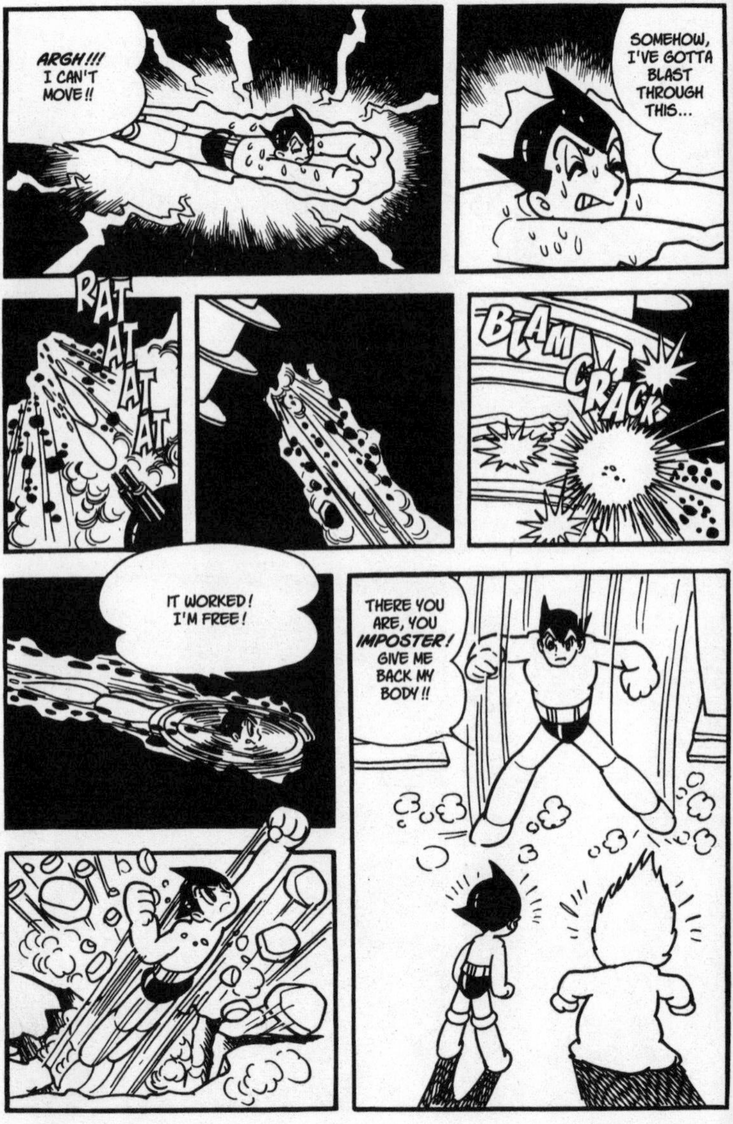
ARGH!!! I CAN'T MOVE!!
SOMEHOW, I'VE GOTTA BLAST THROUGH THIS...
RAT AT AT AT AT
BLAM
CRACK
IT WORKED! I'M FREE!
THERE YOU ARE, YOU IMPOSTER! GIVE ME BACK MY BODY!!

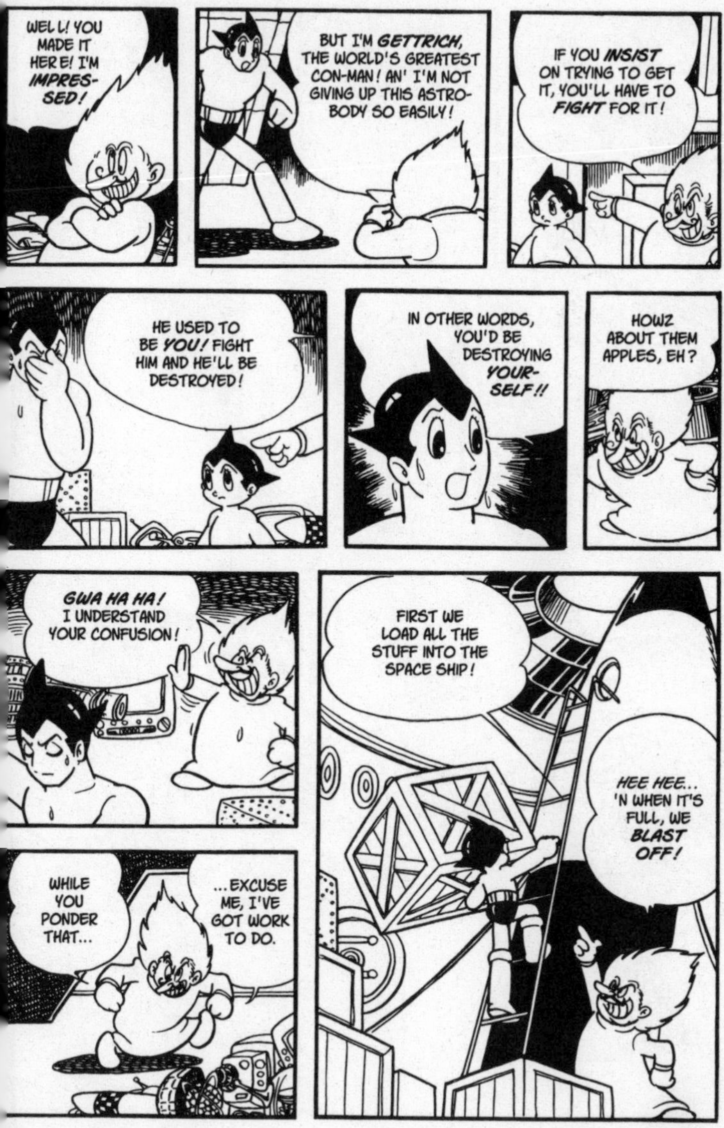
WELL! YOU MADE IT HERE! I'M IMPRESSED!
BUT I'M GETTRICH, THE WORLD'S GREATEST CON-MAN! AN' I'M NOT GIVING UP THIS ASTRO-BODY SO EASILY!
IF YOU INSIST ON TRYING TO GET IT, YOU'LL HAVE TO FIGHT FOR IT!
HE USED TO BE YOU! FIGHT HIM AND HE'LL BE DESTROYED!
IN OTHER WORDS, YOU'D BE DESTROYING YOURSELF!!
HOWZ ABOUT THEM APPLES, EH?
GWA HA HA! I UNDERSTAND YOUR CONFUSION!
WHILE YOU PONDER THAT...
...EXCUSE ME, I'VE GOT WORK TO DO.
FIRST WE LOAD ALL THE STUFF INTO THE SPACE SHIP!
HEE HEE... 'N WHEN IT'S FULL, WE BLAST OFF!

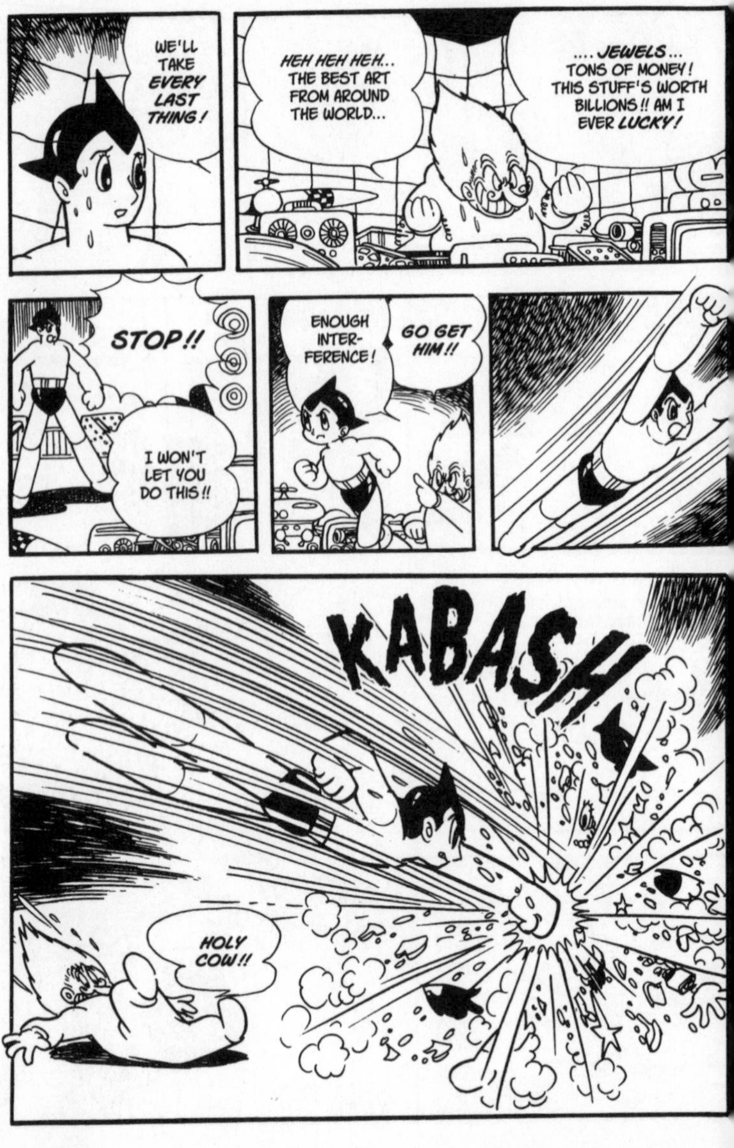

WE'LL TAKE EVERY LAST THING!
HEH HEH HEH... THE BEST ART FROM AROUND THE WORLD...
.... JEWELS... TONS OF MONEY! THIS STUFF'S WORTH BILLIONS!! AM I EVER LUCKY!
STOP!!
I WON'T LET YOU DO THIS!!
ENOUGH INTER-FERENCE!
GO GET HIM!!
KABASH
HOLY COW!!

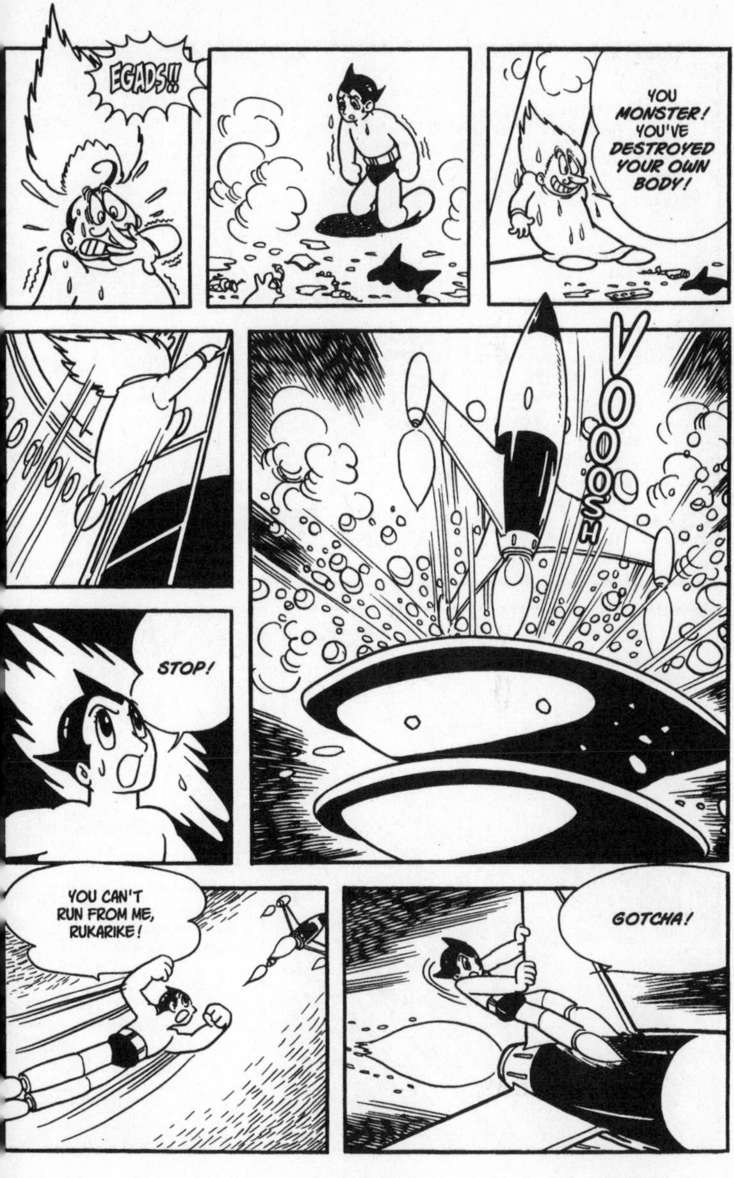
EGADS!!
YOU MONSTER! YOU'VE DESTROYED YOUR OWN BODY!
VOOOOSH
STOP!
YOU CAN'T RUN FROM ME, RUKARIKE!
GOTCHA!

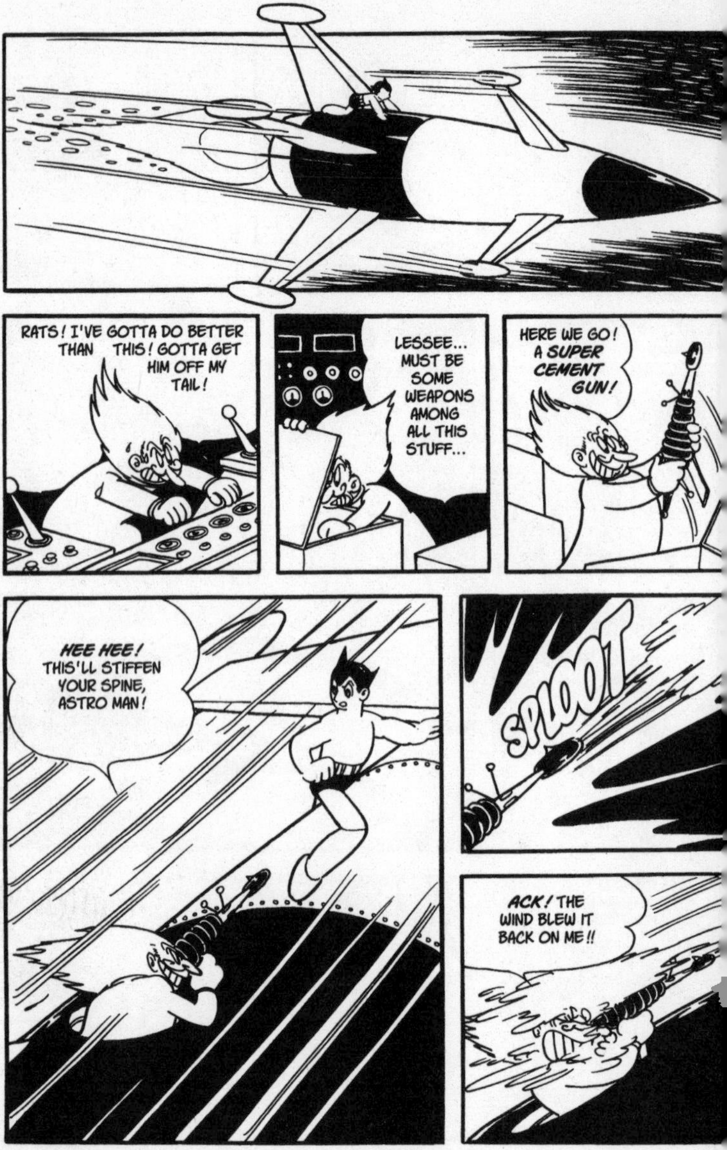
RATS! I'VE GOTTA DO BETTER THAN THIS! GOTTA GET HIM OFF MY TAIL!
LESSEE... MUST BE SOME WEAPONS AMONG ALL THIS STUFF...
HERE WE GO! A SUPER CEMENT GUN!
HEE HEE! THIS'LL STIFFEN YOUR SPINE, ASTRO MAN!
SPLOOT
ACK! THE WIND BLEW IT BACK ON ME!!

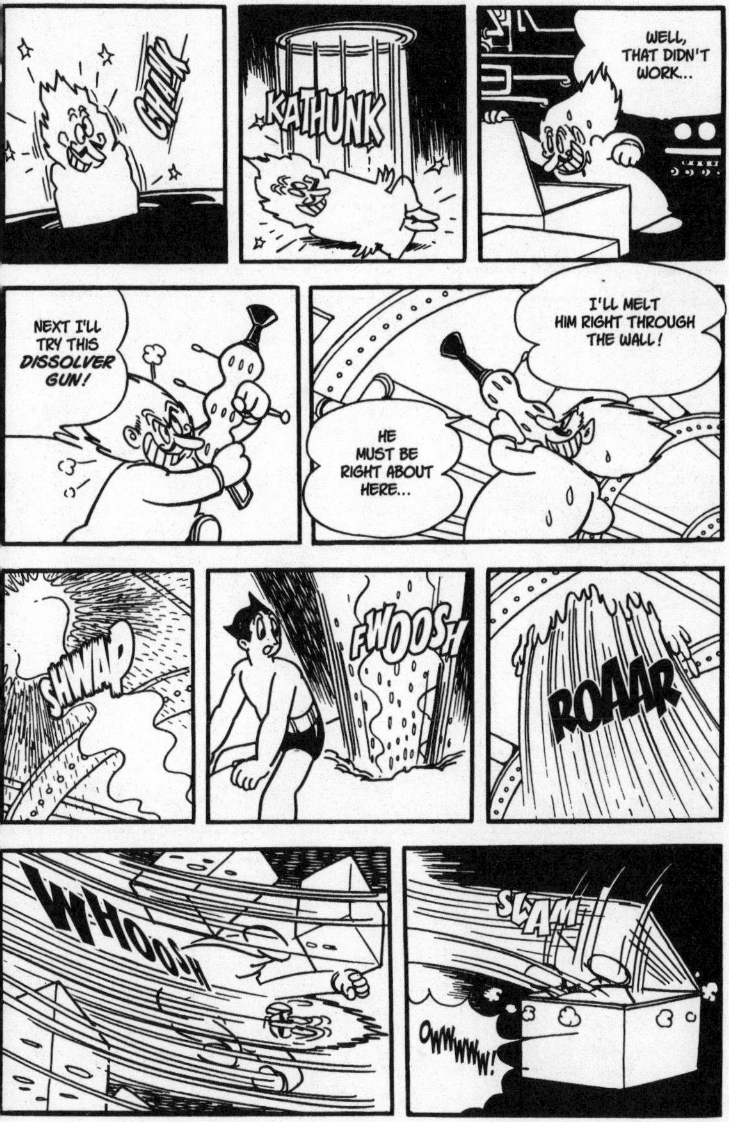

CHAK
KATHUNK
WELL, THAT DIDN'T WORK...
NEXT I'LL TRY THIS *DISSOLVER GUN!*
I'LL MELT HIM RIGHT THROUGH THE WALL!
HE MUST BE RIGHT ABOUT HERE...
SHWAP
FWOOSH
ROAAR
WHOOSH
SLAM
OWWWWW!

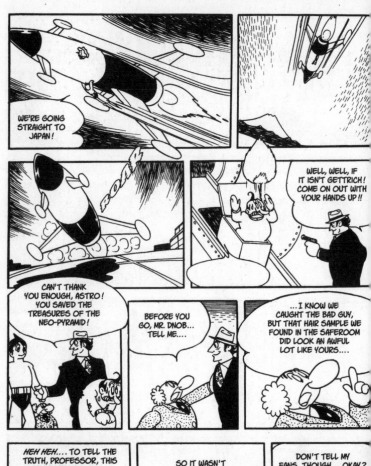

WE'RE GOING STRAIGHT TO JAPAN!

ROAR

WELL, WELL, IF IT ISN'T GETTRICH! COME ON OUT WITH YOUR HANDS UP!!

CAN'T THANK YOU ENOUGH, ASTRO! YOU SAVED THE TREASURES OF THE NEO-PYRAMID!

BEFORE YOU GO, MR. DNOB... TELL ME....

...I KNOW WE CAUGHT THE BAD GUY, BUT THAT HAIR SAMPLE WE FOUND IN THE SAFEROOM DID LOOK AN AWFUL LOT LIKE YOURS....

HEH HEH.... TO TELL THE TRUTH, PROFESSOR, THIS IS ACTUALLY A WIG...

SO IT WASN'T *MY* HAIR...SEE?

DON'T TELL MY FANS, THOUGH... OKAY? BYE NOW!

44

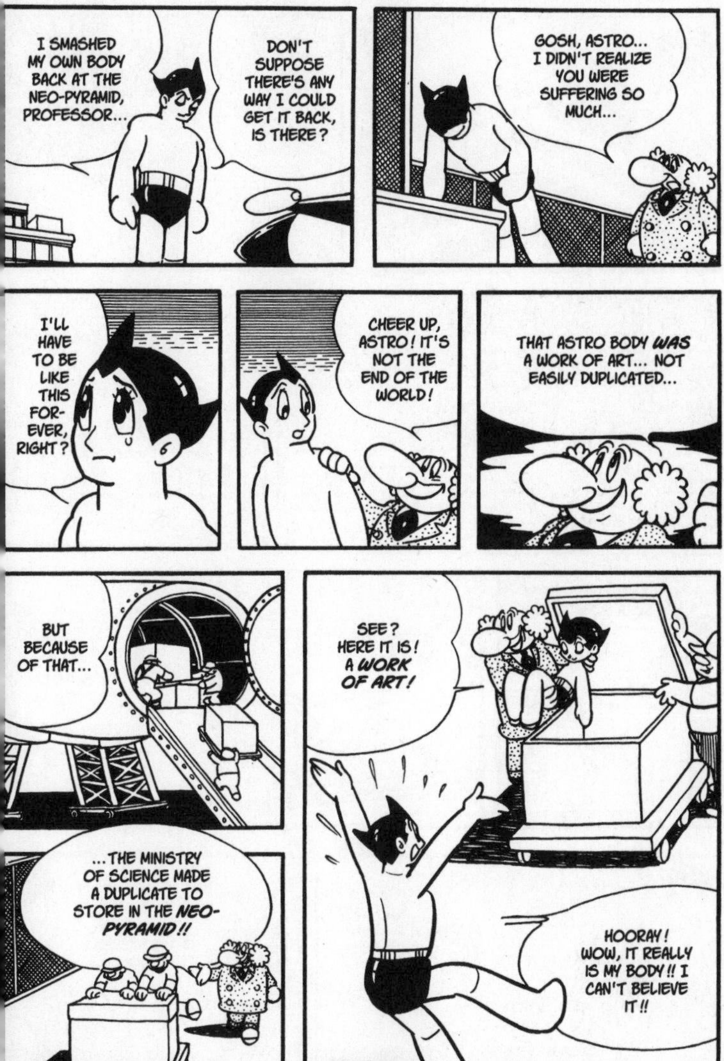
I SMASHED MY OWN BODY BACK AT THE NEO-PYRAMID, PROFESSOR...
DON'T SUPPOSE THERE'S ANY WAY I COULD GET IT BACK, IS THERE?
GOSH, ASTRO... I DIDN'T REALIZE YOU WERE SUFFERING SO MUCH...
I'LL HAVE TO BE LIKE THIS FOR-EVER, RIGHT?
CHEER UP, ASTRO! IT'S NOT THE END OF THE WORLD!
THAT ASTRO BODY *WAS* A WORK OF ART... NOT EASILY DUPLICATED...
BUT BECAUSE OF THAT...
...THE MINISTRY OF SCIENCE MADE A DUPLICATE TO STORE IN THE *NEO-PYRAMID!!*
SEE? HERE IT IS! A *WORK OF ART!*
HOORAY! WOW, IT REALLY IS MY BODY!! I CAN'T BELIEVE IT!!

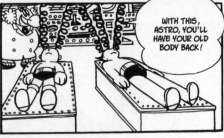

WITH THIS, ASTRO, YOU'LL HAVE YOUR OLD BODY BACK!

WHA?!

PROFESSOR! I'M BACK TO NORMAL! THANKS!

SO ASTRO'S BACK TO HIS OLD SELF NOW....

CONGRAT-ULATIONS, ASTRO!

...AND YOU GOT YOUR ORIGINAL ELECTRO-BRAIN BACK, TOO...

HOW'S THE BODY FEEL, ASTRO?

PERFECT! JUST LIKE IT USED TO!

SO HE'S NOT ME ANYMORE, PROFES-SOR!

HA HA.... THAT'S RIGHT. HE'S A DIFFERENT ROBOT!

46

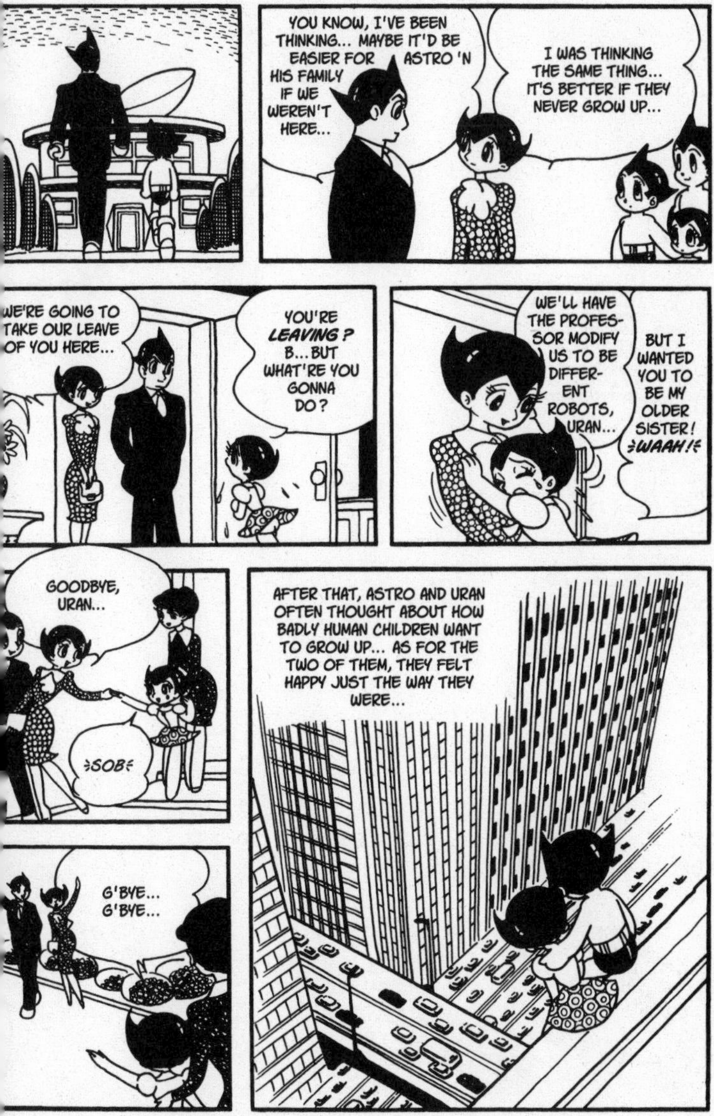

YOU KNOW, I'VE BEEN THINKING... MAYBE IT'D BE EASIER FOR ASTRO 'N HIS FAMILY IF WE WEREN'T HERE...
I WAS THINKING THE SAME THING... IT'S BETTER IF THEY NEVER GROW UP...
WE'RE GOING TO TAKE OUR LEAVE OF YOU HERE...
YOU'RE *LEAVING?* B...BUT WHAT'RE YOU GONNA DO?
WE'LL HAVE THE PROFESSOR MODIFY US TO BE DIFFERENT ROBOTS, URAN...
BUT I WANTED YOU TO BE MY OLDER SISTER! *WAAH!*
GOODBYE, URAN...
SOB
AFTER THAT, ASTRO AND URAN OFTEN THOUGHT ABOUT HOW BADLY HUMAN CHILDREN WANT TO GROW UP... AS FOR THE TWO OF THEM, THEY FELT HAPPY JUST THE WAY THEY WERE...
G'BYE... G'BYE...

THE LAST
DAY ON
EARTH

First serialized from March to June 1964
in *Shonen* magazine.

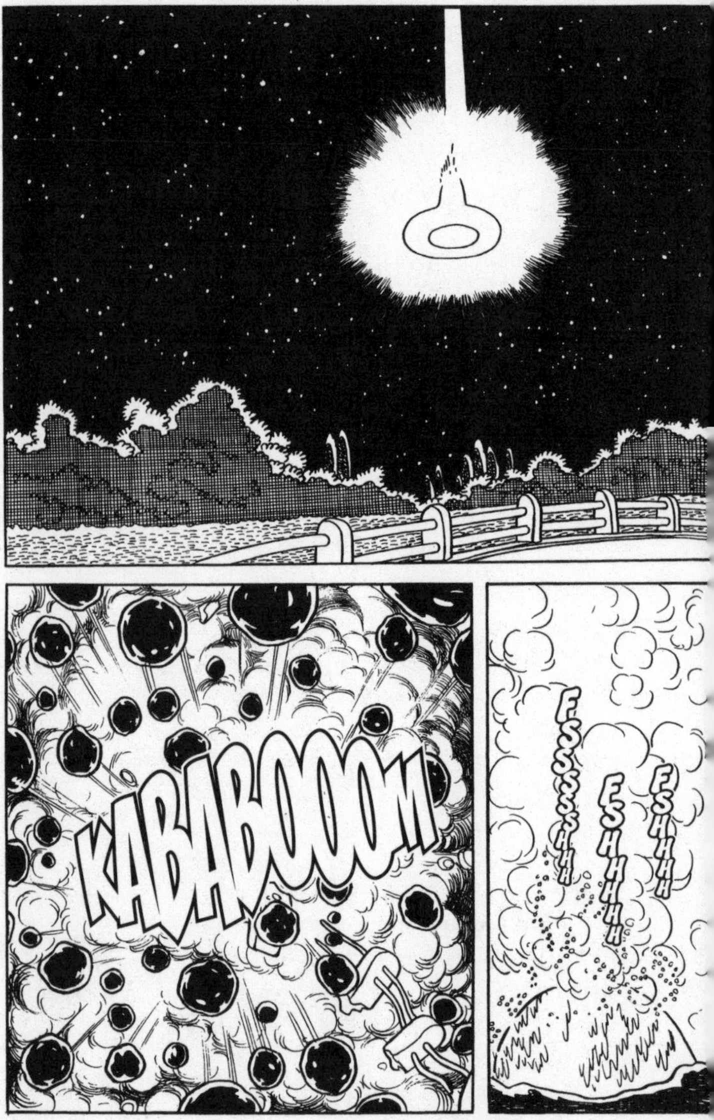
KABABOOOM
FSSSSHHH
FSHHHHH
FSHHHH

CHEEP
CHEEP
CHIRP
CHEEP
CHIRP
WHA?!
WELL I'LL BE... A ***REFRIGERATOR***, FALLEN OUT OF THE SKY, IN THE MIDDLE OF NOWHERE!
MAYBE IT'S FULL OF COLD CANNED FOOD 'N APPLE CIDER!!
HOORAY!
MY LUCKY DAY!
TIME TO OPEN THIS BABY UP!!
YOU MUST NOT OPEN THAT!
HUH?! WHO'RE YOU?!

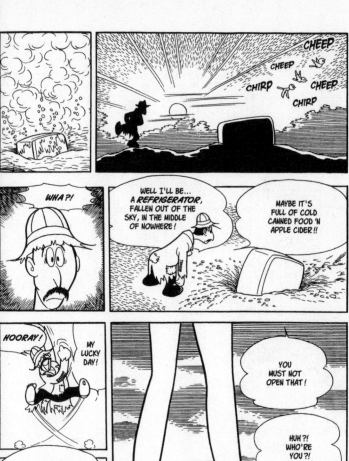

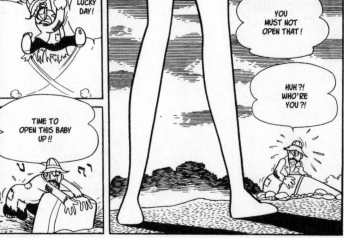

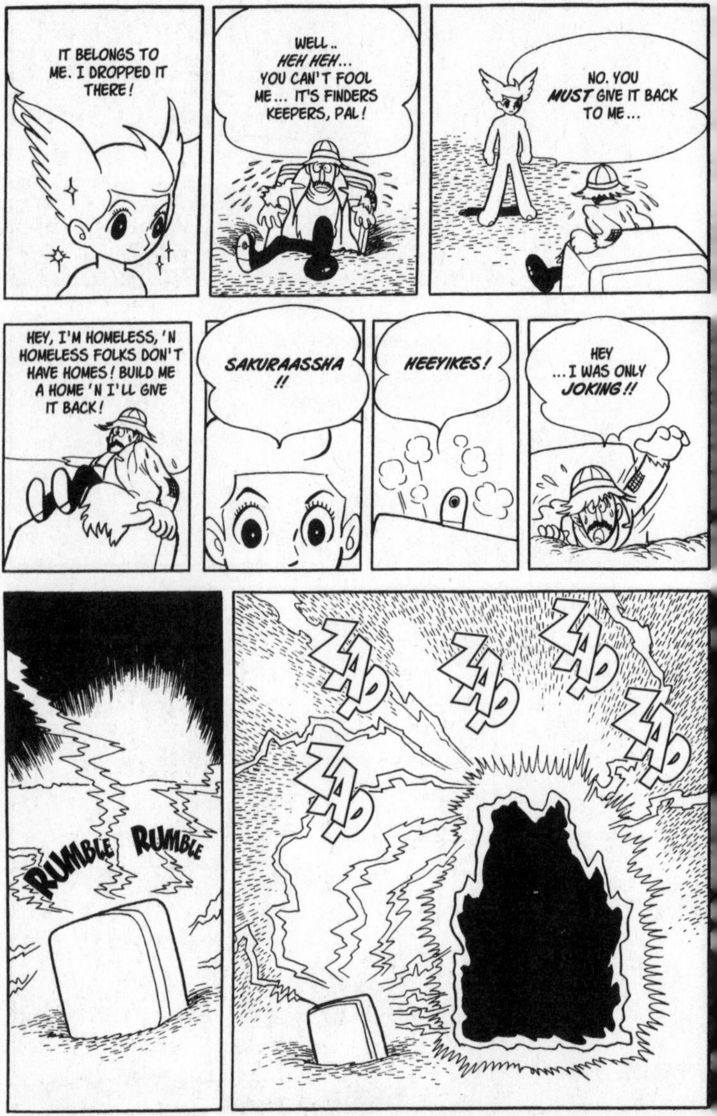
IT BELONGS TO ME. I DROPPED IT THERE!
WELL.. HEH HEH... YOU CAN'T FOOL ME... IT'S FINDERS KEEPERS, PAL!
NO. YOU MUST GIVE IT BACK TO ME...
HEY, I'M HOMELESS, 'N HOMELESS FOLKS DON'T HAVE HOMES! BUILD ME A HOME 'N I'LL GIVE IT BACK!
SAKURAASSHA !!
HEEYIKES!
HEY ...I WAS ONLY JOKING!!
RUMBLE RUMBLE
ZAP
ZAP
ZAP
ZAP
ZAP

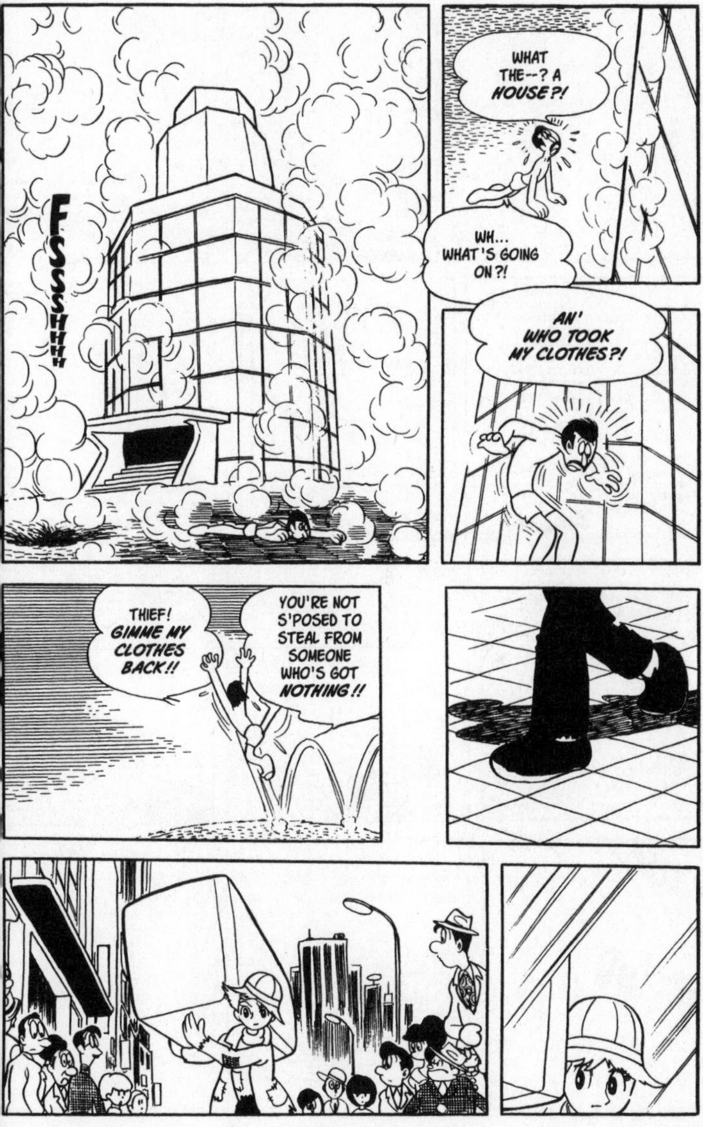
FSSSHHHH
WHAT THE--? A HOUSE?!
WH... WHAT'S GOING ON?!
AN' WHO TOOK MY CLOTHES?!
THIEF! GIMME MY CLOTHES BACK!!
YOU'RE NOT S'POSED TO STEAL FROM SOMEONE WHO'S GOT NOTHING!!

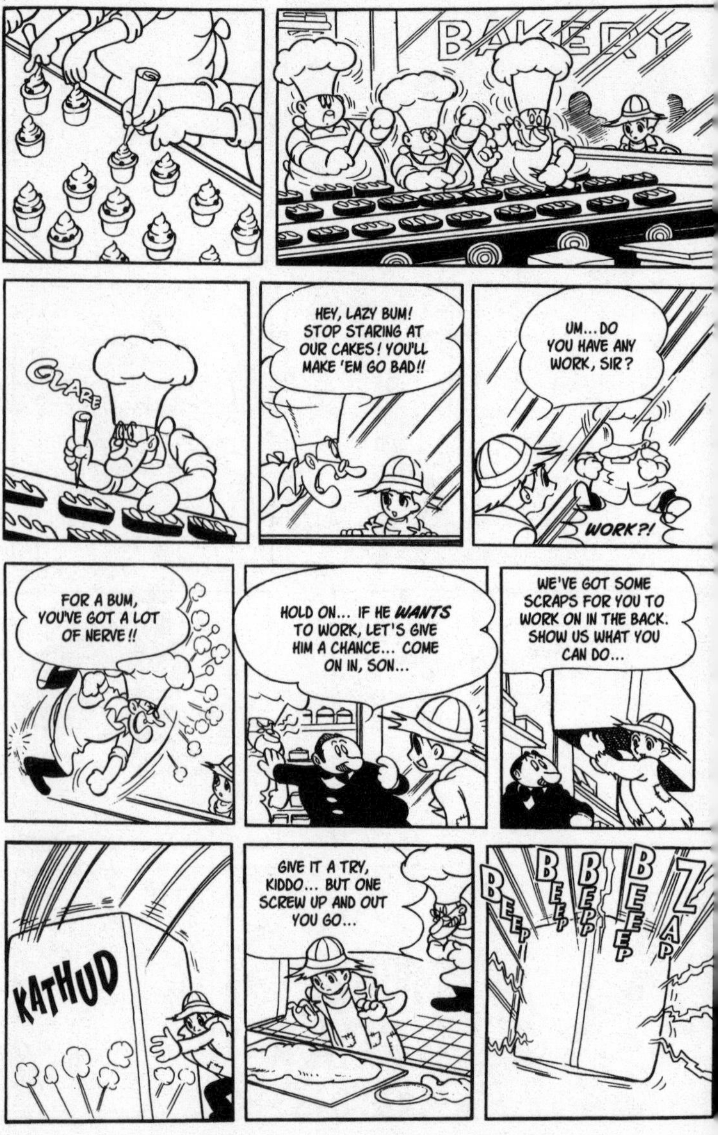
BAKERY
GLARE
HEY, LAZY BUM! STOP STARING AT OUR CAKES! YOU'LL MAKE 'EM GO BAD!!
UM... DO YOU HAVE ANY WORK, SIR?
WORK?!
FOR A BUM, YOU'VE GOT A LOT OF NERVE!!
HOLD ON... IF HE *WANTS* TO WORK, LET'S GIVE HIM A CHANCE... COME ON IN, SON...
WE'VE GOT SOME SCRAPS FOR YOU TO WORK ON IN THE BACK. SHOW US WHAT YOU CAN DO...
KATHUD
GIVE IT A TRY, KIDDO... BUT ONE SCREW UP AND OUT YOU GO...
BEEP
BEEP
BEPP
BEEEP
ZAP

ZUM

FUNK

SHLAP
SHLOOP

HE *DOES* WORK FAST...

WHAT'D HE BRING A FRIDGE FOR, THOUGH? I BETTER CHECK INSIDE...

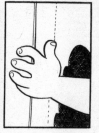

AIEEE!

≶ARGH≶ AIEE..!!

HEY!! WHO GAVE YOU PERMISSION TO OPEN THIS?!

YIKES!

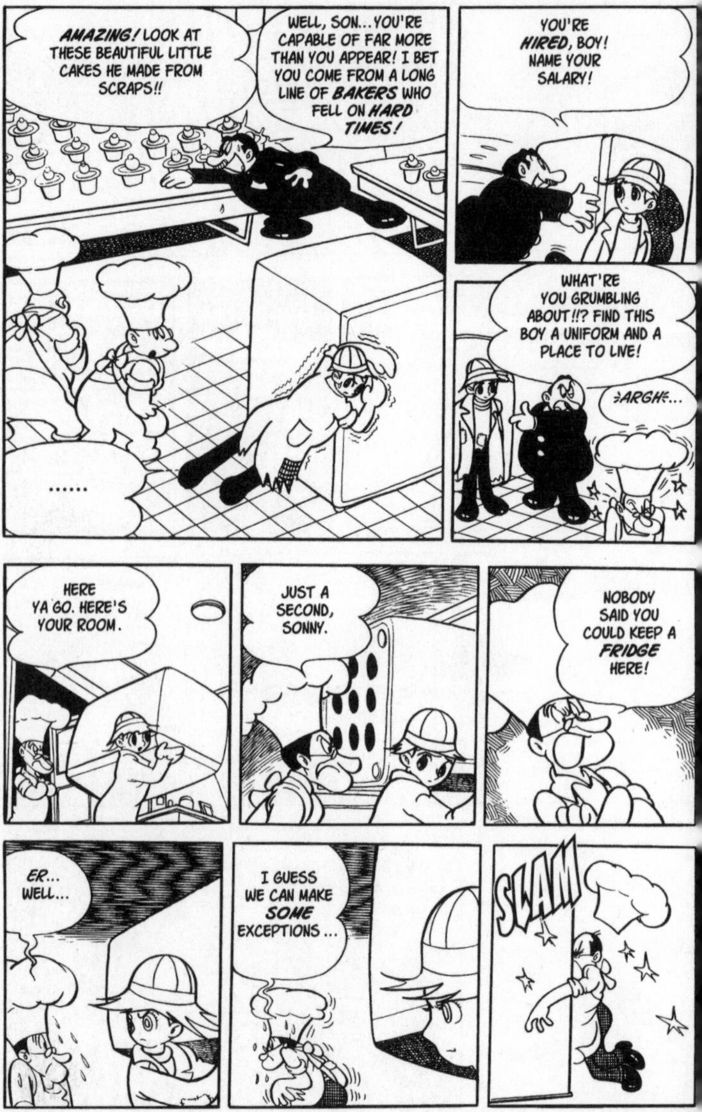
AMAZING! LOOK AT THESE BEAUTIFUL LITTLE CAKES HE MADE FROM SCRAPS!!
WELL, SON... YOU'RE CAPABLE OF FAR MORE THAN YOU APPEAR! I BET YOU COME FROM A LONG LINE OF BAKERS WHO FELL ON HARD TIMES!
......
YOU'RE HIRED, BOY! NAME YOUR SALARY!
WHAT'RE YOU GRUMBLING ABOUT!!? FIND THIS BOY A UNIFORM AND A PLACE TO LIVE!
ARGH...
HERE YA GO. HERE'S YOUR ROOM.
JUST A SECOND, SONNY.
NOBODY SAID YOU COULD KEEP A FRIDGE HERE!
ER... WELL...
I GUESS WE CAN MAKE SOME EXCEPTIONS...
SLAM

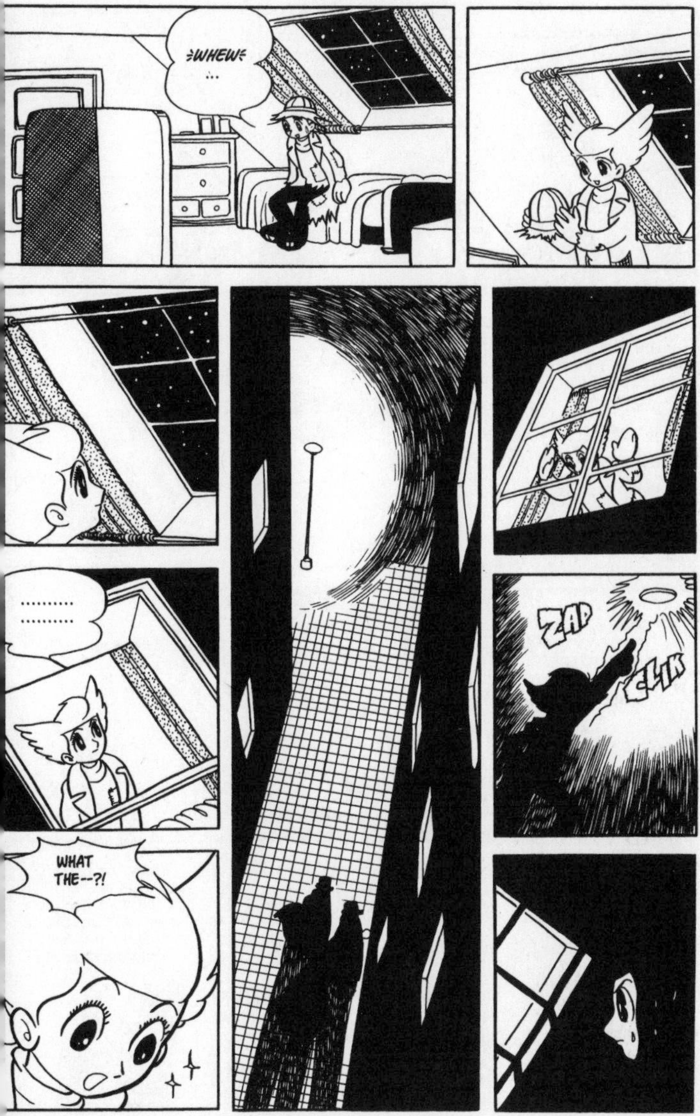
WHEW
...
....
....
WHAT THE--?!
ZAP
CLIK

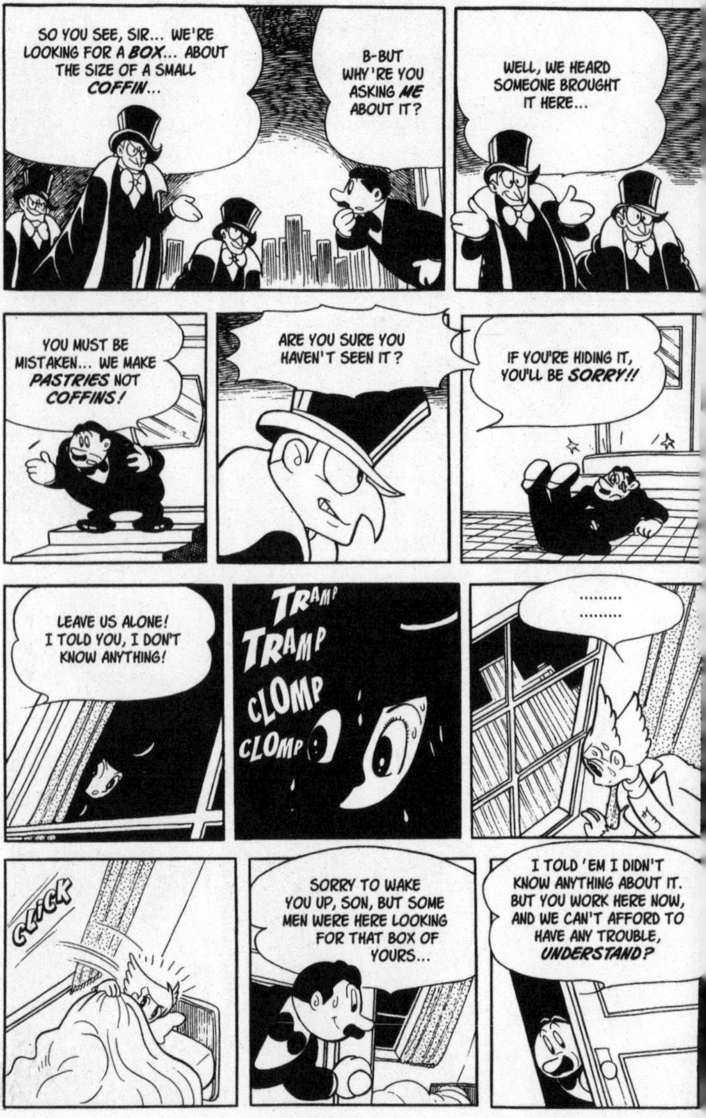
SO YOU SEE, SIR... WE'RE LOOKING FOR A BOX... ABOUT THE SIZE OF A SMALL COFFIN...
B-BUT WHY'RE YOU ASKING ME ABOUT IT?
WELL, WE HEARD SOMEONE BROUGHT IT HERE...
YOU MUST BE MISTAKEN... WE MAKE PASTRIES NOT COFFINS!
ARE YOU SURE YOU HAVEN'T SEEN IT?
IF YOU'RE HIDING IT, YOU'LL BE SORRY!!
LEAVE US ALONE! I TOLD YOU, I DON'T KNOW ANYTHING!
TRAMP
TRAMP
CLOMP
CLOMP
....
....
CLICK
SORRY TO WAKE YOU UP, SON, BUT SOME MEN WERE HERE LOOKING FOR THAT BOX OF YOURS...
I TOLD 'EM I DIDN'T KNOW ANYTHING ABOUT IT. BUT YOU WORK HERE NOW, AND WE CAN'T AFFORD TO HAVE ANY TROUBLE, UNDERSTAND?

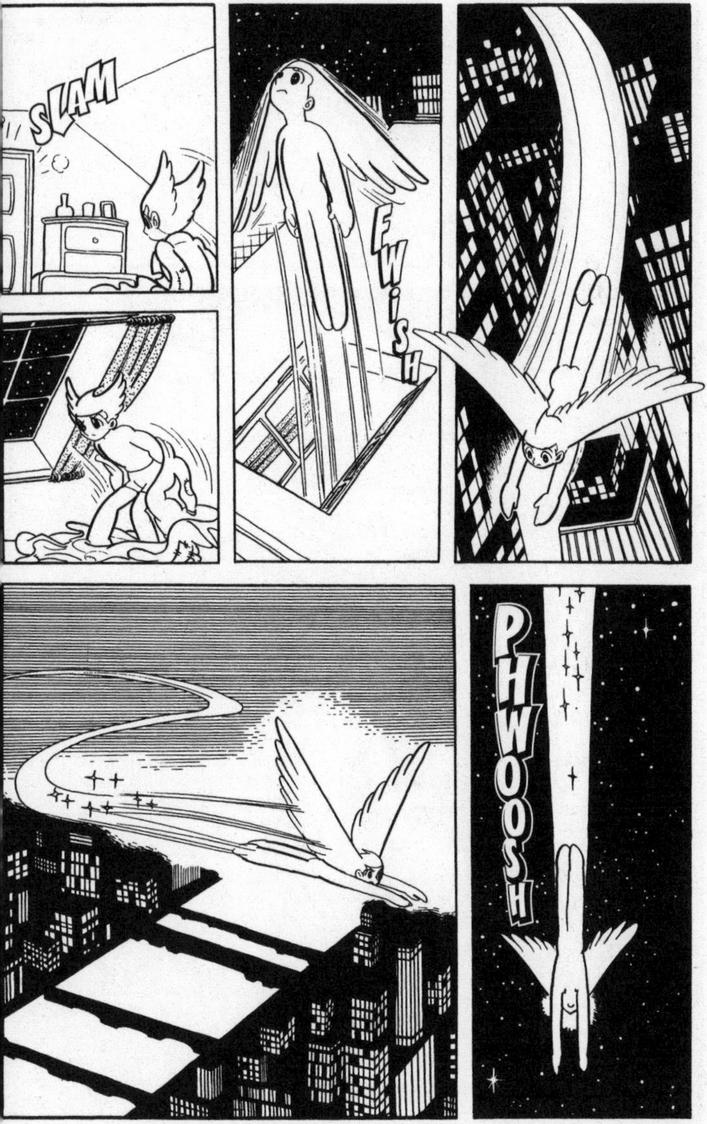

SLAM
FWISH
PHWOOSH

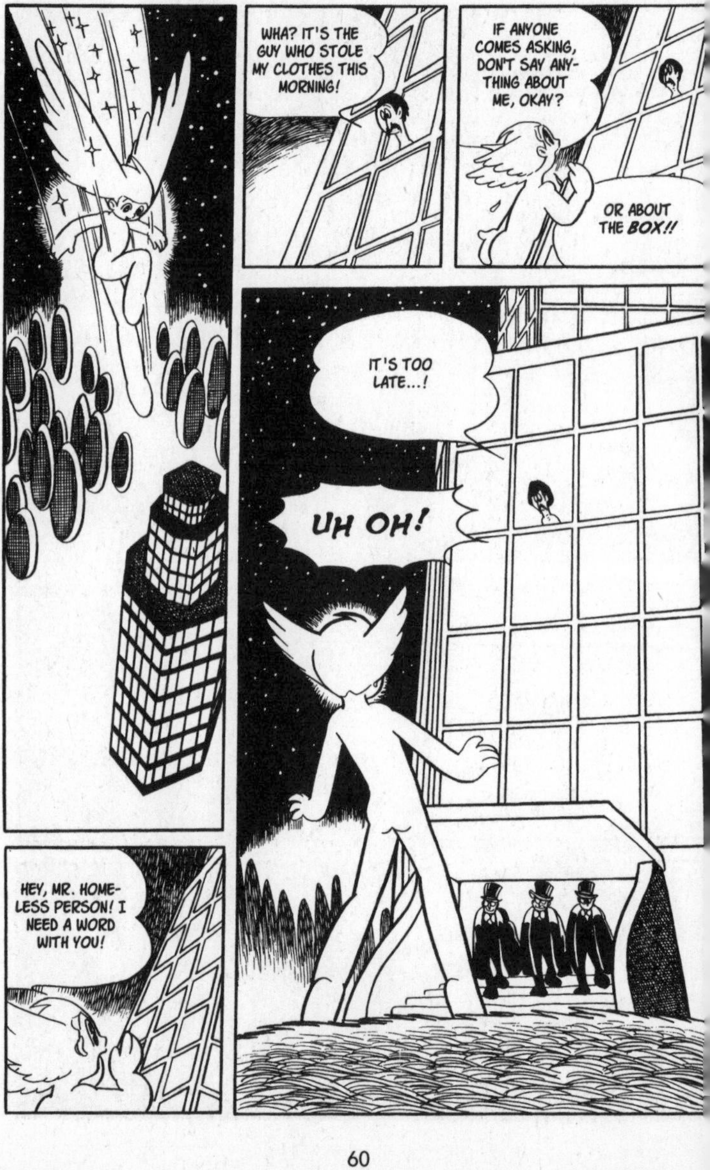
WHA? IT'S THE GUY WHO STOLE MY CLOTHES THIS MORNING!
IF ANYONE COMES ASKING, DON'T SAY ANYTHING ABOUT ME, OKAY?
OR ABOUT THE *BOX!!*
HEY, MR. HOMELESS PERSON! I NEED A WORD WITH YOU!
IT'S TOO LATE...!
UH OH!

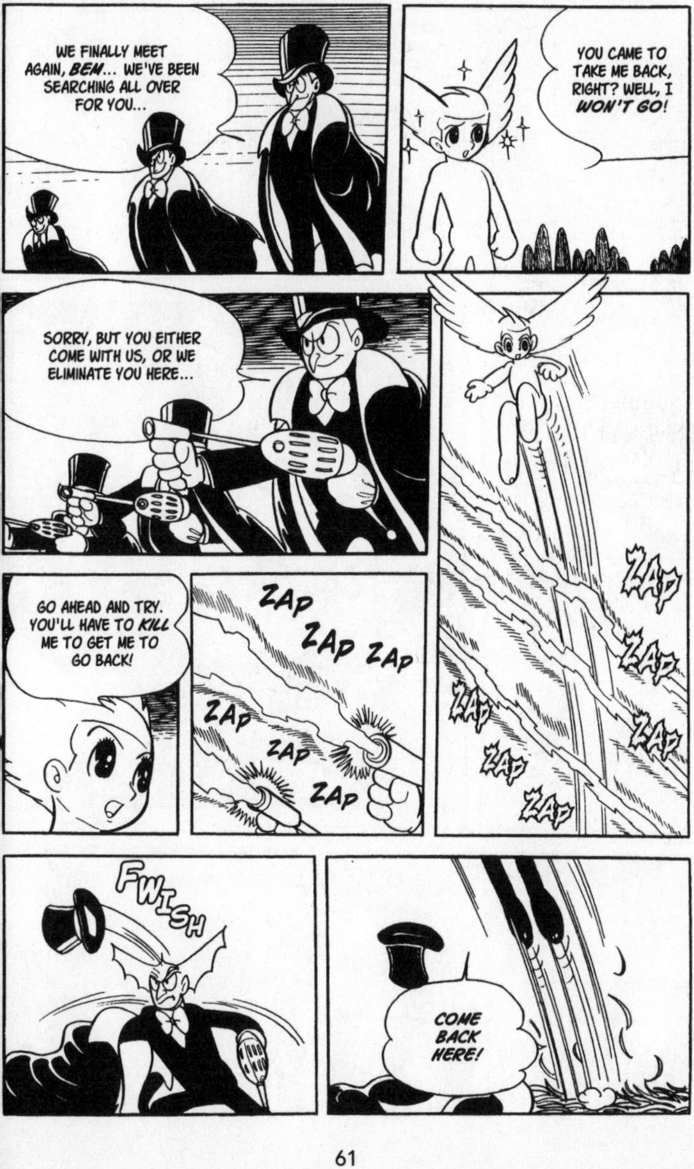
WE FINALLY MEET AGAIN, BEM... WE'VE BEEN SEARCHING ALL OVER FOR YOU...
YOU CAME TO TAKE ME BACK, RIGHT? WELL, I WON'T GO!
SORRY, BUT YOU EITHER COME WITH US, OR WE ELIMINATE YOU HERE...
GO AHEAD AND TRY. YOU'LL HAVE TO KILL ME TO GET ME TO GO BACK!
ZAP
ZAP ZAP
ZAP
ZAP
ZAP
ZAP
ZAP
ZAP
ZAP
ZAP
ZAP
ZAP
FWISH
COME BACK HERE!

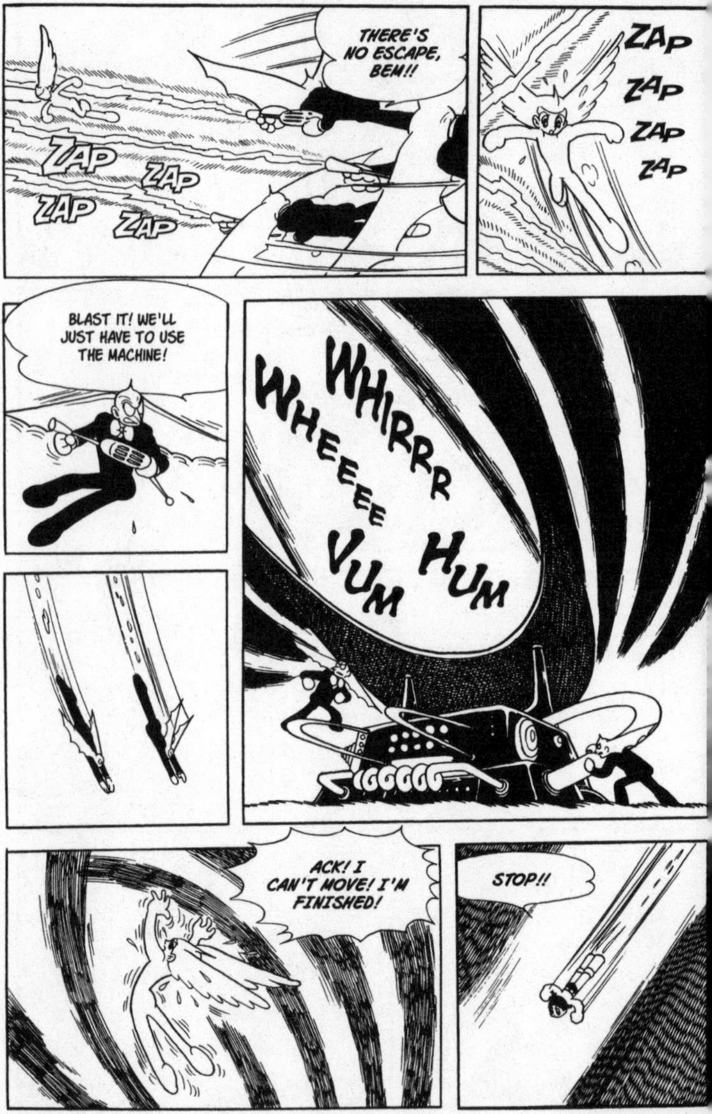
THERE'S NO ESCAPE, BEM!!
ZAP
ZAP
ZAP
ZAP
ZAP
ZAP
ZAP
ZAP
BLAST IT! WE'LL JUST HAVE TO USE THE MACHINE!
WHIRRRR
WHEEEEE
HUM
VUM
ACK! I CAN'T MOVE! I'M FINISHED!
STOP!!

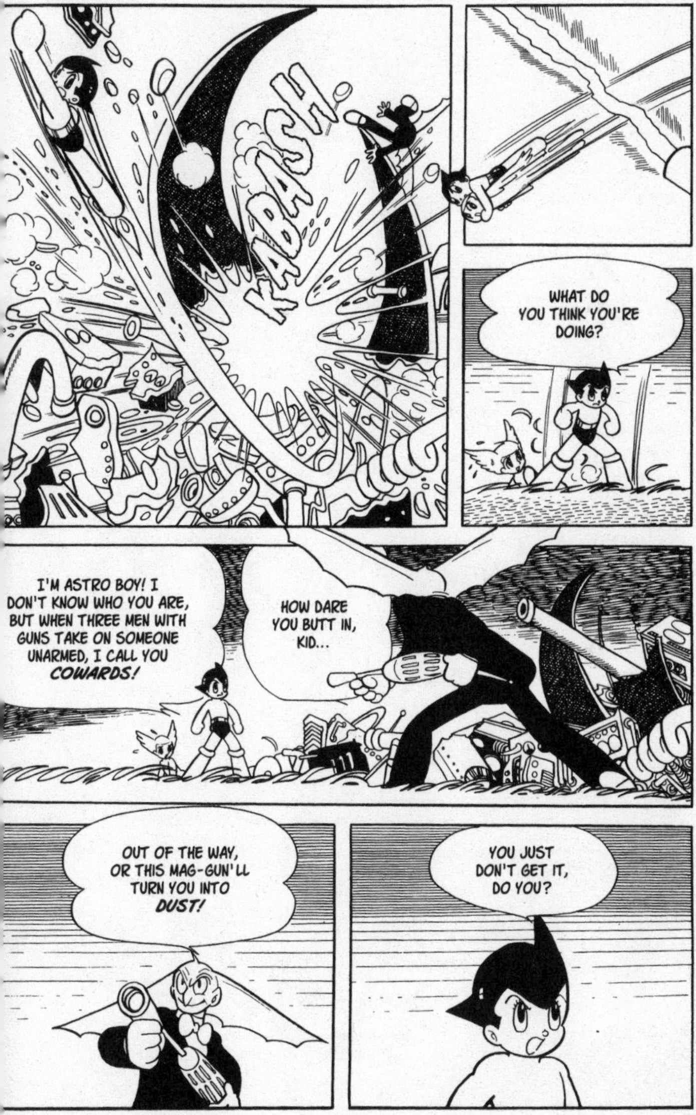
KABASH
WHAT DO YOU THINK YOU'RE DOING?
I'M ASTRO BOY! I DON'T KNOW WHO YOU ARE, BUT WHEN THREE MEN WITH GUNS TAKE ON SOMEONE UNARMED, I CALL YOU COWARDS!
HOW DARE YOU BUTT IN, KID...
OUT OF THE WAY, OR THIS MAG-GUN'LL TURN YOU INTO DUST!
YOU JUST DON'T GET IT, DO YOU?

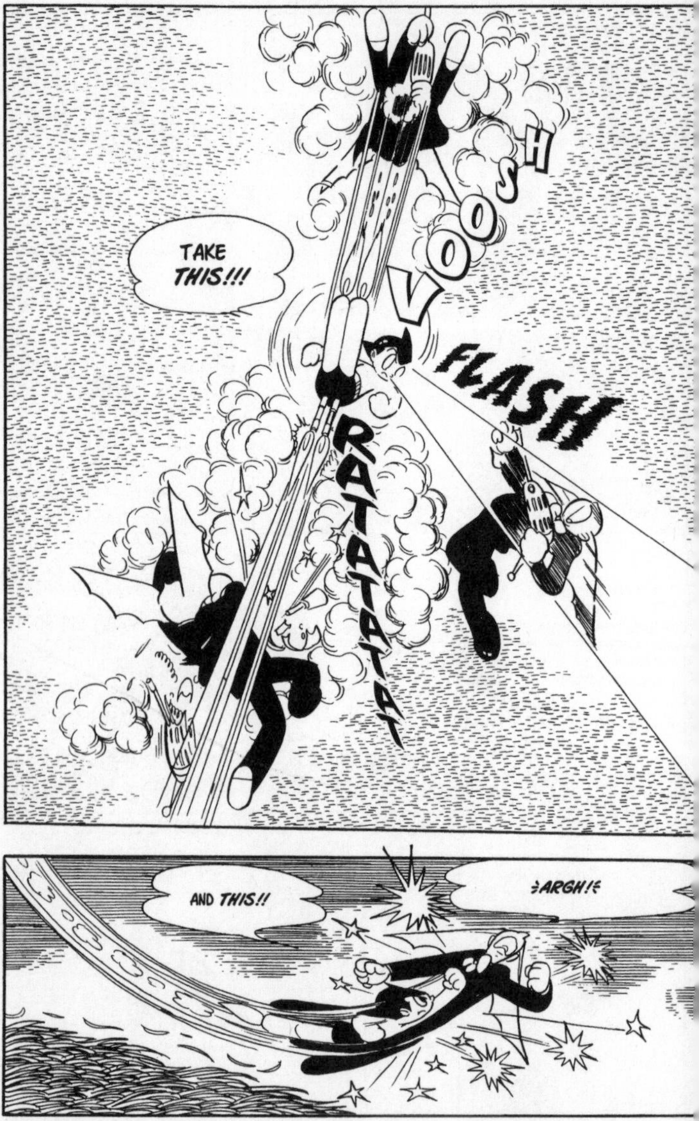

VOOSH
TAKE THIS!!!
FLASH
RATATATAT
AND THIS!!
ARGH!

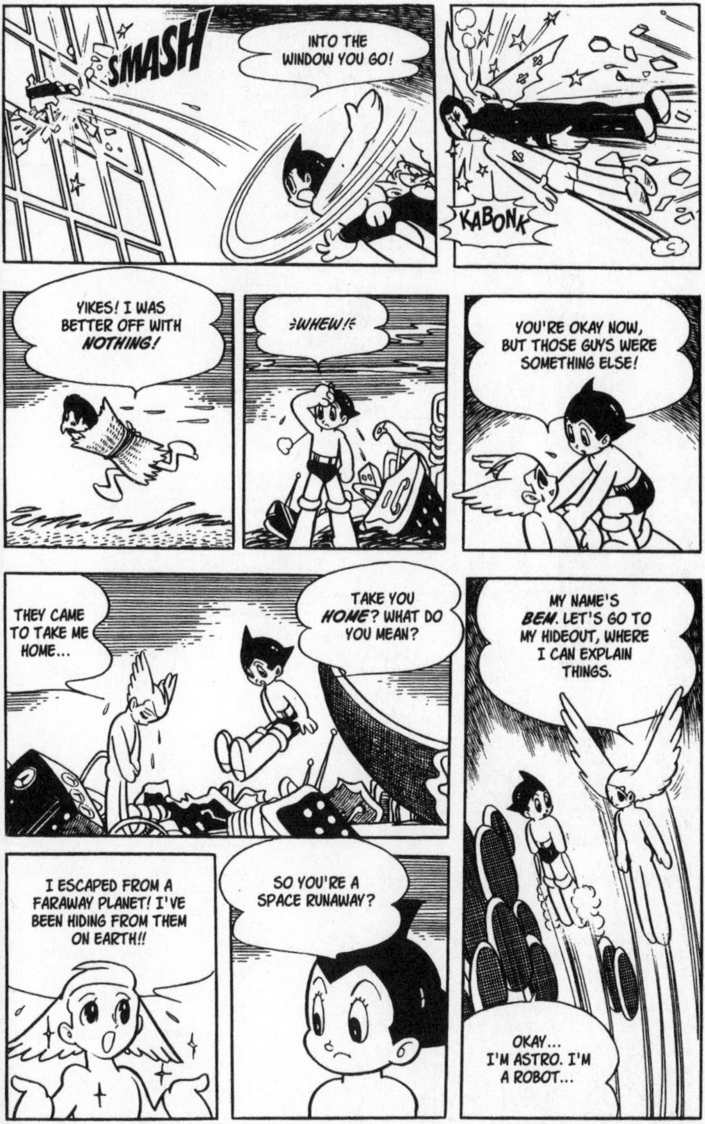
SMASH
INTO THE WINDOW YOU GO!
KABONK
YIKES! I WAS BETTER OFF WITH ***NOTHING!***
≶WHEW!≶
YOU'RE OKAY NOW, BUT THOSE GUYS WERE SOMETHING ELSE!
THEY CAME TO TAKE ME HOME...
TAKE YOU ***HOME***? WHAT DO YOU MEAN?
I ESCAPED FROM A FARAWAY PLANET! I'VE BEEN HIDING FROM THEM ON EARTH!!
SO YOU'RE A SPACE RUNAWAY?
MY NAME'S ***BEM***. LET'S GO TO MY HIDEOUT, WHERE I CAN EXPLAIN THINGS.
OKAY... I'M ASTRO. I'M A ROBOT...

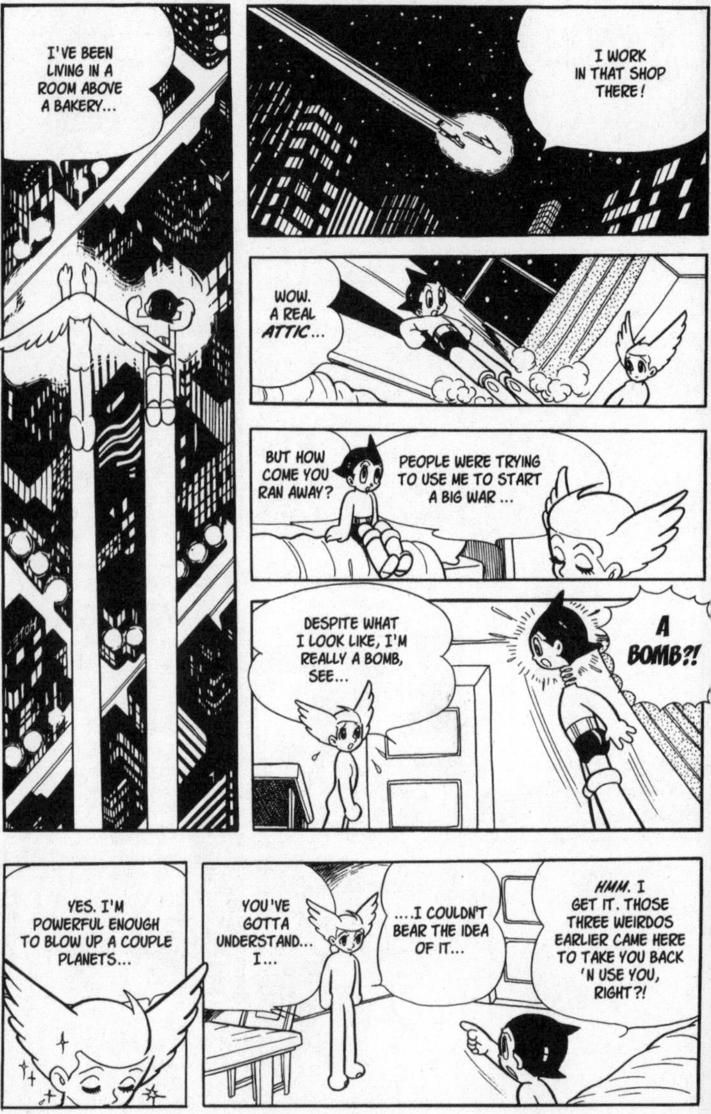
I'VE BEEN LIVING IN A ROOM ABOVE A BAKERY...
I WORK IN THAT SHOP THERE!
WOW. A REAL *ATTIC*...
BUT HOW COME YOU RAN AWAY?
PEOPLE WERE TRYING TO USE ME TO START A BIG WAR ...
DESPITE WHAT I LOOK LIKE, I'M REALLY A BOMB, SEE...
A BOMB?!
YES. I'M POWERFUL ENOUGH TO BLOW UP A COUPLE PLANETS...
YOU'VE GOTTA UNDERSTAND... I...
....I COULDN'T BEAR THE IDEA OF IT...
HMM. I GET IT. THOSE THREE WEIRDOS EARLIER CAME HERE TO TAKE YOU BACK 'N USE YOU, RIGHT?!

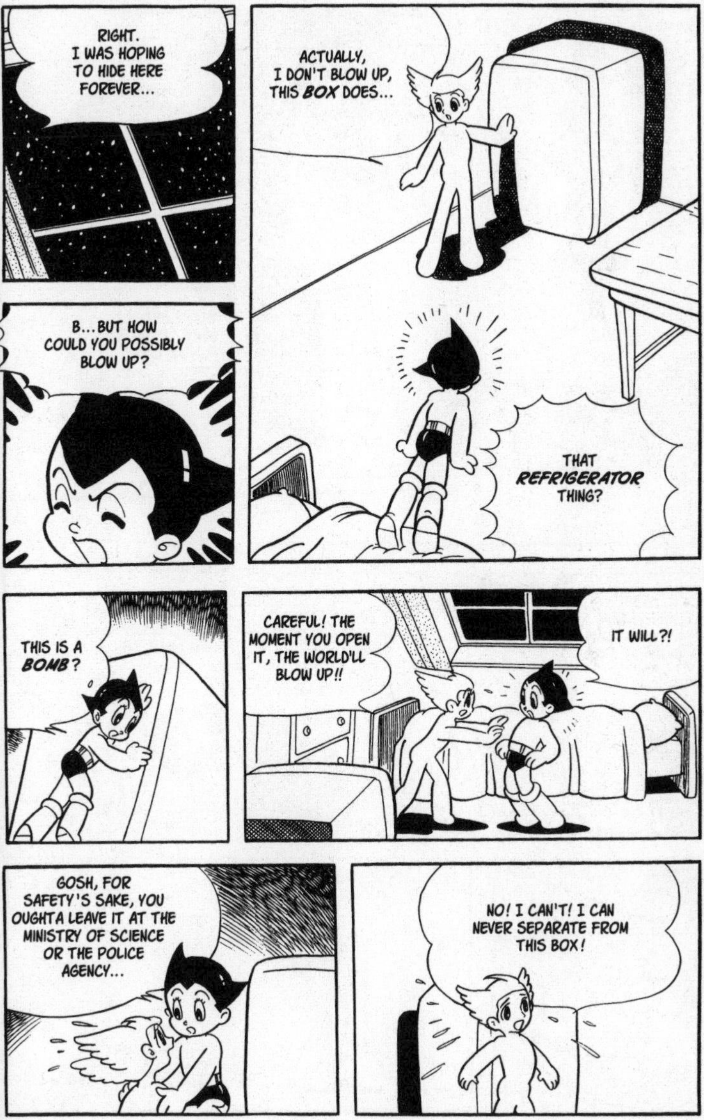
RIGHT. I WAS HOPING TO HIDE HERE FOREVER...
ACTUALLY, I DON'T BLOW UP, THIS *BOX* DOES...
B...BUT HOW COULD YOU POSSIBLY BLOW UP?
THAT *REFRIGERATOR* THING?
THIS IS A *BOMB*?
CAREFUL! THE MOMENT YOU OPEN IT, THE WORLD'LL BLOW UP!!
IT WILL?!
GOSH, FOR SAFETY'S SAKE, YOU OUGHTA LEAVE IT AT THE MINISTRY OF SCIENCE OR THE POLICE AGENCY...
NO! I CAN'T! I CAN NEVER SEPARATE FROM THIS BOX!

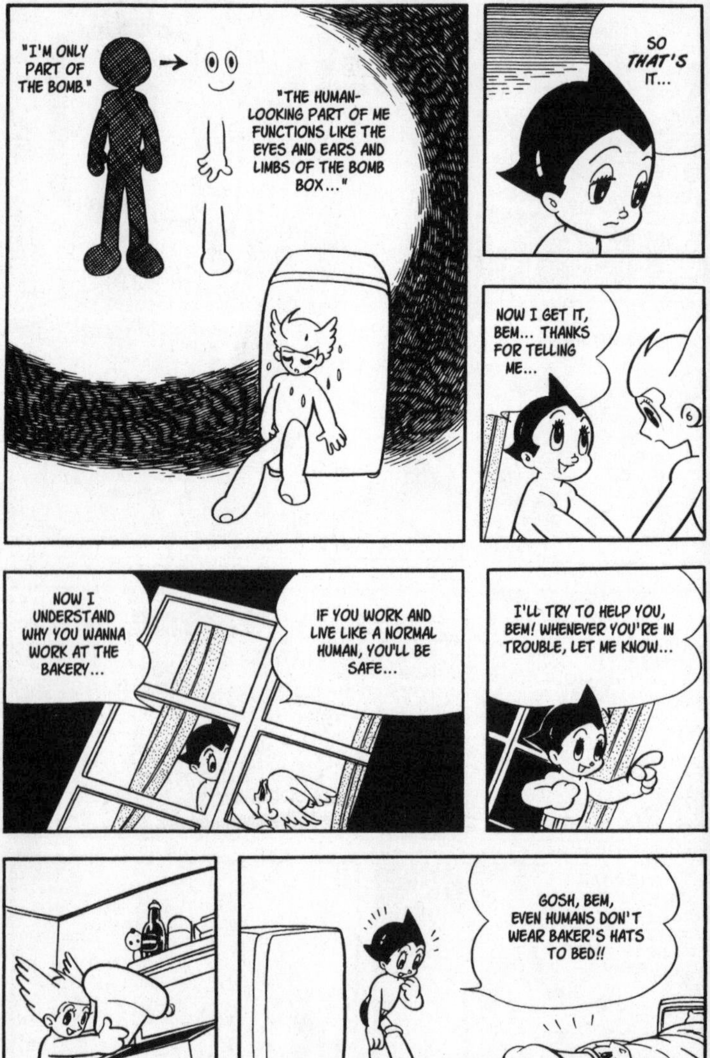
"I'M ONLY PART OF THE BOMB."
"THE HUMAN-LOOKING PART OF ME FUNCTIONS LIKE THE EYES AND EARS AND LIMBS OF THE BOMB BOX..."
SO *THAT'S* IT...
NOW I GET IT, BEM... THANKS FOR TELLING ME...
NOW I UNDERSTAND WHY YOU WANNA WORK AT THE BAKERY...
IF YOU WORK AND LIVE LIKE A NORMAL HUMAN, YOU'LL BE SAFE...
I'LL TRY TO HELP YOU, BEM! WHENEVER YOU'RE IN TROUBLE, LET ME KNOW...
GOSH, BEM, EVEN HUMANS DON'T WEAR BAKER'S HATS TO BED!!

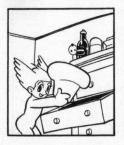

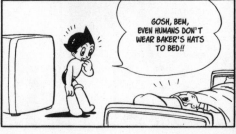

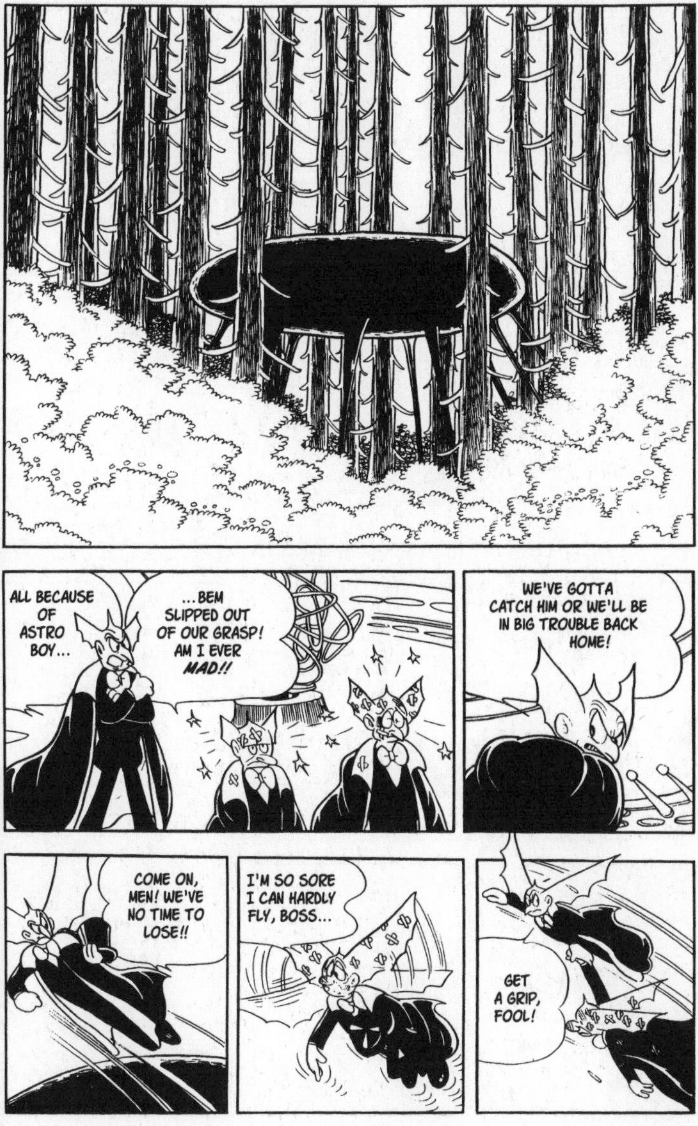
ALL BECAUSE OF ASTRO BOY...
...BEM SLIPPED OUT OF OUR GRASP! AM I EVER *MAD!!*
WE'VE GOTTA CATCH HIM OR WE'LL BE IN BIG TROUBLE BACK HOME!
COME ON, MEN! WE'VE NO TIME TO LOSE!!
I'M SO SORE I CAN HARDLY FLY, BOSS...
GET A GRIP, FOOL!

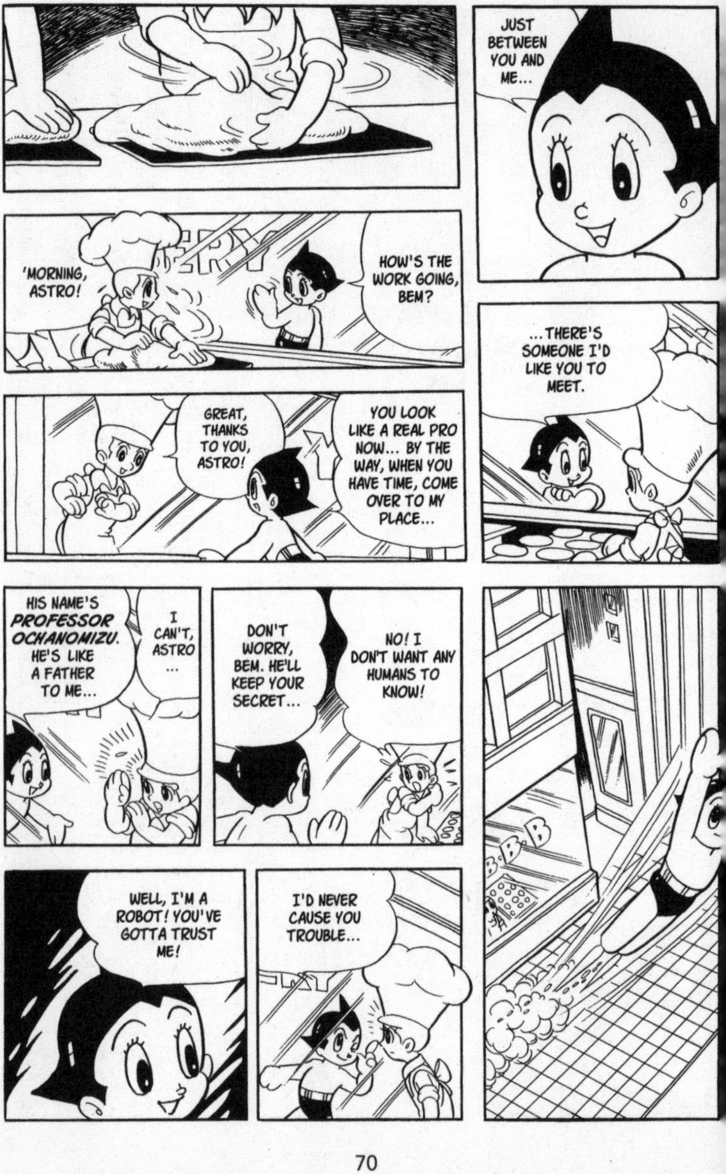
'MORNING, ASTRO!
HOW'S THE WORK GOING, BEM?
GREAT, THANKS TO YOU, ASTRO!
YOU LOOK LIKE A REAL PRO NOW... BY THE WAY, WHEN YOU HAVE TIME, COME OVER TO MY PLACE...
JUST BETWEEN YOU AND ME...
...THERE'S SOMEONE I'D LIKE YOU TO MEET.
HIS NAME'S *PROFESSOR OCHANOMIZU*. HE'S LIKE A FATHER TO ME...
I CAN'T, ASTRO ...
DON'T WORRY, BEM. HE'LL KEEP YOUR SECRET...
NO! I DON'T WANT ANY HUMANS TO KNOW!
WELL, I'M A ROBOT! YOU'VE GOTTA TRUST ME!
I'D NEVER CAUSE YOU TROUBLE...

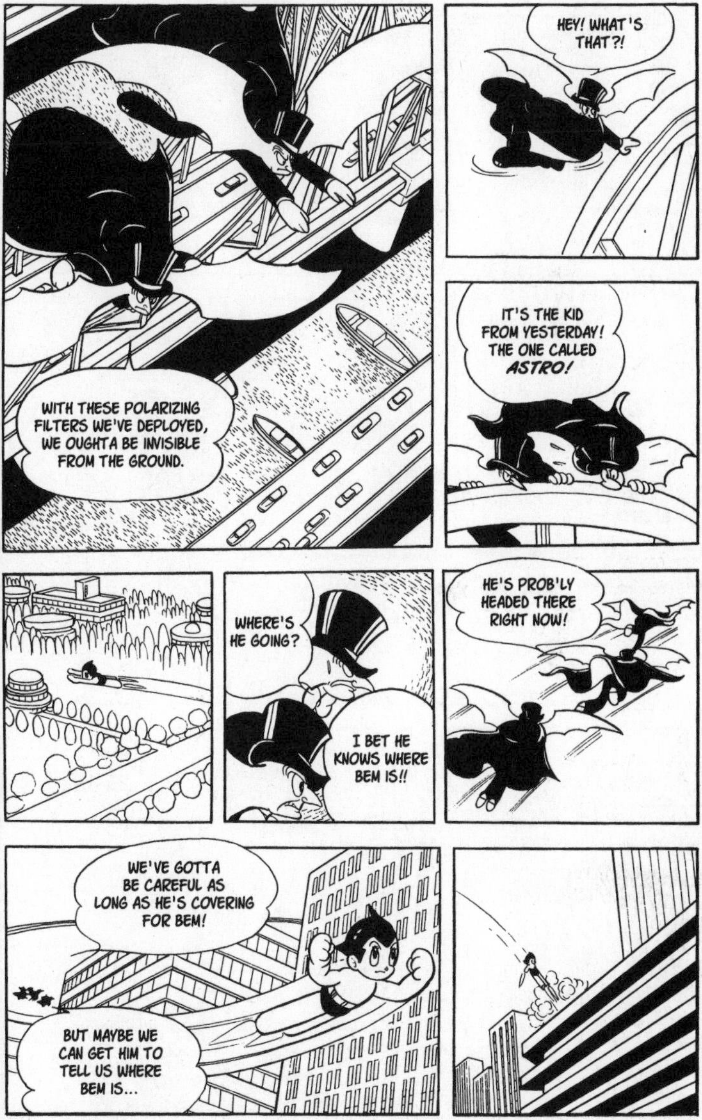
WITH THESE POLARIZING FILTERS WE'VE DEPLOYED, WE OUGHTA BE INVISIBLE FROM THE GROUND.
HEY! WHAT'S THAT?!
IT'S THE KID FROM YESTERDAY! THE ONE CALLED *ASTRO!*
WHERE'S HE GOING?
I BET HE KNOWS WHERE BEM IS!!
HE'S PROB'LY HEADED THERE RIGHT NOW!
WE'VE GOTTA BE CAREFUL AS LONG AS HE'S COVERING FOR BEM!
BUT MAYBE WE CAN GET HIM TO TELL US WHERE BEM IS...

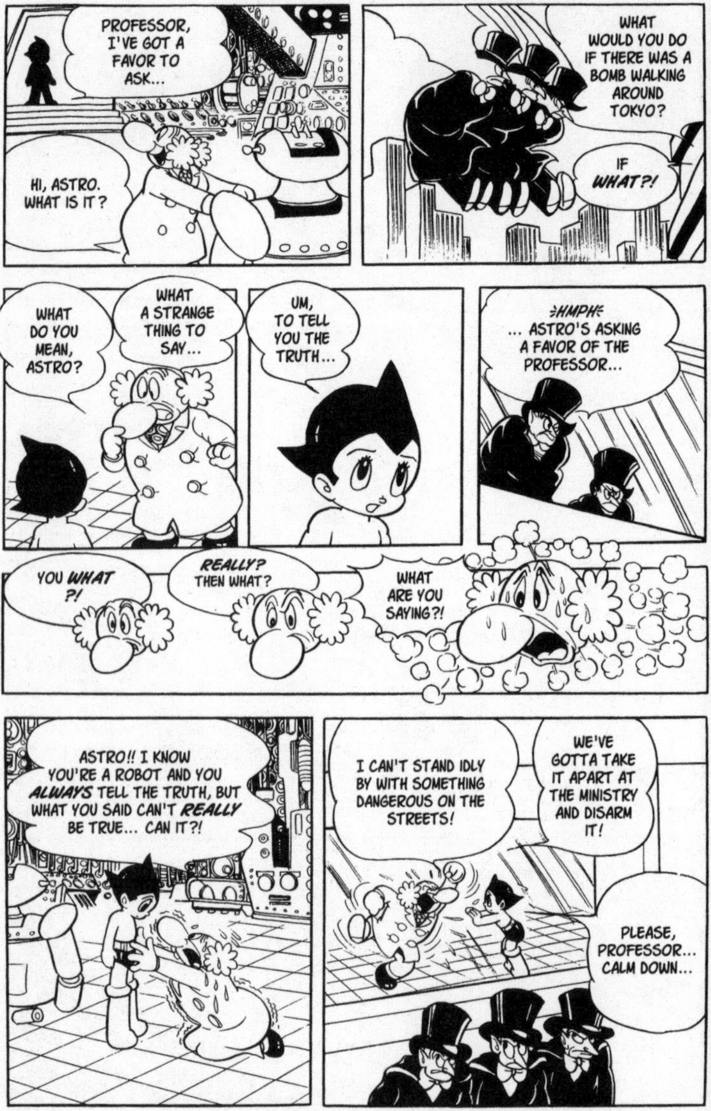
PROFESSOR, I'VE GOT A FAVOR TO ASK...
HI, ASTRO. WHAT IS IT?
WHAT WOULD YOU DO IF THERE WAS A BOMB WALKING AROUND TOKYO?
IF WHAT?!
WHAT DO YOU MEAN, ASTRO?
WHAT A STRANGE THING TO SAY...
UM, TO TELL YOU THE TRUTH...
HMPH
... ASTRO'S ASKING A FAVOR OF THE PROFESSOR...
YOU WHAT ?!
REALLY? THEN WHAT?
WHAT ARE YOU SAYING?!
ASTRO!! I KNOW YOU'RE A ROBOT AND YOU ALWAYS TELL THE TRUTH, BUT WHAT YOU SAID CAN'T REALLY BE TRUE... CAN IT?!
I CAN'T STAND IDLY BY WITH SOMETHING DANGEROUS ON THE STREETS!
WE'VE GOTTA TAKE IT APART AT THE MINISTRY AND DISARM IT!
PLEASE, PROFESSOR... CALM DOWN...

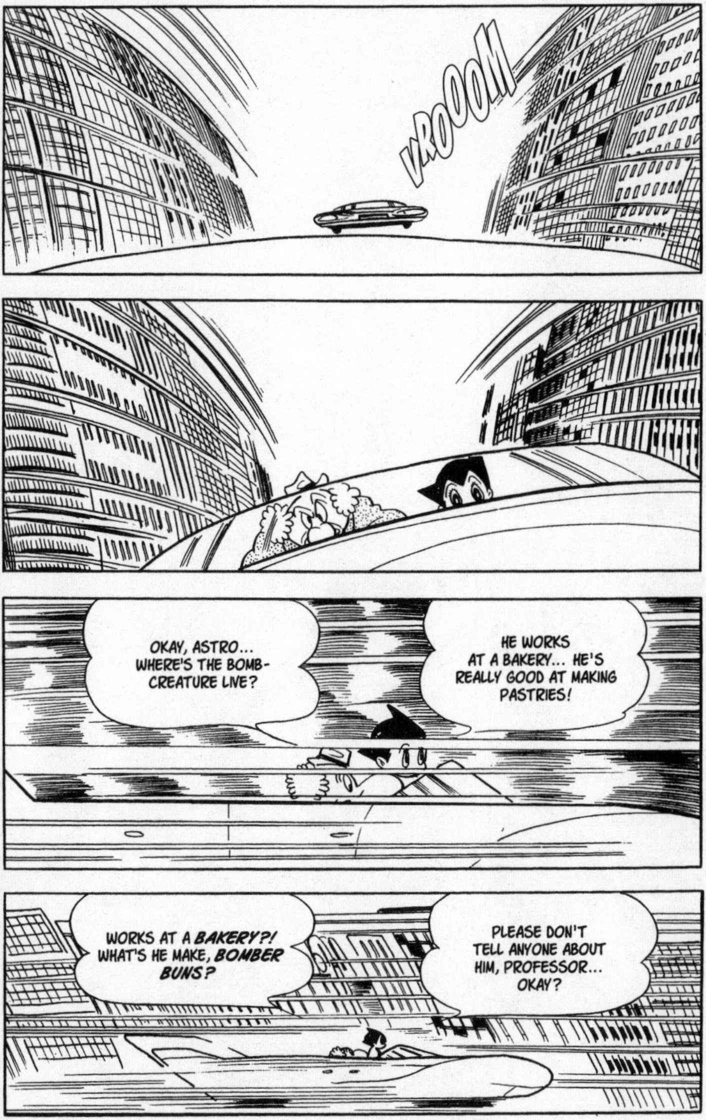
VROOOM
OKAY, ASTRO... WHERE'S THE BOMB-CREATURE LIVE?
HE WORKS AT A BAKERY... HE'S REALLY GOOD AT MAKING PASTRIES!
WORKS AT A *BAKERY?!* WHAT'S HE MAKE, *BOMBER BUNS?*
PLEASE DON'T TELL ANYONE ABOUT HIM, PROFESSOR... OKAY?

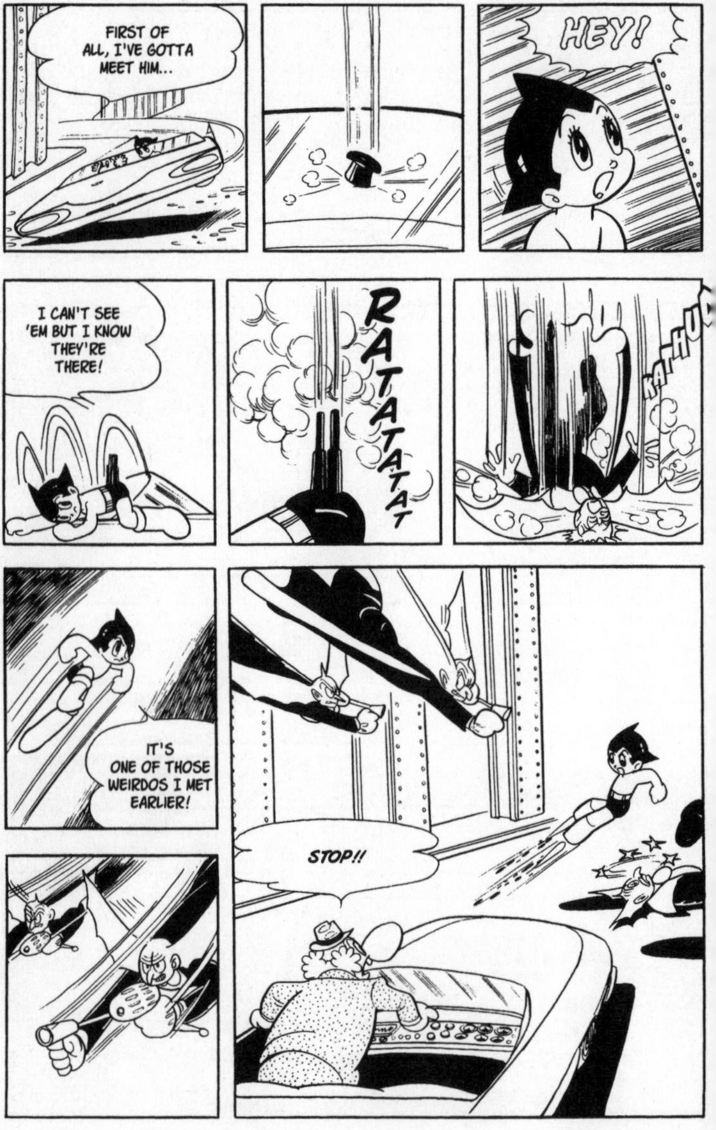

FIRST OF ALL, I'VE GOTTA MEET HIM...
HEY!
I CAN'T SEE 'EM BUT I KNOW THEY'RE THERE!
RATATATATAT
KA-THUD
IT'S ONE OF THOSE WEIRDOS I MET EARLIER!
STOP!!

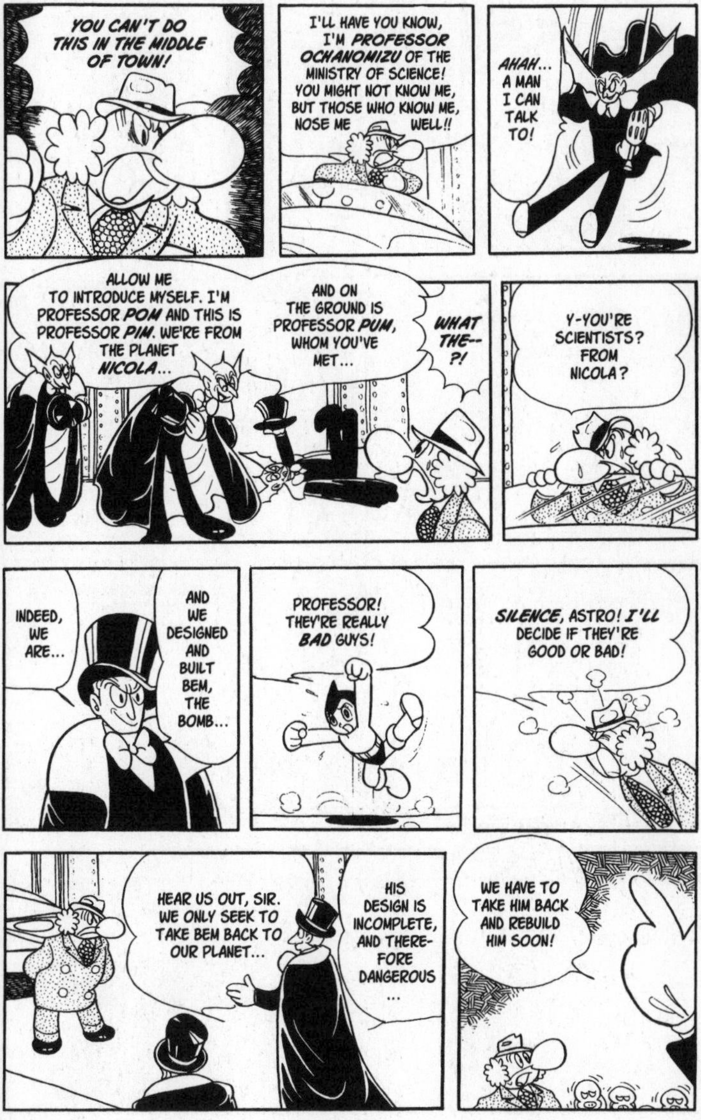

YOU CAN'T DO THIS IN THE MIDDLE OF TOWN!
I'LL HAVE YOU KNOW, I'M PROFESSOR OCHANOMIZU OF THE MINISTRY OF SCIENCE! YOU MIGHT NOT KNOW ME, BUT THOSE WHO KNOW ME, NOSE ME WELL!!
AHAH... A MAN I CAN TALK TO!
ALLOW ME TO INTRODUCE MYSELF. I'M PROFESSOR POM AND THIS IS PROFESSOR PIM. WE'RE FROM THE PLANET NICOLA...
AND ON THE GROUND IS PROFESSOR PUM, WHOM YOU'VE MET...
WHAT THE--?!
Y-YOU'RE SCIENTISTS? FROM NICOLA?
INDEED, WE ARE...
AND WE DESIGNED AND BUILT BEM, THE BOMB...
PROFESSOR! THEY'RE REALLY BAD GUYS!
SILENCE, ASTRO! I'LL DECIDE IF THEY'RE GOOD OR BAD!
HEAR US OUT, SIR. WE ONLY SEEK TO TAKE BEM BACK TO OUR PLANET...
HIS DESIGN IS INCOMPLETE, AND THEREFORE DANGEROUS ...
WE HAVE TO TAKE HIM BACK AND REBUILD HIM SOON!

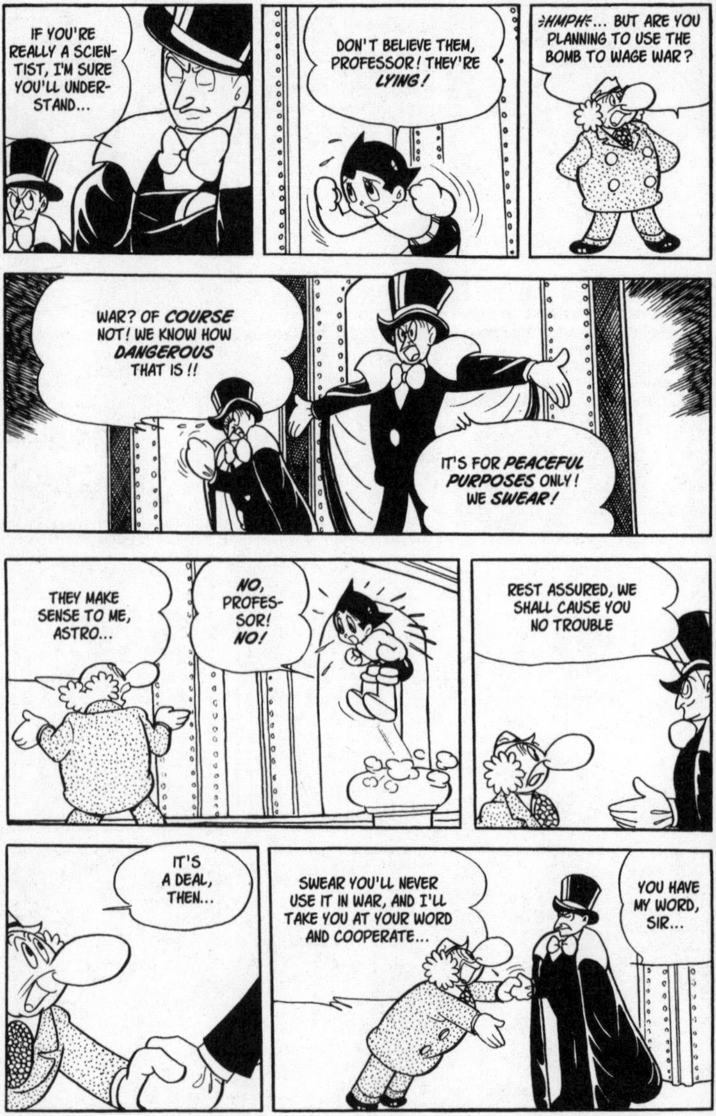
IF YOU'RE REALLY A SCIENTIST, I'M SURE YOU'LL UNDERSTAND...
DON'T BELIEVE THEM, PROFESSOR! THEY'RE *LYING!*
HMPH... BUT ARE YOU PLANNING TO USE THE BOMB TO WAGE WAR?
WAR? OF *COURSE* NOT! WE KNOW HOW *DANGEROUS* THAT IS!!
IT'S FOR *PEACEFUL PURPOSES* ONLY! WE *SWEAR!*
THEY MAKE SENSE TO ME, ASTRO...
NO, PROFESSOR! *NO!*
REST ASSURED, WE SHALL CAUSE YOU NO TROUBLE
IT'S A DEAL, THEN...
SWEAR YOU'LL NEVER USE IT IN WAR, AND I'LL TAKE YOU AT YOUR WORD AND COOPERATE...
YOU HAVE MY WORD, SIR...

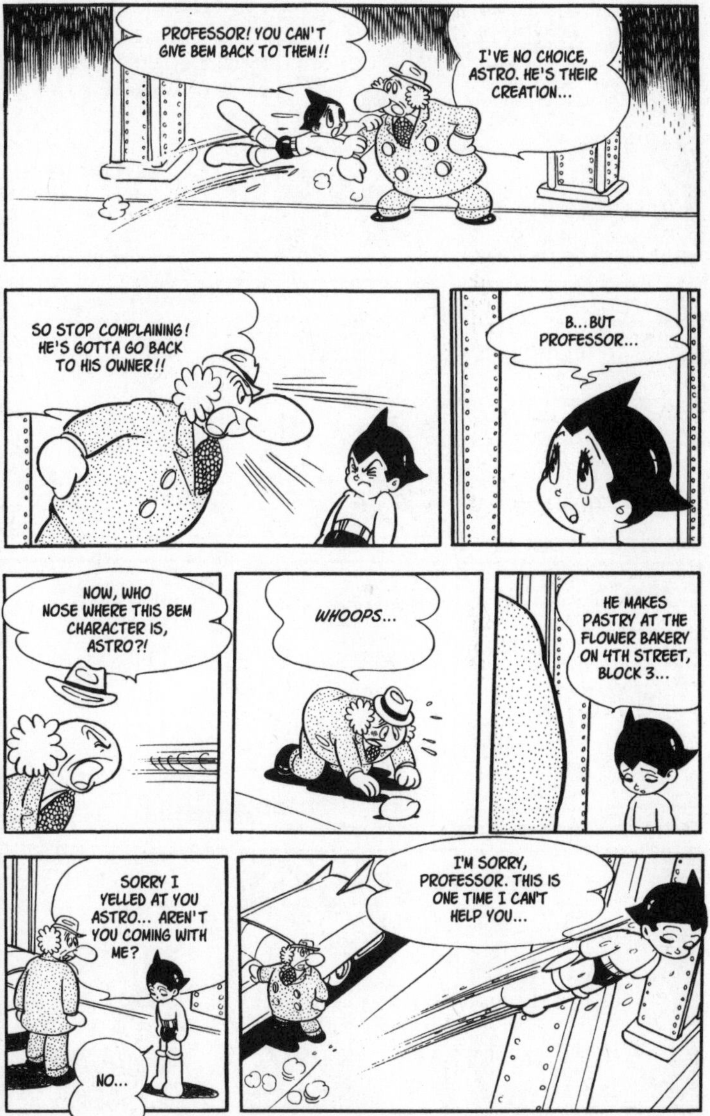
PROFESSOR! YOU CAN'T GIVE BEM BACK TO THEM!!
I'VE NO CHOICE, ASTRO. HE'S THEIR CREATION...
SO STOP COMPLAINING! HE'S GOTTA GO BACK TO HIS OWNER!!
B...BUT PROFESSOR...
NOW, WHO NOSE WHERE THIS BEM CHARACTER IS, ASTRO?!
WHOOPS...
HE MAKES PASTRY AT THE FLOWER BAKERY ON 4TH STREET, BLOCK 3...
SORRY I YELLED AT YOU ASTRO... AREN'T YOU COMING WITH ME?
NO...
I'M SORRY, PROFESSOR. THIS IS ONE TIME I CAN'T HELP YOU...

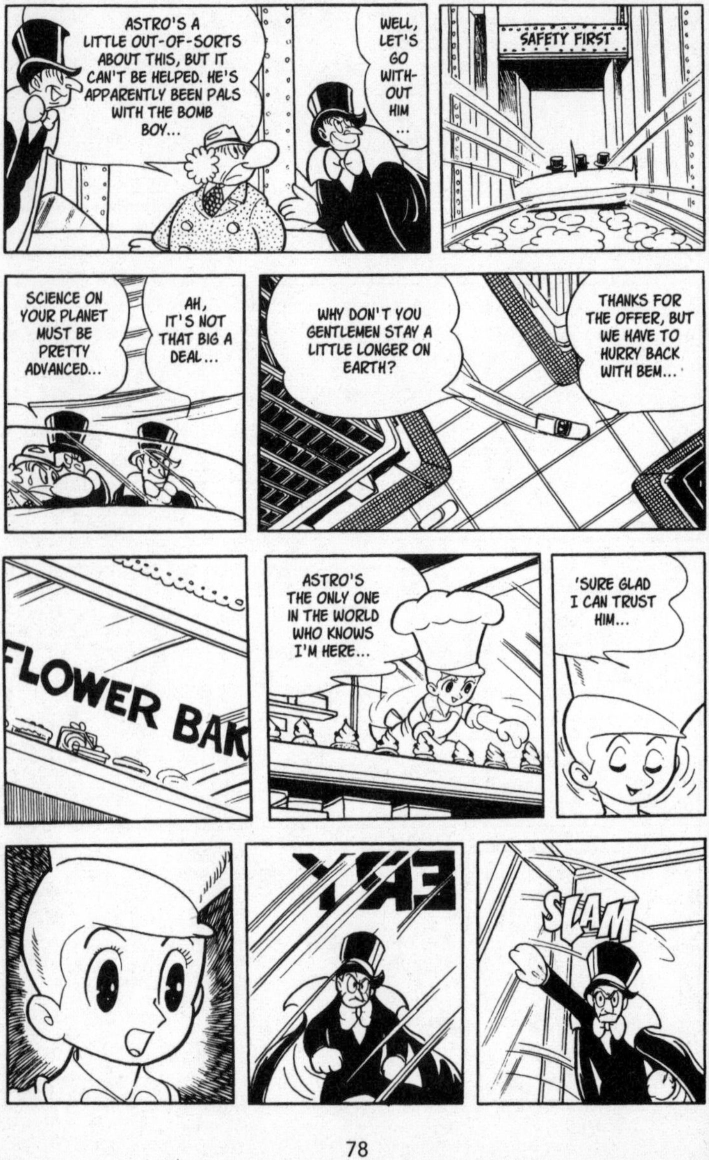
ASTRO'S A LITTLE OUT-OF-SORTS ABOUT THIS, BUT IT CAN'T BE HELPED. HE'S APPARENTLY BEEN PALS WITH THE BOMB BOY...
WELL, LET'S GO WITHOUT HIM ...
SAFETY FIRST
SCIENCE ON YOUR PLANET MUST BE PRETTY ADVANCED...
AH, IT'S NOT THAT BIG A DEAL...
WHY DON'T YOU GENTLEMEN STAY A LITTLE LONGER ON EARTH?
THANKS FOR THE OFFER, BUT WE HAVE TO HURRY BACK WITH BEM...
FLOWER BAK
ASTRO'S THE ONLY ONE IN THE WORLD WHO KNOWS I'M HERE...
'SURE GLAD I CAN TRUST HIM...
SLAM

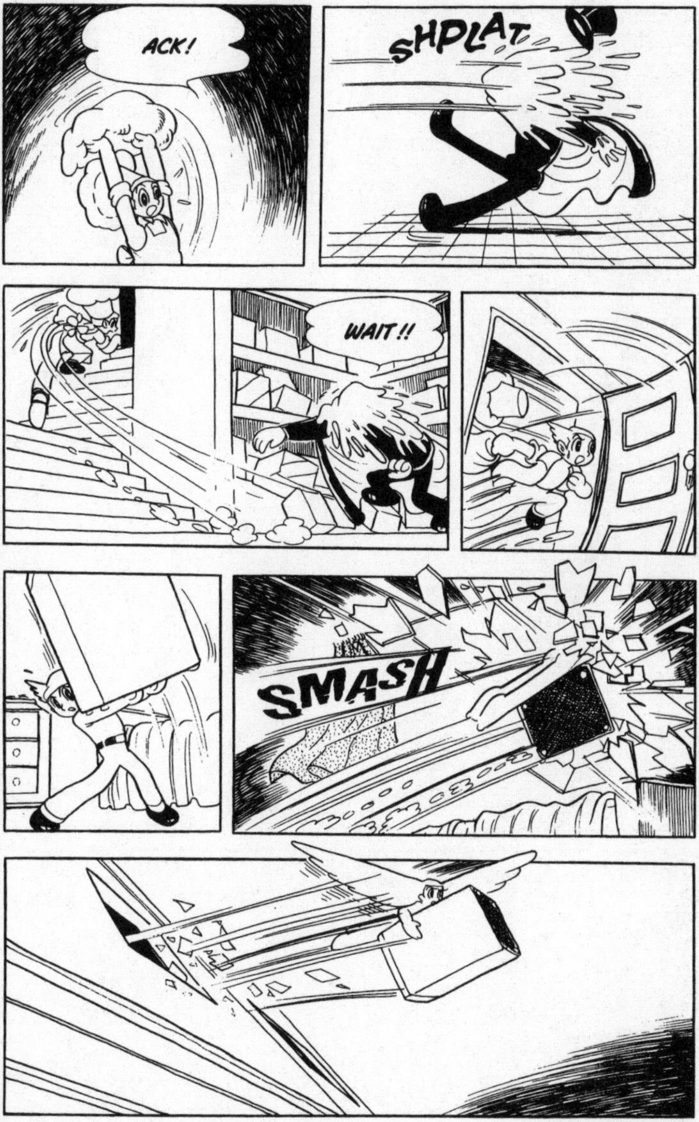
ACK!
SHPLAT
WAIT!!
SMASH

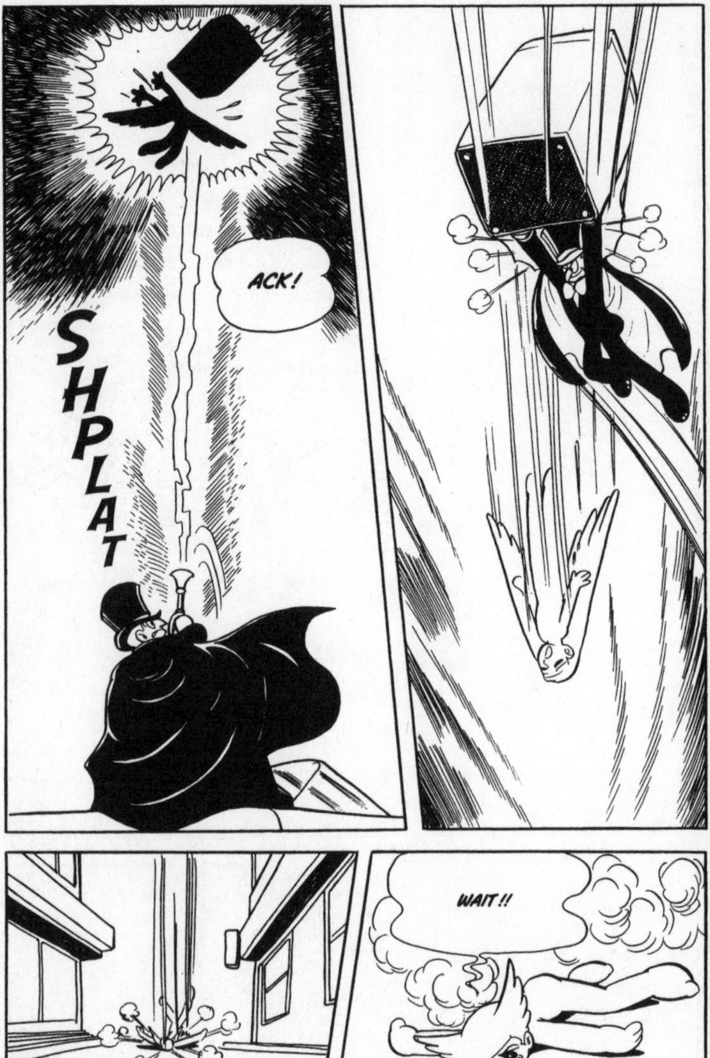
ACK!
SHPLAT
WAIT!!

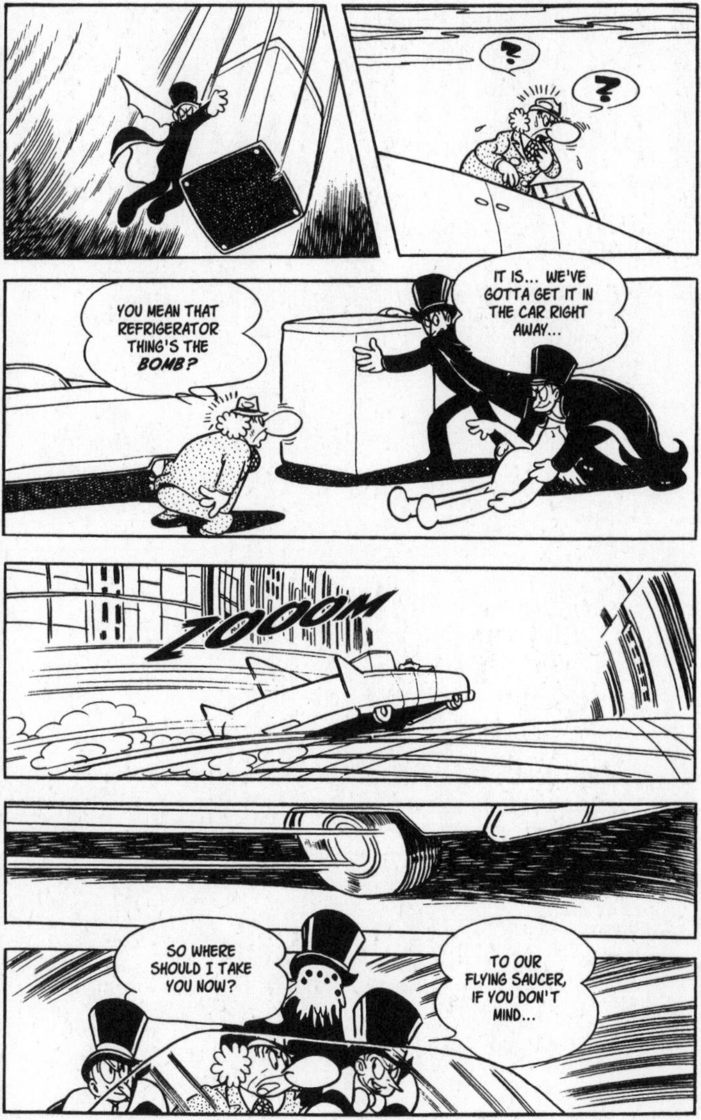
?
?
YOU MEAN THAT REFRIGERATOR THING'S THE *BOMB?*
IT IS... WE'VE GOTTA GET IT IN THE CAR RIGHT AWAY...
ZOOOOM
SO WHERE SHOULD I TAKE YOU NOW?
TO OUR FLYING SAUCER, IF YOU DON'T MIND...

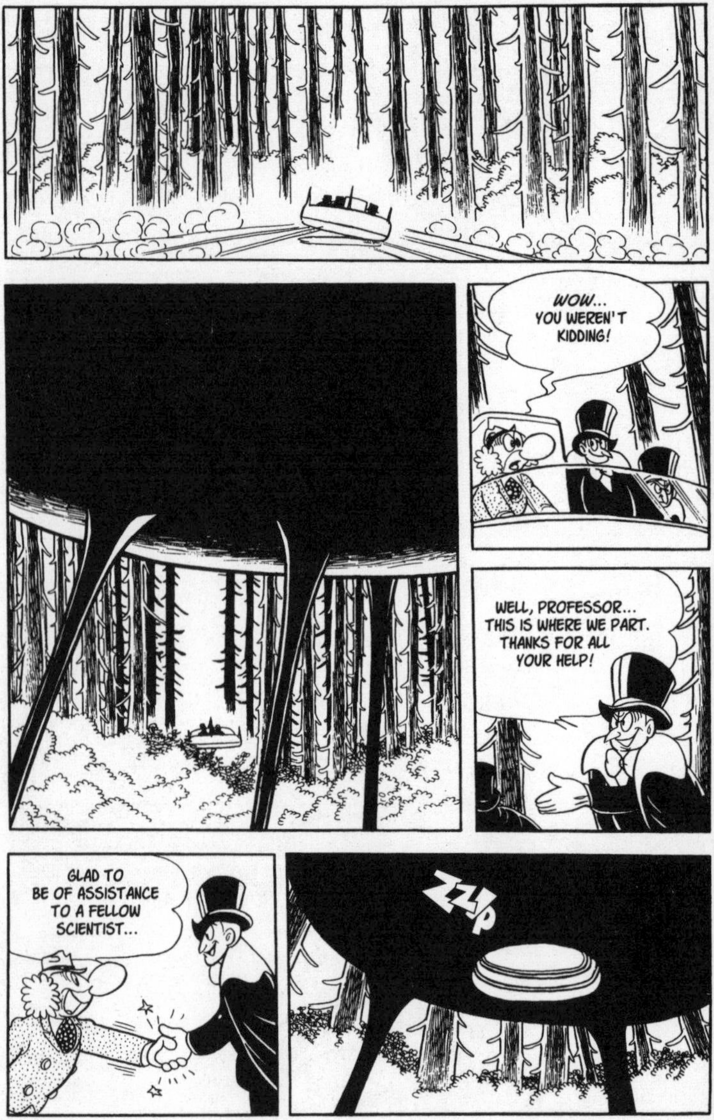
WOW...
YOU WEREN'T KIDDING!
WELL, PROFESSOR... THIS IS WHERE WE PART. THANKS FOR ALL YOUR HELP!
GLAD TO BE OF ASSISTANCE TO A FELLOW SCIENTIST...
ZZIP

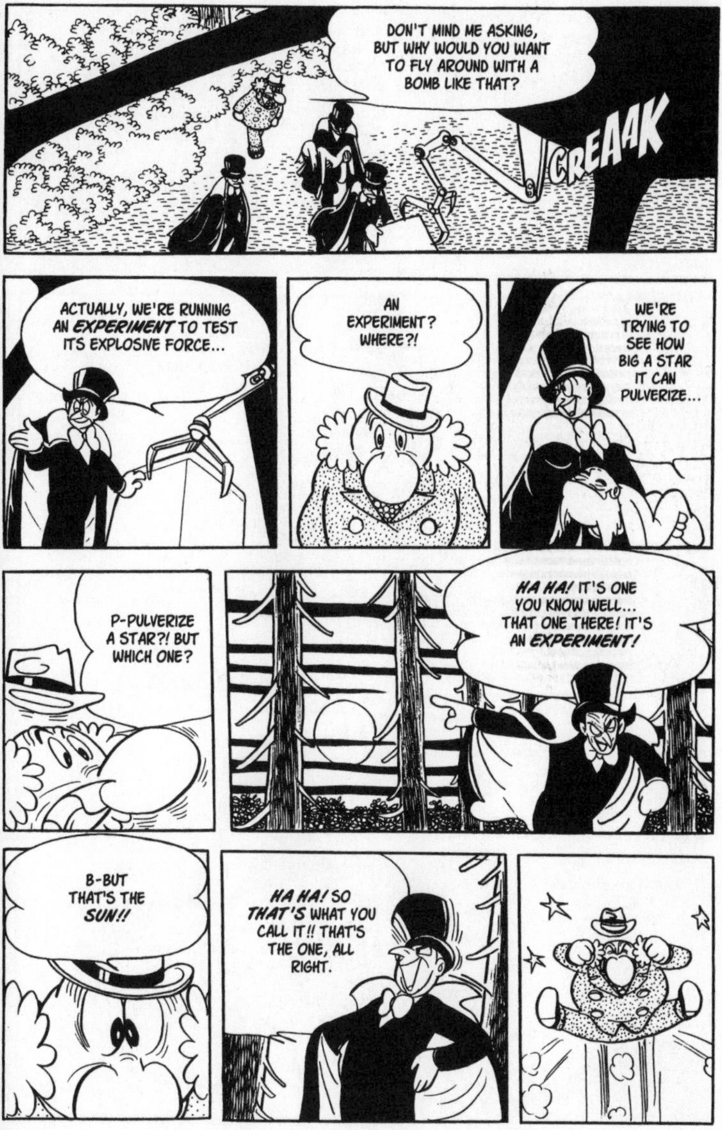
DON'T MIND ME ASKING, BUT WHY WOULD YOU WANT TO FLY AROUND WITH A BOMB LIKE THAT?
CREAAK
ACTUALLY, WE'RE RUNNING AN *EXPERIMENT* TO TEST ITS EXPLOSIVE FORCE...
AN EXPERIMENT? WHERE?!
WE'RE TRYING TO SEE HOW BIG A STAR IT CAN PULVERIZE...
P-PULVERIZE A STAR?! BUT WHICH ONE?
HA HA! IT'S ONE YOU KNOW WELL... THAT ONE THERE! IT'S AN *EXPERIMENT!*
B-BUT THAT'S THE *SUN!!*
HA HA! SO *THAT'S* WHAT YOU CALL IT!! THAT'S THE ONE, ALL RIGHT.

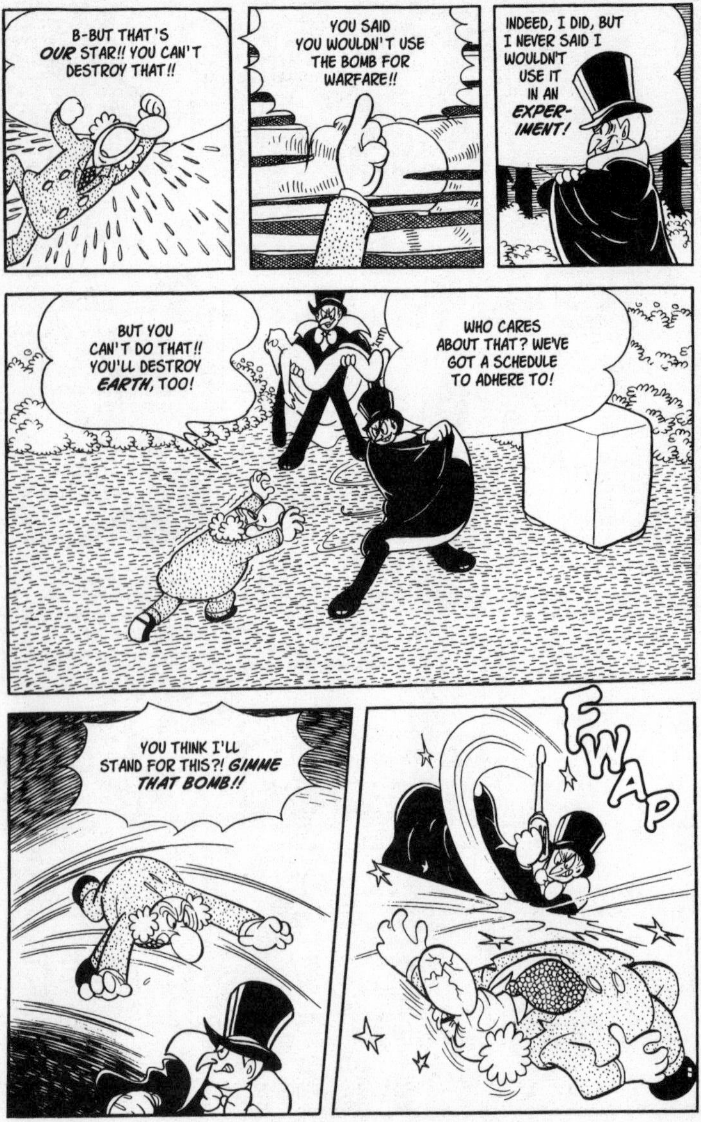
B-BUT THAT'S OUR STAR!! YOU CAN'T DESTROY THAT!!
YOU SAID YOU WOULDN'T USE THE BOMB FOR WARFARE!!
INDEED, I DID, BUT I NEVER SAID I WOULDN'T USE IT IN AN EXPERIMENT!
BUT YOU CAN'T DO THAT!! YOU'LL DESTROY EARTH, TOO!
WHO CARES ABOUT THAT? WE'VE GOT A SCHEDULE TO ADHERE TO!
YOU THINK I'LL STAND FOR THIS?! GIMME THAT BOMB!!
FWAP

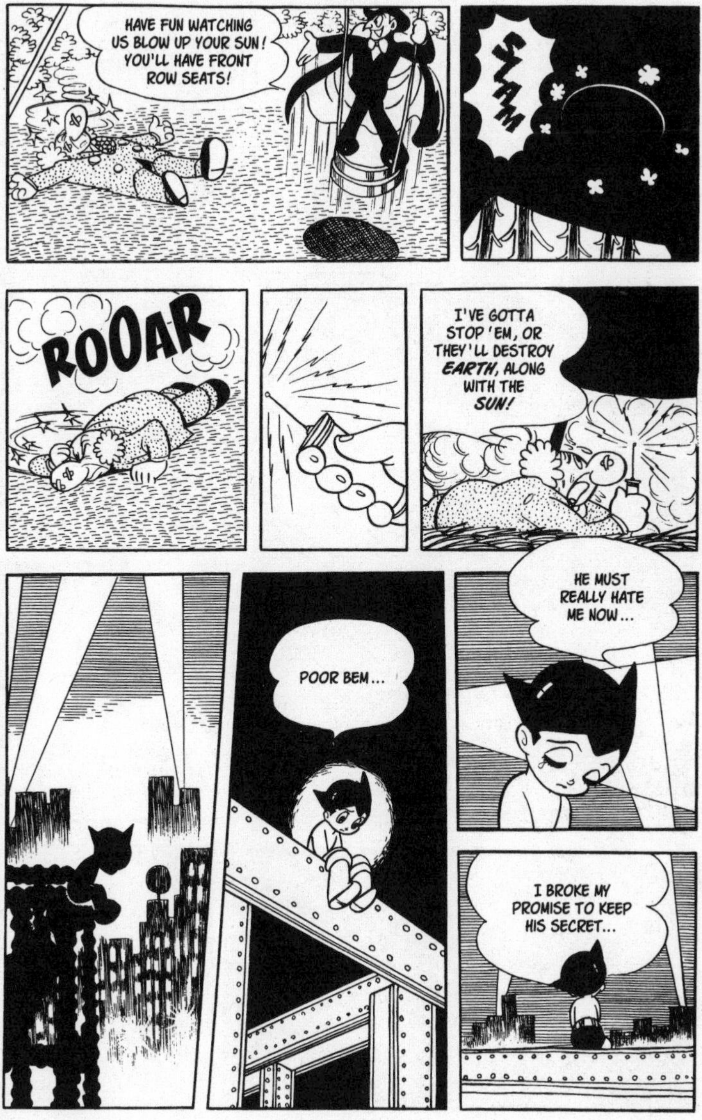
HAVE FUN WATCHING US BLOW UP YOUR SUN! YOU'LL HAVE FRONT ROW SEATS!
SLAM
ROOAR
I'VE GOTTA STOP 'EM, OR THEY'LL DESTROY *EARTH*, ALONG WITH THE *SUN!*
POOR BEM...
HE MUST REALLY HATE ME NOW...
I BROKE MY PROMISE TO KEEP HIS SECRET...

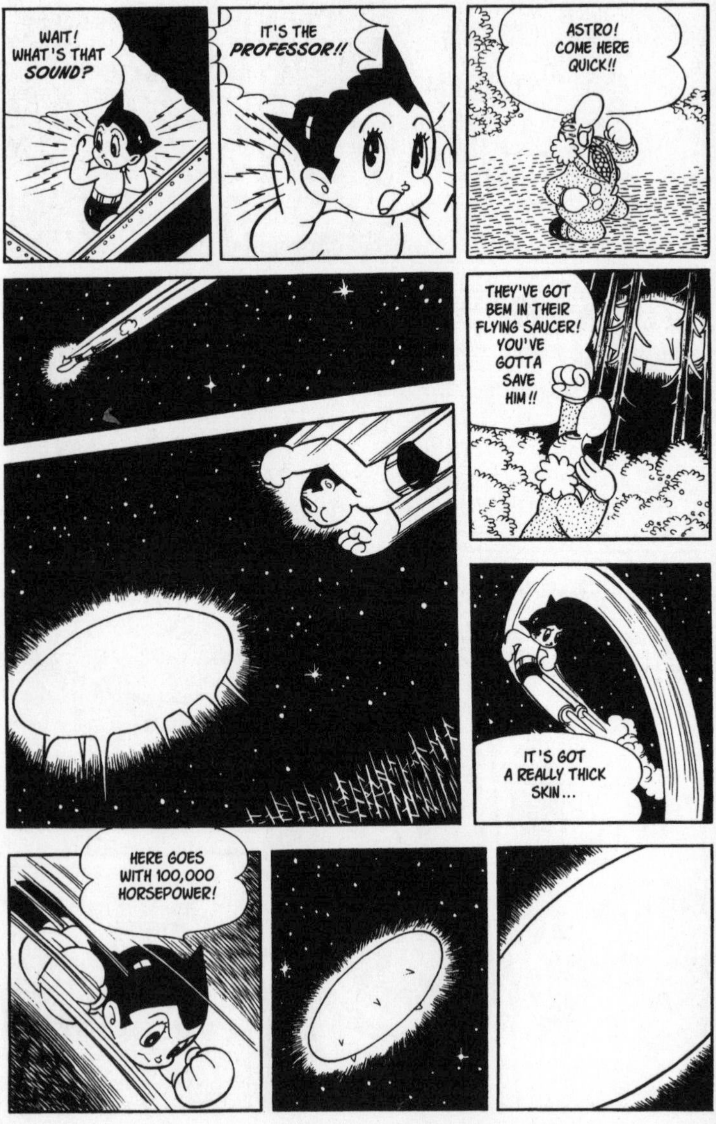
WAIT! WHAT'S THAT *SOUND?*
IT'S THE *PROFESSOR!!*
ASTRO! COME HERE QUICK!!
THEY'VE GOT BEM IN THEIR FLYING SAUCER! YOU'VE GOTTA SAVE HIM!!
IT'S GOT A REALLY THICK SKIN...
HERE GOES WITH 100,000 HORSEPOWER!

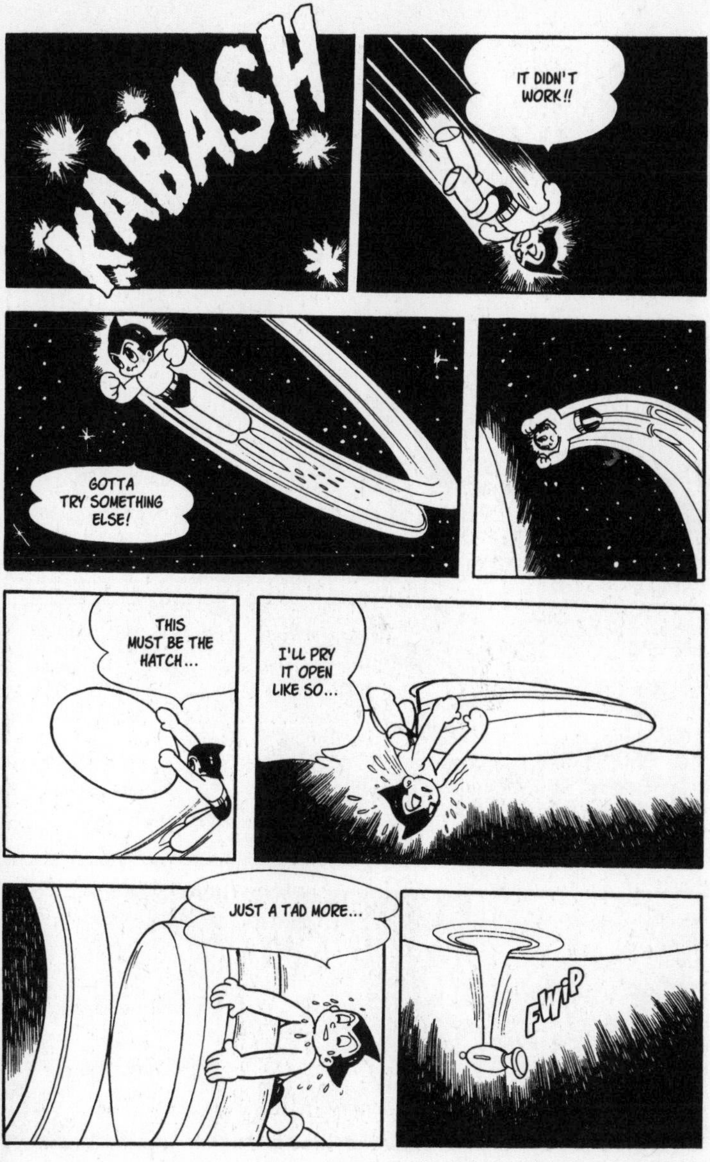
KABASH
IT DIDN'T WORK!!
GOTTA TRY SOMETHING ELSE!
THIS MUST BE THE HATCH...
I'LL PRY IT OPEN LIKE SO...
JUST A TAD MORE...
FWIP

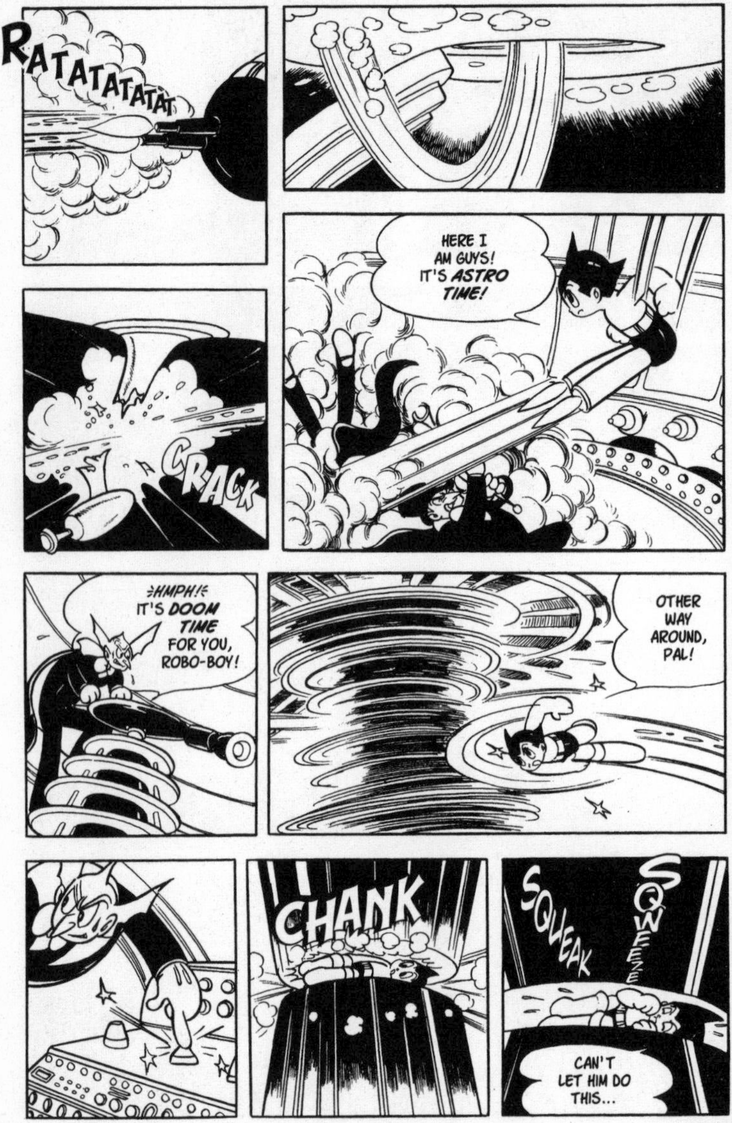
RATATATATATAT
HERE I AM GUYS! IT'S ASTRO TIME!
CRACK
≶HMPH!≶ IT'S DOOM TIME FOR YOU, ROBO-BOY!
OTHER WAY AROUND, PAL!
CHANK
SQUEAK
SQWEEZE
CAN'T LET HIM DO THIS...

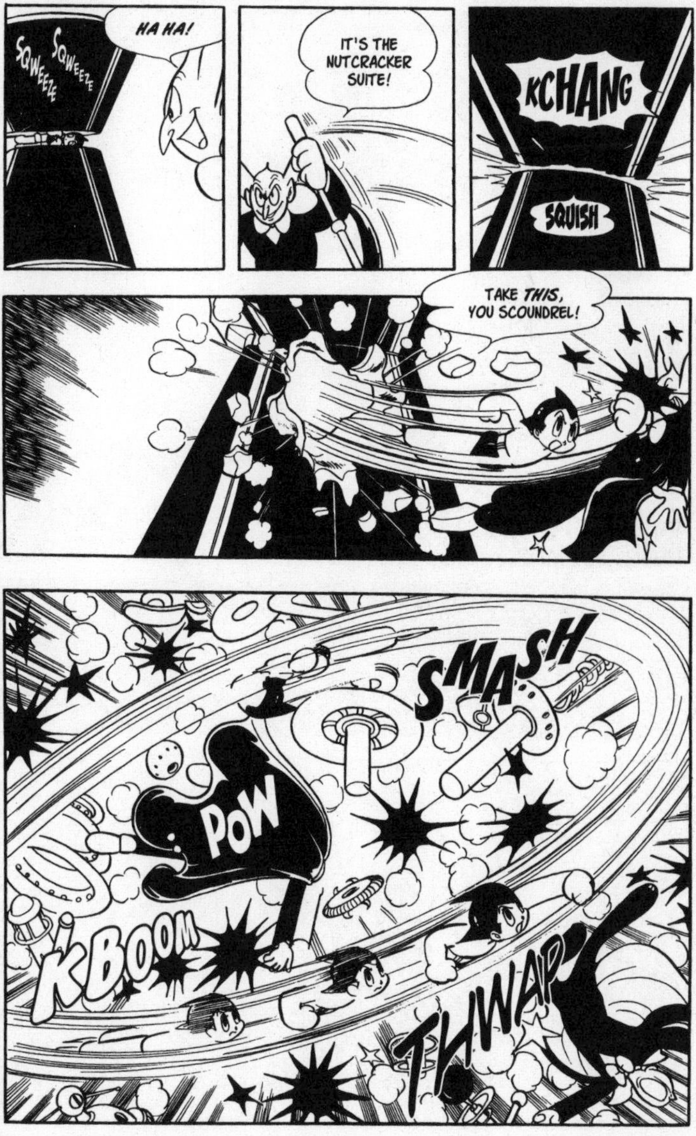
HA HA!
SQWEEZE
SQWEEZE
IT'S THE NUTCRACKER SUITE!
KCHANG
SQUISH
TAKE THIS, YOU SCOUNDREL!
SMASH
POW
KBOOM
THWAP

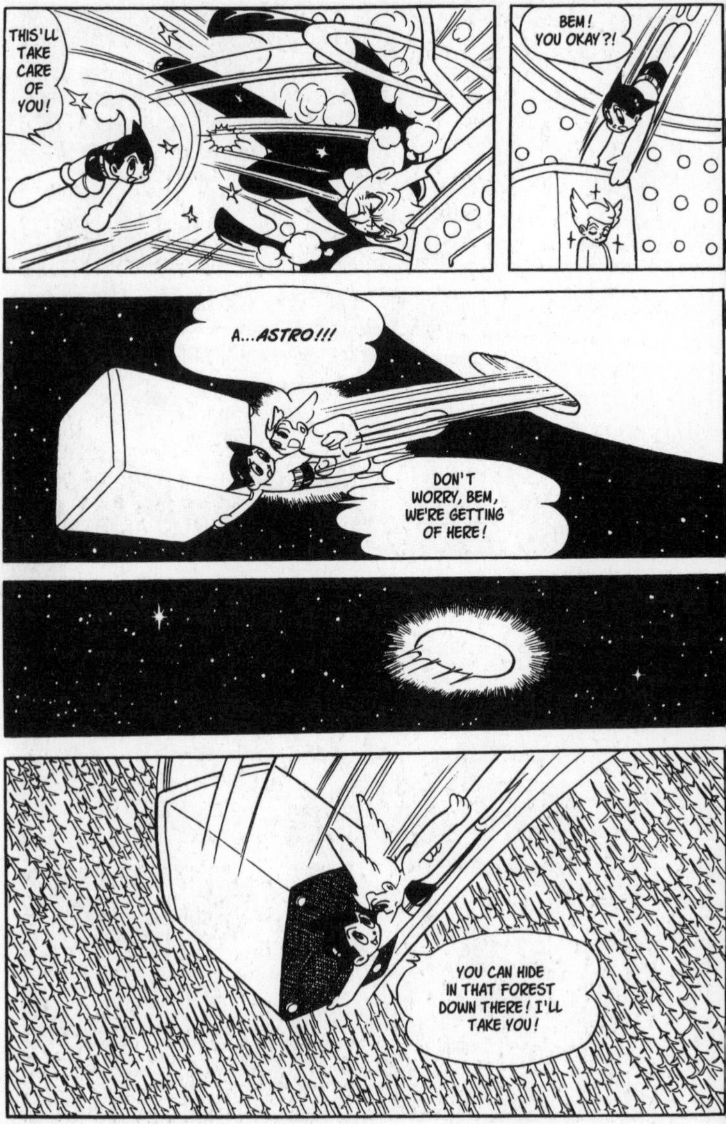
THIS'LL TAKE CARE OF YOU!
BEM! YOU OKAY?!
A...ASTRO!!!
DON'T WORRY, BEM, WE'RE GETTING OF HERE!
YOU CAN HIDE IN THAT FOREST DOWN THERE! I'LL TAKE YOU!

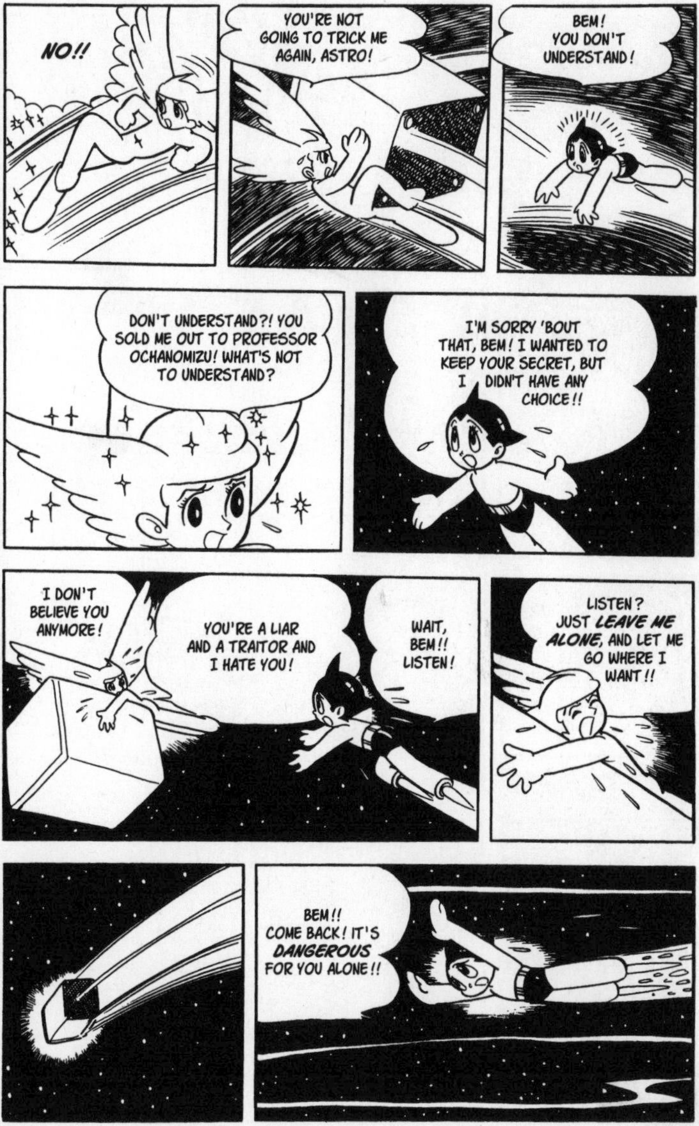
NO!!
YOU'RE NOT GOING TO TRICK ME AGAIN, ASTRO!
BEM! YOU DON'T UNDERSTAND!
DON'T UNDERSTAND?! YOU SOLD ME OUT TO PROFESSOR OCHANOMIZU! WHAT'S NOT TO UNDERSTAND?
I'M SORRY 'BOUT THAT, BEM! I WANTED TO KEEP YOUR SECRET, BUT I DIDN'T HAVE ANY CHOICE!!
I DON'T BELIEVE YOU ANYMORE!
YOU'RE A LIAR AND A TRAITOR AND I HATE YOU!
WAIT, BEM!! LISTEN!
LISTEN? JUST *LEAVE ME ALONE*, AND LET ME GO WHERE I WANT!!
BEM!! COME BACK! IT'S *DANGEROUS* FOR YOU ALONE!!

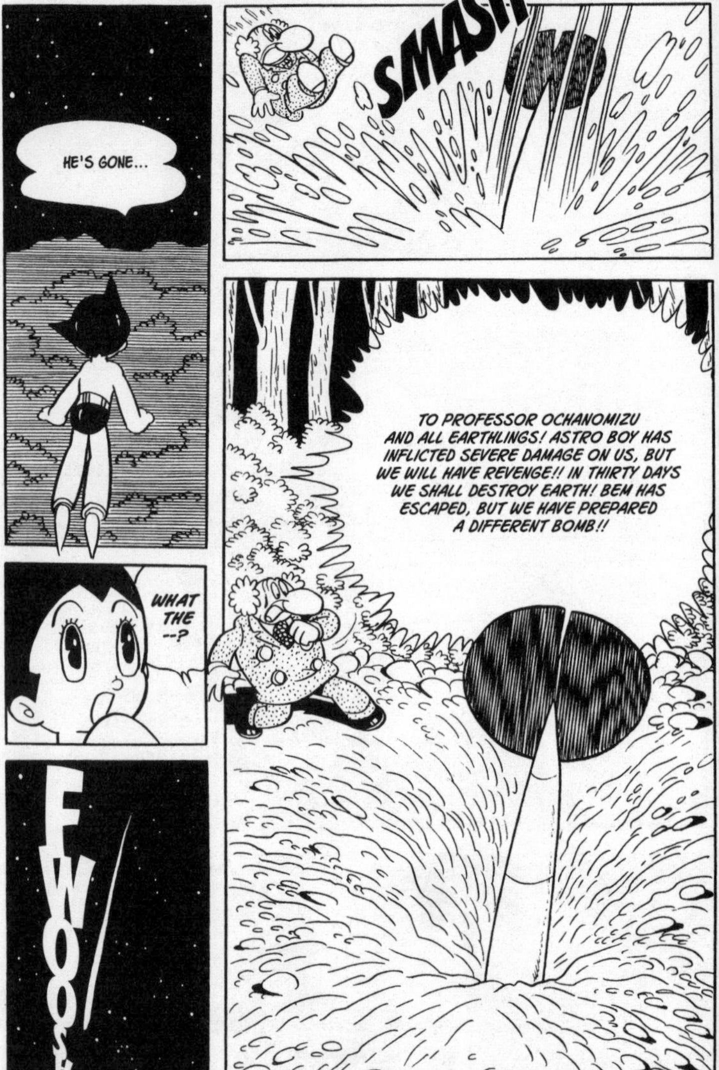
HE'S GONE...
WHAT THE --?
FWOOSH
SMASH
TO PROFESSOR OCHANOMIZU AND ALL EARTHLINGS! ASTRO BOY HAS INFLICTED SEVERE DAMAGE ON US, BUT WE WILL HAVE REVENGE!! IN THIRTY DAYS WE SHALL DESTROY EARTH! BEM HAS ESCAPED, BUT WE HAVE PREPARED A DIFFERENT BOMB!!

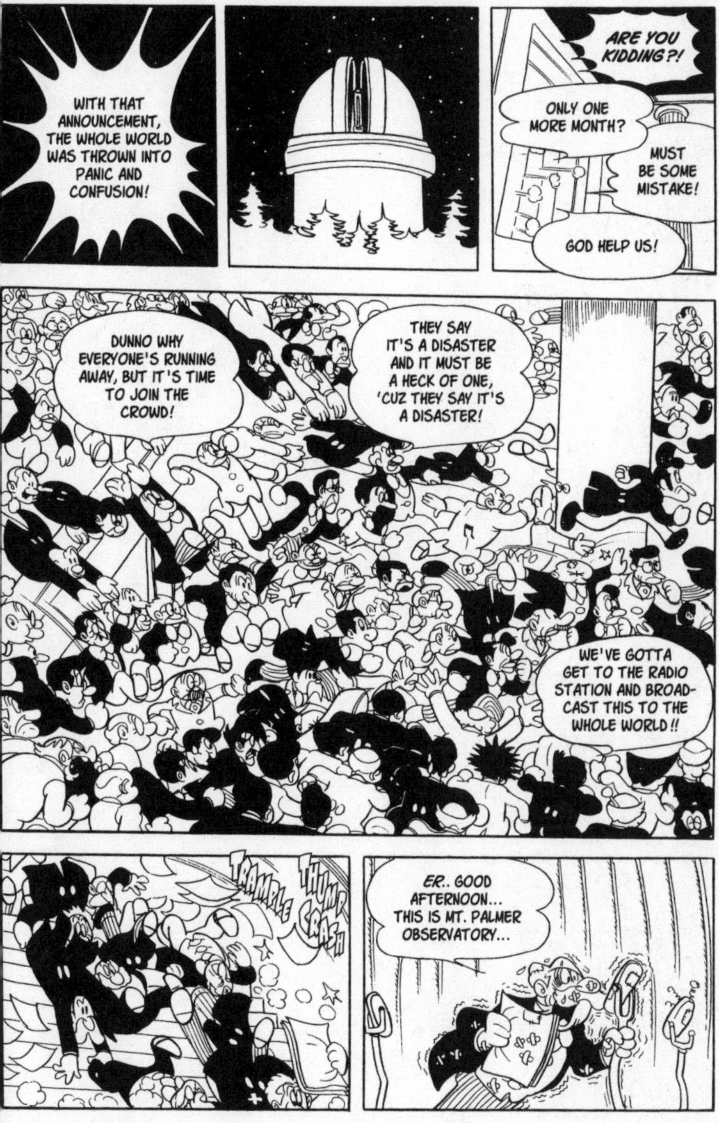
WITH THAT ANNOUNCEMENT, THE WHOLE WORLD WAS THROWN INTO PANIC AND CONFUSION!
ARE YOU KIDDING?!
ONLY ONE MORE MONTH?
MUST BE SOME MISTAKE!
GOD HELP US!
DUNNO WHY EVERYONE'S RUNNING AWAY, BUT IT'S TIME TO JOIN THE CROWD!
THEY SAY IT'S A DISASTER AND IT MUST BE A HECK OF ONE, 'CUZ THEY SAY IT'S A DISASTER!
WE'VE GOTTA GET TO THE RADIO STATION AND BROAD-CAST THIS TO THE WHOLE WORLD!!
TRAMPLE
THUMP
CRASH
ER.. GOOD AFTERNOON... THIS IS MT. PALMER OBSERVATORY...

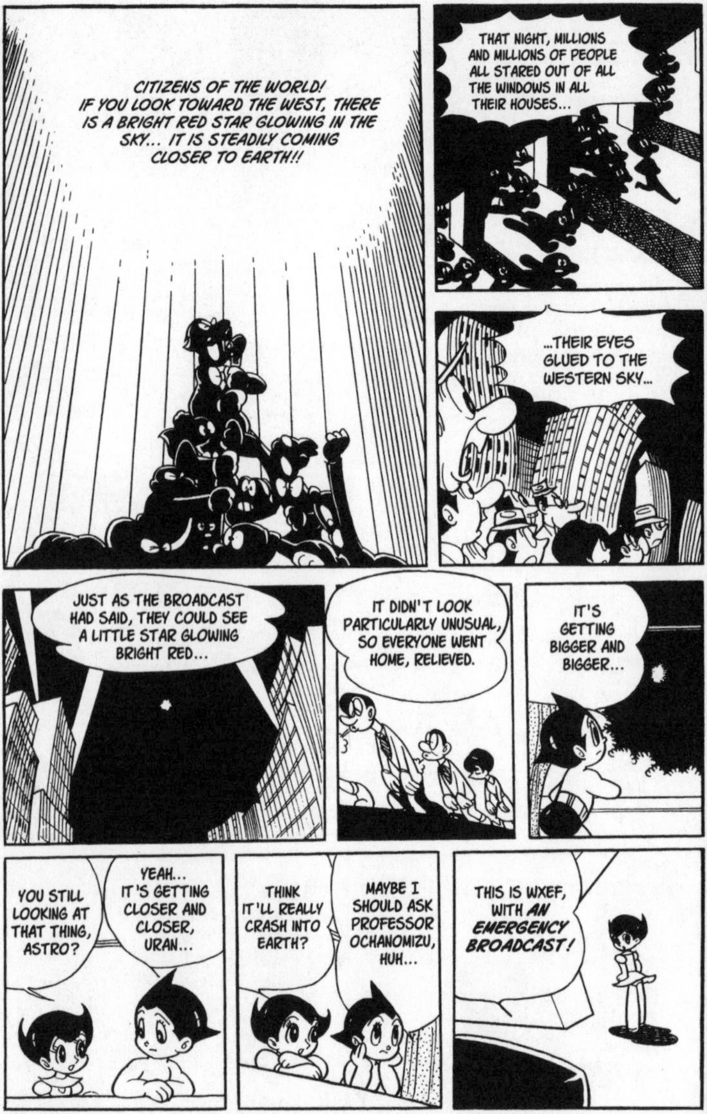
CITIZENS OF THE WORLD! IF YOU LOOK TOWARD THE WEST, THERE IS A BRIGHT RED STAR GLOWING IN THE SKY... IT IS STEADILY COMING CLOSER TO EARTH!!
THAT NIGHT, MILLIONS AND MILLIONS OF PEOPLE ALL STARED OUT OF ALL THE WINDOWS IN ALL THEIR HOUSES...
...THEIR EYES GLUED TO THE WESTERN SKY...
JUST AS THE BROADCAST HAD SAID, THEY COULD SEE A LITTLE STAR GLOWING BRIGHT RED...
IT DIDN'T LOOK PARTICULARLY UNUSUAL, SO EVERYONE WENT HOME, RELIEVED.
IT'S GETTING BIGGER AND BIGGER...
YOU STILL LOOKING AT THAT THING, ASTRO?
YEAH... IT'S GETTING CLOSER AND CLOSER, URAN...
THINK IT'LL REALLY CRASH INTO EARTH?
MAYBE I SHOULD ASK PROFESSOR OCHANOMIZU, HUH...
THIS IS WXEF, WITH AN EMERGENCY BROADCAST!

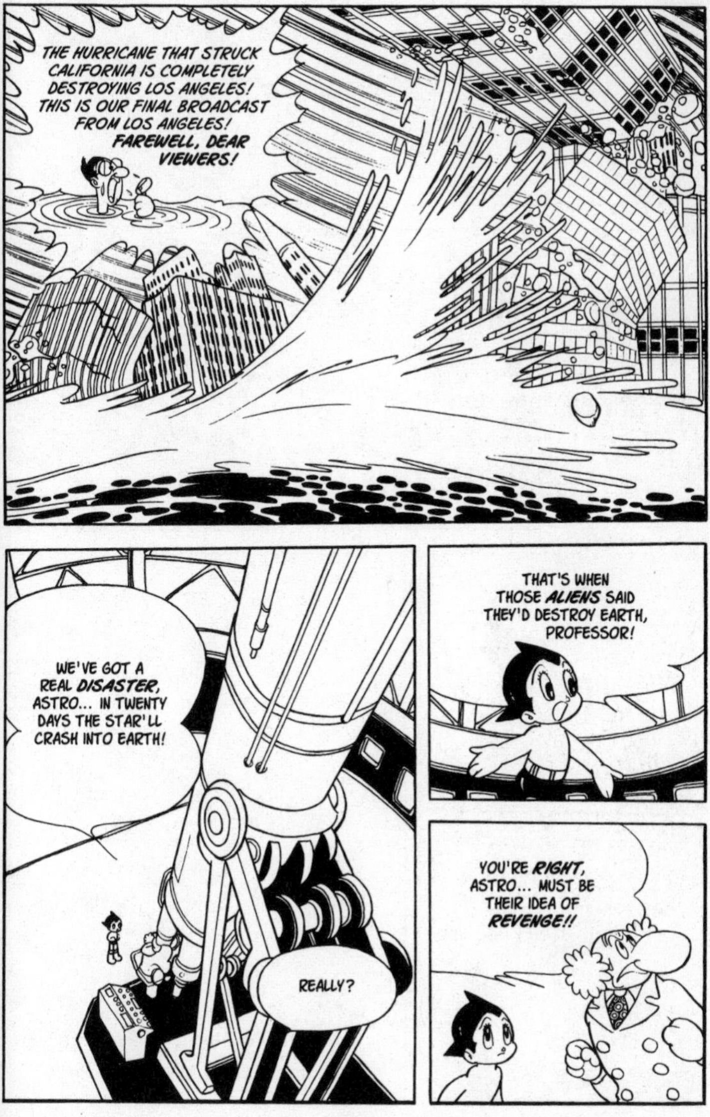
THE HURRICANE THAT STRUCK CALIFORNIA IS COMPLETELY DESTROYING LOS ANGELES! THIS IS OUR FINAL BROADCAST FROM LOS ANGELES! FAREWELL, DEAR VIEWERS!
WE'VE GOT A REAL DISASTER, ASTRO... IN TWENTY DAYS THE STAR'LL CRASH INTO EARTH!
REALLY?
THAT'S WHEN THOSE ALIENS SAID THEY'D DESTROY EARTH, PROFESSOR!
YOU'RE RIGHT, ASTRO... MUST BE THEIR IDEA OF REVENGE!!

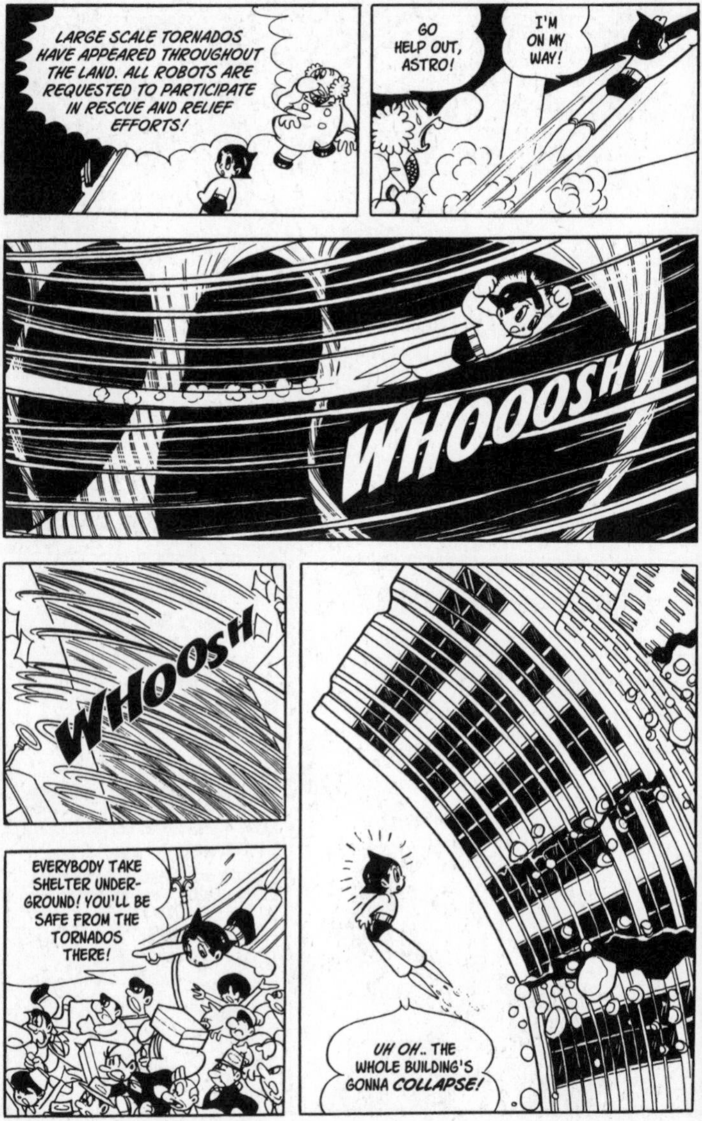
LARGE SCALE TORNADOS HAVE APPEARED THROUGHOUT THE LAND. ALL ROBOTS ARE REQUESTED TO PARTICIPATE IN RESCUE AND RELIEF EFFORTS!
GO HELP OUT, ASTRO!
I'M ON MY WAY!
WHOOOSH
WHOOSH
EVERYBODY TAKE SHELTER UNDER-GROUND! YOU'LL BE SAFE FROM THE TORNADOS THERE!
UH OH.. THE WHOLE BUILDING'S GONNA COLLAPSE!

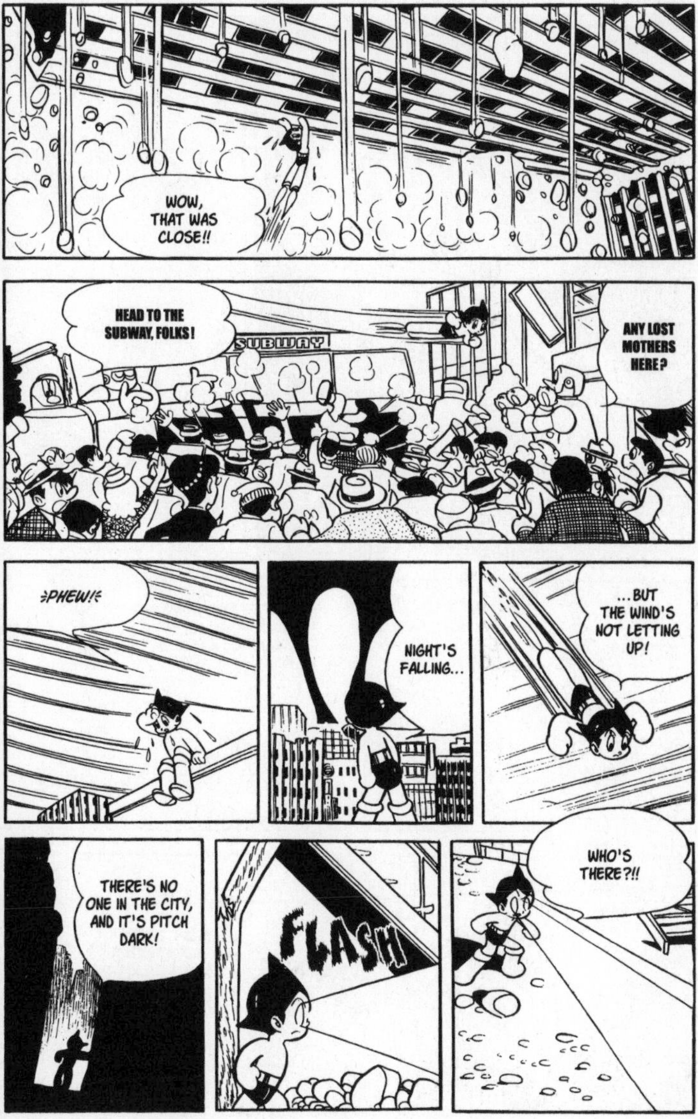
WOW, THAT WAS CLOSE!!
HEAD TO THE SUBWAY, FOLKS!
SUBWAY
ANY LOST MOTHERS HERE?
PHEW!
NIGHT'S FALLING...
...BUT THE WIND'S NOT LETTING UP!
THERE'S NO ONE IN THE CITY, AND IT'S PITCH DARK!
FLASH
WHO'S THERE?!!

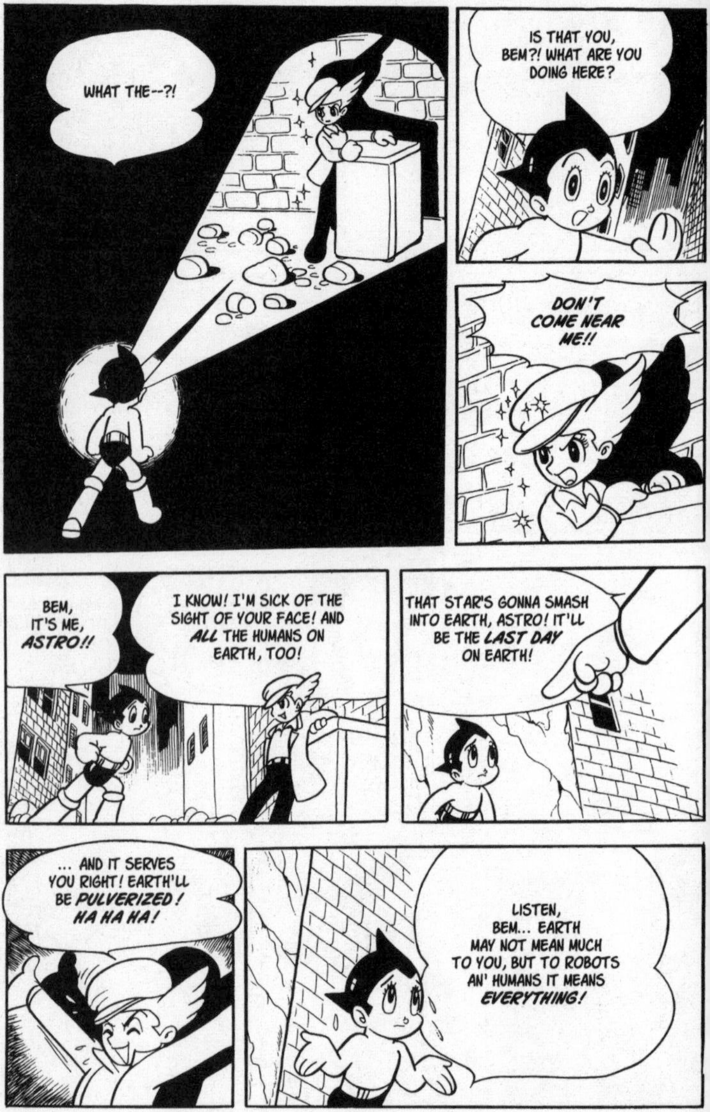
WHAT THE--?!
IS THAT YOU, BEM?! WHAT ARE YOU DOING HERE?
DON'T COME NEAR ME!!
BEM, IT'S ME, ASTRO!!
I KNOW! I'M SICK OF THE SIGHT OF YOUR FACE! AND ALL THE HUMANS ON EARTH, TOO!
THAT STAR'S GONNA SMASH INTO EARTH, ASTRO! IT'LL BE THE LAST DAY ON EARTH!
... AND IT SERVES YOU RIGHT! EARTH'LL BE PULVERIZED! HA HA HA!
LISTEN, BEM... EARTH MAY NOT MEAN MUCH TO YOU, BUT TO ROBOTS AN' HUMANS IT MEANS EVERYTHING!

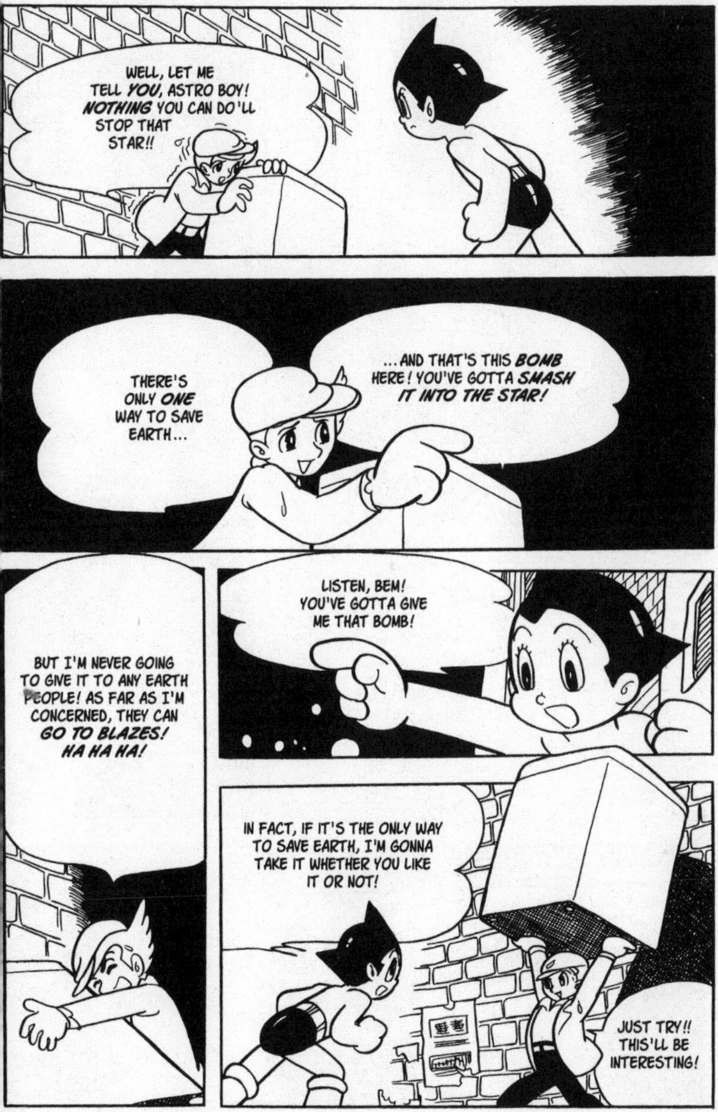
WELL, LET ME TELL *YOU*, ASTRO BOY! *NOTHING* YOU CAN DO'LL STOP THAT STAR!!
THERE'S ONLY *ONE* WAY TO SAVE EARTH...
...AND THAT'S THIS *BOMB* HERE! YOU'VE GOTTA *SMASH IT INTO THE STAR!*
BUT I'M NEVER GOING TO GIVE IT TO ANY EARTH PEOPLE! AS FAR AS I'M CONCERNED, THEY CAN *GO TO BLAZES! HA HA HA!*
LISTEN, BEM! YOU'VE GOTTA GIVE ME THAT BOMB!
IN FACT, IF IT'S THE ONLY WAY TO SAVE EARTH, I'M GONNA TAKE IT WHETHER YOU LIKE IT OR NOT!
JUST TRY!! THIS'LL BE INTERESTING!

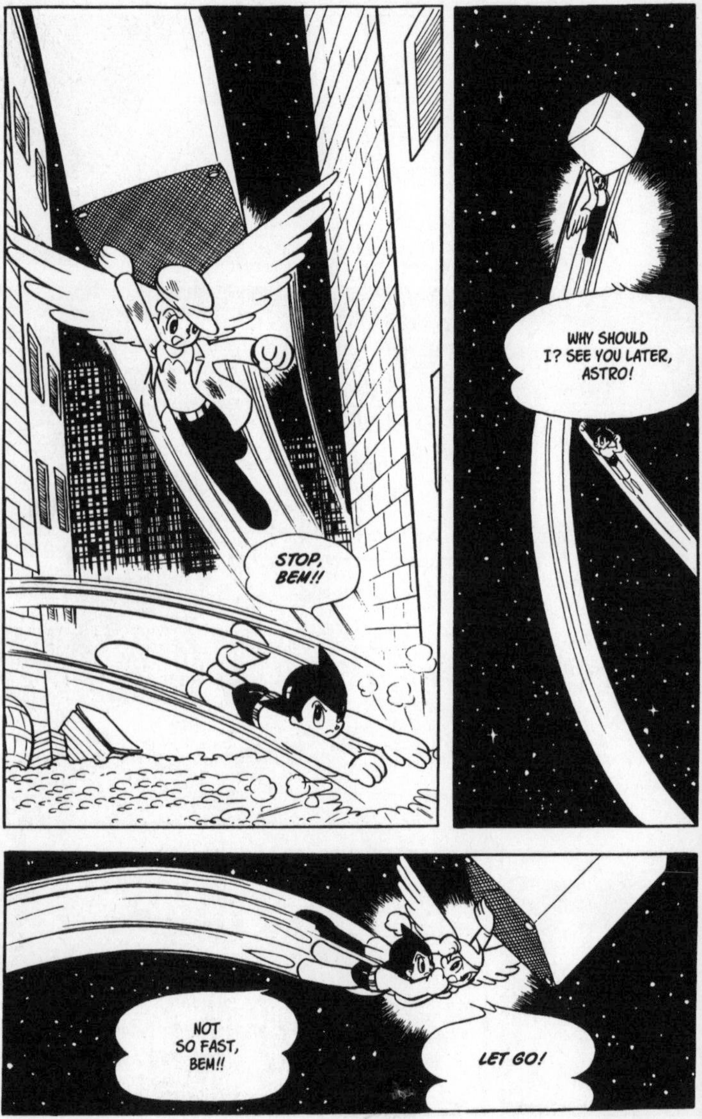
STOP, BEM!!
WHY SHOULD I? SEE YOU LATER, ASTRO!
NOT SO FAST, BEM!!
LET GO!

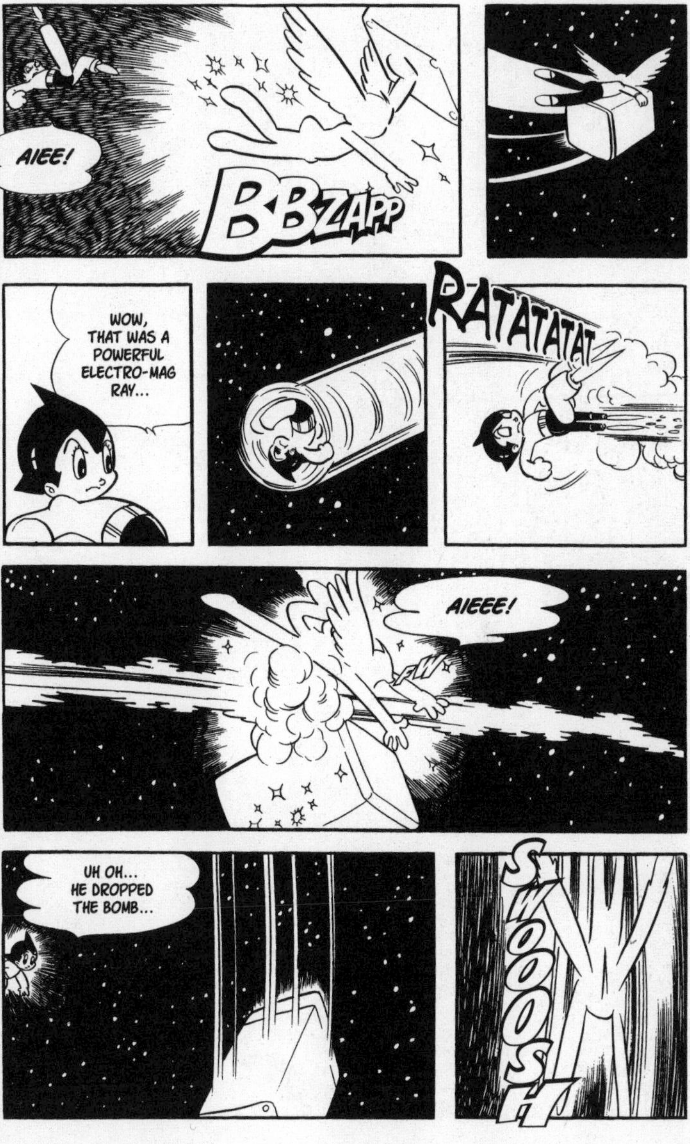
AIEE!
BBZAPP
WOW, THAT WAS A POWERFUL ELECTRO-MAG RAY...
RATATATAT
AIEEE!
FW
UH OH... HE DROPPED THE BOMB...
SWOOOSH

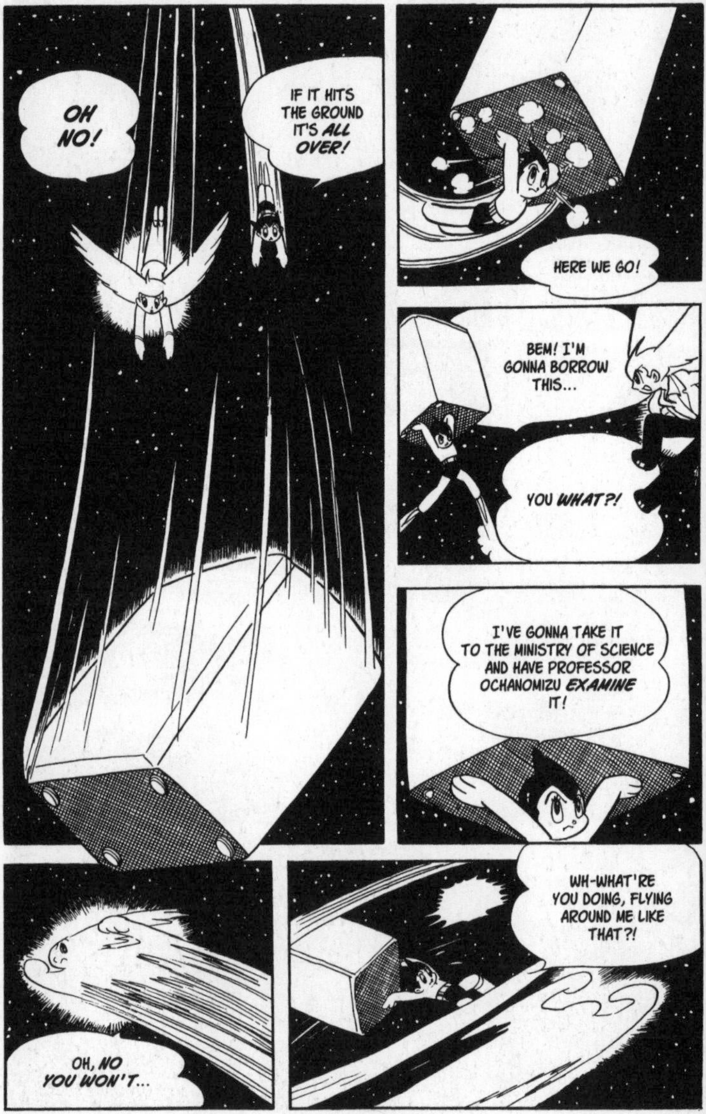
OH NO!
IF IT HITS THE GROUND IT'S *ALL OVER!*
HERE WE GO!
BEM! I'M GONNA BORROW THIS...
YOU *WHAT?!*
I'VE GONNA TAKE IT TO THE MINISTRY OF SCIENCE AND HAVE PROFESSOR OCHANOMIZU *EXAMINE* IT!
OH, NO YOU WON'T...
WH-WHAT'RE YOU DOING, FLYING AROUND ME LIKE THAT?!

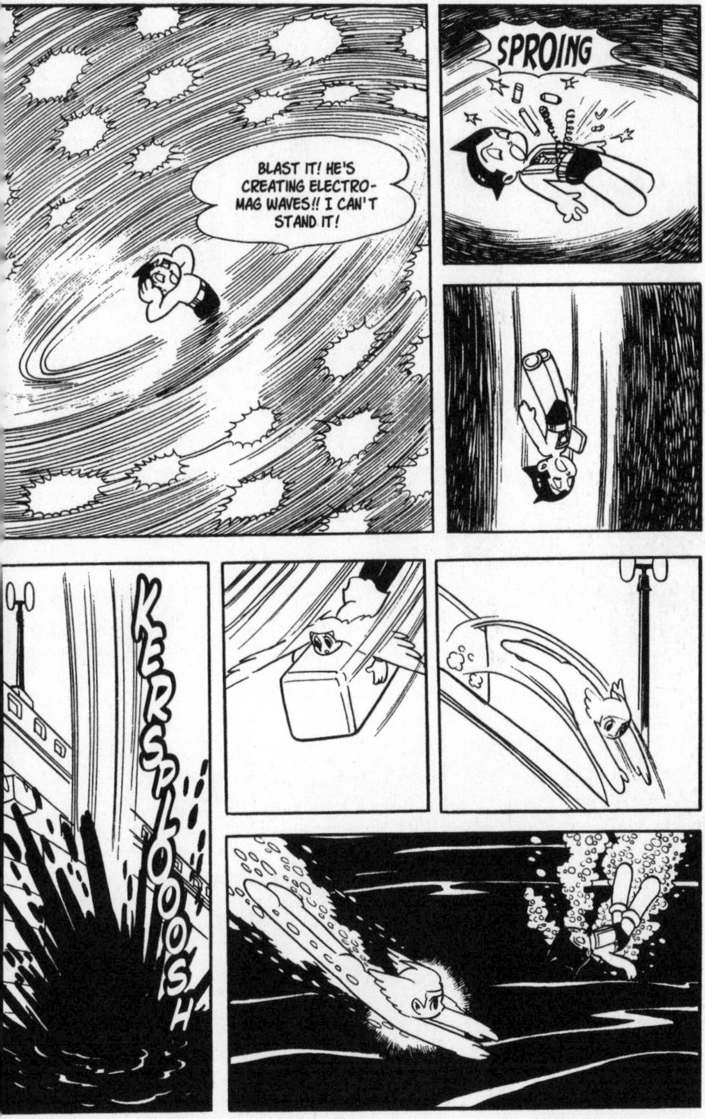

BLAST IT! HE'S CREATING ELECTRO-MAG WAVES!! I CAN'T STAND IT!
SPROING
KERSPLOOOOSH

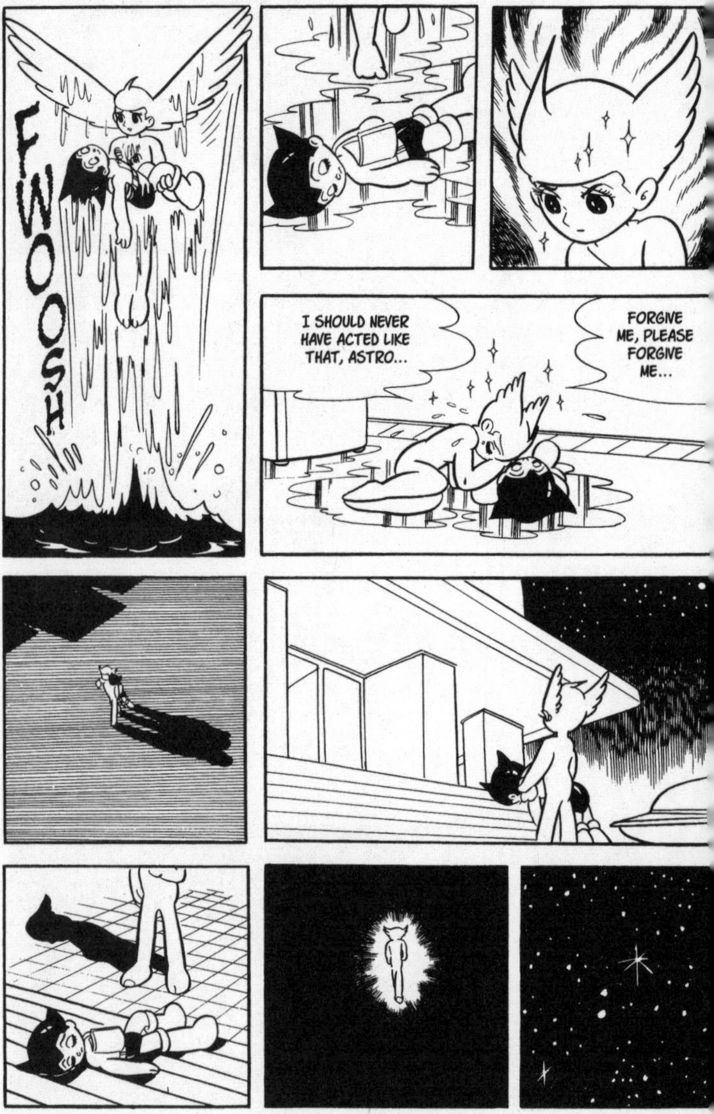

FWOOSH!!
I SHOULD NEVER HAVE ACTED LIKE THAT, ASTRO...
FORGIVE ME, PLEASE FORGIVE ME...

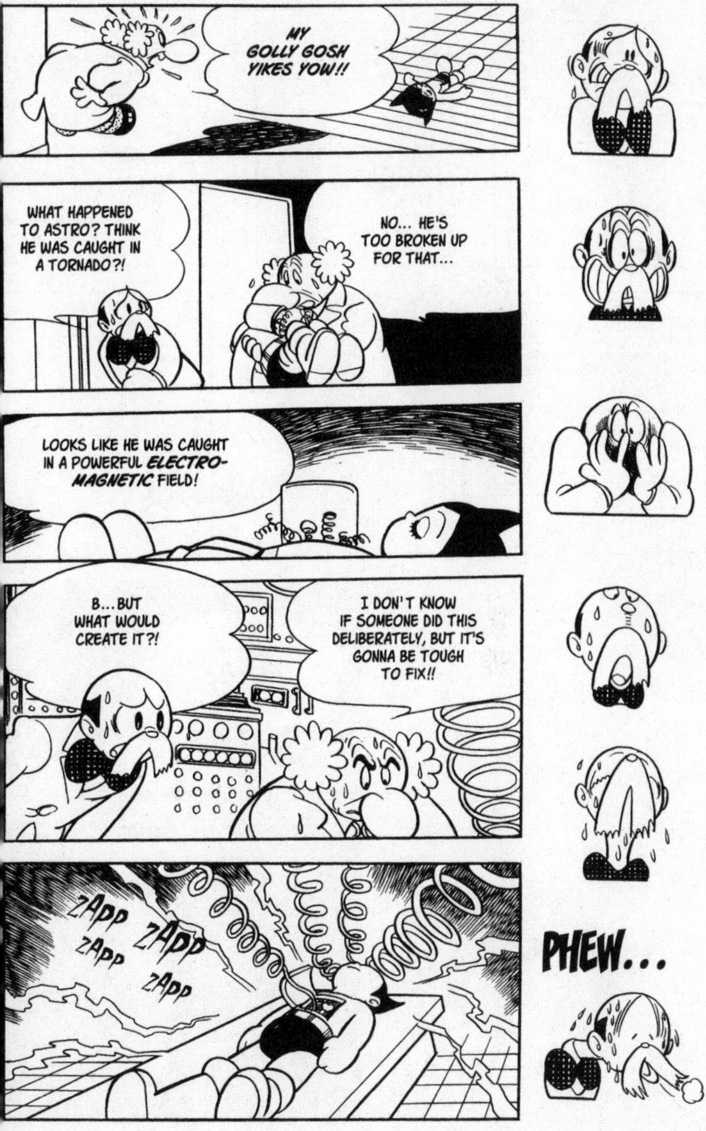

MY GOLLY GOSH YIKES YOW!!
WHAT HAPPENED TO ASTRO? THINK HE WAS CAUGHT IN A TORNADO?!
NO... HE'S TOO BROKEN UP FOR THAT...
LOOKS LIKE HE WAS CAUGHT IN A POWERFUL *ELECTRO-MAGNETIC* FIELD!
B... BUT WHAT WOULD CREATE IT?!
I DON'T KNOW IF SOMEONE DID THIS DELIBERATELY, BUT IT'S GONNA BE TOUGH TO FIX!!
ZAPP
ZAPP
ZAPP
ZAPP
PHEW...

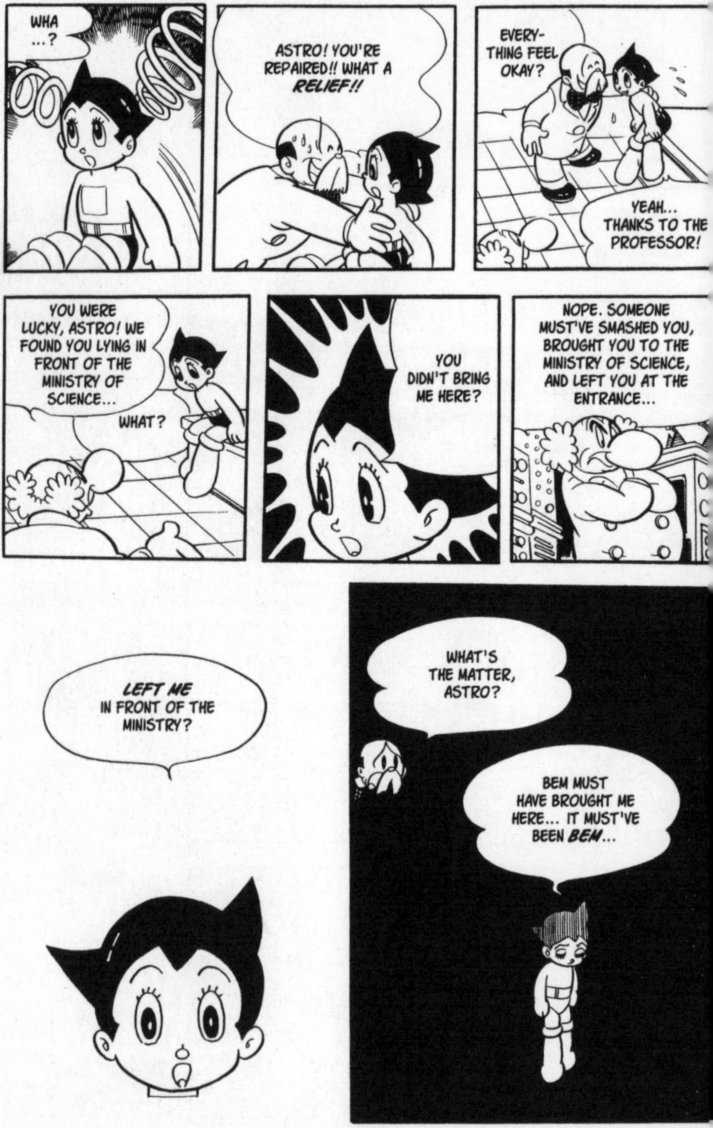
WHA ...?
ASTRO! YOU'RE REPAIRED!! WHAT A RELIEF!!
EVERY-THING FEEL OKAY?
YEAH... THANKS TO THE PROFESSOR!
YOU WERE LUCKY, ASTRO! WE FOUND YOU LYING IN FRONT OF THE MINISTRY OF SCIENCE...
WHAT?
YOU DIDN'T BRING ME HERE?
NOPE. SOMEONE MUST'VE SMASHED YOU, BROUGHT YOU TO THE MINISTRY OF SCIENCE, AND LEFT YOU AT THE ENTRANCE...
LEFT ME IN FRONT OF THE MINISTRY?
WHAT'S THE MATTER, ASTRO?
BEM MUST HAVE BROUGHT ME HERE... IT MUST'VE BEEN BEM...

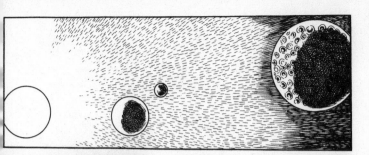

WITH EACH PASSING DAY, THE STRANGE STAR GREW BRIGHTER AND BRIGHTER IN THE WESTERN NIGHT SKY. IT BEGAN TO LOOK LIKE A GIANT EVIL EYE AND TO CAUSE INCREASINGLY VIOLENT CHANGES ON EARTH...

THERE WERE STORMS...

...WITH VIOLENT WINDS UP TO 150 MILES PER HOUR...

POWERFUL EARTHQUAKES SUDDENLY OCCURRED AROUND THE WORLD, CAUSING THE DEATHS OF TENS OF THOUSANDS OF PEOPLE. ALL THESE EVENTS WERE TRIGGERED BY THE STRANGE STAR'S GRAVITY FIELD...

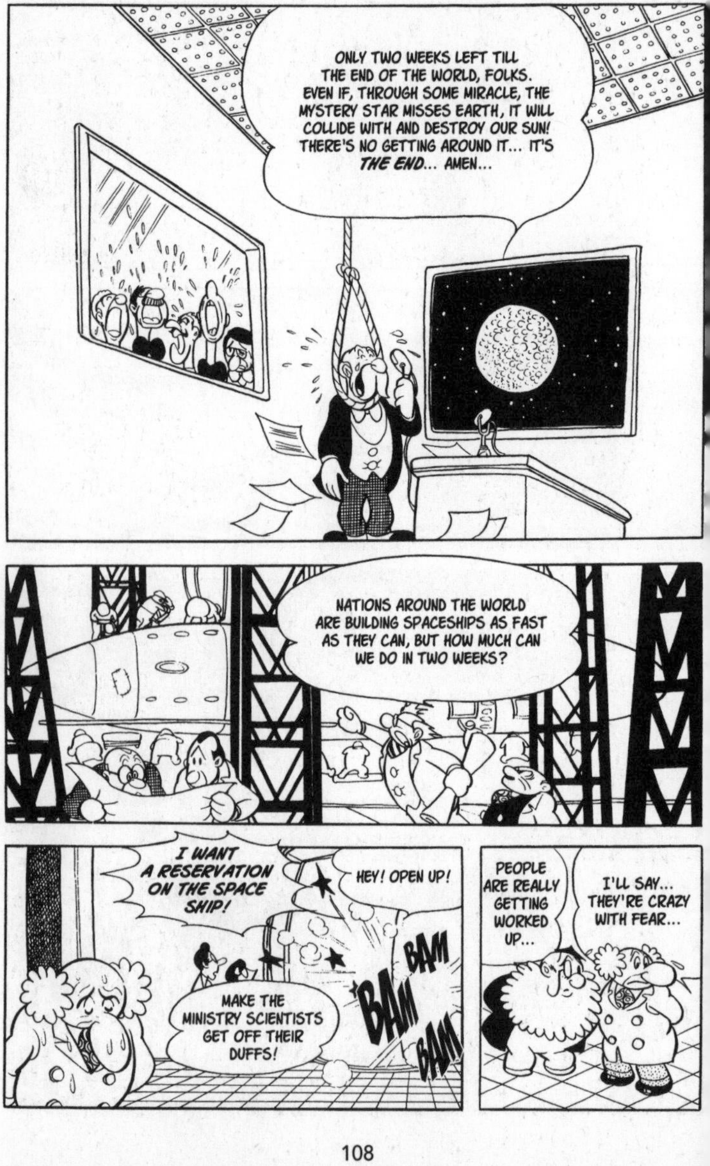
ONLY TWO WEEKS LEFT TILL THE END OF THE WORLD, FOLKS. EVEN IF, THROUGH SOME MIRACLE, THE MYSTERY STAR MISSES EARTH, IT WILL COLLIDE WITH AND DESTROY OUR SUN! THERE'S NO GETTING AROUND IT... IT'S *THE END*... AMEN...
NATIONS AROUND THE WORLD ARE BUILDING SPACESHIPS AS FAST AS THEY CAN, BUT HOW MUCH CAN WE DO IN TWO WEEKS?
I WANT A RESERVATION ON THE SPACE SHIP!
HEY! OPEN UP!
BAM BAM BAM BAM
MAKE THE MINISTRY SCIENTISTS GET OFF THEIR DUFFS!
PEOPLE ARE REALLY GETTING WORKED UP...
I'LL SAY... THEY'RE CRAZY WITH FEAR...

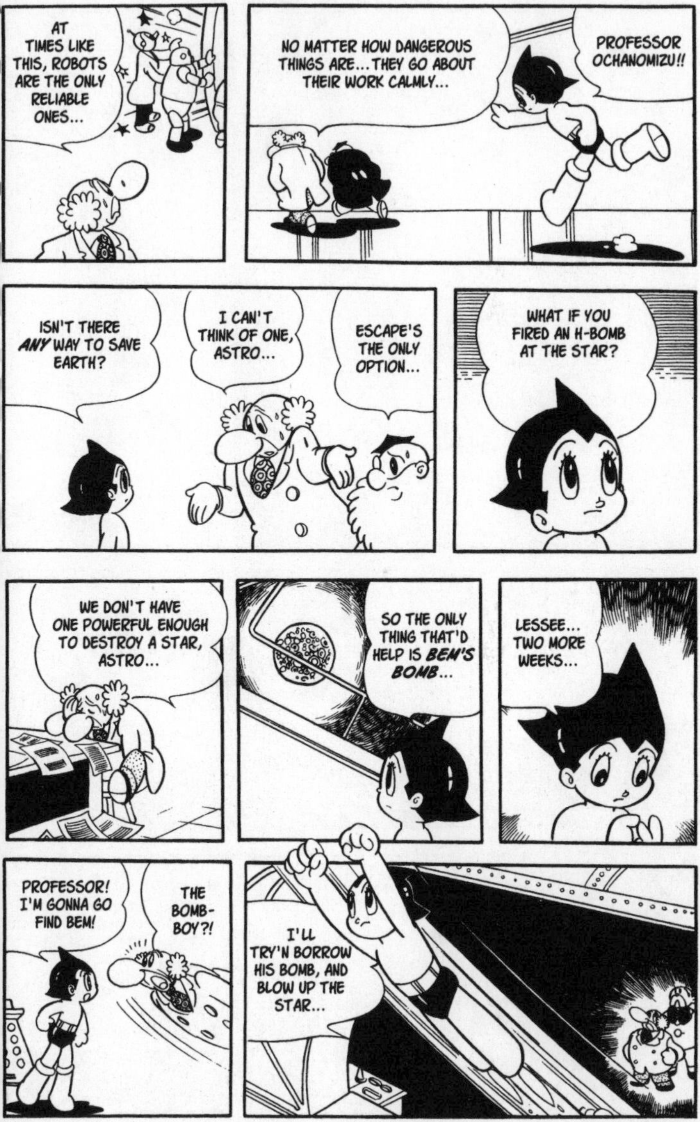

AT TIMES LIKE THIS, ROBOTS ARE THE ONLY RELIABLE ONES...
NO MATTER HOW DANGEROUS THINGS ARE... THEY GO ABOUT THEIR WORK CALMLY...
PROFESSOR OCHANOMIZU!!
ISN'T THERE *ANY* WAY TO SAVE EARTH?
I CAN'T THINK OF ONE, ASTRO...
ESCAPE'S THE ONLY OPTION...
WHAT IF YOU FIRED AN H-BOMB AT THE STAR?
WE DON'T HAVE ONE POWERFUL ENOUGH TO DESTROY A STAR, ASTRO...
SO THE ONLY THING THAT'D HELP IS *BEM'S BOMB*...
LESSEE... TWO MORE WEEKS...
PROFESSOR! I'M GONNA GO FIND BEM!
THE BOMB-BOY?!
I'LL TRY'N BORROW HIS BOMB, AND BLOW UP THE STAR...

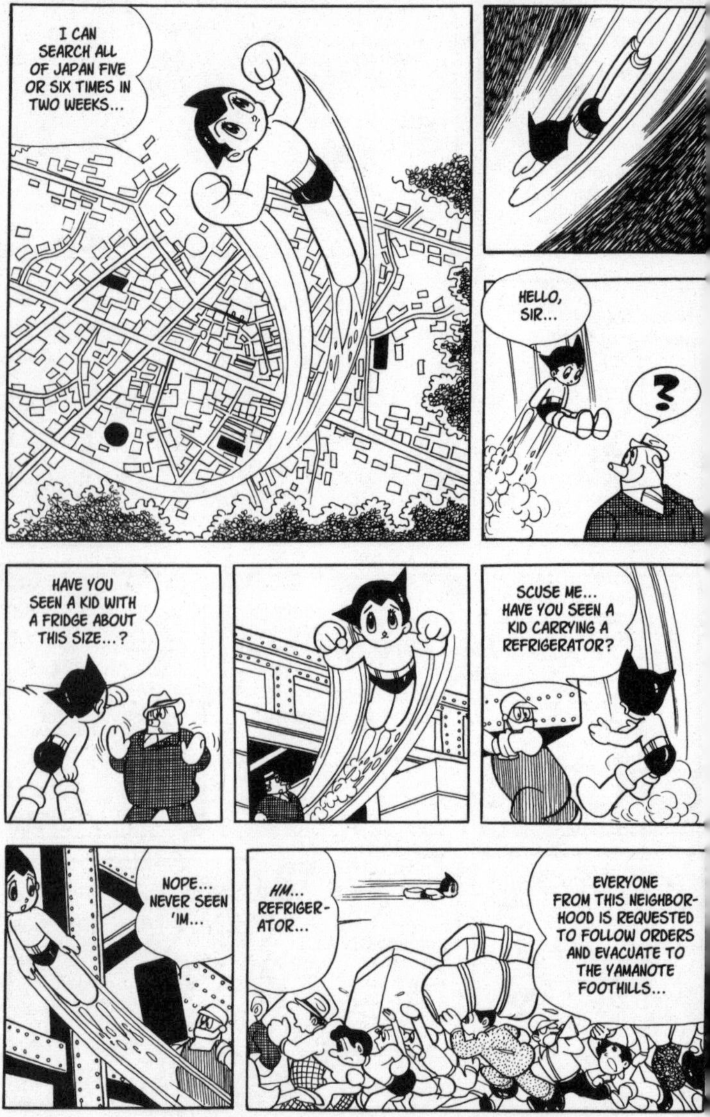
I CAN SEARCH ALL OF JAPAN FIVE OR SIX TIMES IN TWO WEEKS...
HELLO, SIR...
?
HAVE YOU SEEN A KID WITH A FRIDGE ABOUT THIS SIZE...?
SCUSE ME... HAVE YOU SEEN A KID CARRYING A REFRIGERATOR?
NOPE... NEVER SEEN 'IM...
HM... REFRIGER-ATOR...
EVERYONE FROM THIS NEIGHBOR-HOOD IS REQUESTED TO FOLLOW ORDERS AND EVACUATE TO THE YAMANOTE FOOTHILLS...

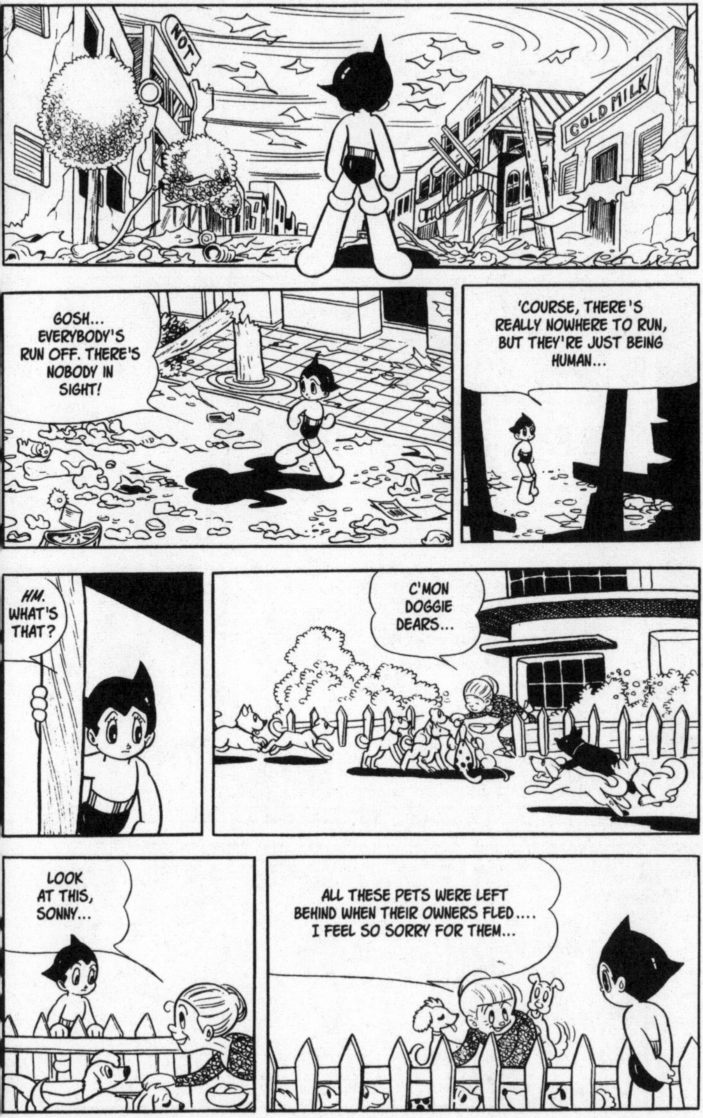
NOT
GOLD MILK
GOSH... EVERYBODY'S RUN OFF. THERE'S NOBODY IN SIGHT!
'COURSE, THERE'S REALLY NOWHERE TO RUN, BUT THEY'RE JUST BEING HUMAN...
HM. WHAT'S THAT?
C'MON DOGGIE DEARS...
LOOK AT THIS, SONNY...
ALL THESE PETS WERE LEFT BEHIND WHEN THEIR OWNERS FLED.... I FEEL SO SORRY FOR THEM...

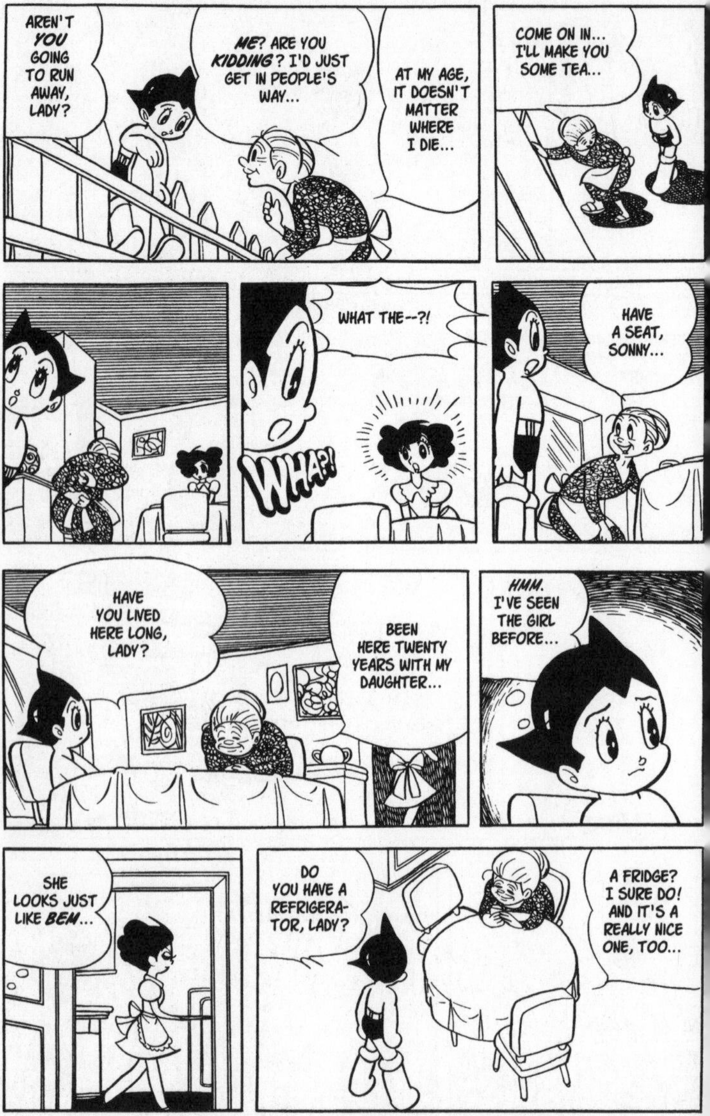
AREN'T YOU GOING TO RUN AWAY, LADY?
ME? ARE YOU KIDDING? I'D JUST GET IN PEOPLE'S WAY...
AT MY AGE, IT DOESN'T MATTER WHERE I DIE...
COME ON IN... I'LL MAKE YOU SOME TEA...
WHAT THE--?!
WHA?!
HAVE A SEAT, SONNY...
HAVE YOU LIVED HERE LONG, LADY?
BEEN HERE TWENTY YEARS WITH MY DAUGHTER...
HMM. I'VE SEEN THE GIRL BEFORE...
SHE LOOKS JUST LIKE BEM...
DO YOU HAVE A REFRIGERA-TOR, LADY?
A FRIDGE? I SURE DO! AND IT'S A REALLY NICE ONE, TOO...

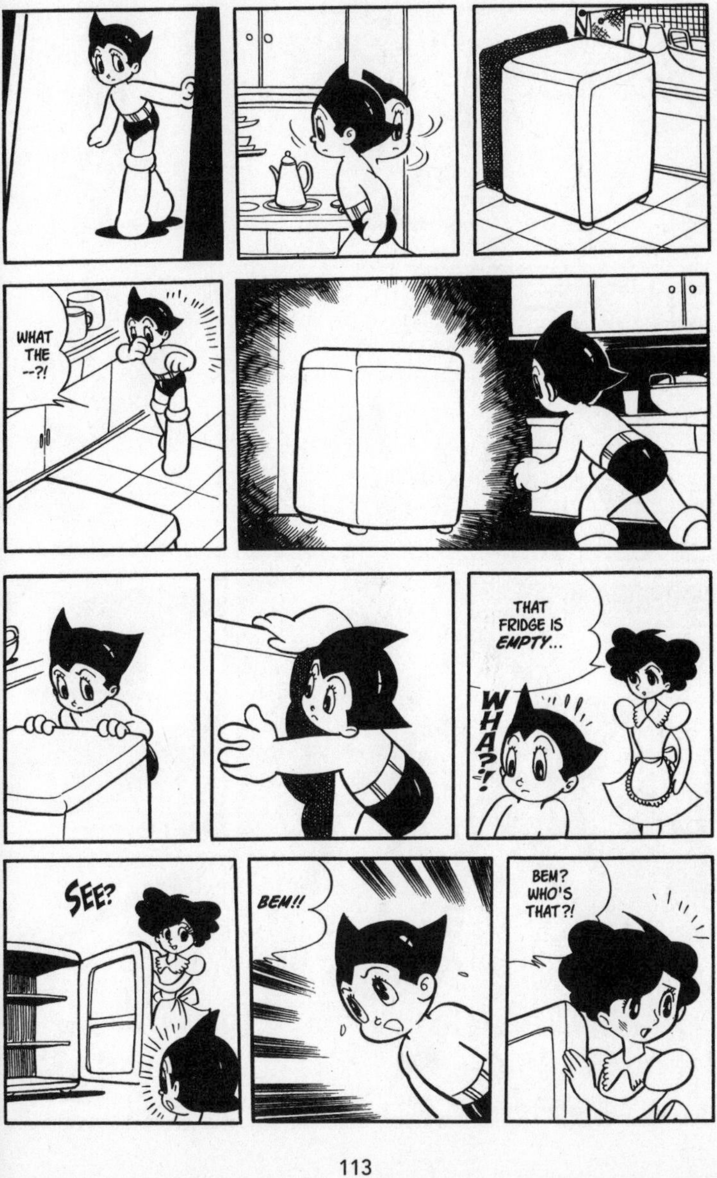
WHAT THE --?!
THAT FRIDGE IS EMPTY...
WHA?!
SEE?
BEM!!
BEM? WHO'S THAT?!

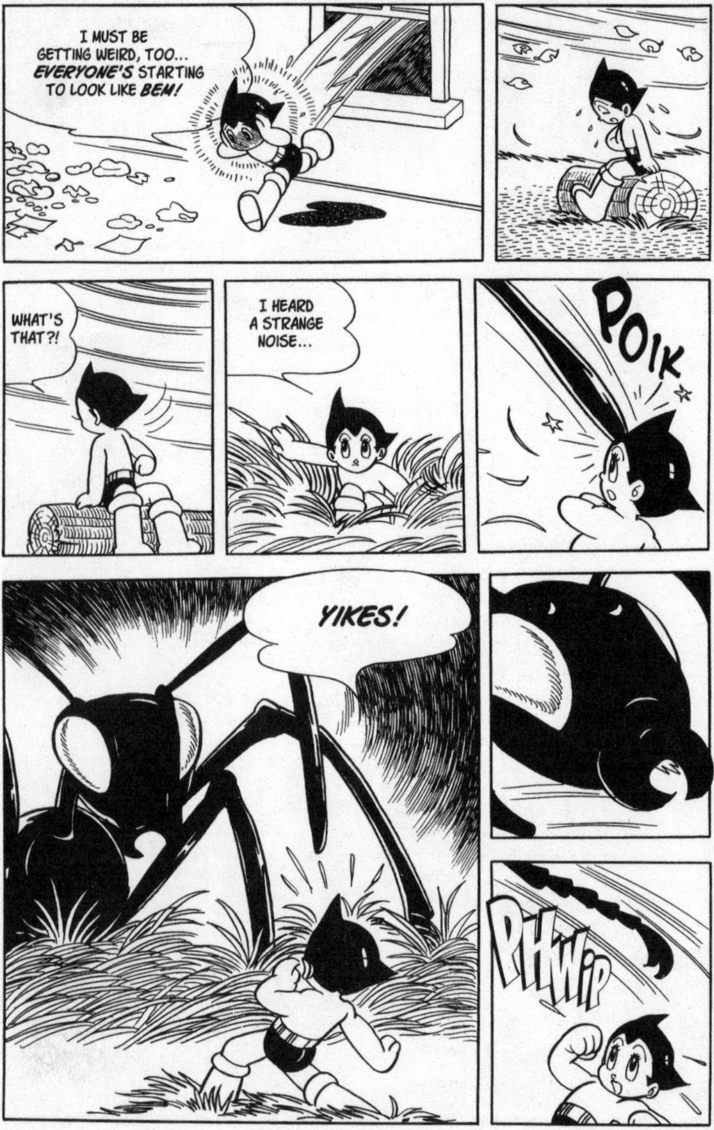
I MUST BE GETTING WEIRD, TOO... *EVERYONE'S* STARTING TO LOOK LIKE *BEM!*
WHAT'S THAT?!
I HEARD A STRANGE NOISE...
POIK
YIKES!
PHWIP

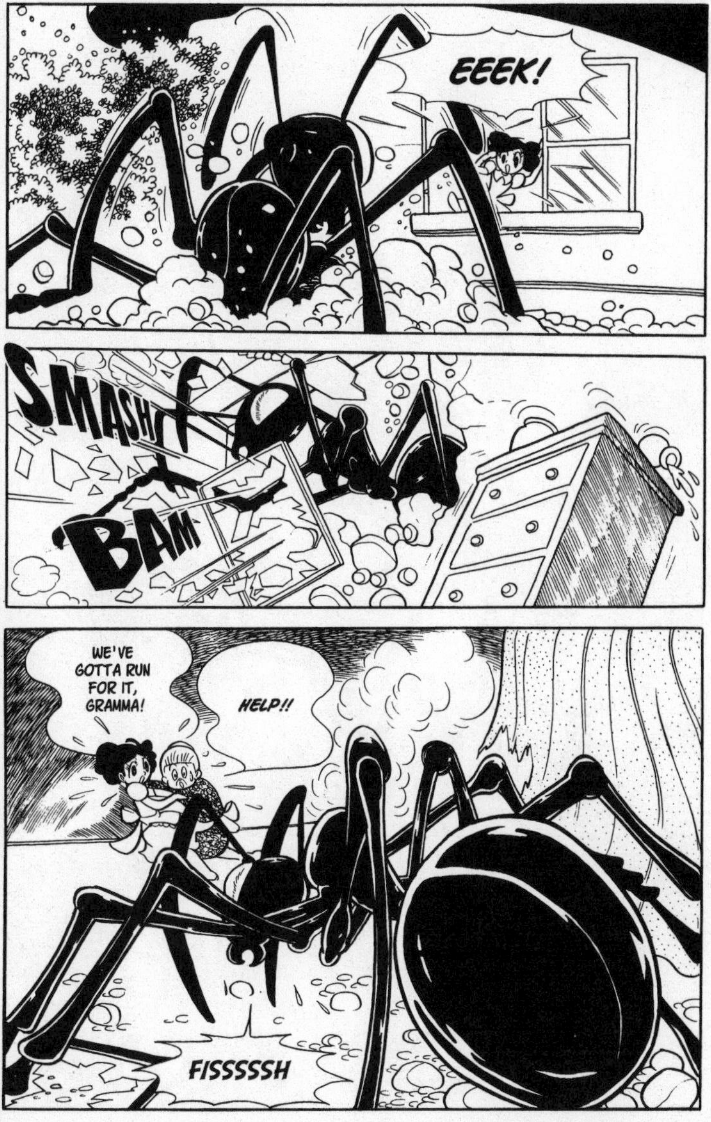
EEEK!
SMASH
BAM
WE'VE GOTTA RUN FOR IT, GRAMMA!
HELP!!
FISSSSSH

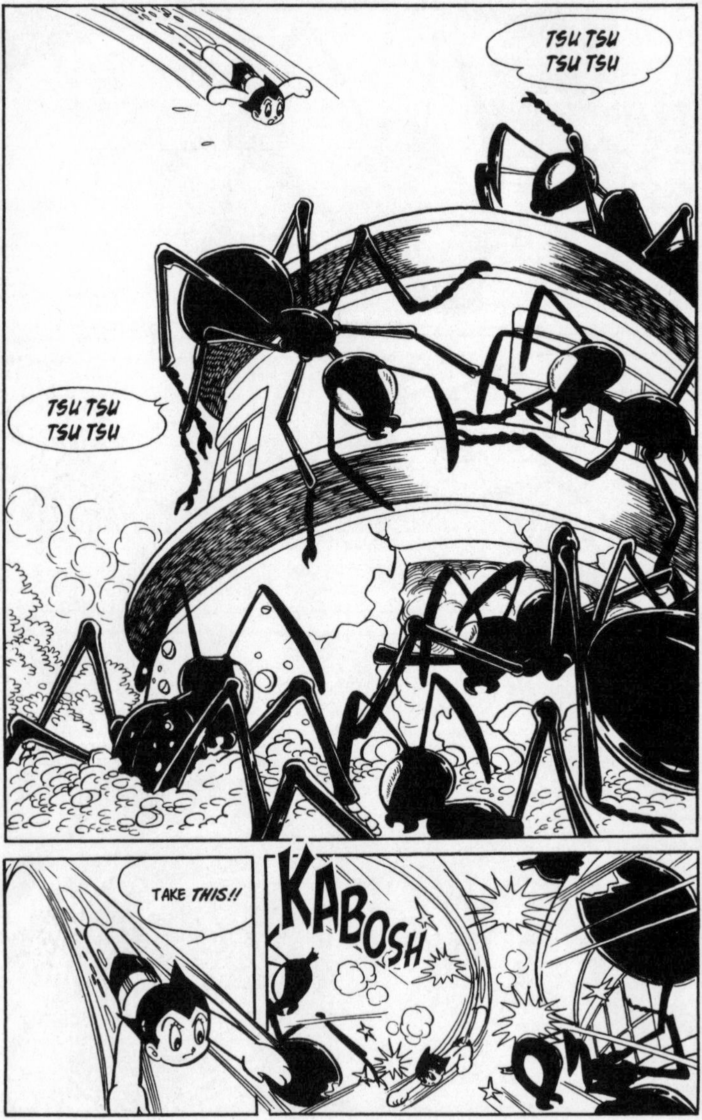
TSU TSU
TSU TSU
TSU TSU
TSU TSU
TAKE THIS!!
KABOSH

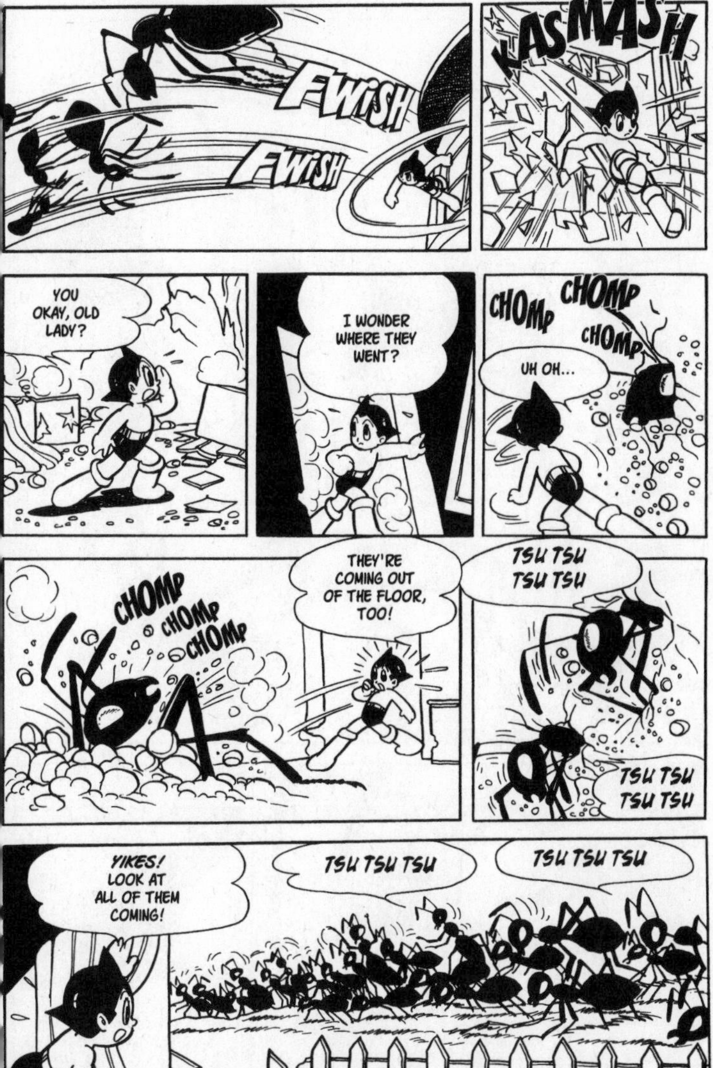
FWISH
FWISH
KASMASH
YOU OKAY, OLD LADY?
I WONDER WHERE THEY WENT?
CHOMP
CHOMP
CHOMP
UH OH...
CHOMP
CHOMP
CHOMP
THEY'RE COMING OUT OF THE FLOOR, TOO!
TSU TSU TSU TSU
TSU TSU TSU TSU
YIKES! LOOK AT ALL OF THEM COMING!
TSU TSU TSU
TSU TSU TSU

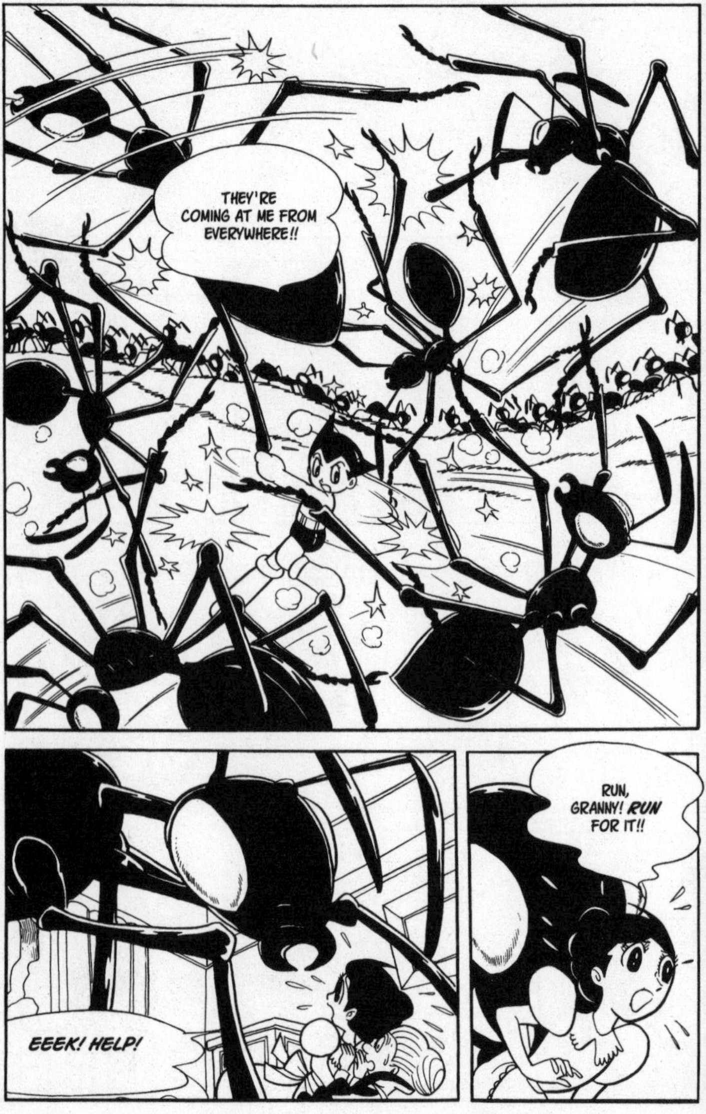
THEY'RE COMING AT ME FROM EVERYWHERE!!
EEEK! HELP!
RUN, GRANNY! *RUN* FOR IT!!

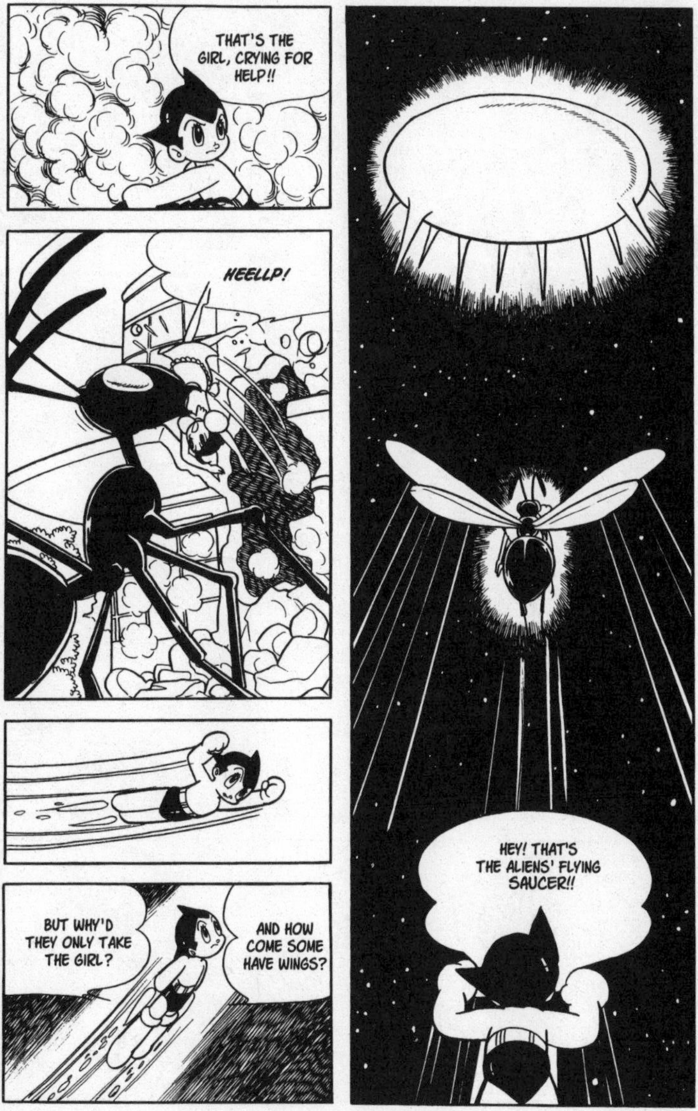
THAT'S THE GIRL, CRYING FOR HELP!!
HEELLP!
BUT WHY'D THEY ONLY TAKE THE GIRL?
AND HOW COME SOME HAVE WINGS?
HEY! THAT'S THE ALIENS' FLYING SAUCER!!

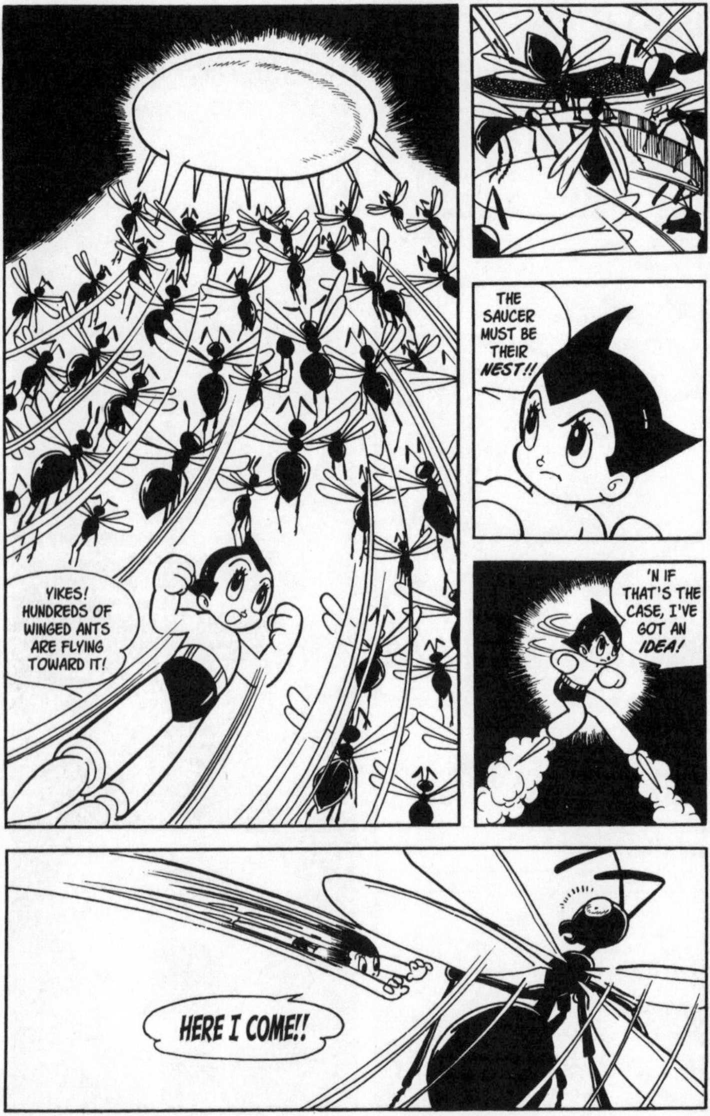
YIKES! HUNDREDS OF WINGED ANTS ARE FLYING TOWARD IT!
THE SAUCER MUST BE THEIR *NEST!!*
'N IF THAT'S THE CASE, I'VE GOT AN *IDEA!*
HERE I COME!!

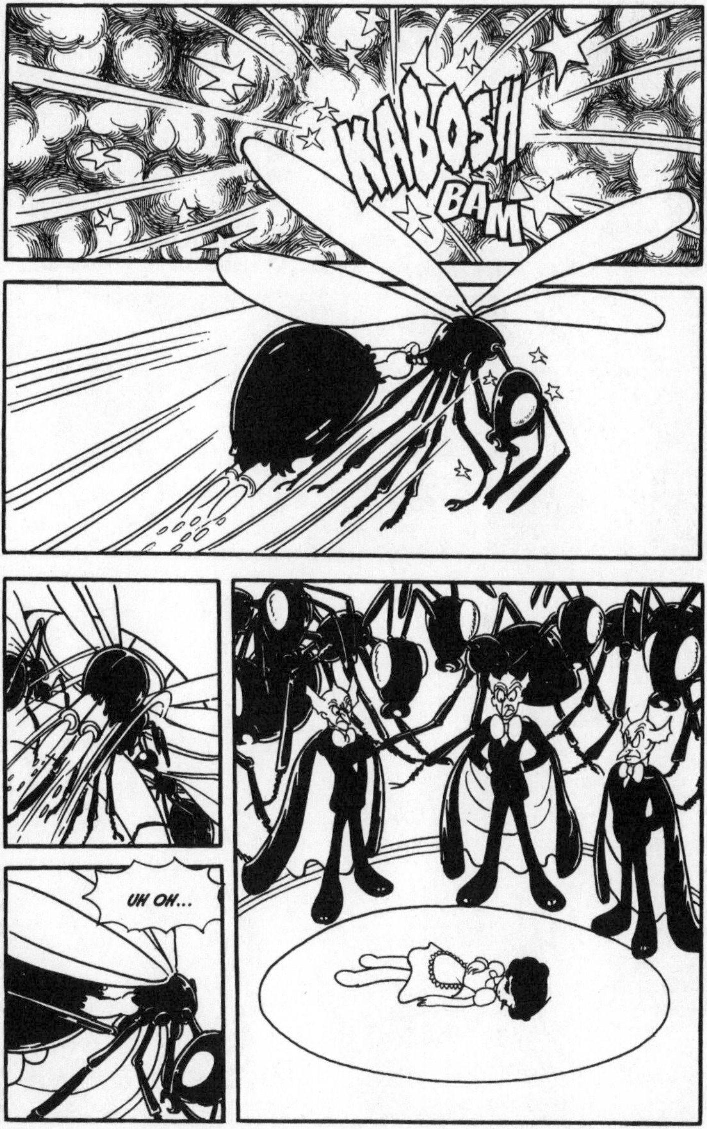
KABOSH
BAM
UH OH...

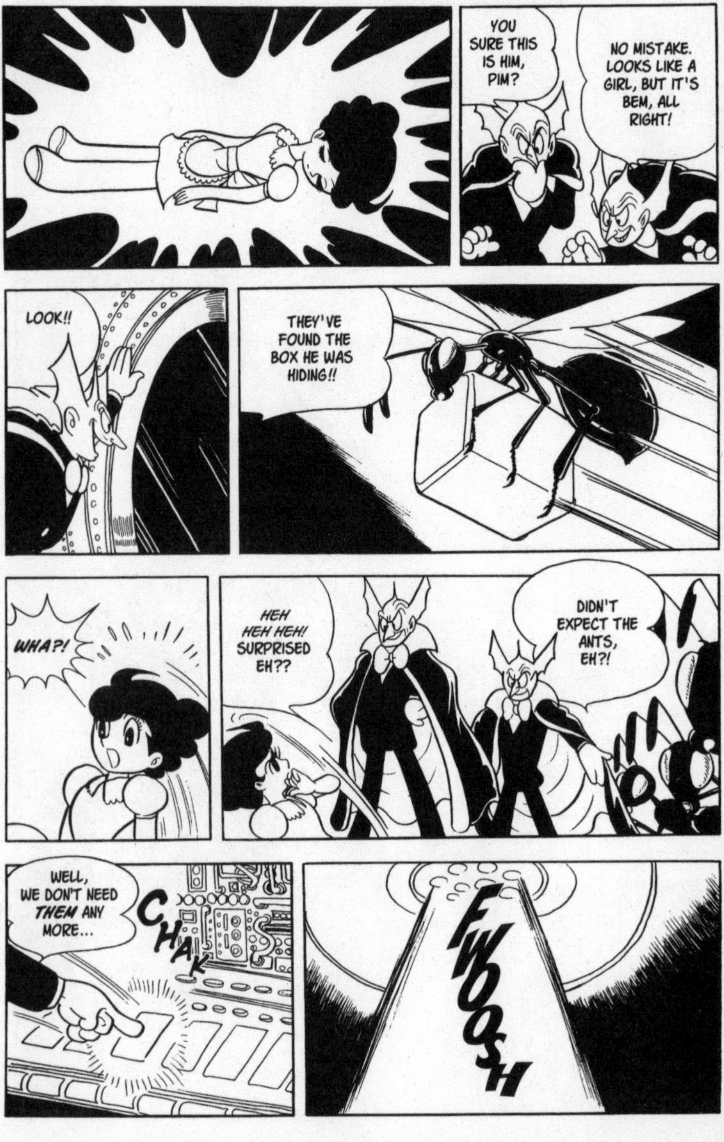
YOU SURE THIS IS HIM, PIM?
NO MISTAKE. LOOKS LIKE A GIRL, BUT IT'S BEM, ALL RIGHT!
LOOK!!
THEY'VE FOUND THE BOX HE WAS HIDING!!
WHA?!
HEH HEH HEH! SURPRISED EH??
DIDN'T EXPECT THE ANTS, EH?!
WELL, WE DON'T NEED THEM ANY MORE...
CHAK
FWOOSH

FLASH

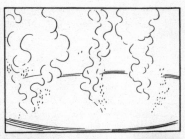

WE FOUND OUT WHERE YOU WERE HIDING, INJECTED *SUPER GROWTH HORMONES* INTO A NEARBY ANT HIVE, AND ENLARGED 'EM!!

THEN WE HIJACKED THEIR BRAINWAVES AND HAD 'EM BRING YOU BACK HERE!! AND THEY BROUGHT THE BOX, TOO!!

YOU DON'T NEED THIS ANY-MORE!

YOU'RE A *BOMB* THAT *WE* MADE!

WHY'D YOU RUN AWAY TO EARTH, ANYWAY?!

YEAH... EARTH'LL BE GONE IN TWO OR THREE DAYS! WHAT'S IT TO YOU?!!

....

LEMME SHOW YOU SOMETHING! *WE* SENT THAT STAR TO CRASH INTO EARTH *AND* THE SUN!

123

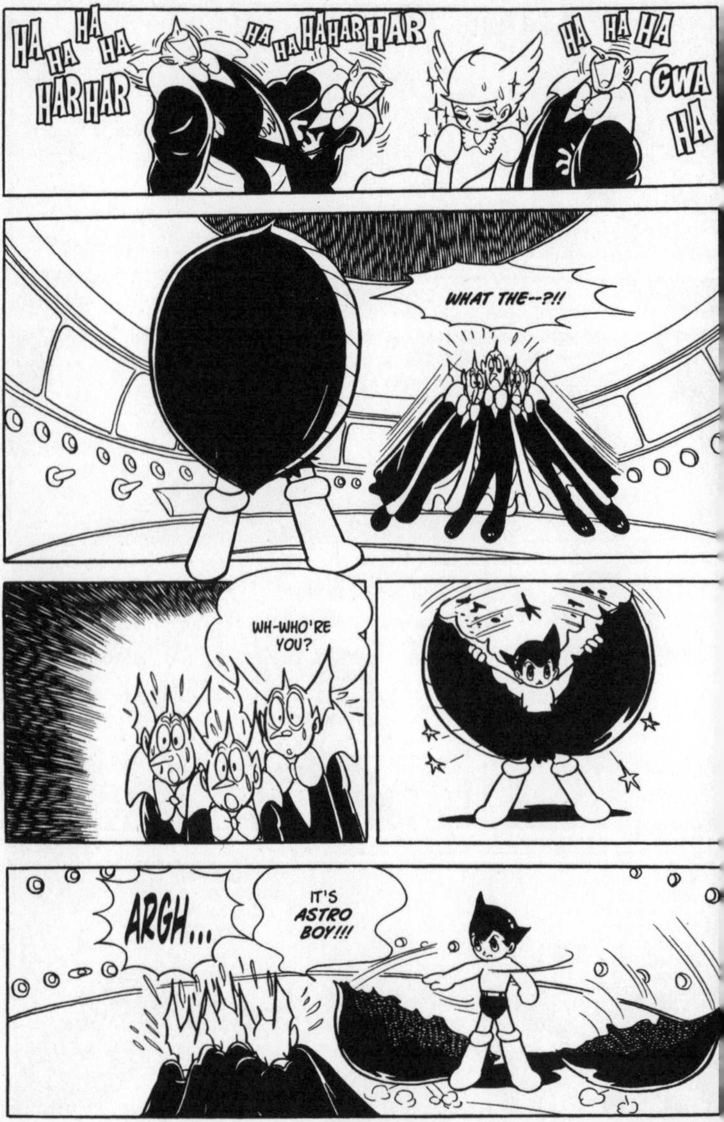
HA HA HA HA HAR HAR
HA HA HA HAR HAR
HA HA HA HA
GWA HA
WHAT THE--?!!
WH-WHO'RE YOU?
ARGH...
IT'S ASTRO BOY!!!

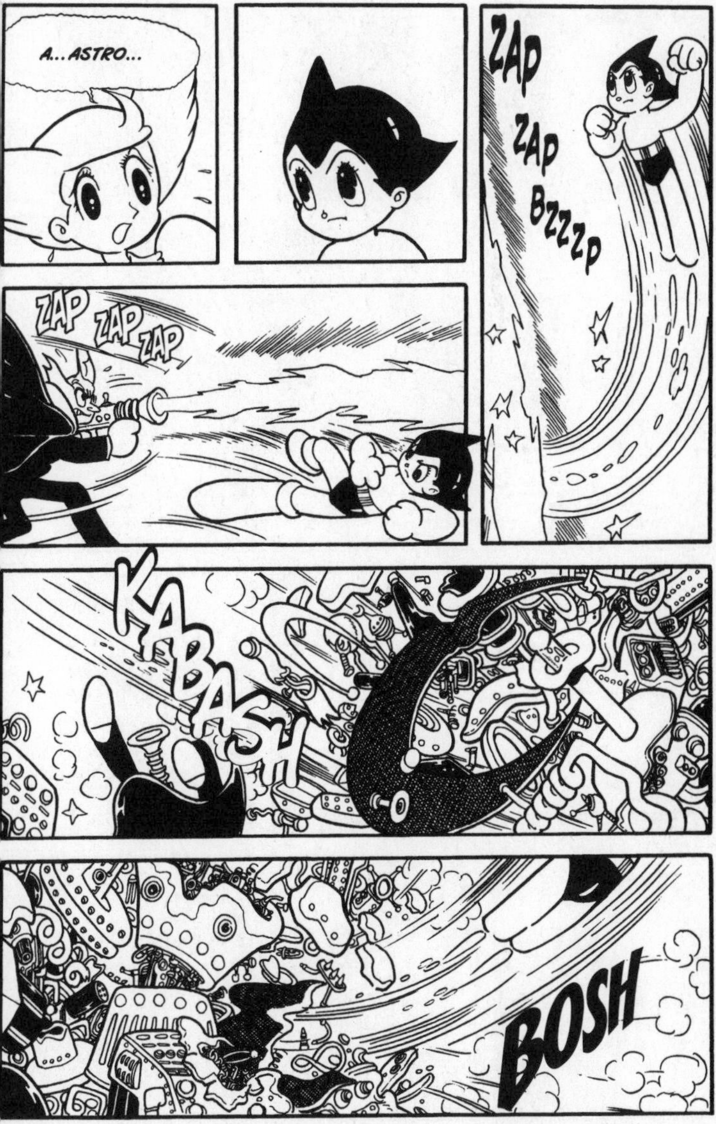
A...ASTRO...
ZAP
ZAP
BZZZZP
ZAP
ZAP
ZAP
KABASH
BOSH

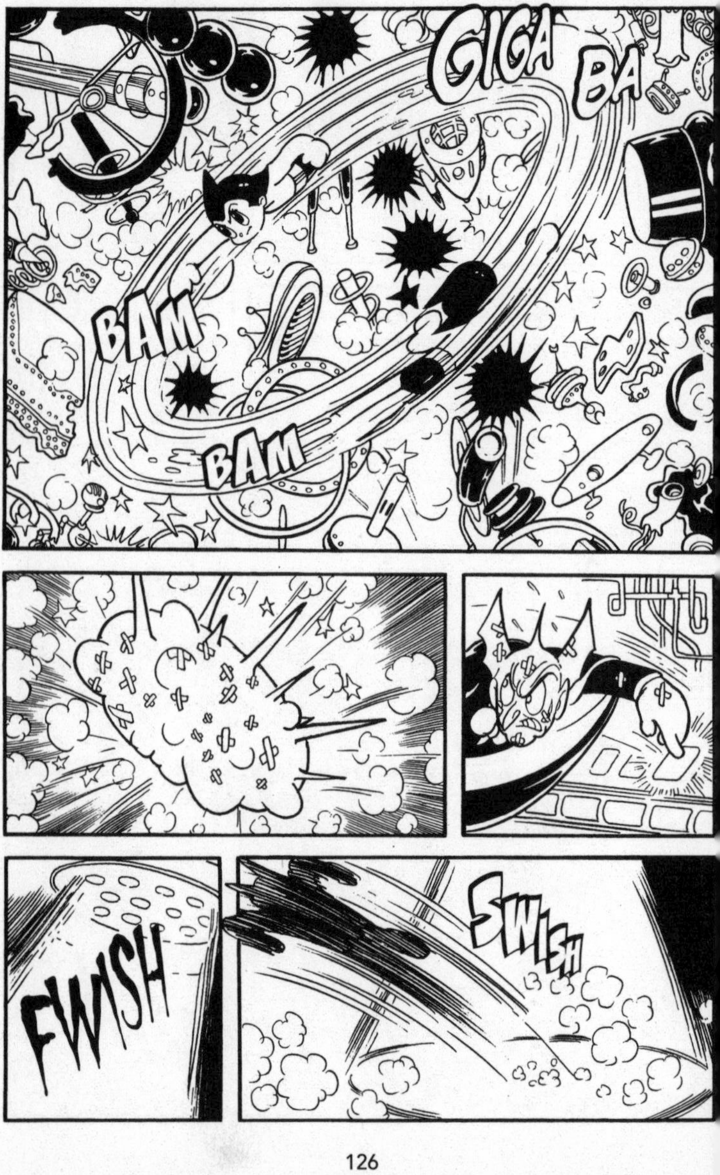
GIGA
BA
BAM
BAM
FWISH
SWISH

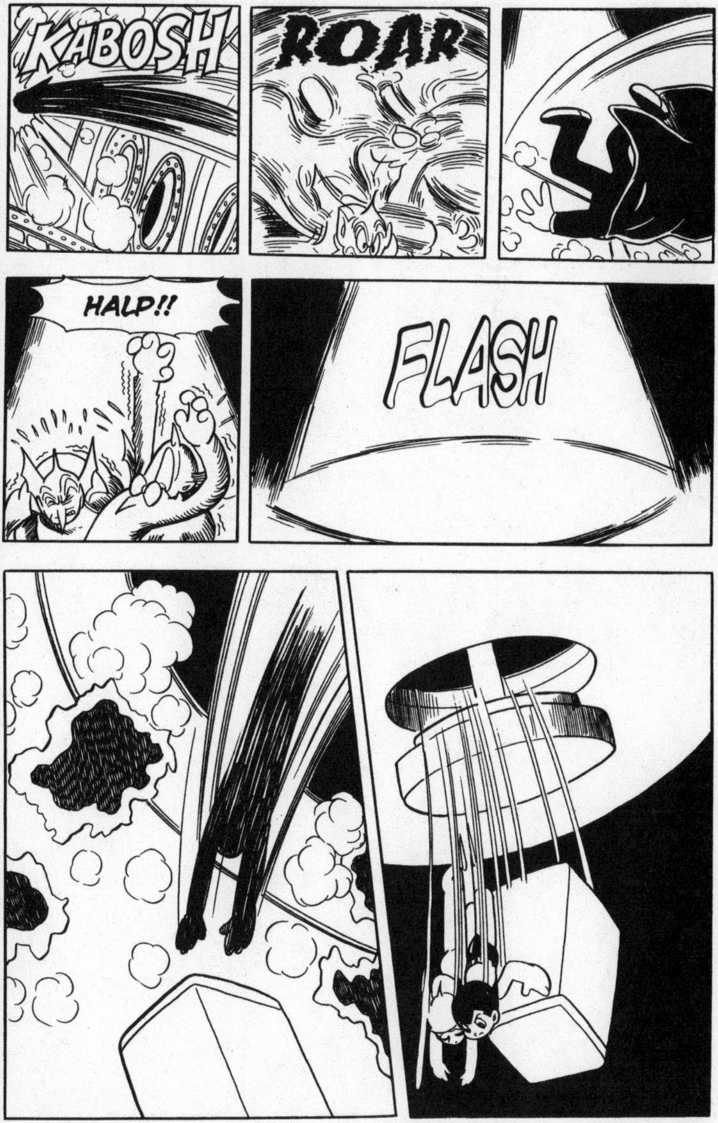
KABOSH
ROAR
HALP!!
FLASH

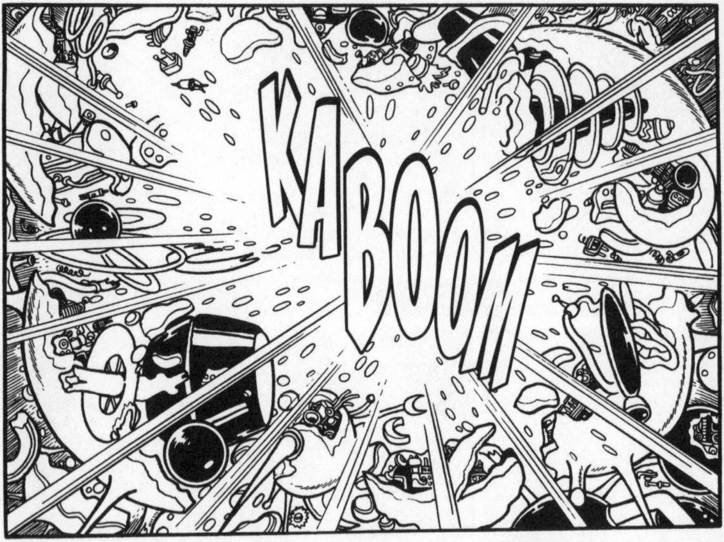
KABOOM
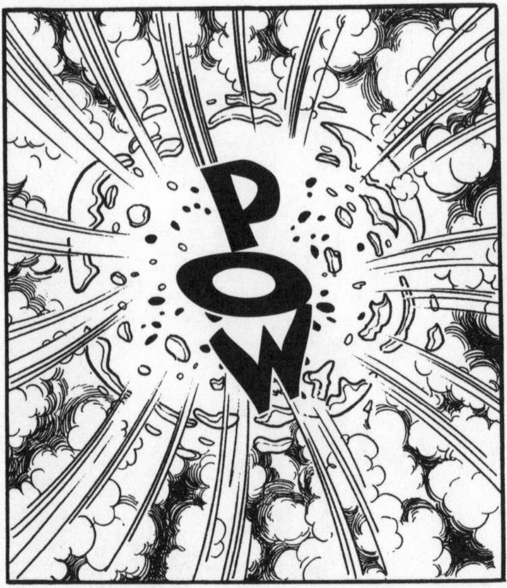
POW
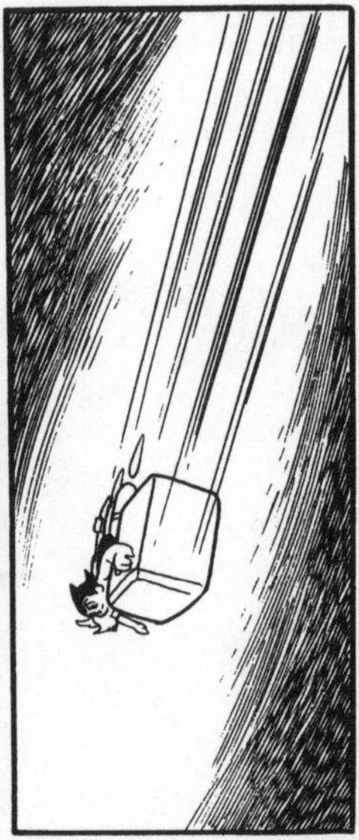

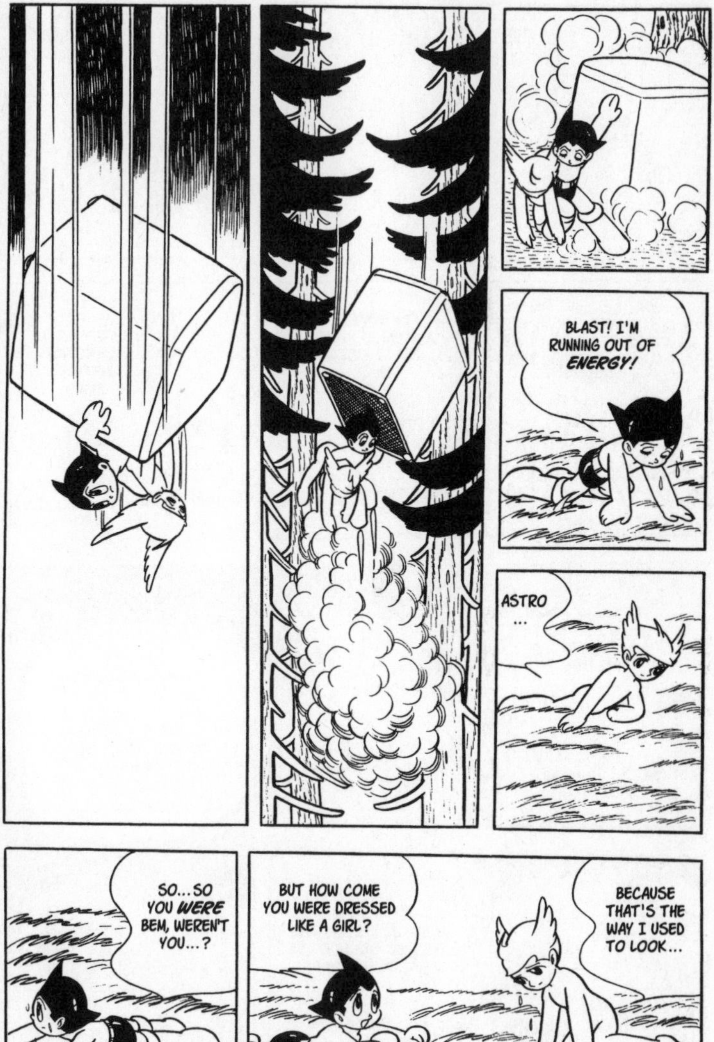
BLAST! I'M RUNNING OUT OF ENERGY!
ASTRO ...
SO...SO YOU WERE BEM, WEREN'T YOU...?
BUT HOW COME YOU WERE DRESSED LIKE A GIRL?
BECAUSE THAT'S THE WAY I USED TO LOOK...

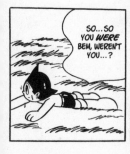

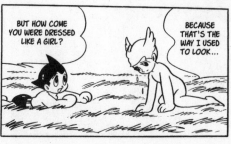

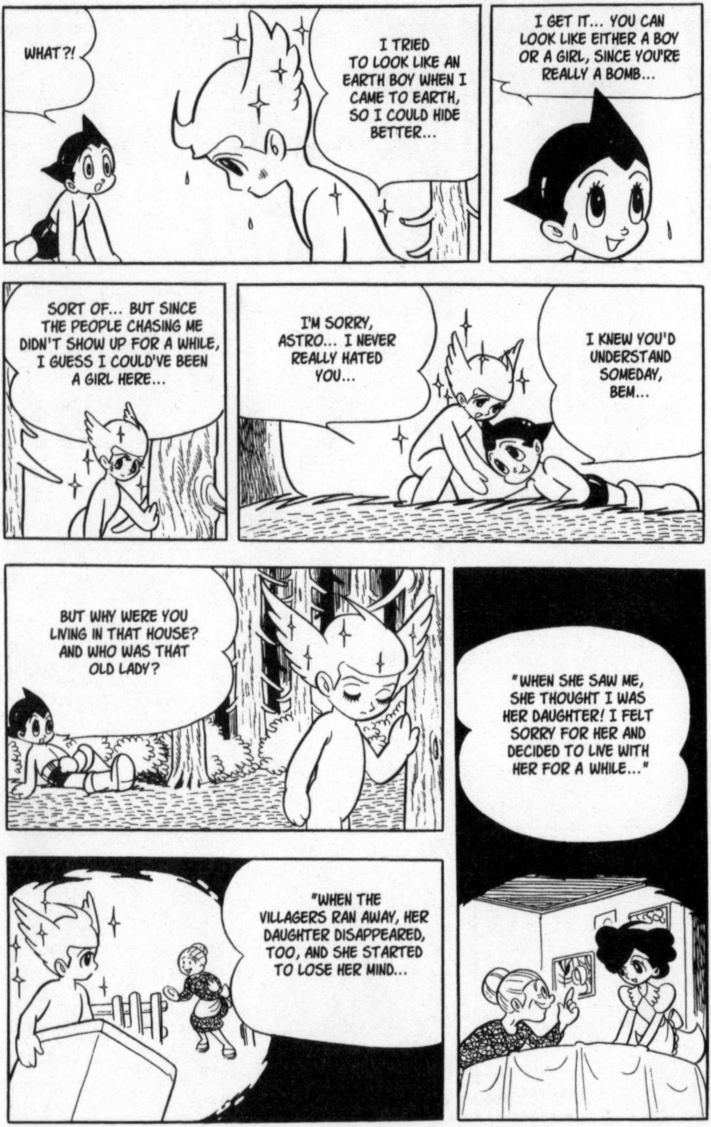

WHAT?!
I TRIED TO LOOK LIKE AN EARTH BOY WHEN I CAME TO EARTH, SO I COULD HIDE BETTER...
I GET IT... YOU CAN LOOK LIKE EITHER A BOY OR A GIRL, SINCE YOU'RE REALLY A BOMB...
SORT OF... BUT SINCE THE PEOPLE CHASING ME DIDN'T SHOW UP FOR A WHILE, I GUESS I COULD'VE BEEN A GIRL HERE...
I'M SORRY, ASTRO... I NEVER REALLY HATED YOU...
I KNEW YOU'D UNDERSTAND SOMEDAY, BEM...
BUT WHY WERE YOU LIVING IN THAT HOUSE? AND WHO WAS THAT OLD LADY?
"WHEN SHE SAW ME, SHE THOUGHT I WAS HER DAUGHTER! I FELT SORRY FOR HER AND DECIDED TO LIVE WITH HER FOR A WHILE..."
"WHEN THE VILLAGERS RAN AWAY, HER DAUGHTER DISAPPEARED, TOO, AND SHE STARTED TO LOSE HER MIND...

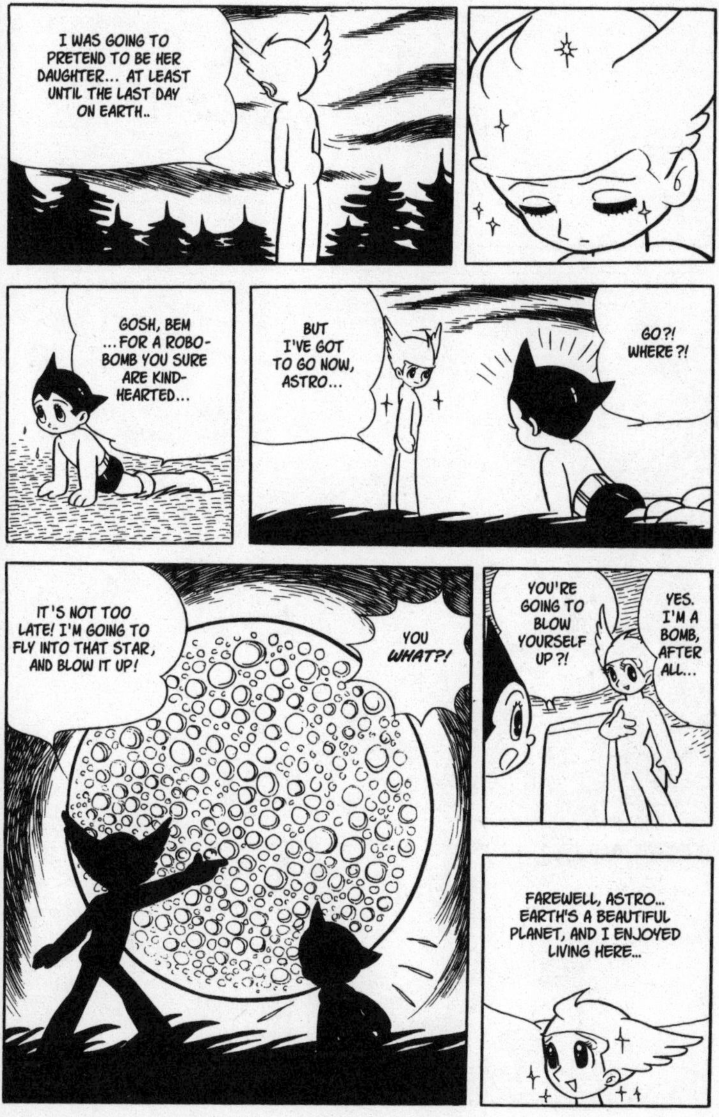

I WAS GOING TO PRETEND TO BE HER DAUGHTER... AT LEAST UNTIL THE LAST DAY ON EARTH..
GOSH, BEM ...FOR A ROBO-BOMB YOU SURE ARE KIND-HEARTED...
BUT I'VE GOT TO GO NOW, ASTRO...
GO?! WHERE?!
IT'S NOT TOO LATE! I'M GOING TO FLY INTO THAT STAR, AND BLOW IT UP!
YOU *WHAT?!*
YOU'RE GOING TO BLOW YOURSELF UP?!
YES. I'M A BOMB, AFTER ALL...
FAREWELL, ASTRO... EARTH'S A BEAUTIFUL PLANET, AND I ENJOYED LIVING HERE...

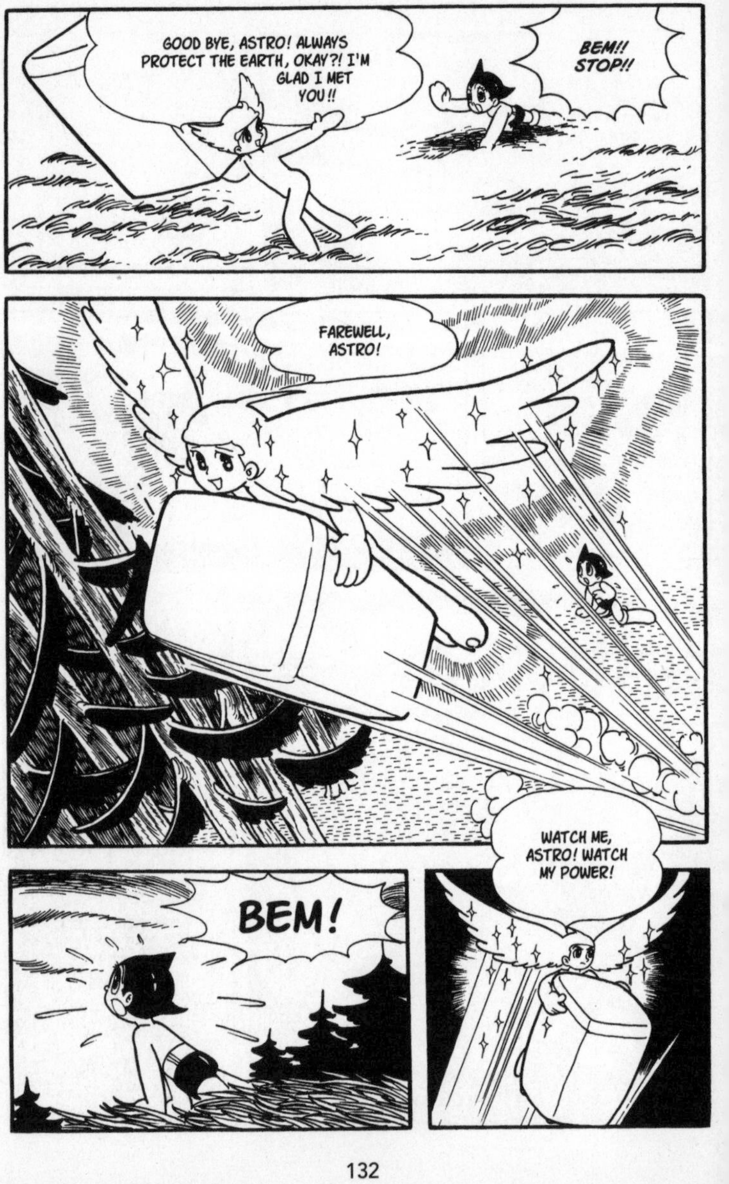
GOOD BYE, ASTRO! ALWAYS PROTECT THE EARTH, OKAY?! I'M GLAD I MET YOU!!
BEM!! STOP!!
FAREWELL, ASTRO!
BEM!
WATCH ME, ASTRO! WATCH MY POWER!

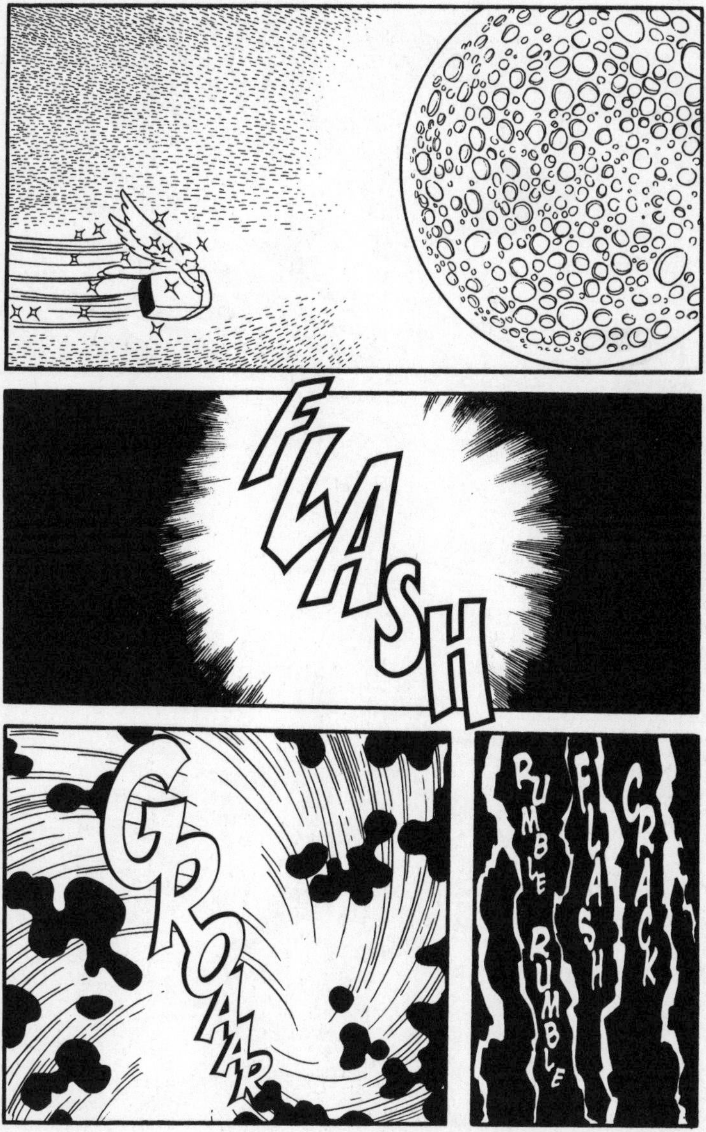
FLASH
GROOAAR
RUMBLE RUMBLE
FLASH
CRACK

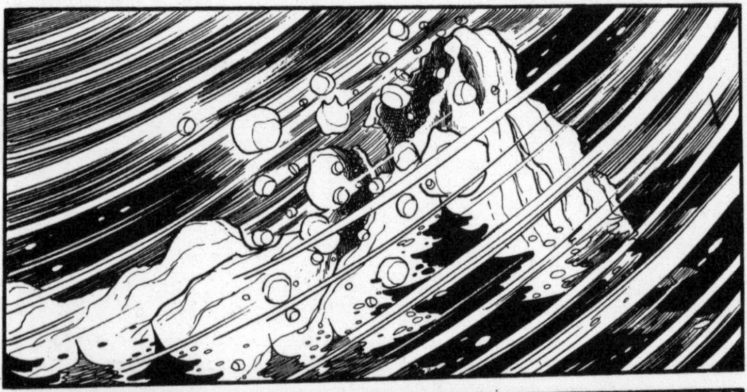

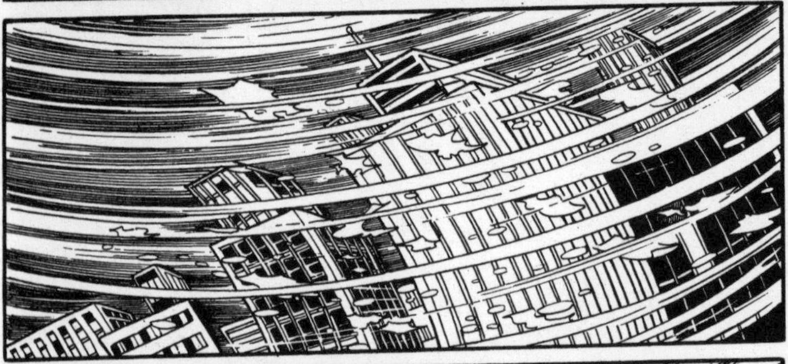

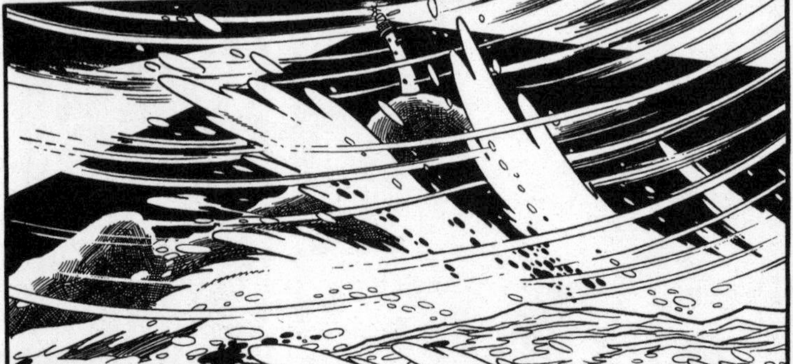

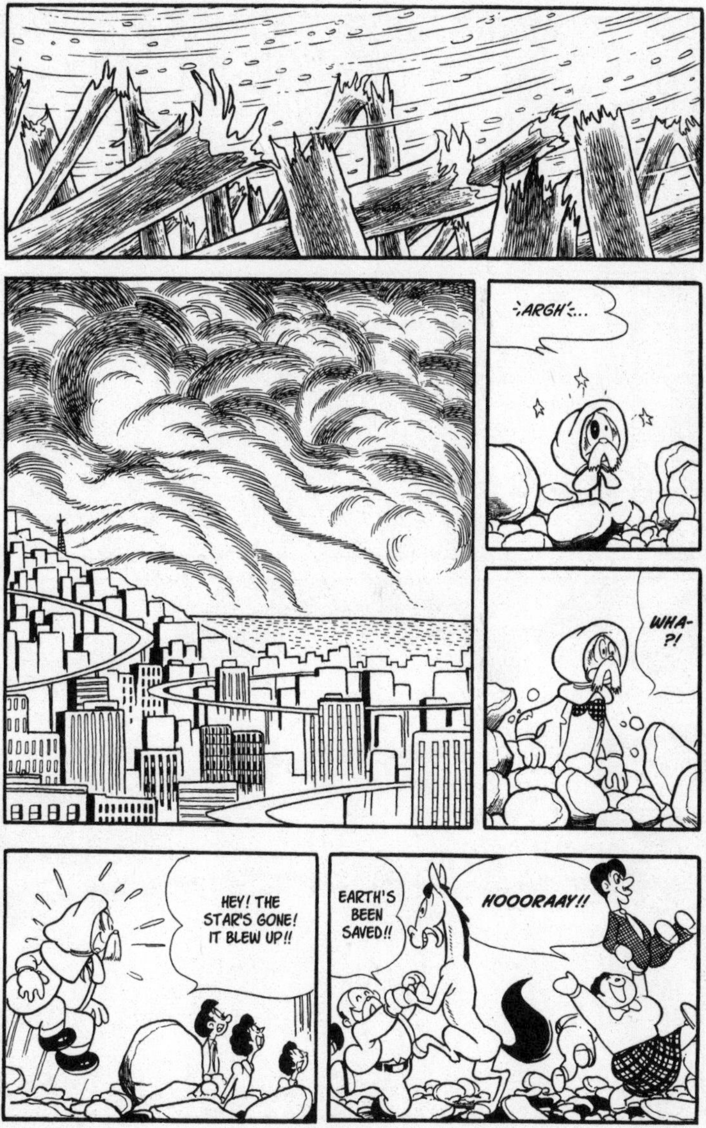
ARGH...
WHA-?!
HEY! THE STAR'S GONE! IT BLEW UP!!
EARTH'S BEEN SAVED!!
HOOORAAY!!

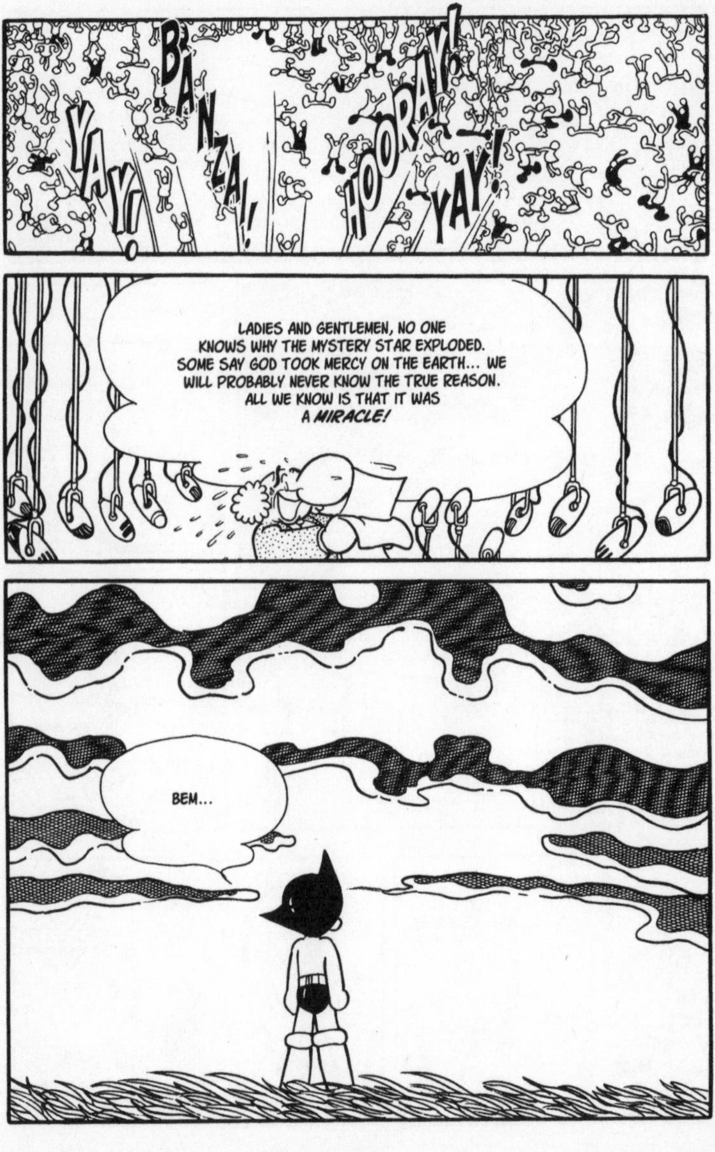
YAY!
BANZAI!
HOORAY!
YAY!
LADIES AND GENTLEMEN, NO ONE KNOWS WHY THE MYSTERY STAR EXPLODED. SOME SAY GOD TOOK MERCY ON THE EARTH... WE WILL PROBABLY NEVER KNOW THE TRUE REASON. ALL WE KNOW IS THAT IT WAS A *MIRACLE!*
BEM...

SUBTERRANEAN TANK

First serialized from October to November 1959
in *Shonen* magazine.

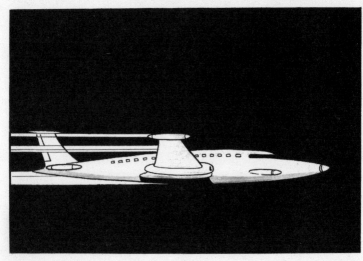

SOME PEOPLE'RE AFRAID TO TRAVEL BY PLANES, BUT NOT *ME*...

NIBBLE *CRUNCH* *NIBBLE*

HECK, FOR ME, FLYING'S A BREEZE!

CRUNCH *NIBBLE* *CRUNCH*

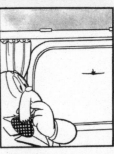

EGADS!

KATHUD

138

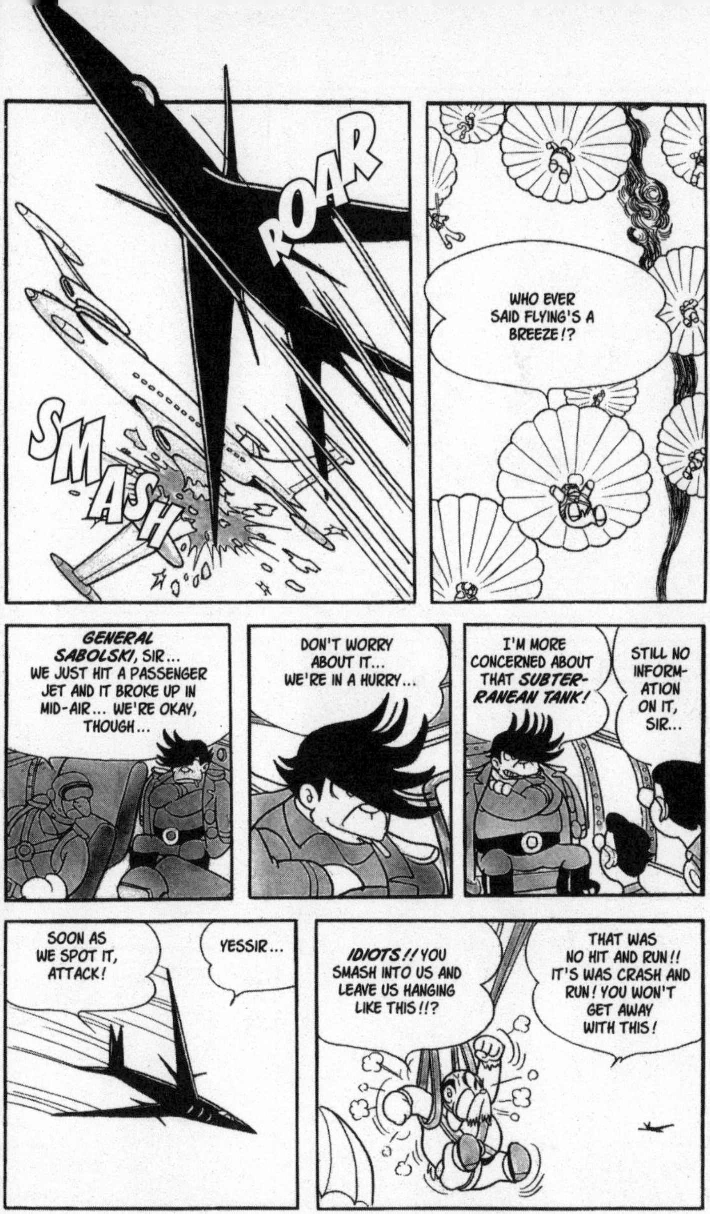
ROAR
SMASH
WHO EVER SAID FLYING'S A BREEZE!?
GENERAL SABOLSKI, SIR... WE JUST HIT A PASSENGER JET AND IT BROKE UP IN MID-AIR... WE'RE OKAY, THOUGH...
DON'T WORRY ABOUT IT... WE'RE IN A HURRY...
I'M MORE CONCERNED ABOUT THAT SUBTERRANEAN TANK!
STILL NO INFORMATION ON IT, SIR...
SOON AS WE SPOT IT, ATTACK!
YESSIR...
IDIOTS!! YOU SMASH INTO US AND LEAVE US HANGING LIKE THIS!!?
THAT WAS NO HIT AND RUN!! IT'S WAS CRASH AND RUN! YOU WON'T GET AWAY WITH THIS!

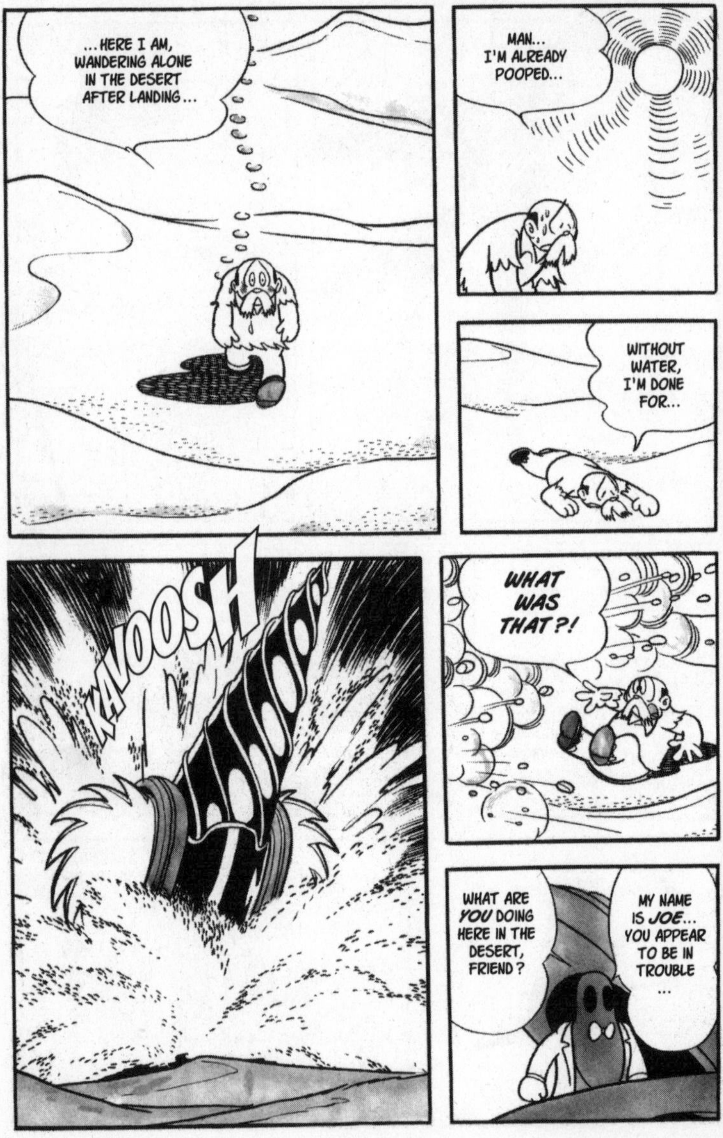

...HERE I AM, WANDERING ALONE IN THE DESERT AFTER LANDING...
MAN... I'M ALREADY POOPED...
WITHOUT WATER, I'M DONE FOR...
KAVOOSH
WHAT WAS THAT?!
WHAT ARE YOU DOING HERE IN THE DESERT, FRIEND?
MY NAME IS JOE... YOU APPEAR TO BE IN TROUBLE ...

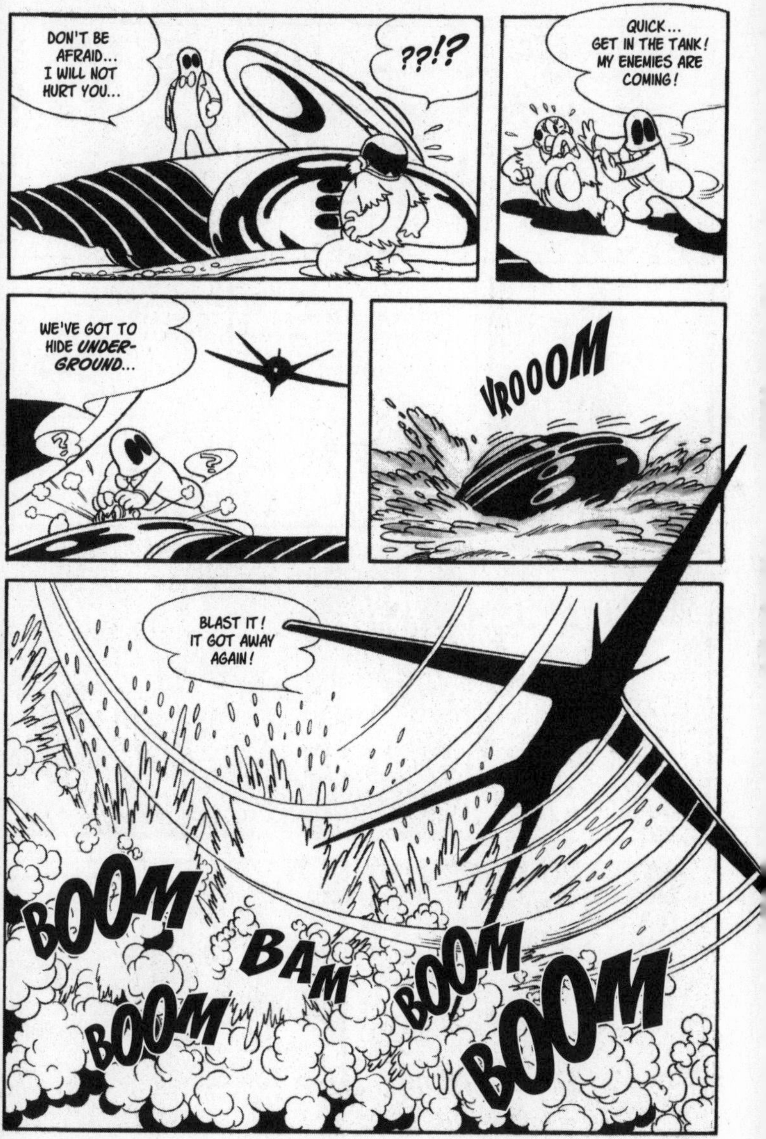

DON'T BE AFRAID... I WILL NOT HURT YOU...
??!?
QUICK... GET IN THE TANK! MY ENEMIES ARE COMING!
WE'VE GOT TO HIDE *UNDER-GROUND*...
VROOOM
BLAST IT! IT GOT AWAY AGAIN!
BOOM
BOOM
BAM
BOOM
BOOM

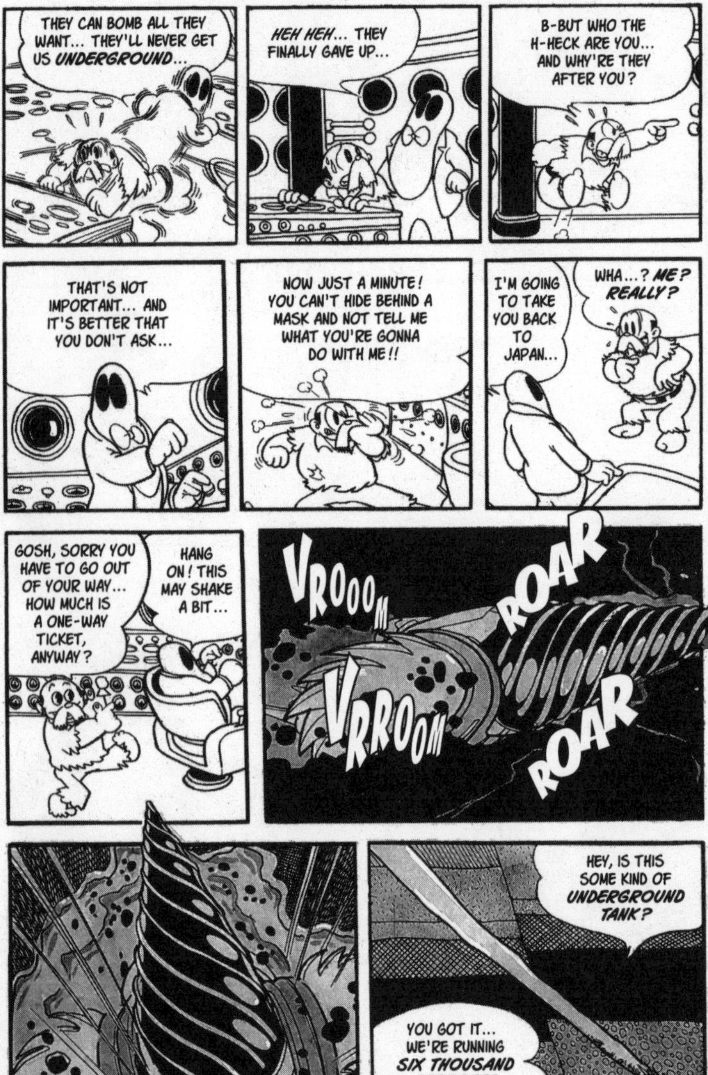
THEY CAN BOMB ALL THEY WANT... THEY'LL NEVER GET US UNDERGROUND...
HEH HEH... THEY FINALLY GAVE UP...
B-BUT WHO THE H-HECK ARE YOU... AND WHY'RE THEY AFTER YOU?
THAT'S NOT IMPORTANT... AND IT'S BETTER THAT YOU DON'T ASK...
NOW JUST A MINUTE! YOU CAN'T HIDE BEHIND A MASK AND NOT TELL ME WHAT YOU'RE GONNA DO WITH ME!!
I'M GOING TO TAKE YOU BACK TO JAPAN...
WHA...? ME? REALLY?
GOSH, SORRY YOU HAVE TO GO OUT OF YOUR WAY... HOW MUCH IS A ONE-WAY TICKET, ANYWAY?
HANG ON! THIS MAY SHAKE A BIT...
VROOOM
ROAR
VRROOM
ROAR
HEY, IS THIS SOME KIND OF UNDERGROUND TANK?
YOU GOT IT... WE'RE RUNNING SIX THOUSAND FEET DEEP NOW...

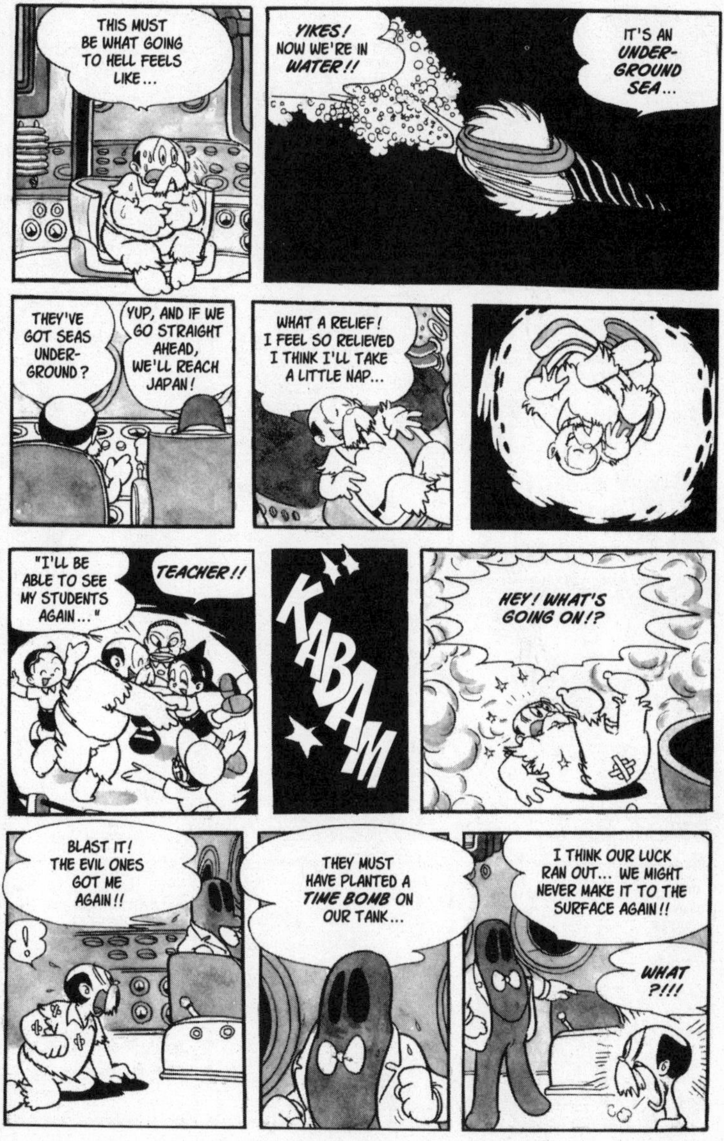
THIS MUST BE WHAT GOING TO HELL FEELS LIKE...
YIKES! NOW WE'RE IN WATER!!
IT'S AN UNDER-GROUND SEA...
THEY'VE GOT SEAS UNDER-GROUND?
YUP, AND IF WE GO STRAIGHT AHEAD, WE'LL REACH JAPAN!
WHAT A RELIEF! I FEEL SO RELIEVED I THINK I'LL TAKE A LITTLE NAP...
"I'LL BE ABLE TO SEE MY STUDENTS AGAIN..."
TEACHER!!
KABAM
HEY! WHAT'S GOING ON!?
BLAST IT! THE EVIL ONES GOT ME AGAIN!!
!
THEY MUST HAVE PLANTED A TIME BOMB ON OUR TANK...
I THINK OUR LUCK RAN OUT... WE MIGHT NEVER MAKE IT TO THE SURFACE AGAIN!!
WHAT?!!!

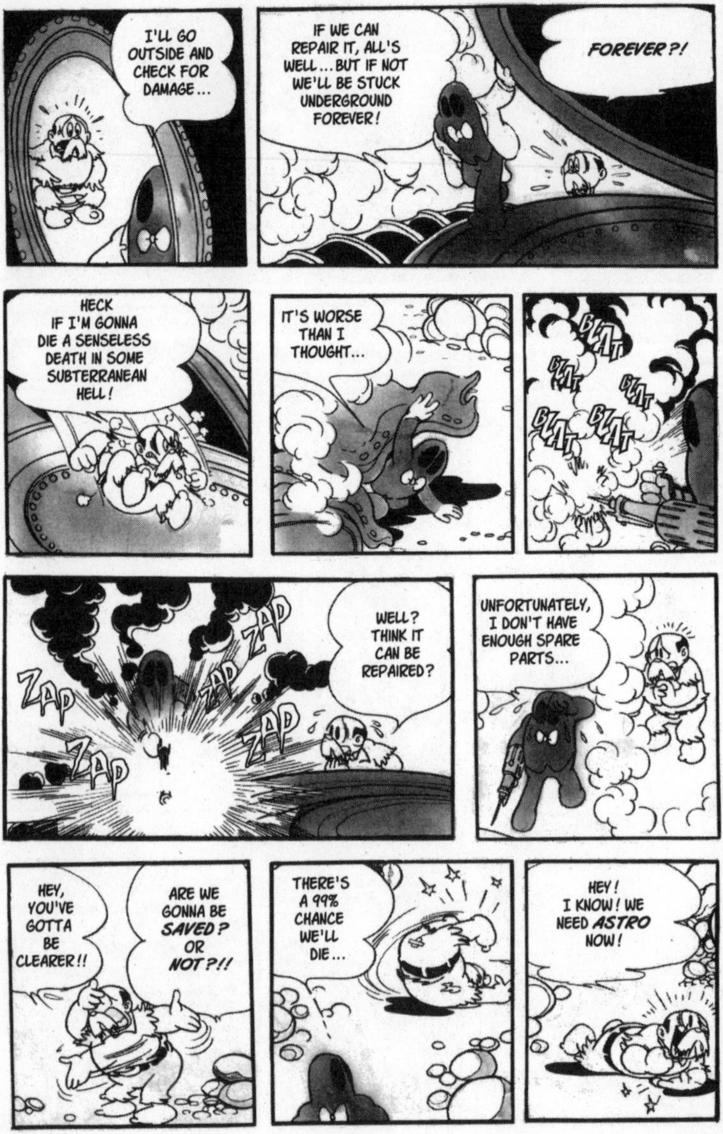

I'LL GO OUTSIDE AND CHECK FOR DAMAGE...
IF WE CAN REPAIR IT, ALL'S WELL...BUT IF NOT WE'LL BE STUCK UNDERGROUND FOREVER!
FOREVER?!
HECK IF I'M GONNA DIE A SENSELESS DEATH IN SOME SUBTERRANEAN HELL!
IT'S WORSE THAN I THOUGHT...
BLAT BLAT BLAT BLAT BLAT
ZAP ZAP ZAP ZAP ZAP ZAP
WELL? THINK IT CAN BE REPAIRED?
UNFORTUNATELY, I DON'T HAVE ENOUGH SPARE PARTS...
HEY, YOU'VE GOTTA BE CLEARER!!
ARE WE GONNA BE SAVED? OR NOT?!!
THERE'S A 99% CHANCE WE'LL DIE...
HEY! I KNOW! WE NEED ASTRO NOW!

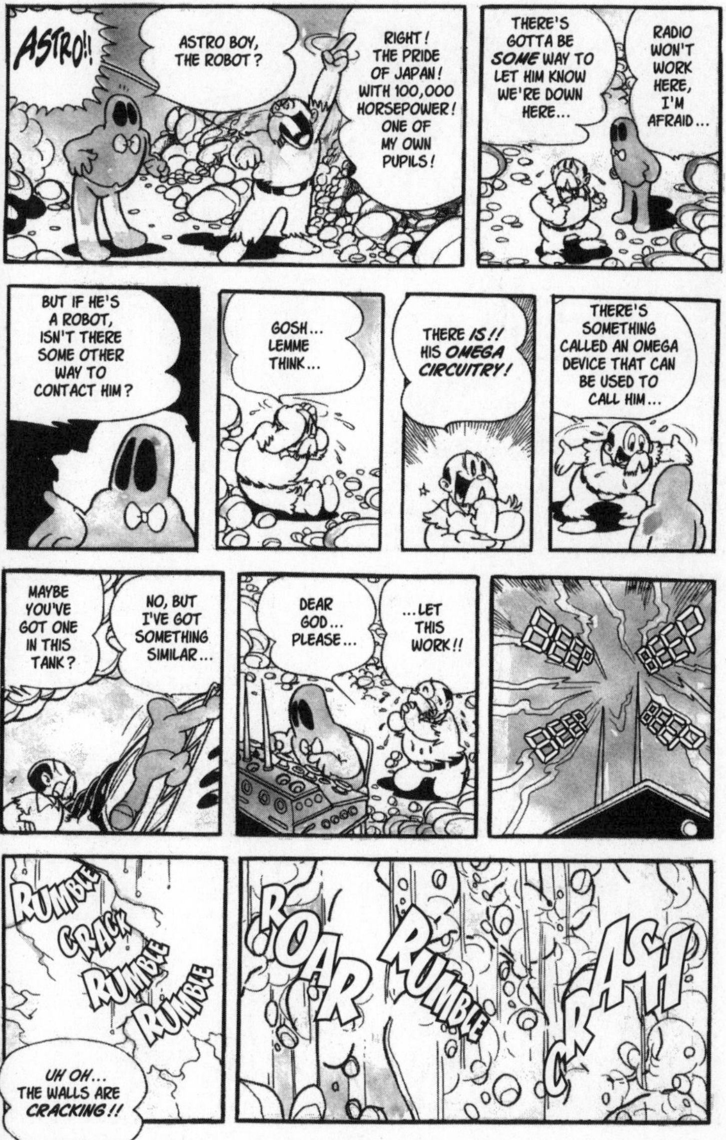

ASTRO!!
ASTRO BOY, THE ROBOT?
RIGHT! THE PRIDE OF JAPAN! WITH 100,000 HORSEPOWER! ONE OF MY OWN PUPILS!
THERE'S GOTTA BE SOME WAY TO LET HIM KNOW WE'RE DOWN HERE...
RADIO WON'T WORK HERE, I'M AFRAID...
BUT IF HE'S A ROBOT, ISN'T THERE SOME OTHER WAY TO CONTACT HIM?
GOSH... LEMME THINK...
THERE IS!! HIS OMEGA CIRCUITRY!
THERE'S SOMETHING CALLED AN OMEGA DEVICE THAT CAN BE USED TO CALL HIM...
MAYBE YOU'VE GOT ONE IN THIS TANK?
NO, BUT I'VE GOT SOMETHING SIMILAR...
DEAR GOD... PLEASE...
...LET THIS WORK!!
BEEP
BEEP
BEEP
BEEP
RUMBLE
CRACK
RUMBLE
RUMBLE
UH OH... THE WALLS ARE CRACKING!!
ROAR
RUMBLE
CRASH

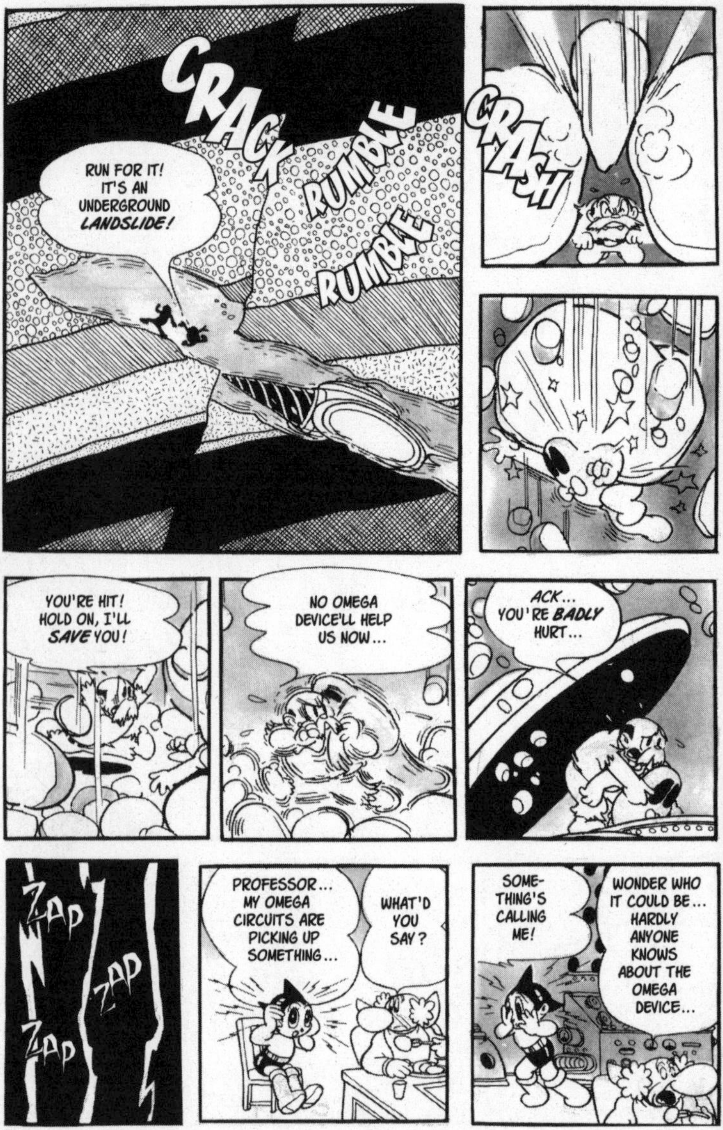
CRACK
RUMBLE
RUMBLE
RUN FOR IT! IT'S AN UNDERGROUND LANDSLIDE!
CRASH
YOU'RE HIT! HOLD ON, I'LL SAVE YOU!
NO OMEGA DEVICE'LL HELP US NOW...
ACK... YOU'RE BADLY HURT...
ZAP
ZAP
ZAP
PROFESSOR... MY OMEGA CIRCUITS ARE PICKING UP SOMETHING...
WHAT'D YOU SAY?
SOME-THING'S CALLING ME!
WONDER WHO IT COULD BE... HARDLY ANYONE KNOWS ABOUT THE OMEGA DEVICE...

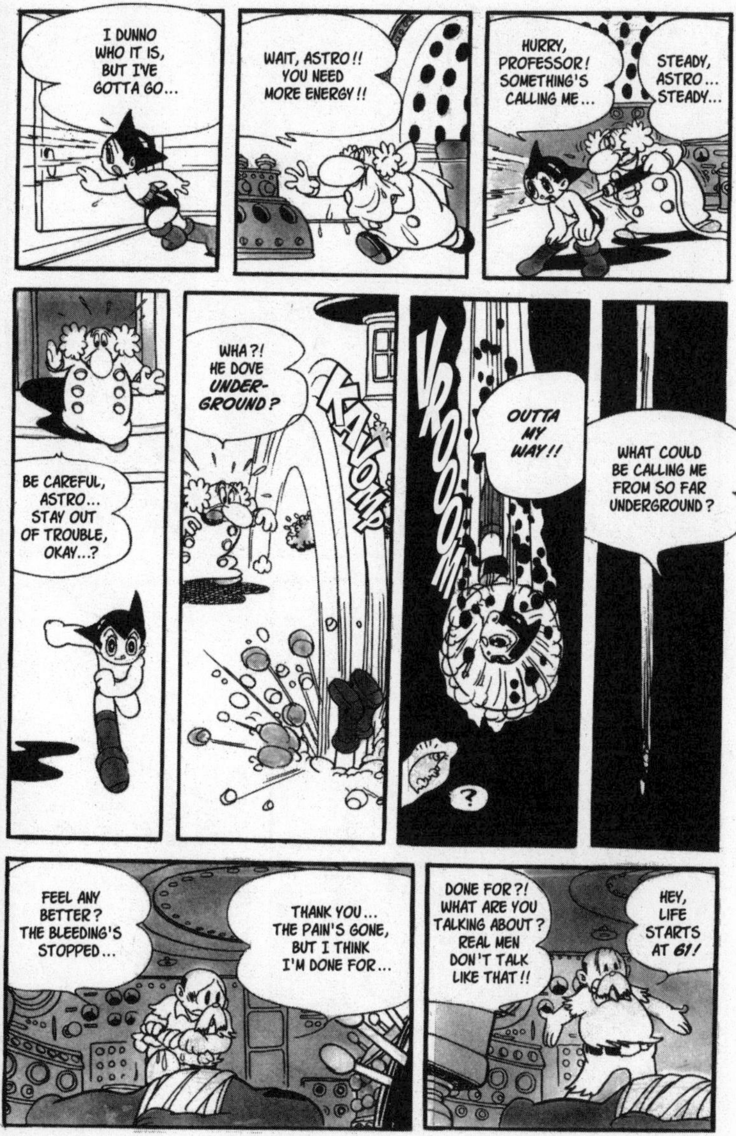
I DUNNO WHO IT IS, BUT I'VE GOTTA GO...
WAIT, ASTRO!! YOU NEED MORE ENERGY!!
HURRY, PROFESSOR! SOMETHING'S CALLING ME...
STEADY, ASTRO... STEADY...
BE CAREFUL, ASTRO... STAY OUT OF TROUBLE, OKAY...?
WHA?! HE DOVE *UNDER-GROUND?*
KAVOMP
VROOOOOM
OUTTA MY WAY!!
?
WHAT COULD BE CALLING ME FROM SO FAR UNDERGROUND?
FEEL ANY BETTER? THE BLEEDING'S STOPPED...
THANK YOU... THE PAIN'S GONE, BUT I THINK I'M DONE FOR...
DONE FOR?! WHAT ARE YOU TALKING ABOUT? REAL MEN DON'T TALK LIKE THAT!!
HEY, LIFE STARTS AT *61!*

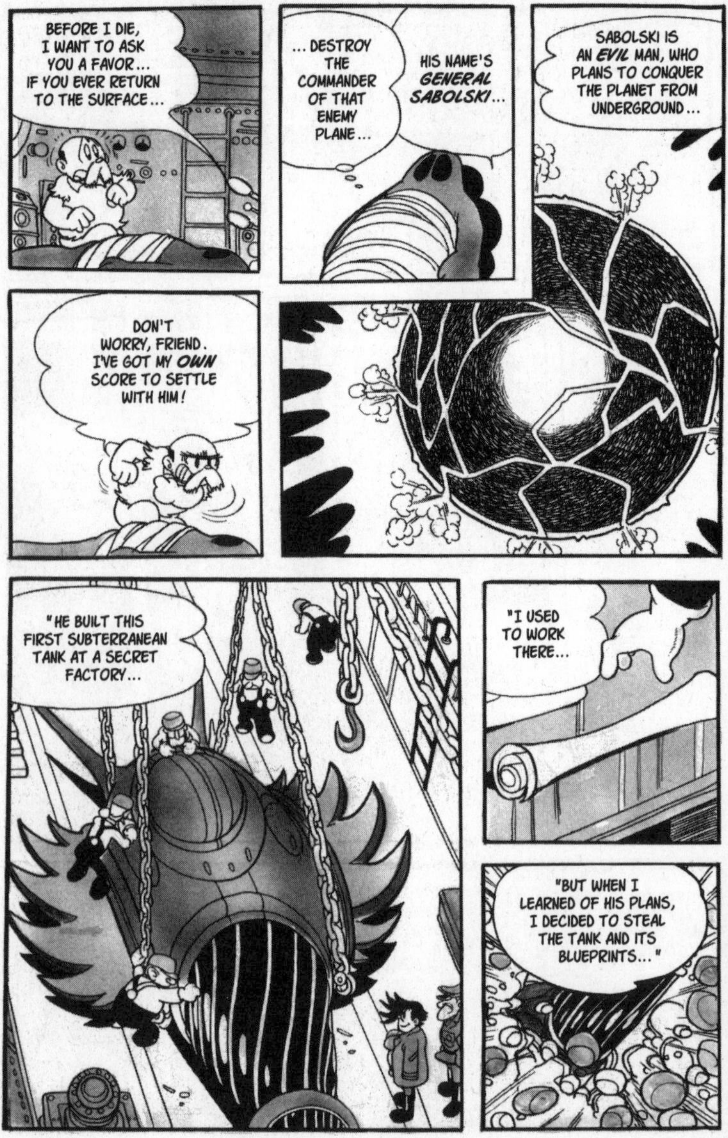
BEFORE I DIE, I WANT TO ASK YOU A FAVOR... IF YOU EVER RETURN TO THE SURFACE...
... DESTROY THE COMMANDER OF THAT ENEMY PLANE...
HIS NAME'S *GENERAL SABOLSKI*...
SABOLSKI IS AN *EVIL* MAN, WHO PLANS TO CONQUER THE PLANET FROM UNDERGROUND...
DON'T WORRY, FRIEND. I'VE GOT MY *OWN* SCORE TO SETTLE WITH HIM!
"HE BUILT THIS FIRST SUBTERRANEAN TANK AT A SECRET FACTORY...
"I USED TO WORK THERE...
"BUT WHEN I LEARNED OF HIS PLANS, I DECIDED TO STEAL THE TANK AND ITS BLUEPRINTS..."

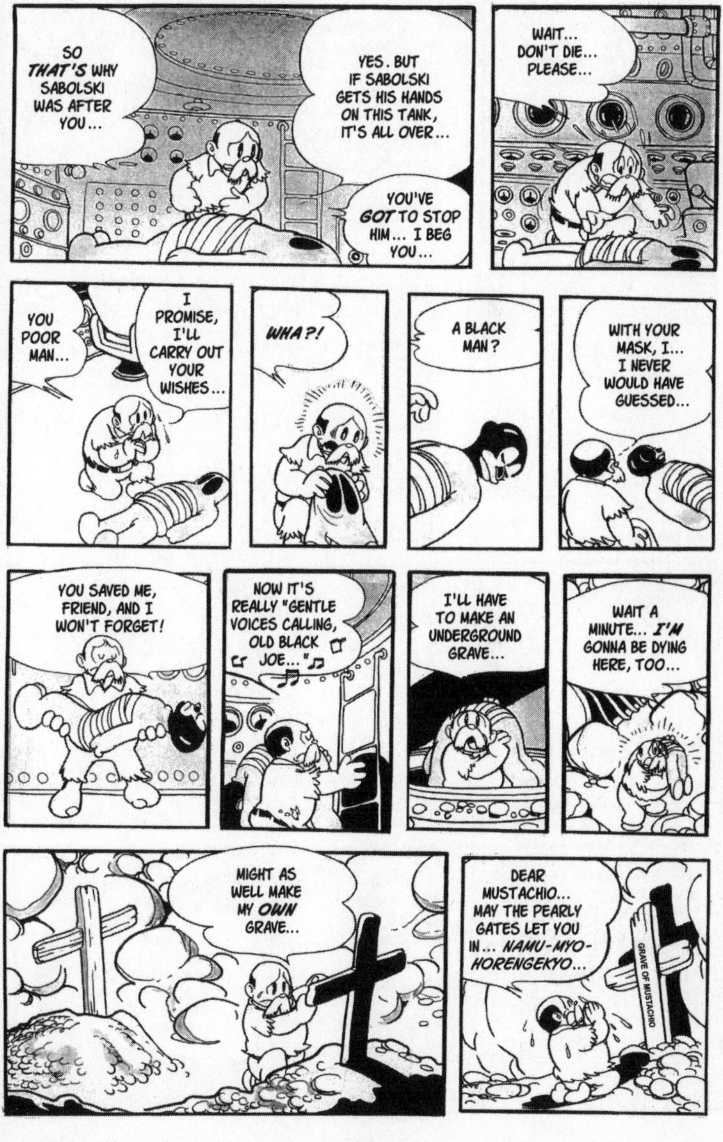
SO *THAT'S* WHY SABOLSKI WAS AFTER YOU...
YES. BUT IF SABOLSKI GETS HIS HANDS ON THIS TANK, IT'S ALL OVER...
YOU'VE *GOT* TO STOP HIM... I BEG YOU...
WAIT... DON'T DIE... PLEASE...
YOU POOR MAN...
I PROMISE, I'LL CARRY OUT YOUR WISHES...
WHA?!
A BLACK MAN?
WITH YOUR MASK, I... I NEVER WOULD HAVE GUESSED...
YOU SAVED ME, FRIEND, AND I WON'T FORGET!
NOW IT'S REALLY "GENTLE VOICES CALLING, OLD BLACK JOE..."
I'LL HAVE TO MAKE AN UNDERGROUND GRAVE...
WAIT A MINUTE... *I'M* GONNA BE DYING HERE, TOO...
MIGHT AS WELL MAKE MY *OWN* GRAVE...
DEAR MUSTACHIO... MAY THE PEARLY GATES LET YOU IN... *NAMU-MYO-HORENGEKYO*...
GRAVE OF MUSTACHIO

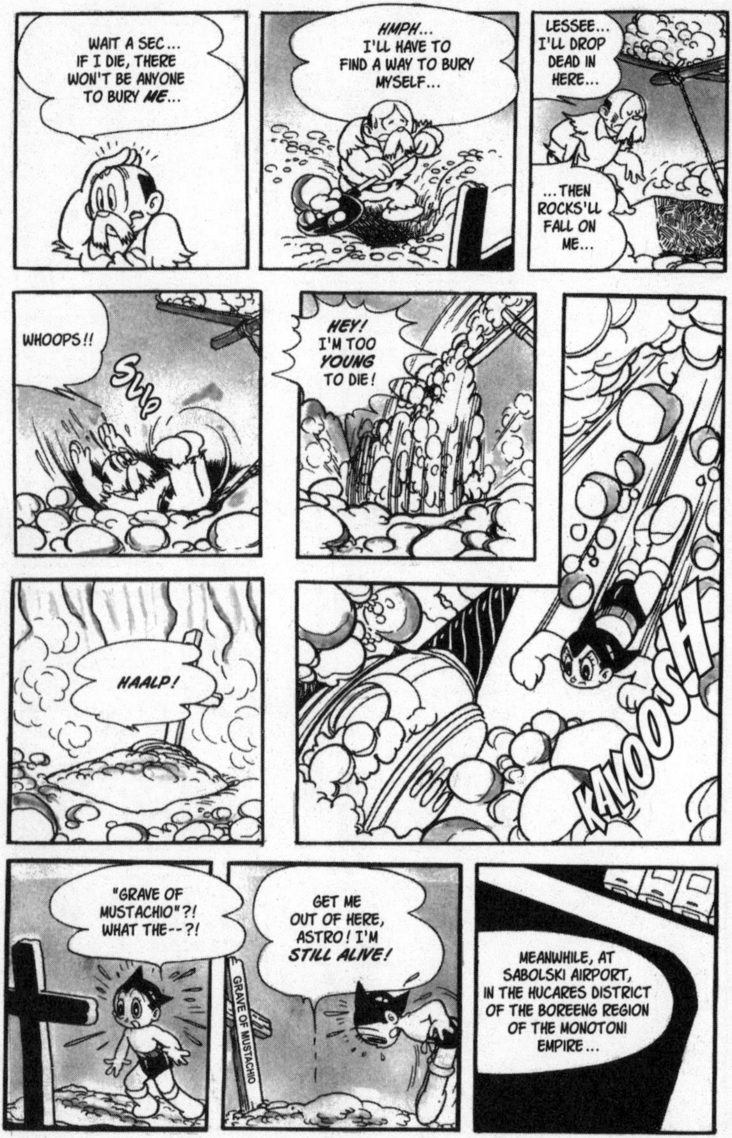

WAIT A SEC... IF I DIE, THERE WON'T BE ANYONE TO BURY *ME*...
HMPH... I'LL HAVE TO FIND A WAY TO BURY MYSELF...
LESSEE... I'LL DROP DEAD IN HERE...
...THEN ROCKS'LL FALL ON ME...
WHOOPS!!
SLIP
HEY! I'M TOO *YOUNG* TO DIE!
HAALP!
KAVOOOSH
"GRAVE OF MUSTACHIO"?! WHAT THE--?!
GRAVE OF MUSTACHIO
GET ME OUT OF HERE, ASTRO! I'M *STILL ALIVE!*
MEANWHILE, AT SABOLSKI AIRPORT, IN THE HUCARES DISTRICT OF THE BOREENG REGION OF THE MONOTONI EMPIRE...

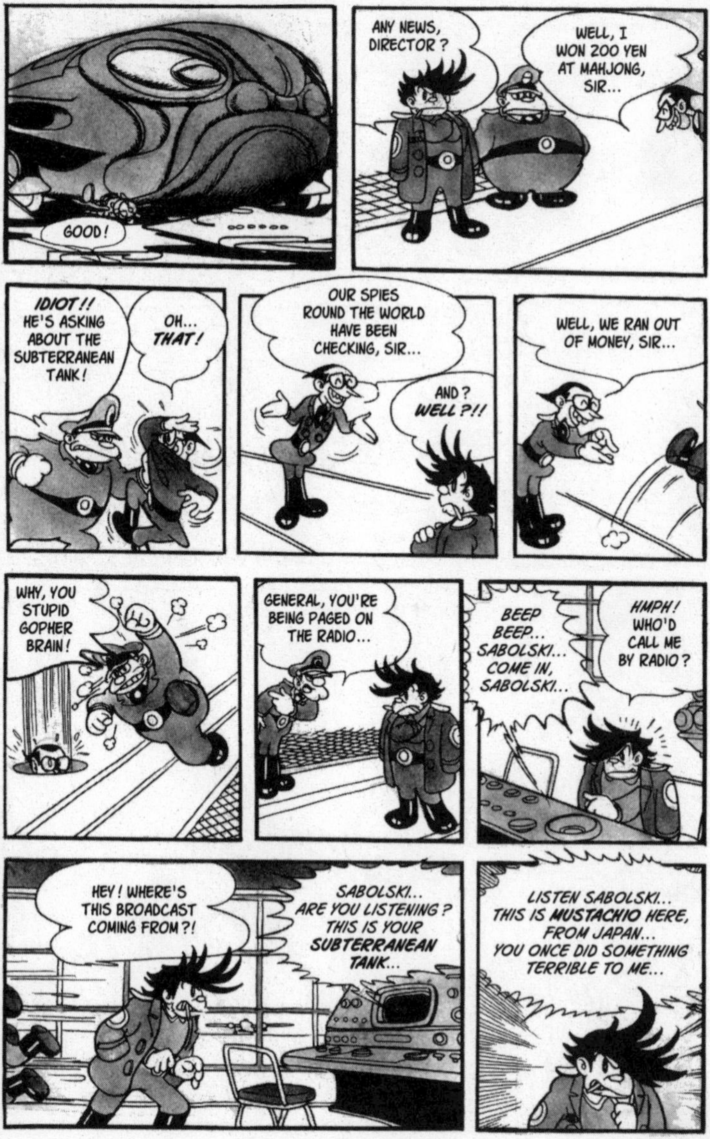

GOOD!
ANY NEWS, DIRECTOR?
WELL, I WON 200 YEN AT MAHJONG, SIR...
IDIOT!! HE'S ASKING ABOUT THE SUBTERRANEAN TANK!
OH... THAT!
OUR SPIES ROUND THE WORLD HAVE BEEN CHECKING, SIR...
AND? WELL?!!
WELL, WE RAN OUT OF MONEY, SIR...
WHY, YOU STUPID GOPHER BRAIN!
GENERAL, YOU'RE BEING PAGED ON THE RADIO...
BEEP BEEP... SABOLSKI... COME IN, SABOLSKI...
HMPH! WHO'D CALL ME BY RADIO?
HEY! WHERE'S THIS BROADCAST COMING FROM?!
SABOLSKI... ARE YOU LISTENING? THIS IS YOUR SUBTERRANEAN TANK...
LISTEN SABOLSKI... THIS IS MUSTACHIO HERE, FROM JAPAN... YOU ONCE DID SOMETHING TERRIBLE TO ME...

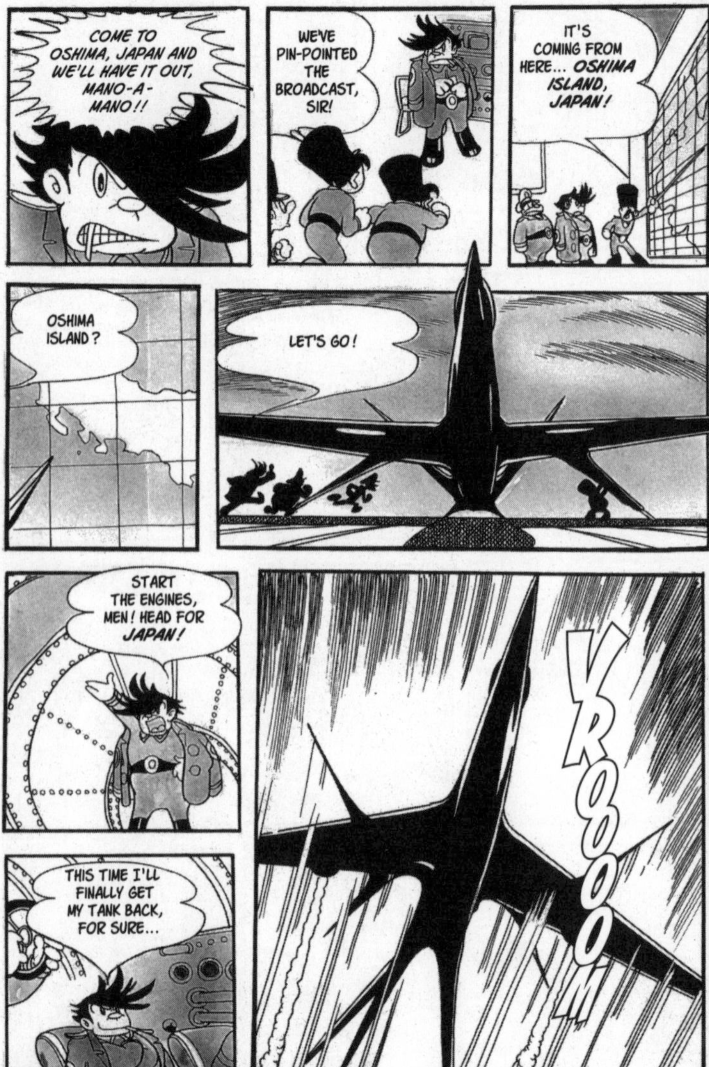
COME TO OSHIMA, JAPAN AND WE'LL HAVE IT OUT, MANO-A-MANO!!
WE'VE PIN-POINTED THE BROADCAST, SIR!
IT'S COMING FROM HERE... OSHIMA ISLAND, JAPAN!
OSHIMA ISLAND?
LET'S GO!
START THE ENGINES, MEN! HEAD FOR JAPAN!
THIS TIME I'LL FINALLY GET MY TANK BACK, FOR SURE...
VROOOOM

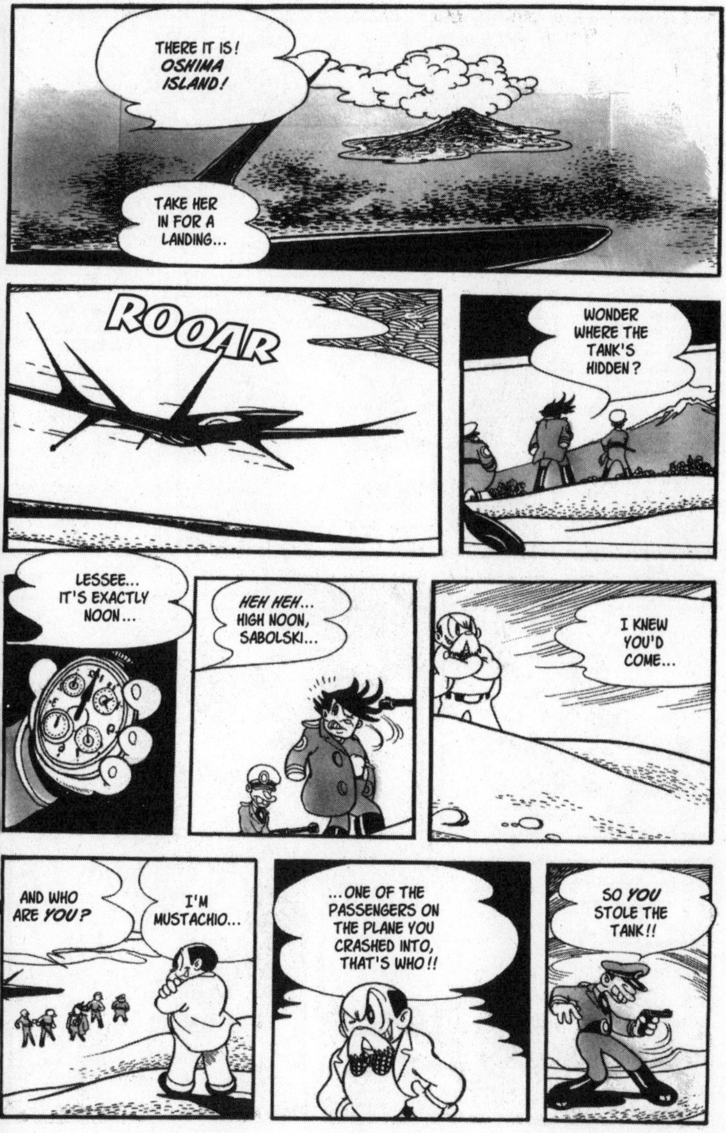
THERE IT IS! OSHIMA ISLAND!
TAKE HER IN FOR A LANDING...
ROOAR
WONDER WHERE THE TANK'S HIDDEN?
LESSEE... IT'S EXACTLY NOON...
HEH HEH... HIGH NOON, SABOLSKI...
I KNEW YOU'D COME...
AND WHO ARE YOU?
I'M MUSTACHIO...
...ONE OF THE PASSENGERS ON THE PLANE YOU CRASHED INTO, THAT'S WHO!!
SO YOU STOLE THE TANK!!

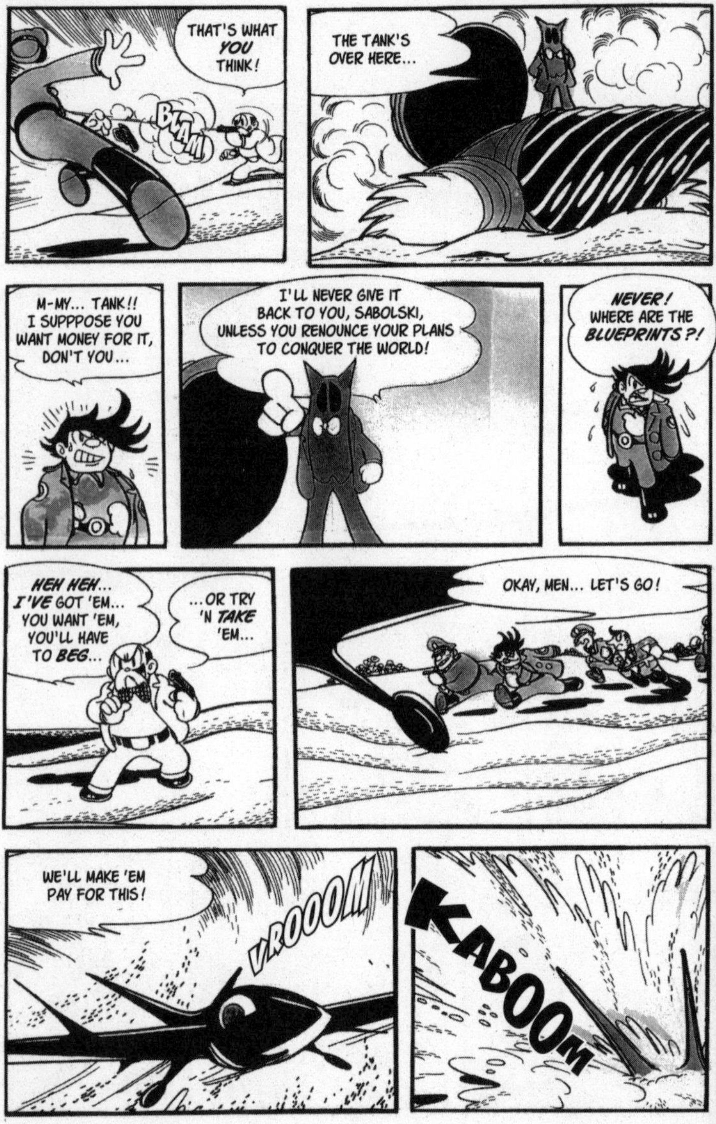
THAT'S WHAT YOU THINK!
BLAM
THE TANK'S OVER HERE...
M-MY... TANK!! I SUPPPOSE YOU WANT MONEY FOR IT, DON'T YOU...
I'LL NEVER GIVE IT BACK TO YOU, SABOLSKI, UNLESS YOU RENOUNCE YOUR PLANS TO CONQUER THE WORLD!
NEVER! WHERE ARE THE BLUEPRINTS?!
HEH HEH... I'VE GOT 'EM... YOU WANT 'EM, YOU'LL HAVE TO BEG...
...OR TRY 'N TAKE 'EM...
OKAY, MEN... LET'S GO!
WE'LL MAKE 'EM PAY FOR THIS!
VROOOM
KABOOOM

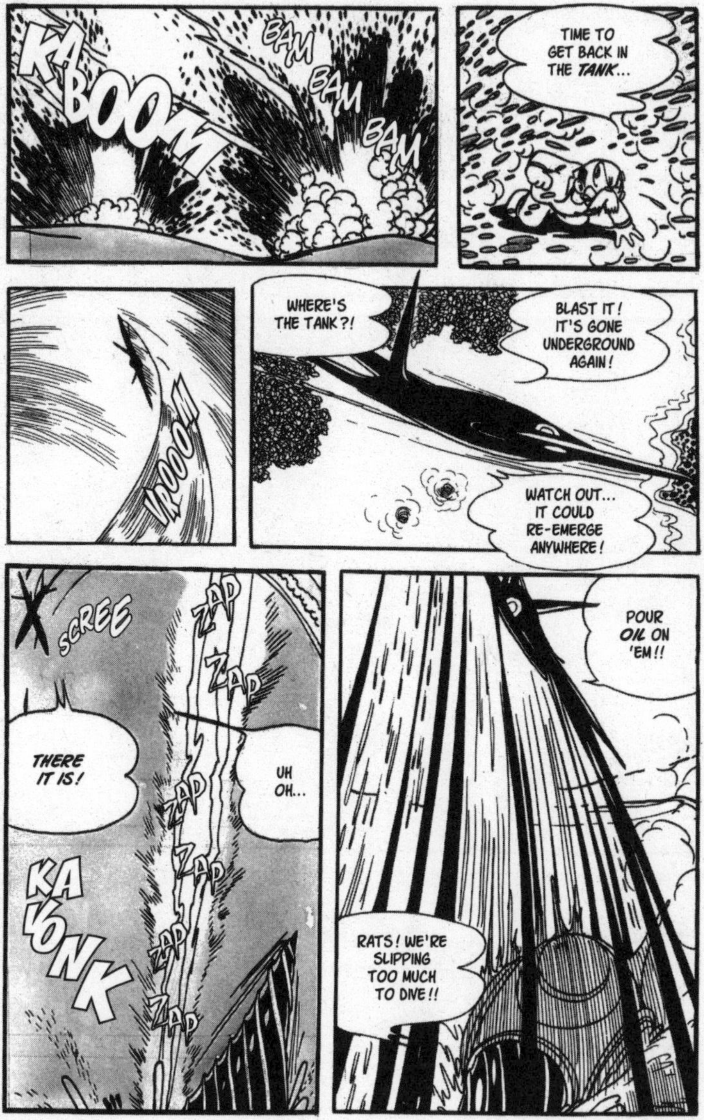
KA BOOM
BAM BAM BAM
TIME TO GET BACK IN THE *TANK*...
VROOOM
WHERE'S THE TANK?!
BLAST IT! IT'S GONE UNDERGROUND AGAIN!
WATCH OUT... IT COULD RE-EMERGE ANYWHERE!
SCREE
ZAP ZAP
THERE IT IS!
UH OH...
ZAP ZAP ZAP ZAP
KA WONK
POUR *OIL* ON 'EM!!
RATS! WE'RE SLIPPING TOO MUCH TO DIVE!!

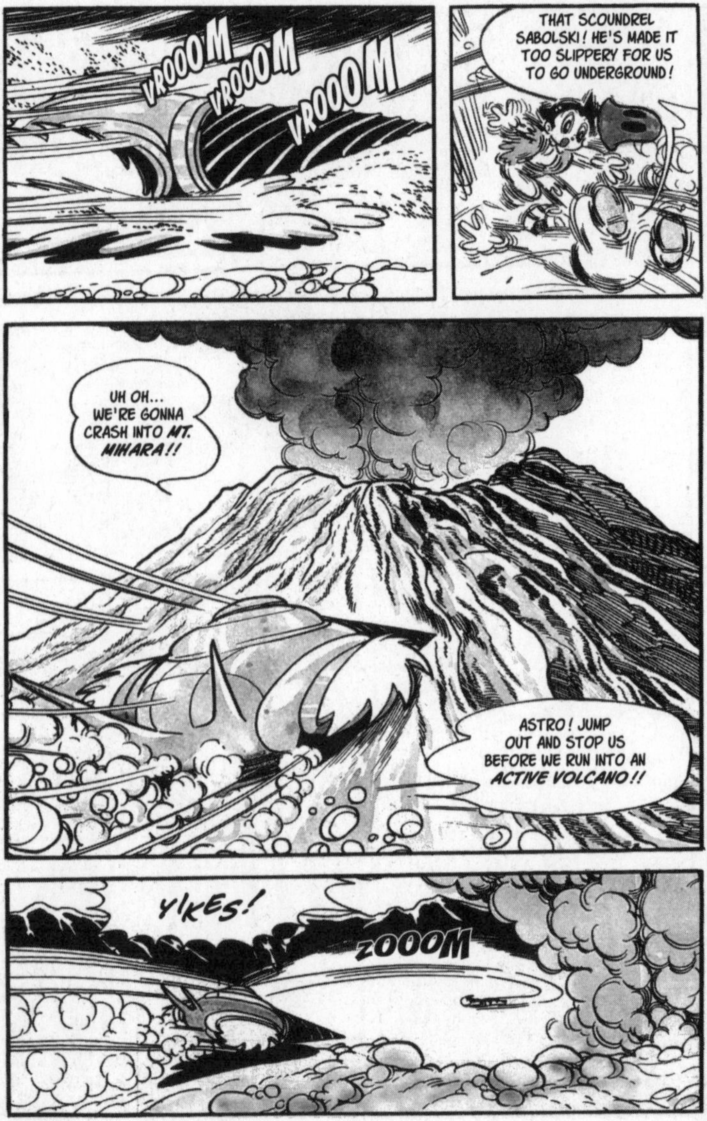
VROOOM VROOOM VROOOM
THAT SCOUNDREL SABOLSKI! HE'S MADE IT TOO SLIPPERY FOR US TO GO UNDERGROUND!
UH OH... WE'RE GONNA CRASH INTO MT. MIHARA!!
ASTRO! JUMP OUT AND STOP US BEFORE WE RUN INTO AN ACTIVE VOLCANO!!
Y'KES!
ZOOOM

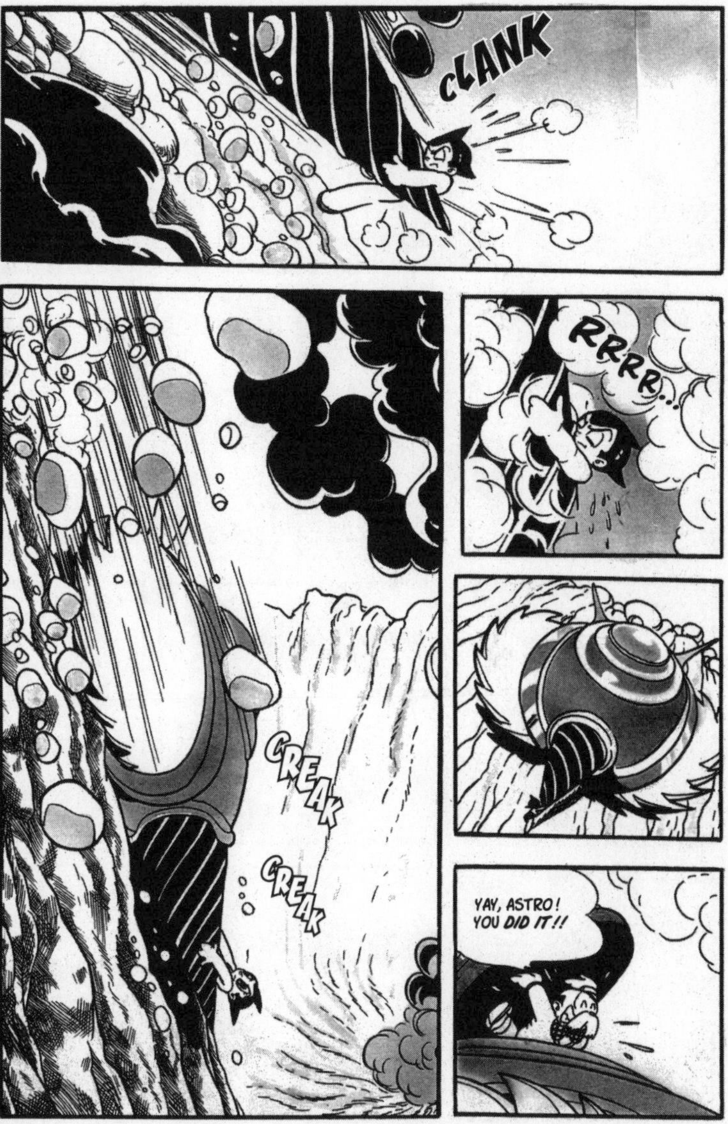
CLANK
CREAK
CREAK
RRRRR...
YAY, ASTRO!
YOU DID IT!!

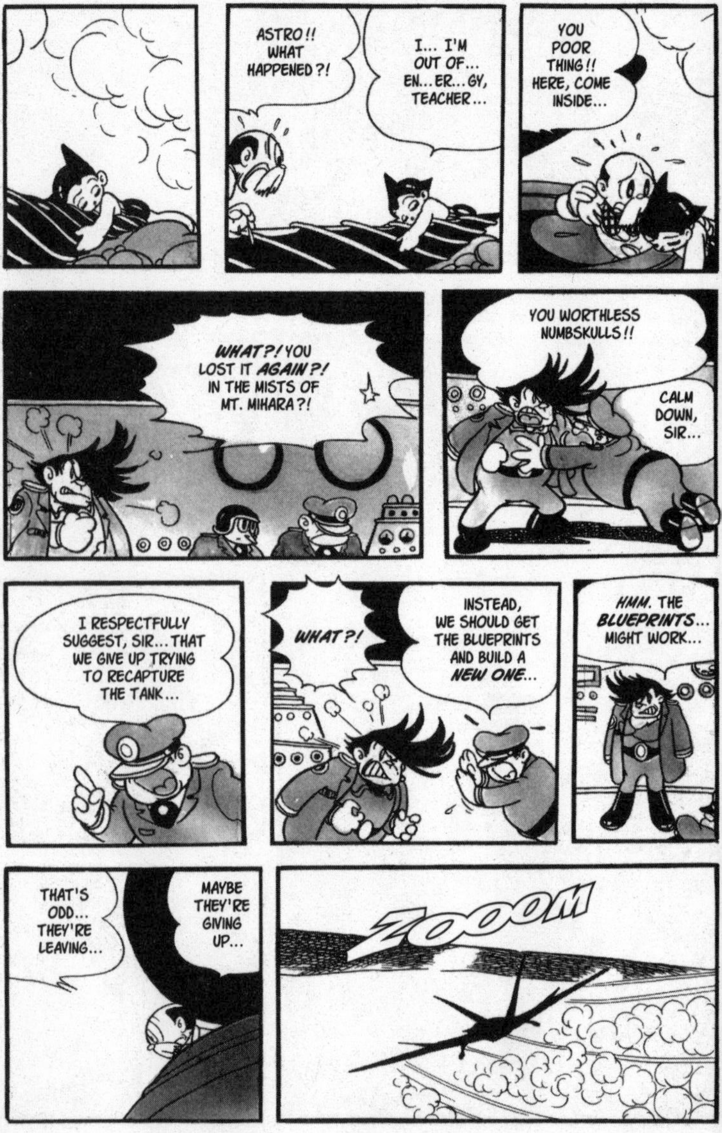
ASTRO!! WHAT HAPPENED?!
I... I'M OUT OF... EN... ER... GY, TEACHER...
YOU POOR THING!! HERE, COME INSIDE...
WHAT?! YOU LOST IT AGAIN?! IN THE MISTS OF MT. MIHARA?!
YOU WORTHLESS NUMBSKULLS!!
CALM DOWN, SIR...
I RESPECTFULLY SUGGEST, SIR... THAT WE GIVE UP TRYING TO RECAPTURE THE TANK...
WHAT?!
INSTEAD, WE SHOULD GET THE BLUEPRINTS AND BUILD A NEW ONE...
HMM. THE BLUEPRINTS... MIGHT WORK...
THAT'S ODD... THEY'RE LEAVING...
MAYBE THEY'RE GIVING UP...
ZOOOM

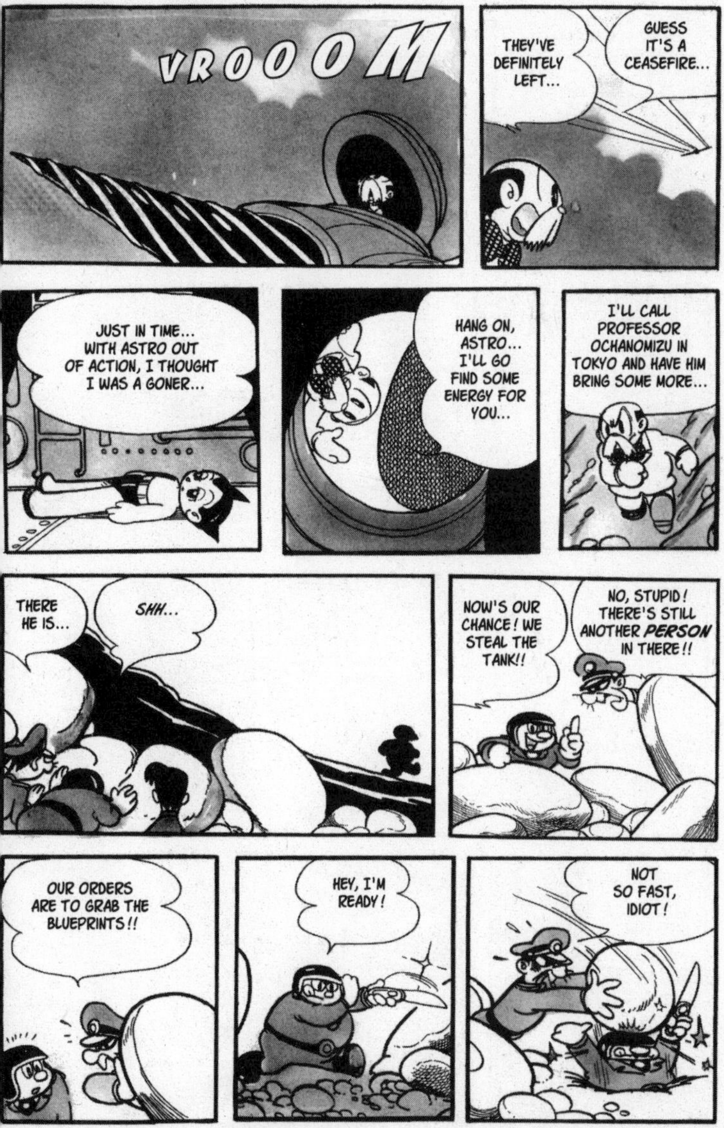
VROOOM
THEY'VE DEFINITELY LEFT...
GUESS IT'S A CEASEFIRE...
JUST IN TIME... WITH ASTRO OUT OF ACTION, I THOUGHT I WAS A GONER...
HANG ON, ASTRO... I'LL GO FIND SOME ENERGY FOR YOU...
I'LL CALL PROFESSOR OCHANOMIZU IN TOKYO AND HAVE HIM BRING SOME MORE...
THERE HE IS...
SHH...
NOW'S OUR CHANCE! WE STEAL THE TANK!!
NO, STUPID! THERE'S STILL ANOTHER ***PERSON*** IN THERE!!
OUR ORDERS ARE TO GRAB THE BLUEPRINTS!!
HEY, I'M READY!
NOT SO FAST, IDIOT!

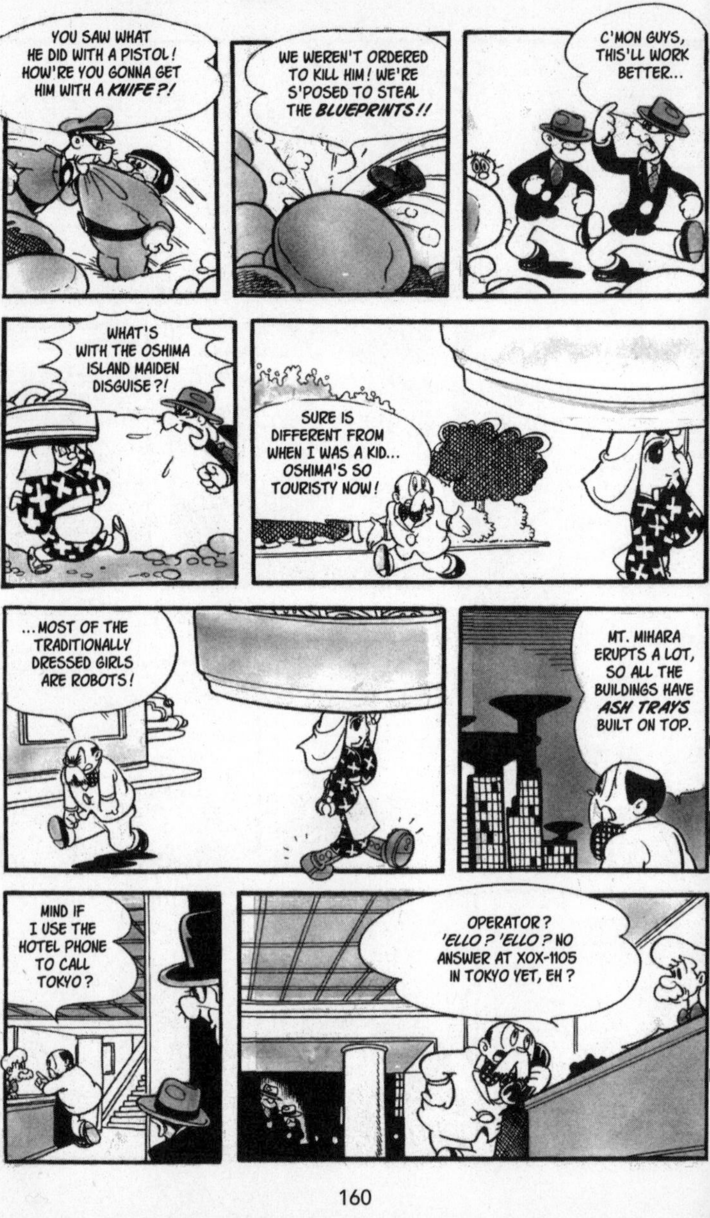
YOU SAW WHAT HE DID WITH A PISTOL! HOW'RE YOU GONNA GET HIM WITH A *KNIFE?!*
WE WEREN'T ORDERED TO KILL HIM! WE'RE S'POSED TO STEAL THE ***BLUEPRINTS!!***
C'MON GUYS, THIS'LL WORK BETTER...
WHAT'S WITH THE OSHIMA ISLAND MAIDEN DISGUISE?!
SURE IS DIFFERENT FROM WHEN I WAS A KID... OSHIMA'S SO TOURISTY NOW!
...MOST OF THE TRADITIONALLY DRESSED GIRLS ARE ROBOTS!
MT. MIHARA ERUPTS A LOT, SO ALL THE BUILDINGS HAVE ***ASH TRAYS*** BUILT ON TOP.
MIND IF I USE THE HOTEL PHONE TO CALL TOKYO?
OPERATOR? *'ELLO? 'ELLO?* NO ANSWER AT XOX-1105 IN TOKYO YET, EH?

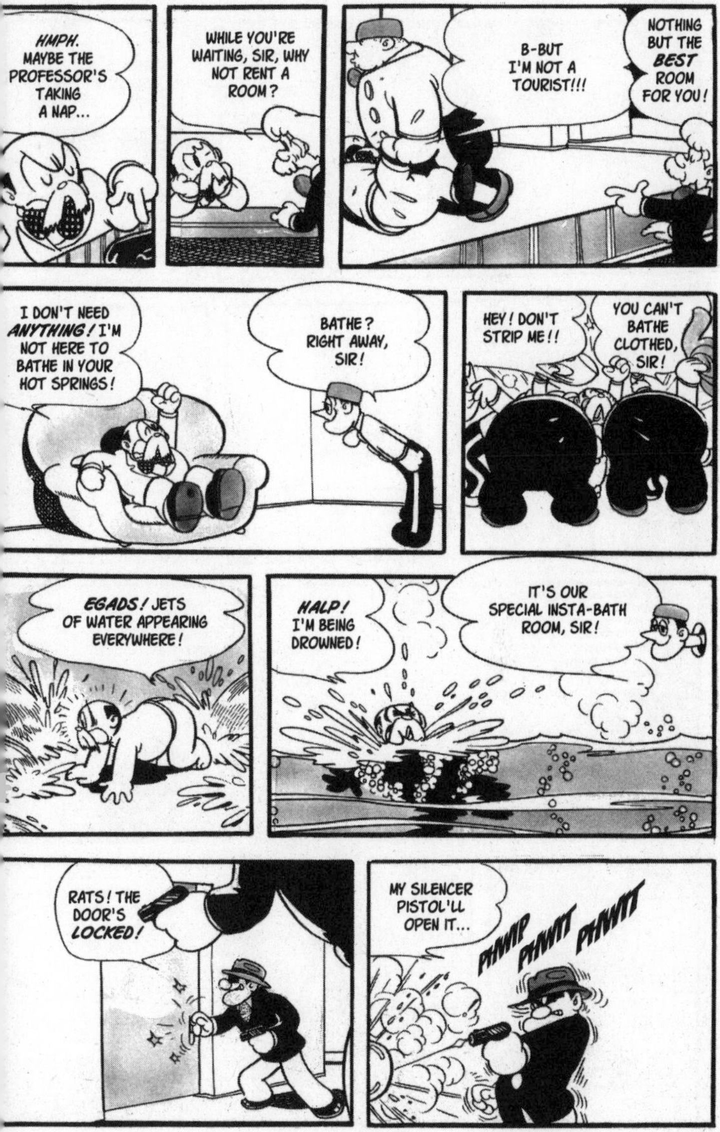
HMPH. MAYBE THE PROFESSOR'S TAKING A NAP...
WHILE YOU'RE WAITING, SIR, WHY NOT RENT A ROOM?
B-BUT I'M NOT A TOURIST!!!
NOTHING BUT THE BEST ROOM FOR YOU!
I DON'T NEED ANYTHING! I'M NOT HERE TO BATHE IN YOUR HOT SPRINGS!
BATHE? RIGHT AWAY, SIR!
HEY! DON'T STRIP ME!!
YOU CAN'T BATHE CLOTHED, SIR!
EGADS! JETS OF WATER APPEARING EVERYWHERE!
HALP! I'M BEING DROWNED!
IT'S OUR SPECIAL INSTA-BATH ROOM, SIR!
RATS! THE DOOR'S LOCKED!
MY SILENCER PISTOL'LL OPEN IT...
PHWIP
PHWIT
PHWIT

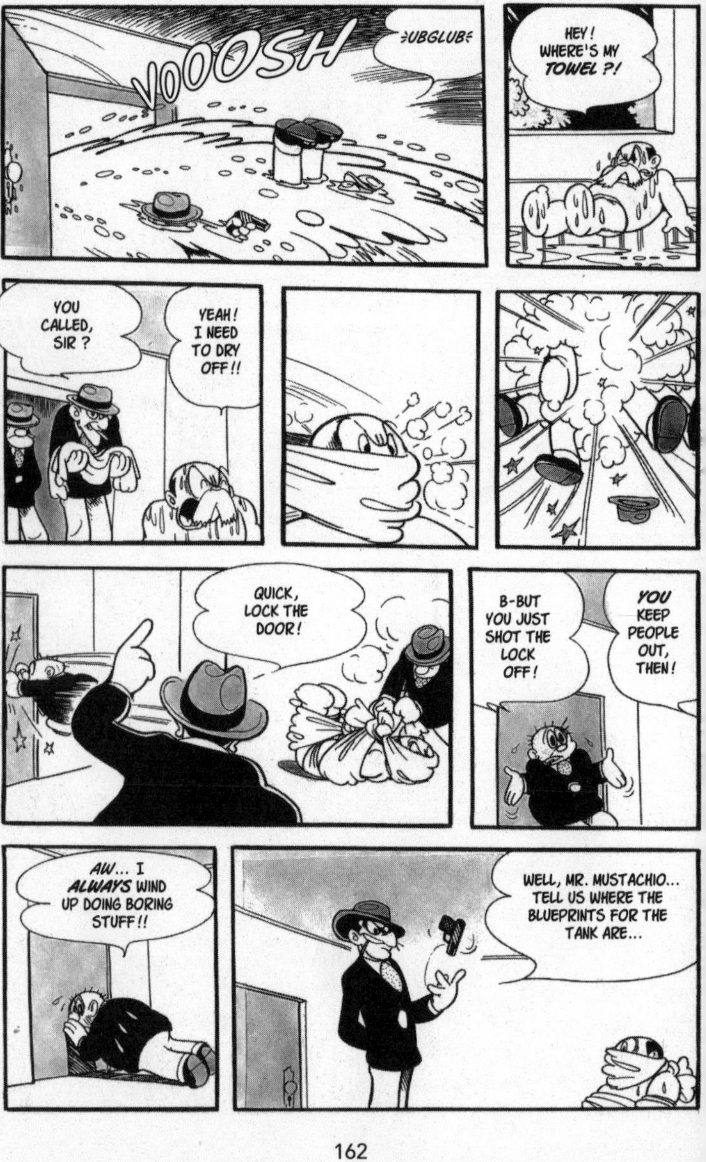
VOOOSH
≶UBGLUB≶
HEY! WHERE'S MY TOWEL ?!
YOU CALLED, SIR ?
YEAH! I NEED TO DRY OFF!!
QUICK, LOCK THE DOOR!
B-BUT YOU JUST SHOT THE LOCK OFF!
YOU KEEP PEOPLE OUT, THEN!
AW... I ALWAYS WIND UP DOING BORING STUFF!!
WELL, MR. MUSTACHIO... TELL US WHERE THE BLUEPRINTS FOR THE TANK ARE...

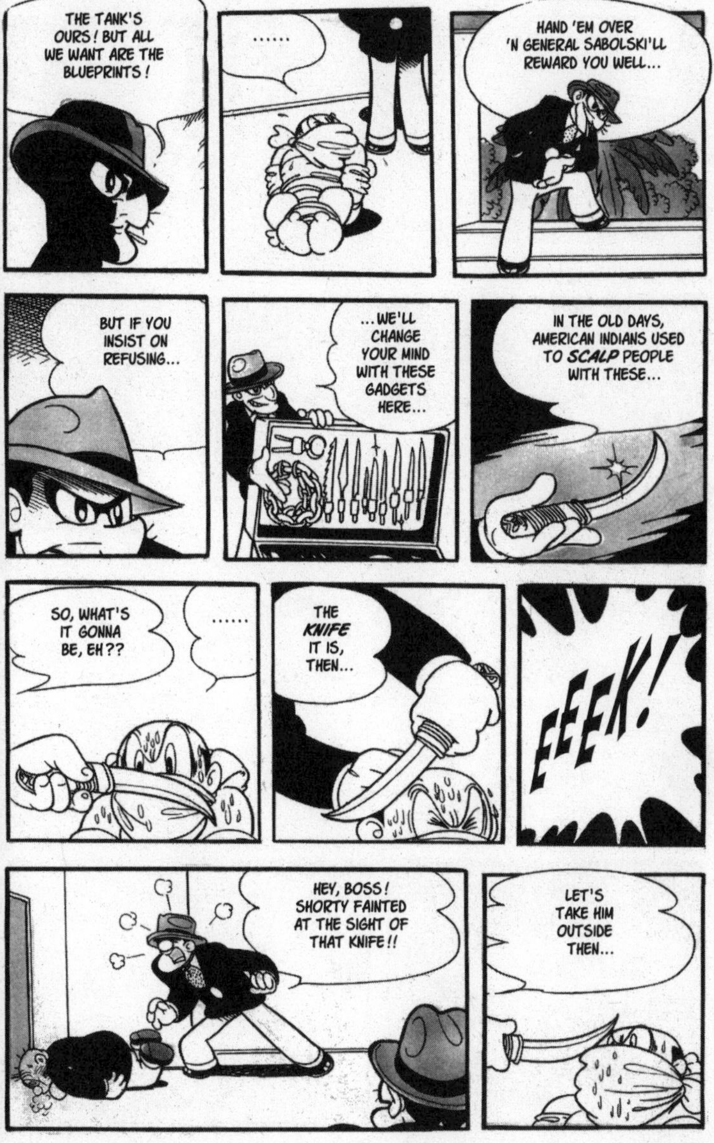
THE TANK'S OURS! BUT ALL WE WANT ARE THE BLUEPRINTS!
......
HAND 'EM OVER 'N GENERAL SABOLSKI'LL REWARD YOU WELL...
BUT IF YOU INSIST ON REFUSING...
...WE'LL CHANGE YOUR MIND WITH THESE GADGETS HERE...
IN THE OLD DAYS, AMERICAN INDIANS USED TO *SCALP* PEOPLE WITH THESE...
SO, WHAT'S IT GONNA BE, EH??
......
THE *KNIFE* IT IS, THEN...
EEEK!
HEY, BOSS! SHORTY FAINTED AT THE SIGHT OF THAT KNIFE!!
LET'S TAKE HIM OUTSIDE THEN...

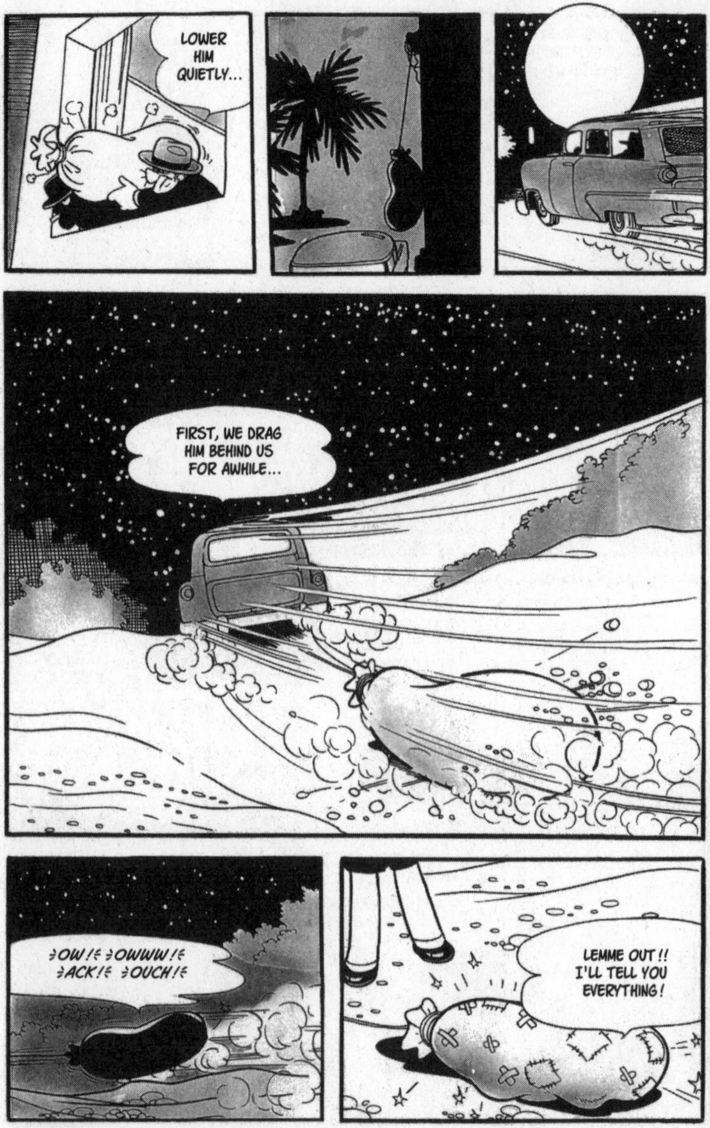
LOWER HIM QUIETLY...
FIRST, WE DRAG HIM BEHIND US FOR AWHILE...
OW! OWWW! ACK! OUCH!
LEMME OUT!! I'LL TELL YOU EVERYTHING!

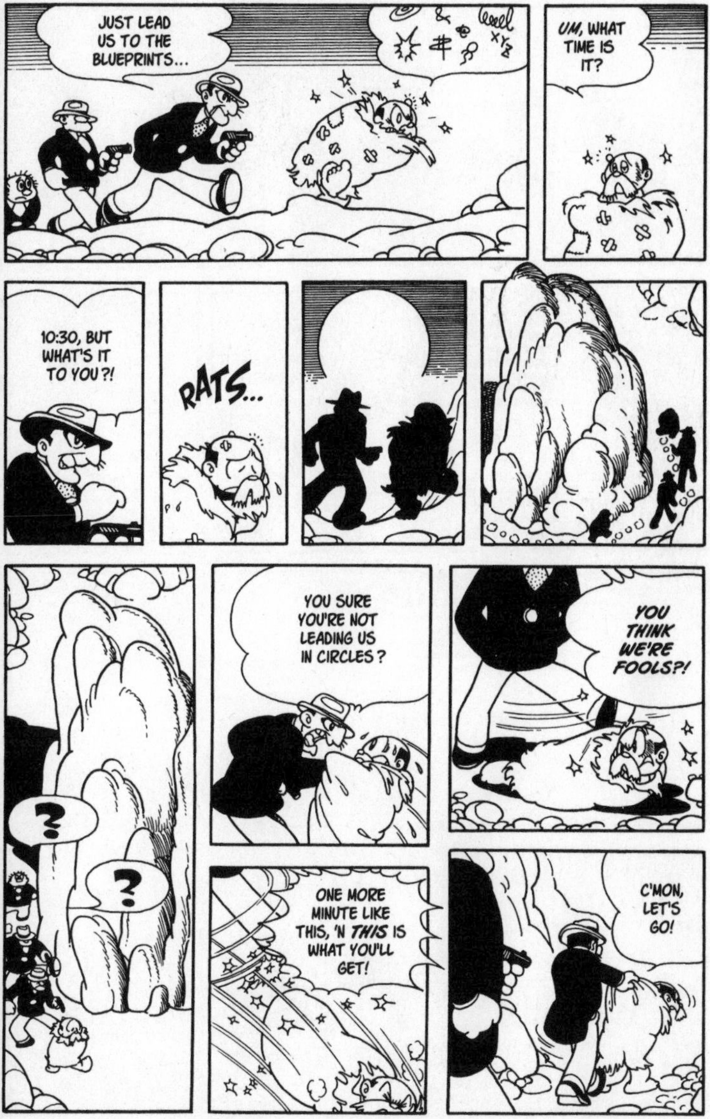
JUST LEAD US TO THE BLUEPRINTS...
UM, WHAT TIME IS IT?
10:30, BUT WHAT'S IT TO YOU?!
RATS...
YOU SURE YOU'RE NOT LEADING US IN CIRCLES?
YOU THINK WE'RE FOOLS?!
?
?
ONE MORE MINUTE LIKE THIS, 'N THIS IS WHAT YOU'LL GET!
C'MON, LET'S GO!

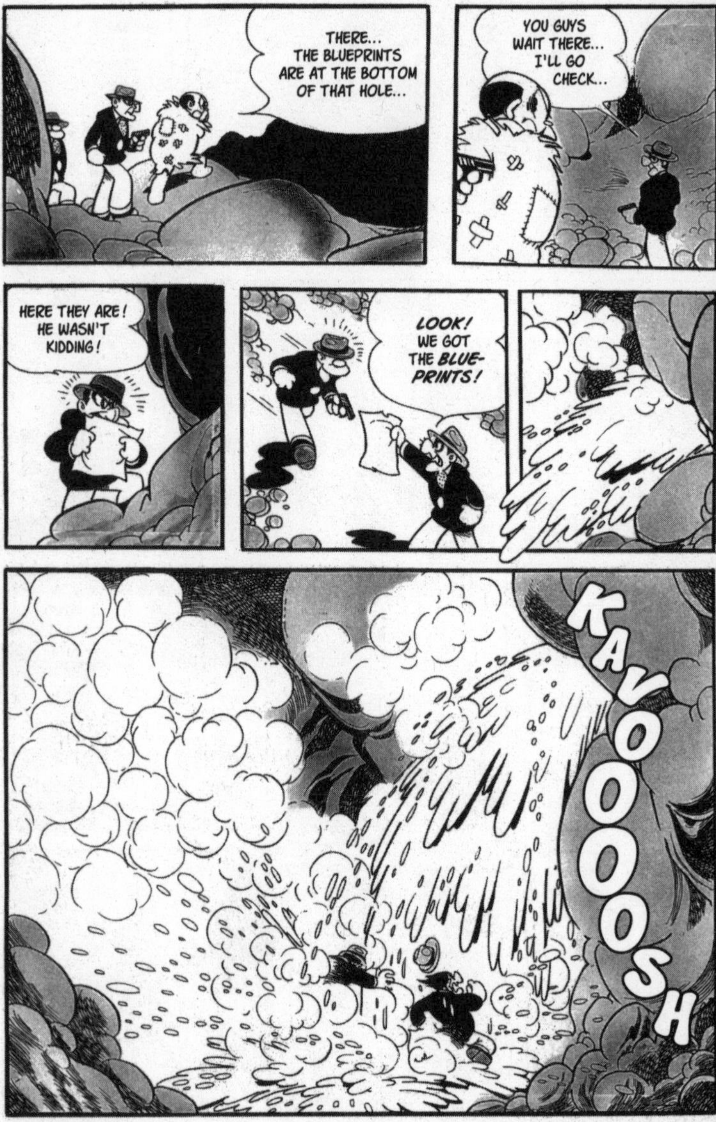
THERE... THE BLUEPRINTS ARE AT THE BOTTOM OF THAT HOLE...
YOU GUYS WAIT THERE... I'LL GO CHECK...
HERE THEY ARE! HE WASN'T KIDDING!
LOOK! WE GOT THE BLUE-PRINTS!
KAVOOOOOSH

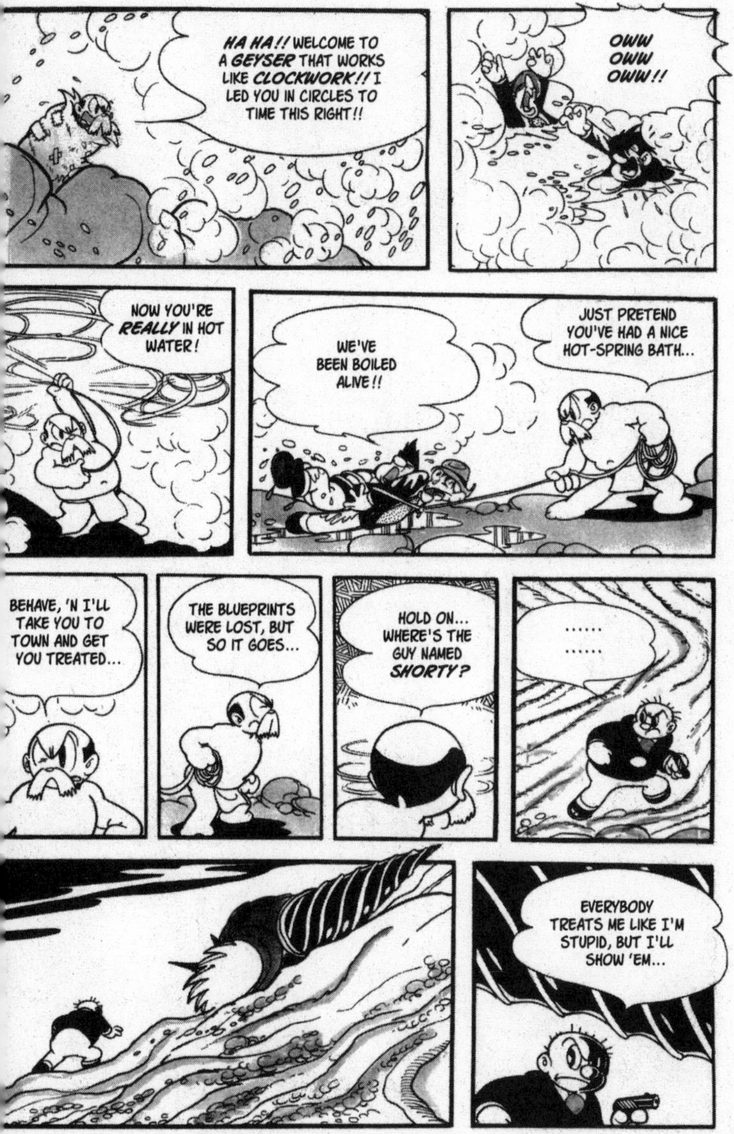
HA HA!! WELCOME TO A GEYSER THAT WORKS LIKE CLOCKWORK!! I LED YOU IN CIRCLES TO TIME THIS RIGHT!!
OWW OWW OWW!!
NOW YOU'RE REALLY IN HOT WATER!
WE'VE BEEN BOILED ALIVE!!
JUST PRETEND YOU'VE HAD A NICE HOT-SPRING BATH...
BEHAVE, 'N I'LL TAKE YOU TO TOWN AND GET YOU TREATED...
THE BLUEPRINTS WERE LOST, BUT SO IT GOES...
HOLD ON... WHERE'S THE GUY NAMED SHORTY?
......
......
EVERYBODY TREATS ME LIKE I'M STUPID, BUT I'LL SHOW 'EM...

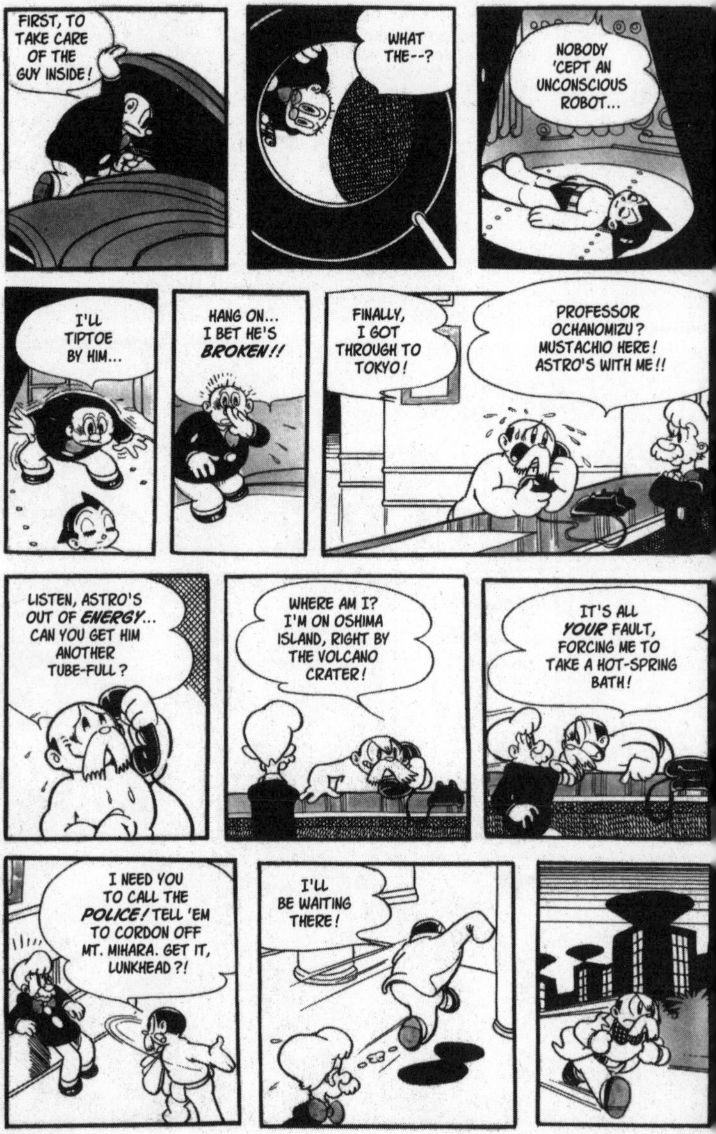
FIRST, TO TAKE CARE OF THE GUY INSIDE!
WHAT THE--?
NOBODY 'CEPT AN UNCONSCIOUS ROBOT...
I'LL TIPTOE BY HIM...
HANG ON... I BET HE'S BROKEN!!
FINALLY, I GOT THROUGH TO TOKYO!
PROFESSOR OCHANOMIZU? MUSTACHIO HERE! ASTRO'S WITH ME!!
LISTEN, ASTRO'S OUT OF ENERGY... CAN YOU GET HIM ANOTHER TUBE-FULL?
WHERE AM I? I'M ON OSHIMA ISLAND, RIGHT BY THE VOLCANO CRATER!
IT'S ALL YOUR FAULT, FORCING ME TO TAKE A HOT-SPRING BATH!
I NEED YOU TO CALL THE POLICE! TELL 'EM TO CORDON OFF MT. MIHARA. GET IT, LUNKHEAD?!
I'LL BE WAITING THERE!

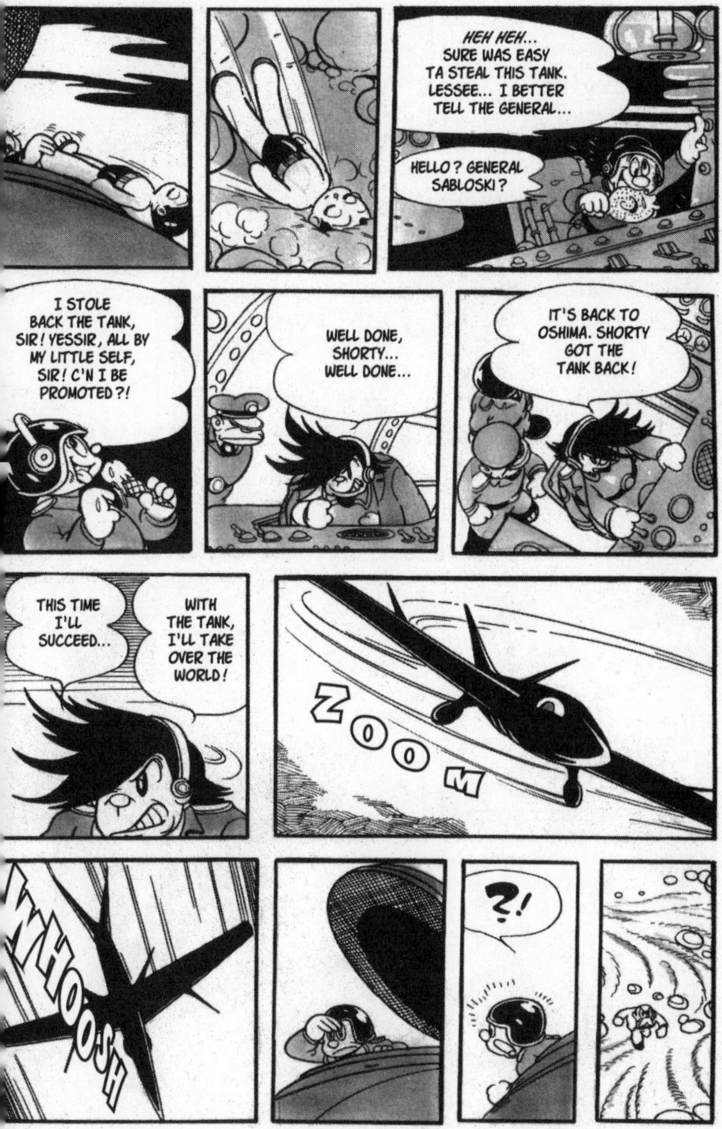
HEH HEH... SURE WAS EASY TA STEAL THIS TANK. LESSEE... I BETTER TELL THE GENERAL...
HELLO? GENERAL SABLOSKI?
I STOLE BACK THE TANK, SIR! YESSIR, ALL BY MY LITTLE SELF, SIR! C'N I BE PROMOTED?!
WELL DONE, SHORTY... WELL DONE...
IT'S BACK TO OSHIMA. SHORTY GOT THE TANK BACK!
THIS TIME I'LL SUCCEED...
WITH THE TANK, I'LL TAKE OVER THE WORLD!
ZOOM
WHOOSH
?!

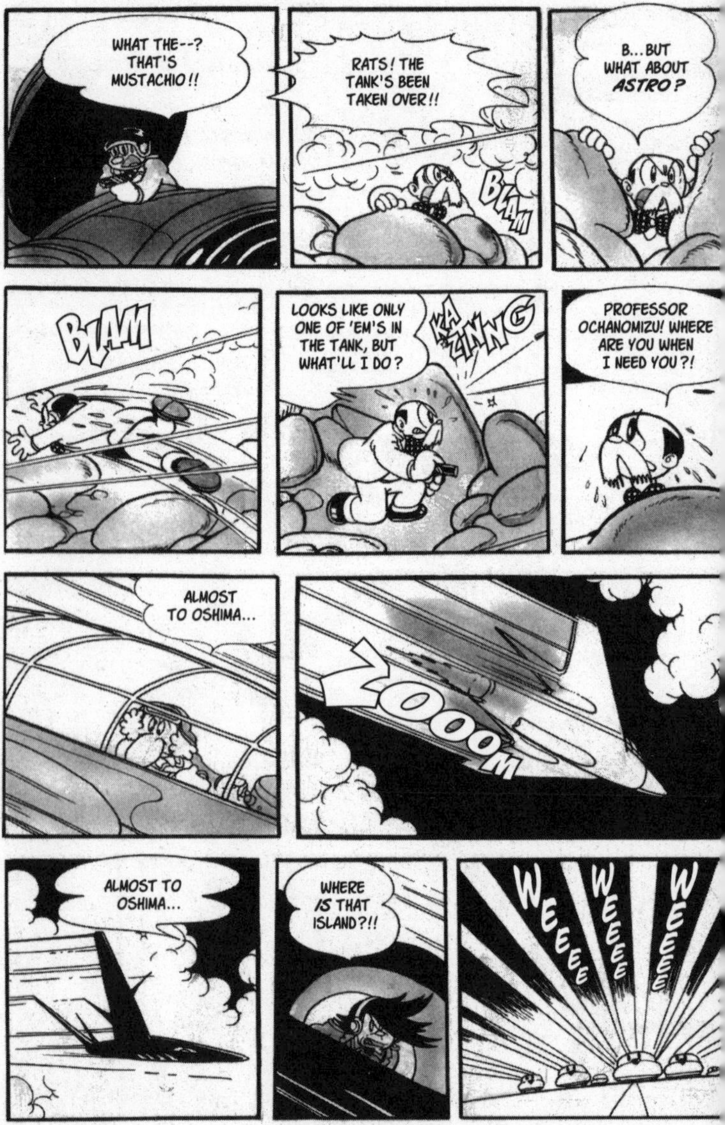

WHAT THE--? THAT'S MUSTACHIO!!
RATS! THE TANK'S BEEN TAKEN OVER!!
BLAM
B...BUT WHAT ABOUT ASTRO?
BLAM
LOOKS LIKE ONLY ONE OF 'EM'S IN THE TANK, BUT WHAT'LL I DO?
KA-ZINNG
PROFESSOR OCHANOMIZU! WHERE ARE YOU WHEN I NEED YOU?!
ALMOST TO OSHIMA...
ZOOOOM
ALMOST TO OSHIMA...
WHERE IS THAT ISLAND?!!
WEEEE
WEEEE
WEEEE

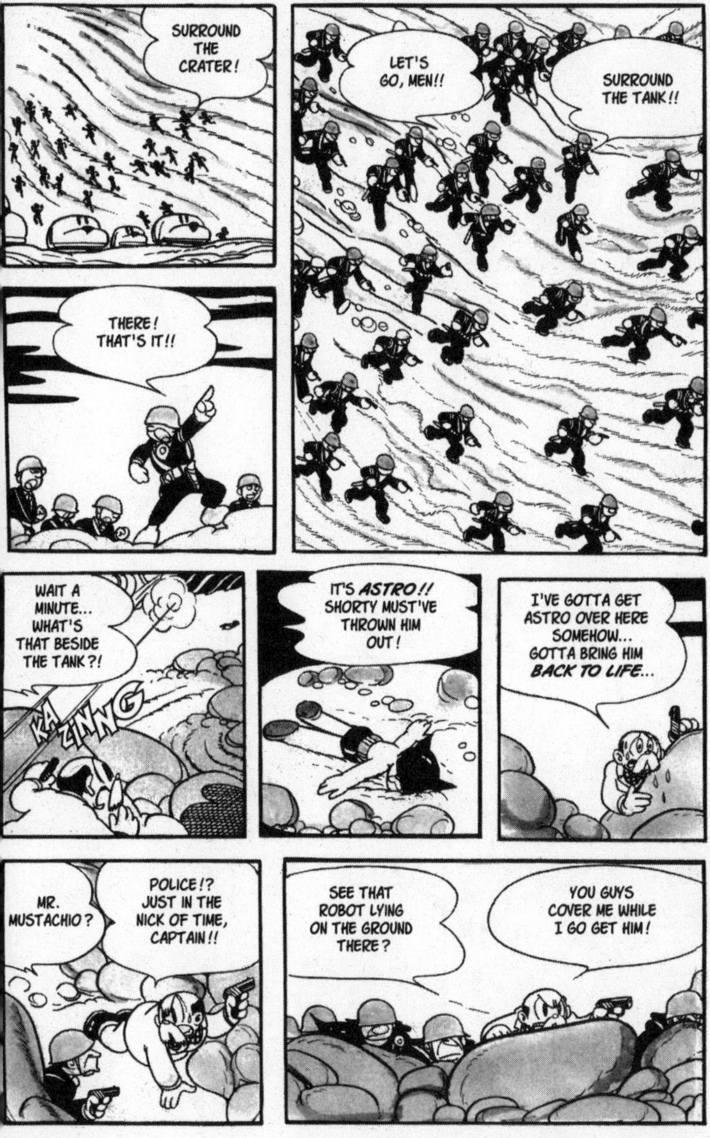
SURROUND THE CRATER!
THERE! THAT'S IT!!
LET'S GO, MEN!!
SURROUND THE TANK!!
WAIT A MINUTE... WHAT'S THAT BESIDE THE TANK?!
KAZINNG
IT'S ASTRO!! SHORTY MUST'VE THROWN HIM OUT!
I'VE GOTTA GET ASTRO OVER HERE SOMEHOW... GOTTA BRING HIM BACK TO LIFE...
MR. MUSTACHIO?
POLICE!? JUST IN THE NICK OF TIME, CAPTAIN!!
SEE THAT ROBOT LYING ON THE GROUND THERE?
YOU GUYS COVER ME WHILE I GO GET HIM!

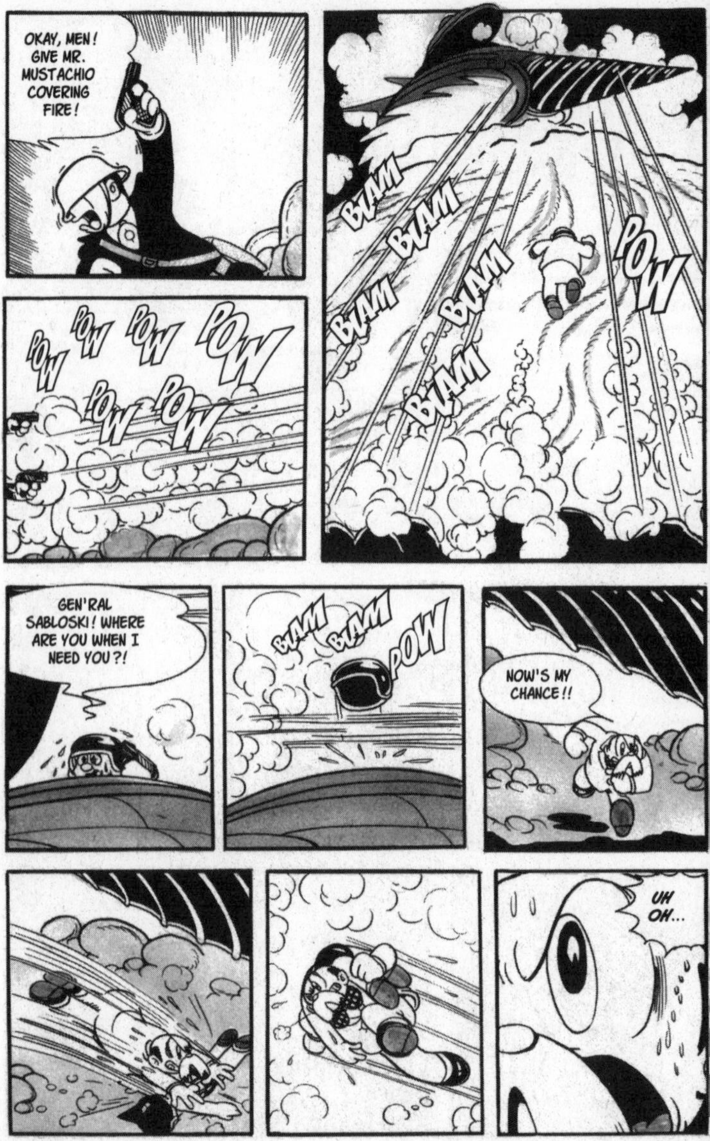
OKAY, MEN! GIVE MR. MUSTACHIO COVERING FIRE!
POW
POW
POW
POW
POW
POW
BLAM
BLAM
BLAM
BLAM
BLAM
BLAM
POW
GEN'RAL SABLOSKI! WHERE ARE YOU WHEN I NEED YOU?!
BLAM
BLAM
POW
NOW'S MY CHANCE!!
UH OH...

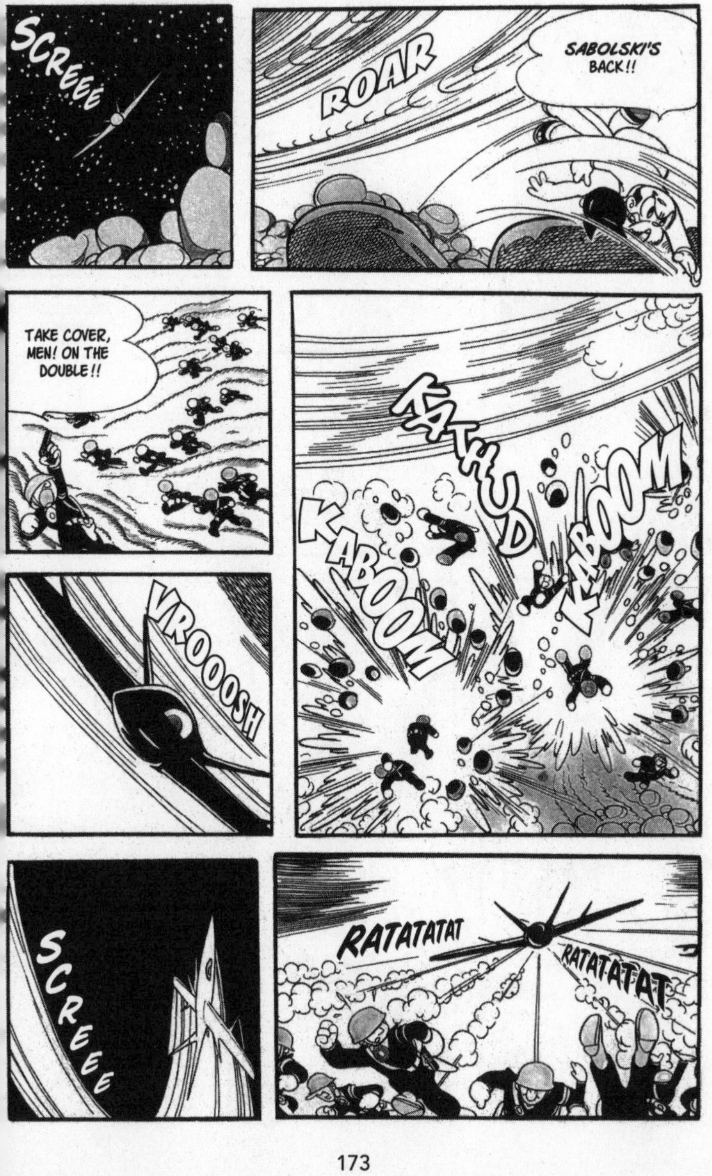
SCREEEE
ROAR
SABOLSKI'S BACK!!
TAKE COVER, MEN! ON THE DOUBLE!!
VROOOOSH
KATHUD
KABOOM
KABOOM
SCREEE
RATATATAT
RATATATAT

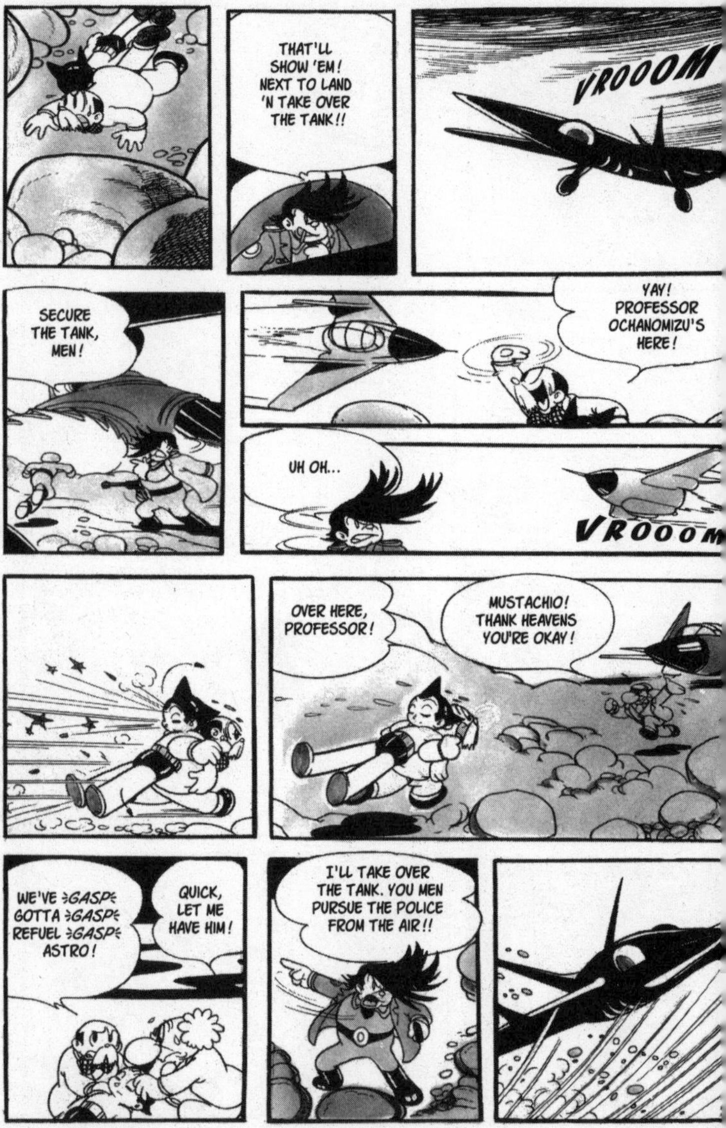
THAT'LL SHOW 'EM! NEXT TO LAND 'N TAKE OVER THE TANK!!
VROOOM
SECURE THE TANK, MEN!
YAY! PROFESSOR OCHANOMIZU'S HERE!
UH OH...
VROOOM
OVER HERE, PROFESSOR!
MUSTACHIO! THANK HEAVENS YOU'RE OKAY!
WE'VE *GASP* GOTTA *GASP* REFUEL *GASP* ASTRO!
QUICK, LET ME HAVE HIM!
I'LL TAKE OVER THE TANK. YOU MEN PURSUE THE POLICE FROM THE AIR!!

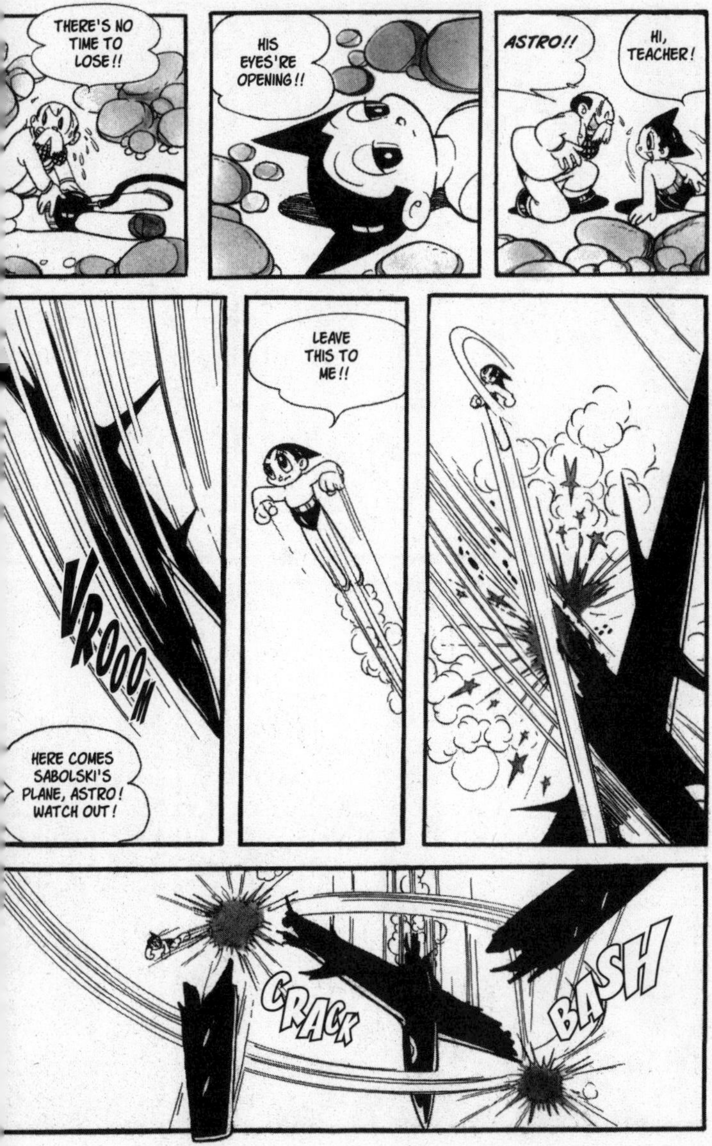
THERE'S NO TIME TO LOSE!!
HIS EYES'RE OPENING!!
ASTRO!!
HI, TEACHER!
VROOOM
HERE COMES SABOLSKI'S PLANE, ASTRO! WATCH OUT!
LEAVE THIS TO ME!!
CRACK
BASH

WHAT THE--?!! OH MY GOSH...

I'LL HAVE TO GO UNDERGROUND IN THE TANK!!

NOT SO FAST, SABOLSKI!

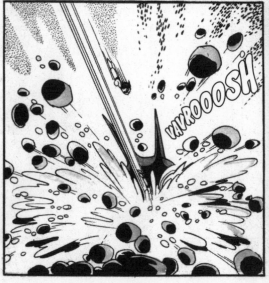

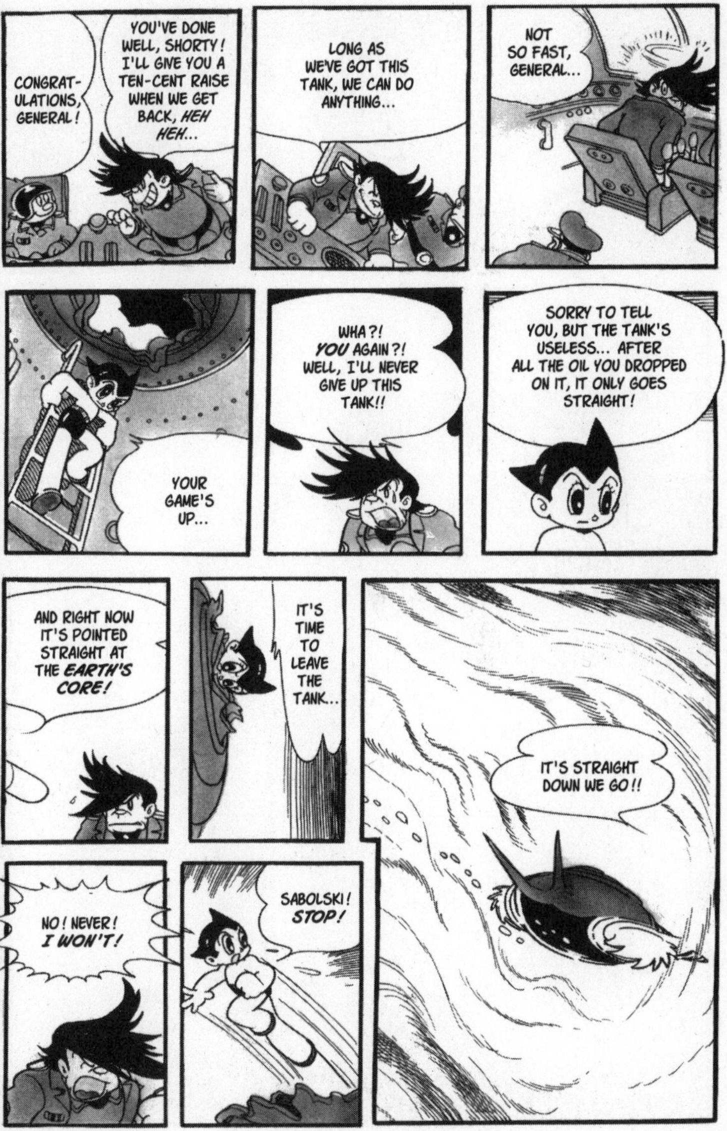
CONGRAT-ULATIONS, GENERAL!
YOU'VE DONE WELL, SHORTY! I'LL GIVE YOU A TEN-CENT RAISE WHEN WE GET BACK, *HEH HEH*...
LONG AS WE'VE GOT THIS TANK, WE CAN DO ANYTHING...
NOT SO FAST, GENERAL...
YOUR GAME'S UP...
WHA?! *YOU* AGAIN?! WELL, I'LL NEVER GIVE UP THIS TANK!!
SORRY TO TELL YOU, BUT THE TANK'S USELESS... AFTER ALL THE OIL YOU DROPPED ON IT, IT ONLY GOES STRAIGHT!
AND RIGHT NOW IT'S POINTED STRAIGHT AT THE *EARTH'S CORE!*
IT'S TIME TO LEAVE THE TANK...
IT'S STRAIGHT DOWN WE GO!!
NO! NEVER! *I WON'T!*
SABOLSKI! *STOP!*

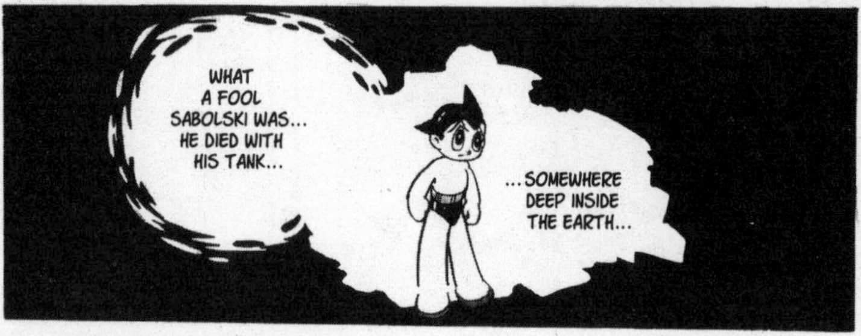
WHAT A FOOL SABOLSKI WAS... HE DIED WITH HIS TANK...
...SOMEWHERE DEEP INSIDE THE EARTH...

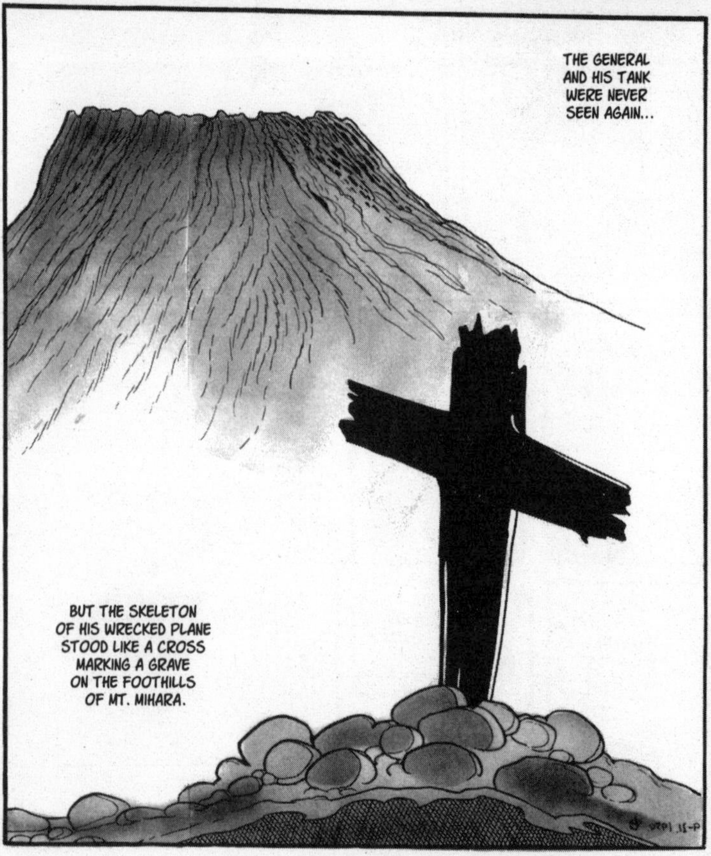
THE GENERAL AND HIS TANK WERE NEVER SEEN AGAIN...
BUT THE SKELETON OF HIS WRECKED PLANE STOOD LIKE A CROSS MARKING A GRAVE ON THE FOOTHILLS OF MT. MIHARA.

THE MAN WHO RETURNED FROM MARS

First serialized from January to March 1969
in *Shonen* magazine.

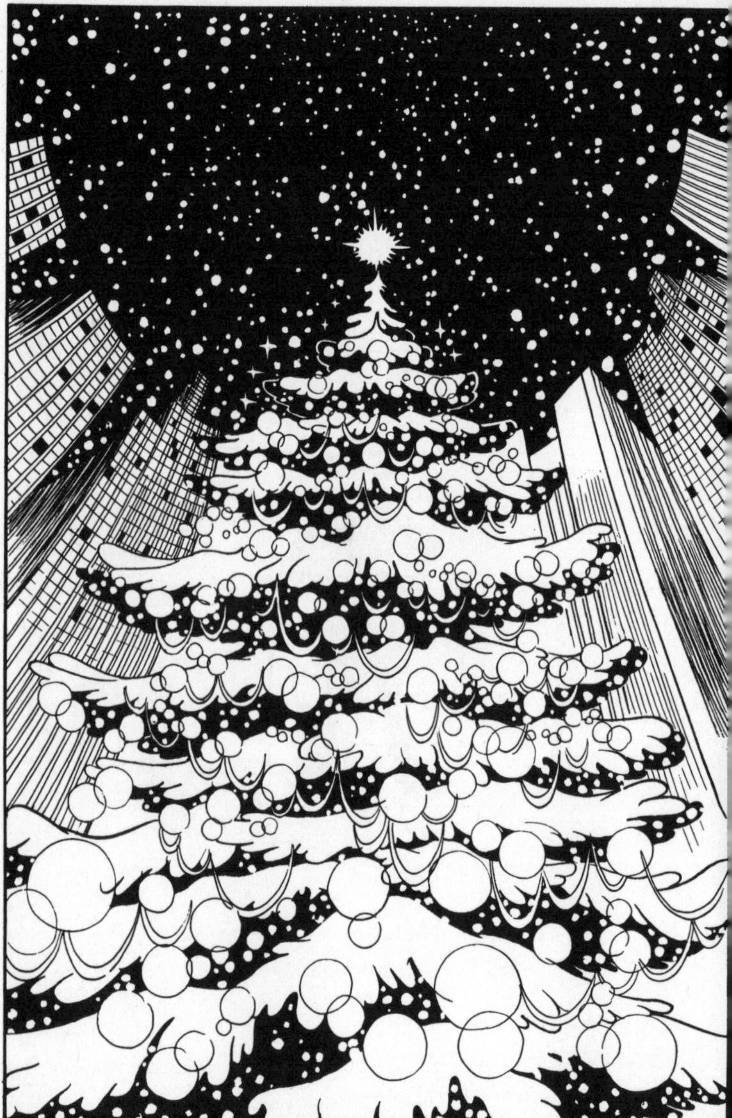

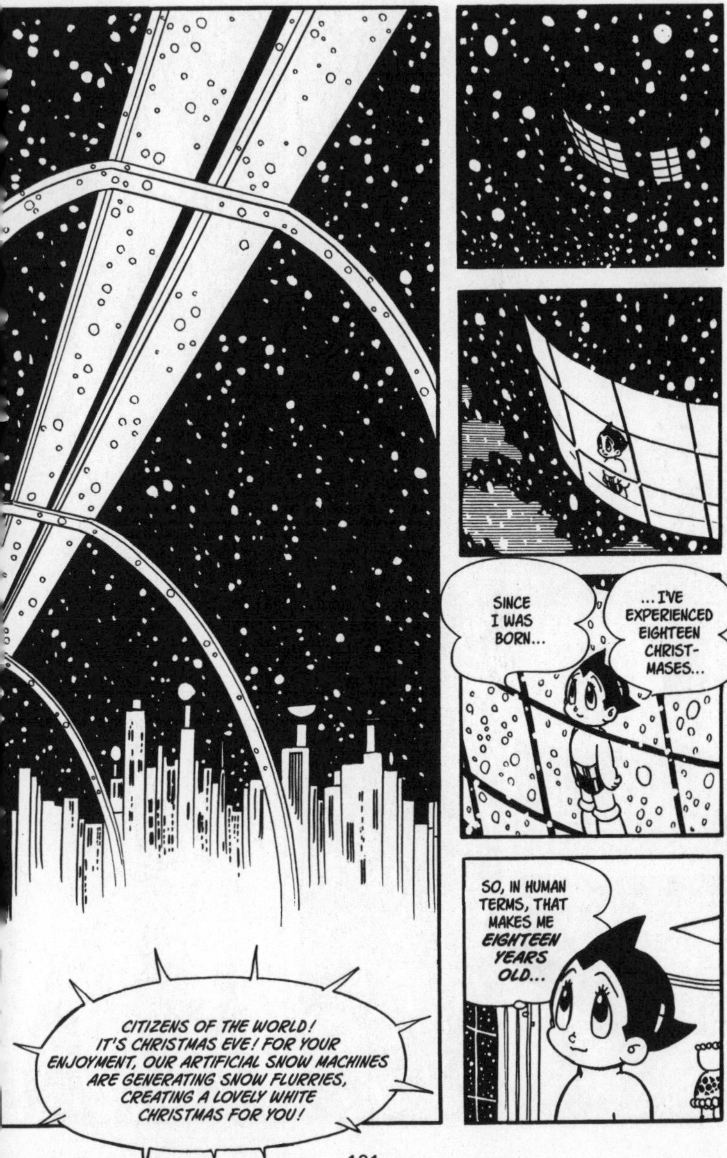
CITIZENS OF THE WORLD! IT'S CHRISTMAS EVE! FOR YOUR ENJOYMENT, OUR ARTIFICIAL SNOW MACHINES ARE GENERATING SNOW FLURRIES, CREATING A LOVELY WHITE CHRISTMAS FOR YOU!
SINCE I WAS BORN...
...I'VE EXPERIENCED EIGHTEEN CHRISTMASES...
SO, IN HUMAN TERMS, THAT MAKES ME *EIGHTEEN YEARS OLD*...

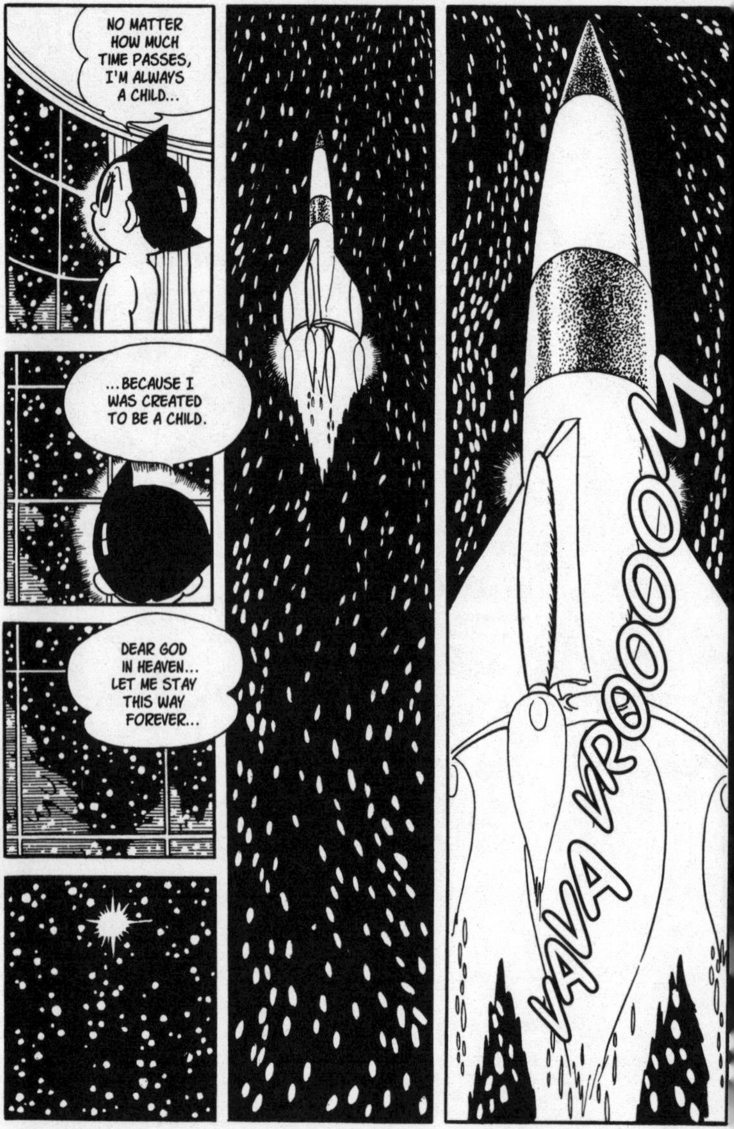
NO MATTER HOW MUCH TIME PASSES, I'M ALWAYS A CHILD...
...BECAUSE I WAS CREATED TO BE A CHILD.
DEAR GOD IN HEAVEN... LET ME STAY THIS WAY FOREVER...
VAVA VROOOOM

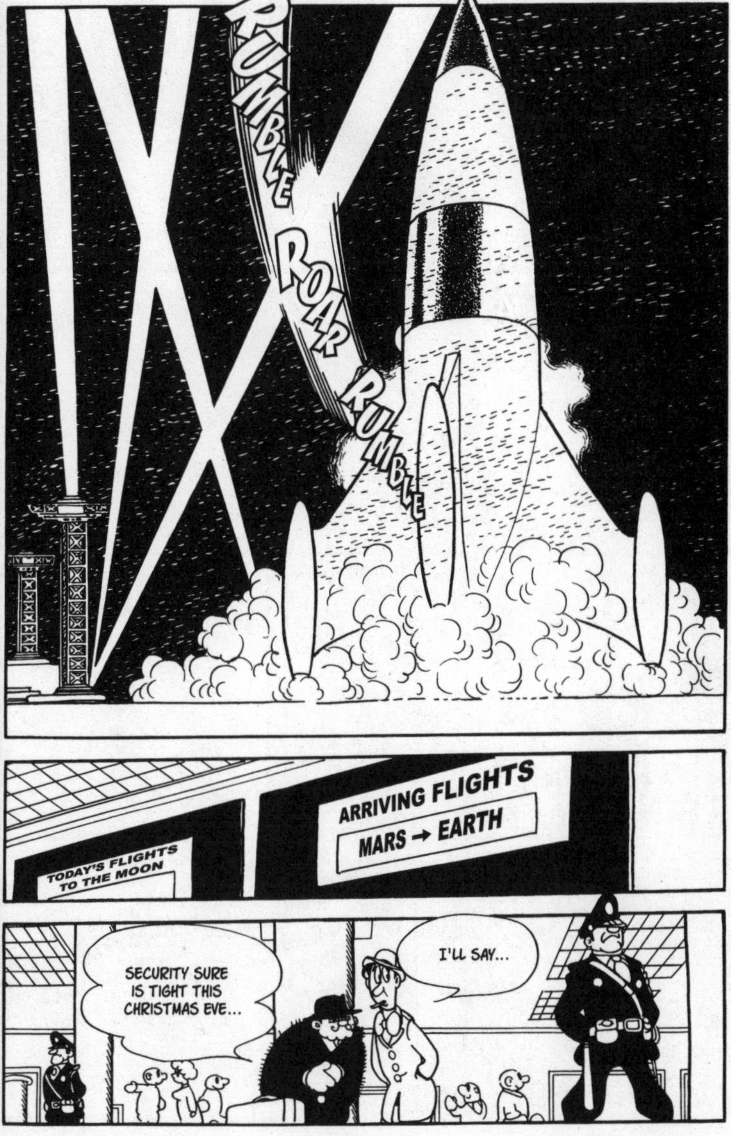
RUMBLE
ROAR
RUMBLE
TODAY'S FLIGHTS TO THE MOON
ARRIVING FLIGHTS
MARS → EARTH
SECURITY SURE IS TIGHT THIS CHRISTMAS EVE...
I'LL SAY...

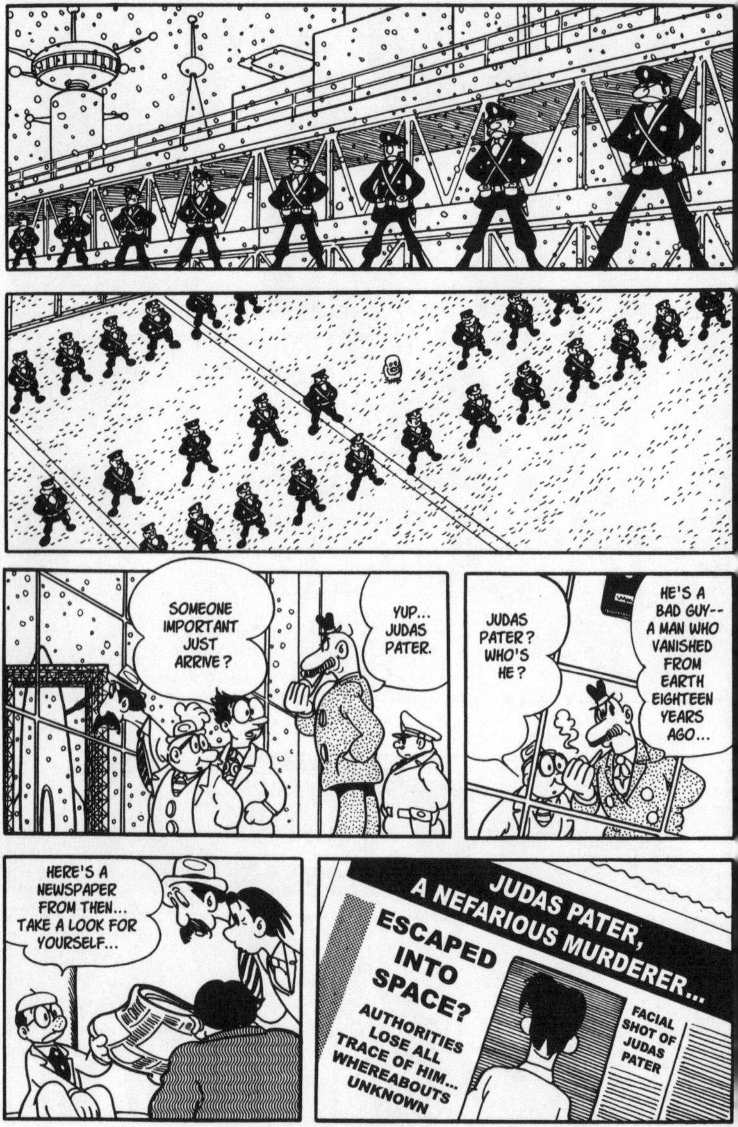

SOMEONE IMPORTANT JUST ARRIVE?
YUP... JUDAS PATER.
JUDAS PATER? WHO'S HE?
HE'S A BAD GUY-- A MAN WHO VANISHED FROM EARTH EIGHTEEN YEARS AGO...
HERE'S A NEWSPAPER FROM THEN... TAKE A LOOK FOR YOURSELF...
JUDAS PATER, A NEFARIOUS MURDERER...
ESCAPED INTO SPACE?
AUTHORITIES LOSE ALL TRACE OF HIM... WHEREABOUTS UNKNOWN
FACIAL SHOT OF JUDAS PATER

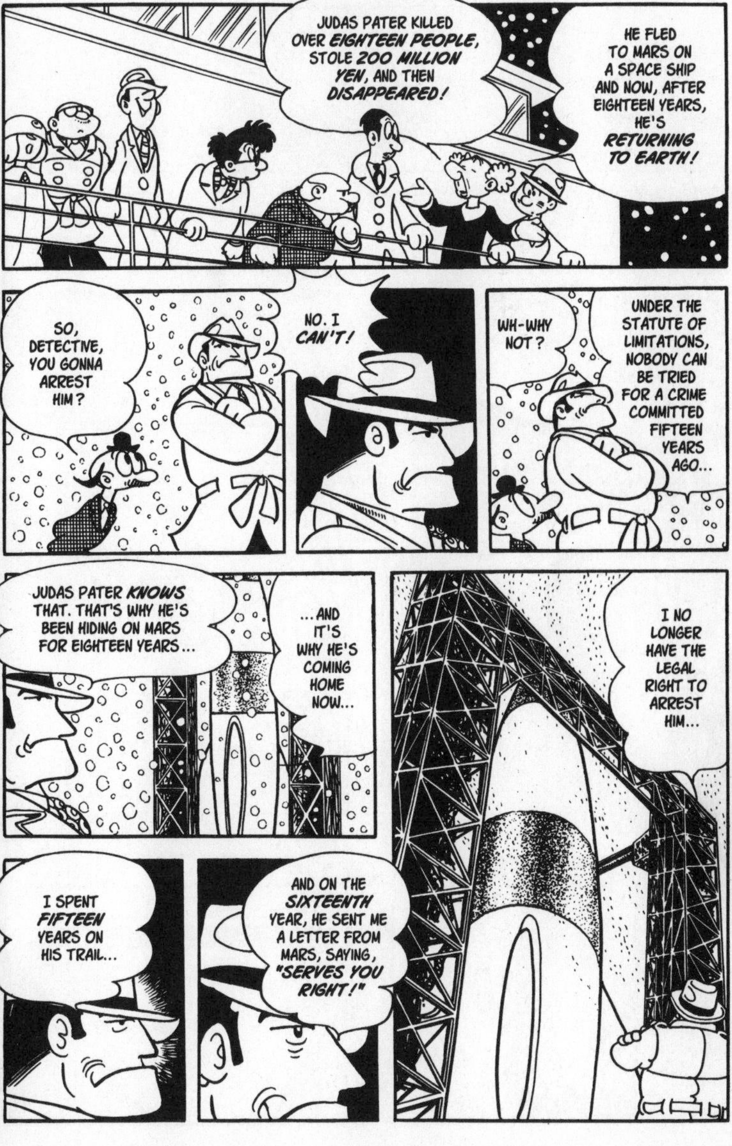
JUDAS PATER KILLED OVER *EIGHTEEN PEOPLE*, STOLE *200 MILLION YEN*, AND THEN *DISAPPEARED!*
HE FLED TO MARS ON A SPACE SHIP AND NOW, AFTER EIGHTEEN YEARS, HE'S *RETURNING TO EARTH!*
SO, DETECTIVE, YOU GONNA ARREST HIM?
NO. I *CAN'T!*
WH-WHY NOT?
UNDER THE STATUTE OF LIMITATIONS, NOBODY CAN BE TRIED FOR A CRIME COMMITTED FIFTEEN YEARS AGO...
JUDAS PATER *KNOWS* THAT. THAT'S WHY HE'S BEEN HIDING ON MARS FOR EIGHTEEN YEARS...
...AND IT'S WHY HE'S COMING HOME NOW...
I NO LONGER HAVE THE LEGAL RIGHT TO ARREST HIM...
I SPENT *FIFTEEN* YEARS ON HIS TRAIL...
AND ON THE *SIXTEENTH* YEAR, HE SENT ME A LETTER FROM MARS, SAYING, *"SERVES YOU RIGHT!"*

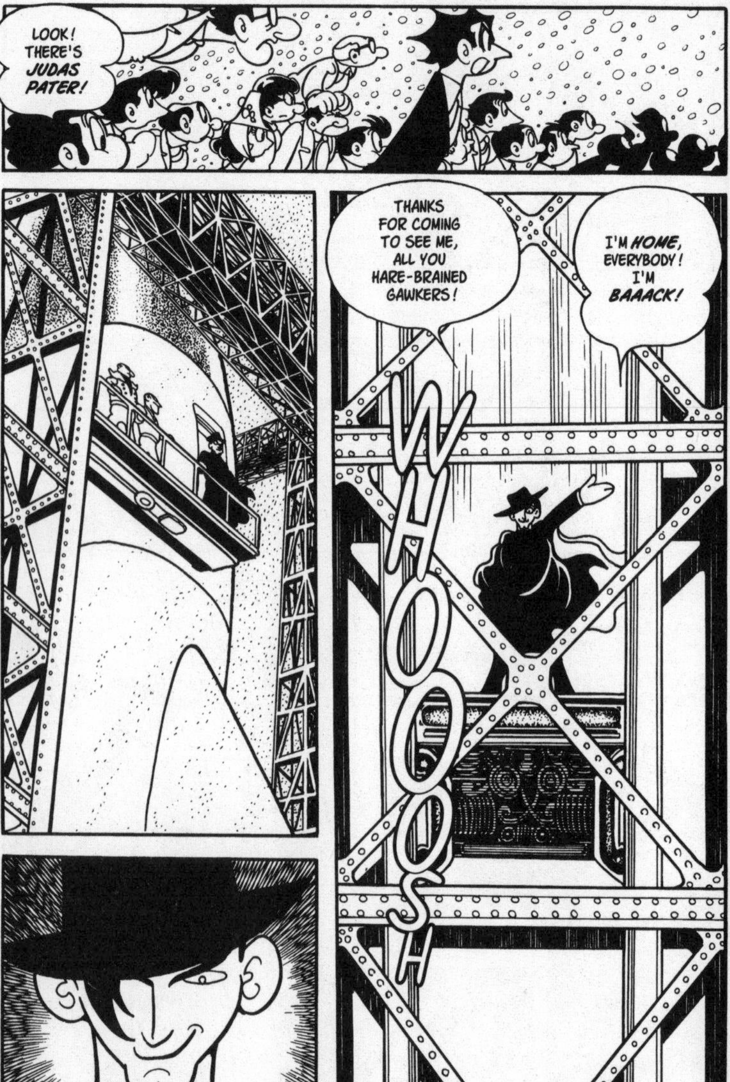
LOOK! THERE'S *JUDAS PATER!*
THANKS FOR COMING TO SEE ME, ALL YOU HARE-BRAINED GAWKERS!
I'M *HOME,* EVERYBODY! I'M *BAAACK!*
WHOOOSH

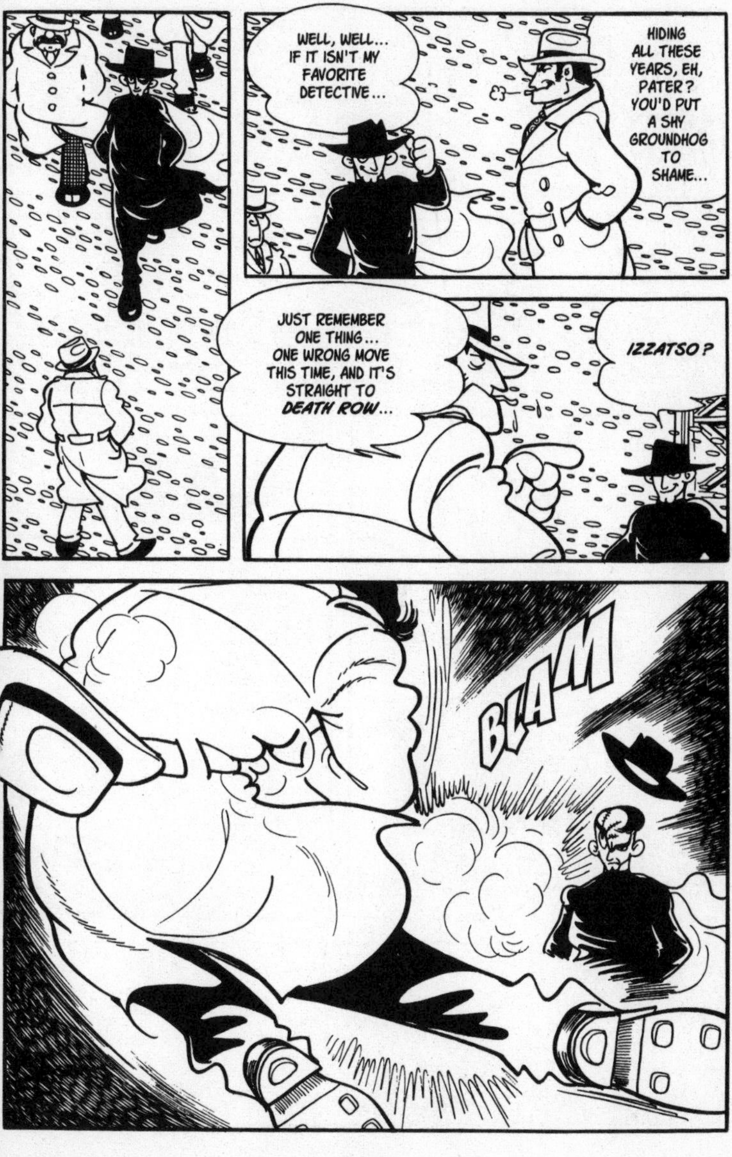
WELL, WELL... IF IT ISN'T MY FAVORITE DETECTIVE...
HIDING ALL THESE YEARS, EH, PATER? YOU'D PUT A SHY GROUNDHOG TO SHAME...
JUST REMEMBER ONE THING... ONE WRONG MOVE THIS TIME, AND IT'S STRAIGHT TO *DEATH ROW*...
IZZATSO?
BLAM

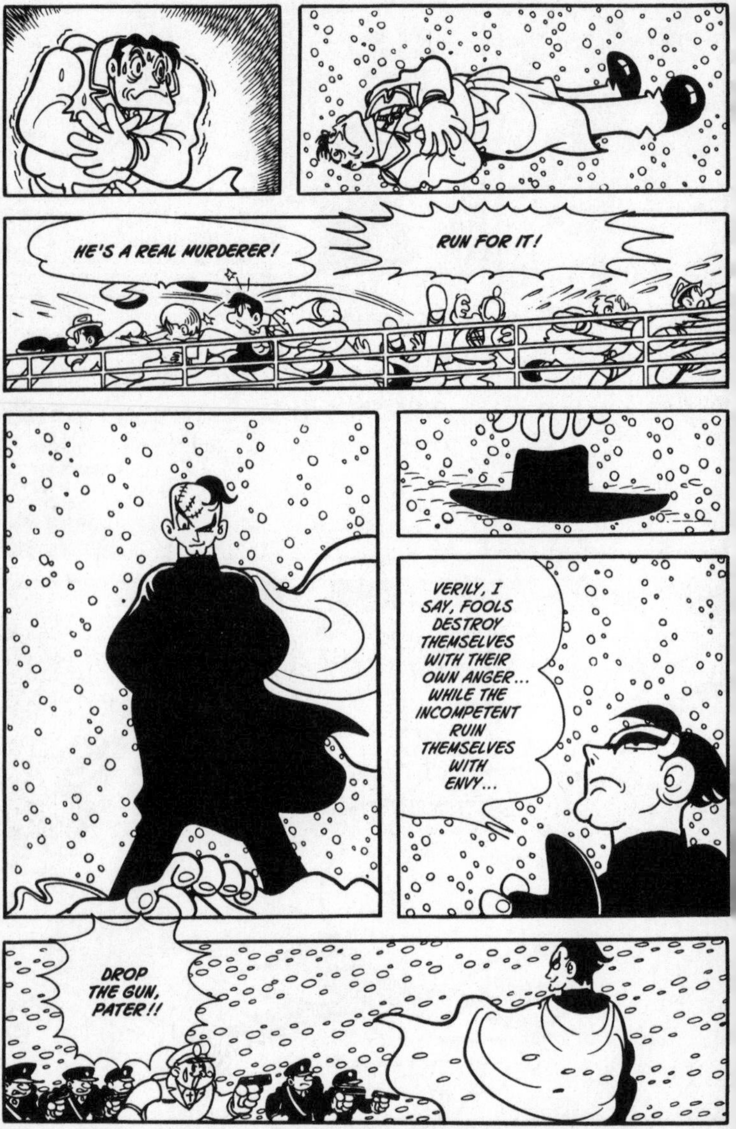
HE'S A REAL MURDERER!
RUN FOR IT!
VERILY, I SAY, FOOLS DESTROY THEMSELVES WITH THEIR OWN ANGER... WHILE THE INCOMPETENT RUIN THEMSELVES WITH ENVY...
DROP THE GUN, PATER!!

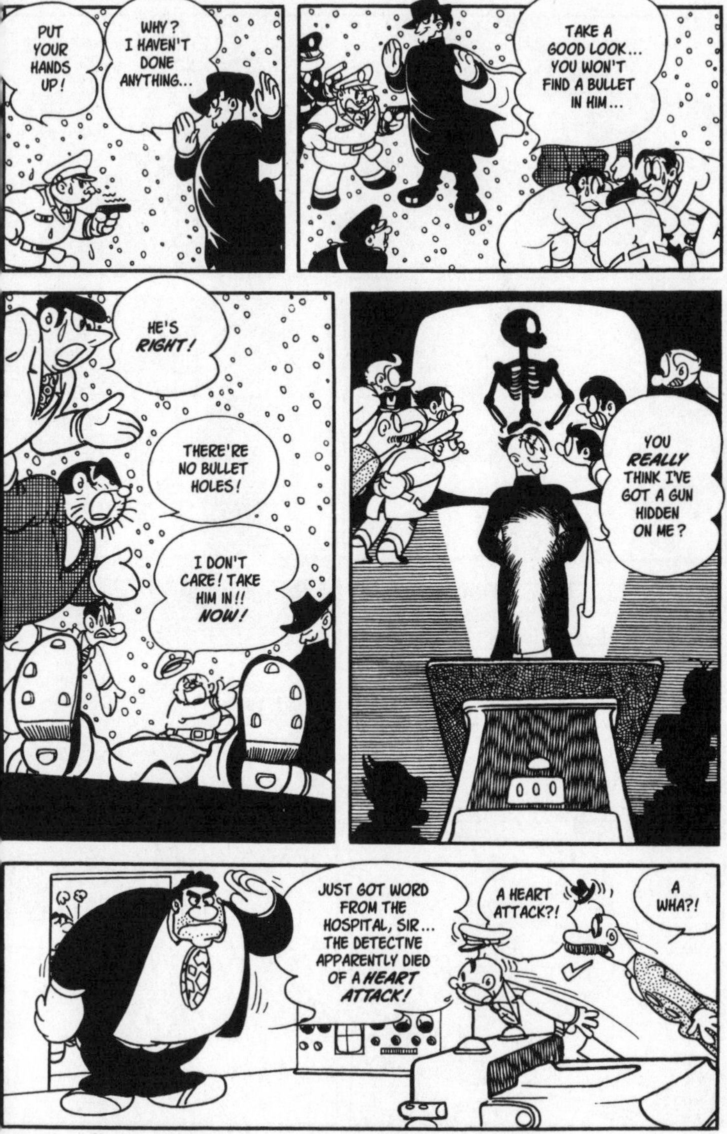
PUT YOUR HANDS UP!
WHY? I HAVEN'T DONE ANYTHING...
TAKE A GOOD LOOK... YOU WON'T FIND A BULLET IN HIM...
HE'S *RIGHT!*
THERE'RE NO BULLET HOLES!
I DON'T CARE! TAKE HIM IN!! *NOW!*
YOU *REALLY* THINK I'VE GOT A GUN HIDDEN ON ME?
JUST GOT WORD FROM THE HOSPITAL, SIR... THE DETECTIVE APPARENTLY DIED OF A *HEART ATTACK!*
A HEART ATTACK?!
A WHA?!

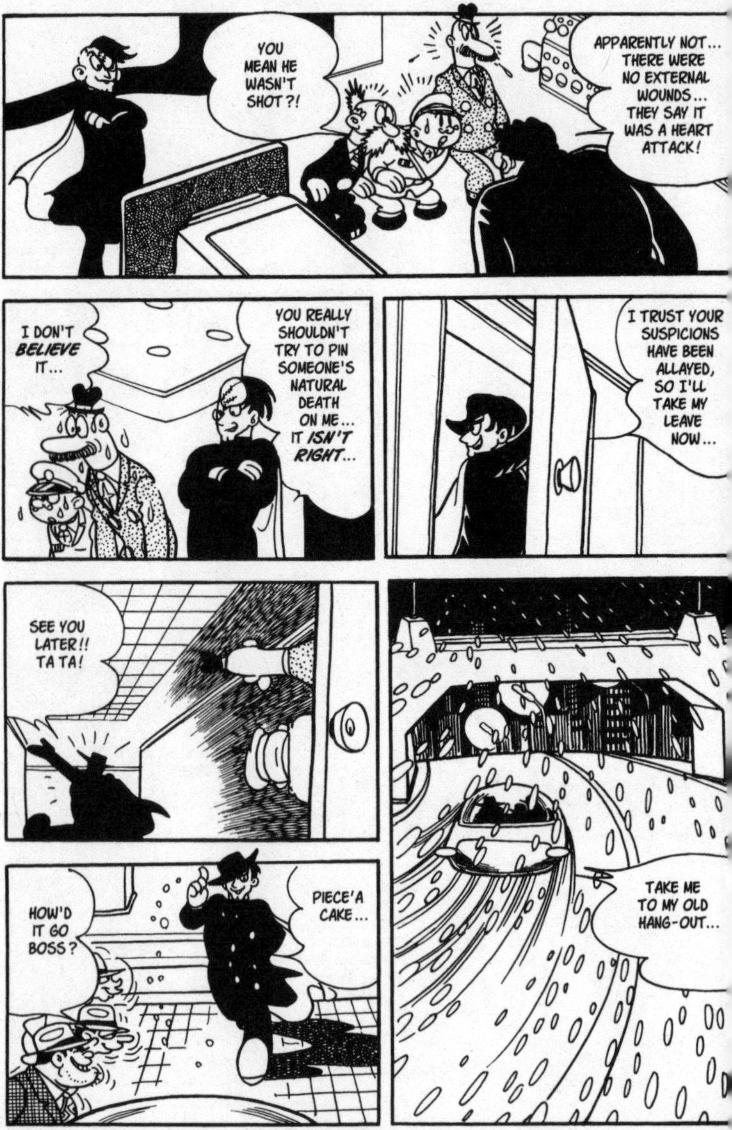
YOU MEAN HE WASN'T SHOT?!
APPARENTLY NOT... THERE WERE NO EXTERNAL WOUNDS... THEY SAY IT WAS A HEART ATTACK!
I DON'T *BELIEVE* IT...
YOU REALLY SHOULDN'T TRY TO PIN SOMEONE'S NATURAL DEATH ON ME... IT *ISN'T RIGHT*...
I TRUST YOUR SUSPICIONS HAVE BEEN ALLAYED, SO I'LL TAKE MY LEAVE NOW...
SEE YOU LATER!! TA TA!
HOW'D IT GO BOSS?
PIECE'A CAKE...
TAKE ME TO MY OLD HANG-OUT...

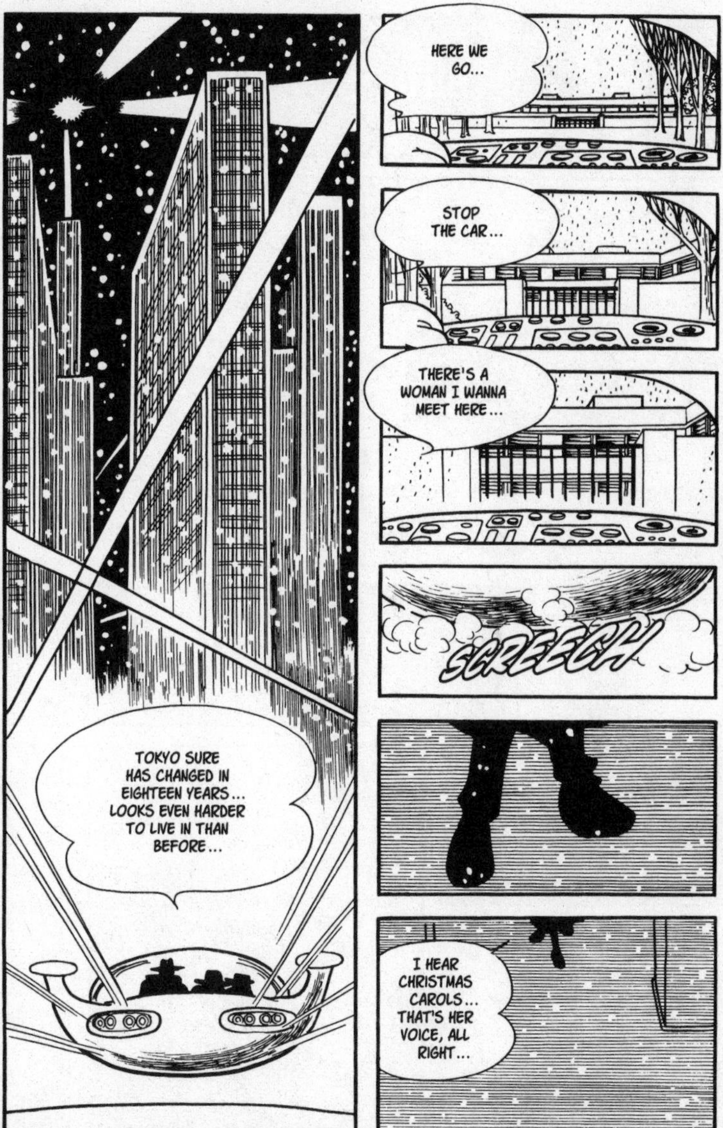
TOKYO SURE HAS CHANGED IN EIGHTEEN YEARS... LOOKS EVEN HARDER TO LIVE IN THAN BEFORE...
HERE WE GO...
STOP THE CAR...
THERE'S A WOMAN I WANNA MEET HERE...
SCREECH
I HEAR CHRISTMAS CAROLS... THAT'S HER VOICE, ALL RIGHT...

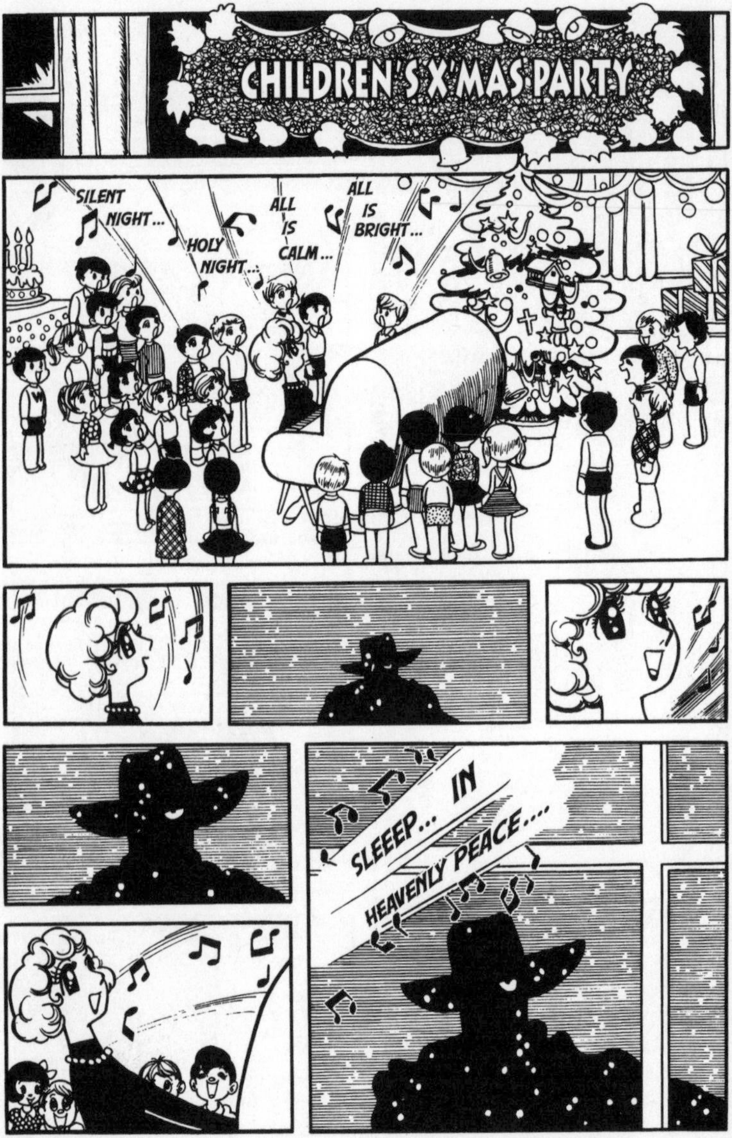
CHILDREN'S X'MAS PARTY
SILENT NIGHT...
HOLY NIGHT...
ALL IS CALM...
ALL IS BRIGHT...
SLEEEP... IN
HEAVENLY PEACE....

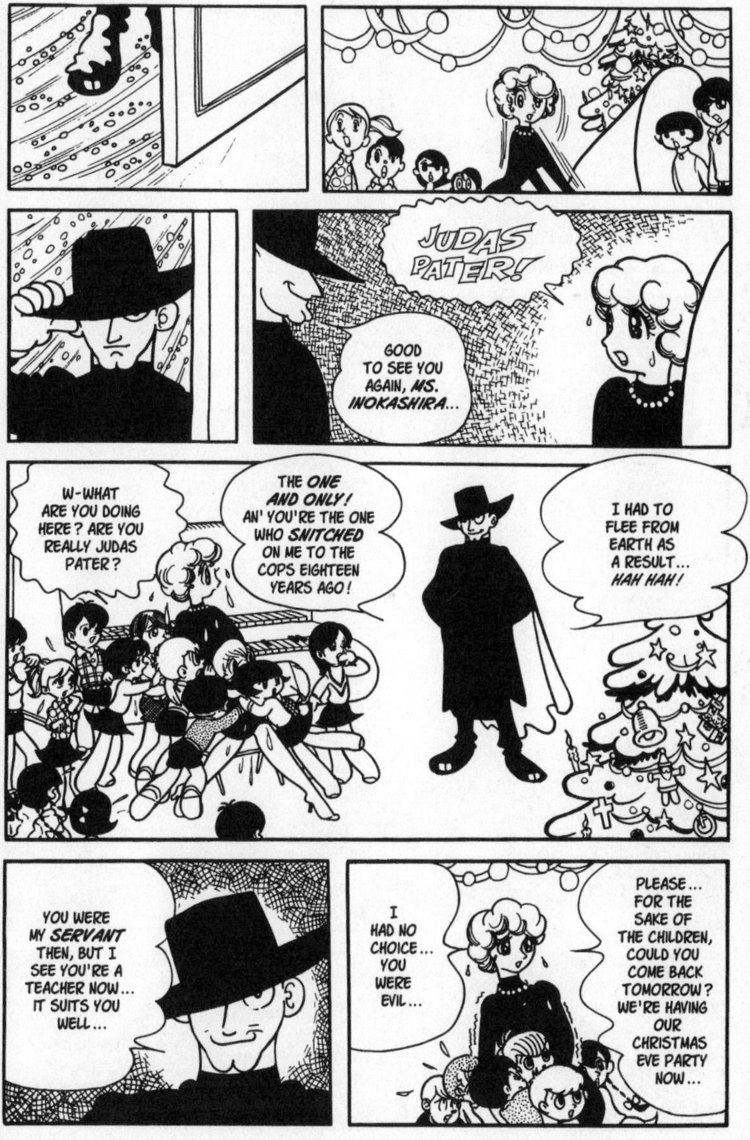
JUDAS PATER!
GOOD TO SEE YOU AGAIN, MS. INOKASHIRA...
W-WHAT ARE YOU DOING HERE? ARE YOU REALLY JUDAS PATER?
THE ONE AND ONLY! AN' YOU'RE THE ONE WHO SNITCHED ON ME TO THE COPS EIGHTEEN YEARS AGO!
I HAD TO FLEE FROM EARTH AS A RESULT... HAH HAH!
YOU WERE MY SERVANT THEN, BUT I SEE YOU'RE A TEACHER NOW... IT SUITS YOU WELL...
I HAD NO CHOICE... YOU WERE EVIL...
PLEASE... FOR THE SAKE OF THE CHILDREN, COULD YOU COME BACK TOMORROW? WE'RE HAVING OUR CHRISTMAS EVE PARTY NOW...

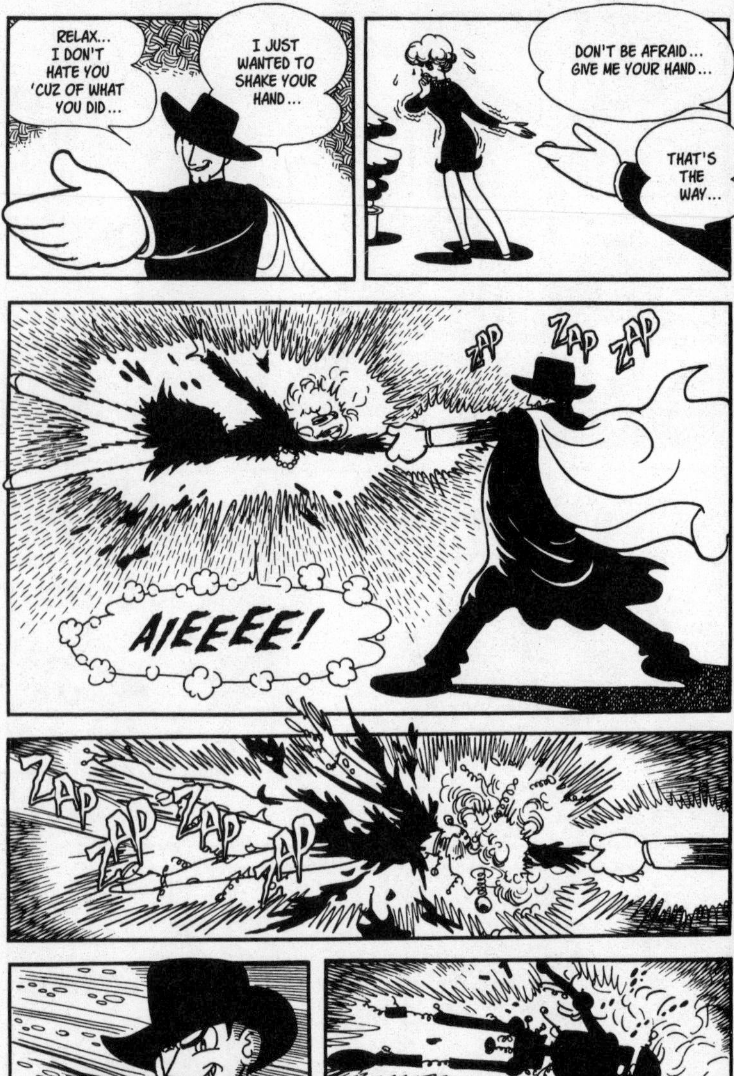
RELAX... I DON'T HATE YOU 'CUZ OF WHAT YOU DID...
I JUST WANTED TO SHAKE YOUR HAND...
DON'T BE AFRAID... GIVE ME YOUR HAND...
THAT'S THE WAY...
ZAP
ZAP
ZAP
AIEEEEE!
ZAP
ZAP
ZAP
ZAP

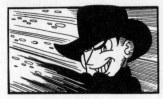

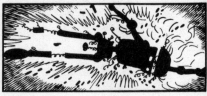

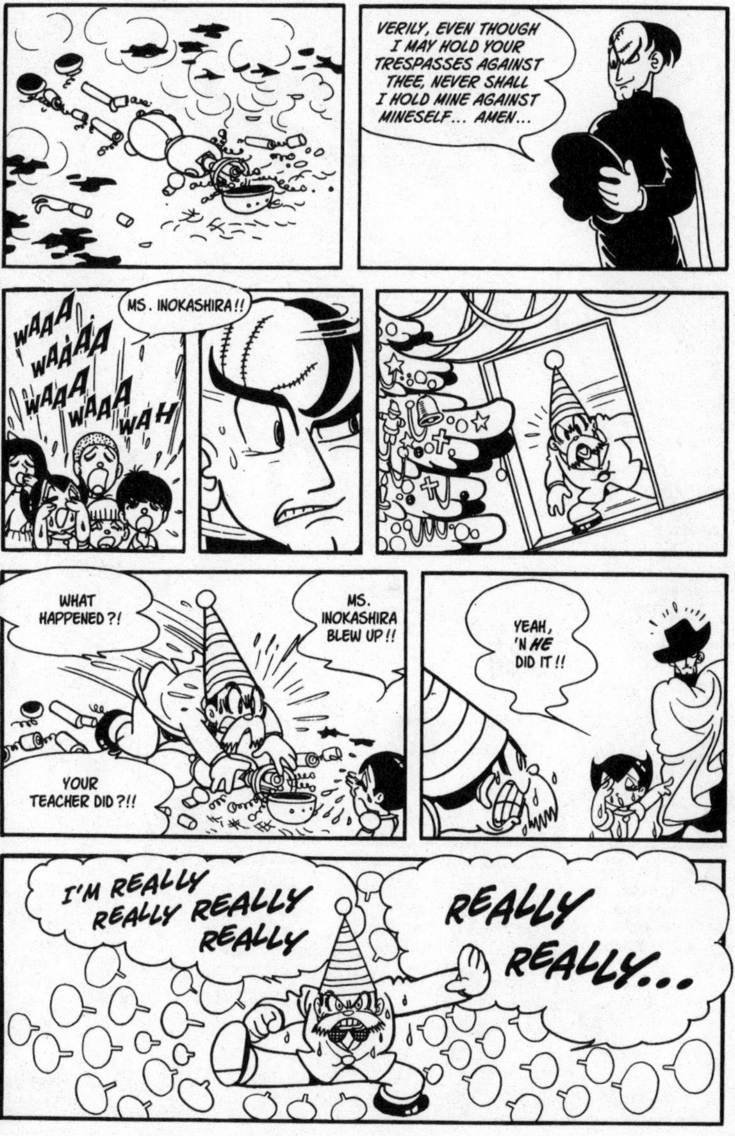
VERILY, EVEN THOUGH I MAY HOLD YOUR TRESPASSES AGAINST THEE, NEVER SHALL I HOLD MINE AGAINST MINESELF... AMEN...
WAAA WAAAA WAAA WAAA WAAA WAH
MS. INOKASHIRA!!
WHAT HAPPENED?!
MS. INOKASHIRA BLEW UP!!
YOUR TEACHER DID?!!
YEAH, 'N HE DID IT!!
I'M REALLY REALLY REALLY REALLY
REALLY REALLY...

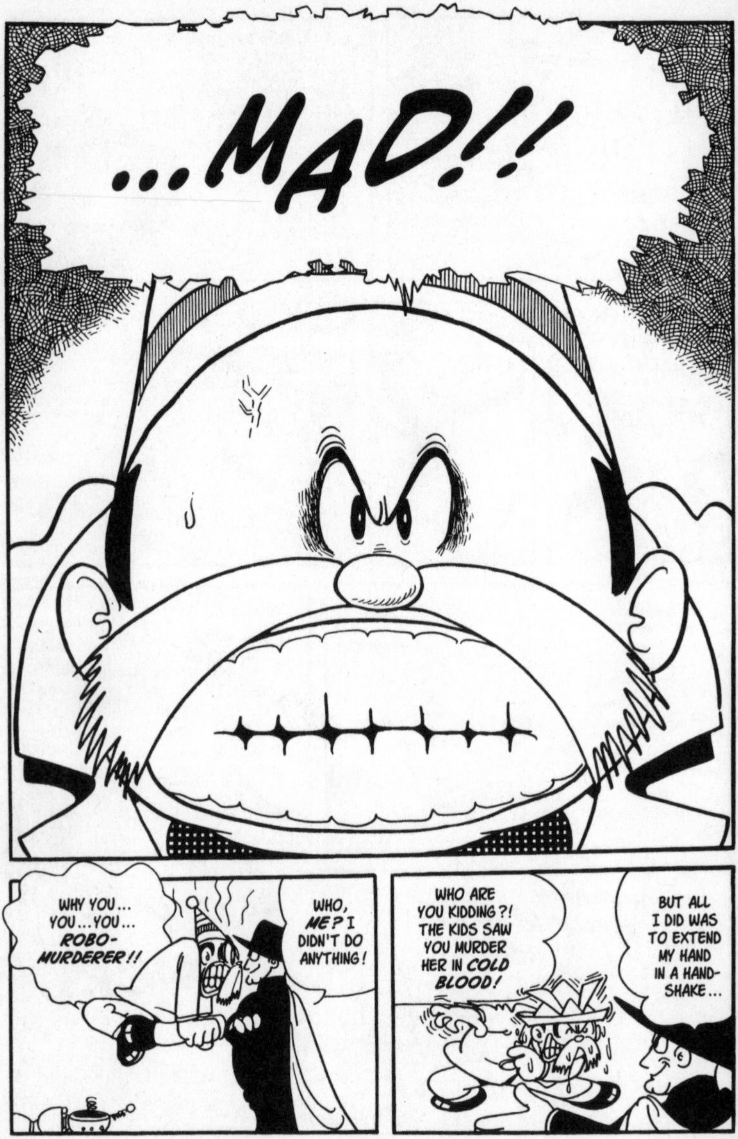
...MAD!!
WHY YOU... YOU...YOU... ROBO-MURDERER!!
WHO, ME? I DIDN'T DO ANYTHING!
WHO ARE YOU KIDDING?! THE KIDS SAW YOU MURDER HER IN COLD BLOOD!
BUT ALL I DID WAS TO EXTEND MY HAND IN A HAND-SHAKE...

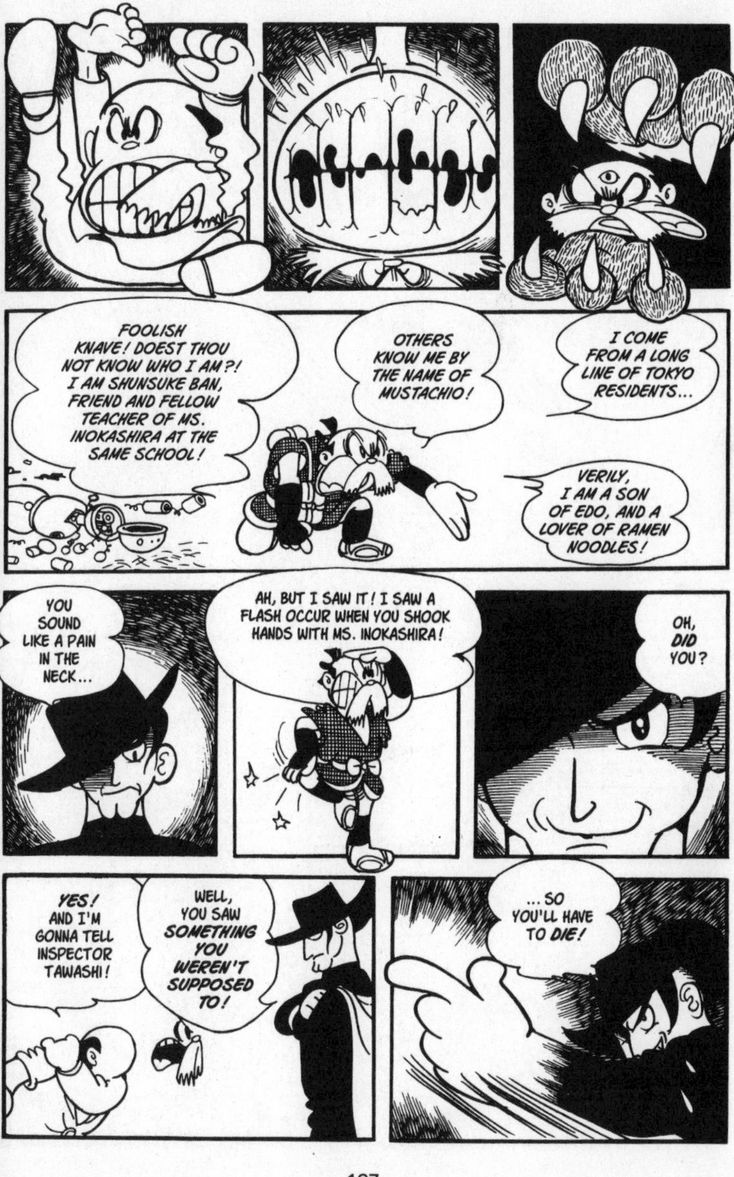
FOOLISH KNAVE! DOEST THOU NOT KNOW WHO I AM?! I AM SHUNSUKE BAN, FRIEND AND FELLOW TEACHER OF MS. INOKASHIRA AT THE SAME SCHOOL!
OTHERS KNOW ME BY THE NAME OF MUSTACHIO!
I COME FROM A LONG LINE OF TOKYO RESIDENTS...
VERILY, I AM A SON OF EDO, AND A LOVER OF RAMEN NOODLES!
YOU SOUND LIKE A PAIN IN THE NECK...
AH, BUT I SAW IT! I SAW A FLASH OCCUR WHEN YOU SHOOK HANDS WITH MS. INOKASHIRA!
OH, *DID* YOU?
YES! AND I'M GONNA TELL INSPECTOR TAWASHI!
WELL, YOU SAW *SOMETHING* YOU *WEREN'T SUPPOSED TO!*
... SO YOU'LL HAVE TO *DIE!*

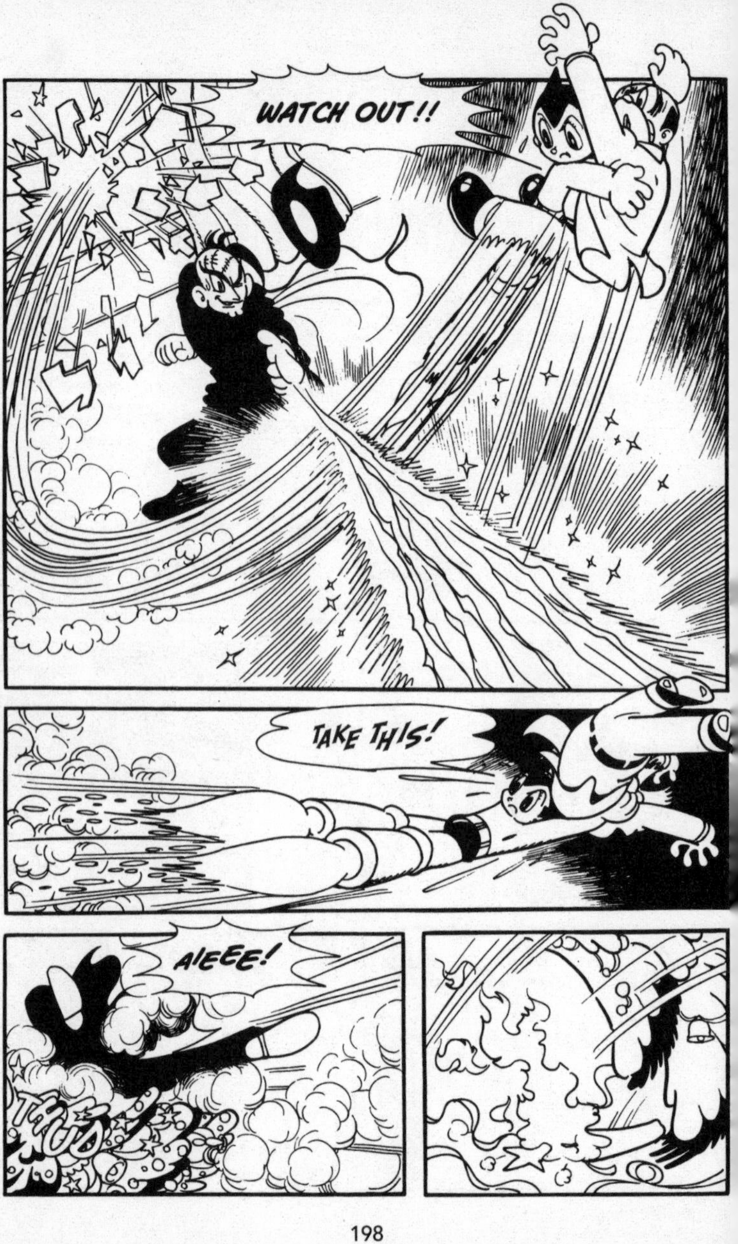
WATCH OUT!!
TAKE THIS!
AIEEE!
THUD

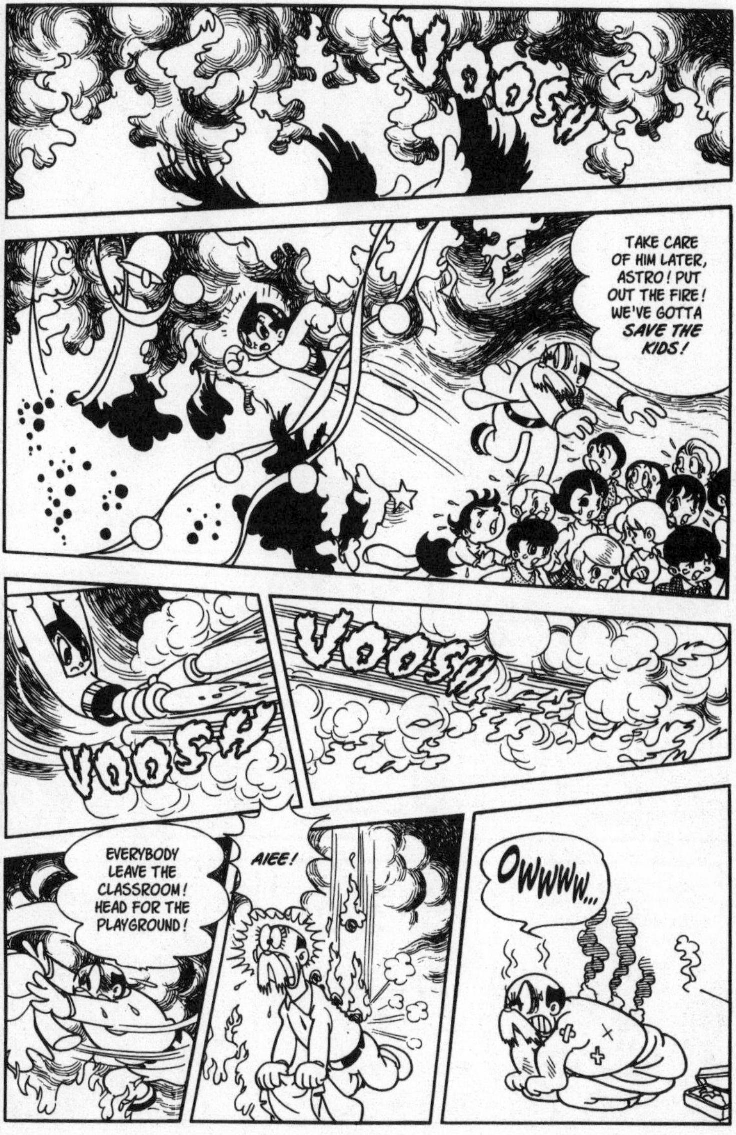
VOOSH
TAKE CARE OF HIM LATER, ASTRO! PUT OUT THE FIRE! WE'VE GOTTA SAVE THE KIDS!
VOOSH
VOOSH
EVERYBODY LEAVE THE CLASSROOM! HEAD FOR THE PLAYGROUND!
AIEE!
OWWWW...

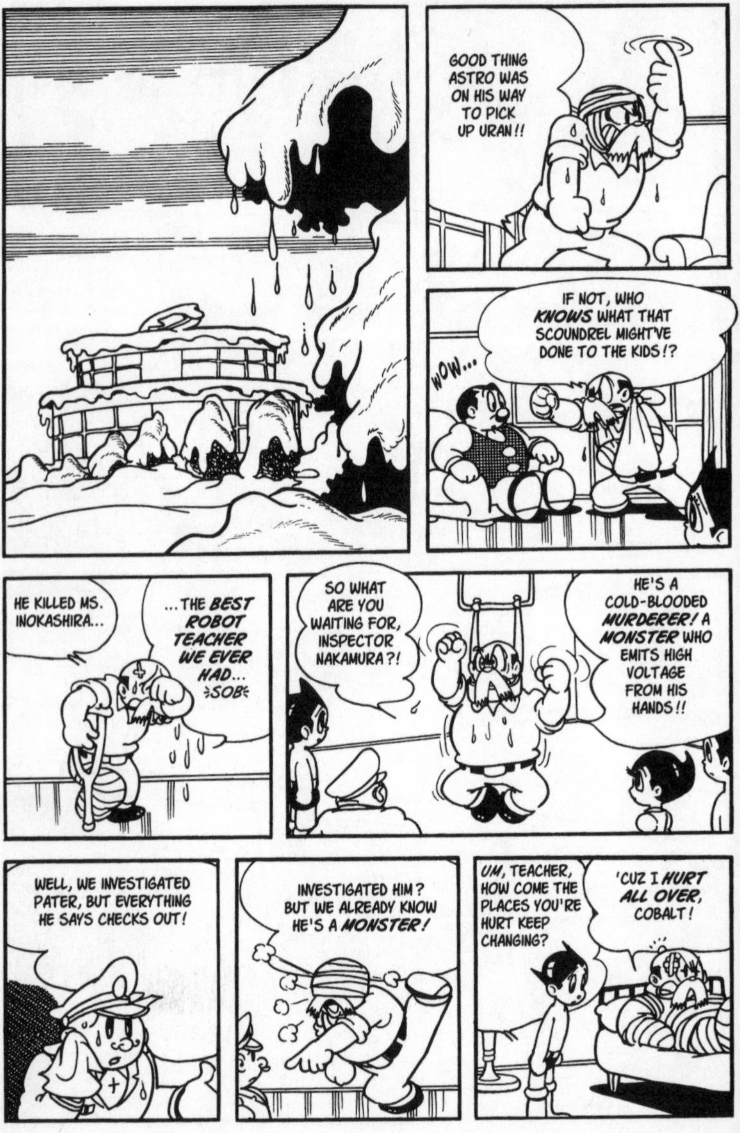

GOOD THING ASTRO WAS ON HIS WAY TO PICK UP URAN!!
IF NOT, WHO KNOWS WHAT THAT SCOUNDREL MIGHT'VE DONE TO THE KIDS!?
WOW...
HE KILLED MS. INOKASHIRA...
...THE BEST ROBOT TEACHER WE EVER HAD... *SOB*
SO WHAT ARE YOU WAITING FOR, INSPECTOR NAKAMURA?!
HE'S A COLD-BLOODED MURDERER! A MONSTER WHO EMITS HIGH VOLTAGE FROM HIS HANDS!!
WELL, WE INVESTIGATED PATER, BUT EVERYTHING HE SAYS CHECKS OUT!
INVESTIGATED HIM? BUT WE ALREADY KNOW HE'S A MONSTER!
UM, TEACHER, HOW COME THE PLACES YOU'RE HURT KEEP CHANGING?
'CUZ I HURT ALL OVER, COBALT!

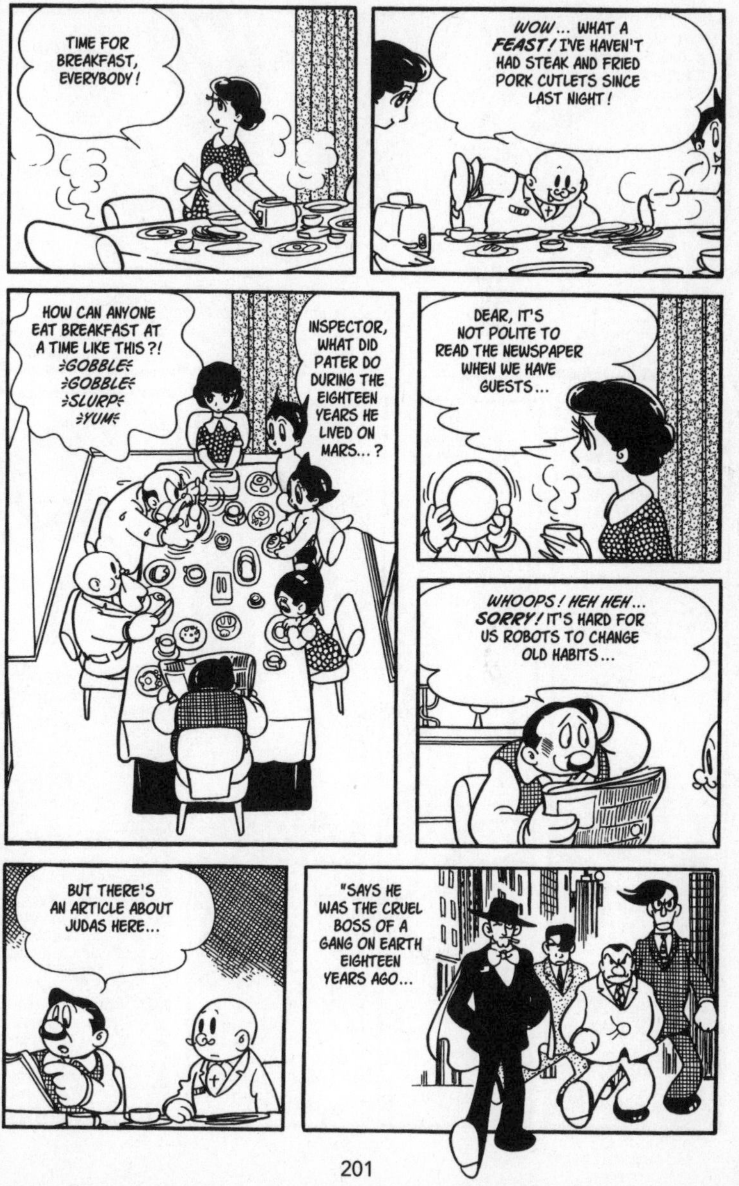

TIME FOR BREAKFAST, EVERYBODY!
WOW... WHAT A FEAST! I'VE HAVEN'T HAD STEAK AND FRIED PORK CUTLETS SINCE LAST NIGHT!
HOW CAN ANYONE EAT BREAKFAST AT A TIME LIKE THIS?! ≡GOBBLE≡ ≡GOBBLE≡ ≡SLURP≡ ≡YUM≡
INSPECTOR, WHAT DID PATER DO DURING THE EIGHTEEN YEARS HE LIVED ON MARS...?
DEAR, IT'S NOT POLITE TO READ THE NEWSPAPER WHEN WE HAVE GUESTS...
WHOOPS! HEH HEH... SORRY! IT'S HARD FOR US ROBOTS TO CHANGE OLD HABITS...
BUT THERE'S AN ARTICLE ABOUT JUDAS HERE...
"SAYS HE WAS THE CRUEL BOSS OF A GANG ON EARTH EIGHTEEN YEARS AGO...

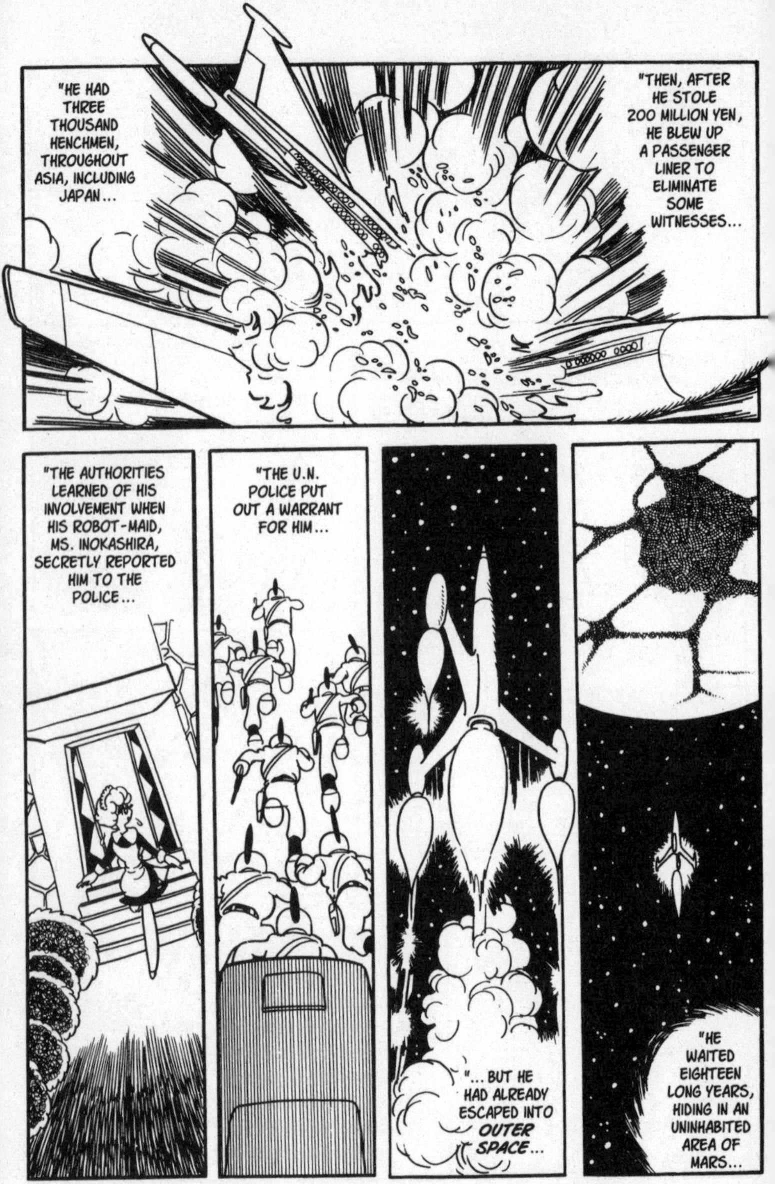
"HE HAD THREE THOUSAND HENCHMEN, THROUGHOUT ASIA, INCLUDING JAPAN...
"THEN, AFTER HE STOLE 200 MILLION YEN, HE BLEW UP A PASSENGER LINER TO ELIMINATE SOME WITNESSES...
"THE AUTHORITIES LEARNED OF HIS INVOLVEMENT WHEN HIS ROBOT-MAID, MS. INOKASHIRA, SECRETLY REPORTED HIM TO THE POLICE...
"THE U.N. POLICE PUT OUT A WARRANT FOR HIM...
"... BUT HE HAD ALREADY ESCAPED INTO *OUTER SPACE*...
"HE WAITED EIGHTEEN LONG YEARS, HIDING IN AN UNINHABITED AREA OF MARS...

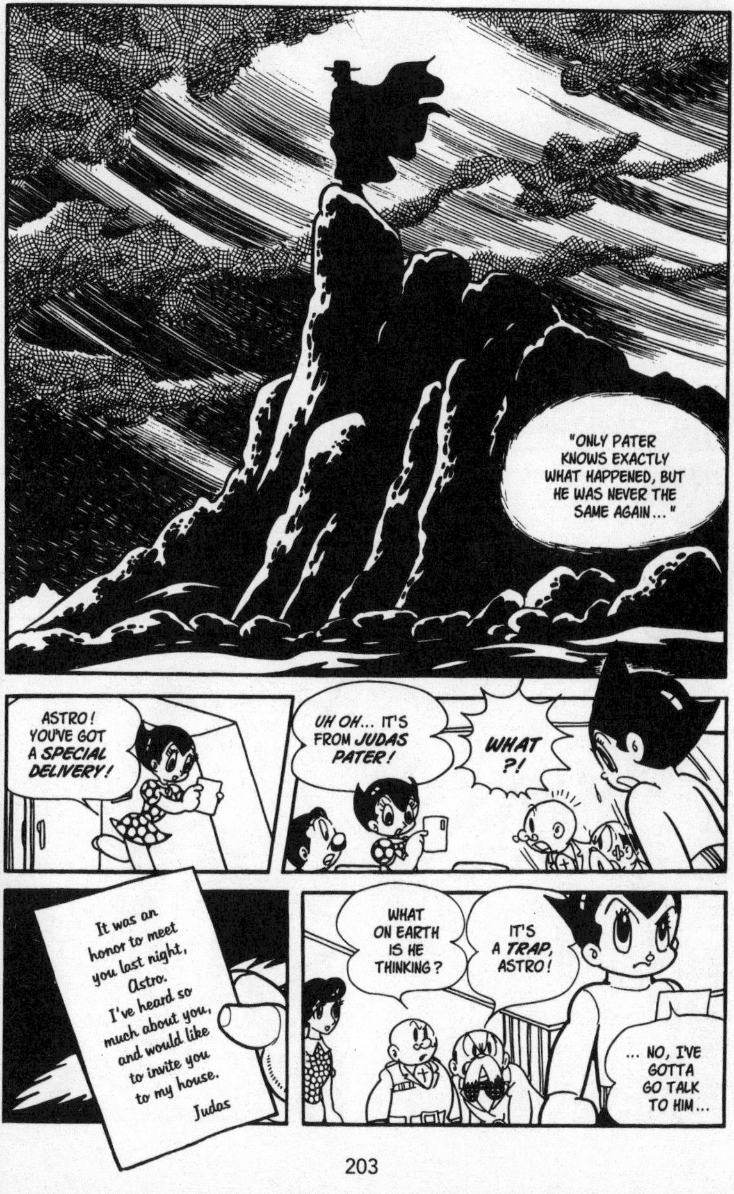

"ONLY PATER KNOWS EXACTLY WHAT HAPPENED, BUT HE WAS NEVER THE SAME AGAIN..."
ASTRO! YOU'VE GOT A SPECIAL DELIVERY!
UH OH... IT'S FROM JUDAS PATER!
WHAT ?!
It was an honor to meet you last night, Astro. I've heard so much about you, and would like to invite you to my house. Judas
WHAT ON EARTH IS HE THINKING?
IT'S A TRAP, ASTRO!
... NO, I'VE GOTTA GO TALK TO HIM...

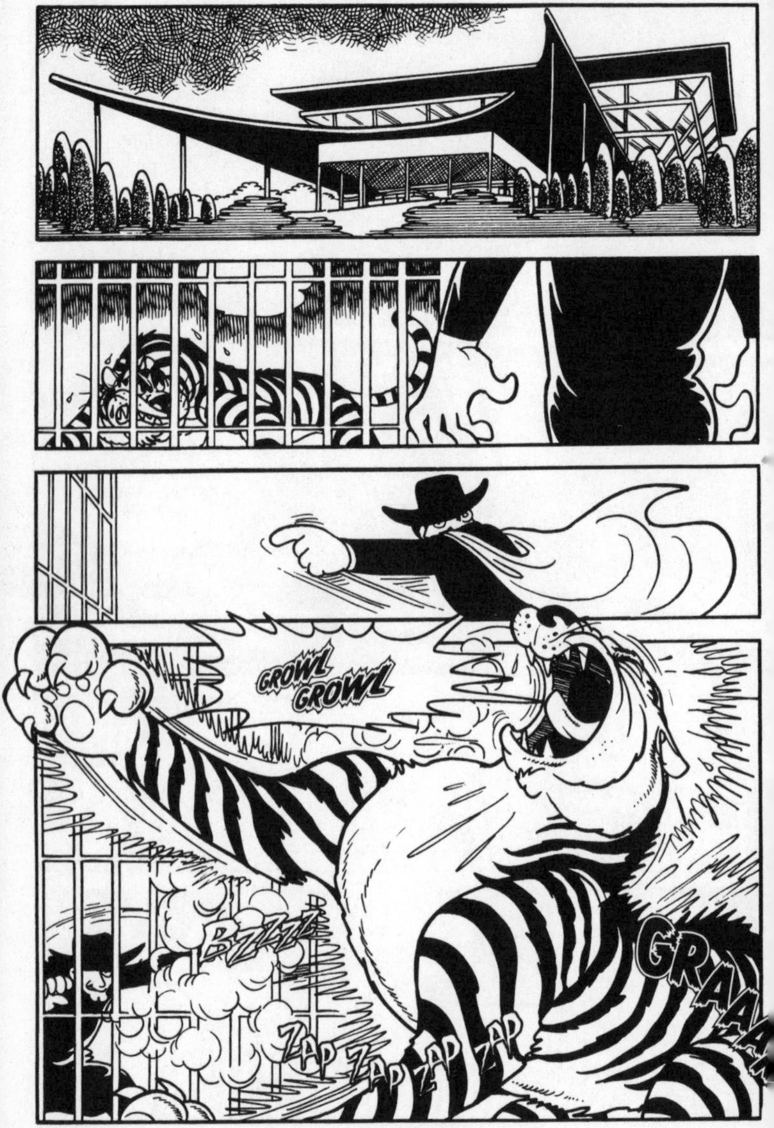
GROWL GROWL
BZZZ
GRAA
ZAP ZAP ZAP ZAP

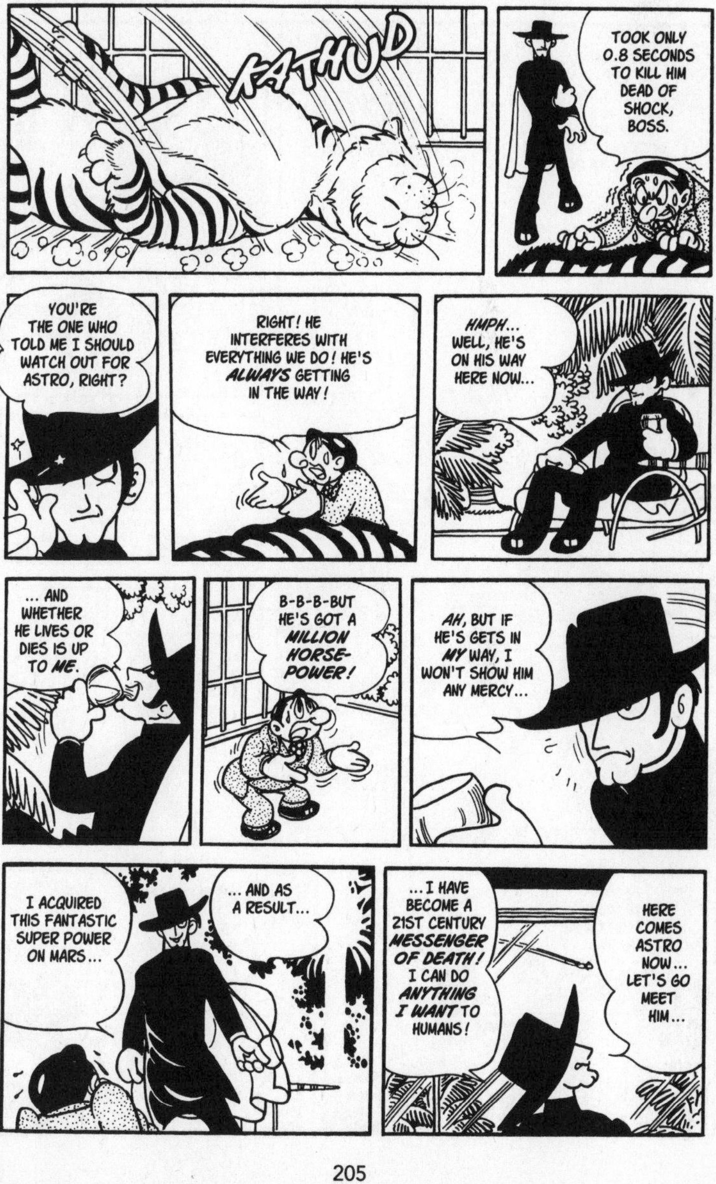
KATHUD
TOOK ONLY 0.8 SECONDS TO KILL HIM DEAD OF SHOCK, BOSS.
YOU'RE THE ONE WHO TOLD ME I SHOULD WATCH OUT FOR ASTRO, RIGHT?
RIGHT! HE INTERFERES WITH EVERYTHING WE DO! HE'S ALWAYS GETTING IN THE WAY!
HMPH... WELL, HE'S ON HIS WAY HERE NOW...
... AND WHETHER HE LIVES OR DIES IS UP TO ME.
B-B-B-BUT HE'S GOT A MILLION HORSE-POWER!
AH, BUT IF HE'S GETS IN MY WAY, I WON'T SHOW HIM ANY MERCY...
I ACQUIRED THIS FANTASTIC SUPER POWER ON MARS...
... AND AS A RESULT...
...I HAVE BECOME A 21ST CENTURY MESSENGER OF DEATH! I CAN DO ANYTHING I WANT TO HUMANS!
HERE COMES ASTRO NOW... LET'S GO MEET HIM...

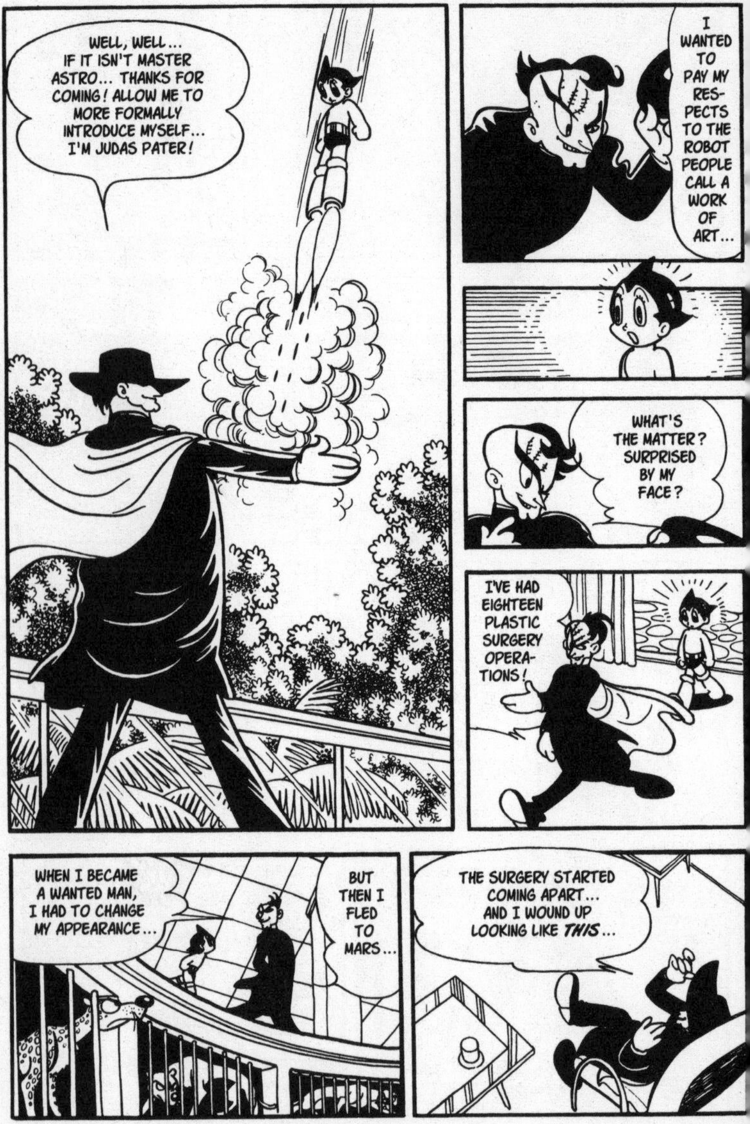
WELL, WELL... IF IT ISN'T MASTER ASTRO... THANKS FOR COMING! ALLOW ME TO MORE FORMALLY INTRODUCE MYSELF... I'M JUDAS PATER!
I WANTED TO PAY MY RES-PECTS TO THE ROBOT PEOPLE CALL A WORK OF ART...
WHAT'S THE MATTER? SURPRISED BY MY FACE?
I'VE HAD EIGHTEEN PLASTIC SURGERY OPERA-TIONS!
WHEN I BECAME A WANTED MAN, I HAD TO CHANGE MY APPEARANCE...
BUT THEN I FLED TO MARS...
THE SURGERY STARTED COMING APART... AND I WOUND UP LOOKING LIKE *THIS*...

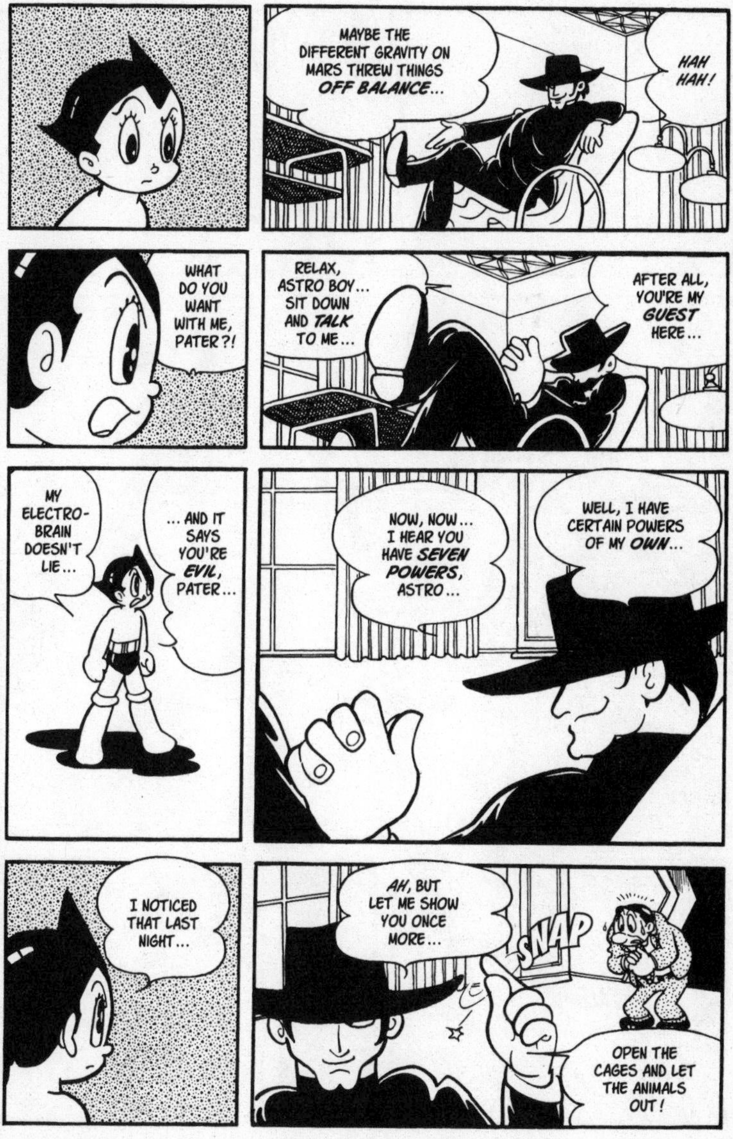

MAYBE THE DIFFERENT GRAVITY ON MARS THREW THINGS OFF BALANCE...
HAH HAH!
WHAT DO YOU WANT WITH ME, PATER?!
RELAX, ASTRO BOY... SIT DOWN AND TALK TO ME...
AFTER ALL, YOU'RE MY GUEST HERE...
MY ELECTRO-BRAIN DOESN'T LIE...
... AND IT SAYS YOU'RE EVIL, PATER...
NOW, NOW... I HEAR YOU HAVE SEVEN POWERS, ASTRO...
WELL, I HAVE CERTAIN POWERS OF MY OWN...
I NOTICED THAT LAST NIGHT...
AH, BUT LET ME SHOW YOU ONCE MORE...
SNAP
OPEN THE CAGES AND LET THE ANIMALS OUT!

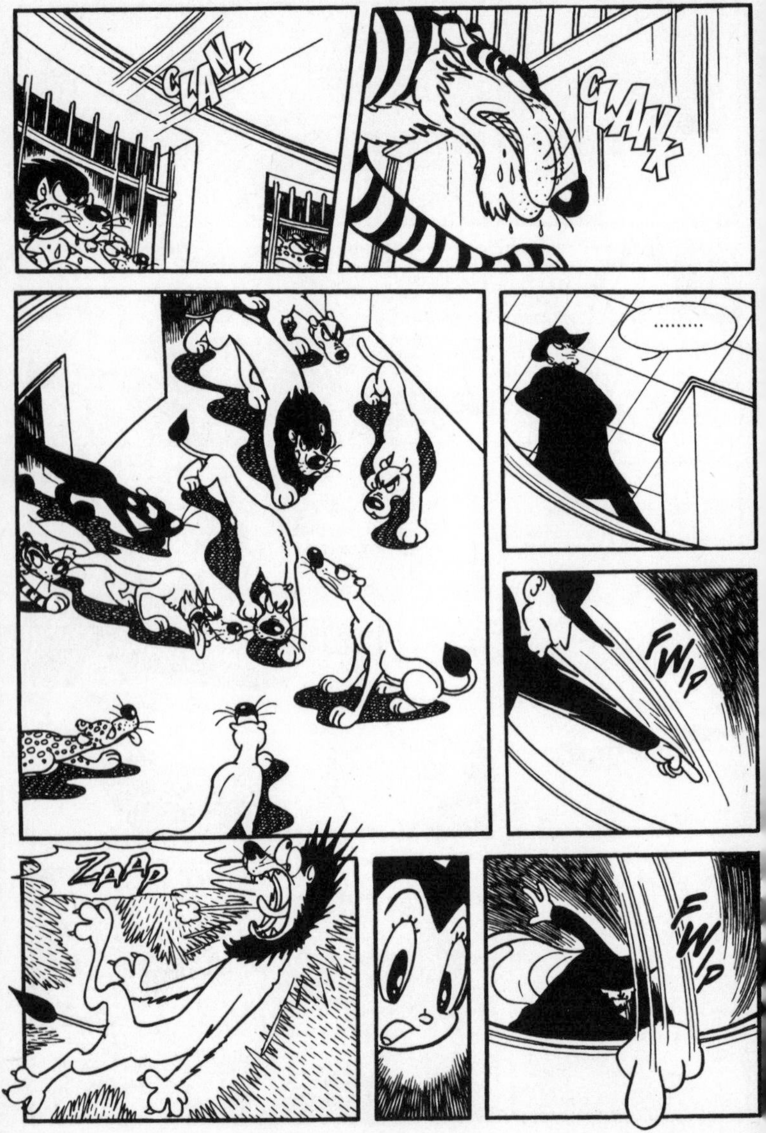
CLANK
CLANK
....
FWIP
ZAAP
FWIP

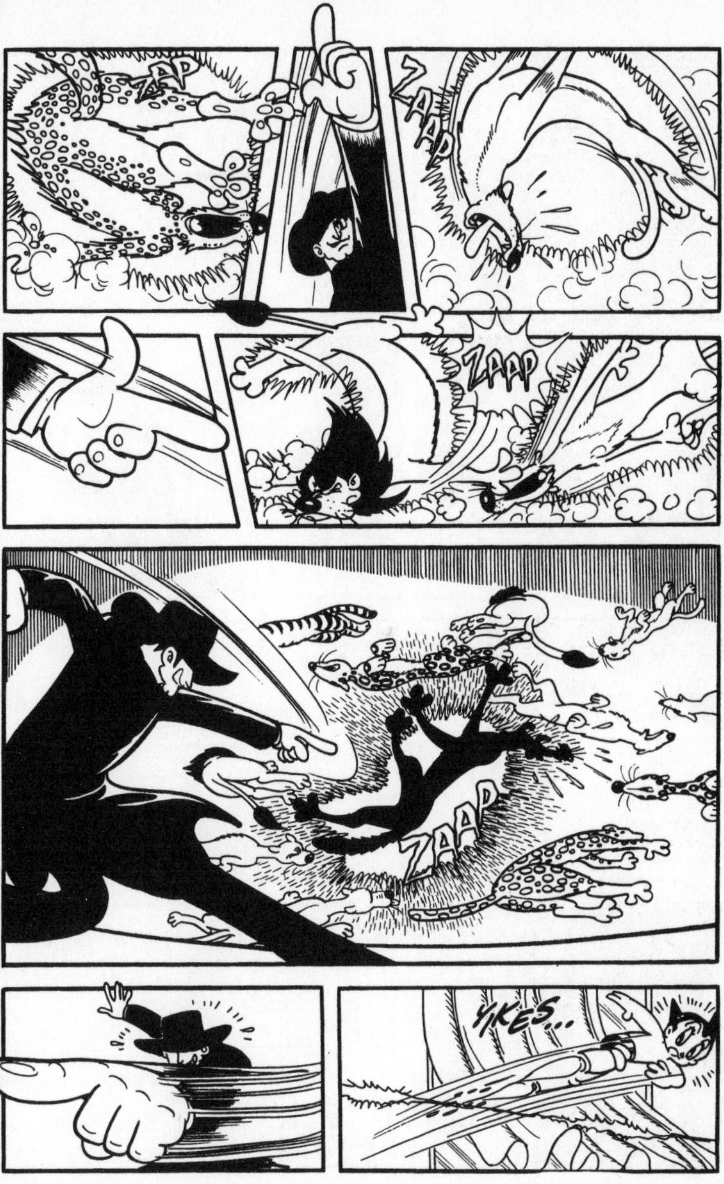
ZAAP
ZAAP
ZAAP
ZAAP
YIKES...

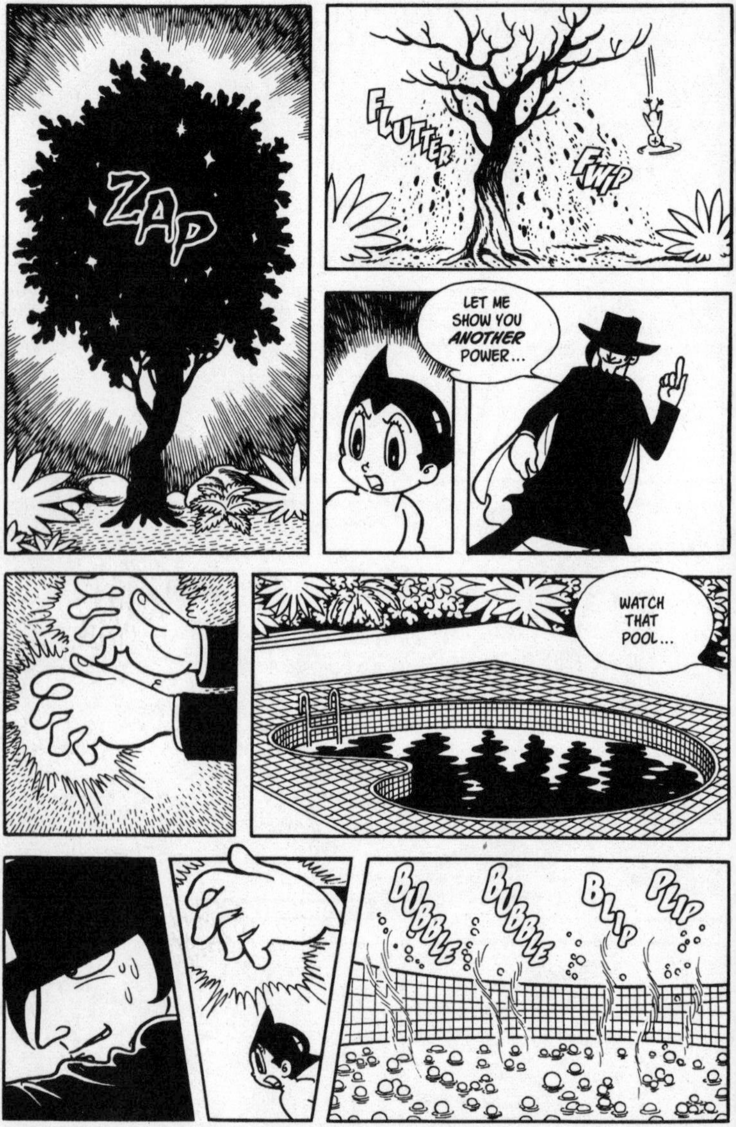
ZAP
FLUTTER
FWIP
LET ME SHOW YOU ANOTHER POWER...
WATCH THAT POOL...
BUBBLE
BUBBLE
BLIP
PLIP

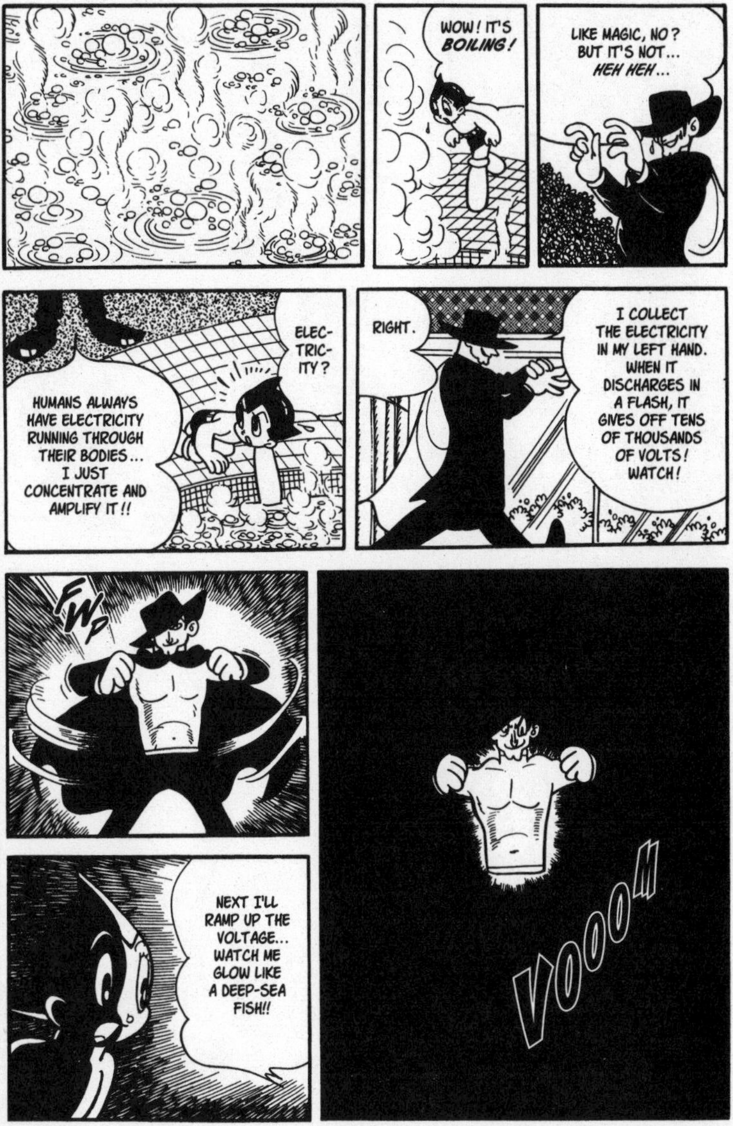
WOW! IT'S *BOILING!*
LIKE MAGIC, NO? BUT IT'S NOT... *HEH HEH...*
HUMANS ALWAYS HAVE ELECTRICITY RUNNING THROUGH THEIR BODIES... I JUST CONCENTRATE AND AMPLIFY IT!!
ELEC-TRIC-ITY?
RIGHT.
I COLLECT THE ELECTRICITY IN MY LEFT HAND. WHEN IT DISCHARGES IN A FLASH, IT GIVES OFF TENS OF THOUSANDS OF VOLTS! WATCH!
FWP
NEXT I'LL RAMP UP THE VOLTAGE... WATCH ME GLOW LIKE A DEEP-SEA FISH!!
VOOOM

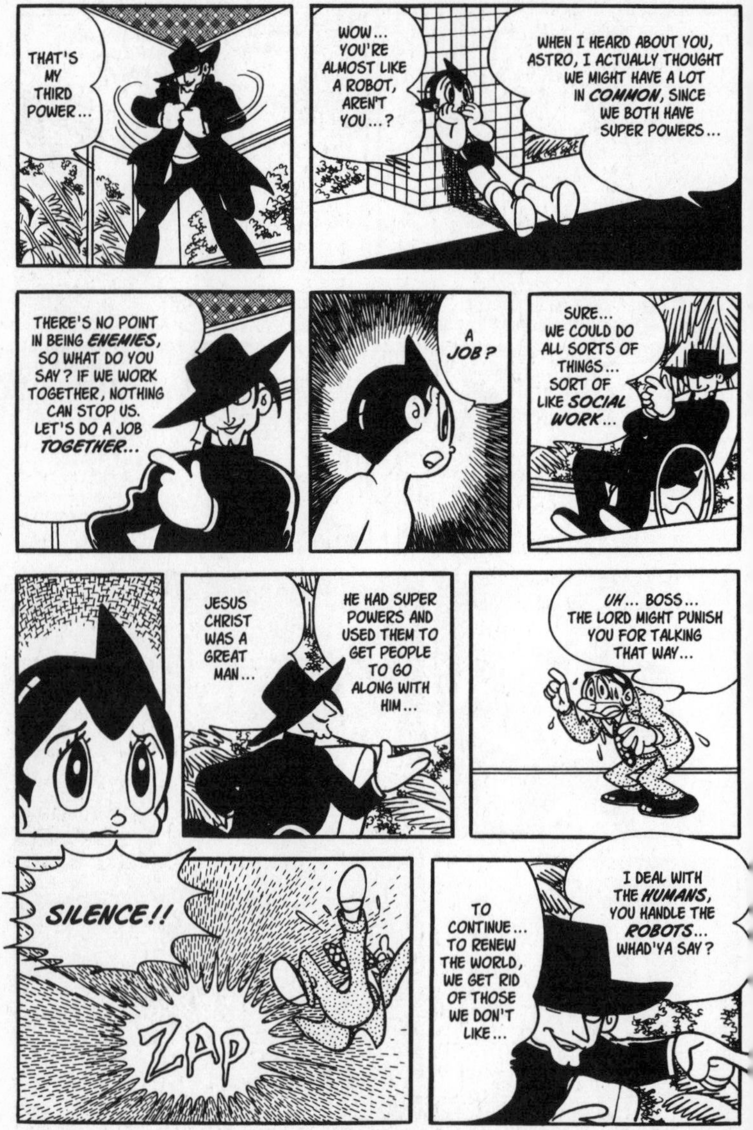
THAT'S MY THIRD POWER...
WOW... YOU'RE ALMOST LIKE A ROBOT, AREN'T YOU...?
WHEN I HEARD ABOUT YOU, ASTRO, I ACTUALLY THOUGHT WE MIGHT HAVE A LOT IN COMMON, SINCE WE BOTH HAVE SUPER POWERS...
THERE'S NO POINT IN BEING ENEMIES, SO WHAT DO YOU SAY? IF WE WORK TOGETHER, NOTHING CAN STOP US. LET'S DO A JOB TOGETHER...
A JOB?
SURE... WE COULD DO ALL SORTS OF THINGS... SORT OF LIKE SOCIAL WORK...
JESUS CHRIST WAS A GREAT MAN...
HE HAD SUPER POWERS AND USED THEM TO GET PEOPLE TO GO ALONG WITH HIM...
UH... BOSS... THE LORD MIGHT PUNISH YOU FOR TALKING THAT WAY...
SILENCE!!
ZAP
TO CONTINUE... TO RENEW THE WORLD, WE GET RID OF THOSE WE DON'T LIKE...
I DEAL WITH THE HUMANS, YOU HANDLE THE ROBOTS... WHAD'YA SAY?

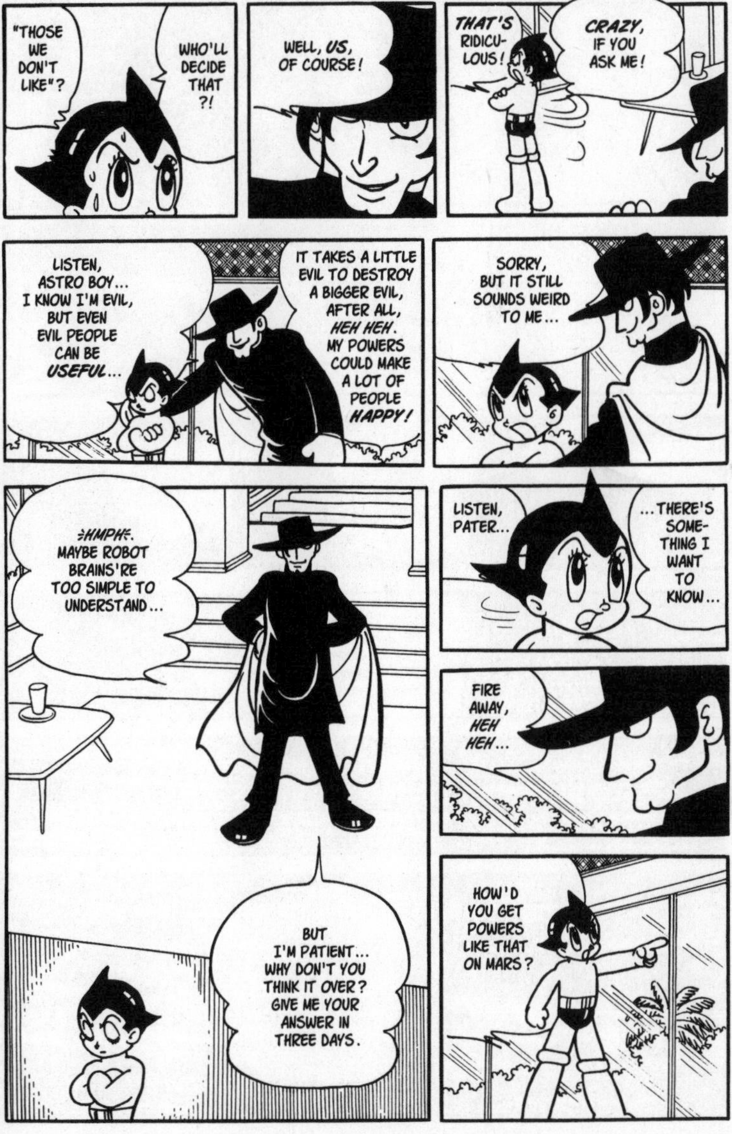
"THOSE WE DON'T LIKE"?
WHO'LL DECIDE THAT ?!
WELL, *US*, OF COURSE!
THAT'S RIDICULOUS!
CRAZY, IF YOU ASK ME!
LISTEN, ASTRO BOY... I KNOW I'M EVIL, BUT EVEN EVIL PEOPLE CAN BE *USEFUL*...
IT TAKES A LITTLE EVIL TO DESTROY A BIGGER EVIL, AFTER ALL, *HEH HEH*. MY POWERS COULD MAKE A LOT OF PEOPLE *HAPPY*!
SORRY, BUT IT STILL SOUNDS WEIRD TO ME...
HMPH. MAYBE ROBOT BRAINS'RE TOO SIMPLE TO UNDERSTAND...
BUT I'M PATIENT... WHY DON'T YOU THINK IT OVER? GIVE ME YOUR ANSWER IN THREE DAYS.
LISTEN, PATER...
...THERE'S SOMETHING I WANT TO KNOW...
FIRE AWAY, *HEH HEH*...
HOW'D YOU GET POWERS LIKE THAT ON MARS?

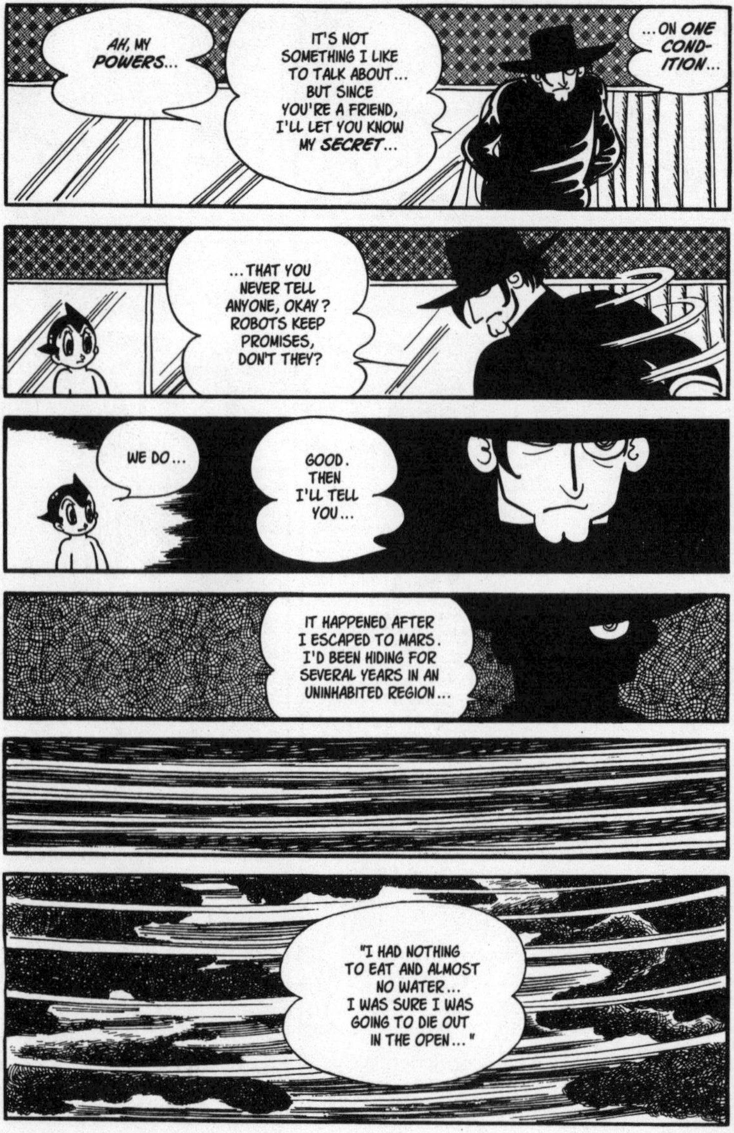
AH, MY POWERS...
IT'S NOT SOMETHING I LIKE TO TALK ABOUT... BUT SINCE YOU'RE A FRIEND, I'LL LET YOU KNOW MY SECRET...
...ON ONE COND- ITION...
...THAT YOU NEVER TELL ANYONE, OKAY? ROBOTS KEEP PROMISES, DON'T THEY?
WE DO...
GOOD. THEN I'LL TELL YOU...
IT HAPPENED AFTER I ESCAPED TO MARS. I'D BEEN HIDING FOR SEVERAL YEARS IN AN UNINHABITED REGION...
"I HAD NOTHING TO EAT AND ALMOST NO WATER... I WAS SURE I WAS GOING TO DIE OUT IN THE OPEN..."

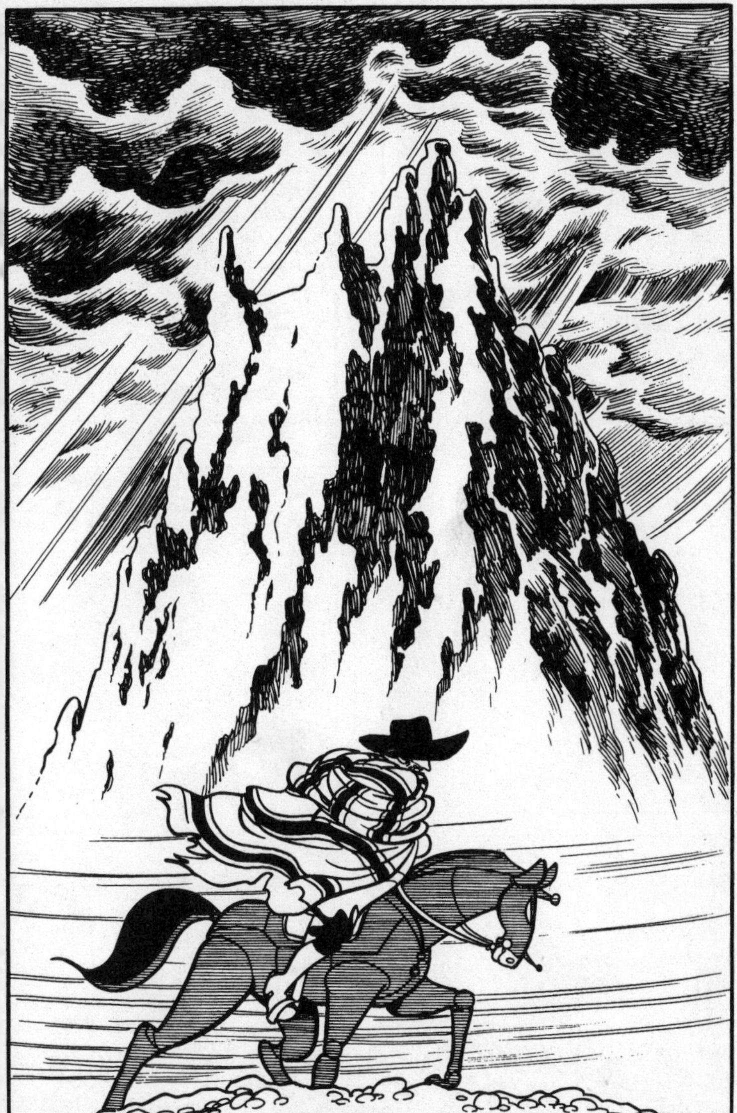

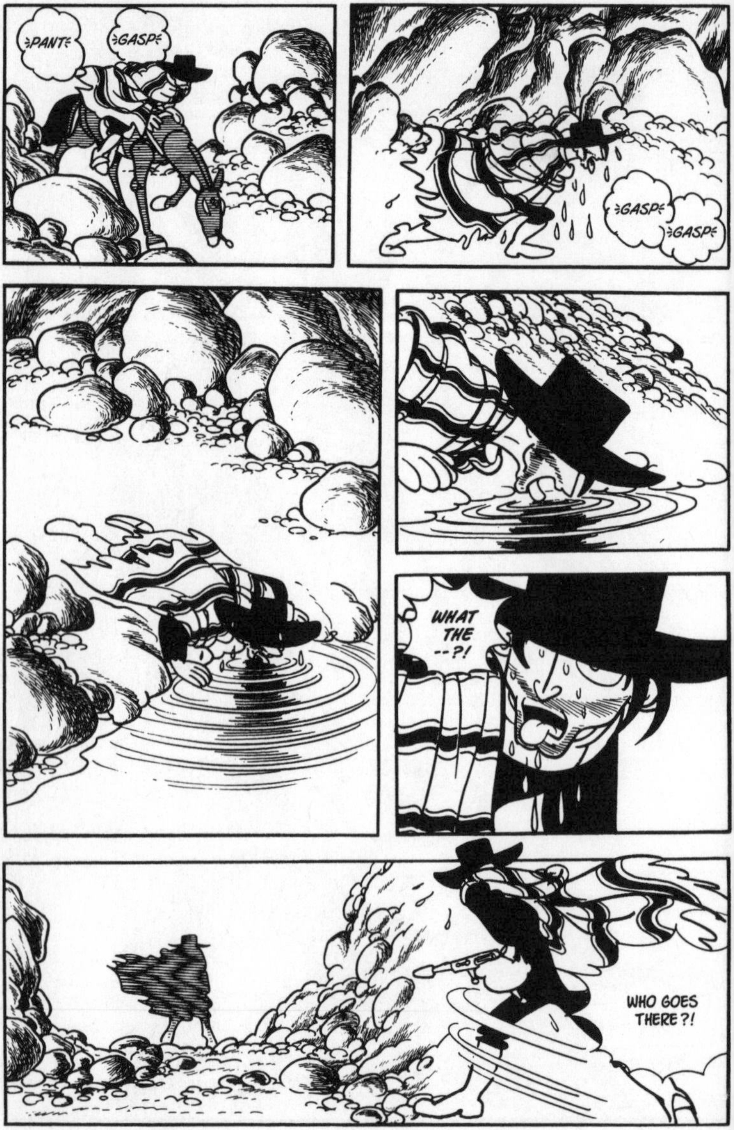
PANT
GASP
GASP
GASP
WHAT THE --?!
WHO GOES THERE?!

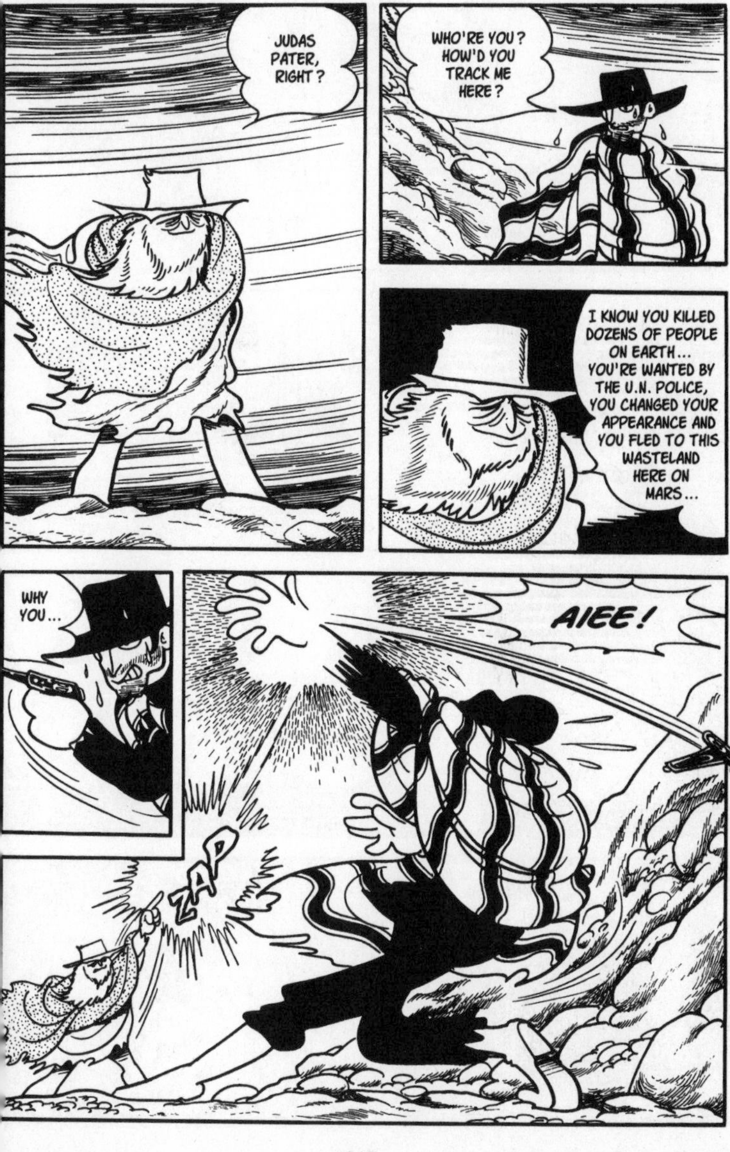
JUDAS PATER, RIGHT ?
WHO'RE YOU ? HOW'D YOU TRACK ME HERE ?
I KNOW YOU KILLED DOZENS OF PEOPLE ON EARTH... YOU'RE WANTED BY THE U.N. POLICE, YOU CHANGED YOUR APPEARANCE AND YOU FLED TO THIS WASTELAND HERE ON MARS...
WHY YOU...
AIEE !
ZAP

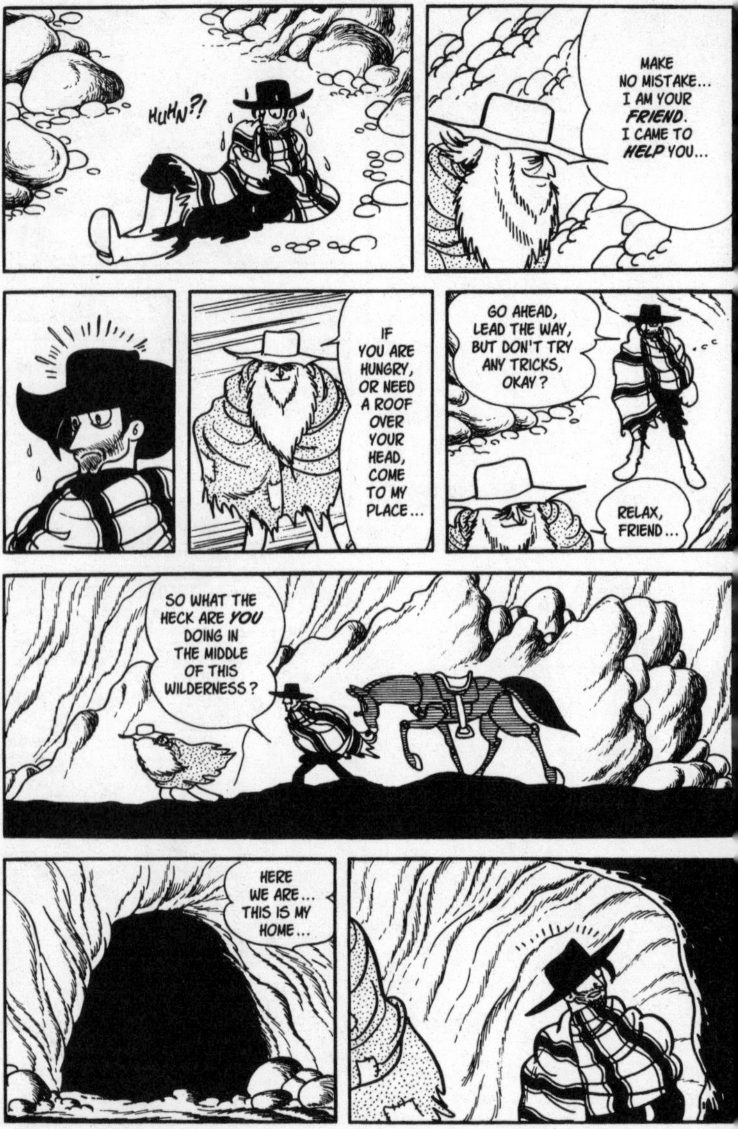
HUHN?!
MAKE NO MISTAKE... I AM YOUR FRIEND. I CAME TO HELP YOU...
IF YOU ARE HUNGRY, OR NEED A ROOF OVER YOUR HEAD, COME TO MY PLACE...
GO AHEAD, LEAD THE WAY, BUT DON'T TRY ANY TRICKS, OKAY?
RELAX, FRIEND...
SO WHAT THE HECK ARE YOU DOING IN THE MIDDLE OF THIS WILDERNESS?
HERE WE ARE... THIS IS MY HOME...

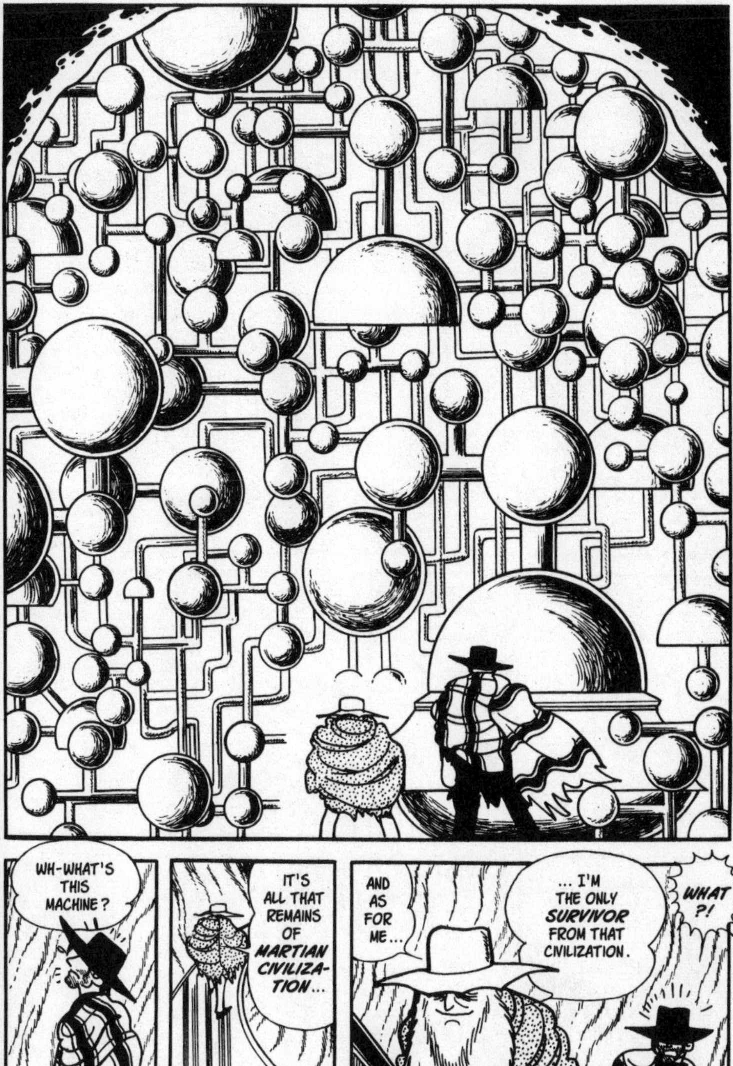
WH-WHAT'S THIS MACHINE?
IT'S ALL THAT REMAINS OF MARTIAN CIVILIZA-TION...
AND AS FOR ME...
... I'M THE ONLY SURVIVOR FROM THAT CIVILIZATION.
WHAT?!

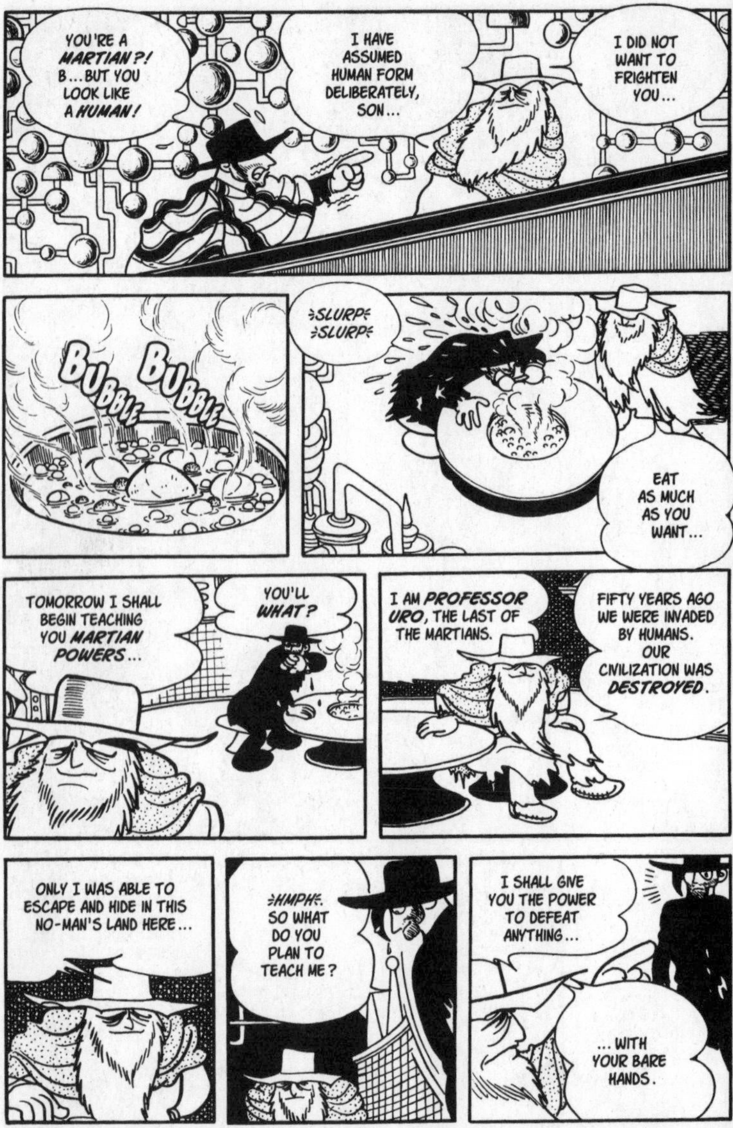
YOU'RE A MARTIAN?! B... BUT YOU LOOK LIKE A HUMAN!
I HAVE ASSUMED HUMAN FORM DELIBERATELY, SON...
I DID NOT WANT TO FRIGHTEN YOU...
BUBBLE BUBBLE
SLURP SLURP
EAT AS MUCH AS YOU WANT...
TOMORROW I SHALL BEGIN TEACHING YOU MARTIAN POWERS...
YOU'LL WHAT?
I AM PROFESSOR URO, THE LAST OF THE MARTIANS.
FIFTY YEARS AGO WE WERE INVADED BY HUMANS. OUR CIVILIZATION WAS DESTROYED.
ONLY I WAS ABLE TO ESCAPE AND HIDE IN THIS NO-MAN'S LAND HERE...
HMPH. SO WHAT DO YOU PLAN TO TEACH ME?
I SHALL GIVE YOU THE POWER TO DEFEAT ANYTHING...
... WITH YOUR BARE HANDS.

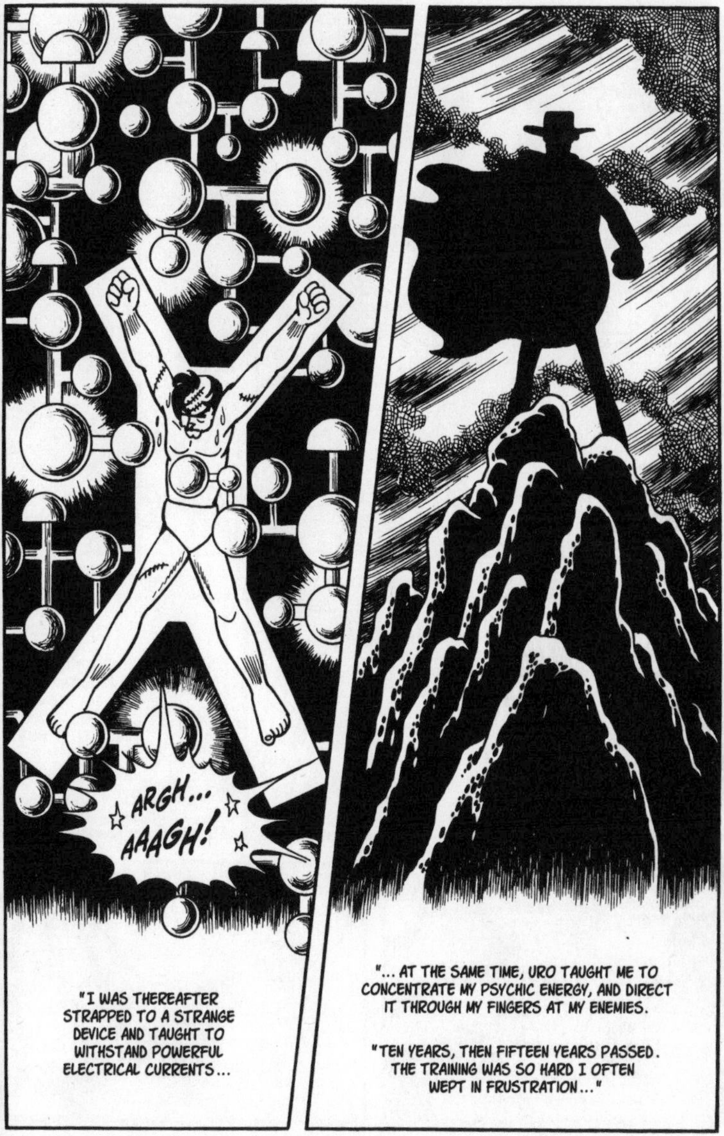
ARGH... AAAGH!
"I WAS THEREAFTER STRAPPED TO A STRANGE DEVICE AND TAUGHT TO WITHSTAND POWERFUL ELECTRICAL CURRENTS...
"... AT THE SAME TIME, URO TAUGHT ME TO CONCENTRATE MY PSYCHIC ENERGY, AND DIRECT IT THROUGH MY FINGERS AT MY ENEMIES.
"TEN YEARS, THEN FIFTEEN YEARS PASSED. THE TRAINING WAS SO HARD I OFTEN WEPT IN FRUSTRATION..."

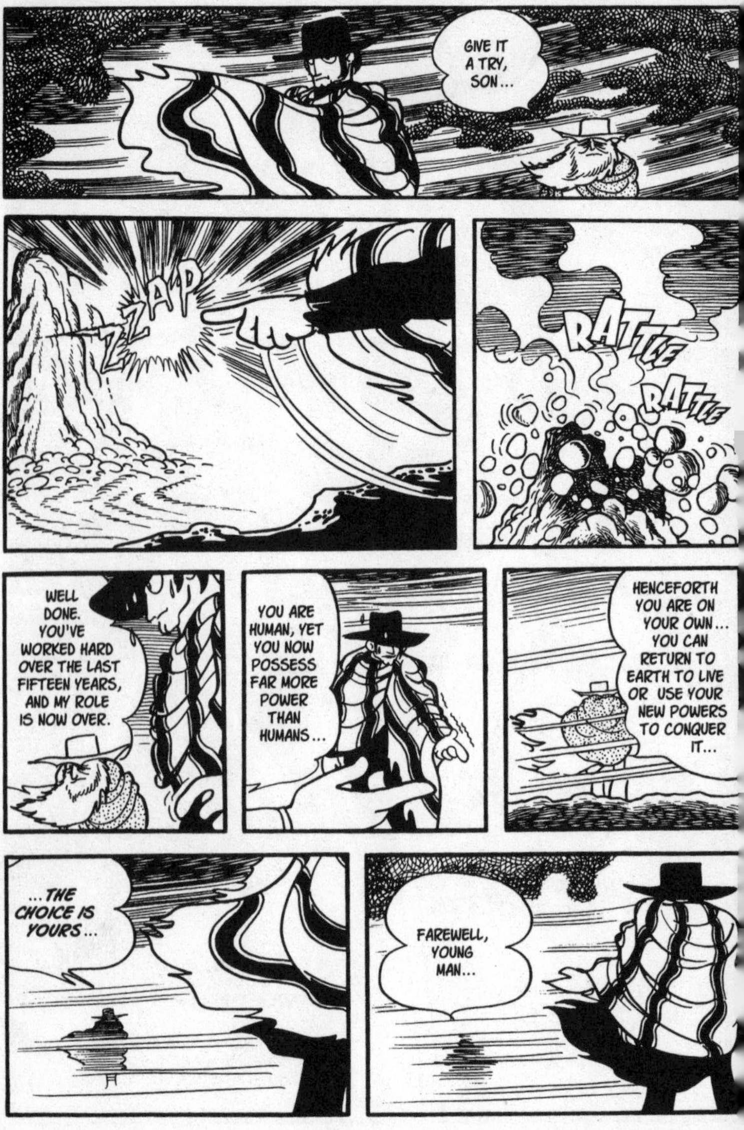

GIVE IT A TRY, SON...
ZZAP
RATTLE
RATTLE
WELL DONE. YOU'VE WORKED HARD OVER THE LAST FIFTEEN YEARS, AND MY ROLE IS NOW OVER.
YOU ARE HUMAN, YET YOU NOW POSSESS FAR MORE POWER THAN HUMANS...
HENCEFORTH YOU ARE ON YOUR OWN... YOU CAN RETURN TO EARTH TO LIVE OR USE YOUR NEW POWERS TO CONQUER IT...
...THE CHOICE IS YOURS...
FAREWELL, YOUNG MAN...

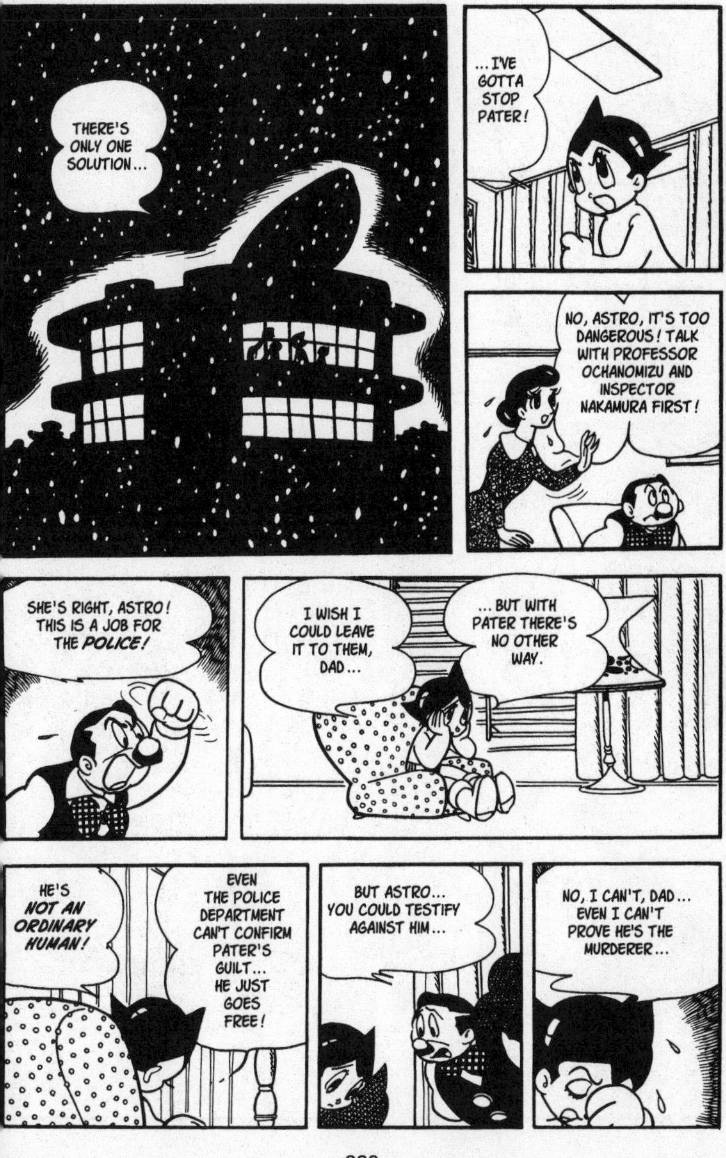
THERE'S ONLY ONE SOLUTION...
...I'VE GOTTA STOP PATER!
NO, ASTRO, IT'S TOO DANGEROUS! TALK WITH PROFESSOR OCHANOMIZU AND INSPECTOR NAKAMURA FIRST!
SHE'S RIGHT, ASTRO! THIS IS A JOB FOR THE POLICE!
I WISH I COULD LEAVE IT TO THEM, DAD...
...BUT WITH PATER THERE'S NO OTHER WAY.
HE'S NOT AN ORDINARY HUMAN!
EVEN THE POLICE DEPARTMENT CAN'T CONFIRM PATER'S GUILT... HE JUST GOES FREE!
BUT ASTRO... YOU COULD TESTIFY AGAINST HIM...
NO, I CAN'T, DAD... EVEN I CAN'T PROVE HE'S THE MURDERER...

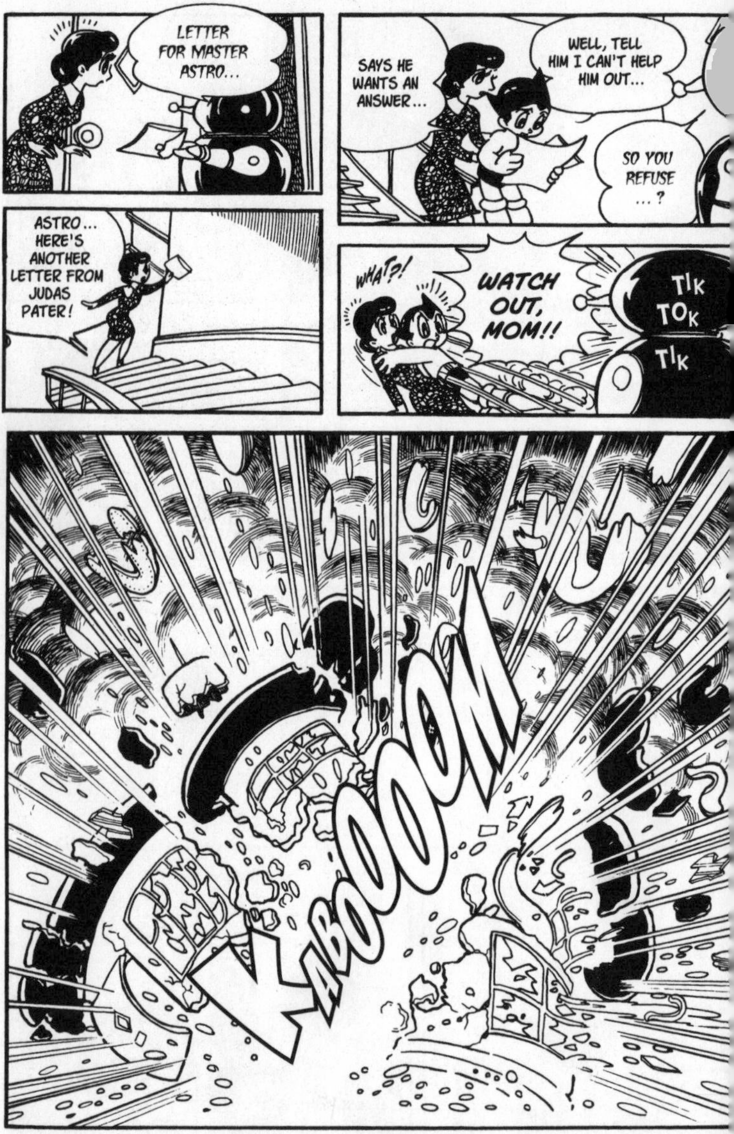
LETTER FOR MASTER ASTRO...
SAYS HE WANTS AN ANSWER...
WELL, TELL HIM I CAN'T HELP HIM OUT...
SO YOU REFUSE ...?
ASTRO... HERE'S ANOTHER LETTER FROM JUDAS PATER!
WHAT?!
WATCH OUT, MOM!!
TIK TOK TIK
KABOOOOOM

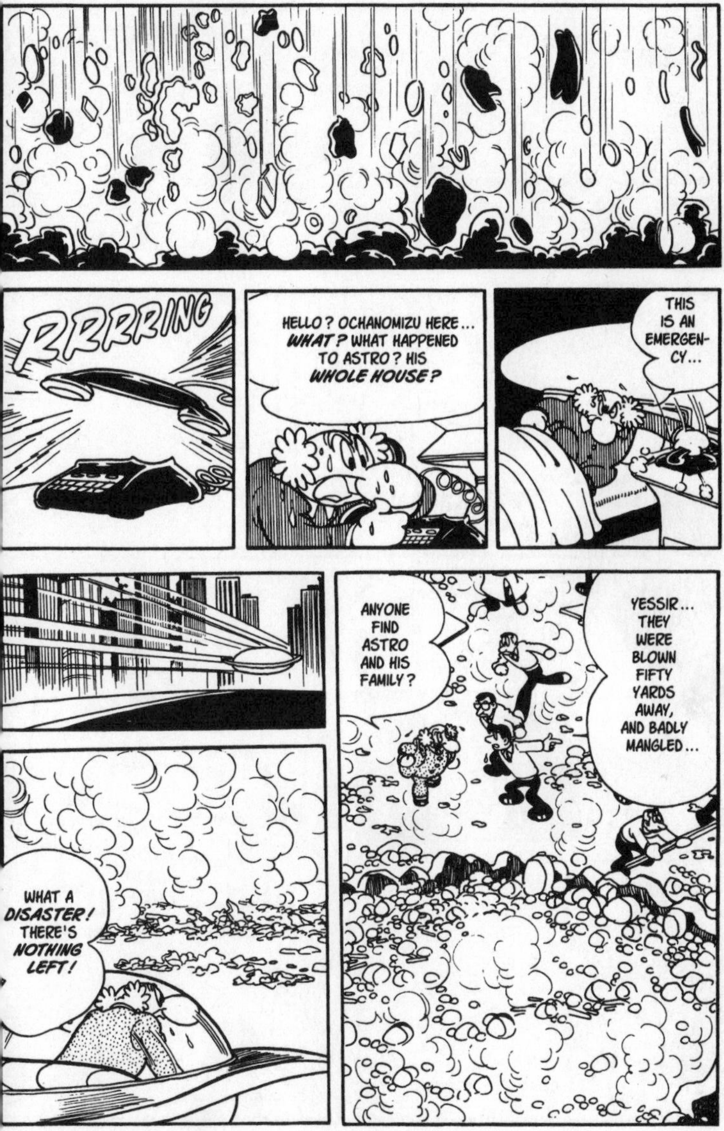
RRRRING
HELLO? OCHANOMIZU HERE... WHAT? WHAT HAPPENED TO ASTRO? HIS WHOLE HOUSE?
THIS IS AN EMERGEN-CY...
WHAT A DISASTER! THERE'S NOTHING LEFT!
ANYONE FIND ASTRO AND HIS FAMILY?
YESSIR... THEY WERE BLOWN FIFTY YARDS AWAY, AND BADLY MANGLED...

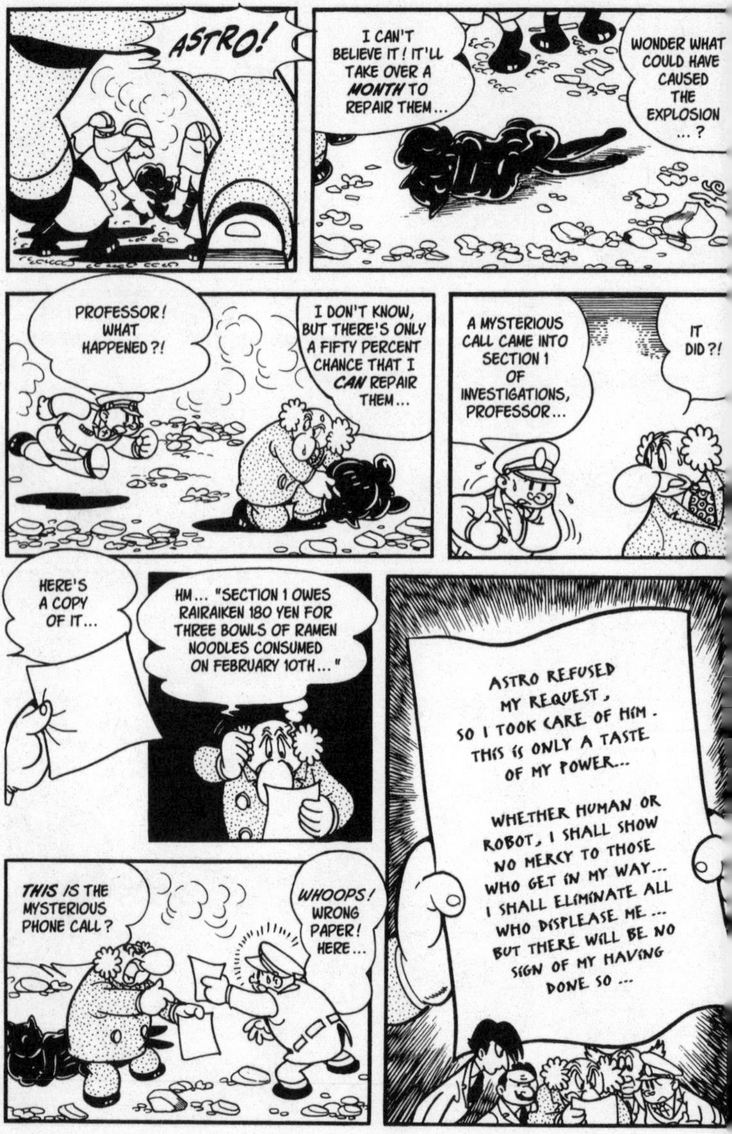
ASTRO!
I CAN'T BELIEVE IT! IT'LL TAKE OVER A MONTH TO REPAIR THEM...
WONDER WHAT COULD HAVE CAUSED THE EXPLOSION ...?
PROFESSOR! WHAT HAPPENED?!
I DON'T KNOW, BUT THERE'S ONLY A FIFTY PERCENT CHANCE THAT I CAN REPAIR THEM...
A MYSTERIOUS CALL CAME INTO SECTION 1 OF INVESTIGATIONS, PROFESSOR...
IT DID?!
HERE'S A COPY OF IT...
HM... "SECTION 1 OWES RAIRAIKEN 180 YEN FOR THREE BOWLS OF RAMEN NOODLES CONSUMED ON FEBRUARY 10TH..."
THIS IS THE MYSTERIOUS PHONE CALL?
WHOOPS! WRONG PAPER! HERE...
ASTRO REFUSED MY REQUEST, SO I TOOK CARE OF HIM. THIS IS ONLY A TASTE OF MY POWER...
WHETHER HUMAN OR ROBOT, I SHALL SHOW NO MERCY TO THOSE WHO GET IN MY WAY... I SHALL ELIMINATE ALL WHO DISPLEASE ME... BUT THERE WILL BE NO SIGN OF MY HAVING DONE SO...

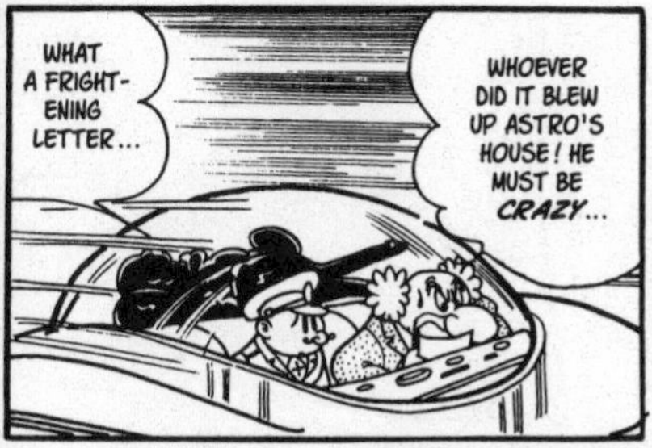
WHAT A FRIGHT-ENING LETTER...
WHOEVER DID IT BLEW UP ASTRO'S HOUSE! HE MUST BE CRAZY...

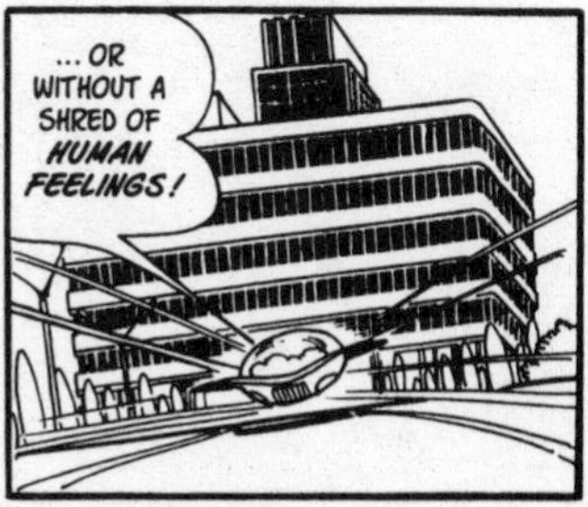
...OR WITHOUT A SHRED OF HUMAN FEELINGS!

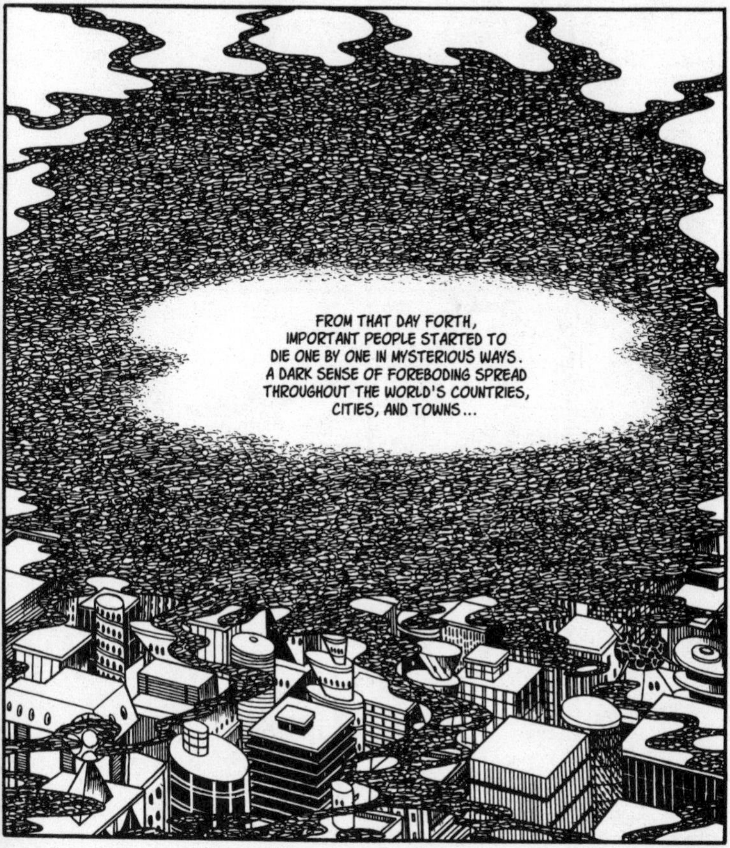
FROM THAT DAY FORTH, IMPORTANT PEOPLE STARTED TO DIE ONE BY ONE IN MYSTERIOUS WAYS. A DARK SENSE OF FOREBODING SPREAD THROUGHOUT THE WORLD'S COUNTRIES, CITIES, AND TOWNS...

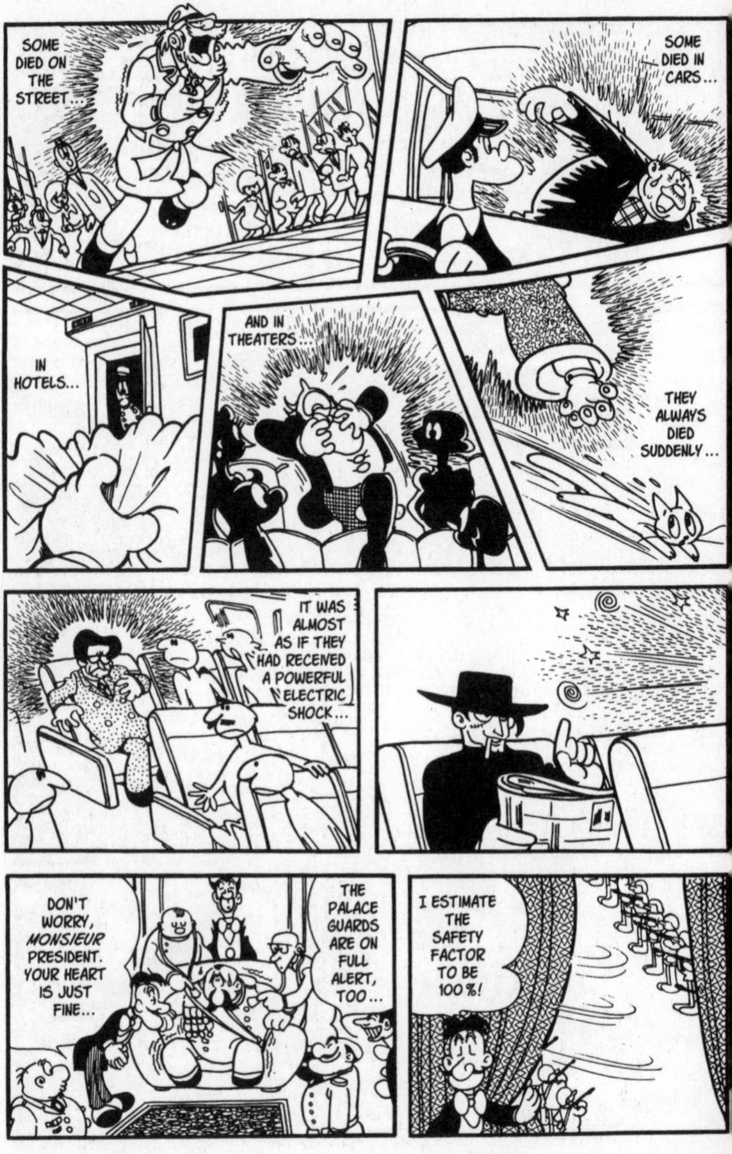
SOME DIED ON THE STREET...
SOME DIED IN CARS...
IN HOTELS...
AND IN THEATERS...
THEY ALWAYS DIED SUDDENLY...
IT WAS ALMOST AS IF THEY HAD RECEIVED A POWERFUL ELECTRIC SHOCK...
DON'T WORRY, *MONSIEUR* PRESIDENT. YOUR HEART IS JUST FINE...
THE PALACE GUARDS ARE ON FULL ALERT, TOO...
I ESTIMATE THE SAFETY FACTOR TO BE 100%!

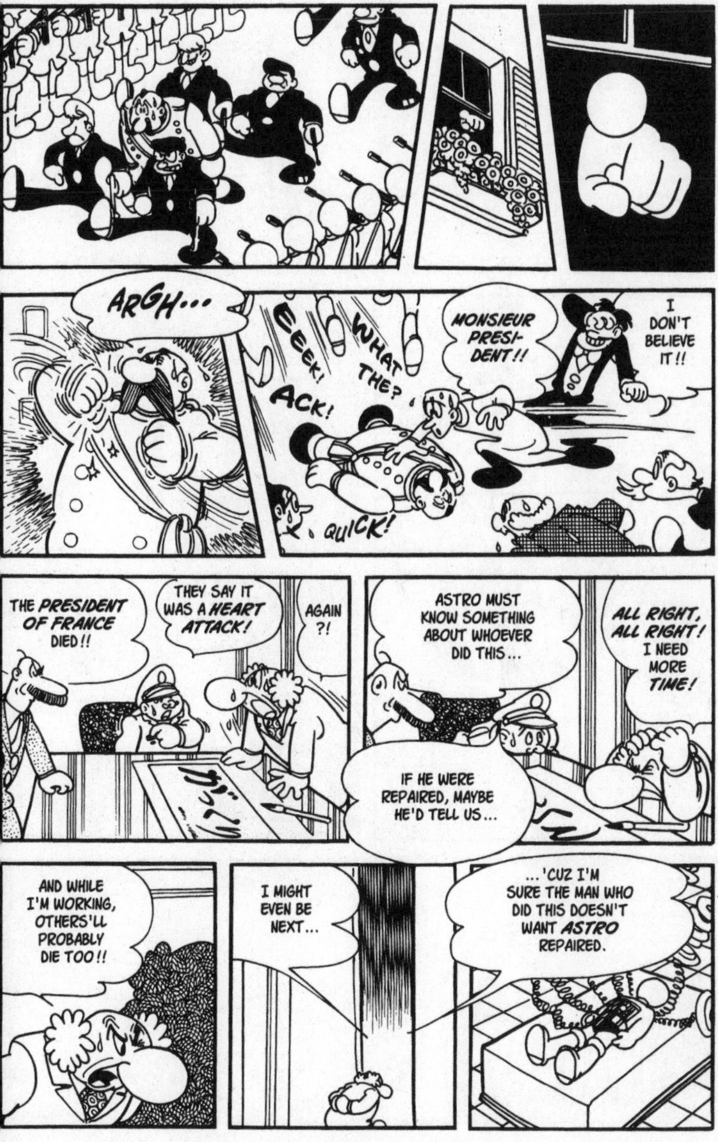
ARGH...
EEEEK!
WHAT THE?
ACK!
MONSIEUR PRESI-DENT!!
I DON'T BELIEVE IT!!
QUICK!
THE PRESIDENT OF FRANCE DIED!!
THEY SAY IT WAS A HEART ATTACK!
AGAIN ?!
ASTRO MUST KNOW SOMETHING ABOUT WHOEVER DID THIS...
ALL RIGHT, ALL RIGHT! I NEED MORE TIME!
IF HE WERE REPAIRED, MAYBE HE'D TELL US...
AND WHILE I'M WORKING, OTHERS'LL PROBABLY DIE TOO!!
I MIGHT EVEN BE NEXT...
...'CUZ I'M SURE THE MAN WHO DID THIS DOESN'T WANT ASTRO REPAIRED.

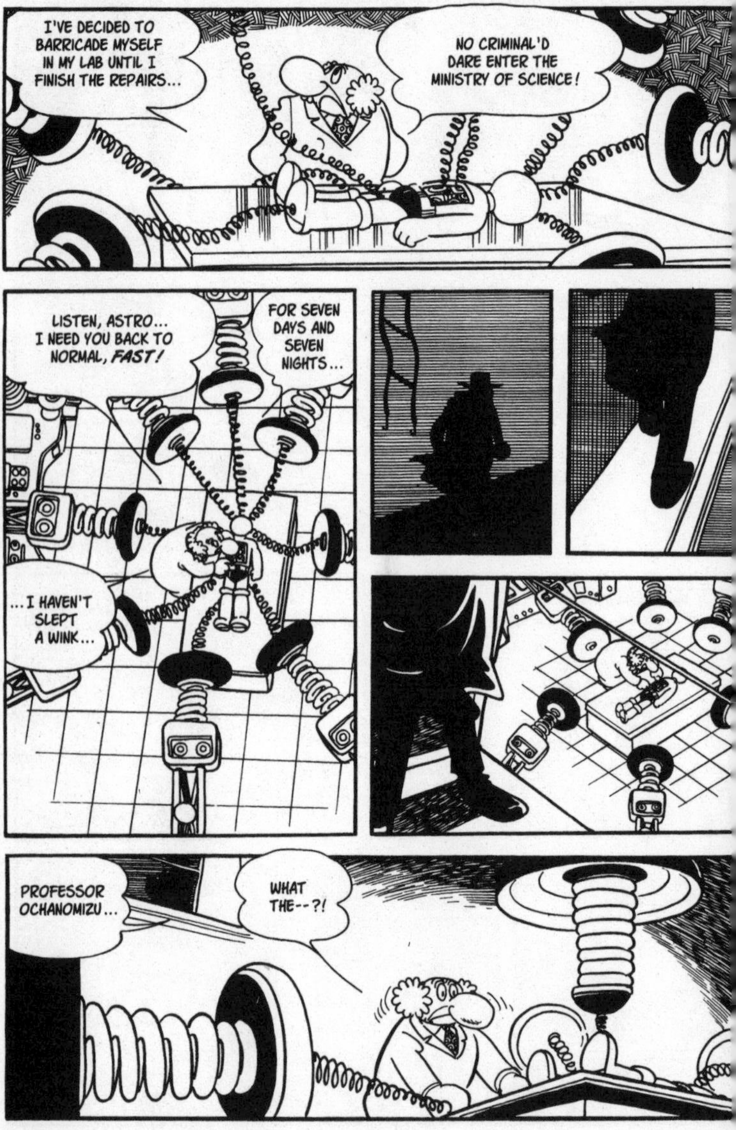
I'VE DECIDED TO BARRICADE MYSELF IN MY LAB UNTIL I FINISH THE REPAIRS...
NO CRIMINAL'D DARE ENTER THE MINISTRY OF SCIENCE!
LISTEN, ASTRO... I NEED YOU BACK TO NORMAL, *FAST!*
FOR SEVEN DAYS AND SEVEN NIGHTS...
...I HAVEN'T SLEPT A WINK...
PROFESSOR OCHANOMIZU...
WHAT THE--?!

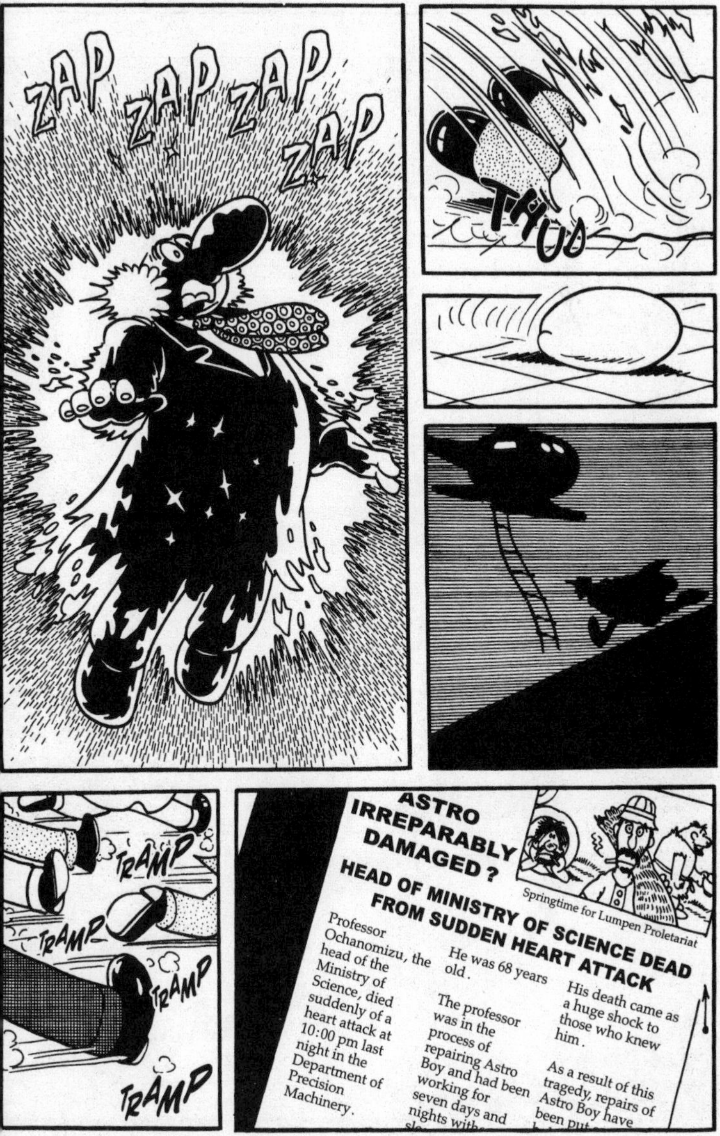
ZAP ZAP ZAP ZAP
THUD
TRAMP
TRAMP
TRAMP
TRAMP
ASTRO IRREPARABLY DAMAGED ?
Springtime for Lumpen Proletariat
HEAD OF MINISTRY OF SCIENCE DEAD FROM SUDDEN HEART ATTACK
Professor Ochanomizu, the head of the Ministry of Science, died suddenly of a heart attack at 10:00 pm last night in the Department of Precision Machinery.
He was 68 years old.
The professor was in the process of repairing Astro Boy and had been working for seven days and nights with
His death came as a huge shock to those who knew him.
As a result of this tragedy, repairs of Astro Boy have been put

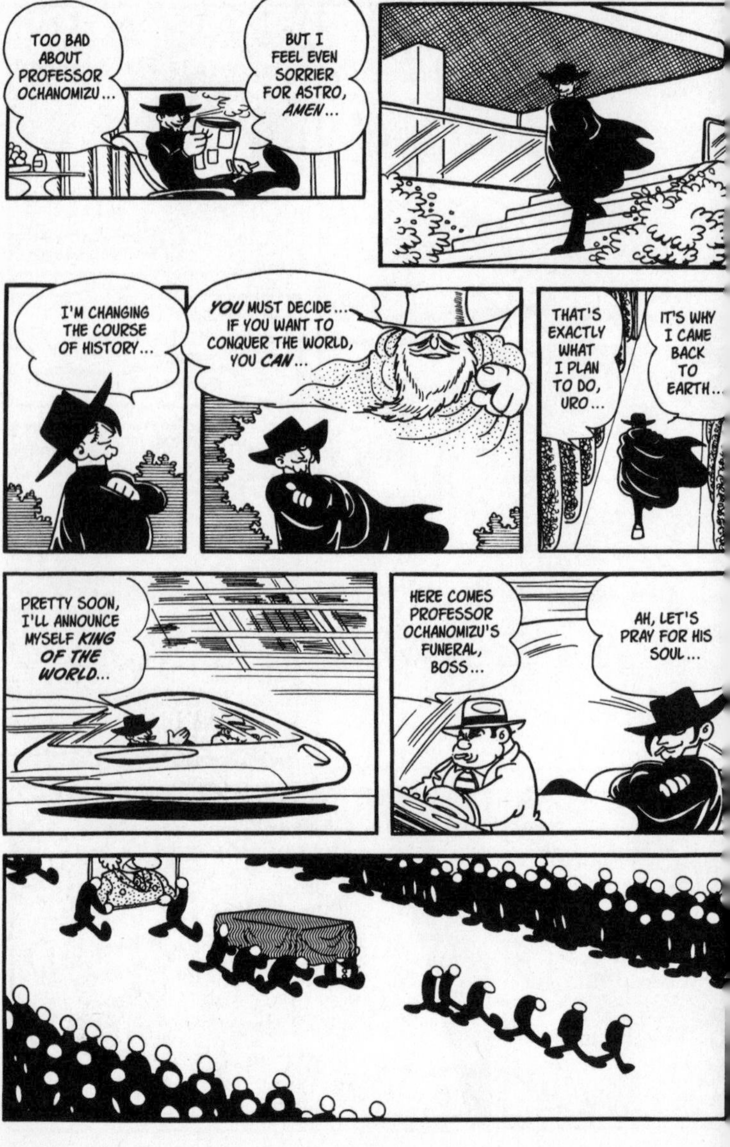
TOO BAD ABOUT PROFESSOR OCHANOMIZU...
BUT I FEEL EVEN SORRIER FOR ASTRO, *AMEN*...
I'M CHANGING THE COURSE OF HISTORY...
YOU MUST DECIDE... IF YOU WANT TO CONQUER THE WORLD, YOU *CAN*...
THAT'S EXACTLY WHAT I PLAN TO DO, URO...
IT'S WHY I CAME BACK TO EARTH...
PRETTY SOON, I'LL ANNOUNCE MYSELF *KING OF THE WORLD*...
HERE COMES PROFESSOR OCHANOMIZU'S FUNERAL, BOSS...
AH, LET'S PRAY FOR HIS SOUL...

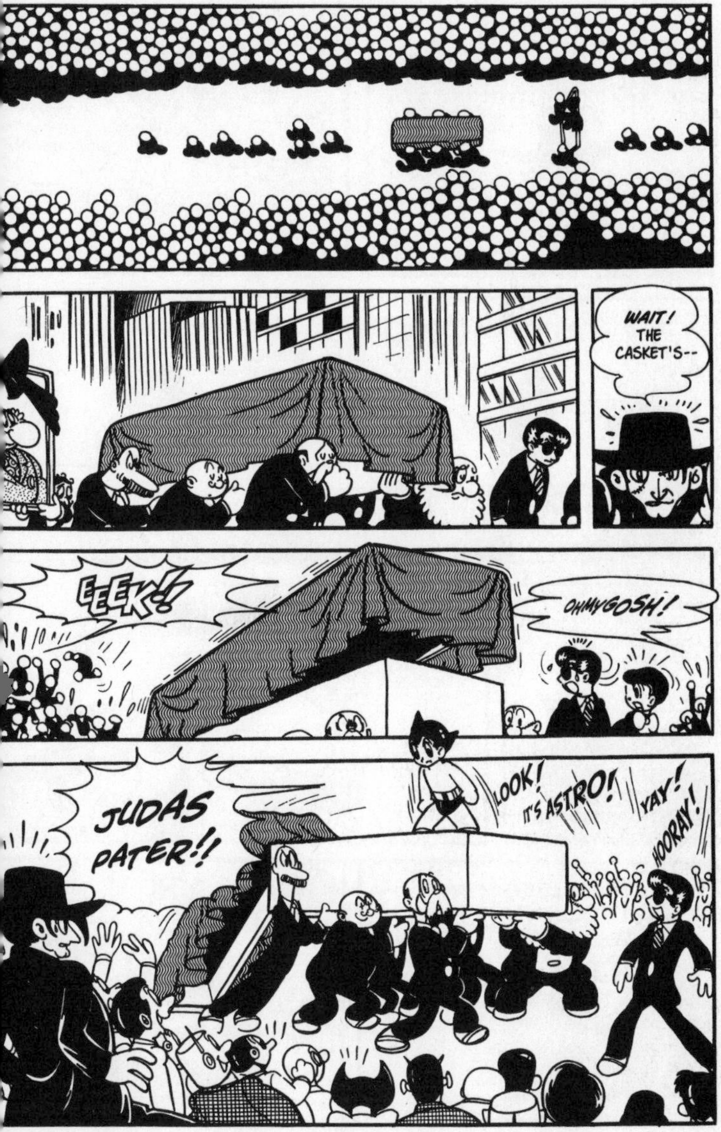
WAIT! THE CASKET'S--
EEEK!!
OHMYGOSH!
JUDAS PATER!!
LOOK!
IT'S ASTRO!
YAY!
HOORAY!

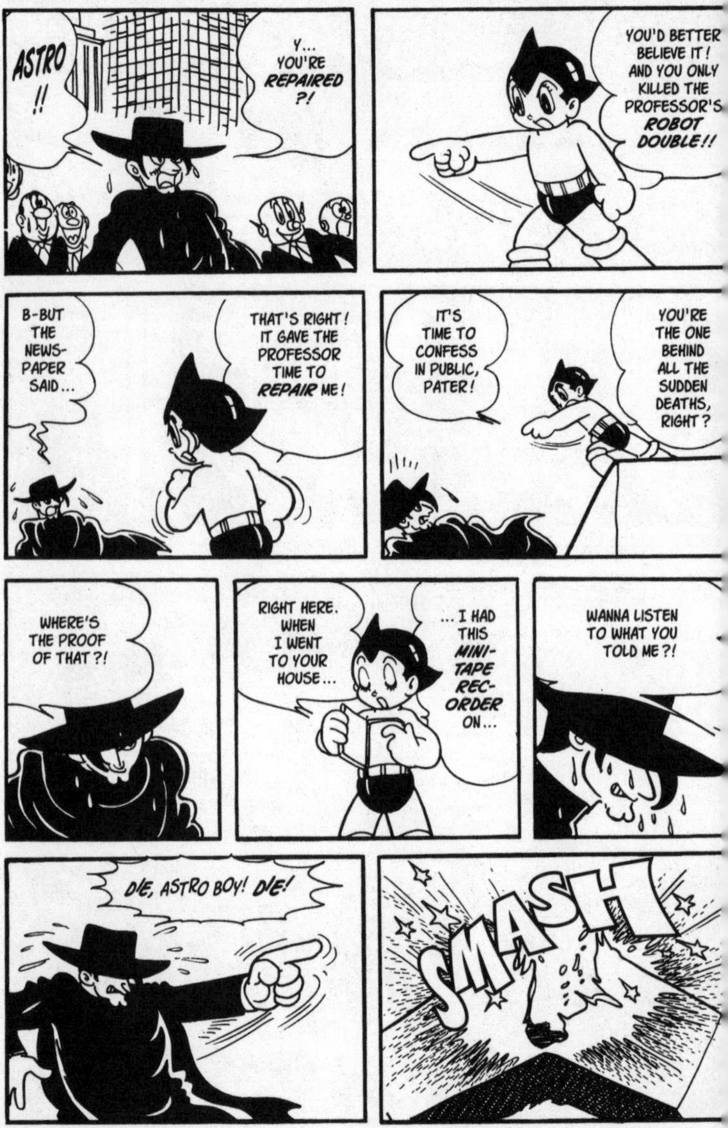
ASTRO !!
Y... YOU'RE REPAIRED ?!
YOU'D BETTER BELIEVE IT! AND YOU ONLY KILLED THE PROFESSOR'S ROBOT DOUBLE!!
B-BUT THE NEWS-PAPER SAID...
THAT'S RIGHT! IT GAVE THE PROFESSOR TIME TO REPAIR ME!
IT'S TIME TO CONFESS IN PUBLIC, PATER!
YOU'RE THE ONE BEHIND ALL THE SUDDEN DEATHS, RIGHT?
WHERE'S THE PROOF OF THAT?!
RIGHT HERE. WHEN I WENT TO YOUR HOUSE...
... I HAD THIS MINI-TAPE REC-ORDER ON...
WANNA LISTEN TO WHAT YOU TOLD ME?!
DIE, ASTRO BOY! DIE!
SMASH

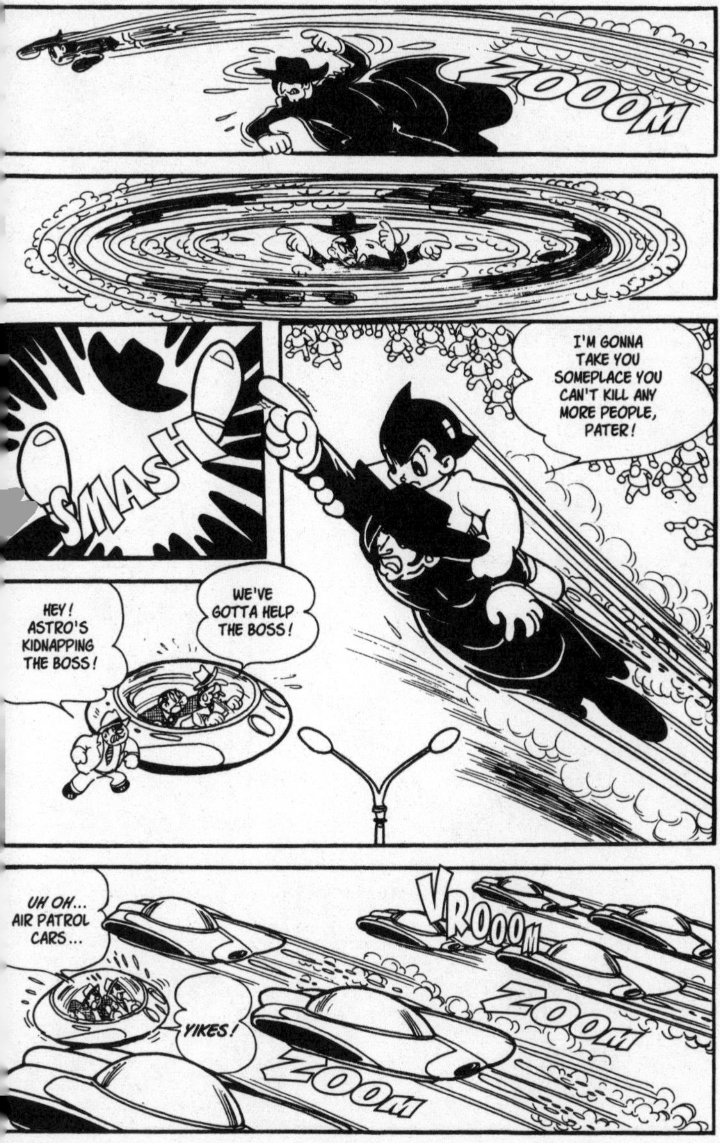
ZOOOOM
SMASH
I'M GONNA TAKE YOU SOMEPLACE YOU CAN'T KILL ANY MORE PEOPLE, PATER!
HEY! ASTRO'S KIDNAPPING THE BOSS!
WE'VE GOTTA HELP THE BOSS!
UH OH... AIR PATROL CARS...
YIKES!
VROOOM
ZOOM
ZOOM

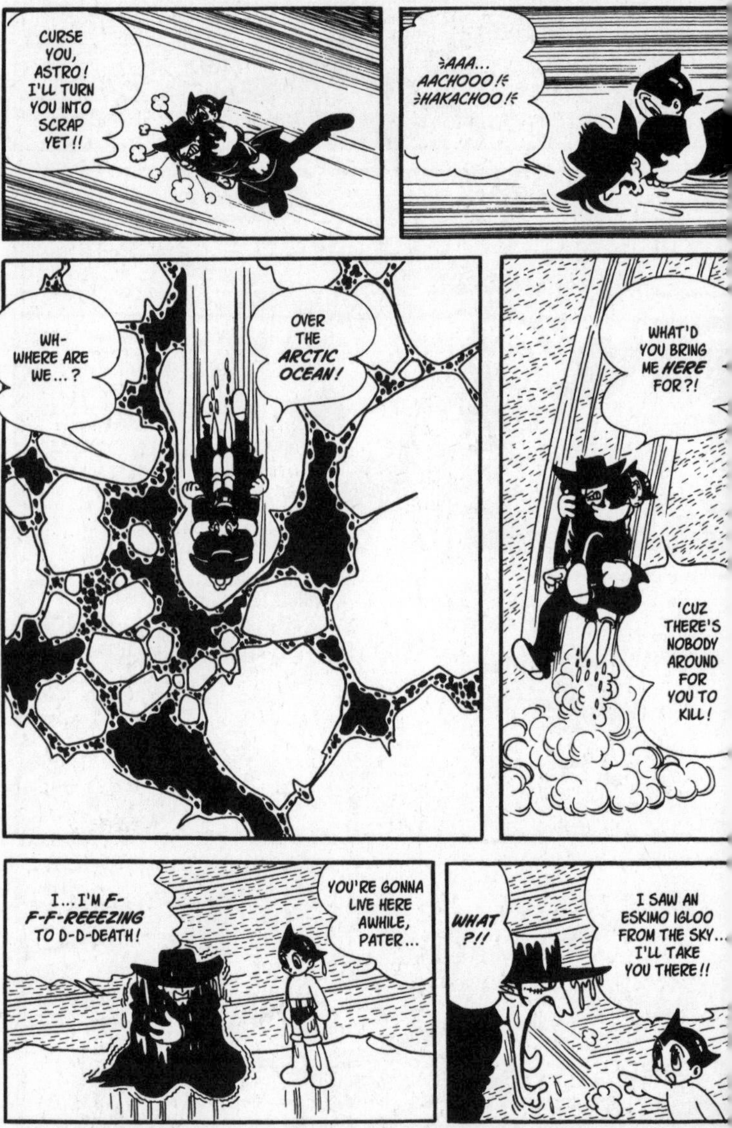
CURSE YOU, ASTRO! I'LL TURN YOU INTO SCRAP YET!!
AAA... AACHOOO!! HAKACHOO!!
WH- WHERE ARE WE...?
OVER THE ARCTIC OCEAN!
WHAT'D YOU BRING ME HERE FOR?!
'CUZ THERE'S NOBODY AROUND FOR YOU TO KILL!
I...I'M F-F-F-REEEZING TO D-D-DEATH!
YOU'RE GONNA LIVE HERE AWHILE, PATER...
WHAT?!!
I SAW AN ESKIMO IGLOO FROM THE SKY... I'LL TAKE YOU THERE!!

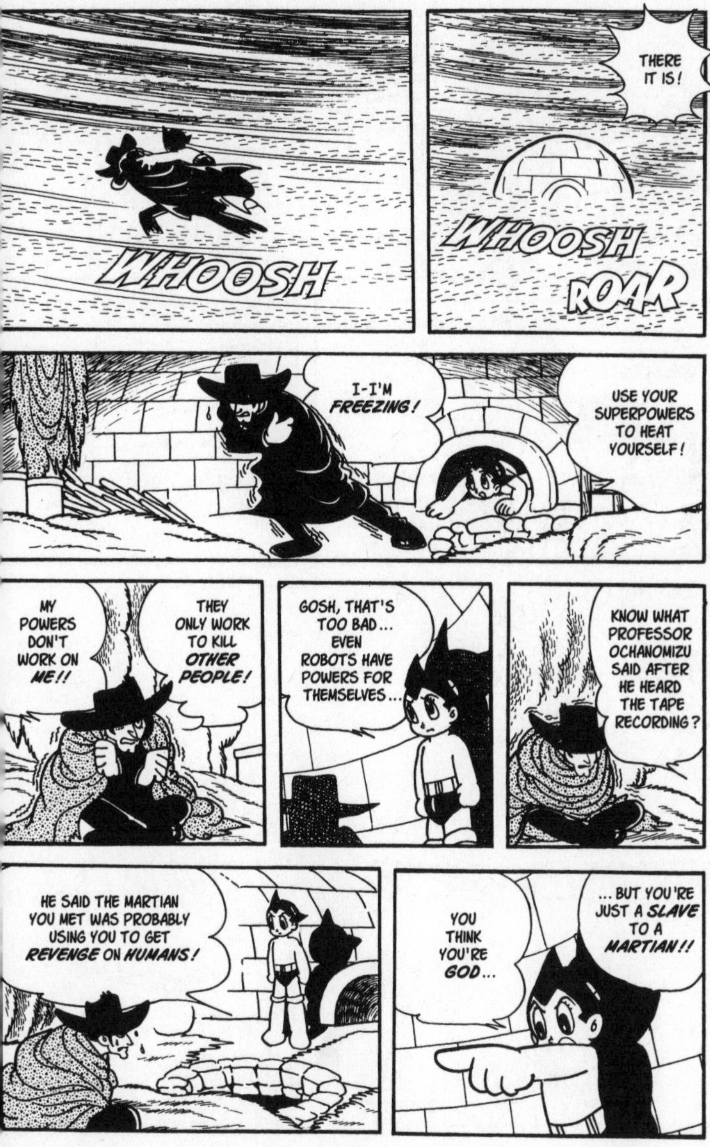
WHOOSH
THERE IT IS!
WHOOSH
ROAR
I-I'M FREEZING!
USE YOUR SUPERPOWERS TO HEAT YOURSELF!
MY POWERS DON'T WORK ON ME!!
THEY ONLY WORK TO KILL OTHER PEOPLE!
GOSH, THAT'S TOO BAD... EVEN ROBOTS HAVE POWERS FOR THEMSELVES...
KNOW WHAT PROFESSOR OCHANOMIZU SAID AFTER HE HEARD THE TAPE RECORDING?
HE SAID THE MARTIAN YOU MET WAS PROBABLY USING YOU TO GET REVENGE ON HUMANS!
YOU THINK YOU'RE GOD...
...BUT YOU'RE JUST A SLAVE TO A MARTIAN!!

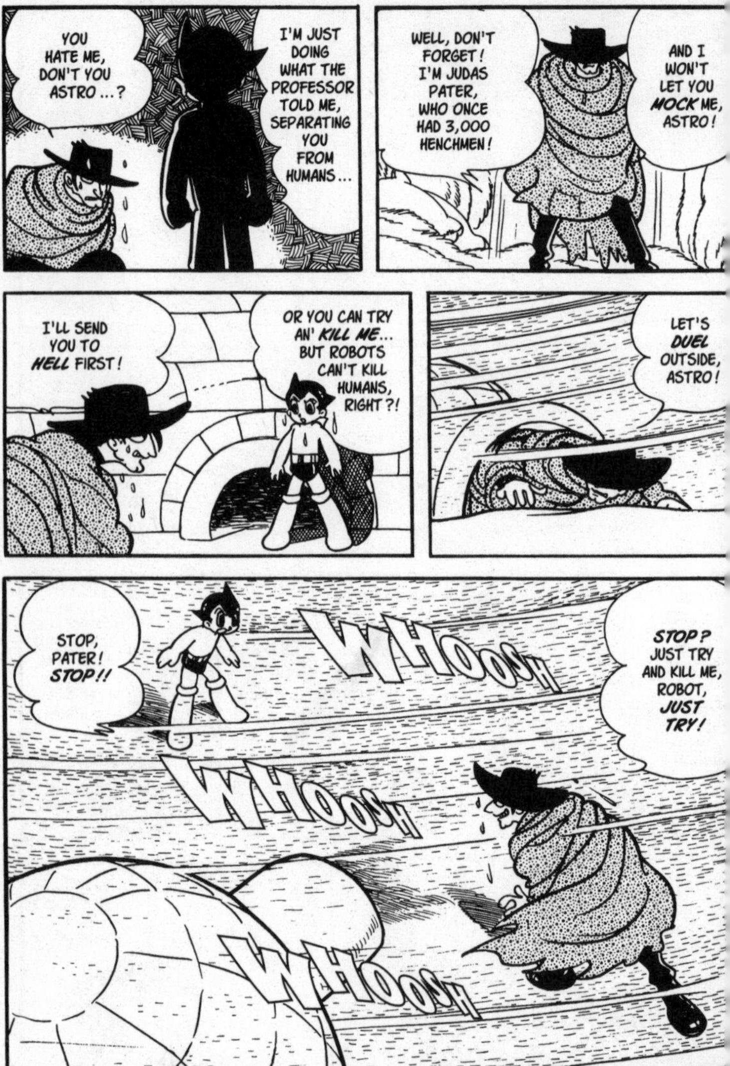
YOU HATE ME, DON'T YOU ASTRO ...?
I'M JUST DOING WHAT THE PROFESSOR TOLD ME, SEPARATING YOU FROM HUMANS ...
WELL, DON'T FORGET! I'M JUDAS PATER, WHO ONCE HAD 3,000 HENCHMEN!
AND I WON'T LET YOU MOCK ME, ASTRO!
I'LL SEND YOU TO HELL FIRST!
OR YOU CAN TRY AN' KILL ME... BUT ROBOTS CAN'T KILL HUMANS, RIGHT?!
LET'S DUEL OUTSIDE, ASTRO!
STOP, PATER! STOP!!
WHOOSH
STOP? JUST TRY AND KILL ME, ROBOT, JUST TRY!
WHOOSH
WHOOSH

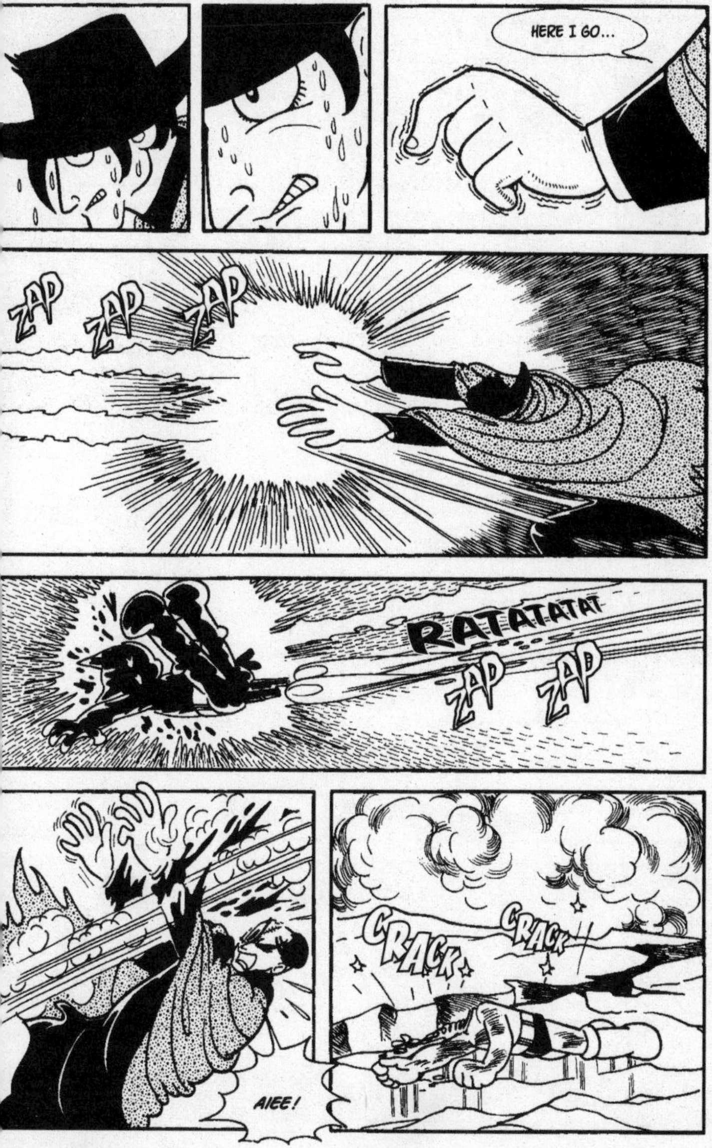
HERE I GO...
ZAP
ZAP
ZAP
RATATATAT
ZAP
ZAP
AIEE!
CRACK
CRACK

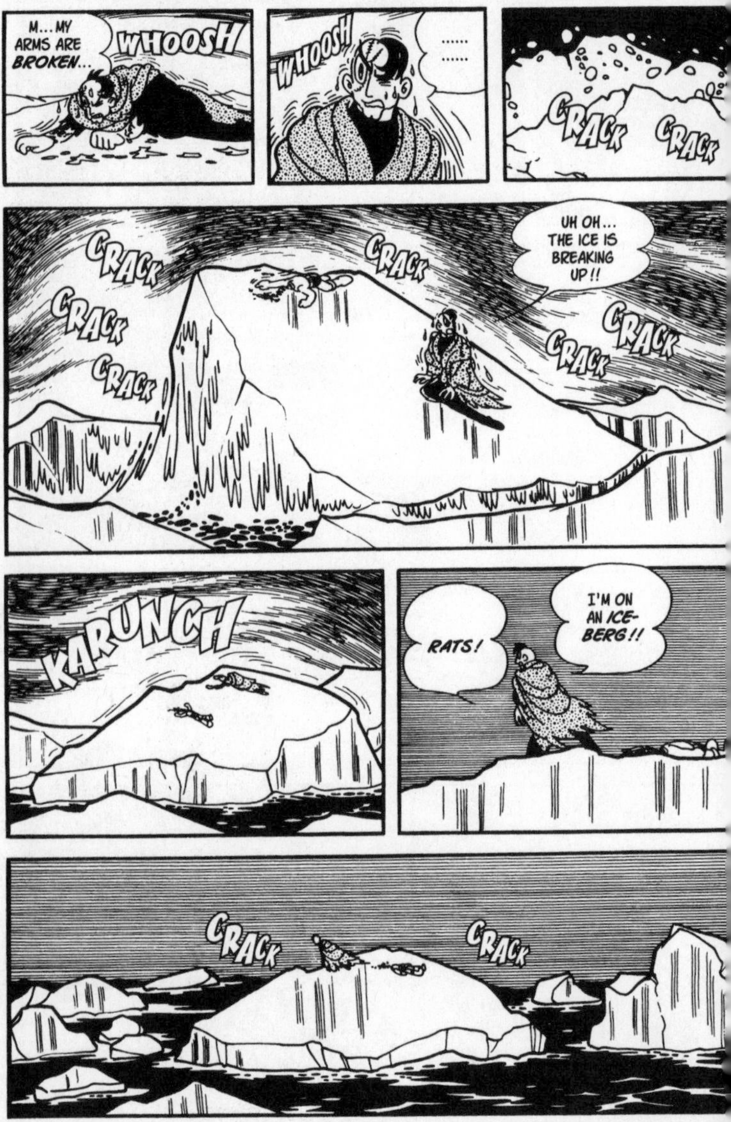
M... MY ARMS ARE BROKEN...
WHOOSH
WHOOSH
......
......
CRACK
CRACK
CRACK
CRACK
CRACK
CRACK
UH OH... THE ICE IS BREAKING UP!!
CRACK
CRACK
KARUNCH
RATS!
I'M ON AN ICE-BERG!!
CRACK
CRACK

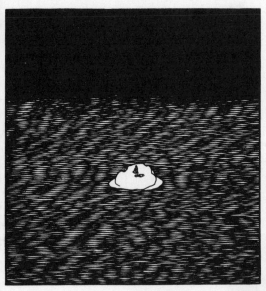

ASTRO, WHEN THIS ICE MELTS, BOTH OF US'LL SINK TO THE BOTTOM OF THE SEA...

WITH BOTH MY ARMS BROKEN, *YOU WIN*...

I CAN FEEL THE FROST-BITE SETTLING IN ALREADY...

BUT YOU... YOU CAN BE REPAIRED AND LIVE ANOTHER DAY...

YOU'RE THE ONE I REALLY *WANTED* TO SURVIVE, ASTRO...

WHAT THE--?

ROOAR

I HEAR A PLANE!

OVER HERE! OVER HERE!

WHY CAN'T THEY SEE US?!

VROOOM

RATS! CAN'T THEY SPOT THIS ICEBERG?!

241

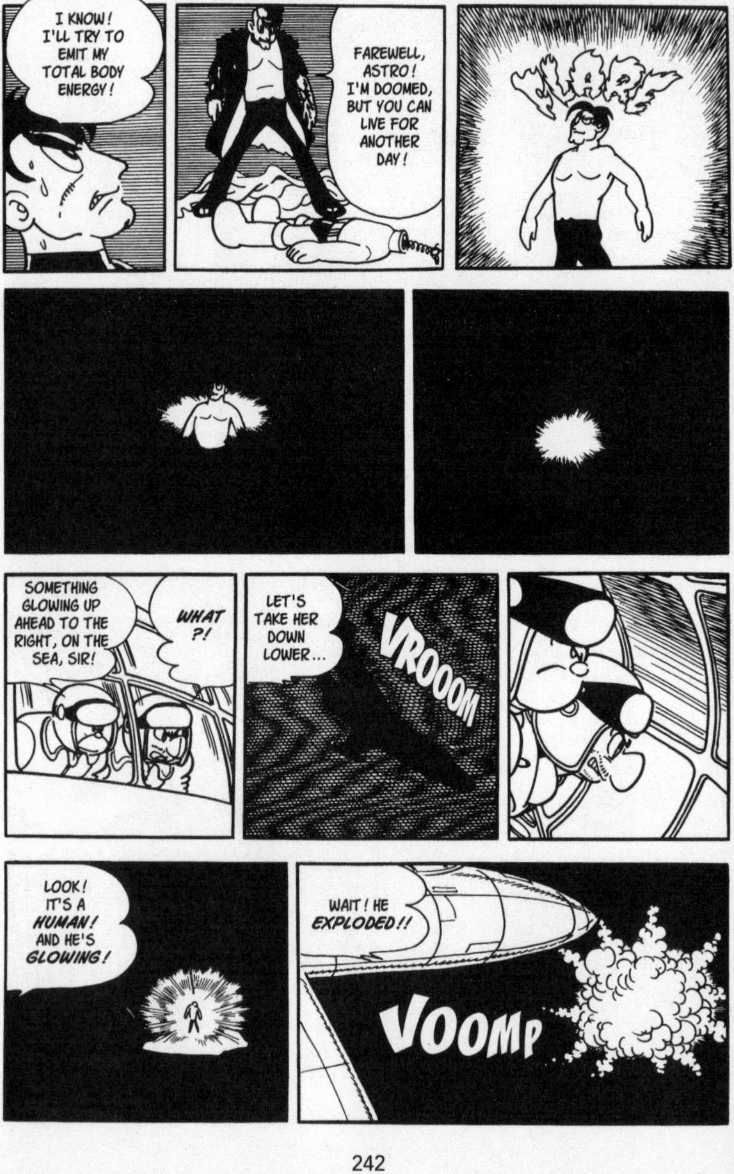
I KNOW! I'LL TRY TO EMIT MY TOTAL BODY ENERGY!
FAREWELL, ASTRO! I'M DOOMED, BUT YOU CAN LIVE FOR ANOTHER DAY!
SOMETHING GLOWING UP AHEAD TO THE RIGHT, ON THE SEA, SIR!
WHAT?!
LET'S TAKE HER DOWN LOWER...
VROOOM
LOOK! IT'S A HUMAN! AND HE'S GLOWING!
WAIT! HE EXPLODED!!
VOOMP

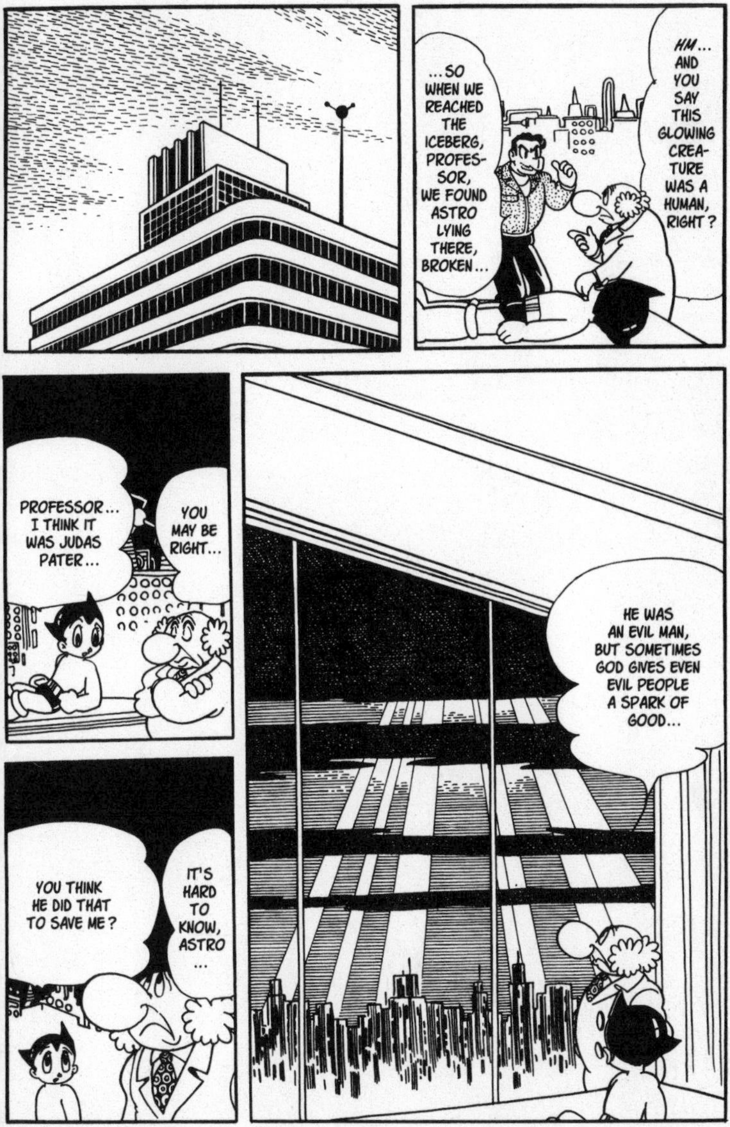
...SO WHEN WE REACHED THE ICEBERG, PROFESSOR, WE FOUND ASTRO LYING THERE, BROKEN...
HM... AND YOU SAY THIS GLOWING CREATURE WAS A HUMAN, RIGHT?
PROFESSOR... I THINK IT WAS JUDAS PATER...
YOU MAY BE RIGHT...
YOU THINK HE DID THAT TO SAVE ME?
IT'S HARD TO KNOW, ASTRO ...
HE WAS AN EVIL MAN, BUT SOMETIMES GOD GIVES EVEN EVIL PEOPLE A SPARK OF GOOD...

THE BLAST
FURNACE
MYSTERY

First appeared in the 1961 summer holiday
expanded edition of *Shonen* magazine.

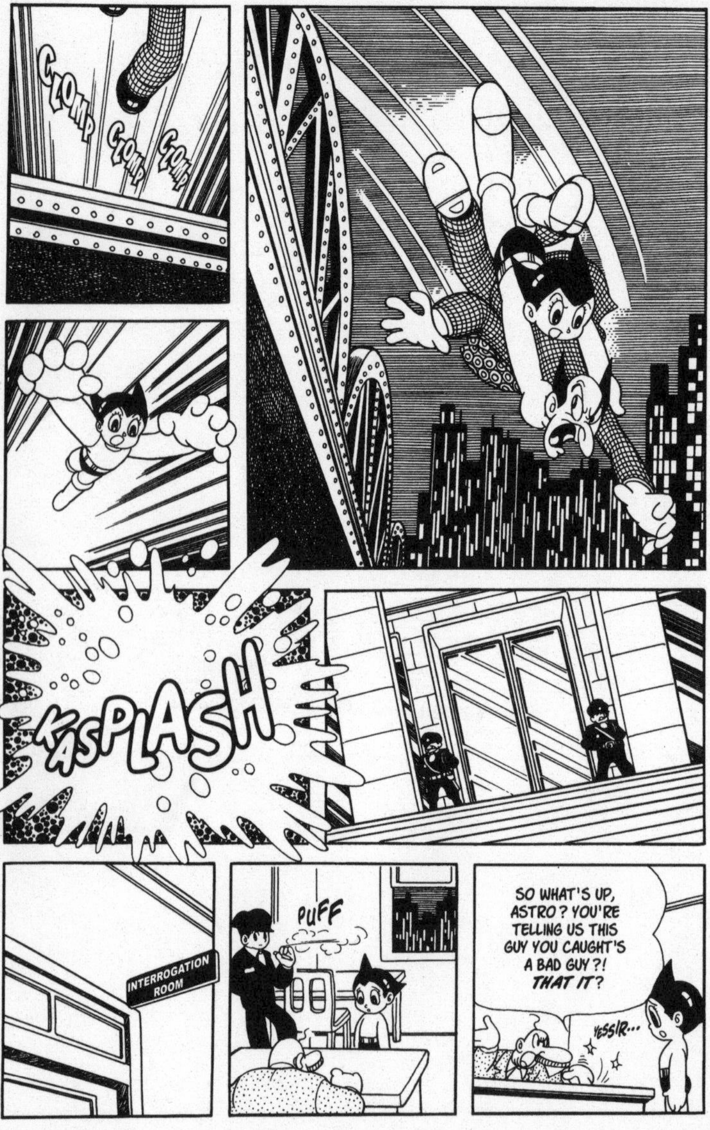
CLOMP
CLOMP
CLOMP
KASPLASH
INTERROGATION ROOM
PUFF
SO WHAT'S UP, ASTRO? YOU'RE TELLING US THIS GUY YOU CAUGHT'S A BAD GUY?! *THAT IT*?
YESSIR...

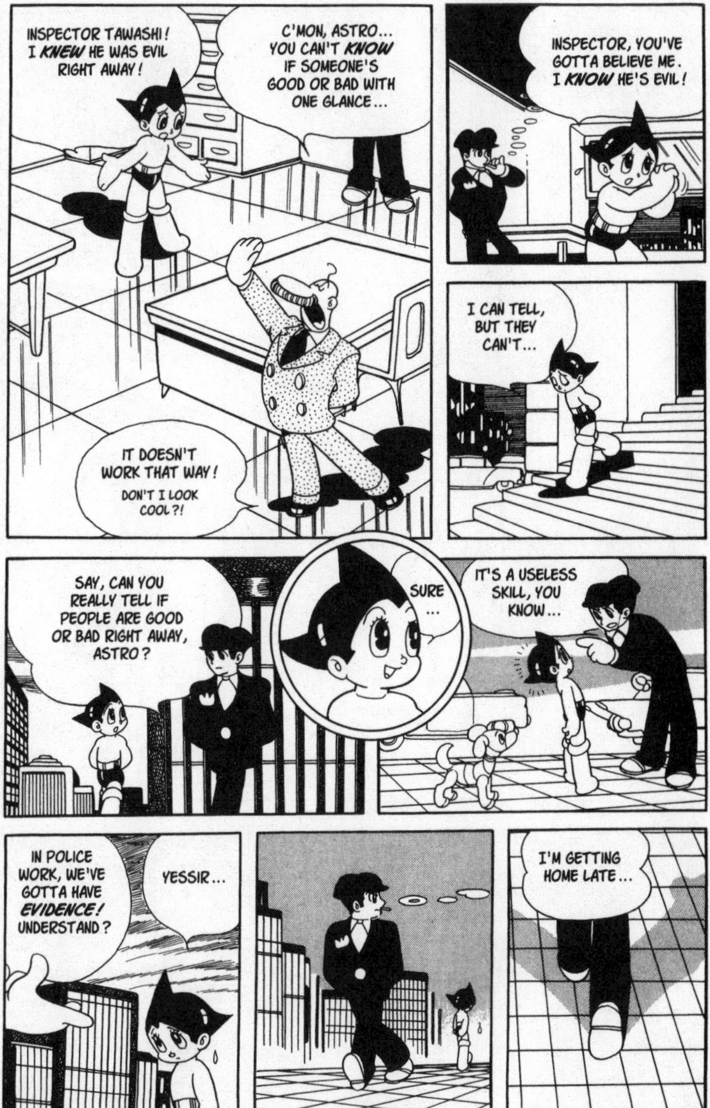
INSPECTOR TAWASHI! I KNEW HE WAS EVIL RIGHT AWAY!
C'MON, ASTRO... YOU CAN'T KNOW IF SOMEONE'S GOOD OR BAD WITH ONE GLANCE...
IT DOESN'T WORK THAT WAY!
DON'T I LOOK COOL?!
INSPECTOR, YOU'VE GOTTA BELIEVE ME. I KNOW HE'S EVIL!
I CAN TELL, BUT THEY CAN'T...
SAY, CAN YOU REALLY TELL IF PEOPLE ARE GOOD OR BAD RIGHT AWAY, ASTRO?
SURE...
IT'S A USELESS SKILL, YOU KNOW...
IN POLICE WORK, WE'VE GOTTA HAVE EVIDENCE! UNDERSTAND?
YESSIR...
I'M GETTING HOME LATE...

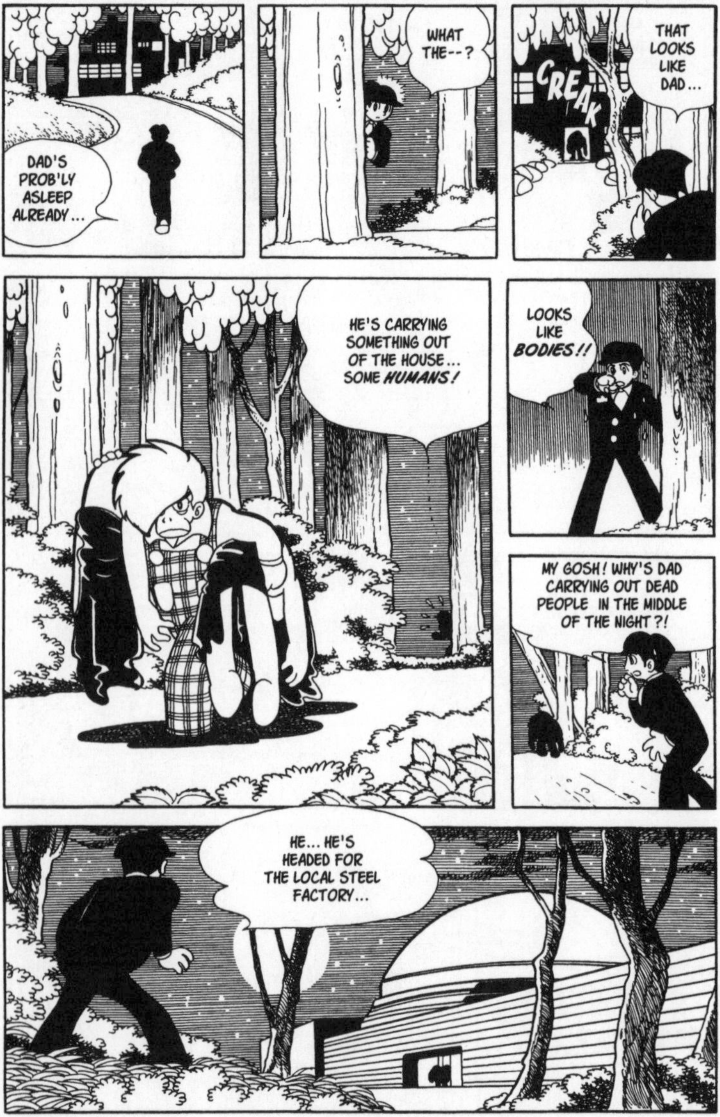
DAD'S PROB'LY ASLEEP ALREADY...
WHAT THE--?
CREAK
THAT LOOKS LIKE DAD...
HE'S CARRYING SOMETHING OUT OF THE HOUSE... SOME HUMANS!
LOOKS LIKE BODIES!!
MY GOSH! WHY'S DAD CARRYING OUT DEAD PEOPLE IN THE MIDDLE OF THE NIGHT?!
HE... HE'S HEADED FOR THE LOCAL STEEL FACTORY...

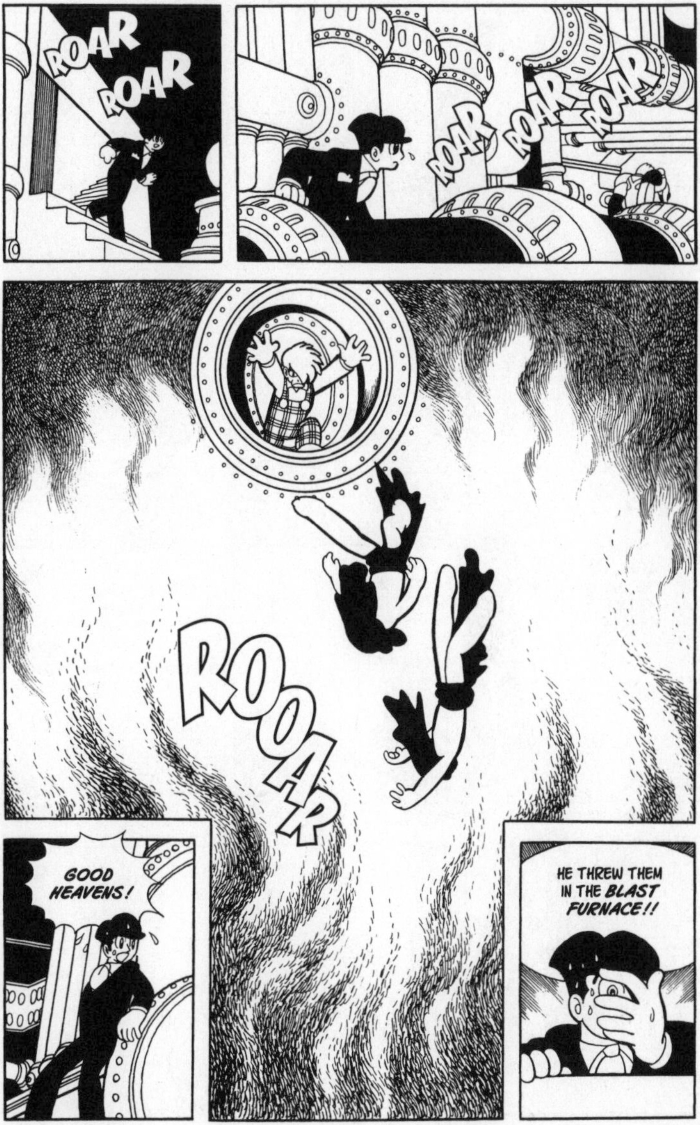
ROAR
ROAR
ROAR
ROAR
ROAR
ROAR
ROOOAR
GOOD HEAVENS!
HE THREW THEM IN THE *BLAST FURNACE!!*

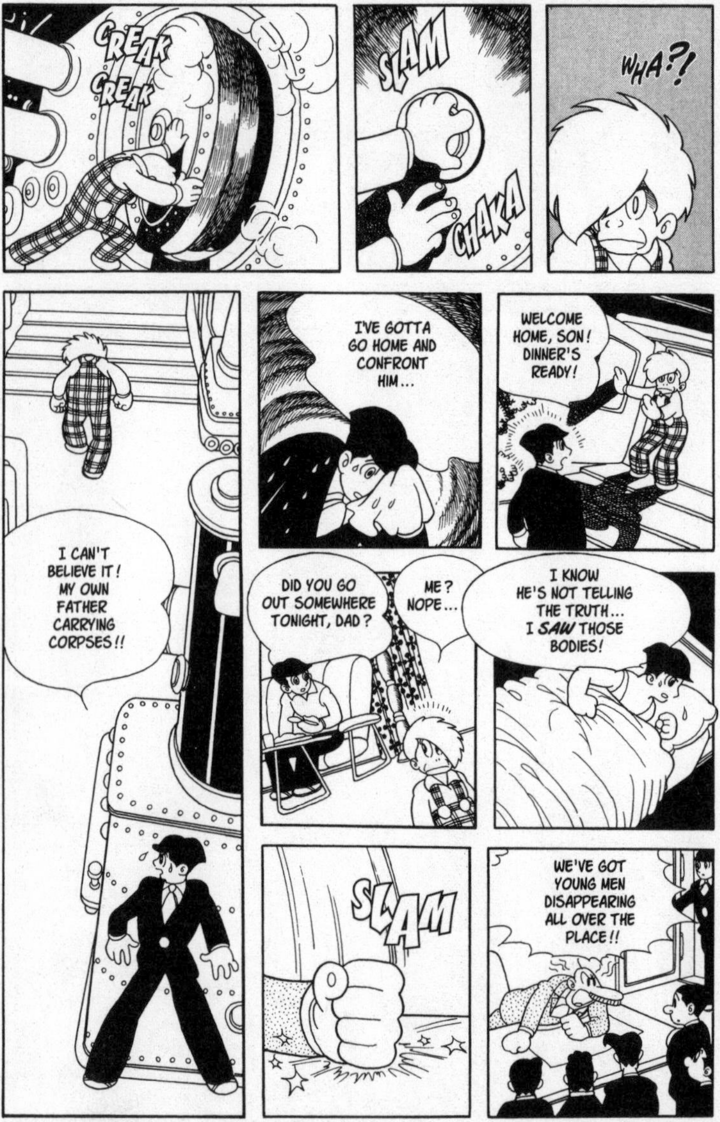
CREAK
CREAK
SLAM
CHAKA
WHA?!
I CAN'T BELIEVE IT! MY OWN FATHER CARRYING CORPSES!!
I'VE GOTTA GO HOME AND CONFRONT HIM...
WELCOME HOME, SON! DINNER'S READY!
DID YOU GO OUT SOMEWHERE TONIGHT, DAD?
ME? NOPE...
I KNOW HE'S NOT TELLING THE TRUTH... I *SAW* THOSE BODIES!
SLAM
WE'VE GOT YOUNG MEN DISAPPEARING ALL OVER THE PLACE!!

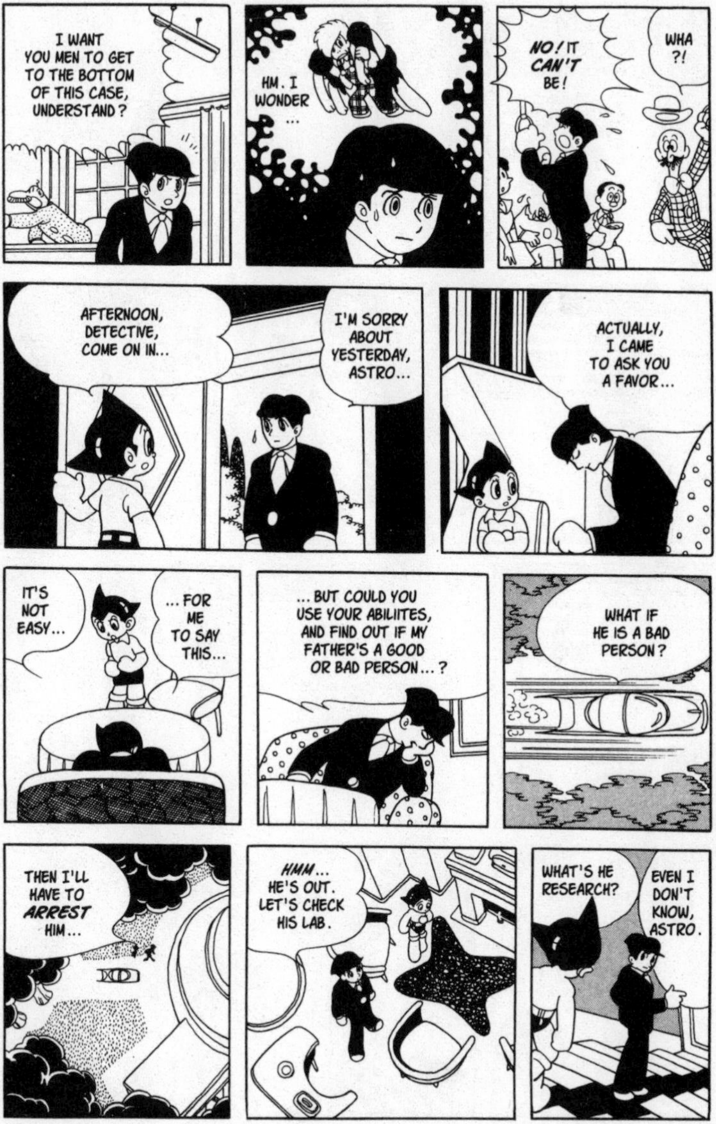
I WANT YOU MEN TO GET TO THE BOTTOM OF THIS CASE, UNDERSTAND?
HM. I WONDER ...
NO! IT CAN'T BE!
WHA ?!
AFTERNOON, DETECTIVE, COME ON IN...
I'M SORRY ABOUT YESTERDAY, ASTRO...
ACTUALLY, I CAME TO ASK YOU A FAVOR...
IT'S NOT EASY...
... FOR ME TO SAY THIS...
... BUT COULD YOU USE YOUR ABILIITES, AND FIND OUT IF MY FATHER'S A GOOD OR BAD PERSON...?
WHAT IF HE IS A BAD PERSON?
THEN I'LL HAVE TO ARREST HIM...
HMM... HE'S OUT. LET'S CHECK HIS LAB.
WHAT'S HE RESEARCH?
EVEN I DON'T KNOW, ASTRO.

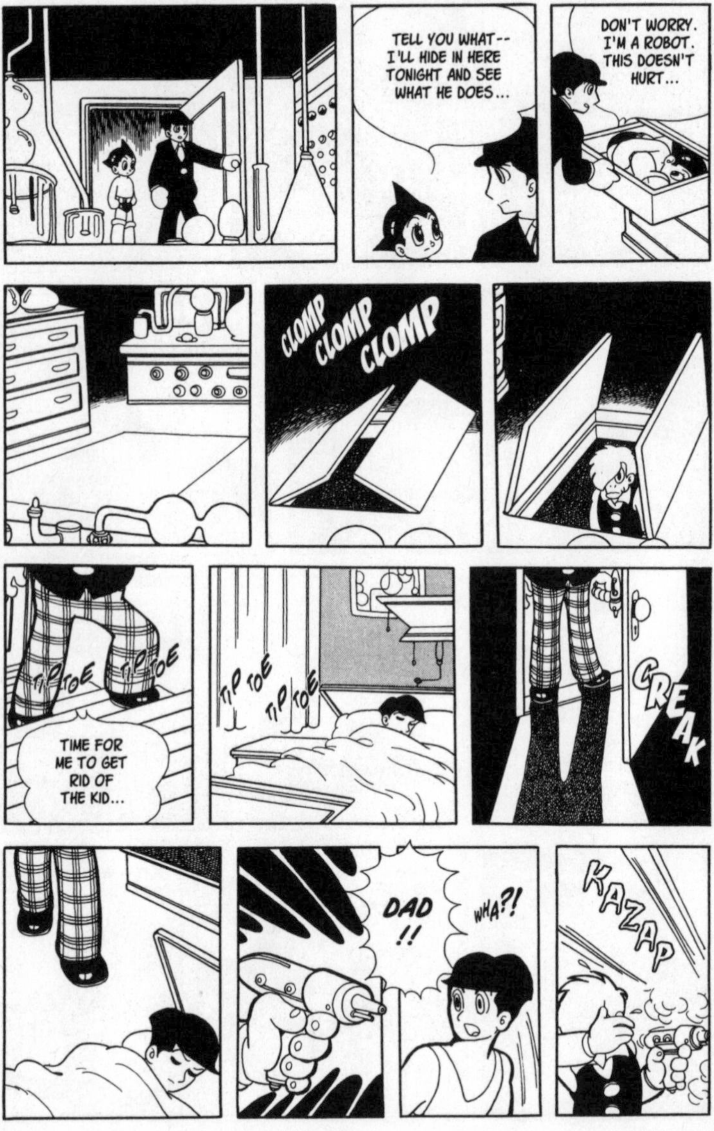
TELL YOU WHAT-- I'LL HIDE IN HERE TONIGHT AND SEE WHAT HE DOES...
DON'T WORRY. I'M A ROBOT. THIS DOESN'T HURT...
CLOMP CLOMP CLOMP
TIP TOE TIP TOE
TIME FOR ME TO GET RID OF THE KID...
TIP TOE TIP TOE
CREAK
DAD !!
WHA?!
KAZAP

KATHUD

FORGIVE ME... IT'S YOUR *LAST* DAY...

IT'S TIME FOR A *NEW* YOU...

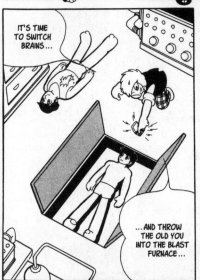
IT'S TIME TO SWITCH BRAINS...

...AND THROW THE OLD YOU INTO THE BLAST FURNACE...

WHEN I FIRST MADE YOU... ...YOU LOOKED LIKE A REGULAR BABY.

I GAVE YOU A NEW AND BIGGER BODY EVERY MONTH...

IT'S NO WONDER YOU THINK YOU'RE A REAL HUMAN...

THIS IS THE 250TH TIME I'VE HAD TO THROW AWAY YOUR OLD BODY...

HUHN--?!

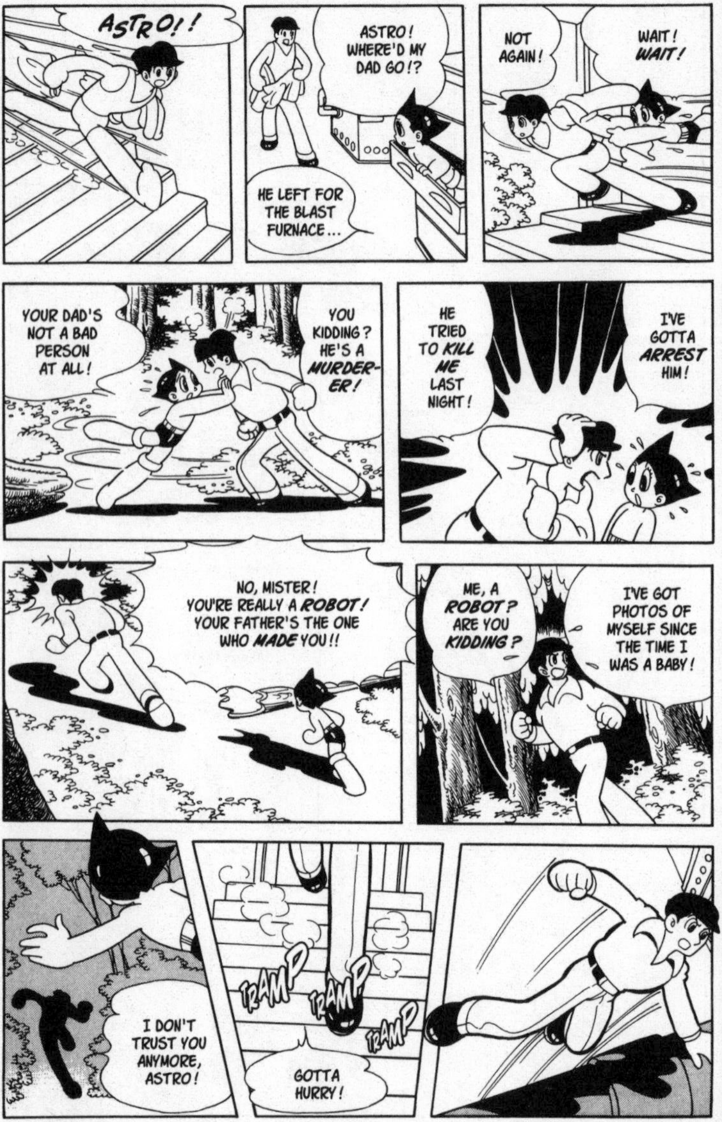
ASTRO!!
ASTRO! WHERE'D MY DAD GO!?
HE LEFT FOR THE BLAST FURNACE...
NOT AGAIN!
WAIT! WAIT!
YOUR DAD'S NOT A BAD PERSON AT ALL!
YOU KIDDING? HE'S A MURDERER!
HE TRIED TO KILL ME LAST NIGHT!
I'VE GOTTA ARREST HIM!
NO, MISTER! YOU'RE REALLY A ROBOT! YOUR FATHER'S THE ONE WHO MADE YOU!!
ME, A ROBOT? ARE YOU KIDDING?
I'VE GOT PHOTOS OF MYSELF SINCE THE TIME I WAS A BABY!
I DON'T TRUST YOU ANYMORE, ASTRO!
TRAMP
TRAMP
TRAMP
GOTTA HURRY!

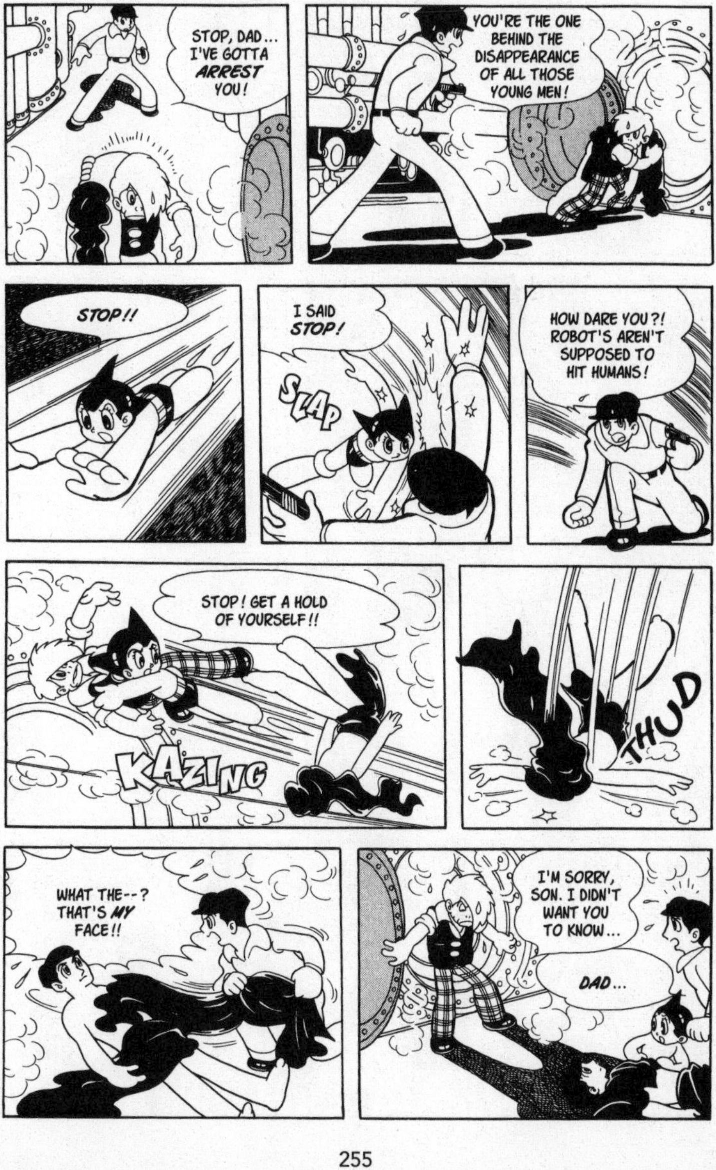
STOP, DAD... I'VE GOTTA ARREST YOU!
YOU'RE THE ONE BEHIND THE DISAPPEARANCE OF ALL THOSE YOUNG MEN!
STOP!!
I SAID STOP!
SLAP
HOW DARE YOU?! ROBOT'S AREN'T SUPPOSED TO HIT HUMANS!
STOP! GET A HOLD OF YOURSELF!!
KAZING
THUD
WHAT THE--? THAT'S MY FACE!!
I'M SORRY, SON. I DIDN'T WANT YOU TO KNOW...
DAD...

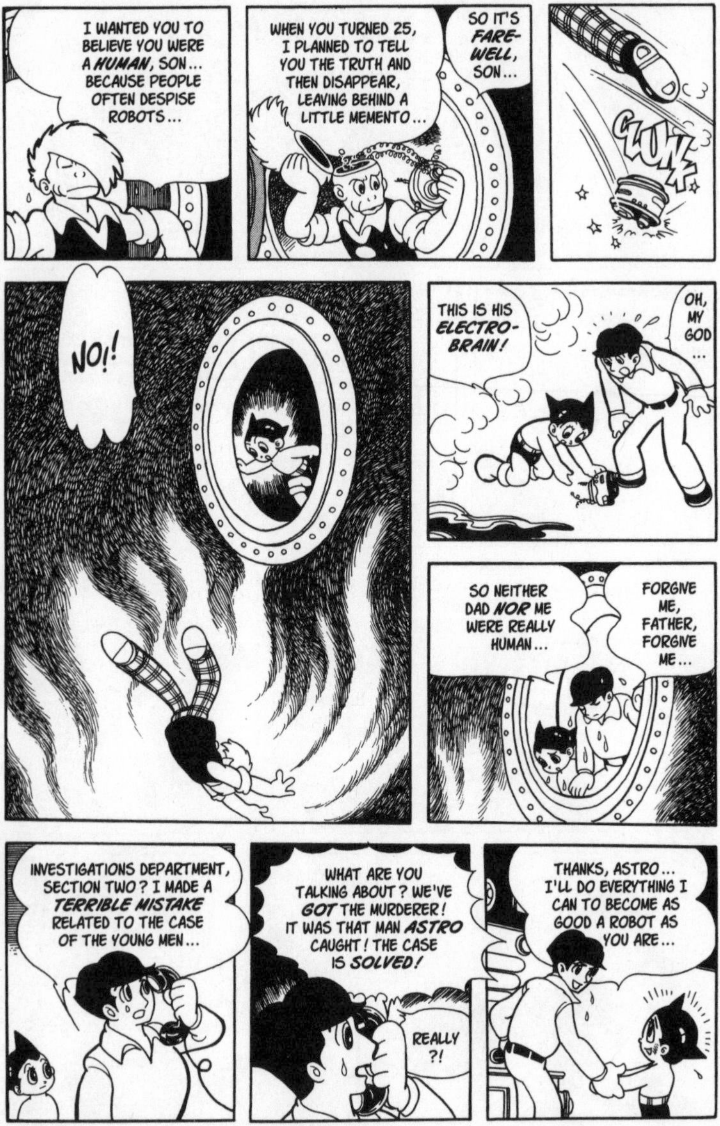
I WANTED YOU TO BELIEVE YOU WERE A *HUMAN*, SON... BECAUSE PEOPLE OFTEN DESPISE ROBOTS...
WHEN YOU TURNED 25, I PLANNED TO TELL YOU THE TRUTH AND THEN DISAPPEAR, LEAVING BEHIND A LITTLE MEMENTO...
SO IT'S *FAREWELL*, SON...
CLUNK
NO!!
THIS IS HIS *ELECTRO-BRAIN!*
OH, MY GOD ...
SO NEITHER DAD *NOR* ME WERE REALLY HUMAN...
FORGIVE ME, FATHER, FORGIVE ME...
INVESTIGATIONS DEPARTMENT, SECTION TWO? I MADE A *TERRIBLE MISTAKE* RELATED TO THE CASE OF THE YOUNG MEN...
WHAT ARE YOU TALKING ABOUT? WE'VE *GOT* THE MURDERER! IT WAS THAT MAN *ASTRO* CAUGHT! THE CASE IS *SOLVED!*
REALLY ?!
THANKS, ASTRO... I'LL DO EVERYTHING I CAN TO BECOME AS GOOD A ROBOT AS YOU ARE...

ROBOIDS

First serialized from January to May 1965
in *Shonen* magazine.

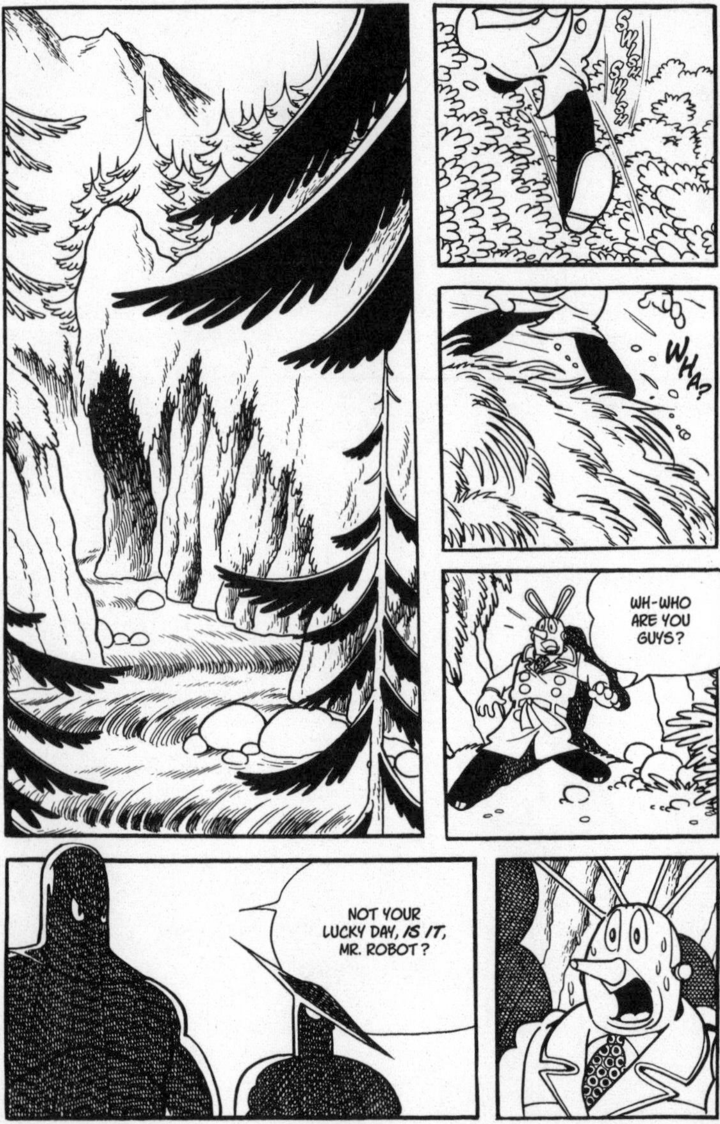
SWISH SWISH SWISH
WHA?
WH-WHO ARE YOU GUYS?
NOT YOUR LUCKY DAY, *IS IT*, MR. ROBOT?

BUT SINCE YOU ASKED, WE'LL ANSWER WHAT'LL BE YOUR FINAL QUESTION IN LIFE... WE'RE *ROBOIDS!!*

WHAT THE--?!

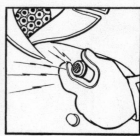

POIK

FWIP

ROAR ROAR

259

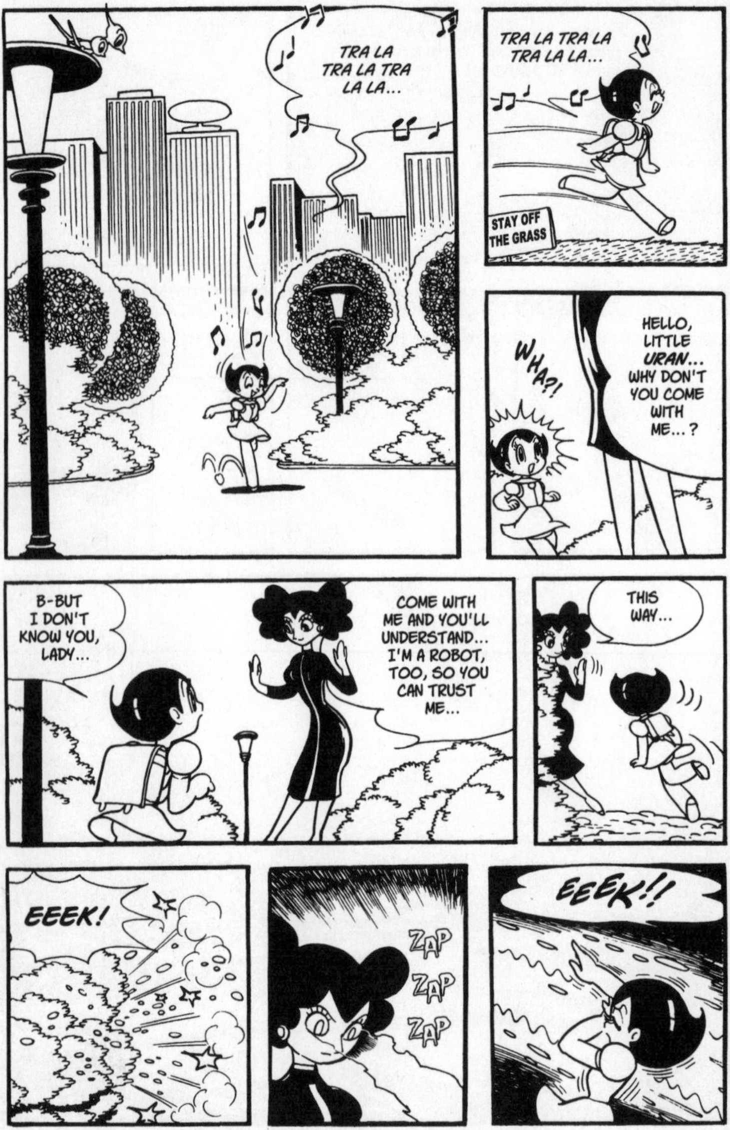

TRA LA
TRA LA TRA
LA LA...
TRA LA TRA LA
TRA LA LA...
STAY OFF
THE GRASS
WHA?!
HELLO, LITTLE URAN... WHY DON'T YOU COME WITH ME...?
B-BUT I DON'T KNOW YOU, LADY...
COME WITH ME AND YOU'LL UNDERSTAND... I'M A ROBOT, TOO, SO YOU CAN TRUST ME...
THIS WAY...
EEEK!
ZAP
ZAP
ZAP
EEEK!!

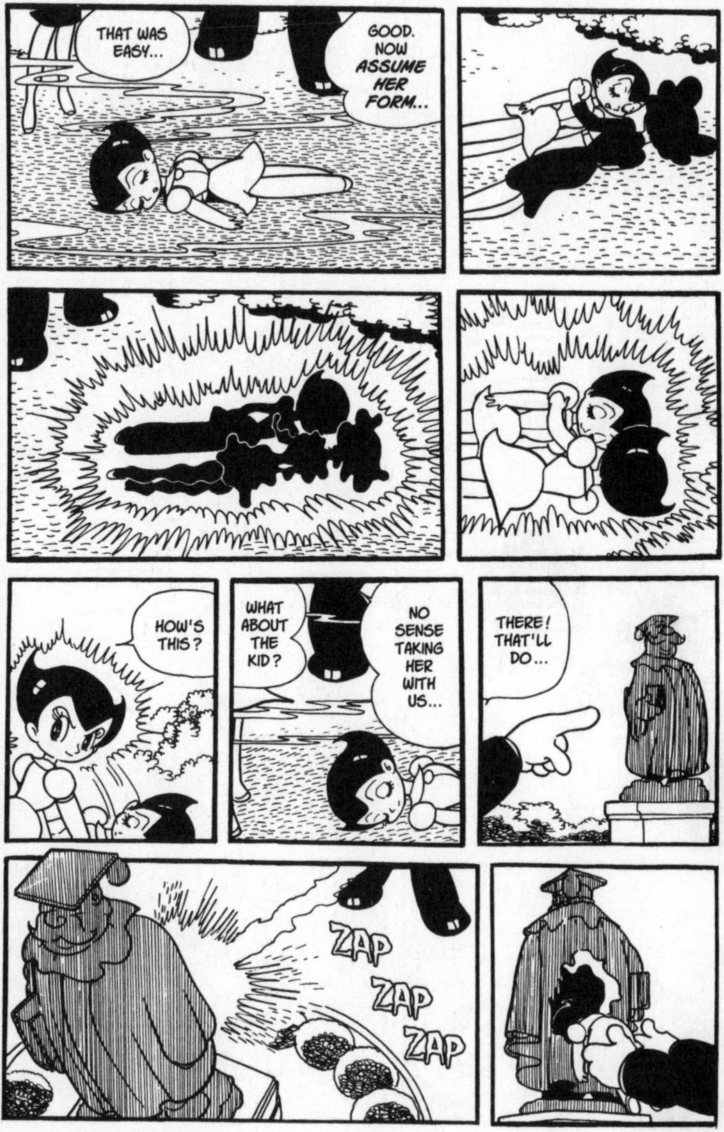
THAT WAS EASY...
GOOD. NOW ASSUME HER FORM...
HOW'S THIS?
WHAT ABOUT THE KID?
NO SENSE TAKING HER WITH US...
THERE! THAT'LL DO...
ZAP
ZAP
ZAP

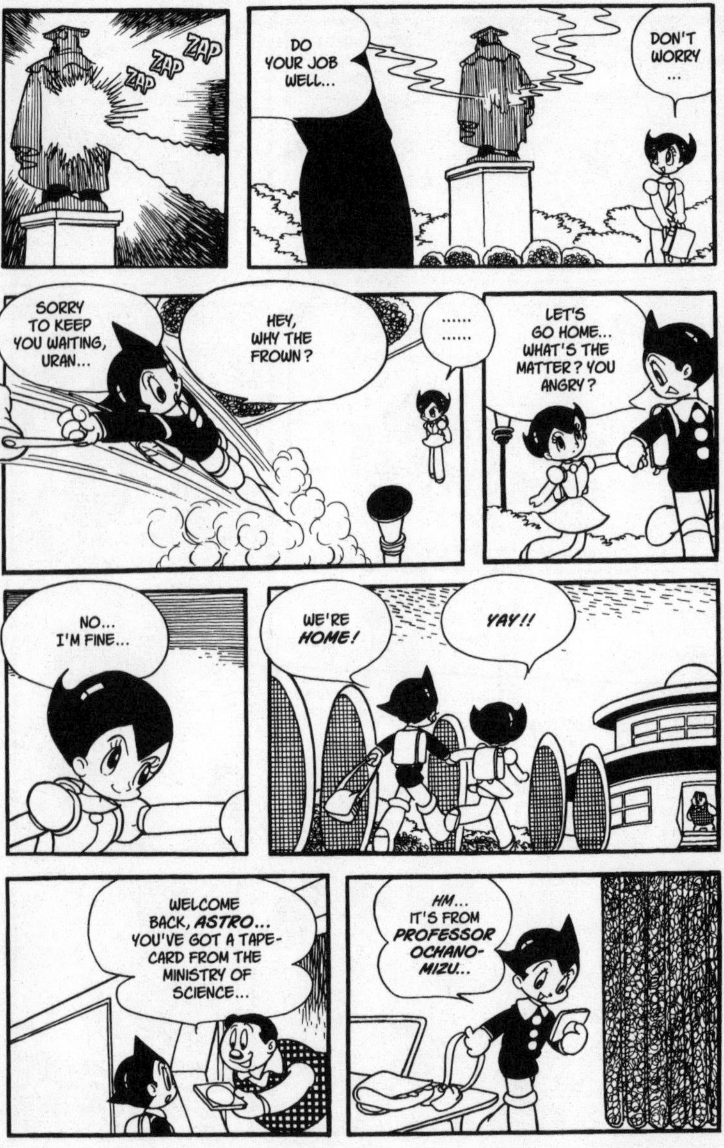
ZAP
ZAP
ZAP
DO YOUR JOB WELL...
DON'T WORRY ...
SORRY TO KEEP YOU WAITING, URAN...
HEY, WHY THE FROWN?
....
LET'S GO HOME... WHAT'S THE MATTER? YOU ANGRY?
NO... I'M FINE...
WE'RE *HOME!*
YAY!!
WELCOME BACK, *ASTRO*... YOU'VE GOT A TAPE-CARD FROM THE MINISTRY OF SCIENCE...
HM... IT'S FROM *PROFESSOR OCHANO-MIZU*...

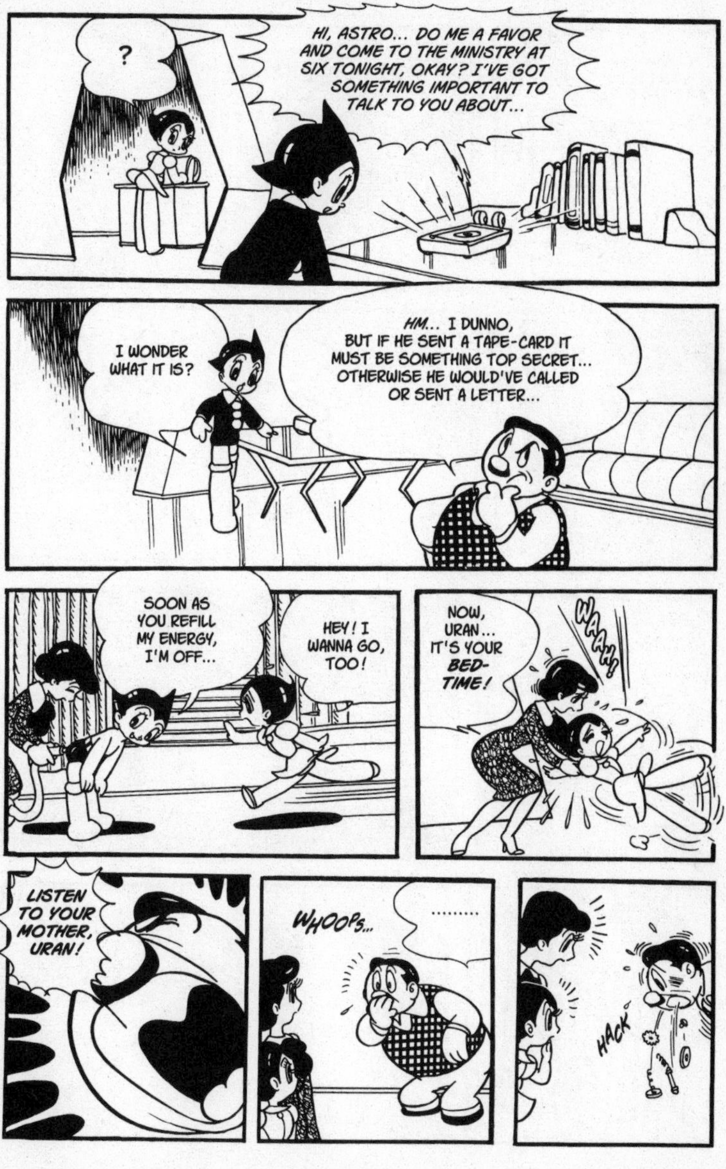
?
HI, ASTRO... DO ME A FAVOR AND COME TO THE MINISTRY AT SIX TONIGHT, OKAY? I'VE GOT SOMETHING IMPORTANT TO TALK TO YOU ABOUT...
I WONDER WHAT IT IS?
HM... I DUNNO, BUT IF HE SENT A TAPE-CARD IT MUST BE SOMETHING TOP SECRET... OTHERWISE HE WOULD'VE CALLED OR SENT A LETTER...
SOON AS YOU REFILL MY ENERGY, I'M OFF...
HEY! I WANNA GO, TOO!
NOW, URAN... IT'S YOUR BED-TIME!
WAAAH!
LISTEN TO YOUR MOTHER, URAN!
WHOOPS...
....
HACK

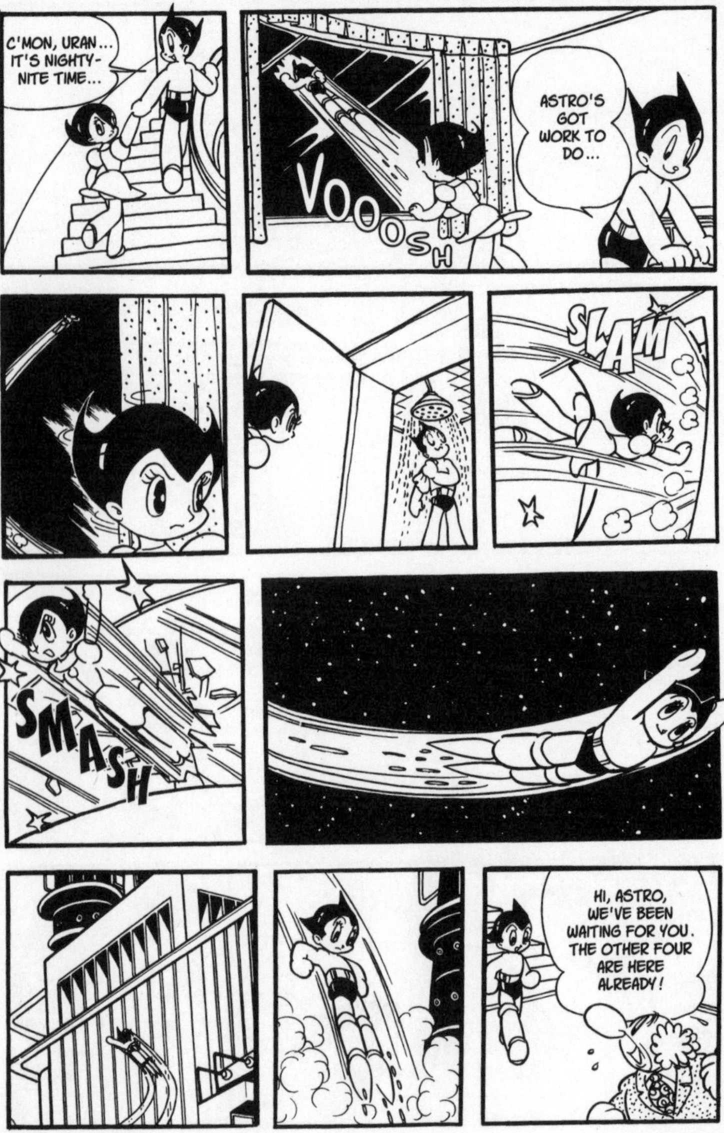
C'MON, URAN... IT'S NIGHTY-NITE TIME...
VOOOSH
ASTRO'S GOT WORK TO DO...
SLAM
SMASH
HI, ASTRO, WE'VE BEEN WAITING FOR YOU. THE OTHER FOUR ARE HERE ALREADY!

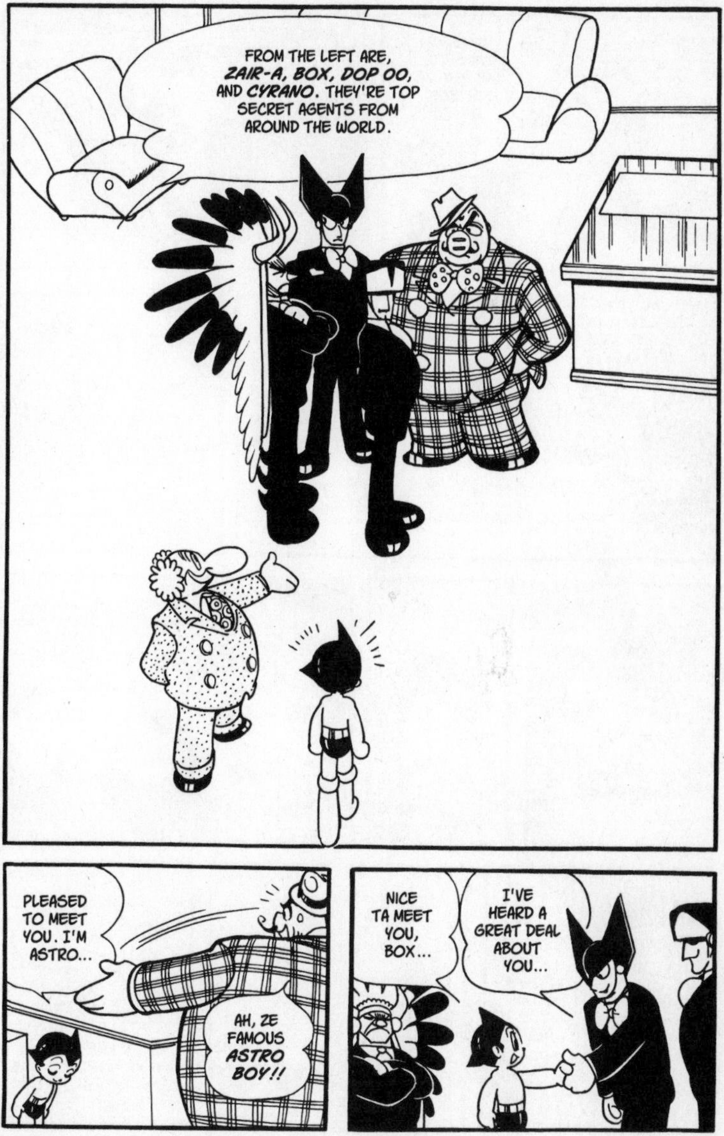
FROM THE LEFT ARE, ZAIR-A, BOX, DOP OO, AND CYRANO. THEY'RE TOP SECRET AGENTS FROM AROUND THE WORLD.
PLEASED TO MEET YOU. I'M ASTRO...
AH, ZE FAMOUS ASTRO BOY!!
NICE TA MEET YOU, BOX...
I'VE HEARD A GREAT DEAL ABOUT YOU...

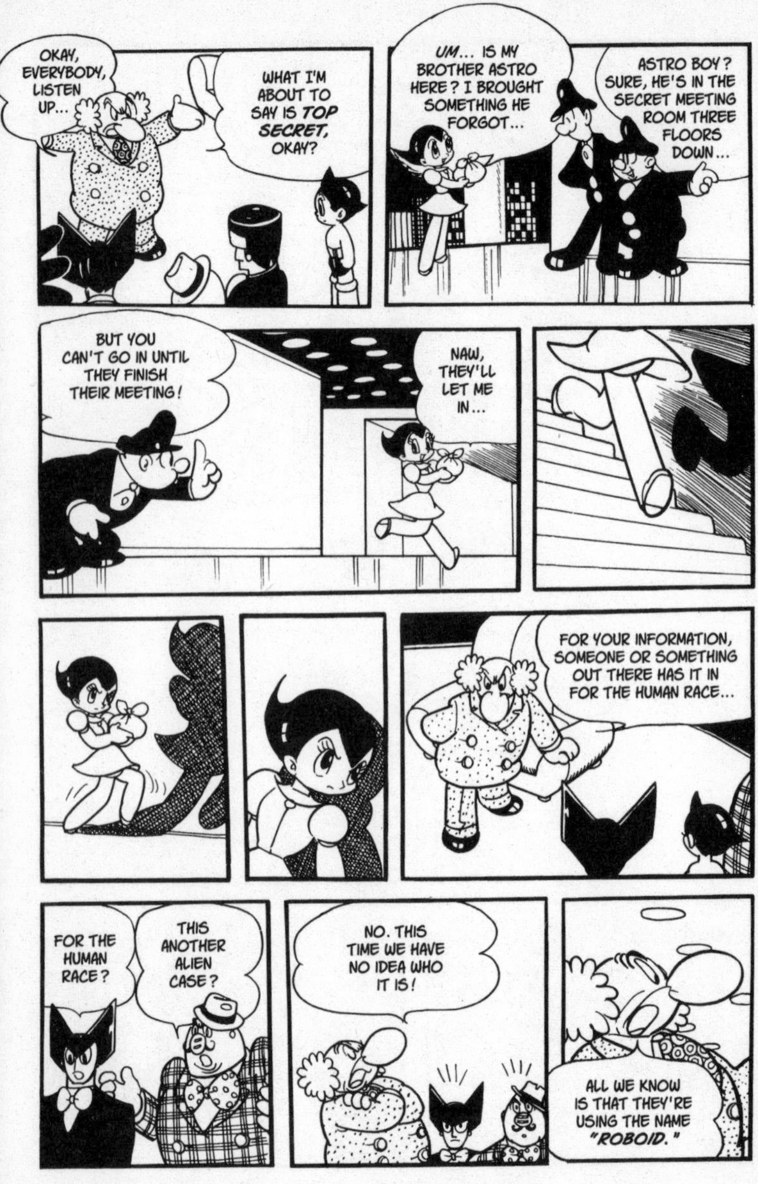
OKAY, EVERYBODY, LISTEN UP...
WHAT I'M ABOUT TO SAY IS *TOP SECRET,* OKAY?
UM... IS MY BROTHER ASTRO HERE? I BROUGHT SOMETHING HE FORGOT...
ASTRO BOY? SURE, HE'S IN THE SECRET MEETING ROOM THREE FLOORS DOWN...
BUT YOU CAN'T GO IN UNTIL THEY FINISH THEIR MEETING!
NAW, THEY'LL LET ME IN...
FOR YOUR INFORMATION, SOMEONE OR SOMETHING OUT THERE HAS IT IN FOR THE HUMAN RACE...
FOR THE HUMAN RACE?
THIS ANOTHER ALIEN CASE?
NO. THIS TIME WE HAVE NO IDEA WHO IT IS!
ALL WE KNOW IS THAT THEY'RE USING THE NAME *"ROBOID."*

WHAT'S A ROBOID??

'ROBOID?!

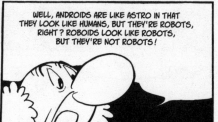

WELL, ANDROIDS ARE LIKE ASTRO IN THAT THEY LOOK LIKE HUMANS, BUT THEY'RE ROBOTS, RIGHT? ROBOIDS LOOK LIKE ROBOTS, BUT THEY'RE NOT ROBOTS!

SO THEY'RE *FAKE* ROBOTS?

WELL, TO PUT IT SIMPLY, YES... BUT THIS IS MUCH SCARIER.... WE KNOW THERE ARE FIVE ROBOIDS INVOLVED, AND WE KNOW THEY'VE INFILTRATED THE ROBOT POPULATION. BUT WE DON'T KNOW *WHAT* ROBOT FORM THEY'VE ASSUMED. AND THEY'RE APPARENTLY PLANNING TO *DESTROY THE ENTIRE HUMAN RACE!!*

BUT *HOW* DO YOU KNOW THIS, PROFESSOR?

A ROBOT FRIEND OF MINE MET A ROBOID AND HEARD IT STRAIGHT FROM HIM...

HE HAD A MINI-TAPE RECORDER IN A BUTTON ON HIS COAT...

HE WAS A NEWSPAPER REPORTER...

JUST BEFORE HE WAS *KILLED*...

FWOOSH

FSSSST

...HE RECORDED THE ROBOIDS SAYING THEY'D COME TO EARTH TO DESTROY HUMANS...

SINCE THE REPORTER HAD A TAPE RECORDER BUTTON GOING RIGHT HERE...

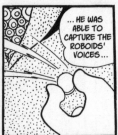

...HE WAS ABLE TO CAPTURE THE ROBOIDS' VOICES...

THEN HE TORE OFF THE BUTTON, AND THREW IT IN THE RIVER!

LUCKILY, THE ROBOIDS DIDN'T SEE IT...

268

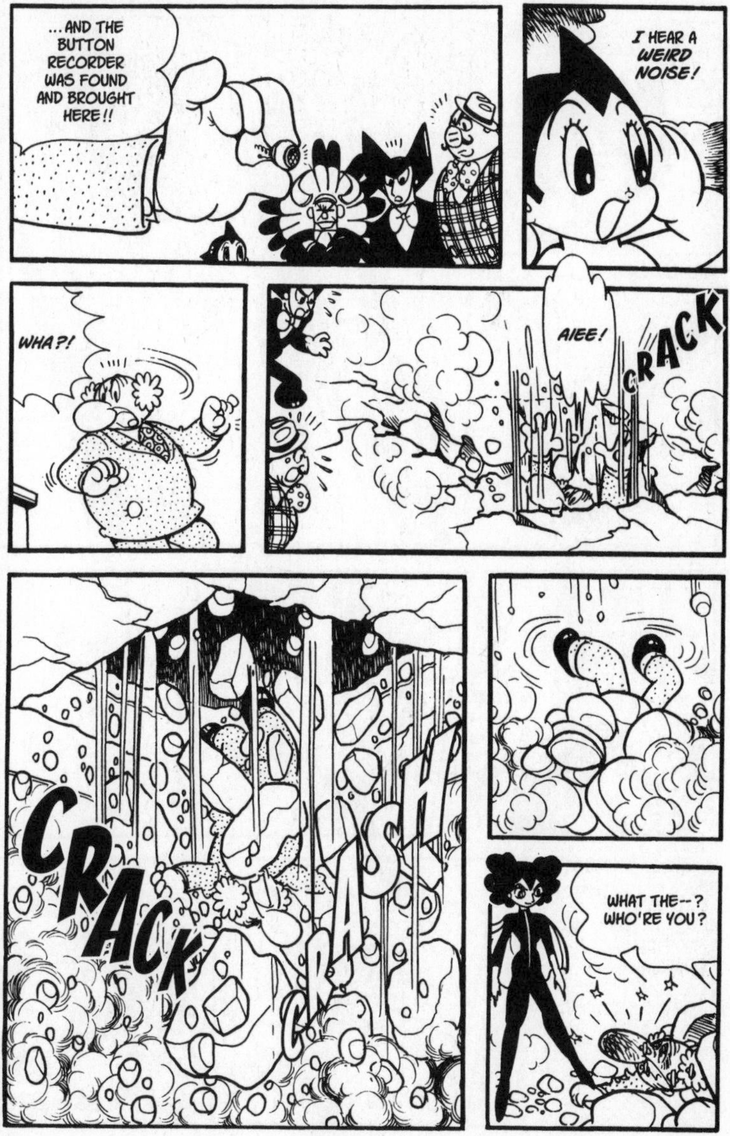
...AND THE BUTTON RECORDER WAS FOUND AND BROUGHT HERE!!
I HEAR A WEIRD NOISE!
WHA?!
AIEE!
CRACK
CRACK
CRASH
WHAT THE--? WHO'RE YOU?

I'M HERE FOR THE *BUTTON-RECORDER*...

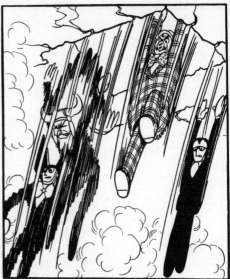

NO!!

GIVE IT TO ME AND I'M GONE...

FWIP

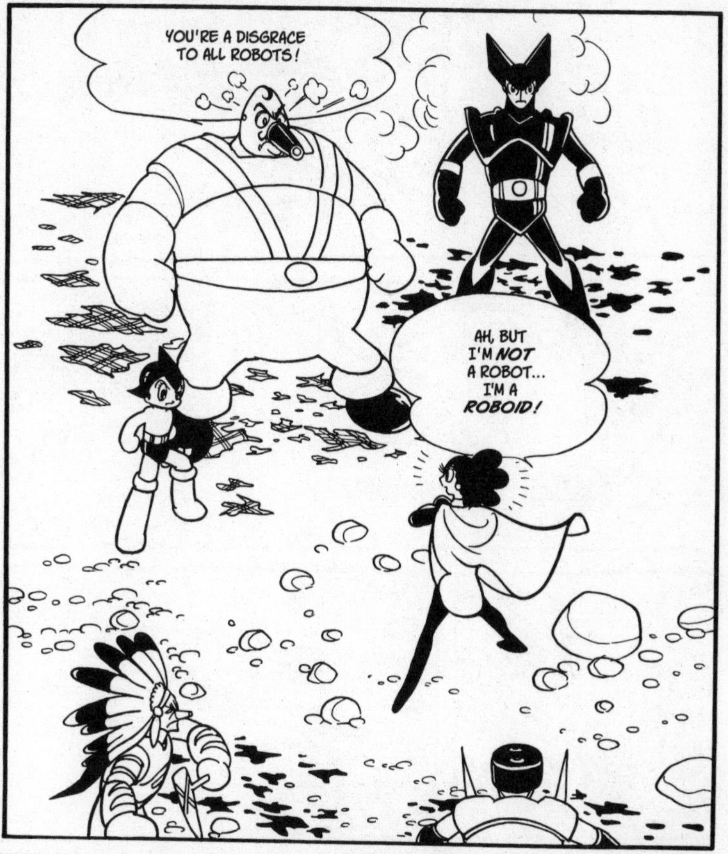
YOU'RE A DISGRACE TO ALL ROBOTS!
AH, BUT I'M NOT A ROBOT... I'M A ROBOID!

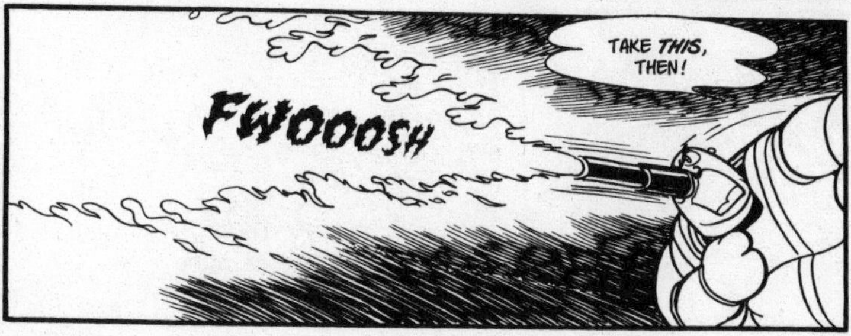
TAKE THIS, THEN!
FWOOOSH

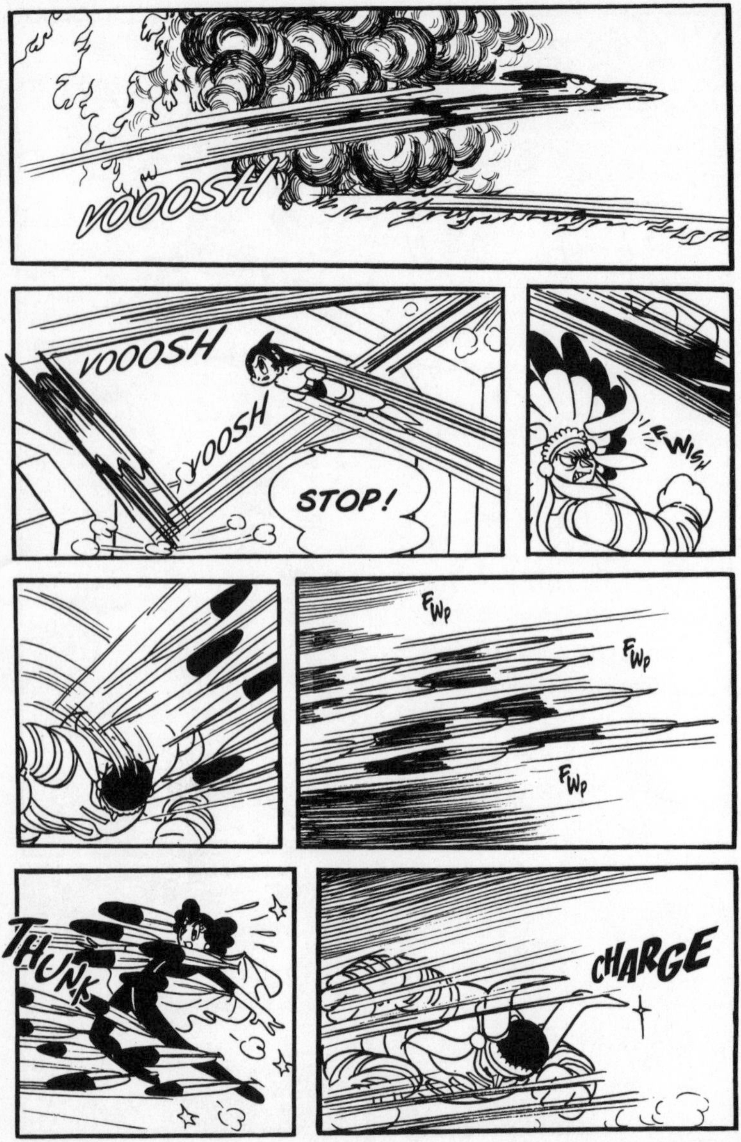
VOOOSH
VOOOSH
YOOSH
STOP!
FWISH
FWp
FWp
FWp
THUNK
CHARGE

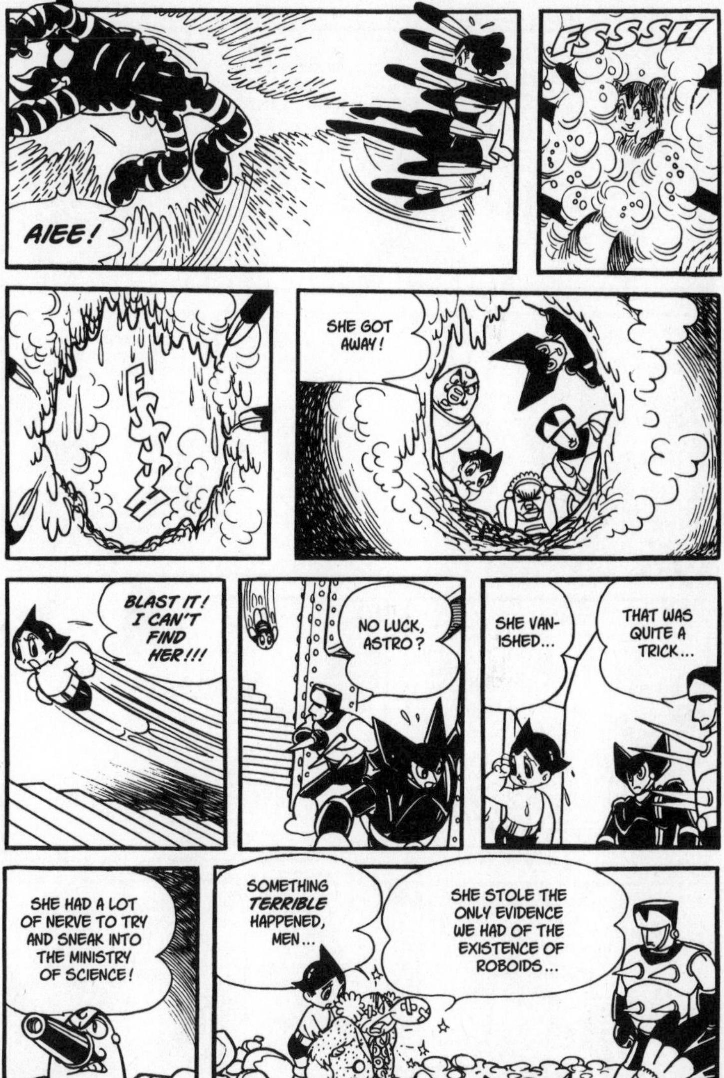
AIEE!
FSSSH
FSSSH
SHE GOT AWAY!
BLAST IT! I CAN'T FIND HER!!!
NO LUCK, ASTRO?
SHE VANISHED...
THAT WAS QUITE A TRICK...
SHE HAD A LOT OF NERVE TO TRY AND SNEAK INTO THE MINISTRY OF SCIENCE!
SOMETHING *TERRIBLE* HAPPENED, MEN...
SHE STOLE THE ONLY EVIDENCE WE HAD OF THE EXISTENCE OF ROBOIDS...

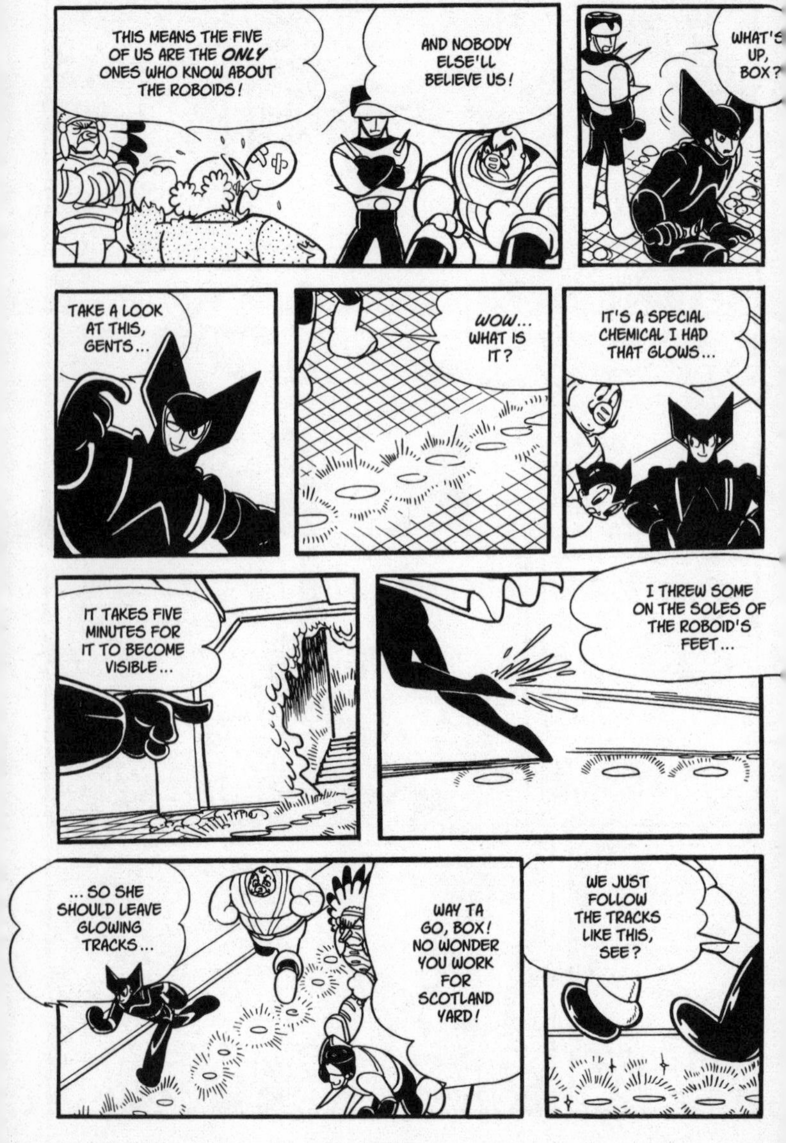
THIS MEANS THE FIVE OF US ARE THE *ONLY* ONES WHO KNOW ABOUT THE ROBOIDS!
AND NOBODY ELSE'LL BELIEVE US!
WHAT'S UP, BOX?
TAKE A LOOK AT THIS, GENTS...
WOW... WHAT IS IT?
IT'S A SPECIAL CHEMICAL I HAD THAT GLOWS...
IT TAKES FIVE MINUTES FOR IT TO BECOME VISIBLE...
I THREW SOME ON THE SOLES OF THE ROBOID'S FEET...
...SO SHE SHOULD LEAVE GLOWING TRACKS...
WAY TA GO, BOX! NO WONDER YOU WORK FOR SCOTLAND YARD!
WE JUST FOLLOW THE TRACKS LIKE THIS, SEE?

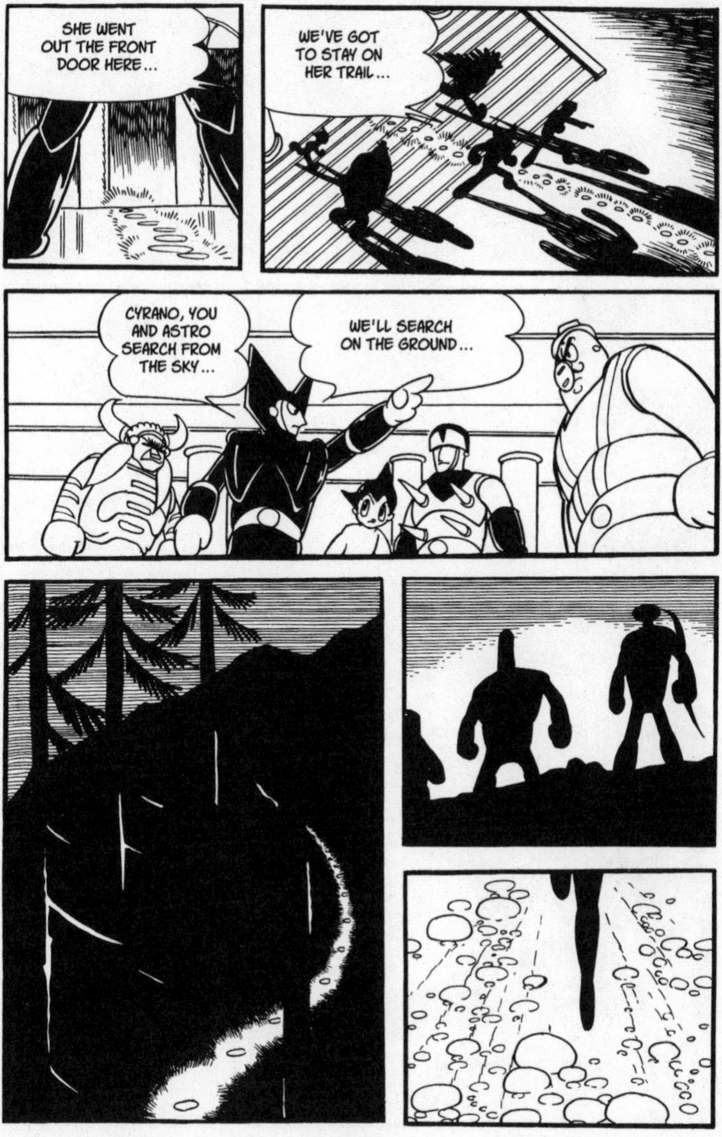
SHE WENT OUT THE FRONT DOOR HERE...
WE'VE GOT TO STAY ON HER TRAIL...
CYRANO, YOU AND ASTRO SEARCH FROM THE SKY...
WE'LL SEARCH ON THE GROUND...

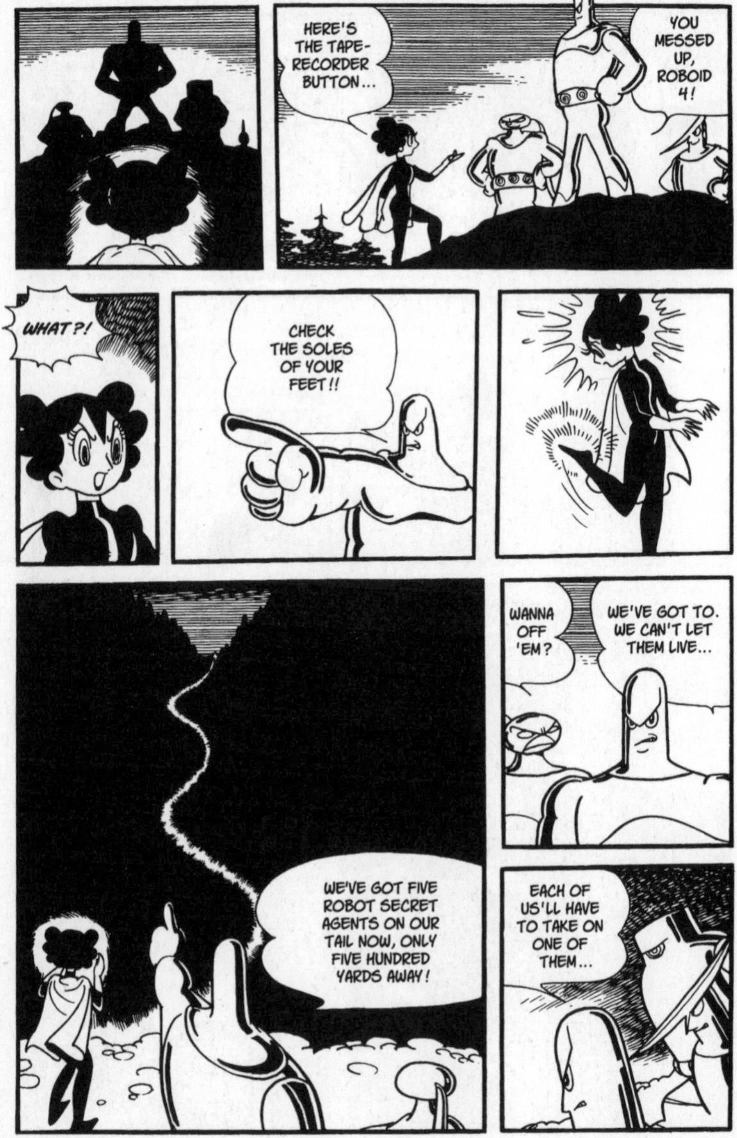
HERE'S THE TAPE-RECORDER BUTTON...
YOU MESSED UP, ROBOID 4!
WHAT?!
CHECK THE SOLES OF YOUR FEET!!
WE'VE GOT FIVE ROBOT SECRET AGENTS ON OUR TAIL NOW, ONLY FIVE HUNDRED YARDS AWAY!
WANNA OFF 'EM?
WE'VE GOT TO. WE CAN'T LET THEM LIVE...
EACH OF US'LL HAVE TO TAKE ON ONE OF THEM...

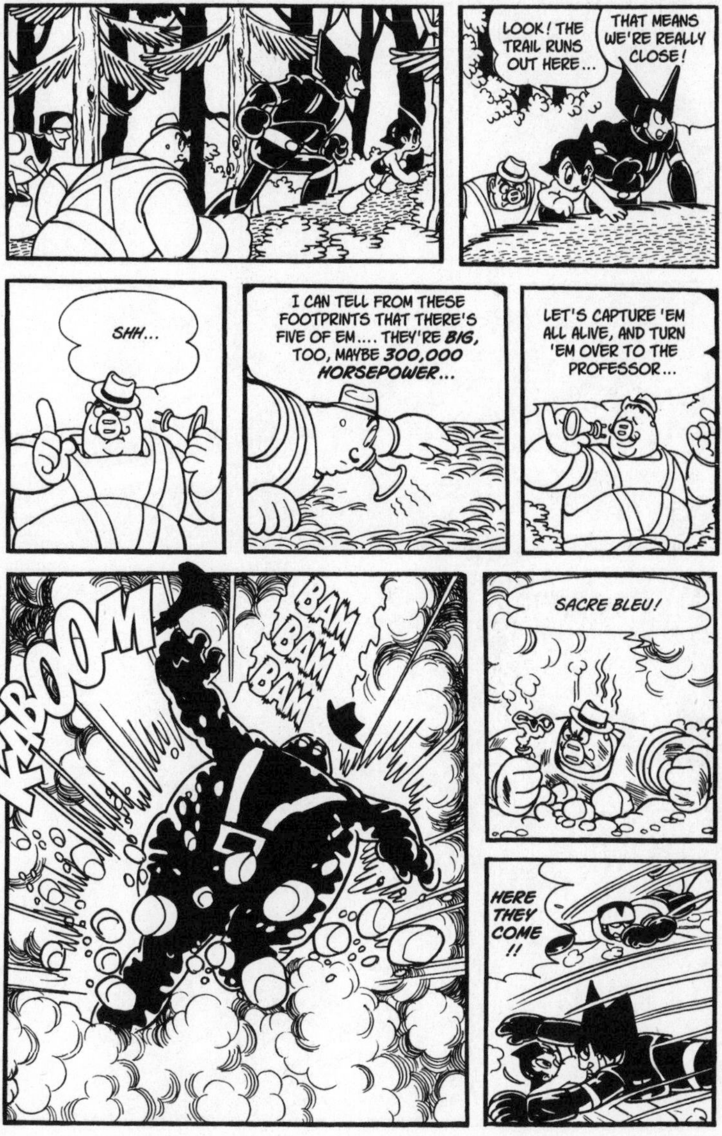
LOOK! THE TRAIL RUNS OUT HERE...
THAT MEANS WE'RE REALLY CLOSE!
SHH...
I CAN TELL FROM THESE FOOTPRINTS THAT THERE'S FIVE OF EM.... THEY'RE BIG, TOO, MAYBE 300,000 HORSEPOWER...
LET'S CAPTURE 'EM ALL ALIVE, AND TURN 'EM OVER TO THE PROFESSOR...
KABOOM
BAM BAM BAM
SACRE BLEU!
HERE THEY COME !!

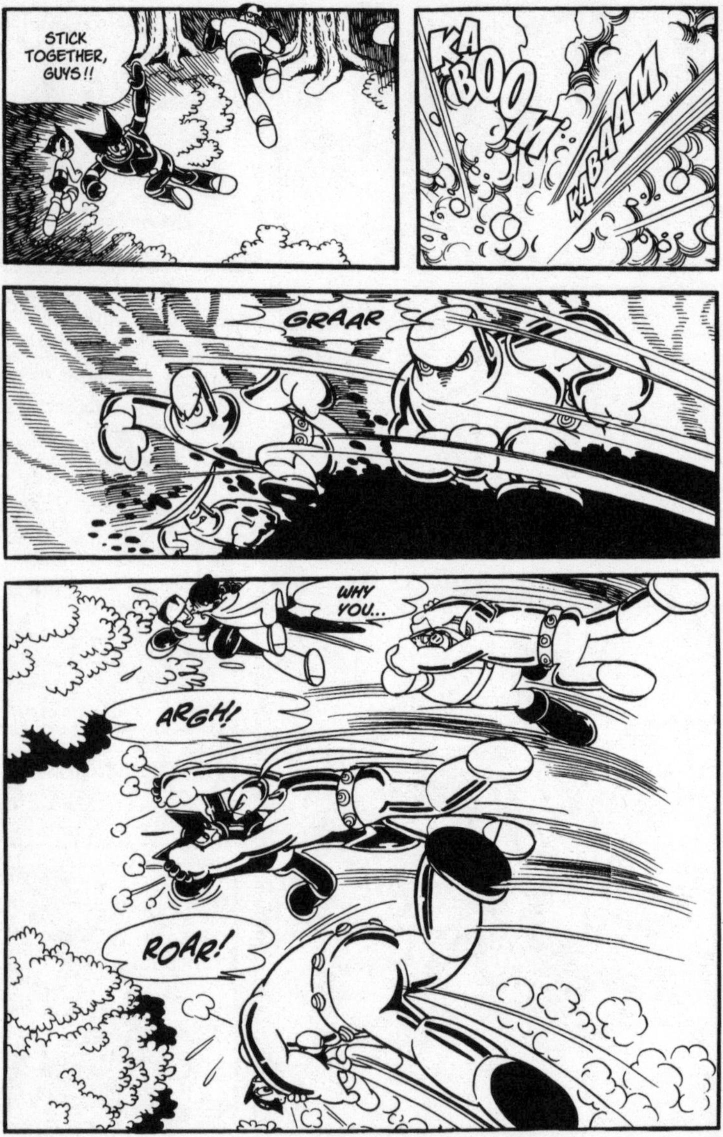

STICK TOGETHER, GUYS!!
KA BOOM
KABAAM
GRAAR
WHY YOU...
ARGH!
ROAR!

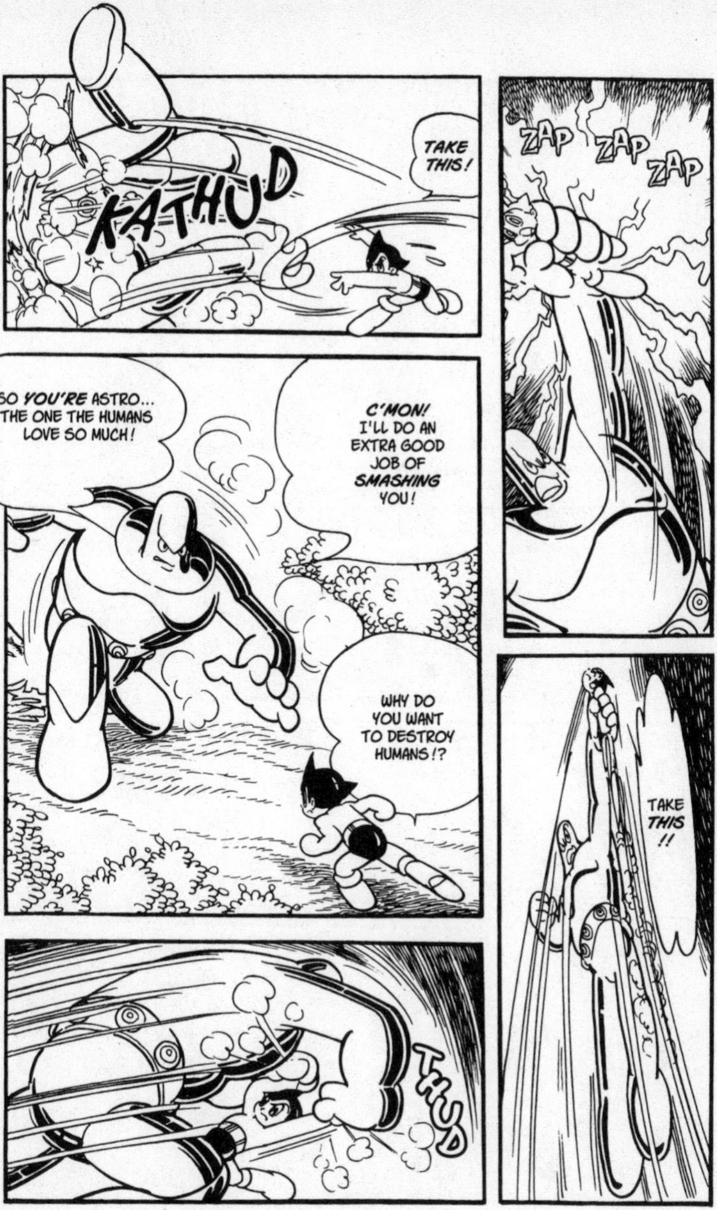
TAKE THIS!
KATHUD
SO YOU'RE ASTRO... THE ONE THE HUMANS LOVE SO MUCH!
C'MON! I'LL DO AN EXTRA GOOD JOB OF SMASHING YOU!
WHY DO YOU WANT TO DESTROY HUMANS!?
THUD
ZAP ZAP ZAP
TAKE THIS!!

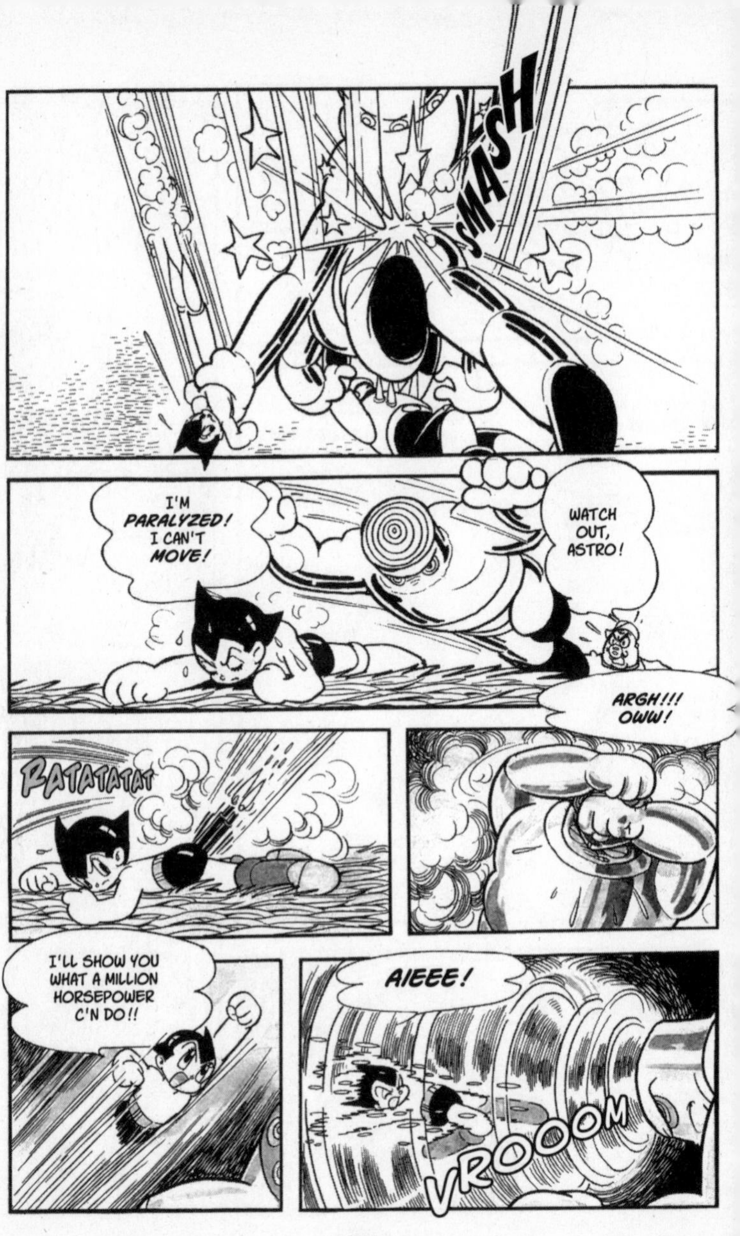
SMASH
I'M PARALYZED! I CAN'T MOVE!
WATCH OUT, ASTRO!
ARGH!!! OWW!
RATATATAT
I'LL SHOW YOU WHAT A MILLION HORSEPOWER C'N DO!!
AIEEE!
VROOOM

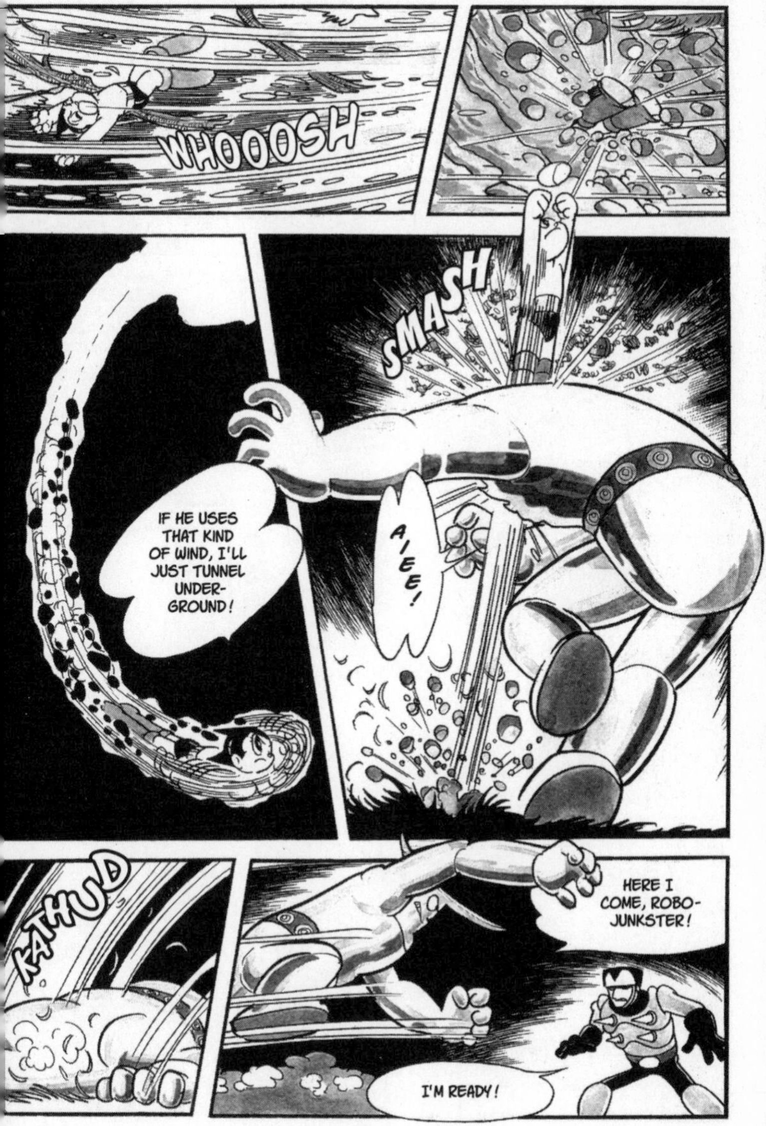
WHOOOSH
SMASH
IF HE USES THAT KIND OF WIND, I'LL JUST TUNNEL UNDER-GROUND!
AIEE!
KATHUD
HERE I COME, ROBO-JUNKSTER!
I'M READY!

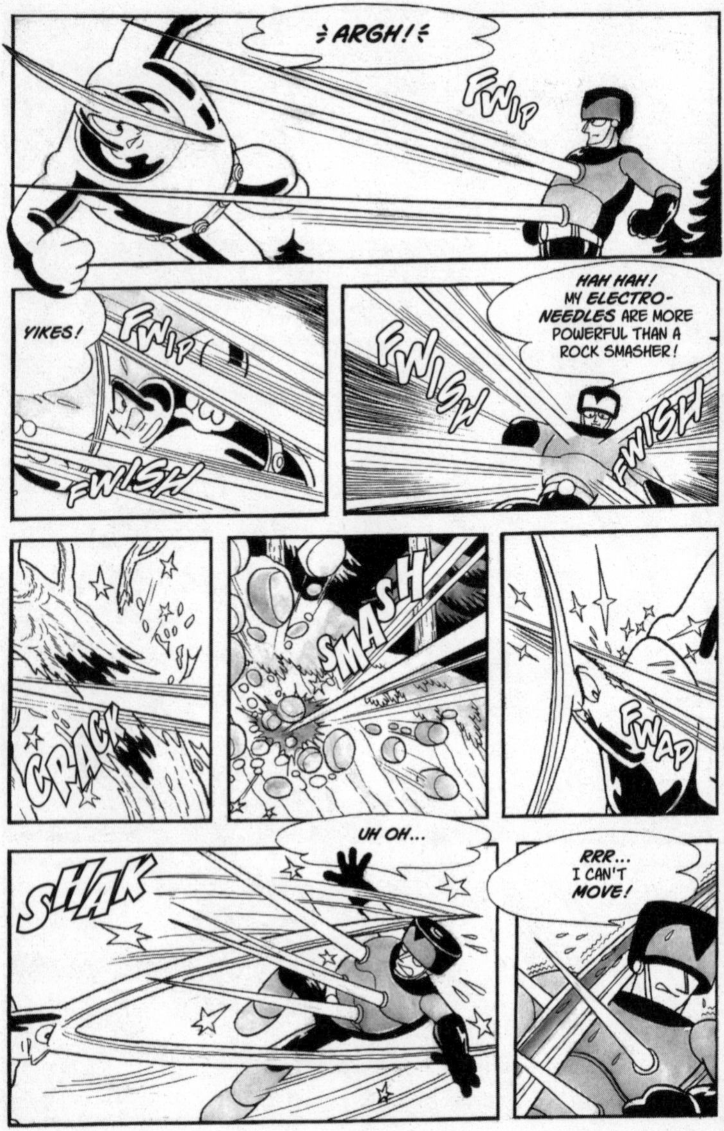
ARGH!
FWIP
YIKES!
FWIP
FWISH
HAH HAH! MY ELECTRO-NEEDLES ARE MORE POWERFUL THAN A ROCK SMASHER!
FWISH
FWISH
CRACK
SMASH
FWAP
SHAK
UH OH...
RRR... I CAN'T MOVE!

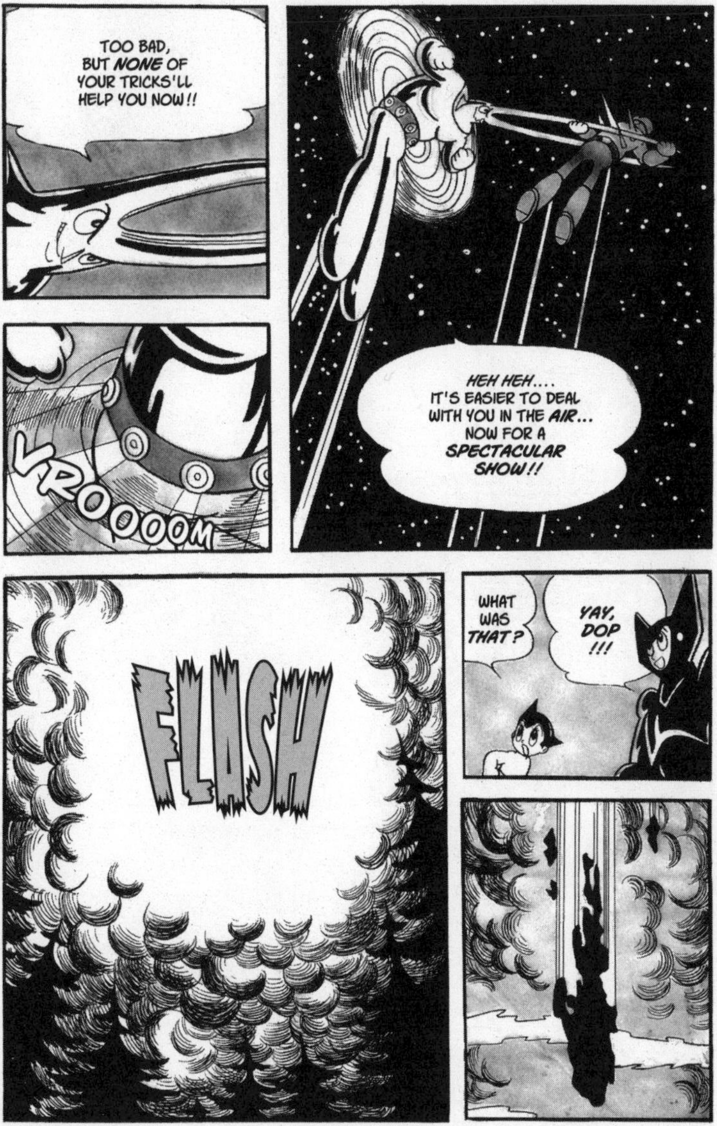
TOO BAD, BUT NONE OF YOUR TRICKS'LL HELP YOU NOW!!
VROOOOM
HEH HEH.... IT'S EASIER TO DEAL WITH YOU IN THE AIR... NOW FOR A SPECTACULAR SHOW!!
FLASH
WHAT WAS THAT?
YAY, DOP !!!

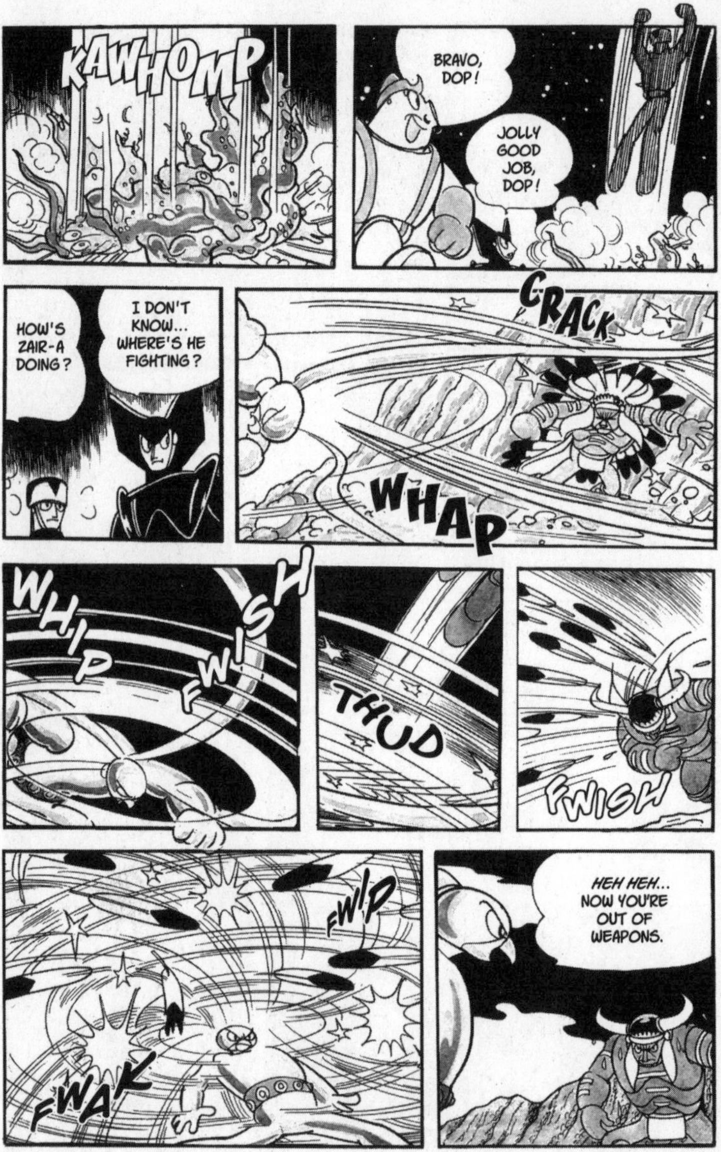
KAWHOMP
BRAVO, DOP!
JOLLY GOOD JOB, DOP!
HOW'S ZAIR-A DOING?
I DON'T KNOW... WHERE'S HE FIGHTING?
CRACK
WHAP
WHIP
FWISH
THUD
FWISH
FWIP
FWAK
HEH HEH... NOW YOU'RE OUT OF WEAPONS.

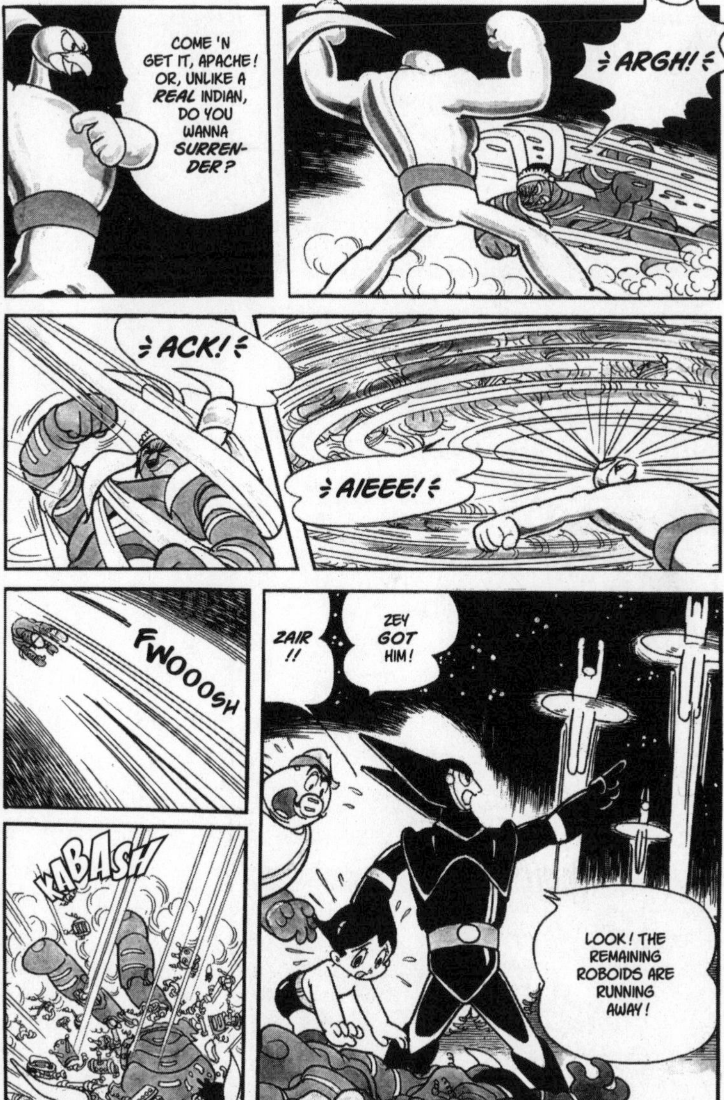
COME 'N GET IT, APACHE! OR, UNLIKE A REAL INDIAN, DO YOU WANNA SURREN-DER?
ARGH!
ACK!
AIEEE!
FWOOOOSH
KABASH
ZAIR !!
ZEY GOT HIM!
LOOK! THE REMAINING ROBOIDS ARE RUNNING AWAY!

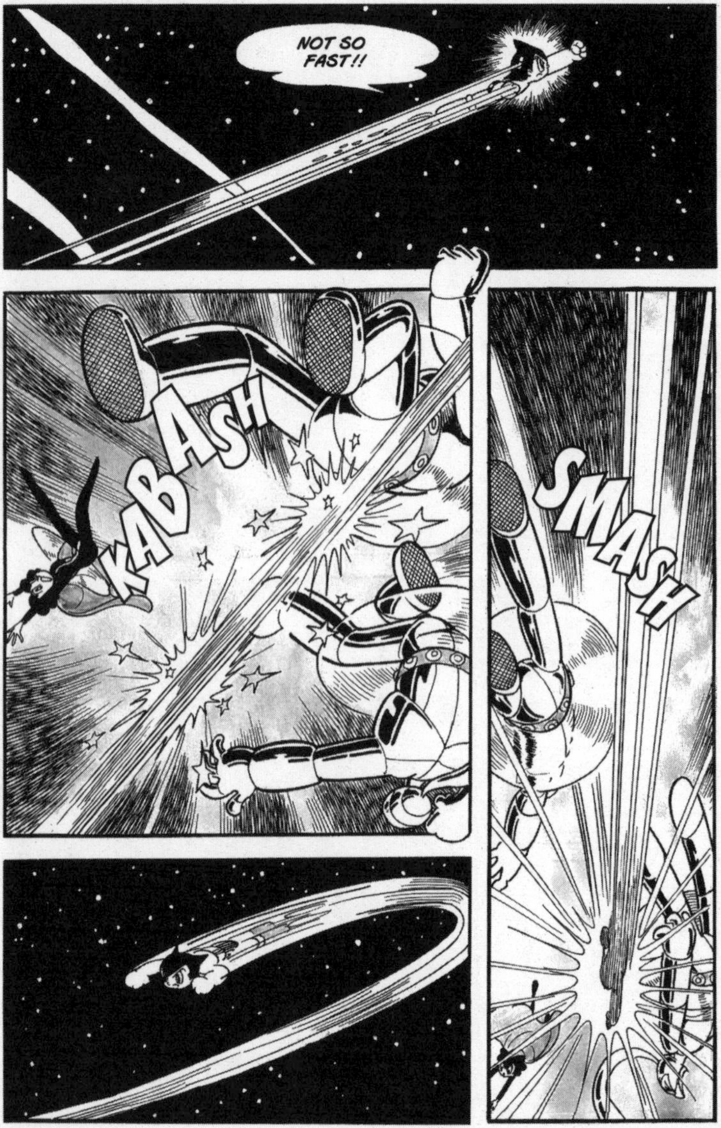
NOT SO FAST!!
KABASH
SMASH

I NOT GONNA LET YOU GET AWAY! I WANNA KNOW WHO YOU *REALLY* ARE!!

CAREFUL, OR YOU'LL GET WHAT YOU *ASK* FOR...

FWP

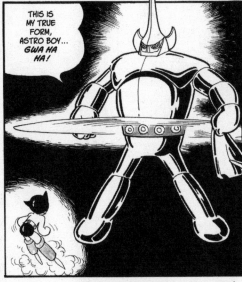
THIS IS MY TRUE FORM, ASTRO BOY... *GWA HA HA!*

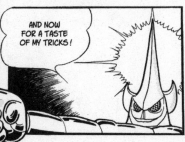
AND NOW FOR A TASTE OF MY TRICKS!

TAKE *THIS!*

287

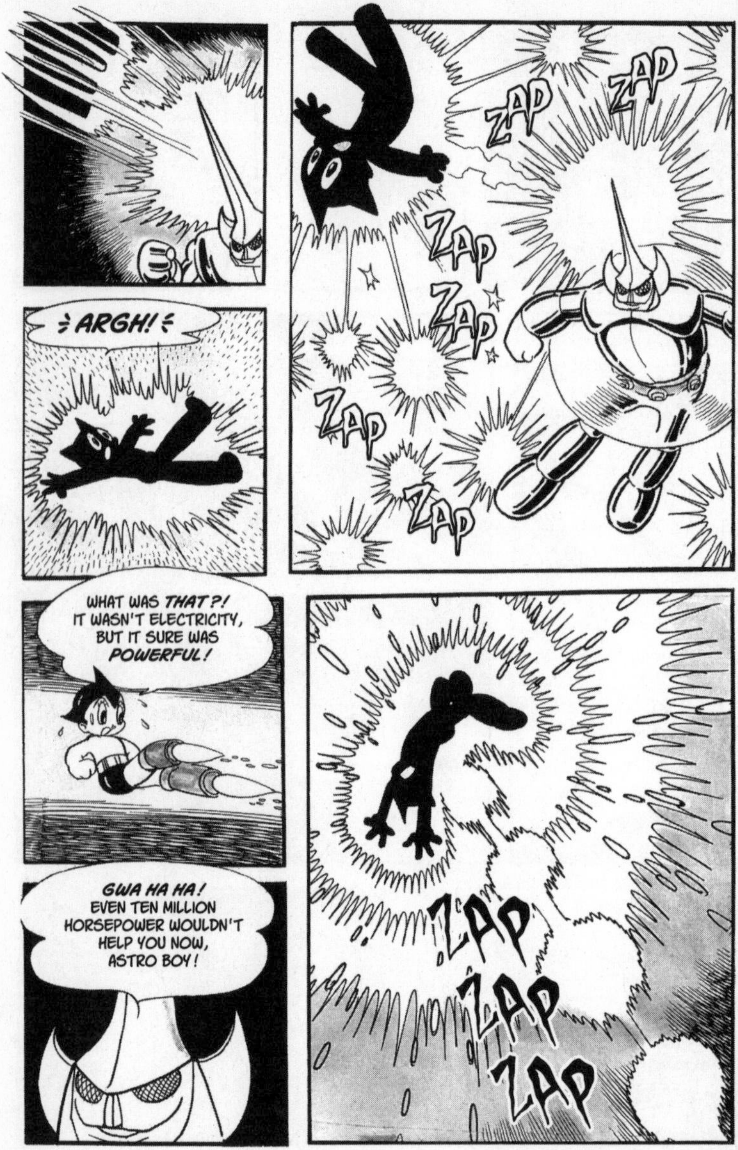
ARGH!
ZAP
ZAP
ZAP
ZAP
ZAP
ZAP
WHAT WAS THAT?! IT WASN'T ELECTRICITY, BUT IT SURE WAS POWERFUL!
GWA HA HA! EVEN TEN MILLION HORSEPOWER WOULDN'T HELP YOU NOW, ASTRO BOY!
ZAP
ZAP
ZAP

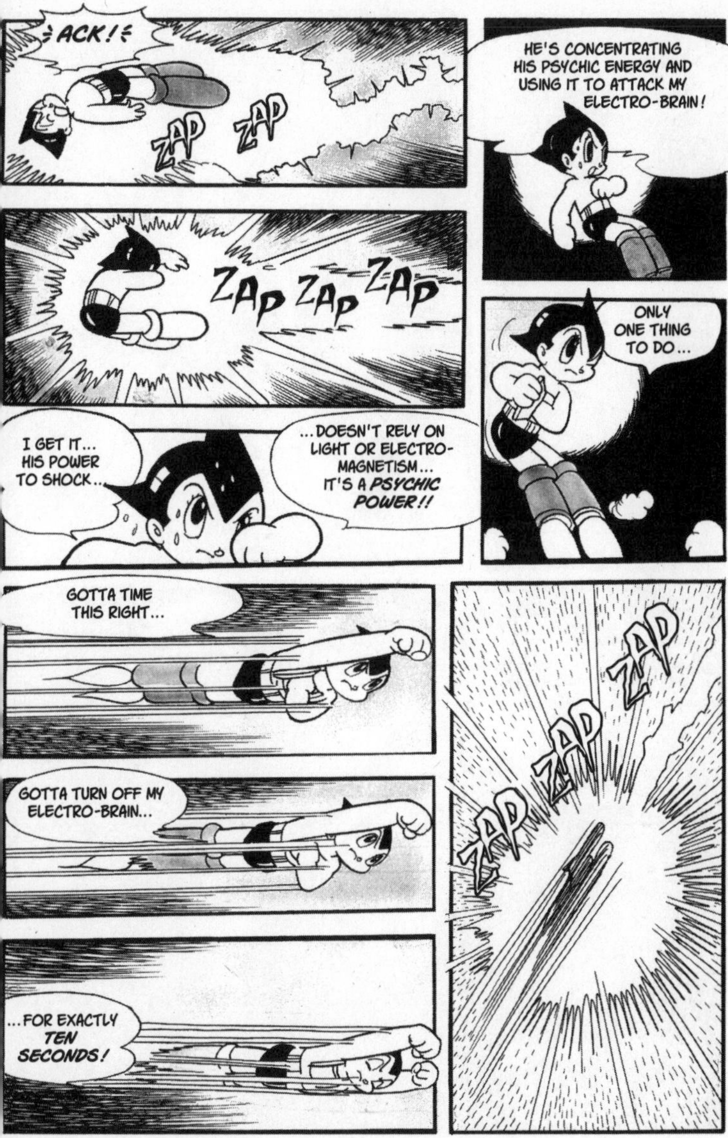
ACK!
ZAP ZAP
HE'S CONCENTRATING HIS PSYCHIC ENERGY AND USING IT TO ATTACK MY ELECTRO-BRAIN!
ZAP ZAP ZAP
ONLY ONE THING TO DO...
I GET IT... HIS POWER TO SHOCK...
...DOESN'T RELY ON LIGHT OR ELECTRO-MAGNETISM... IT'S A PSYCHIC POWER!!
GOTTA TIME THIS RIGHT...
GOTTA TURN OFF MY ELECTRO-BRAIN...
...FOR EXACTLY TEN SECONDS!
ZAP ZAP ZAP

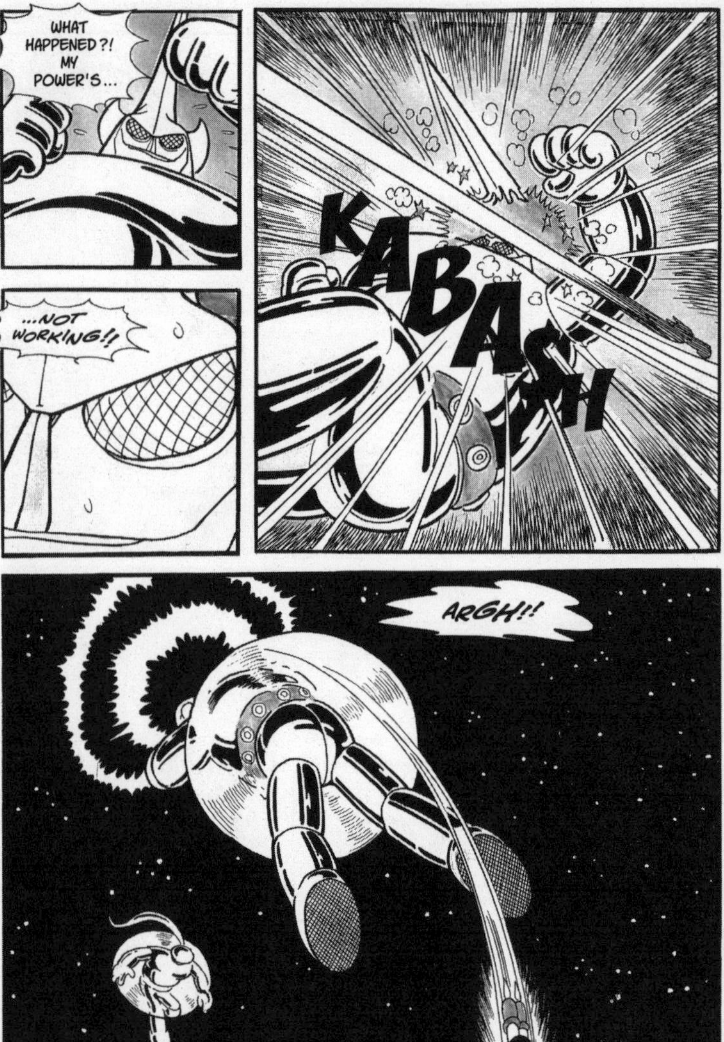
WHAT HAPPENED?! MY POWER'S...
...NOT WORKING!!
KABASH
ARGH!!

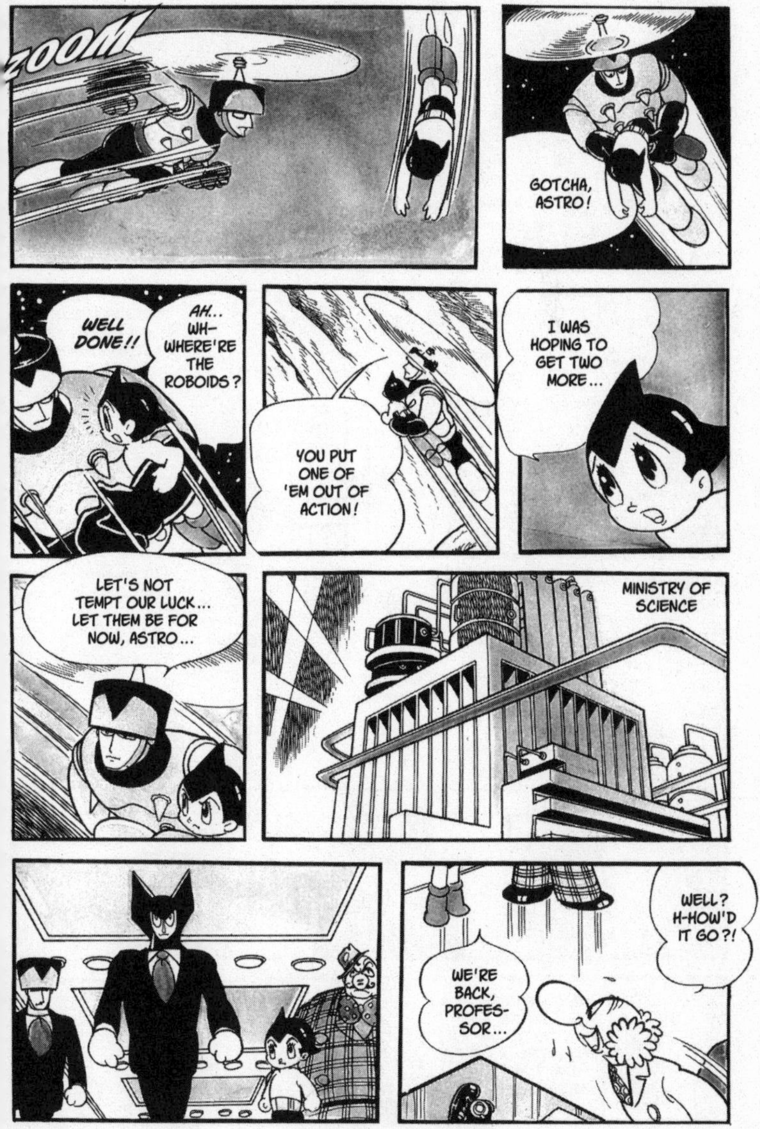
ZOOM
GOTCHA, ASTRO!
WELL DONE!!
AH... WH- WHERE'RE THE ROBOIDS?
YOU PUT ONE OF 'EM OUT OF ACTION!
I WAS HOPING TO GET TWO MORE...
LET'S NOT TEMPT OUR LUCK... LET THEM BE FOR NOW, ASTRO...
MINISTRY OF SCIENCE
WE'RE BACK, PROFES- SOR...
WELL? H-HOW'D IT GO?!

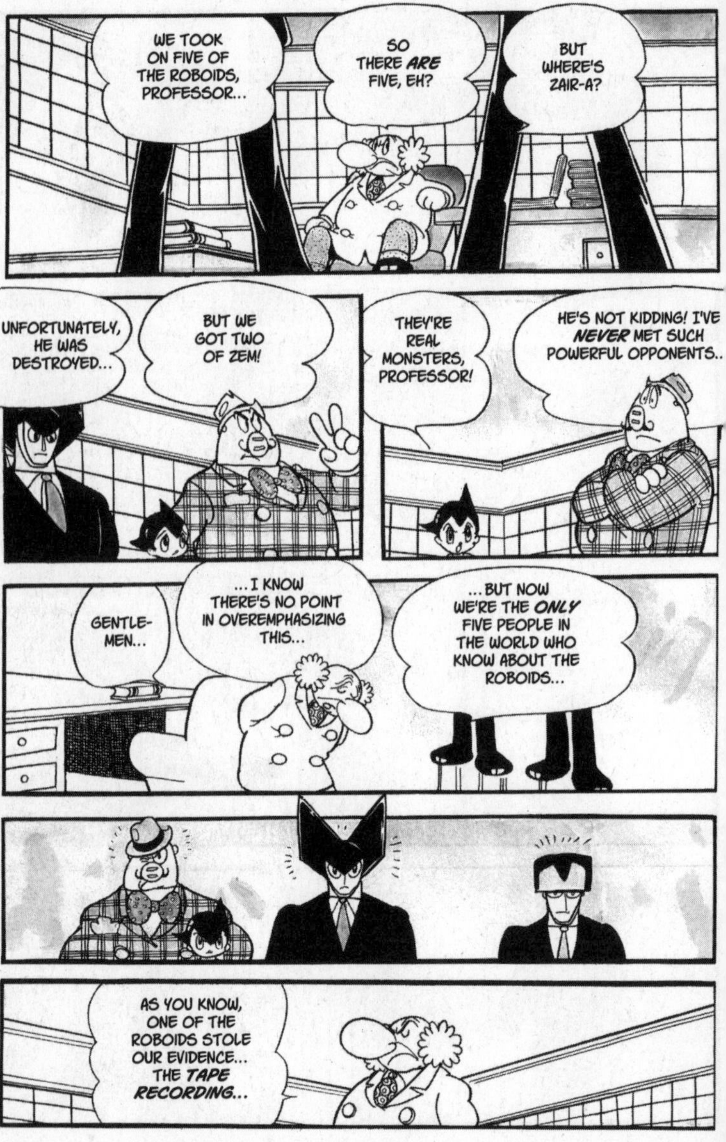
WE TOOK ON FIVE OF THE ROBOIDS, PROFESSOR...
SO THERE *ARE* FIVE, EH?
BUT WHERE'S ZAIR-A?
UNFORTUNATELY, HE WAS DESTROYED...
BUT WE GOT TWO OF ZEM!
THEY'RE REAL MONSTERS, PROFESSOR!
HE'S NOT KIDDING! I'VE *NEVER* MET SUCH POWERFUL OPPONENTS...
GENTLE-MEN...
...I KNOW THERE'S NO POINT IN OVEREMPHASIZING THIS...
...BUT NOW WE'RE THE *ONLY* FIVE PEOPLE IN THE WORLD WHO KNOW ABOUT THE ROBOIDS...
AS YOU KNOW, ONE OF THE ROBOIDS STOLE OUR EVIDENCE... THE *TAPE RECORDING*...

...AND WITHOUT IT, *NO ONE* WILL EVER BELIEVE ME ABOUT THE ROBOID THREAT!

SO THAT MEANS WE'VE GOTTA FIGHT ON *ALONE!*

I WANT TO KNOW WHO THESE ROBOIDS REALLY ARE...

...WHERE THEY'RE FROM, AND WHY THEY WANT TO DESTROY HUMANS!

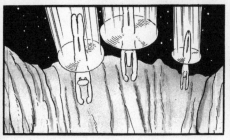

293

CHAK

FSSSH

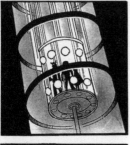

ROBOIDS 1, 3, AND 4 REPORTING!

AND WHAT OF 2 AND 5?

FSSSH

FSSSH

FSSSH

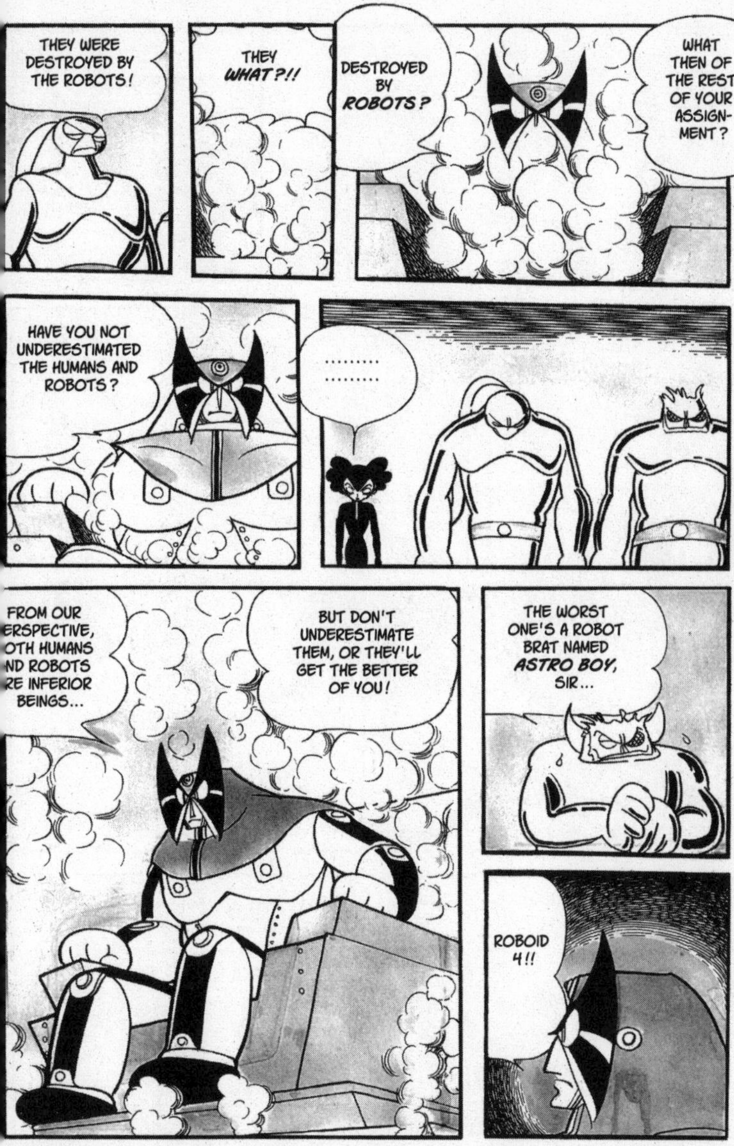
THEY WERE DESTROYED BY THE ROBOTS!
THEY WHAT?!!
DESTROYED BY ROBOTS?
WHAT THEN OF THE REST OF YOUR ASSIGNMENT?
HAVE YOU NOT UNDERESTIMATED THE HUMANS AND ROBOTS?
....
....
FROM OUR ERSPECTIVE, OTH HUMANS ND ROBOTS RE INFERIOR BEINGS...
BUT DON'T UNDERESTIMATE THEM, OR THEY'LL GET THE BETTER OF YOU!
THE WORST ONE'S A ROBOT BRAT NAMED ASTRO BOY, SIR...
ROBOID 4!!

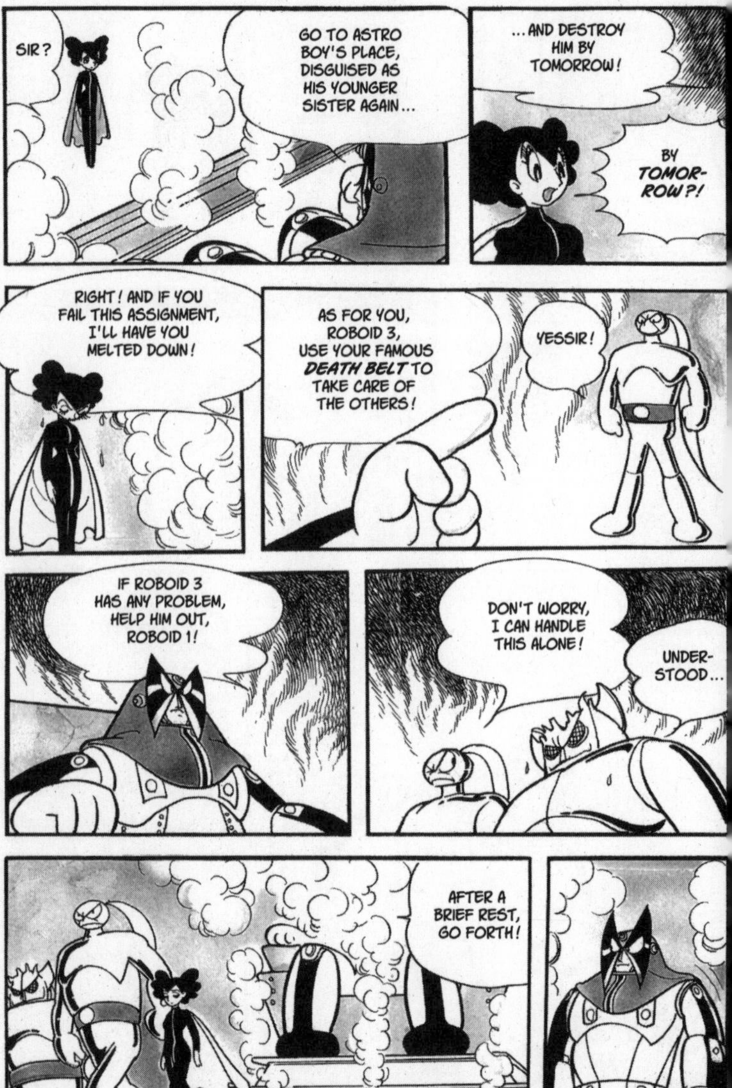
SIR?
GO TO ASTRO BOY'S PLACE, DISGUISED AS HIS YOUNGER SISTER AGAIN...
...AND DESTROY HIM BY TOMORROW!
BY TOMOR-ROW?!
RIGHT! AND IF YOU FAIL THIS ASSIGNMENT, I'LL HAVE YOU MELTED DOWN!
AS FOR YOU, ROBOID 3, USE YOUR FAMOUS DEATH BELT TO TAKE CARE OF THE OTHERS!
YESSIR!
IF ROBOID 3 HAS ANY PROBLEM, HELP HIM OUT, ROBOID 1!
DON'T WORRY, I CAN HANDLE THIS ALONE!
UNDER-STOOD...
AFTER A BRIEF REST, GO FORTH!

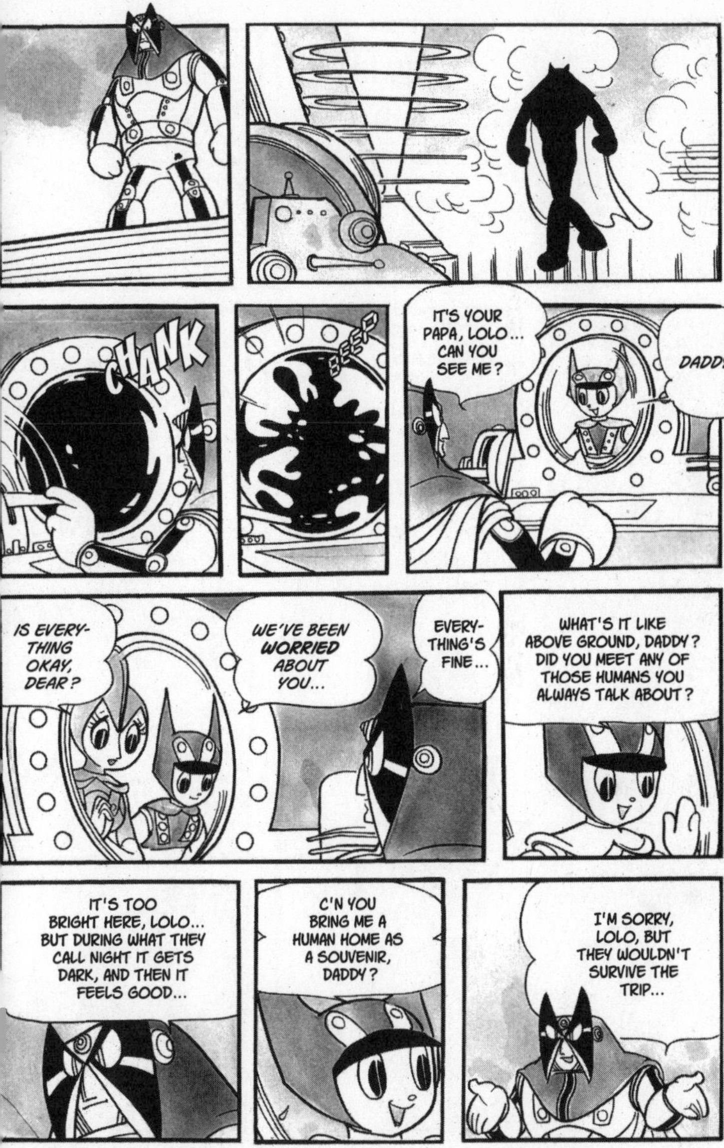
CHANK
BEEP
IT'S YOUR PAPA, LOLO... CAN YOU SEE ME?
DADDY!
IS EVERY-THING OKAY, DEAR?
WE'VE BEEN **WORRIED** ABOUT YOU...
EVERY-THING'S FINE...
WHAT'S IT LIKE ABOVE GROUND, DADDY? DID YOU MEET ANY OF THOSE HUMANS YOU ALWAYS TALK ABOUT?
IT'S TOO BRIGHT HERE, LOLO... BUT DURING WHAT THEY CALL NIGHT IT GETS DARK, AND THEN IT FEELS GOOD...
C'N YOU BRING ME A HUMAN HOME AS A SOUVENIR, DADDY?
I'M SORRY, LOLO, BUT THEY WOULDN'T SURVIVE THE TRIP...

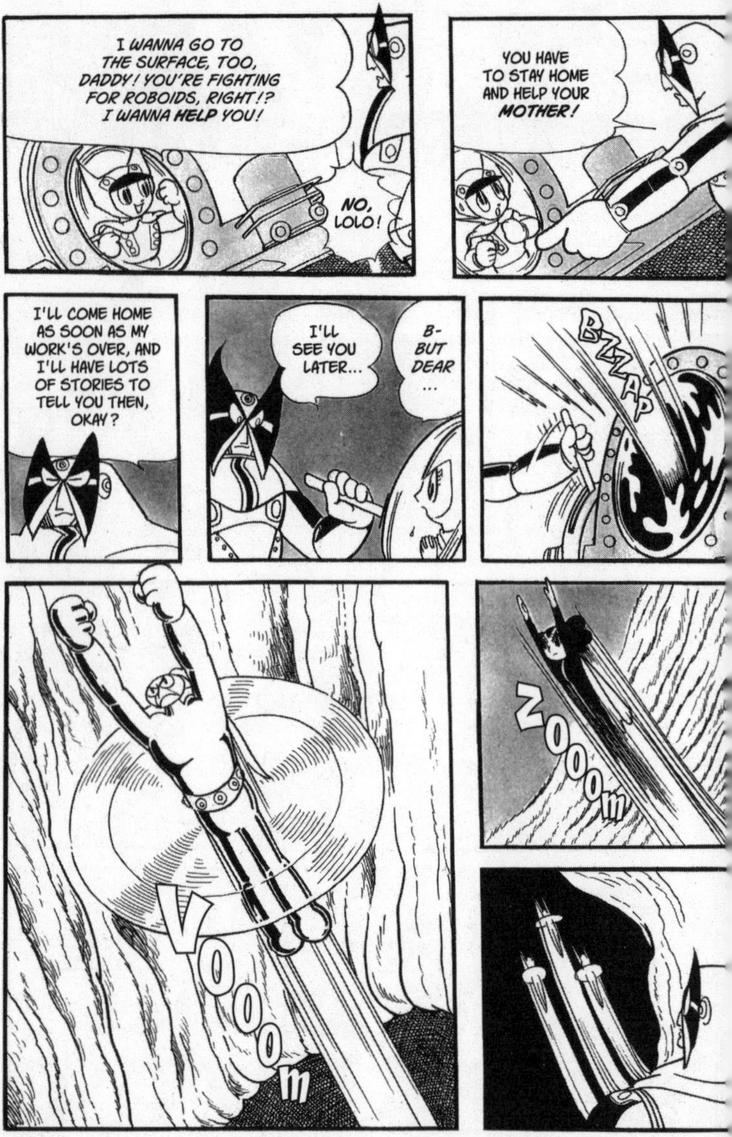
I WANNA GO TO THE SURFACE, TOO, DADDY! YOU'RE FIGHTING FOR ROBOIDS, RIGHT!? I WANNA HELP YOU!
NO, LOLO!
YOU HAVE TO STAY HOME AND HELP YOUR MOTHER!
I'LL COME HOME AS SOON AS MY WORK'S OVER, AND I'LL HAVE LOTS OF STORIES TO TELL YOU THEN, OKAY?
I'LL SEE YOU LATER...
B-BUT DEAR ...
BZZZAP
VOOOOm
ZOOOOm

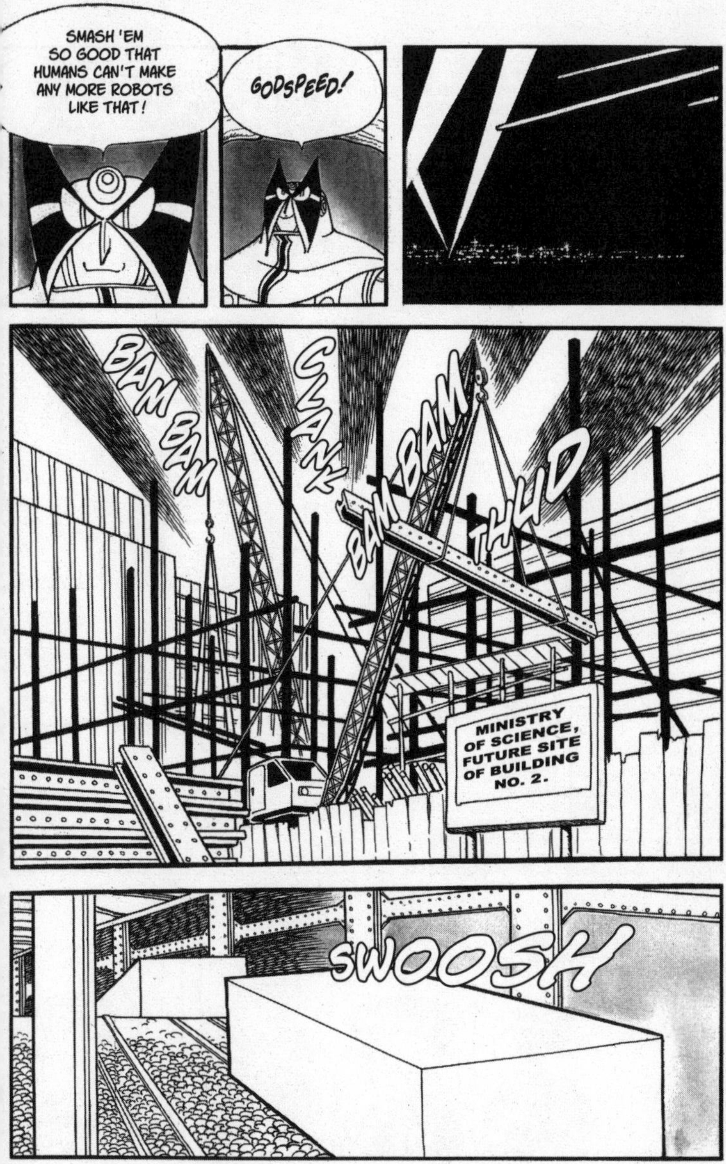
SMASH 'EM SO GOOD THAT HUMANS CAN'T MAKE ANY MORE ROBOTS LIKE THAT!
GODSPEED!
BAM BAM
CLANK
BAM BAM
BAM
THUD
MINISTRY OF SCIENCE, FUTURE SITE OF BUILDING NO. 2.
SWOOSH

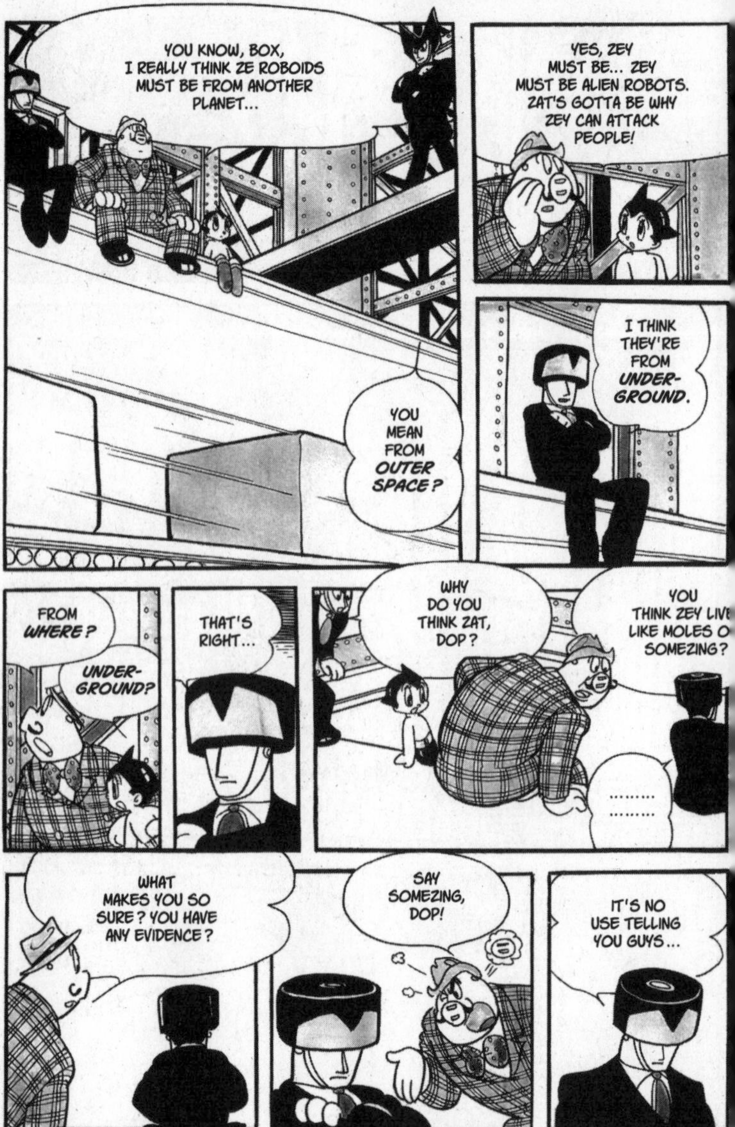

YOU KNOW, BOX, I REALLY THINK ZE ROBOIDS MUST BE FROM ANOTHER PLANET...
YOU MEAN FROM OUTER SPACE?
YES, ZEY MUST BE... ZEY MUST BE ALIEN ROBOTS. ZAT'S GOTTA BE WHY ZEY CAN ATTACK PEOPLE!
I THINK THEY'RE FROM UNDER-GROUND.
FROM WHERE?
UNDER-GROUND?
THAT'S RIGHT...
WHY DO YOU THINK ZAT, DOP?
YOU THINK ZEY LIVE LIKE MOLES OR SOMEZING?
....
....
WHAT MAKES YOU SO SURE? YOU HAVE ANY EVIDENCE?
SAY SOMEZING, DOP!
IT'S NO USE TELLING YOU GUYS...

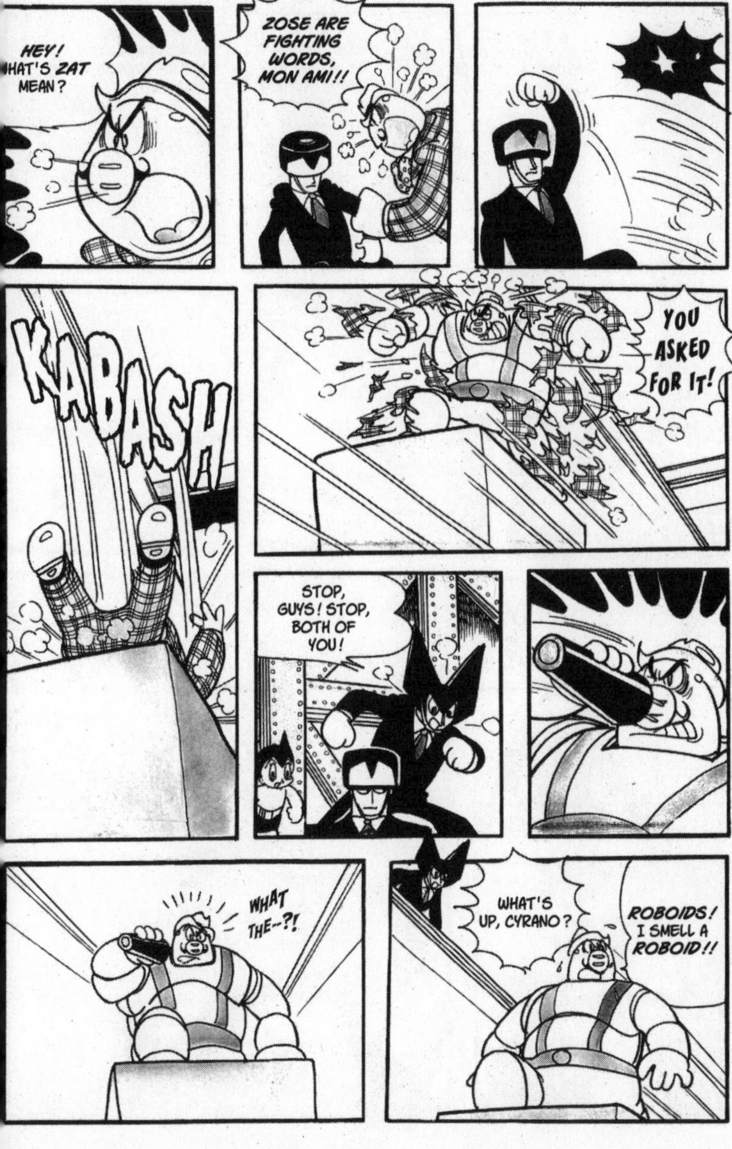
HEY! WHAT'S ZAT MEAN?
ZOSE ARE FIGHTING WORDS, MON AMI!!
KABASH
YOU ASKED FOR IT!
STOP, GUYS! STOP, BOTH OF YOU!
WHAT THE--?!
WHAT'S UP, CYRANO?
ROBOIDS! I SMELL A ROBOID!!

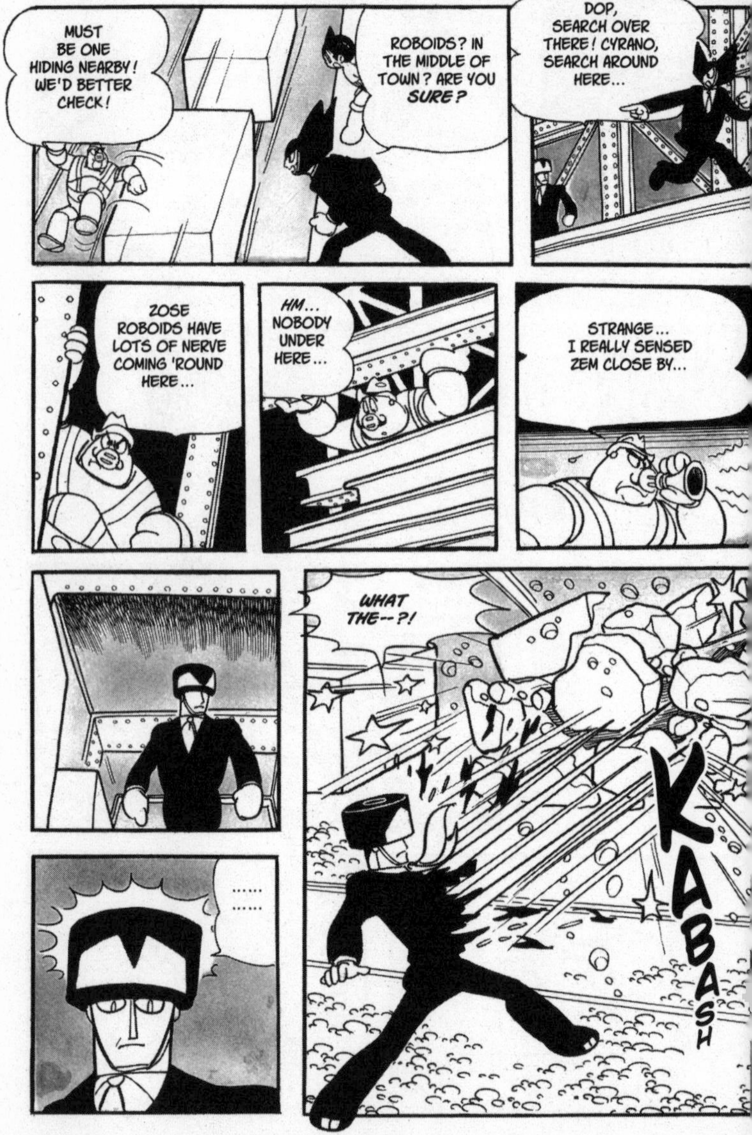
MUST BE ONE HIDING NEARBY! WE'D BETTER CHECK!
ROBOIDS? IN THE MIDDLE OF TOWN? ARE YOU SURE?
DOP, SEARCH OVER THERE! CYRANO, SEARCH AROUND HERE...
ZOSE ROBOIDS HAVE LOTS OF NERVE COMING 'ROUND HERE...
HM... NOBODY UNDER HERE...
STRANGE... I REALLY SENSED ZEM CLOSE BY...
WHAT THE--?!
KABASH
......
......

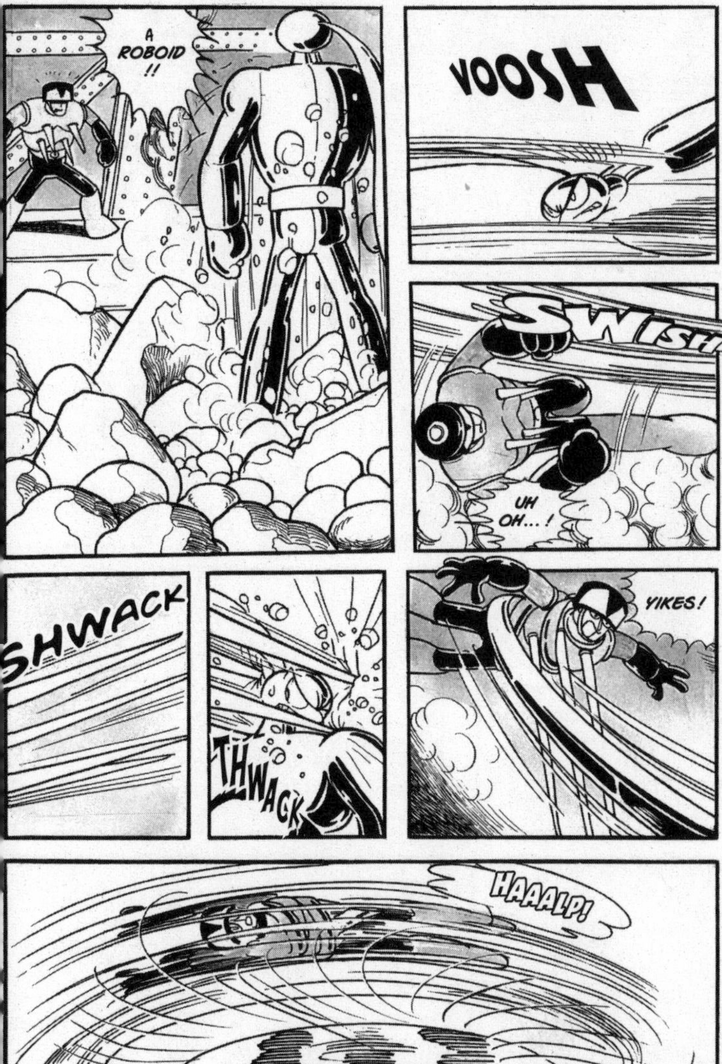
A ROBOID !!
VOOSH
SWISH
UH OH... !
SHWACK
THWACK
YIKES!
HAAALP!

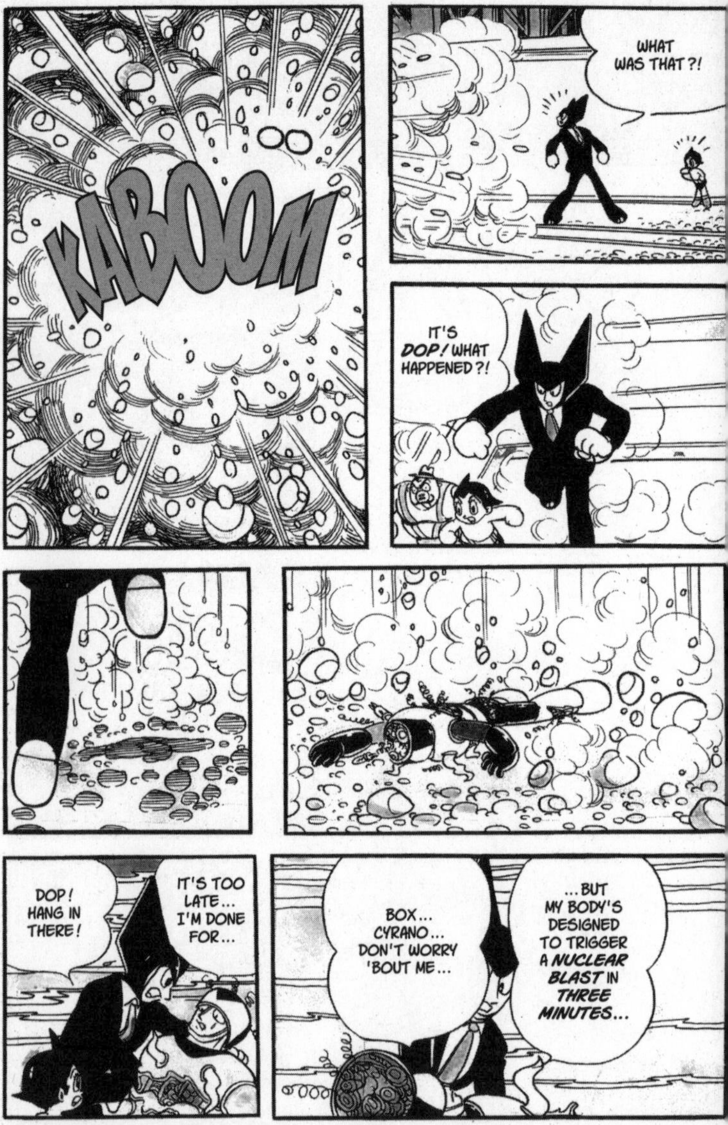
KABOOM
WHAT WAS THAT?!
IT'S DOP! WHAT HAPPENED?!
DOP! HANG IN THERE!
IT'S TOO LATE... I'M DONE FOR...
BOX... CYRANO... DON'T WORRY 'BOUT ME...
...BUT MY BODY'S DESIGNED TO TRIGGER A NUCLEAR BLAST IN THREE MINUTES...

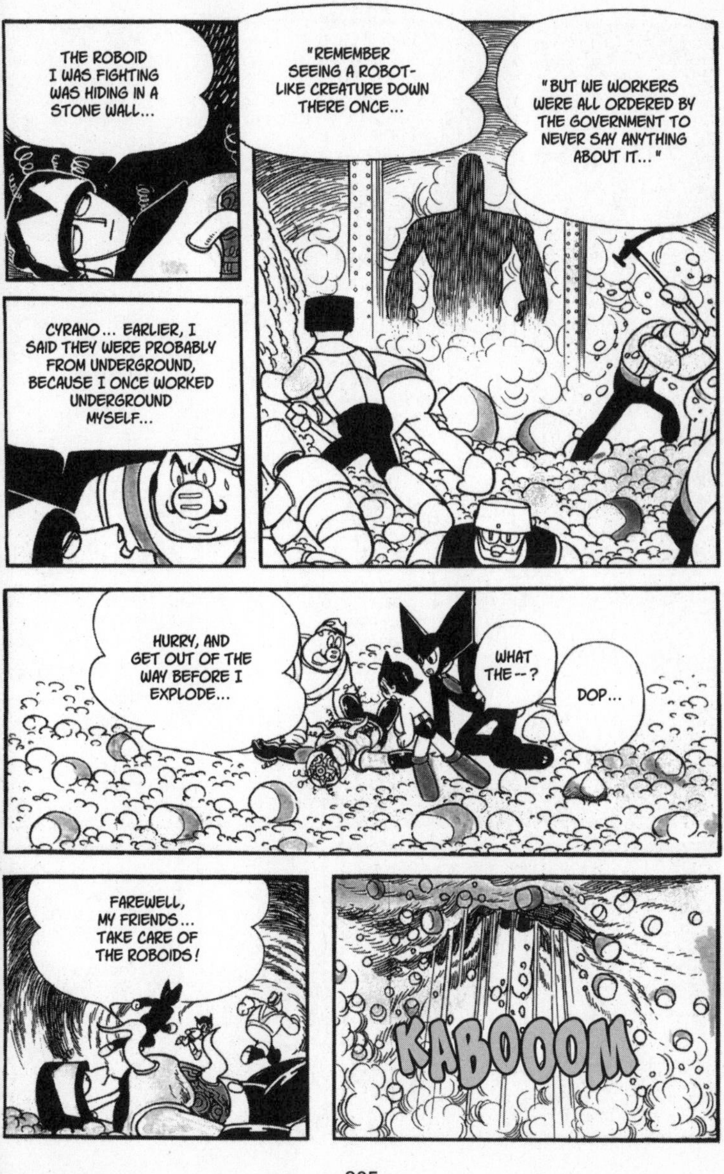
THE ROBOID I WAS FIGHTING WAS HIDING IN A STONE WALL...
"REMEMBER SEEING A ROBOT-LIKE CREATURE DOWN THERE ONCE...
"BUT WE WORKERS WERE ALL ORDERED BY THE GOVERNMENT TO NEVER SAY ANYTHING ABOUT IT..."
CYRANO... EARLIER, I SAID THEY WERE PROBABLY FROM UNDERGROUND, BECAUSE I ONCE WORKED UNDERGROUND MYSELF...
HURRY, AND GET OUT OF THE WAY BEFORE I EXPLODE...
WHAT THE--?
DOP...
FAREWELL, MY FRIENDS... TAKE CARE OF THE ROBOIDS!
KABOOOM

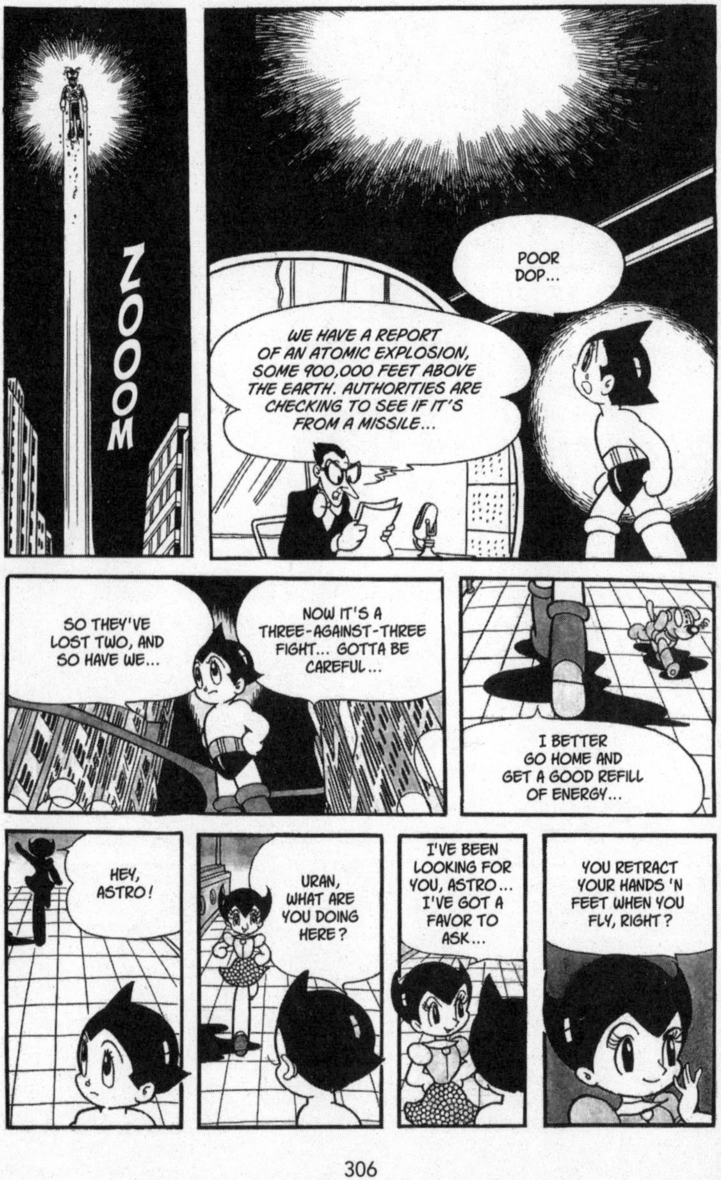
ZOOOM
POOR DOP...
WE HAVE A REPORT OF AN ATOMIC EXPLOSION, SOME 900,000 FEET ABOVE THE EARTH. AUTHORITIES ARE CHECKING TO SEE IF IT'S FROM A MISSILE...
SO THEY'VE LOST TWO, AND SO HAVE WE...
NOW IT'S A THREE-AGAINST-THREE FIGHT... GOTTA BE CAREFUL...
I BETTER GO HOME AND GET A GOOD REFILL OF ENERGY...
HEY, ASTRO!
URAN, WHAT ARE YOU DOING HERE?
I'VE BEEN LOOKING FOR YOU, ASTRO... I'VE GOT A FAVOR TO ASK...
YOU RETRACT YOUR HANDS 'N FEET WHEN YOU FLY, RIGHT?

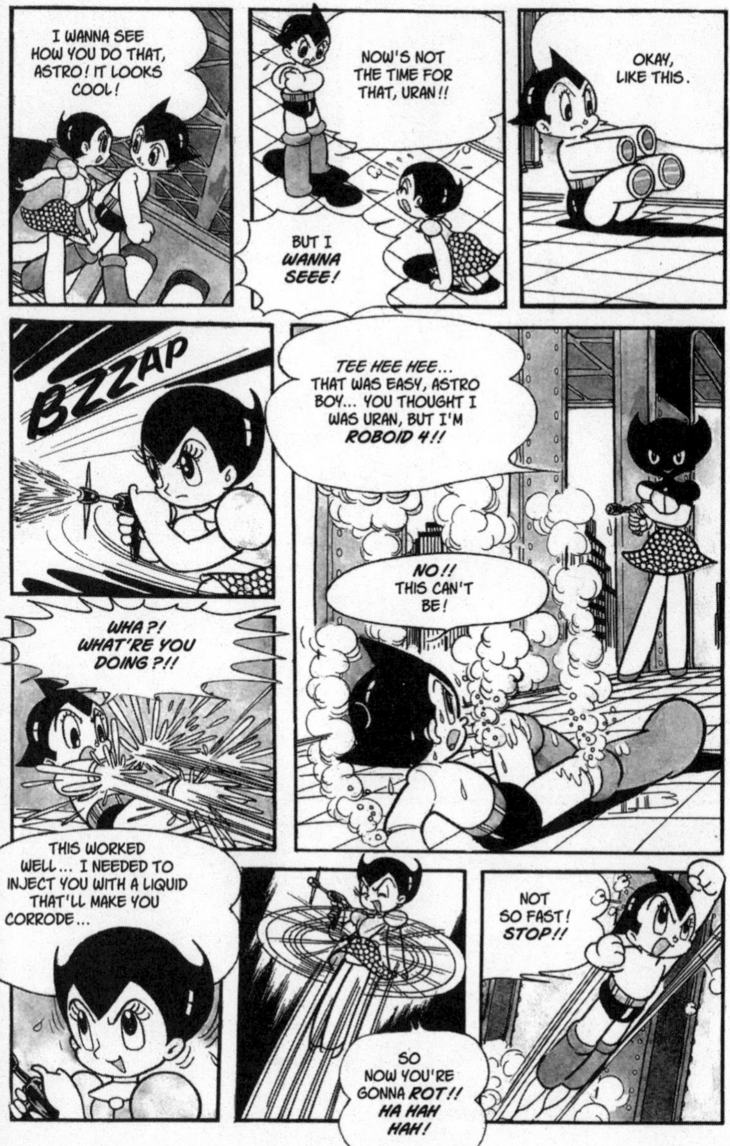
I WANNA SEE HOW YOU DO THAT, ASTRO! IT LOOKS COOL!
NOW'S NOT THE TIME FOR THAT, URAN!!
BUT I WANNA SEEE!
OKAY, LIKE THIS.
BZZAP
TEE HEE HEE... THAT WAS EASY, ASTRO BOY... YOU THOUGHT I WAS URAN, BUT I'M ROBOID 4!!
NO!! THIS CAN'T BE!
WHA?! WHAT'RE YOU DOING?!!
THIS WORKED WELL... I NEEDED TO INJECT YOU WITH A LIQUID THAT'LL MAKE YOU CORRODE...
SO NOW YOU'RE GONNA ROT!! HA HAH HAH!
NOT SO FAST! STOP!!

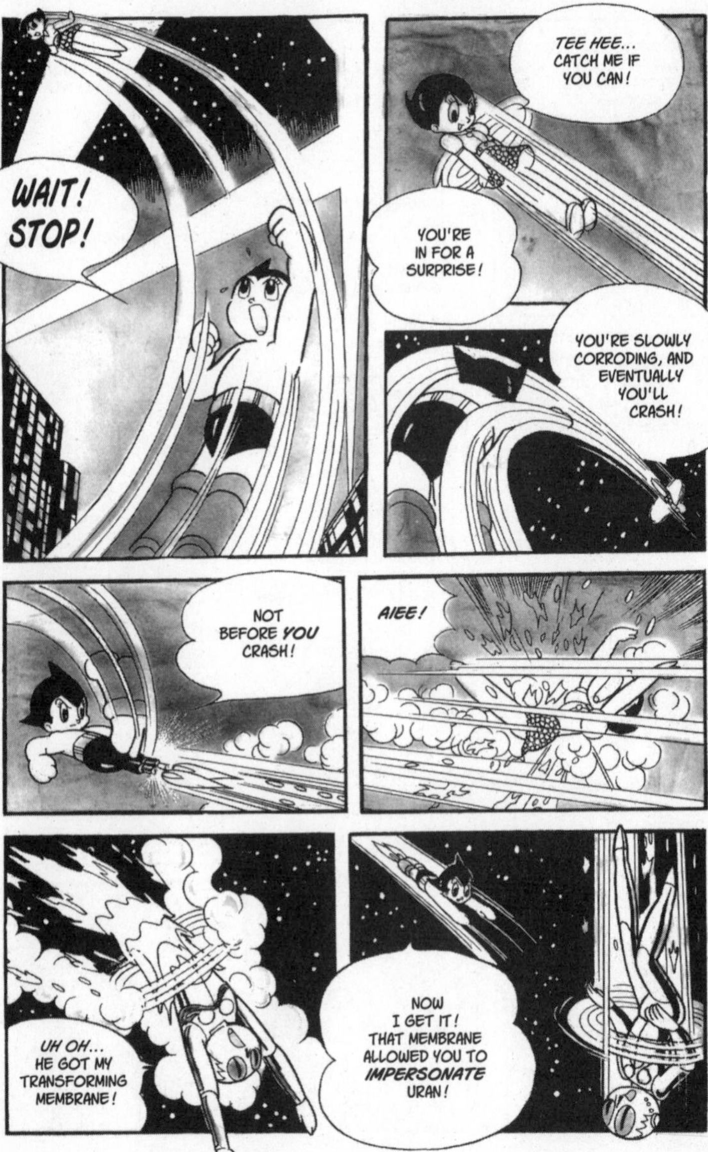
WAIT! STOP!
TEE HEE... CATCH ME IF YOU CAN!
YOU'RE IN FOR A SURPRISE!
YOU'RE SLOWLY CORRODING, AND EVENTUALLY YOU'LL CRASH!
NOT BEFORE *YOU* CRASH!
AIEE!
UH OH... HE GOT MY TRANSFORMING MEMBRANE!
NOW I GET IT! THAT MEMBRANE ALLOWED YOU TO *IMPERSONATE* URAN!

BEEP
BEEP
BEEP
BEEP

ROAR

NO! I'M BEING HIT WITH SOMETHING WEIRD!

FWOOOMP

THESE ARE NAILS!

... AND THEY'RE ALL *MAGNETIZED!*

≶ACK≶, I'M BEING PULLED!

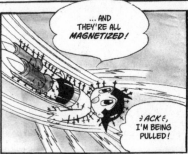

SMACK

HEE HEE... ALL THOSE MAGNETIZED NAILS HAVE NAILED YOU TO AN IRON BEAM!!

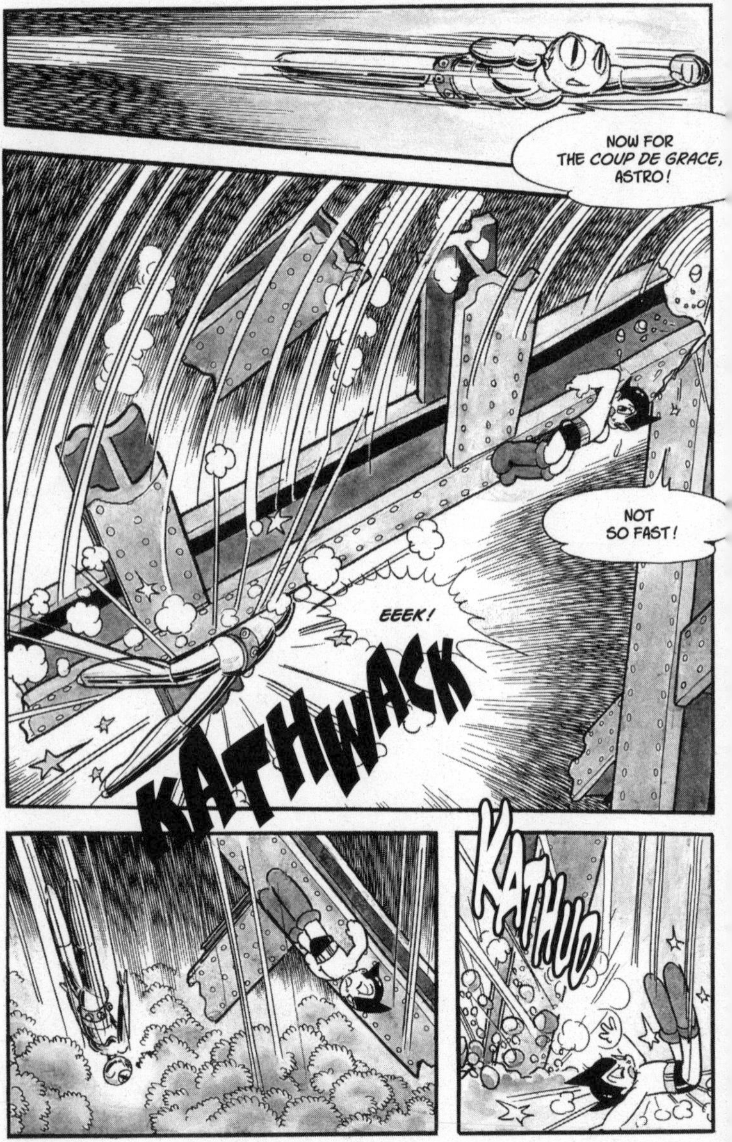
NOW FOR THE COUP DE GRACE, ASTRO!
NOT SO FAST!
EEEK!
KATHWACK
KATHUD

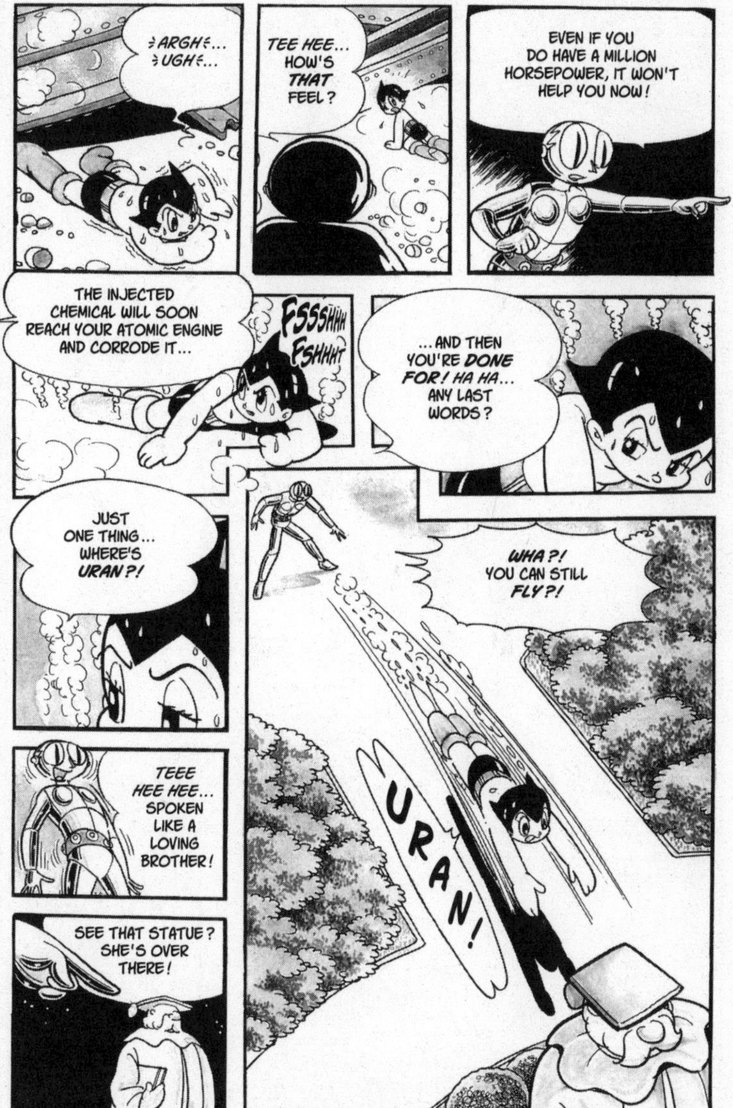

ARGH... UGH...
TEE HEE... HOW'S THAT FEEL?
EVEN IF YOU DO HAVE A MILLION HORSEPOWER, IT WON'T HELP YOU NOW!
THE INJECTED CHEMICAL WILL SOON REACH YOUR ATOMIC ENGINE AND CORRODE IT...
FSSSHHH FSHHHT
...AND THEN YOU'RE DONE FOR! HA HA... ANY LAST WORDS?
JUST ONE THING... WHERE'S URAN?!
WHA?! YOU CAN STILL FLY?!
TEEE HEE HEE... SPOKEN LIKE A LOVING BROTHER!
SEE THAT STATUE? SHE'S OVER THERE!
URAN!

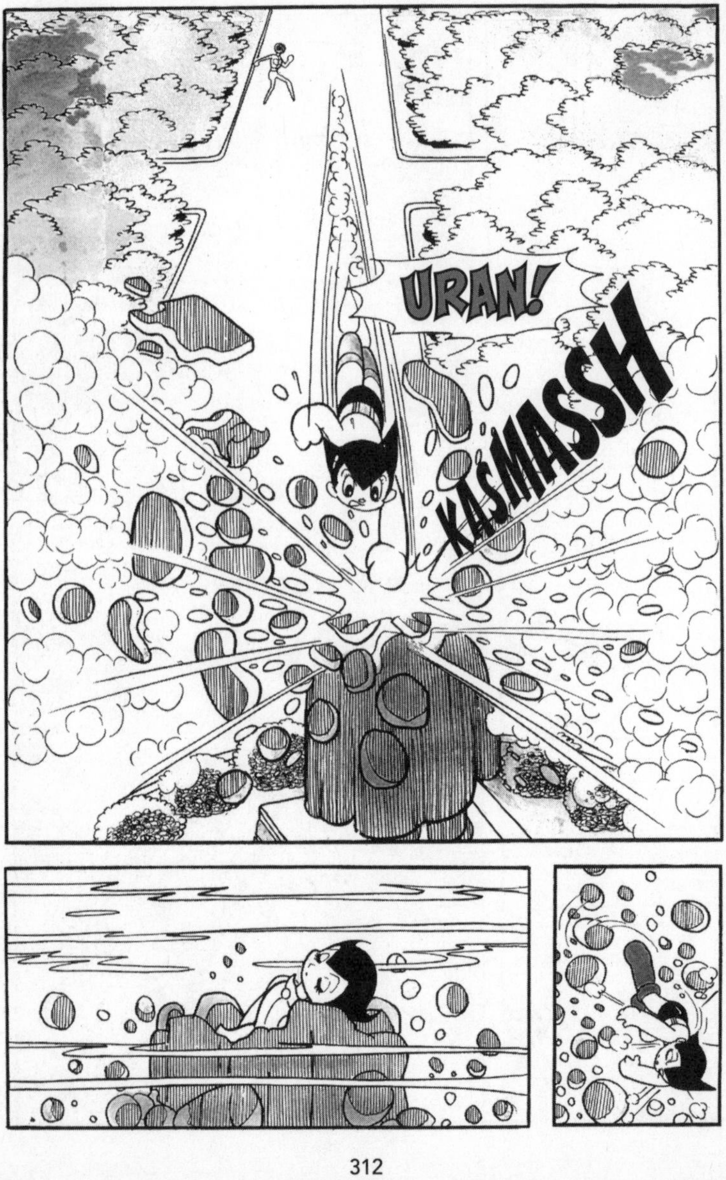
URAN!
KASMASH

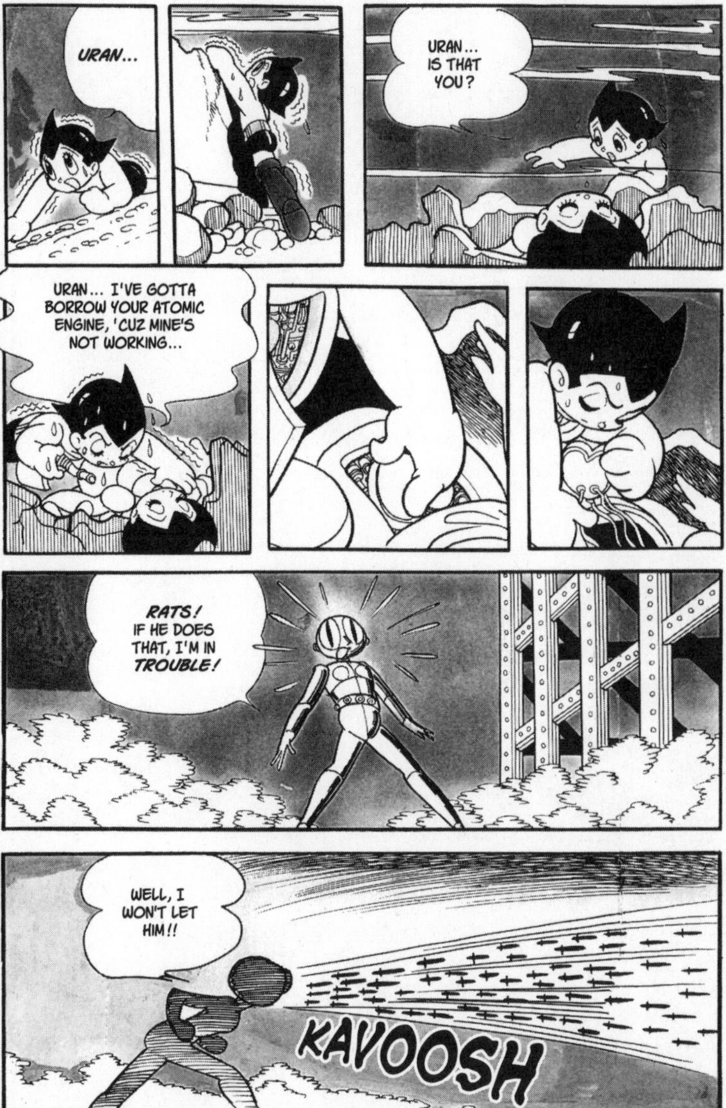
URAN...
URAN... IS THAT YOU?
URAN... I'VE GOTTA BORROW YOUR ATOMIC ENGINE, 'CUZ MINE'S NOT WORKING...
RATS! IF HE DOES THAT, I'M IN TROUBLE!
WELL, I WON'T LET HIM!!
KAVOOSH

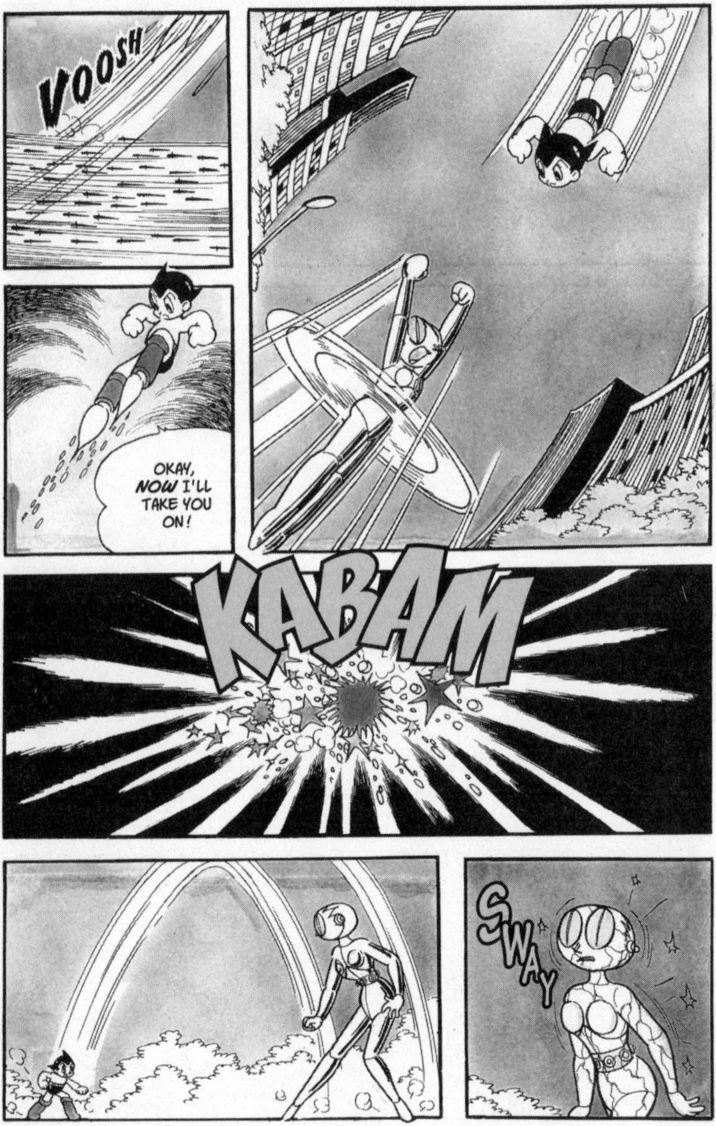
VOOSH
OKAY, NOW I'LL TAKE YOU ON!
KABAM
SWAY

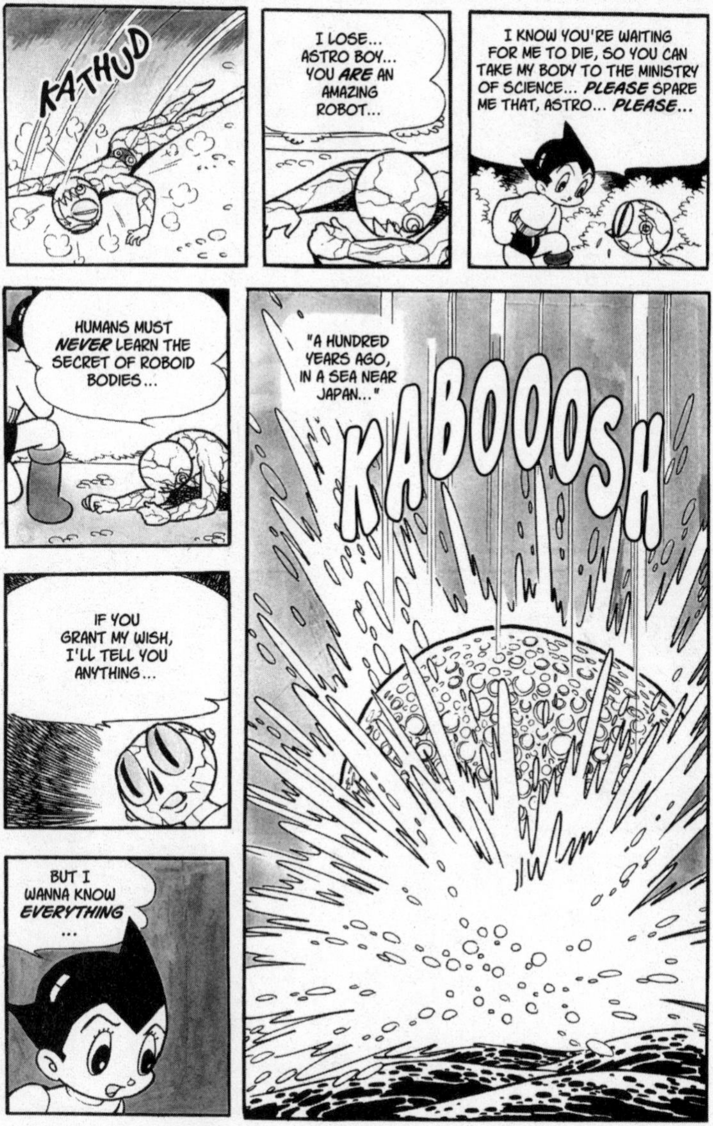
KATHUD
I LOSE... ASTRO BOY... YOU ARE AN AMAZING ROBOT...
I KNOW YOU'RE WAITING FOR ME TO DIE, SO YOU CAN TAKE MY BODY TO THE MINISTRY OF SCIENCE... PLEASE SPARE ME THAT, ASTRO... PLEASE...
HUMANS MUST NEVER LEARN THE SECRET OF ROBOID BODIES...
IF YOU GRANT MY WISH, I'LL TELL YOU ANYTHING...
BUT I WANNA KNOW EVERYTHING ...
"A HUNDRED YEARS AGO, IN A SEA NEAR JAPAN..."
KABOOOSH

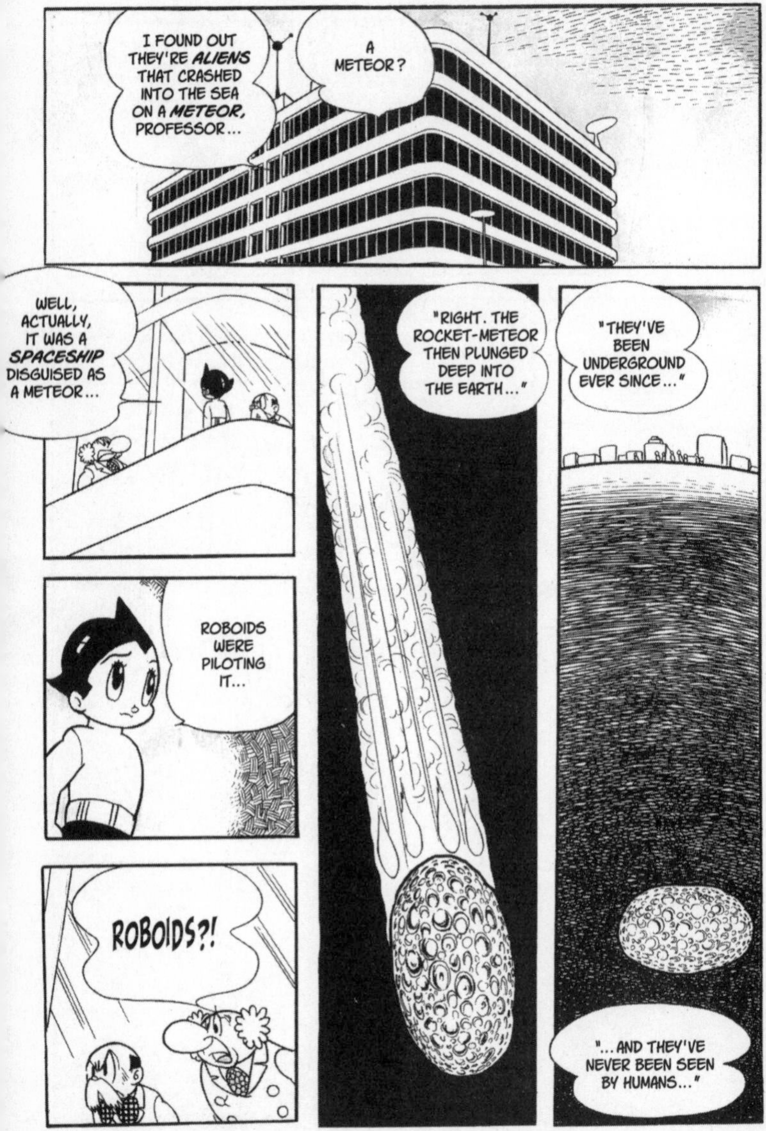
I FOUND OUT THEY'RE *ALIENS* THAT CRASHED INTO THE SEA ON A *METEOR,* PROFESSOR...
A METEOR?
WELL, ACTUALLY, IT WAS A *SPACESHIP* DISGUISED AS A METEOR...
ROBOIDS WERE PILOTING IT...
ROBOIDS?!
"RIGHT. THE ROCKET-METEOR THEN PLUNGED DEEP INTO THE EARTH..."
"THEY'VE BEEN UNDERGROUND EVER SINCE..."
"...AND THEY'VE NEVER BEEN SEEN BY HUMANS..."

B-BUT WHERE'RE ZE ROBOIDS REALLY FROM?

WELL, ON A CERTAIN STAR...

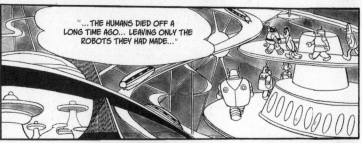

"...THE HUMANS DIED OFF A LONG TIME AGO... LEAVING ONLY THE ROBOTS THEY HAD MADE..."

"THE ROBOTS KEPT MAKING NEW ROBOTS, AND *EVOLVING*..."

THEY WERE BORN AND DIED, JUST LIKE HUMANS, AND THEY COULD APPARENTLY HAVE *CHILDREN*, TOO...

ROBOTS HAVING CHILDREN? *HAH!* I'LL BELIEVE IT WHEN I SEE IT!

317

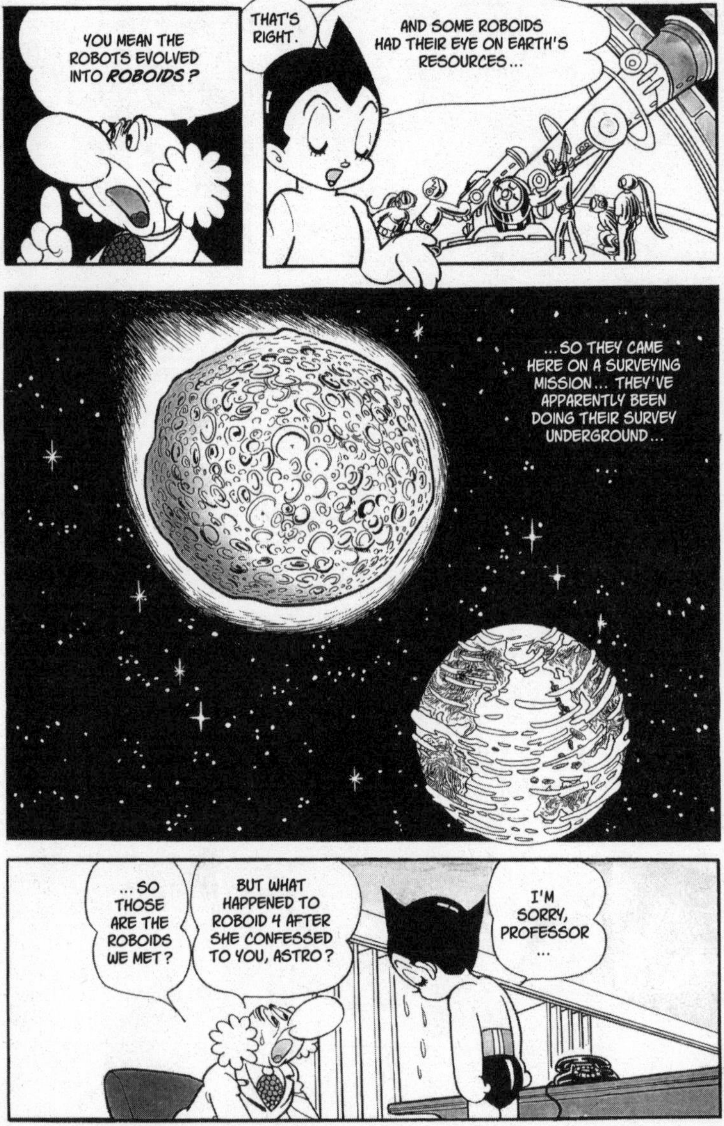
YOU MEAN THE ROBOTS EVOLVED INTO ROBOIDS?
THAT'S RIGHT.
AND SOME ROBOIDS HAD THEIR EYE ON EARTH'S RESOURCES...
...SO THEY CAME HERE ON A SURVEYING MISSION... THEY'VE APPARENTLY BEEN DOING THEIR SURVEY UNDERGROUND...
...SO THOSE ARE THE ROBOIDS WE MET?
BUT WHAT HAPPENED TO ROBOID 4 AFTER SHE CONFESSED TO YOU, ASTRO?
I'M SORRY, PROFESSOR ...

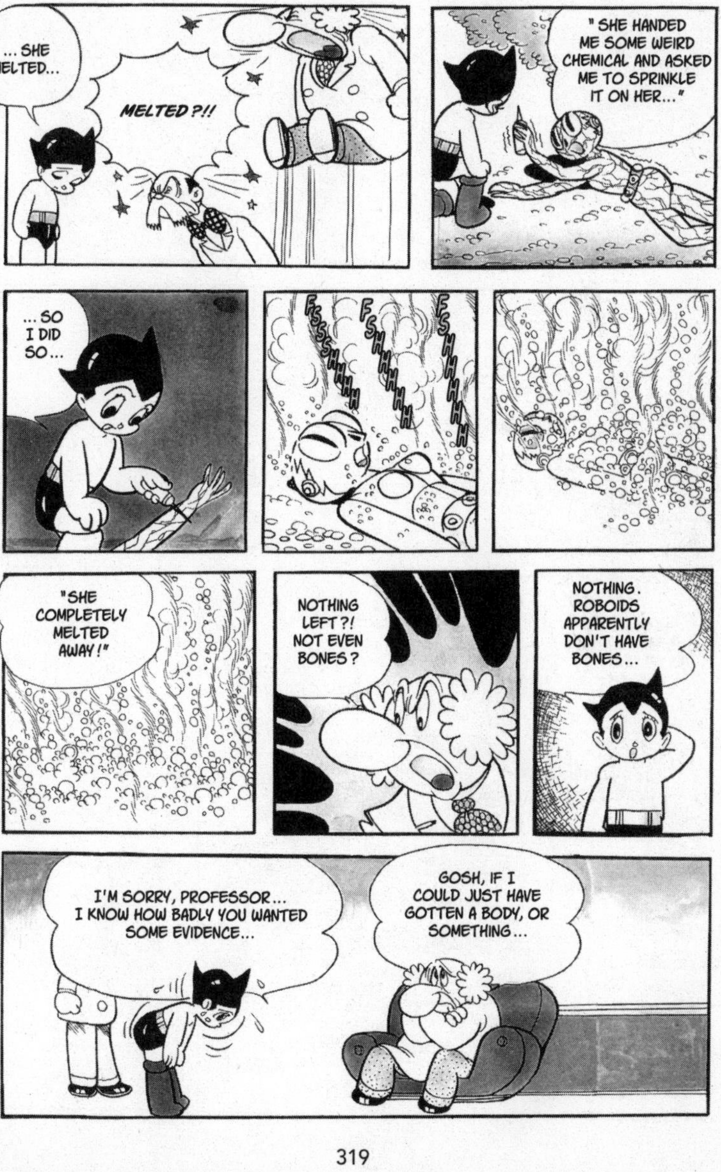
...SHE MELTED...
MELTED?!!
"SHE HANDED ME SOME WEIRD CHEMICAL AND ASKED ME TO SPRINKLE IT ON HER..."
...SO I DID SO...
FSSSHHHH
FSHHHHHH
FSHHHHHHH
"SHE COMPLETELY MELTED AWAY!"
NOTHING LEFT?! NOT EVEN BONES?
NOTHING. ROBOIDS APPARENTLY DON'T HAVE BONES...
I'M SORRY, PROFESSOR... I KNOW HOW BADLY YOU WANTED SOME EVIDENCE...
GOSH, IF I COULD JUST HAVE GOTTEN A BODY, OR SOMETHING...

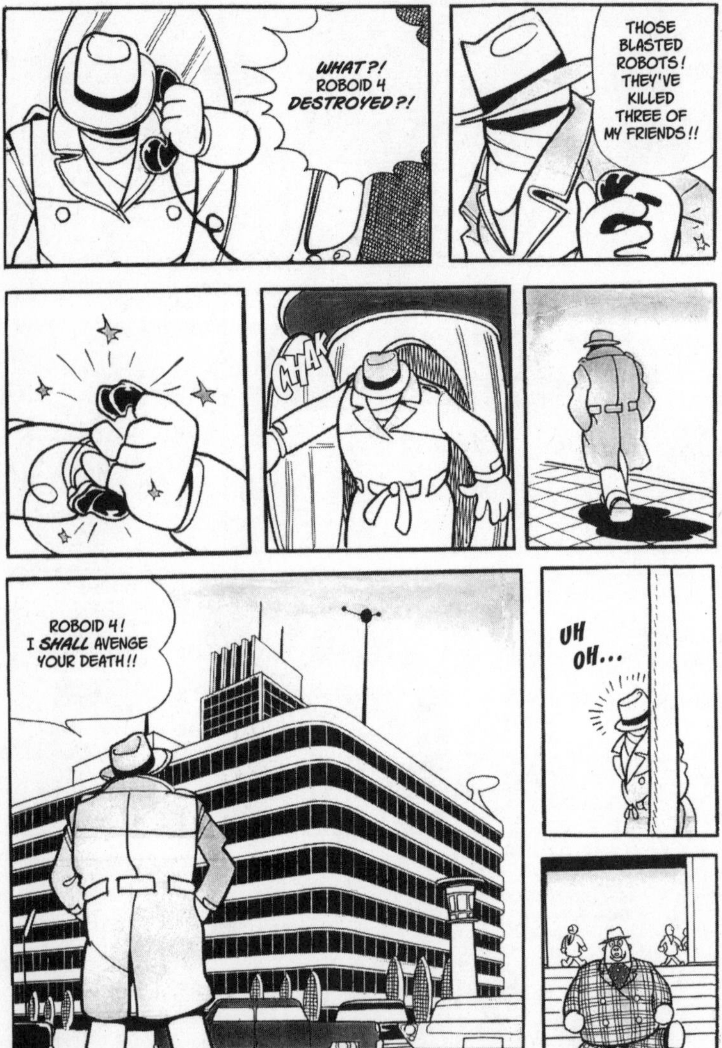
WHAT?! ROBOID 4 DESTROYED?!
THOSE BLASTED ROBOTS! THEY'VE KILLED THREE OF MY FRIENDS!!
CHAK
ROBOID 4! I SHALL AVENGE YOUR DEATH!!
UH OH...

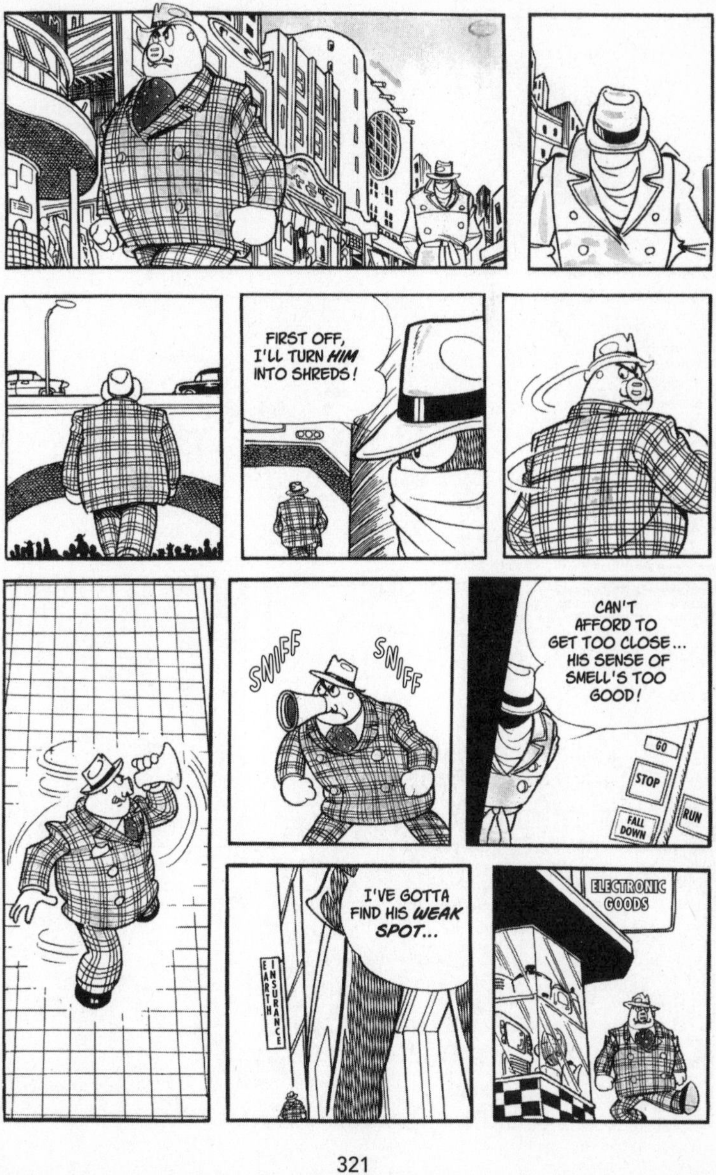
FIRST OFF, I'LL TURN *HIM* INTO SHREDS!
SNIFF
SNIFF
CAN'T AFFORD TO GET TOO CLOSE... HIS SENSE OF SMELL'S TOO GOOD!
GO
STOP
RUN
FALL DOWN
I'VE GOTTA FIND HIS *WEAK* *SPOT*...
EARTH INSURANCE
ELECTRONIC GOODS

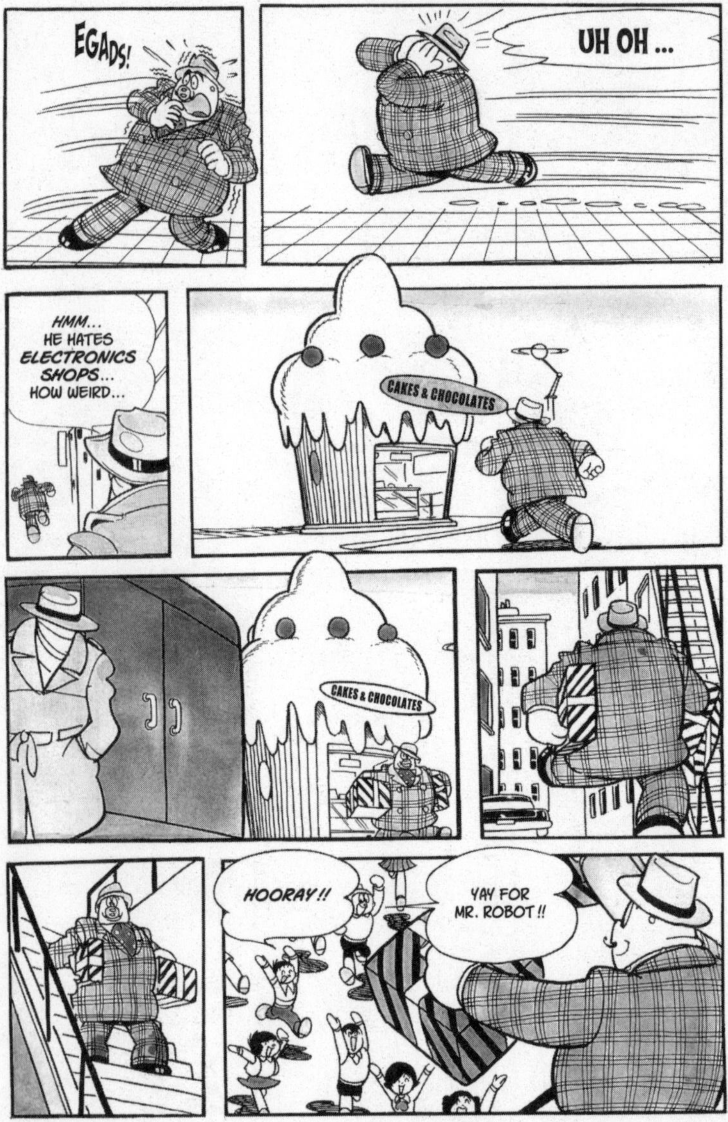
EGADS!
UH OH ...
HMM... HE HATES ELECTRONICS SHOPS... HOW WEIRD...
CAKES & CHOCOLATES
CAKES & CHOCOLATES
HOORAY!!
YAY FOR MR. ROBOT!!

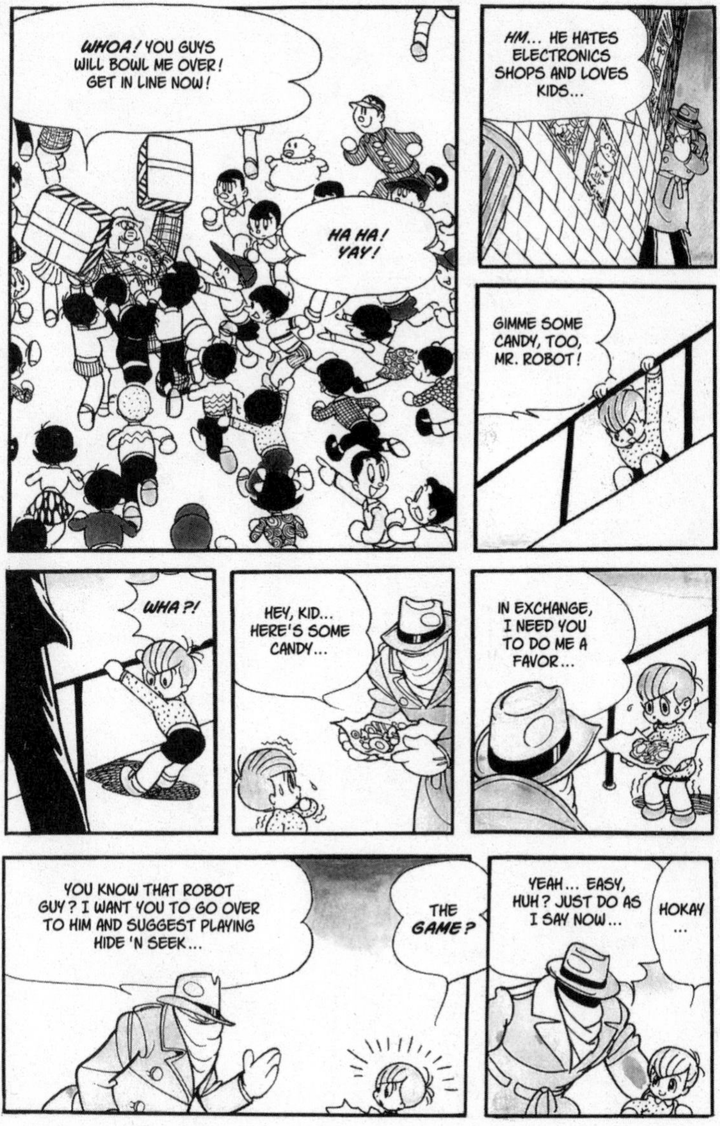
WHOA! YOU GUYS WILL BOWL ME OVER! GET IN LINE NOW!
HA HA! YAY!
HM... HE HATES ELECTRONICS SHOPS AND LOVES KIDS...
GIMME SOME CANDY, TOO, MR. ROBOT!
WHA?!
HEY, KID... HERE'S SOME CANDY...
IN EXCHANGE, I NEED YOU TO DO ME A FAVOR...
YOU KNOW THAT ROBOT GUY? I WANT YOU TO GO OVER TO HIM AND SUGGEST PLAYING HIDE 'N SEEK...
THE GAME?
YEAH... EASY, HUH? JUST DO AS I SAY NOW...
HOKAY ...

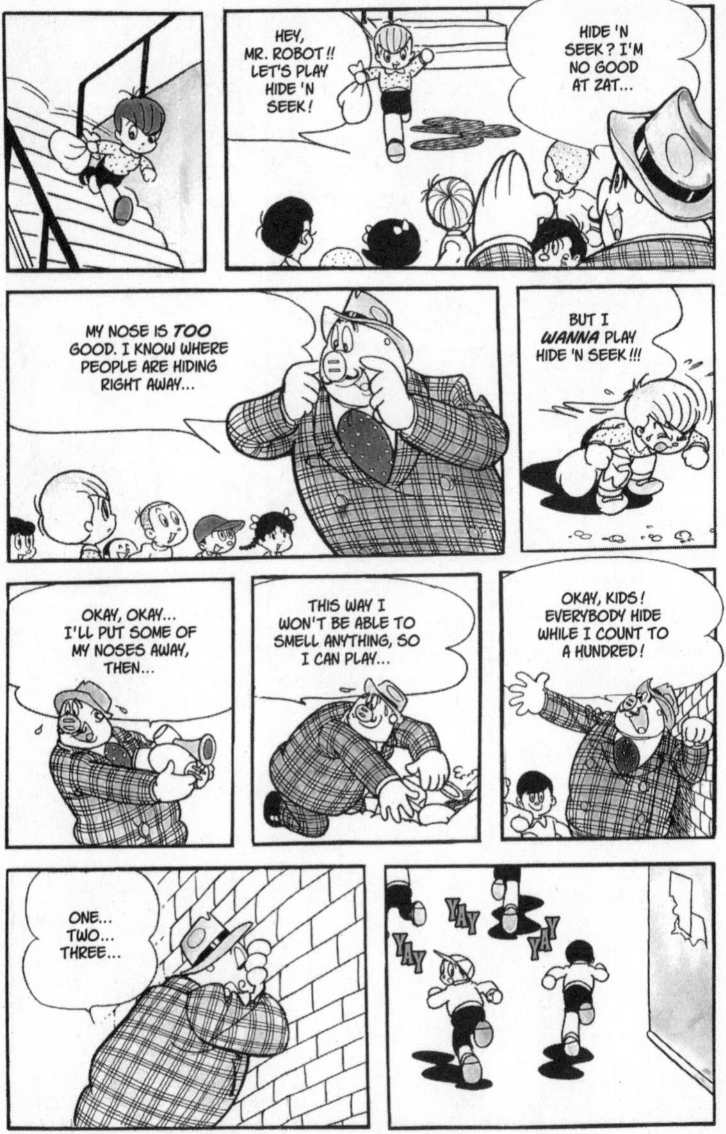
HEY, MR. ROBOT!! LET'S PLAY HIDE 'N SEEK!
HIDE 'N SEEK? I'M NO GOOD AT ZAT...
MY NOSE IS *TOO* GOOD. I KNOW WHERE PEOPLE ARE HIDING RIGHT AWAY...
BUT I *WANNA* PLAY HIDE 'N SEEK!!!
OKAY, OKAY... I'LL PUT SOME OF MY NOSES AWAY, THEN...
THIS WAY I WON'T BE ABLE TO SMELL ANYTHING, SO I CAN PLAY...
OKAY, KIDS! EVERYBODY HIDE WHILE I COUNT TO A HUNDRED!
ONE... TWO... THREE...
YAY
YAY
YAY

FIFTY...
FIFTY-ONE...
FIFTY-TWO...

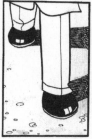

...ONE HUNDRED.

WHA ?!

A-ARE YOU A ROBOID?!

INDEED, I AM... TOO BAD YOU DIDN'T SENSE ME COMING...

WHY YOU...

SLAP

HEH HEH HEH...

325

MAYBE I DID LET MY GUARD DOWN...

...BUT YOU ARE STILL DEALING WITH ME! WITH *CYRANO*!!

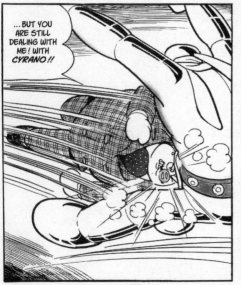

ZAP ZAP
ZAP ZAP

SMASH

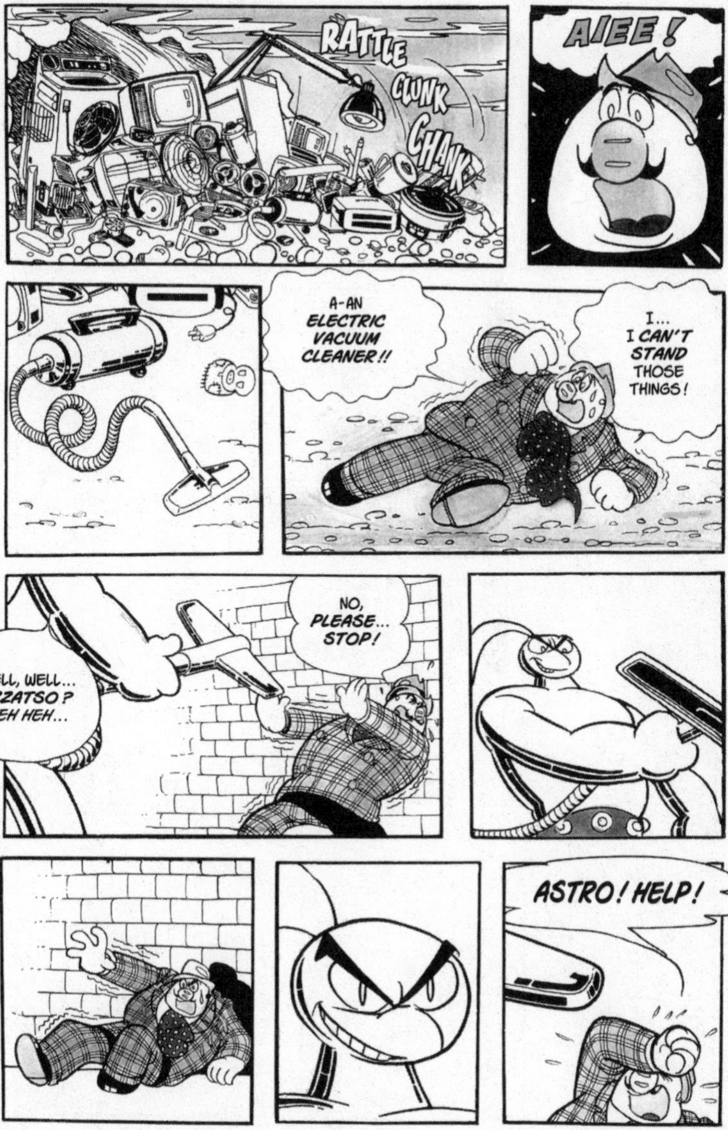
RATTLE
CLUNK
CHANK
AIEE!
A-AN ELECTRIC VACUUM CLEANER!!
I... I CAN'T STAND THOSE THINGS!
WELL, WELL... IZZATSO? HEH HEH...
NO, PLEASE... STOP!
ASTRO! HELP!

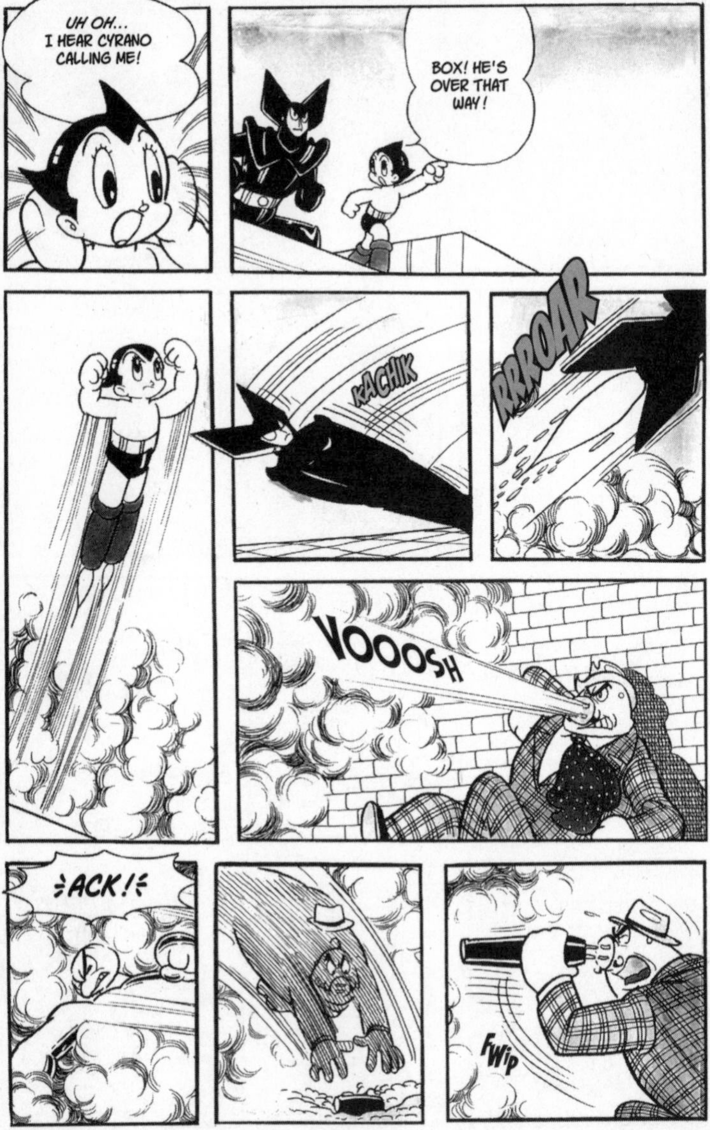
UH OH...
I HEAR CYRANO
CALLING ME!
BOX! HE'S
OVER THAT
WAY!
KACHIK
RRROAR
VOOOSH
ACK!
FWIP

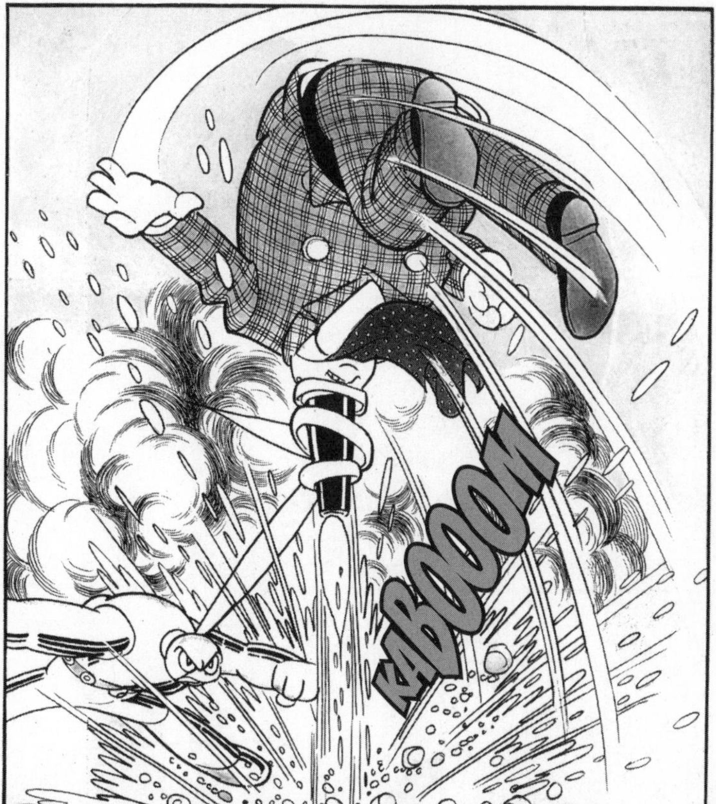
KABOOOM
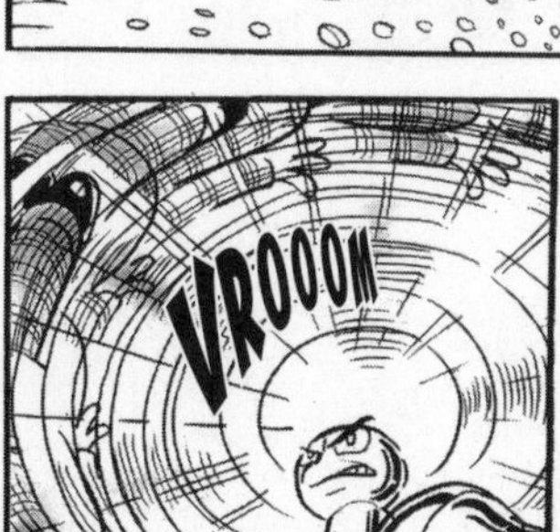
VROOOM
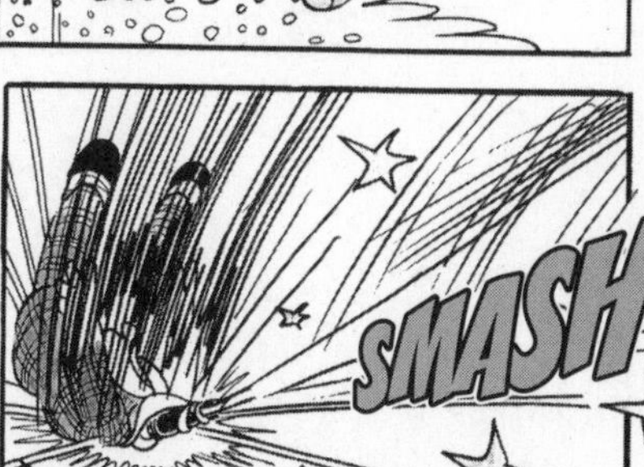
SMASH

NOW IT'S TWO AGAINST TWO....

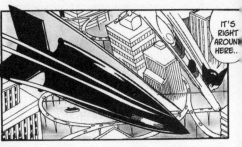

IT'S RIGHT AROUND HERE..

LOOK! THERE'S *CYRANO!*

WONDER WHAT HE'S DOING?

HOW COME YOU'RE STILL STANDING LIKE THAT, MR. ROBOT?

YEAH, WE FINISHED PLAYING HIDE 'N SEEK...

YOU C'N LOOK NOW, MISTER!

HEY, CYRANO!

WHAT THE--?!

NOOO!!

330

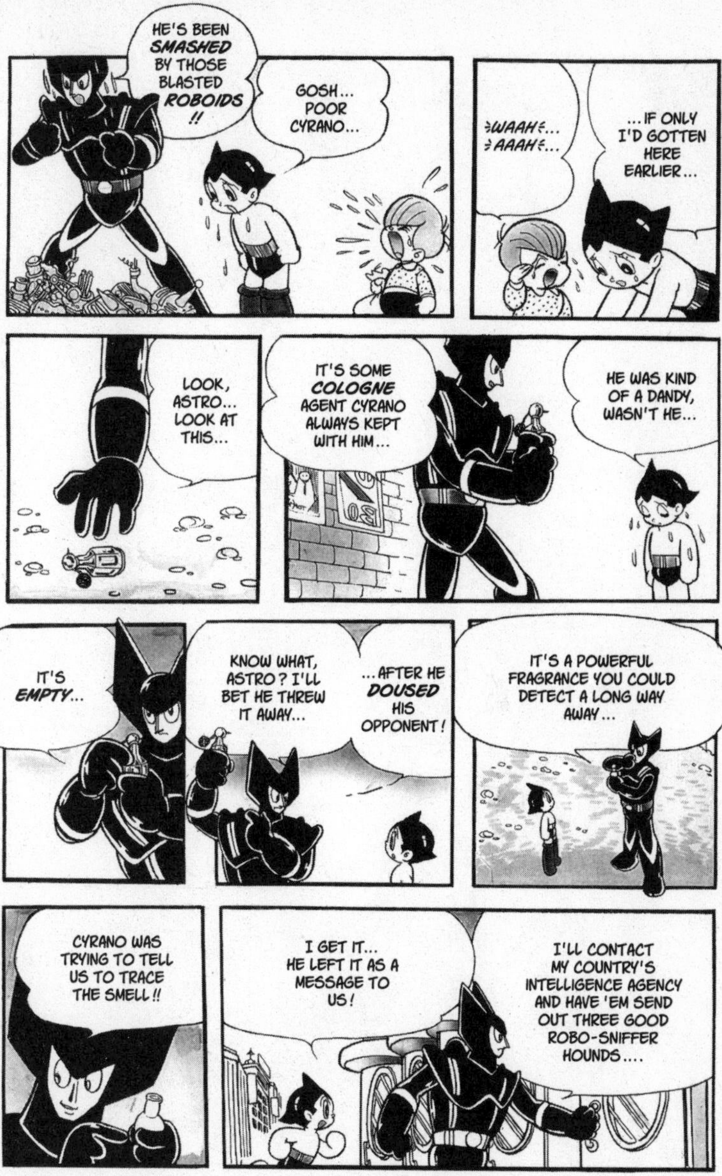
HE'S BEEN *SMASHED* BY THOSE BLASTED *ROBOIDS* !!
GOSH... POOR CYRANO...
WAAH... AAAH...
...IF ONLY I'D GOTTEN HERE EARLIER...
LOOK, ASTRO... LOOK AT THIS...
IT'S SOME *COLOGNE* AGENT CYRANO ALWAYS KEPT WITH HIM...
HE WAS KIND OF A DANDY, WASN'T HE...
IT'S *EMPTY*...
KNOW WHAT, ASTRO? I'LL BET HE THREW IT AWAY...
...AFTER HE *DOUSED* HIS OPPONENT!
IT'S A POWERFUL FRAGRANCE YOU COULD DETECT A LONG WAY AWAY...
CYRANO WAS TRYING TO TELL US TO TRACE THE SMELL!!
I GET IT... HE LEFT IT AS A MESSAGE TO US!
I'LL CONTACT MY COUNTRY'S INTELLIGENCE AGENCY AND HAVE 'EM SEND OUT THREE GOOD ROBO-SNIFFER HOUNDS....

WITH THIS SMELL, THE ROBOIDS'LL NEVER BE ABLE TO HIDE FROM US!

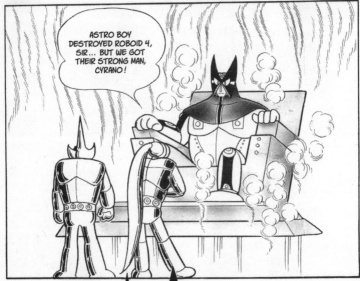

ASTRO BOY DESTROYED ROBOID 4, SIR... BUT WE GOT THEIR STRONG MAN, CYRANO!

I DON'T CARE ABOUT THAT!!

I WANT TO KNOW WHY YOU *STINK* SO MUCH?!

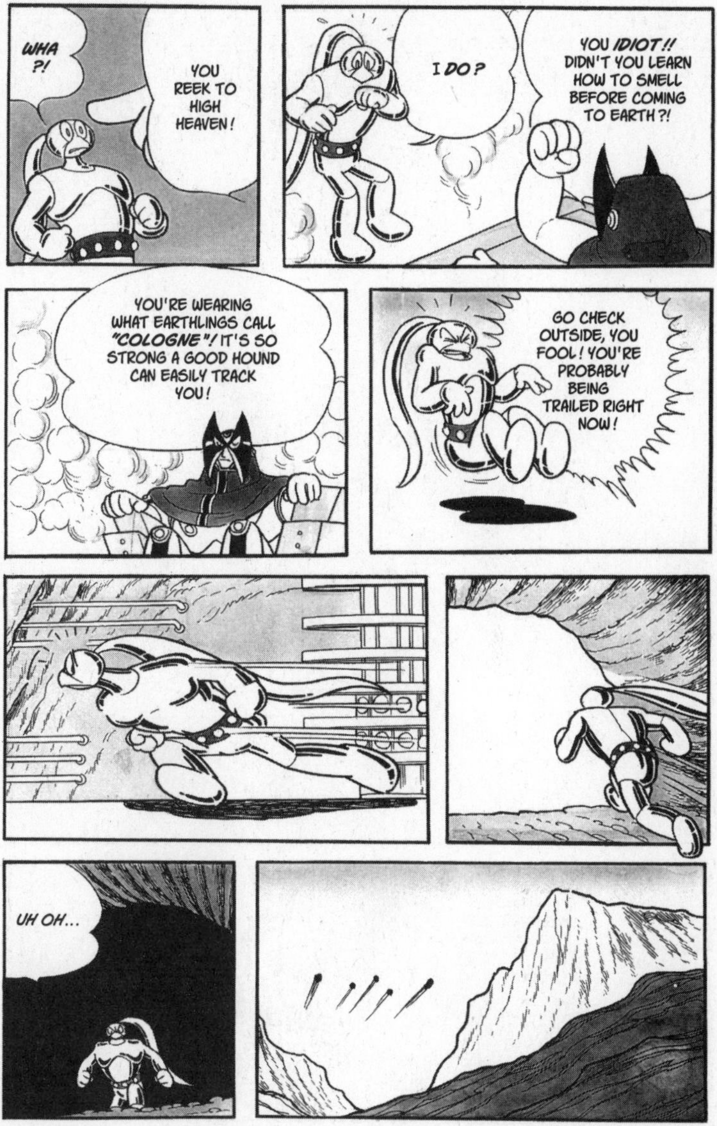
WHA ?!
YOU REEK TO HIGH HEAVEN!
I DO?
YOU IDIOT!! DIDN'T YOU LEARN HOW TO SMELL BEFORE COMING TO EARTH?!
YOU'RE WEARING WHAT EARTHLINGS CALL "COLOGNE"! IT'S SO STRONG A GOOD HOUND CAN EASILY TRACK YOU!
GO CHECK OUTSIDE, YOU FOOL! YOU'RE PROBABLY BEING TRAILED RIGHT NOW!
UH OH...

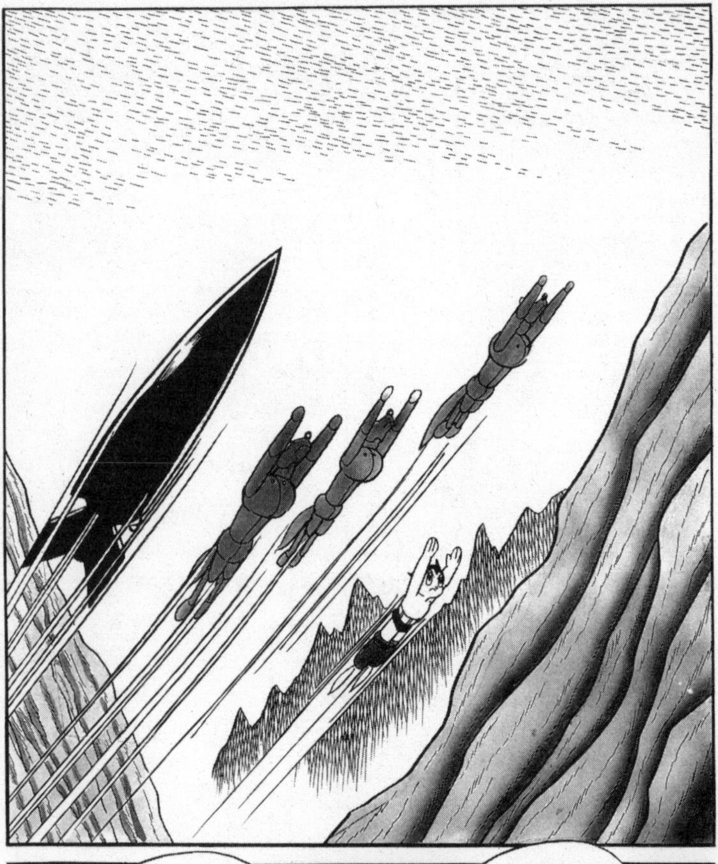

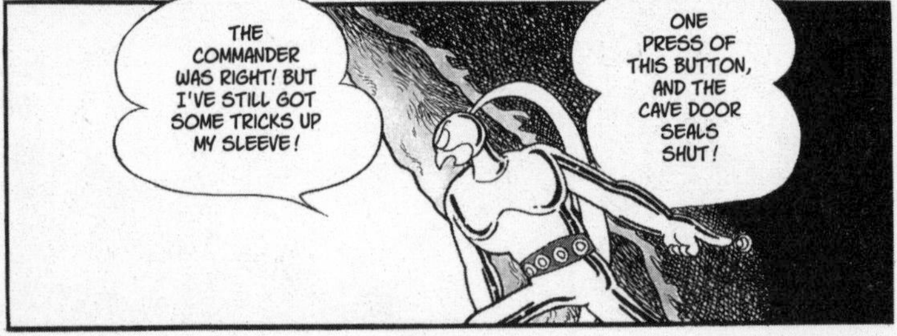
THE COMMANDER WAS RIGHT! BUT I'VE STILL GOT SOME TRICKS UP MY SLEEVE!
ONE PRESS OF THIS BUTTON, AND THE CAVE DOOR SEALS SHUT!

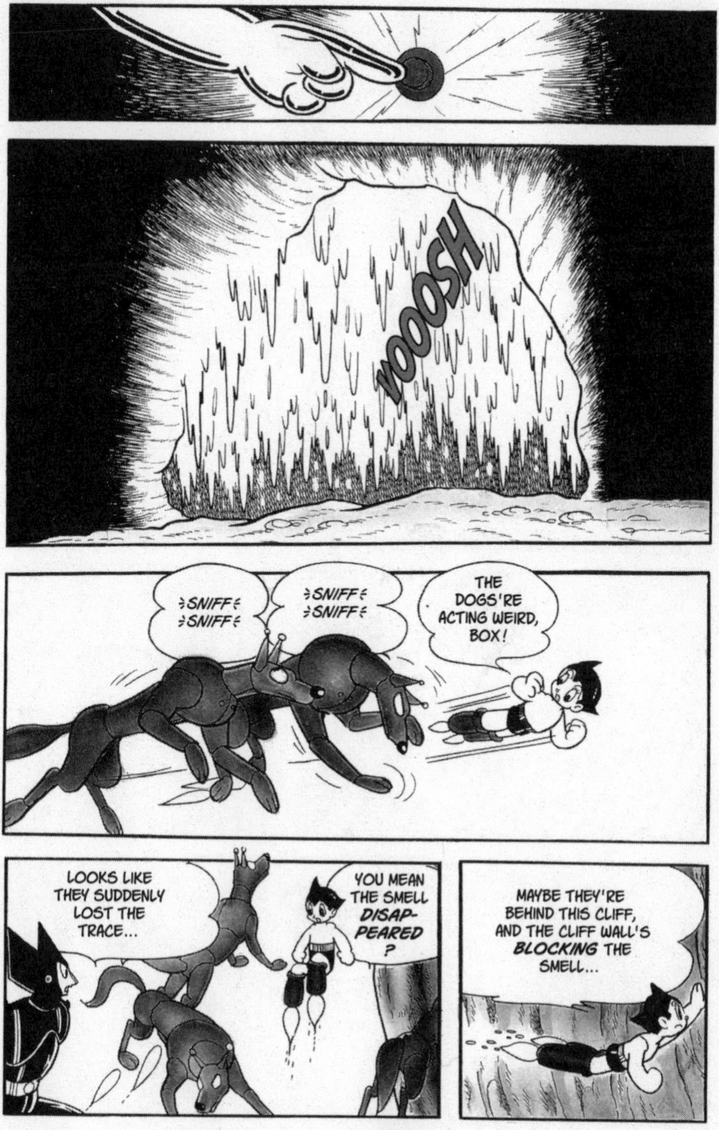

VOOOSH
SNIFF SNIFF
SNIFF SNIFF
THE DOGS'RE ACTING WEIRD, BOX!
LOOKS LIKE THEY SUDDENLY LOST THE TRACE...
YOU MEAN THE SMELL *DISAPPEARED*?
MAYBE THEY'RE BEHIND THIS CLIFF, AND THE CLIFF WALL'S *BLOCKING* THE SMELL...

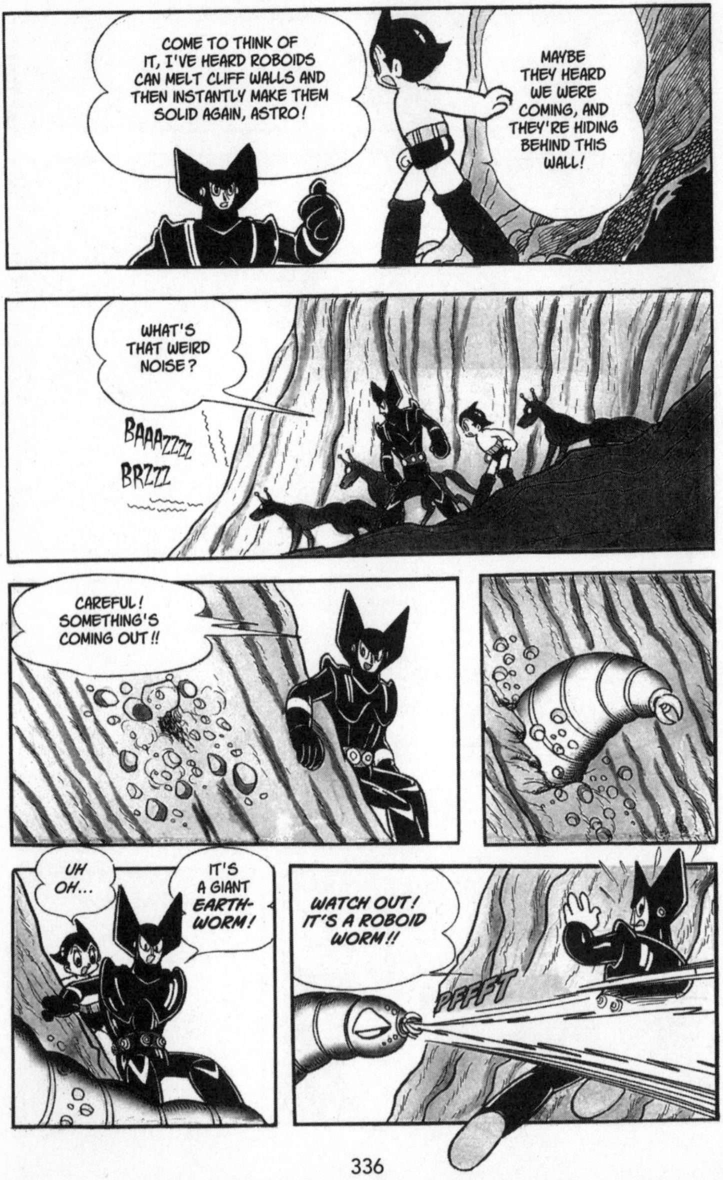
COME TO THINK OF IT, I'VE HEARD ROBOIDS CAN MELT CLIFF WALLS AND THEN INSTANTLY MAKE THEM SOLID AGAIN, ASTRO!
MAYBE THEY HEARD WE WERE COMING, AND THEY'RE HIDING BEHIND THIS WALL!
WHAT'S THAT WEIRD NOISE?
BAAAZZZZ
BRZZZ
CAREFUL! SOMETHING'S COMING OUT!!
UH OH...
IT'S A GIANT EARTH-WORM!
WATCH OUT! IT'S A ROBOID WORM!!
PFFFT

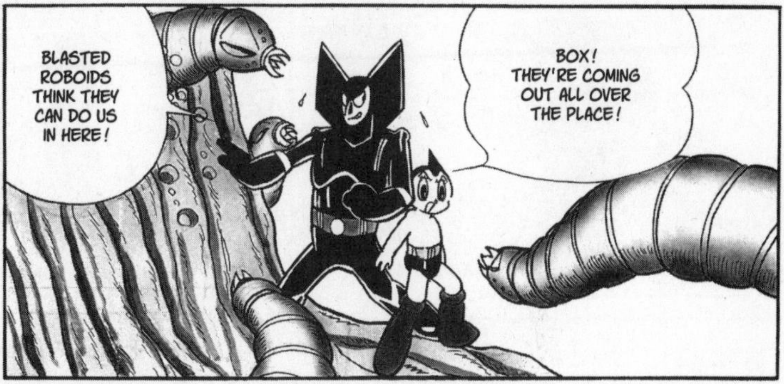
BLASTED ROBOIDS THINK THEY CAN DO US IN HERE!
BOX! THEY'RE COMING OUT ALL OVER THE PLACE!

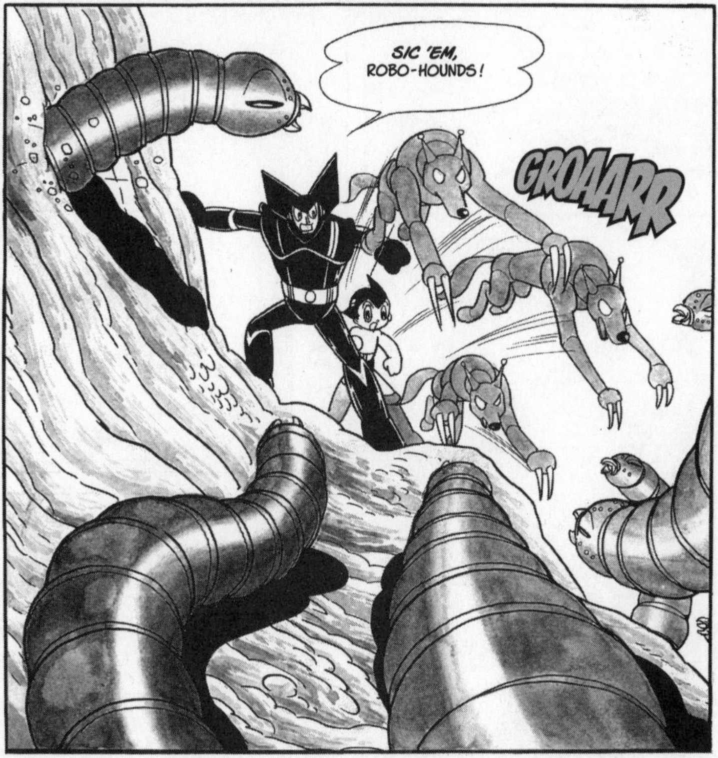
SIC 'EM, ROBO-HOUNDS!
GROAARR

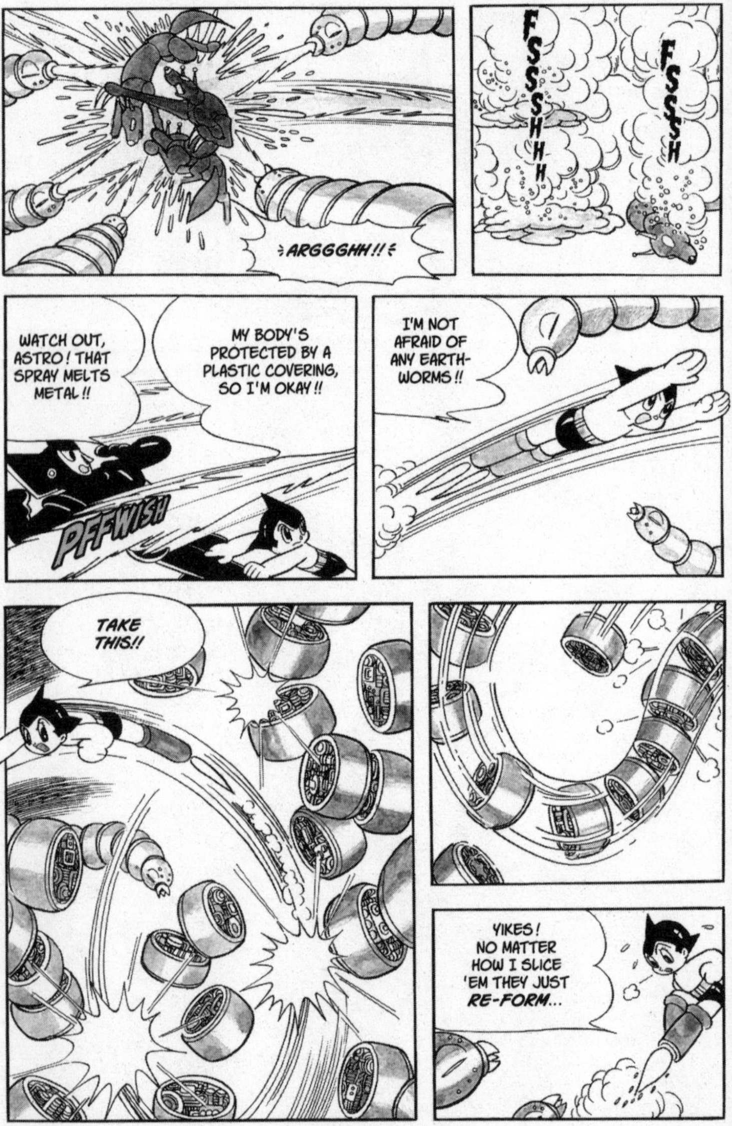
ARGGGHH!!
FSSSHHH
FSSSH
WATCH OUT, ASTRO! THAT SPRAY MELTS METAL!!
MY BODY'S PROTECTED BY A PLASTIC COVERING, SO I'M OKAY!!
PFFWISH
I'M NOT AFRAID OF ANY EARTH-WORMS!!
TAKE THIS!!
YIKES! NO MATTER HOW I SLICE 'EM THEY JUST RE-FORM...

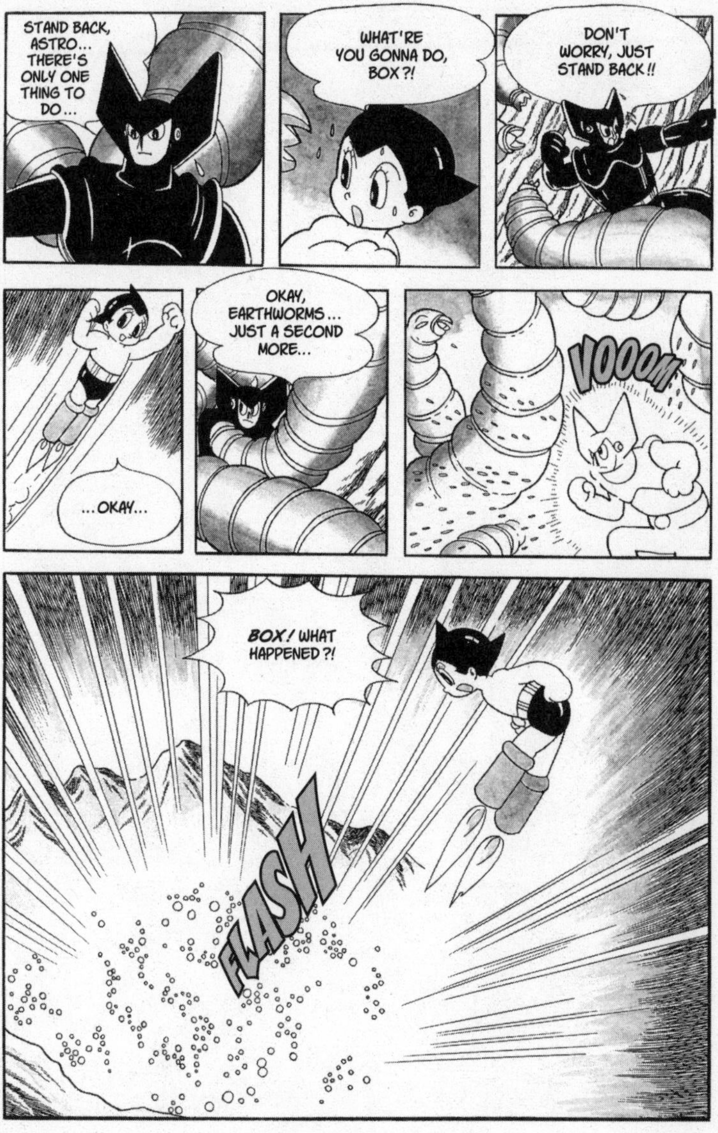
STAND BACK, ASTRO... THERE'S ONLY ONE THING TO DO...
WHAT'RE YOU GONNA DO, BOX?!
DON'T WORRY, JUST STAND BACK!!
...OKAY...
OKAY, EARTHWORMS... JUST A SECOND MORE...
VOOOM
BOX! WHAT HAPPENED?!
FLASH

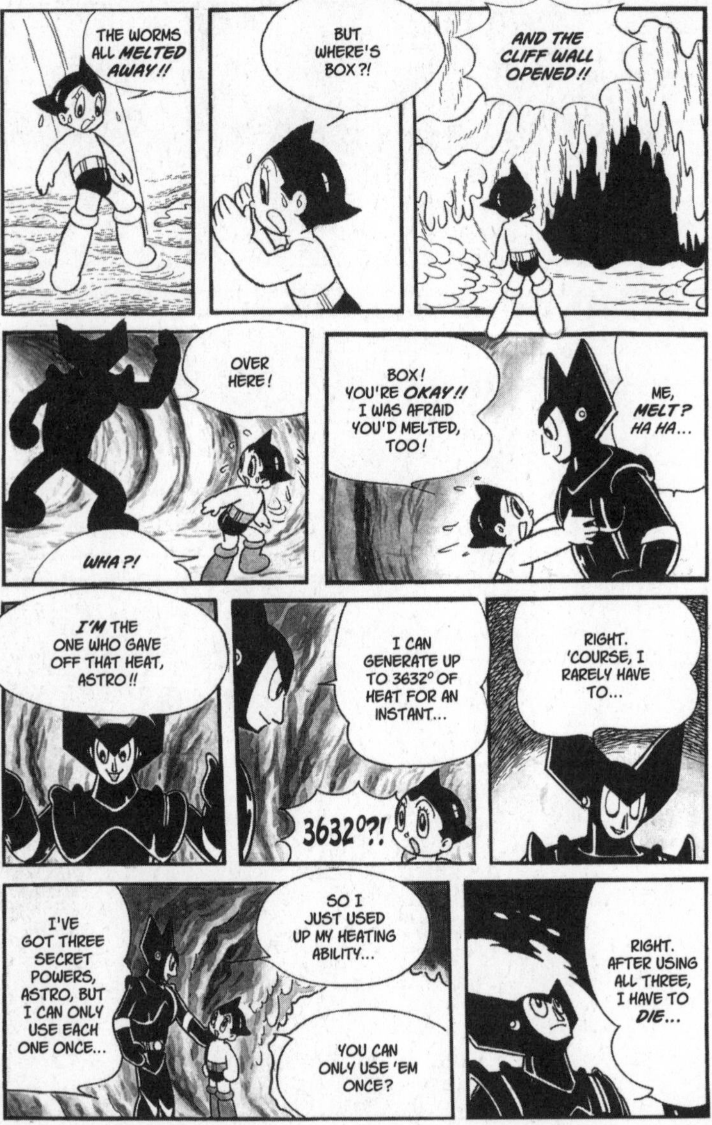
THE WORMS ALL MELTED AWAY!!
BUT WHERE'S BOX?!
AND THE CLIFF WALL OPENED!!
OVER HERE!
WHA?!
BOX! YOU'RE OKAY!! I WAS AFRAID YOU'D MELTED, TOO!
ME, MELT? HA HA...
I'M THE ONE WHO GAVE OFF THAT HEAT, ASTRO!!
I CAN GENERATE UP TO 3632° OF HEAT FOR AN INSTANT...
3632°?!
RIGHT. 'COURSE, I RARELY HAVE TO...
I'VE GOT THREE SECRET POWERS, ASTRO, BUT I CAN ONLY USE EACH ONE ONCE...
SO I JUST USED UP MY HEATING ABILITY...
YOU CAN ONLY USE 'EM ONCE?
RIGHT. AFTER USING ALL THREE, I HAVE TO DIE...

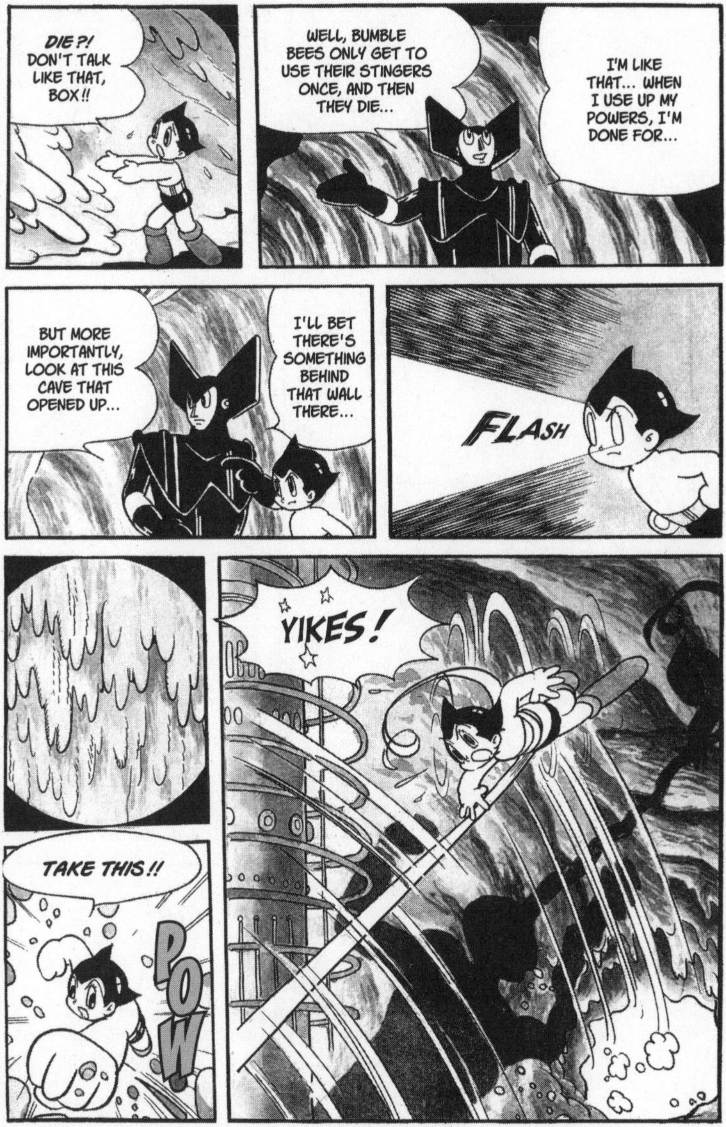
DIE?! DON'T TALK LIKE THAT, BOX!!
WELL, BUMBLE BEES ONLY GET TO USE THEIR STINGERS ONCE, AND THEN THEY DIE...
I'M LIKE THAT... WHEN I USE UP MY POWERS, I'M DONE FOR...
BUT MORE IMPORTANTLY, LOOK AT THIS CAVE THAT OPENED UP...
I'LL BET THERE'S SOMETHING BEHIND THAT WALL THERE...
FLASH
TAKE THIS!!
POW
YIKES!

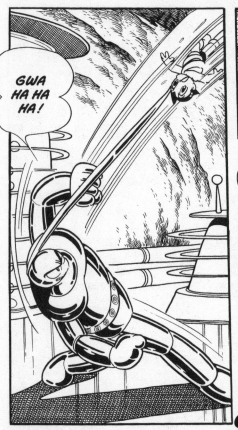

GWA HA HA HA!

I'VE BEEN WAITING FOR YOU, ASTRO BOY! *WELCOME TO YOUR GRAVE!!*

SMACK

WHAP

ASTRO!!

ZAAP

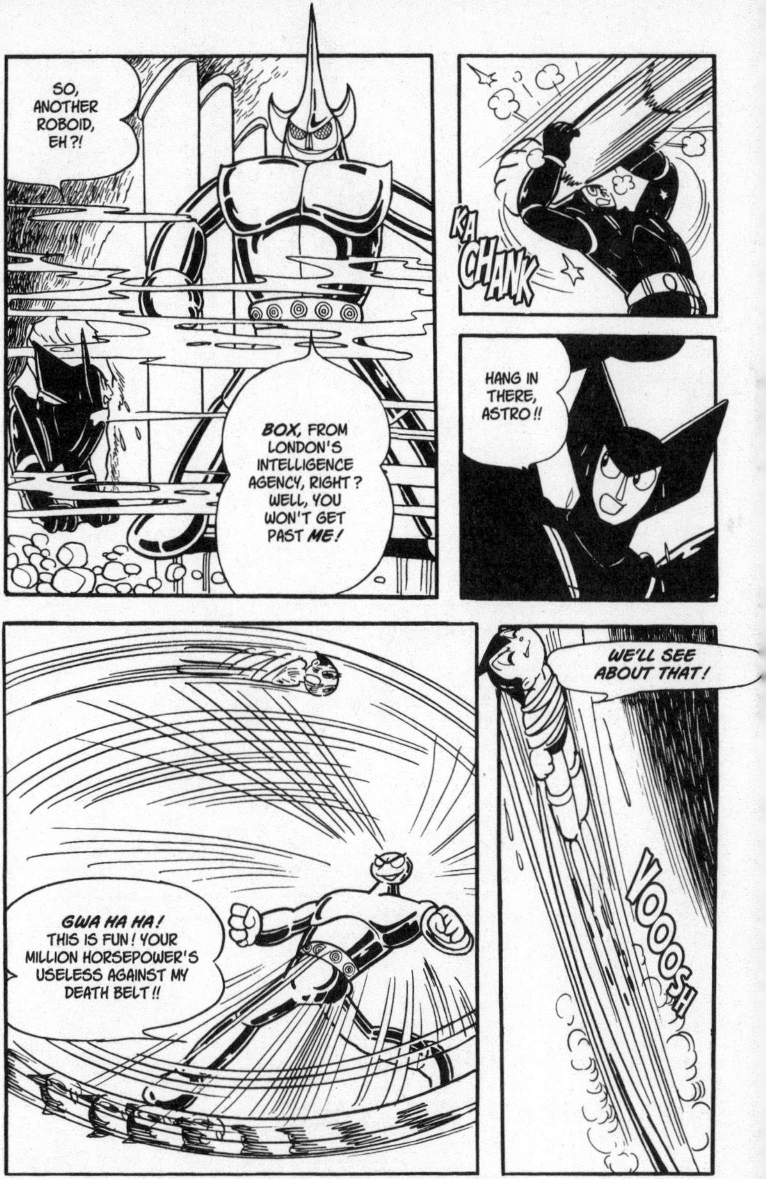
SO, ANOTHER ROBOID, EH?!
BOX, FROM LONDON'S INTELLIGENCE AGENCY, RIGHT? WELL, YOU WON'T GET PAST ME!
KA CHANK
HANG IN THERE, ASTRO!!
GWA HA HA! THIS IS FUN! YOUR MILLION HORSEPOWER'S USELESS AGAINST MY DEATH BELT!!
WE'LL SEE ABOUT THAT!
VOOOOSH

KATHUD
CRASH
STOP!!
WHA?!
HUMM
BEEP BEEEP
BEEEP
BUZZZ BUZZ
YOU COWARD !!

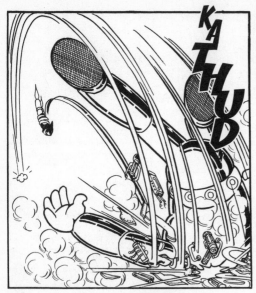

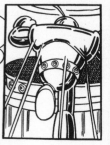

BZZZ
BEEP
BZZZ
BEEEP
BEEP
BZZ
FWP
YIKES!
FWAP
WELCOME TO OUR MULTIPLIER MACHINE! HA HA!
FWP
ARGH ...

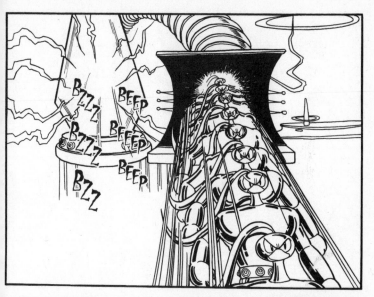

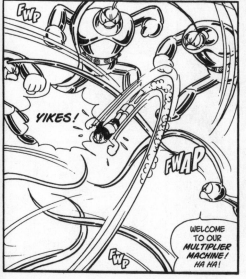

NOW TO RIP YOU TO SHREDS, ASTRO!

CHAK

SHOOTING US WON'T WORK, SUCKER!

I'VE GOT A DIFFERENT TARGET!!

KABASH

RATATATAT

KABABOOOM

FSSHHHH

FCSHHHH

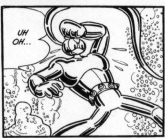

UH OH...

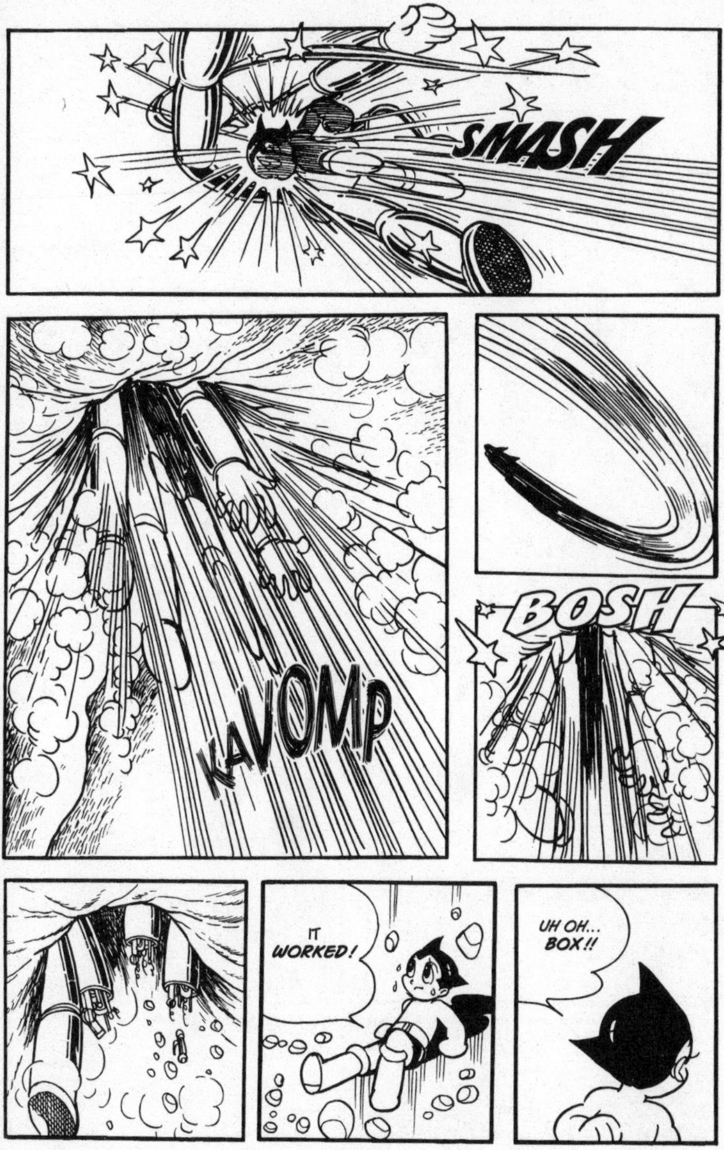
SMASH
KAVOMP
BOSH
IT WORKED!
UH OH... BOX!!

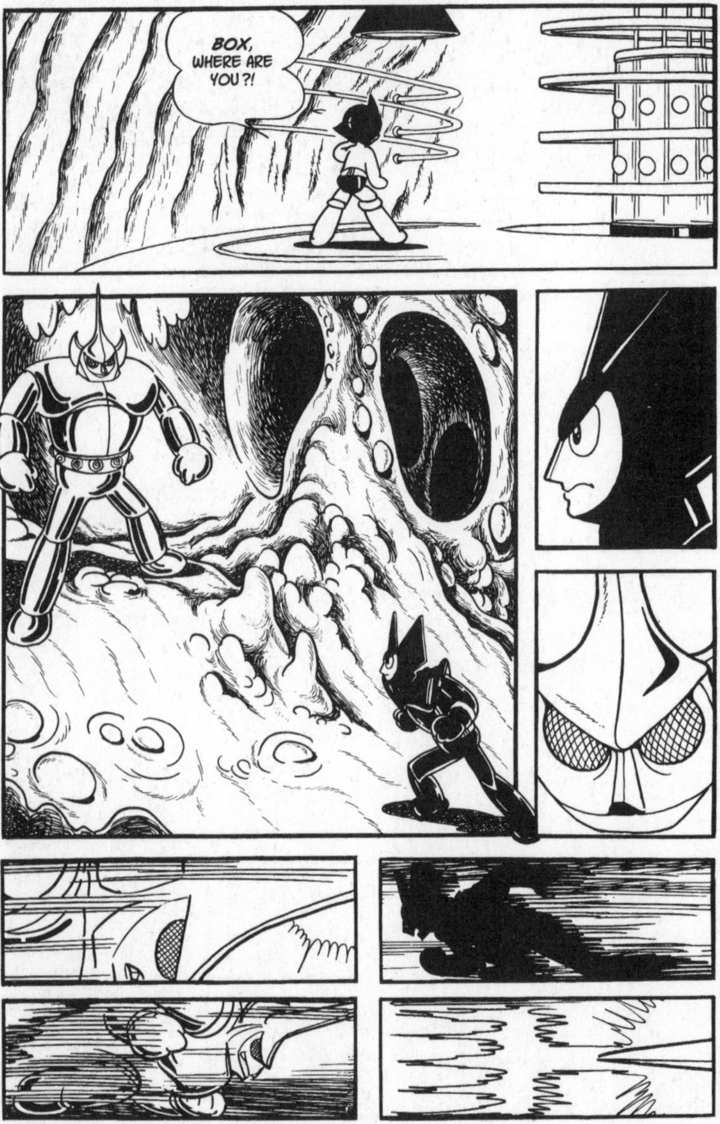
BOX, WHERE ARE YOU?!

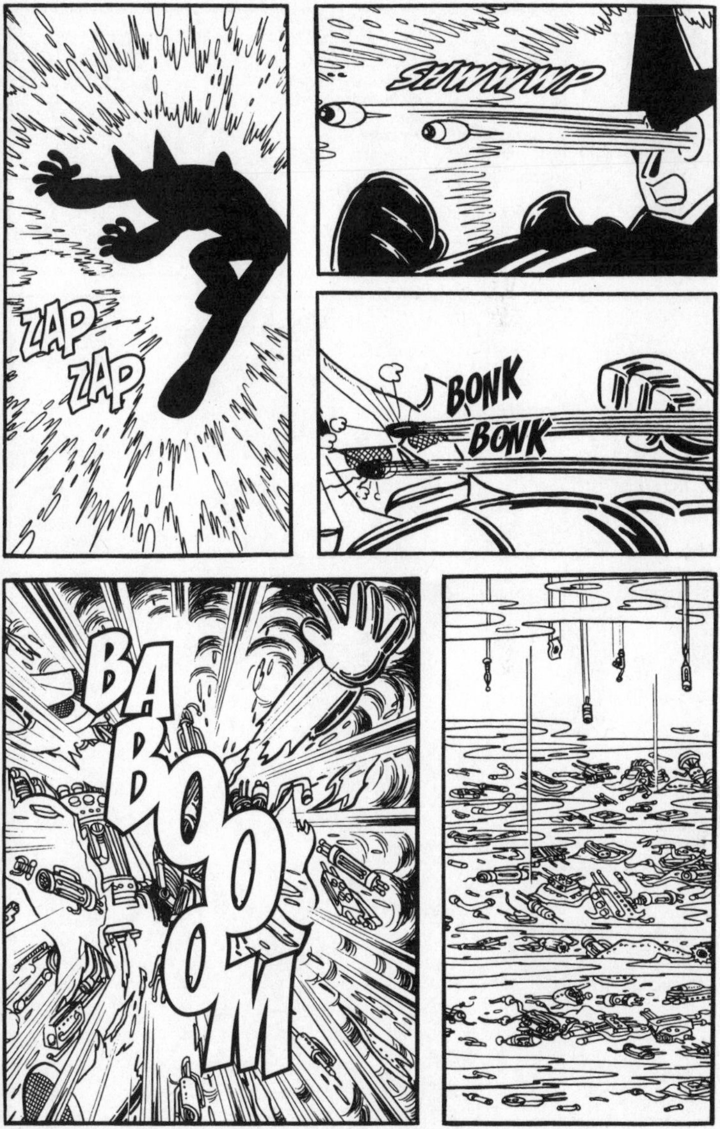
ZAP
ZAP
SHWWWWP
BONK
BONK
BA
BOOOM

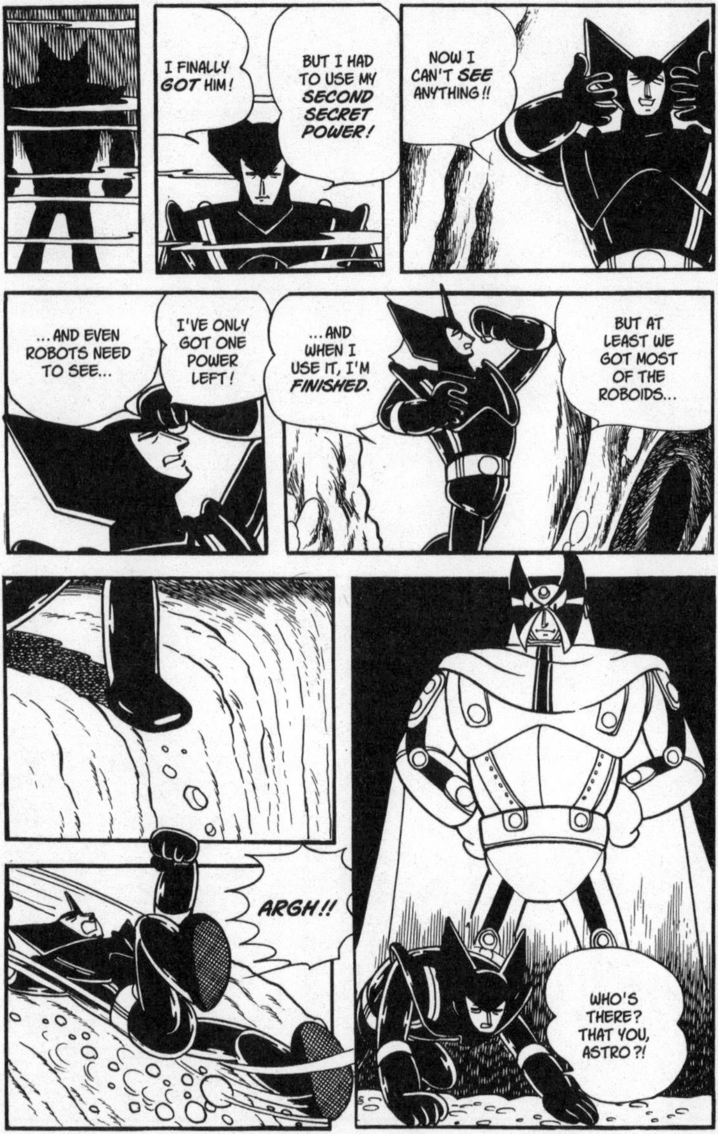
I FINALLY GOT HIM!
BUT I HAD TO USE MY SECOND SECRET POWER!
NOW I CAN'T SEE ANYTHING!!
...AND EVEN ROBOTS NEED TO SEE...
I'VE ONLY GOT ONE POWER LEFT!
...AND WHEN I USE IT, I'M FINISHED.
BUT AT LEAST WE GOT MOST OF THE ROBOIDS...
ARGH!!
WHO'S THERE? THAT YOU, ASTRO?!

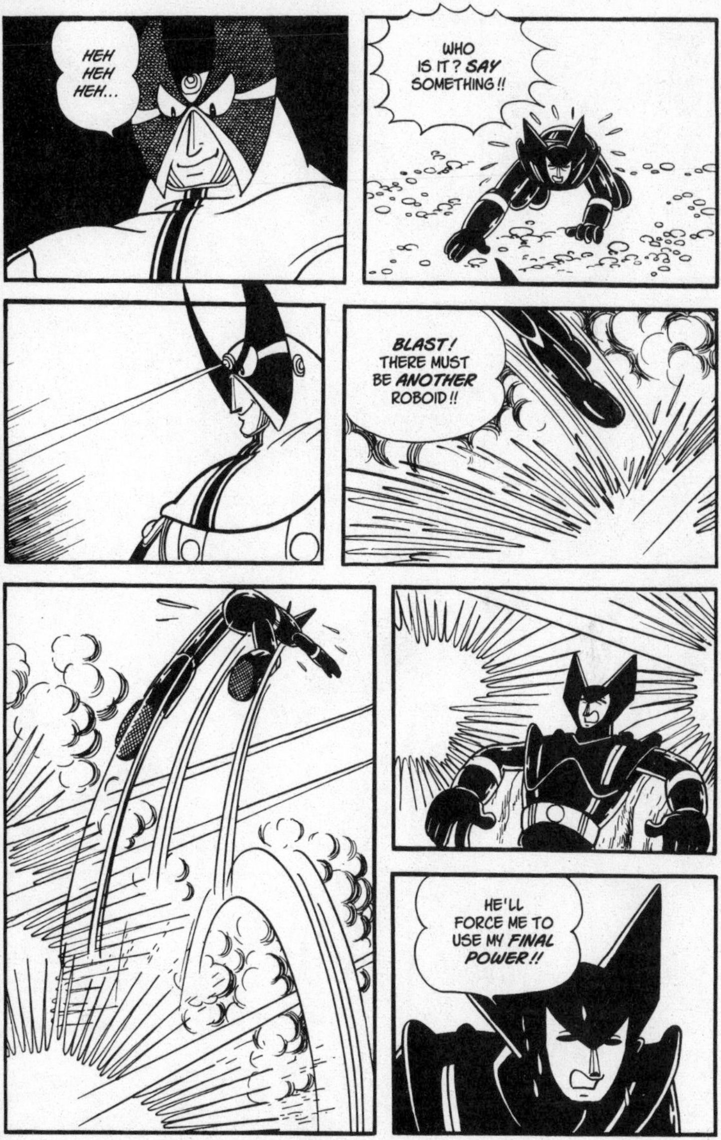
HEH HEH HEH...
WHO IS IT? SAY SOMETHING!!
BLAST! THERE MUST BE ANOTHER ROBOID!!
HE'LL FORCE ME TO USE MY FINAL POWER!!

IF I DO THIS, I'LL DIE! BUT I'LL TAKE YOU WITH ME!!

PREPARE FOR THE *END*, ROBOID!!

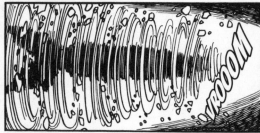

VROOOM

BASH!

ROAR

352

≥HMPH!≤ THAT WAS A STUPID PARLOR TRICK...

BOX! WHERE ARE YOU?

BOX... WHA?

?

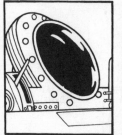

CHAK

WHA?!

WHO'RE YOU?

WHO'RE YOU?!

353

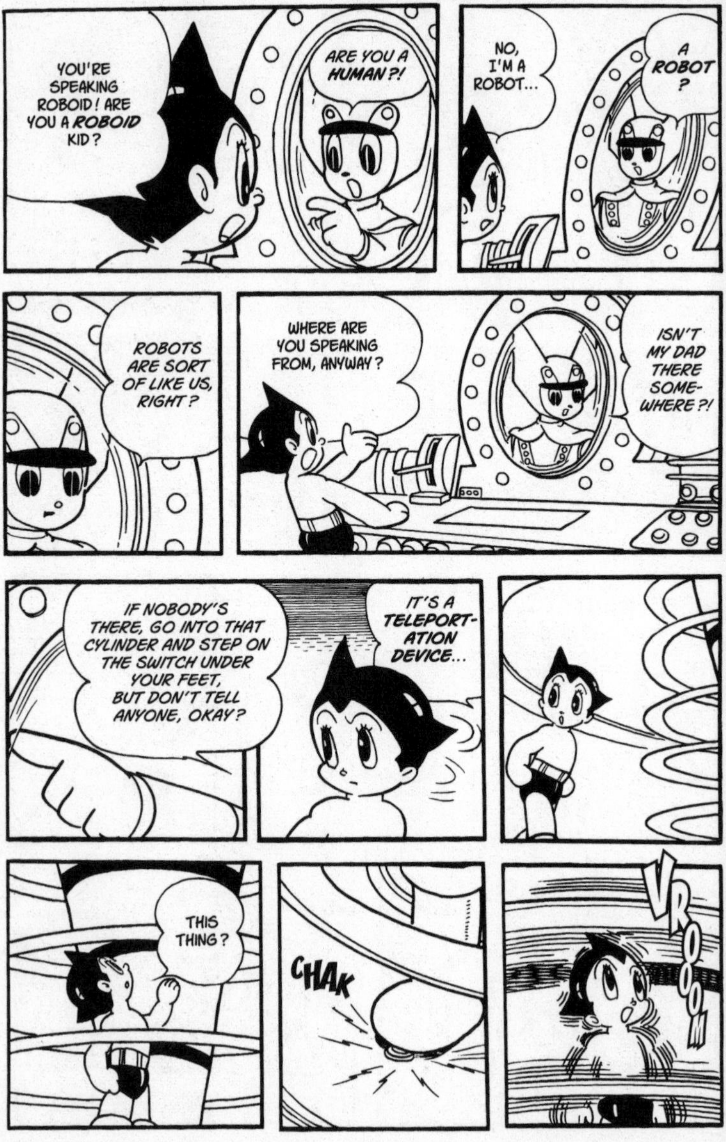
YOU'RE SPEAKING ROBOID! ARE YOU A ROBOID KID?
ARE YOU A HUMAN?!
NO, I'M A ROBOT...
A ROBOT?
ROBOTS ARE SORT OF LIKE US, RIGHT?
WHERE ARE YOU SPEAKING FROM, ANYWAY?
ISN'T MY DAD THERE SOMEWHERE?!
IF NOBODY'S THERE, GO INTO THAT CYLINDER AND STEP ON THE SWITCH UNDER YOUR FEET, BUT DON'T TELL ANYONE, OKAY?
IT'S A TELEPORTATION DEVICE...
THIS THING?
CHAK
VROOOOM

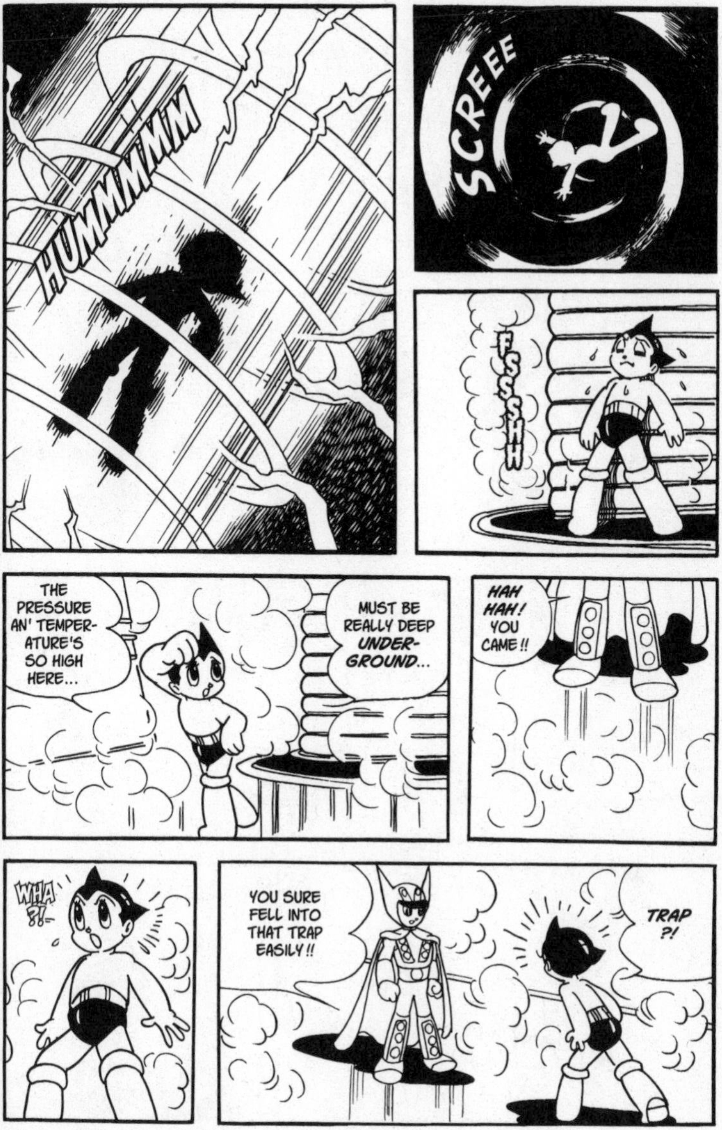
HUMMMMM
SCREEE
FSSSHH
THE PRESSURE AN' TEMPERATURE'S SO HIGH HERE...
MUST BE REALLY DEEP UNDERGROUND...
HAH HAH! YOU CAME!!
WHA ?!
YOU SURE FELL INTO THAT TRAP EASILY!!
TRAP ?!

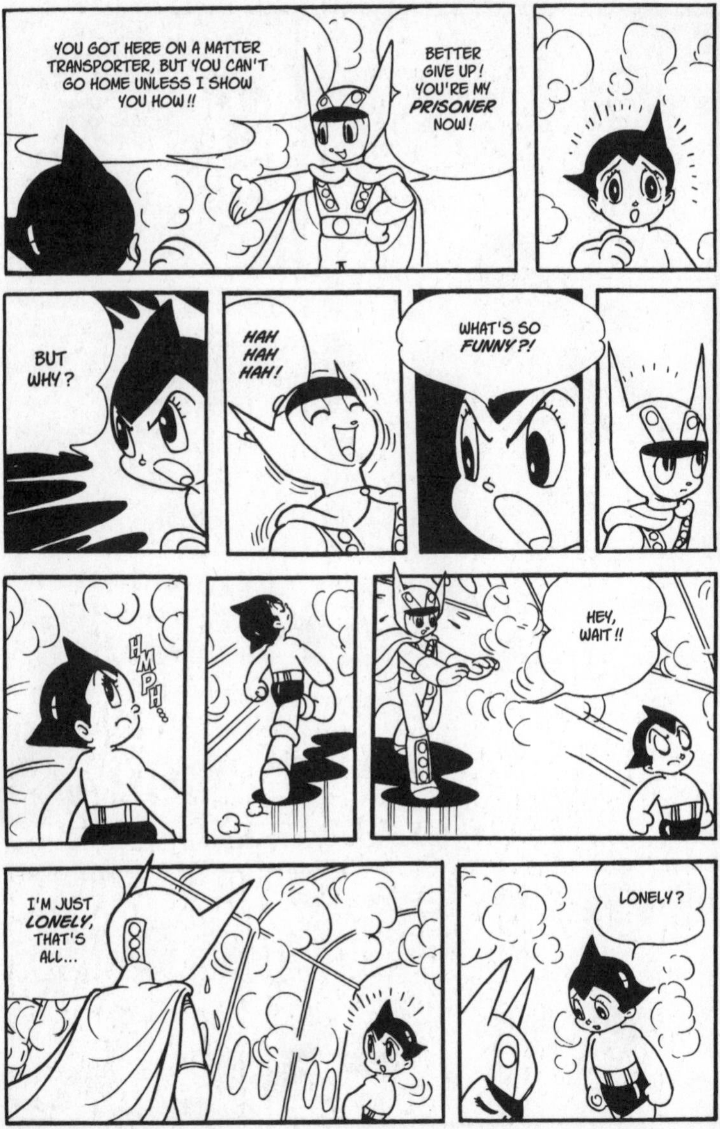
YOU GOT HERE ON A MATTER TRANSPORTER, BUT YOU CAN'T GO HOME UNLESS I SHOW YOU HOW!!
BETTER GIVE UP! YOU'RE MY PRISONER NOW!
BUT WHY?
HAH HAH HAH!
WHAT'S SO FUNNY?!
HMPH...
HEY, WAIT!!
I'M JUST LONELY, THAT'S ALL...
LONELY?

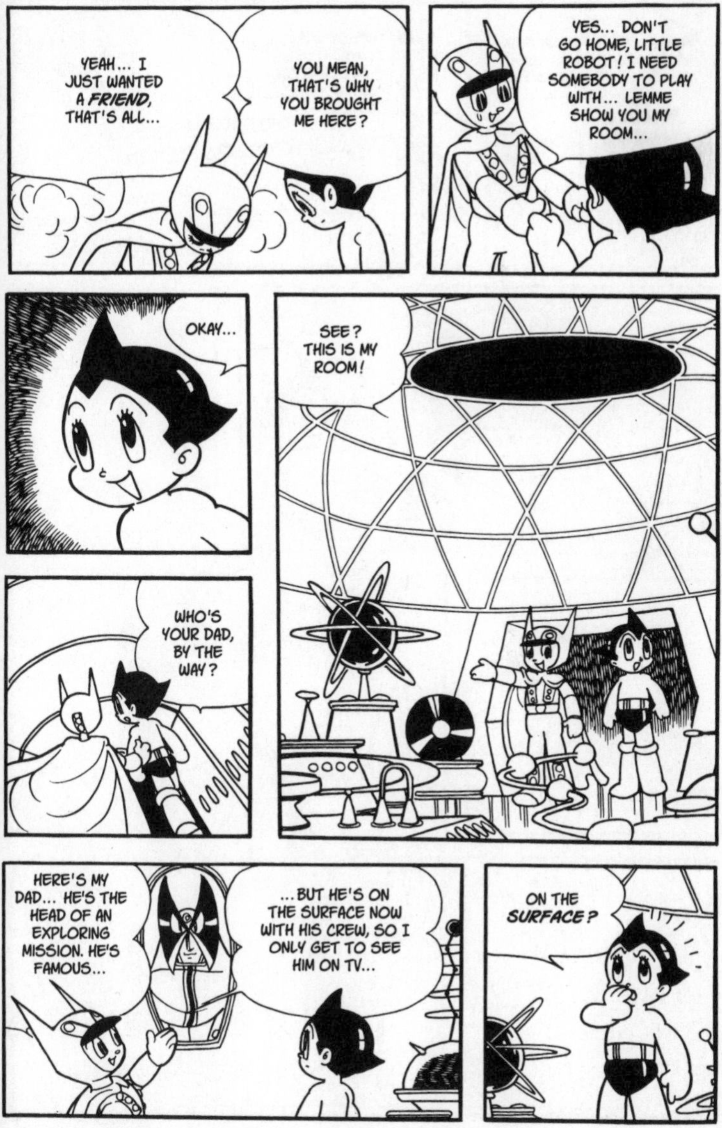
YEAH... I JUST WANTED A *FRIEND*, THAT'S ALL...
YOU MEAN, THAT'S WHY YOU BROUGHT ME HERE?
YES... DON'T GO HOME, LITTLE ROBOT! I NEED SOMEBODY TO PLAY WITH... LEMME SHOW YOU MY ROOM...
OKAY...
WHO'S YOUR DAD, BY THE WAY?
SEE? THIS IS MY ROOM!
HERE'S MY DAD... HE'S THE HEAD OF AN EXPLORING MISSION. HE'S FAMOUS...
...BUT HE'S ON THE SURFACE NOW WITH HIS CREW, SO I ONLY GET TO SEE HIM ON TV...
ON THE *SURFACE*?

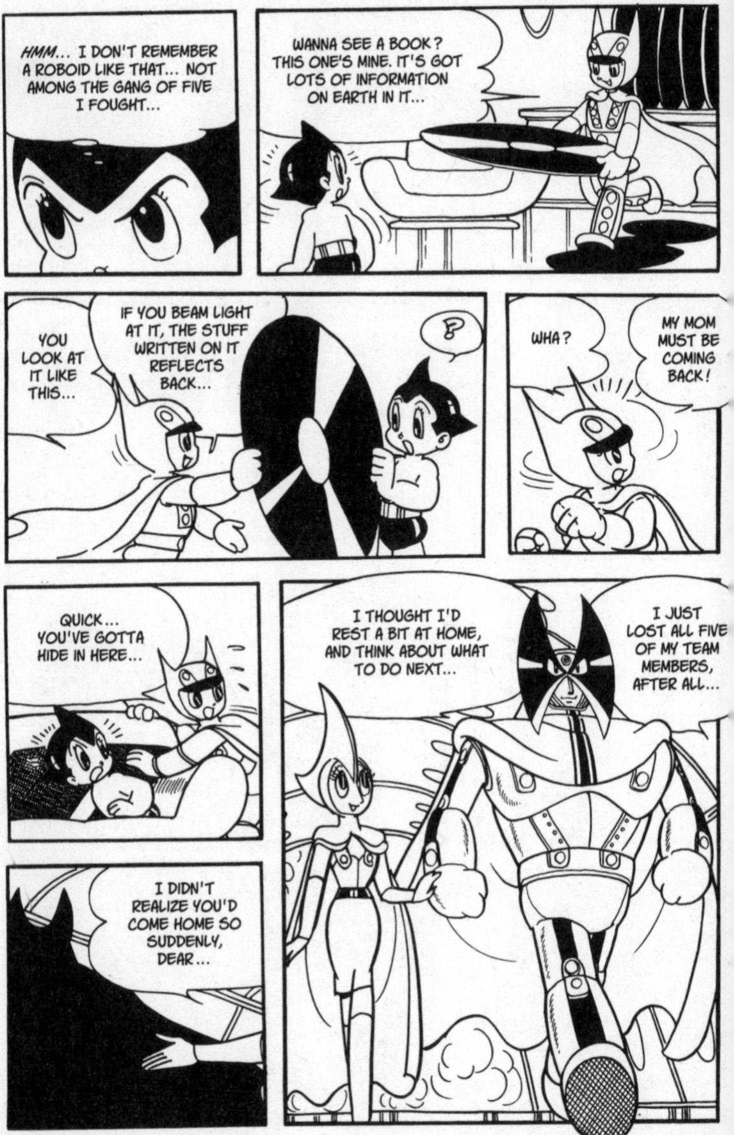
HMM... I DON'T REMEMBER A ROBOID LIKE THAT... NOT AMONG THE GANG OF FIVE I FOUGHT...
WANNA SEE A BOOK? THIS ONE'S MINE. IT'S GOT LOTS OF INFORMATION ON EARTH IN IT...
YOU LOOK AT IT LIKE THIS...
IF YOU BEAM LIGHT AT IT, THE STUFF WRITTEN ON IT REFLECTS BACK...
?
WHA?
MY MOM MUST BE COMING BACK!
QUICK... YOU'VE GOTTA HIDE IN HERE...
I DIDN'T REALIZE YOU'D COME HOME SO SUDDENLY, DEAR...
I THOUGHT I'D REST A BIT AT HOME, AND THINK ABOUT WHAT TO DO NEXT...
I JUST LOST ALL FIVE OF MY TEAM MEMBERS, AFTER ALL...

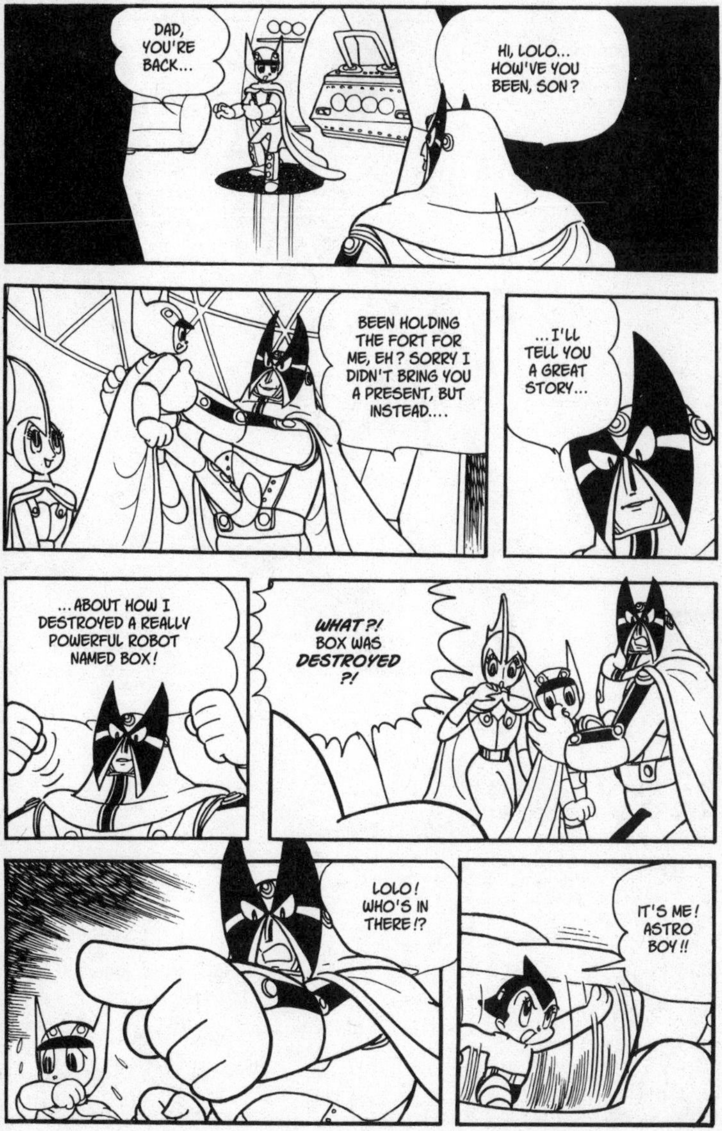
DAD, YOU'RE BACK...
HI, LOLO... HOW'VE YOU BEEN, SON?
BEEN HOLDING THE FORT FOR ME, EH? SORRY I DIDN'T BRING YOU A PRESENT, BUT INSTEAD....
...I'LL TELL YOU A GREAT STORY...
...ABOUT HOW I DESTROYED A REALLY POWERFUL ROBOT NAMED BOX!
WHAT?! BOX WAS DESTROYED ?!
LOLO! WHO'S IN THERE!?
IT'S ME! ASTRO BOY!!

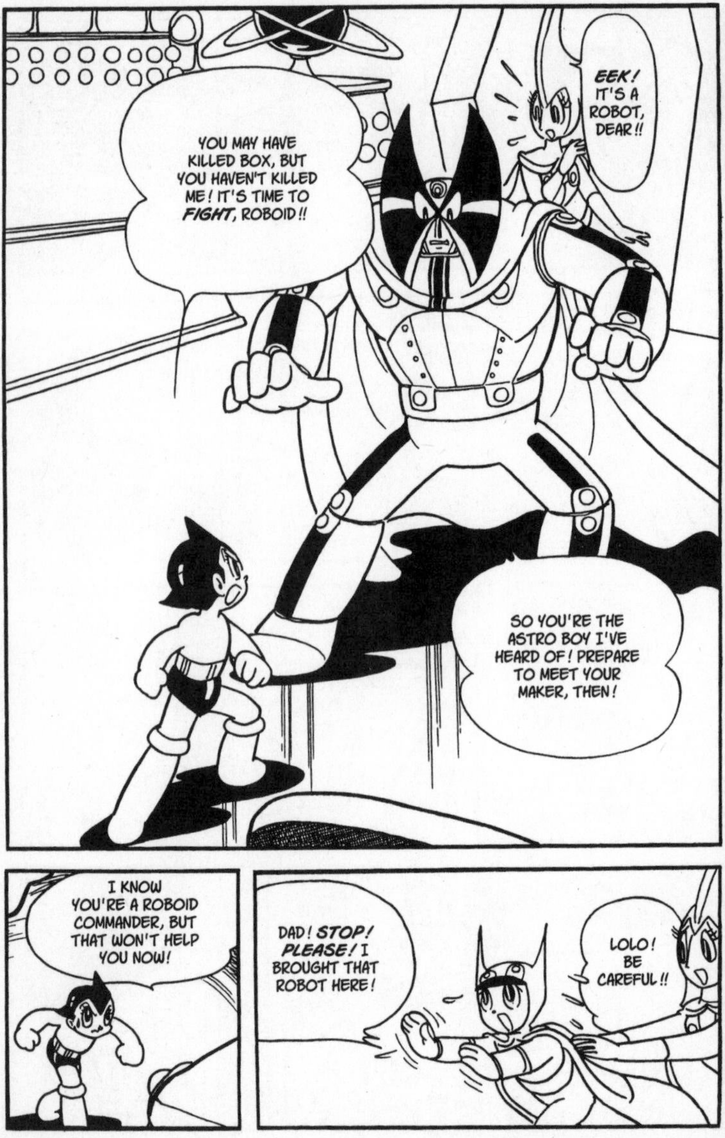
YOU MAY HAVE KILLED BOX, BUT YOU HAVEN'T KILLED ME! IT'S TIME TO FIGHT, ROBOID!!
EEK! IT'S A ROBOT, DEAR!!
SO YOU'RE THE ASTRO BOY I'VE HEARD OF! PREPARE TO MEET YOUR MAKER, THEN!
I KNOW YOU'RE A ROBOID COMMANDER, BUT THAT WON'T HELP YOU NOW!
DAD! STOP! PLEASE! I BROUGHT THAT ROBOT HERE!
LOLO! BE CAREFUL!!

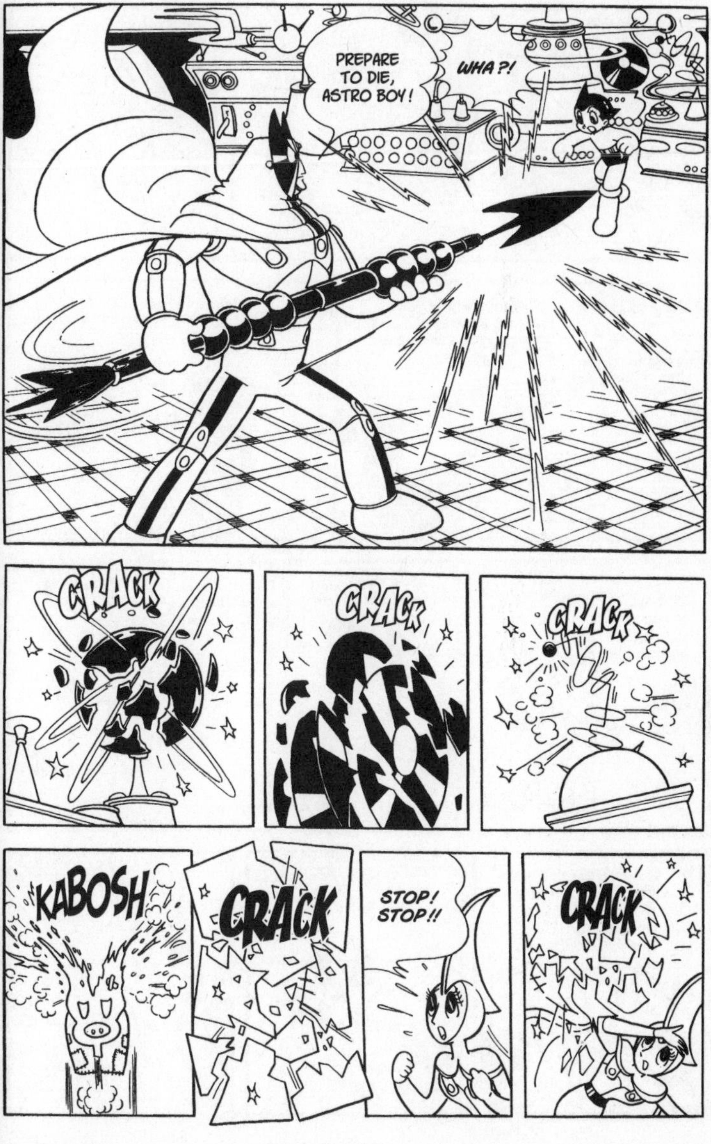
PREPARE TO DIE, ASTRO BOY!
WHA?!
CRACK
CRACK
CRACK
KABOSH
CRACK
STOP! STOP!!
CRACK

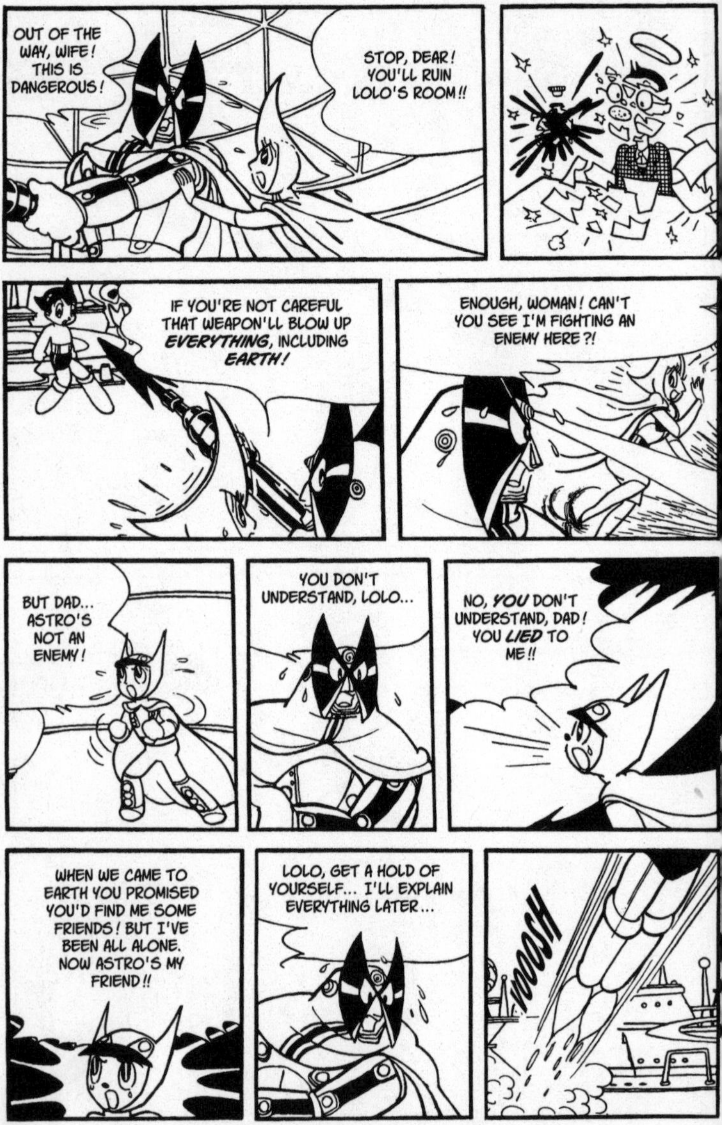
OUT OF THE WAY, WIFE! THIS IS DANGEROUS!
STOP, DEAR! YOU'LL RUIN LOLO'S ROOM!!
IF YOU'RE NOT CAREFUL THAT WEAPON'LL BLOW UP *EVERYTHING*, INCLUDING *EARTH!*
ENOUGH, WOMAN! CAN'T YOU SEE I'M FIGHTING AN ENEMY HERE?!
BUT DAD... ASTRO'S NOT AN ENEMY!
YOU DON'T UNDERSTAND, LOLO...
NO, *YOU* DON'T UNDERSTAND, DAD! YOU *LIED* TO ME!!
WHEN WE CAME TO EARTH YOU PROMISED YOU'D FIND ME SOME FRIENDS! BUT I'VE BEEN ALL ALONE. NOW ASTRO'S MY FRIEND!!
LOLO, GET A HOLD OF YOURSELF... I'LL EXPLAIN EVERYTHING LATER...
WHOOOSH

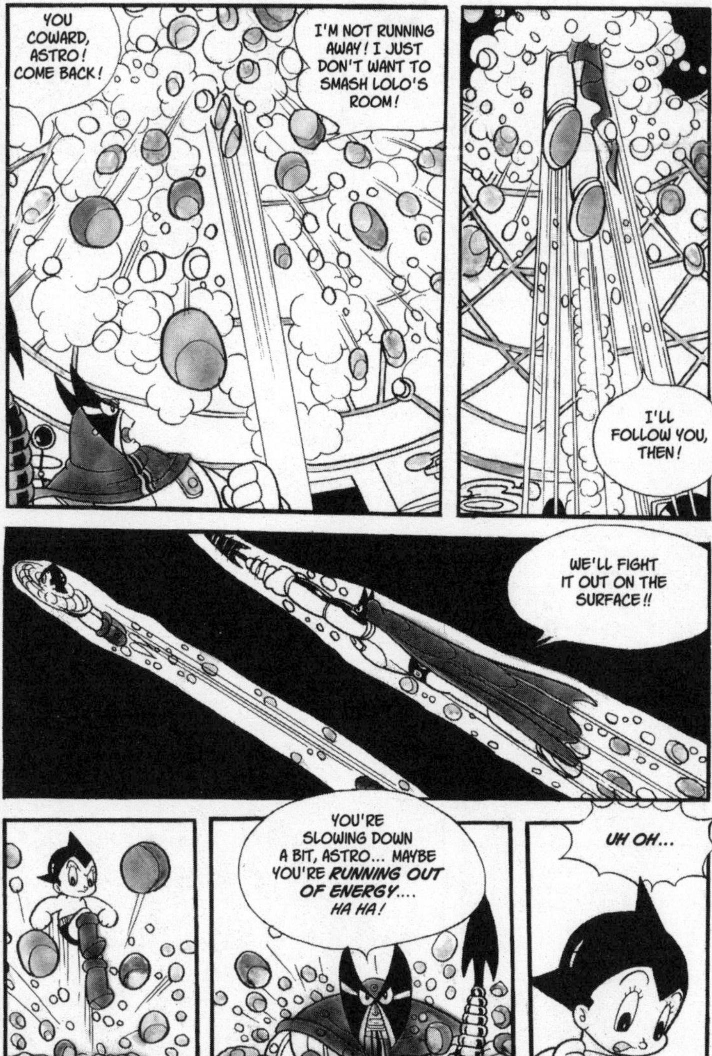
YOU COWARD, ASTRO! COME BACK!
I'M NOT RUNNING AWAY! I JUST DON'T WANT TO SMASH LOLO'S ROOM!
I'LL FOLLOW YOU, THEN!
WE'LL FIGHT IT OUT ON THE SURFACE!!
YOU'RE SLOWING DOWN A BIT, ASTRO... MAYBE YOU'RE *RUNNING OUT OF ENERGY*.... *HA HA!*
UH OH...

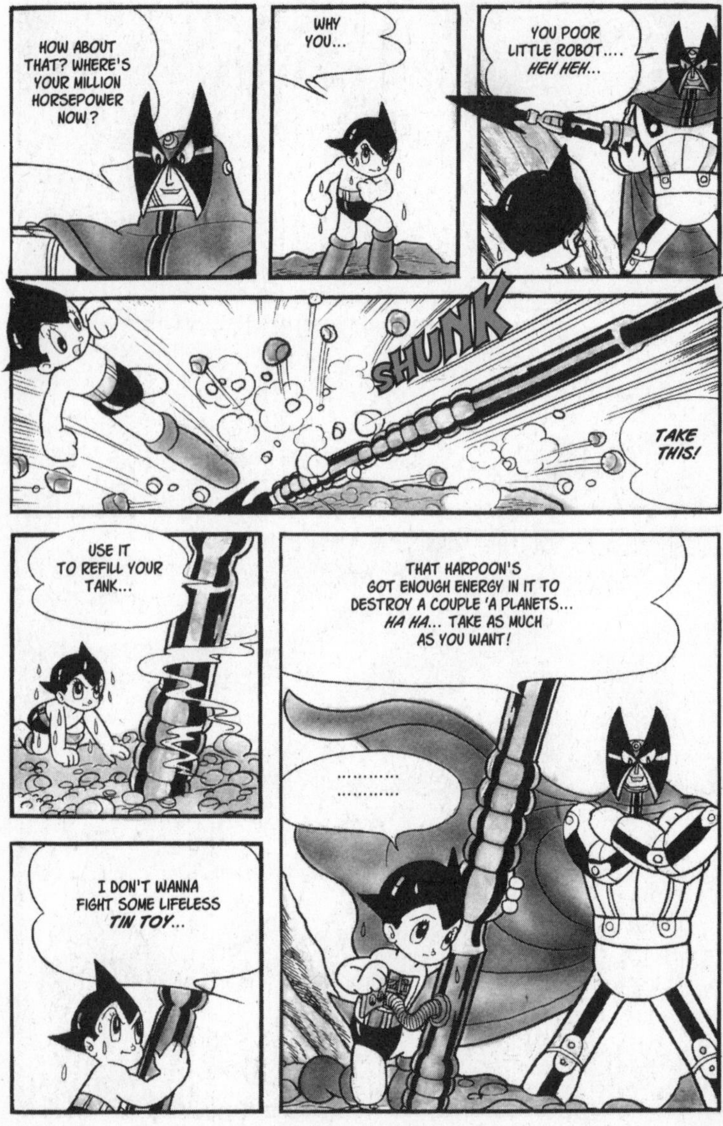
HOW ABOUT THAT? WHERE'S YOUR MILLION HORSEPOWER NOW?
WHY YOU...
YOU POOR LITTLE ROBOT.... HEH HEH...
SHUNK
TAKE THIS!
USE IT TO REFILL YOUR TANK...
I DON'T WANNA FIGHT SOME LIFELESS TIN TOY...
THAT HARPOON'S GOT ENOUGH ENERGY IN IT TO DESTROY A COUPLE 'A PLANETS... HA HA... TAKE AS MUCH AS YOU WANT!
....
....

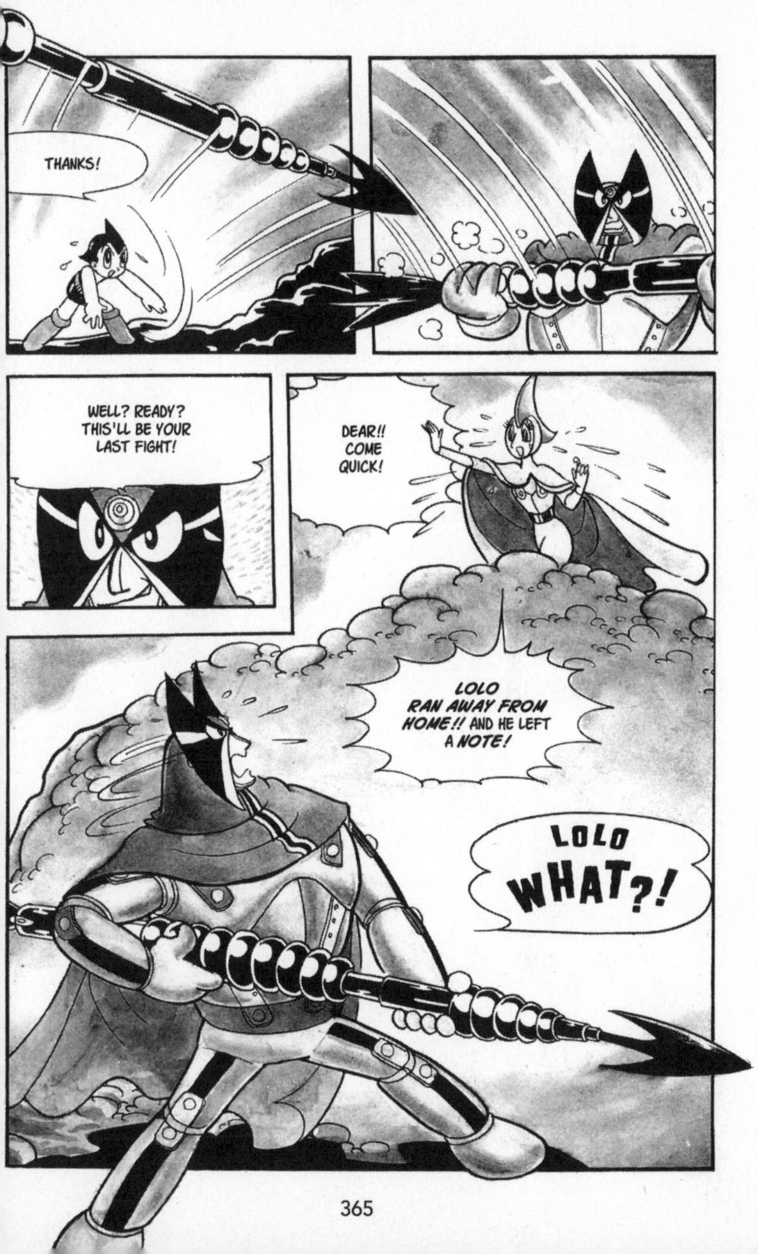
THANKS!
WELL? READY? THIS'LL BE YOUR LAST FIGHT!
DEAR!! COME QUICK!
LOLO RAN AWAY FROM HOME!! AND HE LEFT A NOTE!
LOLO WHAT?!

HOW'D HE GET OUT OF OUR PLACE?

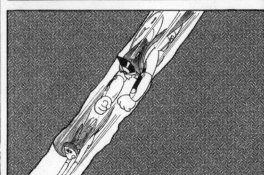

HE USED THE TELEPORTATION DEVICE!

HE WHAT?!

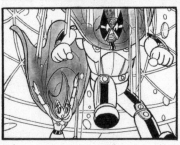

366

SO HE USED THIS THING?!
HE DIDN'T SAY ANYTHING?
HERE, HE WROTE A NOTE ON THIS!
DEAR MOM AND DAD. I CAN'T STAND IT ANYMORE. JUST WHEN I MAKE FRIENDS WITH ASTRO BOY, DAD DRIVES HIM AWAY. DAD LIED TO ME. HE SAID HE'D SHOW ME LOTS OF INTERESTING STUFF WHEN WE CAME TO EARTH, BUT HE'S NEVER TAKEN ME TO THE SURFACE, NOT EVEN ONCE!!

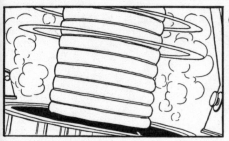

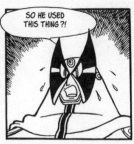

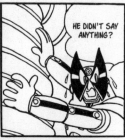

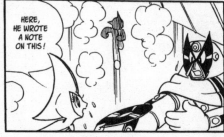

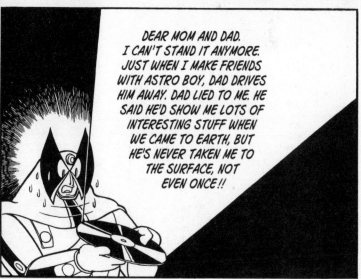

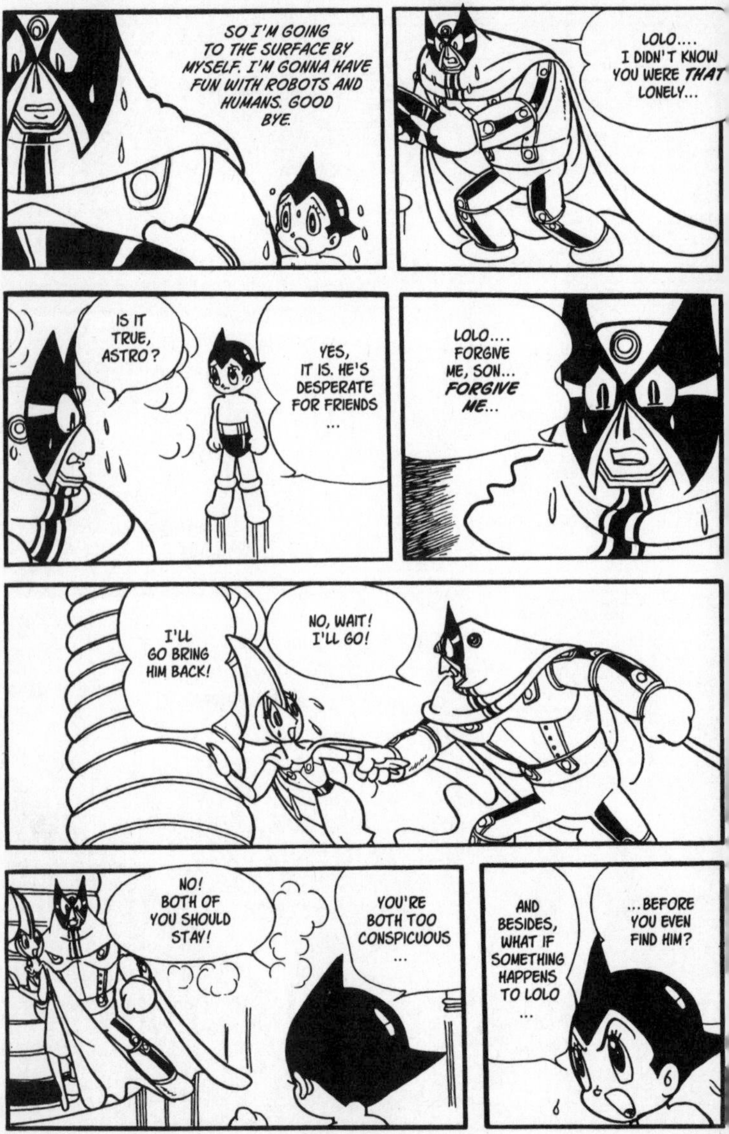
SO I'M GOING TO THE SURFACE BY MYSELF. I'M GONNA HAVE FUN WITH ROBOTS AND HUMANS. GOOD BYE.
LOLO.... I DIDN'T KNOW YOU WERE *THAT* LONELY...
IS IT TRUE, ASTRO?
YES, IT IS. HE'S DESPERATE FOR FRIENDS ...
LOLO.... FORGIVE ME, SON... ***FORGIVE ME***...
I'LL GO BRING HIM BACK!
NO, WAIT! I'LL GO!
NO! BOTH OF YOU SHOULD STAY!
YOU'RE BOTH TOO CONSPICUOUS ...
AND BESIDES, WHAT IF SOMETHING HAPPENS TO LOLO ...
...BEFORE YOU EVEN FIND HIM?

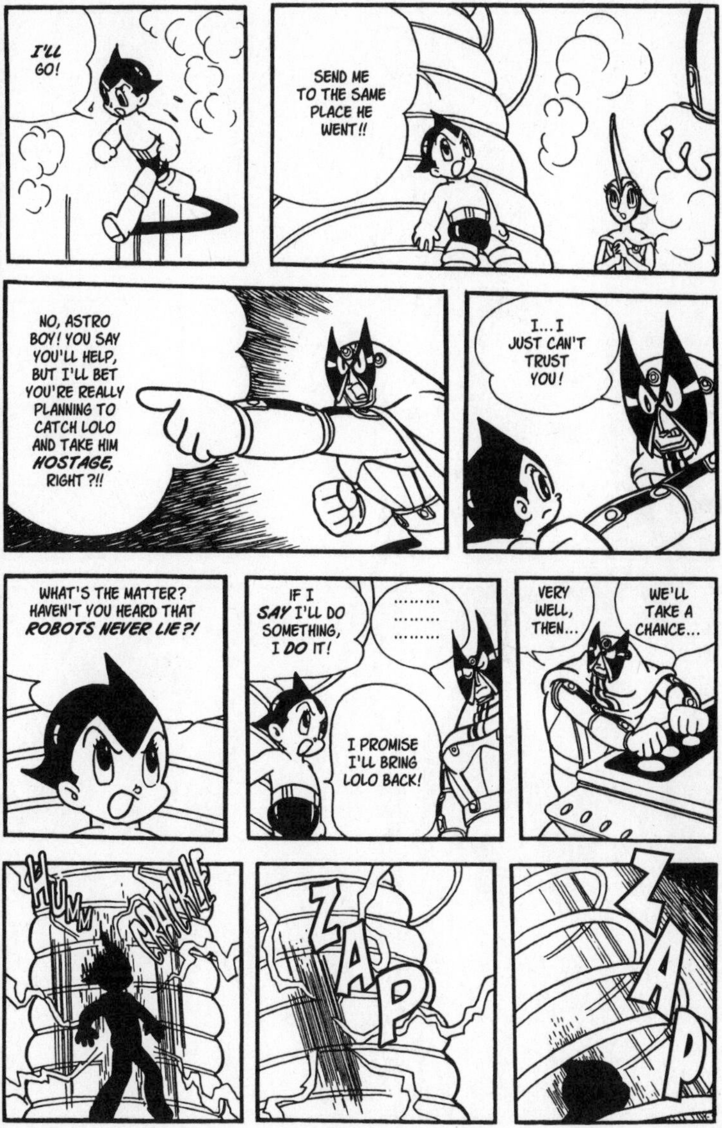

I'LL GO!
SEND ME TO THE SAME PLACE HE WENT!!
NO, ASTRO BOY! YOU SAY YOU'LL HELP, BUT I'LL BET YOU'RE REALLY PLANNING TO CATCH LOLO AND TAKE HIM HOSTAGE, RIGHT?!!
I... I JUST CAN'T TRUST YOU!
WHAT'S THE MATTER? HAVEN'T YOU HEARD THAT ROBOTS NEVER LIE?!
IF I SAY I'LL DO SOMETHING, I DO IT!
....
....
....
I PROMISE I'LL BRING LOLO BACK!
VERY WELL, THEN...
WE'LL TAKE A CHANCE...
HUMM
CRACKLE
ZAP
ZAP

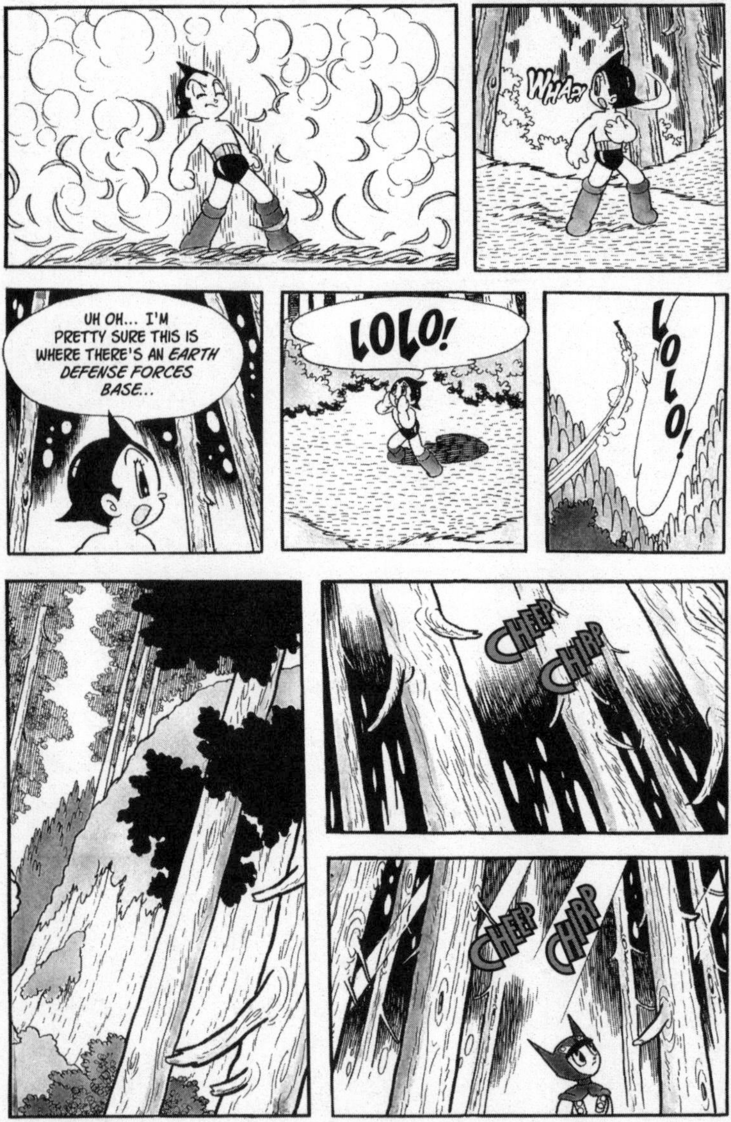
WHA?
UH OH... I'M PRETTY SURE THIS IS WHERE THERE'S AN *EARTH DEFENSE FORCES* BASE...
LOLO!
LOLO!
CHEEP
CHIRP
CHEEP
CHIRP

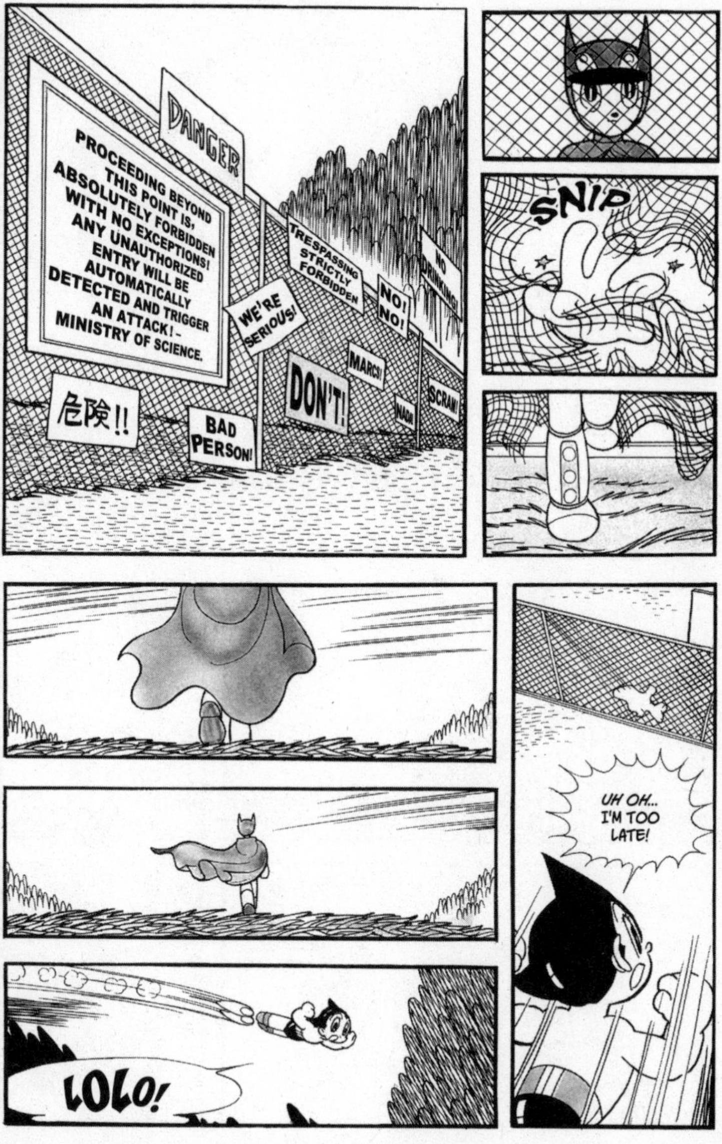
DANGER
PROCEEDING BEYOND THIS POINT IS, ABSOLUTELY FORBIDDEN WITH NO EXCEPTIONS! ANY UNAUTHORIZED ENTRY WILL BE AUTOMATICALLY DETECTED AND TRIGGER AN ATTACK! – MINISTRY OF SCIENCE.
TRESPASSING STRICTLY FORBIDDEN
NO DRINKING!
NO! NO!
WE'RE SERIOUS!
MARCS!
DON'T!
NADA
SCRAM!
危険!!
BAD PERSON!
SNIP
LOLO!
UH OH... I'M TOO LATE!

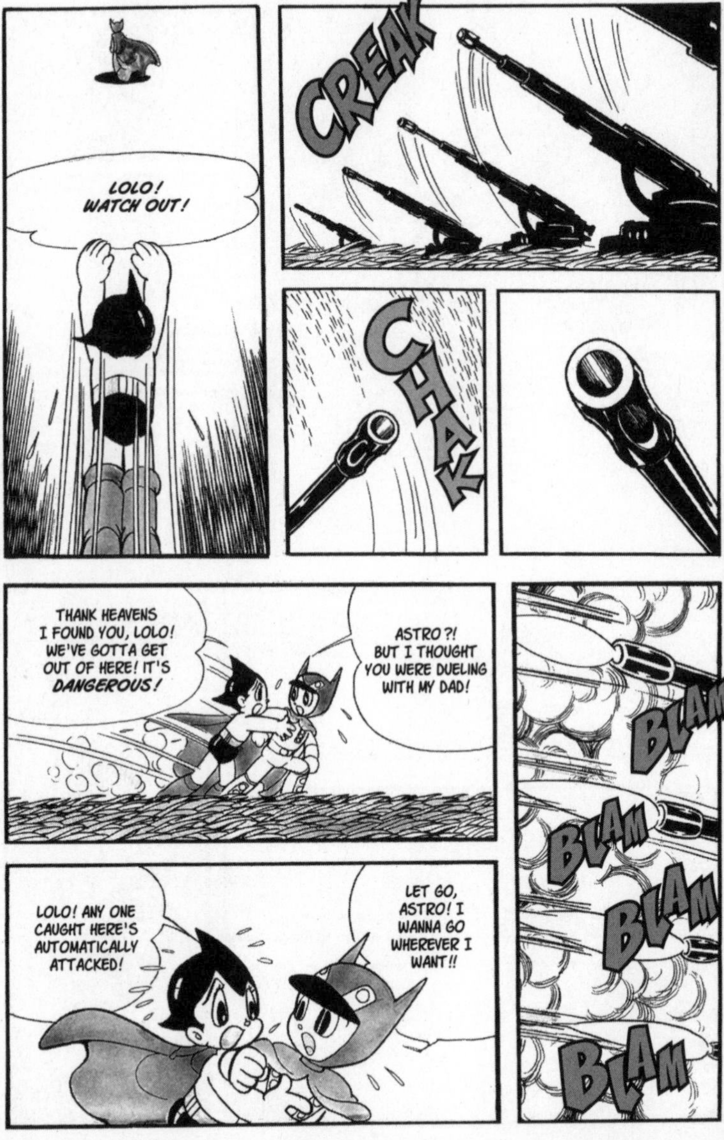
LOLO! WATCH OUT!
CREAK
CHAK
THANK HEAVENS I FOUND YOU, LOLO! WE'VE GOTTA GET OUT OF HERE! IT'S *DANGEROUS!*
ASTRO?! BUT I THOUGHT YOU WERE DUELING WITH MY DAD!
LOLO! ANY ONE CAUGHT HERE'S AUTOMATICALLY ATTACKED!
LET GO, ASTRO! I WANNA GO WHEREVER I WANT!!
BLAM
BLAM
BLAM
BLAM

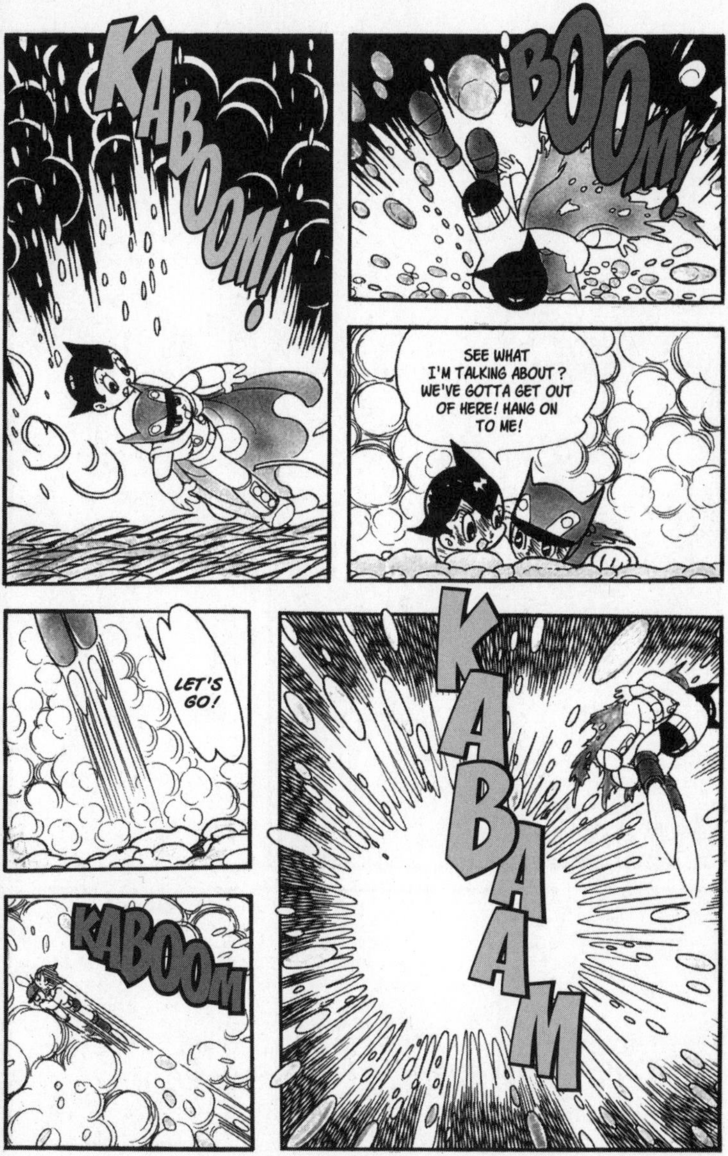
KABOOM!
BOOOM!
SEE WHAT I'M TALKING ABOUT? WE'VE GOTTA GET OUT OF HERE! HANG ON TO ME!
LET'S GO!
KABAAM
KABOOM

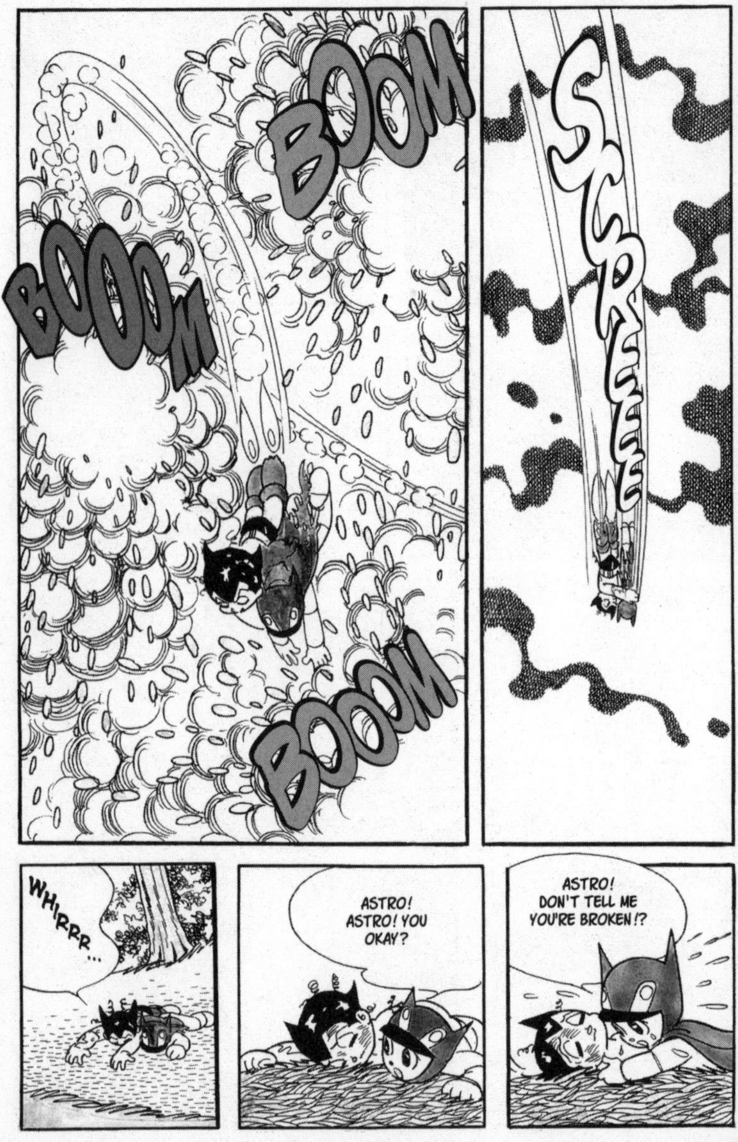
BOOM
BOOOM
BOOOM
WHIRRR...
ASTRO! ASTRO! YOU OKAY?
ASTRO! DON'T TELL ME YOU'RE BROKEN!?

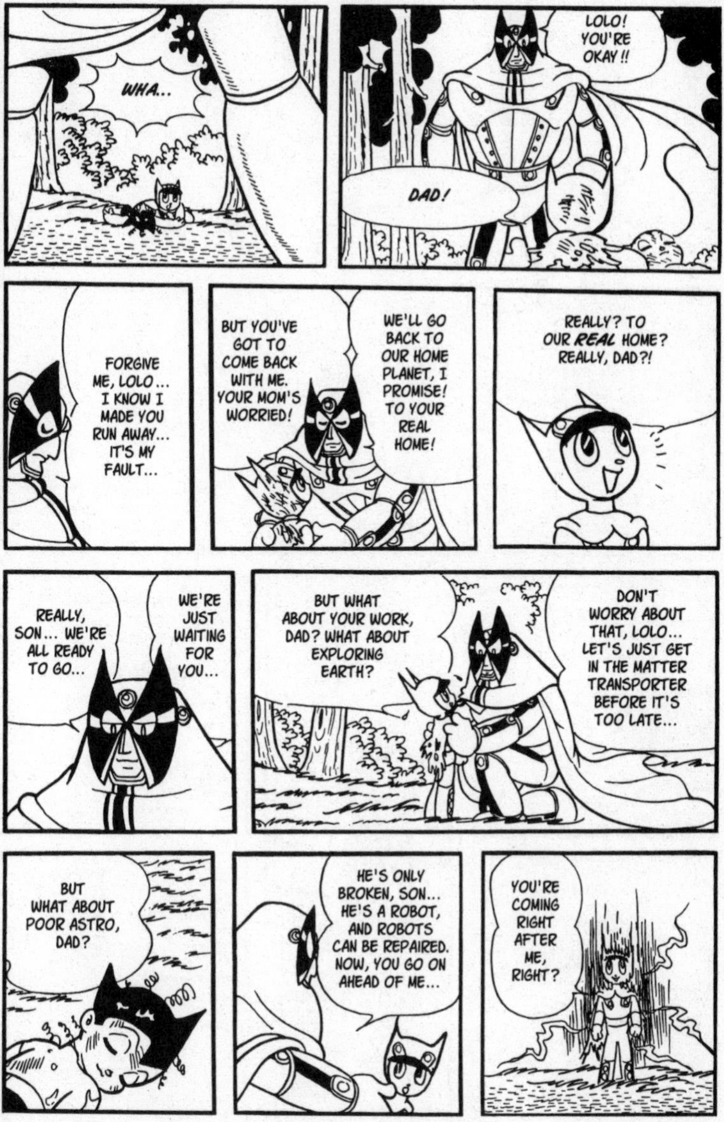
WHA...
LOLO! YOU'RE OKAY!!
DAD!
FORGIVE ME, LOLO... I KNOW I MADE YOU RUN AWAY... IT'S MY FAULT...
BUT YOU'VE GOT TO COME BACK WITH ME. YOUR MOM'S WORRIED!
WE'LL GO BACK TO OUR HOME PLANET, I PROMISE! TO YOUR REAL HOME!
REALLY? TO OUR REAL HOME? REALLY, DAD?!
REALLY, SON... WE'RE ALL READY TO GO...
WE'RE JUST WAITING FOR YOU...
BUT WHAT ABOUT YOUR WORK, DAD? WHAT ABOUT EXPLORING EARTH?
DON'T WORRY ABOUT THAT, LOLO... LET'S JUST GET IN THE MATTER TRANSPORTER BEFORE IT'S TOO LATE...
BUT WHAT ABOUT POOR ASTRO, DAD?
HE'S ONLY BROKEN, SON... HE'S A ROBOT, AND ROBOTS CAN BE REPAIRED. NOW, YOU GO ON AHEAD OF ME...
YOU'RE COMING RIGHT AFTER ME, RIGHT?

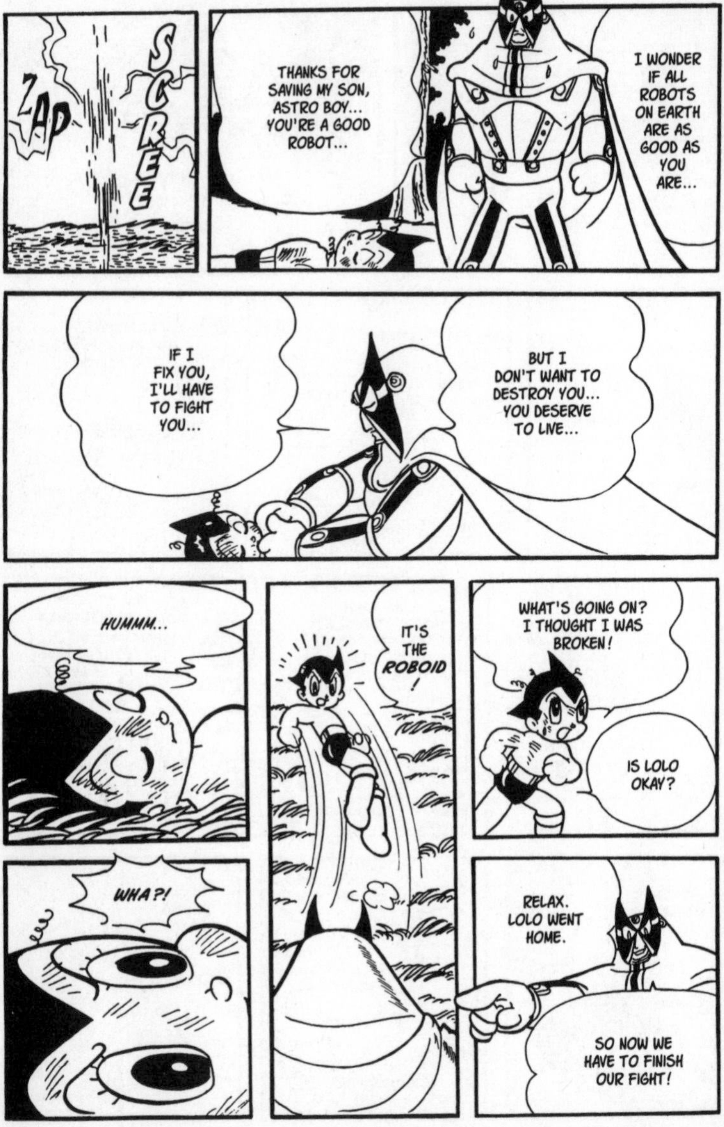
ZAP
SCREE
THANKS FOR SAVING MY SON, ASTRO BOY... YOU'RE A GOOD ROBOT...
I WONDER IF ALL ROBOTS ON EARTH ARE AS GOOD AS YOU ARE...
IF I FIX YOU, I'LL HAVE TO FIGHT YOU...
BUT I DON'T WANT TO DESTROY YOU... YOU DESERVE TO LIVE...
HUMMM...
WHA?!
IT'S THE ROBOID!
WHAT'S GOING ON? I THOUGHT I WAS BROKEN!
IS LOLO OKAY?
RELAX. LOLO WENT HOME.
SO NOW WE HAVE TO FINISH OUR FIGHT!

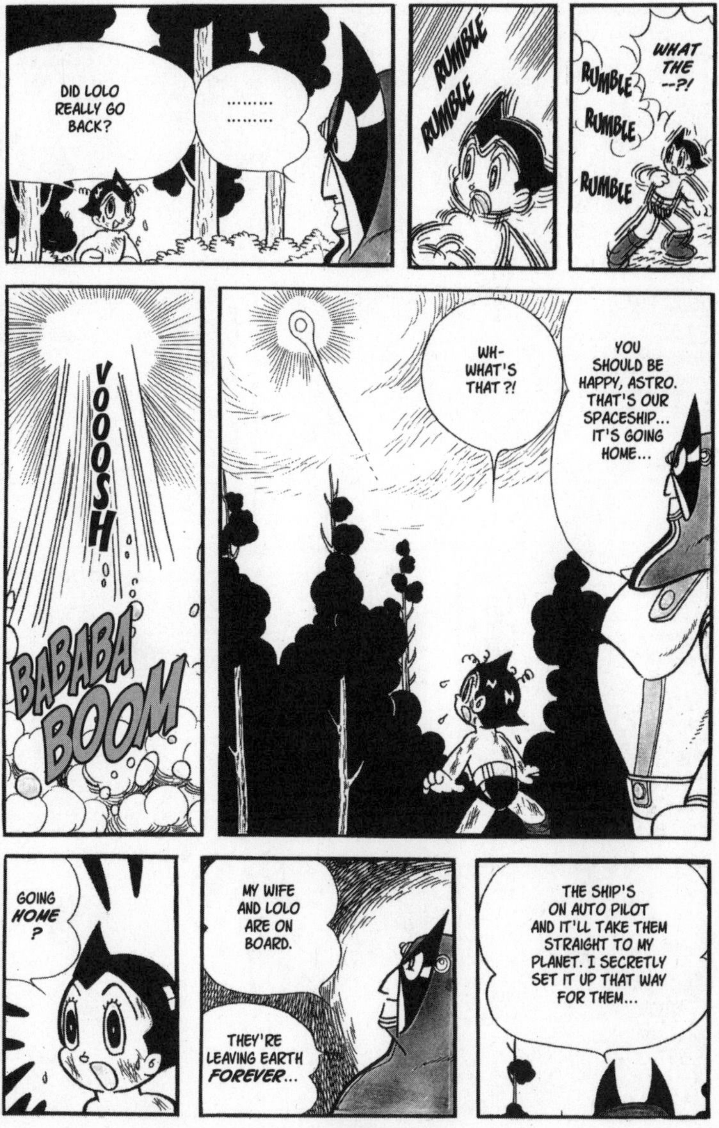
DID LOLO REALLY GO BACK?
....
....
RUMBLE
RUMBLE
RUMBLE
WHAT THE --?!
RUMBLE
RUMBLE
VOOOOSH
BABABA BOOM
WH- WHAT'S THAT ?!
YOU SHOULD BE HAPPY, ASTRO. THAT'S OUR SPACESHIP... IT'S GOING HOME...
GOING *HOME* ?
MY WIFE AND LOLO ARE ON BOARD.
THEY'RE LEAVING EARTH *FOREVER*...
THE SHIP'S ON AUTO PILOT AND IT'LL TAKE THEM STRAIGHT TO MY PLANET. I SECRETLY SET IT UP THAT WAY FOR THEM...

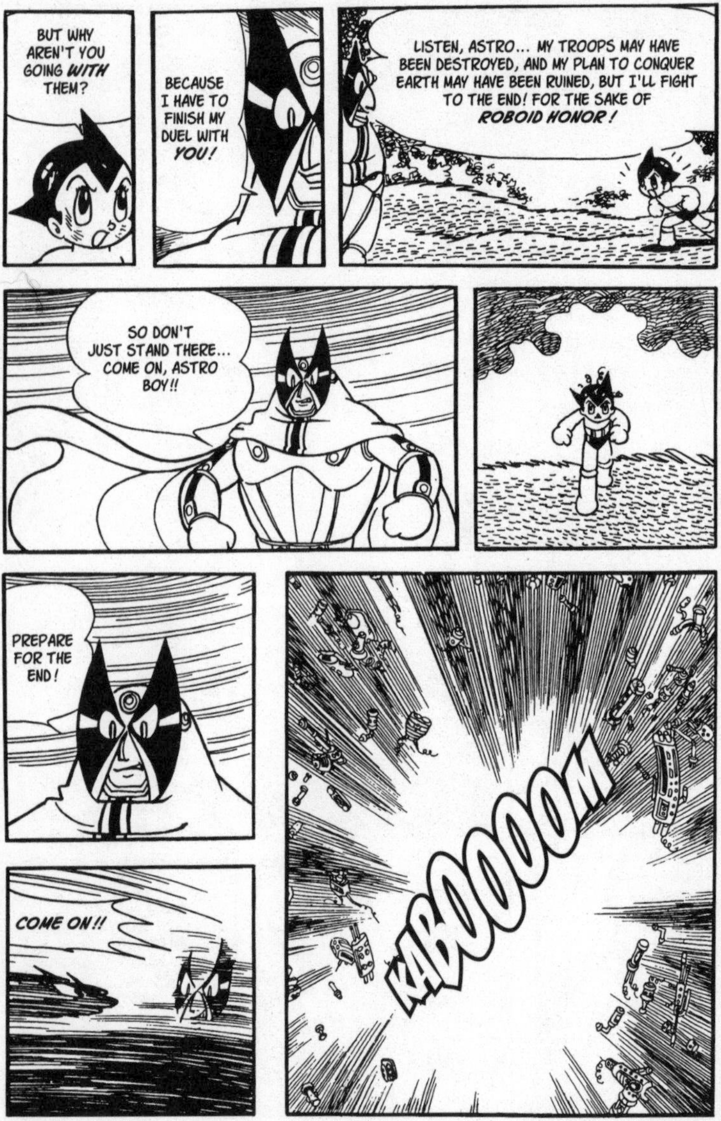
BUT WHY AREN'T YOU GOING WITH THEM?
BECAUSE I HAVE TO FINISH MY DUEL WITH YOU!
LISTEN, ASTRO... MY TROOPS MAY HAVE BEEN DESTROYED, AND MY PLAN TO CONQUER EARTH MAY HAVE BEEN RUINED, BUT I'LL FIGHT TO THE END! FOR THE SAKE OF ROBOID HONOR!
SO DON'T JUST STAND THERE... COME ON, ASTRO BOY!!
PREPARE FOR THE END!
COME ON!!
KABOOOOOM

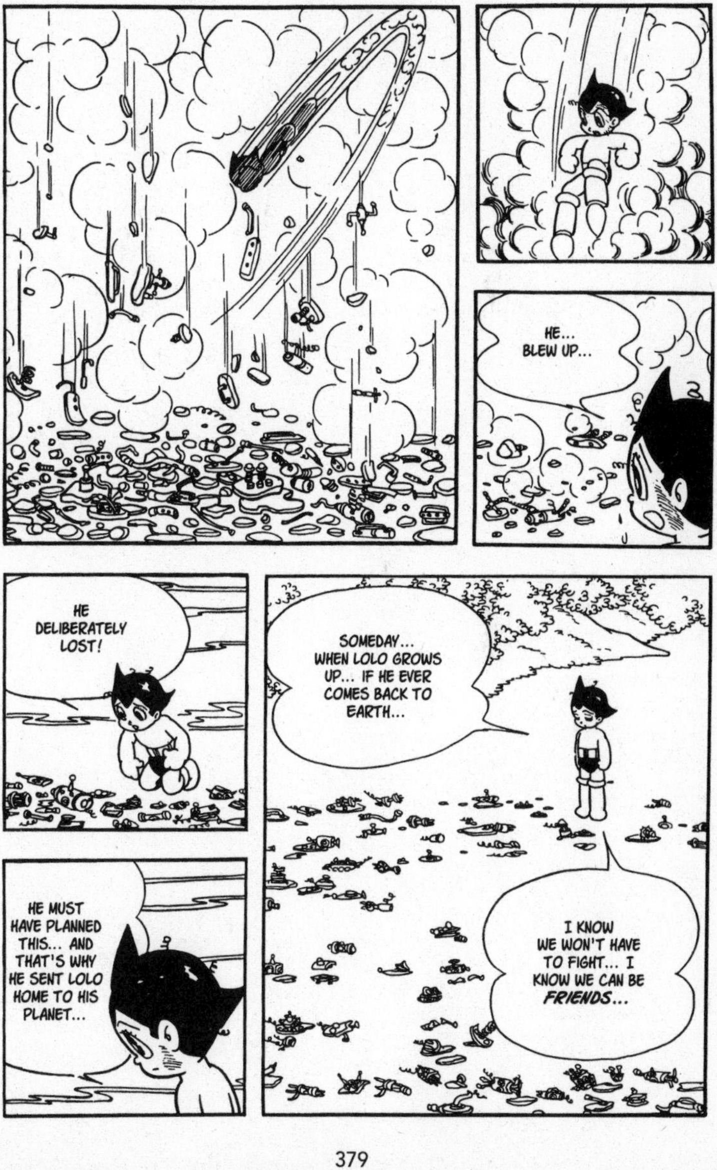
HE... BLEW UP...
HE DELIBERATELY LOST!
HE MUST HAVE PLANNED THIS... AND THAT'S WHY HE SENT LOLO HOME TO HIS PLANET...
SOMEDAY... WHEN LOLO GROWS UP... IF HE EVER COMES BACK TO EARTH...
I KNOW WE WON'T HAVE TO FIGHT... I KNOW WE CAN BE ***FRIENDS***...

THE EYES OF CHRIST

First appeared in the January 1965 supplement
of *Shonen* magazine.

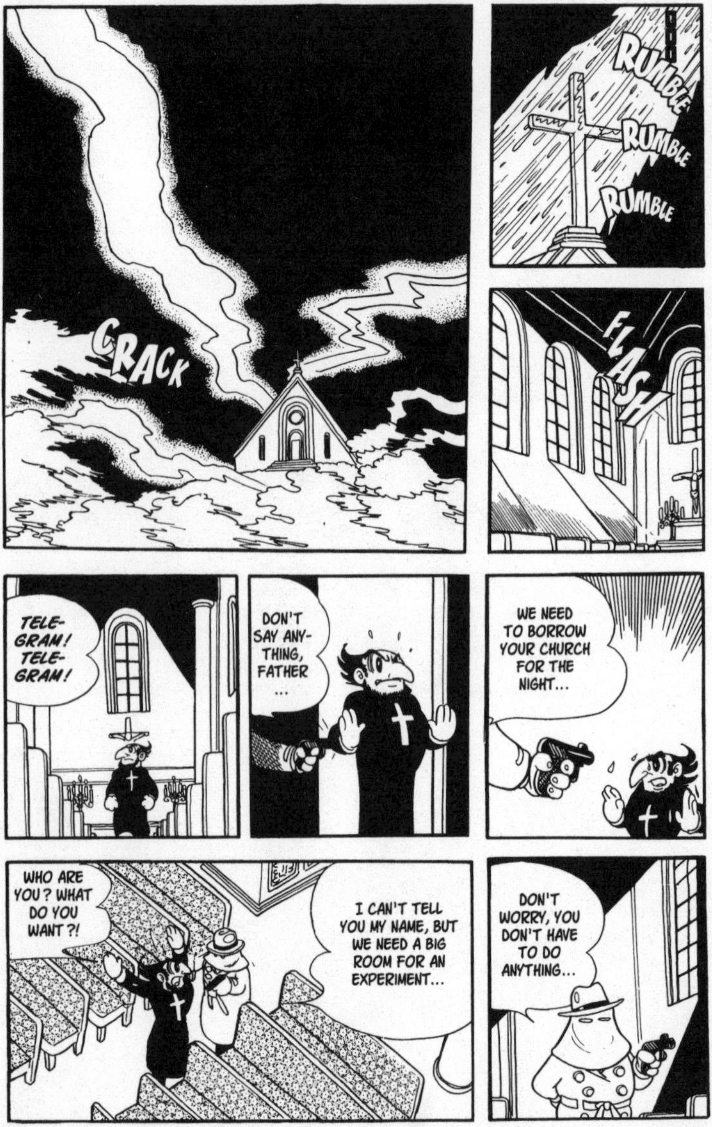
CRACK
RUMBLE
RUMBLE
RUMBLE
FLASH
TELE-GRAM! TELE-GRAM!
DON'T SAY ANY-THING, FATHER ...
WE NEED TO BORROW YOUR CHURCH FOR THE NIGHT...
WHO ARE YOU? WHAT DO YOU WANT?!
I CAN'T TELL YOU MY NAME, BUT WE NEED A BIG ROOM FOR AN EXPERIMENT...
DON'T WORRY, YOU DON'T HAVE TO DO ANYTHING...

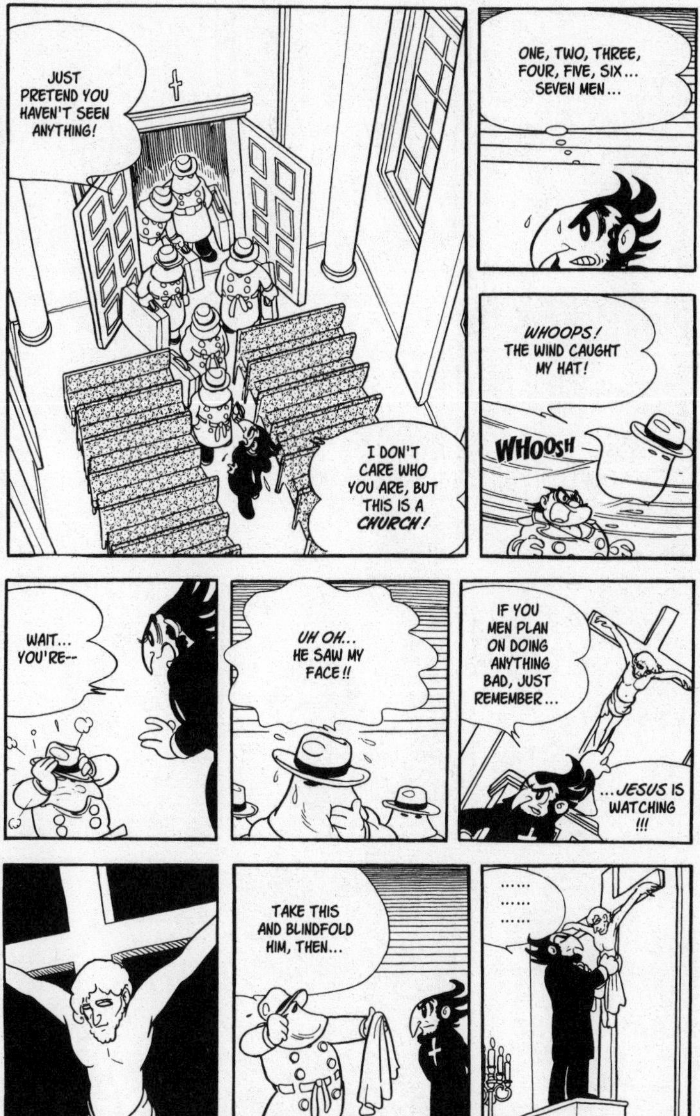
JUST PRETEND YOU HAVEN'T SEEN ANYTHING!
I DON'T CARE WHO YOU ARE, BUT THIS IS A CHURCH!
ONE, TWO, THREE, FOUR, FIVE, SIX... SEVEN MEN...
WHOOPS! THE WIND CAUGHT MY HAT!
WHOOSH
WAIT... YOU'RE--
UH OH... HE SAW MY FACE!!
IF YOU MEN PLAN ON DOING ANYTHING BAD, JUST REMEMBER...
...JESUS IS WATCHING!!!
TAKE THIS AND BLINDFOLD HIM, THEN...
......
......
......

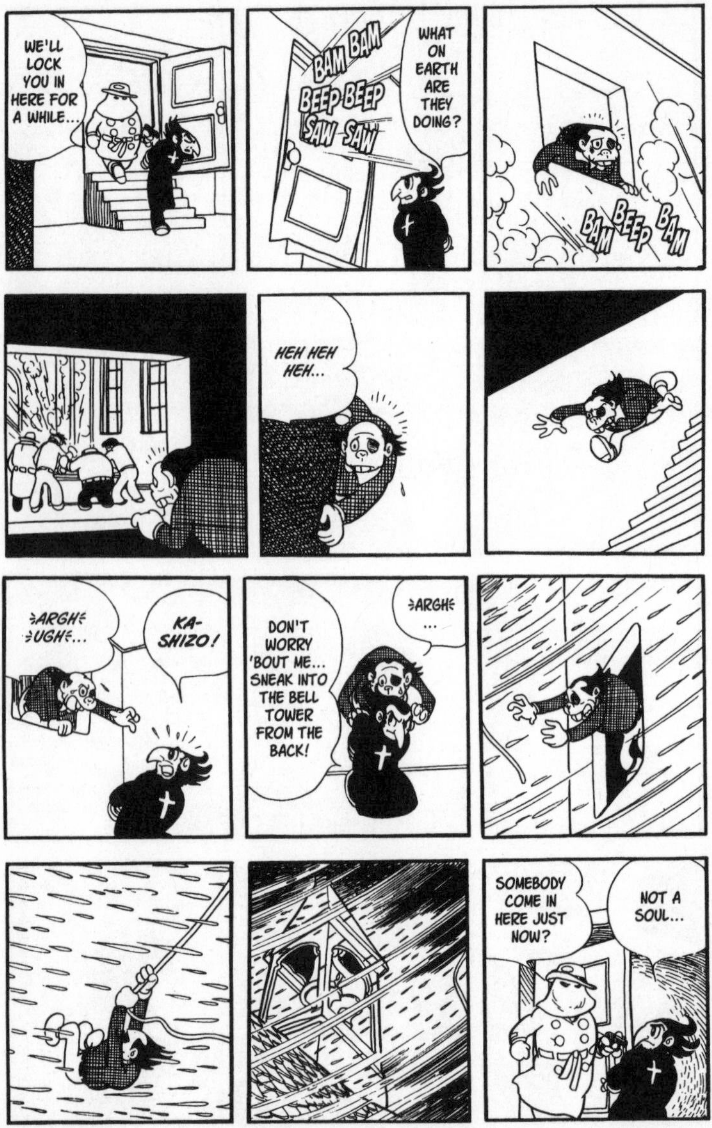
WE'LL LOCK YOU IN HERE FOR A WHILE...
BAM BAM
BEEP BEEP
SAW SAW
WHAT ON EARTH ARE THEY DOING?
BAM BEEP BAM
HEH HEH HEH...
ARGH UGH...
KA-SHIZO!
ARGH ...
DON'T WORRY 'BOUT ME... SNEAK INTO THE BELL TOWER FROM THE BACK!
SOMEBODY COME IN HERE JUST NOW?
NOT A SOUL...

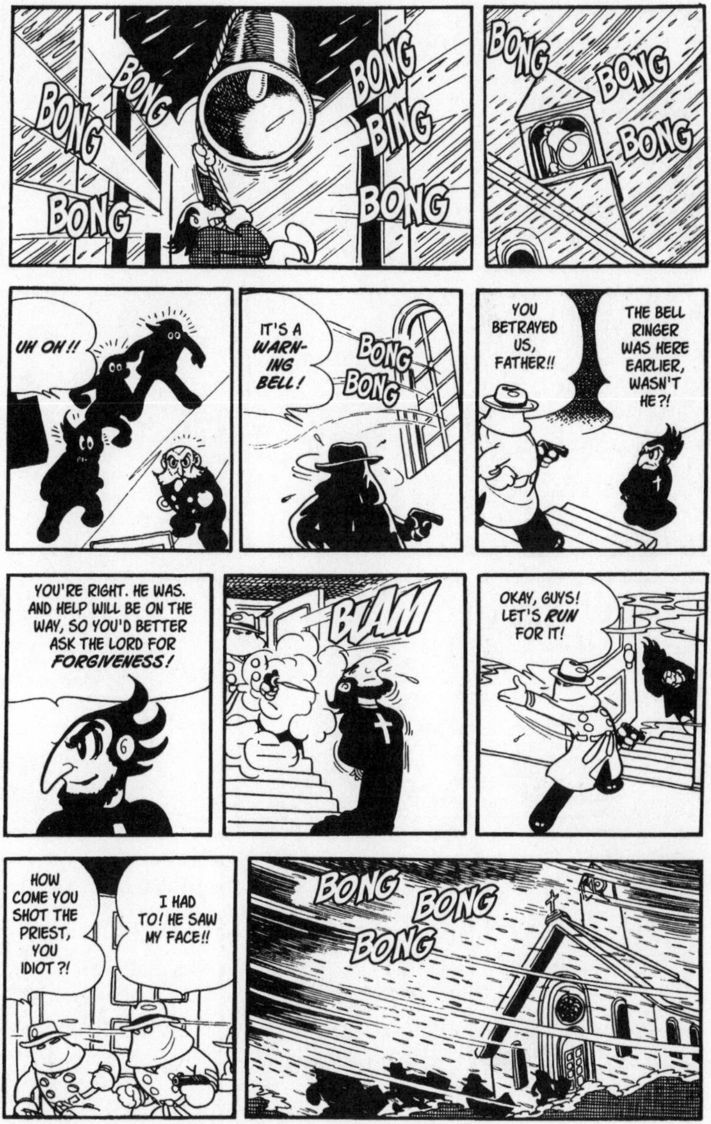
BONG
BONG
BONG
BONG
BING
BONG
BONG
BONG
BONG
BONG
UH OH!!
IT'S A WARNING BELL!
BONG
BONG
YOU BETRAYED US, FATHER!!
THE BELL RINGER WAS HERE EARLIER, WASN'T HE?!
YOU'RE RIGHT. HE WAS. AND HELP WILL BE ON THE WAY, SO YOU'D BETTER ASK THE LORD FOR FORGIVENESS!
BLAM
OKAY, GUYS! LET'S RUN FOR IT!
HOW COME YOU SHOT THE PRIEST, YOU IDIOT?!
I HAD TO! HE SAW MY FACE!!
BONG
BONG
BONG

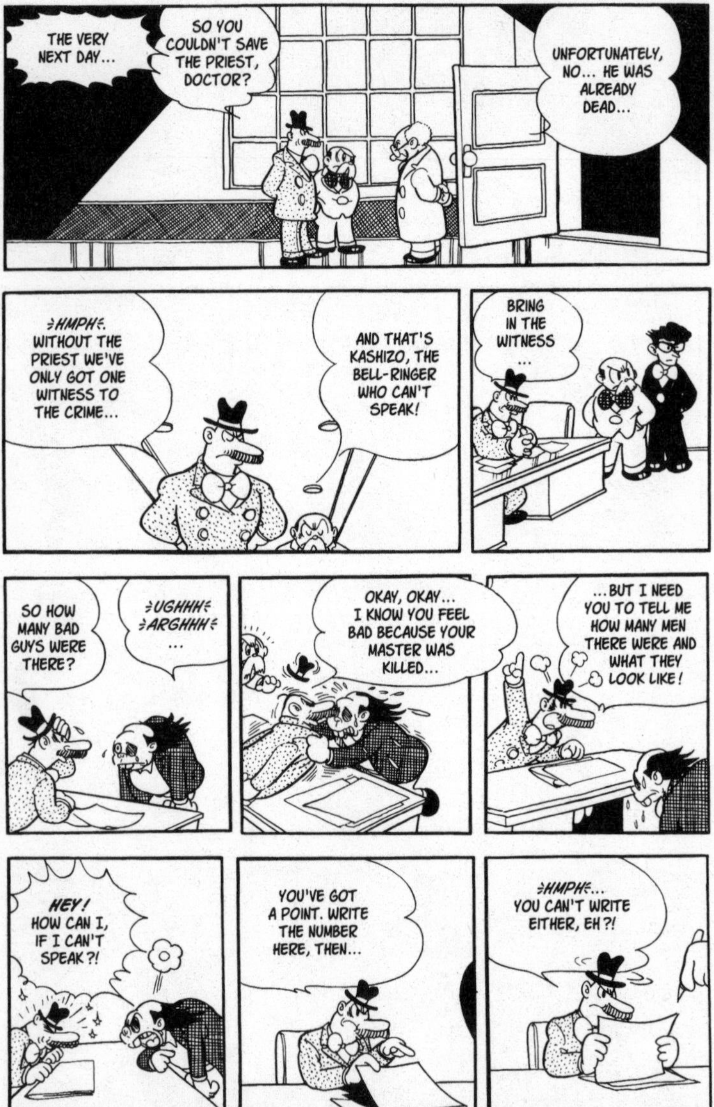
THE VERY NEXT DAY...
SO YOU COULDN'T SAVE THE PRIEST, DOCTOR?
UNFORTUNATELY, NO... HE WAS ALREADY DEAD...
HMPH. WITHOUT THE PRIEST WE'VE ONLY GOT ONE WITNESS TO THE CRIME...
AND THAT'S KASHIZO, THE BELL-RINGER WHO CAN'T SPEAK!
BRING IN THE WITNESS ...
SO HOW MANY BAD GUYS WERE THERE?
UGHHH *ARGHHH* ...
OKAY, OKAY... I KNOW YOU FEEL BAD BECAUSE YOUR MASTER WAS KILLED...
...BUT I NEED YOU TO TELL ME HOW MANY MEN THERE WERE AND WHAT THEY LOOK LIKE!
HEY! HOW CAN I, IF I CAN'T SPEAK?!
YOU'VE GOT A POINT. WRITE THE NUMBER HERE, THEN...
HMPH... YOU CAN'T WRITE EITHER, EH?!

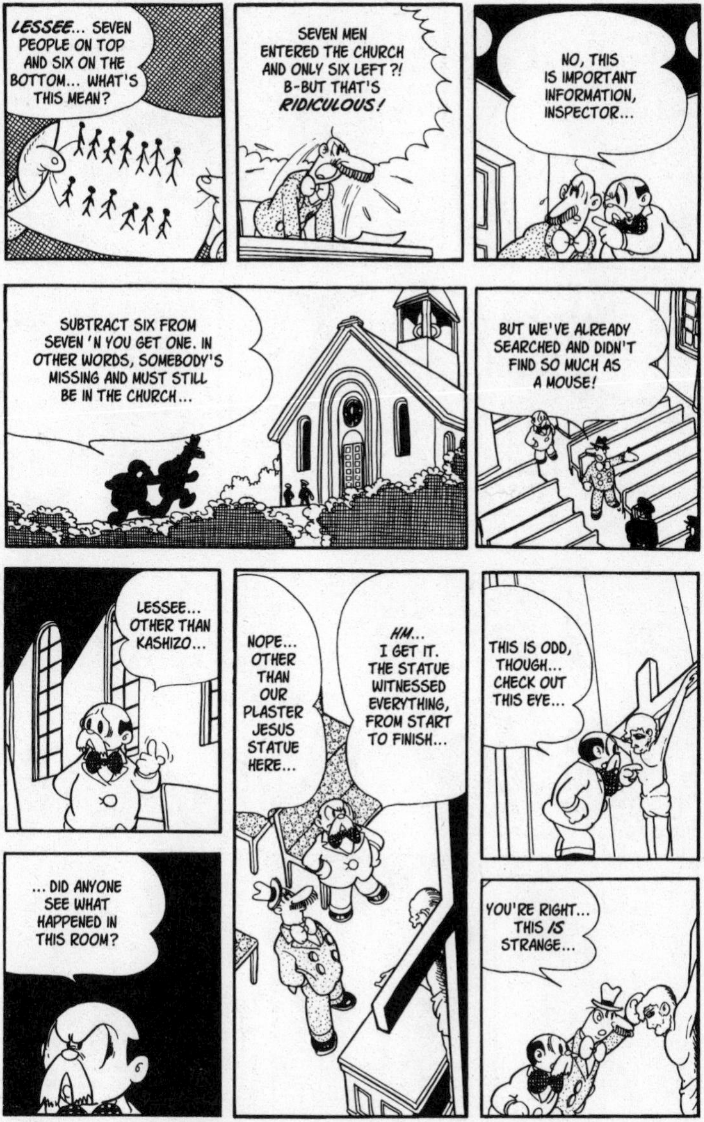
LESSEE... SEVEN PEOPLE ON TOP AND SIX ON THE BOTTOM... WHAT'S THIS MEAN?
SEVEN MEN ENTERED THE CHURCH AND ONLY SIX LEFT?! B-BUT THAT'S *RIDICULOUS!*
NO, THIS IS IMPORTANT INFORMATION, INSPECTOR...
SUBTRACT SIX FROM SEVEN 'N YOU GET ONE. IN OTHER WORDS, SOMEBODY'S MISSING AND MUST STILL BE IN THE CHURCH...
BUT WE'VE ALREADY SEARCHED AND DIDN'T FIND SO MUCH AS A MOUSE!
LESSEE... OTHER THAN KASHIZO...
... DID ANYONE SEE WHAT HAPPENED IN THIS ROOM?
NOPE... OTHER THAN OUR PLASTER JESUS STATUE HERE...
HM... I GET IT. THE STATUE WITNESSED EVERYTHING, FROM START TO FINISH...
THIS IS ODD, THOUGH... CHECK OUT THIS EYE...
YOU'RE RIGHT... THIS *IS* STRANGE...

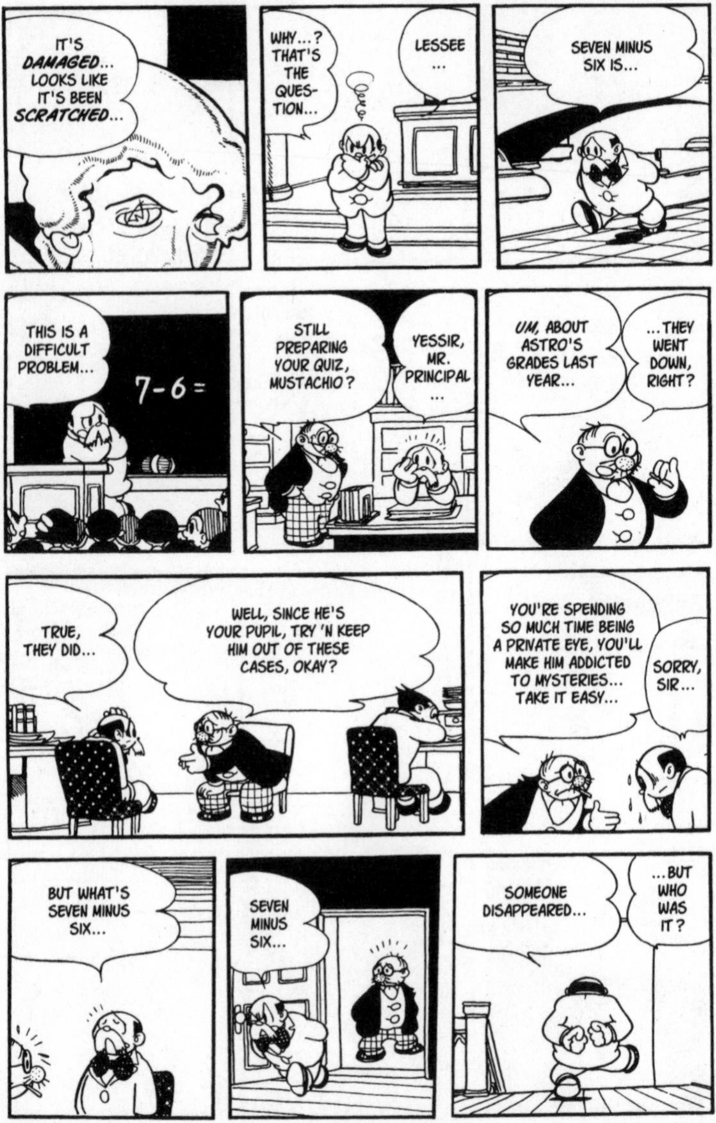
IT'S *DAMAGED*... LOOKS LIKE IT'S BEEN *SCRATCHED*...
WHY...? THAT'S THE QUES-TION...
LESSEE ...
SEVEN MINUS SIX IS...
THIS IS A DIFFICULT PROBLEM...
7-6=
STILL PREPARING YOUR QUIZ, MUSTACHIO?
YESSIR, MR. PRINCIPAL ...
UM, ABOUT ASTRO'S GRADES LAST YEAR...
...THEY WENT DOWN, RIGHT?
TRUE, THEY DID...
WELL, SINCE HE'S YOUR PUPIL, TRY 'N KEEP HIM OUT OF THESE CASES, OKAY?
YOU'RE SPENDING SO MUCH TIME BEING A PRIVATE EYE, YOU'LL MAKE HIM ADDICTED TO MYSTERIES... TAKE IT EASY...
SORRY, SIR...
BUT WHAT'S SEVEN MINUS SIX...
SEVEN MINUS SIX...
SOMEONE DISAPPEARED...
...BUT WHO WAS IT?

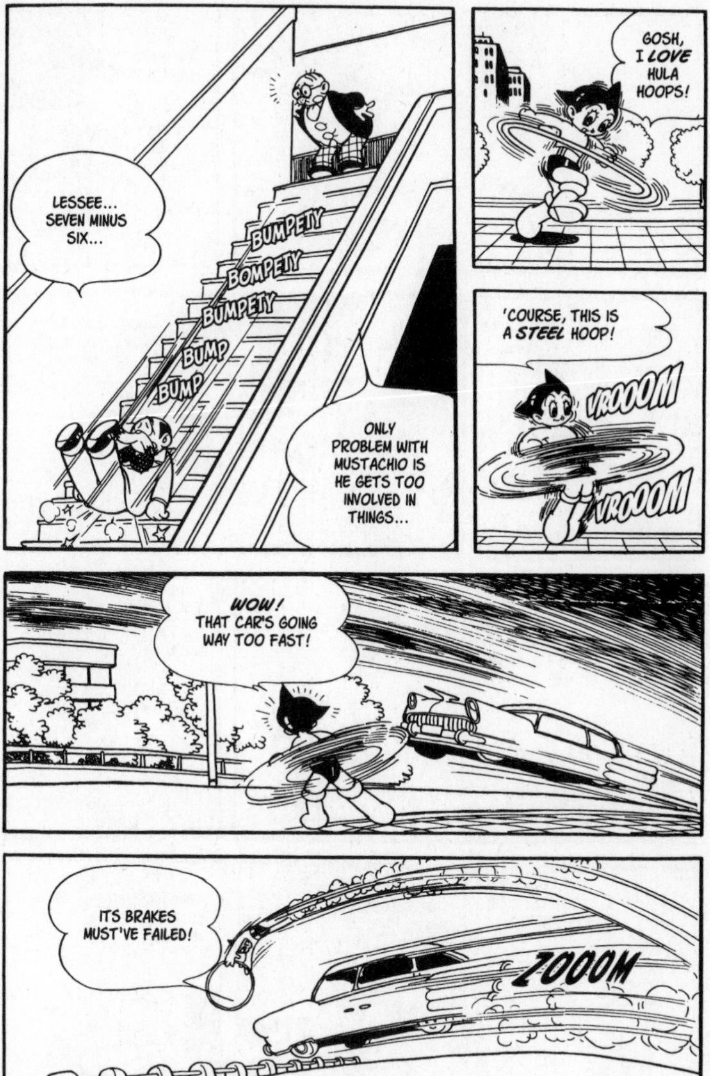
LESSEE... SEVEN MINUS SIX...
BUMPETY
BOMPETY
BUMPETY
BUMP
BUMP
ONLY PROBLEM WITH MUSTACHIO IS HE GETS TOO INVOLVED IN THINGS...
GOSH, I LOVE HULA HOOPS!
'COURSE, THIS IS A STEEL HOOP!
VROOOM
VROOOM
WOW! THAT CAR'S GOING WAY TOO FAST!
ITS BRAKES MUST'VE FAILED!
ZOOOM

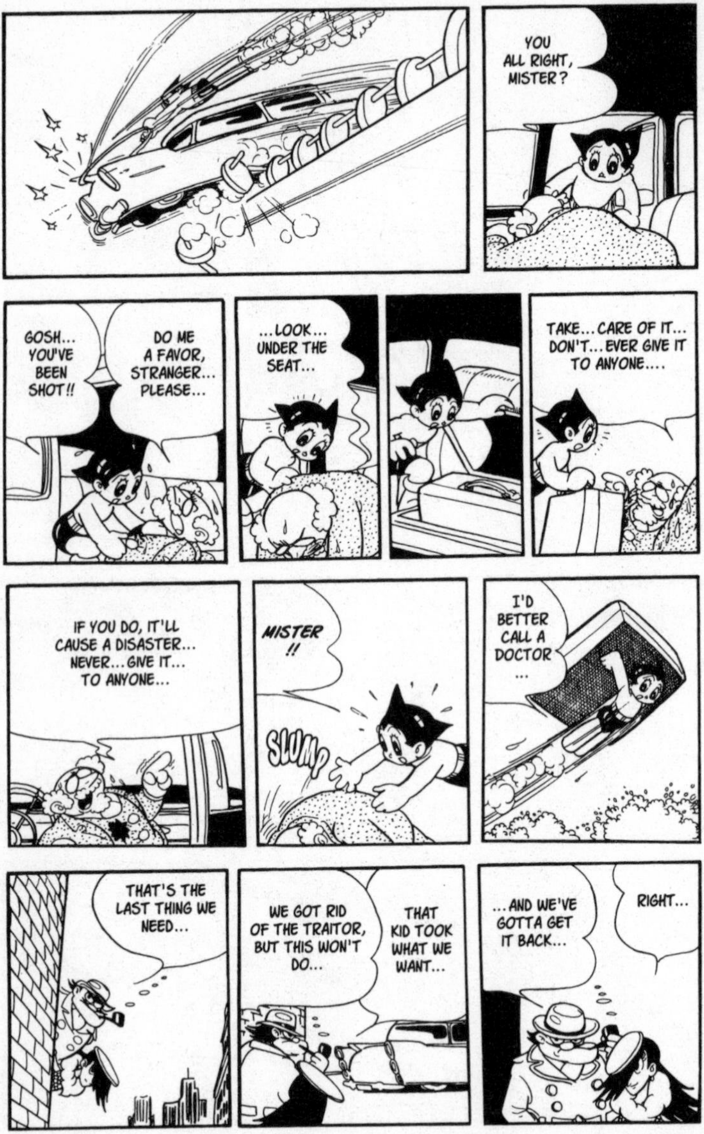
YOU ALL RIGHT, MISTER?
GOSH... YOU'VE BEEN SHOT!!
DO ME A FAVOR, STRANGER... PLEASE...
...LOOK... UNDER THE SEAT...
TAKE... CARE OF IT... DON'T... EVER GIVE IT TO ANYONE....
IF YOU DO, IT'LL CAUSE A DISASTER... NEVER... GIVE IT... TO ANYONE...
MISTER !!
SLUMP
I'D BETTER CALL A DOCTOR ...
THAT'S THE LAST THING WE NEED...
WE GOT RID OF THE TRAITOR, BUT THIS WON'T DO...
THAT KID TOOK WHAT WE WANT...
...AND WE'VE GOTTA GET IT BACK...
RIGHT...

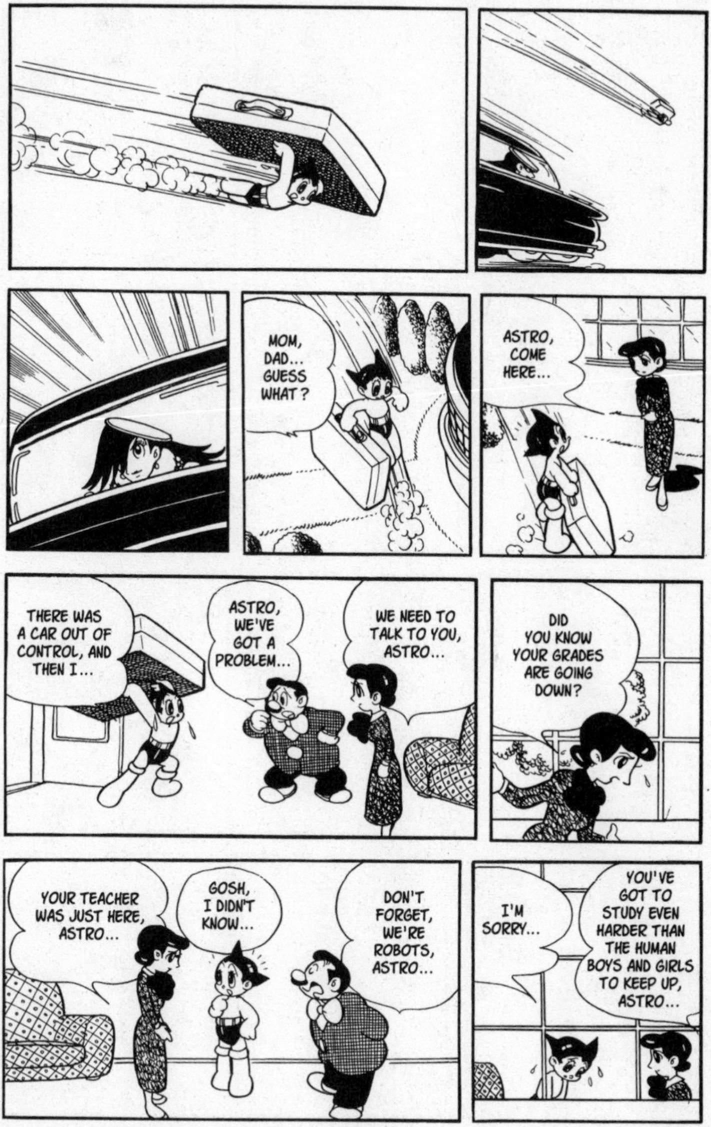

MOM, DAD... GUESS WHAT?
ASTRO, COME HERE...
THERE WAS A CAR OUT OF CONTROL, AND THEN I...
ASTRO, WE'VE GOT A PROBLEM...
WE NEED TO TALK TO YOU, ASTRO...
DID YOU KNOW YOUR GRADES ARE GOING DOWN?
YOUR TEACHER WAS JUST HERE, ASTRO...
GOSH, I DIDN'T KNOW...
DON'T FORGET, WE'RE ROBOTS, ASTRO...
I'M SORRY...
YOU'VE GOT TO STUDY EVEN HARDER THAN THE HUMAN BOYS AND GIRLS TO KEEP UP, ASTRO...

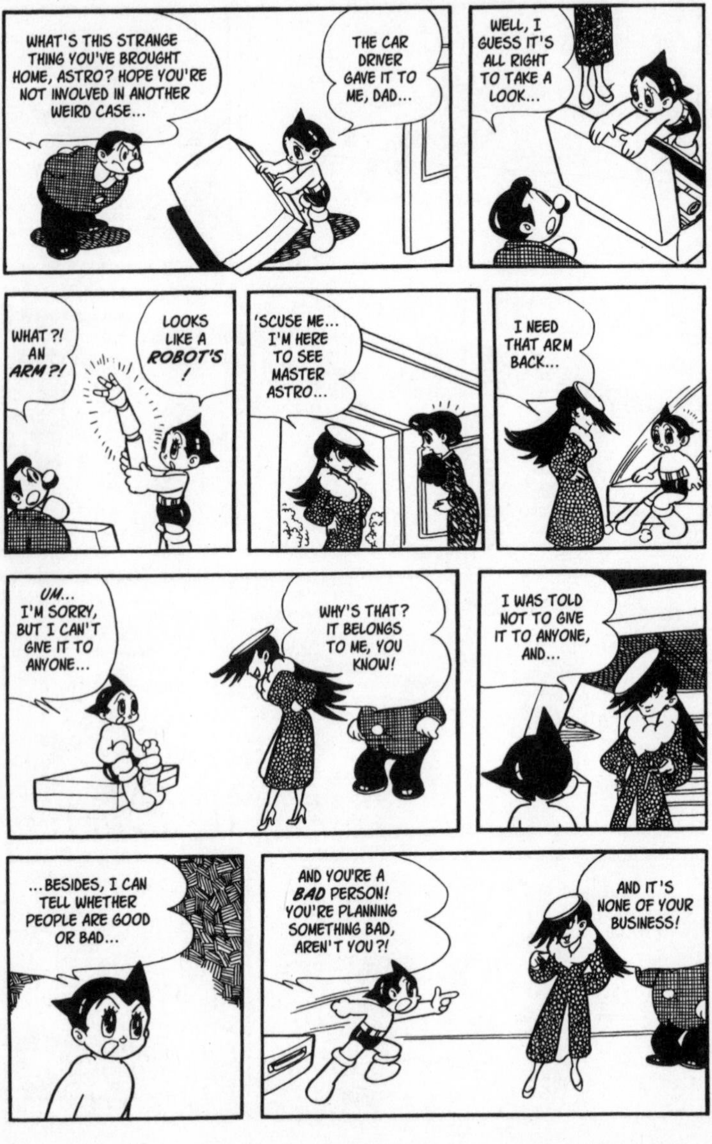
WHAT'S THIS STRANGE THING YOU'VE BROUGHT HOME, ASTRO? HOPE YOU'RE NOT INVOLVED IN ANOTHER WEIRD CASE...
THE CAR DRIVER GAVE IT TO ME, DAD...
WELL, I GUESS IT'S ALL RIGHT TO TAKE A LOOK...
WHAT?! AN *ARM?!*
LOOKS LIKE A *ROBOT'S*!
'SCUSE ME... I'M HERE TO SEE MASTER ASTRO...
I NEED THAT ARM BACK...
UM... I'M SORRY, BUT I CAN'T GIVE IT TO ANYONE...
WHY'S THAT? IT BELONGS TO ME, YOU KNOW!
I WAS TOLD NOT TO GIVE IT TO ANYONE, AND...
...BESIDES, I CAN TELL WHETHER PEOPLE ARE GOOD OR BAD...
AND YOU'RE A *BAD* PERSON! YOU'RE PLANNING SOMETHING BAD, AREN'T YOU?!
AND IT'S NONE OF YOUR BUSINESS!

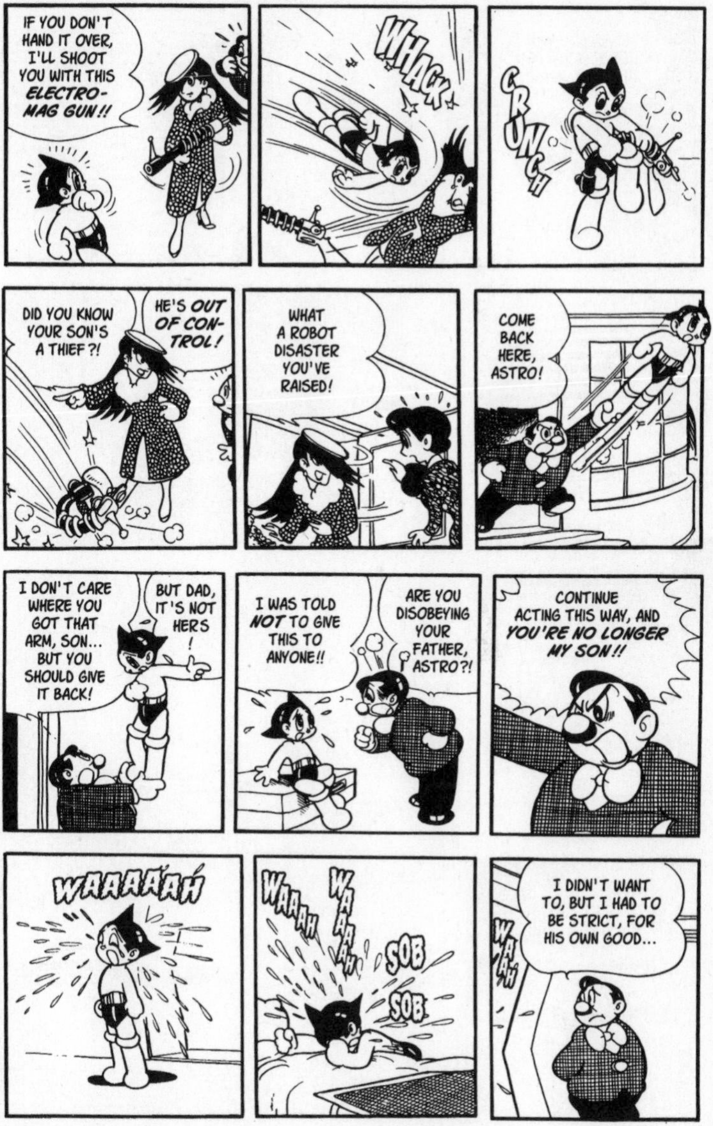
IF YOU DON'T HAND IT OVER, I'LL SHOOT YOU WITH THIS ELECTRO-MAG GUN!!
WHACK
CRUNCH
DID YOU KNOW YOUR SON'S A THIEF?!
HE'S OUT OF CON-TROL!
WHAT A ROBOT DISASTER YOU'VE RAISED!
COME BACK HERE, ASTRO!
I DON'T CARE WHERE YOU GOT THAT ARM, SON... BUT YOU SHOULD GIVE IT BACK!
BUT DAD, IT'S NOT HERS!
I WAS TOLD NOT TO GIVE THIS TO ANYONE!!
ARE YOU DISOBEYING YOUR FATHER, ASTRO?!
CONTINUE ACTING THIS WAY, AND YOU'RE NO LONGER MY SON!!
WAAAAAAH
WAAAAH
WAAAAAH
SOB
SOB
WAAH
I DIDN'T WANT TO, BUT I HAD TO BE STRICT, FOR HIS OWN GOOD...

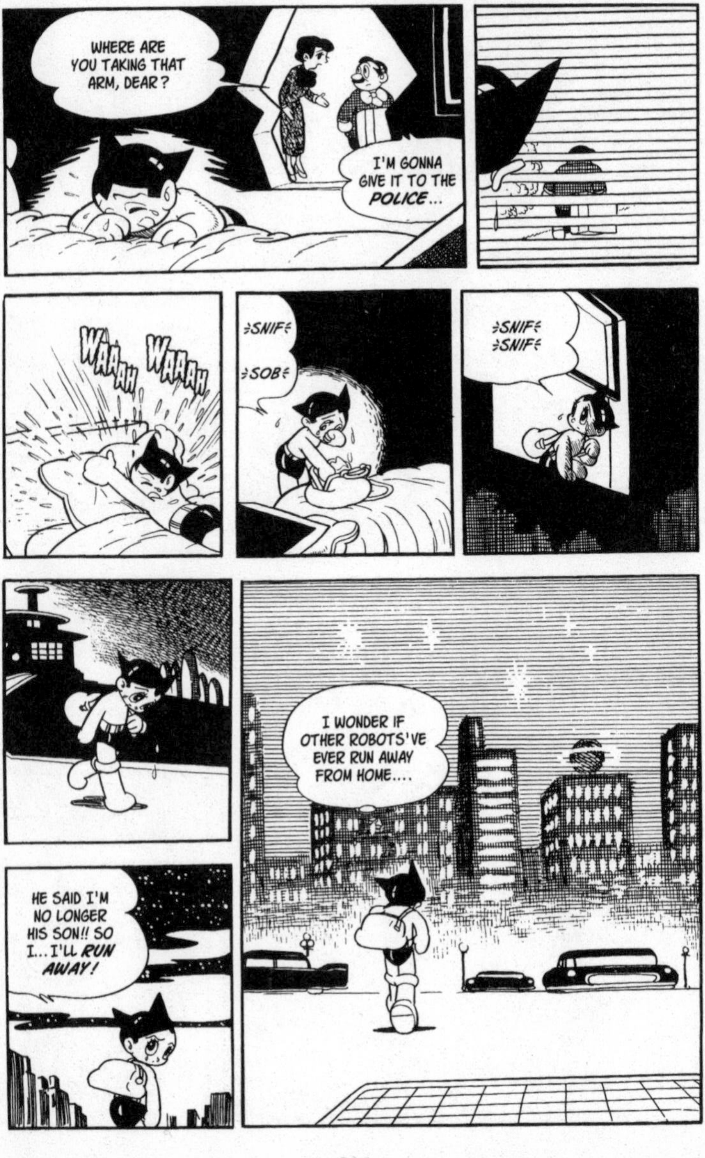
WHERE ARE YOU TAKING THAT ARM, DEAR?
I'M GONNA GIVE IT TO THE POLICE...
WAAAH WAAAH
SNIF
SOB
SNIF SNIF
HE SAID I'M NO LONGER HIS SON!! SO I... I'LL RUN AWAY!
I WONDER IF OTHER ROBOTS'VE EVER RUN AWAY FROM HOME....

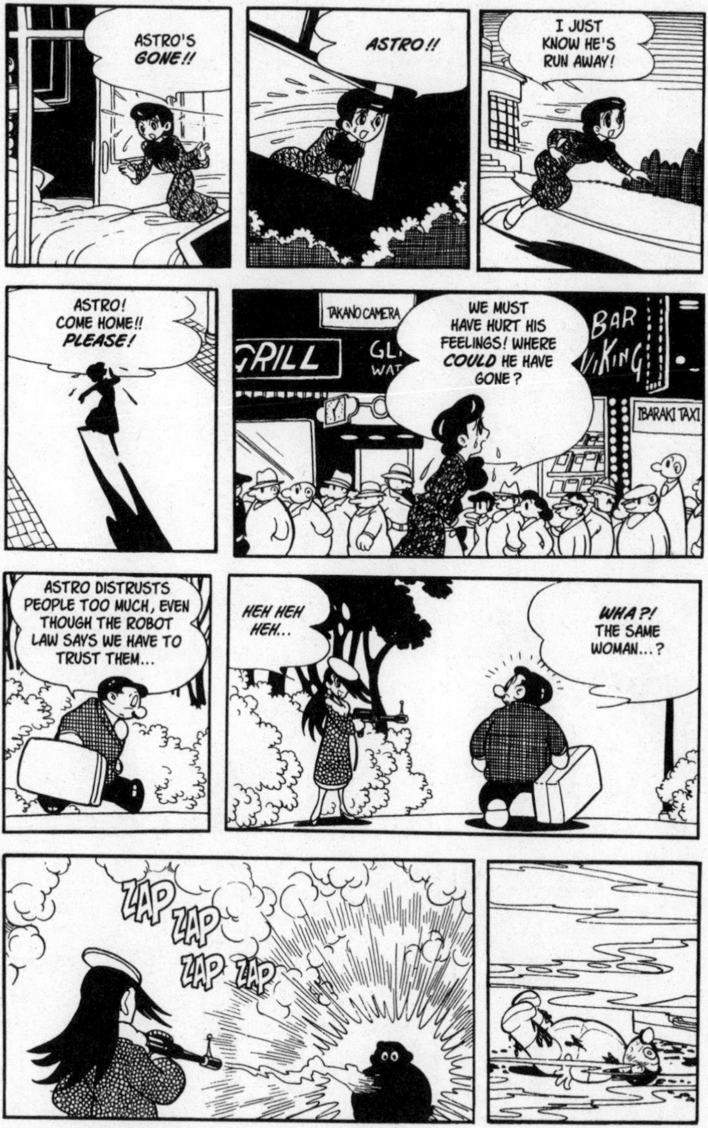
ASTRO'S GONE!!
ASTRO!!
I JUST KNOW HE'S RUN AWAY!
ASTRO! COME HOME!! PLEASE!
TAKANO CAMERA
GRILL
BAR VIKING
WE MUST HAVE HURT HIS FEELINGS! WHERE COULD HE HAVE GONE?
IBARAKI TAXI
ASTRO DISTRUSTS PEOPLE TOO MUCH, EVEN THOUGH THE ROBOT LAW SAYS WE HAVE TO TRUST THEM...
HEH HEH HEH...
WHA?! THE SAME WOMAN...?
ZAP ZAP ZAP ZAP

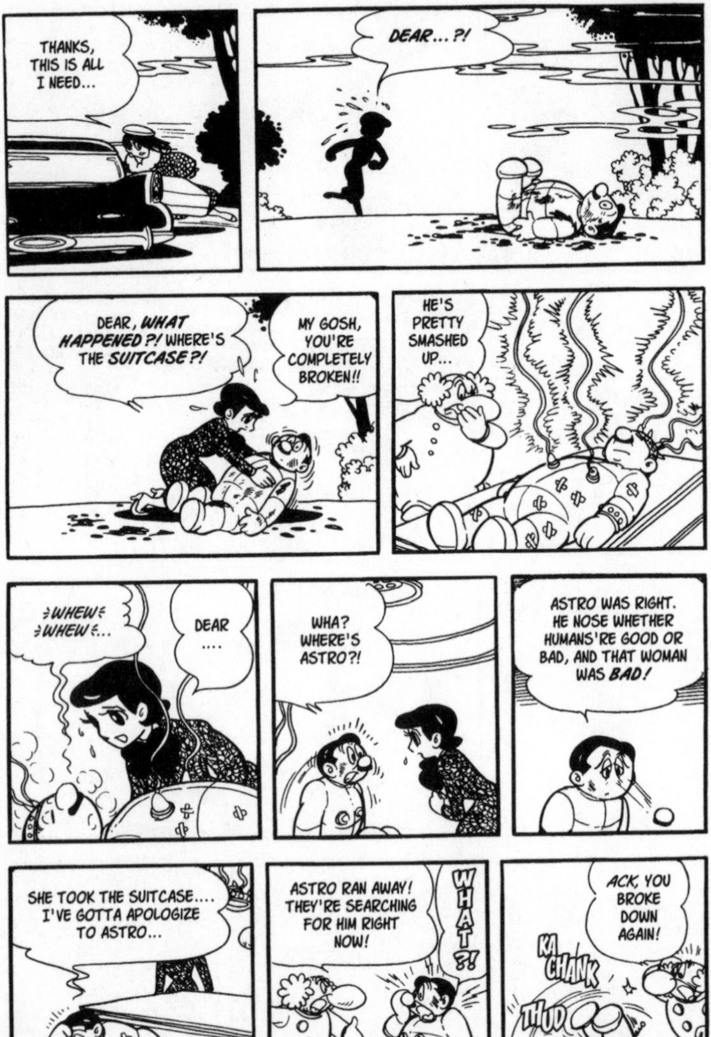
THANKS, THIS IS ALL I NEED...
DEAR...?!
DEAR, WHAT HAPPENED?! WHERE'S THE SUITCASE?!
MY GOSH, YOU'RE COMPLETELY BROKEN!!
HE'S PRETTY SMASHED UP...
WHEW WHEW...
DEAR ....
WHA? WHERE'S ASTRO?!
ASTRO WAS RIGHT. HE NOSE WHETHER HUMANS'RE GOOD OR BAD, AND THAT WOMAN WAS BAD!
SHE TOOK THE SUITCASE.... I'VE GOTTA APOLOGIZE TO ASTRO...
ASTRO RAN AWAY! THEY'RE SEARCHING FOR HIM RIGHT NOW!
WHAT?!
ACK, YOU BROKE DOWN AGAIN!
KA CHANK
THUD

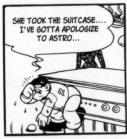

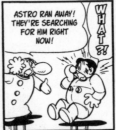

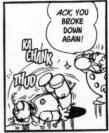

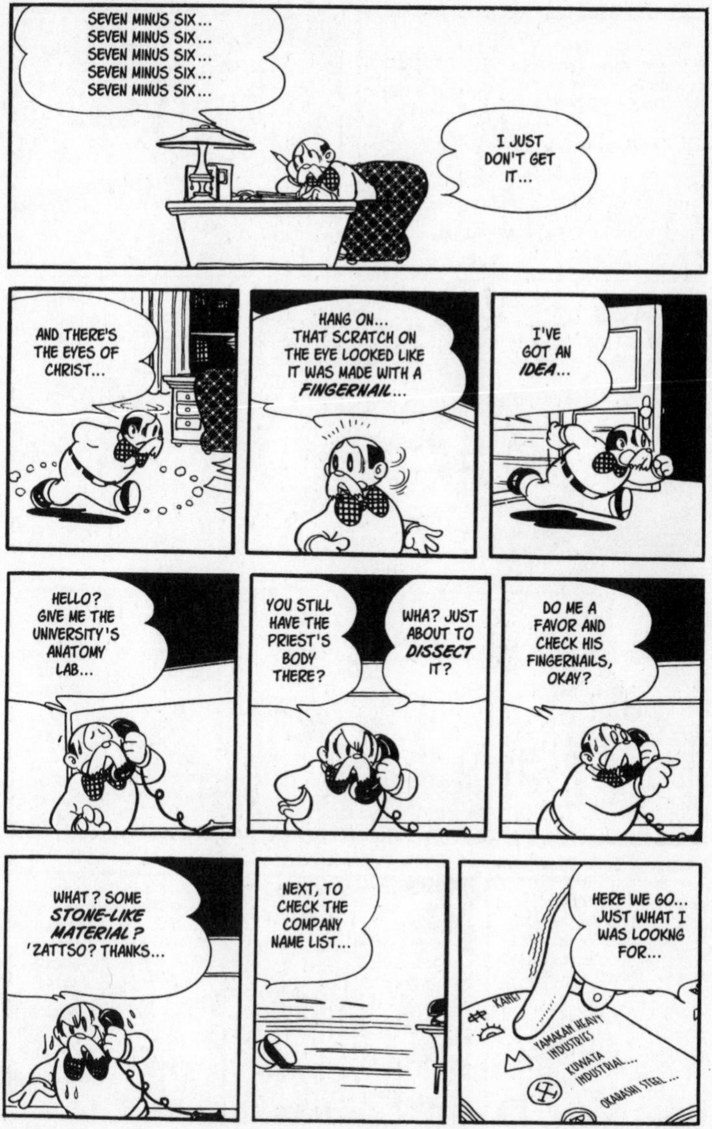
SEVEN MINUS SIX...
SEVEN MINUS SIX...
SEVEN MINUS SIX...
SEVEN MINUS SIX...
SEVEN MINUS SIX...
I JUST DON'T GET IT...
AND THERE'S THE EYES OF CHRIST...
HANG ON... THAT SCRATCH ON THE EYE LOOKED LIKE IT WAS MADE WITH A *FINGERNAIL*...
I'VE GOT AN *IDEA*...
HELLO? GIVE ME THE UNIVERSITY'S ANATOMY LAB...
YOU STILL HAVE THE PRIEST'S BODY THERE?
WHA? JUST ABOUT TO *DISSECT* IT?
DO ME A FAVOR AND CHECK HIS FINGERNAILS, OKAY?
WHAT? SOME *STONE-LIKE MATERIAL?* 'ZATTSO? THANKS...
NEXT, TO CHECK THE COMPANY NAME LIST...
HERE WE GO... JUST WHAT I WAS LOOKNG FOR...
KANEI
YAMAKAN HEAVY INDUSTRIES
KUWATA INDUSTRIAL...
OKABASHI STEEL...

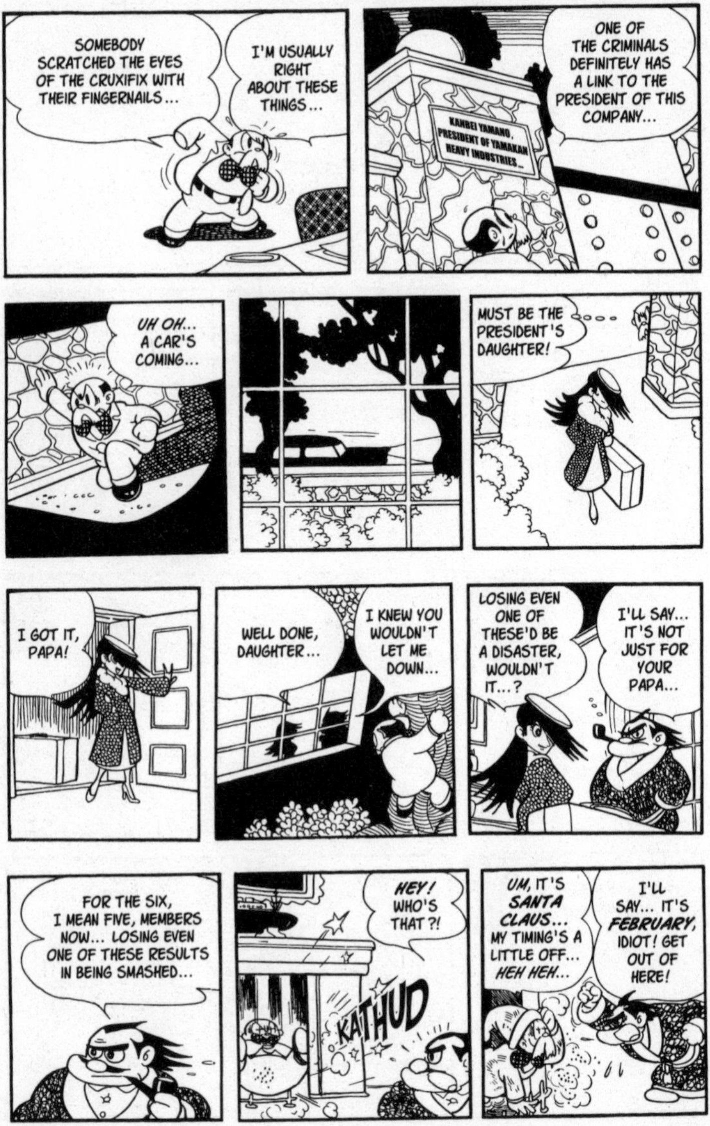

SOMEBODY SCRATCHED THE EYES OF THE CRUXIFIX WITH THEIR FINGERNAILS...
I'M USUALLY RIGHT ABOUT THESE THINGS...
KANBEI YAMANO, PRESIDENT OF YAMAKAN HEAVY INDUSTRIES...
ONE OF THE CRIMINALS DEFINITELY HAS A LINK TO THE PRESIDENT OF THIS COMPANY...
UH OH... A CAR'S COMING...
MUST BE THE PRESIDENT'S DAUGHTER!
I GOT IT, PAPA!
WELL DONE, DAUGHTER...
I KNEW YOU WOULDN'T LET ME DOWN...
LOSING EVEN ONE OF THESE'D BE A DISASTER, WOULDN'T IT...?
I'LL SAY... IT'S NOT JUST FOR YOUR PAPA...
FOR THE SIX, I MEAN FIVE, MEMBERS NOW... LOSING EVEN ONE OF THESE RESULTS IN BEING SMASHED...
HEY! WHO'S THAT?!
KATHUD
UM, IT'S SANTA CLAUS... MY TIMING'S A LITTLE OFF... HEH HEH...
I'LL SAY... IT'S FEBRUARY, IDIOT! GET OUT OF HERE!

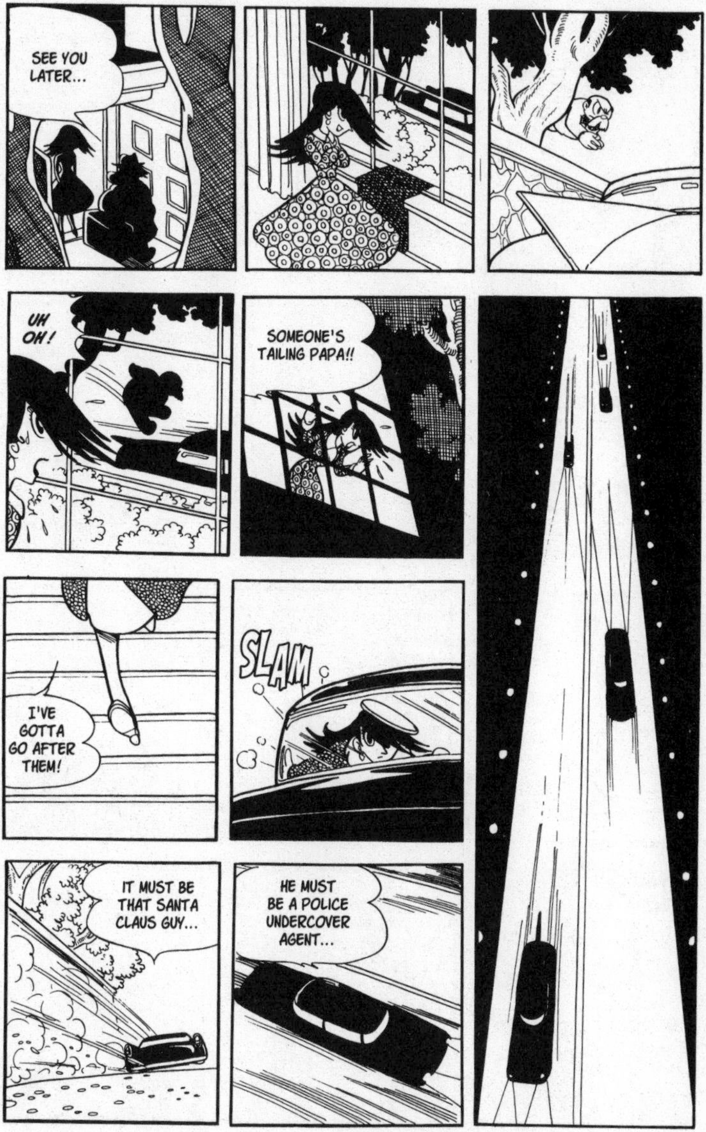
SEE YOU LATER...
UH OH!
SOMEONE'S TAILING PAPA!!
I'VE GOTTA GO AFTER THEM!
SLAM
IT MUST BE THAT SANTA CLAUS GUY...
HE MUST BE A POLICE UNDERCOVER AGENT...

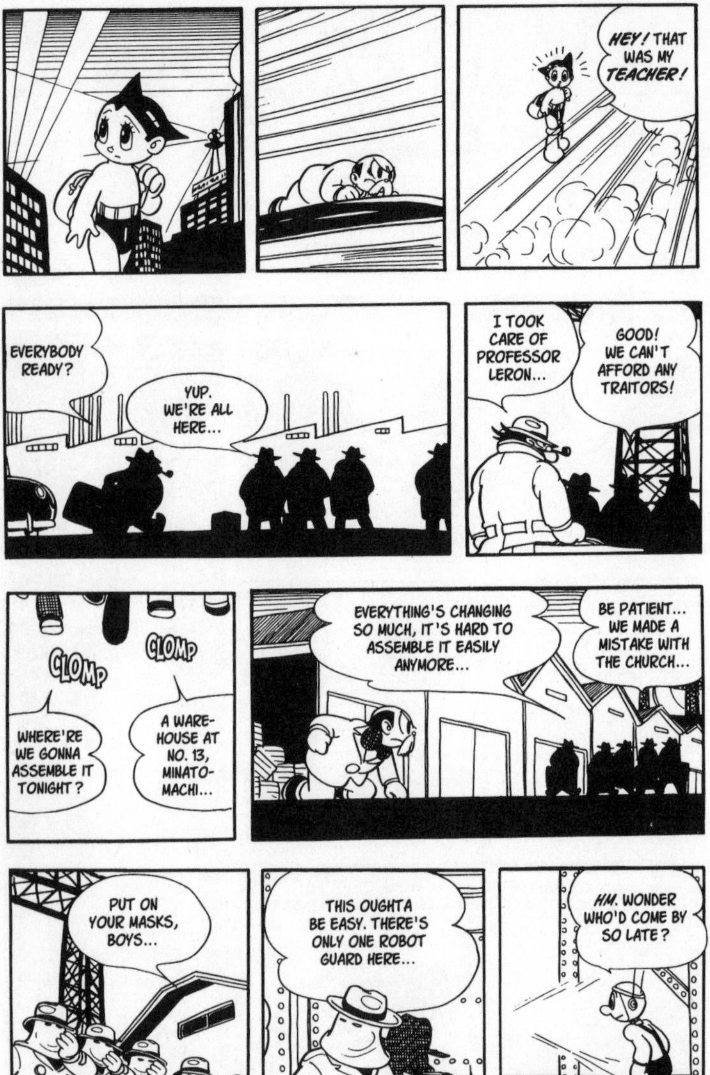
HEY! THAT WAS MY TEACHER!
EVERYBODY READY?
YUP. WE'RE ALL HERE...
I TOOK CARE OF PROFESSOR LERON...
GOOD! WE CAN'T AFFORD ANY TRAITORS!
CLOMP
CLOMP
WHERE'RE WE GONNA ASSEMBLE IT TONIGHT?
A WARE-HOUSE AT NO. 13, MINATO-MACHI...
EVERYTHING'S CHANGING SO MUCH, IT'S HARD TO ASSEMBLE IT EASILY ANYMORE...
BE PATIENT... WE MADE A MISTAKE WITH THE CHURCH...
PUT ON YOUR MASKS, BOYS...
THIS OUGHTA BE EASY. THERE'S ONLY ONE ROBOT GUARD HERE...
HM. WONDER WHO'D COME BY SO LATE?

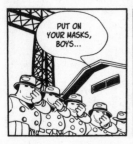

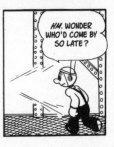

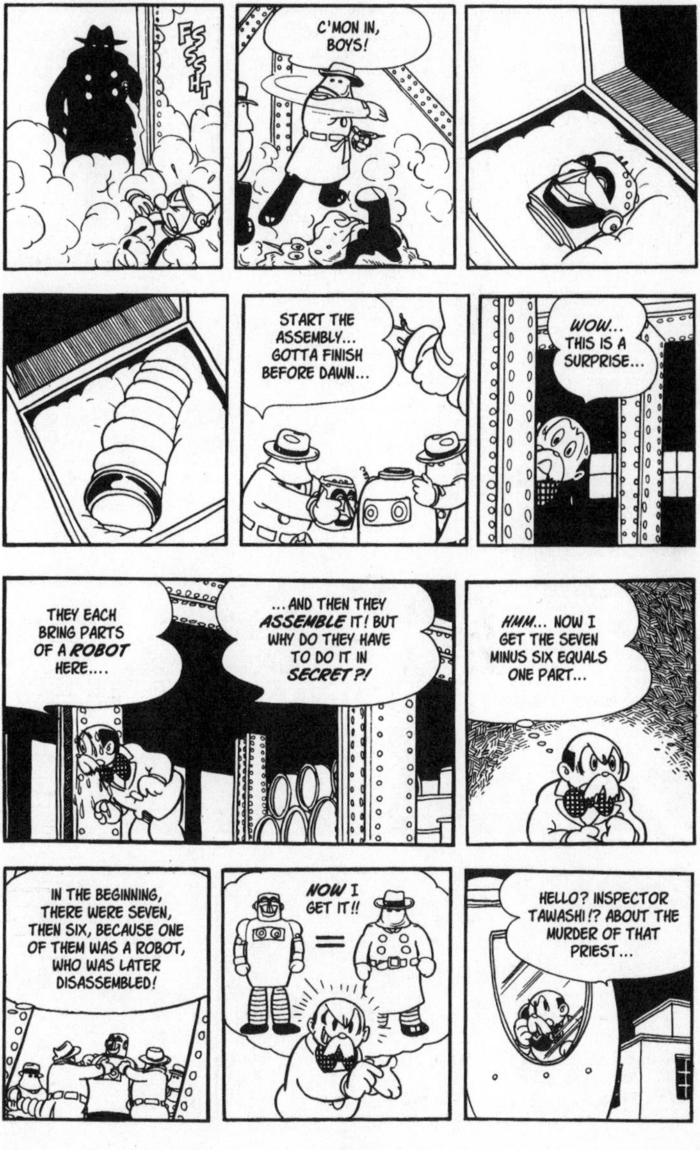
FSSSHT
C'MON IN, BOYS!
START THE ASSEMBLY... GOTTA FINISH BEFORE DAWN...
WOW... THIS IS A SURPRISE...
THEY EACH BRING PARTS OF A ROBOT HERE....
...AND THEN THEY ASSEMBLE IT! BUT WHY DO THEY HAVE TO DO IT IN SECRET?!
HMM... NOW I GET THE SEVEN MINUS SIX EQUALS ONE PART...
IN THE BEGINNING, THERE WERE SEVEN, THEN SIX, BECAUSE ONE OF THEM WAS A ROBOT, WHO WAS LATER DISASSEMBLED!
NOW I GET IT!!
HELLO? INSPECTOR TAWASHI!? ABOUT THE MURDER OF THAT PRIEST...

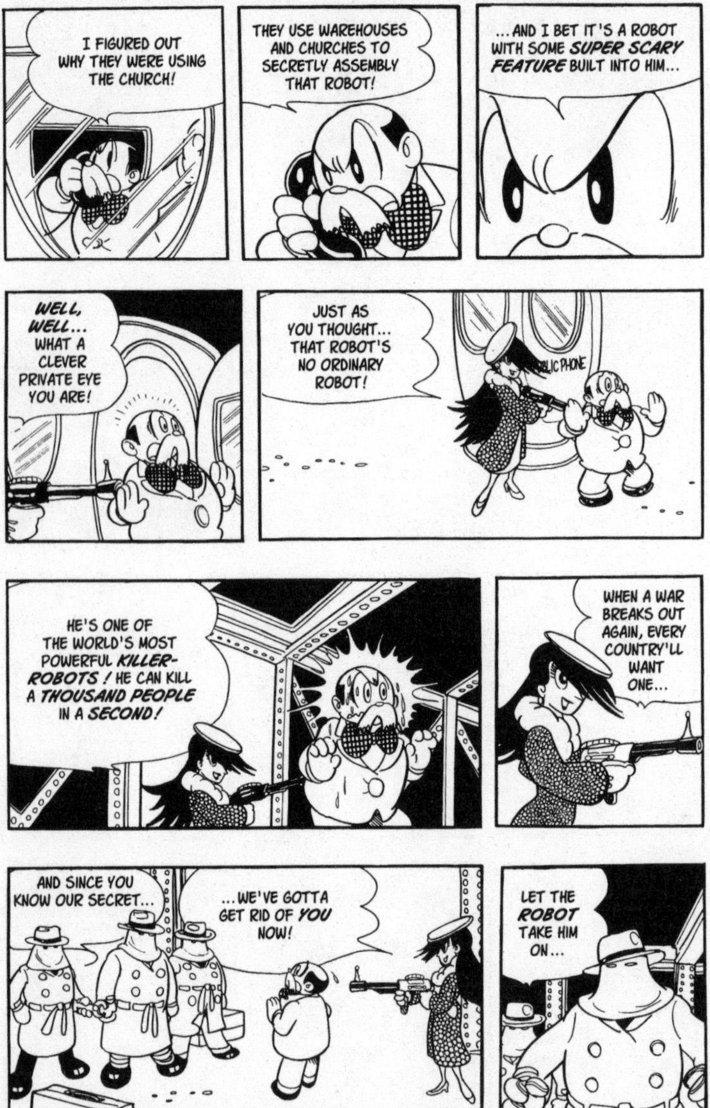
I FIGURED OUT WHY THEY WERE USING THE CHURCH!
THEY USE WAREHOUSES AND CHURCHES TO SECRETLY ASSEMBLY THAT ROBOT!
...AND I BET IT'S A ROBOT WITH SOME SUPER SCARY FEATURE BUILT INTO HIM...
WELL, WELL... WHAT A CLEVER PRIVATE EYE YOU ARE!
JUST AS YOU THOUGHT... THAT ROBOT'S NO ORDINARY ROBOT!
BLIC PHONE
HE'S ONE OF THE WORLD'S MOST POWERFUL KILLER-ROBOTS! HE CAN KILL A THOUSAND PEOPLE IN A SECOND!
WHEN A WAR BREAKS OUT AGAIN, EVERY COUNTRY'LL WANT ONE...
AND SINCE YOU KNOW OUR SECRET...
...WE'VE GOTTA GET RID OF YOU NOW!
LET THE ROBOT TAKE HIM ON...

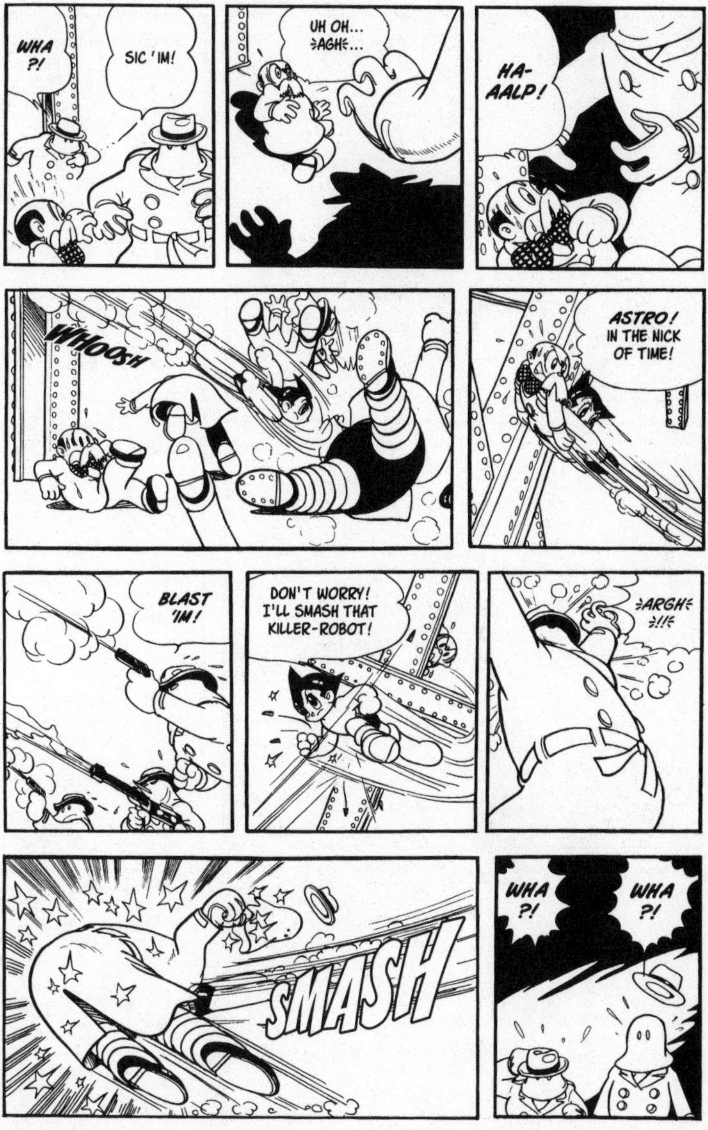
WHA ?!
SIC 'IM!
UH OH... AGH...
HA-AALP!
WHOOSH
ASTRO! IN THE NICK OF TIME!
BLAST 'IM!
DON'T WORRY! I'LL SMASH THAT KILLER-ROBOT!
ARGH !!!
SMASH
WHA ?!
WHA ?!

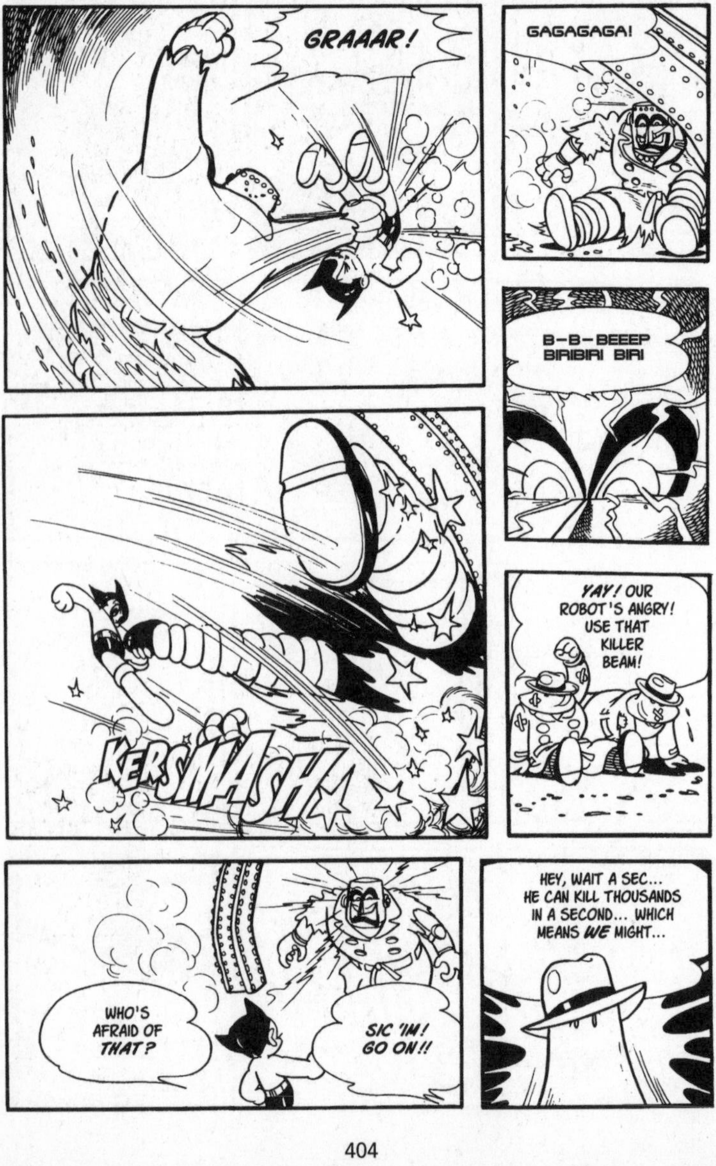
GRAAAR!
KERSMASH
GAGAGAGA!
B-B-BEEEP BIRIBIRI BIRI
YAY! OUR ROBOT'S ANGRY! USE THAT KILLER BEAM!
WHO'S AFRAID OF THAT?
SIC 'IM! GO ON!!
HEY, WAIT A SEC... HE CAN KILL THOUSANDS IN A SECOND... WHICH MEANS WE MIGHT...

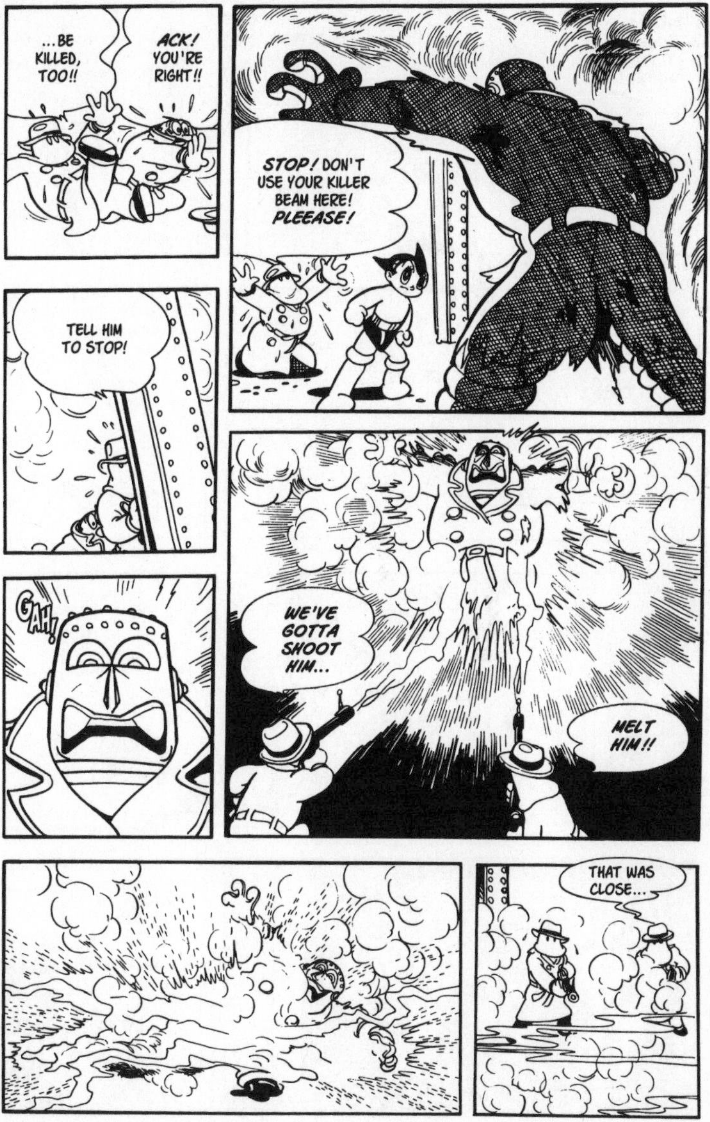
...BE KILLED, TOO!!
ACK! YOU'RE RIGHT!!
STOP! DON'T USE YOUR KILLER BEAM HERE! PLEEASE!
TELL HIM TO STOP!
GAH!
WE'VE GOTTA SHOOT HIM...
MELT HIM!!
THAT WAS CLOSE...

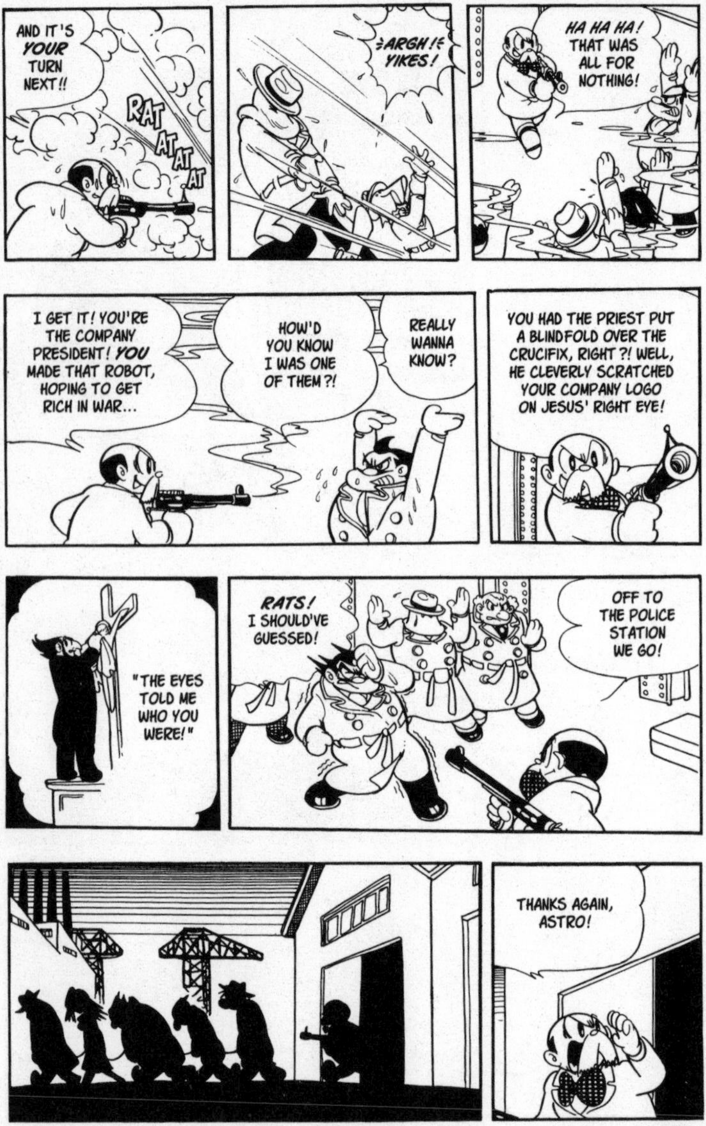

AND IT'S *YOUR* TURN NEXT!!
RAT AT AT AT
ARGH! YIKES!
HA HA HA! THAT WAS ALL FOR NOTHING!
I GET IT! YOU'RE THE COMPANY PRESIDENT! *YOU* MADE THAT ROBOT, HOPING TO GET RICH IN WAR...
HOW'D YOU KNOW I WAS ONE OF THEM?!
REALLY WANNA KNOW?
YOU HAD THE PRIEST PUT A BLINDFOLD OVER THE CRUCIFIX, RIGHT?! WELL, HE CLEVERLY SCRATCHED YOUR COMPANY LOGO ON JESUS' RIGHT EYE!
"THE EYES TOLD ME WHO YOU WERE!"
RATS! I SHOULD'VE GUESSED!
OFF TO THE POLICE STATION WE GO!
THANKS AGAIN, ASTRO!

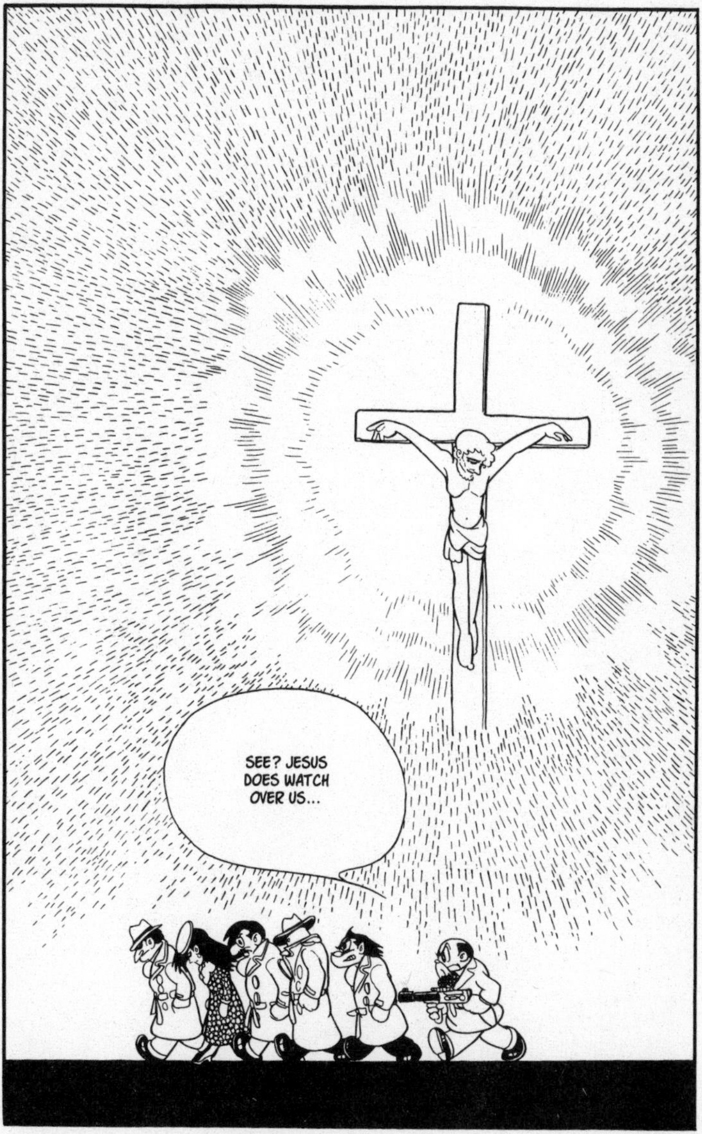
SEE? JESUS DOES WATCH OVER US...

YOUTH GAS

First serialized from February to September 1955
in *Shonen* magazine.

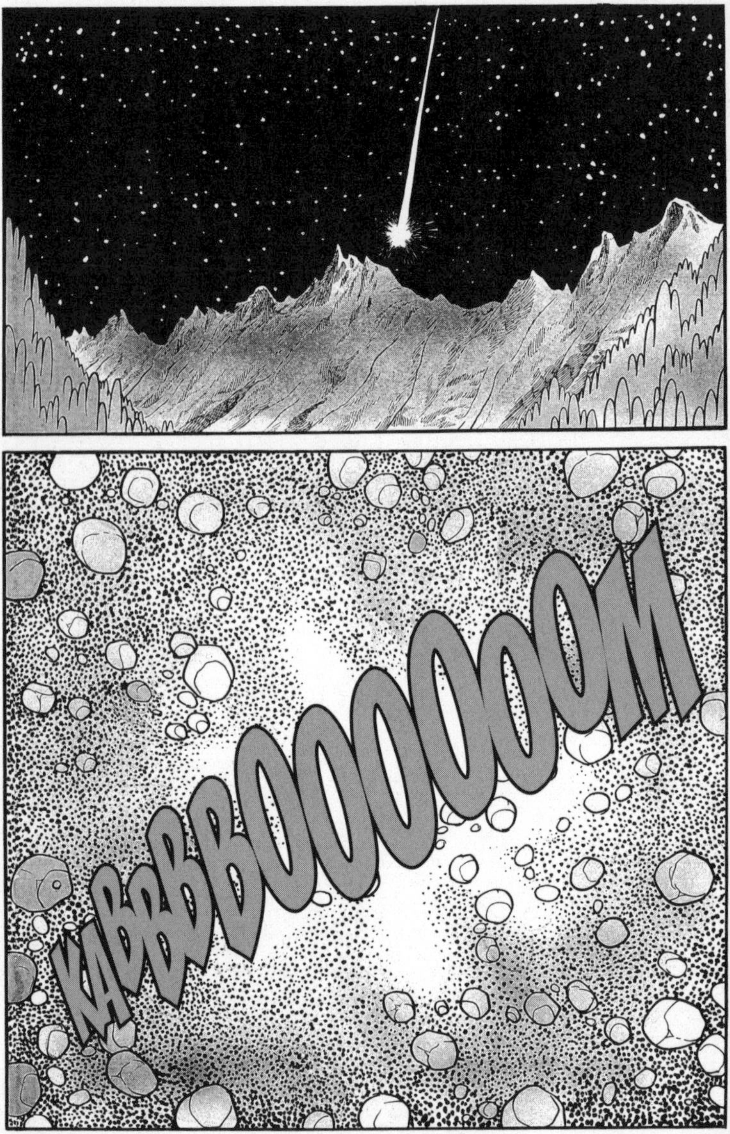
KABBBOOOOOOOM

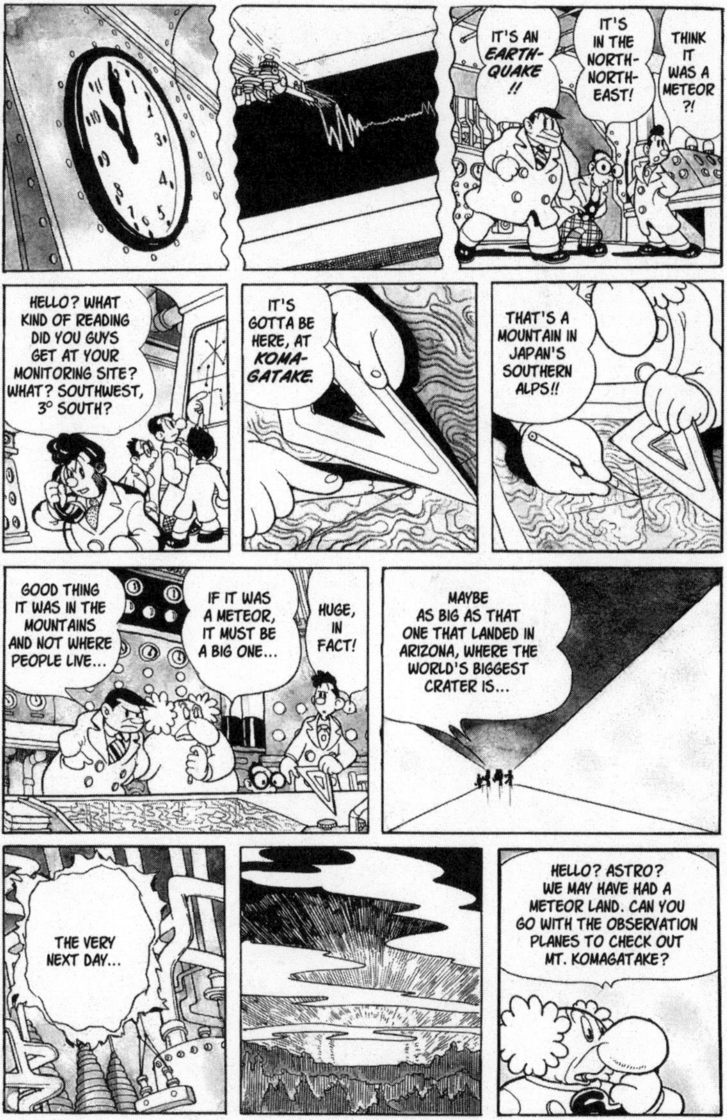
IT'S AN EARTH-QUAKE !!
IT'S IN THE NORTH-NORTH-EAST!
THINK IT WAS A METEOR ?!
HELLO? WHAT KIND OF READING DID YOU GUYS GET AT YOUR MONITORING SITE? WHAT? SOUTHWEST, 3° SOUTH?
IT'S GOTTA BE HERE, AT KOMA-GATAKE.
THAT'S A MOUNTAIN IN JAPAN'S SOUTHERN ALPS!!
GOOD THING IT WAS IN THE MOUNTAINS AND NOT WHERE PEOPLE LIVE...
IF IT WAS A METEOR, IT MUST BE A BIG ONE...
HUGE, IN FACT!
MAYBE AS BIG AS THAT ONE THAT LANDED IN ARIZONA, WHERE THE WORLD'S BIGGEST CRATER IS...
THE VERY NEXT DAY...
HELLO? ASTRO? WE MAY HAVE HAD A METEOR LAND. CAN YOU GO WITH THE OBSERVATION PLANES TO CHECK OUT MT. KOMAGATAKE?

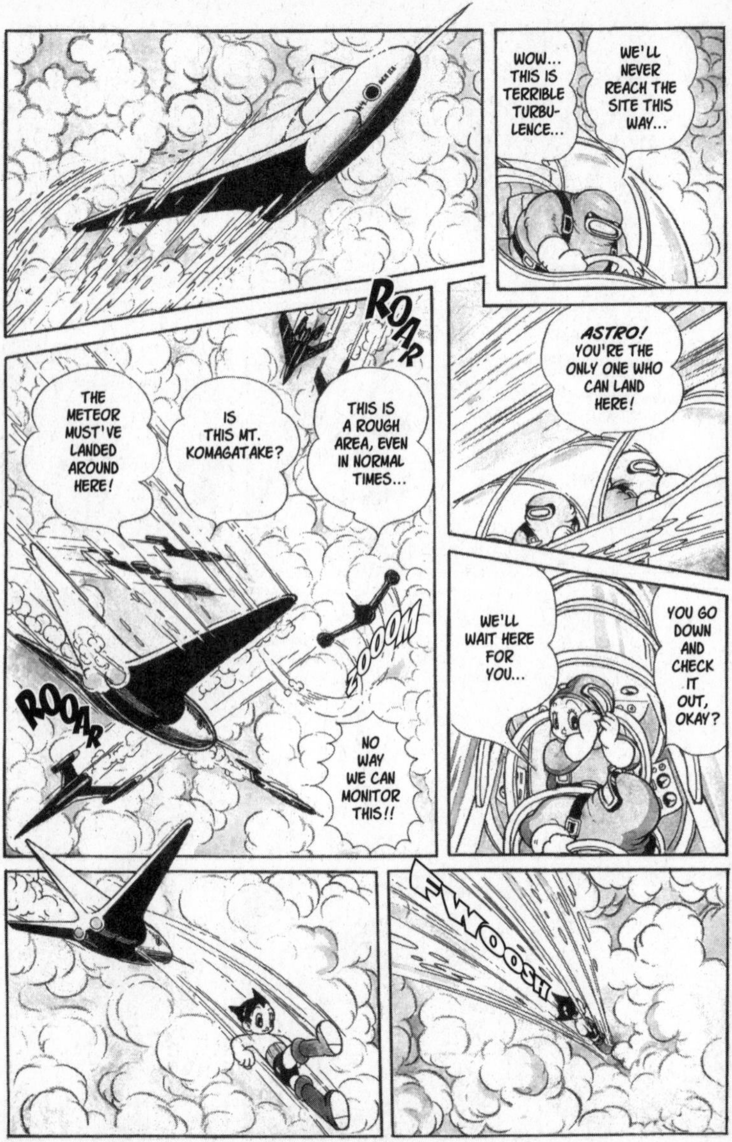
WOW... THIS IS TERRIBLE TURBULENCE...
WE'LL NEVER REACH THE SITE THIS WAY...
ROAR
THE METEOR MUST'VE LANDED AROUND HERE!
IS THIS MT. KOMAGATAKE?
THIS IS A ROUGH AREA, EVEN IN NORMAL TIMES...
ZOOOM
ROOOAR
NO WAY WE CAN MONITOR THIS!!
ASTRO! YOU'RE THE ONLY ONE WHO CAN LAND HERE!
WE'LL WAIT HERE FOR YOU...
YOU GO DOWN AND CHECK IT OUT, OKAY?
FWOOSH

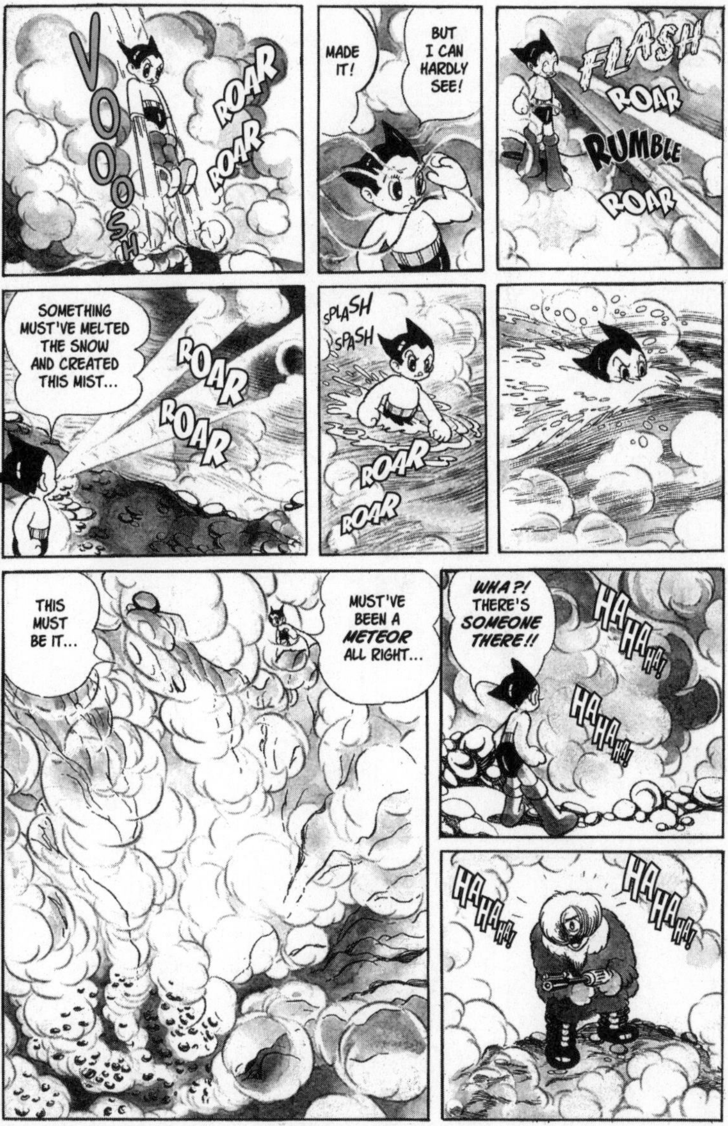
VOOOSH
ROAR
ROAR
MADE IT!
BUT I CAN HARDLY SEE!
FLASH
ROAR
RUMBLE
ROAR
SOMETHING MUST'VE MELTED THE SNOW AND CREATED THIS MIST...
ROAR
ROAR
SPLASH
SPASH
ROAR
ROAR
THIS MUST BE IT...
MUST'VE BEEN A *METEOR* ALL RIGHT...
WHA?! THERE'S *SOMEONE THERE!!*
HAHAHA!
HAHAHAHA!
HAHAHAHA!
HAHAHAHA!

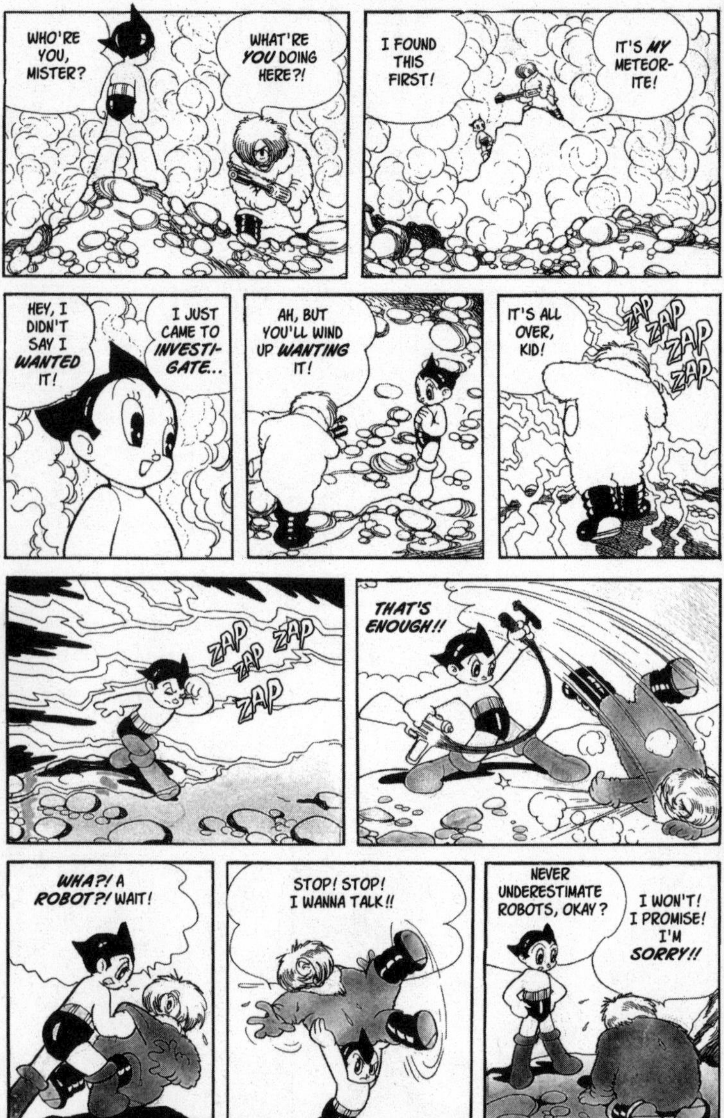
WHO'RE YOU, MISTER?
WHAT'RE *YOU* DOING HERE?!
I FOUND THIS FIRST!
IT'S *MY* METEORITE!
HEY, I DIDN'T SAY I *WANTED* IT!
I JUST CAME TO *INVESTIGATE...*
AH, BUT YOU'LL WIND UP *WANTING* IT!
IT'S ALL OVER, KID!
ZAP ZAP ZAP ZAP
ZAP ZAP ZAP ZAP
THAT'S ENOUGH!!
WHA?! A ROBOT?! WAIT!
STOP! STOP! I WANNA TALK!!
NEVER UNDERESTIMATE ROBOTS, OKAY?
I WON'T! I PROMISE! I'M *SORRY!!*

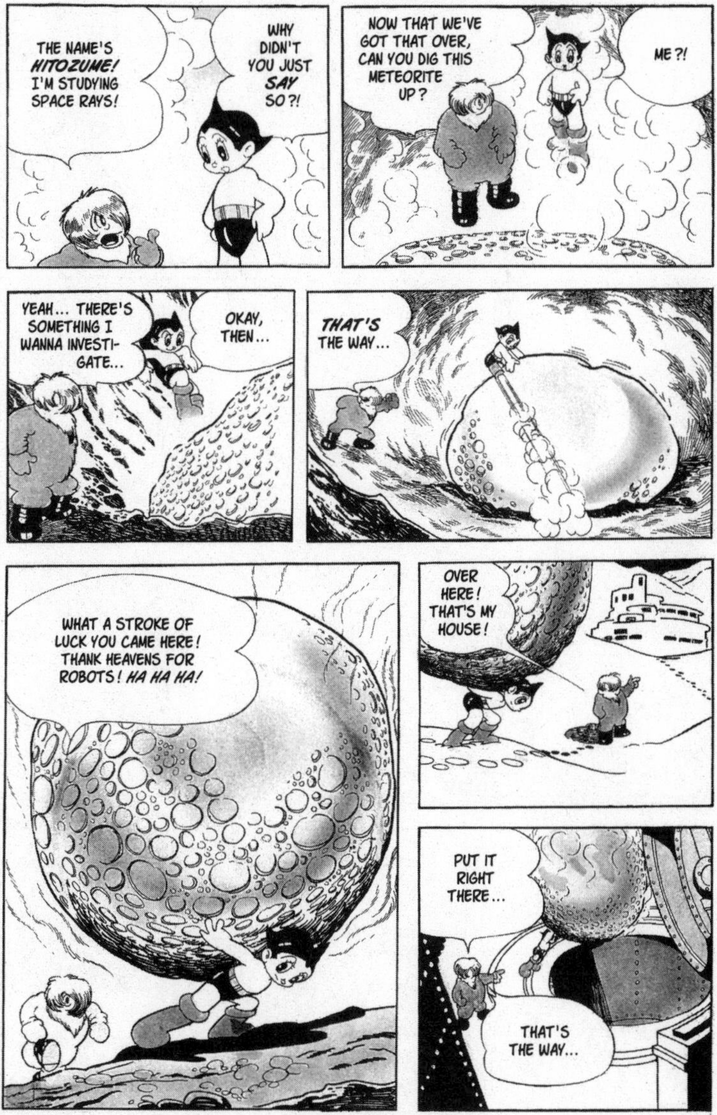
THE NAME'S *HITOZUME!* I'M STUDYING SPACE RAYS!
WHY DIDN'T YOU JUST *SAY* SO?!
NOW THAT WE'VE GOT THAT OVER, CAN YOU DIG THIS METEORITE UP?
ME?!
YEAH... THERE'S SOMETHING I WANNA INVESTI-GATE...
OKAY, THEN...
THAT'S THE WAY...
WHAT A STROKE OF LUCK YOU CAME HERE! THANK HEAVENS FOR ROBOTS! *HA HA HA!*
OVER HERE! THAT'S MY HOUSE!
PUT IT RIGHT THERE...
THAT'S THE WAY...

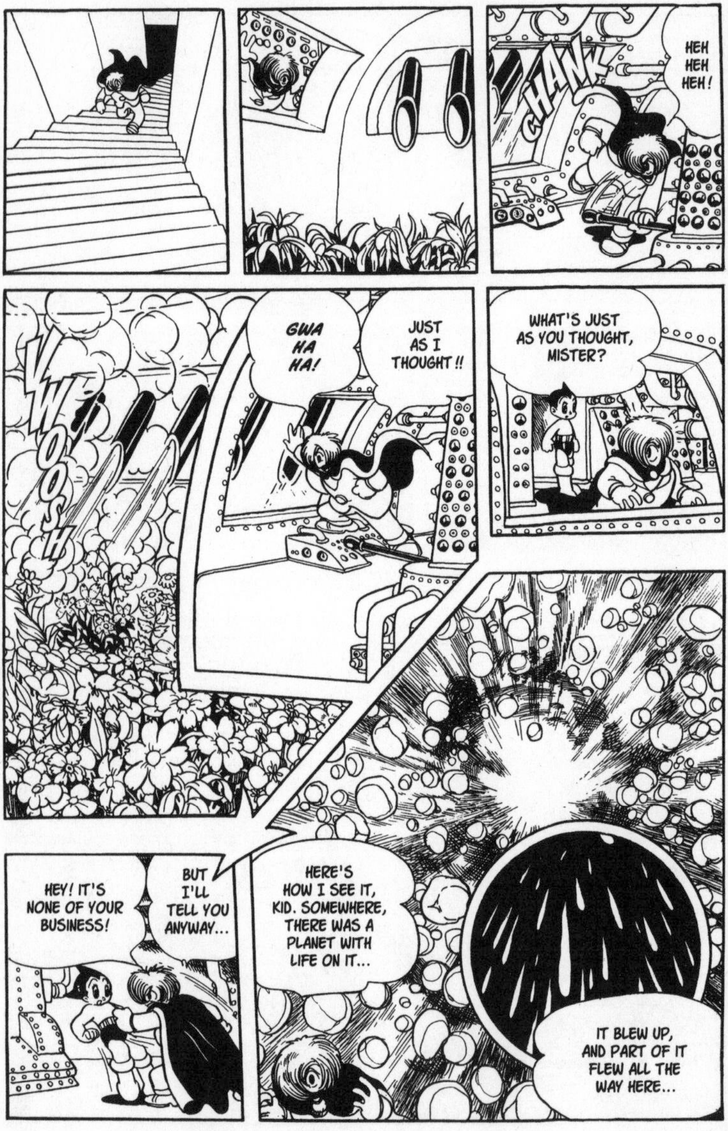
CHANK
HEH HEH HEH!
VWOOSH
GWA HA HA!
JUST AS I THOUGHT!!
WHAT'S JUST AS YOU THOUGHT, MISTER?
HEY! IT'S NONE OF YOUR BUSINESS!
BUT I'LL TELL YOU ANYWAY...
HERE'S HOW I SEE IT, KID. SOMEWHERE, THERE WAS A PLANET WITH LIFE ON IT...
IT BLEW UP, AND PART OF IT FLEW ALL THE WAY HERE...

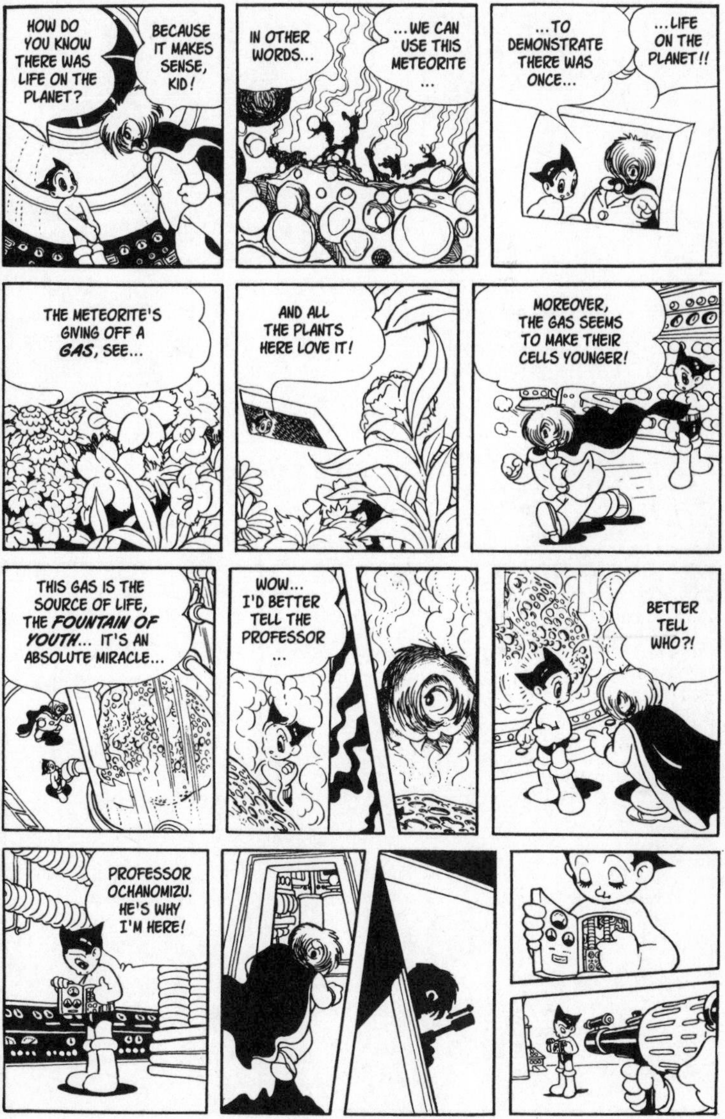
HOW DO YOU KNOW THERE WAS LIFE ON THE PLANET?
BECAUSE IT MAKES SENSE, KID!
IN OTHER WORDS...
...WE CAN USE THIS METEORITE ...
...TO DEMONSTRATE THERE WAS ONCE...
...LIFE ON THE PLANET!!
THE METEORITE'S GIVING OFF A GAS, SEE...
AND ALL THE PLANTS HERE LOVE IT!
MOREOVER, THE GAS SEEMS TO MAKE THEIR CELLS YOUNGER!
THIS GAS IS THE SOURCE OF LIFE, THE FOUNTAIN OF YOUTH... IT'S AN ABSOLUTE MIRACLE...
WOW... I'D BETTER TELL THE PROFESSOR ...
BETTER TELL WHO?!
PROFESSOR OCHANOMIZU. HE'S WHY I'M HERE!

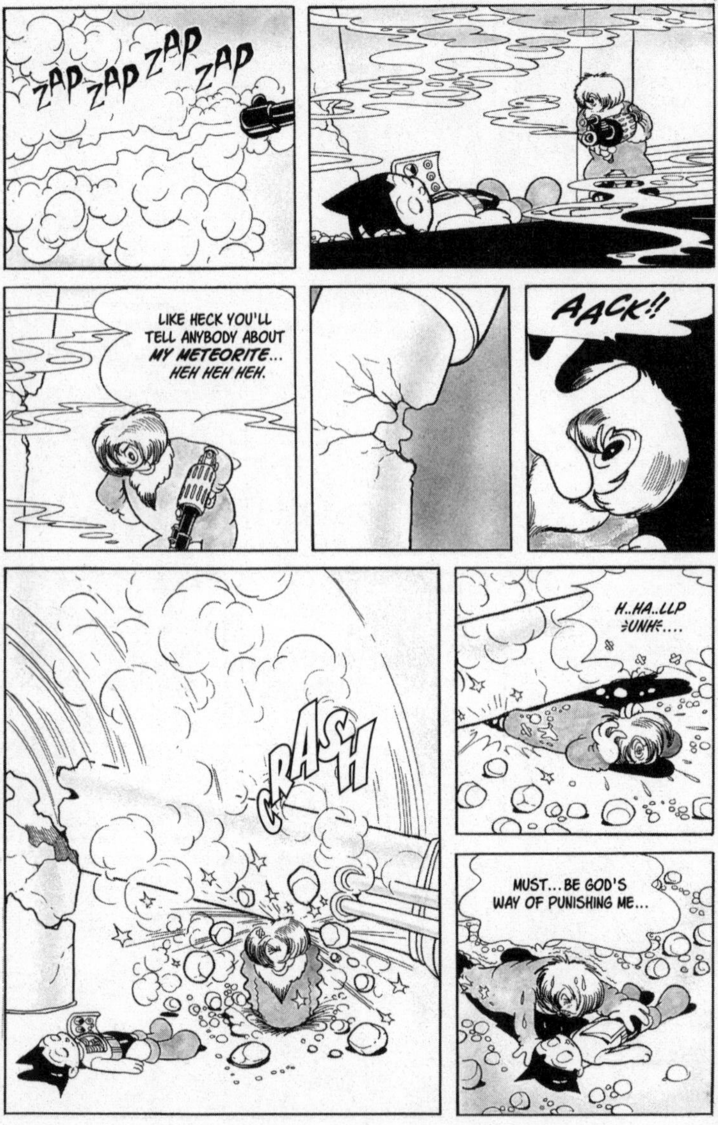
ZAP ZAP ZAP ZAP
LIKE HECK YOU'LL TELL ANYBODY ABOUT *MY METEORITE*... *HEH HEH HEH.*
AACK!!
CRASH
H..HA..LLP
UNH....
MUST... BE GOD'S WAY OF PUNISHING ME...

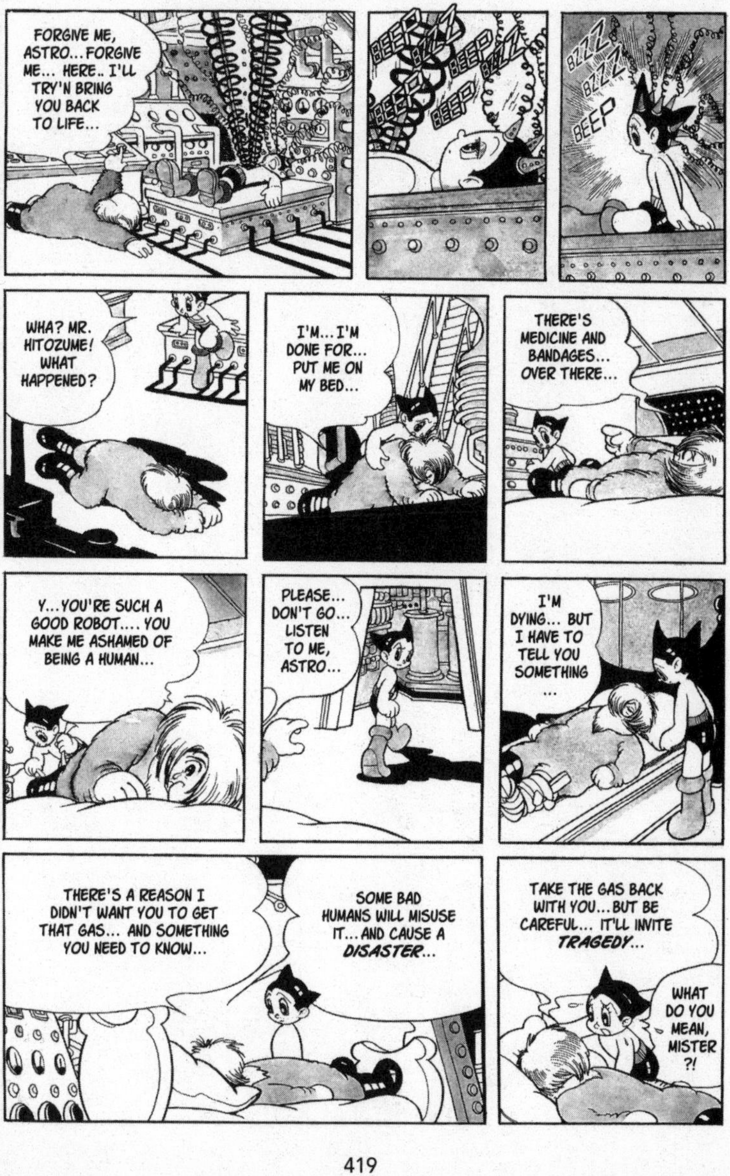
FORGIVE ME, ASTRO...FORGIVE ME... HERE.. I'LL TRY'N BRING YOU BACK TO LIFE...
BEEP BZZZ BEEP BEEP BEEP BZZZ
BZZZ BZZZ BEEP
WHA? MR. HITOZUME! WHAT HAPPENED?
I'M...I'M DONE FOR... PUT ME ON MY BED...
THERE'S MEDICINE AND BANDAGES... OVER THERE...
Y...YOU'RE SUCH A GOOD ROBOT.... YOU MAKE ME ASHAMED OF BEING A HUMAN...
PLEASE... DON'T GO... LISTEN TO ME, ASTRO...
I'M DYING... BUT I HAVE TO TELL YOU SOMETHING ...
THERE'S A REASON I DIDN'T WANT YOU TO GET THAT GAS... AND SOMETHING YOU NEED TO KNOW...
SOME BAD HUMANS WILL MISUSE IT...AND CAUSE A *DISASTER*...
TAKE THE GAS BACK WITH YOU...BUT BE CAREFUL... IT'LL INVITE *TRAGEDY*...
WHAT DO YOU MEAN, MISTER ?!

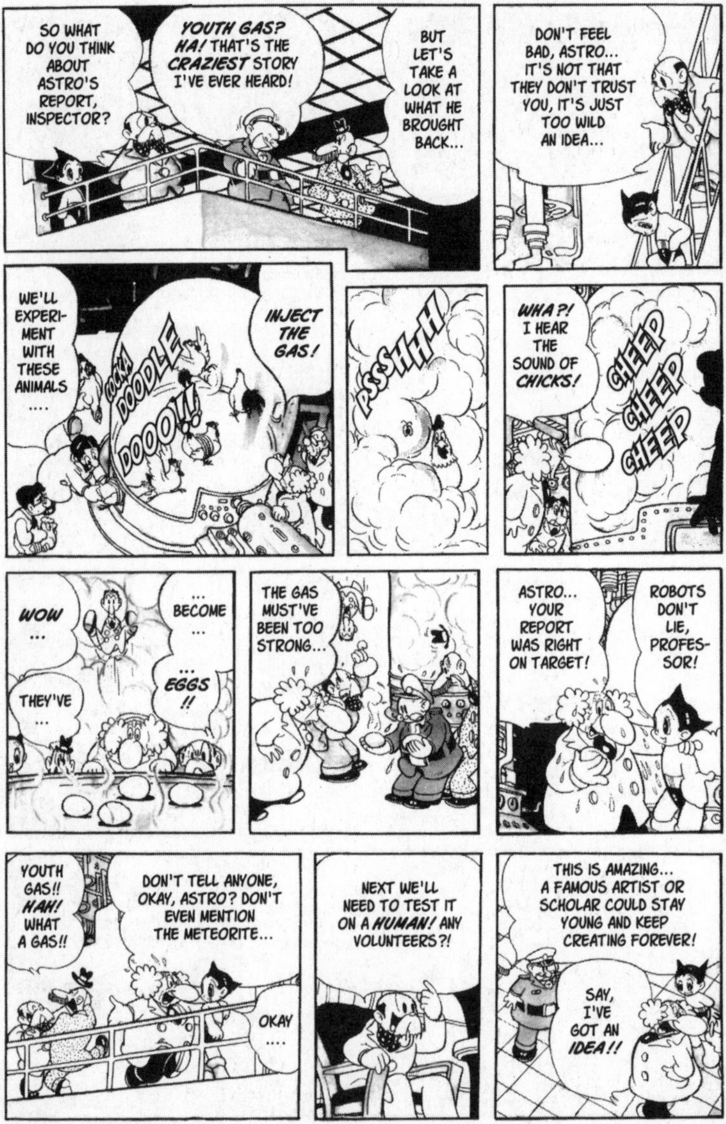
SO WHAT DO YOU THINK ABOUT ASTRO'S REPORT, INSPECTOR?
YOUTH GAS? HA! THAT'S THE CRAZIEST STORY I'VE EVER HEARD!
BUT LET'S TAKE A LOOK AT WHAT HE BROUGHT BACK...
DON'T FEEL BAD, ASTRO... IT'S NOT THAT THEY DON'T TRUST YOU, IT'S JUST TOO WILD AN IDEA...
WE'LL EXPERIMENT WITH THESE ANIMALS ....
COCKA DOODLE DOOO!!
INJECT THE GAS!
PSSSHHH
WHA?! I HEAR THE SOUND OF CHICKS!
CHEEP CHEEP CHEEP
WOW ...
THEY'VE ...
... BECOME ...
... EGGS !!
THE GAS MUST'VE BEEN TOO STRONG...
ASTRO... YOUR REPORT WAS RIGHT ON TARGET!
ROBOTS DON'T LIE, PROFESSOR!
YOUTH GAS!! HAH! WHAT A GAS!!
DON'T TELL ANYONE, OKAY, ASTRO? DON'T EVEN MENTION THE METEORITE...
OKAY ....
NEXT WE'LL NEED TO TEST IT ON A HUMAN! ANY VOLUNTEERS?!
THIS IS AMAZING... A FAMOUS ARTIST OR SCHOLAR COULD STAY YOUNG AND KEEP CREATING FOREVER!
SAY, I'VE GOT AN IDEA!!

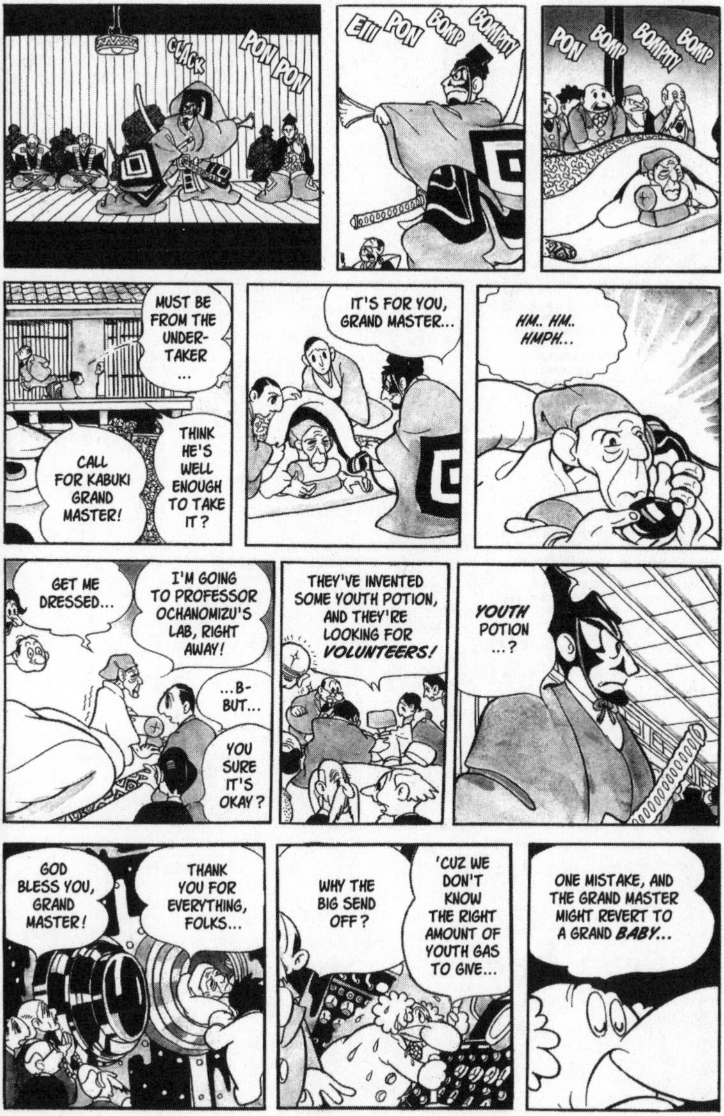
CLACK
PON PON
EIII PON BOMP BOMPITY
PON BOMP BOMPITY BOMP
MUST BE FROM THE UNDER-TAKER ...
CALL FOR KABUKI GRAND MASTER!
THINK HE'S WELL ENOUGH TO TAKE IT?
IT'S FOR YOU, GRAND MASTER...
HM.. HM.. HMPH...
GET ME DRESSED...
I'M GOING TO PROFESSOR OCHANOMIZU'S LAB, RIGHT AWAY!
...B-BUT...
YOU SURE IT'S OKAY?
THEY'VE INVENTED SOME YOUTH POTION, AND THEY'RE LOOKING FOR VOLUNTEERS!
YOUTH POTION ...?
GOD BLESS YOU, GRAND MASTER!
THANK YOU FOR EVERYTHING, FOLKS...
WHY THE BIG SEND OFF?
'CUZ WE DON'T KNOW THE RIGHT AMOUNT OF YOUTH GAS TO GIVE...
ONE MISTAKE, AND THE GRAND MASTER MIGHT REVERT TO A GRAND BABY...

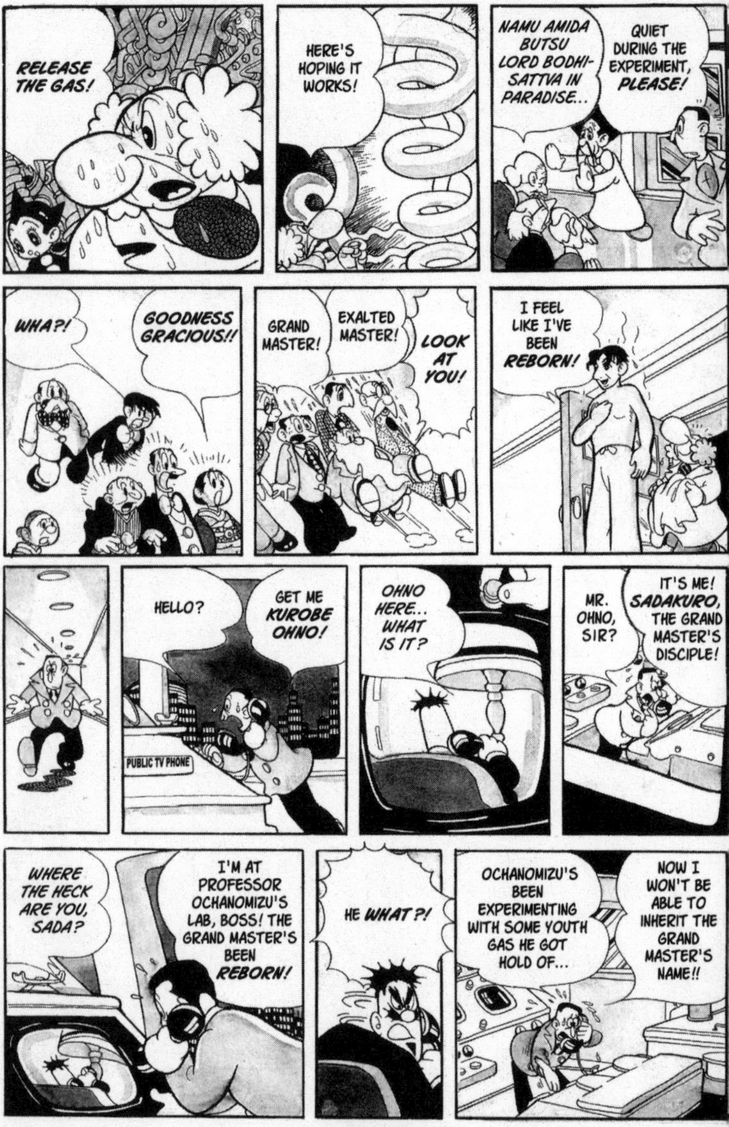
RELEASE THE GAS!
HERE'S HOPING IT WORKS!
NAMU AMIDA BUTSU LORD BODHI-SATTVA IN PARADISE...
QUIET DURING THE EXPERIMENT, PLEASE!
WHA?!
GOODNESS GRACIOUS!!
GRAND MASTER!
EXALTED MASTER!
LOOK AT YOU!
I FEEL LIKE I'VE BEEN REBORN!
HELLO?
GET ME KUROBE OHNO!
PUBLIC TV PHONE
OHNO HERE... WHAT IS IT?
MR. OHNO, SIR?
IT'S ME! SADAKURO, THE GRAND MASTER'S DISCIPLE!
WHERE THE HECK ARE YOU, SADA?
I'M AT PROFESSOR OCHANOMIZU'S LAB, BOSS! THE GRAND MASTER'S BEEN REBORN!
HE WHAT?!
OCHANOMIZU'S BEEN EXPERIMENTING WITH SOME YOUTH GAS HE GOT HOLD OF...
NOW I WON'T BE ABLE TO INHERIT THE GRAND MASTER'S NAME!!

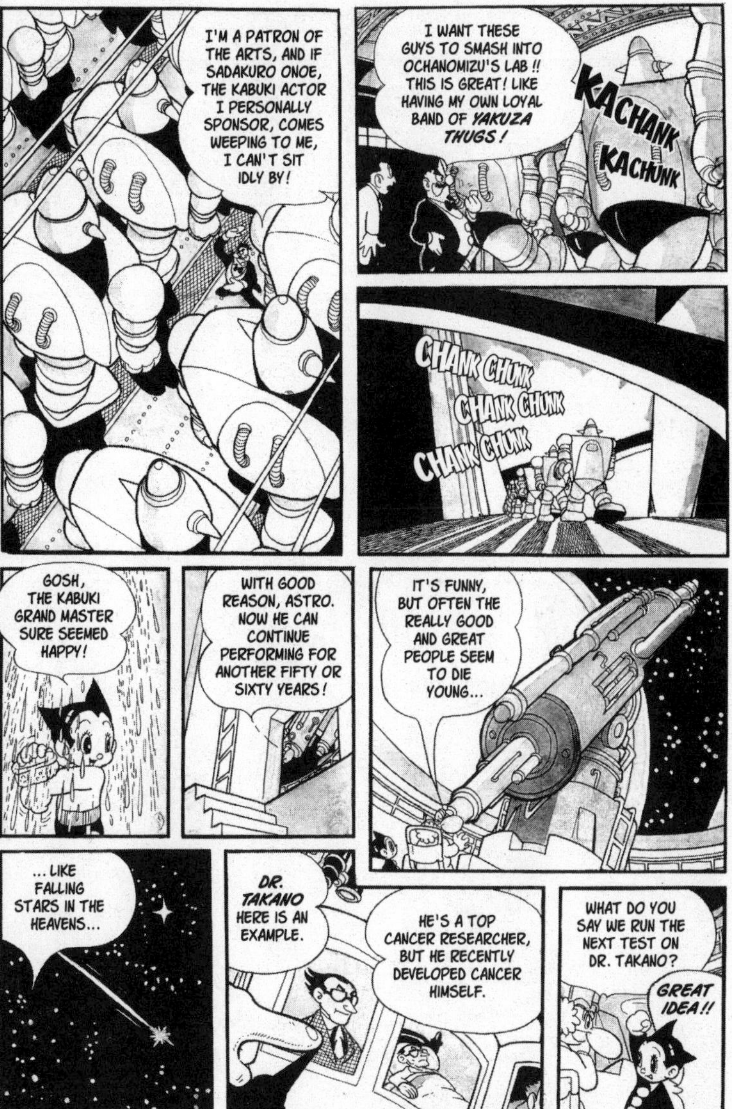
I'M A PATRON OF THE ARTS, AND IF SADAKURO ONOE, THE KABUKI ACTOR I PERSONALLY SPONSOR, COMES WEEPING TO ME, I CAN'T SIT IDLY BY!
I WANT THESE GUYS TO SMASH INTO OCHANOMIZU'S LAB !! THIS IS GREAT! LIKE HAVING MY OWN LOYAL BAND OF *YAKUZA THUGS* !
KACHANK
KACHUNK
CHANK CHUNK
CHANK CHUNK
CHANK CHUNK
GOSH, THE KABUKI GRAND MASTER SURE SEEMED HAPPY!
WITH GOOD REASON, ASTRO. NOW HE CAN CONTINUE PERFORMING FOR ANOTHER FIFTY OR SIXTY YEARS!
IT'S FUNNY, BUT OFTEN THE REALLY GOOD AND GREAT PEOPLE SEEM TO DIE YOUNG...
... LIKE FALLING STARS IN THE HEAVENS...
DR. TAKANO HERE IS AN EXAMPLE.
HE'S A TOP CANCER RESEARCHER, BUT HE RECENTLY DEVELOPED CANCER HIMSELF.
WHAT DO YOU SAY WE RUN THE NEXT TEST ON DR. TAKANO?
GREAT IDEA!!

G'NITE ASTRO! SEE YOU LATER...

G'NITE, PROFESSOR...

♪♫♪♫

CARI CARI
CIRIRIRI
OWAA

CRASH

EEII!

I BETTER SEE WHAT'S GOING ON...

ZOOOM

GOSH! IT'S THE LABORATORY!

PROFESSOR!!!

≠UNK≠...
≠ARGH≠...

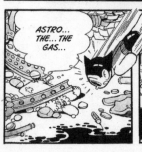

ASTRO... THE... THE GAS...

YIKES! THEY'RE STEALING THE GAS!

424

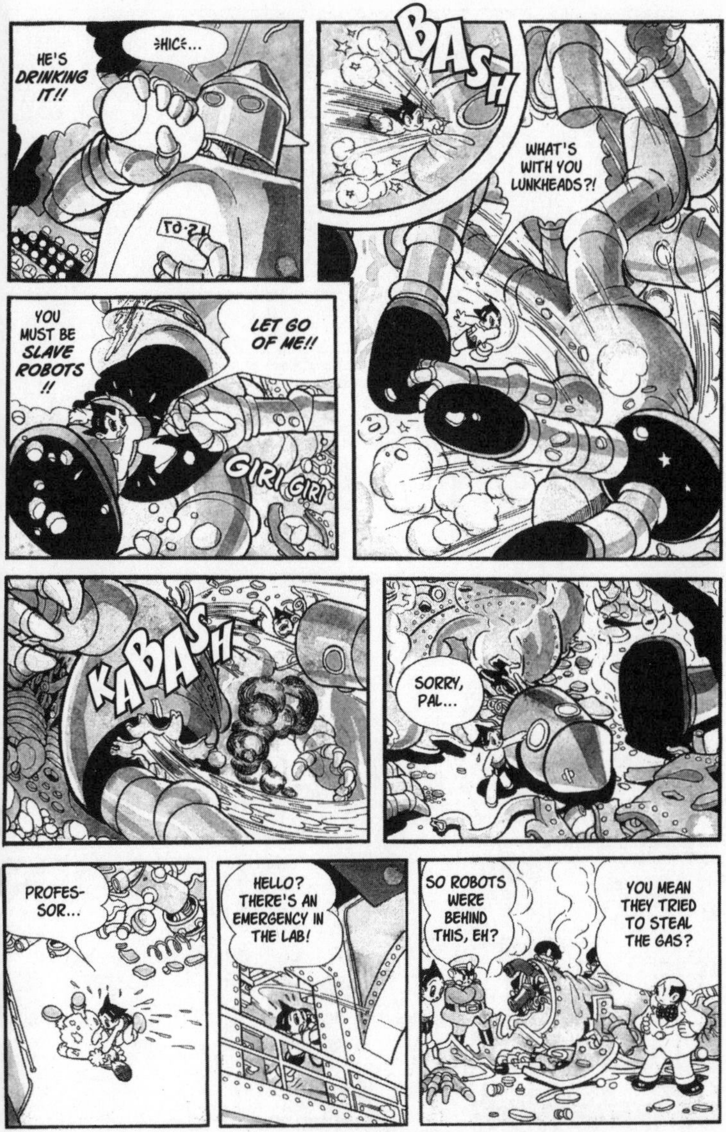

HE'S DRINKING IT!!
HIC...
YOU MUST BE SLAVE ROBOTS!!
LET GO OF ME!!
GIRI GIRI
BASH
WHAT'S WITH YOU LUNKHEADS?!
KABASH
SORRY, PAL...
PROFES-SOR...
HELLO? THERE'S AN EMERGENCY IN THE LAB!
SO ROBOTS WERE BEHIND THIS, EH?
YOU MEAN THEY TRIED TO STEAL THE GAS?

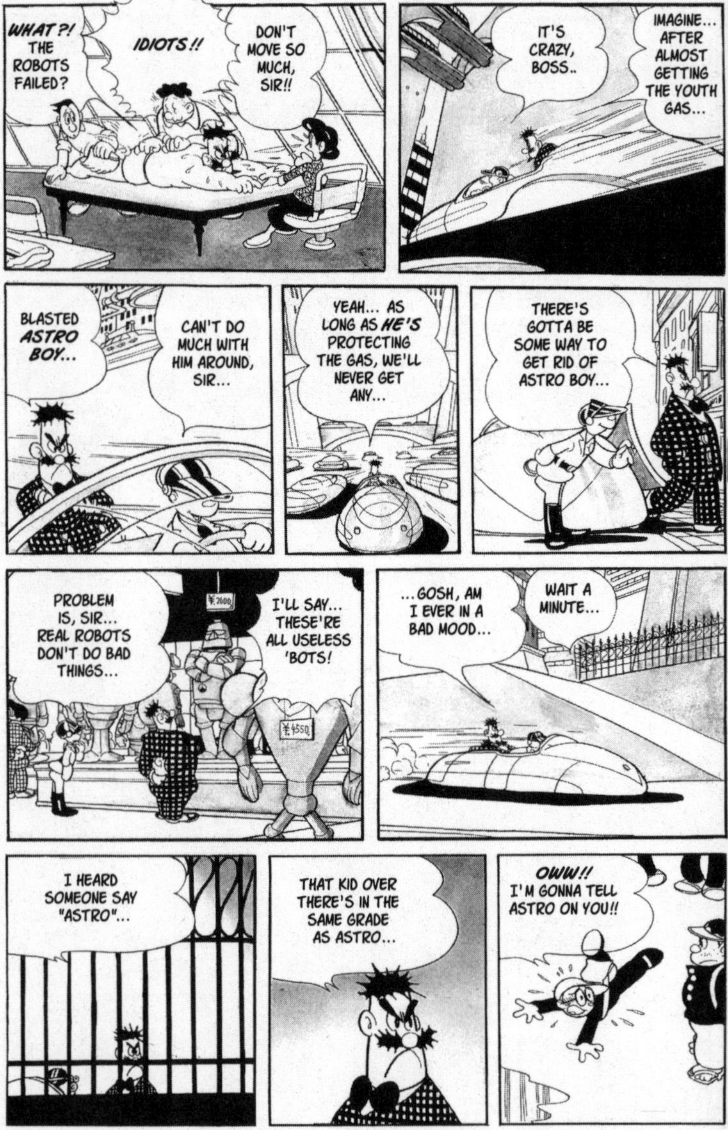
WHAT?! THE ROBOTS FAILED?
IDIOTS!!
DON'T MOVE SO MUCH, SIR!!
IT'S CRAZY, BOSS..
IMAGINE... AFTER ALMOST GETTING THE YOUTH GAS...
BLASTED ASTRO BOY...
CAN'T DO MUCH WITH HIM AROUND, SIR...
YEAH... AS LONG AS HE'S PROTECTING THE GAS, WE'LL NEVER GET ANY...
THERE'S GOTTA BE SOME WAY TO GET RID OF ASTRO BOY...
PROBLEM IS, SIR... REAL ROBOTS DON'T DO BAD THINGS...
¥2600
I'LL SAY... THESE'RE ALL USELESS 'BOTS!
¥4550
...GOSH, AM I EVER IN A BAD MOOD...
WAIT A MINUTE...
I HEARD SOMEONE SAY "ASTRO"...
THAT KID OVER THERE'S IN THE SAME GRADE AS ASTRO...
OWW!! I'M GONNA TELL ASTRO ON YOU!!

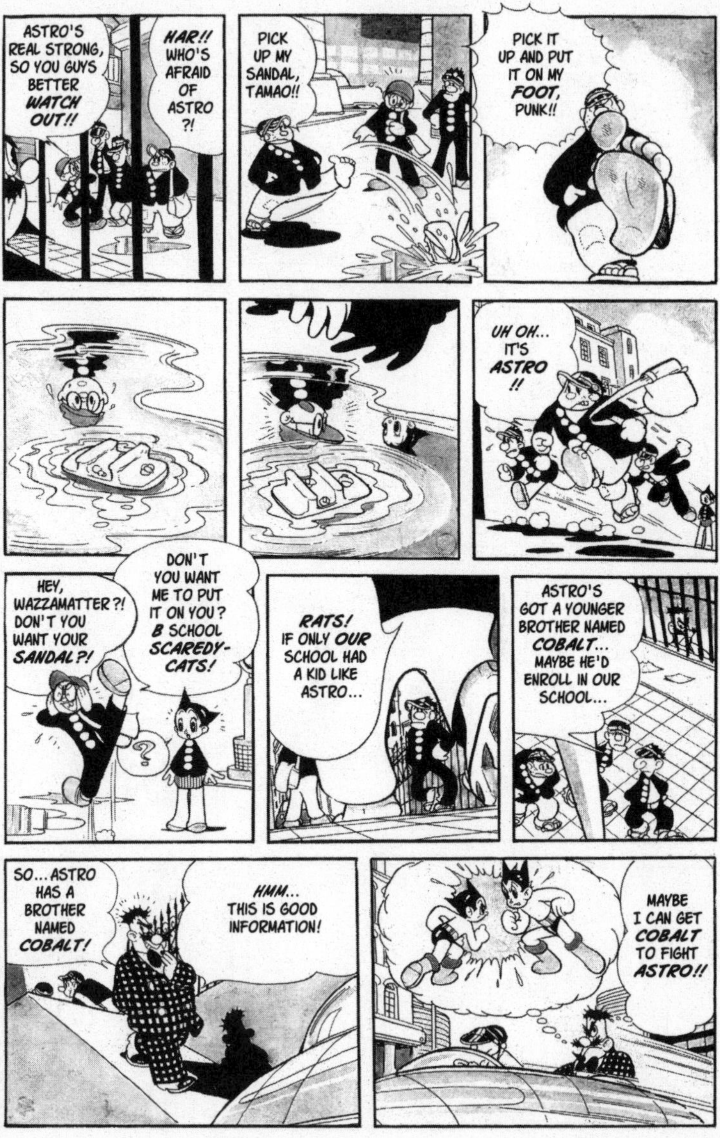
ASTRO'S REAL STRONG, SO YOU GUYS BETTER WATCH OUT!!
HAR!! WHO'S AFRAID OF ASTRO ?!
PICK UP MY SANDAL, TAMAO!!
PICK IT UP AND PUT IT ON MY FOOT, PUNK!!
UH OH... IT'S ASTRO !!
HEY, WAZZAMATTER?! DON'T YOU WANT YOUR SANDAL?!
DON'T YOU WANT ME TO PUT IT ON YOU? B SCHOOL SCAREDY-CATS!
RATS! IF ONLY OUR SCHOOL HAD A KID LIKE ASTRO...
ASTRO'S GOT A YOUNGER BROTHER NAMED COBALT... MAYBE HE'D ENROLL IN OUR SCHOOL...
SO... ASTRO HAS A BROTHER NAMED COBALT!
HMM... THIS IS GOOD INFORMATION!
MAYBE I CAN GET COBALT TO FIGHT ASTRO!!

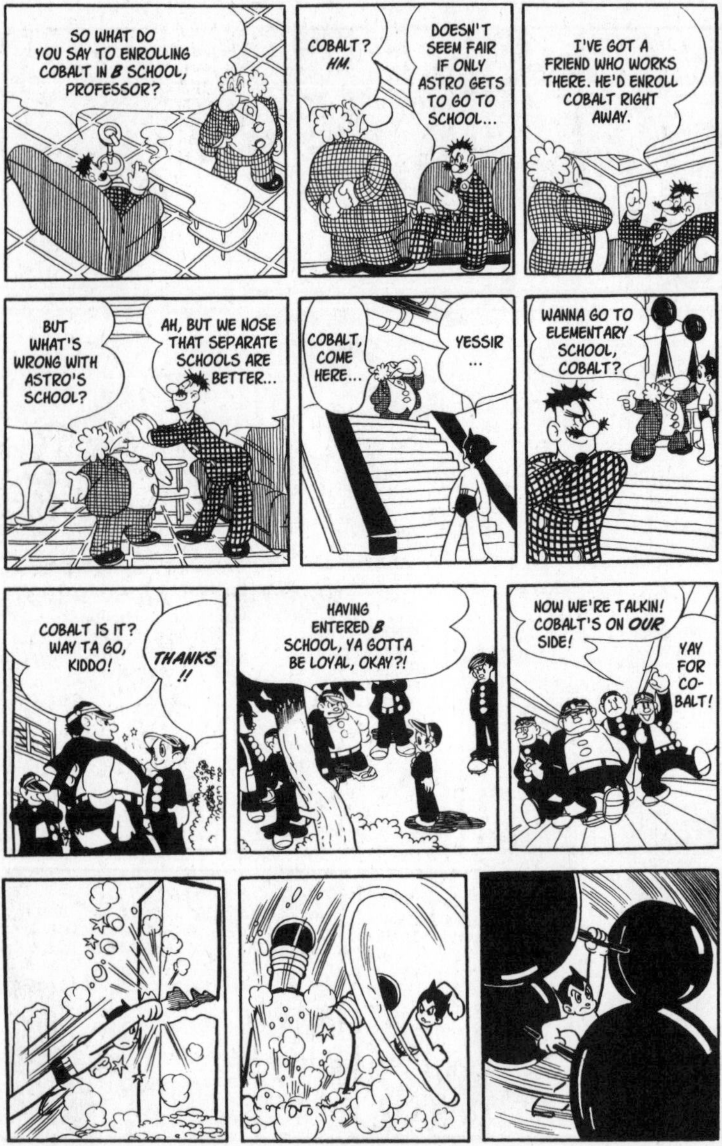
SO WHAT DO YOU SAY TO ENROLLING COBALT IN B SCHOOL, PROFESSOR?
COBALT? HM.
DOESN'T SEEM FAIR IF ONLY ASTRO GETS TO GO TO SCHOOL...
I'VE GOT A FRIEND WHO WORKS THERE. HE'D ENROLL COBALT RIGHT AWAY.
BUT WHAT'S WRONG WITH ASTRO'S SCHOOL?
AH, BUT WE NOSE THAT SEPARATE SCHOOLS ARE BETTER...
COBALT, COME HERE...
YESSIR ...
WANNA GO TO ELEMENTARY SCHOOL, COBALT?
COBALT IS IT? WAY TA GO, KIDDO!
THANKS !!
HAVING ENTERED B SCHOOL, YA GOTTA BE LOYAL, OKAY?!
NOW WE'RE TALKIN! COBALT'S ON OUR SIDE!
YAY FOR CO-BALT!

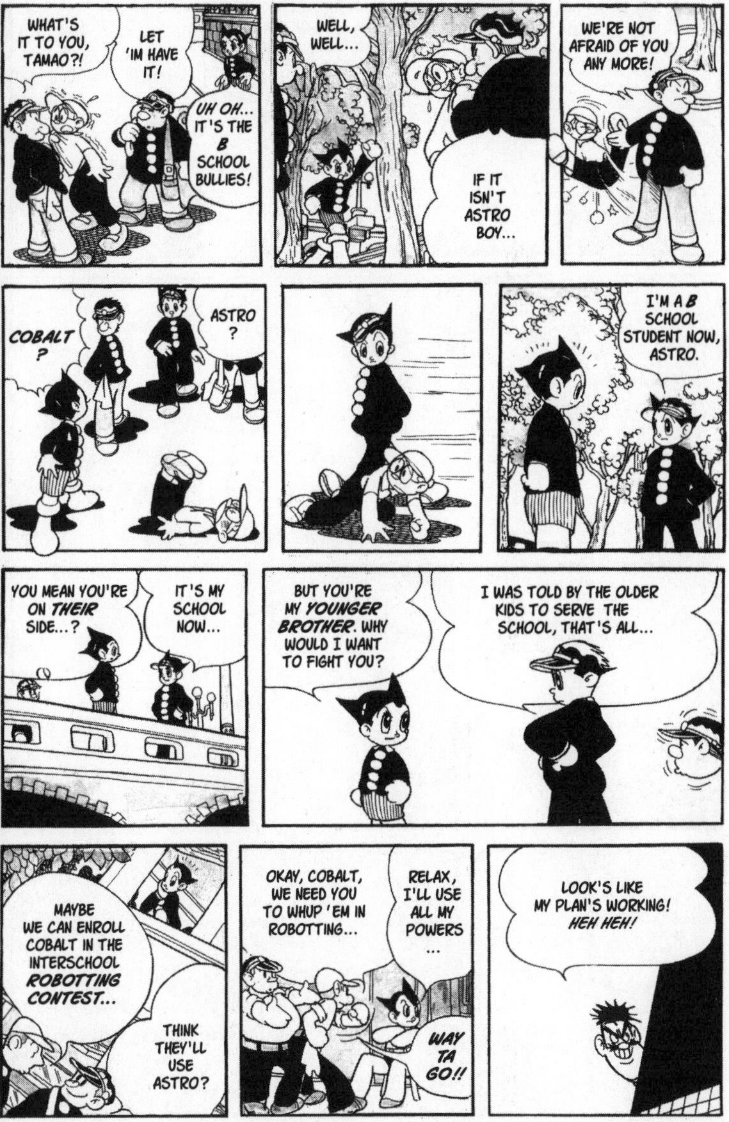
WHAT'S IT TO YOU, TAMAO?!
LET 'IM HAVE IT!
UH OH... IT'S THE B SCHOOL BULLIES!
WELL, WELL...
IF IT ISN'T ASTRO BOY...
WE'RE NOT AFRAID OF YOU ANY MORE!
COBALT?
ASTRO?
I'M A B SCHOOL STUDENT NOW, ASTRO.
YOU MEAN YOU'RE ON THEIR SIDE...?
IT'S MY SCHOOL NOW...
BUT YOU'RE MY YOUNGER BROTHER. WHY WOULD I WANT TO FIGHT YOU?
I WAS TOLD BY THE OLDER KIDS TO SERVE THE SCHOOL, THAT'S ALL...
MAYBE WE CAN ENROLL COBALT IN THE INTERSCHOOL ROBOTTING CONTEST...
THINK THEY'LL USE ASTRO?
OKAY, COBALT, WE NEED YOU TO WHUP 'EM IN ROBOTTING...
RELAX, I'LL USE ALL MY POWERS...
WAY TA GO!!
LOOK'S LIKE MY PLAN'S WORKING! HEH HEH!

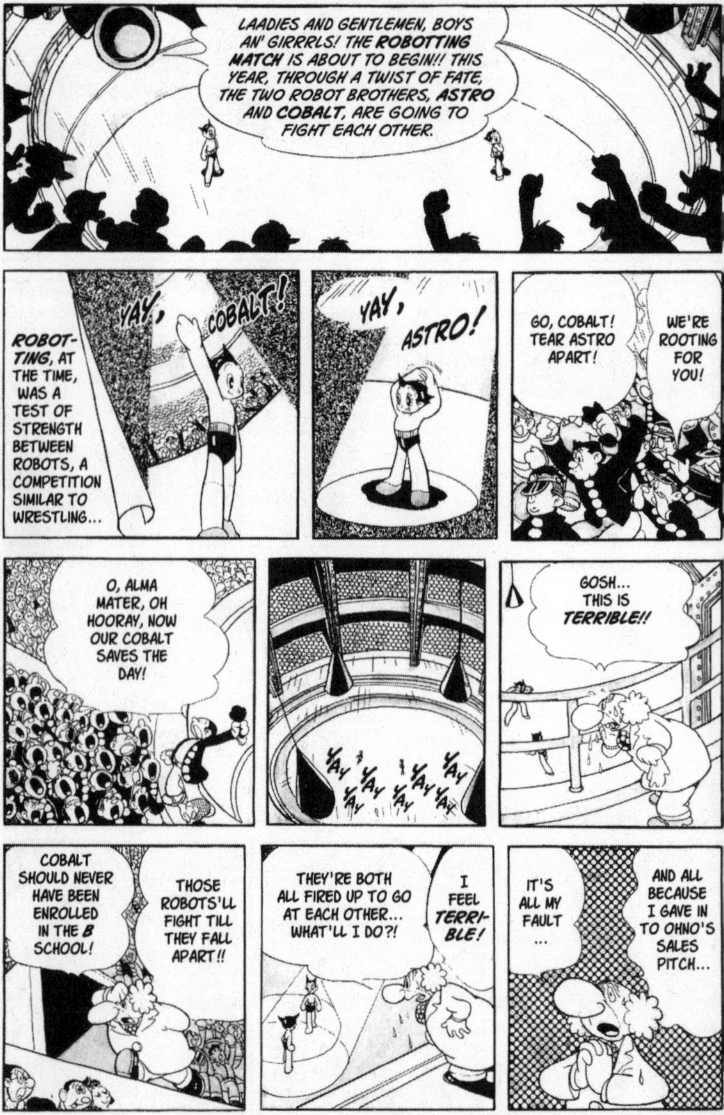
LAADIES AND GENTLEMEN, BOYS AN' GIRRRLS! THE ROBOTTING MATCH IS ABOUT TO BEGIN!! THIS YEAR, THROUGH A TWIST OF FATE, THE TWO ROBOT BROTHERS, ASTRO AND COBALT, ARE GOING TO FIGHT EACH OTHER.
ROBOTTING, AT THE TIME, WAS A TEST OF STRENGTH BETWEEN ROBOTS, A COMPETITION SIMILAR TO WRESTLING...
YAY, COBALT!
YAY, ASTRO!
GO, COBALT! TEAR ASTRO APART!
WE'RE ROOTING FOR YOU!
O, ALMA MATER, OH HOORAY, NOW OUR COBALT SAVES THE DAY!
YAY YAY YAY YAY YAY YAY YAY YAY
GOSH... THIS IS TERRIBLE!!
COBALT SHOULD NEVER HAVE BEEN ENROLLED IN THE B SCHOOL!
THOSE ROBOTS'LL FIGHT TILL THEY FALL APART!!
THEY'RE BOTH ALL FIRED UP TO GO AT EACH OTHER... WHAT'LL I DO?!
I FEEL TERRIBLE!
IT'S ALL MY FAULT ...
AND ALL BECAUSE I GAVE IN TO OHNO'S SALES PITCH...

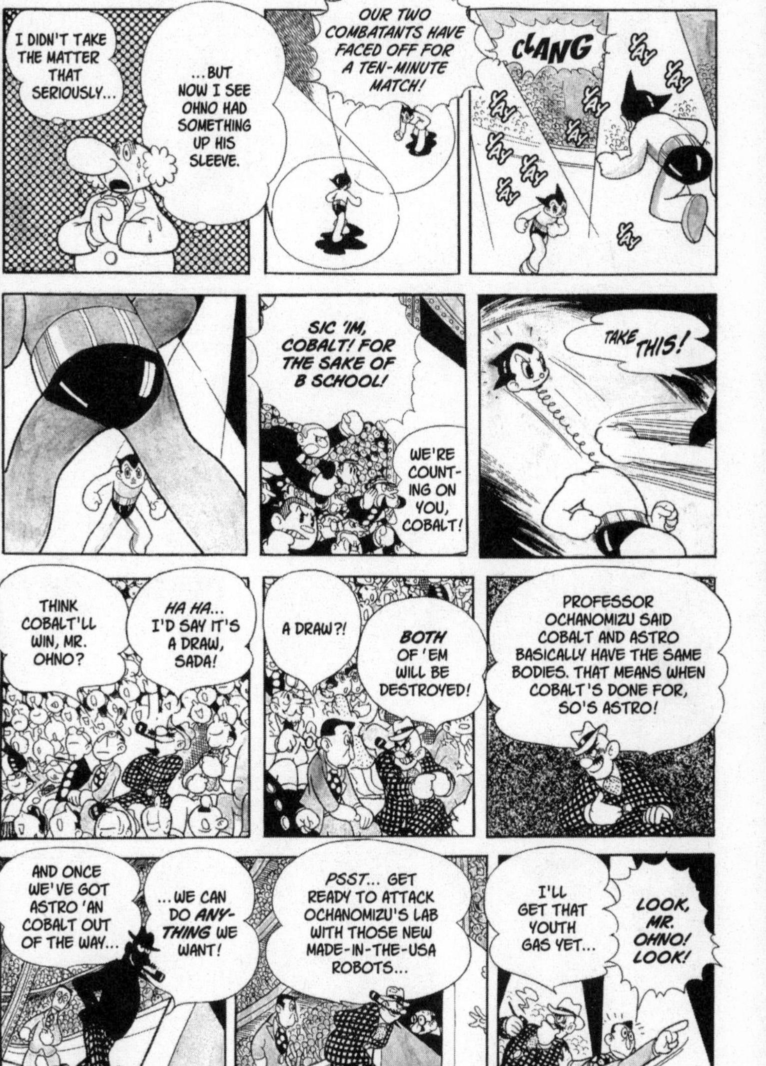
I DIDN'T TAKE THE MATTER THAT SERIOUSLY...
...BUT NOW I SEE OHNO HAD SOMETHING UP HIS SLEEVE.
OUR TWO COMBATANTS HAVE FACED OFF FOR A TEN-MINUTE MATCH!
CLANG
YAY YAY YAY YAY YAY YAY YAY YAY YAY YAY
SIC 'IM, COBALT! FOR THE SAKE OF B SCHOOL!
WE'RE COUNTING ON YOU, COBALT!
TAKE THIS!
THINK COBALT'LL WIN, MR. OHNO?
HA HA... I'D SAY IT'S A DRAW, SADA!
A DRAW?!
BOTH OF 'EM WILL BE DESTROYED!
PROFESSOR OCHANOMIZU SAID COBALT AND ASTRO BASICALLY HAVE THE SAME BODIES. THAT MEANS WHEN COBALT'S DONE FOR, SO'S ASTRO!
AND ONCE WE'VE GOT ASTRO 'AN COBALT OUT OF THE WAY...
...WE CAN DO ANYTHING WE WANT!
PSST... GET READY TO ATTACK OCHANOMIZU'S LAB WITH THOSE NEW MADE-IN-THE-USA ROBOTS...
I'LL GET THAT YOUTH GAS YET...
LOOK, MR. OHNO! LOOK!

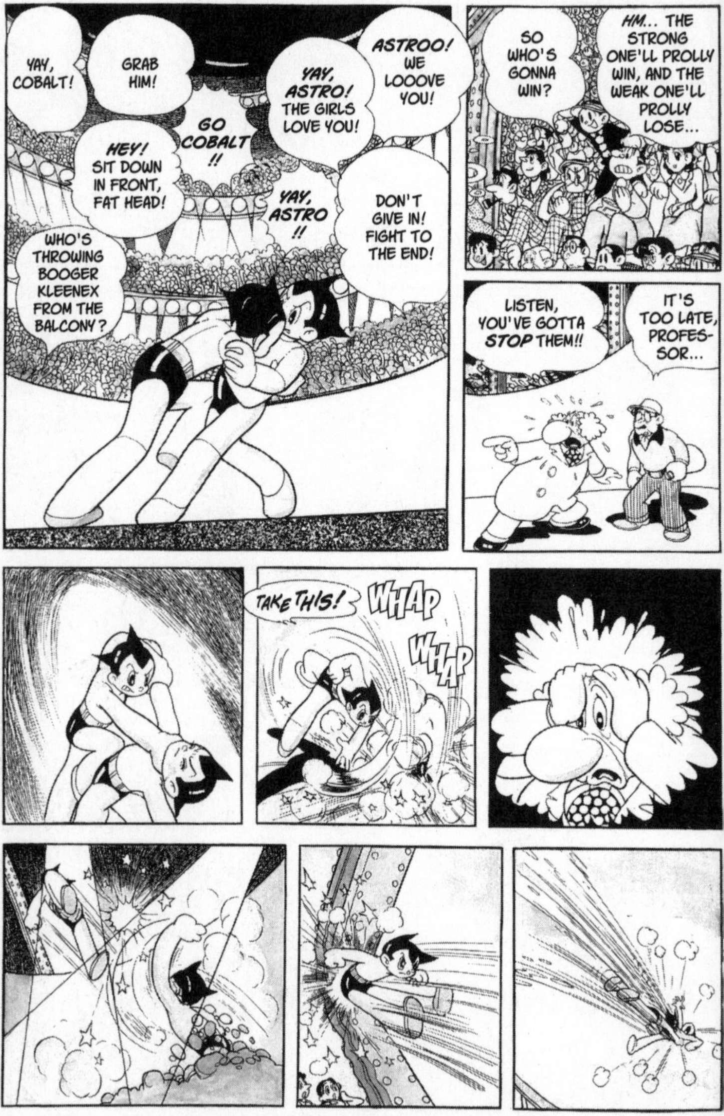
YAY, COBALT!
GRAB HIM!
HEY! SIT DOWN IN FRONT, FAT HEAD!
GO COBALT !!
YAY, ASTRO! THE GIRLS LOVE YOU!
ASTROO! WE LOOOVE YOU!
WHO'S THROWING BOOGER KLEENEX FROM THE BALCONY?
YAY, ASTRO !!
DON'T GIVE IN! FIGHT TO THE END!
SO WHO'S GONNA WIN?
HM... THE STRONG ONE'LL PROLLY WIN, AND THE WEAK ONE'LL PROLLY LOSE...
LISTEN, YOU'VE GOTTA STOP THEM!!
IT'S TOO LATE, PROFESSOR...
TAKE THIS!
WHAP
WHAP

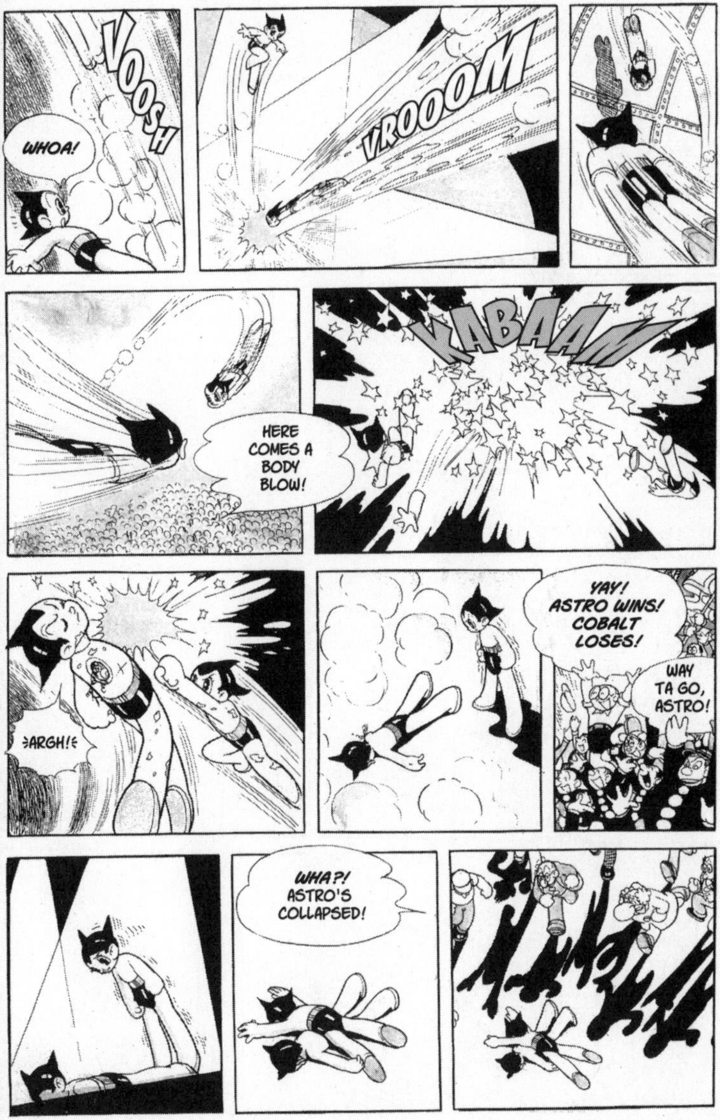
VOOSH
WHOA!
VROOOM
HERE COMES A BODY BLOW!
KABAAM
ARGH!
YAY! ASTRO WINS! COBALT LOSES!
WAY TA GO, ASTRO!
WHA?! ASTRO'S COLLAPSED!

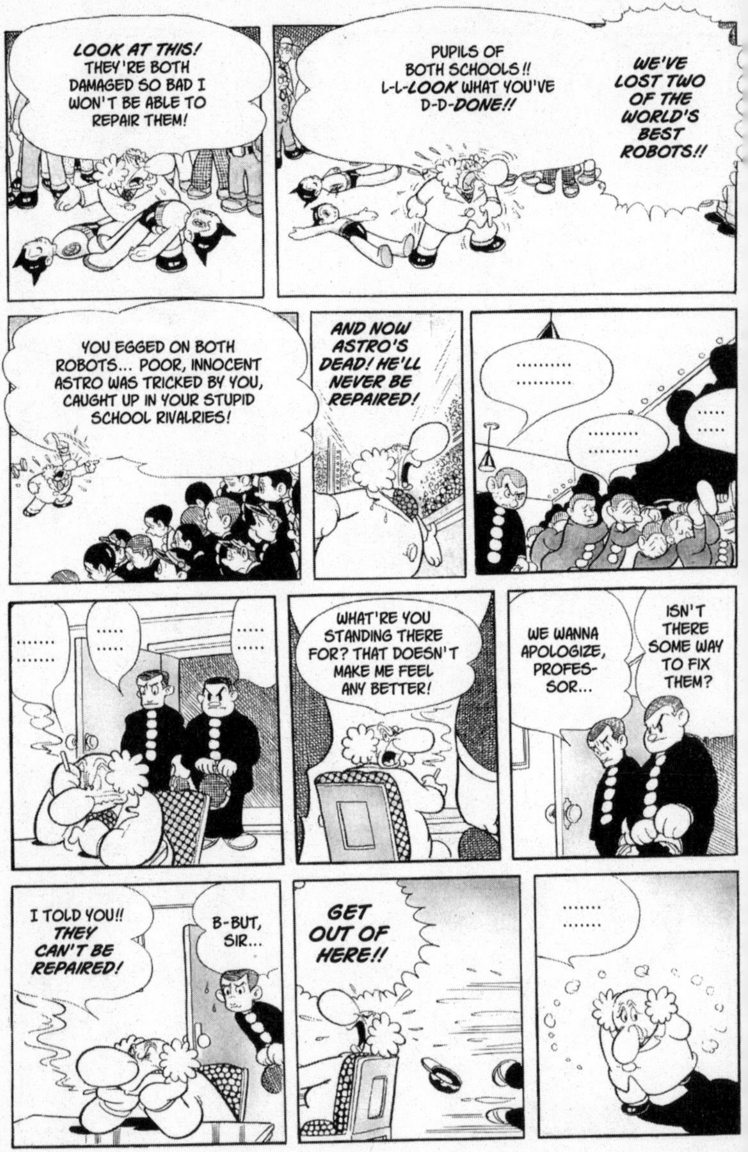

LOOK AT THIS! THEY'RE BOTH DAMAGED SO BAD I WON'T BE ABLE TO REPAIR THEM!
PUPILS OF BOTH SCHOOLS!! L-L-LOOK WHAT YOU'VE D-D-DONE!!
WE'VE LOST TWO OF THE WORLD'S BEST ROBOTS!!
YOU EGGED ON BOTH ROBOTS... POOR, INNOCENT ASTRO WAS TRICKED BY YOU, CAUGHT UP IN YOUR STUPID SCHOOL RIVALRIES!
AND NOW ASTRO'S DEAD! HE'LL NEVER BE REPAIRED!
WHAT'RE YOU STANDING THERE FOR? THAT DOESN'T MAKE ME FEEL ANY BETTER!
WE WANNA APOLOGIZE, PROFES-SOR...
ISN'T THERE SOME WAY TO FIX THEM?
I TOLD YOU!! THEY CAN'T BE REPAIRED!
B-BUT, SIR...
GET OUT OF HERE!!

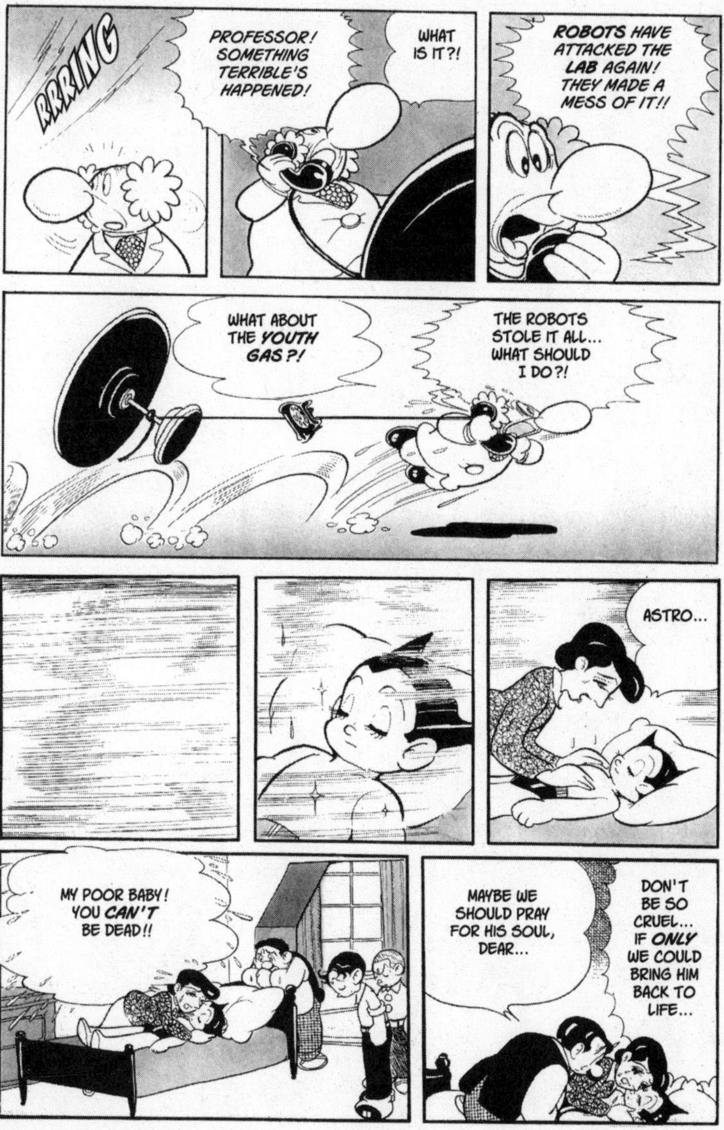
RRRING
PROFESSOR! SOMETHING TERRIBLE'S HAPPENED!
WHAT IS IT?!
ROBOTS HAVE ATTACKED THE LAB AGAIN! THEY MADE A MESS OF IT!!
WHAT ABOUT THE YOUTH GAS?!
THE ROBOTS STOLE IT ALL... WHAT SHOULD I DO?!
ASTRO...
MY POOR BABY! YOU CAN'T BE DEAD!!
MAYBE WE SHOULD PRAY FOR HIS SOUL, DEAR...
DON'T BE SO CRUEL... IF ONLY WE COULD BRING HIM BACK TO LIFE...

ASTRO SURE WAS A GOOD PAL...

AND BRAVE, TOO!

HEY, KEN! C'MERE QUICK!

WHAT? YOU SAW *GIANT ROBOTS* IN OUR POND?

YEAH! LOOKS LIKE THE SAME ONE THAT ATTACKED THE PROFESSOR'S LAB!!

WE'VE GOTTA TELL THE *POLICE!*

NOT SO FAST!

YOU'RE NEAR-SIGHTED AND THAT POND'S DEEP... YOU SURE YOU DIDN'T SEE SOME OLD DRUM CANS?

LET'S GO DOUBLE-CHECK, GUYS!

THE POND'S RIGHT NEXT TO THE PROFESSOR'S LAB...

GREEN BELT TREAT NATURE WITH CARE PROTECT TOKYO NATURAL BEAUTY

I WAS FISHING, AND SUDDENLY SAW IT...

NOT MUCH OF A POND...

I'LL CHECK UNDERWATER...

BE CAREFUL, TANAKA...

436

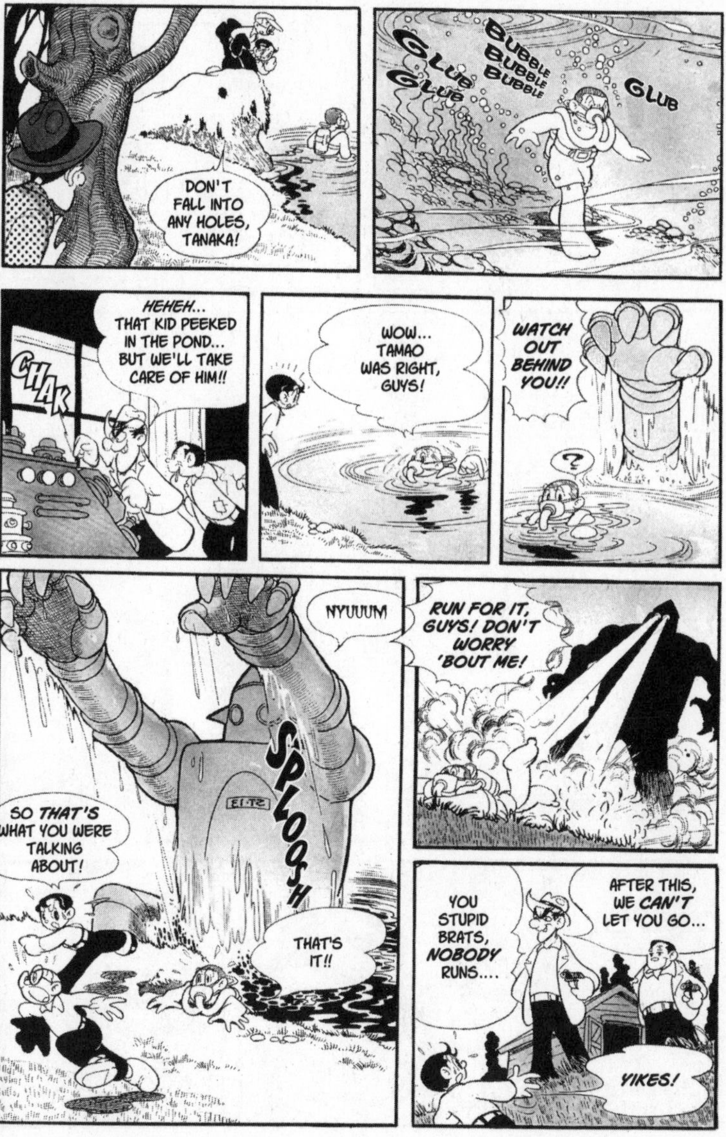
DON'T FALL INTO ANY HOLES, TANAKA!
BUBBLE BUBBLE BUBBLE
GLUB GLUB
GLUB
HEHEH... THAT KID PEEKED IN THE POND... BUT WE'LL TAKE CARE OF HIM!!
CHAK
WOW... TAMAO WAS RIGHT, GUYS!
WATCH OUT BEHIND YOU!!
?
NYUUUM
SPLOOSH
SO THAT'S WHAT YOU WERE TALKING ABOUT!
THAT'S IT!!
RUN FOR IT, GUYS! DON'T WORRY 'BOUT ME!
YOU STUPID BRATS, NOBODY RUNS....
AFTER THIS, WE CAN'T LET YOU GO...
YIKES!

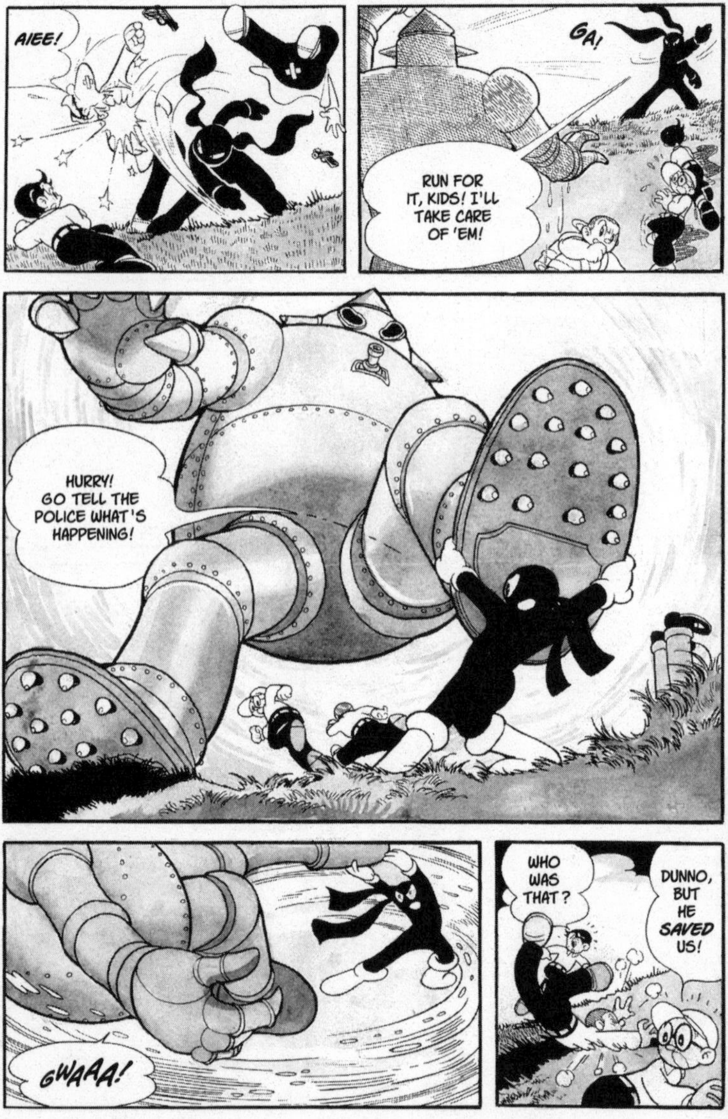
AIEE!
GA!
RUN FOR IT, KIDS! I'LL TAKE CARE OF 'EM!
HURRY! GO TELL THE POLICE WHAT'S HAPPENING!
GWAAA!
WHO WAS THAT?
DUNNO, BUT HE SAVED US!

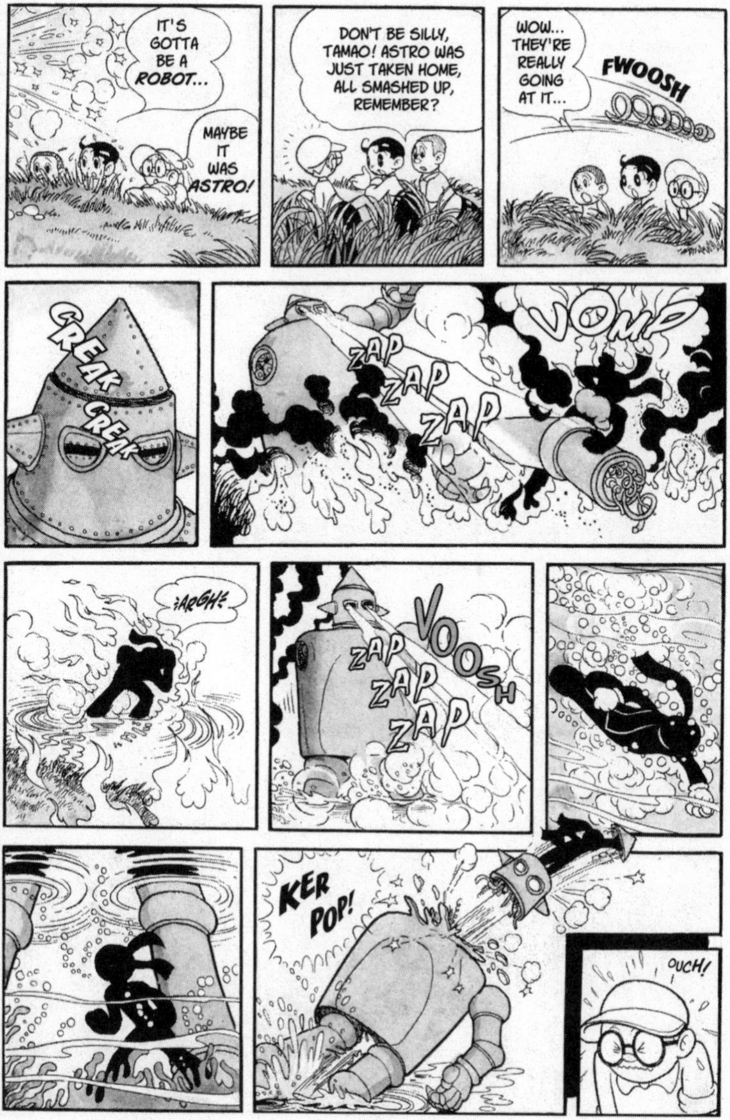
IT'S GOTTA BE A ROBOT...
MAYBE IT WAS ASTRO!
DON'T BE SILLY, TAMAO! ASTRO WAS JUST TAKEN HOME, ALL SMASHED UP, REMEMBER?
WOW... THEY'RE REALLY GOING AT IT...
FWOOSH
CREAK CREAK
ZAP ZAP ZAP
VOMP
ARGH
ZAP ZAP ZAP
VOOSH
KER POP!
OUCH!

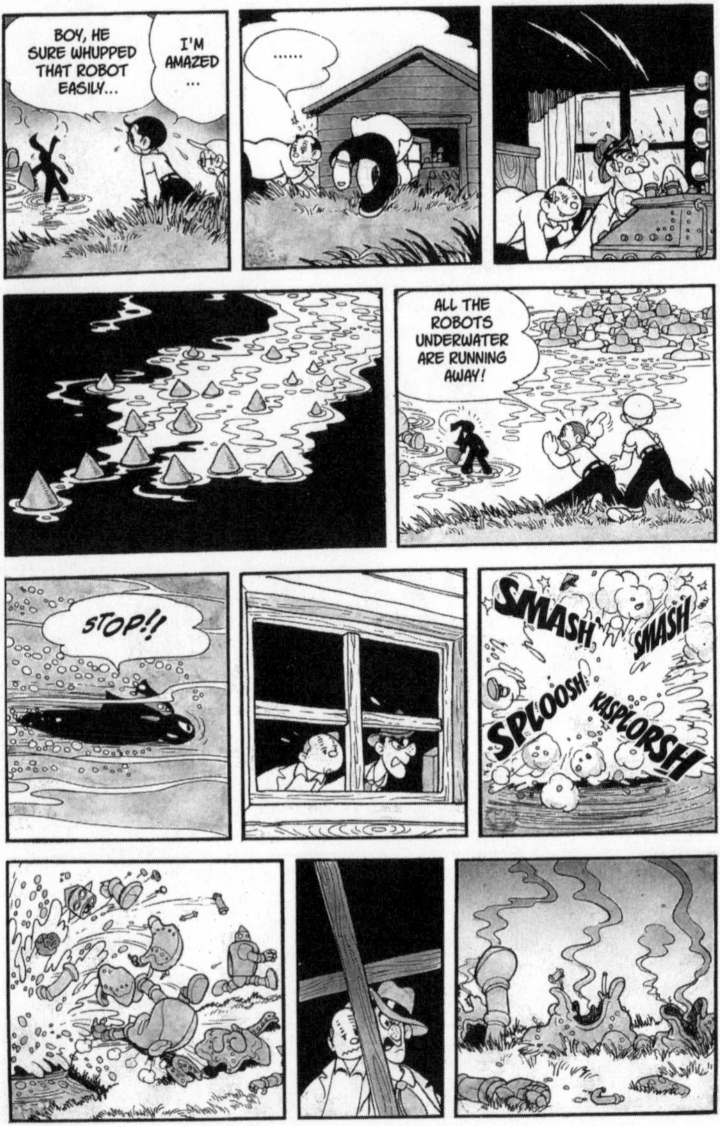
BOY, HE SURE WHUPPED THAT ROBOT EASILY...
I'M AMAZED ...
......
ALL THE ROBOTS UNDERWATER ARE RUNNING AWAY!
STOP!!
SMASH
SMASH
SPLOOSH
KASPLORSH

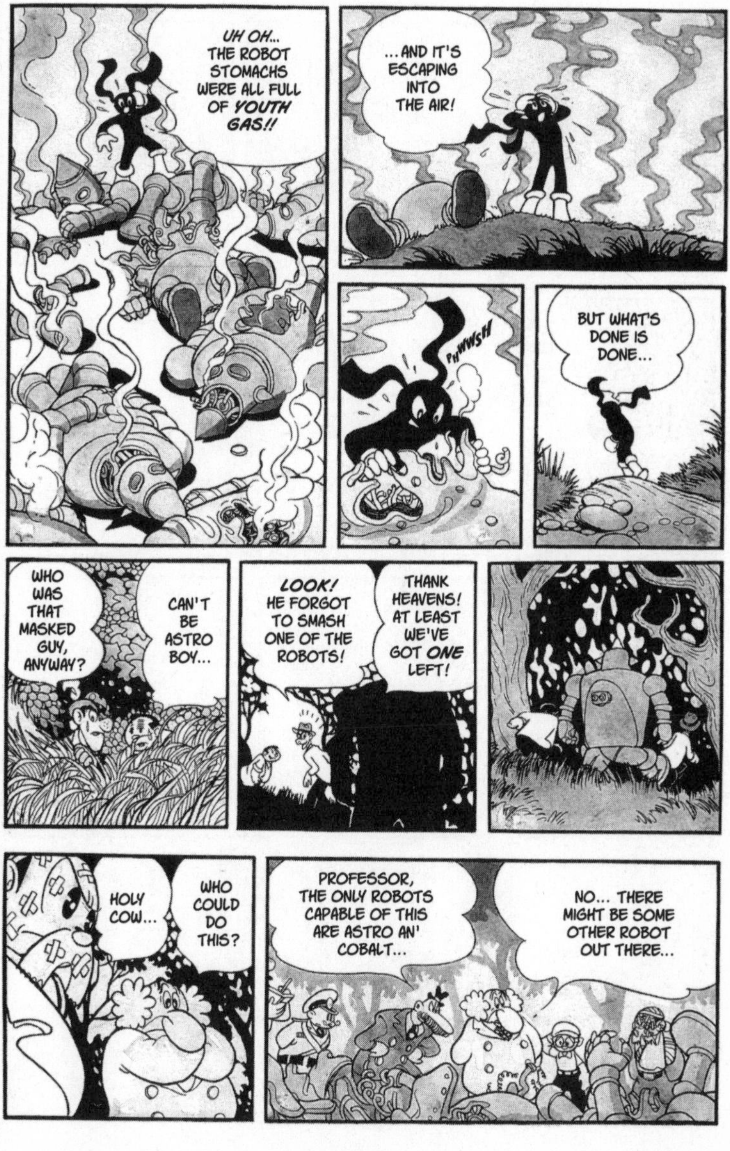
UH OH... THE ROBOT STOMACHS WERE ALL FULL OF YOUTH GAS!!
...AND IT'S ESCAPING INTO THE AIR!
PHWWSH
BUT WHAT'S DONE IS DONE...
WHO WAS THAT MASKED GUY, ANYWAY?
CAN'T BE ASTRO BOY...
LOOK! HE FORGOT TO SMASH ONE OF THE ROBOTS!
THANK HEAVENS! AT LEAST WE'VE GOT ONE LEFT!
HOLY COW...
WHO COULD DO THIS?
PROFESSOR, THE ONLY ROBOTS CAPABLE OF THIS ARE ASTRO AN' COBALT...
NO... THERE MIGHT BE SOME OTHER ROBOT OUT THERE...

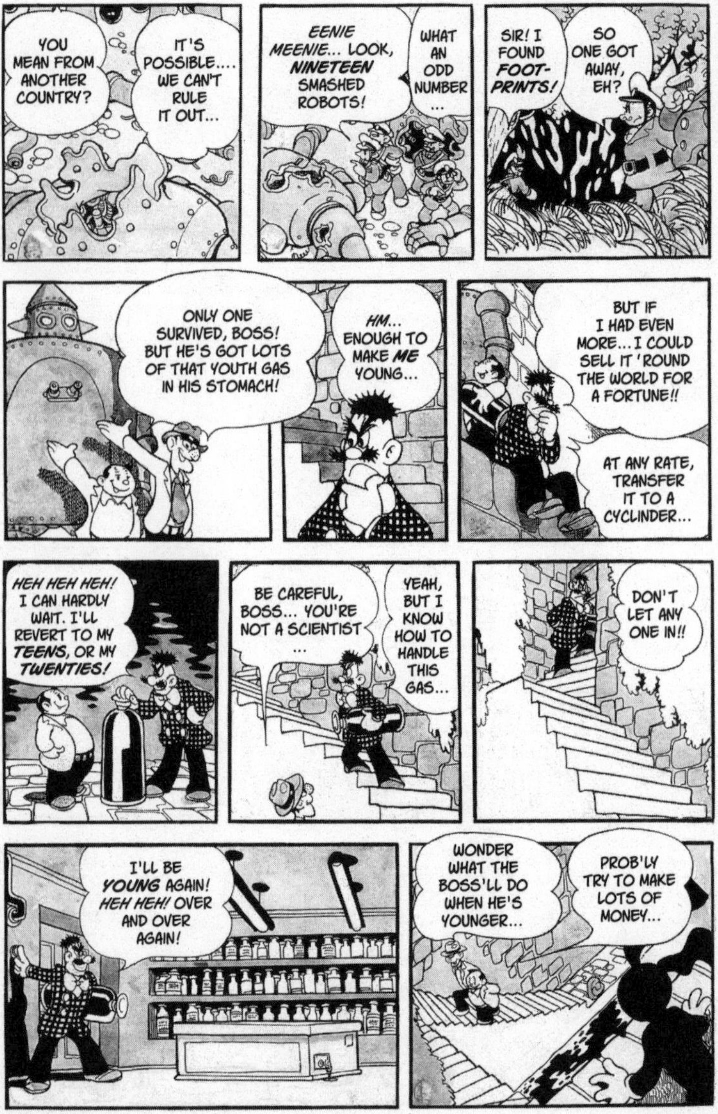
YOU MEAN FROM ANOTHER COUNTRY?
IT'S POSSIBLE.... WE CAN'T RULE IT OUT...
EENIE MEENIE... LOOK, NINETEEN SMASHED ROBOTS!
WHAT AN ODD NUMBER ...
SIR! I FOUND FOOT-PRINTS!
SO ONE GOT AWAY, EH?
ONLY ONE SURVIVED, BOSS! BUT HE'S GOT LOTS OF THAT YOUTH GAS IN HIS STOMACH!
HM... ENOUGH TO MAKE ME YOUNG...
BUT IF I HAD EVEN MORE... I COULD SELL IT 'ROUND THE WORLD FOR A FORTUNE!!
AT ANY RATE, TRANSFER IT TO A CYCLINDER...
HEH HEH HEH! I CAN HARDLY WAIT. I'LL REVERT TO MY TEENS, OR MY TWENTIES!
BE CAREFUL, BOSS... YOU'RE NOT A SCIENTIST ...
YEAH, BUT I KNOW HOW TO HANDLE THIS GAS...
DON'T LET ANY ONE IN!!
I'LL BE YOUNG AGAIN! HEH HEH! OVER AND OVER AGAIN!
WONDER WHAT THE BOSS'LL DO WHEN HE'S YOUNGER...
PROB'LY TRY TO MAKE LOTS OF MONEY...

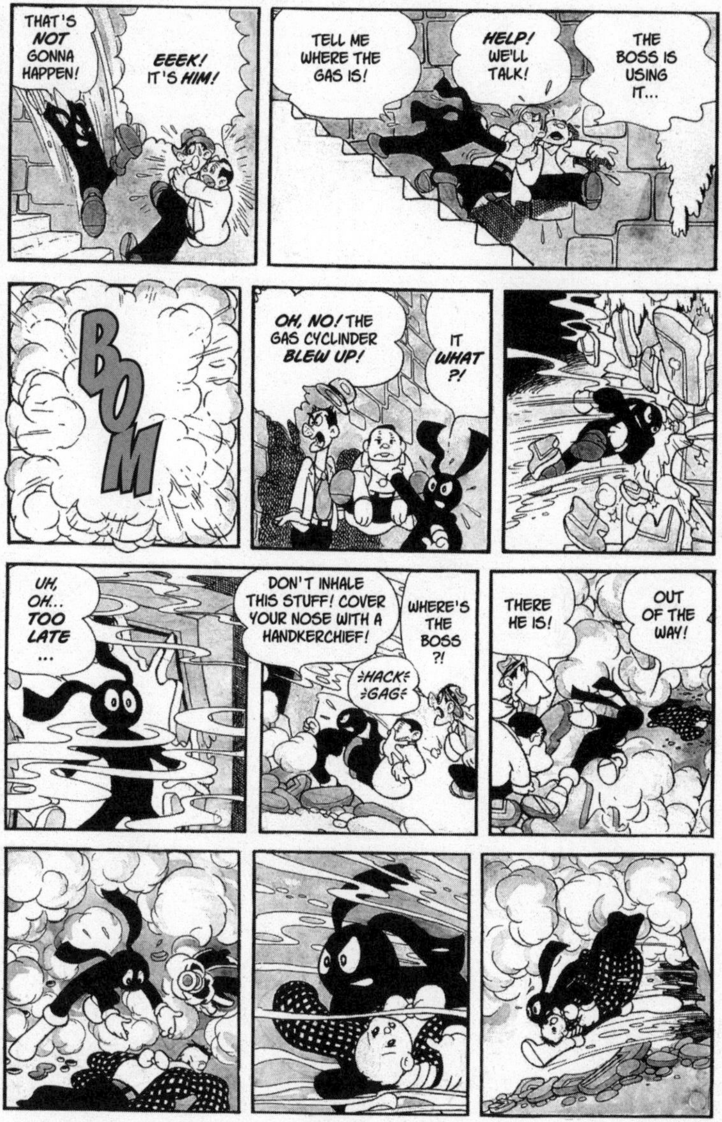
THAT'S NOT GONNA HAPPEN!
EEEK! IT'S HIM!
TELL ME WHERE THE GAS IS!
HELP! WE'LL TALK!
THE BOSS IS USING IT...
BOOM
OH, NO! THE GAS CYCLINDER BLEW UP!
IT WHAT?!
UH, OH... TOO LATE ...
DON'T INHALE THIS STUFF! COVER YOUR NOSE WITH A HANDKERCHIEF!
WHERE'S THE BOSS ?!
HACK
GAG
THERE HE IS!
OUT OF THE WAY!

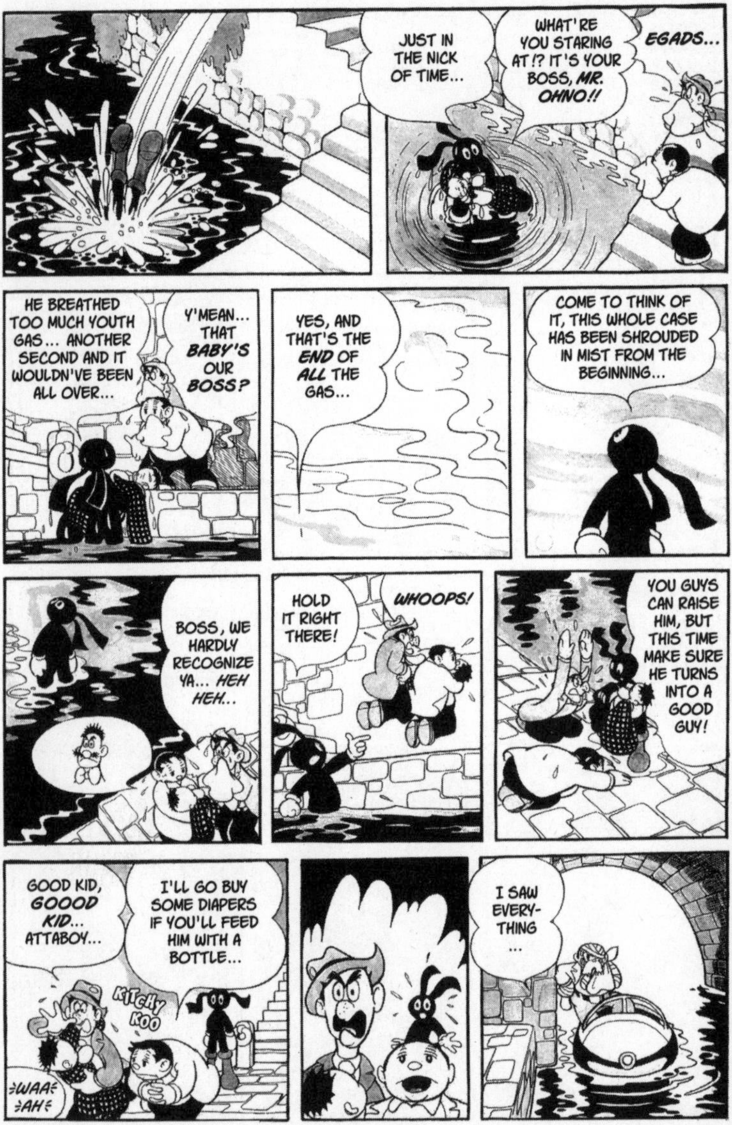
JUST IN THE NICK OF TIME...
WHAT'RE YOU STARING AT!? IT'S YOUR BOSS, MR. OHNO!!
EGADS...
HE BREATHED TOO MUCH YOUTH GAS... ANOTHER SECOND AND IT WOULDN'VE BEEN ALL OVER...
Y'MEAN... THAT BABY'S OUR BOSS?
YES, AND THAT'S THE END OF ALL THE GAS...
COME TO THINK OF IT, THIS WHOLE CASE HAS BEEN SHROUDED IN MIST FROM THE BEGINNING...
BOSS, WE HARDLY RECOGNIZE YA... HEH HEH...
HOLD IT RIGHT THERE!
WHOOPS!
YOU GUYS CAN RAISE HIM, BUT THIS TIME MAKE SURE HE TURNS INTO A GOOD GUY!
GOOD KID, GOOOD KID... ATTABOY...
I'LL GO BUY SOME DIAPERS IF YOU'LL FEED HIM WITH A BOTTLE...
KITCHY KOO
WAA AH
I SAW EVERY-THING ...

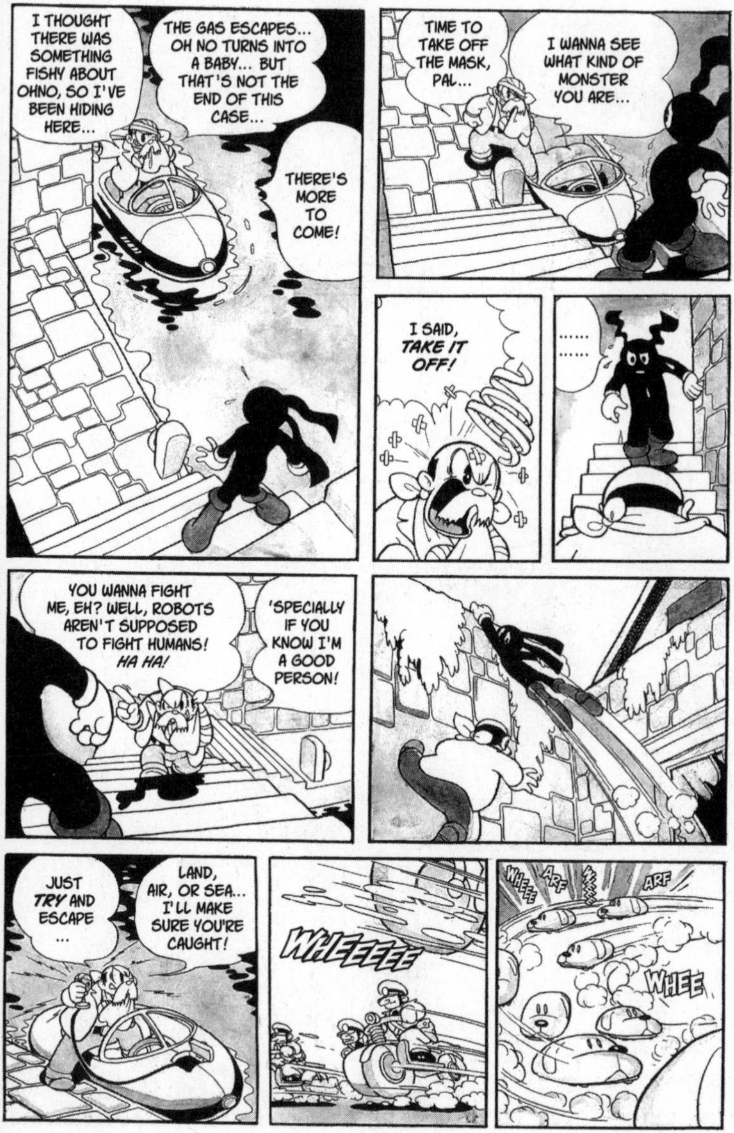
I THOUGHT THERE WAS SOMETHING FISHY ABOUT OHNO, SO I'VE BEEN HIDING HERE...
THE GAS ESCAPES... OH NO TURNS INTO A BABY... BUT THAT'S NOT THE END OF THIS CASE...
THERE'S MORE TO COME!
TIME TO TAKE OFF THE MASK, PAL...
I WANNA SEE WHAT KIND OF MONSTER YOU ARE...
I SAID, *TAKE IT OFF!*
......
......
YOU WANNA FIGHT ME, EH? WELL, ROBOTS AREN'T SUPPOSED TO FIGHT HUMANS! *HA HA!*
'SPECIALLY IF YOU KNOW I'M A GOOD PERSON!
JUST *TRY* AND ESCAPE ...
LAND, AIR, OR SEA... I'LL MAKE SURE YOU'RE CAUGHT!
WHEEEEEE
WHEEE
ARF
WHEEE
ARF
WHEE

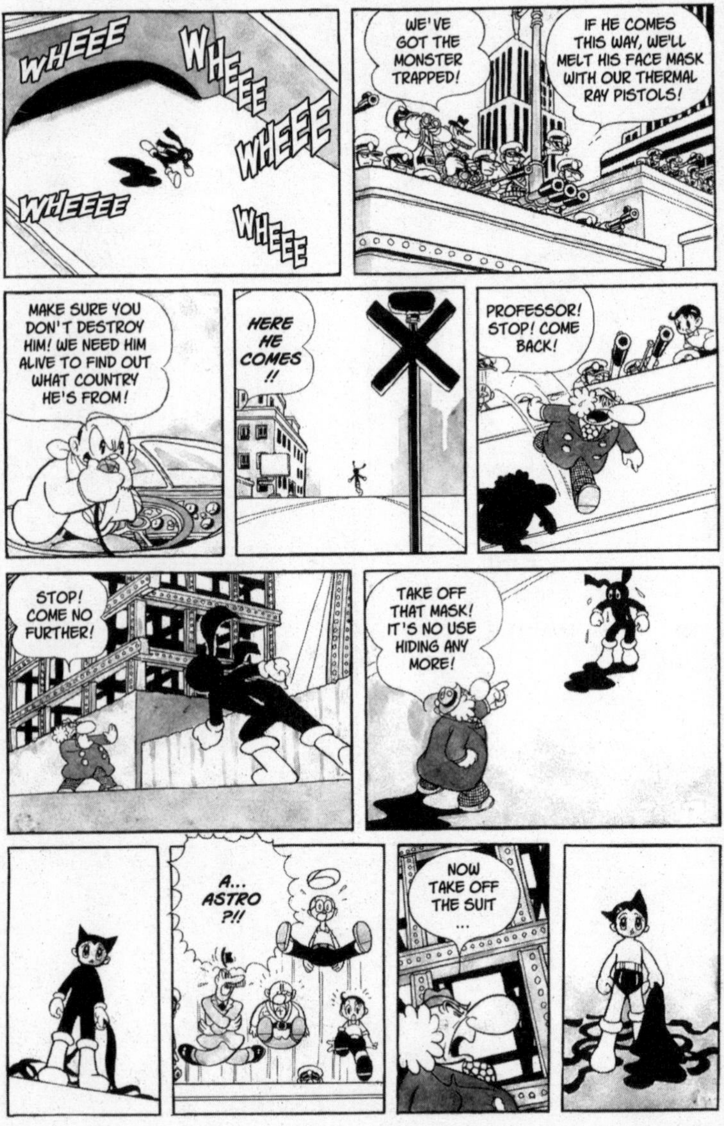
WHEEE
WHEEE
WHEEE
WHEEEE
WHEEE
WE'VE GOT THE MONSTER TRAPPED!
IF HE COMES THIS WAY, WE'LL MELT HIS FACE MASK WITH OUR THERMAL RAY PISTOLS!
MAKE SURE YOU DON'T DESTROY HIM! WE NEED HIM ALIVE TO FIND OUT WHAT COUNTRY HE'S FROM!
HERE HE COMES !!
PROFESSOR! STOP! COME BACK!
STOP! COME NO FURTHER!
TAKE OFF THAT MASK! IT'S NO USE HIDING ANY MORE!
A... ASTRO ?!!
NOW TAKE OFF THE SUIT ...

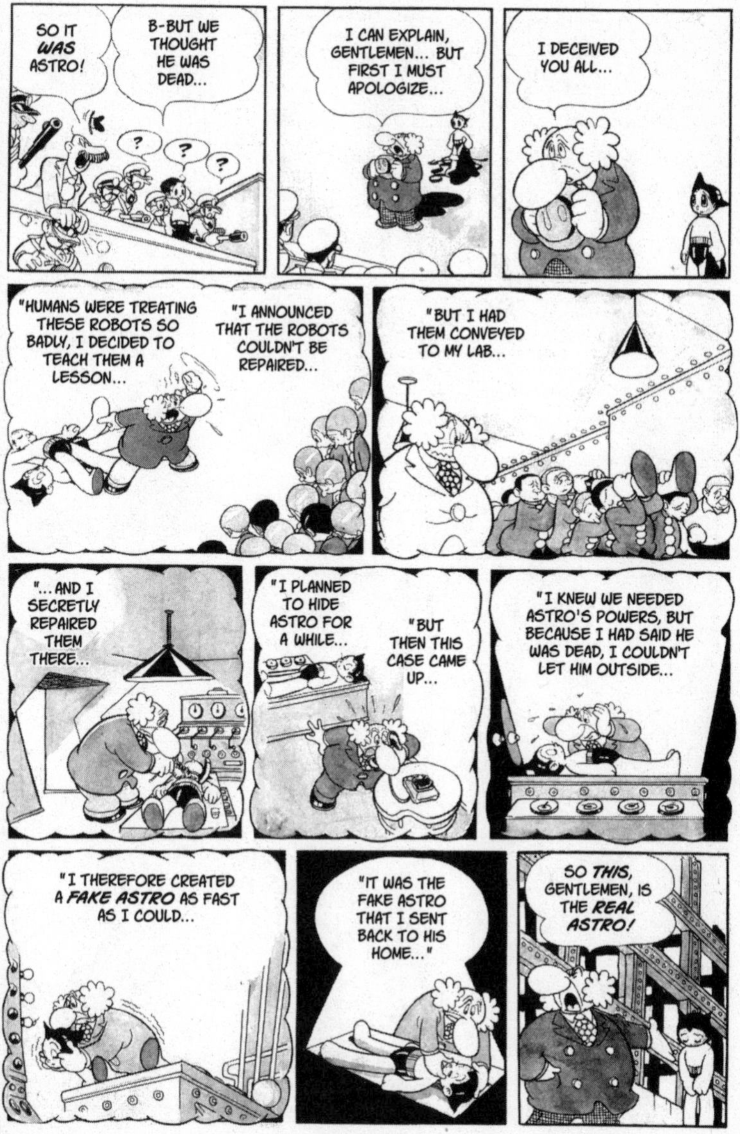
SO IT WAS ASTRO!
B-BUT WE THOUGHT HE WAS DEAD...
?
?
?
I CAN EXPLAIN, GENTLEMEN... BUT FIRST I MUST APOLOGIZE...
I DECEIVED YOU ALL...
"HUMANS WERE TREATING THESE ROBOTS SO BADLY, I DECIDED TO TEACH THEM A LESSON...
"I ANNOUNCED THAT THE ROBOTS COULDN'T BE REPAIRED...
"BUT I HAD THEM CONVEYED TO MY LAB...
"...AND I SECRETLY REPAIRED THEM THERE...
"I PLANNED TO HIDE ASTRO FOR A WHILE...
"BUT THEN THIS CASE CAME UP...
"I KNEW WE NEEDED ASTRO'S POWERS, BUT BECAUSE I HAD SAID HE WAS DEAD, I COULDN'T LET HIM OUTSIDE...
"I THEREFORE CREATED A FAKE ASTRO AS FAST AS I COULD...
"IT WAS THE FAKE ASTRO THAT I SENT BACK TO HIS HOME..."
SO THIS, GENTLEMEN, IS THE REAL ASTRO!

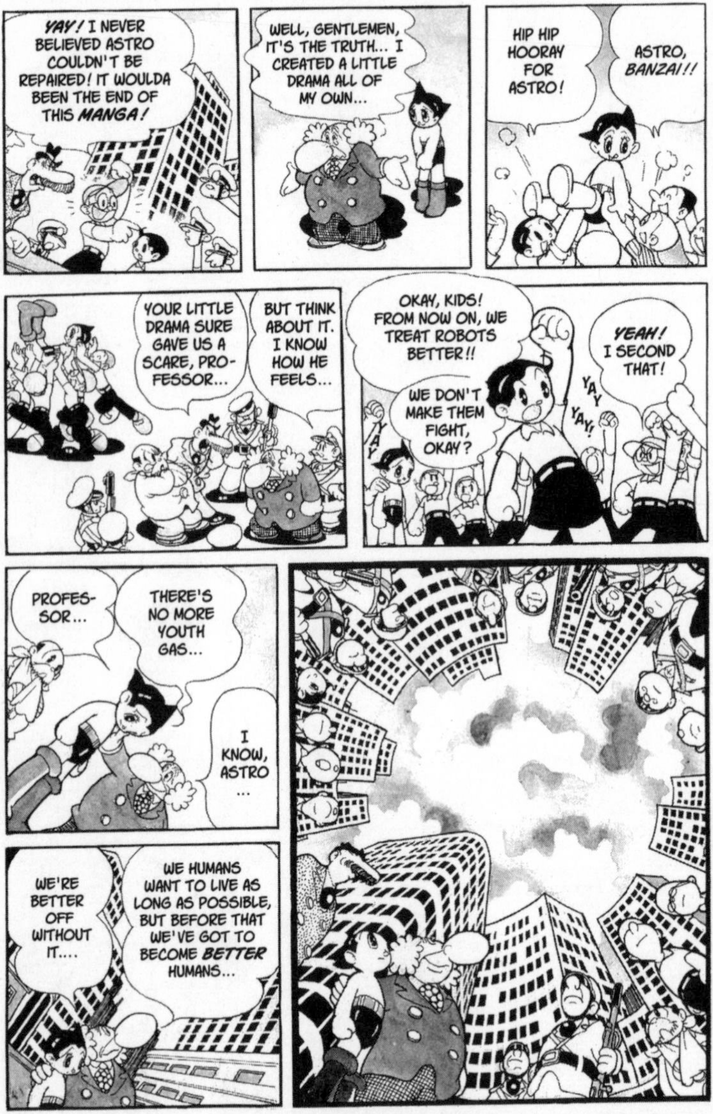
YAY! I NEVER BELIEVED ASTRO COULDN'T BE REPAIRED! IT WOULDA BEEN THE END OF THIS MANGA!
WELL, GENTLEMEN, IT'S THE TRUTH... I CREATED A LITTLE DRAMA ALL OF MY OWN...
HIP HIP HOORAY FOR ASTRO!
ASTRO, BANZAI!!
YOUR LITTLE DRAMA SURE GAVE US A SCARE, PROFESSOR...
BUT THINK ABOUT IT. I KNOW HOW HE FEELS...
OKAY, KIDS! FROM NOW ON, WE TREAT ROBOTS BETTER!!
YAY
WE DON'T MAKE THEM FIGHT, OKAY?
YAY
YAY!
YEAH! I SECOND THAT!
PROFESSOR...
THERE'S NO MORE YOUTH GAS...
I KNOW, ASTRO...
WE'RE BETTER OFF WITHOUT IT....
WE HUMANS WANT TO LIVE AS LONG AS POSSIBLE, BUT BEFORE THAT WE'VE GOT TO BECOME BETTER HUMANS...

BROADCASTS FROM OUTER SPACE

First serialized in the December 1965 and January
1966 editions of *Tetsuwan Atom Kurabu*.

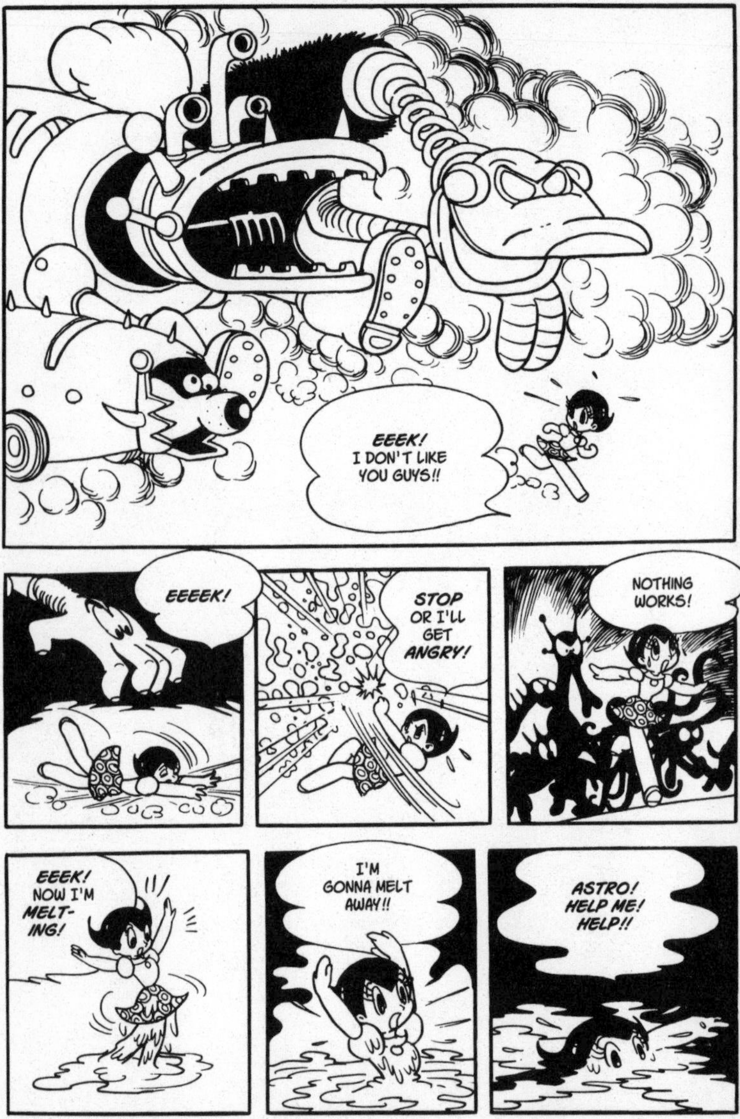
EEEK! I DON'T LIKE YOU GUYS!!
EEEEK!
STOP OR I'LL GET ANGRY!
NOTHING WORKS!
EEEK! NOW I'M MELT-ING!
I'M GONNA MELT AWAY!!
ASTRO! HELP ME! HELP!!

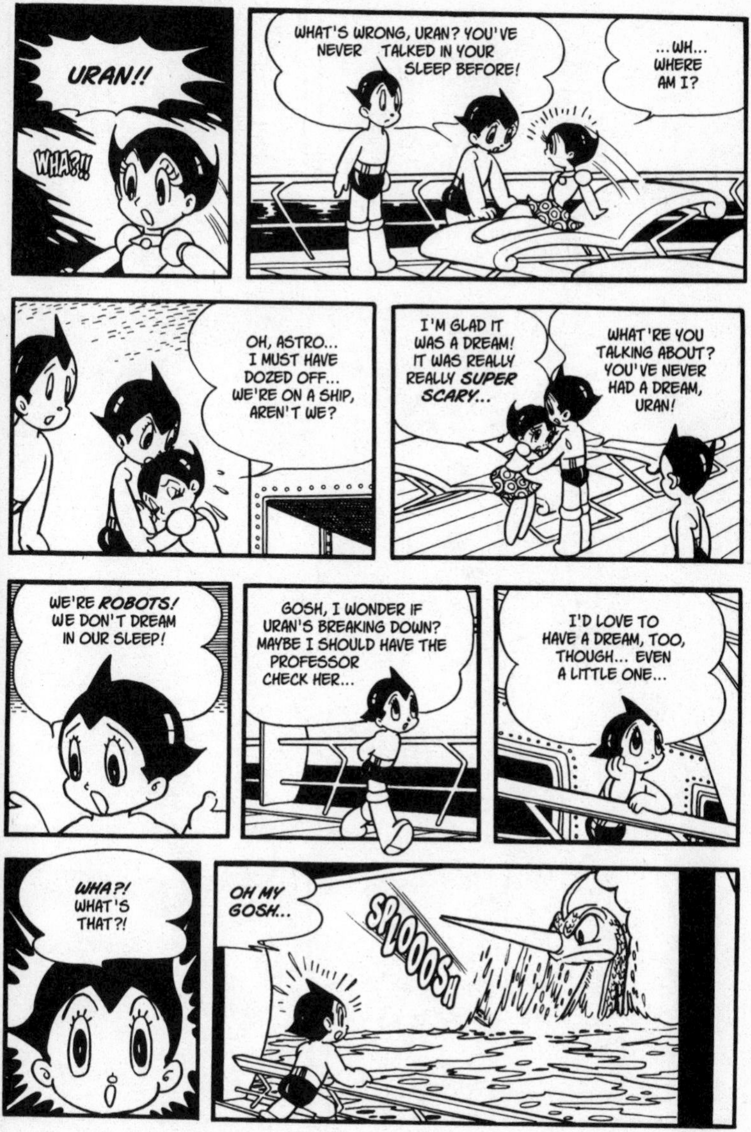
URAN!!
WHA?!!
WHAT'S WRONG, URAN? YOU'VE NEVER TALKED IN YOUR SLEEP BEFORE!
...WH... WHERE AM I?
OH, ASTRO... I MUST HAVE DOZED OFF... WE'RE ON A SHIP, AREN'T WE?
I'M GLAD IT WAS A DREAM! IT WAS REALLY REALLY SUPER SCARY...
WHAT'RE YOU TALKING ABOUT? YOU'VE NEVER HAD A DREAM, URAN!
WE'RE ROBOTS! WE DON'T DREAM IN OUR SLEEP!
GOSH, I WONDER IF URAN'S BREAKING DOWN? MAYBE I SHOULD HAVE THE PROFESSOR CHECK HER...
I'D LOVE TO HAVE A DREAM, TOO, THOUGH... EVEN A LITTLE ONE...
WHA?! WHAT'S THAT?!
OH MY GOSH...
SPLOOOSH

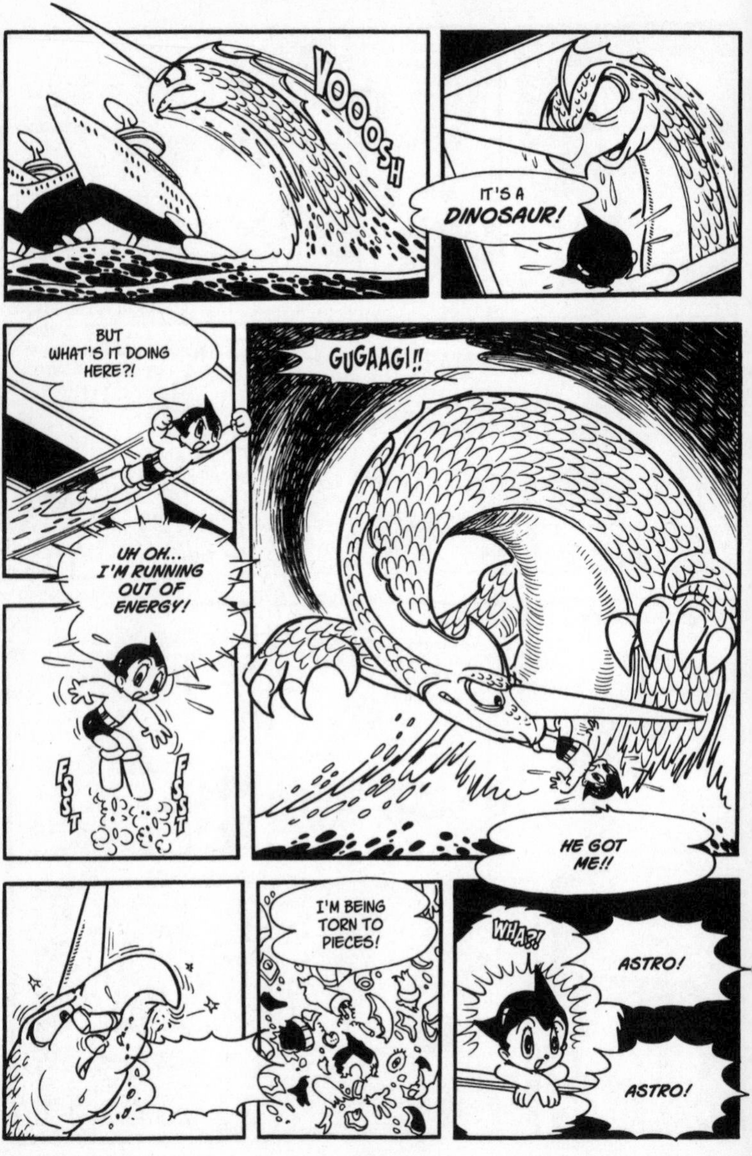

VOOOOSH
IT'S A DINOSAUR!
BUT WHAT'S IT DOING HERE?!
UH OH... I'M RUNNING OUT OF ENERGY!
FSST
FSST
GUGAAGI!!
HE GOT ME!!
I'M BEING TORN TO PIECES!
WHA?!
ASTRO!
ASTRO!

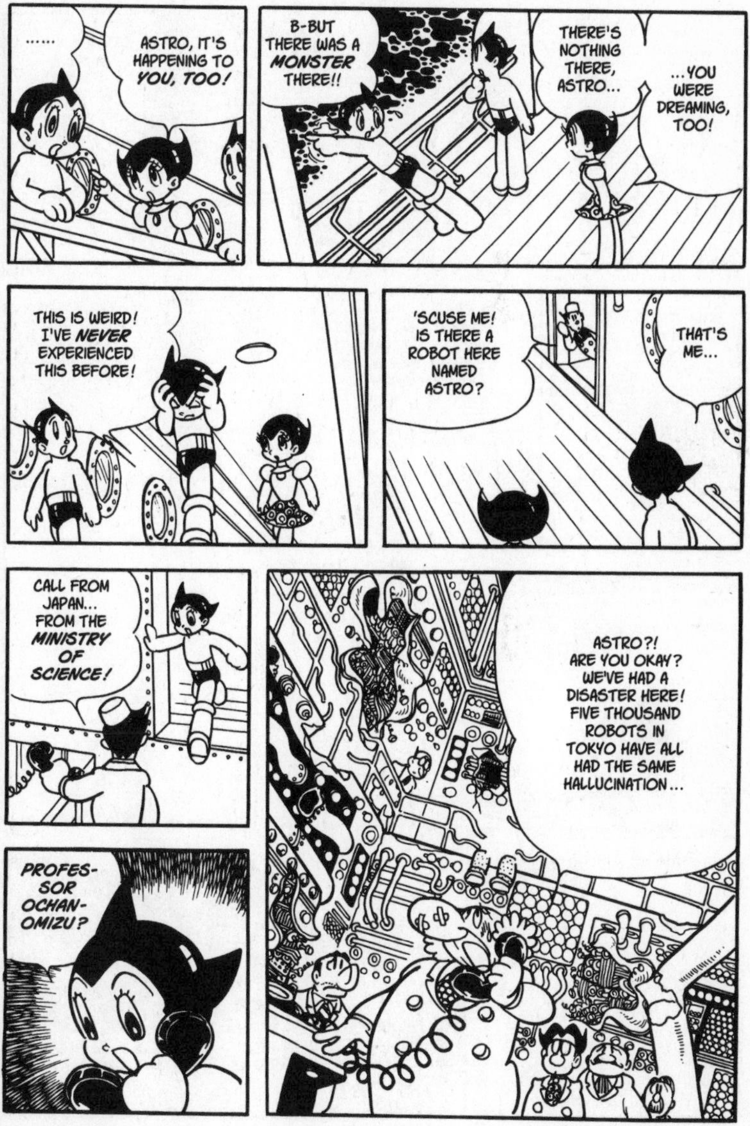
......
ASTRO, IT'S HAPPENING TO YOU, TOO!
B-BUT THERE WAS A MONSTER THERE!!
THERE'S NOTHING THERE, ASTRO...
...YOU WERE DREAMING, TOO!
THIS IS WEIRD! I'VE NEVER EXPERIENCED THIS BEFORE!
'SCUSE ME! IS THERE A ROBOT HERE NAMED ASTRO?
THAT'S ME...
CALL FROM JAPAN... FROM THE MINISTRY OF SCIENCE!
PROFES-SOR OCHAN-OMIZU?
ASTRO?! ARE YOU OKAY? WE'VE HAD A DISASTER HERE! FIVE THOUSAND ROBOTS IN TOKYO HAVE ALL HAD THE SAME HALLUCINATION...

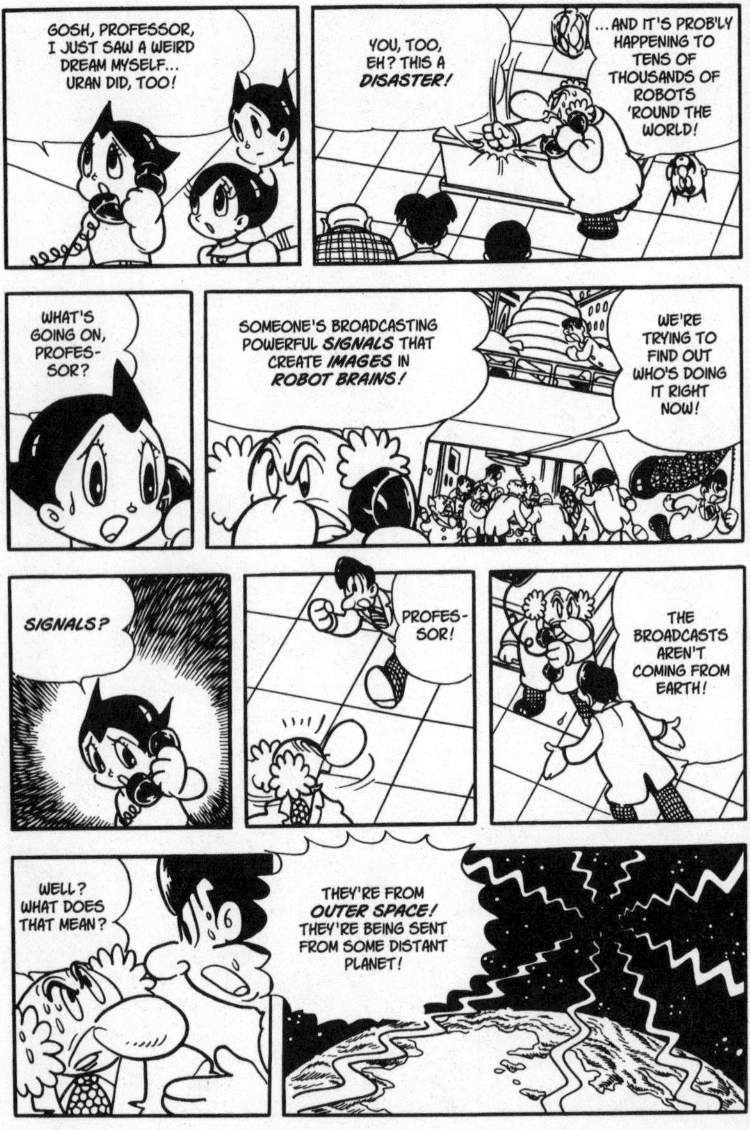
GOSH, PROFESSOR, I JUST SAW A WEIRD DREAM MYSELF... URAN DID, TOO!
YOU, TOO, EH? THIS A *DISASTER!*
...AND IT'S PROB'LY HAPPENING TO TENS OF THOUSANDS OF ROBOTS 'ROUND THE WORLD!
WHAT'S GOING ON, PROFES-SOR?
SOMEONE'S BROADCASTING POWERFUL *SIGNALS* THAT CREATE *IMAGES* IN *ROBOT BRAINS!*
WE'RE TRYING TO FIND OUT WHO'S DOING IT RIGHT NOW!
SIGNALS?
PROFES-SOR!
THE BROADCASTS AREN'T COMING FROM EARTH!
WELL? WHAT DOES THAT MEAN?
THEY'RE FROM *OUTER SPACE!* THEY'RE BEING SENT FROM SOME DISTANT PLANET!

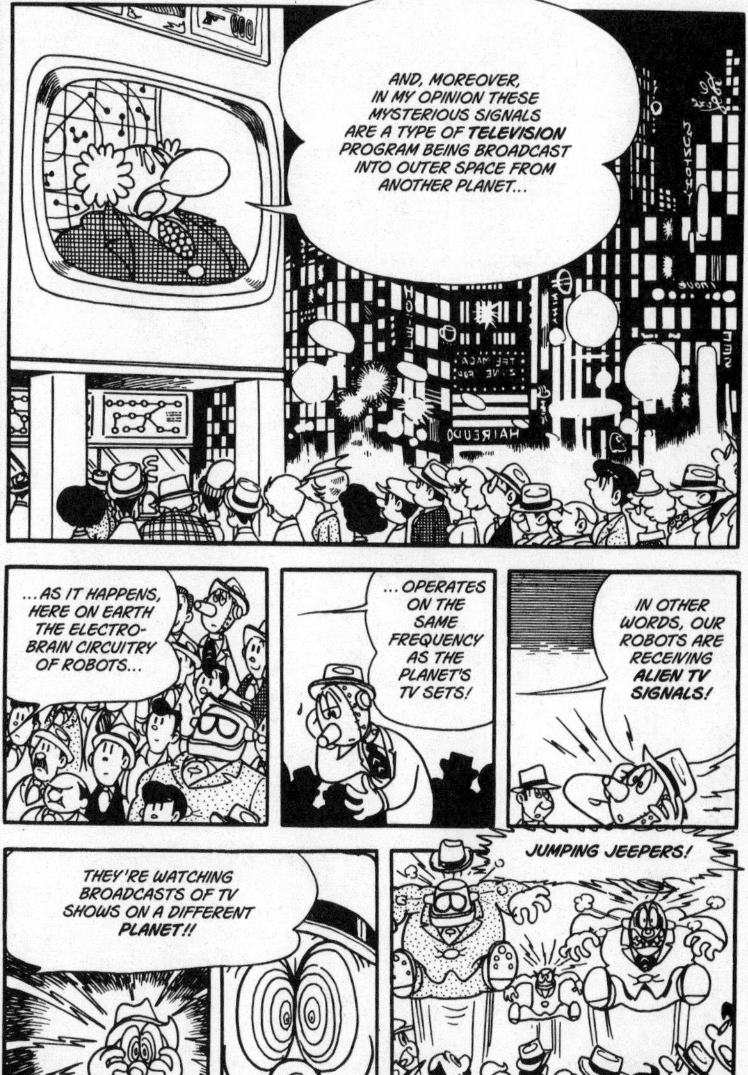

AND, MOREOVER, IN MY OPINION THESE MYSTERIOUS SIGNALS ARE A TYPE OF TELEVISION PROGRAM BEING BROADCAST INTO OUTER SPACE FROM ANOTHER PLANET...
...AS IT HAPPENS, HERE ON EARTH THE ELECTRO-BRAIN CIRCUITRY OF ROBOTS...
...OPERATES ON THE SAME FREQUENCY AS THE PLANET'S TV SETS!
IN OTHER WORDS, OUR ROBOTS ARE RECEIVING ALIEN TV SIGNALS!
THEY'RE WATCHING BROADCASTS OF TV SHOWS ON A DIFFERENT PLANET!!
JUMPING JEEPERS!

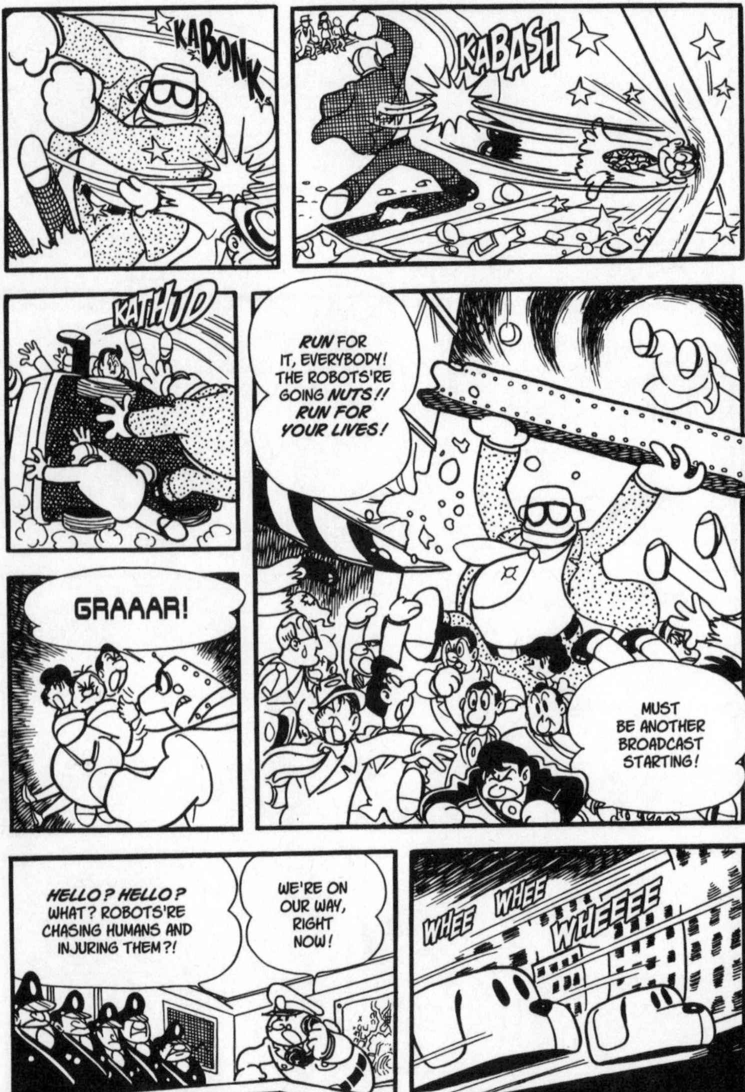
KABONK
KABASH
KATHUD
RUN FOR IT, EVERYBODY! THE ROBOTS'RE GOING NUTS!! RUN FOR YOUR LIVES!
GRAAAR!
MUST BE ANOTHER BROADCAST STARTING!
HELLO? HELLO? WHAT? ROBOTS'RE CHASING HUMANS AND INJURING THEM?!
WE'RE ON OUR WAY, RIGHT NOW!
WHEE WHEE WHEEEE

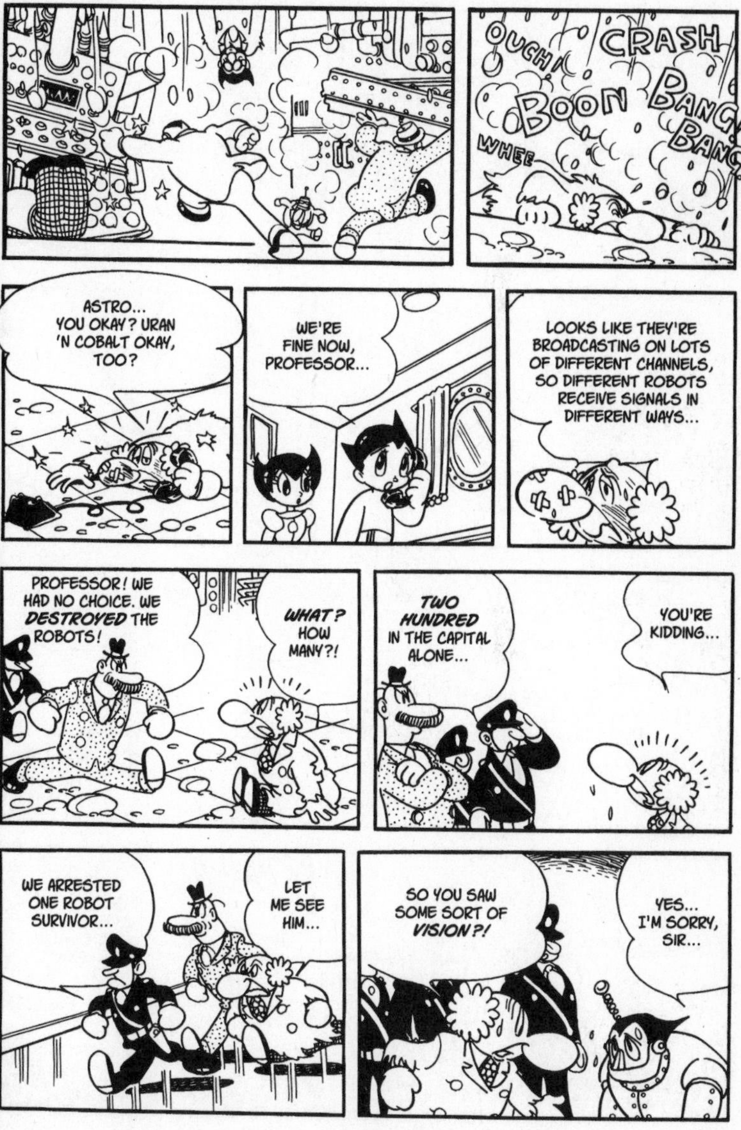
OUCH!
CRASH
BOON
BANG!
BANG!
WHEE
ASTRO... YOU OKAY? URAN 'N COBALT OKAY, TOO?
WE'RE FINE NOW, PROFESSOR...
LOOKS LIKE THEY'RE BROADCASTING ON LOTS OF DIFFERENT CHANNELS, SO DIFFERENT ROBOTS RECEIVE SIGNALS IN DIFFERENT WAYS...
PROFESSOR! WE HAD NO CHOICE. WE *DESTROYED* THE ROBOTS!
WHAT? HOW MANY?!
TWO HUNDRED IN THE CAPITAL ALONE...
YOU'RE KIDDING...
WE ARRESTED ONE ROBOT SURVIVOR...
LET ME SEE HIM...
SO YOU SAW SOME SORT OF *VISION?!*
YES... I'M SORRY, SIR...

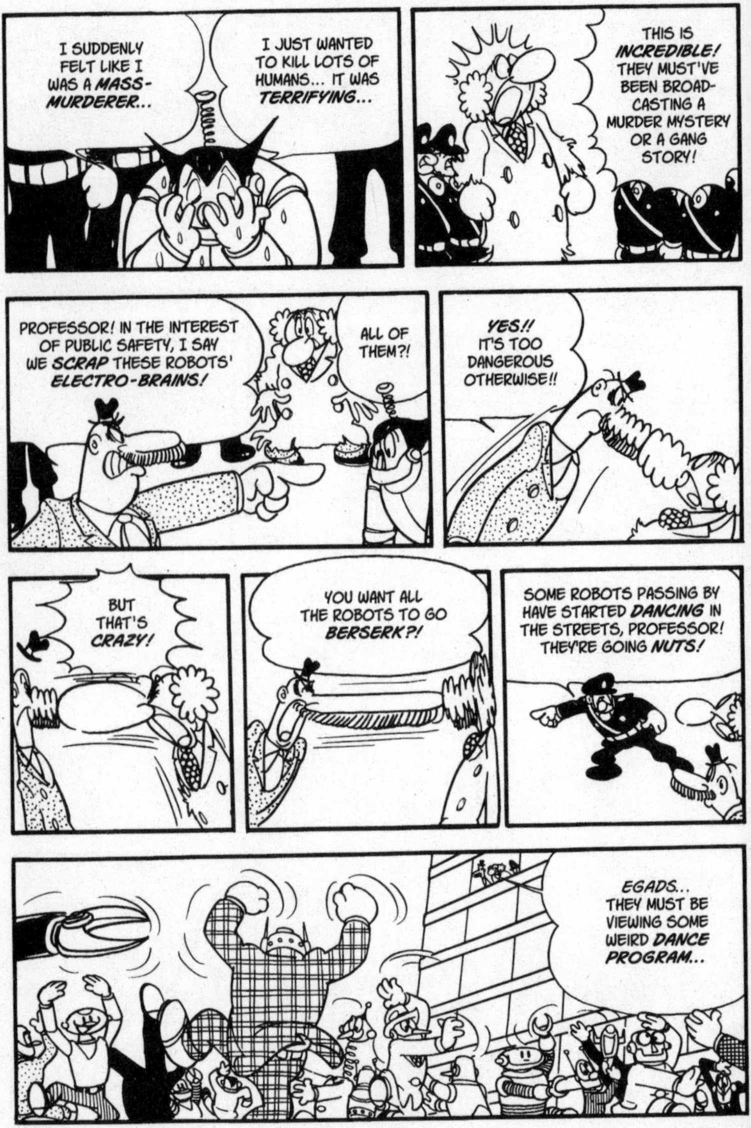
I SUDDENLY FELT LIKE I WAS A *MASS-MURDERER...*
I JUST WANTED TO KILL LOTS OF HUMANS... IT WAS *TERRIFYING...*
THIS IS *INCREDIBLE!* THEY MUST'VE BEEN BROAD-CASTING A MURDER MYSTERY OR A GANG STORY!
PROFESSOR! IN THE INTEREST OF PUBLIC SAFETY, I SAY WE *SCRAP* THESE ROBOTS' *ELECTRO-BRAINS!*
ALL OF THEM?!
YES!! IT'S TOO DANGEROUS OTHERWISE!!
BUT THAT'S *CRAZY!*
YOU WANT ALL THE ROBOTS TO GO *BERSERK?!*
SOME ROBOTS PASSING BY HAVE STARTED *DANCING* IN THE STREETS, PROFESSOR! THEY'RE GOING *NUTS!*
EGADS... THEY MUST BE VIEWING SOME WEIRD *DANCE PROGRAM...*

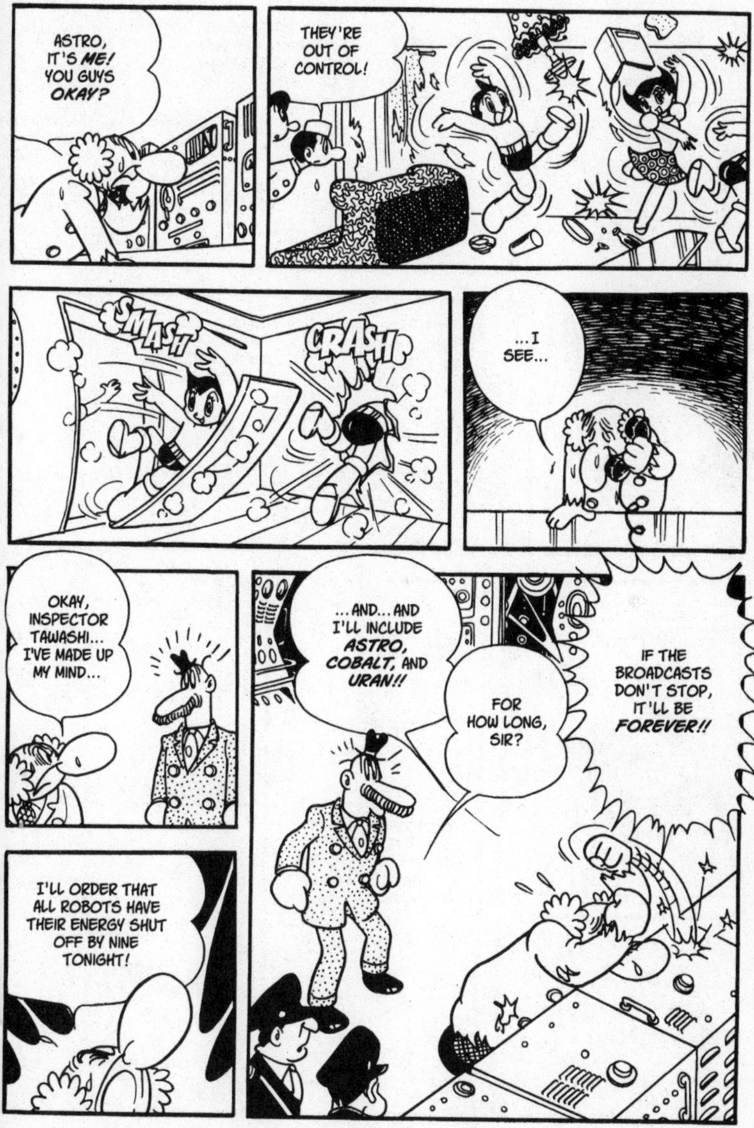
ASTRO, IT'S ME! YOU GUYS OKAY?
THEY'RE OUT OF CONTROL!
SMASH
CRASH
...I SEE...
OKAY, INSPECTOR TAWASHI... I'VE MADE UP MY MIND...
I'LL ORDER THAT ALL ROBOTS HAVE THEIR ENERGY SHUT OFF BY NINE TONIGHT!
...AND...AND I'LL INCLUDE ASTRO, COBALT, AND URAN!!
FOR HOW LONG, SIR?
IF THE BROADCASTS DON'T STOP, IT'LL BE FOREVER!!

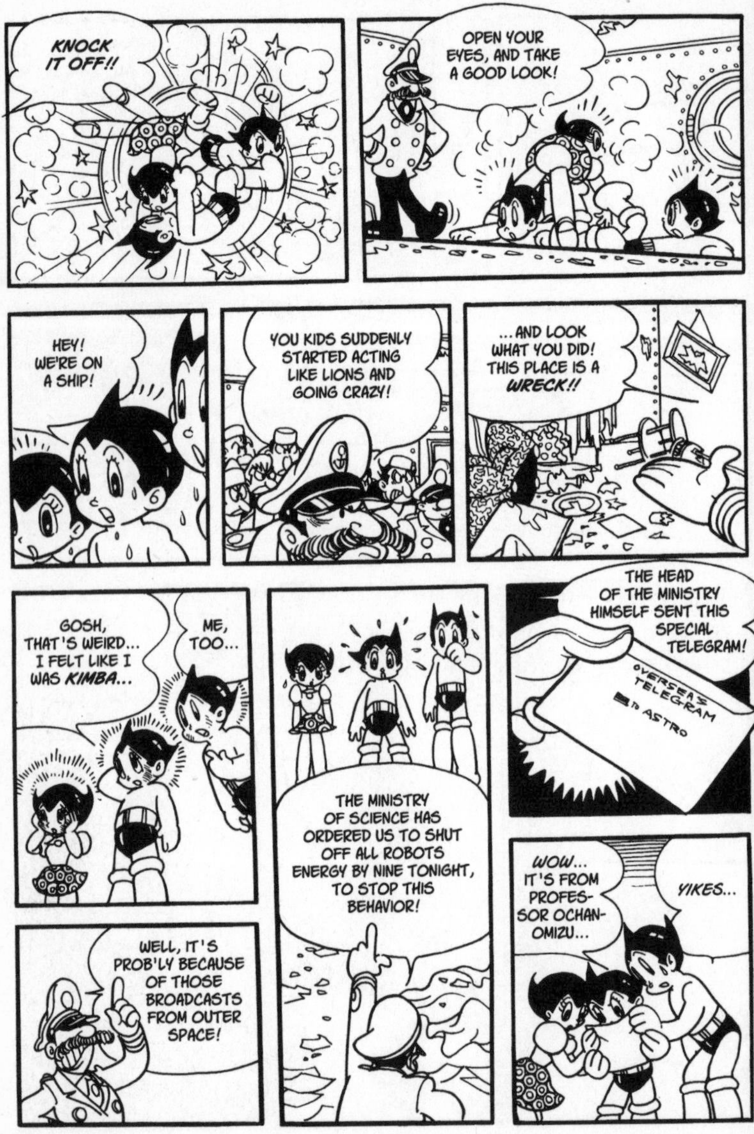
KNOCK IT OFF!!
OPEN YOUR EYES, AND TAKE A GOOD LOOK!
HEY! WE'RE ON A SHIP!
YOU KIDS SUDDENLY STARTED ACTING LIKE LIONS AND GOING CRAZY!
...AND LOOK WHAT YOU DID! THIS PLACE IS A WRECK!!
GOSH, THAT'S WEIRD... I FELT LIKE I WAS KIMBA...
ME, TOO...
WELL, IT'S PROB'LY BECAUSE OF THOSE BROADCASTS FROM OUTER SPACE!
THE MINISTRY OF SCIENCE HAS ORDERED US TO SHUT OFF ALL ROBOTS ENERGY BY NINE TONIGHT, TO STOP THIS BEHAVIOR!
THE HEAD OF THE MINISTRY HIMSELF SENT THIS SPECIAL TELEGRAM!
OVERSEAS TELEGRAM
TO ASTRO
WOW... IT'S FROM PROFES-SOR OCHAN-OMIZU...
YIKES...

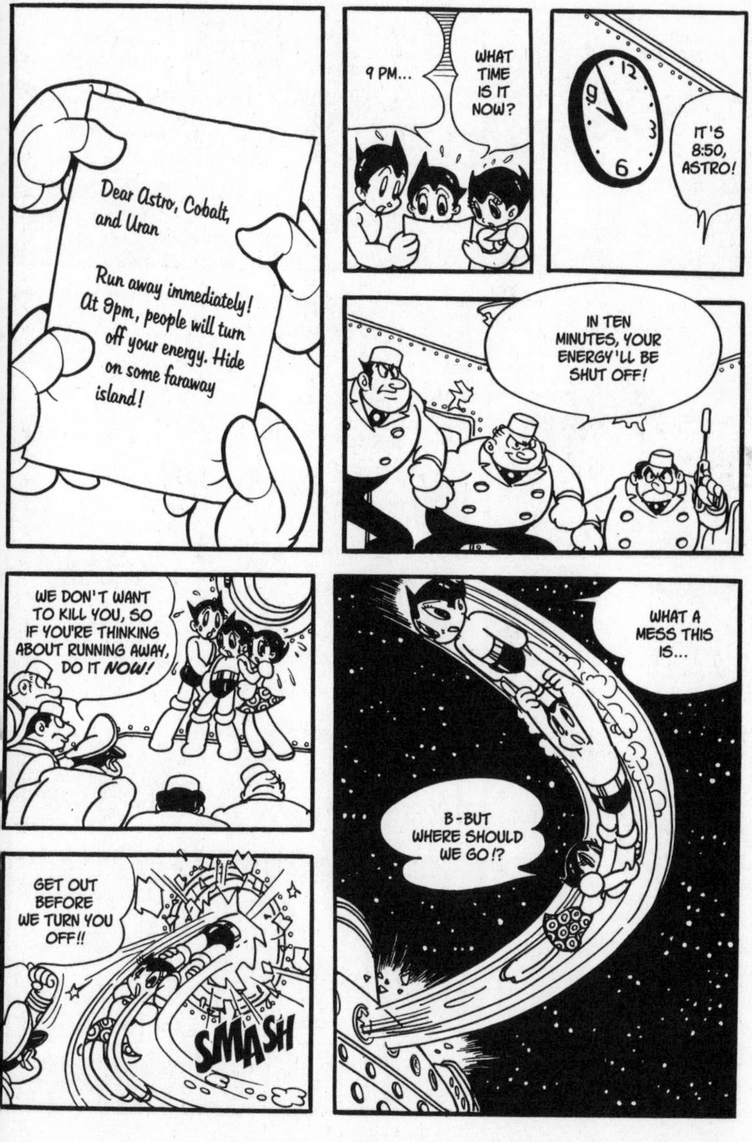

Dear Astro, Cobalt, and Uran
Run away immediately! At 9pm, people will turn off your energy. Hide on some faraway island!
WHAT TIME IS IT NOW?
9 PM...
IT'S 8:50, ASTRO!
IN TEN MINUTES, YOUR ENERGY'LL BE SHUT OFF!
WE DON'T WANT TO KILL YOU, SO IF YOU'RE THINKING ABOUT RUNNING AWAY, DO IT NOW!
GET OUT BEFORE WE TURN YOU OFF!!
SMASH
WHAT A MESS THIS IS...
B-BUT WHERE SHOULD WE GO!?

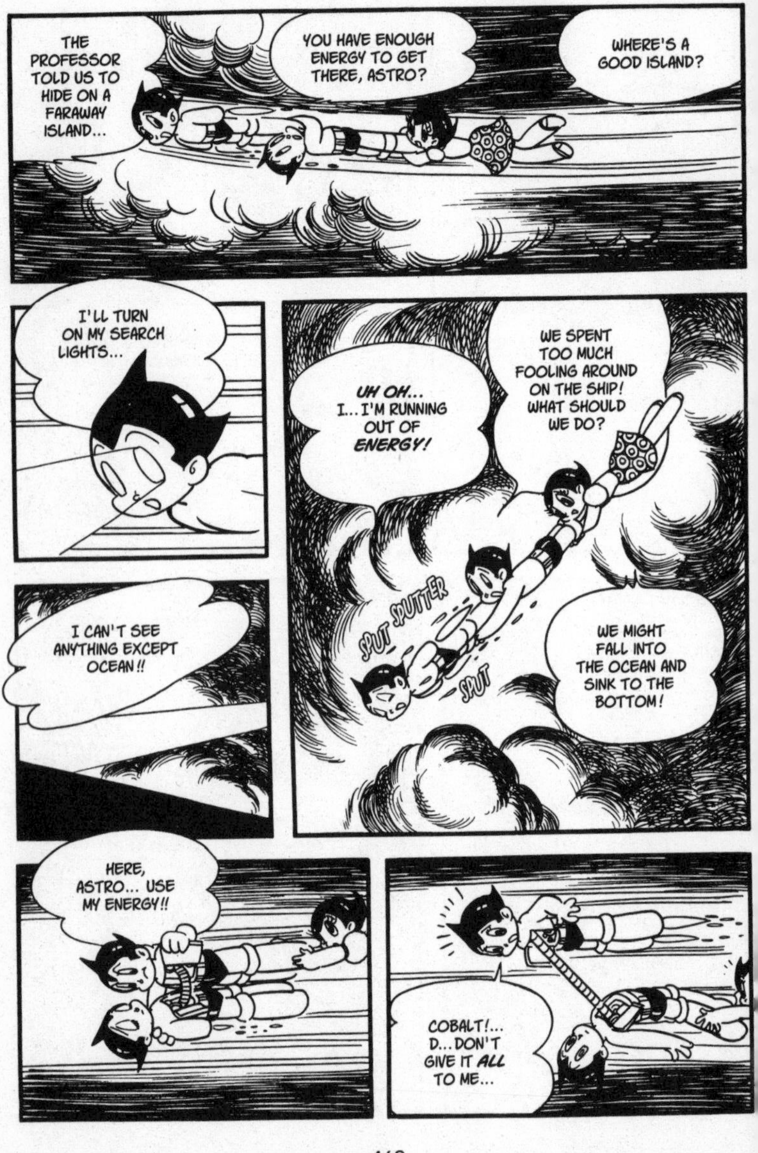
THE PROFESSOR TOLD US TO HIDE ON A FARAWAY ISLAND...
YOU HAVE ENOUGH ENERGY TO GET THERE, ASTRO?
WHERE'S A GOOD ISLAND?
I'LL TURN ON MY SEARCH LIGHTS...
I CAN'T SEE ANYTHING EXCEPT OCEAN!!
WE SPENT TOO MUCH FOOLING AROUND ON THE SHIP! WHAT SHOULD WE DO?
UH OH... I...I'M RUNNING OUT OF ENERGY!
SPUT SPUTTER
SPUT
WE MIGHT FALL INTO THE OCEAN AND SINK TO THE BOTTOM!
HERE, ASTRO... USE MY ENERGY!!
COBALT!... D...DON'T GIVE IT ALL TO ME...

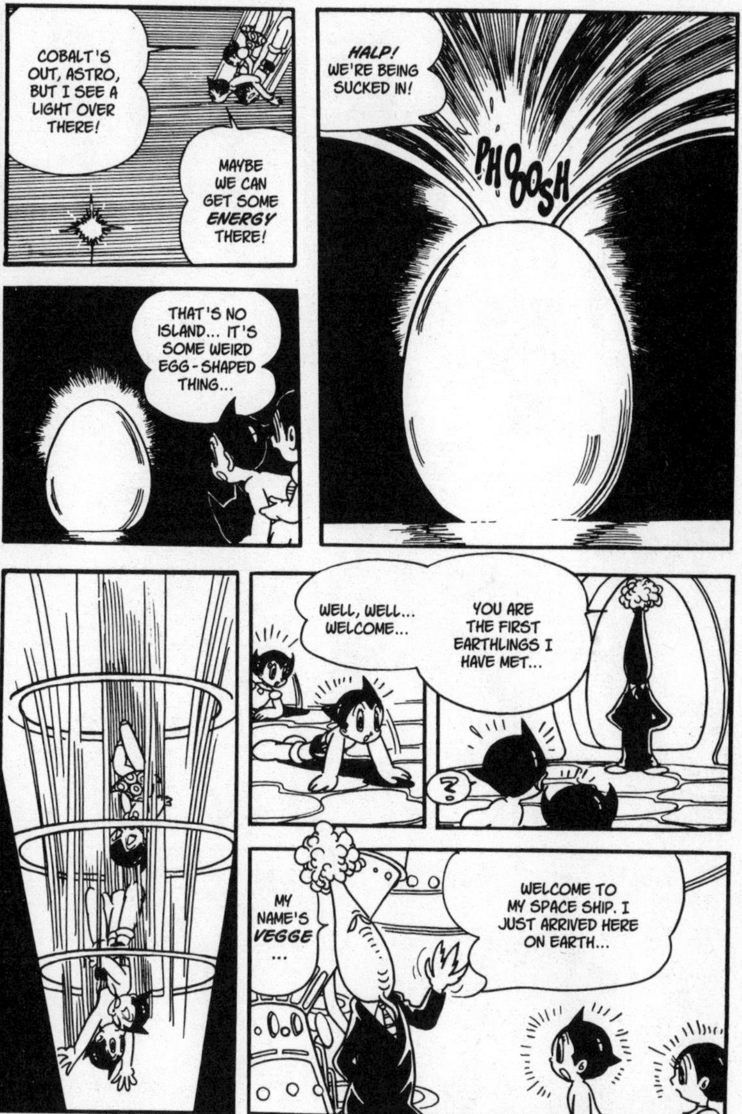
COBALT'S OUT, ASTRO, BUT I SEE A LIGHT OVER THERE!
MAYBE WE CAN GET SOME ENERGY THERE!
THAT'S NO ISLAND... IT'S SOME WEIRD EGG-SHAPED THING...
HALP! WE'RE BEING SUCKED IN!
PHOOOSH
WELL, WELL... WELCOME...
YOU ARE THE FIRST EARTHLINGS I HAVE MET...
?
MY NAME'S VEGGE ...
WELCOME TO MY SPACE SHIP. I JUST ARRIVED HERE ON EARTH...

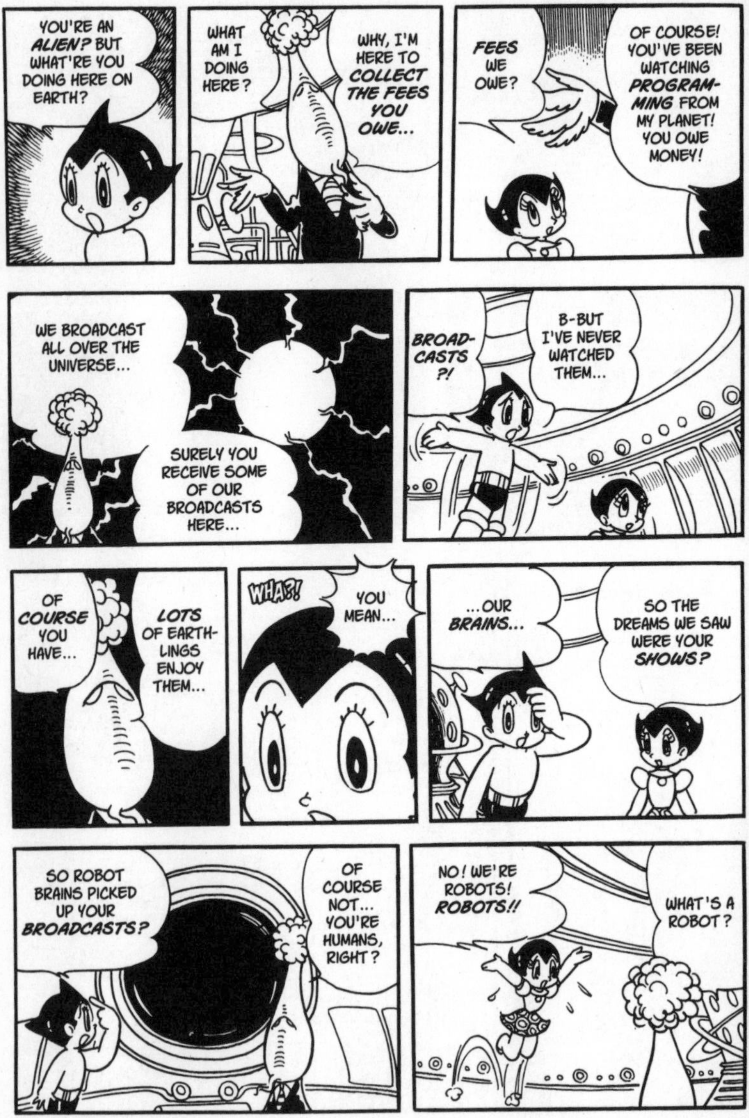
YOU'RE AN ALIEN? BUT WHAT'RE YOU DOING HERE ON EARTH?
WHAT AM I DOING HERE?
WHY, I'M HERE TO COLLECT THE FEES YOU OWE...
FEES WE OWE?
OF COURSE! YOU'VE BEEN WATCHING PROGRAMMING FROM MY PLANET! YOU OWE MONEY!
WE BROADCAST ALL OVER THE UNIVERSE...
SURELY YOU RECEIVE SOME OF OUR BROADCASTS HERE...
BROADCASTS?!
B-BUT I'VE NEVER WATCHED THEM...
OF COURSE YOU HAVE...
LOTS OF EARTHLINGS ENJOY THEM...
WHA?!
YOU MEAN...
...OUR BRAINS...
SO THE DREAMS WE SAW WERE YOUR SHOWS?
SO ROBOT BRAINS PICKED UP YOUR BROADCASTS?
OF COURSE NOT... YOU'RE HUMANS, RIGHT?
NO! WE'RE ROBOTS! ROBOTS!!
WHAT'S A ROBOT?

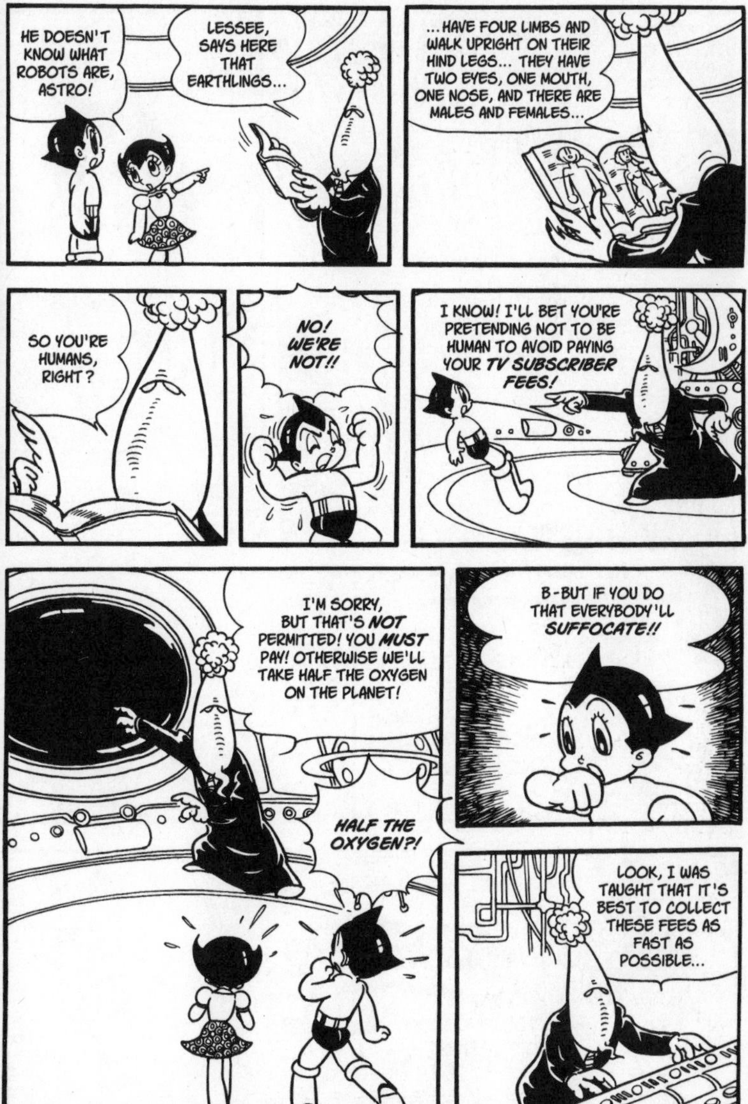
HE DOESN'T KNOW WHAT ROBOTS ARE, ASTRO!
LESSEE, SAYS HERE THAT EARTHLINGS...
...HAVE FOUR LIMBS AND WALK UPRIGHT ON THEIR HIND LEGS... THEY HAVE TWO EYES, ONE MOUTH, ONE NOSE, AND THERE ARE MALES AND FEMALES...
SO YOU'RE HUMANS, RIGHT?
NO! WE'RE NOT!!
I KNOW! I'LL BET YOU'RE PRETENDING NOT TO BE HUMAN TO AVOID PAYING YOUR TV SUBSCRIBER FEES!
I'M SORRY, BUT THAT'S NOT PERMITTED! YOU MUST PAY! OTHERWISE WE'LL TAKE HALF THE OXYGEN ON THE PLANET!
HALF THE OXYGEN?!
B-BUT IF YOU DO THAT EVERYBODY'LL SUFFOCATE!!
LOOK, I WAS TAUGHT THAT IT'S BEST TO COLLECT THESE FEES AS FAST AS POSSIBLE...

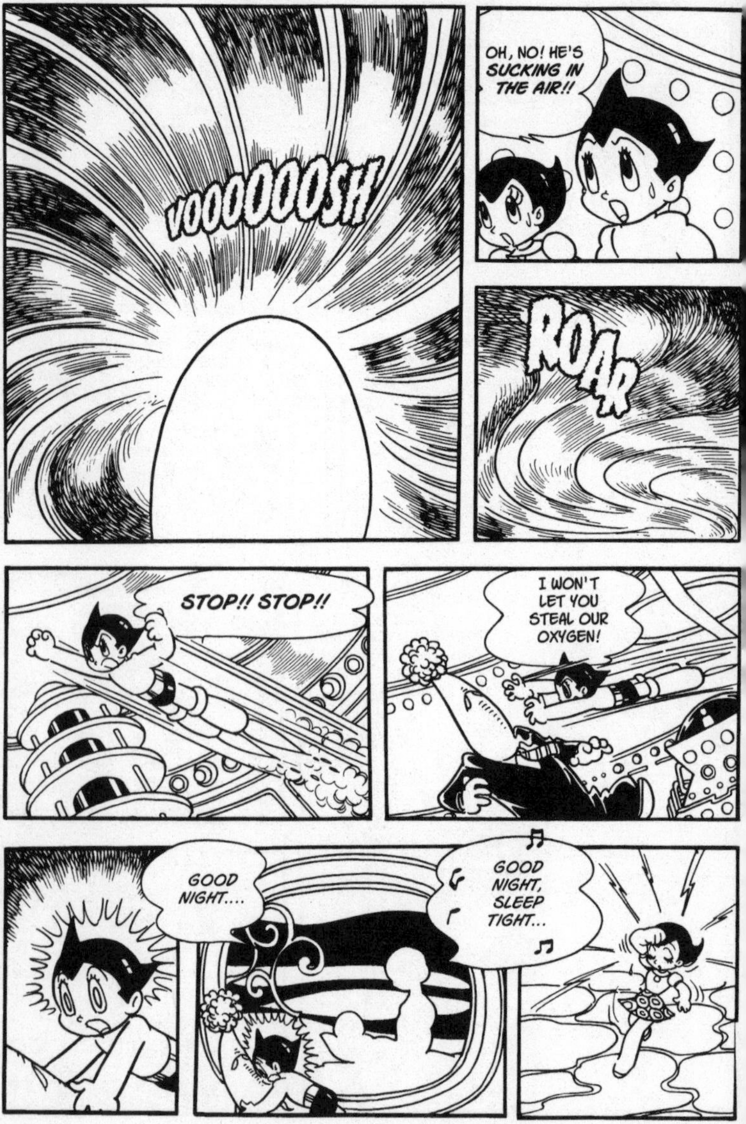
VOOOOOOSH
OH, NO! HE'S SUCKING IN THE AIR!!
ROAR
STOP!! STOP!!
I WON'T LET YOU STEAL OUR OXYGEN!
GOOD NIGHT....
GOOD NIGHT, SLEEP TIGHT...

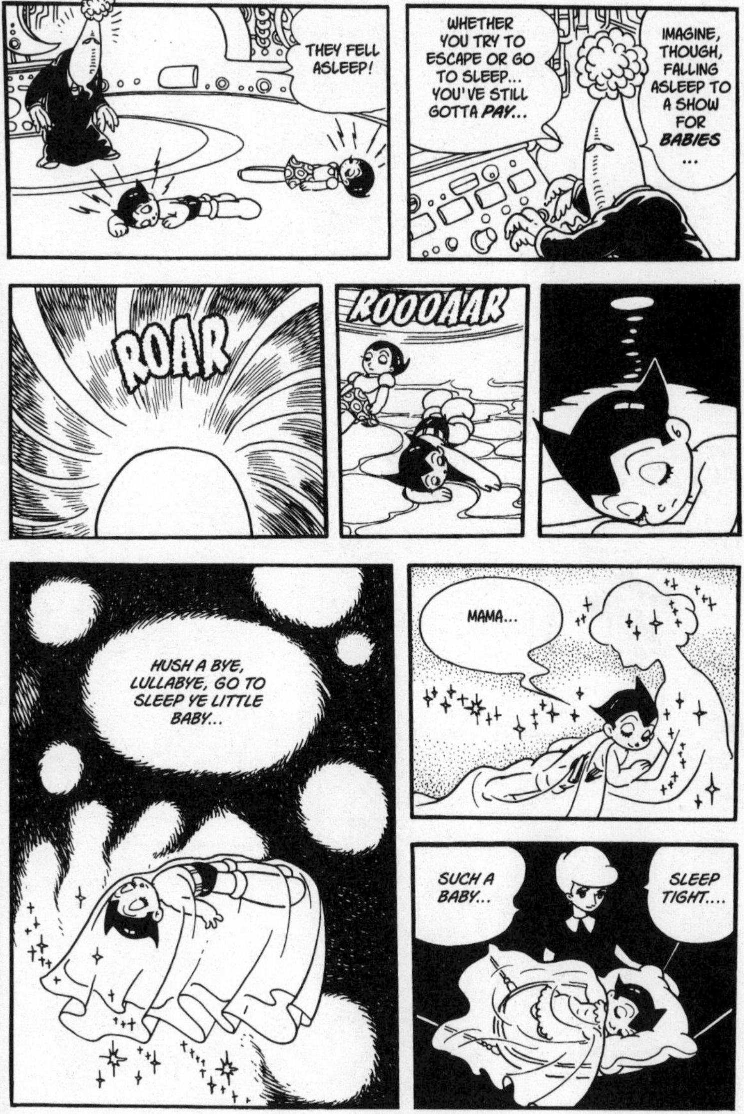
THEY FELL ASLEEP!
WHETHER YOU TRY TO ESCAPE OR GO TO SLEEP... YOU'VE STILL GOTTA *PAY*...
IMAGINE, THOUGH, FALLING ASLEEP TO A SHOW FOR *BABIES* ...
ROAR
ROOOAAR
HUSH A BYE, LULLABYE, GO TO SLEEP YE LITTLE BABY...
MAMA...
SUCH A BABY...
SLEEP TIGHT....

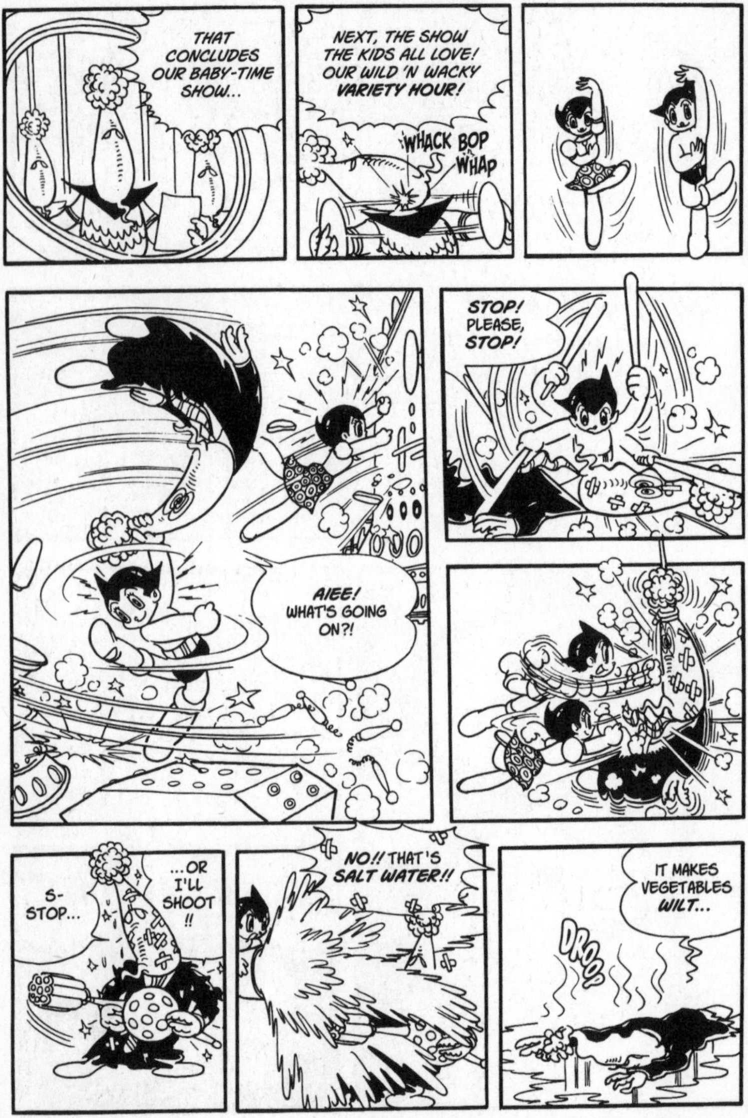
THAT CONCLUDES OUR BABY-TIME SHOW...
NEXT, THE SHOW THE KIDS ALL LOVE! OUR WILD 'N WACKY VARIETY HOUR!
WHACK BOP WHAP
AIEE! WHAT'S GOING ON?!
STOP! PLEASE, STOP!
S- STOP...
...OR I'LL SHOOT !!
NO!! THAT'S SALT WATER!!
IT MAKES VEGETABLES WILT...
DROOP

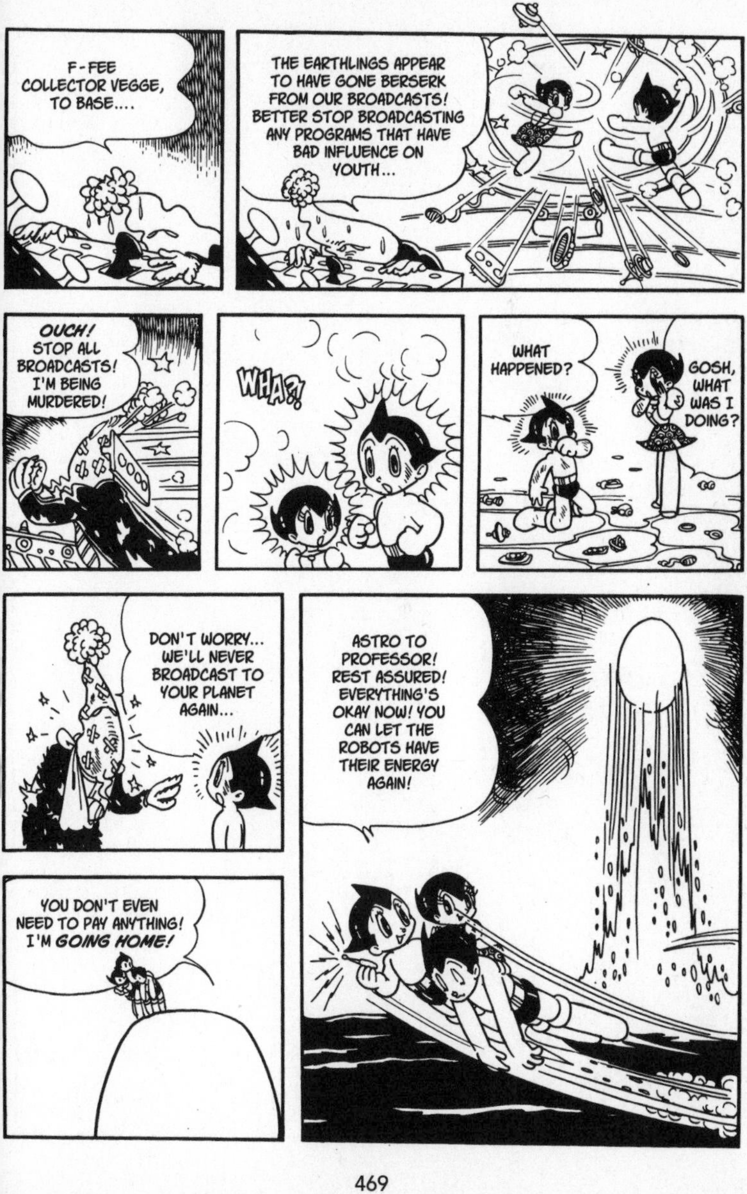
F-FEE COLLECTOR VEGGE, TO BASE....
THE EARTHLINGS APPEAR TO HAVE GONE BERSERK FROM OUR BROADCASTS! BETTER STOP BROADCASTING ANY PROGRAMS THAT HAVE BAD INFLUENCE ON YOUTH...
OUCH! STOP ALL BROADCASTS! I'M BEING MURDERED!
WHA?!
WHAT HAPPENED?
GOSH, WHAT WAS I DOING?
DON'T WORRY... WE'LL NEVER BROADCAST TO YOUR PLANET AGAIN...
YOU DON'T EVEN NEED TO PAY ANYTHING! I'M GOING HOME!
ASTRO TO PROFESSOR! REST ASSURED! EVERYTHING'S OKAY NOW! YOU CAN LET THE ROBOTS HAVE THEIR ENERGY AGAIN!

ZOLOMON'S
JEWELS

First serialized from May to December 1967
in *Shonen* magazine.

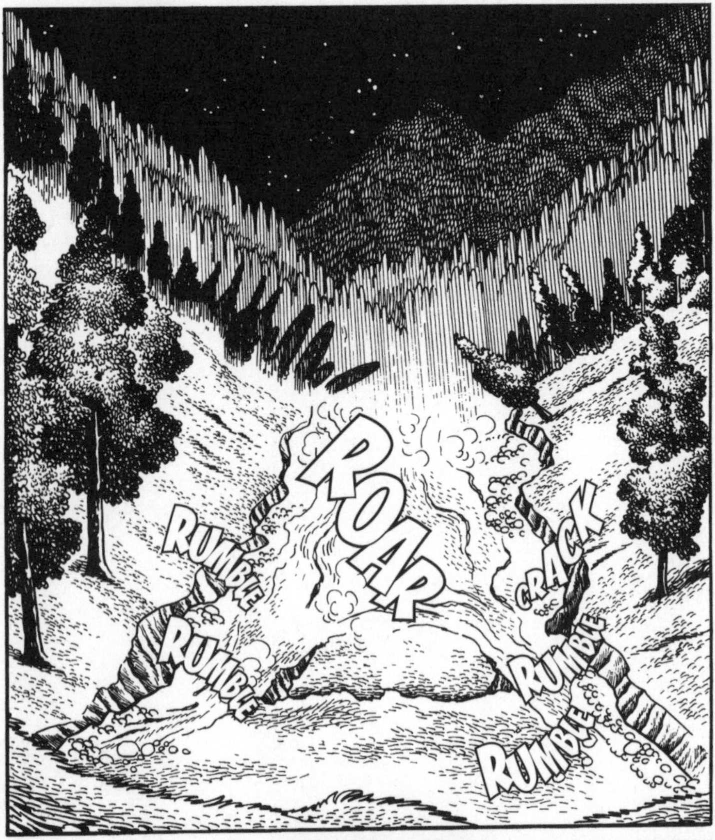
ROAR
RUMBLE
RUMBLE
CRACK
RUMBLE
RUMBLE

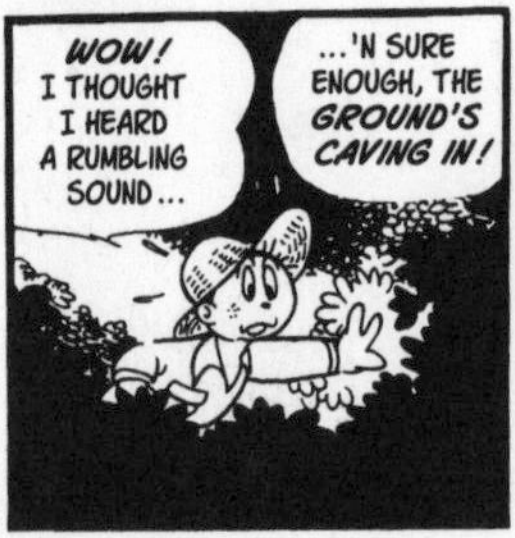
WOW! I THOUGHT I HEARD A RUMBLING SOUND...
...'N SURE ENOUGH, THE GROUND'S CAVING IN!

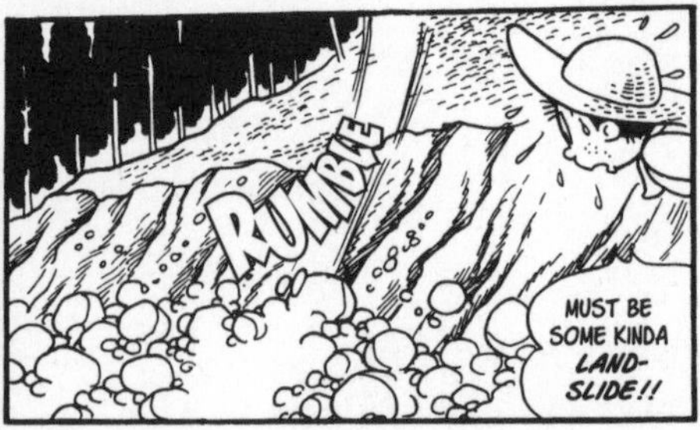
RUMBLE
MUST BE SOME KINDA LAND-SLIDE!!

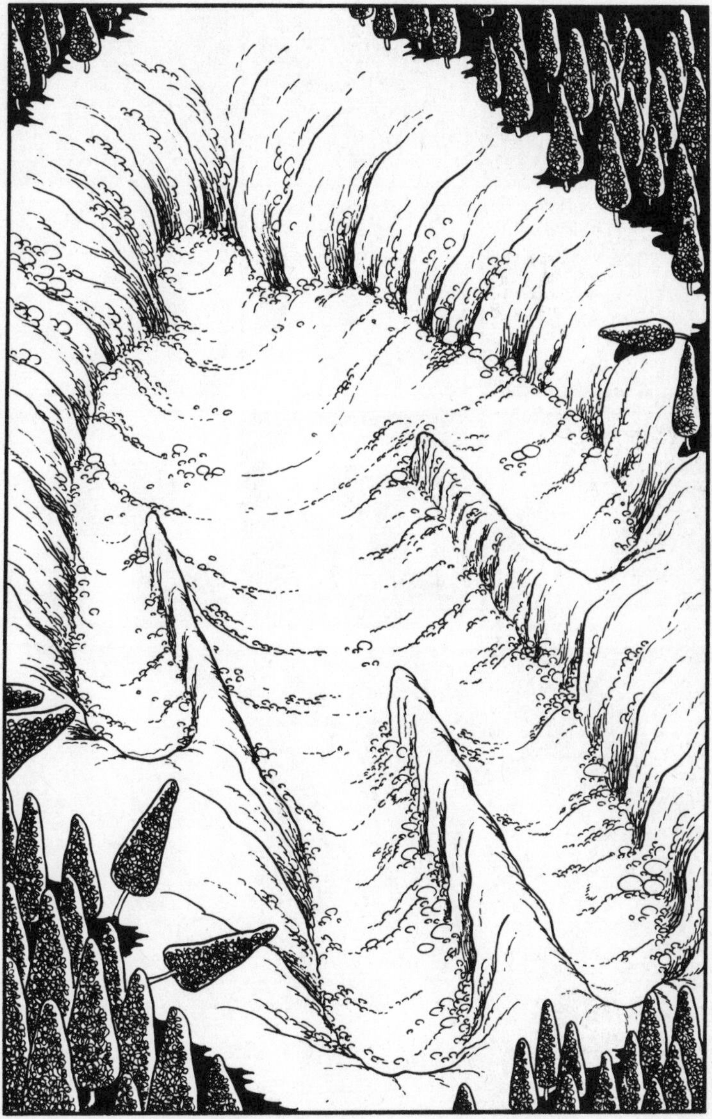

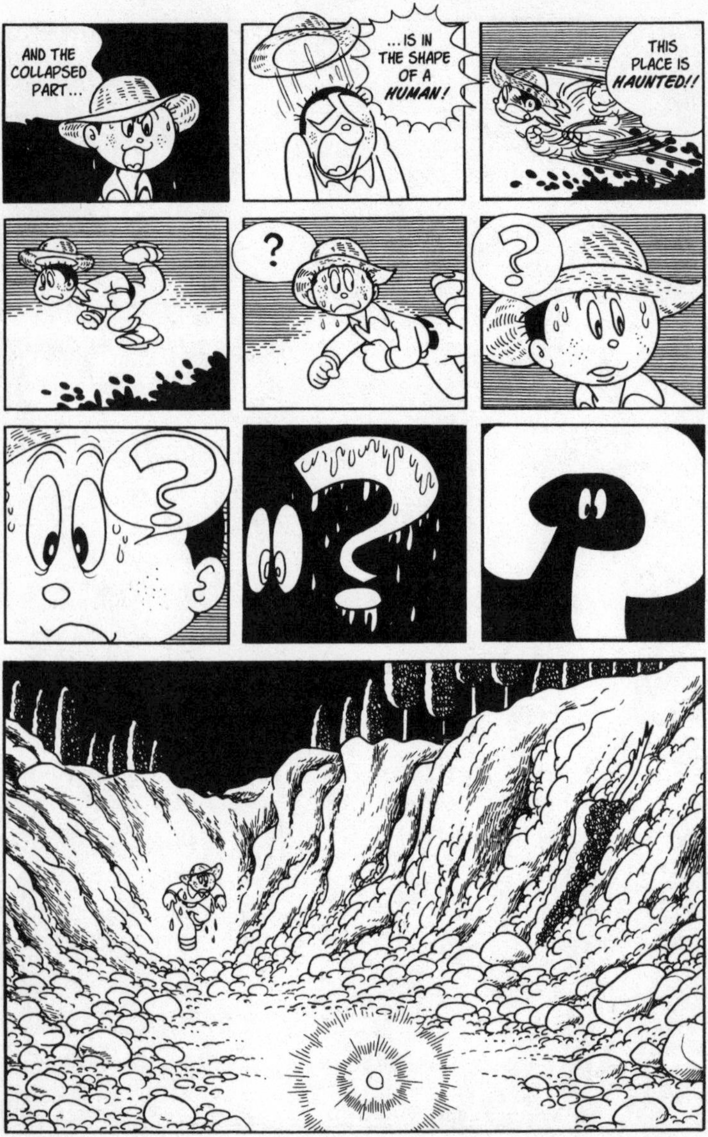
AND THE COLLAPSED PART...
...IS IN THE SHAPE OF A HUMAN!
THIS PLACE IS HAUNTED!!
?
?
?

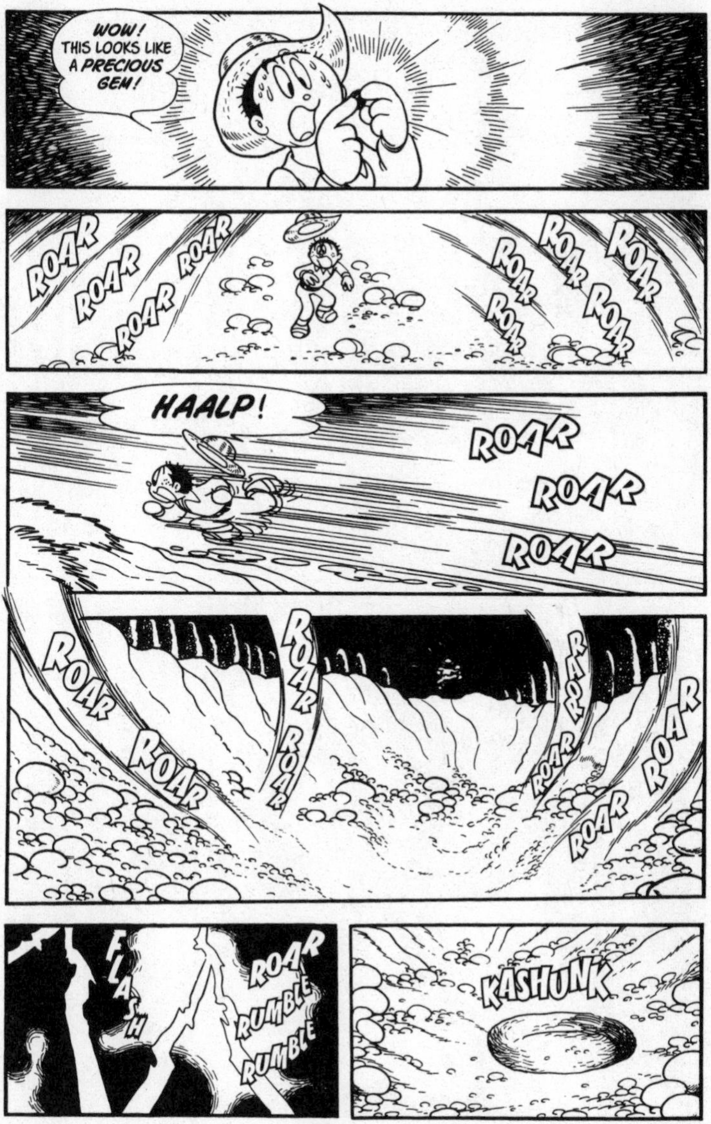
WOW! THIS LOOKS LIKE A PRECIOUS GEM!
ROAR
ROAR
ROAR
ROAR
ROAR
ROAR
ROAR
ROAR
ROAR
HAALP!
ROAR
ROAR
ROAR
ROAR
ROAR
ROAR
ROAR
ROAR
ROAR
ROAR
ROAR
FLASH
ROAR
RUMBLE
RUMBLE
KASHUNK

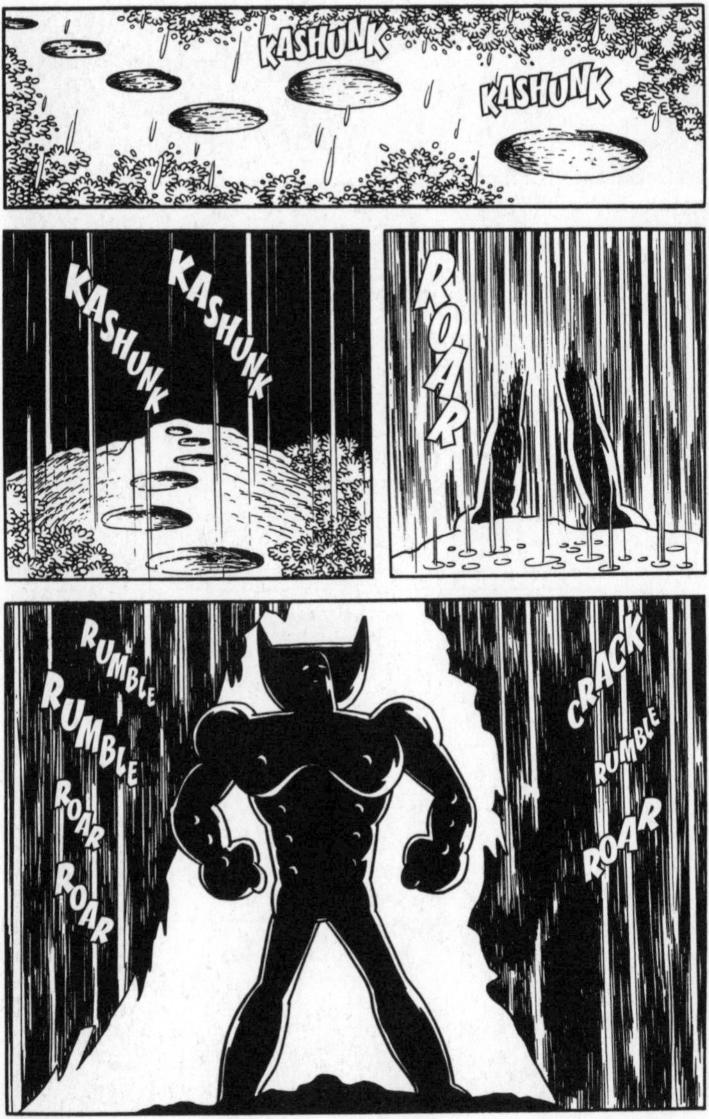
KASHUNK
KASHUNK
KASHUNK
KASHUNK
ROAR
RUMBLE
RUMBLE
ROAR
ROAR
CRACK
RUMBLE
ROAR

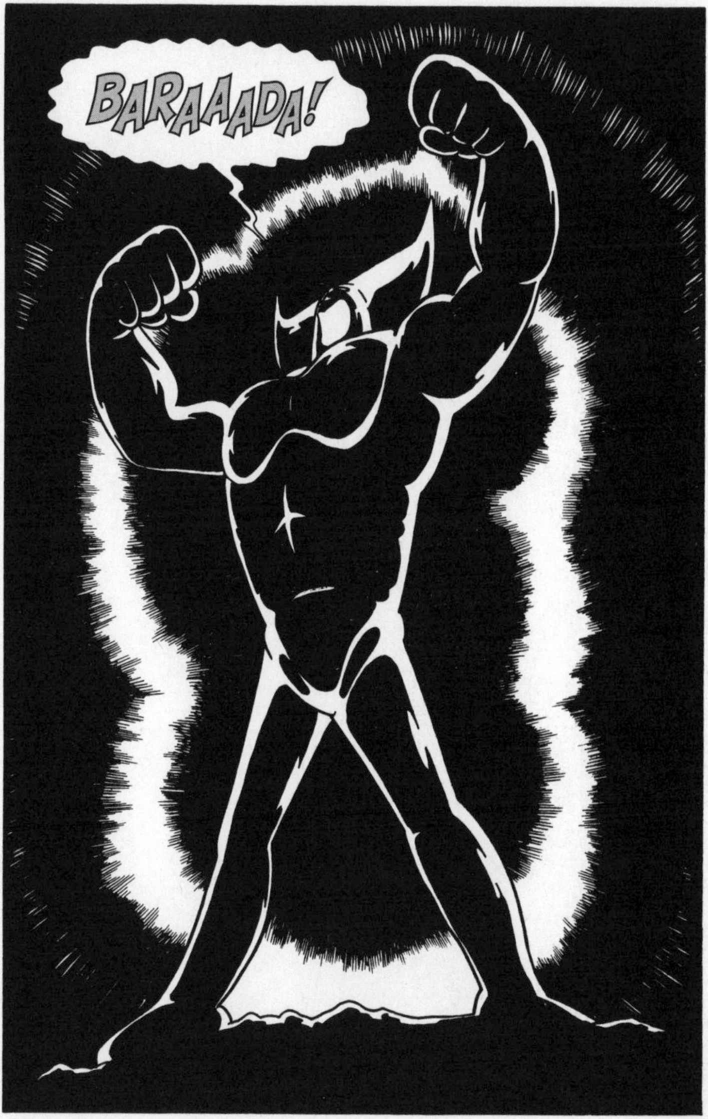
BARAAADA!

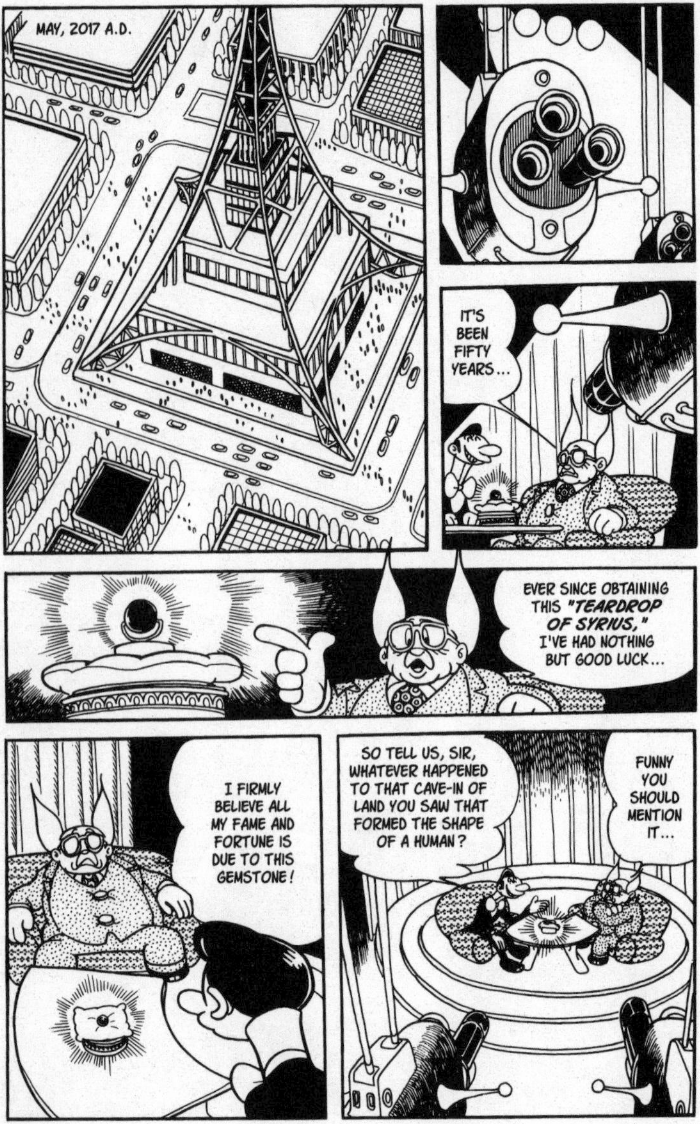
MAY, 2017 A.D.
IT'S BEEN FIFTY YEARS...
EVER SINCE OBTAINING THIS "TEARDROP OF SYRIUS," I'VE HAD NOTHING BUT GOOD LUCK...
I FIRMLY BELIEVE ALL MY FAME AND FORTUNE IS DUE TO THIS GEMSTONE!
SO TELL US, SIR, WHATEVER HAPPENED TO THAT CAVE-IN OF LAND YOU SAW THAT FORMED THE SHAPE OF A HUMAN?
FUNNY YOU SHOULD MENTION IT...

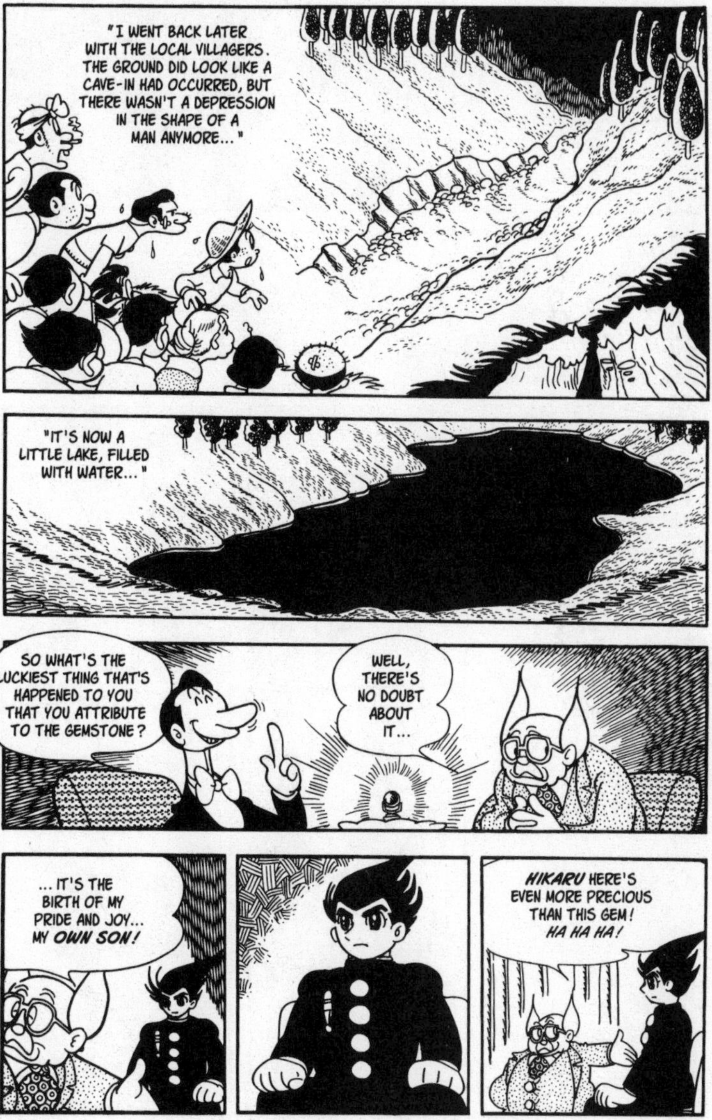
"I WENT BACK LATER WITH THE LOCAL VILLAGERS. THE GROUND DID LOOK LIKE A CAVE-IN HAD OCCURRED, BUT THERE WASN'T A DEPRESSION IN THE SHAPE OF A MAN ANYMORE..."
"IT'S NOW A LITTLE LAKE, FILLED WITH WATER..."
SO WHAT'S THE LUCKIEST THING THAT'S HAPPENED TO YOU THAT YOU ATTRIBUTE TO THE GEMSTONE?
WELL, THERE'S NO DOUBT ABOUT IT...
... IT'S THE BIRTH OF MY PRIDE AND JOY... MY OWN SON!
HIKARU HERE'S EVEN MORE PRECIOUS THAN THIS GEM! HA HA HA!

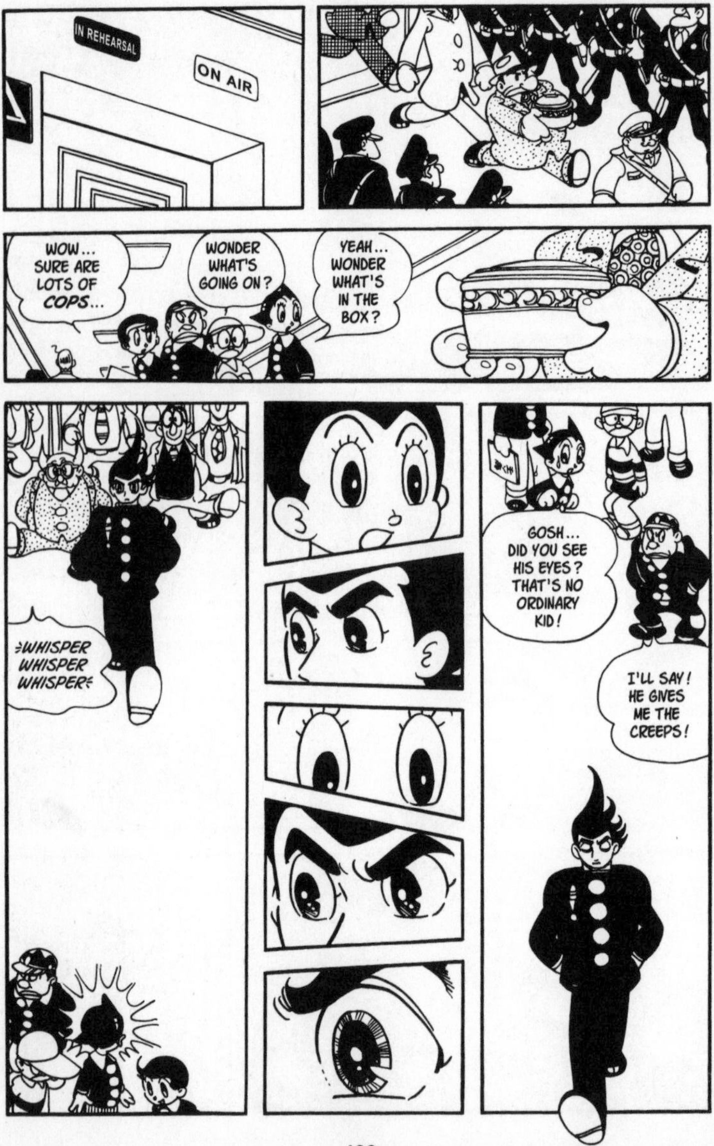
IN REHEARSAL
ON AIR
WOW... SURE ARE LOTS OF COPS...
WONDER WHAT'S GOING ON?
YEAH... WONDER WHAT'S IN THE BOX?
WHISPER WHISPER WHISPER
GOSH... DID YOU SEE HIS EYES? THAT'S NO ORDINARY KID!
I'LL SAY! HE GIVES ME THE CREEPS!

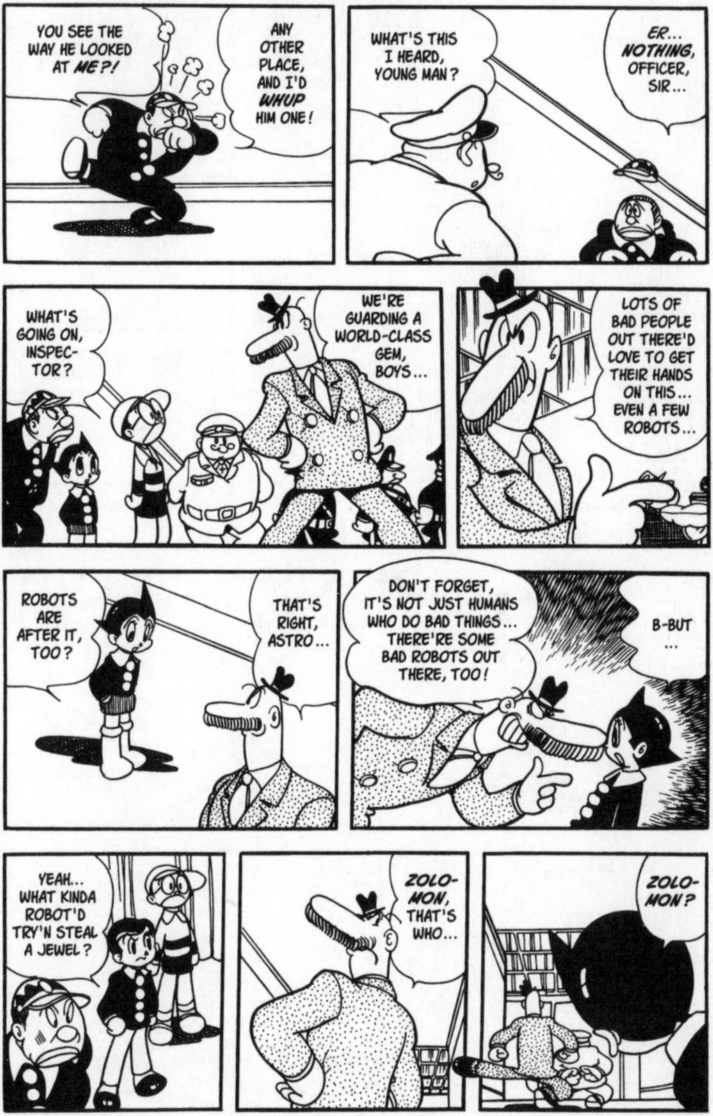
YOU SEE THE WAY HE LOOKED AT ME?!
ANY OTHER PLACE, AND I'D WHUP HIM ONE!
WHAT'S THIS I HEARD, YOUNG MAN?
ER... NOTHING, OFFICER, SIR...
WHAT'S GOING ON, INSPEC-TOR?
WE'RE GUARDING A WORLD-CLASS GEM, BOYS...
LOTS OF BAD PEOPLE OUT THERE'D LOVE TO GET THEIR HANDS ON THIS... EVEN A FEW ROBOTS...
ROBOTS ARE AFTER IT, TOO?
THAT'S RIGHT, ASTRO...
DON'T FORGET, IT'S NOT JUST HUMANS WHO DO BAD THINGS... THERE'RE SOME BAD ROBOTS OUT THERE, TOO!
B-BUT ...
YEAH... WHAT KINDA ROBOT'D TRY'N STEAL A JEWEL?
ZOLO-MON, THAT'S WHO...
ZOLO-MON?

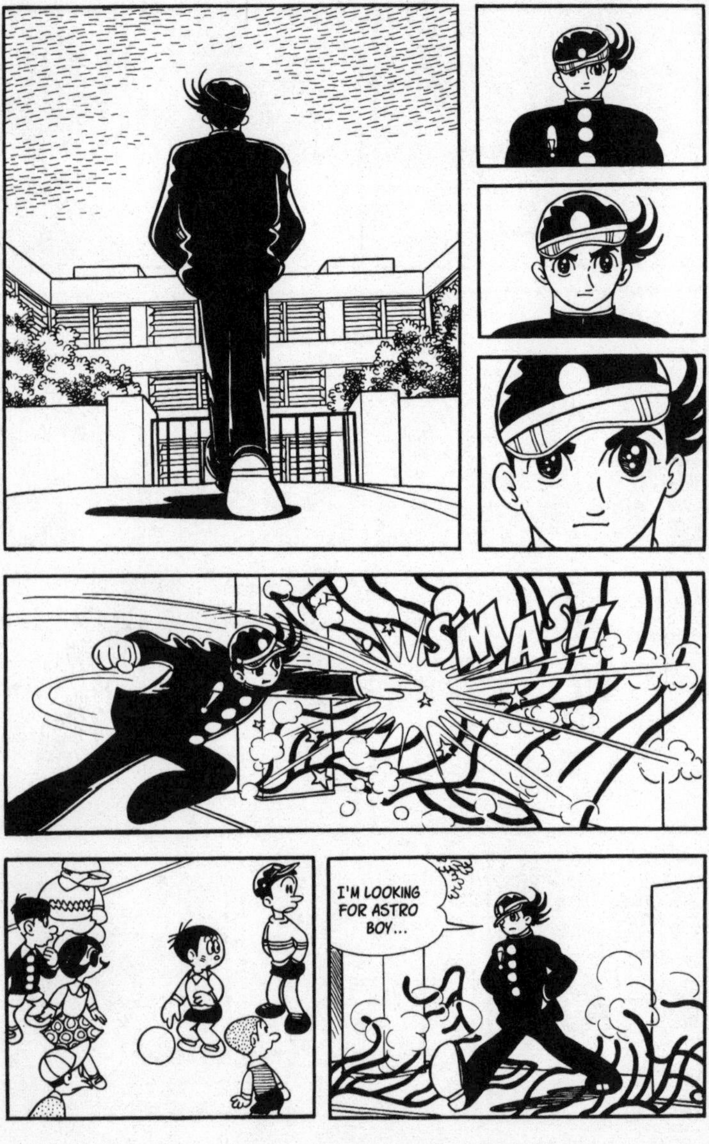
SMASH
I'M LOOKING FOR ASTRO BOY...

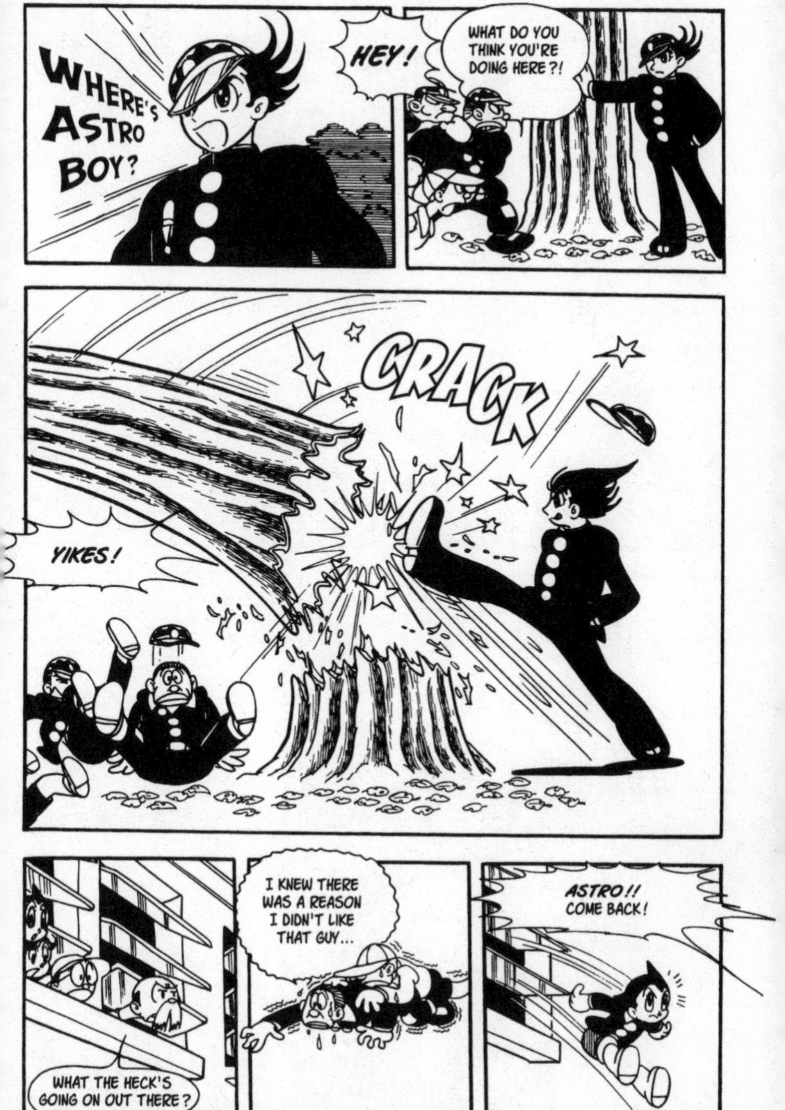
WHERE'S ASTRO BOY?
HEY!
WHAT DO YOU THINK YOU'RE DOING HERE?!
CRACK
YIKES!
WHAT THE HECK'S GOING ON OUT THERE?
I KNEW THERE WAS A REASON I DIDN'T LIKE THAT GUY...
ASTRO!! COME BACK!

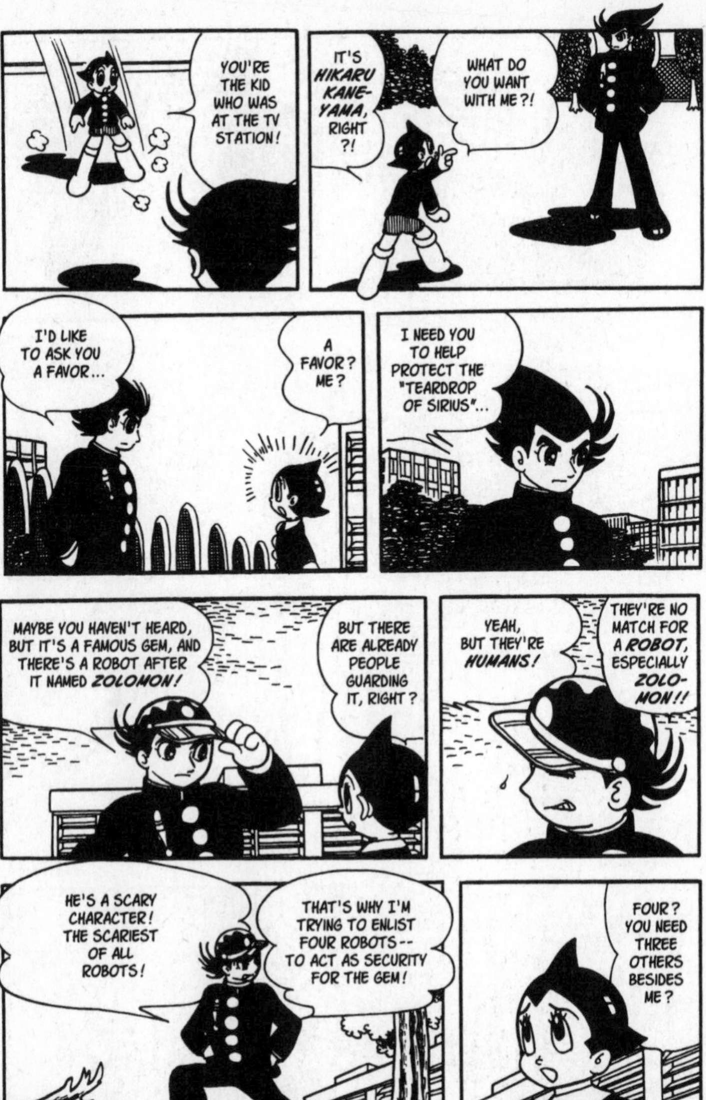
YOU'RE THE KID WHO WAS AT THE TV STATION!
IT'S HIKARU KANE-YAMA, RIGHT?!
WHAT DO YOU WANT WITH ME?!
I'D LIKE TO ASK YOU A FAVOR...
A FAVOR? ME?
I NEED YOU TO HELP PROTECT THE "TEARDROP OF SIRIUS"...
MAYBE YOU HAVEN'T HEARD, BUT IT'S A FAMOUS GEM, AND THERE'S A ROBOT AFTER IT NAMED ZOLOMON!
BUT THERE ARE ALREADY PEOPLE GUARDING IT, RIGHT?
YEAH, BUT THEY'RE HUMANS!
THEY'RE NO MATCH FOR A ROBOT, ESPECIALLY ZOLO-MON!!
HE'S A SCARY CHARACTER! THE SCARIEST OF ALL ROBOTS!
THAT'S WHY I'M TRYING TO ENLIST FOUR ROBOTS-- TO ACT AS SECURITY FOR THE GEM!
FOUR? YOU NEED THREE OTHERS BESIDES ME?

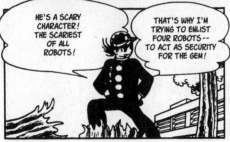

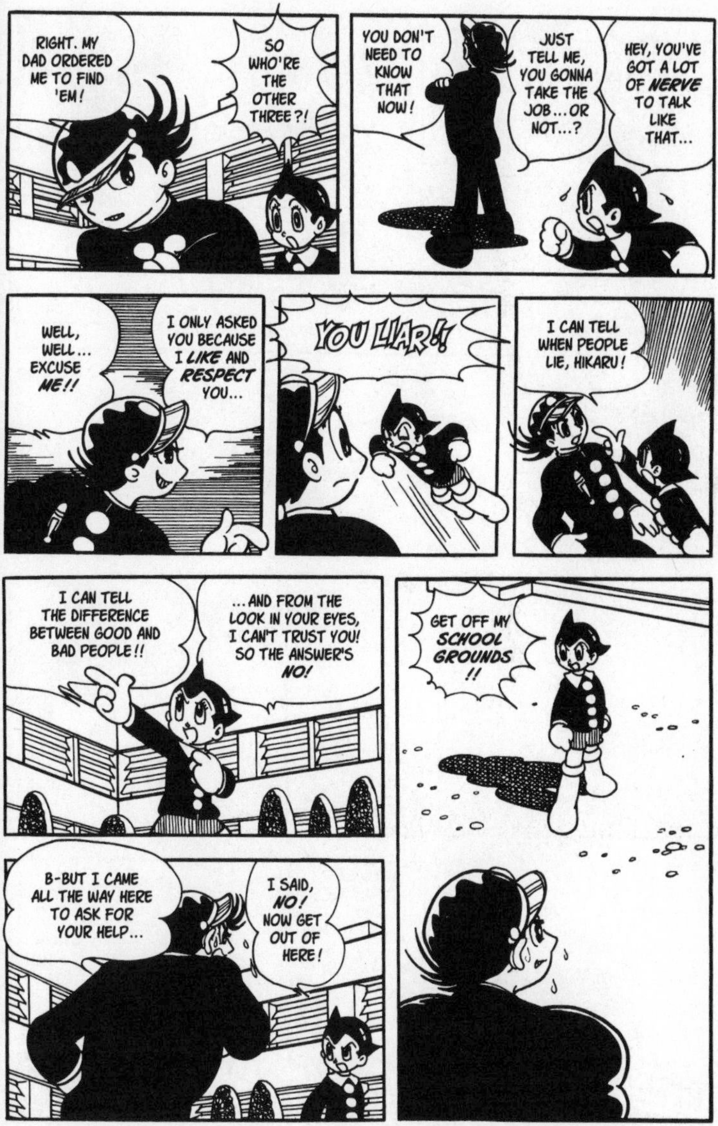
RIGHT. MY DAD ORDERED ME TO FIND 'EM!
SO WHO'RE THE OTHER THREE?!
YOU DON'T NEED TO KNOW THAT NOW!
JUST TELL ME, YOU GONNA TAKE THE JOB... OR NOT...?
HEY, YOU'VE GOT A LOT OF NERVE TO TALK LIKE THAT...
WELL, WELL... EXCUSE ME!!
I ONLY ASKED YOU BECAUSE I LIKE AND RESPECT YOU...
YOU LIAR!!
I CAN TELL WHEN PEOPLE LIE, HIKARU!
I CAN TELL THE DIFFERENCE BETWEEN GOOD AND BAD PEOPLE!!
...AND FROM THE LOOK IN YOUR EYES, I CAN'T TRUST YOU! SO THE ANSWER'S NO!
B-BUT I CAME ALL THE WAY HERE TO ASK FOR YOUR HELP...
I SAID, NO! NOW GET OUT OF HERE!
GET OFF MY SCHOOL GROUNDS!!

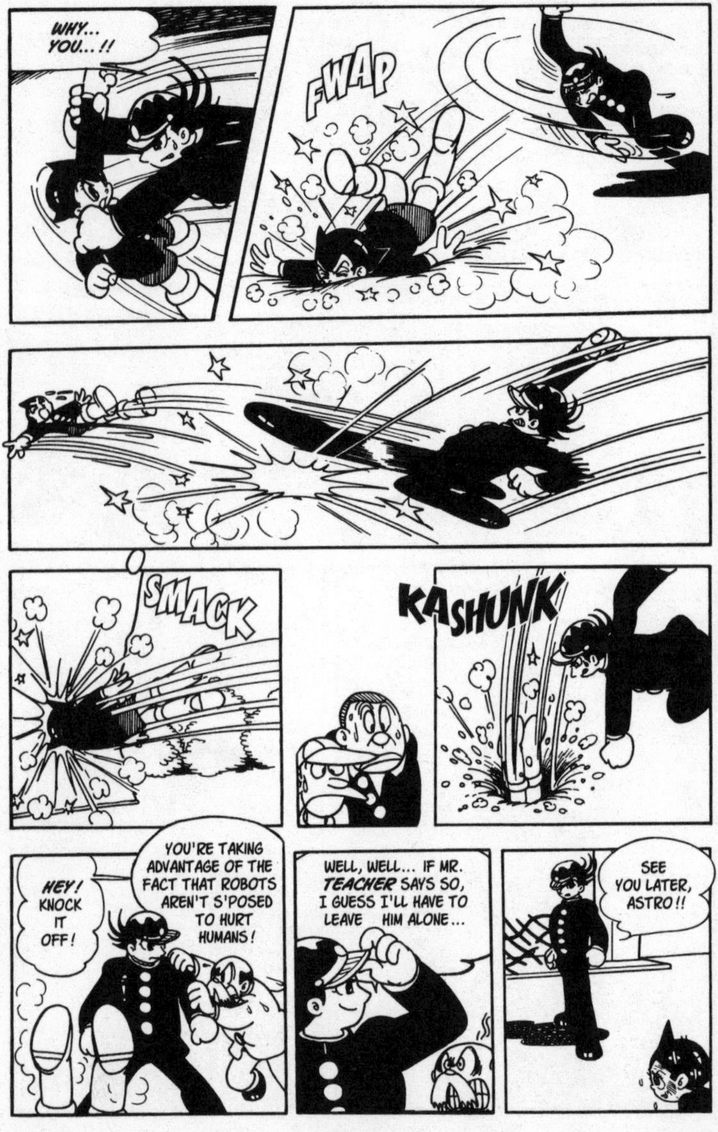
WHY...
YOU...!!
FWAP
SMACK
KASHUNK
HEY! KNOCK IT OFF!
YOU'RE TAKING ADVANTAGE OF THE FACT THAT ROBOTS AREN'T S'POSED TO HURT HUMANS!
WELL, WELL... IF MR. TEACHER SAYS SO, I GUESS I'LL HAVE TO LEAVE HIM ALONE...
SEE YOU LATER, ASTRO!!

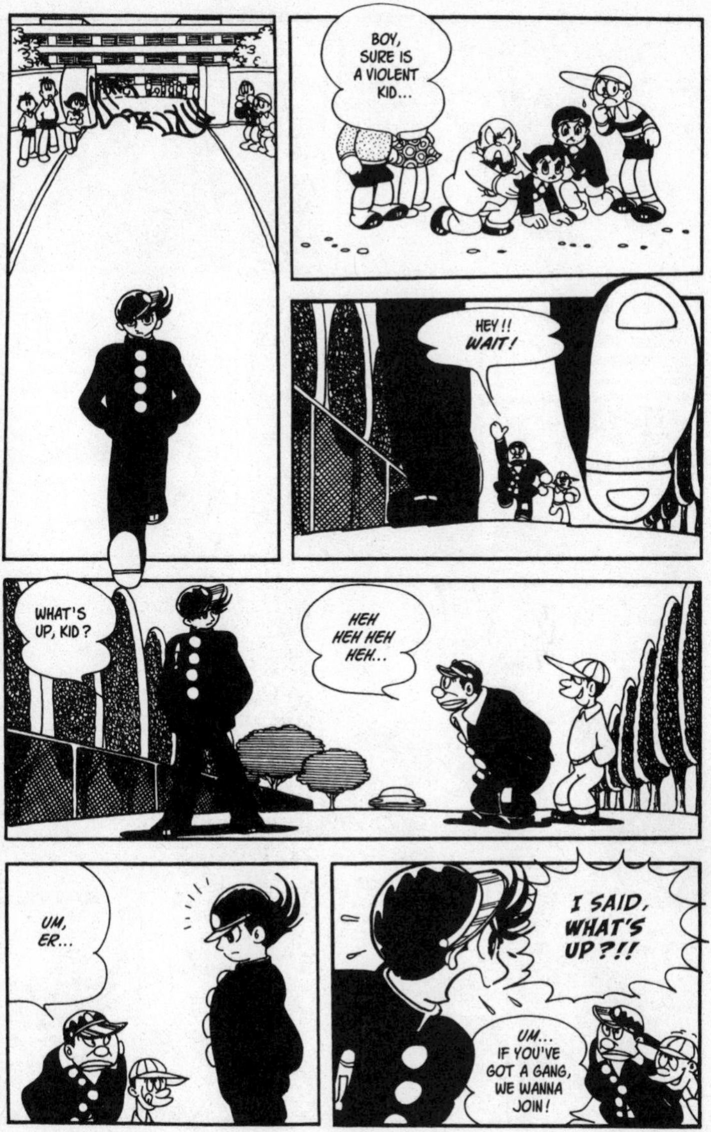
BOY, SURE IS A VIOLENT KID...
HEY!! WAIT!
WHAT'S UP, KID?
HEH HEH HEH HEH...
UM, ER...
I SAID, WHAT'S UP?!!
UM... IF YOU'VE GOT A GANG, WE WANNA JOIN!

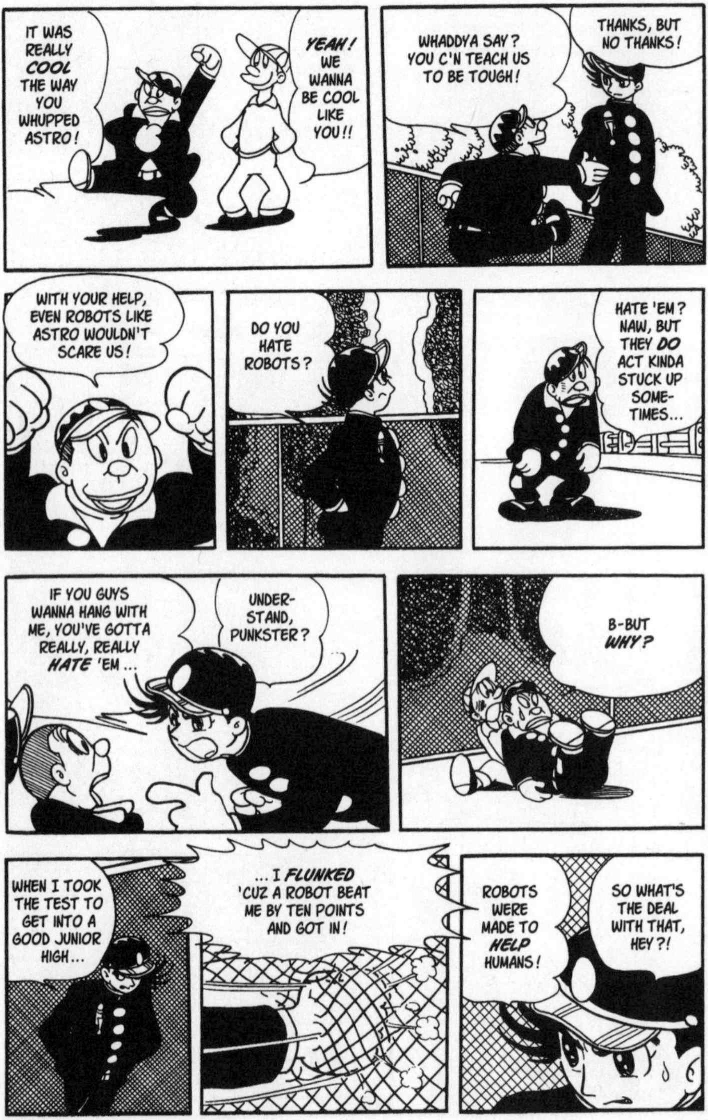
IT WAS REALLY COOL THE WAY YOU WHUPPED ASTRO!
YEAH! WE WANNA BE COOL LIKE YOU!!
WHADDYA SAY? YOU C'N TEACH US TO BE TOUGH!
THANKS, BUT NO THANKS!
WITH YOUR HELP, EVEN ROBOTS LIKE ASTRO WOULDN'T SCARE US!
DO YOU HATE ROBOTS?
HATE 'EM? NAW, BUT THEY DO ACT KINDA STUCK UP SOME-TIMES...
IF YOU GUYS WANNA HANG WITH ME, YOU'VE GOTTA REALLY, REALLY HATE 'EM...
UNDER-STAND, PUNKSTER?
B-BUT WHY?
WHEN I TOOK THE TEST TO GET INTO A GOOD JUNIOR HIGH...
... I FLUNKED 'CUZ A ROBOT BEAT ME BY TEN POINTS AND GOT IN!
ROBOTS WERE MADE TO HELP HUMANS!
SO WHAT'S THE DEAL WITH THAT, HEY?!

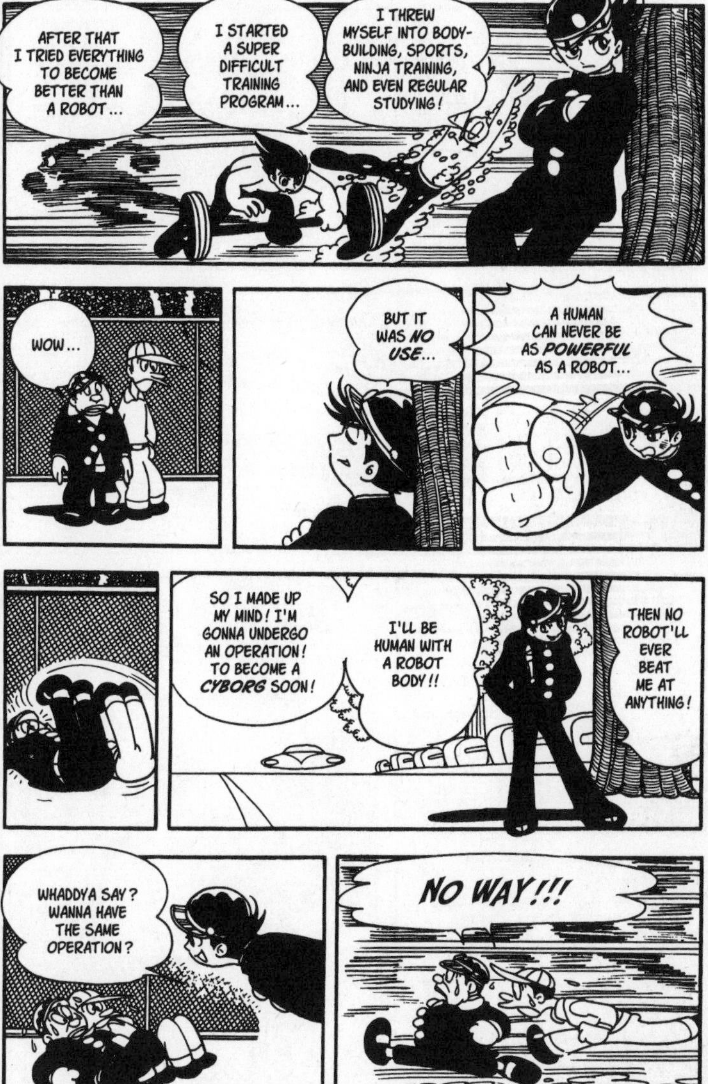
AFTER THAT I TRIED EVERYTHING TO BECOME BETTER THAN A ROBOT...
I STARTED A SUPER DIFFICULT TRAINING PROGRAM...
I THREW MYSELF INTO BODY-BUILDING, SPORTS, NINJA TRAINING, AND EVEN REGULAR STUDYING!
WOW...
BUT IT WAS NO USE...
A HUMAN CAN NEVER BE AS POWERFUL AS A ROBOT...
SO I MADE UP MY MIND! I'M GONNA UNDERGO AN OPERATION! TO BECOME A CYBORG SOON!
I'LL BE HUMAN WITH A ROBOT BODY!!
THEN NO ROBOT'LL EVER BEAT ME AT ANYTHING!
WHADDYA SAY? WANNA HAVE THE SAME OPERATION?
NO WAY!!!

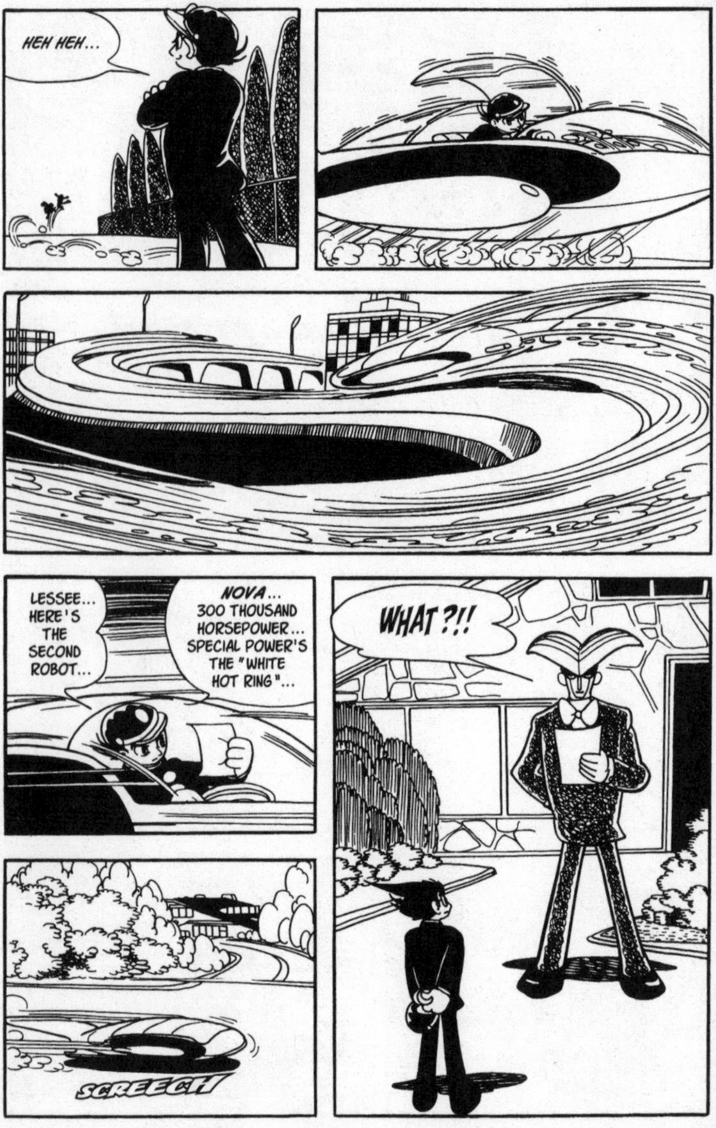
HEH HEH...
LESSEE... HERE'S THE SECOND ROBOT...
NOVA... 300 THOUSAND HORSEPOWER... SPECIAL POWER'S THE "WHITE HOT RING"...
WHAT?!!
SCREECH

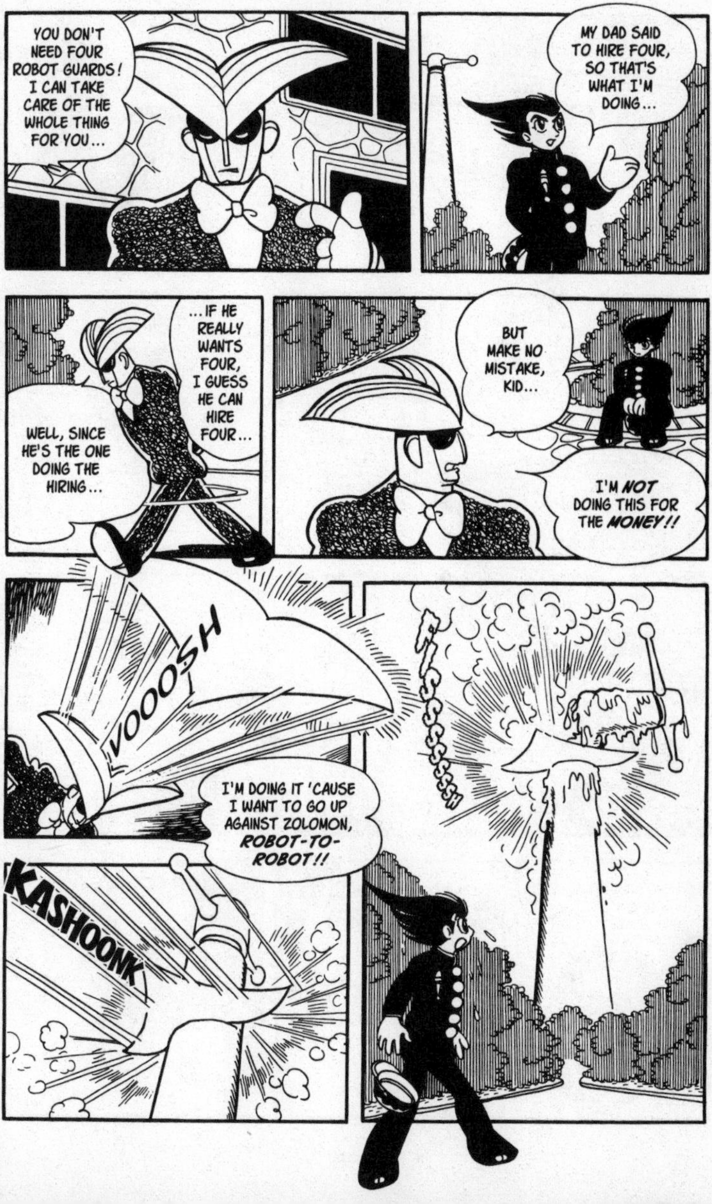
YOU DON'T NEED FOUR ROBOT GUARDS! I CAN TAKE CARE OF THE WHOLE THING FOR YOU...
MY DAD SAID TO HIRE FOUR, SO THAT'S WHAT I'M DOING...
WELL, SINCE HE'S THE ONE DOING THE HIRING...
...IF HE REALLY WANTS FOUR, I GUESS HE CAN HIRE FOUR...
BUT MAKE NO MISTAKE, KID...
I'M *NOT* DOING THIS FOR THE *MONEY!!*
VOOOSH
I'M DOING IT 'CAUSE I WANT TO GO UP AGAINST ZOLOMON, *ROBOT-TO-ROBOT!!*
KASHOONK
FISSSSSSH

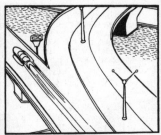

SCREECH

L-44

ZOLOMON?!

WHAT'S THE MATTER? AFRAID?

I'VE HEARD HE'S *AWFULLY* POWER-FUL...

WE NEED *YOUR* SUPER POWER, L-44...

...AND MY DAD SAYS HE'S WILLING TO *PAY* FOR IT!!

ENOUGH FOR ME TO BECOME A HUMAN?

I'VE HEARD THERE'S AN OPERATION THAT CAN CHANGE ROBOTS INTO HUMANS, AND I WANT IT...

Y-YOU WANT TO BECOME A *HUMAN?* B-BUT WHY?

492

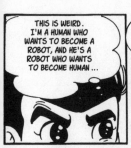

THIS IS WEIRD. I'M A HUMAN WHO WANTS TO BECOME A ROBOT, AND HE'S A ROBOT WHO WANTS TO BECOME HUMAN...

I'M JUST AFRAID THE OPERATION MIGHT NOT WORK ON A REAL ROBOT LIKE ME...

HEY, IT'D PROBABLY WORK, AT LEAST SUPERFICIALLY... I HEAR THEY'VE EVEN GOT ARTIFICIAL CELLS THESE DAYS...

THEN COUNT ME IN, YOUNG MAN...

I'LL DO MY BEST TO PROTECT THE GEM FROM ZOLOMON!

....
....

AH, WHY WAS I MADE TO BE A *ROBOT*...? I'D GIVE ANYTHING TO BE A FLESH AND BLOOD *HUMAN*...

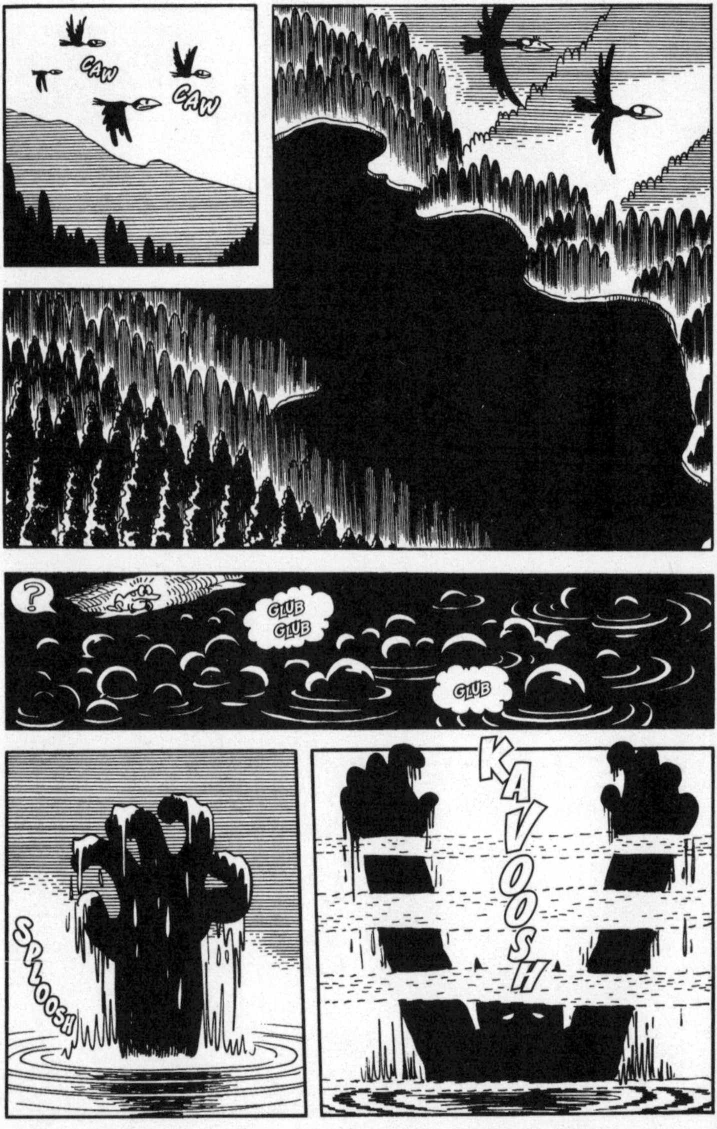
CAW
CAW
?
GLUB GLUB
GLUB
SPLOOSH
KAVOOSH

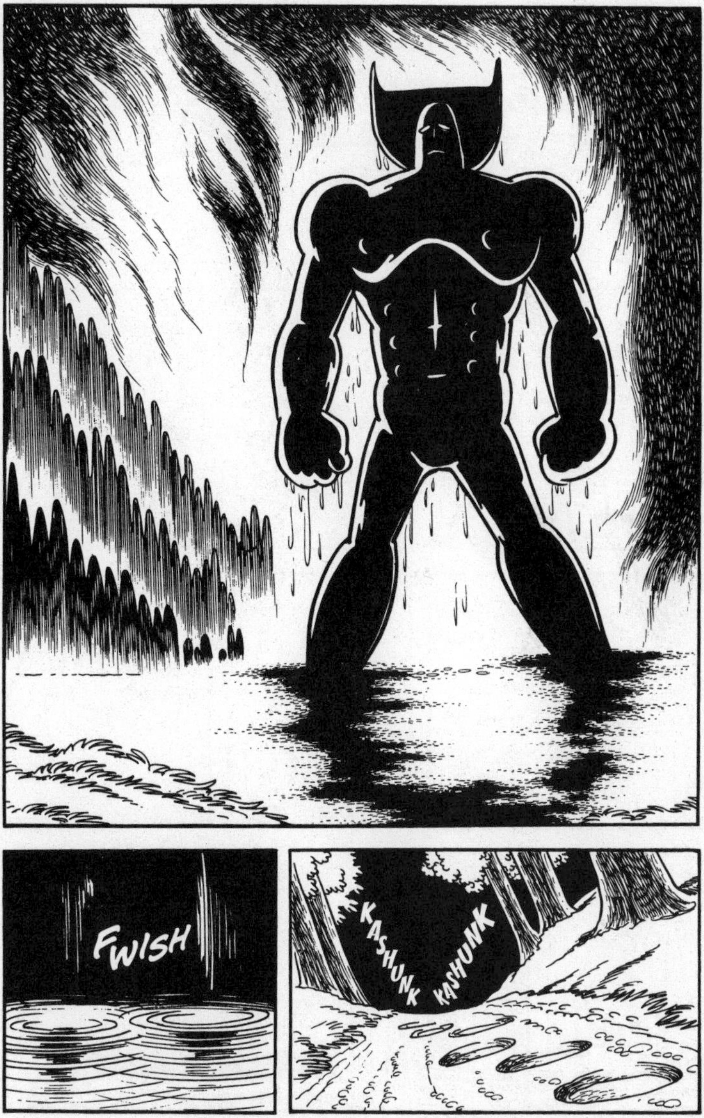
FWISH
KASHUNK
KASHUNK

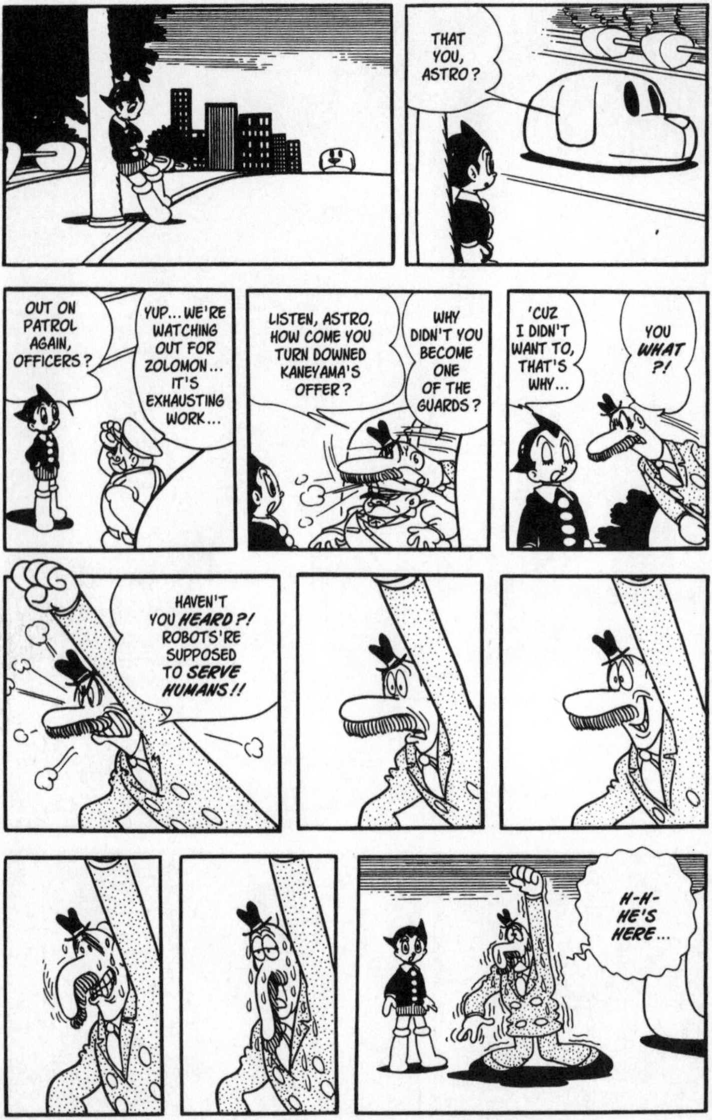
THAT YOU, ASTRO?
OUT ON PATROL AGAIN, OFFICERS?
YUP... WE'RE WATCHING OUT FOR ZOLOMON... IT'S EXHAUSTING WORK...
LISTEN, ASTRO, HOW COME YOU TURN DOWNED KANEYAMA'S OFFER?
WHY DIDN'T YOU BECOME ONE OF THE GUARDS?
'CUZ I DIDN'T WANT TO, THAT'S WHY...
YOU WHAT?!
HAVEN'T YOU HEARD?! ROBOTS'RE SUPPOSED TO SERVE HUMANS!!
H-H-HE'S HERE...

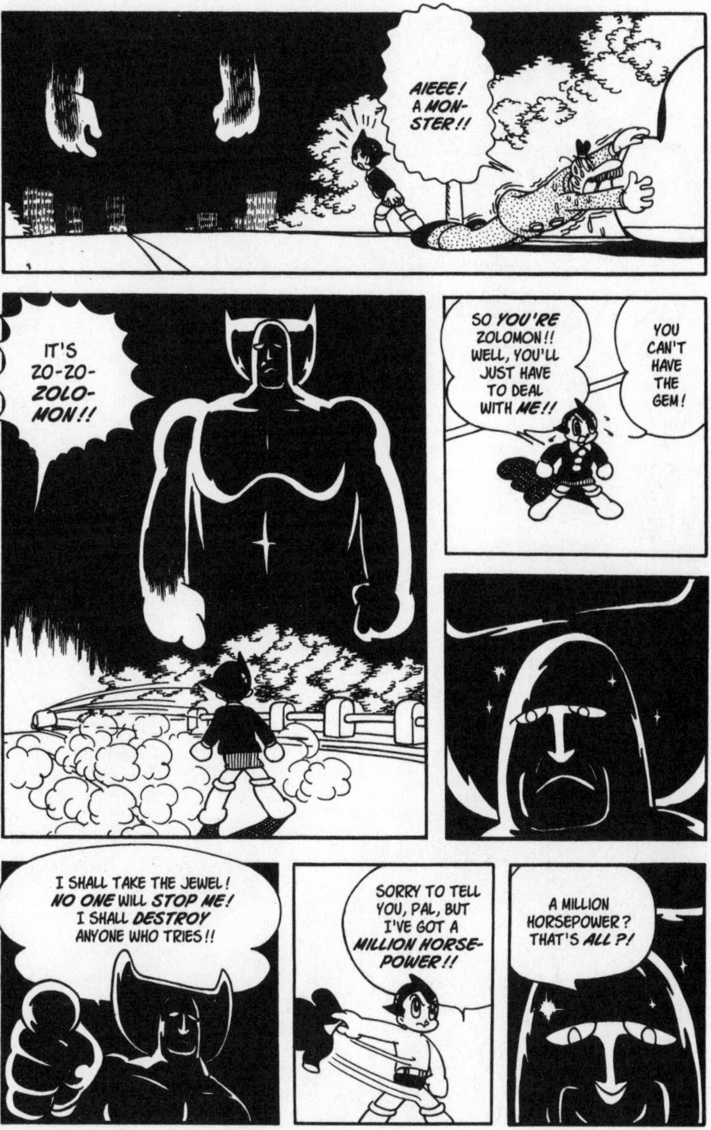
AIEEE! A MON-STER!!
IT'S ZO-ZO-ZOLO-MON!!
SO YOU'RE ZOLOMON!! WELL, YOU'LL JUST HAVE TO DEAL WITH ME!!
YOU CAN'T HAVE THE GEM!
I SHALL TAKE THE JEWEL! NO ONE WILL STOP ME! I SHALL DESTROY ANYONE WHO TRIES!!
SORRY TO TELL YOU, PAL, BUT I'VE GOT A MILLION HORSE-POWER!!
A MILLION HORSEPOWER? THAT'S ALL?!

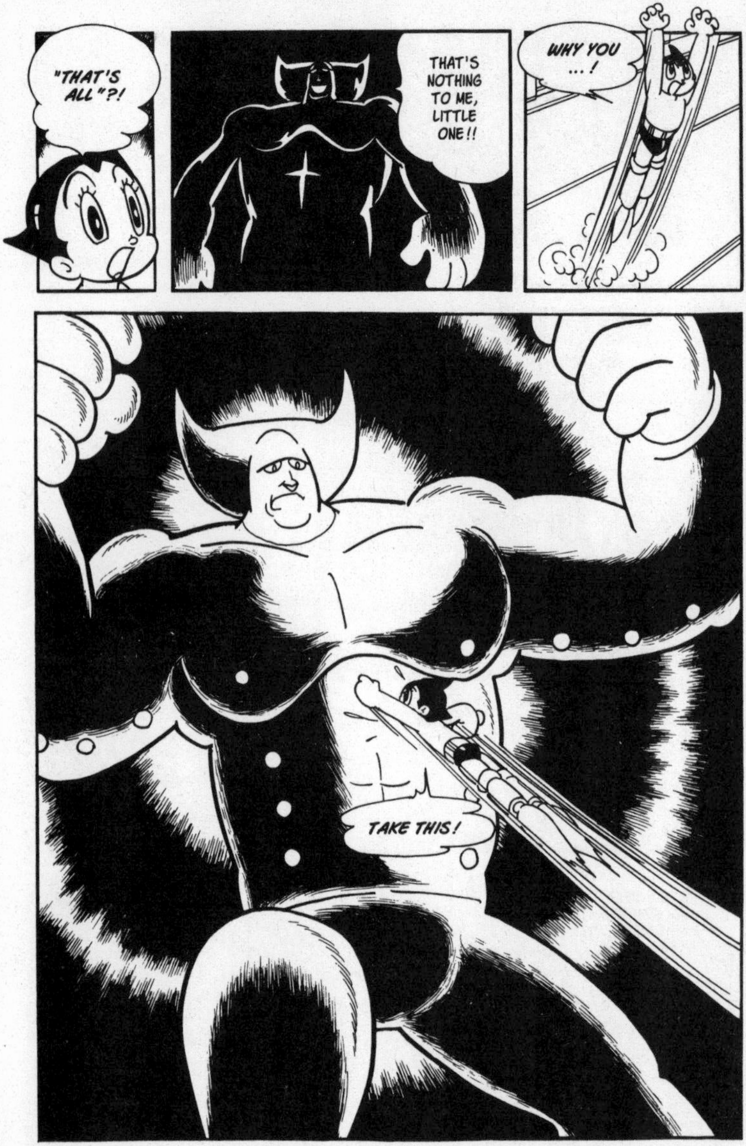
"THAT'S ALL"?!
THAT'S NOTHING TO ME, LITTLE ONE!!
WHY YOU ...!
TAKE THIS!

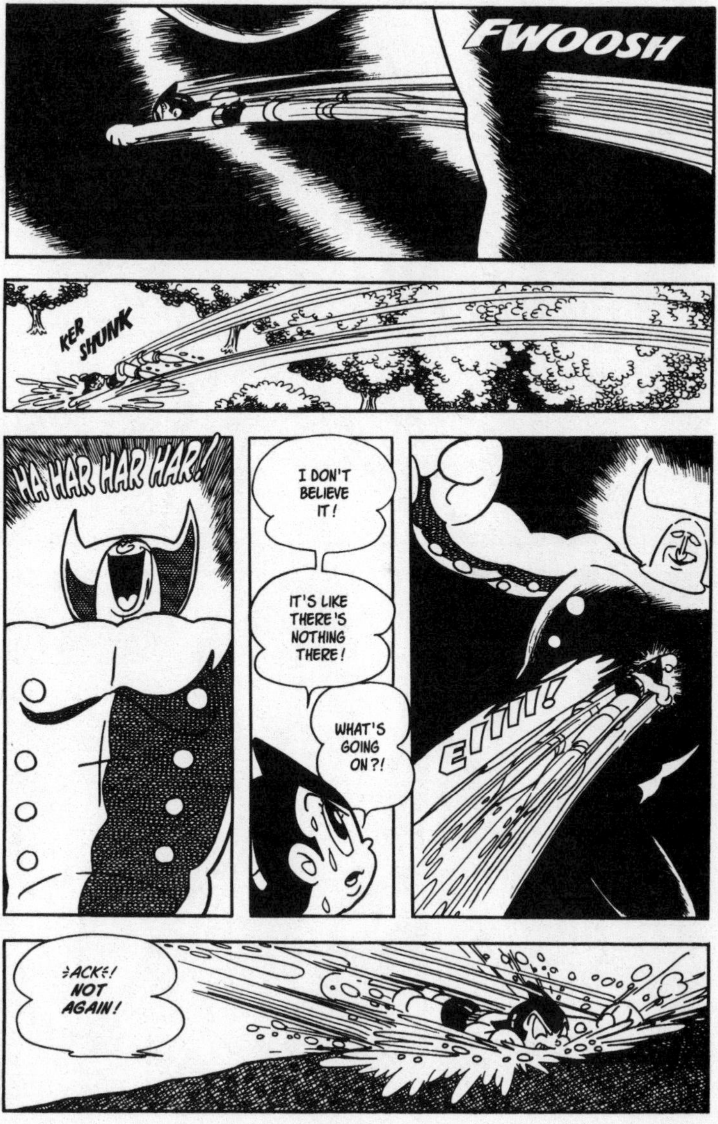
FWOOSH
KER SHUNK
HA HAR HAR HAR!
I DON'T BELIEVE IT!
IT'S LIKE THERE'S NOTHING THERE!
WHAT'S GOING ON?!
EIIIII!
ACK! NOT AGAIN!

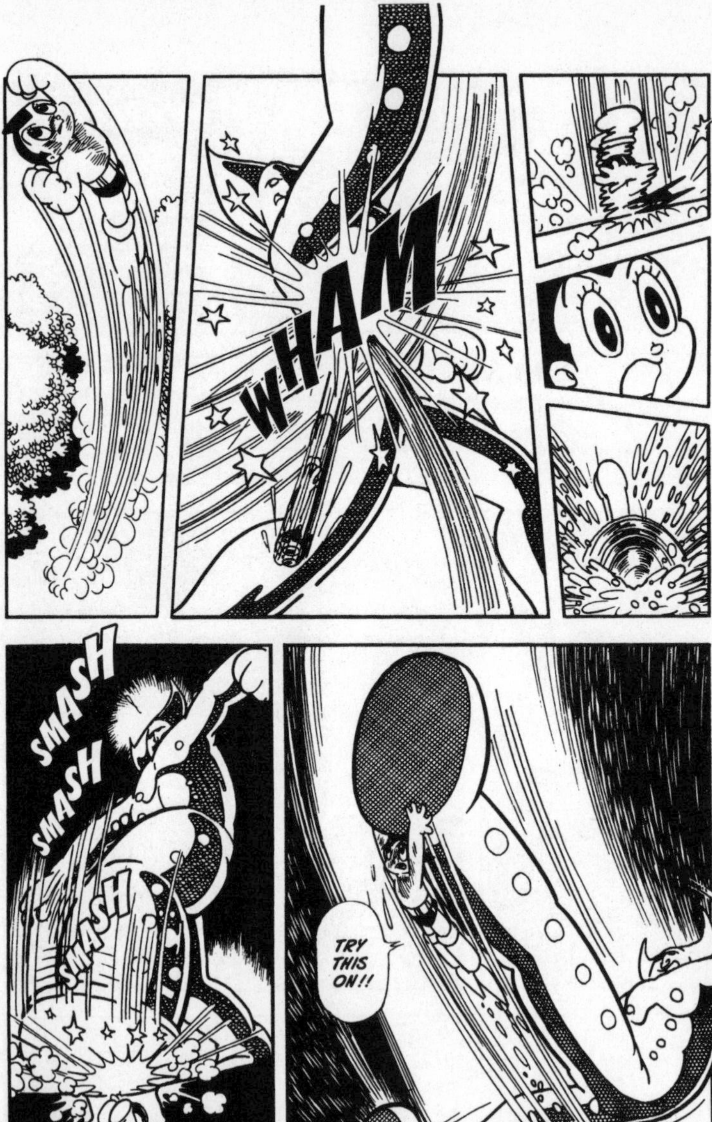
WHAM
SMASH
SMASH
SMASH
SMASH
TRY THIS ON!!

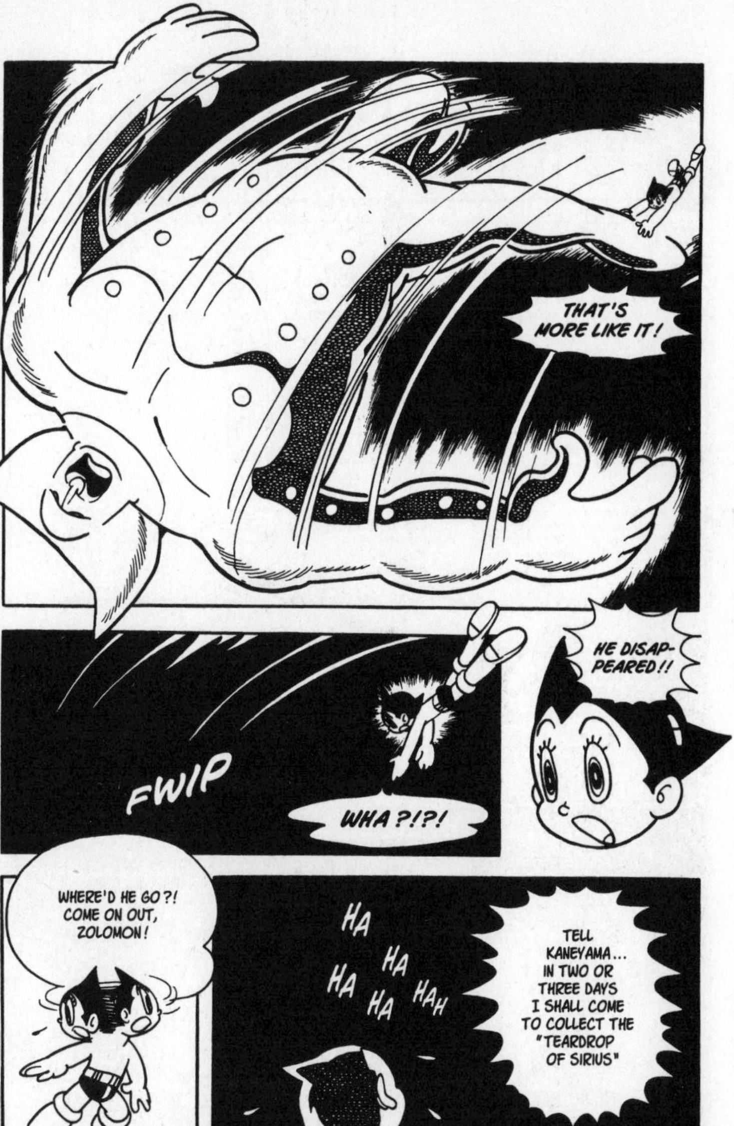
THAT'S MORE LIKE IT!
FWIP
WHA?!?!
HE DISAP-PEARED!!
WHERE'D HE GO?! COME ON OUT, ZOLOMON!
HA HA HA HA HAH
TELL KANEYAMA... IN TWO OR THREE DAYS I SHALL COME TO COLLECT THE "TEARDROP OF SIRIUS"

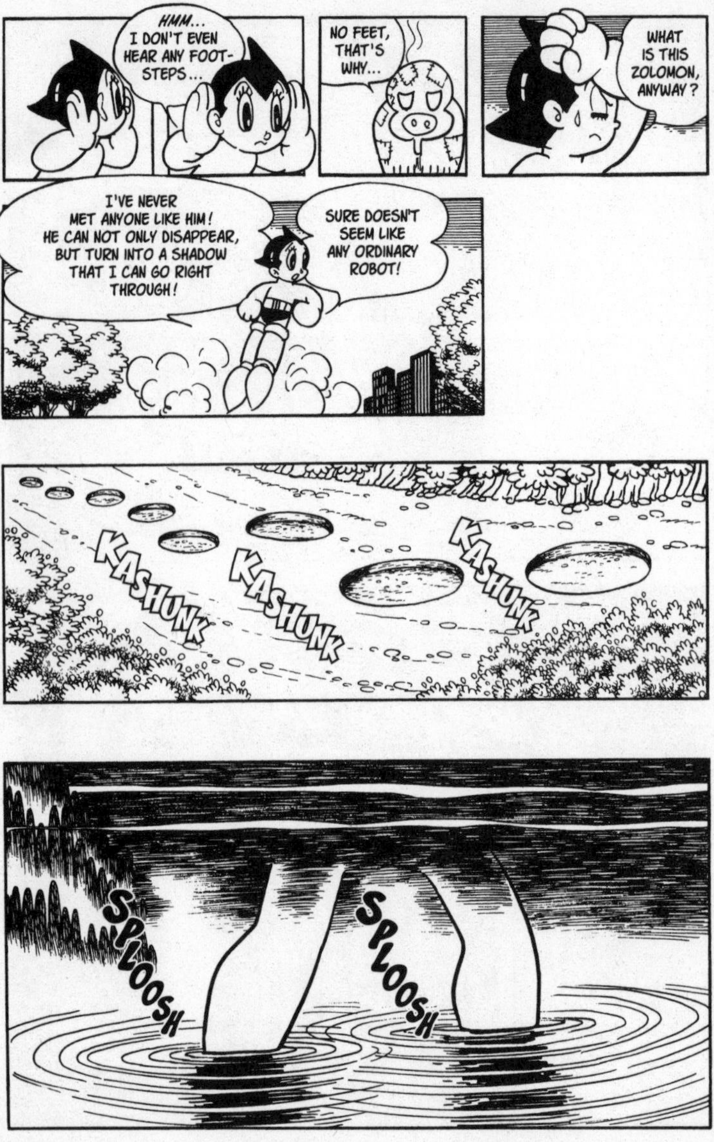
HMM...
I DON'T EVEN HEAR ANY FOOT-STEPS...
NO FEET, THAT'S WHY...
WHAT IS THIS ZOLOMON, ANYWAY?
I'VE NEVER MET ANYONE LIKE HIM! HE CAN NOT ONLY DISAPPEAR, BUT TURN INTO A SHADOW THAT I CAN GO RIGHT THROUGH!
SURE DOESN'T SEEM LIKE ANY ORDINARY ROBOT!
KASHUNK
KASHUNK
KASHUNK
SPLOOSH
SPLOOSH

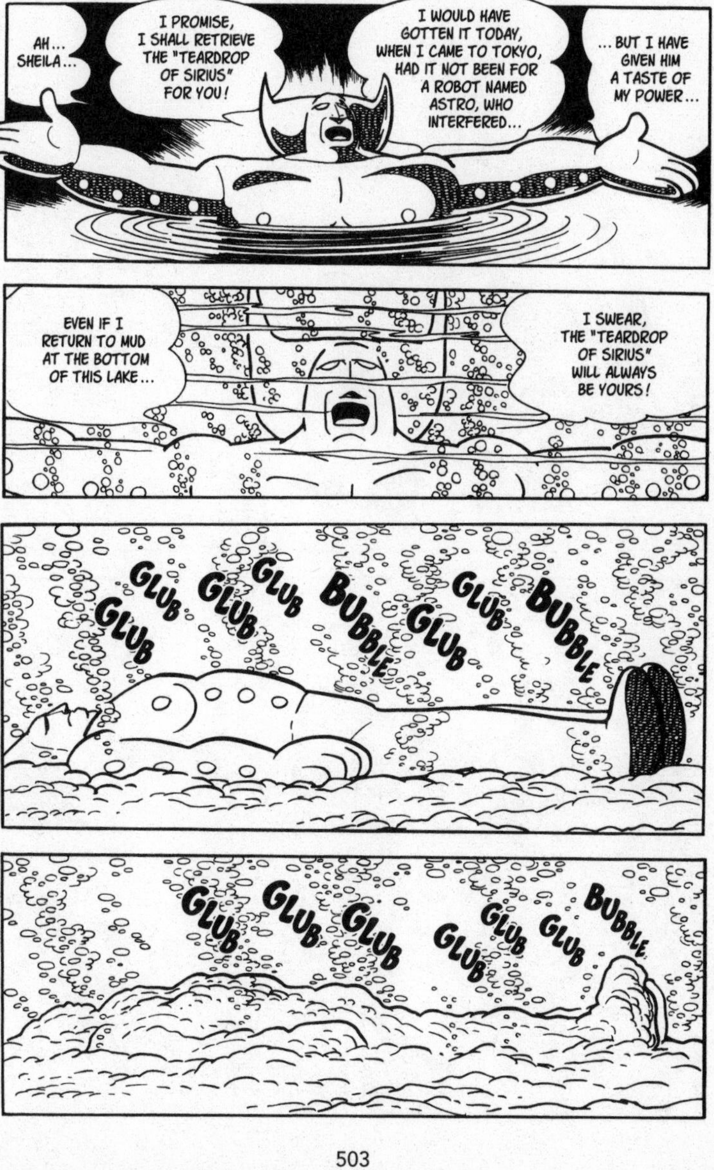
AH... SHEILA...
I PROMISE, I SHALL RETRIEVE THE "TEARDROP OF SIRIUS" FOR YOU!
I WOULD HAVE GOTTEN IT TODAY, WHEN I CAME TO TOKYO, HAD IT NOT BEEN FOR A ROBOT NAMED ASTRO, WHO INTERFERED...
... BUT I HAVE GIVEN HIM A TASTE OF MY POWER...
EVEN IF I RETURN TO MUD AT THE BOTTOM OF THIS LAKE...
I SWEAR, THE "TEARDROP OF SIRIUS" WILL ALWAYS BE YOURS!
GLUB
GLUB
GLUB
GLUB
BUBBLE
GLUB
GLUB
BUBBLE
GLUB
GLUB
GLUB
GLUB
GLUB
GLUB
BUBBLE

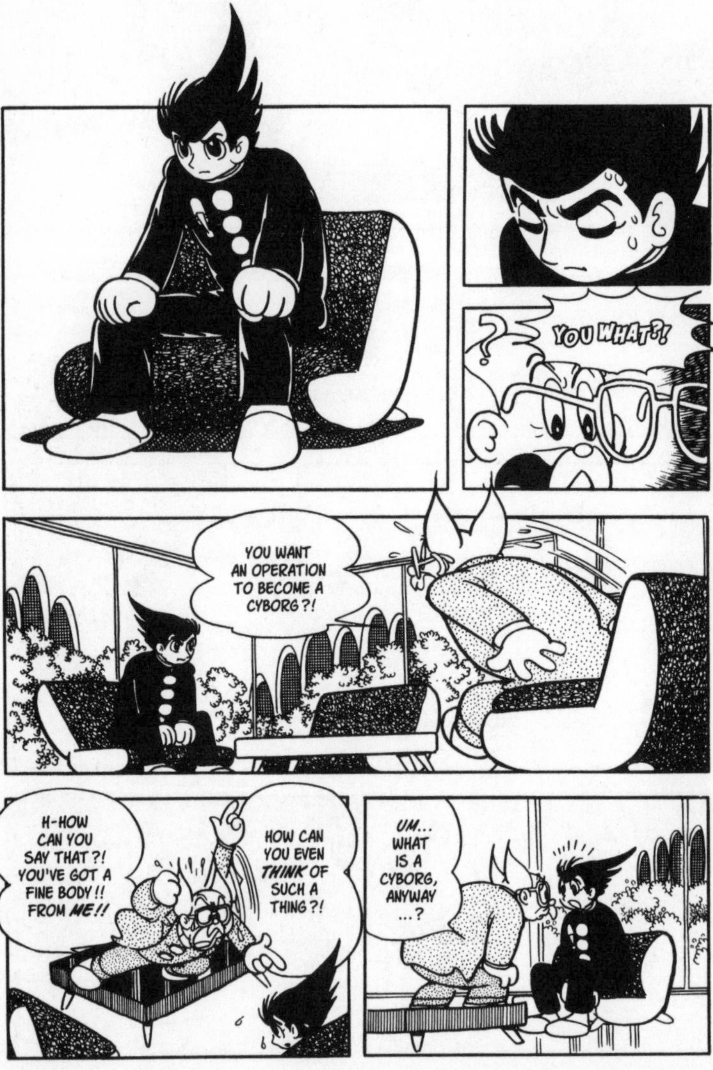
YOU WHAT?!
YOU WANT AN OPERATION TO BECOME A CYBORG?!
H-HOW CAN YOU SAY THAT?! YOU'VE GOT A FINE BODY!! FROM *ME!!*
HOW CAN YOU EVEN *THINK* OF SUCH A THING?!
UM... WHAT IS A CYBORG, ANYWAY ...?

LESSEE... CY... CY... CYBORG... CYBORG...
"A HUMAN WITH PARTS OF HIS OR HER BODY MODIFIED TO BE A ROBOT, OFTEN DONE TO FACILITATE LIFE IN OUTER SPACE..."
THAT SETTLES IT, HIKARU!
I ABSOLUTELY WON'T PERMIT IT!!
NOT EVEN OVER MY DEAD BODY!!!
BLAST IT! EVEN IF I GOT A PART-TIME JOB...
...I'D STILL NEVER MAKE ENOUGH MONEY TO PAY FOR THE OPERATION BY MYSELF...
ROBOT PLASTIC SURGERY CLINIC

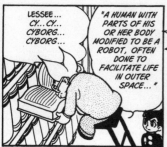

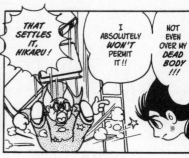

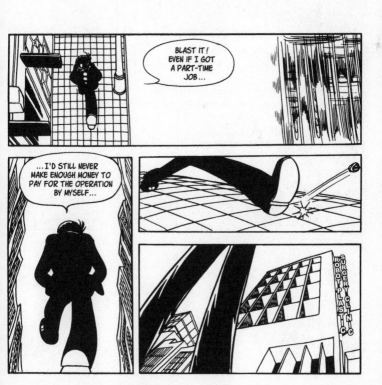

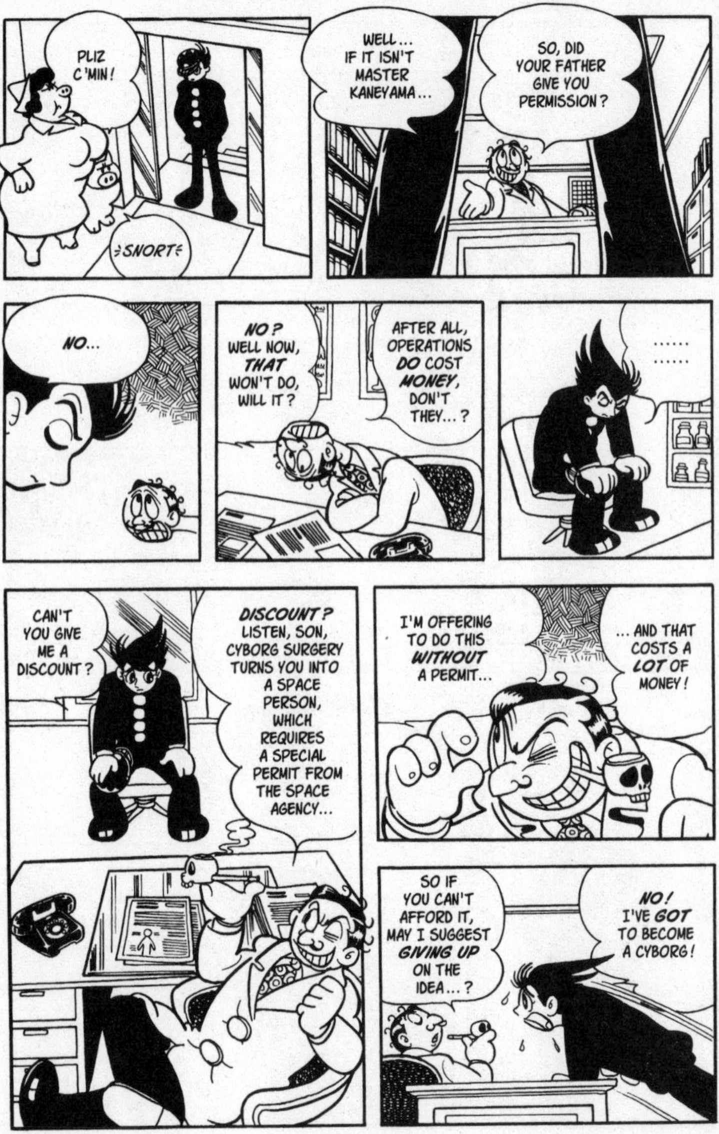
PLIZ C'MIN!
SNORT
WELL... IF IT ISN'T MASTER KANEYAMA...
SO, DID YOUR FATHER GIVE YOU PERMISSION?
NO...
NO? WELL NOW, THAT WON'T DO, WILL IT?
AFTER ALL, OPERATIONS DO COST MONEY, DON'T THEY...?
......
......
CAN'T YOU GIVE ME A DISCOUNT?
DISCOUNT? LISTEN, SON, CYBORG SURGERY TURNS YOU INTO A SPACE PERSON, WHICH REQUIRES A SPECIAL PERMIT FROM THE SPACE AGENCY...
I'M OFFERING TO DO THIS WITHOUT A PERMIT...
...AND THAT COSTS A LOT OF MONEY!
SO IF YOU CAN'T AFFORD IT, MAY I SUGGEST GIVING UP ON THE IDEA...?
NO! I'VE GOT TO BECOME A CYBORG!

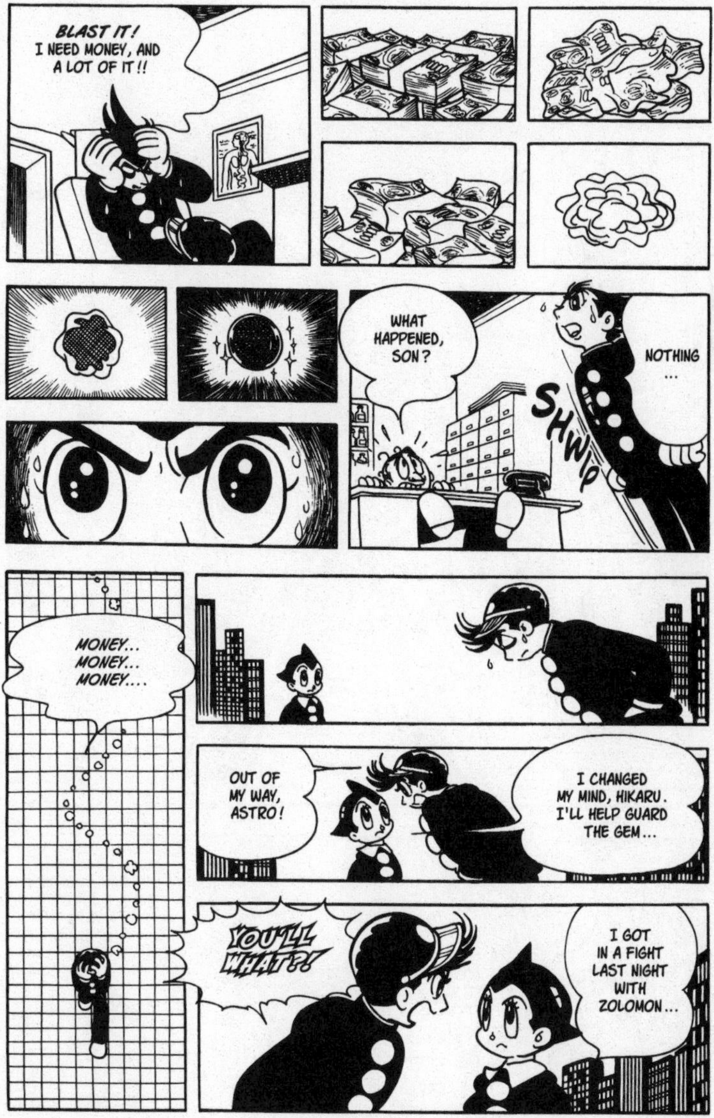
BLAST IT! I NEED MONEY, AND A LOT OF IT!!
WHAT HAPPENED, SON?
NOTHING ...
SHWIP
MONEY... MONEY... MONEY....
OUT OF MY WAY, ASTRO!
I CHANGED MY MIND, HIKARU. I'LL HELP GUARD THE GEM...
YOU'LL WHAT?!
I GOT IN A FIGHT LAST NIGHT WITH ZOLOMON...

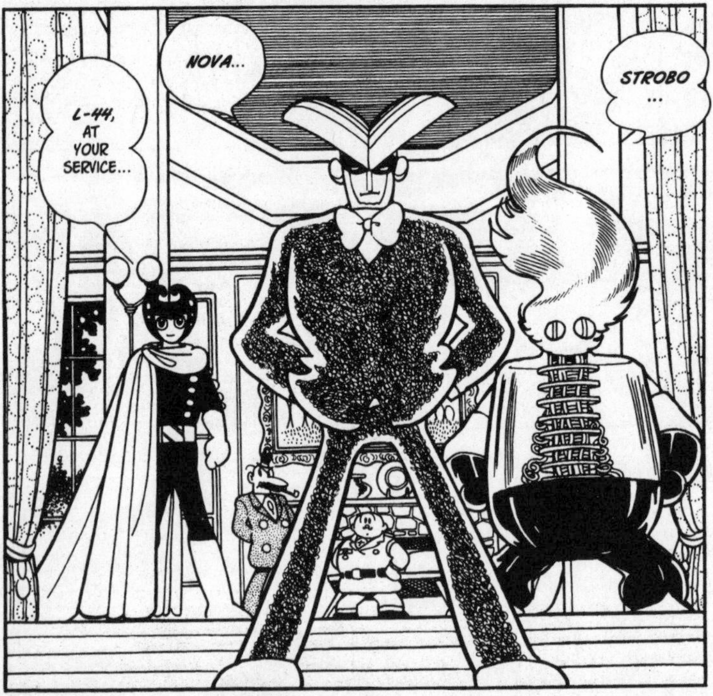
L-44, AT YOUR SERVICE...
NOVA...
STROBO ...
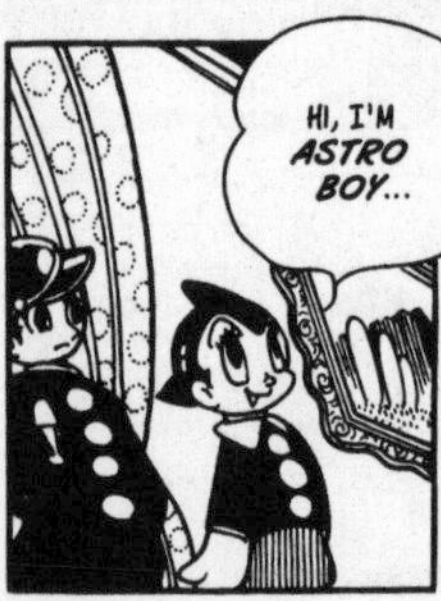
HI, I'M ASTRO BOY...
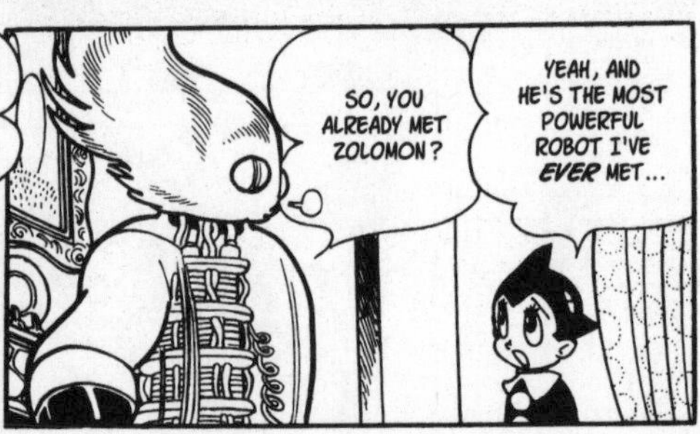
SO, YOU ALREADY MET ZOLOMON?
YEAH, AND HE'S THE MOST POWERFUL ROBOT I'VE EVER MET...

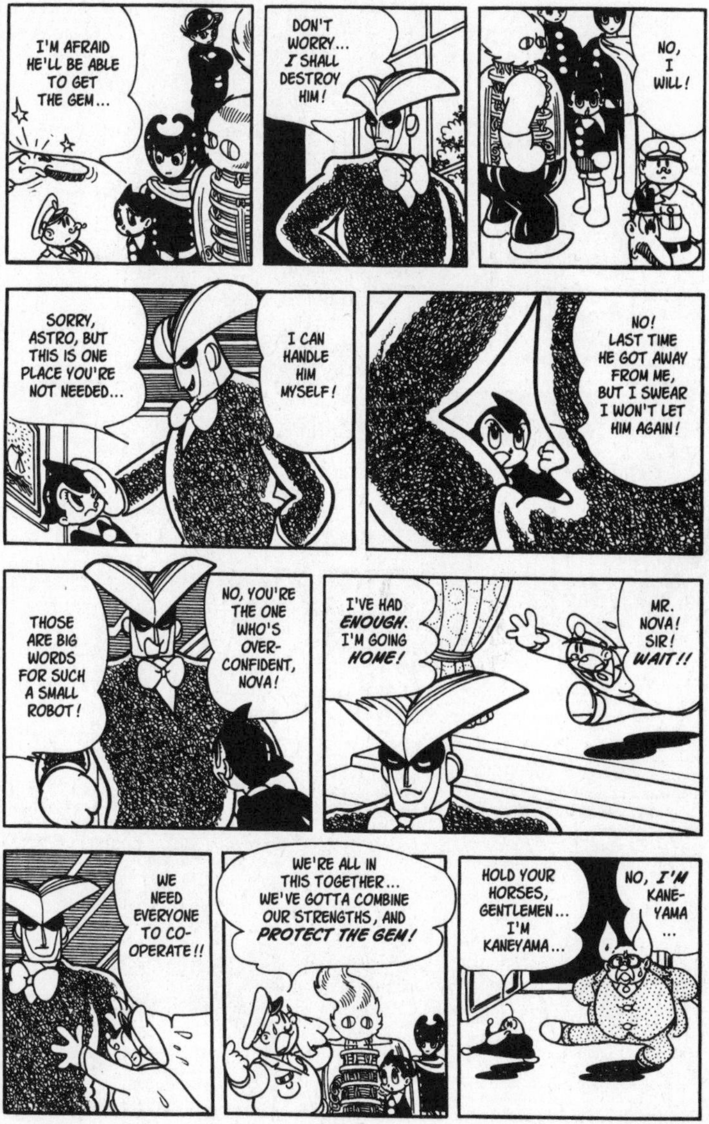
I'M AFRAID HE'LL BE ABLE TO GET THE GEM...
DON'T WORRY... I SHALL DESTROY HIM!
NO, I WILL!
SORRY, ASTRO, BUT THIS IS ONE PLACE YOU'RE NOT NEEDED...
I CAN HANDLE HIM MYSELF!
NO! LAST TIME HE GOT AWAY FROM ME, BUT I SWEAR I WON'T LET HIM AGAIN!
THOSE ARE BIG WORDS FOR SUCH A SMALL ROBOT!
NO, YOU'RE THE ONE WHO'S OVER-CONFIDENT, NOVA!
I'VE HAD ENOUGH. I'M GOING HOME!
MR. NOVA! SIR! WAIT!!
WE NEED EVERYONE TO CO-OPERATE!!
WE'RE ALL IN THIS TOGETHER... WE'VE GOTTA COMBINE OUR STRENGTHS, AND PROTECT THE GEM!
HOLD YOUR HORSES, GENTLEMEN... I'M KANEYAMA...
NO, I'M KANE-YAMA ...

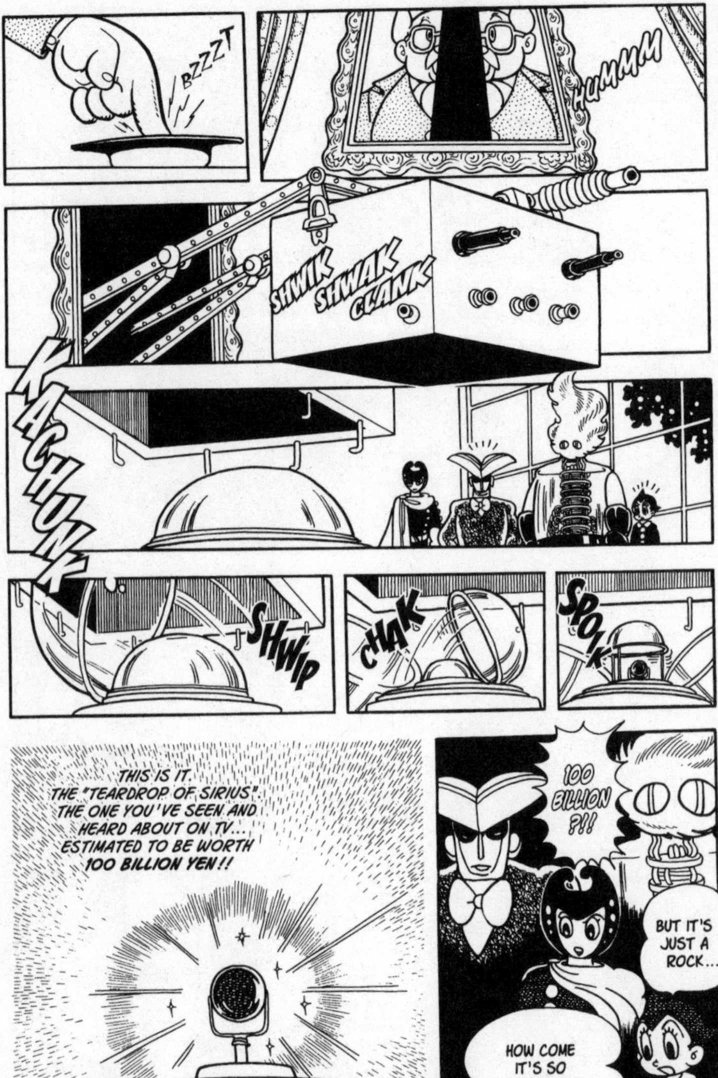
BZZZT
HUMMM
SHWIK
SHWAK
CLANK
KACHUNK
SHWIP
CHAK
SPOIK
THIS IS IT. THE "TEARDROP OF SIRIUS". THE ONE YOU'VE SEEN AND HEARD ABOUT ON TV... ESTIMATED TO BE WORTH 100 BILLION YEN!!
100 BILLION ?!!
BUT IT'S JUST A ROCK...
HOW COME IT'S SO EXPENSIVE?

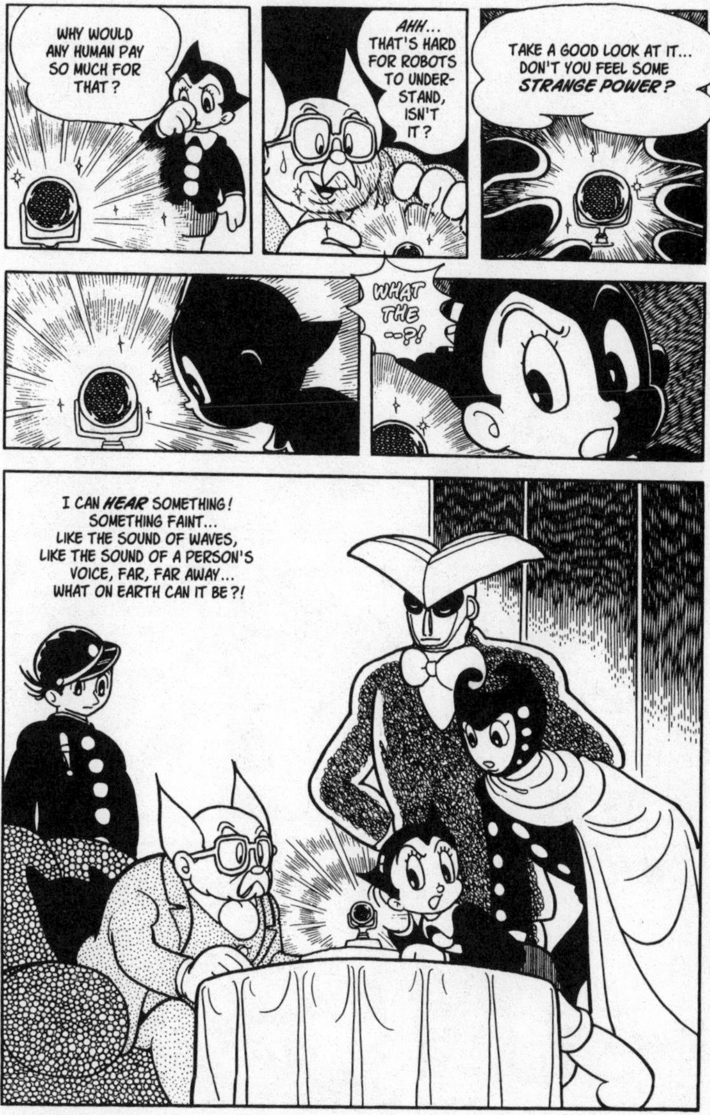
WHY WOULD ANY HUMAN PAY SO MUCH FOR THAT?
AHH... THAT'S HARD FOR ROBOTS TO UNDERSTAND, ISN'T IT?
TAKE A GOOD LOOK AT IT... DON'T YOU FEEL SOME STRANGE POWER?
WHAT THE --?!
I CAN HEAR SOMETHING! SOMETHING FAINT... LIKE THE SOUND OF WAVES, LIKE THE SOUND OF A PERSON'S VOICE, FAR, FAR AWAY... WHAT ON EARTH CAN IT BE?!

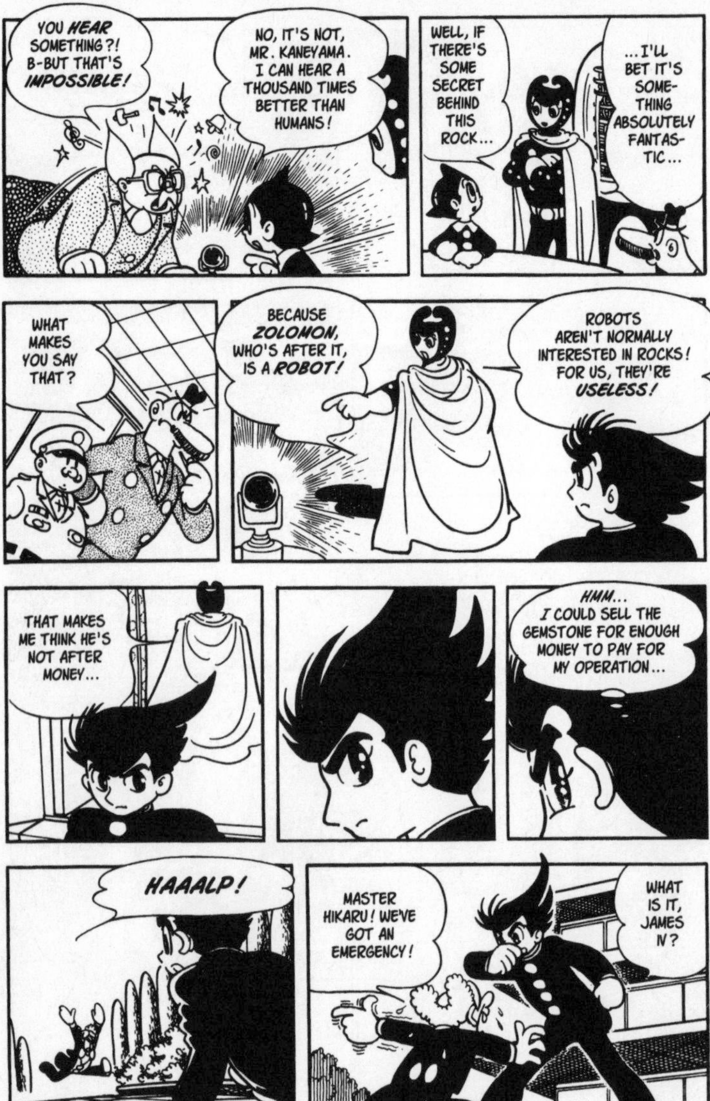
YOU HEAR SOMETHING?! B-BUT THAT'S IMPOSSIBLE!
NO, IT'S NOT, MR. KANEYAMA. I CAN HEAR A THOUSAND TIMES BETTER THAN HUMANS!
WELL, IF THERE'S SOME SECRET BEHIND THIS ROCK...
...I'LL BET IT'S SOMETHING ABSOLUTELY FANTASTIC...
WHAT MAKES YOU SAY THAT?
BECAUSE ZOLOMON, WHO'S AFTER IT, IS A ROBOT!
ROBOTS AREN'T NORMALLY INTERESTED IN ROCKS! FOR US, THEY'RE USELESS!
THAT MAKES ME THINK HE'S NOT AFTER MONEY...
HMM... I COULD SELL THE GEMSTONE FOR ENOUGH MONEY TO PAY FOR MY OPERATION...
HAAALP!
MASTER HIKARU! WE'VE GOT AN EMERGENCY!
WHAT IS IT, JAMES IV?

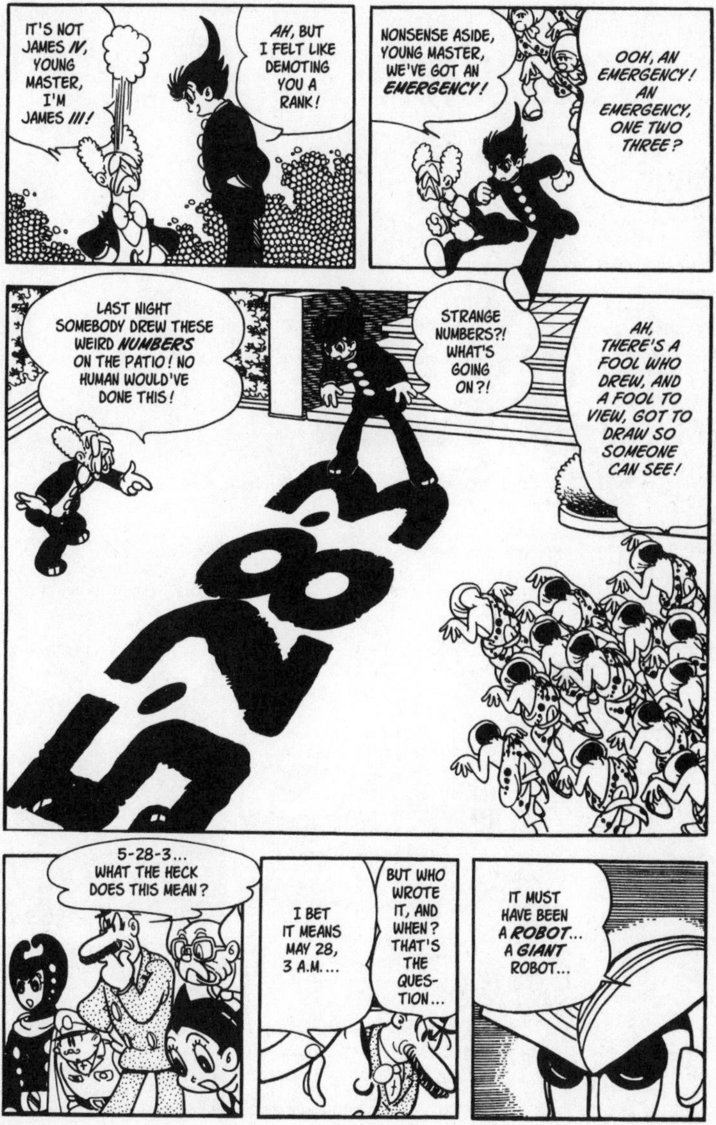

IT'S NOT JAMES IV, YOUNG MASTER, I'M JAMES III!
AH, BUT I FELT LIKE DEMOTING YOU A RANK!
NONSENSE ASIDE, YOUNG MASTER, WE'VE GOT AN EMERGENCY!
OOH, AN EMERGENCY! AN EMERGENCY, ONE TWO THREE?
LAST NIGHT SOMEBODY DREW THESE WEIRD NUMBERS ON THE PATIO! NO HUMAN WOULD'VE DONE THIS!
STRANGE NUMBERS?! WHAT'S GOING ON?!
AH, THERE'S A FOOL WHO DREW, AND A FOOL TO VIEW, GOT TO DRAW SO SOMEONE CAN SEE!
5-28-3...
5-28-3... WHAT THE HECK DOES THIS MEAN?
I BET IT MEANS MAY 28, 3 A.M....
BUT WHO WROTE IT, AND WHEN? THAT'S THE QUES-TION...
IT MUST HAVE BEEN A ROBOT... A GIANT ROBOT...

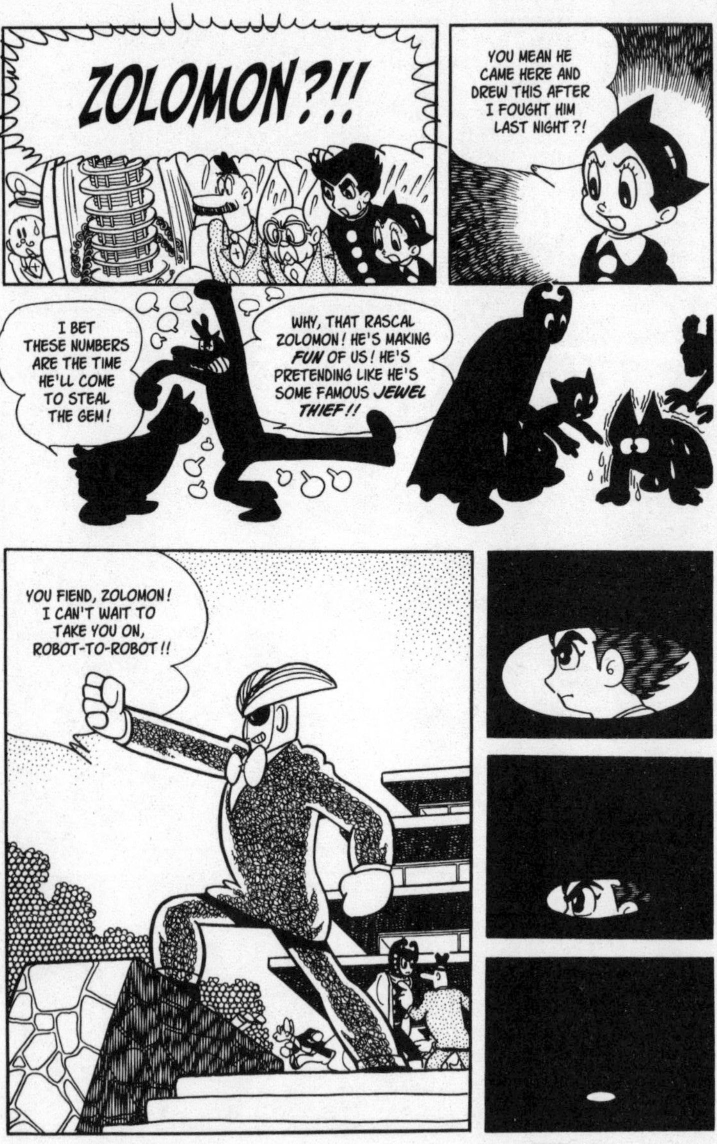

ZOLOMON?!!
YOU MEAN HE CAME HERE AND DREW THIS AFTER I FOUGHT HIM LAST NIGHT?!
I BET THESE NUMBERS ARE THE TIME HE'LL COME TO STEAL THE GEM!
WHY, THAT RASCAL ZOLOMON! HE'S MAKING FUN OF US! HE'S PRETENDING LIKE HE'S SOME FAMOUS JEWEL THIEF!!
YOU FIEND, ZOLOMON! I CAN'T WAIT TO TAKE YOU ON, ROBOT-TO-ROBOT!!

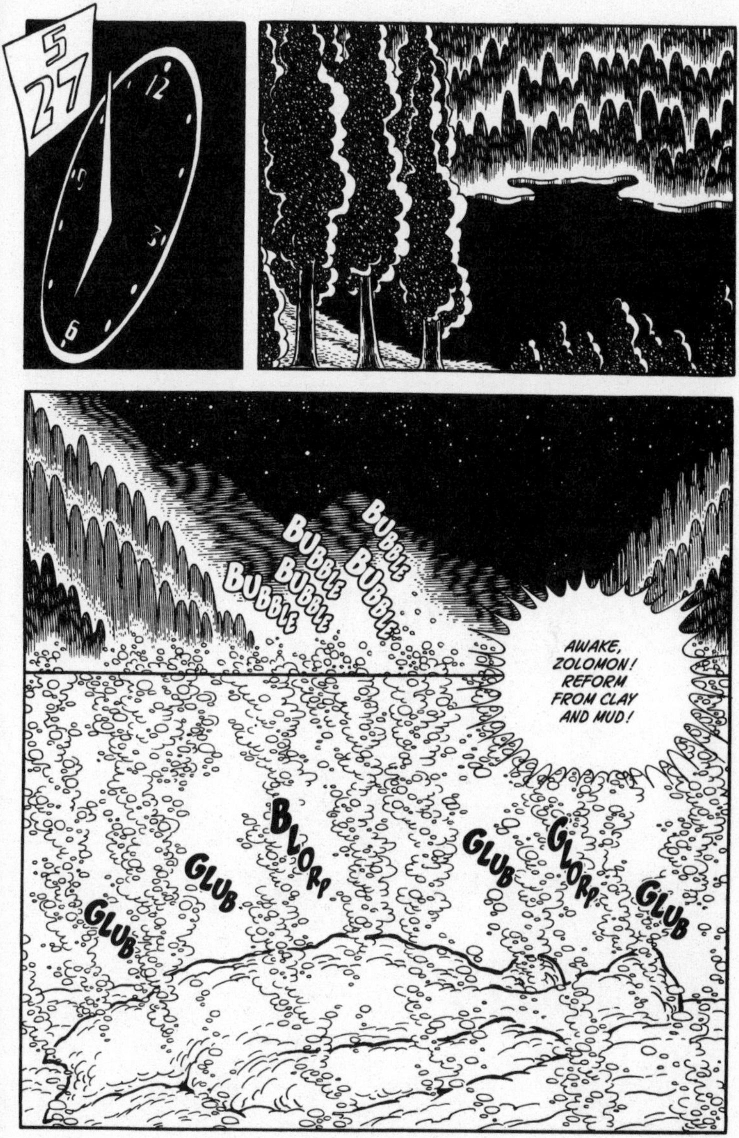
5
27
BUBBLE
BUBBLE
BUBBLE
BUBBLE
BUBBLE
AWAKE, ZOLOMON! REFORM FROM CLAY AND MUD!
GLUB
GLUB
BLORP
GLUB
GLORP
GLUB

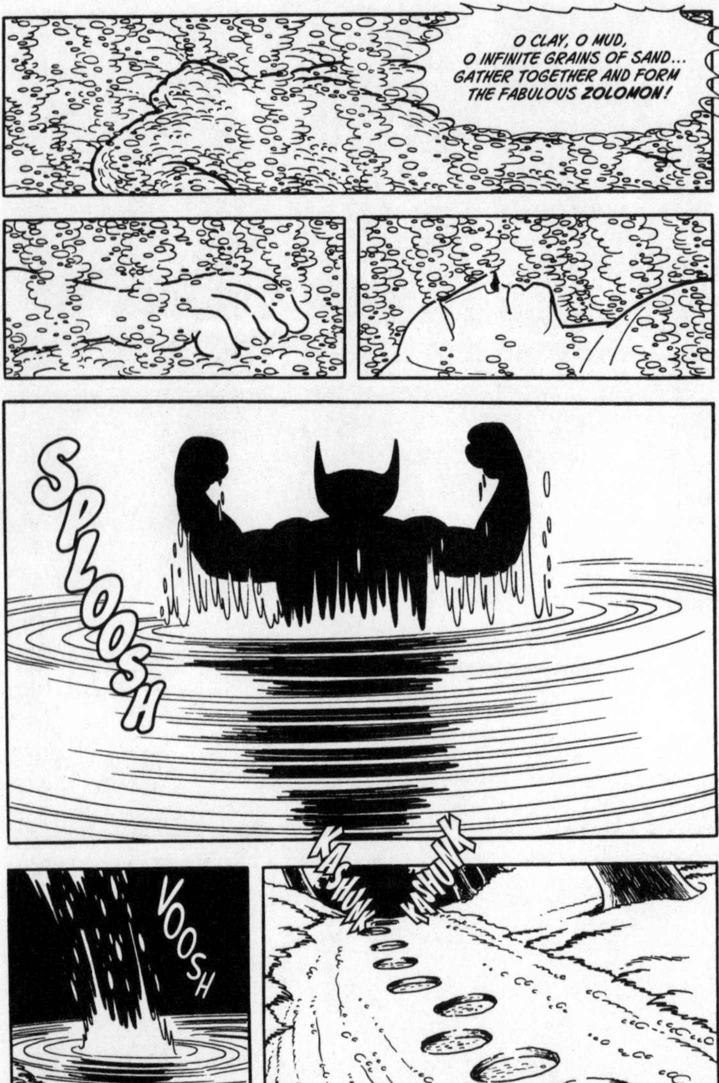
O CLAY, O MUD, O INFINITE GRAINS OF SAND... GATHER TOGETHER AND FORM THE FABULOUS ZOLOMON!
SPLOOSH
VOOSH
KASHUNK
KASHUNK

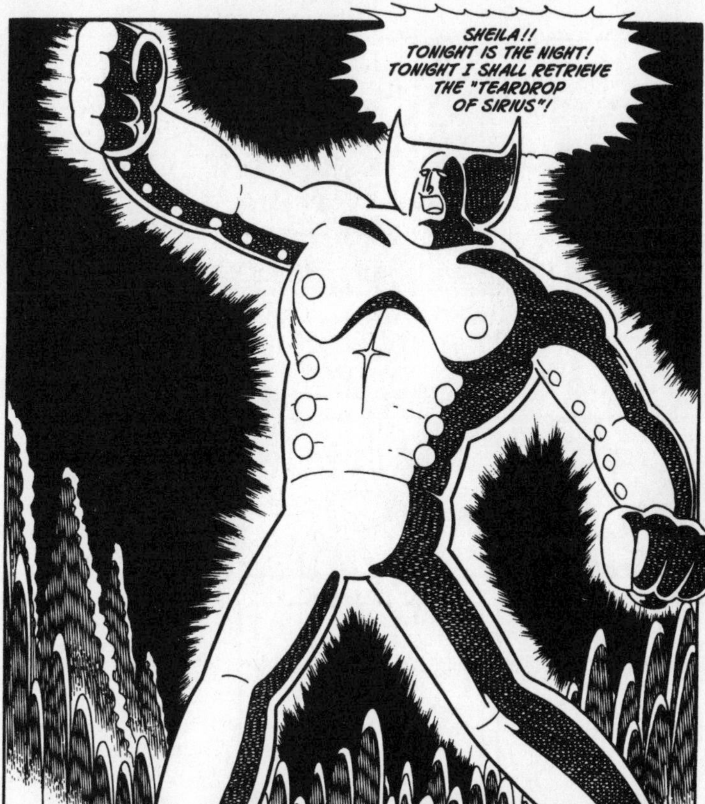
SHEILA!! TONIGHT IS THE NIGHT! TONIGHT I SHALL RETRIEVE THE "TEARDROP OF SIRIUS"!

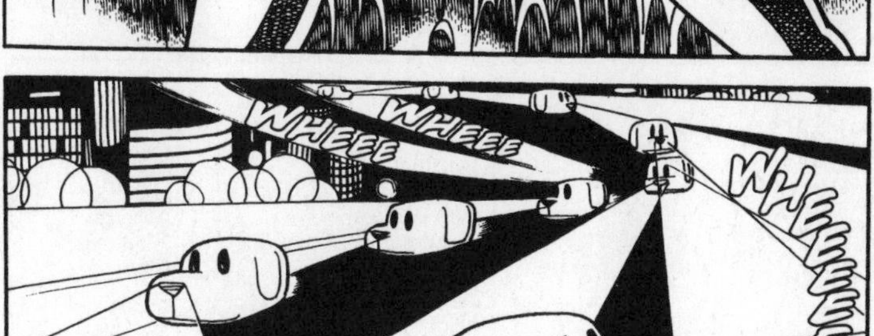
WHEEEE
WHEEEE
WHEEEEEEEEE

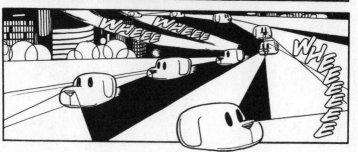

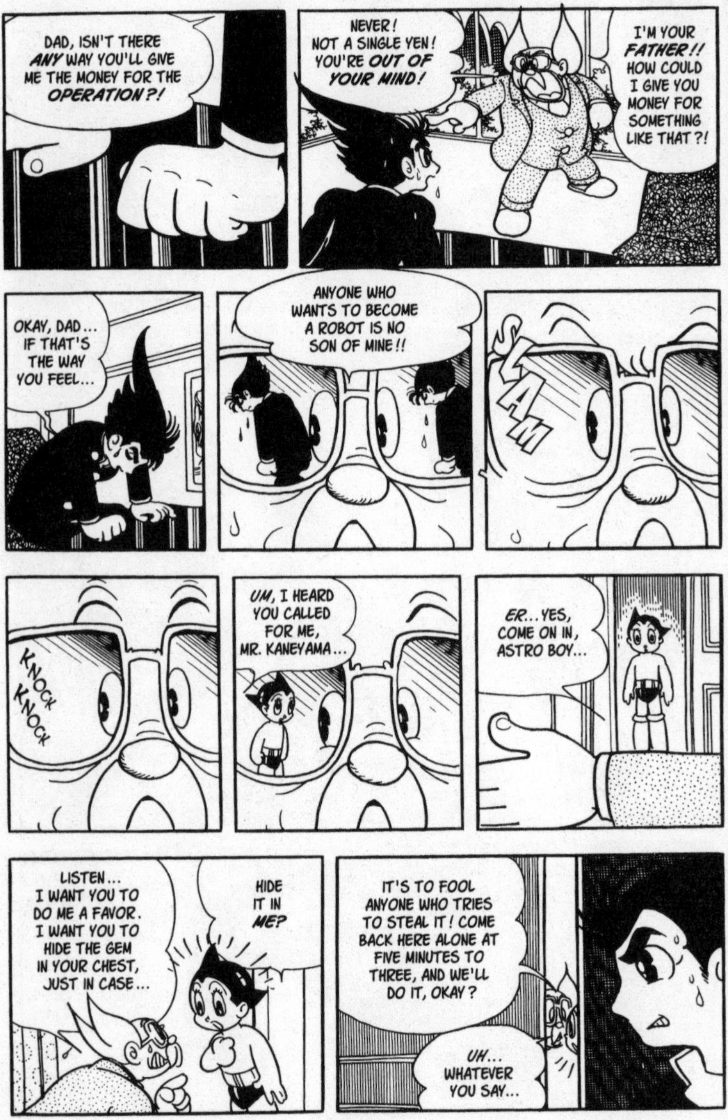
DAD, ISN'T THERE ANY WAY YOU'LL GIVE ME THE MONEY FOR THE OPERATION?!
NEVER! NOT A SINGLE YEN! YOU'RE OUT OF YOUR MIND!
I'M YOUR FATHER!! HOW COULD I GIVE YOU MONEY FOR SOMETHING LIKE THAT?!
OKAY, DAD... IF THAT'S THE WAY YOU FEEL...
ANYONE WHO WANTS TO BECOME A ROBOT IS NO SON OF MINE!!
SLAM
KNOCK KNOCK
UM, I HEARD YOU CALLED FOR ME, MR. KANEYAMA...
ER... YES, COME ON IN, ASTRO BOY...
LISTEN... I WANT YOU TO DO ME A FAVOR. I WANT YOU TO HIDE THE GEM IN YOUR CHEST, JUST IN CASE...
HIDE IT IN ME?
IT'S TO FOOL ANYONE WHO TRIES TO STEAL IT! COME BACK HERE ALONE AT FIVE MINUTES TO THREE, AND WE'LL DO IT, OKAY?
UH... WHATEVER YOU SAY...

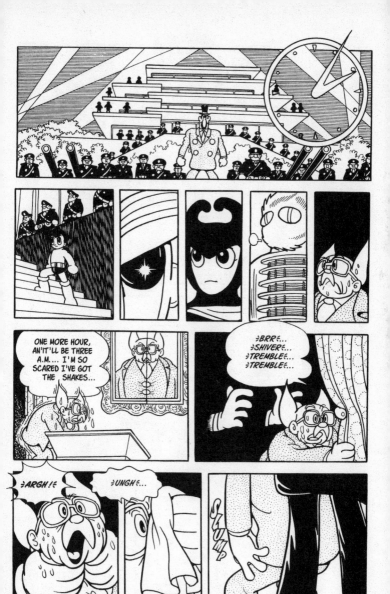

ONE MORE HOUR, AN'IT'LL BE THREE A.M.... I'M SO SCARED I'VE GOT THE SHAKES...

≥BRR≤...
≥SHIVER≤...
≥TREMBLE≤...
≥TREMBLE≤...

≥ARGH!≤

≥UNGH≤...

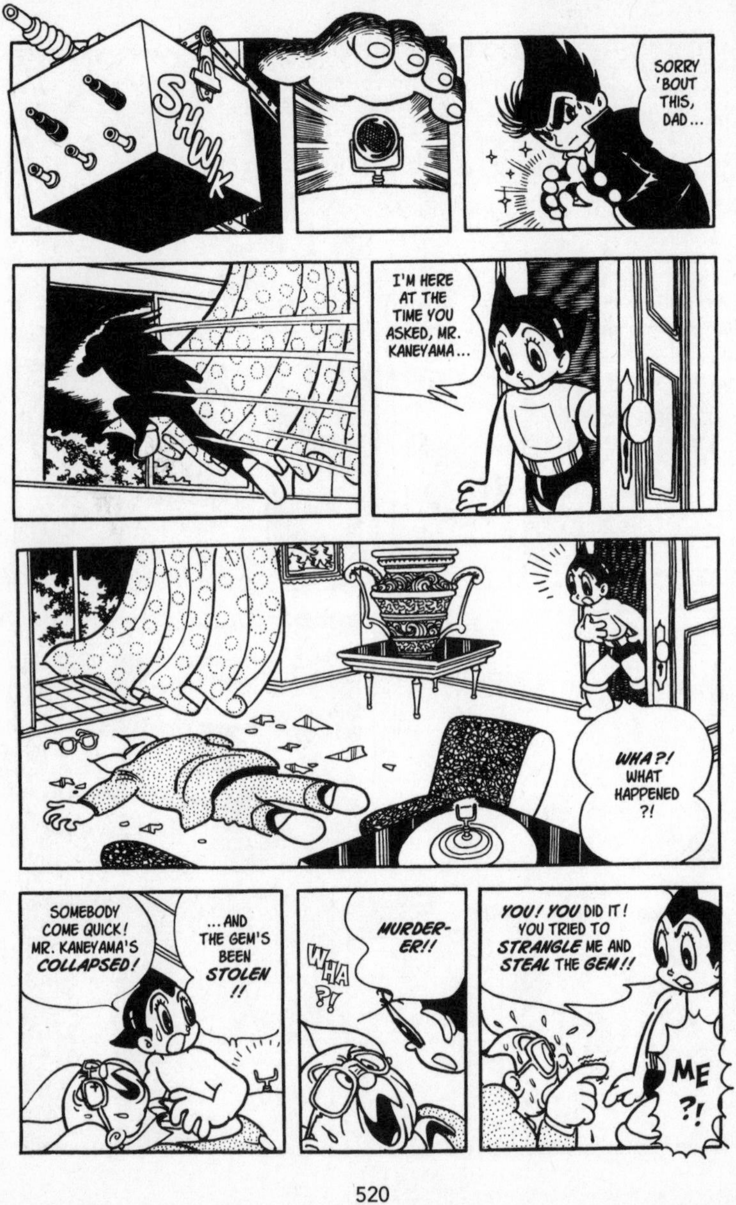
SHWIK
SORRY 'BOUT THIS, DAD...
I'M HERE AT THE TIME YOU ASKED, MR. KANEYAMA...
WHA?! WHAT HAPPENED ?!
SOMEBODY COME QUICK! MR. KANEYAMA'S COLLAPSED!
...AND THE GEM'S BEEN STOLEN !!
WHA ?!
MURDER-ER!!
YOU! YOU DID IT! YOU TRIED TO STRANGLE ME AND STEAL THE GEM!!
ME ?!

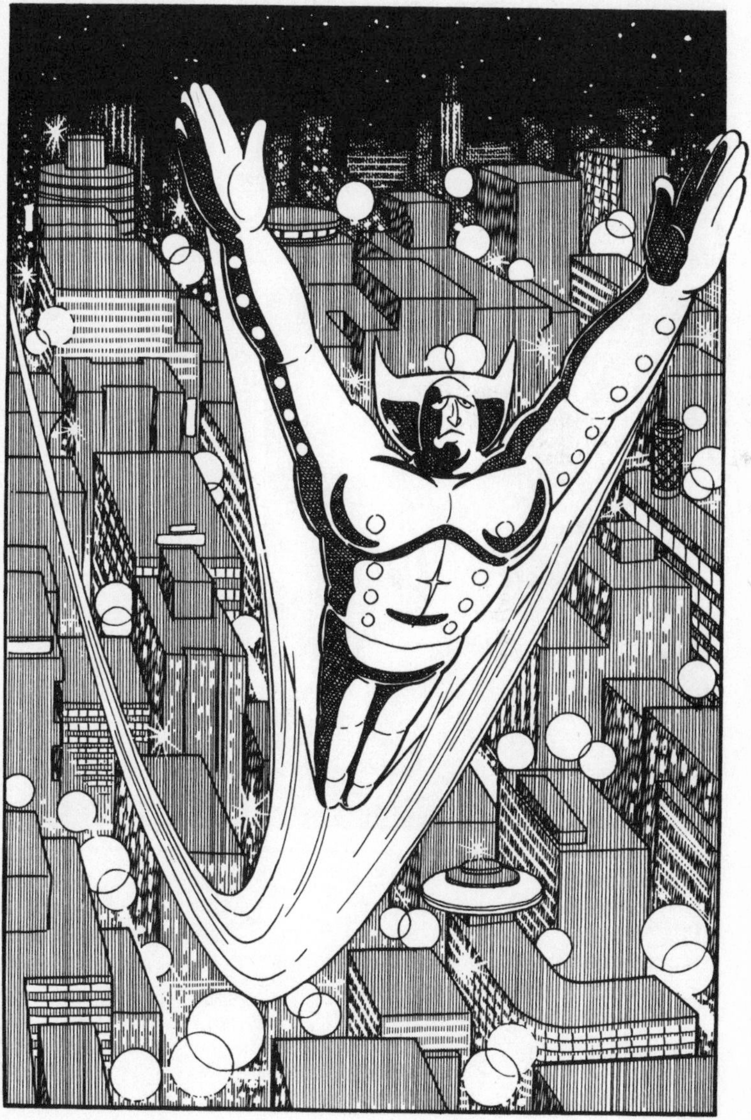

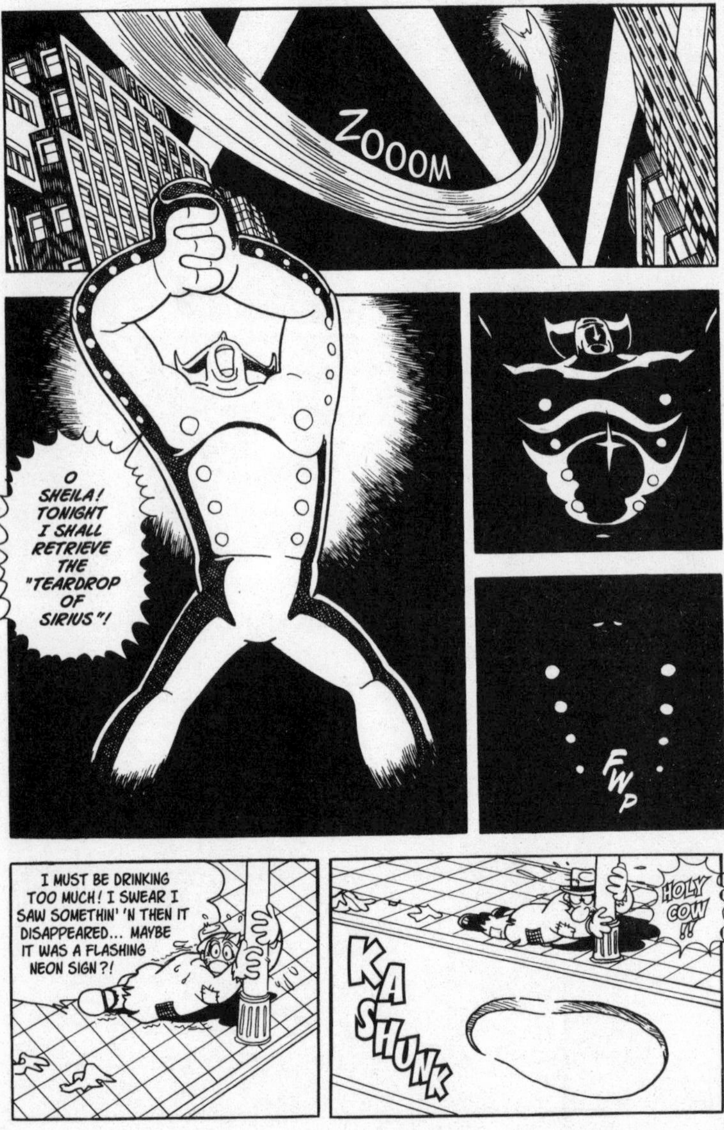
ZOOOM
O SHEILA! TONIGHT I SHALL RETRIEVE THE "TEARDROP OF SIRIUS"!
FWP
I MUST BE DRINKING TOO MUCH! I SWEAR I SAW SOMETHIN' 'N THEN IT DISAPPEARED... MAYBE IT WAS A FLASHING NEON SIGN?!
HOLY COW!!
KASHUNK

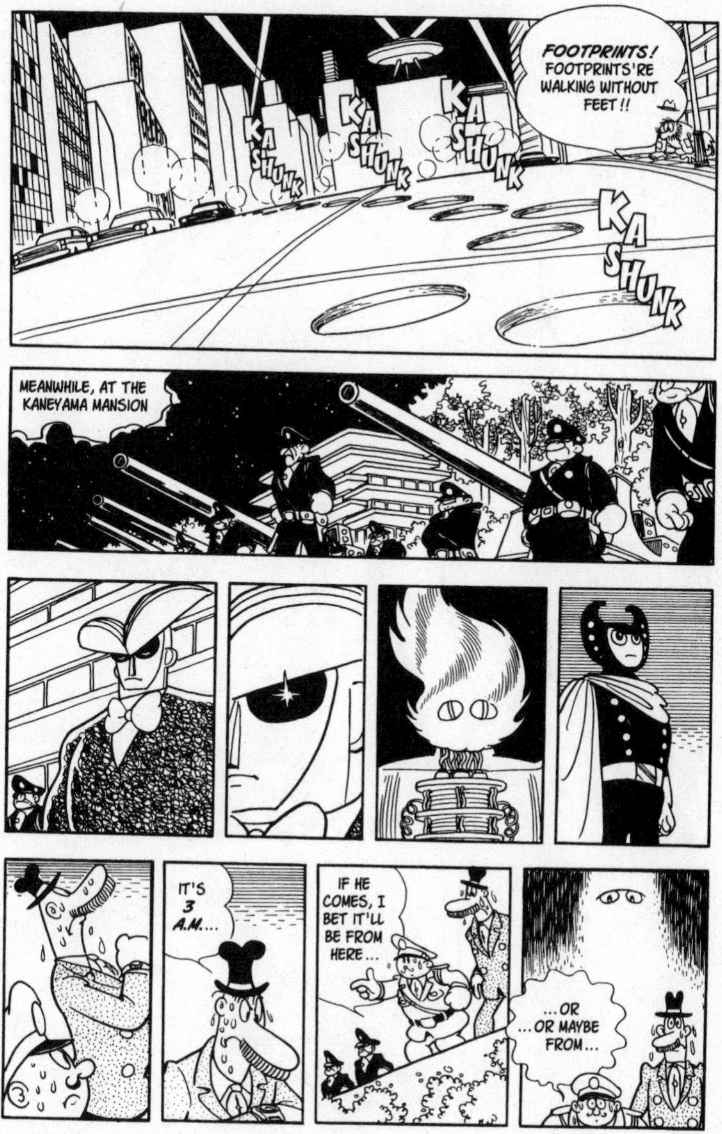
KA SHUNK
KA SHUNK
KA SHUNK
FOOTPRINTS! FOOTPRINTS'RE WALKING WITHOUT FEET!!
KA SHUNK
MEANWHILE, AT THE KANEYAMA MANSION
IT'S 3 A.M....
IF HE COMES, I BET IT'LL BE FROM HERE...
...OR ...OR MAYBE FROM...

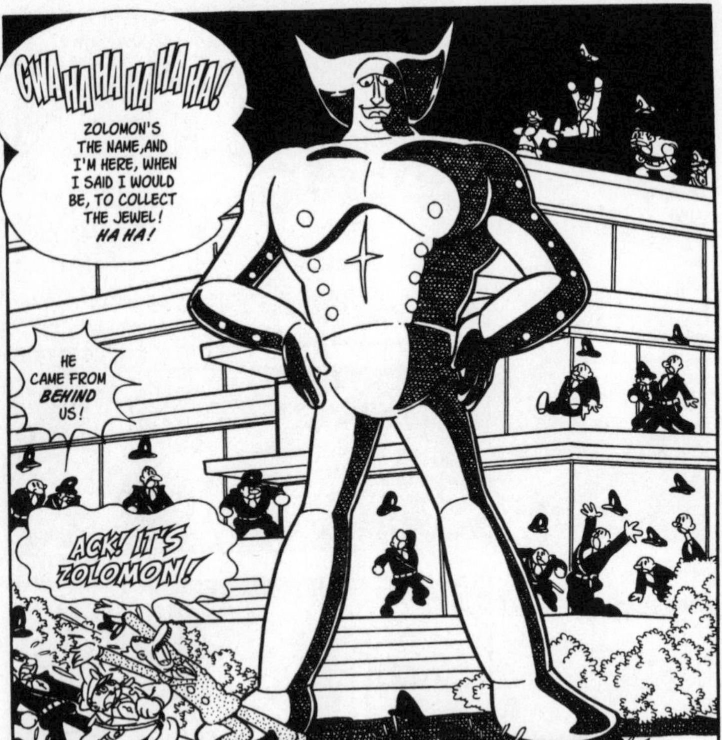
GWAHAHAHAHAHAHA!
ZOLOMON'S THE NAME, AND I'M HERE, WHEN I SAID I WOULD BE, TO COLLECT THE JEWEL! HA HA!
HE CAME FROM BEHIND US!
ACK! IT'S ZOLOMON!
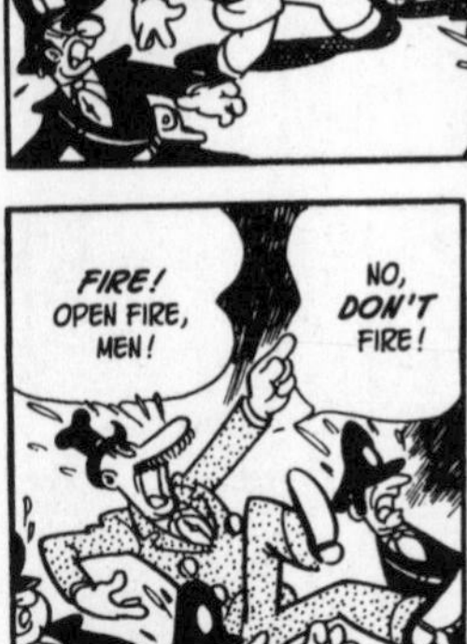
FIRE! OPEN FIRE, MEN!
NO, DON'T FIRE!
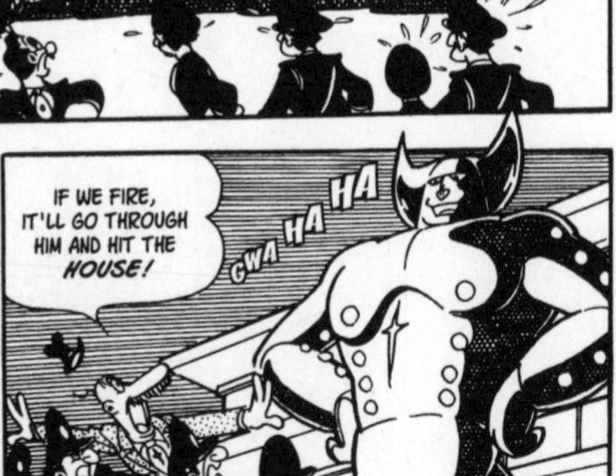
IF WE FIRE, IT'LL GO THROUGH HIM AND HIT THE HOUSE!
GWA HA HA

WH-WHADDA YOU THINK YOU'RE DOING, YOU BIG BALDY? YOU'RE TOO BIG TO EVEN *ENTER* THE HOUSE!

OWW, TAWASHI! GET YOUR HAND OFF MY HEAD!

...AN' BESIDES, YOU'D NEVER BE ABLE TO FIND THE GEM... *HA!* SERVES YOU RIGHT, YOU *USELESS LUNKHEAD!*

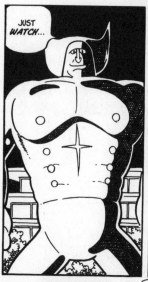

JUST *WATCH...*

WHAT THE --?!

HEY! THIS GUY CAN BE ANY SIZE HE WANTS!

STILL THINK I CAN'T ENTER THE HOUSE?

ROBO-GUARDS! NOW'S THE TIME! SHOW US WHAT YOU CAN DO!

FWOOSH

KERSHMASH

KID STUFF LIKE THAT WON'T WORK ON ME...

"KID STUFF" ...?

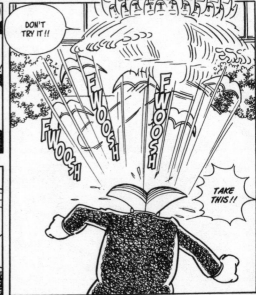

DON'T TRY IT!!

FWOOSH

FWOOSH

FWOOSH

TAKE THIS!!

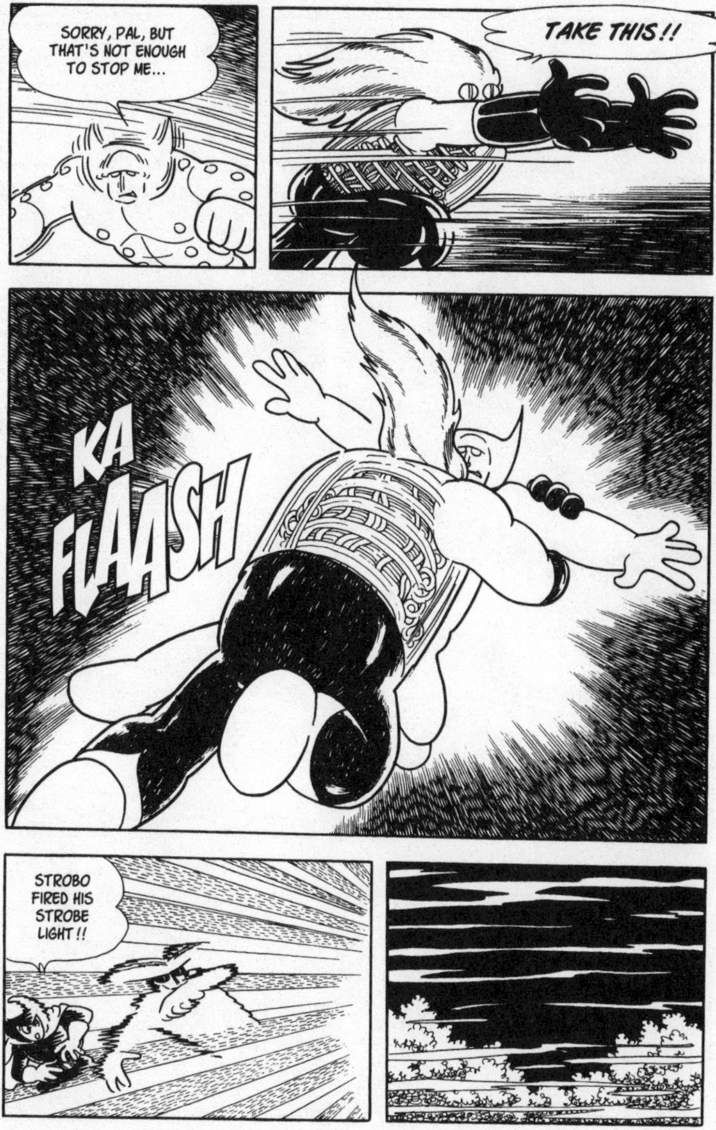
SORRY, PAL, BUT THAT'S NOT ENOUGH TO STOP ME...
TAKE THIS!!
KA FLAASH
STROBO FIRED HIS STROBE LIGHT!!

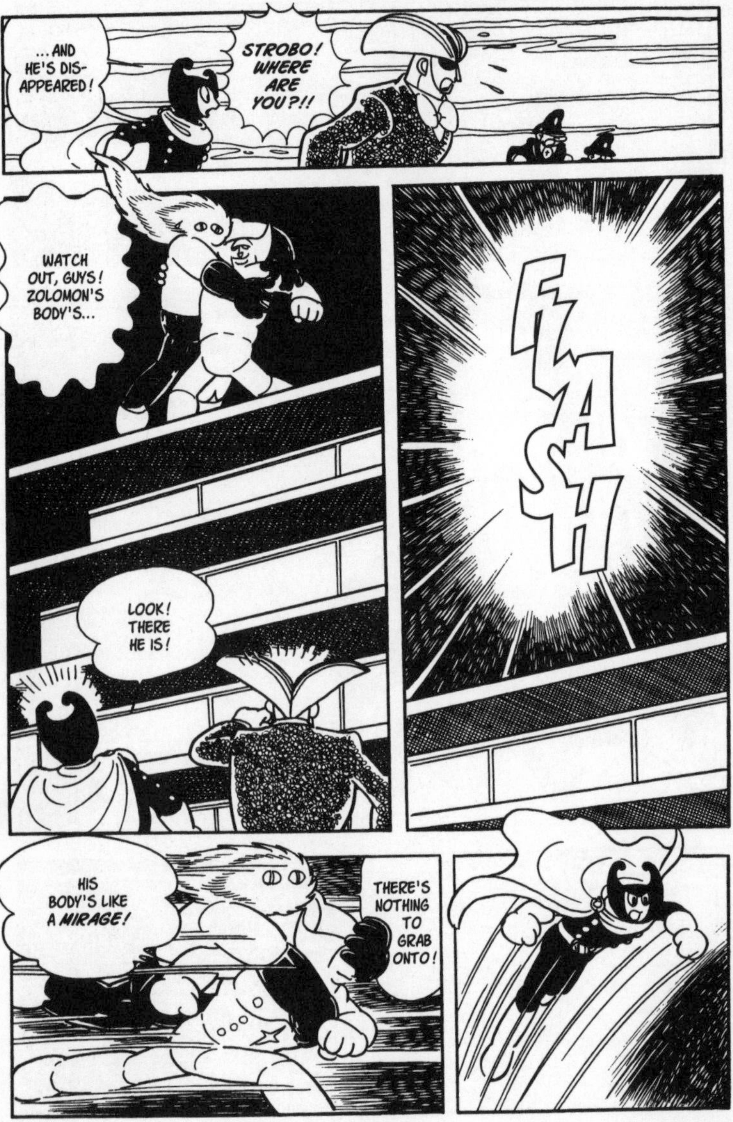
...AND HE'S DIS-APPEARED!
STROBO! WHERE ARE YOU?!!
WATCH OUT, GUYS! ZOLOMON'S BODY'S...
LOOK! THERE HE IS!
FLASH
HIS BODY'S LIKE A *MIRAGE!*
THERE'S NOTHING TO GRAB ONTO!

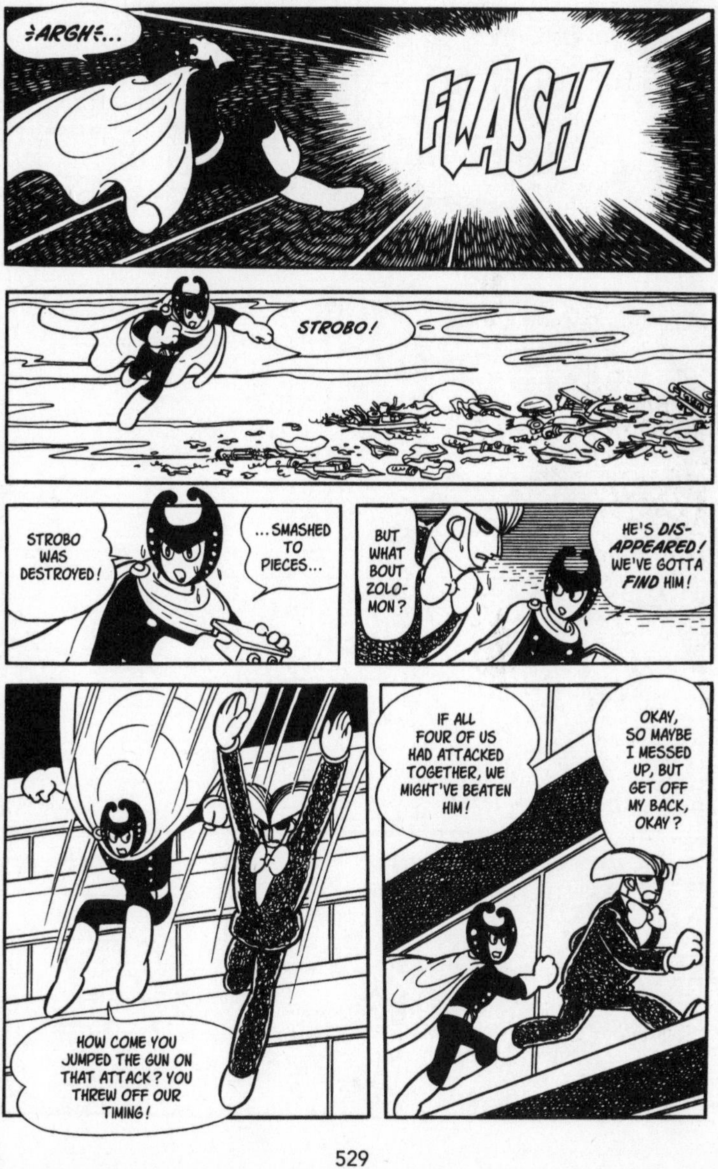

ARGH...
FLASH
STROBO!
STROBO WAS DESTROYED!
...SMASHED TO PIECES...
BUT WHAT BOUT ZOLOMON?
HE'S DISAPPEARED! WE'VE GOTTA FIND HIM!
HOW COME YOU JUMPED THE GUN ON THAT ATTACK? YOU THREW OFF OUR TIMING!
IF ALL FOUR OF US HAD ATTACKED TOGETHER, WE MIGHT'VE BEATEN HIM!
OKAY, SO MAYBE I MESSED UP, BUT GET OFF MY BACK, OKAY?

I THOUGHT I'D BE ABLE TO HANDLE HIM BY MYSELF!!

BUT WHERE'S ASTRO?!

HOW COME HE'S OFF ON HIS OWN, JUST WHEN WE NEED HIM?

GUARD THE INSIDE OF THE BUILDING! ZOLOMON MAY HAVE GOTTEN INSIDE!

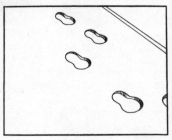

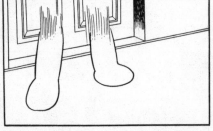

ARE YOU MR. YAMAMORI KANEYAMA? WHERE IS THE "TEARDROP OF SIRIUS"?

HAALP! DON'T KILL ME!

530

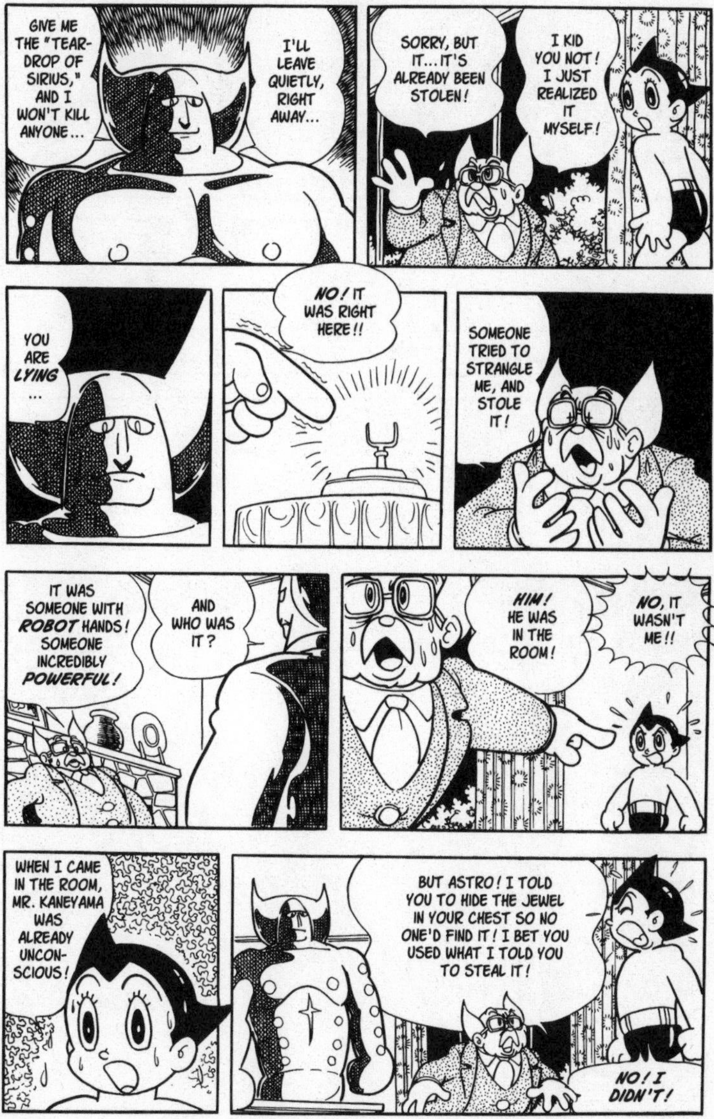
GIVE ME THE "TEAR-DROP OF SIRIUS," AND I WON'T KILL ANYONE...
I'LL LEAVE QUIETLY, RIGHT AWAY...
SORRY, BUT IT... IT'S ALREADY BEEN STOLEN!
I KID YOU NOT! I JUST REALIZED IT MYSELF!
YOU ARE LYING ...
NO! IT WAS RIGHT HERE!!
SOMEONE TRIED TO STRANGLE ME, AND STOLE IT!
IT WAS SOMEONE WITH ROBOT HANDS! SOMEONE INCREDIBLY POWERFUL!
AND WHO WAS IT?
HIM! HE WAS IN THE ROOM!
NO, IT WASN'T ME!!
WHEN I CAME IN THE ROOM, MR. KANEYAMA WAS ALREADY UNCON-SCIOUS!
BUT ASTRO! I TOLD YOU TO HIDE THE JEWEL IN YOUR CHEST SO NO ONE'D FIND IT! I BET YOU USED WHAT I TOLD YOU TO STEAL IT!
NO! I DIDN'T!

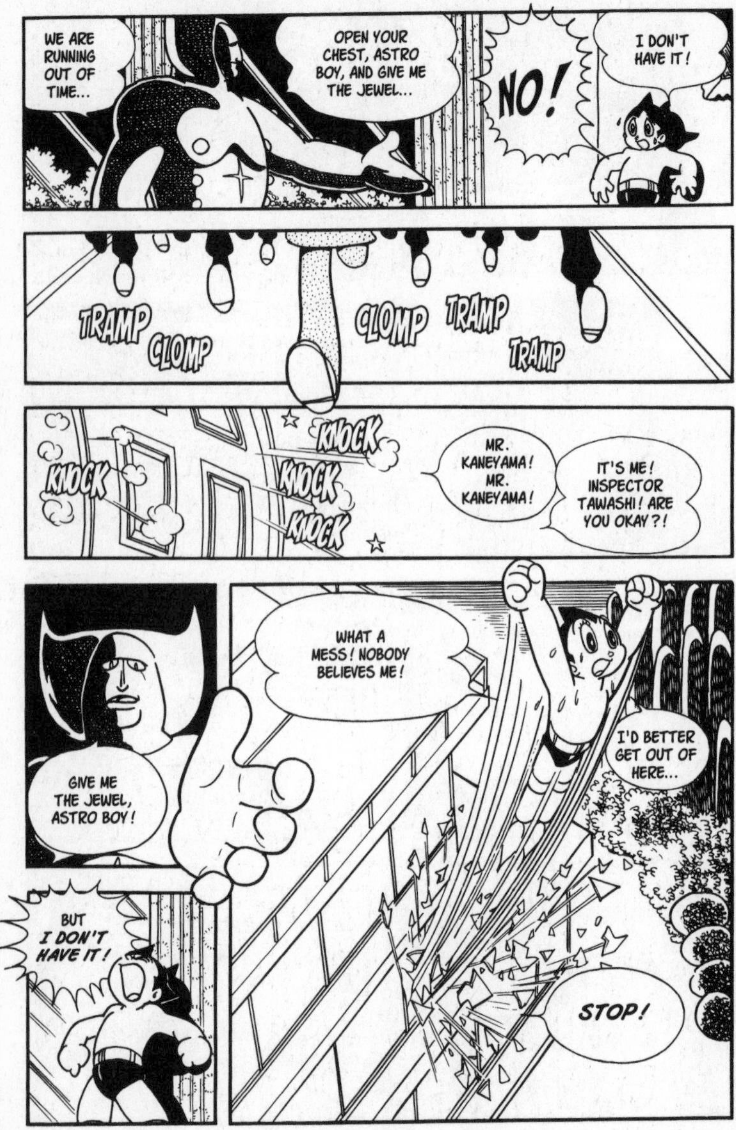
WE ARE RUNNING OUT OF TIME...
OPEN YOUR CHEST, ASTRO BOY, AND GIVE ME THE JEWEL...
NO!
I DON'T HAVE IT!
TRAMP
CLOMP
CLOMP
TRAMP
TRAMP
KNOCK
KNOCK
KNOCK
KNOCK
MR. KANEYAMA! MR. KANEYAMA!
IT'S ME! INSPECTOR TAWASHI! ARE YOU OKAY?!
GIVE ME THE JEWEL, ASTRO BOY!
BUT I DON'T HAVE IT!
WHAT A MESS! NOBODY BELIEVES ME!
I'D BETTER GET OUT OF HERE...
STOP!

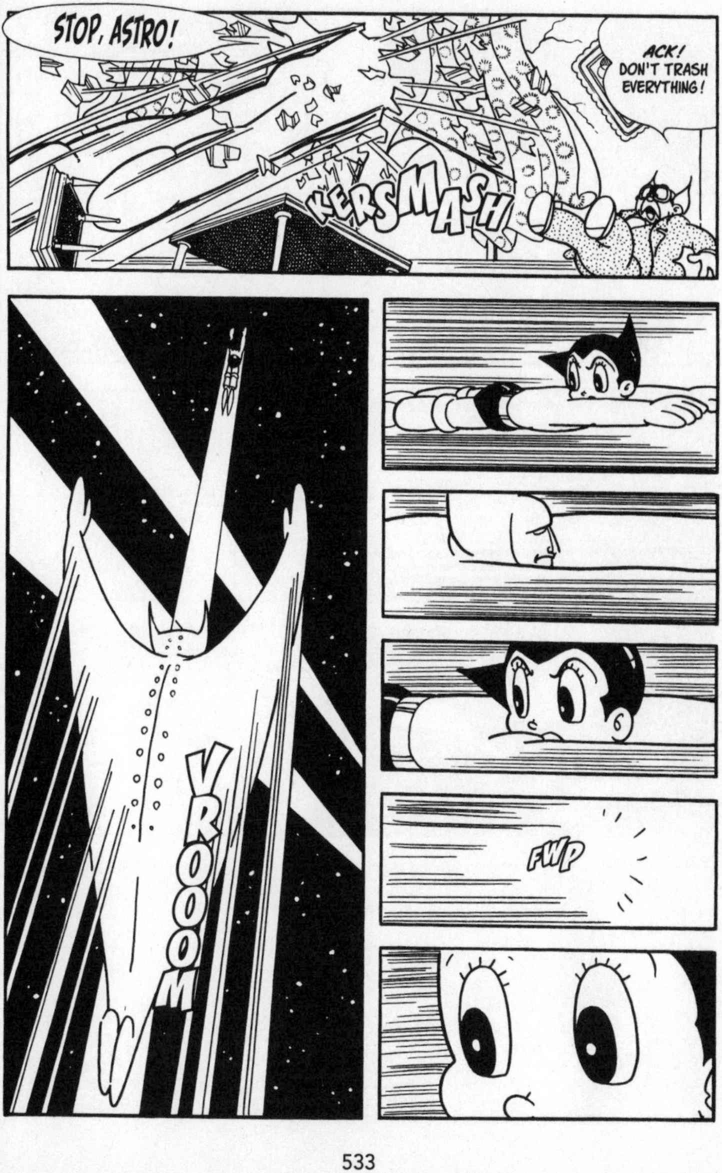
STOP, ASTRO!
ACK! DON'T TRASH EVERYTHING!
KERSMASH
VROOOM
FWP

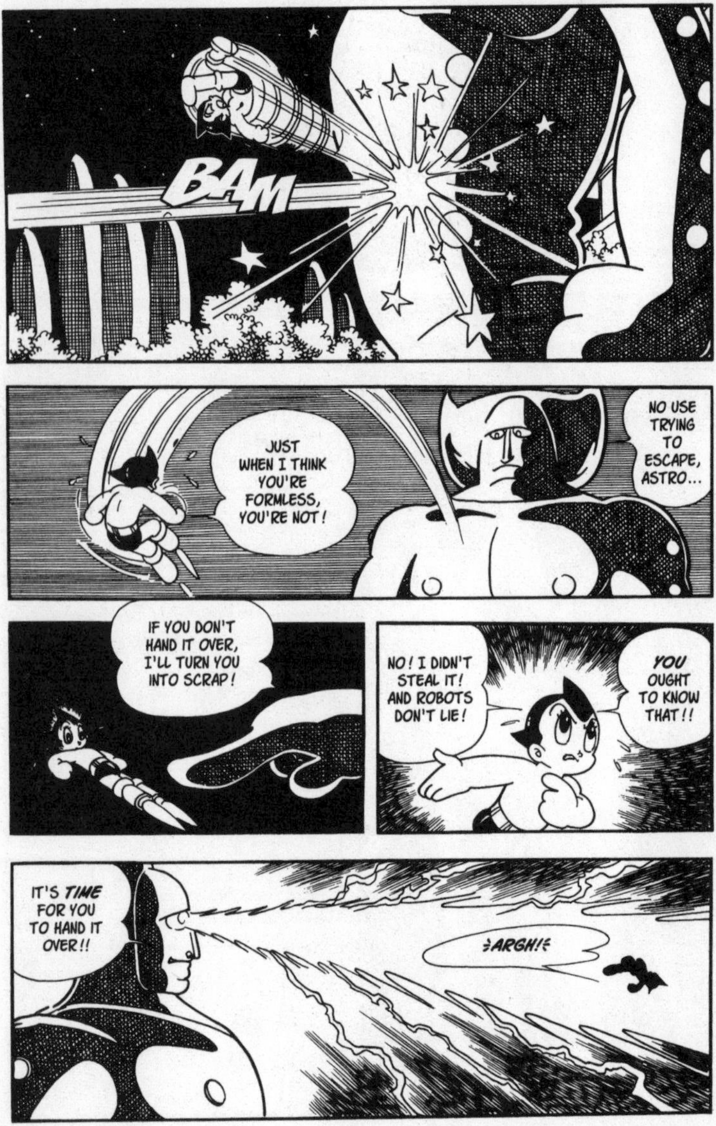
BAM
JUST WHEN I THINK YOU'RE FORMLESS, YOU'RE NOT!
NO USE TRYING TO ESCAPE, ASTRO...
IF YOU DON'T HAND IT OVER, I'LL TURN YOU INTO SCRAP!
NO! I DIDN'T STEAL IT! AND ROBOTS DON'T LIE!
YOU OUGHT TO KNOW THAT!!
IT'S TIME FOR YOU TO HAND IT OVER!!
ARGH!

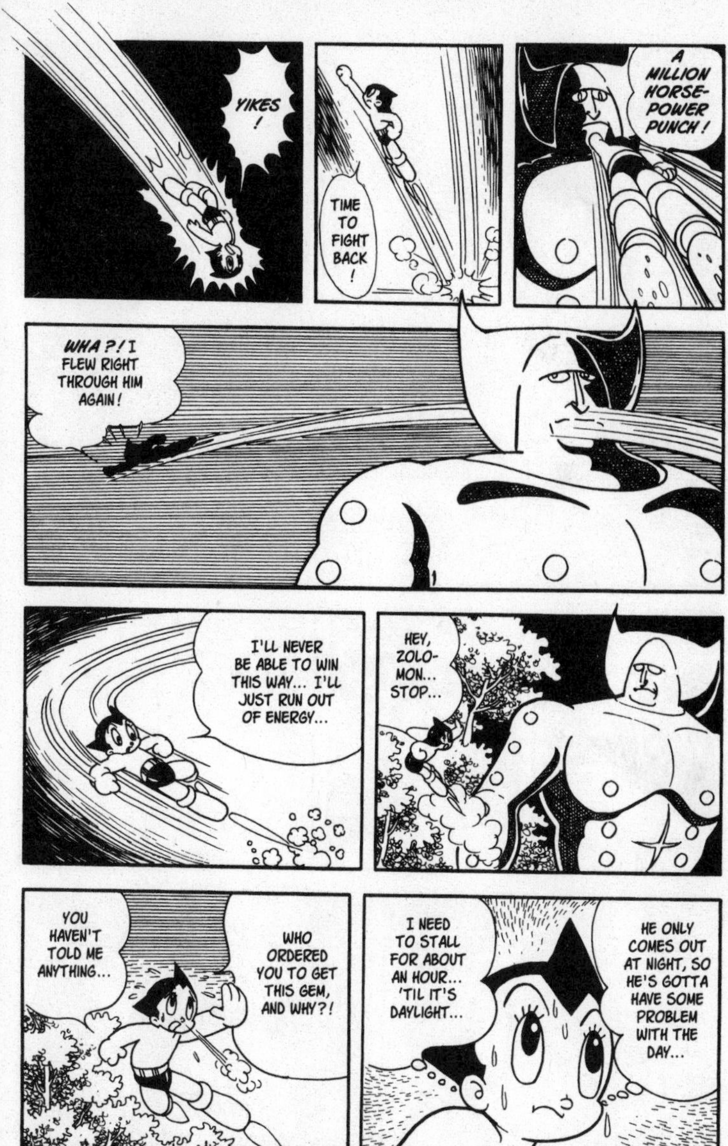
YIKES !
TIME TO FIGHT BACK !
A MILLION HORSE-POWER PUNCH !
WHA ?! I FLEW RIGHT THROUGH HIM AGAIN !
I'LL NEVER BE ABLE TO WIN THIS WAY... I'LL JUST RUN OUT OF ENERGY...
HEY, ZOLO-MON... STOP...
YOU HAVEN'T TOLD ME ANYTHING...
WHO ORDERED YOU TO GET THIS GEM, AND WHY?!
I NEED TO STALL FOR ABOUT AN HOUR... 'TIL IT'S DAYLIGHT...
HE ONLY COMES OUT AT NIGHT, SO HE'S GOTTA HAVE SOME PROBLEM WITH THE DAY...

WHO ORDERED ME?

SHEILA DID.

WHO'S SHEILA?

MY MISTRESS...

I KNOW THERE'S SOMETHING WEIRD ABOUT THAT ROCK...

I CAN HEAR VOICES COMING FROM IT... AND STRANGE SOUNDS LIKE THE OCEAN...

YOU HAVE GOOD EARS...

SO WHAT'S THE DEAL WITH THE JEWEL, ZOLOMON? IT'S NOT REALLY A JEWEL, RIGHT?

....

YOU CAN TELL ME, ZOLOMON! I WON'T TELL ANYONE ELSE!

....

C'MON, TELL ME... AS LONG AS IT'S NOT SOMETHING BAD, I'LL GIVE IT BACK TO YOU...

YOU WOULDN'T BELIEVE ME...

NO, I WILL, ZOLOMON, I WILL...

WELL, IT'S A WHOLE WORLD...

536

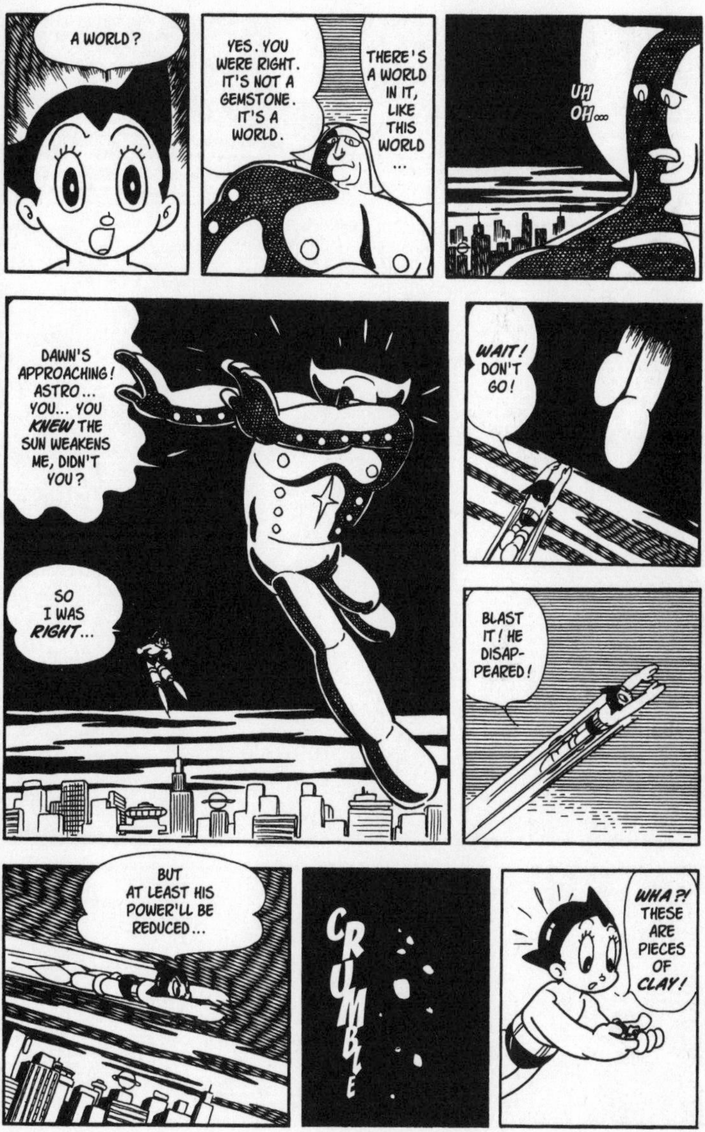
A WORLD?
YES. YOU WERE RIGHT. IT'S NOT A GEMSTONE. IT'S A WORLD.
THERE'S A WORLD IN IT, LIKE THIS WORLD...
UH OH...
DAWN'S APPROACHING! ASTRO... YOU... YOU *KNEW* THE SUN WEAKENS ME, DIDN'T YOU?
SO I WAS *RIGHT*...
WAIT! DON'T GO!
BLAST IT! HE DISAPPEARED!
BUT AT LEAST HIS POWER'LL BE REDUCED...
CRUMBLE
WHA?! THESE ARE PIECES OF *CLAY!*

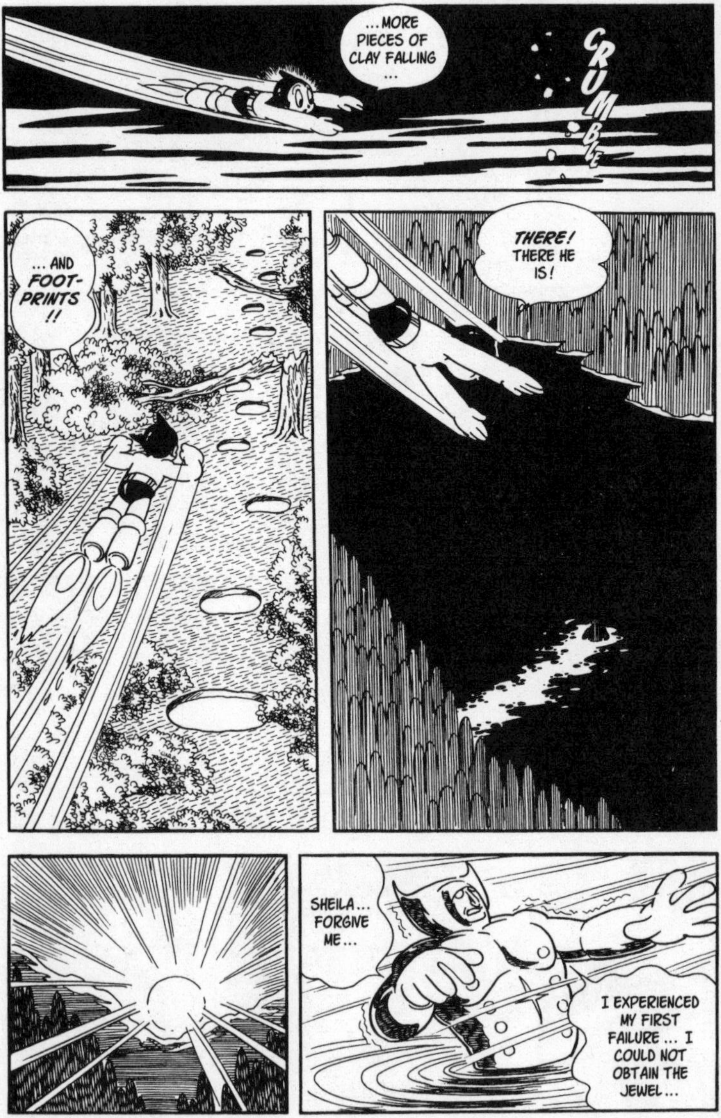
...MORE PIECES OF CLAY FALLING ...
CRUMBLE
... AND FOOT-PRINTS !!
THERE! THERE HE IS!
SHEILA... FORGIVE ME...
I EXPERIENCED MY FIRST FAILURE ... I COULD NOT OBTAIN THE JEWEL...

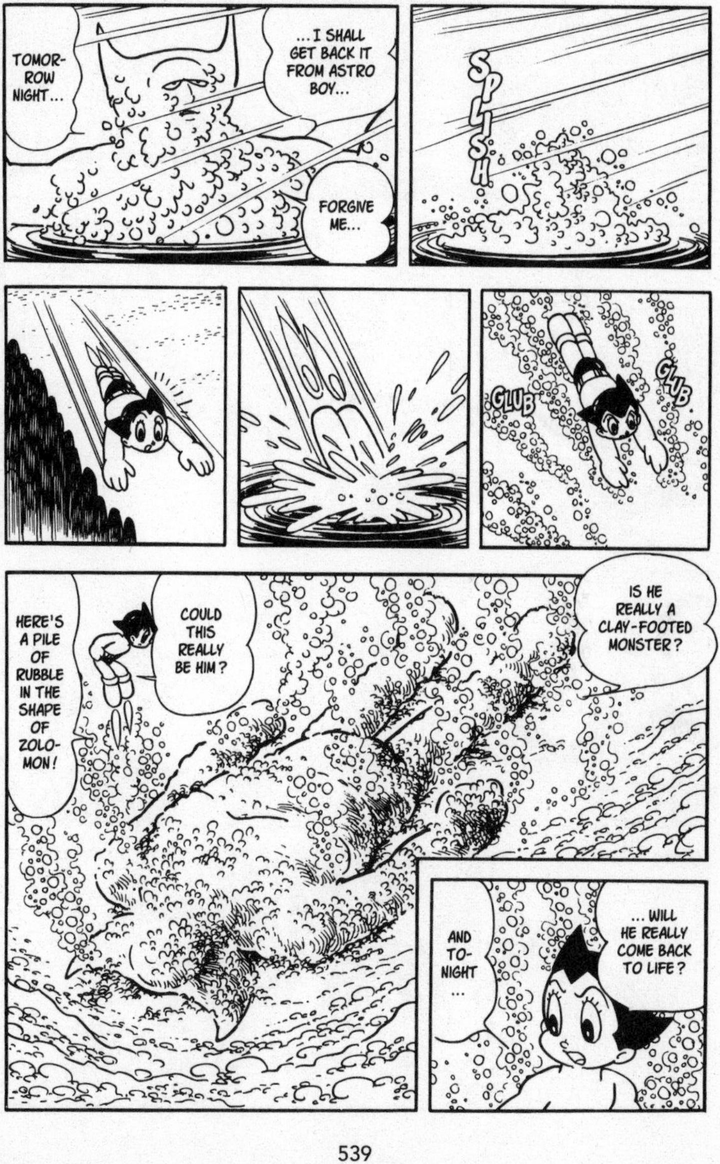
TOMOR-ROW NIGHT...
...I SHALL GET BACK IT FROM ASTRO BOY...
FORGIVE ME...
SPLISH
GLUB
GLUB
HERE'S A PILE OF RUBBLE IN THE SHAPE OF ZOLO-MON!
COULD THIS REALLY BE HIM?
IS HE REALLY A CLAY-FOOTED MONSTER?
AND TO-NIGHT ...
...WILL HE REALLY COME BACK TO LIFE?

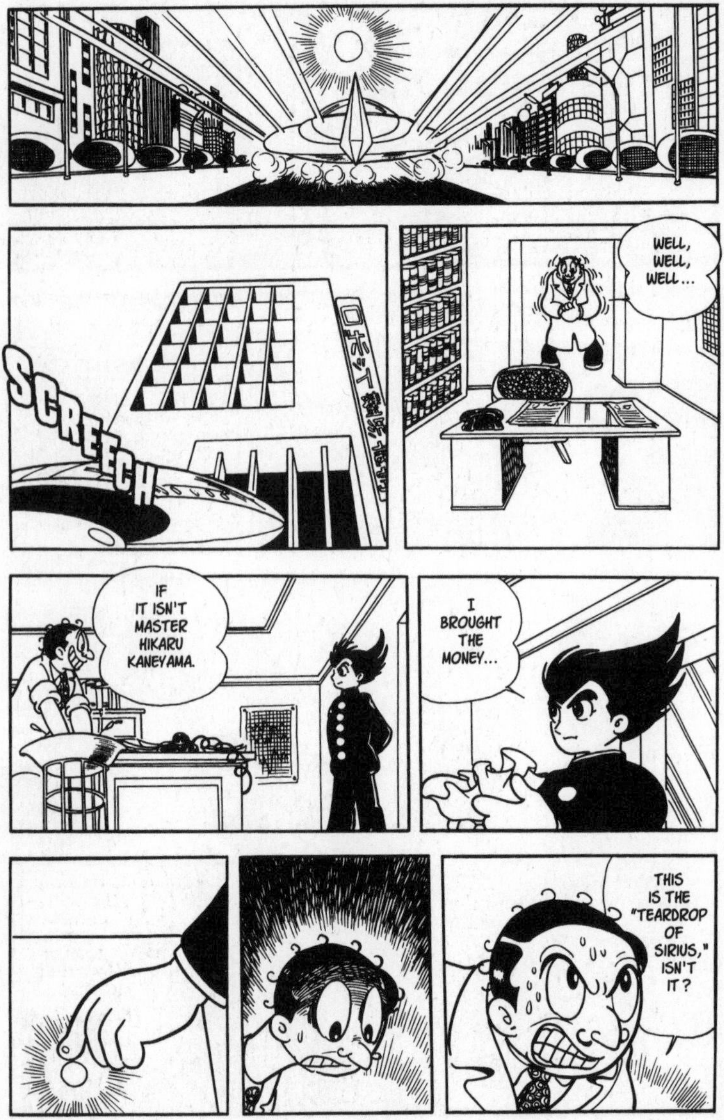
SCREECH
WELL, WELL, WELL...
IF IT ISN'T MASTER HIKARU KANEYAMA.
I BROUGHT THE MONEY...
THIS IS THE "TEARDROP OF SIRIUS," ISN'T IT?

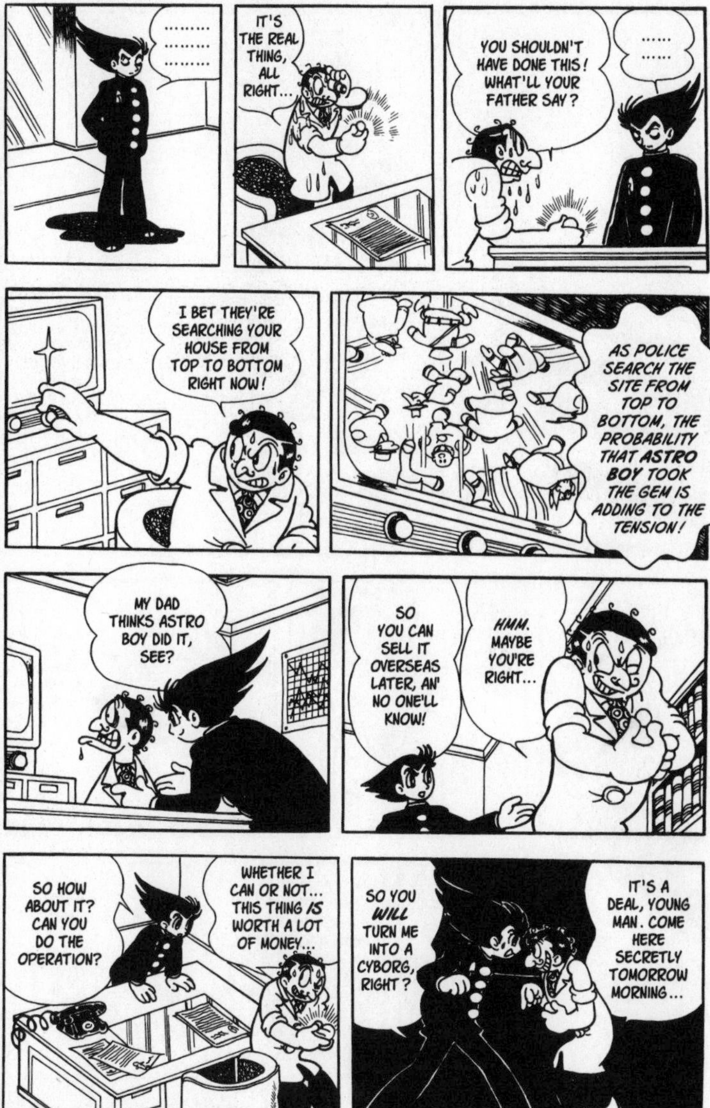

....
....
....
IT'S THE REAL THING, ALL RIGHT...
YOU SHOULDN'T HAVE DONE THIS! WHAT'LL YOUR FATHER SAY?
......
......
I BET THEY'RE SEARCHING YOUR HOUSE FROM TOP TO BOTTOM RIGHT NOW!
AS POLICE SEARCH THE SITE FROM TOP TO BOTTOM, THE PROBABILITY THAT ASTRO BOY TOOK THE GEM IS ADDING TO THE TENSION!
MY DAD THINKS ASTRO BOY DID IT, SEE?
SO YOU CAN SELL IT OVERSEAS LATER, AN' NO ONE'LL KNOW!
HMM. MAYBE YOU'RE RIGHT...
SO HOW ABOUT IT? CAN YOU DO THE OPERATION?
WHETHER I CAN OR NOT... THIS THING IS WORTH A LOT OF MONEY...
SO YOU WILL TURN ME INTO A CYBORG, RIGHT?
IT'S A DEAL, YOUNG MAN. COME HERE SECRETLY TOMORROW MORNING...

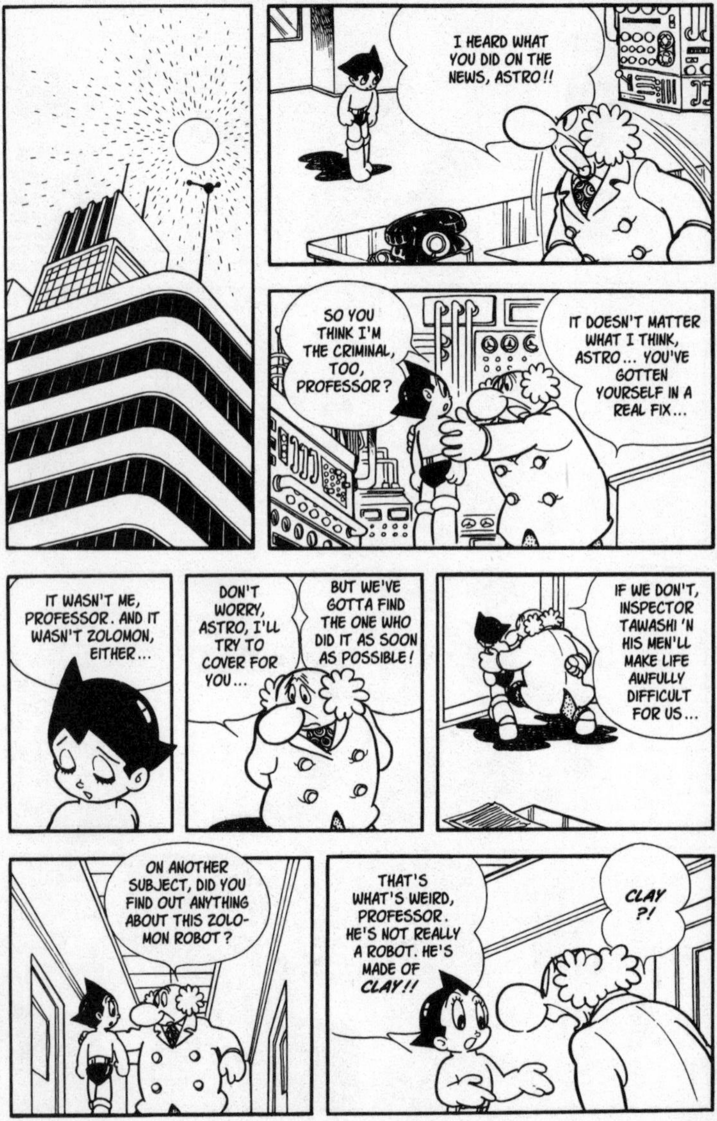
I HEARD WHAT YOU DID ON THE NEWS, ASTRO!!
SO YOU THINK I'M THE CRIMINAL, TOO, PROFESSOR?
IT DOESN'T MATTER WHAT I THINK, ASTRO... YOU'VE GOTTEN YOURSELF IN A REAL FIX...
IT WASN'T ME, PROFESSOR. AND IT WASN'T ZOLOMON, EITHER...
DON'T WORRY, ASTRO, I'LL TRY TO COVER FOR YOU...
BUT WE'VE GOTTA FIND THE ONE WHO DID IT AS SOON AS POSSIBLE!
IF WE DON'T, INSPECTOR TAWASHI 'N HIS MEN'LL MAKE LIFE AWFULLY DIFFICULT FOR US...
ON ANOTHER SUBJECT, DID YOU FIND OUT ANYTHING ABOUT THIS ZOLO-MON ROBOT?
THAT'S WHAT'S WEIRD, PROFESSOR. HE'S NOT REALLY A ROBOT. HE'S MADE OF CLAY!!
CLAY?!

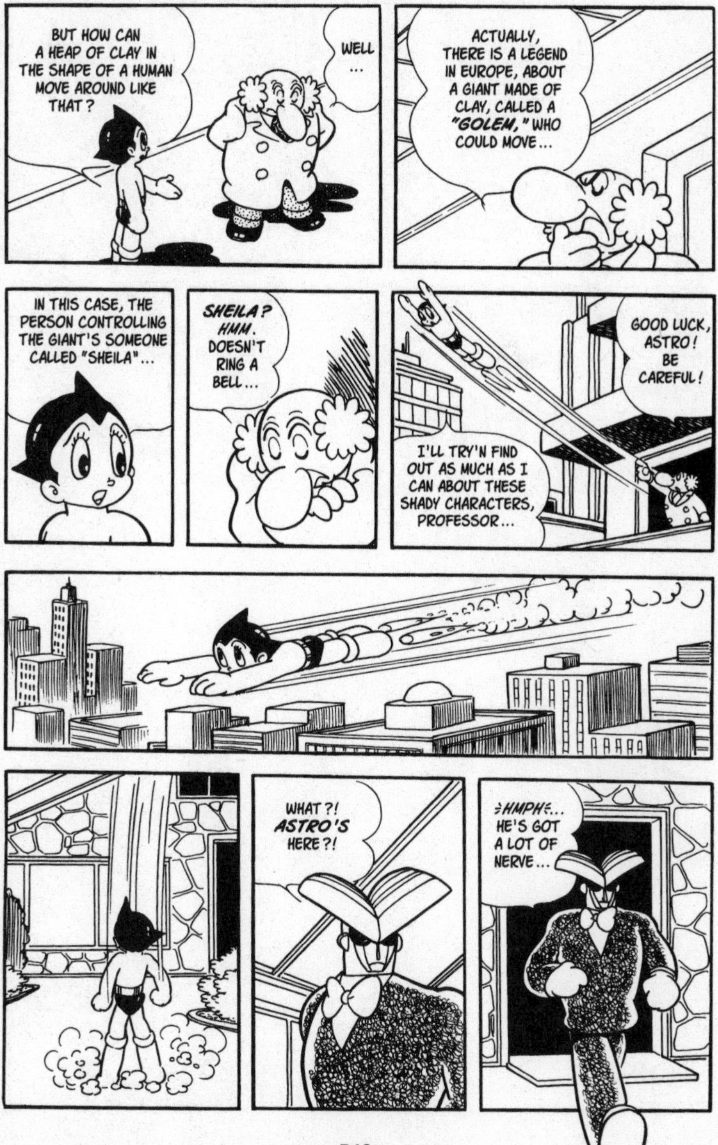
BUT HOW CAN A HEAP OF CLAY IN THE SHAPE OF A HUMAN MOVE AROUND LIKE THAT?
WELL ...
ACTUALLY, THERE IS A LEGEND IN EUROPE, ABOUT A GIANT MADE OF CLAY, CALLED A "GOLEM," WHO COULD MOVE...
IN THIS CASE, THE PERSON CONTROLLING THE GIANT'S SOMEONE CALLED "SHEILA"...
SHEILA? HMM. DOESN'T RING A BELL...
GOOD LUCK, ASTRO! BE CAREFUL!
I'LL TRY'N FIND OUT AS MUCH AS I CAN ABOUT THESE SHADY CHARACTERS, PROFESSOR...
WHAT?! ASTRO'S HERE?!
HMPH... HE'S GOT A LOT OF NERVE...

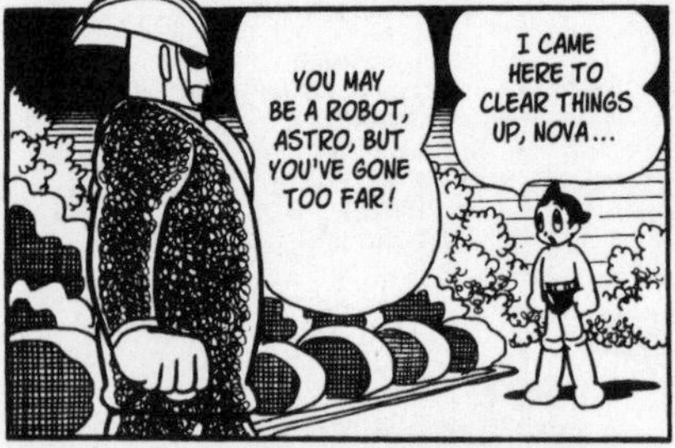
YOU MAY BE A ROBOT, ASTRO, BUT YOU'VE GONE TOO FAR!
I CAME HERE TO CLEAR THINGS UP, NOVA...
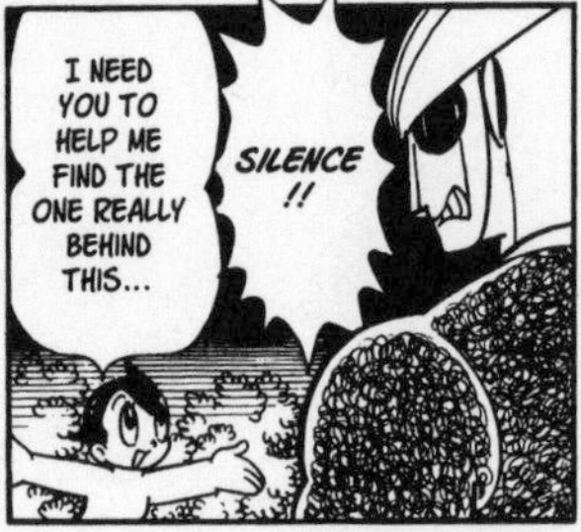
I NEED YOU TO HELP ME FIND THE ONE REALLY BEHIND THIS...
SILENCE!!
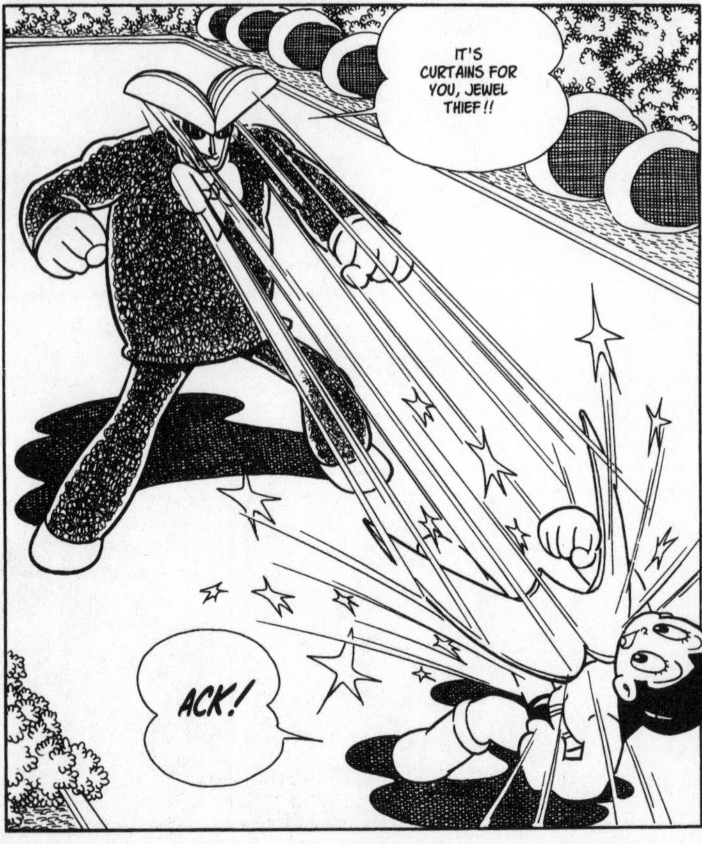
IT'S CURTAINS FOR YOU, JEWEL THIEF!!
ACK!

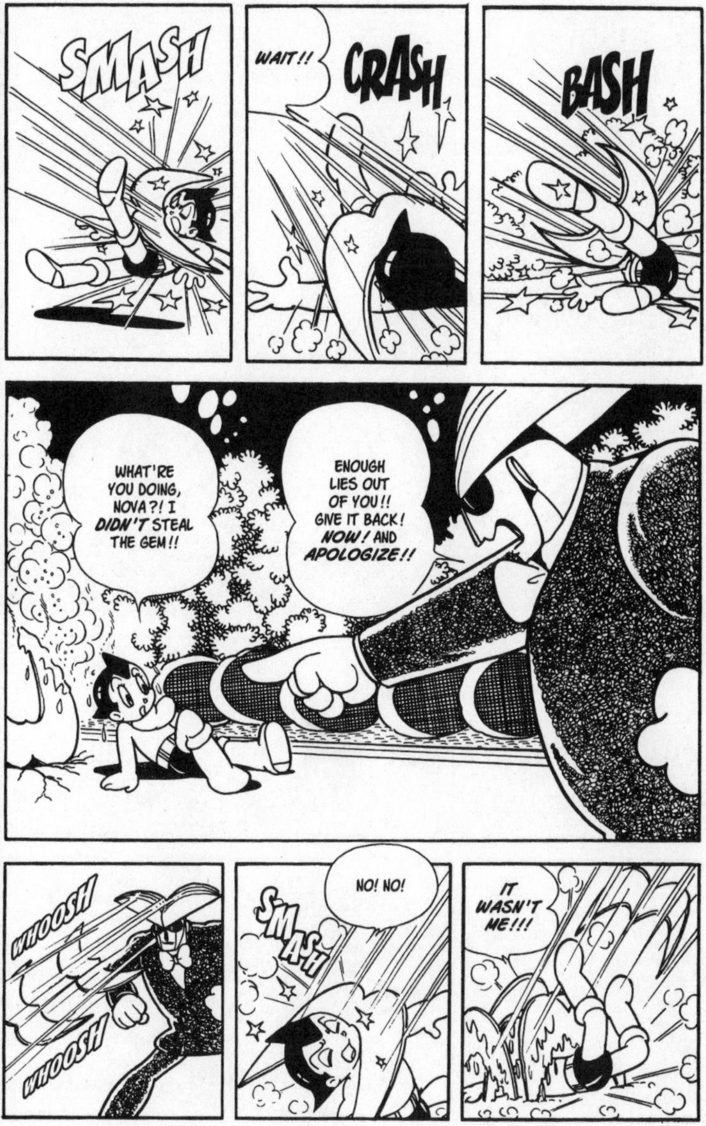
SMASH
WAIT!!
CRASH
BASH
WHAT'RE YOU DOING, NOVA?! I DIDN'T STEAL THE GEM!!
ENOUGH LIES OUT OF YOU!! GIVE IT BACK! NOW! AND APOLOGIZE!!
WHOOSH
WHOOSH
SMASH
NO! NO!
IT WASN'T ME!!!

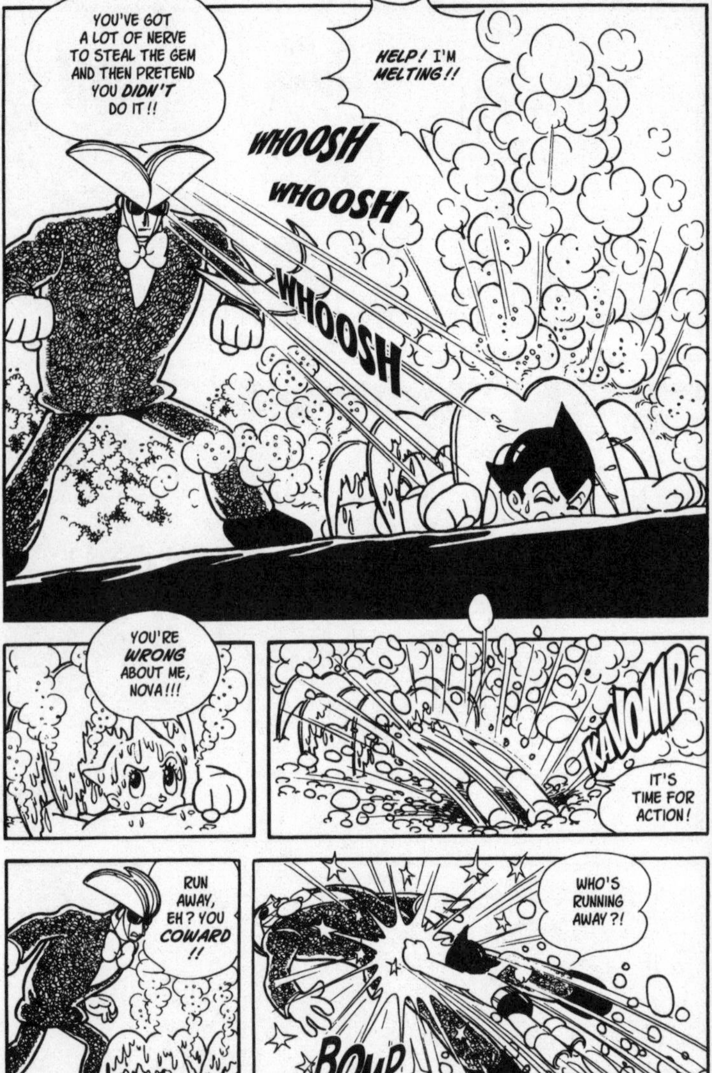
YOU'VE GOT A LOT OF NERVE TO STEAL THE GEM AND THEN PRETEND YOU DIDN'T DO IT!!
HELP! I'M MELTING!!
WHOOSH
WHOOSH
WHOOSH
YOU'RE WRONG ABOUT ME, NOVA!!!
KAVOMP
IT'S TIME FOR ACTION!
RUN AWAY, EH? YOU COWARD!!
WHO'S RUNNING AWAY?!
BOMP

ZIP
ZIP

KAPOW

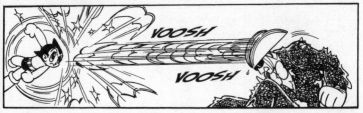

VOOSH

VOOSH

TAKE THIS!

GRUNCH

OW OW OW!

SORRY, BUT YOU JUST DON'T GET IT, DO YOU!?

≷ACK≷ ≷ACK≷ ≷OW≷

I CAME HERE TO ASK FOR YOUR HELP! BUT AFTER THIS, *FORGET IT!!*

ASK PROFESSOR OCHANOMIZU AT THE MINISTRY OF SCIENCE TO REPAIR YOU!!

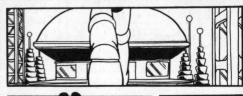

WHAT THE--?!

IT'S ME, L-44... ASTRO!

I NEED TO ASK YOU A FAVOR. IT'S ABOUT THE JEWEL THIEF!

BUT I THOUGHT IT WAS *YOU!*

REALLY? SO YOU THOUGHT SO, TOO?

OPEN YOUR CHEST, ASTRO BOY!

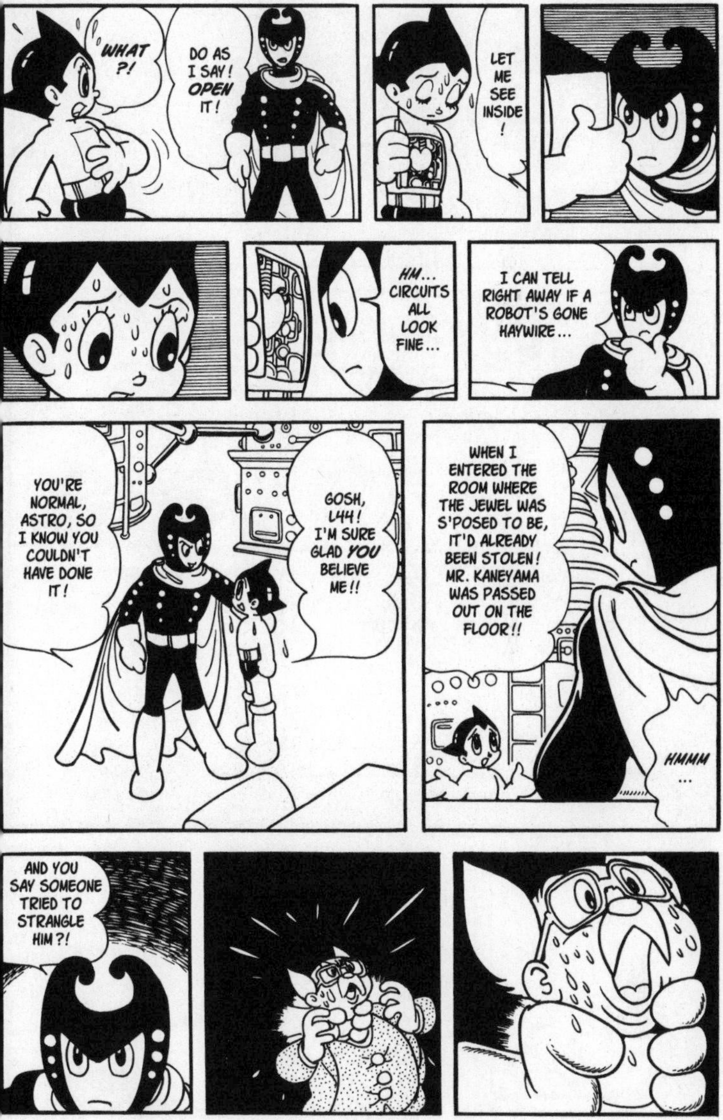
WHAT ?!
DO AS I SAY! OPEN IT!
LET ME SEE INSIDE !
HM... CIRCUITS ALL LOOK FINE...
I CAN TELL RIGHT AWAY IF A ROBOT'S GONE HAYWIRE...
YOU'RE NORMAL, ASTRO, SO I KNOW YOU COULDN'T HAVE DONE IT!
GOSH, L44! I'M SURE GLAD YOU BELIEVE ME!!
WHEN I ENTERED THE ROOM WHERE THE JEWEL WAS S'POSED TO BE, IT'D ALREADY BEEN STOLEN! MR. KANEYAMA WAS PASSED OUT ON THE FLOOR!!
HMMM...
AND YOU SAY SOMEONE TRIED TO STRANGLE HIM?!

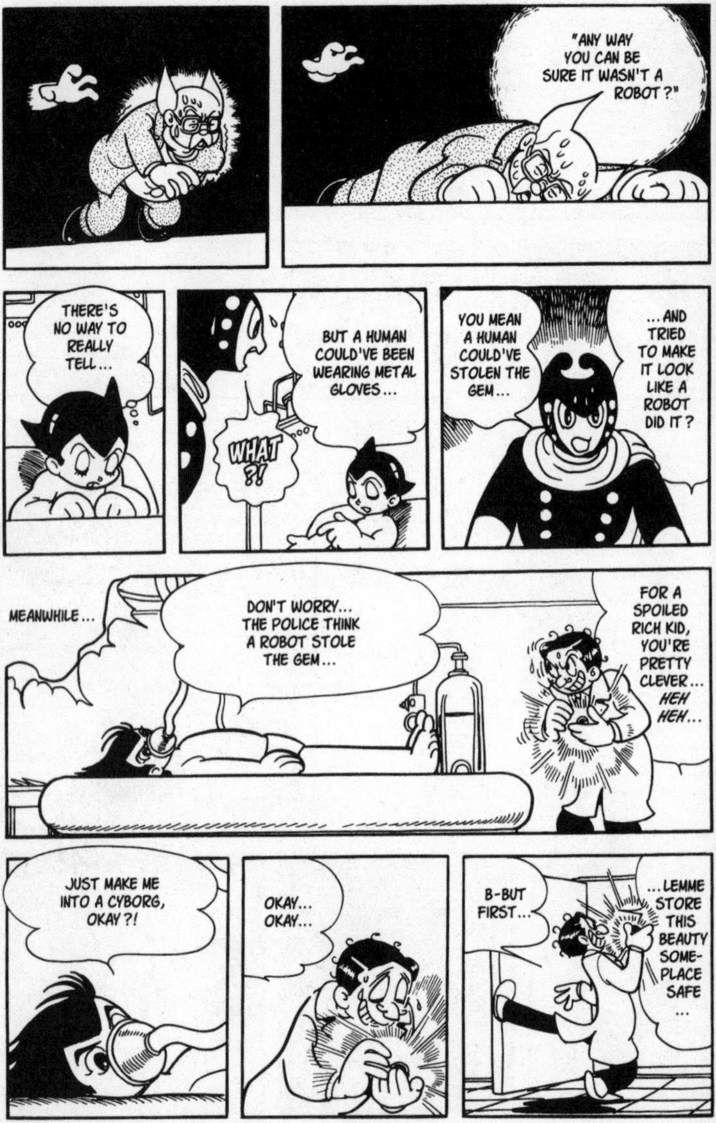
"ANY WAY YOU CAN BE SURE IT WASN'T A ROBOT?"
THERE'S NO WAY TO REALLY TELL...
BUT A HUMAN COULD'VE BEEN WEARING METAL GLOVES...
WHAT ?!
YOU MEAN A HUMAN COULD'VE STOLEN THE GEM...
...AND TRIED TO MAKE IT LOOK LIKE A ROBOT DID IT?
MEANWHILE...
DON'T WORRY... THE POLICE THINK A ROBOT STOLE THE GEM...
FOR A SPOILED RICH KID, YOU'RE PRETTY CLEVER... HEH HEH...
JUST MAKE ME INTO A CYBORG, OKAY?!
OKAY... OKAY...
B-BUT FIRST...
...LEMME STORE THIS BEAUTY SOME-PLACE SAFE ...

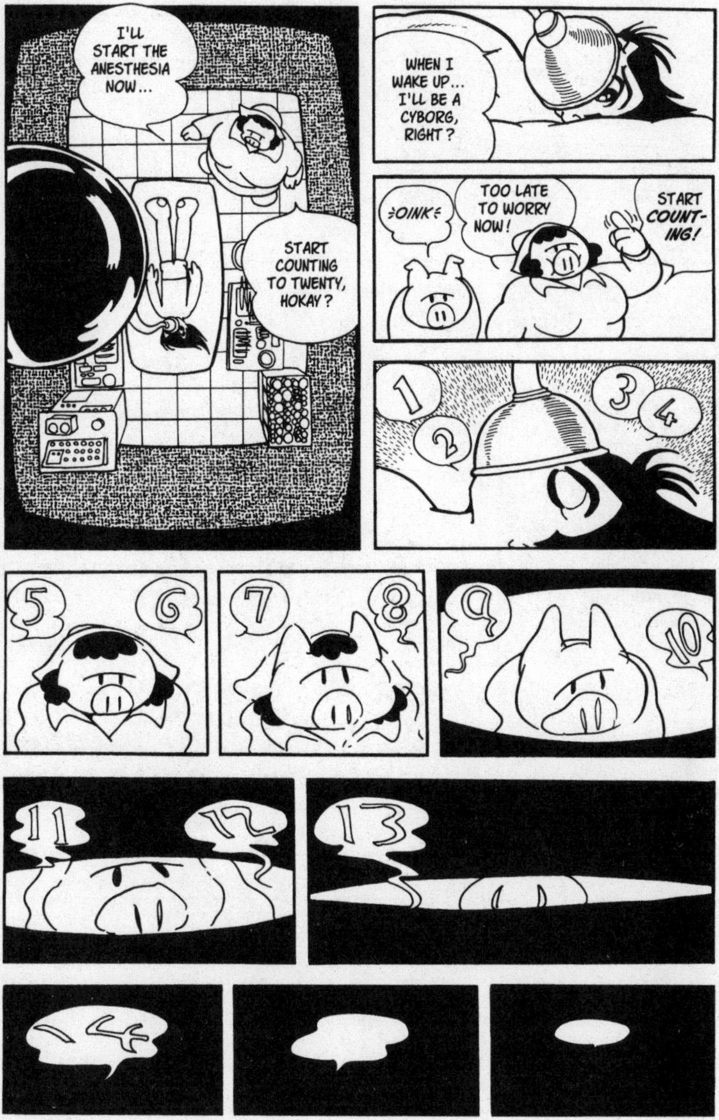
I'LL START THE ANESTHESIA NOW...
START COUNTING TO TWENTY, HOKAY?
WHEN I WAKE UP... I'LL BE A CYBORG, RIGHT?
OINK
TOO LATE TO WORRY NOW!
START COUNTING!
1
2
3
4
5
6
7
8
9
10
11
12
13
14

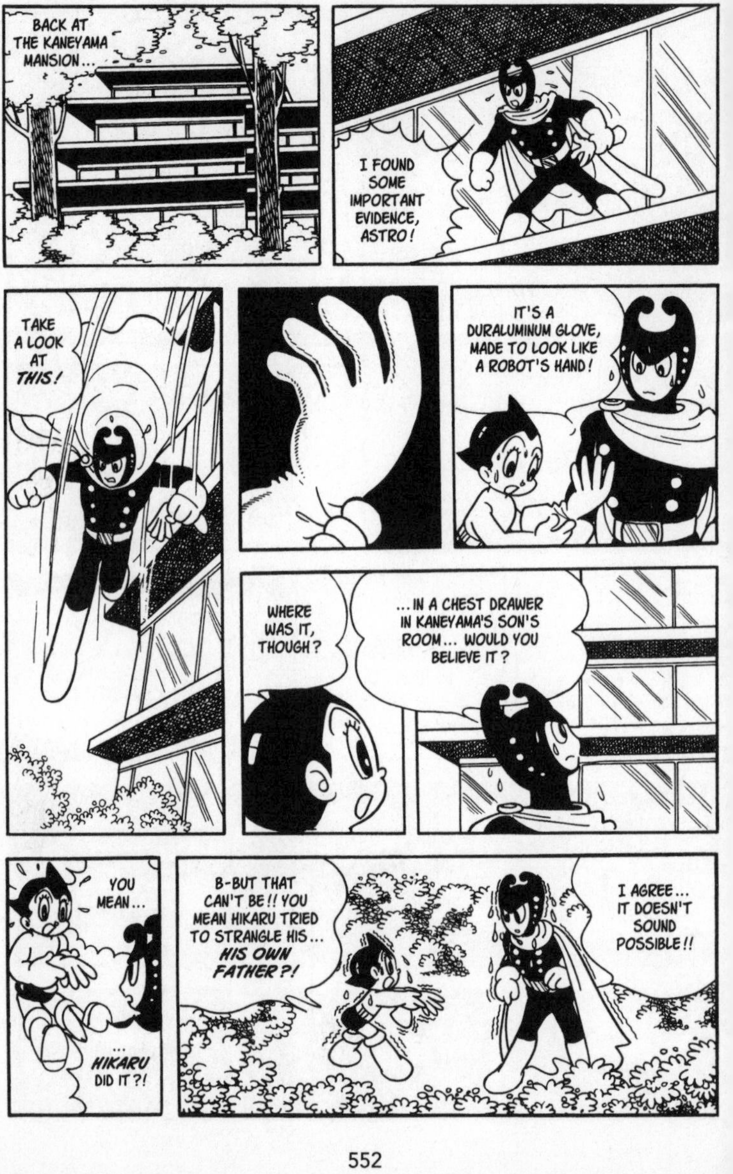
BACK AT THE KANEYAMA MANSION...
I FOUND SOME IMPORTANT EVIDENCE, ASTRO!
TAKE A LOOK AT *THIS!*
IT'S A DURALUMINUM GLOVE, MADE TO LOOK LIKE A ROBOT'S HAND!
WHERE WAS IT, THOUGH?
...IN A CHEST DRAWER IN KANEYAMA'S SON'S ROOM... WOULD YOU BELIEVE IT?
YOU MEAN...
... *HIKARU* DID IT?!
B-BUT THAT CAN'T BE!! YOU MEAN HIKARU TRIED TO STRANGLE HIS... *HIS OWN FATHER?!*
I AGREE... IT DOESN'T SOUND POSSIBLE!!

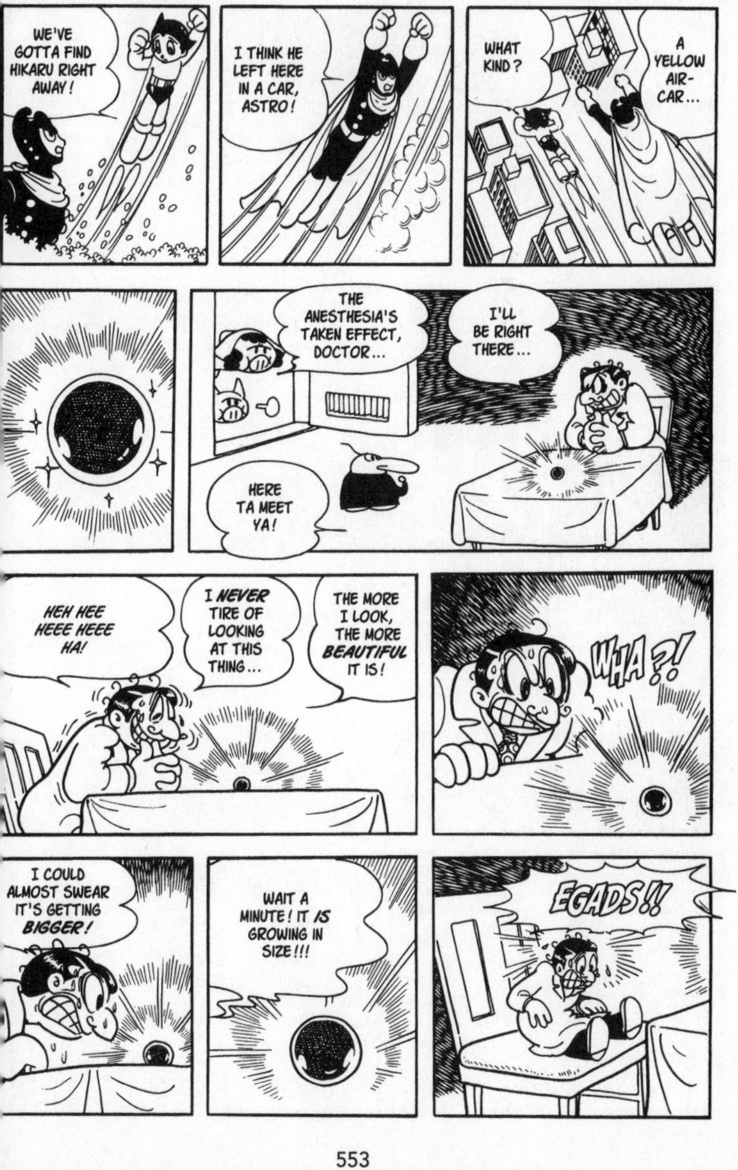
WE'VE GOTTA FIND HIKARU RIGHT AWAY!
I THINK HE LEFT HERE IN A CAR, ASTRO!
WHAT KIND?
A YELLOW AIR-CAR...
THE ANESTHESIA'S TAKEN EFFECT, DOCTOR...
I'LL BE RIGHT THERE...
HERE TA MEET YA!
HEH HEE HEEE HEEE HA!
I NEVER TIRE OF LOOKING AT THIS THING...
THE MORE I LOOK, THE MORE BEAUTIFUL IT IS!
WHA?!
I COULD ALMOST SWEAR IT'S GETTING BIGGER!
WAIT A MINUTE! IT IS GROWING IN SIZE!!!
EGADS!!

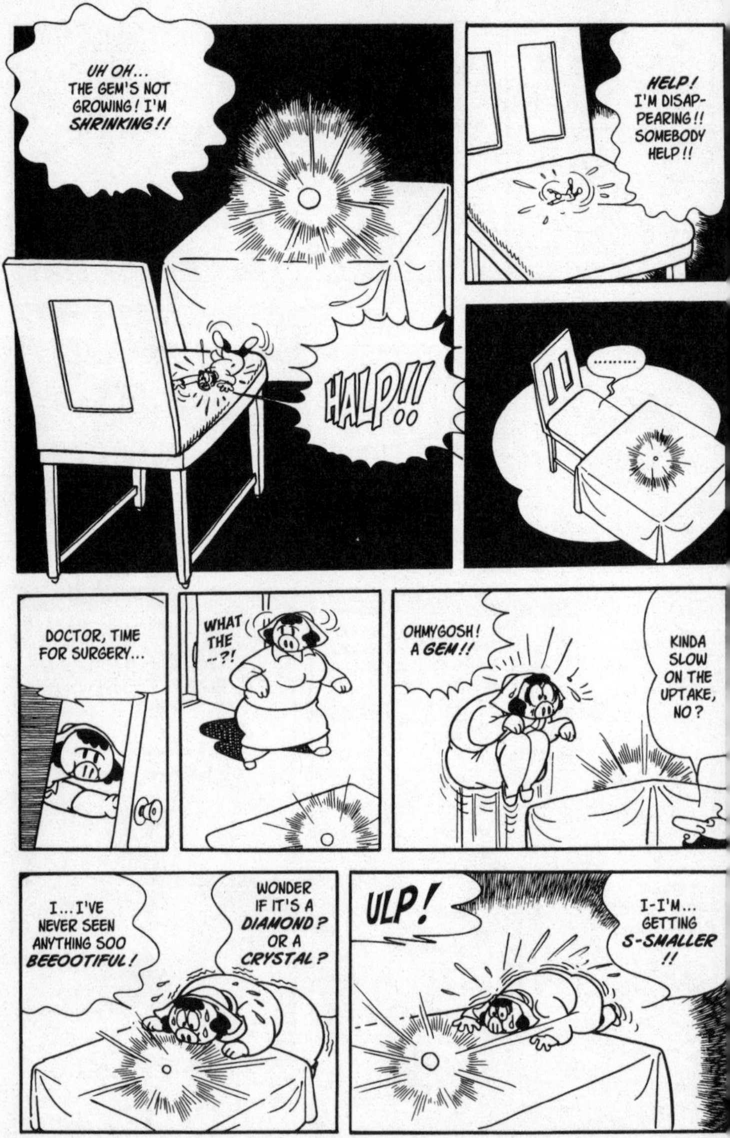
UH OH... THE GEM'S NOT GROWING! I'M SHRINKING!!
HALP!!
HELP! I'M DISAP-PEARING!! SOMEBODY HELP!!
....
DOCTOR, TIME FOR SURGERY...
WHAT THE --?!
OHMYGOSH! A GEM!!
KINDA SLOW ON THE UPTAKE, NO?
I...I'VE NEVER SEEN ANYTHING SOO BEEOOTIFUL!
WONDER IF IT'S A DIAMOND? OR A CRYSTAL?
ULP!
I-I'M... GETTING S-SMALLER!!

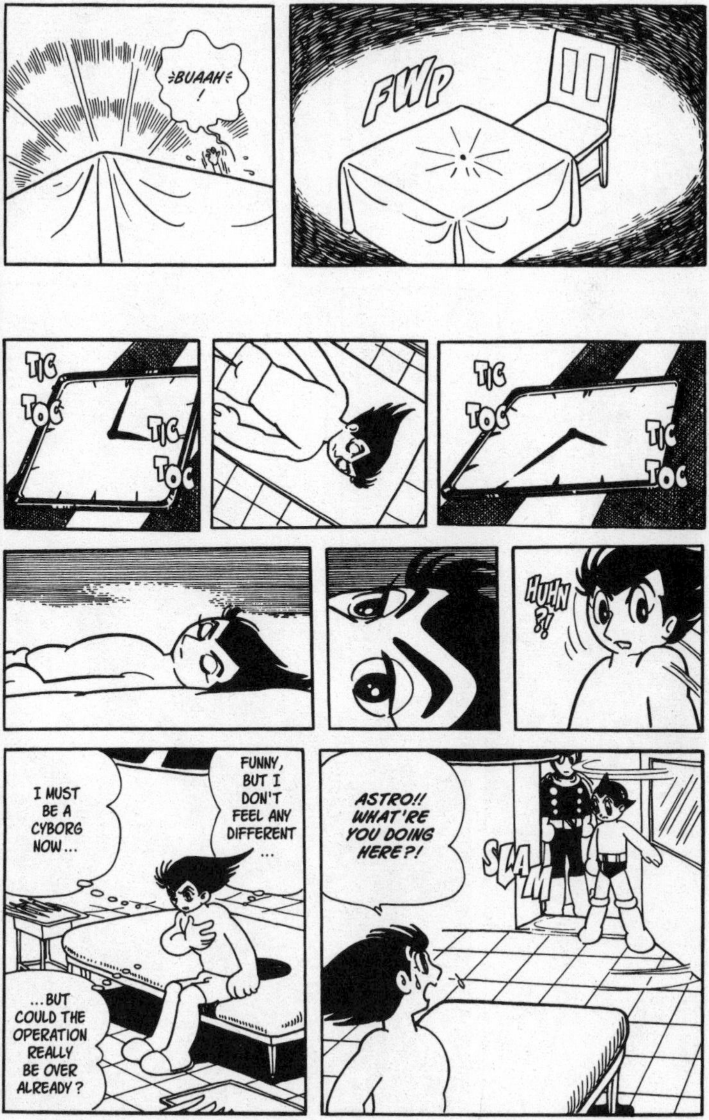
BUAAH
!
FWP
TIC
TOC
TIC
TOC
TIC
TOC
TIC
TOC
HUHN
?!
I MUST BE A CYBORG NOW...
FUNNY, BUT I DON'T FEEL ANY DIFFERENT ...
...BUT COULD THE OPERATION REALLY BE OVER ALREADY?
ASTRO!! WHAT'RE YOU DOING HERE?!
SLAM

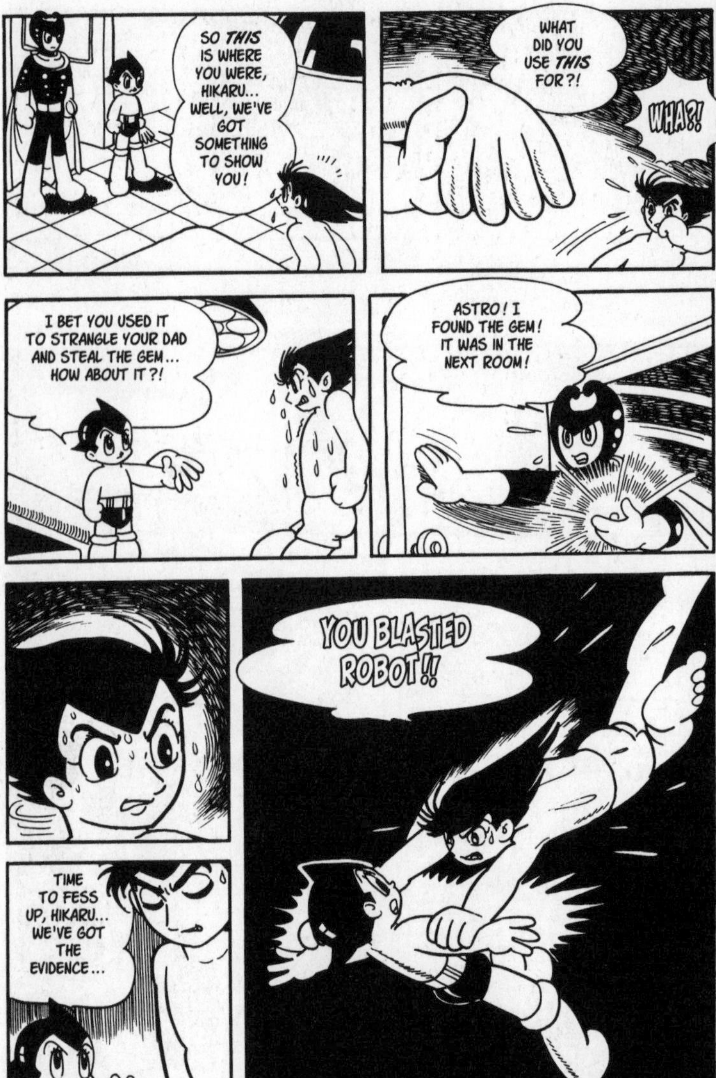

SO *THIS* IS WHERE YOU WERE, HIKARU... WELL, WE'VE GOT SOMETHING TO SHOW YOU!
WHAT DID YOU USE *THIS* FOR?!
WHA?!
I BET YOU USED IT TO STRANGLE YOUR DAD AND STEAL THE GEM... HOW ABOUT IT?!
ASTRO! I FOUND THE GEM! IT WAS IN THE NEXT ROOM!
TIME TO FESS UP, HIKARU... WE'VE GOT THE EVIDENCE...
YOU BLASTED ROBOT!!

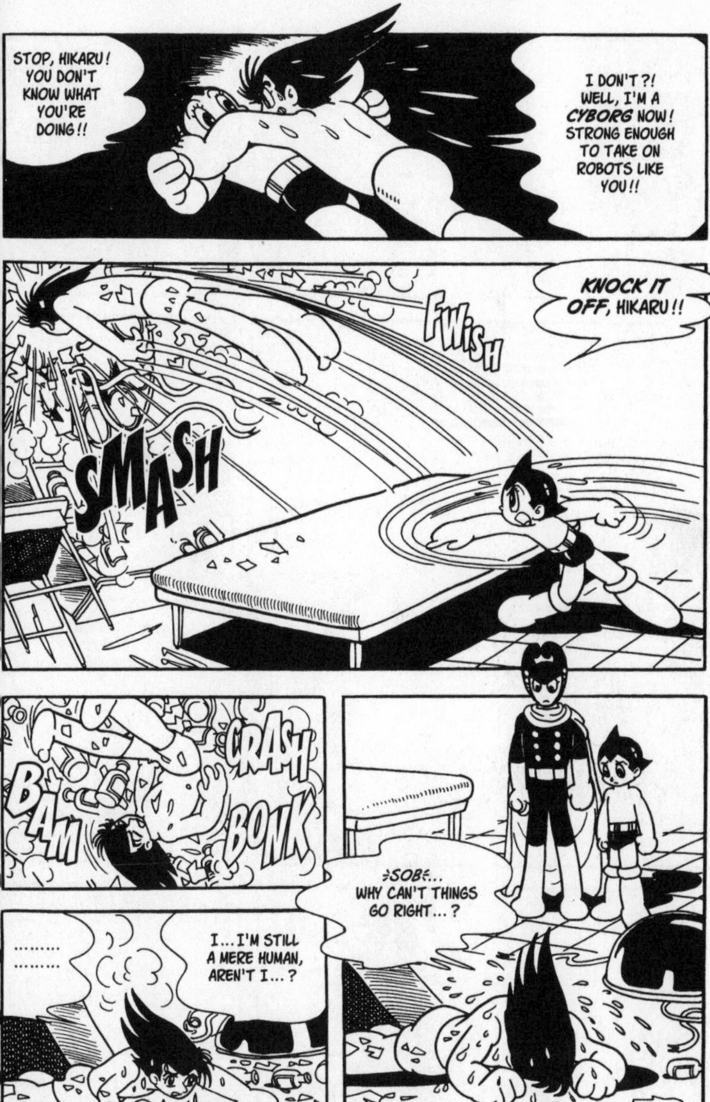
STOP, HIKARU! YOU DON'T KNOW WHAT YOU'RE DOING!!
I DON'T?! WELL, I'M A *CYBORG* NOW! STRONG ENOUGH TO TAKE ON ROBOTS LIKE YOU!!
FWISH
KNOCK IT OFF, HIKARU!!
SMASH
CRASH
BAM
BONK
....
....
I... I'M STILL A MERE HUMAN, AREN'T I...?
SOB... WHY CAN'T THINGS GO RIGHT...?

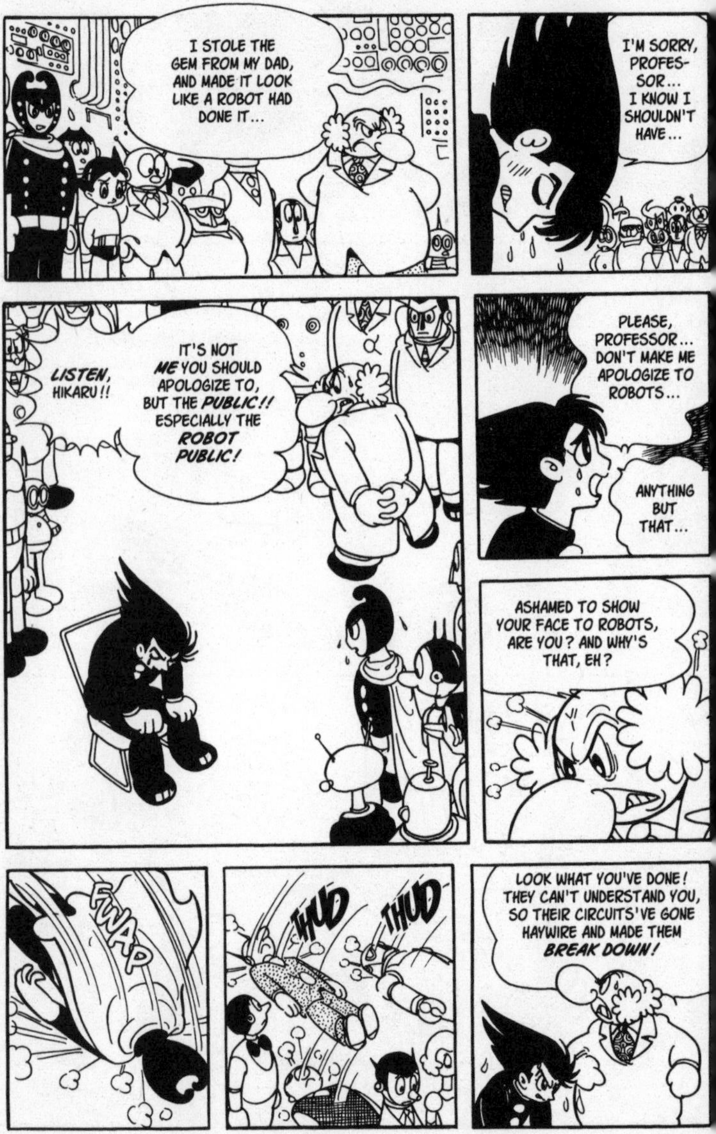
I STOLE THE GEM FROM MY DAD, AND MADE IT LOOK LIKE A ROBOT HAD DONE IT...
I'M SORRY, PROFES-SOR... I KNOW I SHOULDN'T HAVE...
LISTEN, HIKARU!!
IT'S NOT ME YOU SHOULD APOLOGIZE TO, BUT THE PUBLIC!! ESPECIALLY THE ROBOT PUBLIC!
PLEASE, PROFESSOR... DON'T MAKE ME APOLOGIZE TO ROBOTS...
ANYTHING BUT THAT...
ASHAMED TO SHOW YOUR FACE TO ROBOTS, ARE YOU? AND WHY'S THAT, EH?
FWAP
THUD
THUD
LOOK WHAT YOU'VE DONE! THEY CAN'T UNDERSTAND YOU, SO THEIR CIRCUITS'VE GONE HAYWIRE AND MADE THEM BREAK DOWN!

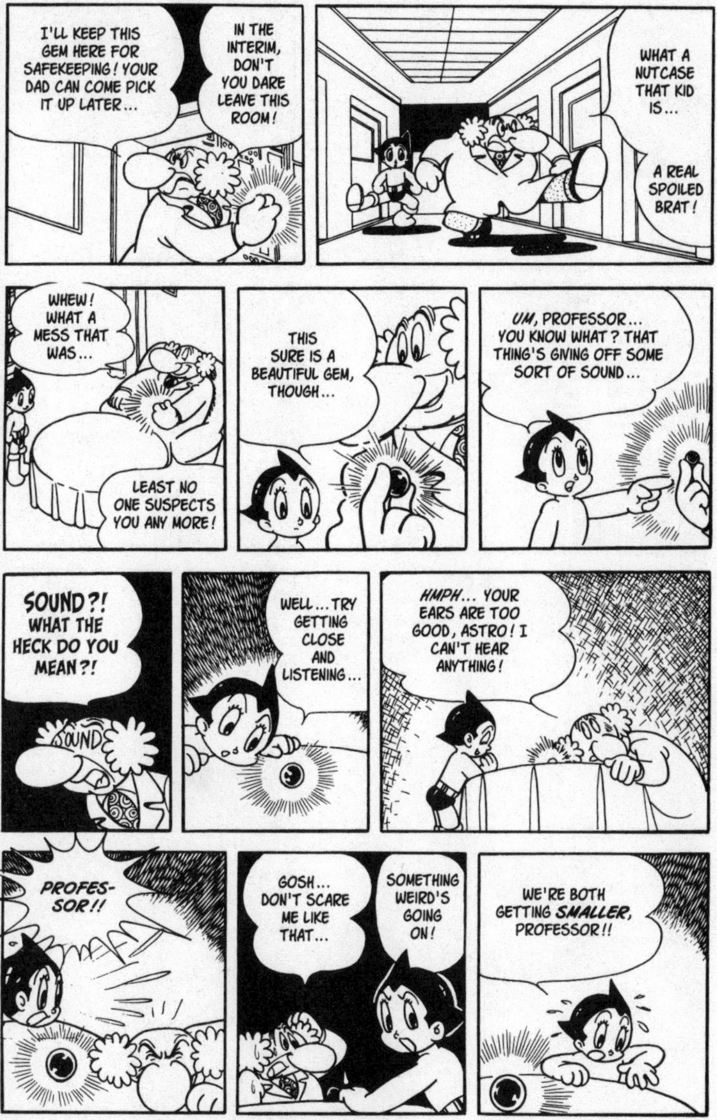
I'LL KEEP THIS GEM HERE FOR SAFEKEEPING! YOUR DAD CAN COME PICK IT UP LATER...
IN THE INTERIM, DON'T YOU DARE LEAVE THIS ROOM!
WHAT A NUTCASE THAT KID IS...
A REAL SPOILED BRAT!
WHEW! WHAT A MESS THAT WAS...
LEAST NO ONE SUSPECTS YOU ANY MORE!
THIS SURE IS A BEAUTIFUL GEM, THOUGH...
UM, PROFESSOR... YOU KNOW WHAT? THAT THING'S GIVING OFF SOME SORT OF SOUND...
SOUND?! WHAT THE HECK DO YOU MEAN?!
SOUND
WELL... TRY GETTING CLOSE AND LISTENING...
HMPH... YOUR EARS ARE TOO GOOD, ASTRO! I CAN'T HEAR ANYTHING!
PROFES-SOR!!
GOSH... DON'T SCARE ME LIKE THAT...
SOMETHING WEIRD'S GOING ON!
WE'RE BOTH GETTING SMALLER, PROFESSOR!!

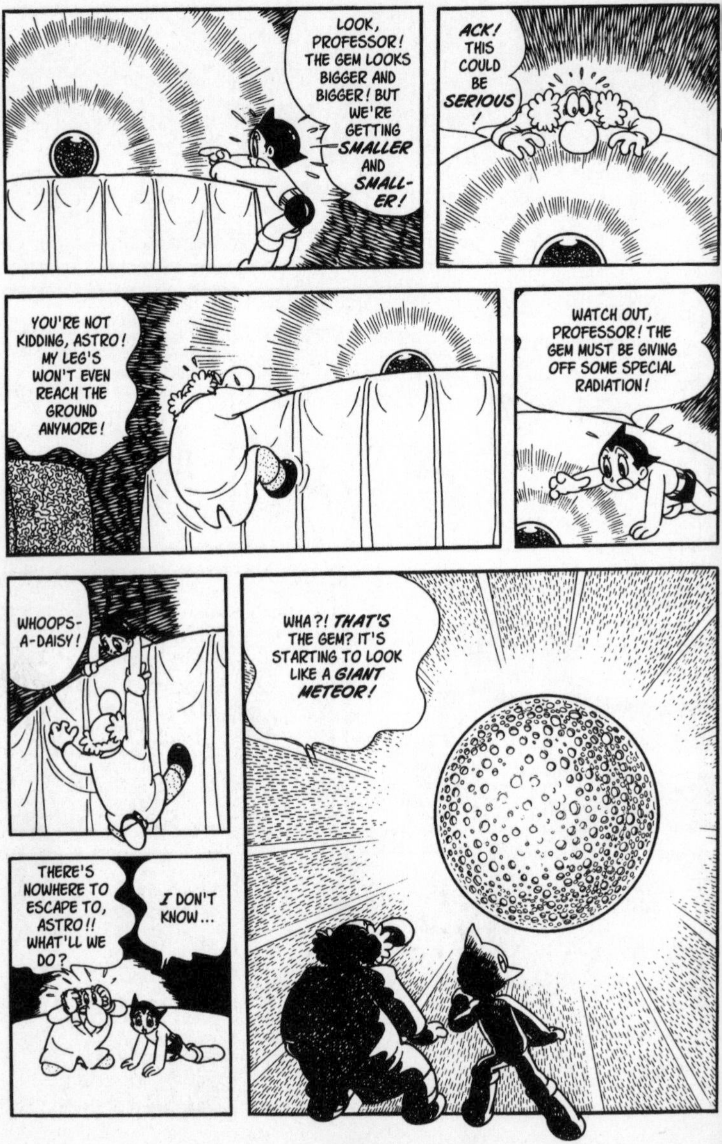
LOOK, PROFESSOR! THE GEM LOOKS BIGGER AND BIGGER! BUT WE'RE GETTING SMALLER AND SMALLER!
ACK! THIS COULD BE SERIOUS!
YOU'RE NOT KIDDING, ASTRO! MY LEG'S WON'T EVEN REACH THE GROUND ANYMORE!
WATCH OUT, PROFESSOR! THE GEM MUST BE GIVING OFF SOME SPECIAL RADIATION!
WHOOPS-A-DAISY!
WHA?! THAT'S THE GEM? IT'S STARTING TO LOOK LIKE A GIANT METEOR!
THERE'S NOWHERE TO ESCAPE TO, ASTRO!! WHAT'LL WE DO?
I DON'T KNOW...

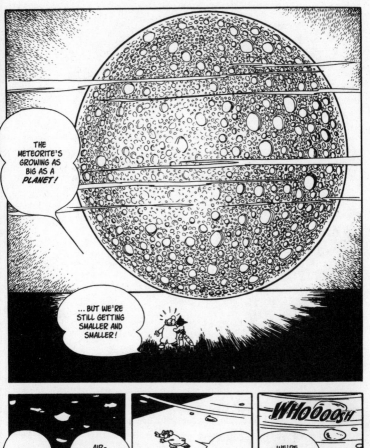

THE METEORITE'S GROWING AS BIG AS A *PLANET!*

...BUT WE'RE STILL GETTING SMALLER AND SMALLER!

WONDER WHAT THIS IS?

AIR-BORNE DUST PARTICLES, THAT'S WHAT!!

WATCH OUT, ASTRO!

WHOOOOSH

WE'RE BEING DRAWN INTO THAT GIANT ORB!

561

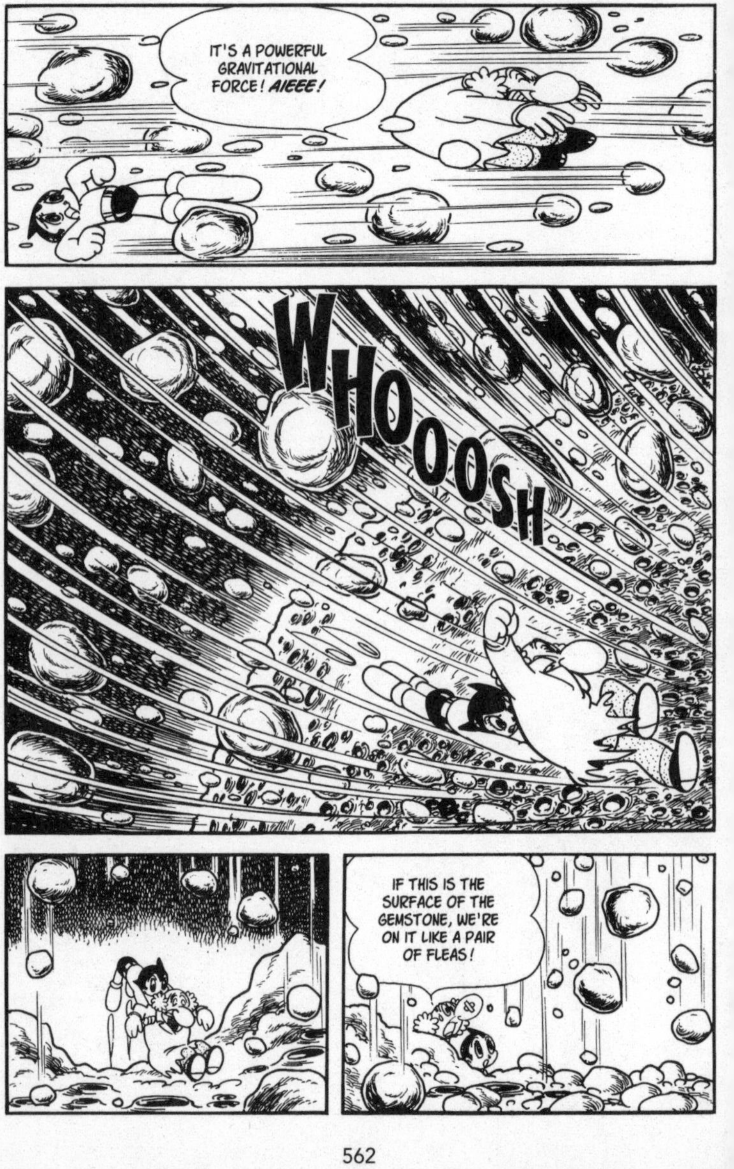
IT'S A POWERFUL GRAVITATIONAL FORCE! AIEEE!
WHOOOSH
IF THIS IS THE SURFACE OF THE GEMSTONE, WE'RE ON IT LIKE A PAIR OF FLEAS!

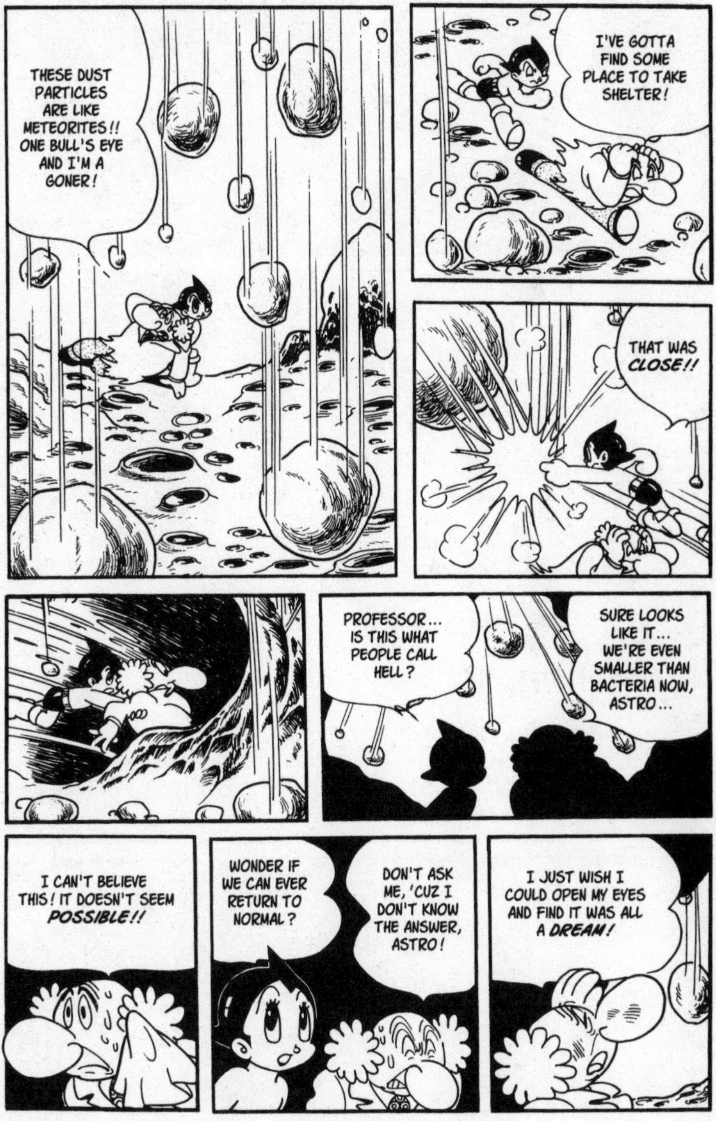
THESE DUST PARTICLES ARE LIKE METEORITES!! ONE BULL'S EYE AND I'M A GONER!
I'VE GOTTA FIND SOME PLACE TO TAKE SHELTER!
THAT WAS *CLOSE!!*
PROFESSOR... IS THIS WHAT PEOPLE CALL HELL?
SURE LOOKS LIKE IT... WE'RE EVEN SMALLER THAN BACTERIA NOW, ASTRO...
I CAN'T BELIEVE THIS! IT DOESN'T SEEM *POSSIBLE!!*
WONDER IF WE CAN EVER RETURN TO NORMAL?
DON'T ASK ME, 'CUZ I DON'T KNOW THE ANSWER, ASTRO!
I JUST WISH I COULD OPEN MY EYES AND FIND IT WAS ALL A *DREAM!*

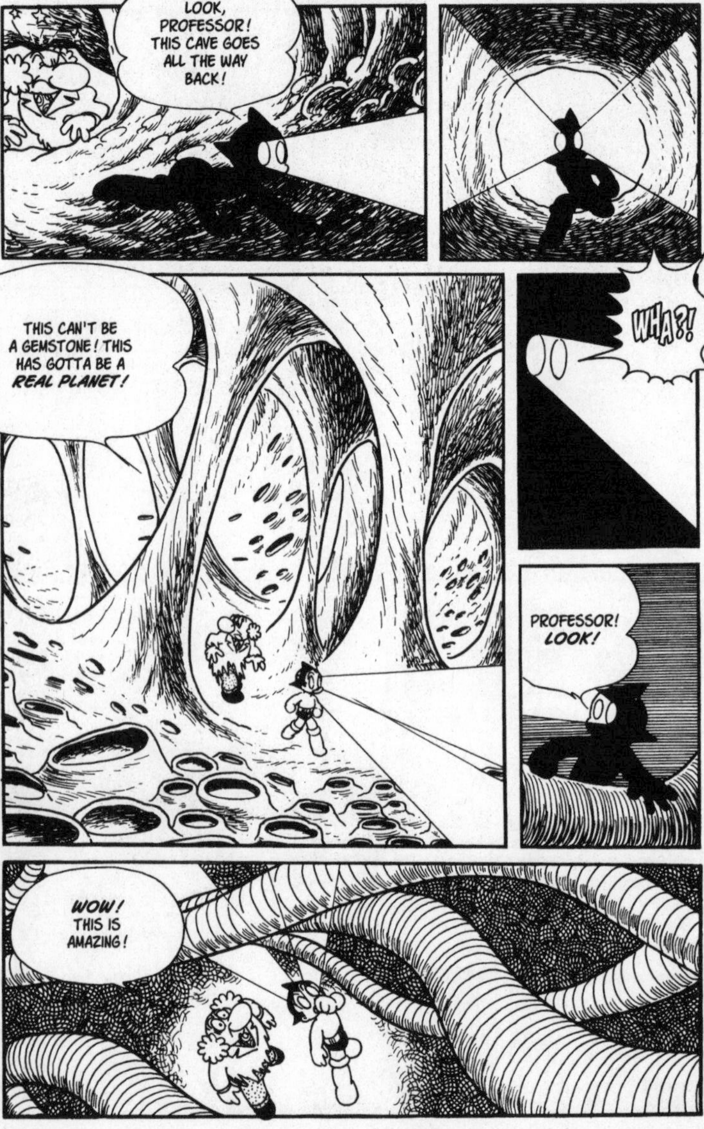
LOOK, PROFESSOR! THIS CAVE GOES ALL THE WAY BACK!
THIS CAN'T BE A GEMSTONE! THIS HAS GOTTA BE A REAL PLANET!
WHA?!
PROFESSOR! LOOK!
WOW! THIS IS AMAZING!

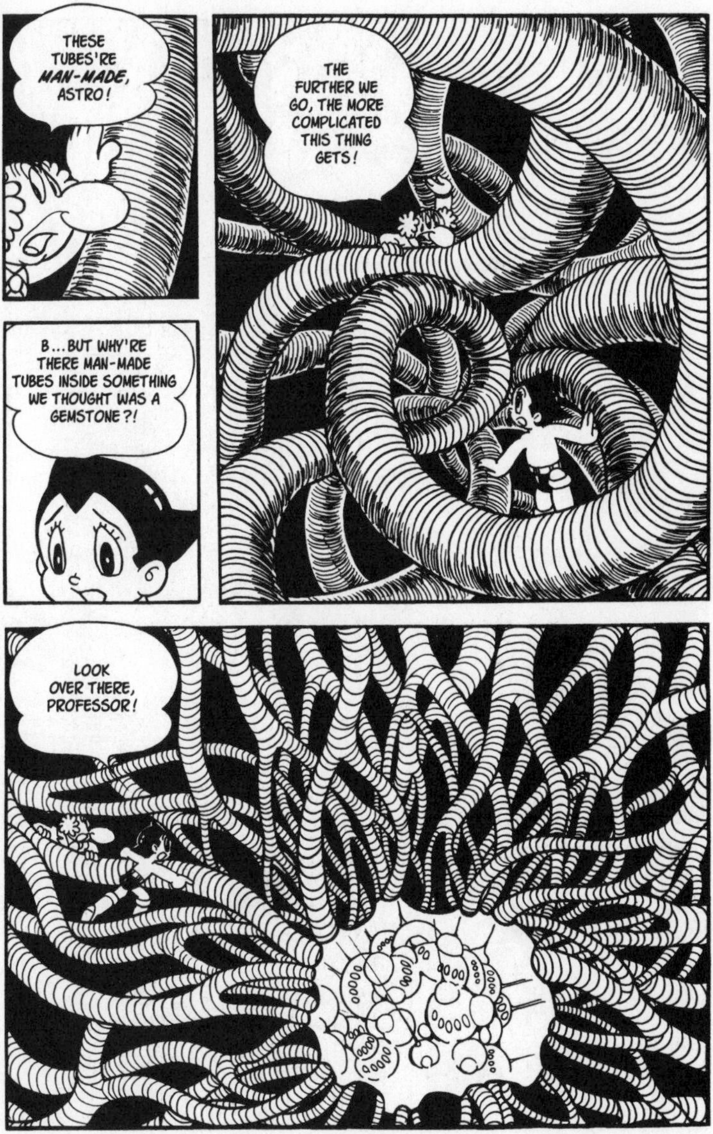
THESE TUBES'RE *MAN-MADE*, ASTRO!
B...BUT WHY'RE THERE MAN-MADE TUBES INSIDE SOMETHING WE THOUGHT WAS A GEMSTONE?!
THE FURTHER WE GO, THE MORE COMPLICATED THIS THING GETS!
LOOK OVER THERE, PROFESSOR!

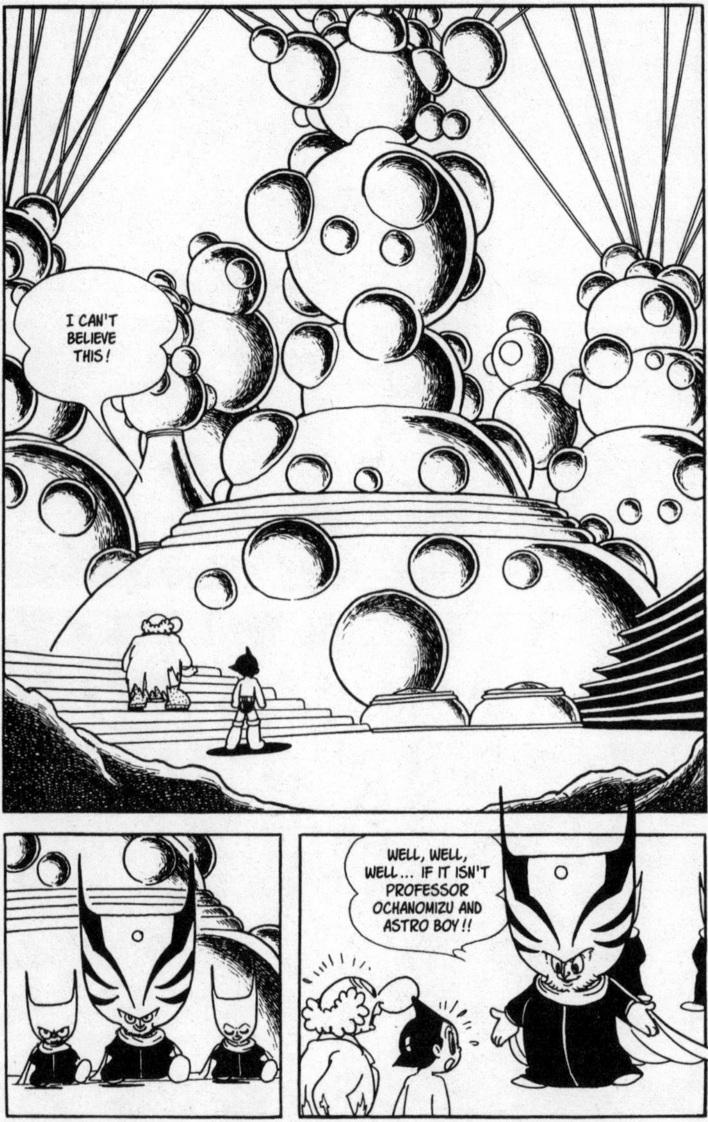
I CAN'T BELIEVE THIS!
WELL, WELL, WELL... IF IT ISN'T PROFESSOR OCHANOMIZU AND ASTRO BOY!!

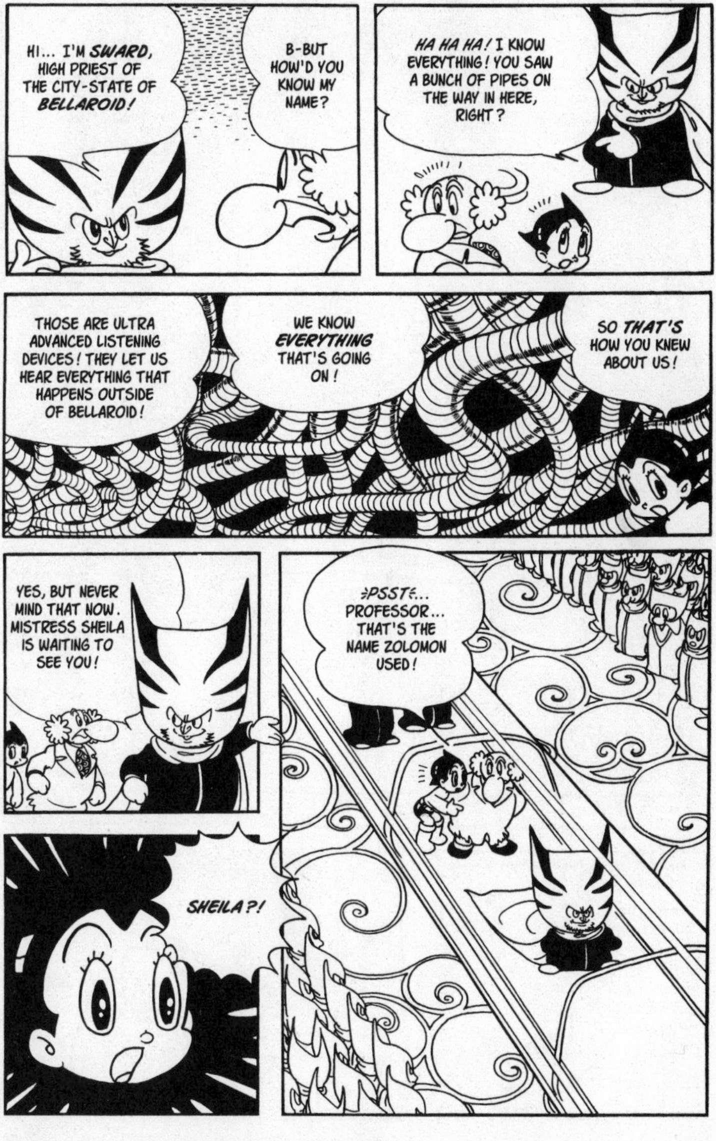
HI... I'M SWARD, HIGH PRIEST OF THE CITY-STATE OF BELLAROID!
B-BUT HOW'D YOU KNOW MY NAME?
HA HA HA! I KNOW EVERYTHING! YOU SAW A BUNCH OF PIPES ON THE WAY IN HERE, RIGHT?
THOSE ARE ULTRA ADVANCED LISTENING DEVICES! THEY LET US HEAR EVERYTHING THAT HAPPENS OUTSIDE OF BELLAROID!
WE KNOW EVERYTHING THAT'S GOING ON!
SO THAT'S HOW YOU KNEW ABOUT US!
YES, BUT NEVER MIND THAT NOW. MISTRESS SHEILA IS WAITING TO SEE YOU!
PSST... PROFESSOR... THAT'S THE NAME ZOLOMON USED!
SHEILA?!

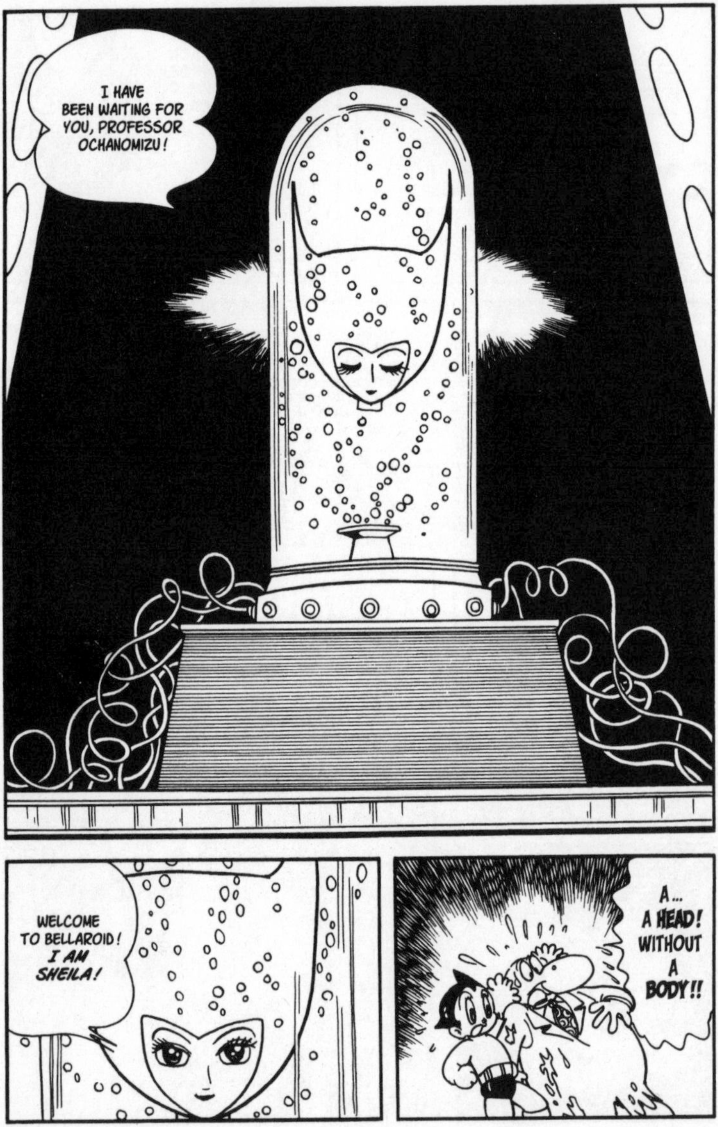

I HAVE BEEN WAITING FOR YOU, PROFESSOR OCHANOMIZU!
WELCOME TO BELLAROID! I AM SHEILA!
A... A HEAD! WITHOUT A BODY!!

HA HA HA HA! SO MY FORM SURPRISES YOU?!

I SUPPOSE IT WOULD, WOULDN'T IT?! HA HA!

LISTEN, I NEED SOME ANSWERS! WHAT *IS* BELLAROID? AND WHY DON'T YOU HAVE A *BODY*?!

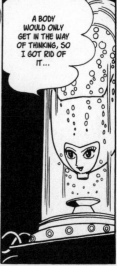

A BODY WOULD ONLY GET IN THE WAY OF THINKING, SO I GOT RID OF IT...

GOT RID OF IT?!

THERE'S AN OPERATION TO DO THAT?

SIT DOWN. LET ME EXPLAIN...

FWID

FWP

MANY TRAGEDIES OCCUR IN THIS UNIVERSE...

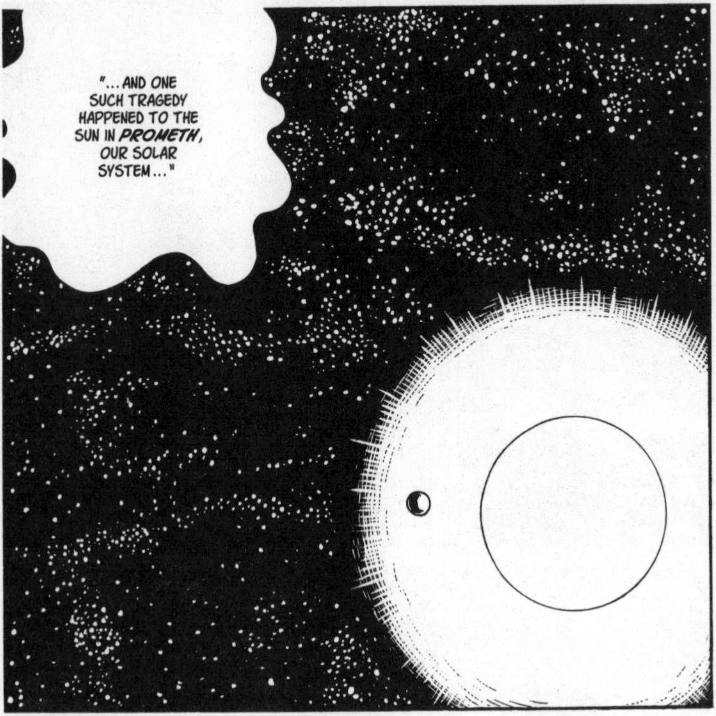
"... AND ONE SUCH TRAGEDY HAPPENED TO THE SUN IN *PROMETH*, OUR SOLAR SYSTEM ..."

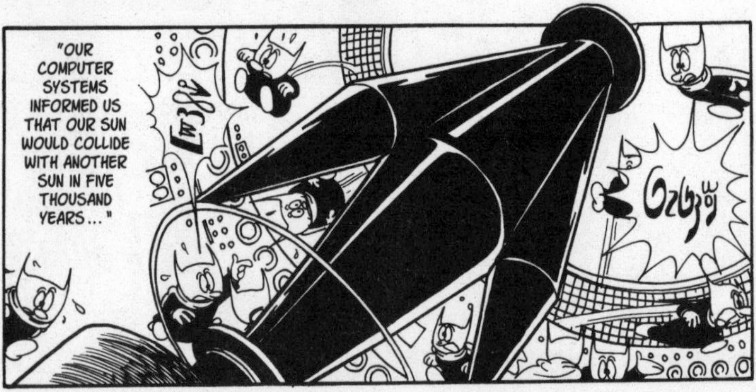
"OUR COMPUTER SYSTEMS INFORMED US THAT OUR SUN WOULD COLLIDE WITH ANOTHER SUN IN FIVE THOUSAND YEARS ..."

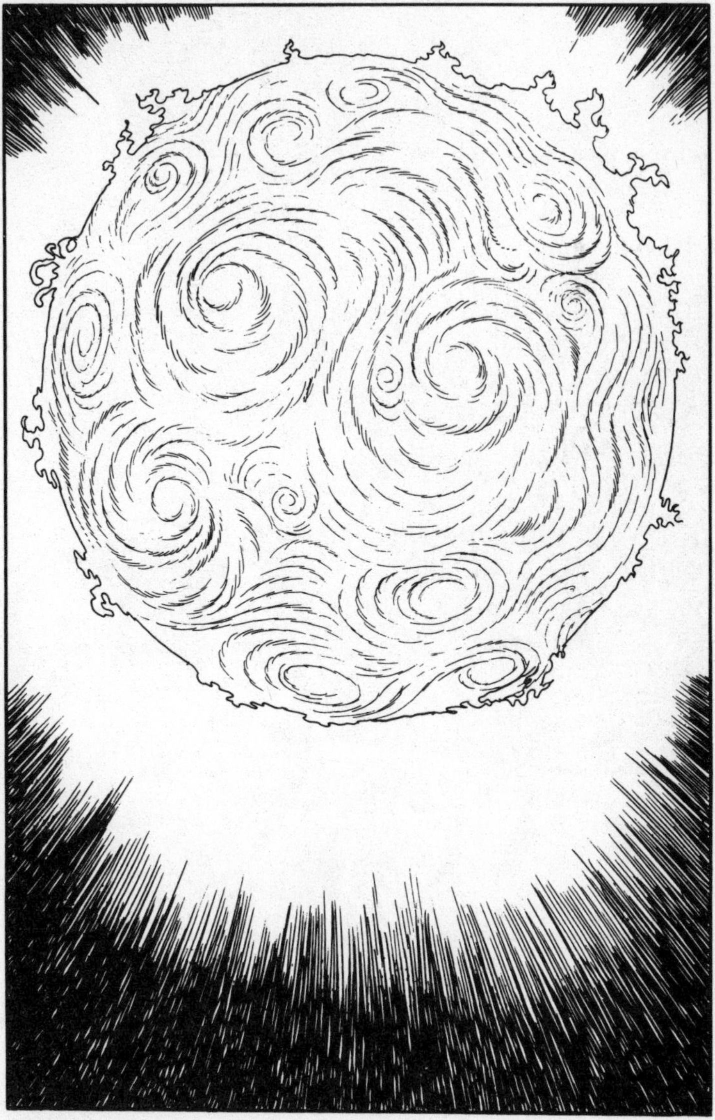

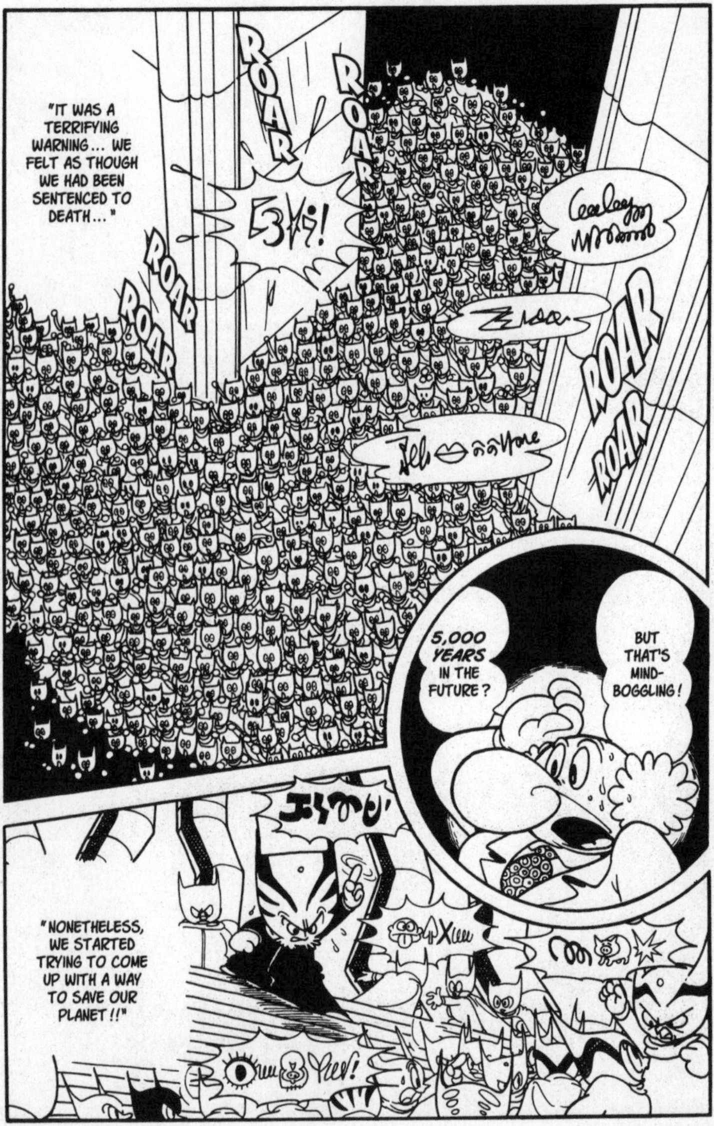
"IT WAS A TERRIFYING WARNING... WE FELT AS THOUGH WE HAD BEEN SENTENCED TO DEATH..."
ROAR
ROAR
ROAR
ROAR
ROAR
ROAR
5,000 YEARS IN THE FUTURE?
BUT THAT'S MIND-BOGGLING!
"NONETHELESS, WE STARTED TRYING TO COME UP WITH A WAY TO SAVE OUR PLANET!!"

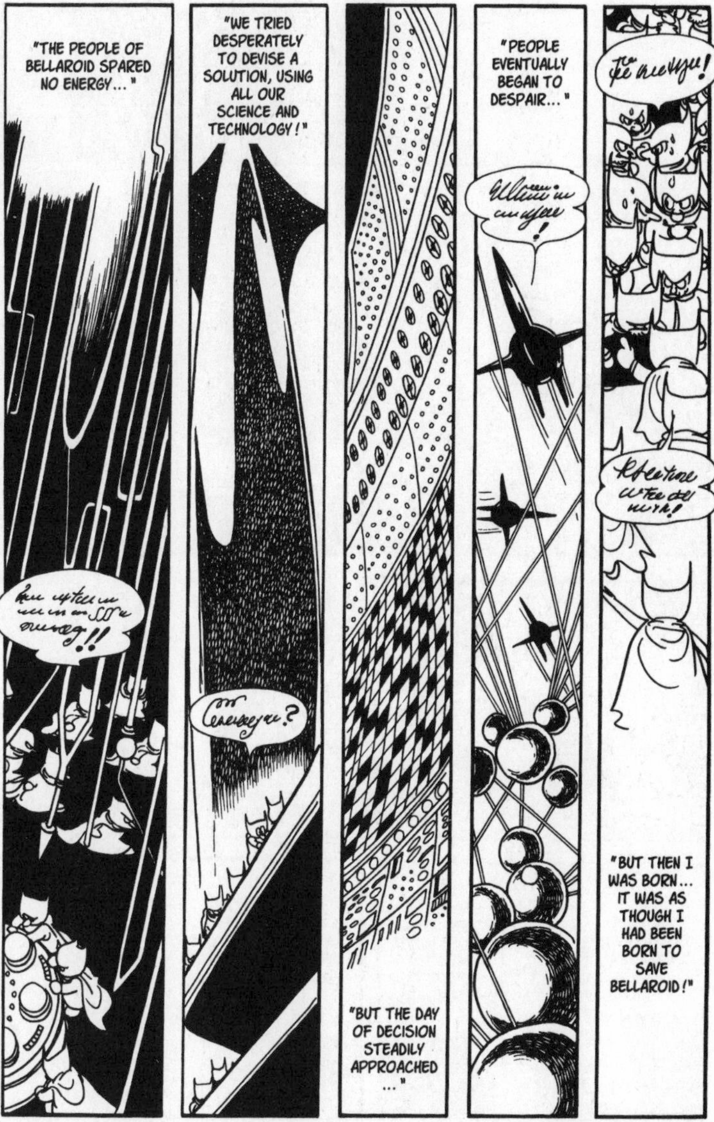
"THE PEOPLE OF BELLAROID SPARED NO ENERGY..."
"WE TRIED DESPERATELY TO DEVISE A SOLUTION, USING ALL OUR SCIENCE AND TECHNOLOGY!"
"BUT THE DAY OF DECISION STEADILY APPROACHED..."
"PEOPLE EVENTUALLY BEGAN TO DESPAIR..."
"BUT THEN I WAS BORN... IT WAS AS THOUGH I HAD BEEN BORN TO SAVE BELLAROID!"

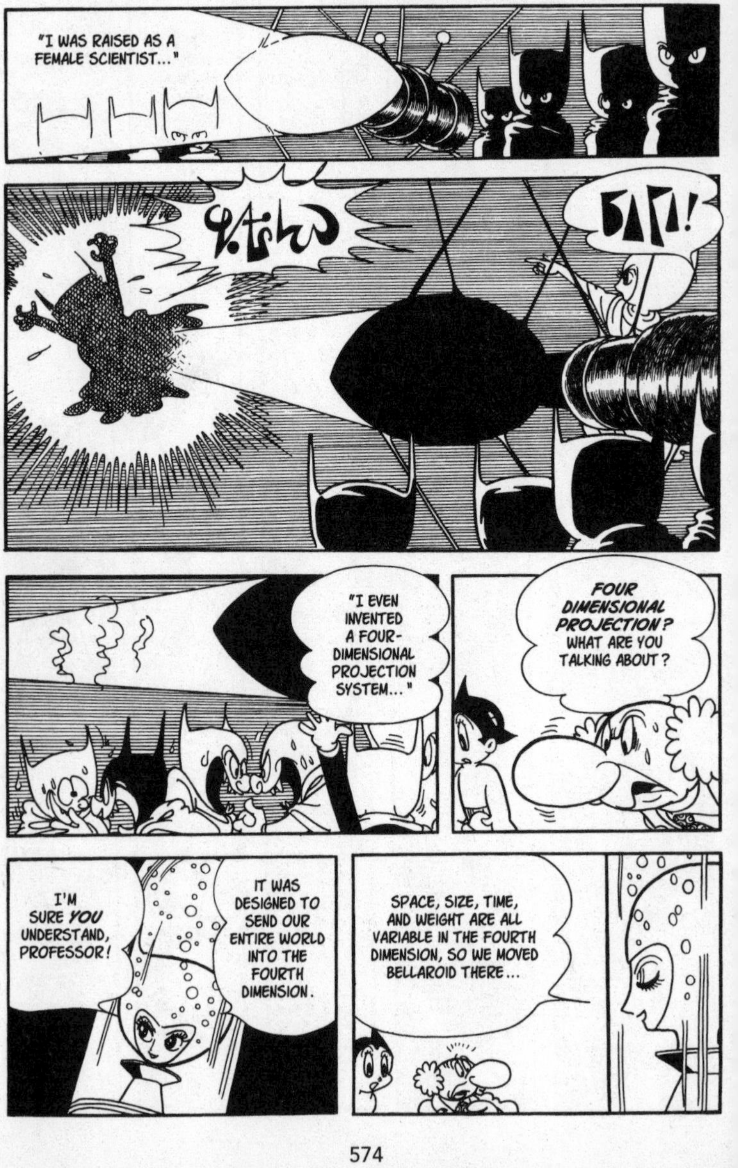
"I WAS RAISED AS A FEMALE SCIENTIST..."
"I EVEN INVENTED A FOUR-DIMENSIONAL PROJECTION SYSTEM..."
FOUR DIMENSIONAL PROJECTION? WHAT ARE YOU TALKING ABOUT?
I'M SURE *YOU* UNDERSTAND, PROFESSOR!
IT WAS DESIGNED TO SEND OUR ENTIRE WORLD INTO THE FOURTH DIMENSION.
SPACE, SIZE, TIME, AND WEIGHT ARE ALL VARIABLE IN THE FOURTH DIMENSION, SO WE MOVED BELLAROID THERE...

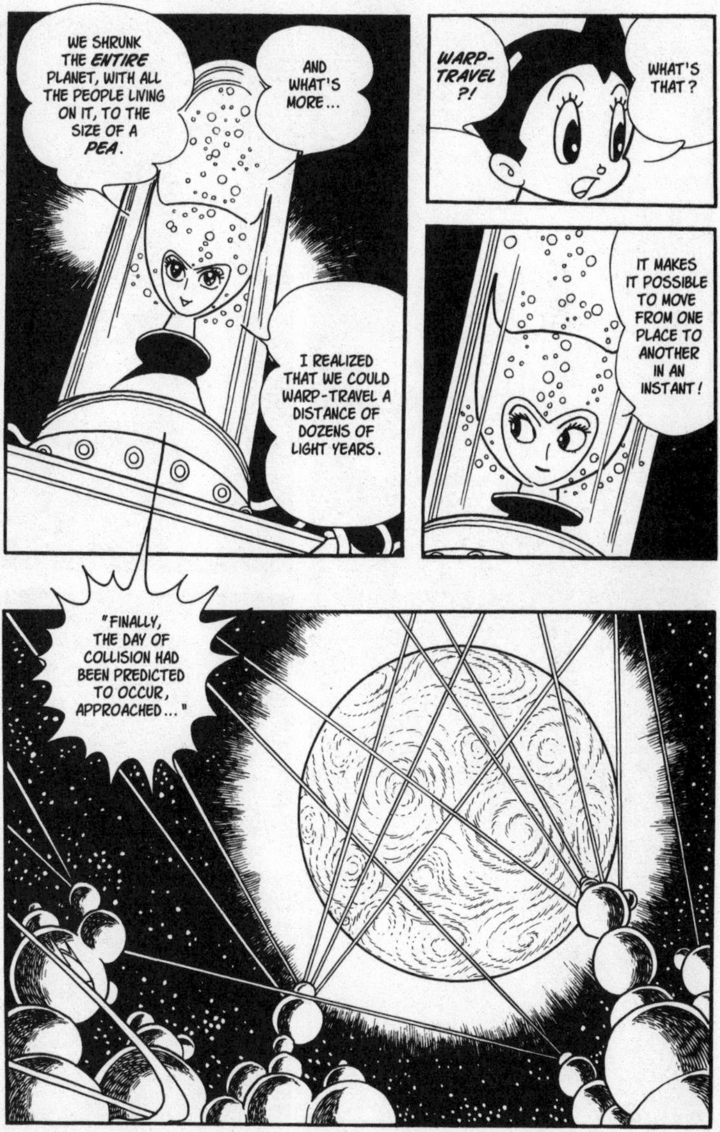
WE SHRUNK THE *ENTIRE* PLANET, WITH ALL THE PEOPLE LIVING ON IT, TO THE SIZE OF A *PEA*.
AND WHAT'S MORE...
I REALIZED THAT WE COULD WARP-TRAVEL A DISTANCE OF DOZENS OF LIGHT YEARS.
WARP-TRAVEL?!
WHAT'S THAT?
IT MAKES IT POSSIBLE TO MOVE FROM ONE PLACE TO ANOTHER IN AN INSTANT!
"FINALLY, THE DAY OF COLLISION HAD BEEN PREDICTED TO OCCUR, APPROACHED..."

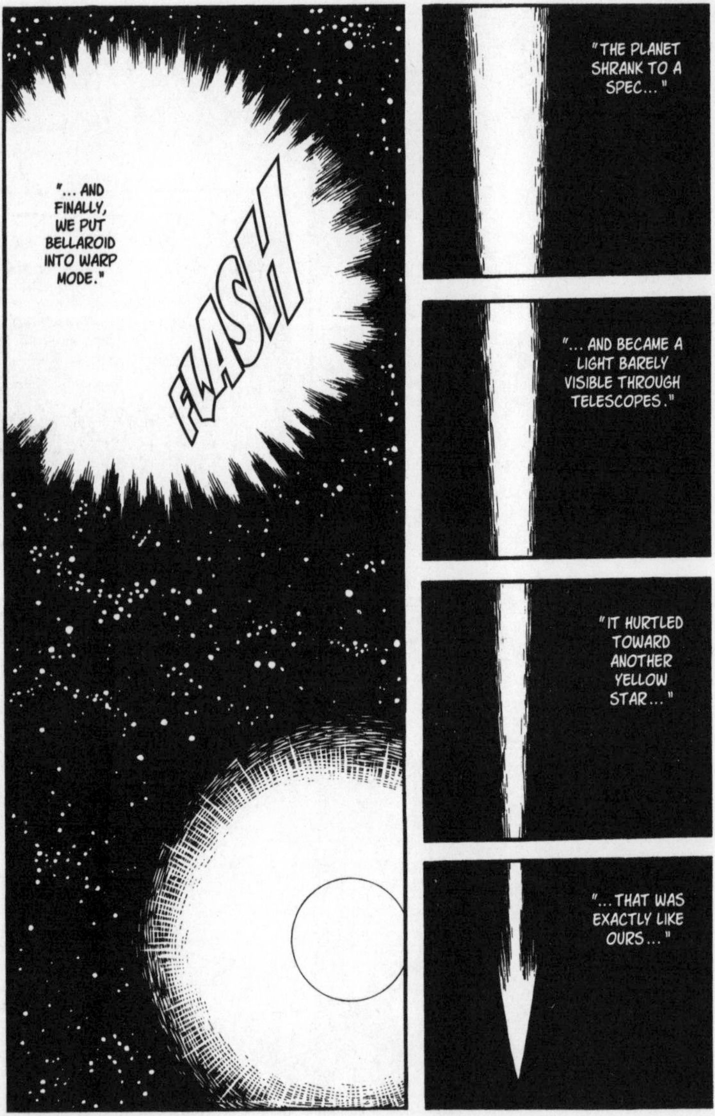
"... AND FINALLY, WE PUT BELLAROID INTO WARP MODE."
FLASH
"THE PLANET SHRANK TO A SPEC..."
"... AND BECAME A LIGHT BARELY VISIBLE THROUGH TELESCOPES."
"IT HURTLED TOWARD ANOTHER YELLOW STAR..."
"... THAT WAS EXACTLY LIKE OURS..."

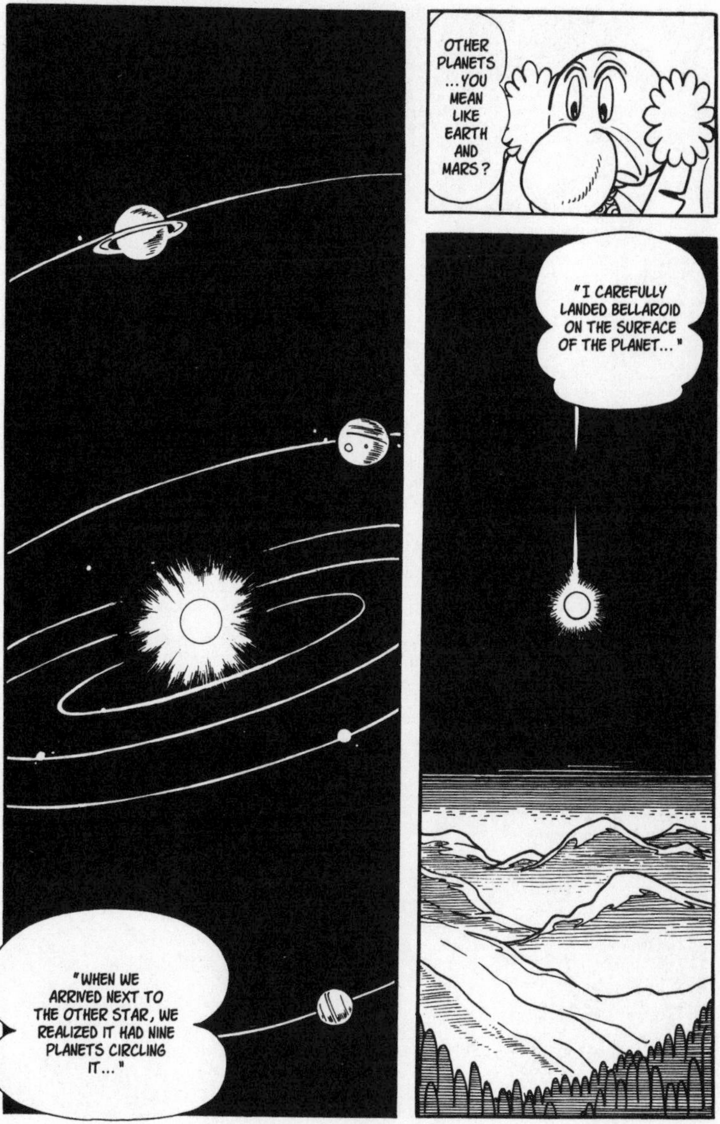
"WHEN WE ARRIVED NEXT TO THE OTHER STAR, WE REALIZED IT HAD NINE PLANETS CIRCLING IT..."
OTHER PLANETS ...YOU MEAN LIKE EARTH AND MARS?
"I CAREFULLY LANDED BELLAROID ON THE SURFACE OF THE PLANET..."

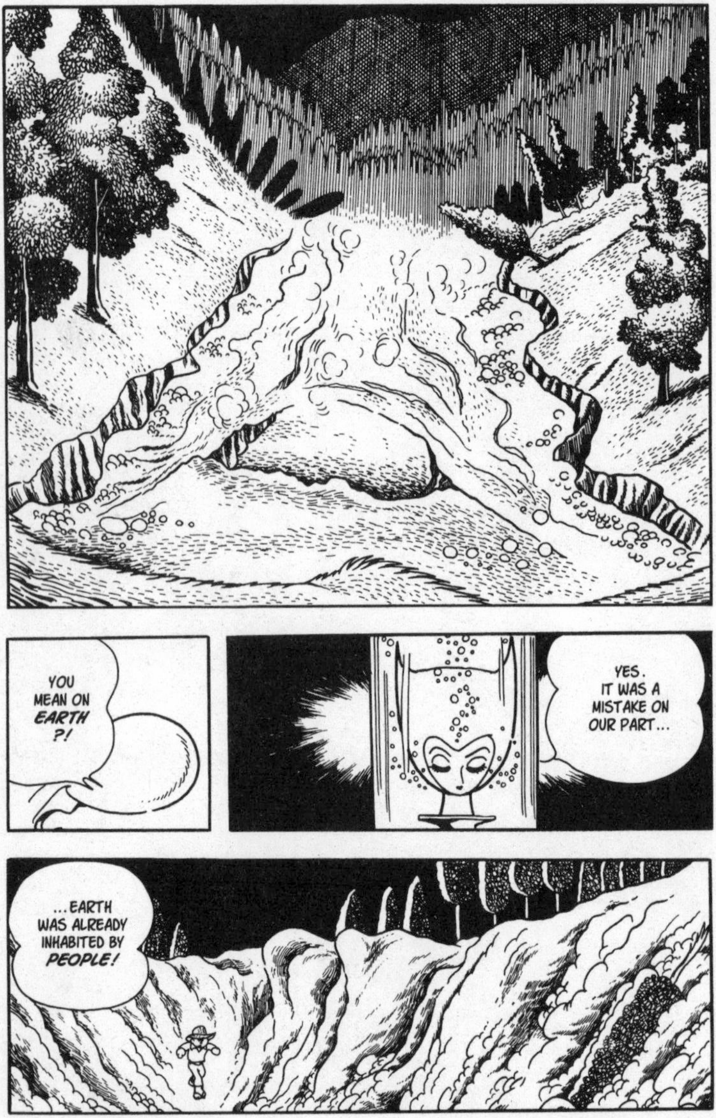
YOU MEAN ON EARTH ?!
YES. IT WAS A MISTAKE ON OUR PART...
...EARTH WAS ALREADY INHABITED BY PEOPLE!

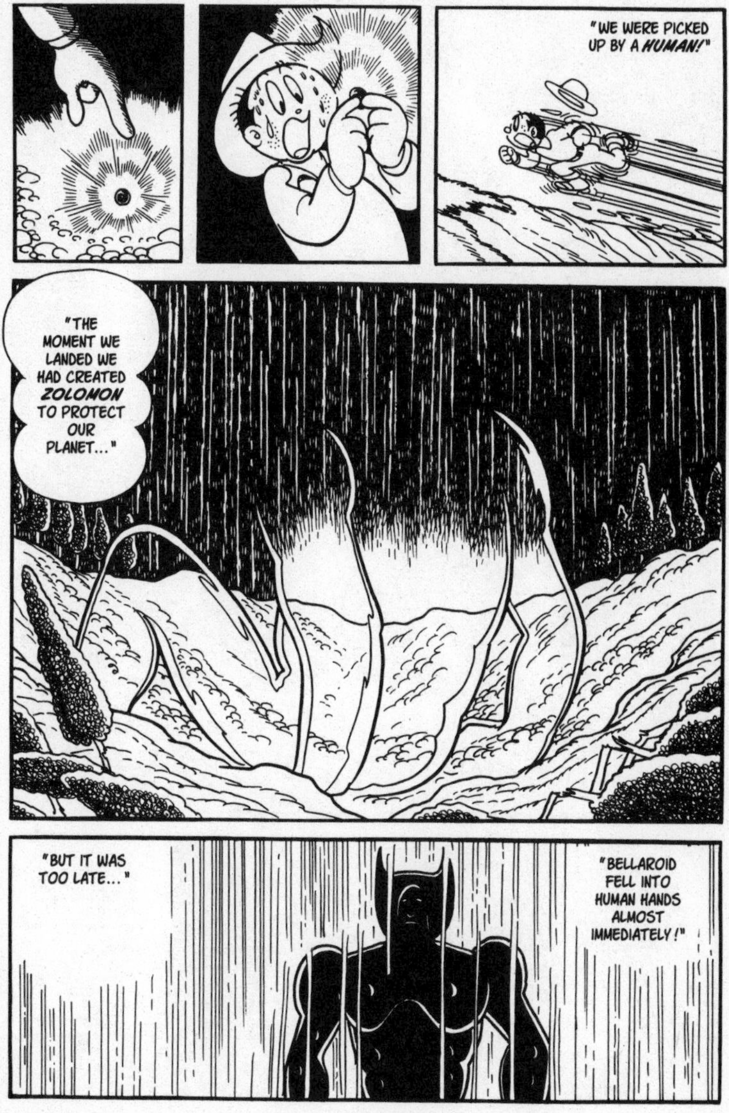
"WE WERE PICKED UP BY A HUMAN!"
"THE MOMENT WE LANDED WE HAD CREATED ZOLOMON TO PROTECT OUR PLANET..."
"BUT IT WAS TOO LATE..."
"BELLAROID FELL INTO HUMAN HANDS ALMOST IMMEDIATELY!"

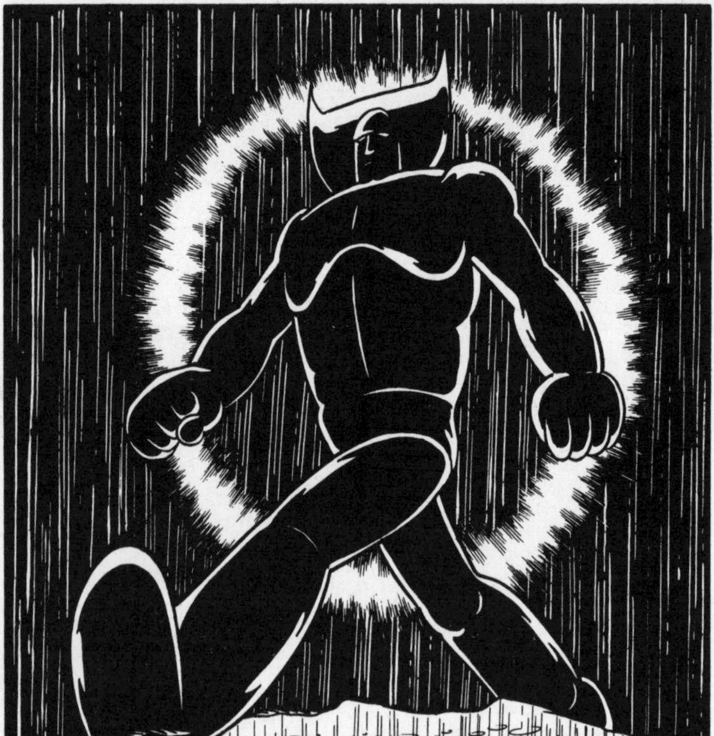

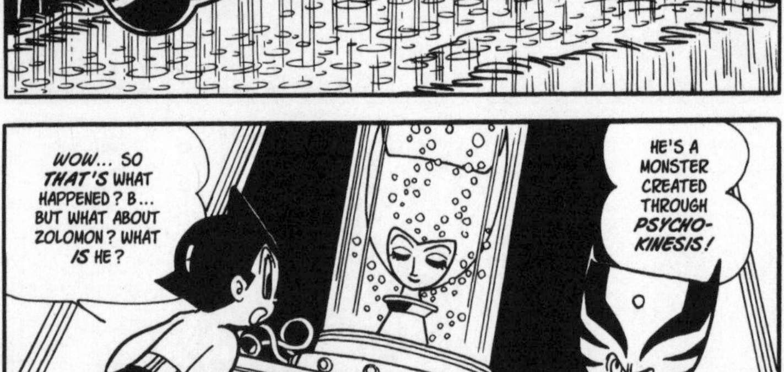
WOW... SO THAT'S WHAT HAPPENED? B... BUT WHAT ABOUT ZOLOMON? WHAT IS HE?
HE'S A MONSTER CREATED THROUGH PSYCHO-KINESIS!

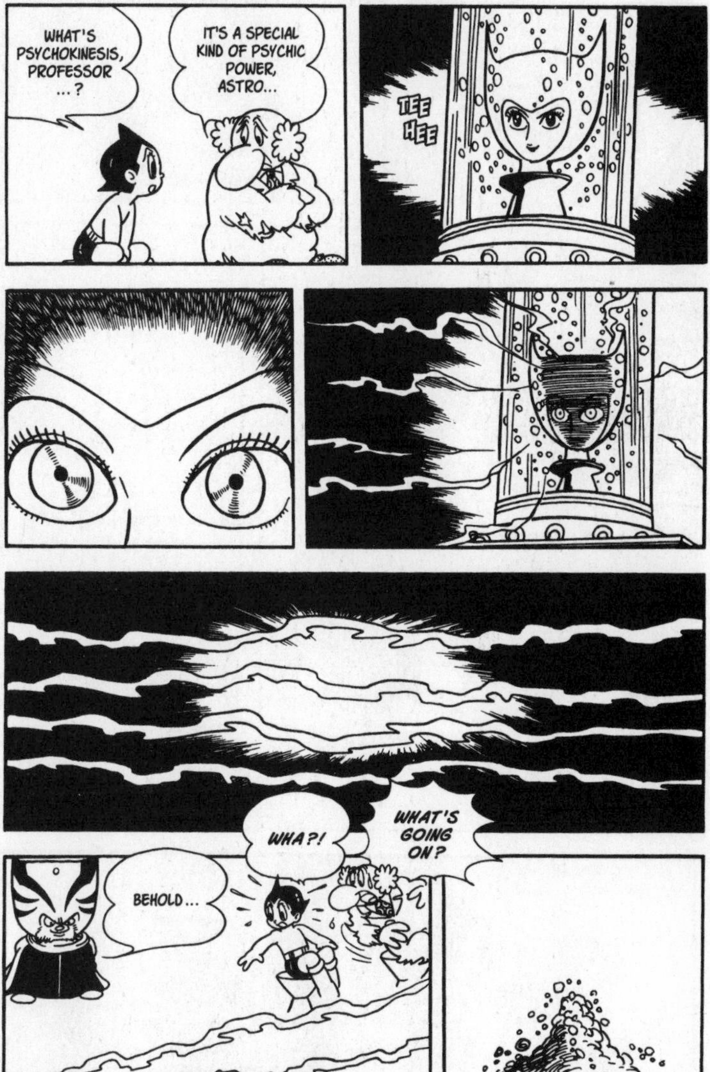
WHAT'S PSYCHOKINESIS, PROFESSOR ... ?
IT'S A SPECIAL KIND OF PSYCHIC POWER, ASTRO...
TEE HEE
BEHOLD...
WHA?!
WHAT'S GOING ON?

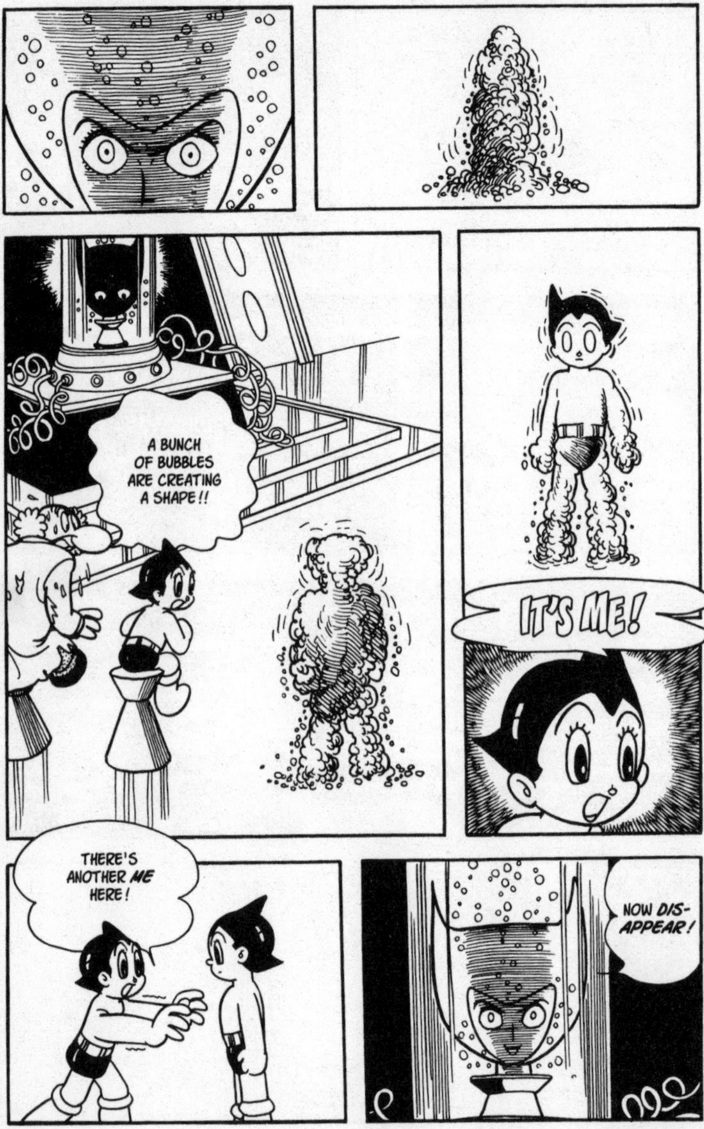
A BUNCH OF BUBBLES ARE CREATING A SHAPE!!
IT'S ME!
THERE'S ANOTHER ME HERE!
NOW DIS- APPEAR!

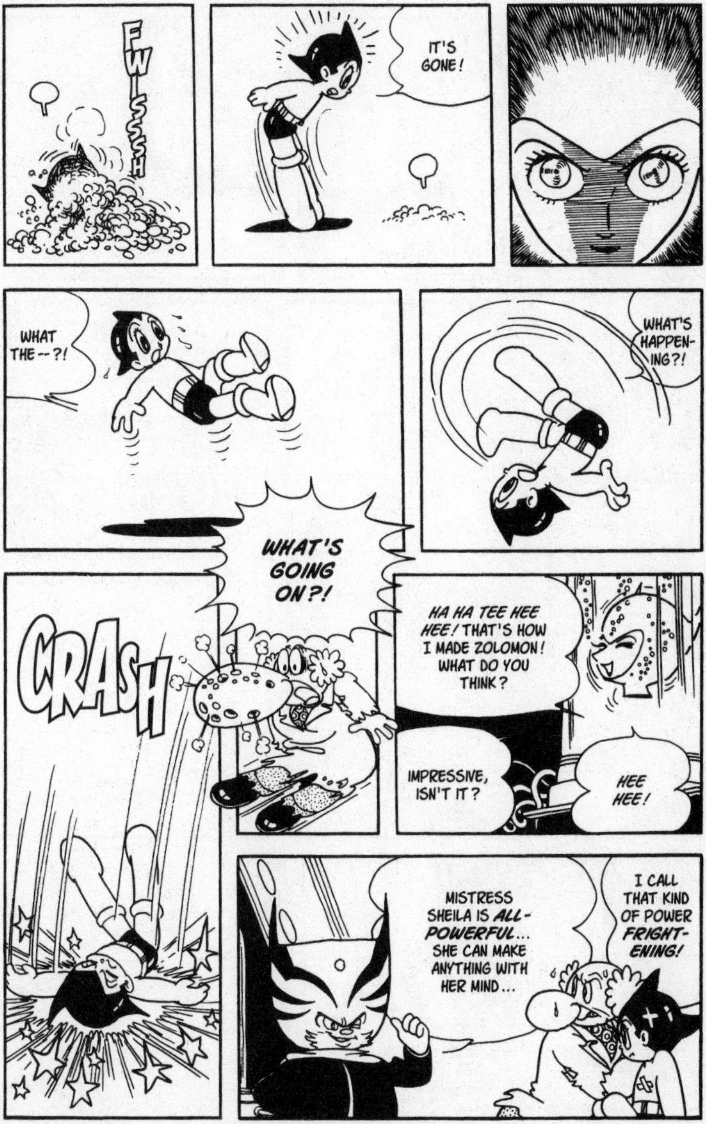
FWISSSH
IT'S GONE!
WHAT THE--?!
WHAT'S HAPPENING?!
WHAT'S GOING ON?!
CRASH
HA HA TEE HEE HEE! THAT'S HOW I MADE ZOLOMON! WHAT DO YOU THINK?
IMPRESSIVE, ISN'T IT?
HEE HEE!
MISTRESS SHEILA IS ALL-POWERFUL... SHE CAN MAKE ANYTHING WITH HER MIND...
I CALL THAT KIND OF POWER FRIGHTENING!

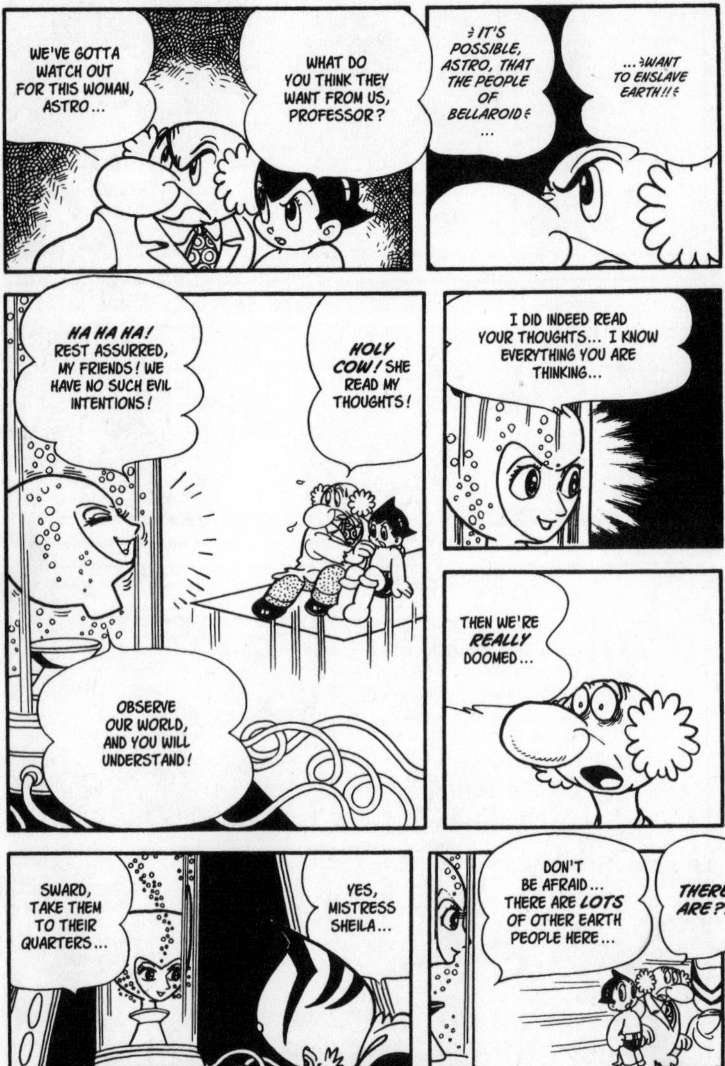

WE'VE GOTTA WATCH OUT FOR THIS WOMAN, ASTRO...
WHAT DO YOU THINK THEY WANT FROM US, PROFESSOR?
IT'S POSSIBLE, ASTRO, THAT THE PEOPLE OF BELLAROID...
...WANT TO ENSLAVE EARTH!!
HA HA HA! REST ASSURRED, MY FRIENDS! WE HAVE NO SUCH EVIL INTENTIONS!
HOLY COW! SHE READ MY THOUGHTS!
OBSERVE OUR WORLD, AND YOU WILL UNDERSTAND!
I DID INDEED READ YOUR THOUGHTS... I KNOW EVERYTHING YOU ARE THINKING...
THEN WE'RE REALLY DOOMED...
SWARD, TAKE THEM TO THEIR QUARTERS...
YES, MISTRESS SHEILA...
DON'T BE AFRAID... THERE ARE LOTS OF OTHER EARTH PEOPLE HERE...
THERE ARE?!

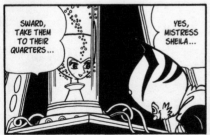

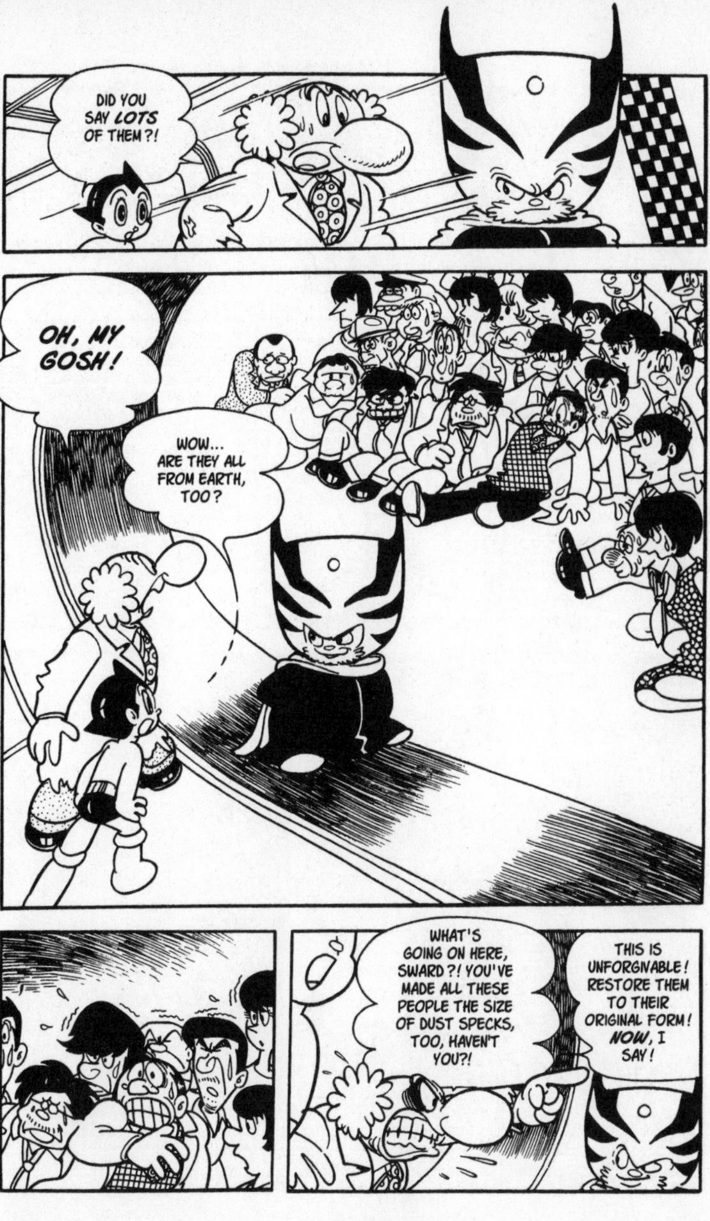
DID YOU SAY LOTS OF THEM?!
OH, MY GOSH!
WOW... ARE THEY ALL FROM EARTH, TOO?
WHAT'S GOING ON HERE, SWARD?! YOU'VE MADE ALL THESE PEOPLE THE SIZE OF DUST SPECKS, TOO, HAVEN'T YOU?!
THIS IS UNFORGIVABLE! RESTORE THEM TO THEIR ORIGINAL FORM! NOW, I SAY!

SORRY, BUT WE CAN'T DO THAT... THEY HAVE TO STAY HERE!

...BECAUSE THEY KNOW THE SECRET OF THIS PLANET... OF THIS GEMSTONE!

IF YOU DON'T MIND, I'D LIKE YOU TO EXPLAIN THINGS SIMPLY TO THEM...

NO! THIS ISN'T *FAIR!*

SOMETHING WEIRD'S GOING ON HERE, ASTRO! SOMETHING REALLY, *REALLY* WEIRD! THEY'RE TRYING TO *USE* US!

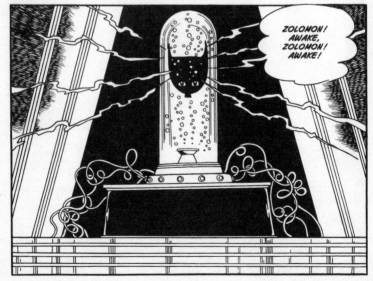

ZOLOMON! AWAKE, ZOLOMON! AWAKE!

GLUB
GOBO
BLUB
GOBO
GLUB
GLUB
GOBO
BLUB
GOBO
GLUB
GLUB
GLUB
SPLOOOSH
AT YOUR COMMAND, MISTRESS SHEILA!

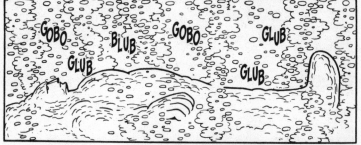

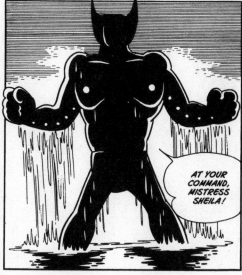

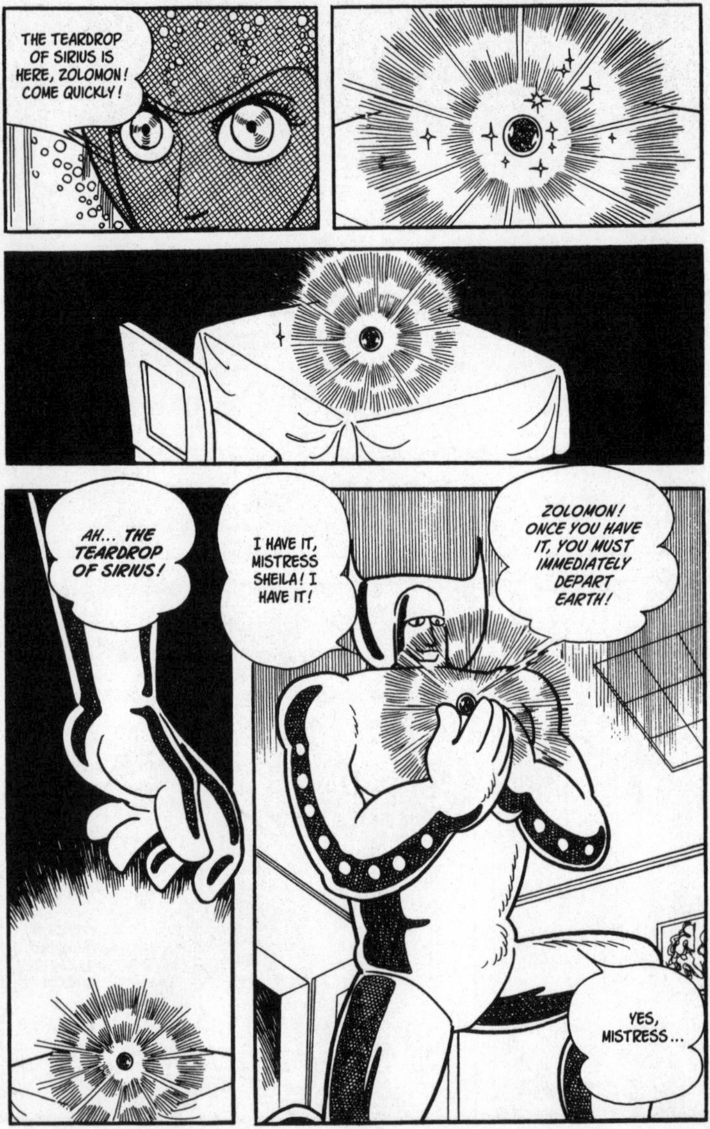
THE TEARDROP OF SIRIUS IS HERE, ZOLOMON! COME QUICKLY!
AH... THE TEARDROP OF SIRIUS!
I HAVE IT, MISTRESS SHEILA! I HAVE IT!
ZOLOMON! ONCE YOU HAVE IT, YOU MUST IMMEDIATELY DEPART EARTH!
YES, MISTRESS...

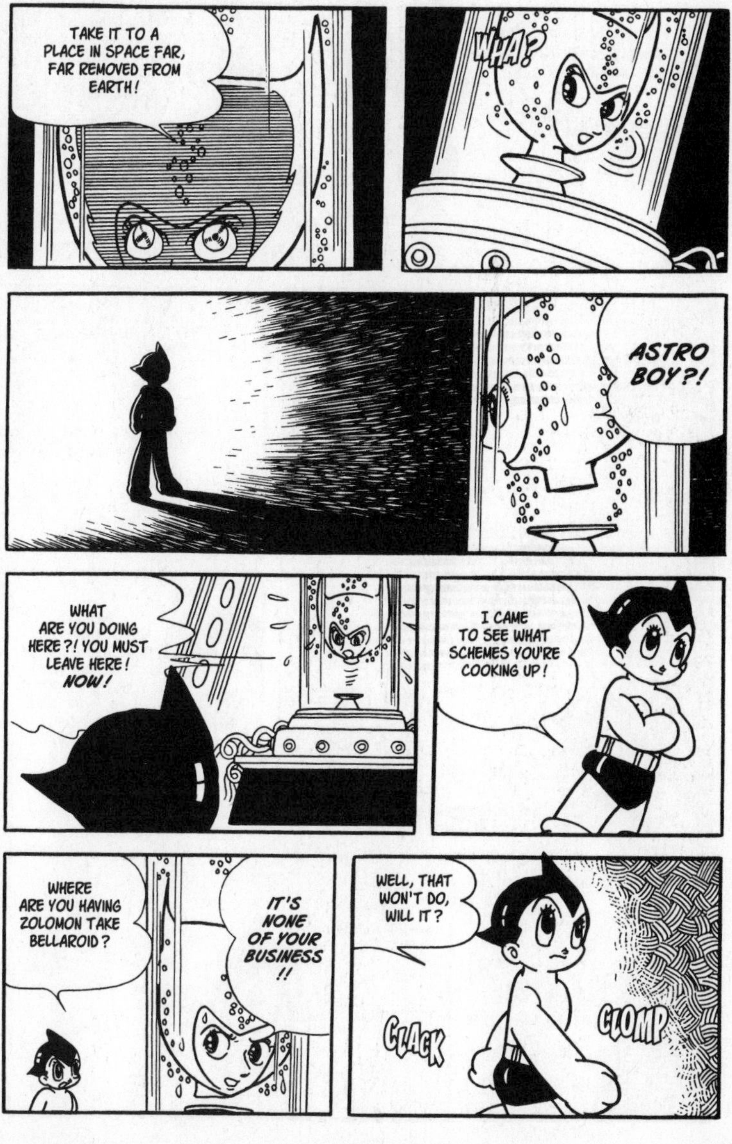
TAKE IT TO A PLACE IN SPACE FAR, FAR REMOVED FROM EARTH!
WHA?
ASTRO BOY?!
WHAT ARE YOU DOING HERE?! YOU MUST LEAVE HERE! NOW!
I CAME TO SEE WHAT SCHEMES YOU'RE COOKING UP!
WHERE ARE YOU HAVING ZOLOMON TAKE BELLAROID?
IT'S NONE OF YOUR BUSINESS!!
WELL, THAT WON'T DO, WILL IT?
CLACK
CLOMP

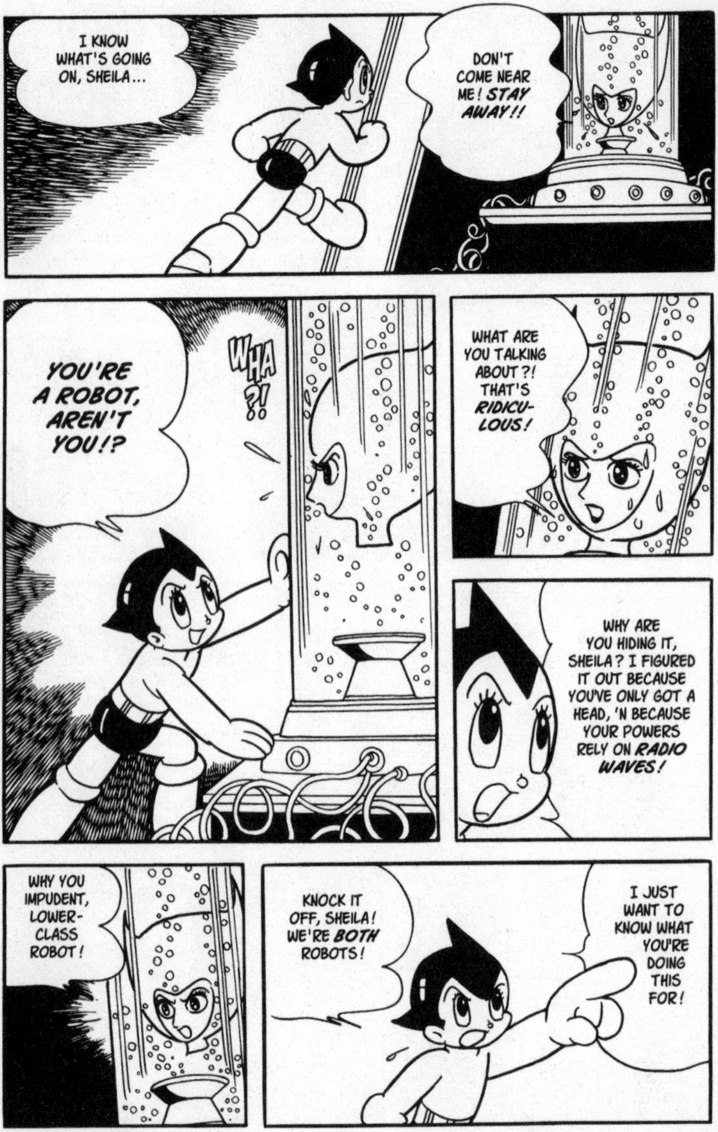
I KNOW WHAT'S GOING ON, SHEILA...
DON'T COME NEAR ME! STAY AWAY!!
YOU'RE A ROBOT, AREN'T YOU!?
WHA ?!
WHAT ARE YOU TALKING ABOUT?! THAT'S RIDICULOUS!
WHY ARE YOU HIDING IT, SHEILA? I FIGURED IT OUT BECAUSE YOU'VE ONLY GOT A HEAD, 'N BECAUSE YOUR POWERS RELY ON RADIO WAVES!
WHY YOU IMPUDENT, LOWER-CLASS ROBOT!
KNOCK IT OFF, SHEILA! WE'RE BOTH ROBOTS!
I JUST WANT TO KNOW WHAT YOU'RE DOING THIS FOR!

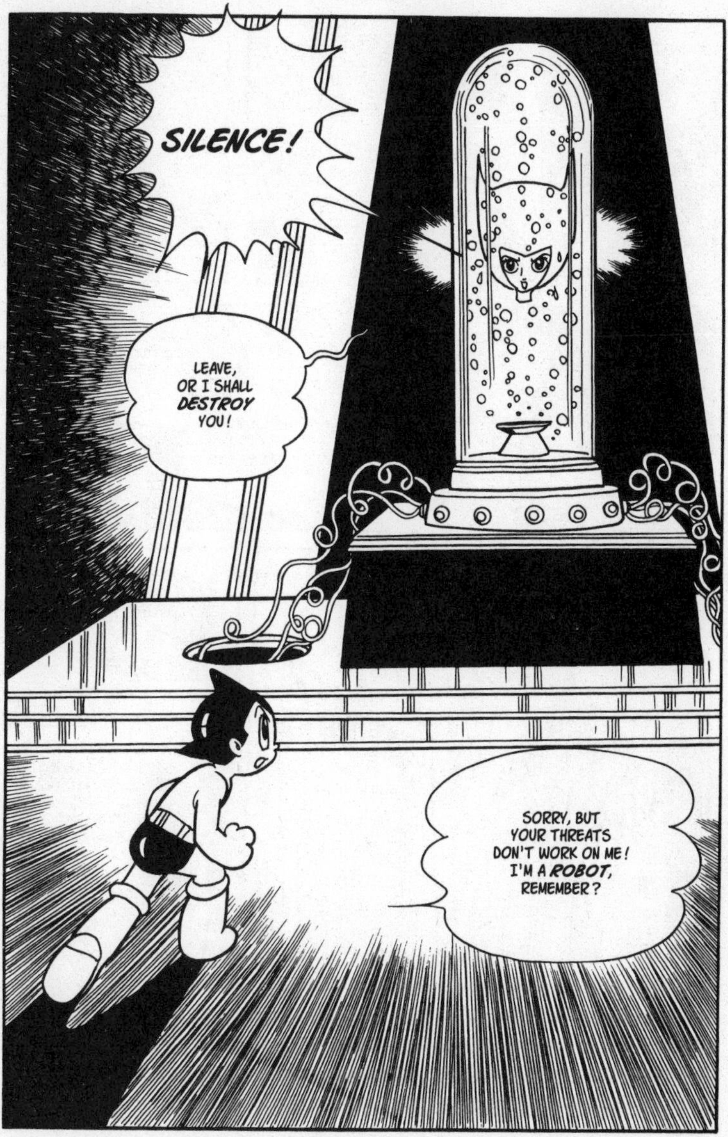
SILENCE!
LEAVE, OR I SHALL DESTROY YOU!
SORRY, BUT YOUR THREATS DON'T WORK ON ME! I'M A ROBOT, REMEMBER?

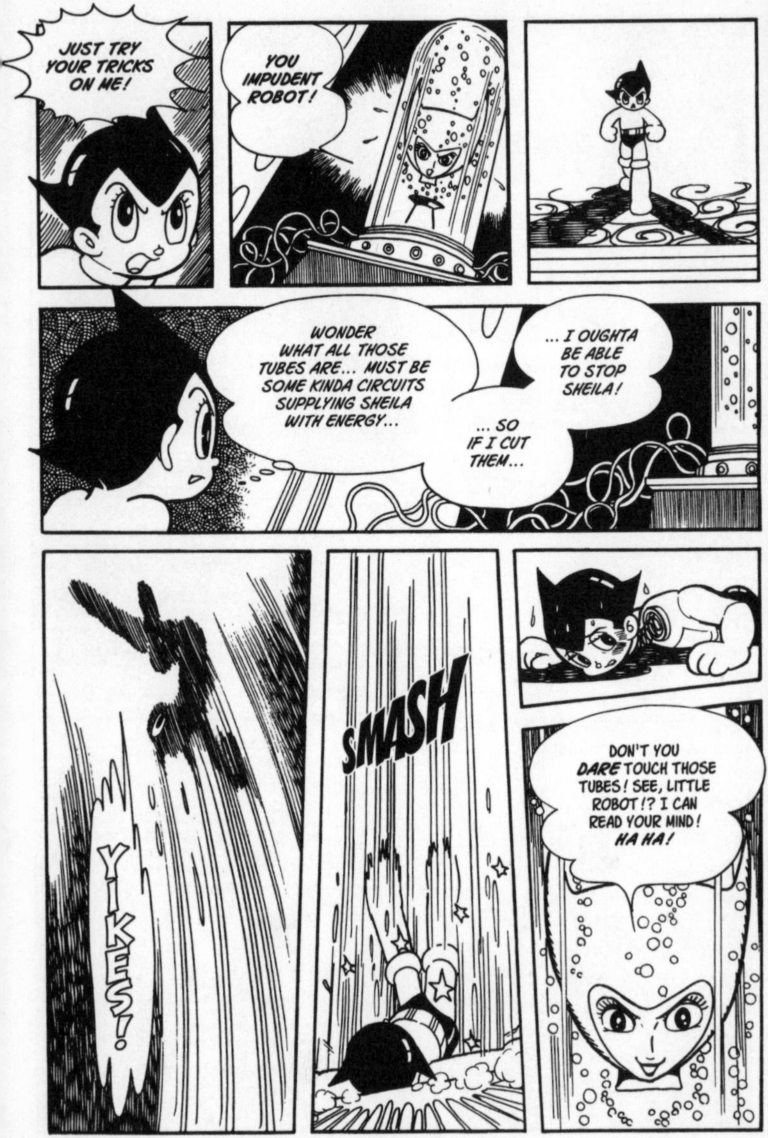
JUST TRY YOUR TRICKS ON ME!
YOU IMPUDENT ROBOT!
WONDER WHAT ALL THOSE TUBES ARE... MUST BE SOME KINDA CIRCUITS SUPPLYING SHEILA WITH ENERGY...
... SO IF I CUT THEM...
... I OUGHTA BE ABLE TO STOP SHEILA!
YIKES!
SMASH
DON'T YOU DARE TOUCH THOSE TUBES! SEE, LITTLE ROBOT!? I CAN READ YOUR MIND! HA HA!

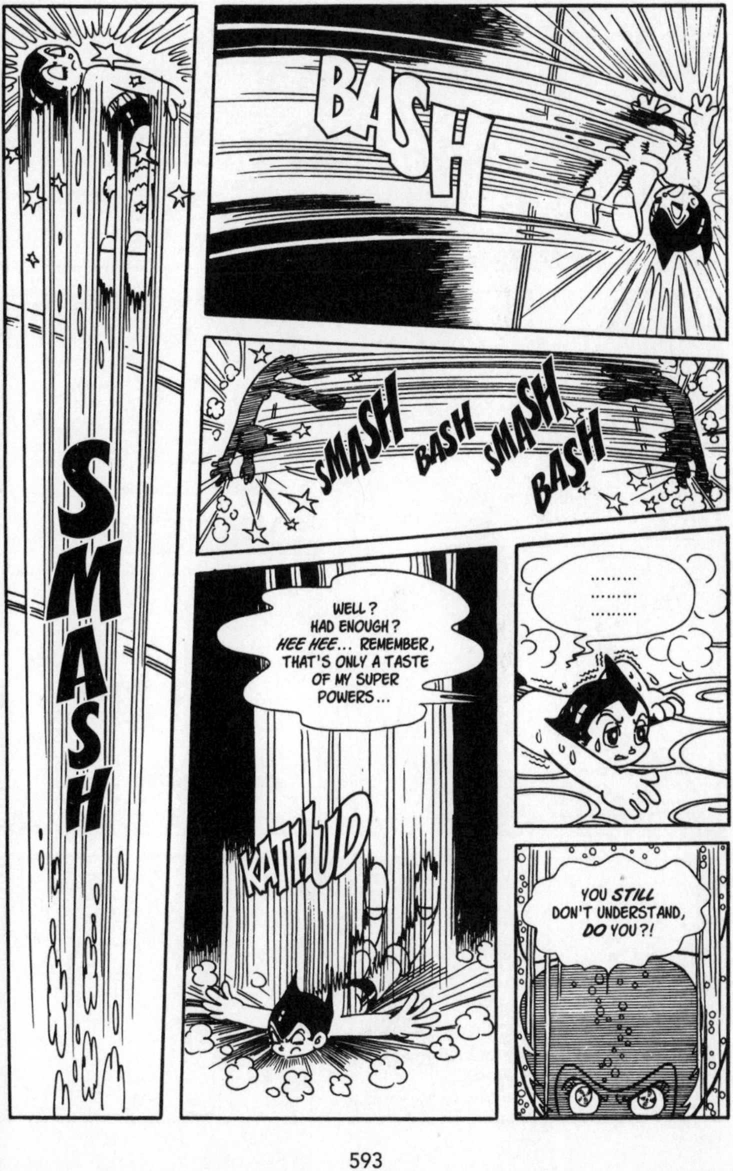
SMASH
BASH
SMASH
BASH
SMASH
BASH
WELL? HAD ENOUGH? *HEE HEE*... REMEMBER, THAT'S ONLY A TASTE OF MY SUPER POWERS...
KATHUD
....
....
....
YOU *STILL* DON'T UNDERSTAND, *DO* YOU?!

TIME FOR A *SPIN!*

YIKES!

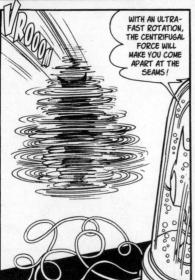

VROOOM

WITH AN ULTRA-FAST ROTATION, THE CENTRIFUGAL FORCE WILL MAKE YOU COME APART AT THE SEAMS!

SLAM

BASH

594

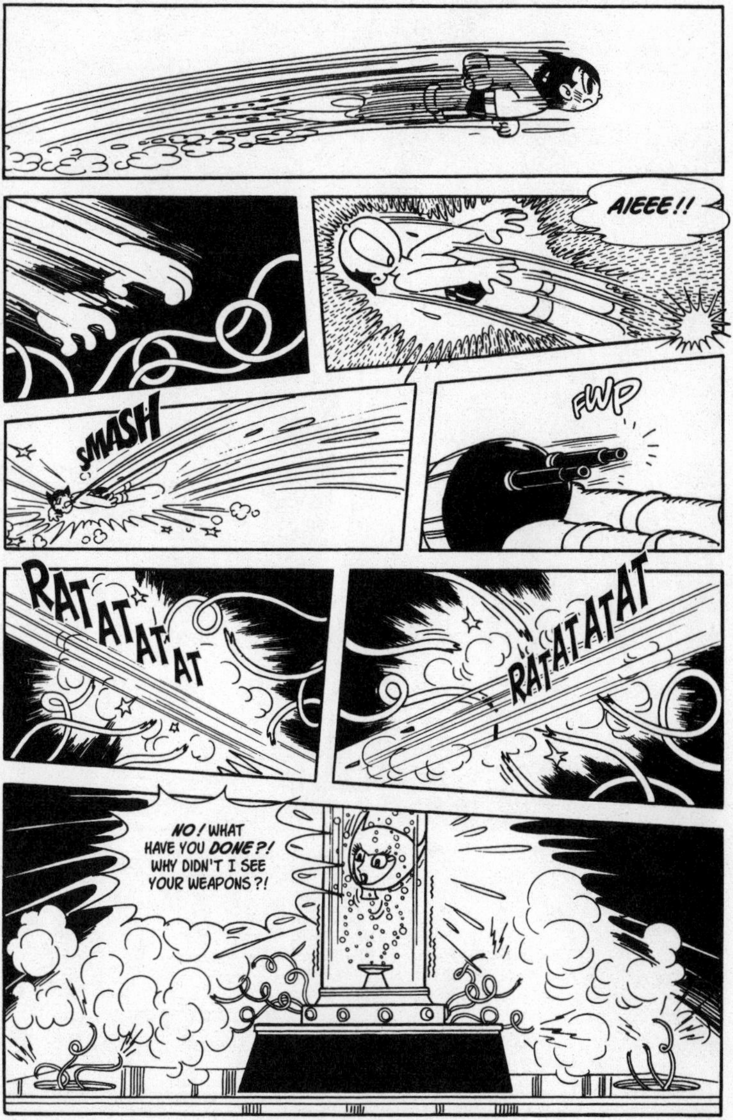
AIEEE!!
SMASH
FWP
RATATATAT
RATATATAT
NO! WHAT HAVE YOU DONE?! WHY DIDN'T I SEE YOUR WEAPONS?!

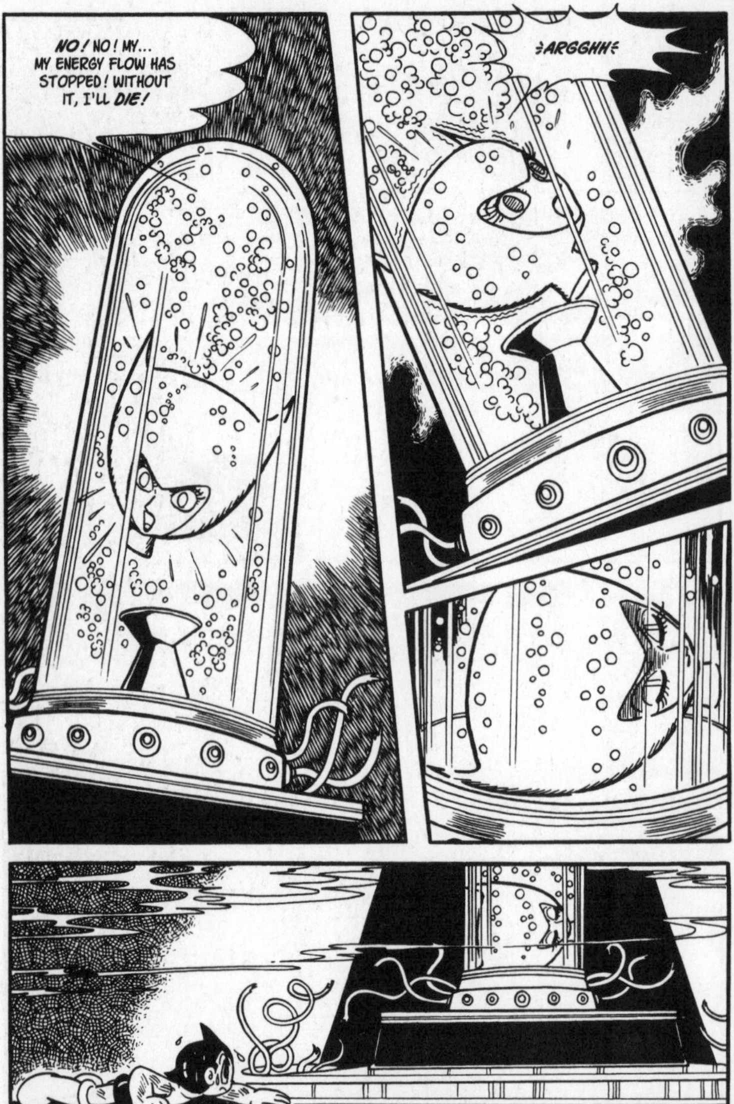
NO! NO! MY... MY ENERGY FLOW HAS STOPPED! WITHOUT IT, I'LL DIE!
ARGGHH

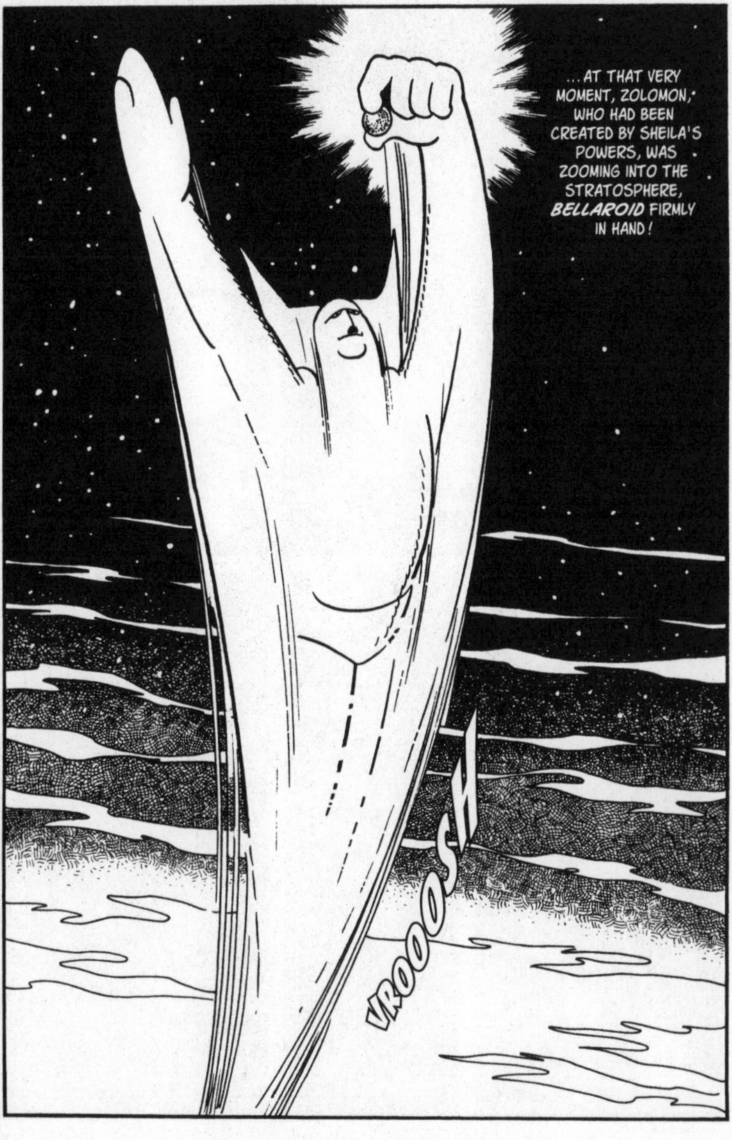
...AT THAT VERY MOMENT, ZOLOMON, WHO HAD BEEN CREATED BY SHEILA'S POWERS, WAS ZOOMING INTO THE STRATOSPHERE, *BELLAROID* FIRMLY IN HAND!
VROOOOSH

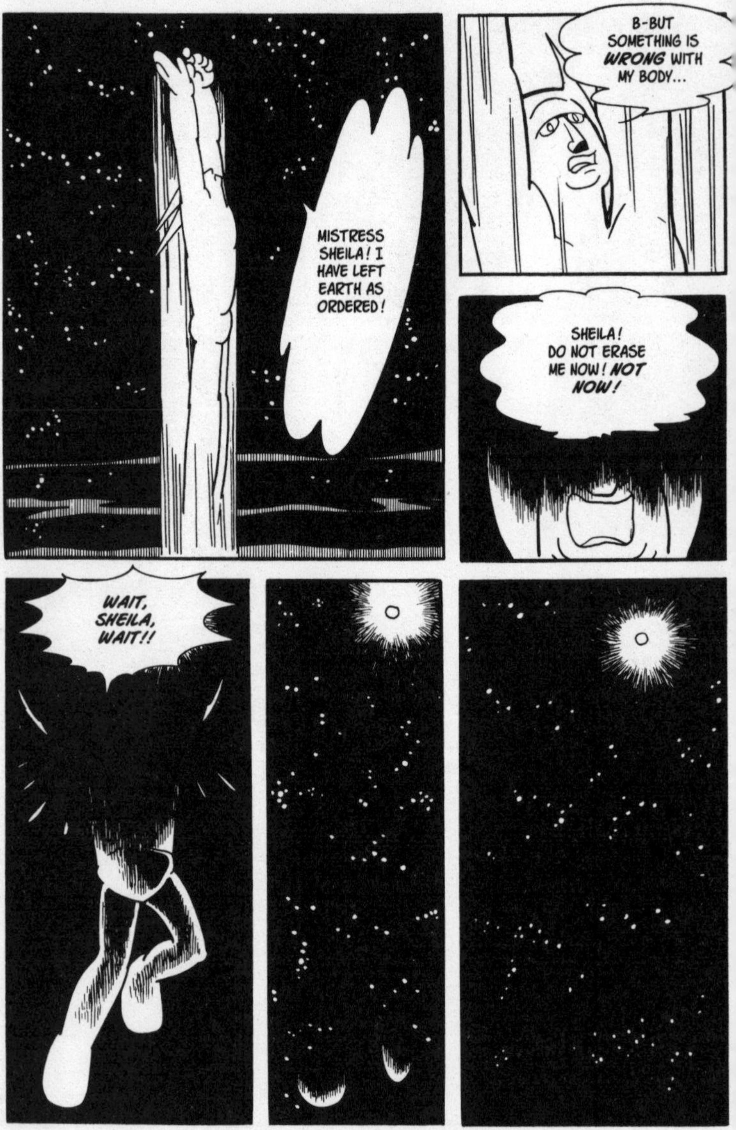
MISTRESS SHEILA! I HAVE LEFT EARTH AS ORDERED!
B-BUT SOMETHING IS ***WRONG*** WITH MY BODY...
SHEILA! DO NOT ERASE ME NOW! ***NOT NOW!***
WAIT, SHEILA, WAIT!!

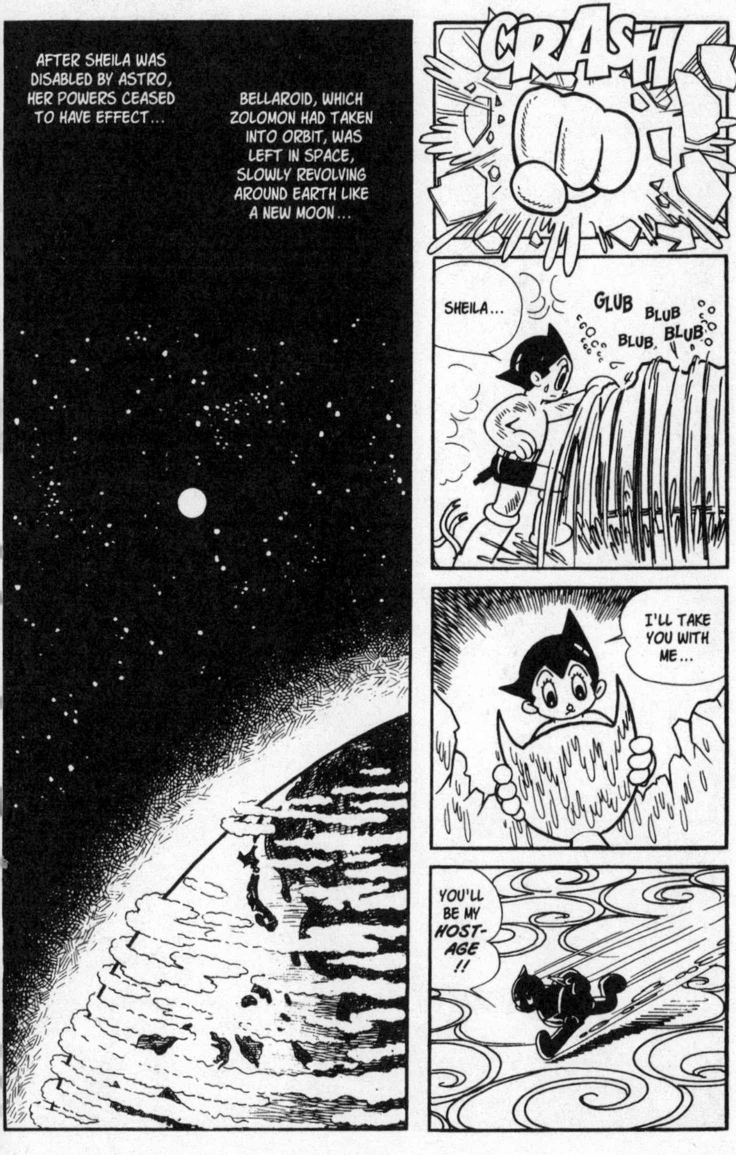
AFTER SHEILA WAS DISABLED BY ASTRO, HER POWERS CEASED TO HAVE EFFECT...
BELLAROID, WHICH ZOLOMON HAD TAKEN INTO ORBIT, WAS LEFT IN SPACE, SLOWLY REVOLVING AROUND EARTH LIKE A NEW MOON...
CRASH
SHEILA...
GLUB
BLUB
BLUB
BLUB
I'LL TAKE YOU WITH ME...
YOU'LL BE MY *HOST-AGE* !!

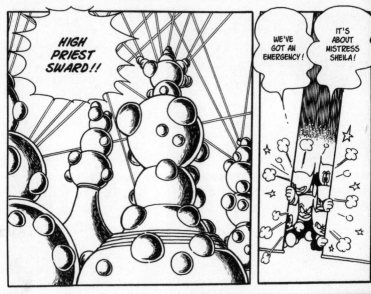

HIGH PRIEST SWARD!!

WE'VE GOT AN EMERGENCY!

IT'S ABOUT MISTRESS SHEILA!

WHAT? YOU SAY SHE'S *GONE*?!

IT'S TRUE! AN' HER CAPSULE'S BEEN SMASHED!

B-BUT WHAT ABOUT BELLAROID?!

IF WE DON'T *DO* SOMETHING, WE'LL BE DRAGGED OUT OF ORBIT BY THE EARTH'S GRAVITY AND BURN UP AS WE ENTER THE ATMOSPHERE!

I FOUND THE PERSON WHO KIDNAPPED MISTRESS SHEILA, SIR!

WHERE? WHERE IS HE?

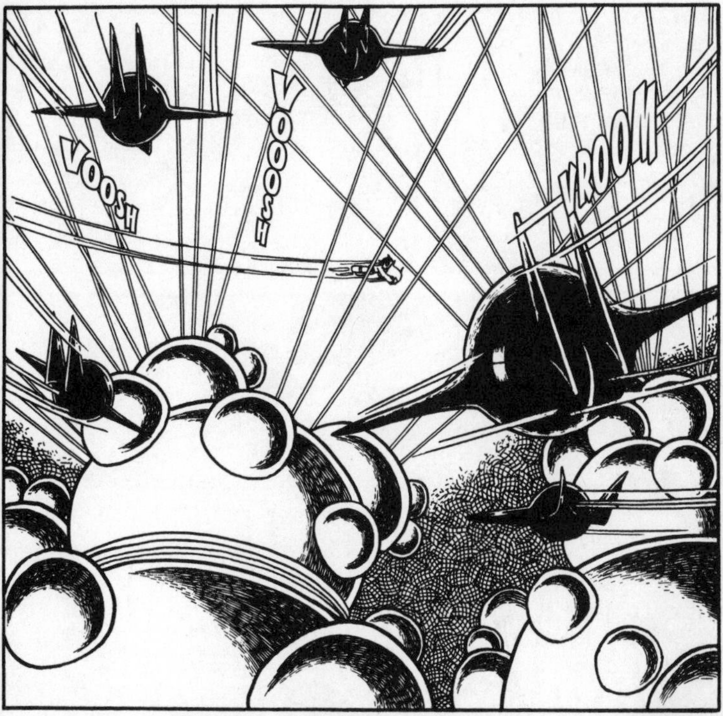
VOOSH
VOOOOSH
VROOM
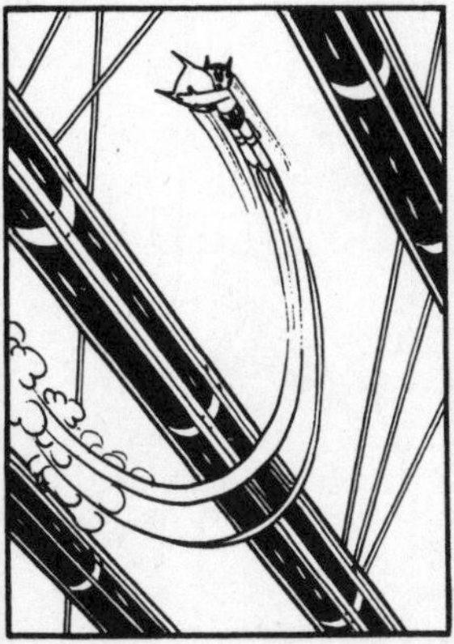
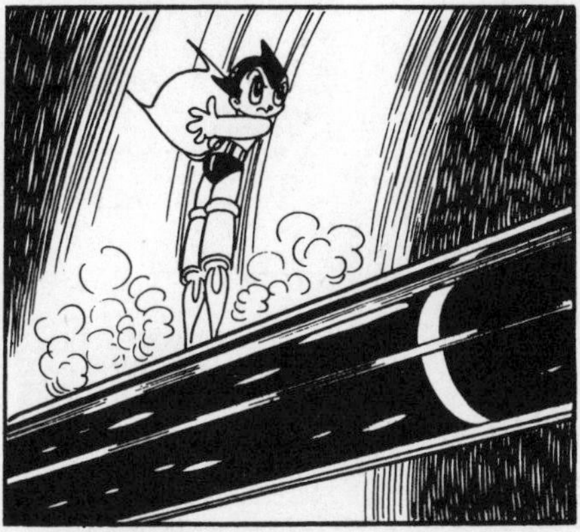

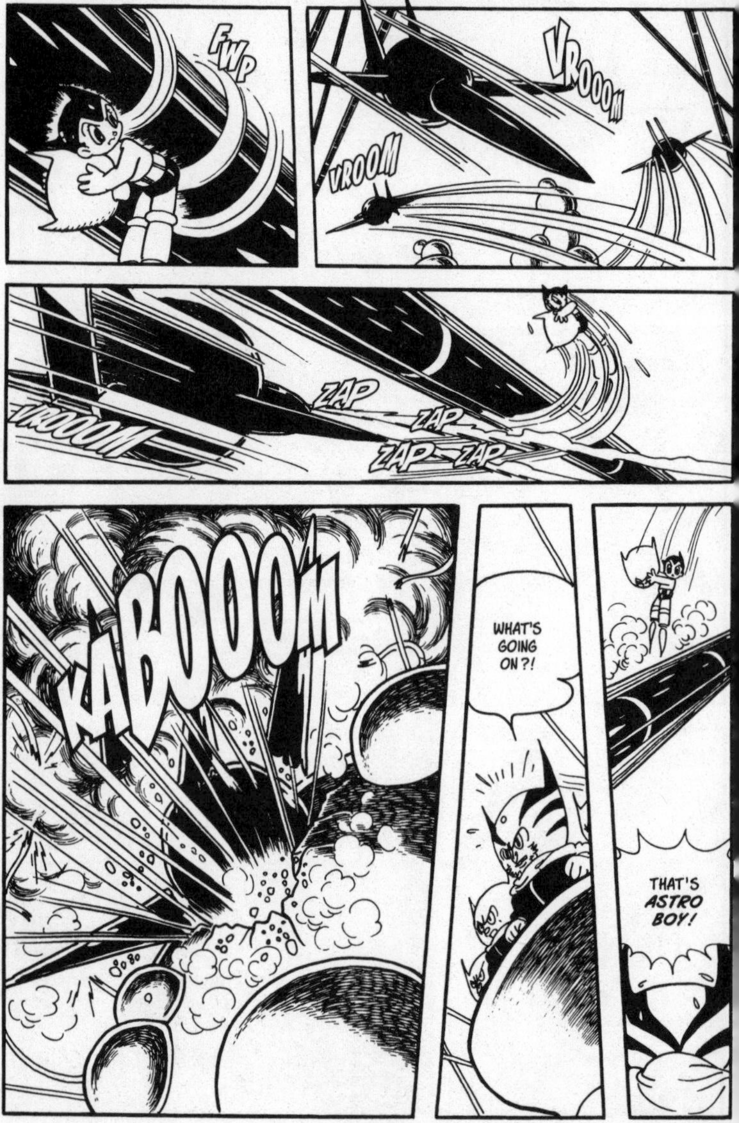
FWP
VROOOM
VROOM
ZAP
ZAP
ZAP
ZAP
VROOOOM
KABOOOM
WHAT'S GOING ON?!
THAT'S ASTRO BOY!

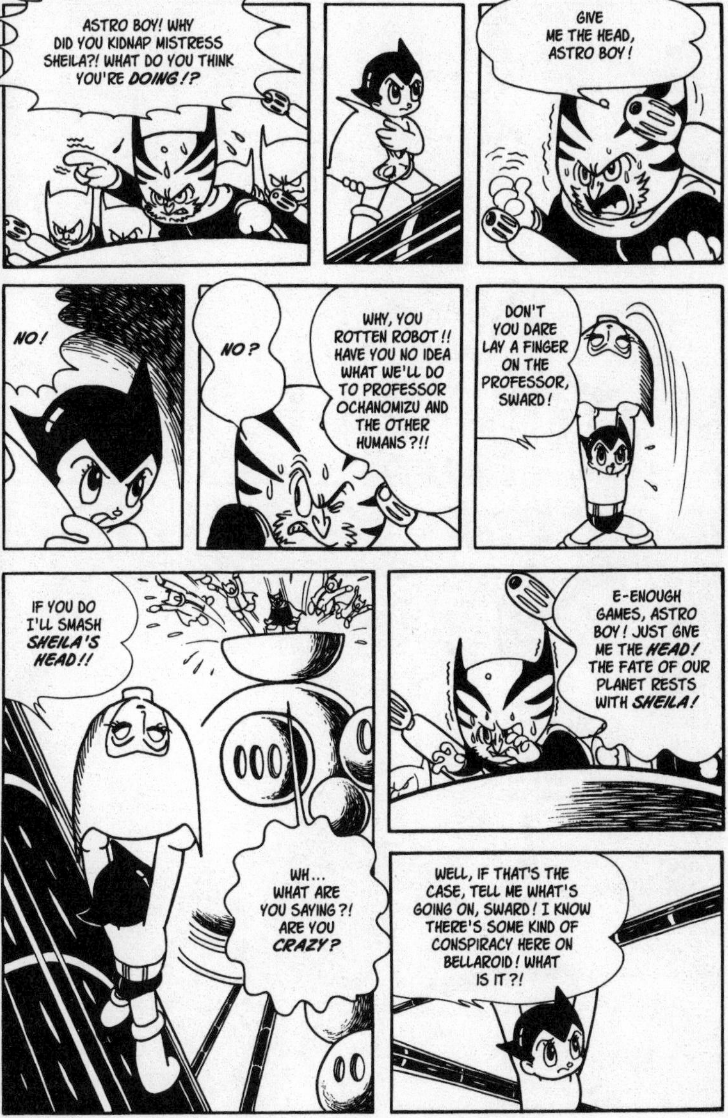
ASTRO BOY! WHY DID YOU KIDNAP MISTRESS SHEILA?! WHAT DO YOU THINK YOU'RE **DOING!?**
GIVE ME THE HEAD, ASTRO BOY!
NO!
NO?
WHY, YOU ROTTEN ROBOT!! HAVE YOU NO IDEA WHAT WE'LL DO TO PROFESSOR OCHANOMIZU AND THE OTHER HUMANS?!!
DON'T YOU DARE LAY A FINGER ON THE PROFESSOR, SWARD!
IF YOU DO I'LL SMASH ***SHEILA'S HEAD!!***
WH... WHAT ARE YOU SAYING?! ARE YOU ***CRAZY?***
E-ENOUGH GAMES, ASTRO BOY! JUST GIVE ME THE ***HEAD!*** THE FATE OF OUR PLANET RESTS WITH ***SHEILA!***
WELL, IF THAT'S THE CASE, TELL ME WHAT'S GOING ON, SWARD! I KNOW THERE'S SOME KIND OF CONSPIRACY HERE ON BELLAROID! WHAT IS IT?!

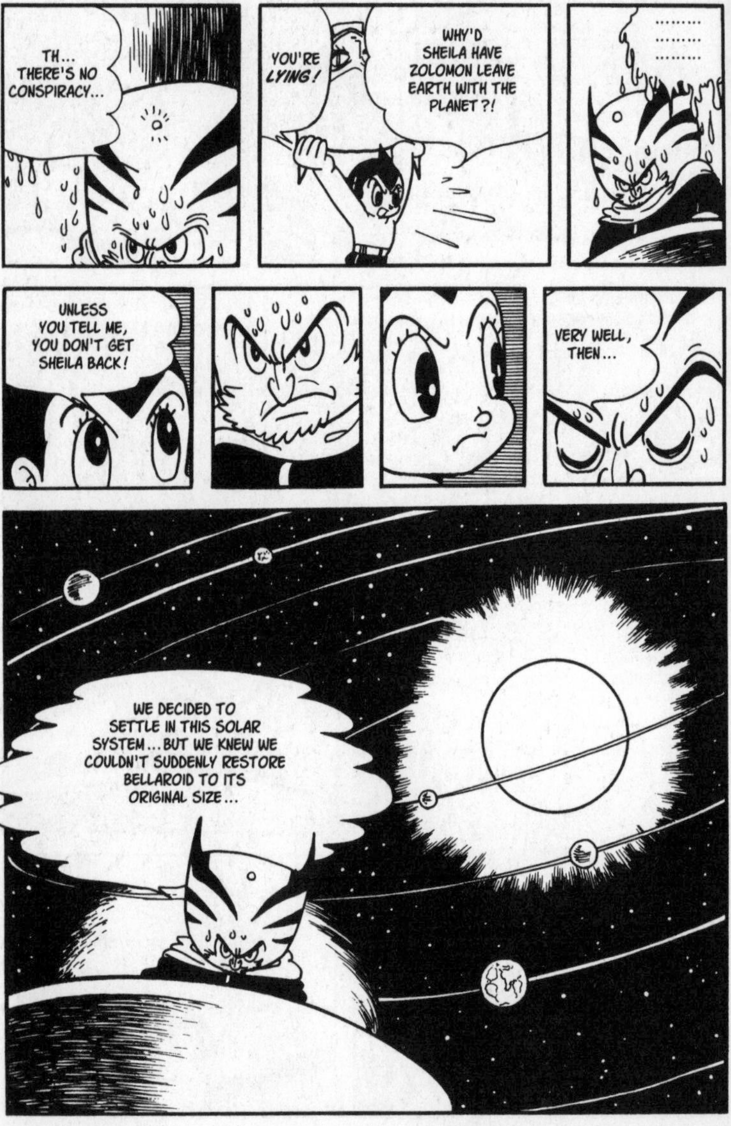

TH... THERE'S NO CONSPIRACY...
YOU'RE LYING!
WHY'D SHEILA HAVE ZOLOMON LEAVE EARTH WITH THE PLANET?!
....
....
....
UNLESS YOU TELL ME, YOU DON'T GET SHEILA BACK!
VERY WELL, THEN...
WE DECIDED TO SETTLE IN THIS SOLAR SYSTEM...BUT WE KNEW WE COULDN'T SUDDENLY RESTORE BELLAROID TO ITS ORIGINAL SIZE...

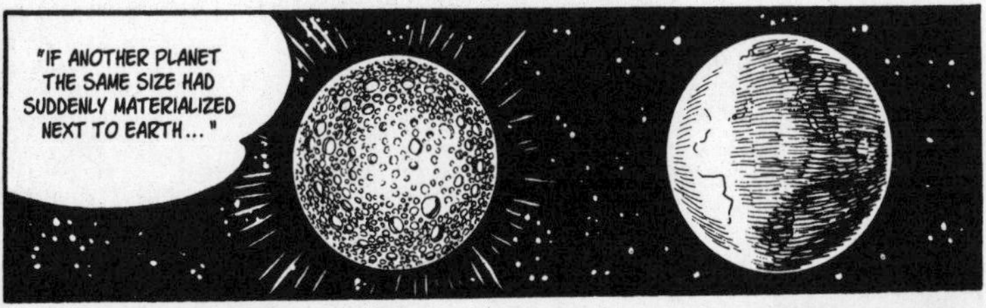
"IF ANOTHER PLANET THE SAME SIZE HAD SUDDENLY MATERIALIZED NEXT TO EARTH..."
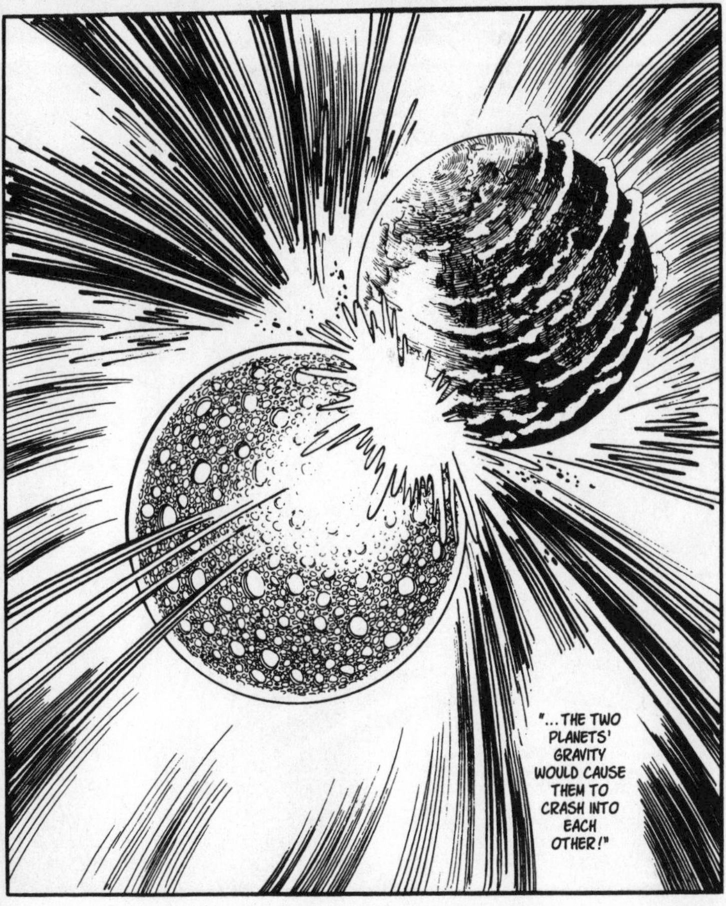
"...THE TWO PLANETS' GRAVITY WOULD CAUSE THEM TO CRASH INTO EACH OTHER!"

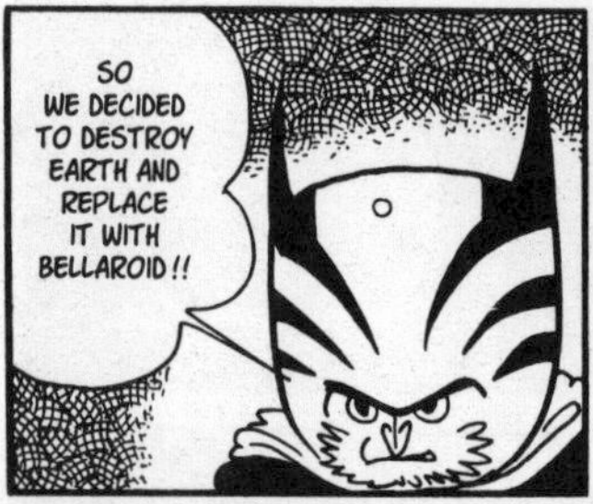
SO WE DECIDED TO DESTROY EARTH AND REPLACE IT WITH BELLAROID!!

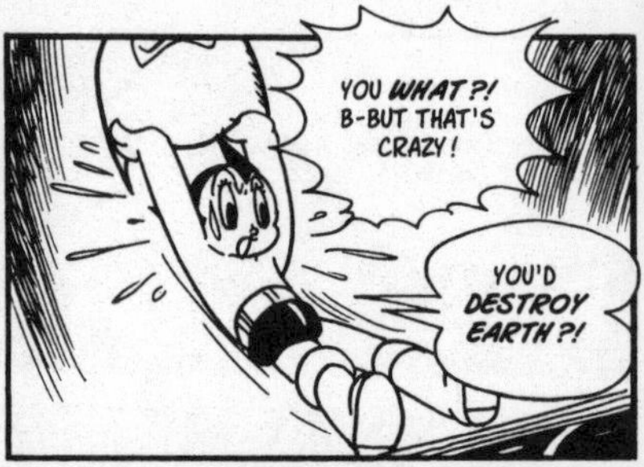
YOU **WHAT?!** B-BUT THAT'S CRAZY!
YOU'D ***DESTROY EARTH?!***

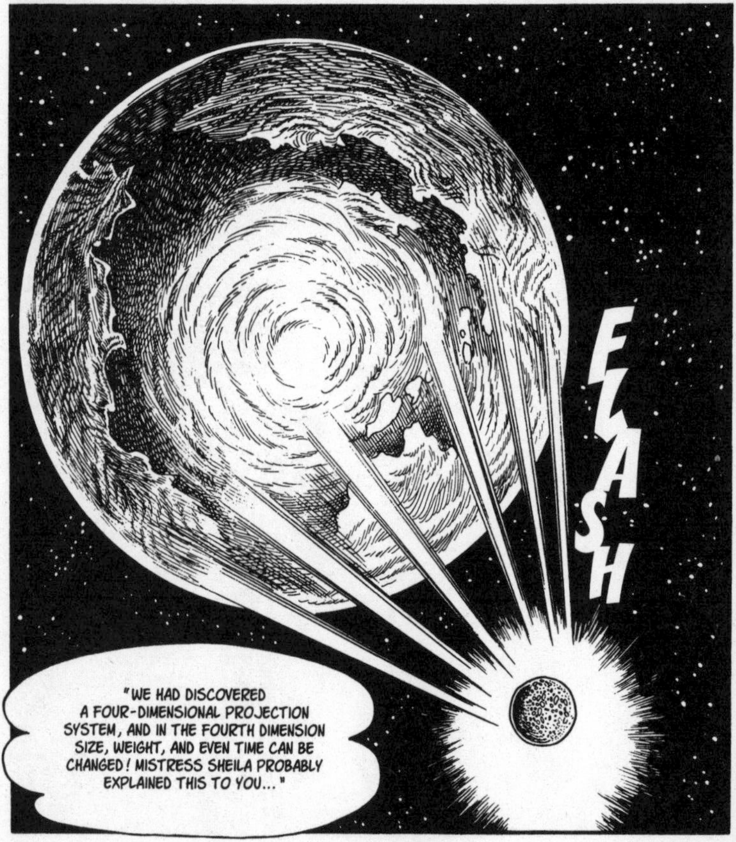
FLASH
"WE HAD DISCOVERED A FOUR-DIMENSIONAL PROJECTION SYSTEM, AND IN THE FOURTH DIMENSION SIZE, WEIGHT, AND EVEN TIME CAN BE CHANGED! MISTRESS SHEILA PROBABLY EXPLAINED THIS TO YOU..."

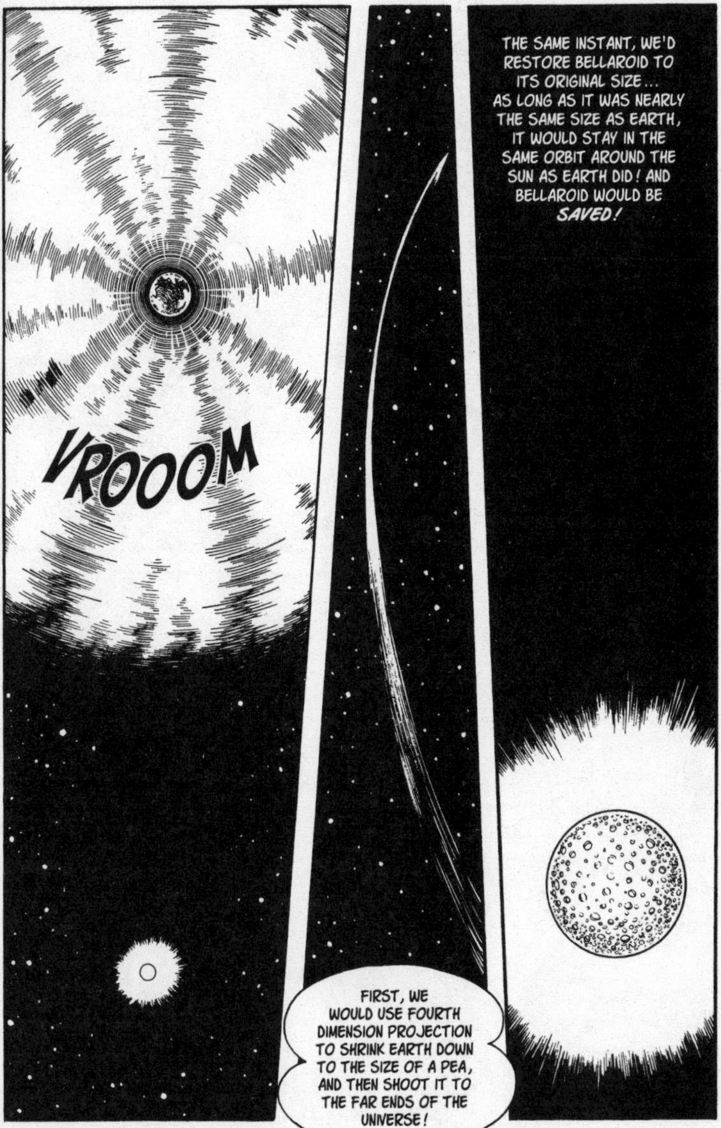
VROOOM
FIRST, WE WOULD USE FOURTH DIMENSION PROJECTION TO SHRINK EARTH DOWN TO THE SIZE OF A PEA, AND THEN SHOOT IT TO THE FAR ENDS OF THE UNIVERSE!
THE SAME INSTANT, WE'D RESTORE BELLAROID TO ITS ORIGINAL SIZE... AS LONG AS IT WAS NEARLY THE SAME SIZE AS EARTH, IT WOULD STAY IN THE SAME ORBIT AROUND THE SUN AS EARTH DID! AND BELLAROID WOULD BE SAVED!

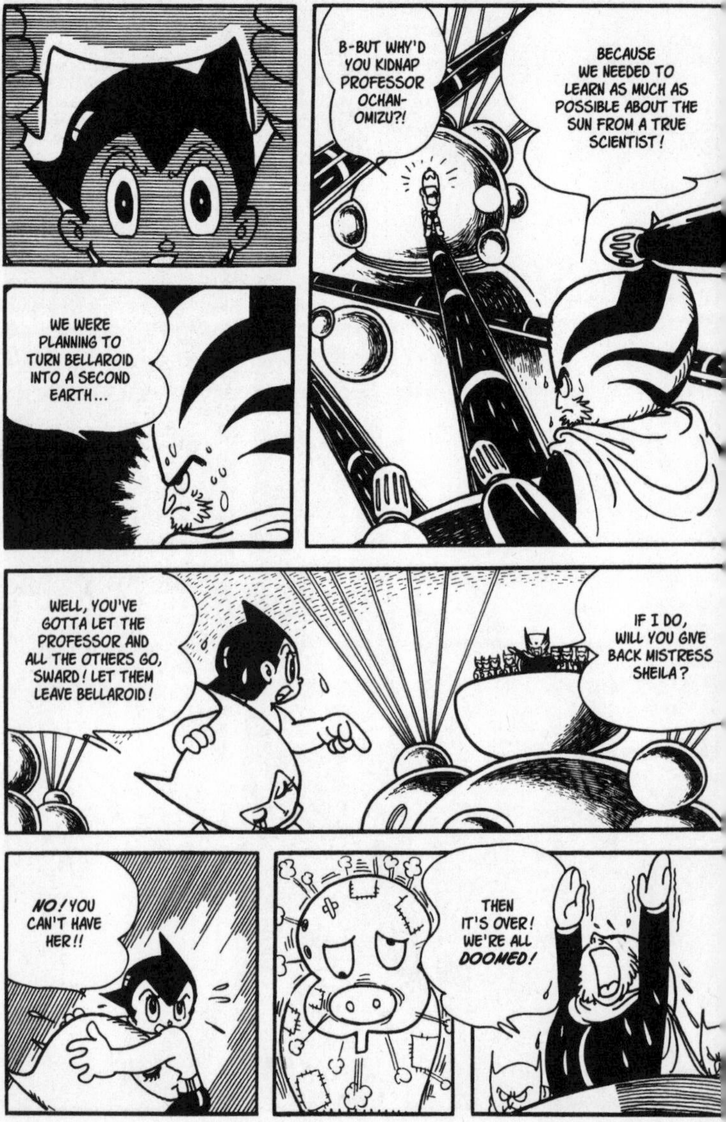
B-BUT WHY'D YOU KIDNAP PROFESSOR OCHAN-OMIZU?!
BECAUSE WE NEEDED TO LEARN AS MUCH AS POSSIBLE ABOUT THE SUN FROM A TRUE SCIENTIST!
WE WERE PLANNING TO TURN BELLAROID INTO A SECOND EARTH...
WELL, YOU'VE GOTTA LET THE PROFESSOR AND ALL THE OTHERS GO, SWARD! LET THEM LEAVE BELLAROID!
IF I DO, WILL YOU GIVE BACK MISTRESS SHEILA?
NO! YOU CAN'T HAVE HER!!
THEN IT'S OVER! WE'RE ALL DOOMED!

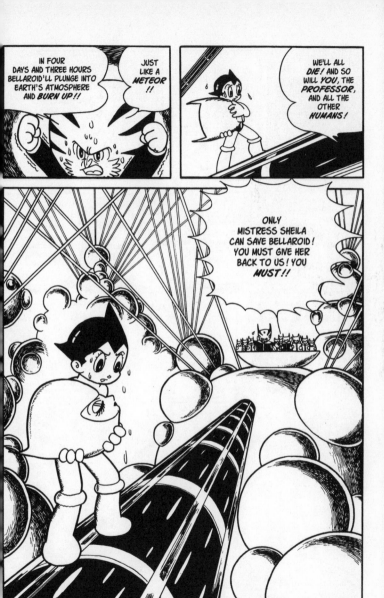

IN FOUR DAYS AND THREE HOURS BELLAROID'LL PLUNGE INTO EARTH'S ATMOSPHERE AND *BURN UP!!*

JUST LIKE A *METEOR!!*

WE'LL ALL *DIE!* AND SO WILL *YOU,* THE *PROFESSOR,* AND ALL THE OTHER *HUMANS!*

ONLY MISTRESS SHEILA CAN SAVE BELLAROID! YOU MUST GIVE HER BACK TO US! YOU *MUST!!*

I KNOW!

I'LL HAVE THE PROFESSOR *REBUILD* SHEILA! SHE CAN KEEP HER SUPER POWERS...

... BUT HE CAN MODIFY HER TO BE A ROBOT THAT LOVES EARTH AND IS A *FRIEND* OF HUMANS!

NO EARTH SCIENTIST COULD EVER *MODIFY* MISTRESS SHEILA!

EVEN TRYING'S A WASTE OF TIME!

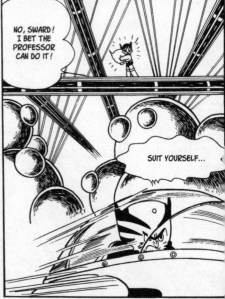

NO, SWARD! I BET THE PROFESSOR CAN DO IT!

SUIT YOURSELF...

610

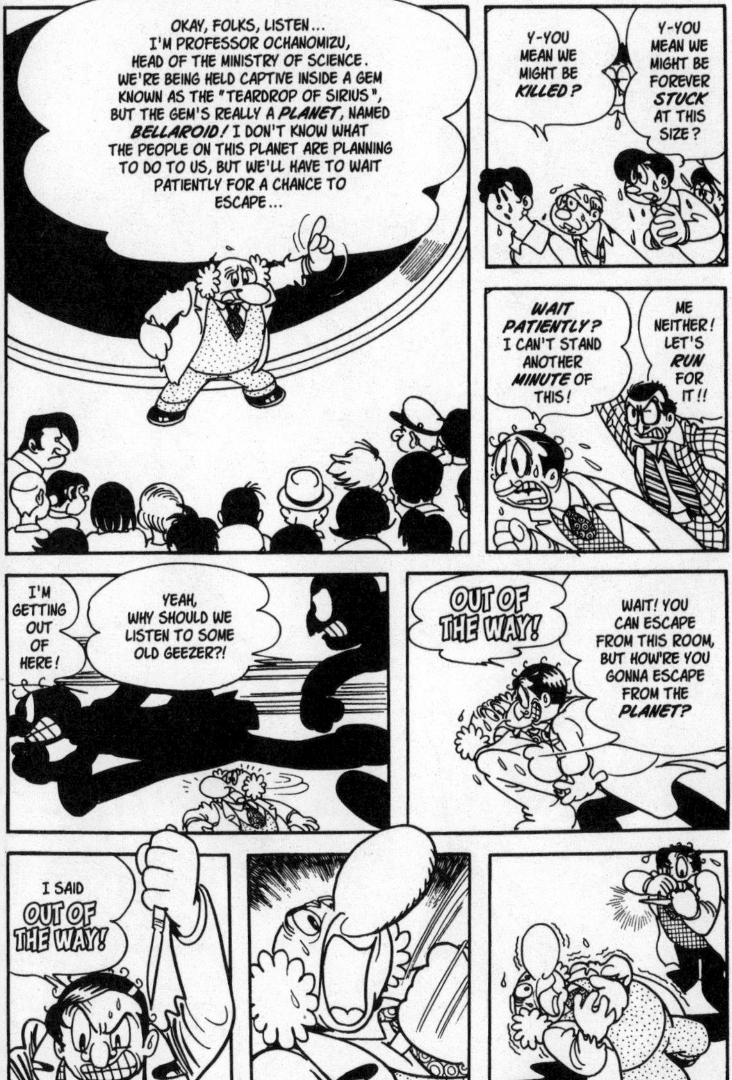

OKAY, FOLKS, LISTEN... I'M PROFESSOR OCHANOMIZU, HEAD OF THE MINISTRY OF SCIENCE. WE'RE BEING HELD CAPTIVE INSIDE A GEM KNOWN AS THE "TEARDROP OF SIRIUS", BUT THE GEM'S REALLY A PLANET, NAMED BELLAROID! I DON'T KNOW WHAT THE PEOPLE ON THIS PLANET ARE PLANNING TO DO TO US, BUT WE'LL HAVE TO WAIT PATIENTLY FOR A CHANCE TO ESCAPE...
Y-YOU MEAN WE MIGHT BE KILLED?
Y-YOU MEAN WE MIGHT BE FOREVER STUCK AT THIS SIZE?
WAIT PATIENTLY? I CAN'T STAND ANOTHER MINUTE OF THIS!
ME NEITHER! LET'S RUN FOR IT!!
I'M GETTING OUT OF HERE!
YEAH, WHY SHOULD WE LISTEN TO SOME OLD GEEZER?!
OUT OF THE WAY!
WAIT! YOU CAN ESCAPE FROM THIS ROOM, BUT HOW'RE YOU GONNA ESCAPE FROM THE PLANET?
I SAID OUT OF THE WAY!

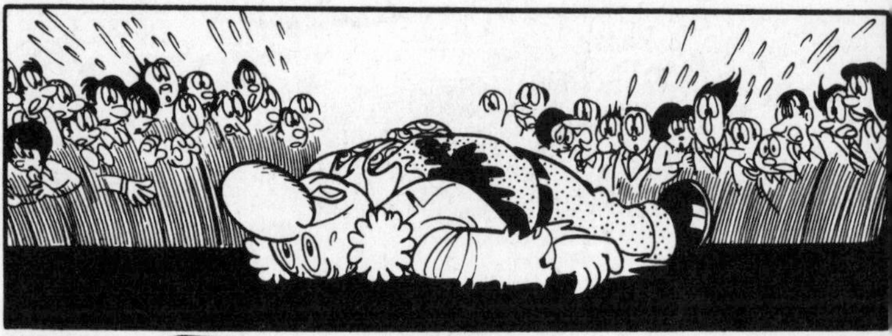

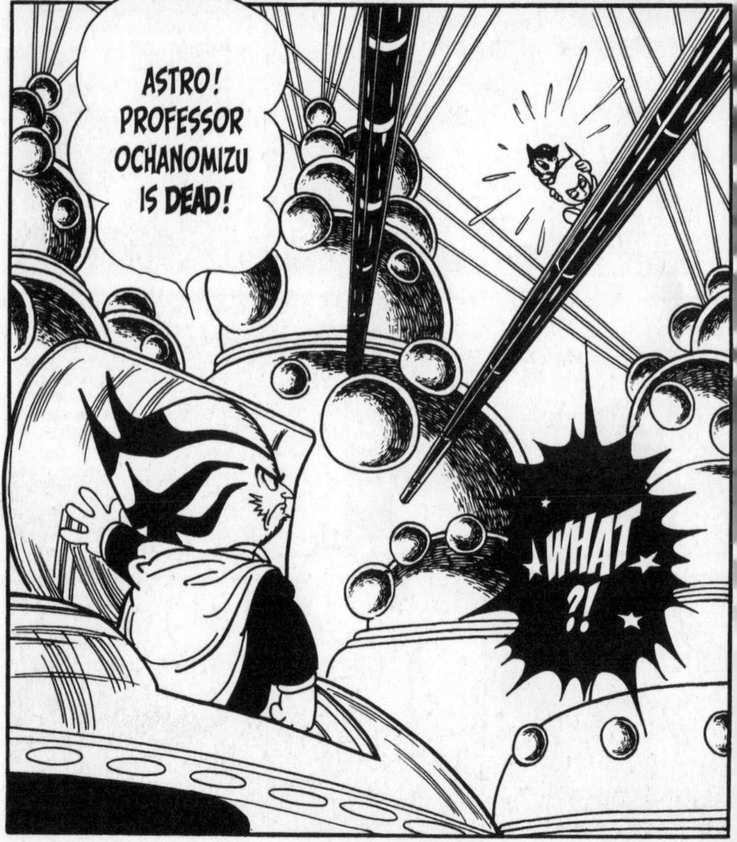
ASTRO! PROFESSOR OCHANOMIZU IS DEAD!
WHAT ?!

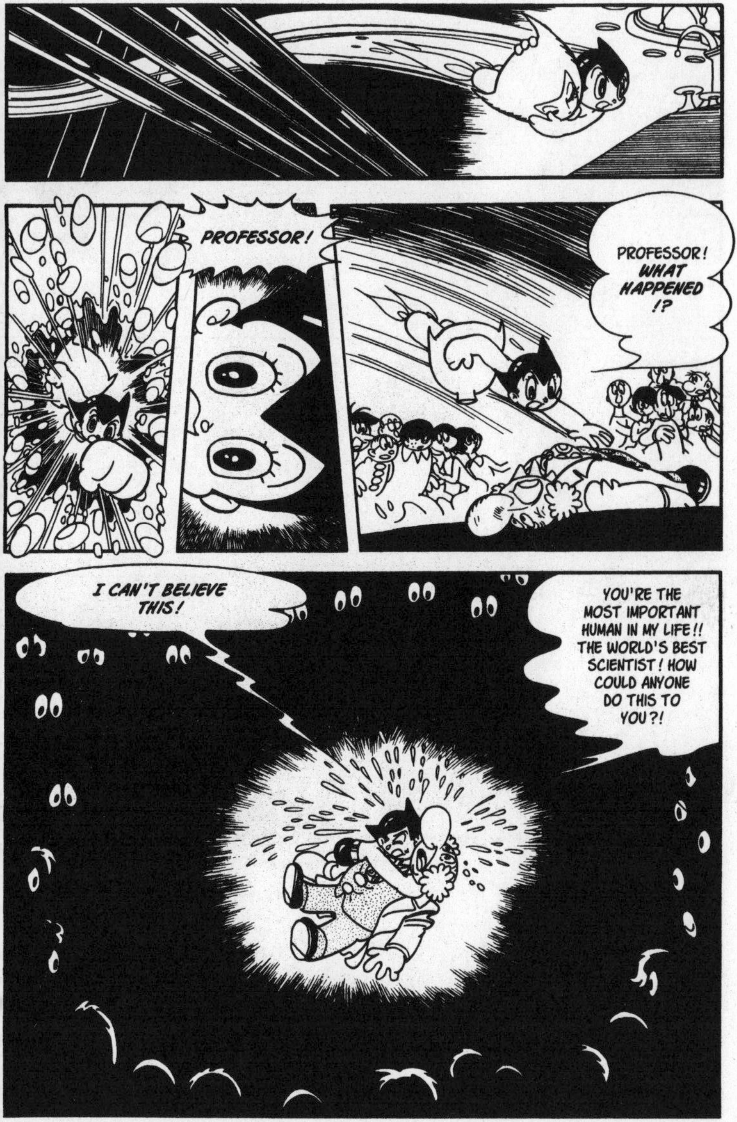
PROFESSOR!
PROFESSOR! WHAT HAPPENED !?
I CAN'T BELIEVE THIS!
YOU'RE THE MOST IMPORTANT HUMAN IN MY LIFE!! THE WORLD'S BEST SCIENTIST! HOW COULD ANYONE DO THIS TO YOU?!

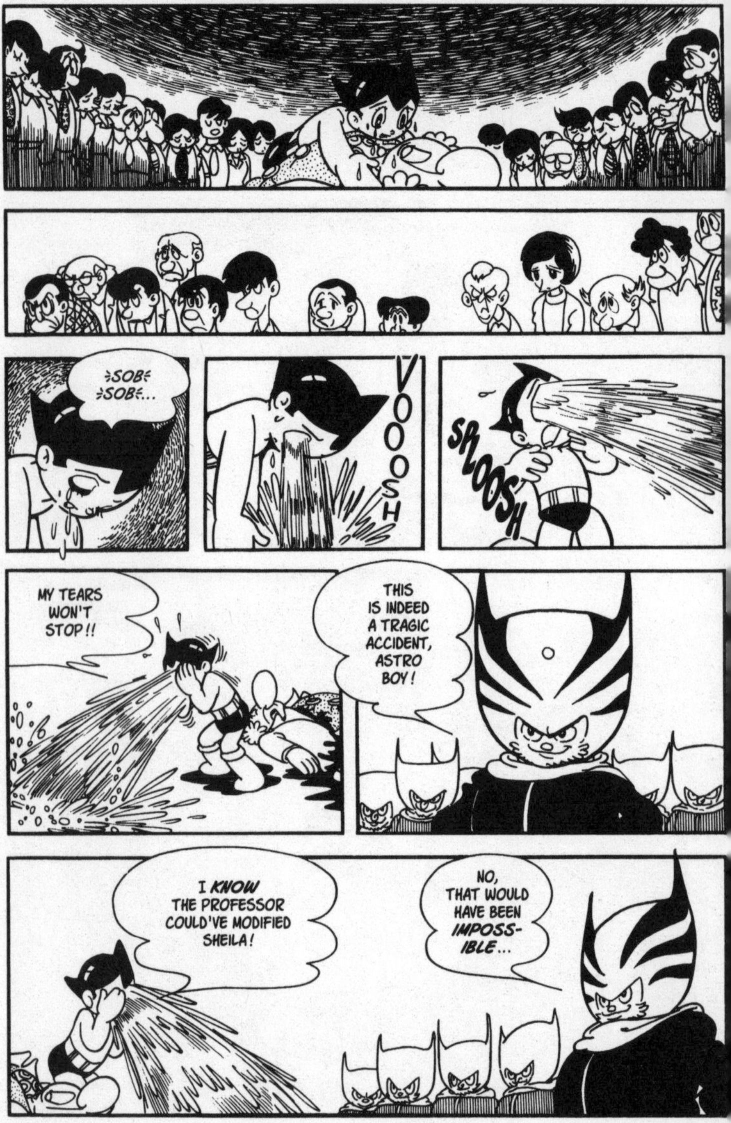

SOB SOB...
VOOOOSH
SPLOOSH
MY TEARS WON'T STOP!!
THIS IS INDEED A TRAGIC ACCIDENT, ASTRO BOY!
I *KNOW* THE PROFESSOR COULD'VE MODIFIED SHEILA!
NO, THAT WOULD HAVE BEEN *IMPOSS-IBLE*...

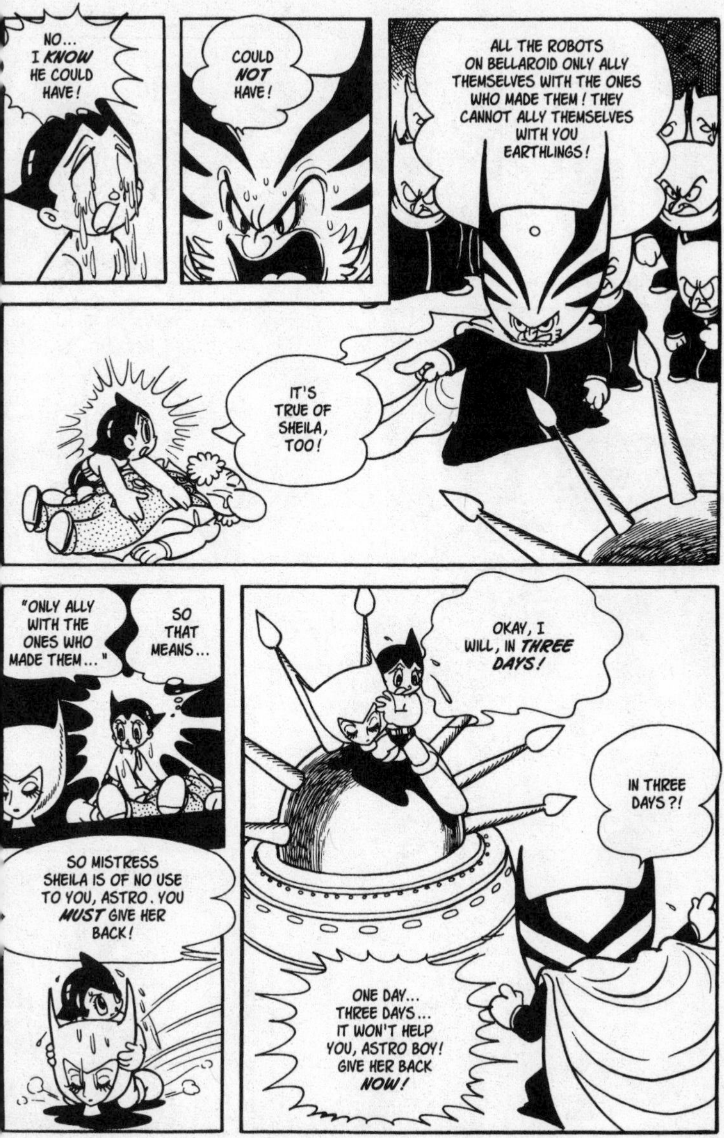
NO... I KNOW HE COULD HAVE!
COULD NOT HAVE!
ALL THE ROBOTS ON BELLAROID ONLY ALLY THEMSELVES WITH THE ONES WHO MADE THEM! THEY CANNOT ALLY THEMSELVES WITH YOU EARTHLINGS!
IT'S TRUE OF SHEILA, TOO!
"ONLY ALLY WITH THE ONES WHO MADE THEM..."
SO THAT MEANS...
SO MISTRESS SHEILA IS OF NO USE TO YOU, ASTRO. YOU MUST GIVE HER BACK!
OKAY, I WILL, IN THREE DAYS!
IN THREE DAYS?!
ONE DAY... THREE DAYS... IT WON'T HELP YOU, ASTRO BOY! GIVE HER BACK NOW!

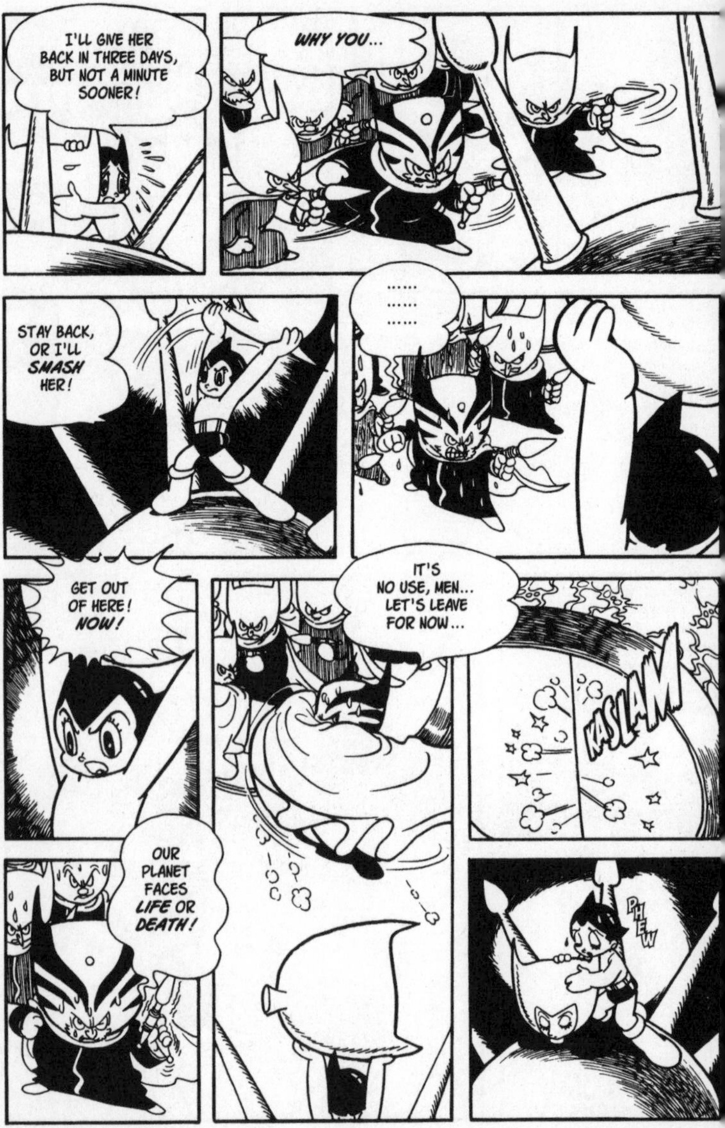
I'LL GIVE HER BACK IN THREE DAYS, BUT NOT A MINUTE SOONER!
WHY YOU...
STAY BACK, OR I'LL SMASH HER!
....
GET OUT OF HERE! NOW!
OUR PLANET FACES LIFE OR DEATH!
IT'S NO USE, MEN... LET'S LEAVE FOR NOW...
KASLAM
PHEW

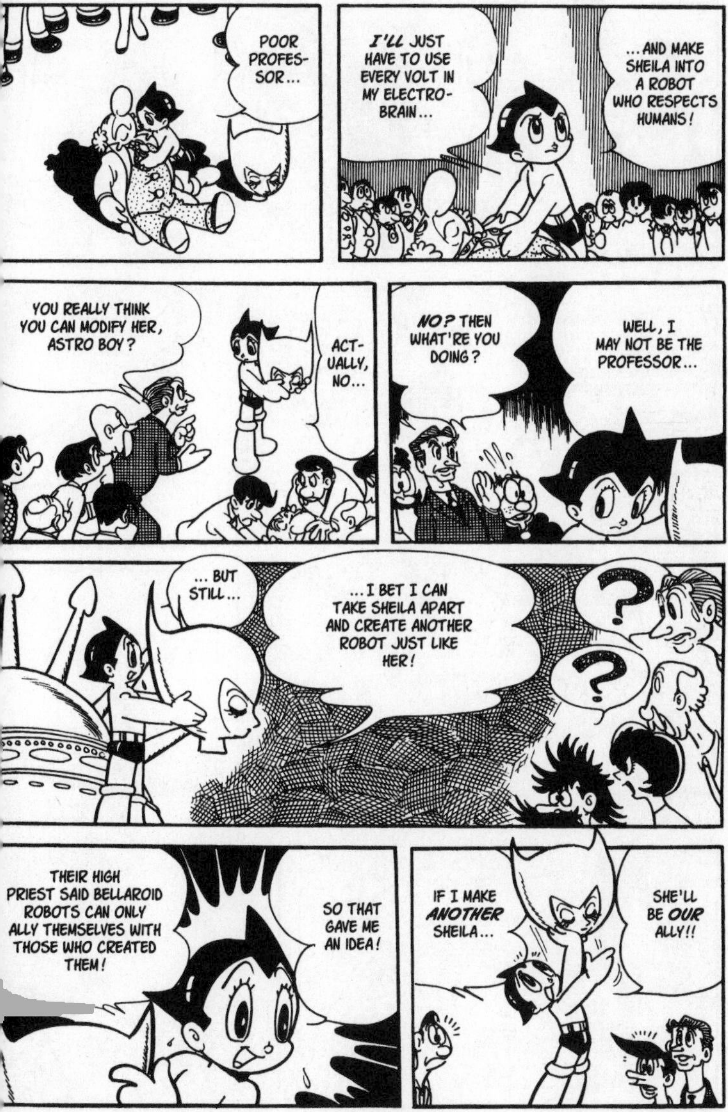
POOR PROFES-SOR...
I'LL JUST HAVE TO USE EVERY VOLT IN MY ELECTRO-BRAIN...
...AND MAKE SHEILA INTO A ROBOT WHO RESPECTS HUMANS!
YOU REALLY THINK YOU CAN MODIFY HER, ASTRO BOY?
ACT-UALLY, NO...
NO? THEN WHAT'RE YOU DOING?
WELL, I MAY NOT BE THE PROFESSOR...
...BUT STILL...
...I BET I CAN TAKE SHEILA APART AND CREATE ANOTHER ROBOT JUST LIKE HER!
?
?
THEIR HIGH PRIEST SAID BELLAROID ROBOTS CAN ONLY ALLY THEMSELVES WITH THOSE WHO CREATED THEM!
SO THAT GAVE ME AN IDEA!
IF I MAKE ANOTHER SHEILA...
SHE'LL BE OUR ALLY!!

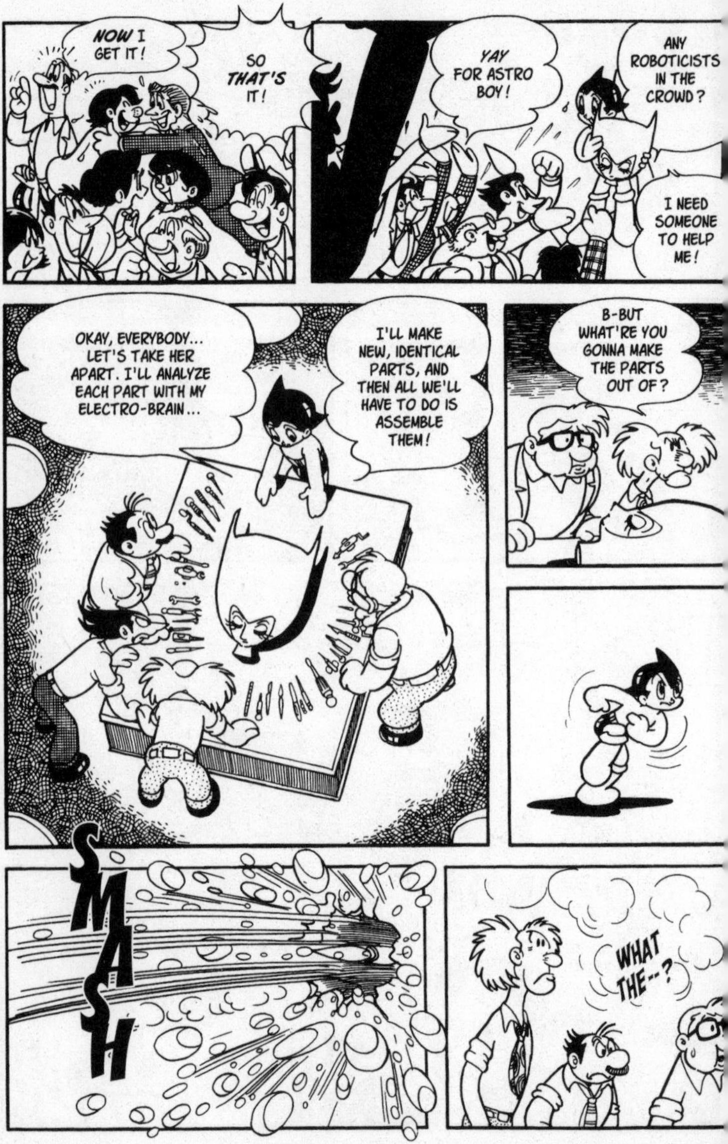
NOW I GET IT!
SO THAT'S IT!
YAY FOR ASTRO BOY!
ANY ROBOTICISTS IN THE CROWD?
I NEED SOMEONE TO HELP ME!
OKAY, EVERYBODY... LET'S TAKE HER APART. I'LL ANALYZE EACH PART WITH MY ELECTRO-BRAIN...
I'LL MAKE NEW, IDENTICAL PARTS, AND THEN ALL WE'LL HAVE TO DO IS ASSEMBLE THEM!
B-BUT WHAT'RE YOU GONNA MAKE THE PARTS OUT OF?
SMASH
WHAT THE--?

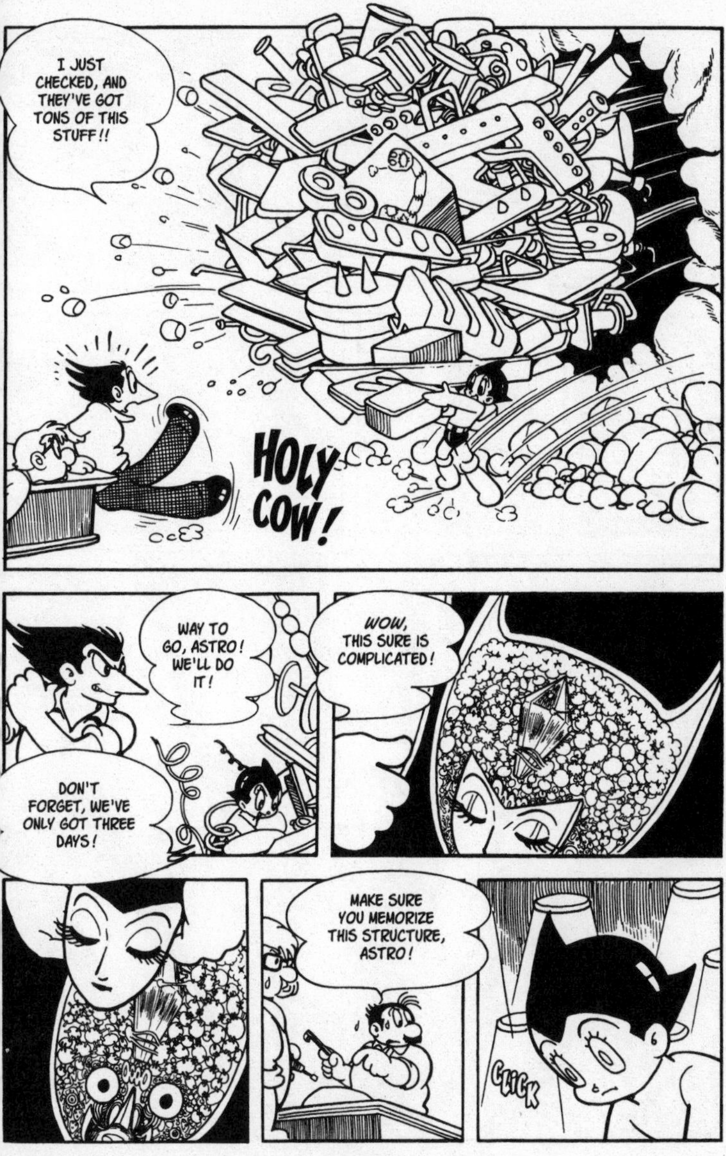
I JUST CHECKED, AND THEY'VE GOT TONS OF THIS STUFF!!
HOLY COW!
WAY TO GO, ASTRO! WE'LL DO IT!
DON'T FORGET, WE'VE ONLY GOT THREE DAYS!
WOW, THIS SURE IS COMPLICATED!
MAKE SURE YOU MEMORIZE THIS STRUCTURE, ASTRO!
CLICK

OKAY, ASTRO... EACH ONE OF THESE THINGS...

...IS APPARENTLY ONE OF HER BRAIN SPHERES... THINK CAN YOU ANALYZE THEM?

I'LL TRY...

I'LL PUT 'EM IN HERE...

...AND MY COMPUTER'LL ANALYZE 'EM IN TEN SECONDS!

BZZZT

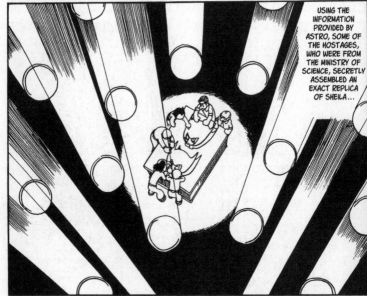

USING THE INFORMATION PROVIDED BY ASTRO, SOME OF THE HOSTAGES, WHO WERE FROM THE MINISTRY OF SCIENCE, SECRETLY ASSEMBLED AN EXACT REPLICA OF SHEILA...

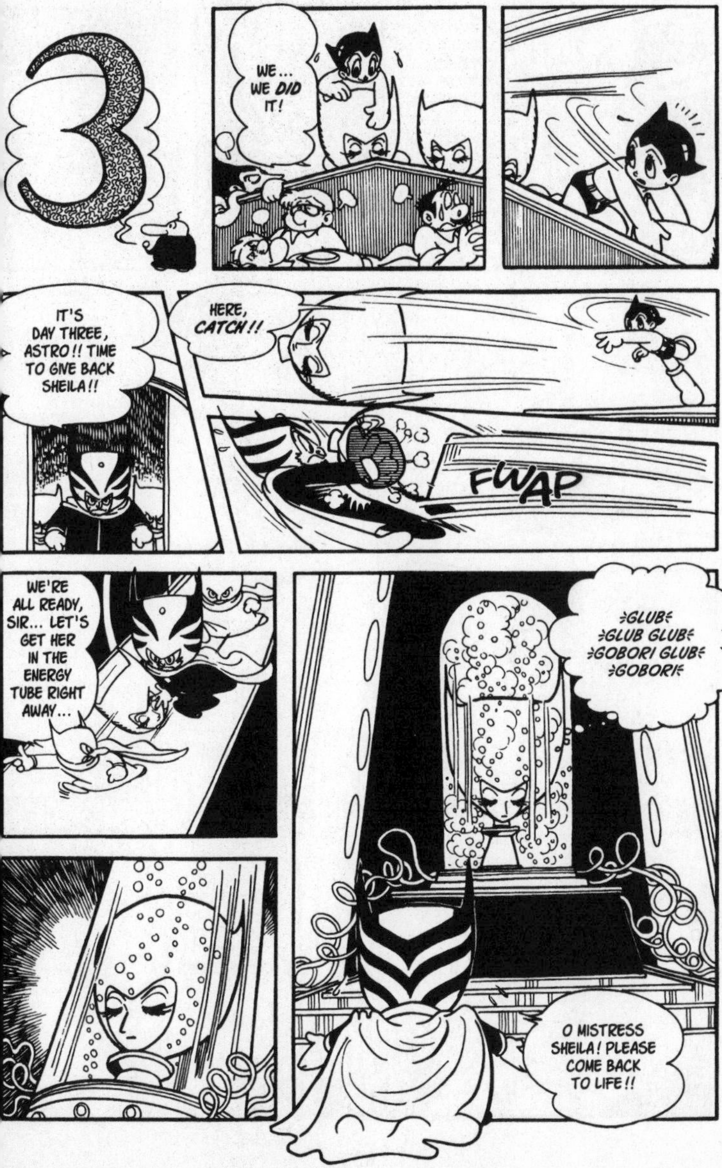
3
WE... WE DID IT!
IT'S DAY THREE, ASTRO!! TIME TO GIVE BACK SHEILA!!
HERE, CATCH!!
FWAP
WE'RE ALL READY, SIR... LET'S GET HER IN THE ENERGY TUBE RIGHT AWAY...
GLUB GLUB GLUB GOBORI GLUB GOBORI
O MISTRESS SHEILA! PLEASE COME BACK TO LIFE!!

GLUB GLUB GLUG GLUB GLUG GLUB GLUB

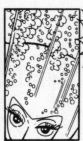

YOU'RE BACK!!

YOU'VE FINALLY COME TO AGAIN!

DO YOU RECOGNIZE ME, MISTRESS?

HIGH PRIEST SWARD...

THANK GOD! YOU SEEM TO BE ALL RIGHT!

FIRST OF ALL, I NEED YOU TO USE YOUR PSYCHIC POWERS AND TEACH THAT UPSTART ASTRO BOY AND THE EARTHLINGS WITH HIM A LESSON!!

NO!

WH- WHAT?!

I REFUSE! I SHALL *NOT* "TEACH ASTRO A LESSON"!!

AND I WON'T ALLOW YOU TO HURT HIM, EITHER!

B-B-BUT MISTRESS SHEILA!! WHAT HAPPENED?! ASTRO IS YOUR *ENEMY!* THE ENEMY OF *ALL BELLA-ROID!*

NO! HE IS OUR *FRIEND!!*

MISTRESS SHEILA'S LOST HER MIND!

AND ASTRO MUST BE BEHIND THIS!

PULL THE PLUG ON HER, MEN!

STOP!

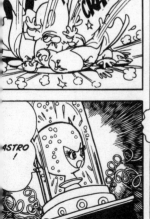

THUD

CRASH!

ASTRO!

YOU OKAY, SHEILA?

DON'T WORRY, ASTRO! I'M FINE!

THAT BLASTED ROBOT!!

623

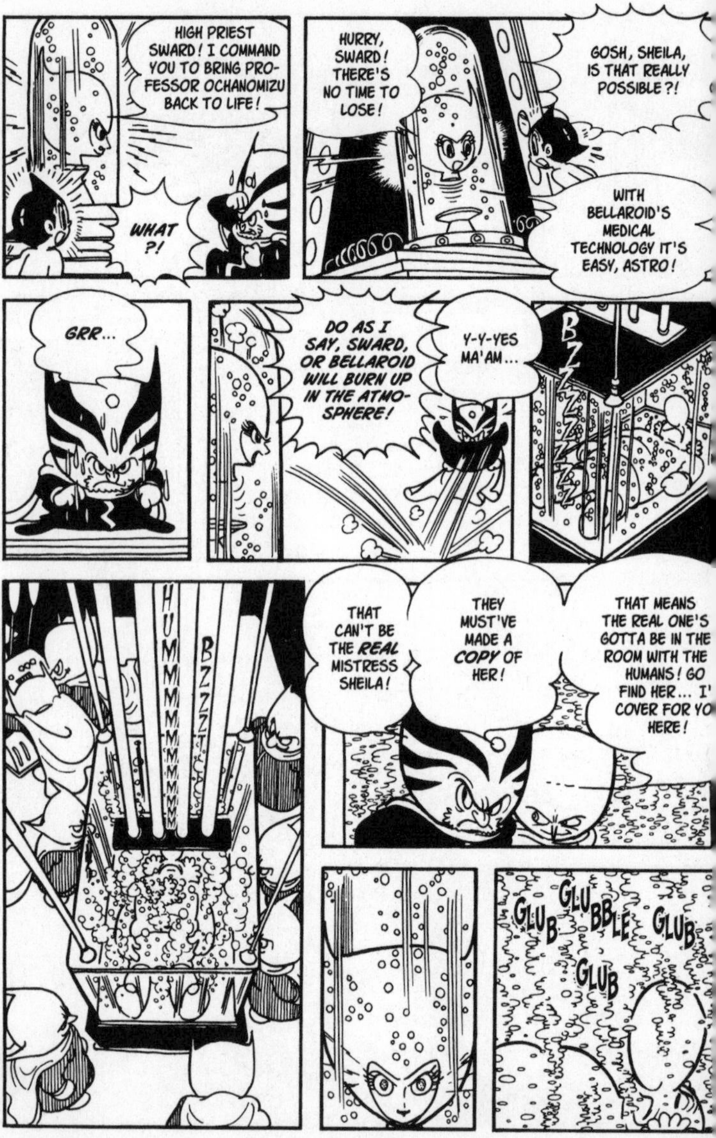
HIGH PRIEST SWARD! I COMMAND YOU TO BRING PROFESSOR OCHANOMIZU BACK TO LIFE!
WHAT?!
HURRY, SWARD! THERE'S NO TIME TO LOSE!
GOSH, SHEILA, IS THAT REALLY POSSIBLE?!
WITH BELLAROID'S MEDICAL TECHNOLOGY IT'S EASY, ASTRO!
GRR...
DO AS I SAY, SWARD, OR BELLAROID WILL BURN UP IN THE ATMOSPHERE!
Y-Y-YES MA'AM...
BZZZZZZ
HUMMMMMMMMMMM
BZZZT
THAT CAN'T BE THE *REAL* MISTRESS SHEILA!
THEY MUST'VE MADE A *COPY* OF HER!
THAT MEANS THE REAL ONE'S GOTTA BE IN THE ROOM WITH THE HUMANS! GO FIND HER... I' COVER FOR YO HERE!
GLUB GLUBBLE GLUB
GLUB

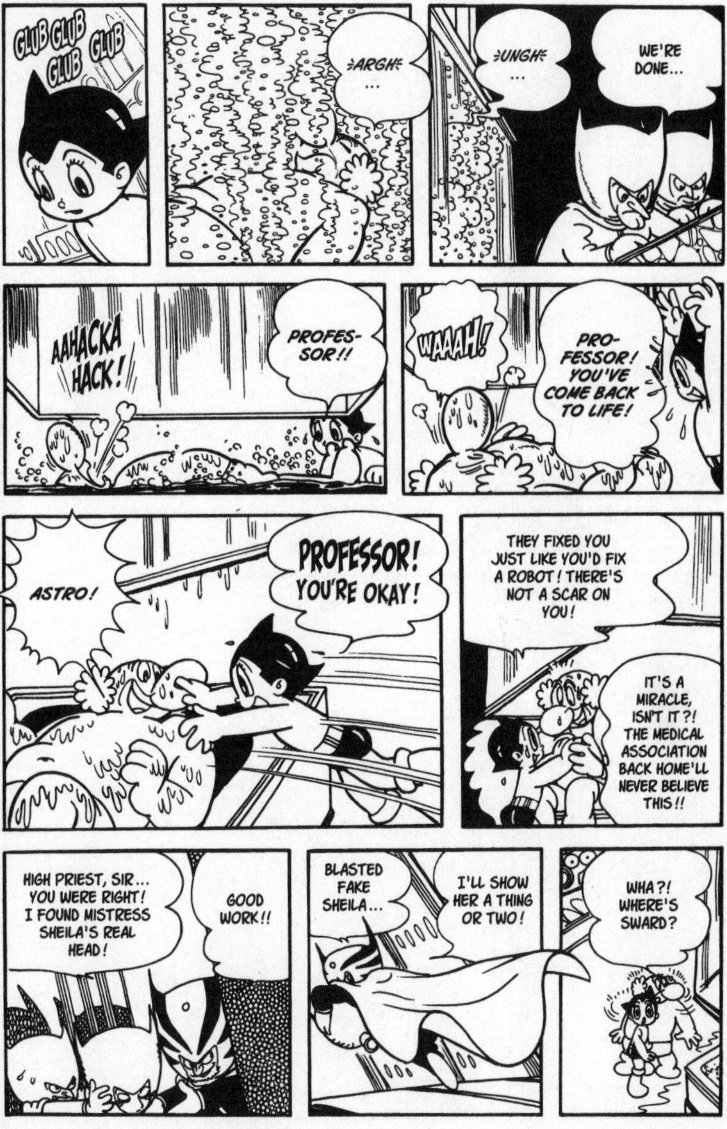
GLUB GLUB GLUB GLUB
ARGH ...
UNGH ...
WE'RE DONE...
AAHACKA HACK!
PROFES-SOR!!
WAAAH!
PRO-FESSOR! YOU'VE COME BACK TO LIFE!
ASTRO!
PROFESSOR! YOU'RE OKAY!
THEY FIXED YOU JUST LIKE YOU'D FIX A ROBOT! THERE'S NOT A SCAR ON YOU!
IT'S A MIRACLE, ISN'T IT?! THE MEDICAL ASSOCIATION BACK HOME'LL NEVER BELIEVE THIS!!
HIGH PRIEST, SIR... YOU WERE RIGHT! I FOUND MISTRESS SHEILA'S REAL HEAD!
GOOD WORK!!
BLASTED FAKE SHEILA...
I'LL SHOW HER A THING OR TWO!
WHA?! WHERE'S SWARD?

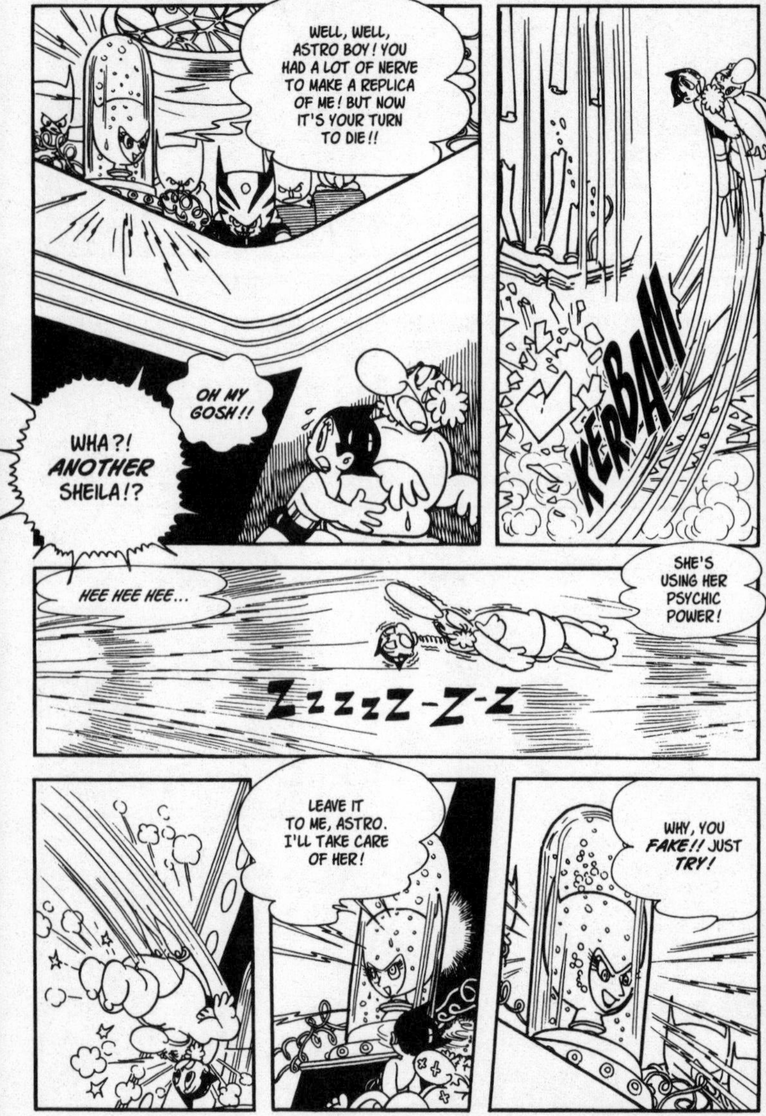
WELL, WELL, ASTRO BOY! YOU HAD A LOT OF NERVE TO MAKE A REPLICA OF ME! BUT NOW IT'S YOUR TURN TO DIE!!
OH MY GOSH!!
WHA?! ANOTHER SHEILA!?
KERBAM
HEE HEE HEE...
SHE'S USING HER PSYCHIC POWER!
ZzzzZ-Z-Z
LEAVE IT TO ME, ASTRO. I'LL TAKE CARE OF HER!
WHY, YOU FAKE!! JUST TRY!

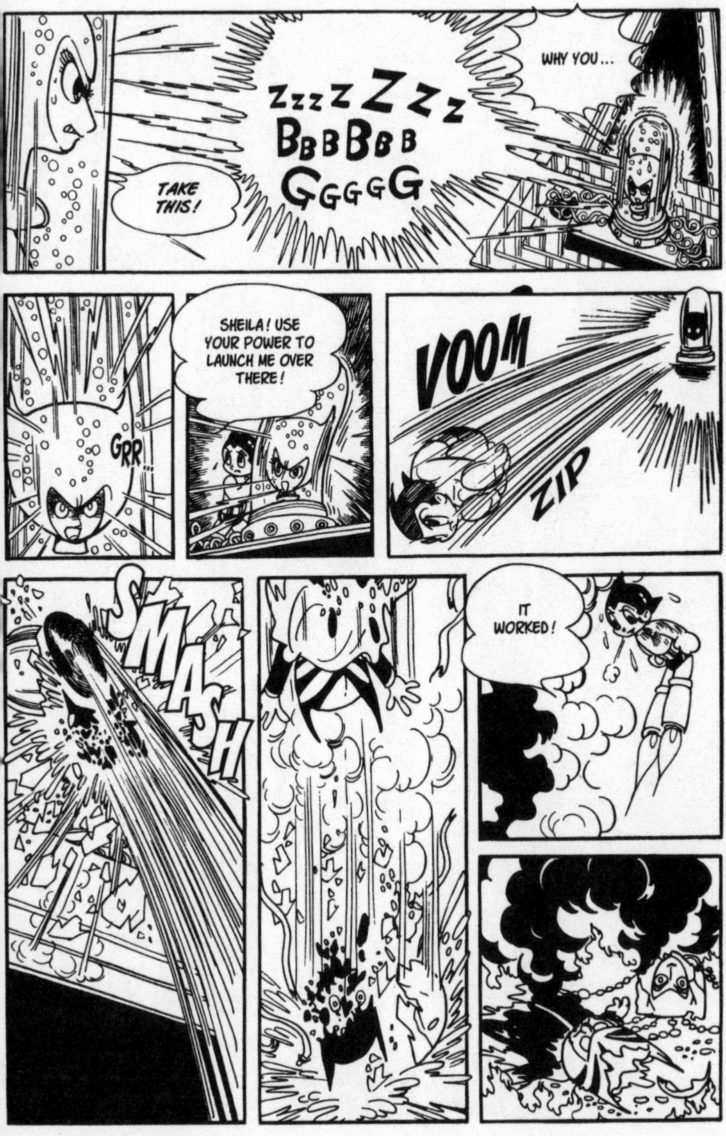
TAKE THIS!
ZzzZZZz
BBBBBB
GGGGG
WHY YOU...
GRR...
SHEILA! USE YOUR POWER TO LAUNCH ME OVER THERE!
VOOM
ZIP
SMASH
IT WORKED!

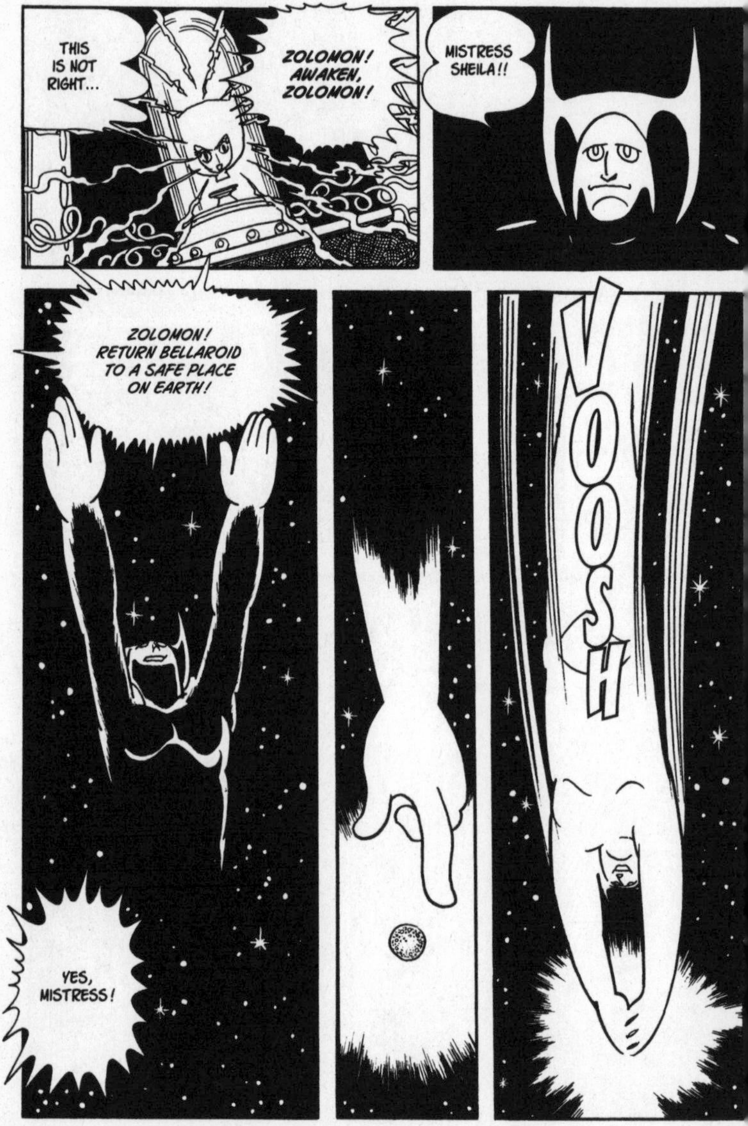
THIS IS NOT RIGHT...
ZOLOMON! AWAKEN, ZOLOMON!
MISTRESS SHEILA!!
ZOLOMON! RETURN BELLAROID TO A SAFE PLACE ON EARTH!
YES, MISTRESS!
VOOOSH

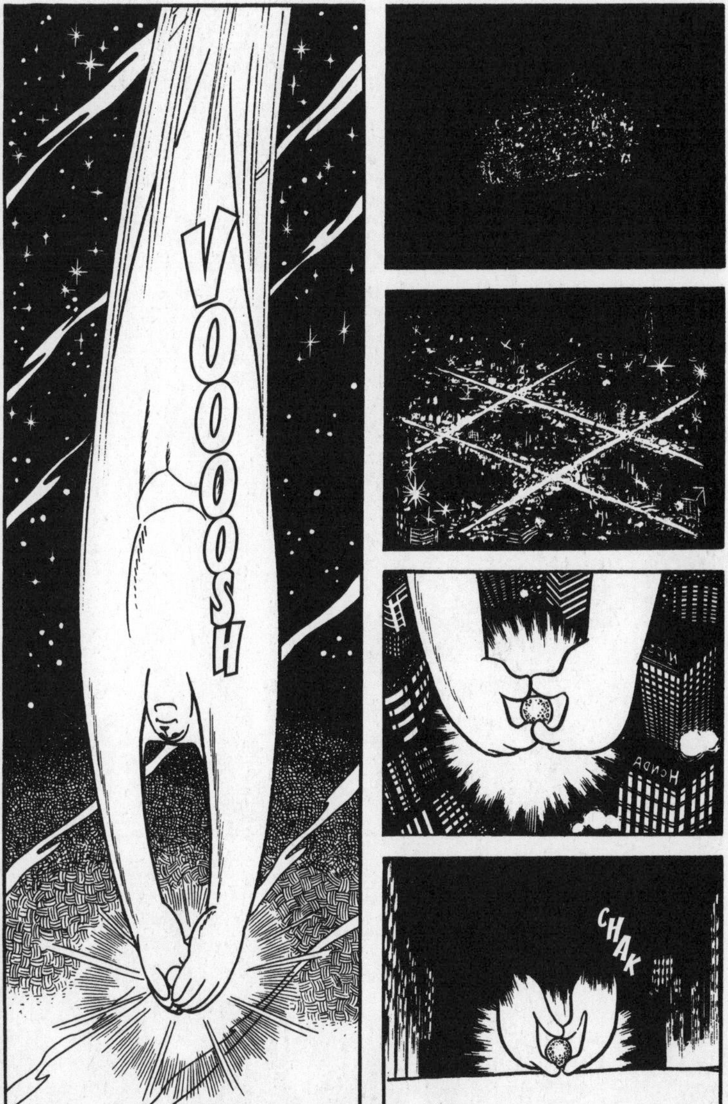
VOOOOSH
HONDA
CHAK

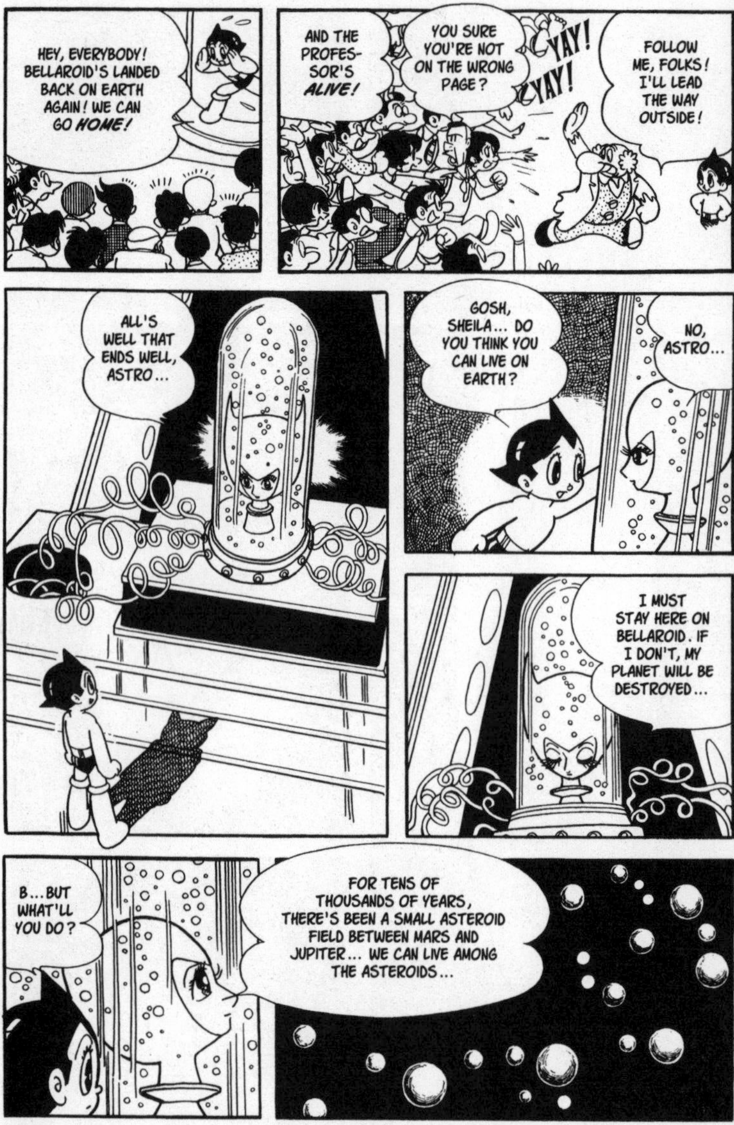
HEY, EVERYBODY! BELLAROID'S LANDED BACK ON EARTH AGAIN! WE CAN GO **HOME!**
AND THE PROFES-SOR'S **ALIVE!**
YOU SURE YOU'RE NOT ON THE WRONG PAGE?
YAY!
YAY!
FOLLOW ME, FOLKS! I'LL LEAD THE WAY OUTSIDE!
ALL'S WELL THAT ENDS WELL, ASTRO...
GOSH, SHEILA... DO YOU THINK YOU CAN LIVE ON EARTH?
NO, ASTRO...
I MUST STAY HERE ON BELLAROID. IF I DON'T, MY PLANET WILL BE DESTROYED...
B... BUT WHAT'LL YOU DO?
FOR TENS OF THOUSANDS OF YEARS, THERE'S BEEN A SMALL ASTEROID FIELD BETWEEN MARS AND JUPITER... WE CAN LIVE AMONG THE ASTEROIDS...

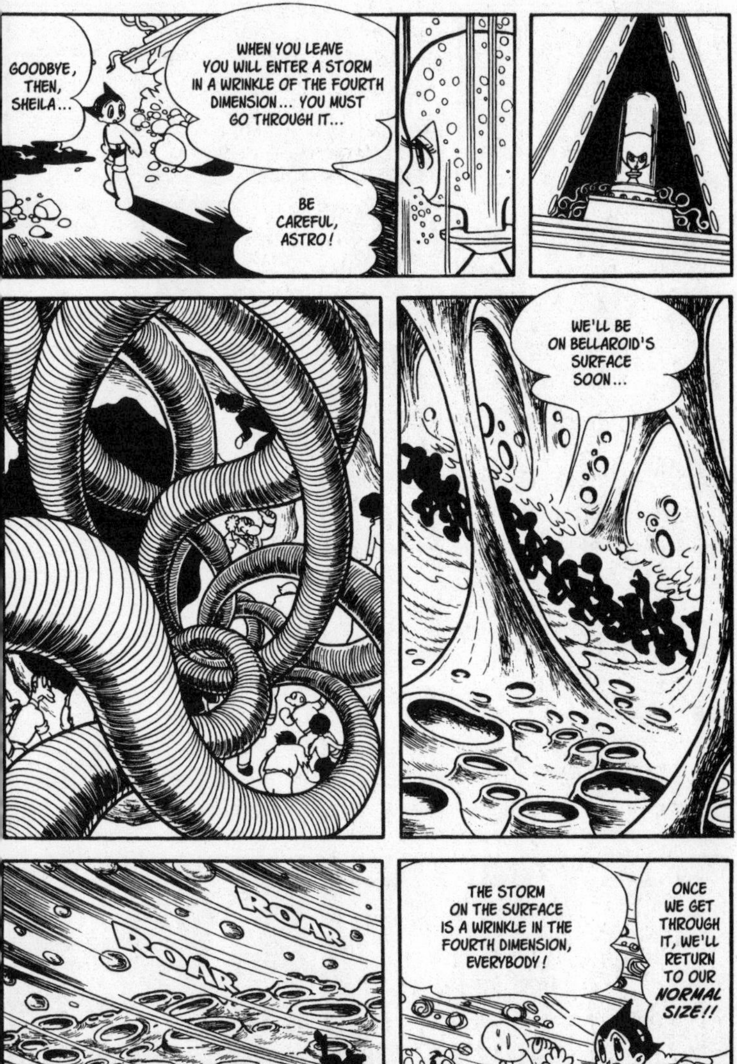
GOODBYE, THEN, SHEILA...
WHEN YOU LEAVE YOU WILL ENTER A STORM IN A WRINKLE OF THE FOURTH DIMENSION... YOU MUST GO THROUGH IT...
BE CAREFUL, ASTRO!
WE'LL BE ON BELLAROID'S SURFACE SOON...
ROAR
ROAR
THE STORM ON THE SURFACE IS A WRINKLE IN THE FOURTH DIMENSION, EVERYBODY!
ONCE WE GET THROUGH IT, WE'LL RETURN TO OUR *NORMAL SIZE!!*

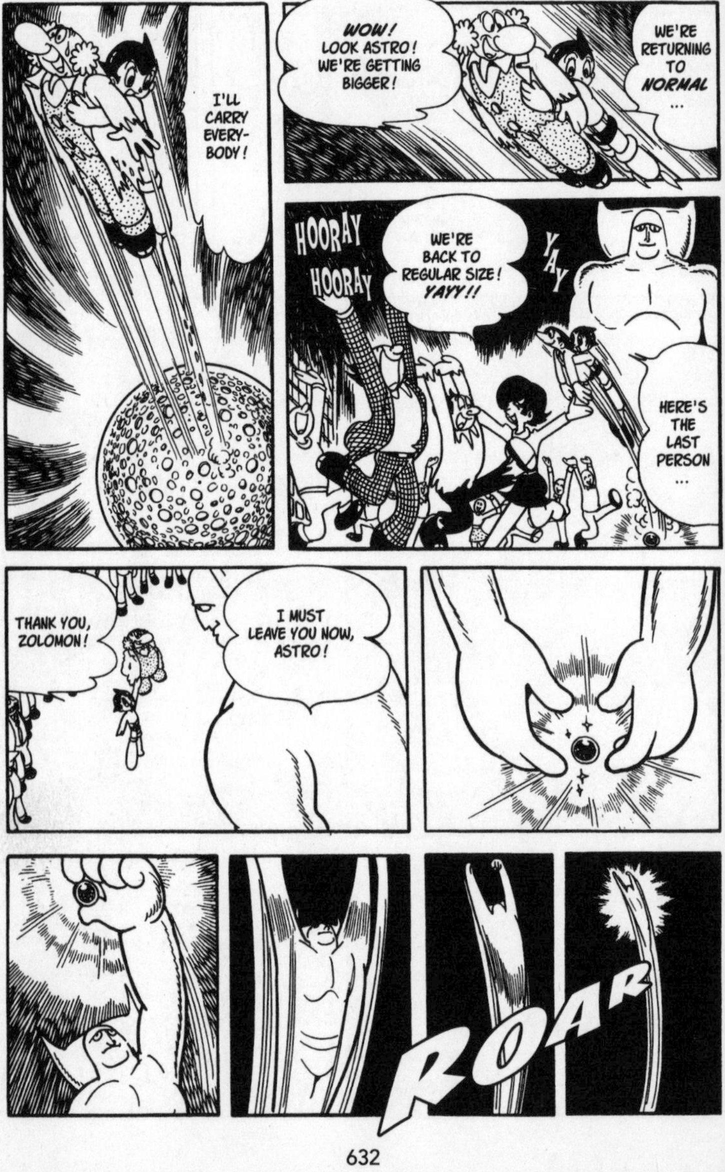
I'LL CARRY EVERY-BODY!
WOW! LOOK ASTRO! WE'RE GETTING BIGGER!
WE'RE RETURNING TO NORMAL ...
HOORAY HOORAY
WE'RE BACK TO REGULAR SIZE! YAYY!!
YAY
HERE'S THE LAST PERSON ...
THANK YOU, ZOLOMON!
I MUST LEAVE YOU NOW, ASTRO!
ROAR

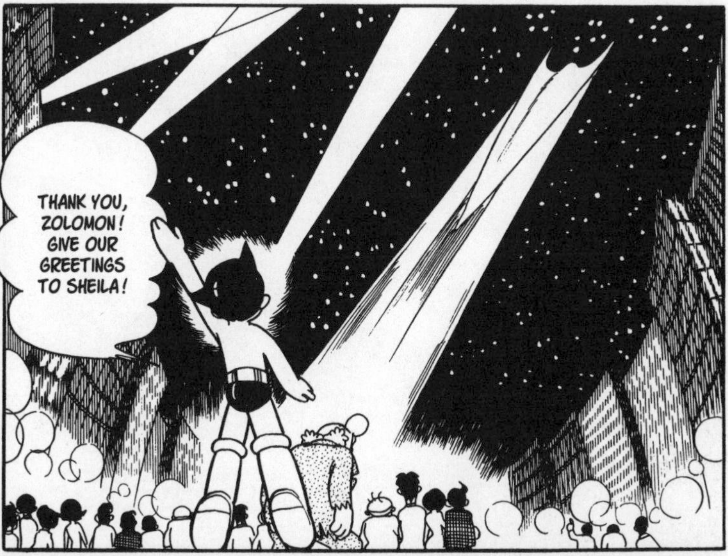
THANK YOU, ZOLOMON! GIVE OUR GREETINGS TO SHEILA!
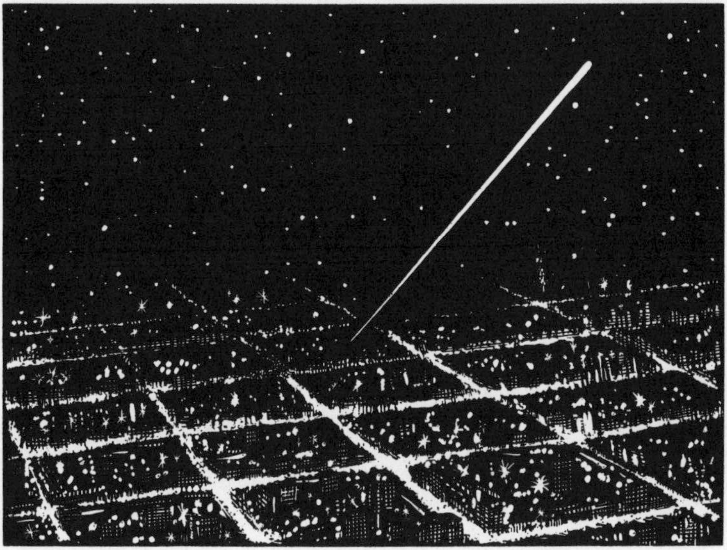

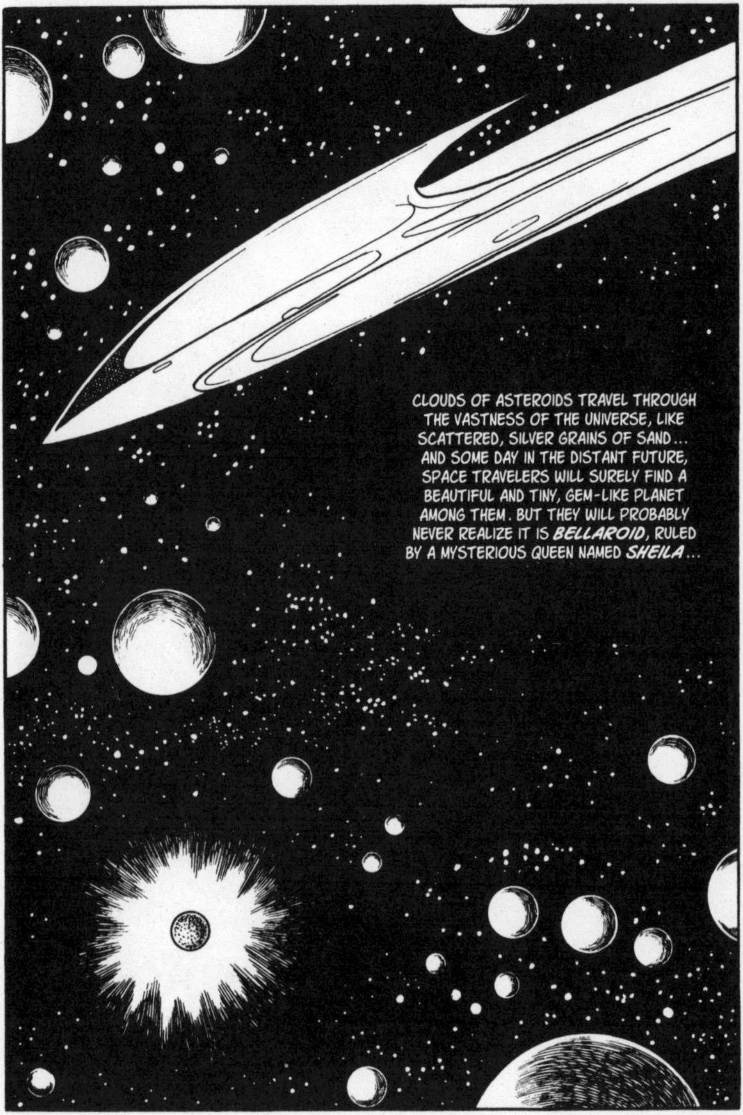
CLOUDS OF ASTEROIDS TRAVEL THROUGH THE VASTNESS OF THE UNIVERSE, LIKE SCATTERED, SILVER GRAINS OF SAND... AND SOME DAY IN THE DISTANT FUTURE, SPACE TRAVELERS WILL SURELY FIND A BEAUTIFUL AND TINY, GEM-LIKE PLANET AMONG THEM. BUT THEY WILL PROBABLY NEVER REALIZE IT IS *BELLAROID*, RULED BY A MYSTERIOUS QUEEN NAMED *SHEILA*...

SHOOTOUT

IN THE ALPS

First appeared in the January 1956 supplement
of *Shonen* magazine.

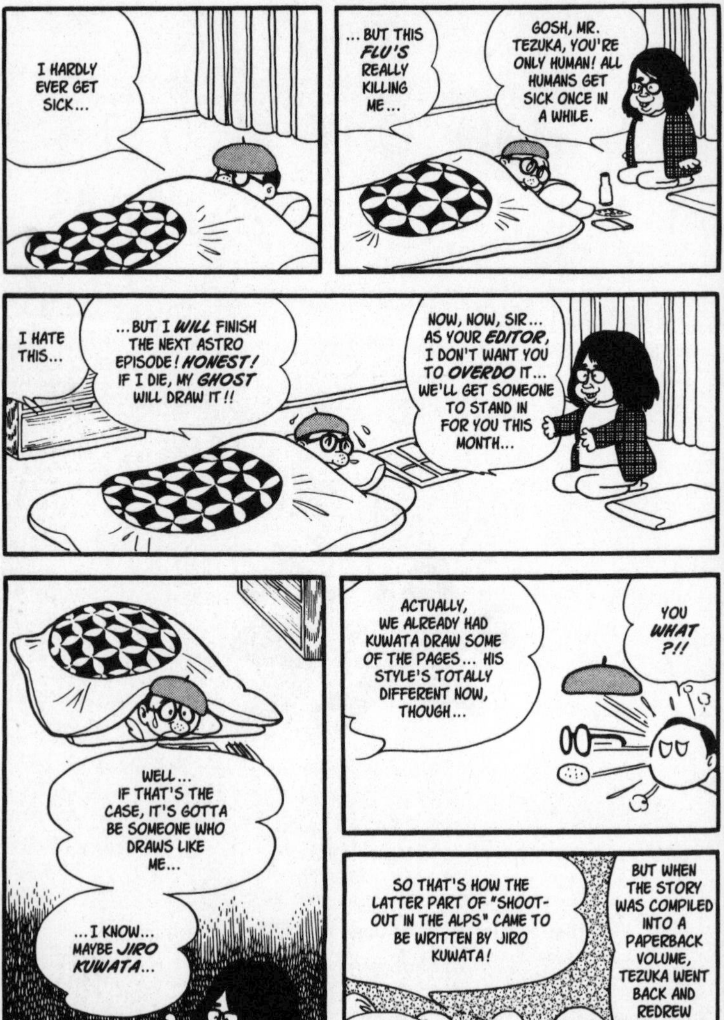

I HARDLY EVER GET SICK...
...BUT THIS FLU'S REALLY KILLING ME...
GOSH, MR. TEZUKA, YOU'RE ONLY HUMAN! ALL HUMANS GET SICK ONCE IN A WHILE.
I HATE THIS...
...BUT I WILL FINISH THE NEXT ASTRO EPISODE! HONEST! IF I DIE, MY GHOST WILL DRAW IT!!
NOW, NOW, SIR... AS YOUR EDITOR, I DON'T WANT YOU TO OVERDO IT... WE'LL GET SOMEONE TO STAND IN FOR YOU THIS MONTH...
WELL... IF THAT'S THE CASE, IT'S GOTTA BE SOMEONE WHO DRAWS LIKE ME...
...I KNOW... MAYBE JIRO KUWATA...
ACTUALLY, WE ALREADY HAD KUWATA DRAW SOME OF THE PAGES... HIS STYLE'S TOTALLY DIFFERENT NOW, THOUGH...
YOU WHAT?!!
SO THAT'S HOW THE LATTER PART OF "SHOOT-OUT IN THE ALPS" CAME TO BE WRITTEN BY JIRO KUWATA!
SO WE WERE DRAWN BY A STAND-IN!
BUT WHEN THE STORY WAS COMPILED INTO A PAPERBACK VOLUME, TEZUKA WENT BACK AND REDREW MOST OF THE PAGES, SO IT COMES OUT THE SAME!

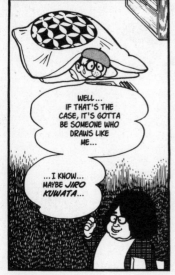

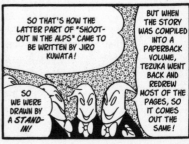

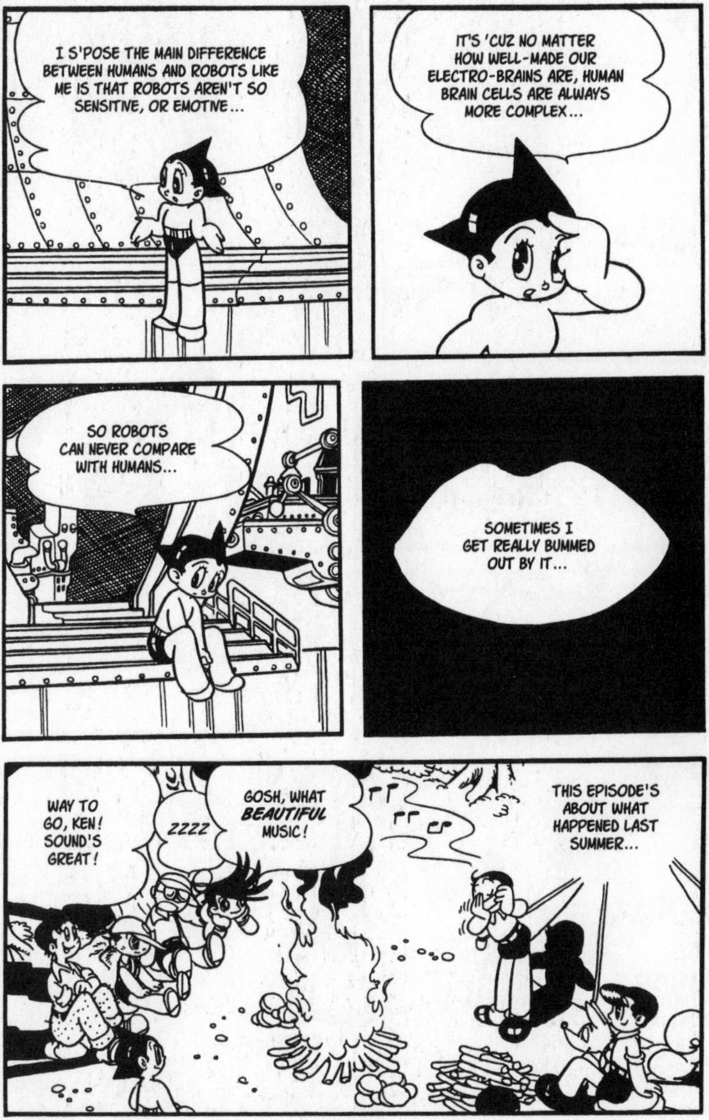
I S'POSE THE MAIN DIFFERENCE BETWEEN HUMANS AND ROBOTS LIKE ME IS THAT ROBOTS AREN'T SO SENSITIVE, OR EMOTIVE...
IT'S 'CUZ NO MATTER HOW WELL-MADE OUR ELECTRO-BRAINS ARE, HUMAN BRAIN CELLS ARE ALWAYS MORE COMPLEX...
SO ROBOTS CAN NEVER COMPARE WITH HUMANS...
SOMETIMES I GET REALLY BUMMED OUT BY IT...
WAY TO GO, KEN! SOUND'S GREAT!
ZZZZ
GOSH, WHAT *BEAUTIFUL* MUSIC!
THIS EPISODE'S ABOUT WHAT HAPPENED LAST SUMMER...

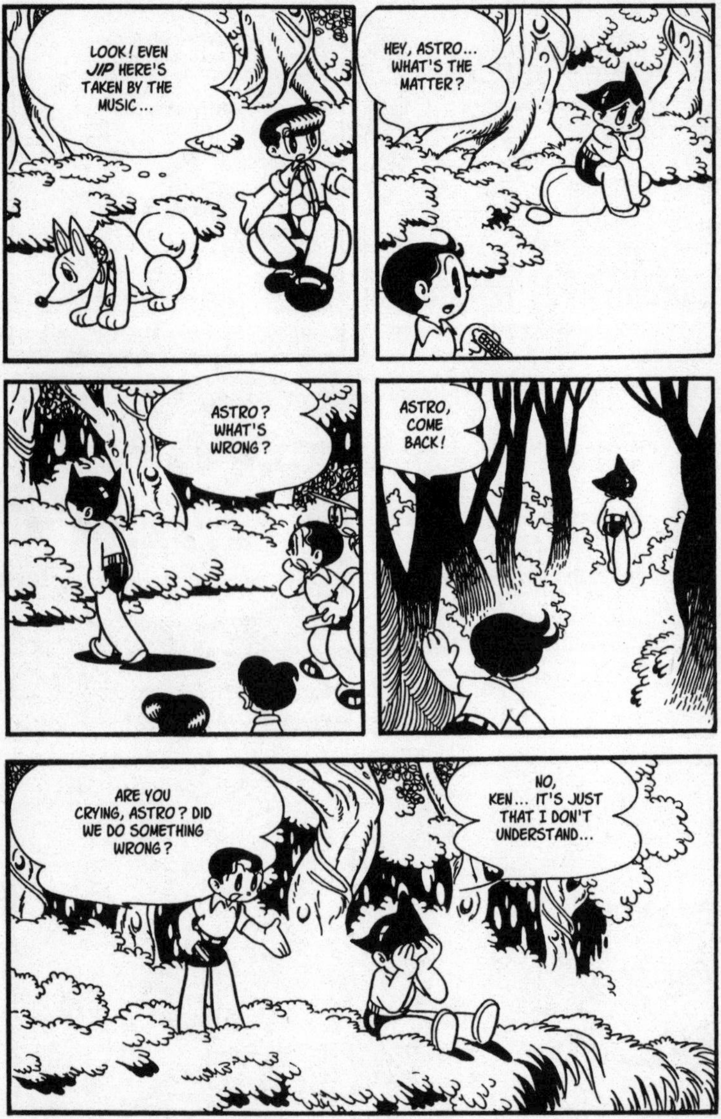
LOOK! EVEN JIP HERE'S TAKEN BY THE MUSIC...
HEY, ASTRO... WHAT'S THE MATTER?
ASTRO? WHAT'S WRONG?
ASTRO, COME BACK!
ARE YOU CRYING, ASTRO? DID WE DO SOMETHING WRONG?
NO, KEN... IT'S JUST THAT I DON'T UNDERSTAND...

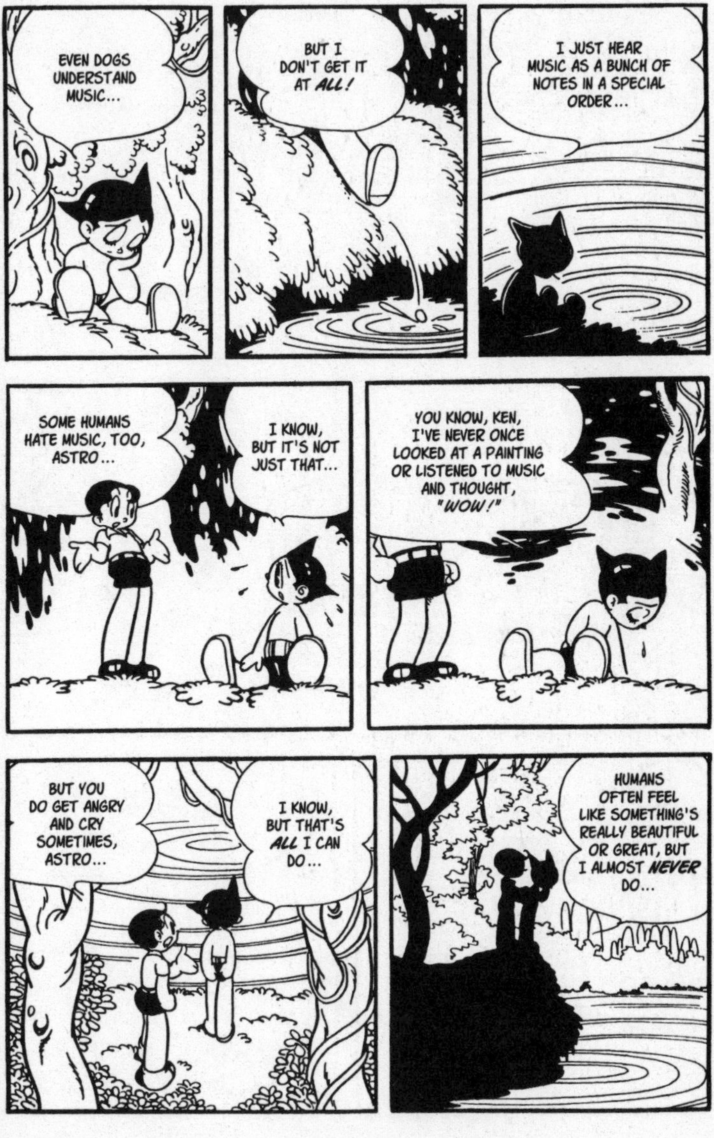
EVEN DOGS UNDERSTAND MUSIC...
BUT I DON'T GET IT AT ALL!
I JUST HEAR MUSIC AS A BUNCH OF NOTES IN A SPECIAL ORDER...
SOME HUMANS HATE MUSIC, TOO, ASTRO...
I KNOW, BUT IT'S NOT JUST THAT...
YOU KNOW, KEN, I'VE NEVER ONCE LOOKED AT A PAINTING OR LISTENED TO MUSIC AND THOUGHT, "WOW!"
BUT YOU DO GET ANGRY AND CRY SOMETIMES, ASTRO...
I KNOW, BUT THAT'S ALL I CAN DO...
HUMANS OFTEN FEEL LIKE SOMETHING'S REALLY BEAUTIFUL OR GREAT, BUT I ALMOST NEVER DO...

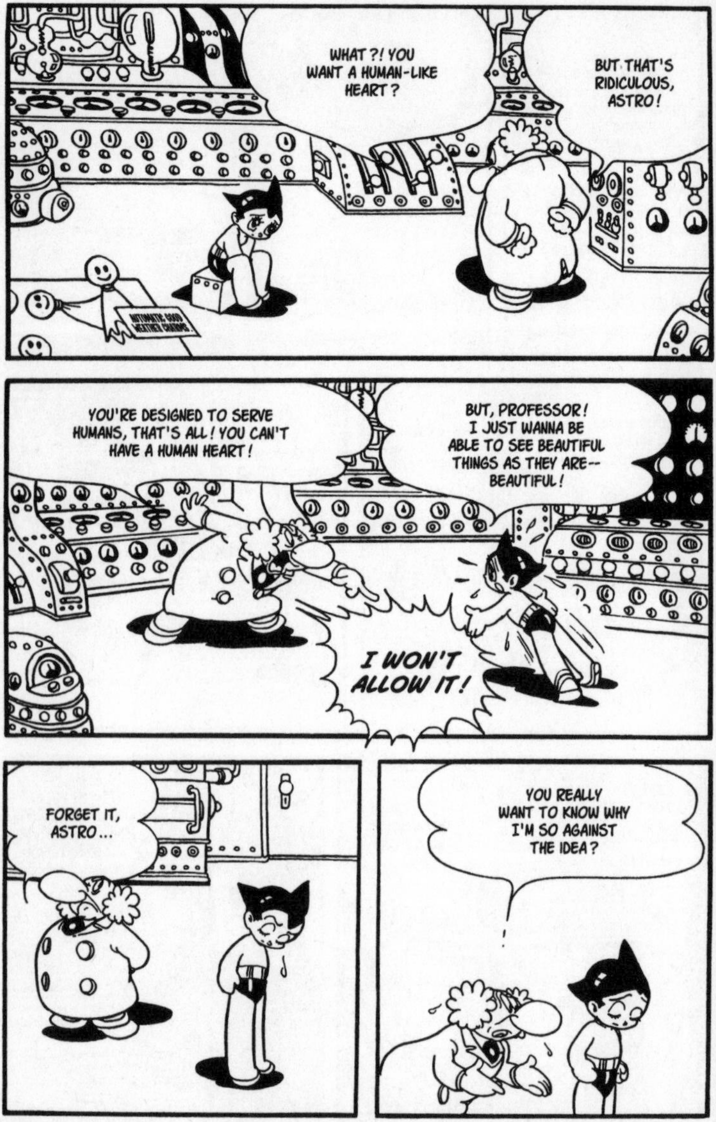
WHAT?! YOU WANT A HUMAN-LIKE HEART?
BUT THAT'S RIDICULOUS, ASTRO!
YOU'RE DESIGNED TO SERVE HUMANS, THAT'S ALL! YOU CAN'T HAVE A HUMAN HEART!
BUT, PROFESSOR! I JUST WANNA BE ABLE TO SEE BEAUTIFUL THINGS AS THEY ARE-- BEAUTIFUL!
I WON'T ALLOW IT!
FORGET IT, ASTRO...
YOU REALLY WANT TO KNOW WHY I'M SO AGAINST THE IDEA?

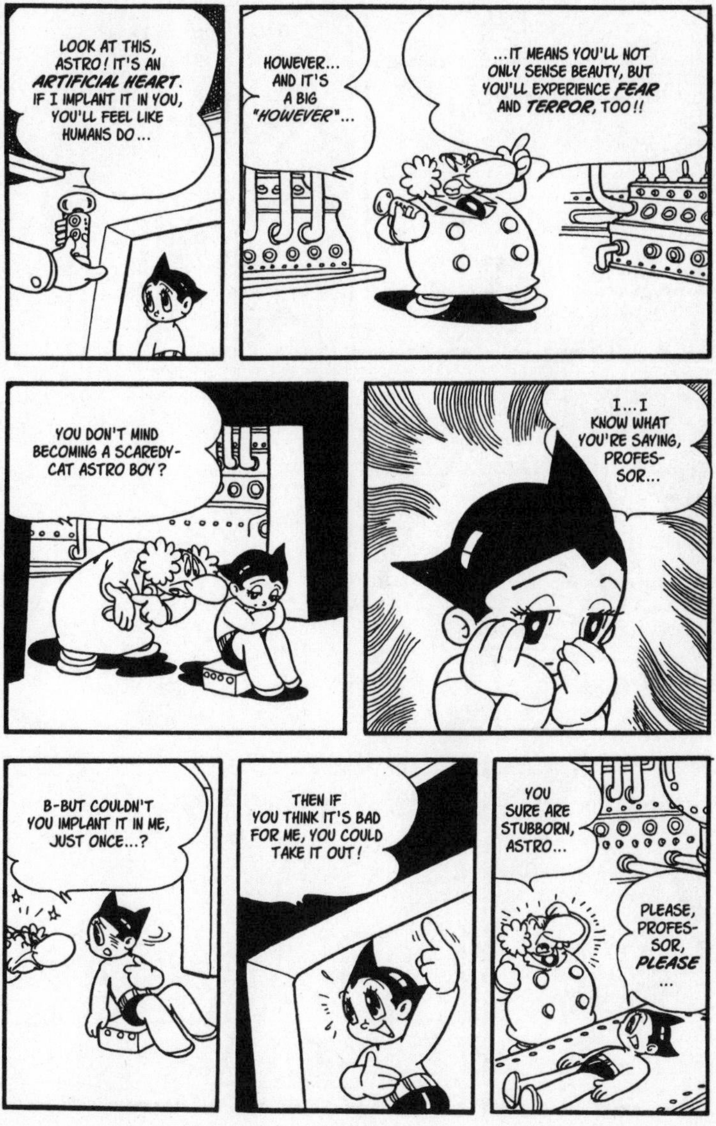
LOOK AT THIS, ASTRO! IT'S AN ***ARTIFICIAL HEART***. IF I IMPLANT IT IN YOU, YOU'LL FEEL LIKE HUMANS DO...
HOWEVER... AND IT'S A BIG "***HOWEVER***"...
...IT MEANS YOU'LL NOT ONLY SENSE BEAUTY, BUT YOU'LL EXPERIENCE ***FEAR*** AND ***TERROR***, TOO!!
YOU DON'T MIND BECOMING A SCAREDY-CAT ASTRO BOY?
I...I KNOW WHAT YOU'RE SAYING, PROFES-SOR...
B-BUT COULDN'T YOU IMPLANT IT IN ME, JUST ONCE...?
THEN IF YOU THINK IT'S BAD FOR ME, YOU COULD TAKE IT OUT!
YOU SURE ARE STUBBORN, ASTRO...
PLEASE, PROFES-SOR, ***PLEASE***...

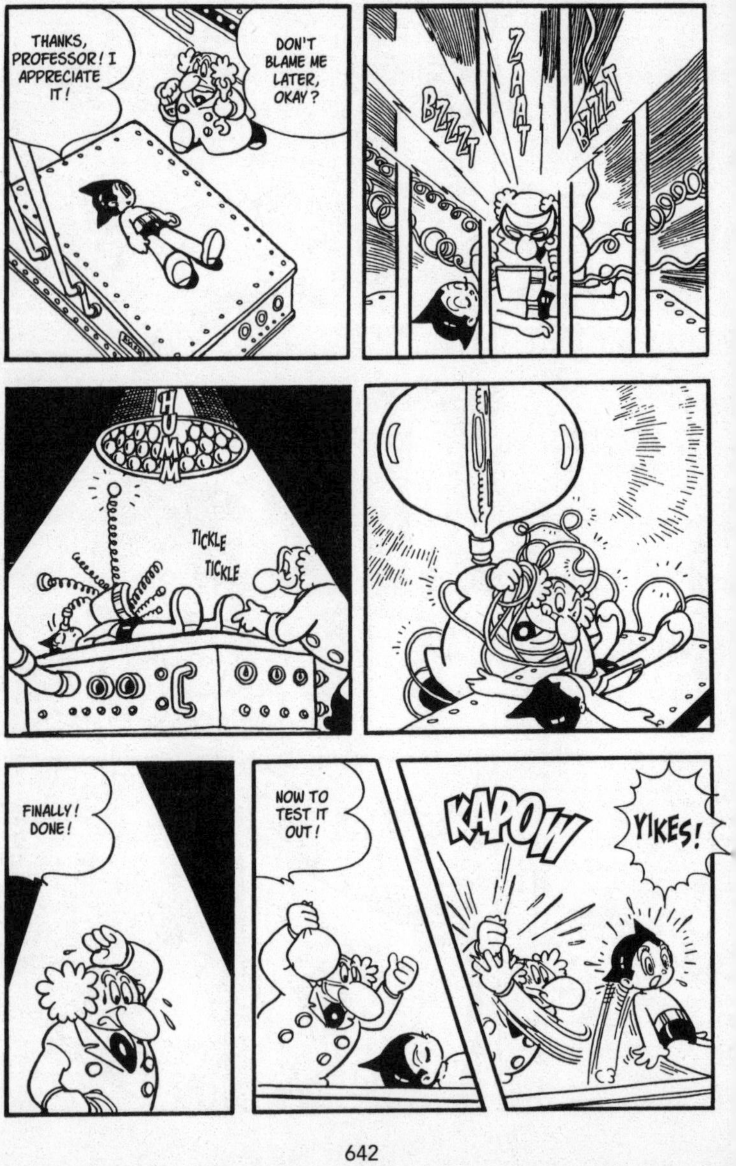

THANKS, PROFESSOR! I APPRECIATE IT!
DON'T BLAME ME LATER, OKAY?
BZZZT
ZAAAT
BZZZT
HUMM
TICKLE
TICKLE
FINALLY! DONE!
NOW TO TEST IT OUT!
KAPOW
YIKES!

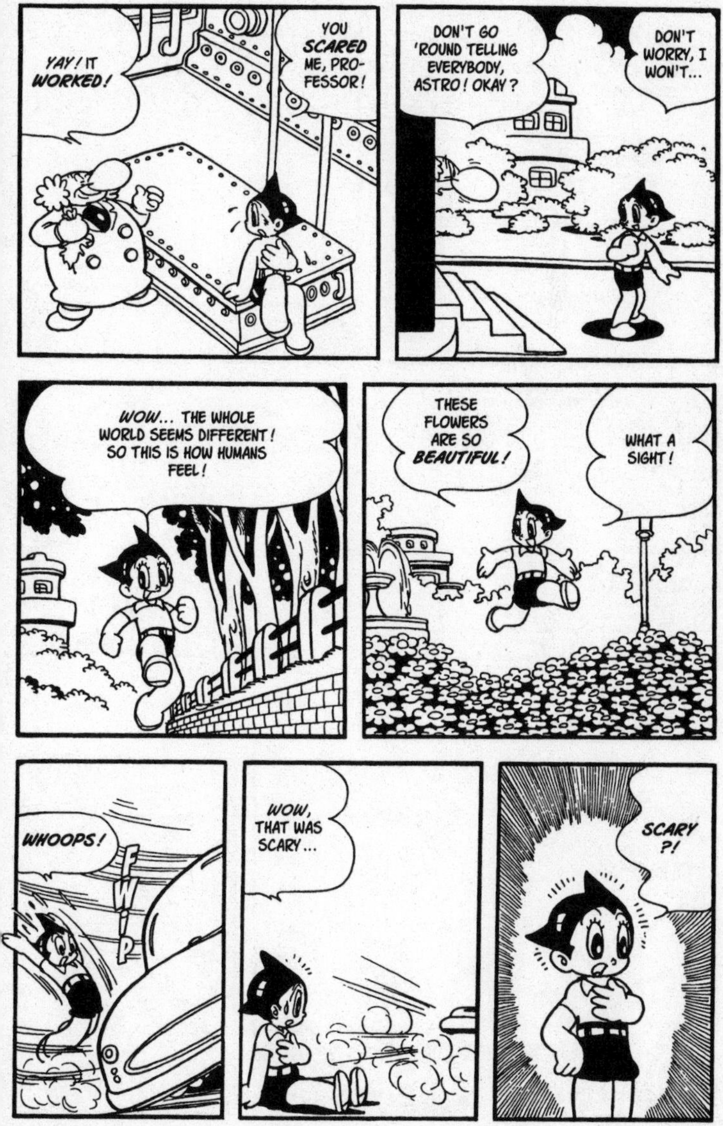
YAY! IT WORKED!
YOU SCARED ME, PRO-FESSOR!
DON'T GO 'ROUND TELLING EVERYBODY, ASTRO! OKAY?
DON'T WORRY, I WON'T...
WOW... THE WHOLE WORLD SEEMS DIFFERENT! SO THIS IS HOW HUMANS FEEL!
THESE FLOWERS ARE SO BEAUTIFUL!
WHAT A SIGHT!
WHOOPS!
FWIP
WOW, THAT WAS SCARY...
SCARY ?!

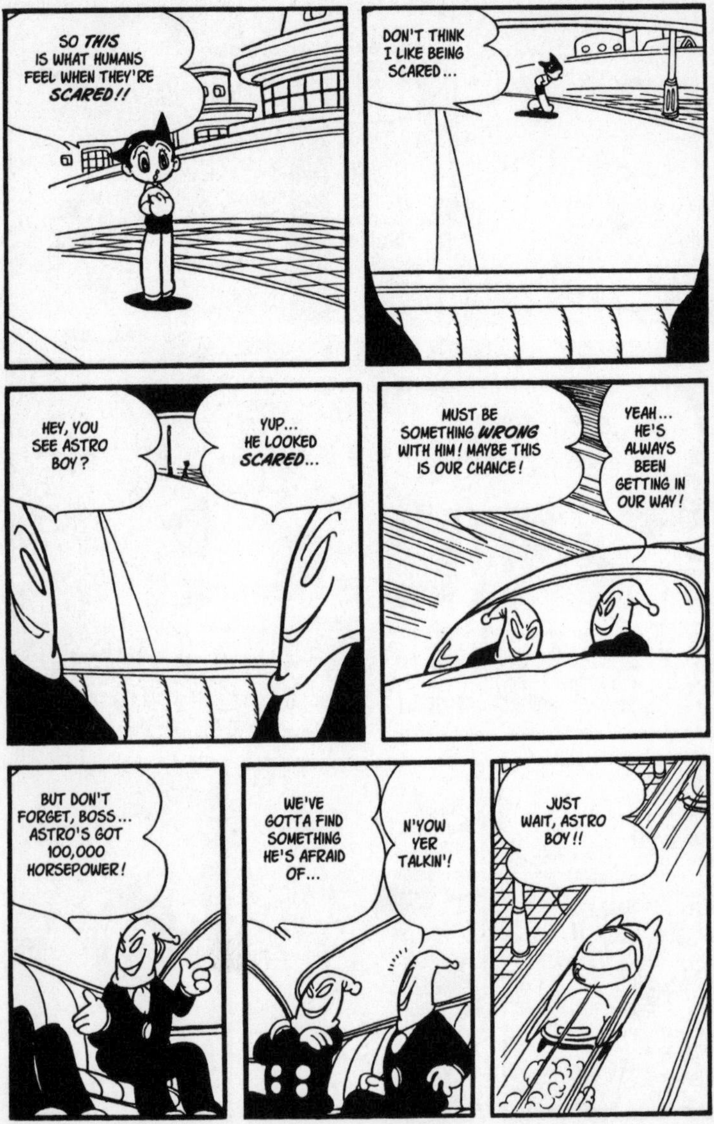

SO THIS IS WHAT HUMANS FEEL WHEN THEY'RE SCARED!!
DON'T THINK I LIKE BEING SCARED...
HEY, YOU SEE ASTRO BOY?
YUP... HE LOOKED SCARED...
MUST BE SOMETHING WRONG WITH HIM! MAYBE THIS IS OUR CHANCE!
YEAH... HE'S ALWAYS BEEN GETTING IN OUR WAY!
BUT DON'T FORGET, BOSS... ASTRO'S GOT 100,000 HORSEPOWER!
WE'VE GOTTA FIND SOMETHING HE'S AFRAID OF...
N'YOW YER TALKIN'!
JUST WAIT, ASTRO BOY!!

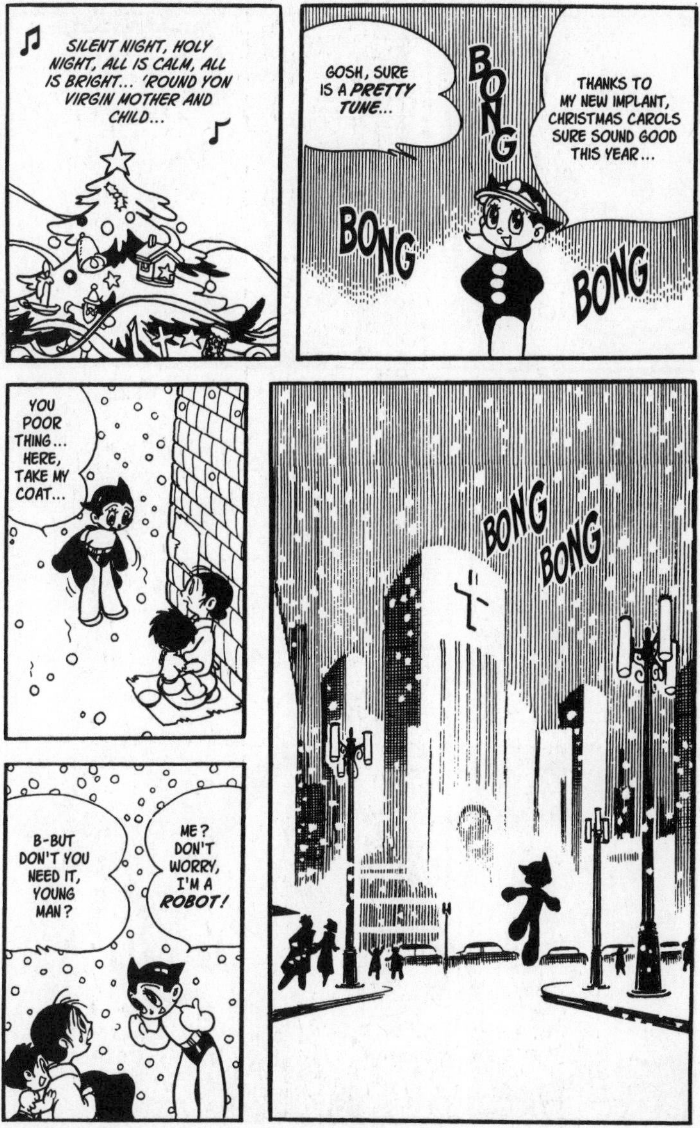
♫ SILENT NIGHT, HOLY NIGHT, ALL IS CALM, ALL IS BRIGHT... 'ROUND YON VIRGIN MOTHER AND CHILD... ♪
GOSH, SURE IS A *PRETTY TUNE*...
BONG
THANKS TO MY NEW IMPLANT, CHRISTMAS CAROLS SURE SOUND GOOD THIS YEAR...
BONG
BONG
YOU POOR THING... HERE, TAKE MY COAT...
B-BUT DON'T YOU NEED IT, YOUNG MAN?
ME? DON'T WORRY, I'M A *ROBOT!*
BONG
BONG

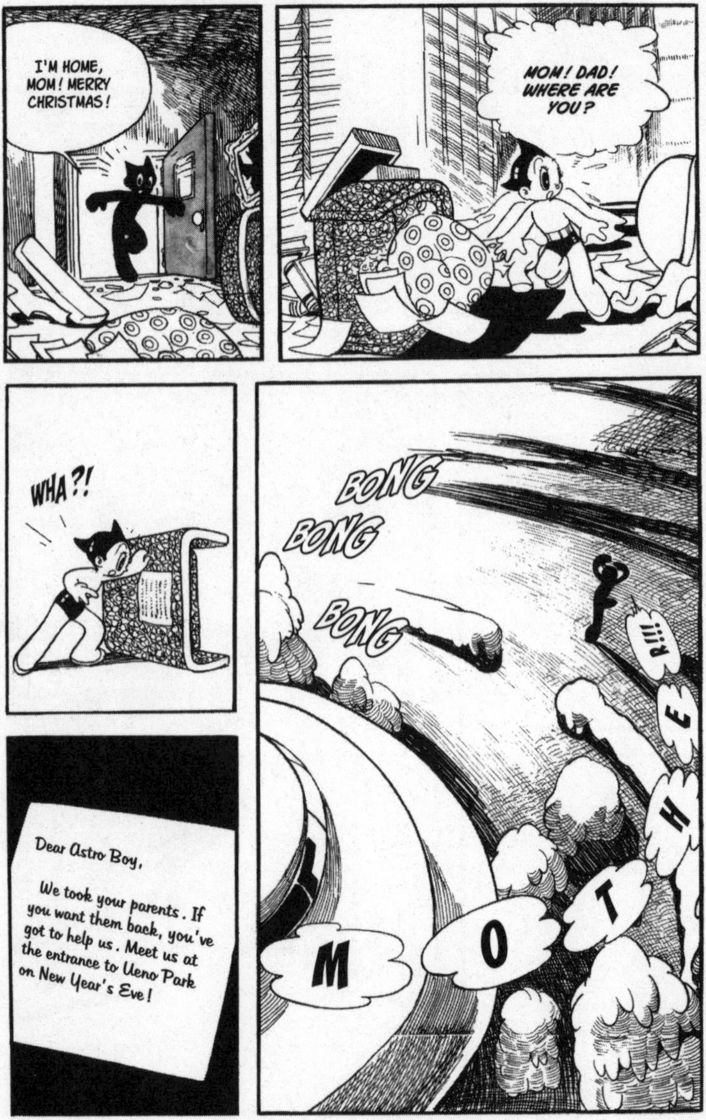

I'M HOME, MOM! MERRY CHRISTMAS!
MOM! DAD! WHERE ARE YOU?
WHA?!
Dear Astro Boy,
We took your parents. If you want them back, you've got to help us. Meet us at the entrance to Ueno Park on New Year's Eve!
BONG
BONG
BONG
M O T H E R!!!

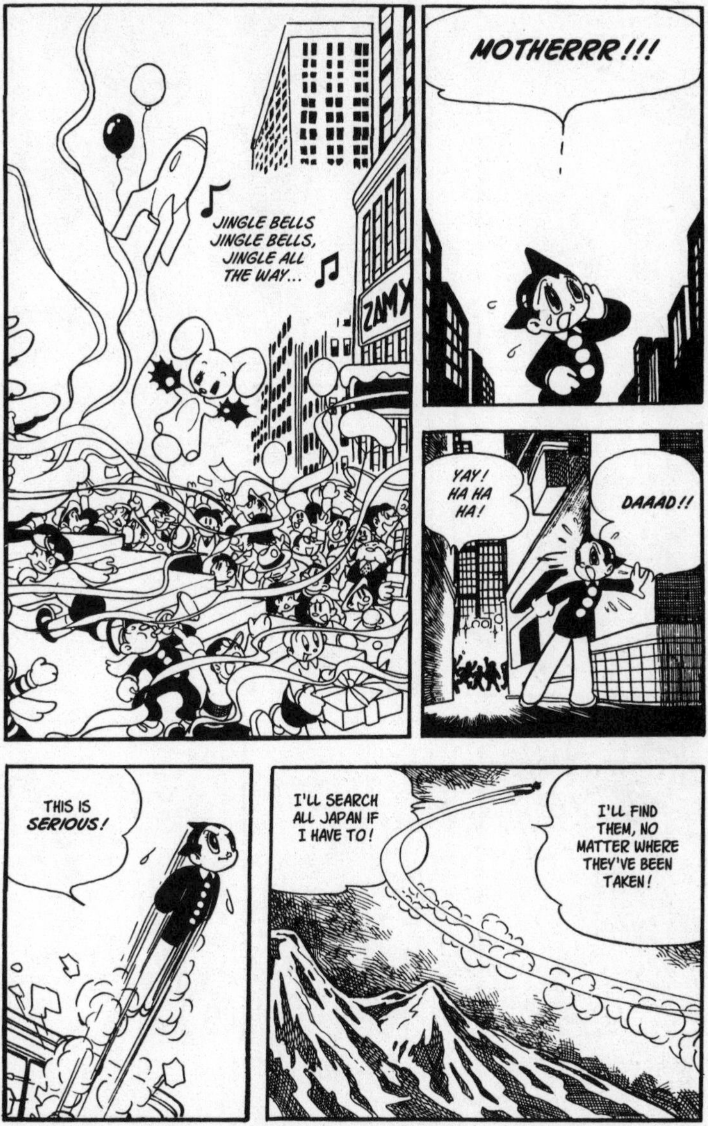
JINGLE BELLS
JINGLE BELLS,
JINGLE ALL
THE WAY...
ZAMX
MOTHERRR!!!
YAY! HA HA HA!
DAAAD!!
THIS IS SERIOUS!
I'LL SEARCH ALL JAPAN IF I HAVE TO!
I'LL FIND THEM, NO MATTER WHERE THEY'VE BEEN TAKEN!

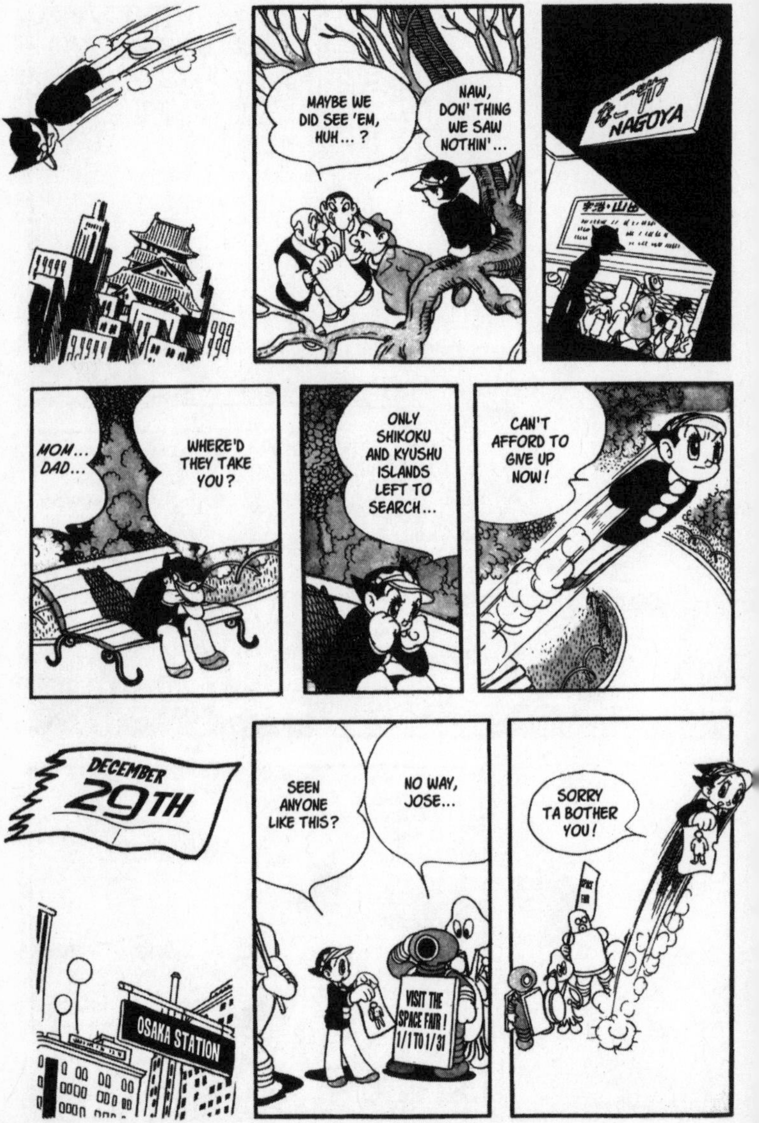
MAYBE WE DID SEE 'EM, HUH... ?
NAW, DON' THING WE SAW NOTHIN'...
NAGOYA
MOM... DAD...
WHERE'D THEY TAKE YOU?
ONLY SHIKOKU AND KYUSHU ISLANDS LEFT TO SEARCH...
CAN'T AFFORD TO GIVE UP NOW!
DECEMBER 29TH
OSAKA STATION
SEEN ANYONE LIKE THIS?
NO WAY, JOSE...
VISIT THE SPACE FAIR! 1/1 TO 1/31
SORRY TA BOTHER YOU!
SPACE FAIR

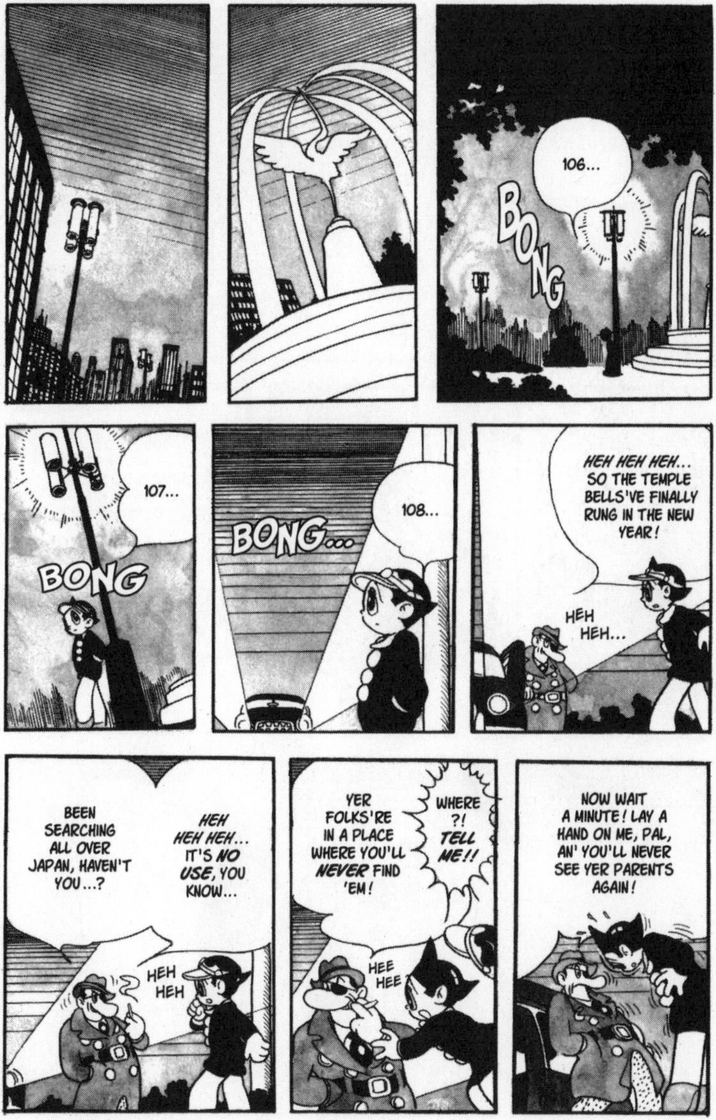
106...
BONG
107...
BONG
108...
BONG...
HEH HEH HEH... SO THE TEMPLE BELLS'VE FINALLY RUNG IN THE NEW YEAR!
HEH HEH...
BEEN SEARCHING ALL OVER JAPAN, HAVEN'T YOU...?
HEH HEH HEH... IT'S NO USE, YOU KNOW...
HEH HEH
YER FOLKS'RE IN A PLACE WHERE YOU'LL NEVER FIND 'EM!
WHERE ?! TELL ME!!
HEE HEE
NOW WAIT A MINUTE! LAY A HAND ON ME, PAL, AN' YOU'LL NEVER SEE YER PARENTS AGAIN!

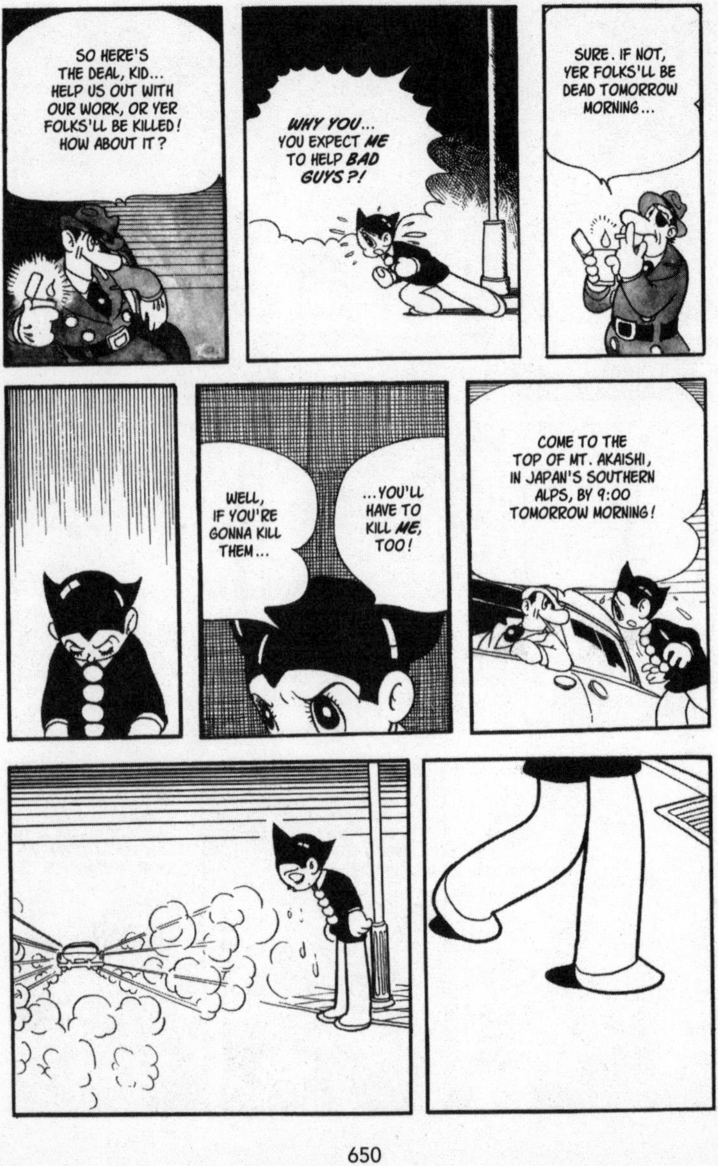
SO HERE'S THE DEAL, KID... HELP US OUT WITH OUR WORK, OR YER FOLKS'LL BE KILLED! HOW ABOUT IT?
WHY YOU... YOU EXPECT ME TO HELP BAD GUYS?!
SURE. IF NOT, YER FOLKS'LL BE DEAD TOMORROW MORNING...
WELL, IF YOU'RE GONNA KILL THEM...
...YOU'LL HAVE TO KILL ME, TOO!
COME TO THE TOP OF MT. AKAISHI, IN JAPAN'S SOUTHERN ALPS, BY 9:00 TOMORROW MORNING!

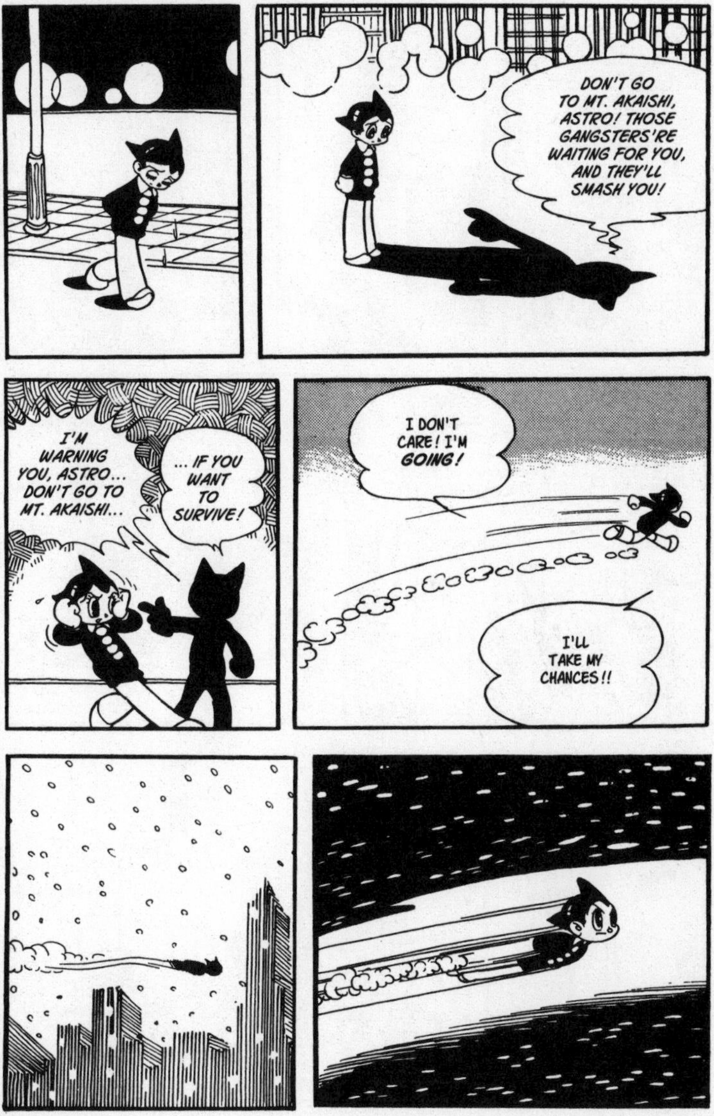
DON'T GO TO MT. AKAISHI, ASTRO! THOSE GANGSTERS'RE WAITING FOR YOU, AND THEY'LL SMASH YOU!
I'M WARNING YOU, ASTRO... DON'T GO TO MT. AKAISHI...
...IF YOU WANT TO SURVIVE!
I DON'T CARE! I'M GOING!
I'LL TAKE MY CHANCES!!

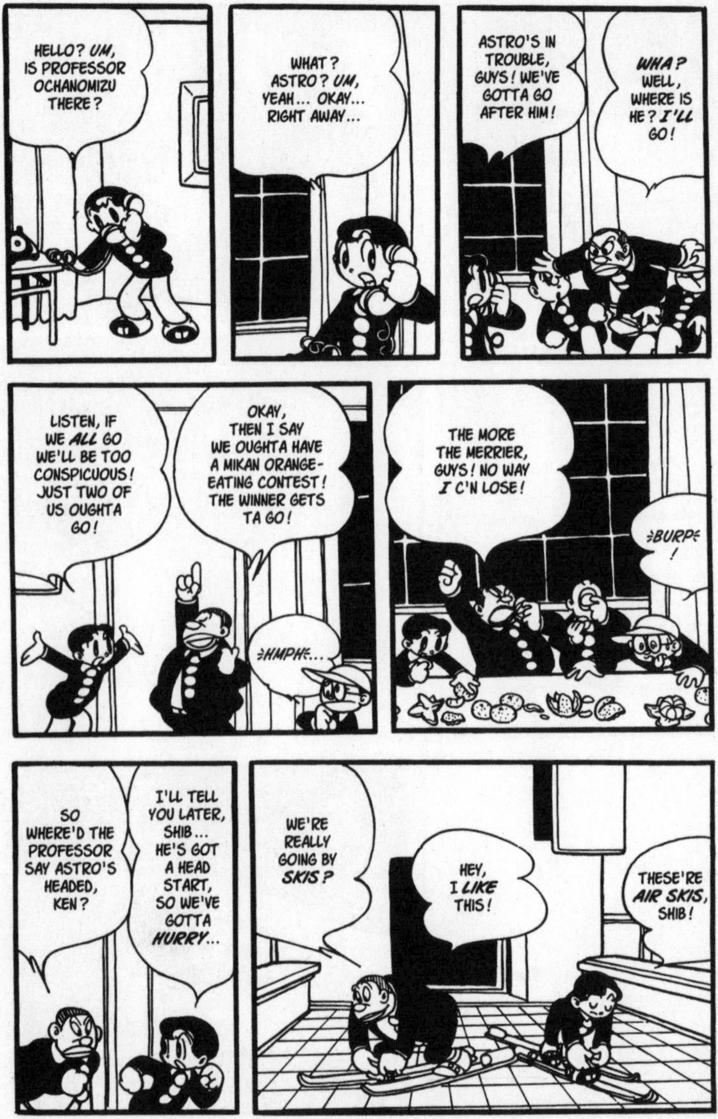
HELLO? UM, IS PROFESSOR OCHANOMIZU THERE?
WHAT? ASTRO? UM, YEAH... OKAY... RIGHT AWAY...
ASTRO'S IN TROUBLE, GUYS! WE'VE GOTTA GO AFTER HIM!
WHA? WELL, WHERE IS HE? I'LL GO!
LISTEN, IF WE ALL GO WE'LL BE TOO CONSPICUOUS! JUST TWO OF US OUGHTA GO!
OKAY, THEN I SAY WE OUGHTA HAVE A MIKAN ORANGE-EATING CONTEST! THE WINNER GETS TA GO!
HMPH...
THE MORE THE MERRIER, GUYS! NO WAY I C'N LOSE!
BURP!
SO WHERE'D THE PROFESSOR SAY ASTRO'S HEADED, KEN?
I'LL TELL YOU LATER, SHIB... HE'S GOT A HEAD START, SO WE'VE GOTTA HURRY...
WE'RE REALLY GOING BY SKIS?
HEY, I LIKE THIS!
THESE'RE AIR SKIS, SHIB!

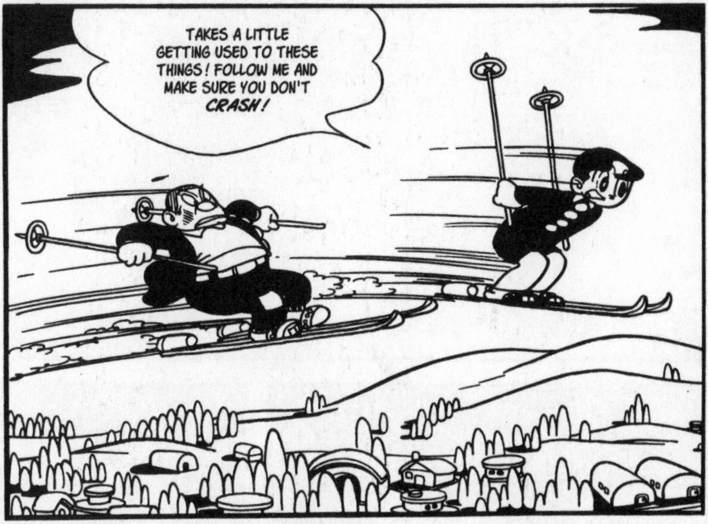
TAKES A LITTLE GETTING USED TO THESE THINGS! FOLLOW ME AND MAKE SURE YOU DON'T CRASH!

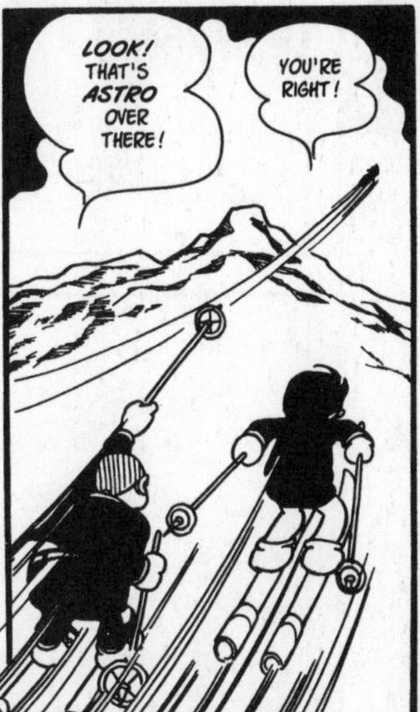
LOOK! THAT'S ASTRO OVER THERE!
YOU'RE RIGHT!

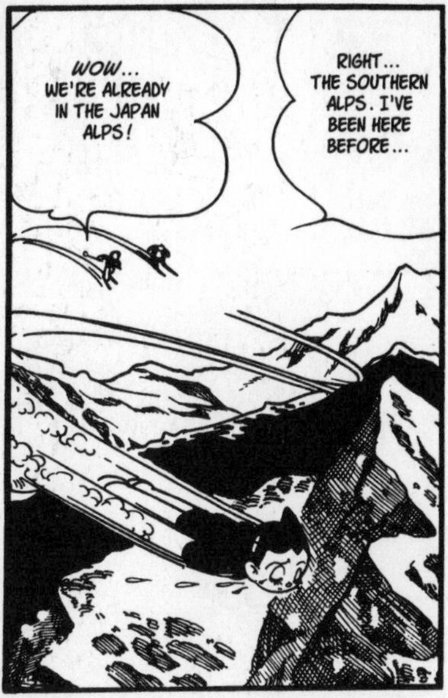
WOW... WE'RE ALREADY IN THE JAPAN ALPS!
RIGHT... THE SOUTHERN ALPS. I'VE BEEN HERE BEFORE...

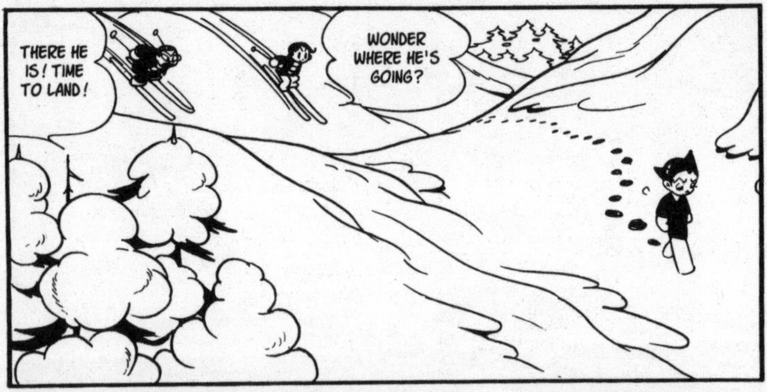
THERE HE IS! TIME TO LAND!
WONDER WHERE HE'S GOING?

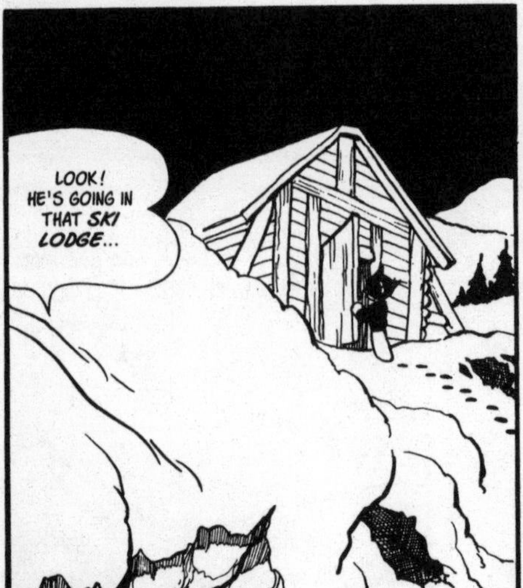
LOOK! HE'S GOING IN THAT *SKI LODGE*...

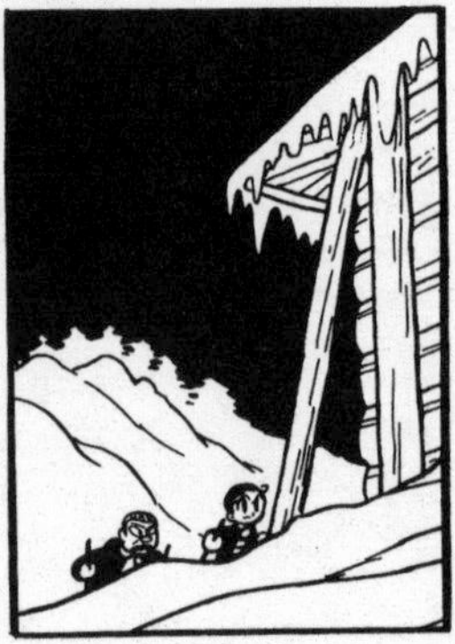

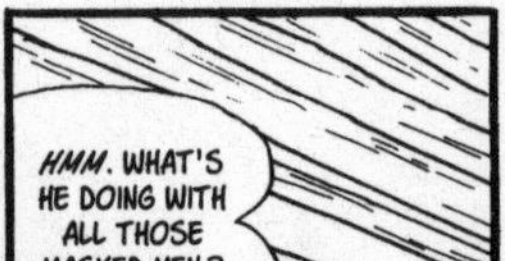
HMM. WHAT'S HE DOING WITH ALL THOSE MASKED MEN?

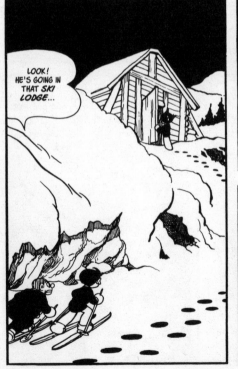

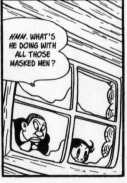

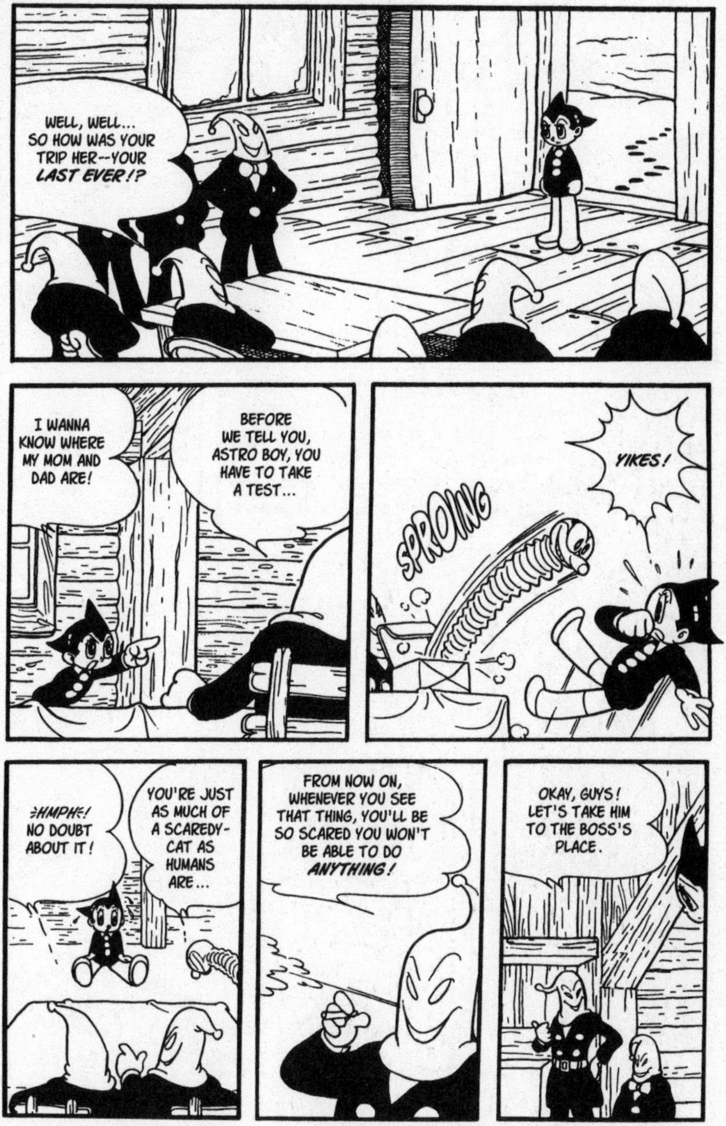
WELL, WELL... SO HOW WAS YOUR TRIP HER--YOUR LAST EVER!?
I WANNA KNOW WHERE MY MOM AND DAD ARE!
BEFORE WE TELL YOU, ASTRO BOY, YOU HAVE TO TAKE A TEST...
SPROING
YIKES!
≥HMPH≤! NO DOUBT ABOUT IT!
YOU'RE JUST AS MUCH OF A SCAREDY-CAT AS HUMANS ARE...
FROM NOW ON, WHENEVER YOU SEE THAT THING, YOU'LL BE SO SCARED YOU WON'T BE ABLE TO DO ANYTHING!
OKAY, GUYS! LET'S TAKE HIM TO THE BOSS'S PLACE.

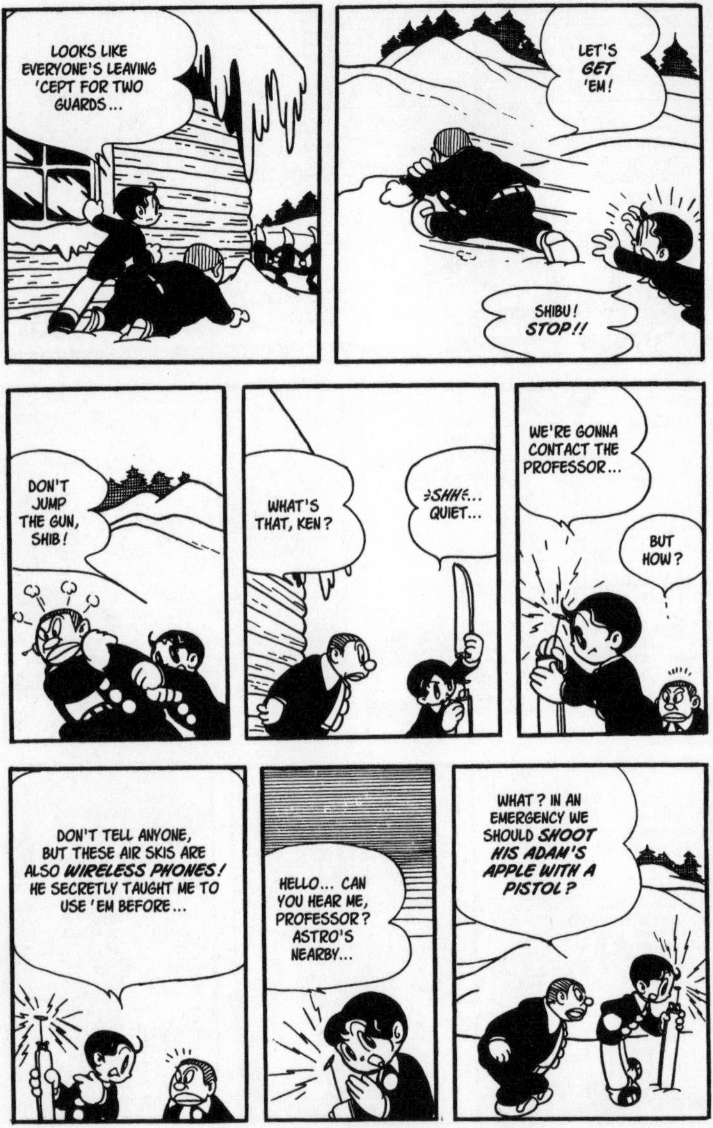
LOOKS LIKE EVERYONE'S LEAVING 'CEPT FOR TWO GUARDS...
LET'S *GET* 'EM!
SHIBU! **STOP!!**
DON'T JUMP THE GUN, SHIB!
WHAT'S THAT, KEN?
≶SHH≶... QUIET...
WE'RE GONNA CONTACT THE PROFESSOR...
BUT HOW?
DON'T TELL ANYONE, BUT THESE AIR SKIS ARE ALSO ***WIRELESS PHONES!*** HE SECRETLY TAUGHT ME TO USE 'EM BEFORE...
HELLO... CAN YOU HEAR ME, PROFESSOR? ASTRO'S NEARBY...
WHAT? IN AN EMERGENCY WE SHOULD ***SHOOT HIS ADAM'S APPLE WITH A PISTOL?***

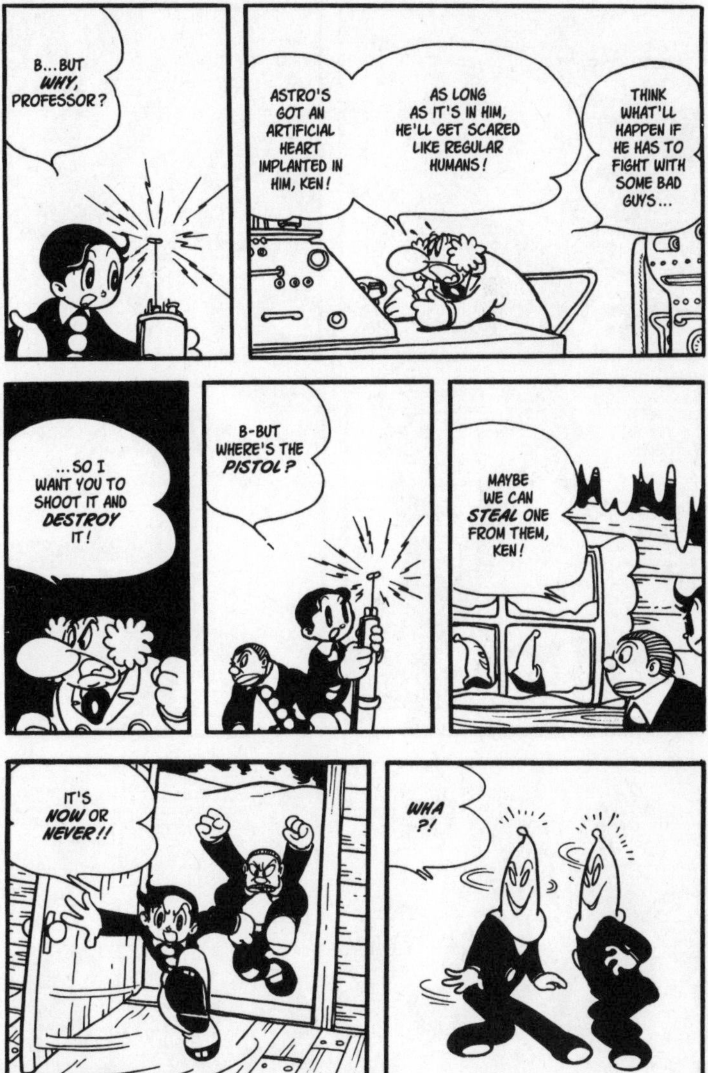

B...BUT *WHY,* PROFESSOR?
ASTRO'S GOT AN ARTIFICIAL HEART IMPLANTED IN HIM, KEN!
AS LONG AS IT'S IN HIM, HE'LL GET SCARED LIKE REGULAR HUMANS!
THINK WHAT'LL HAPPEN IF HE HAS TO FIGHT WITH SOME BAD GUYS...
...SO I WANT YOU TO SHOOT IT AND *DESTROY* IT!
B-BUT WHERE'S THE *PISTOL?*
MAYBE WE CAN *STEAL* ONE FROM THEM, KEN!
IT'S *NOW* OR *NEVER!!*
WHA ?!

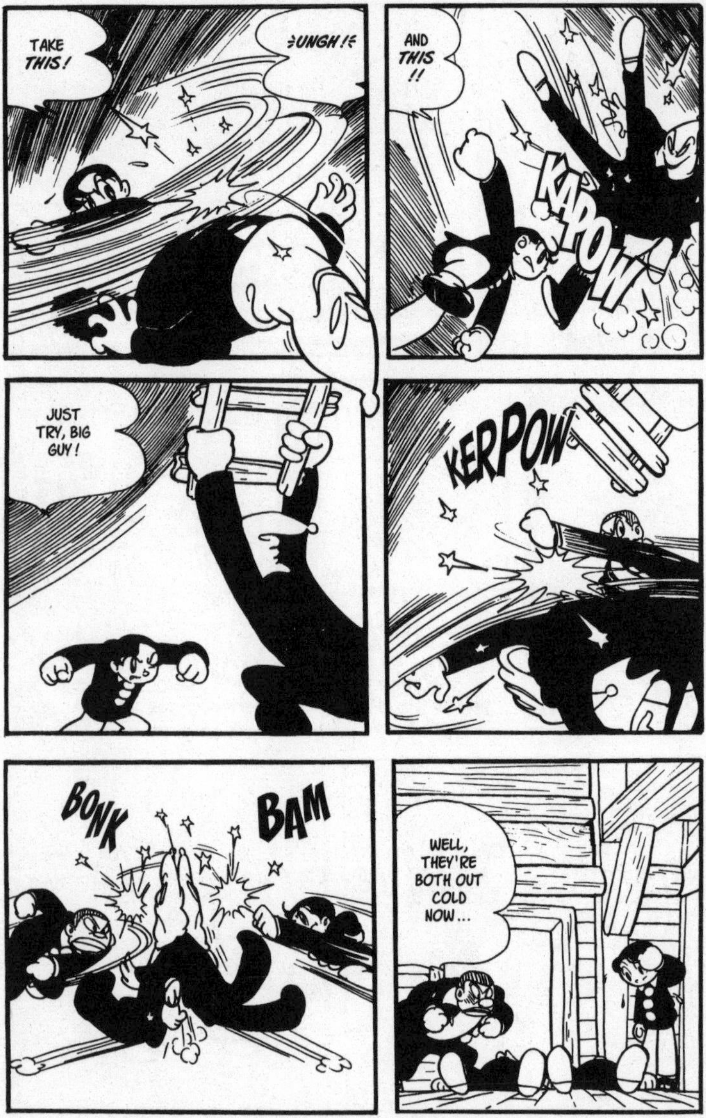
TAKE THIS!
UNGH!
AND THIS!!
KAPOW
JUST TRY, BIG GUY!
KERPOW
BONK
BAM
WELL, THEY'RE BOTH OUT COLD NOW...

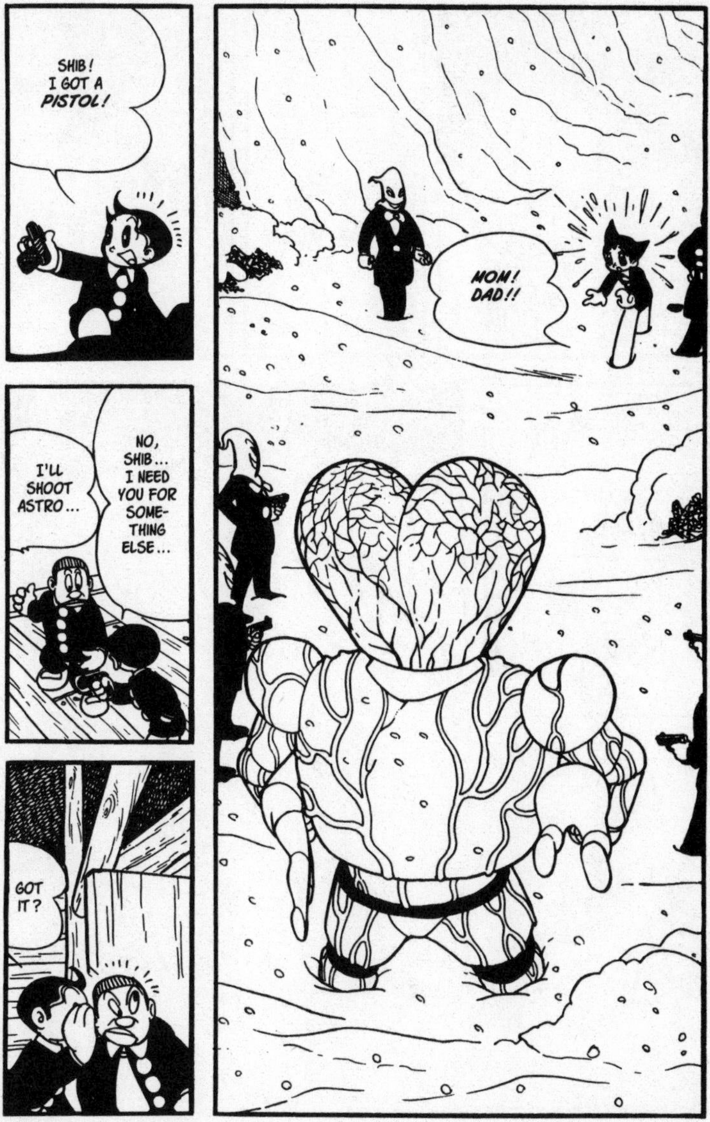
SHIB! I GOT A *PISTOL!*
I'LL SHOOT ASTRO...
NO, SHIB... I NEED YOU FOR SOME-THING ELSE...
GOT IT?
MOM! DAD!!

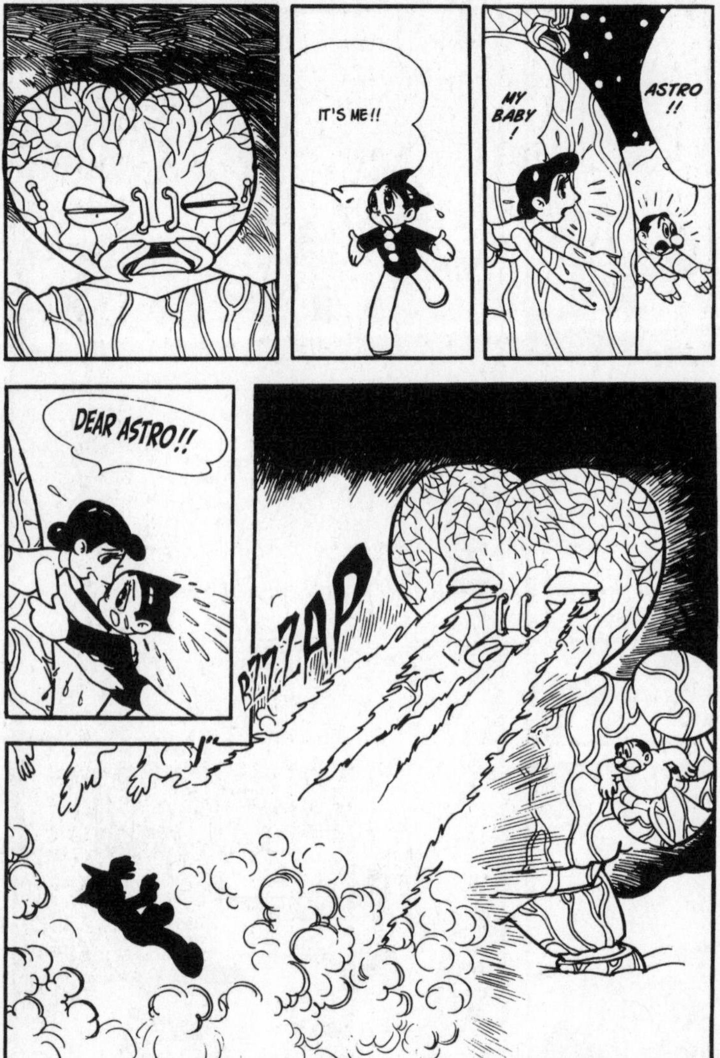
IT'S ME!!
MY BABY !
ASTRO !!
DEAR ASTRO!!
BZZZAP

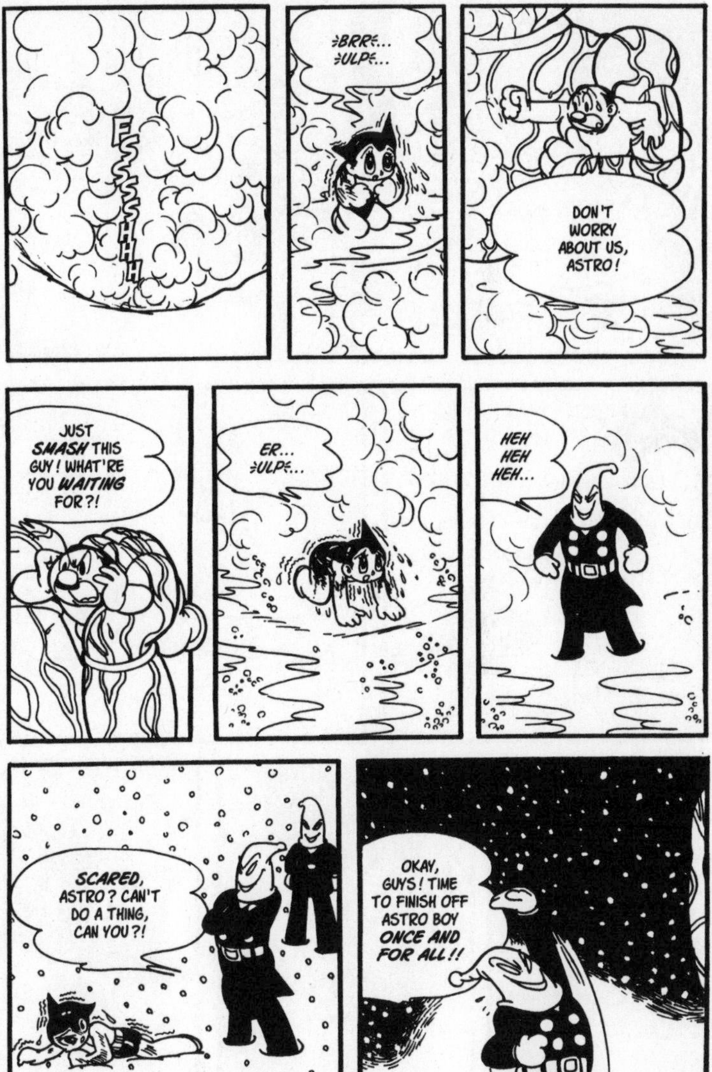
FSSSSHHH
BRR... ULP...
DON'T WORRY ABOUT US, ASTRO!
JUST SMASH THIS GUY! WHAT'RE YOU WAITING FOR?!
ER... ULP...
HEH HEH HEH...
SCARED, ASTRO? CAN'T DO A THING, CAN YOU?!
OKAY, GUYS! TIME TO FINISH OFF ASTRO BOY ONCE AND FOR ALL!!

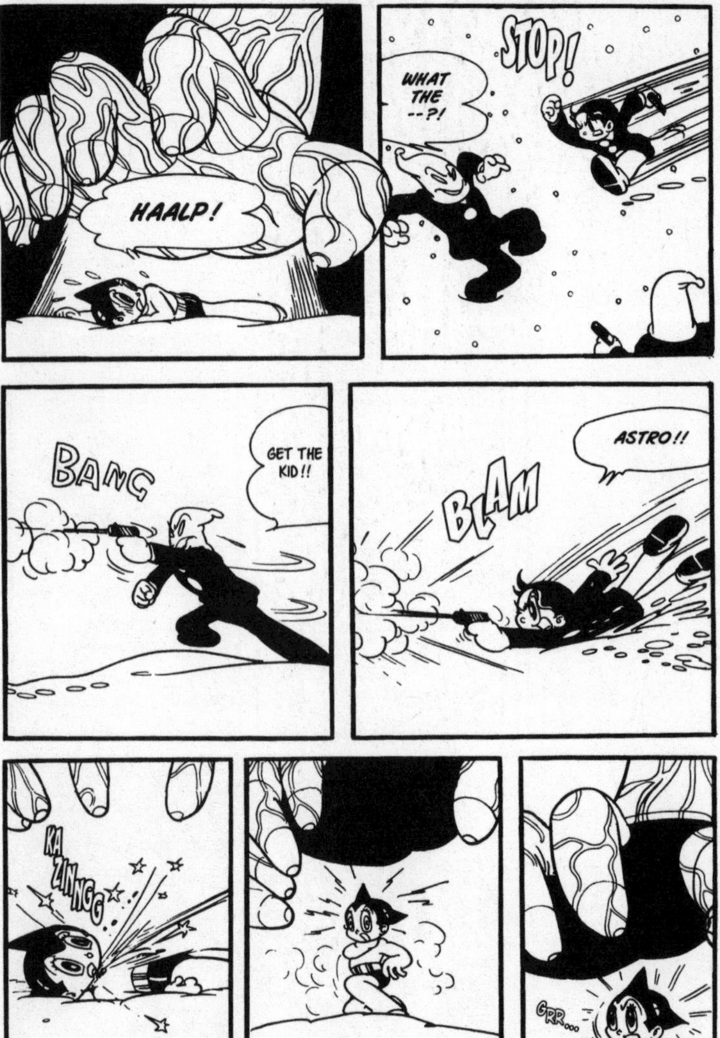
HAALP!
WHAT THE --?!
STOP!
BANG
GET THE KID!!
ASTRO!!
BLAM
KA ZINNGG
GRR...

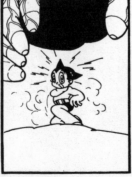

UH OH! RUN FOR IT!

TAKE THIS!!
KABLOOSH

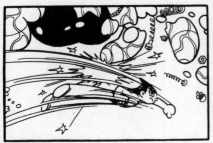

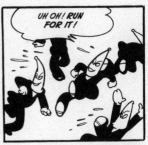

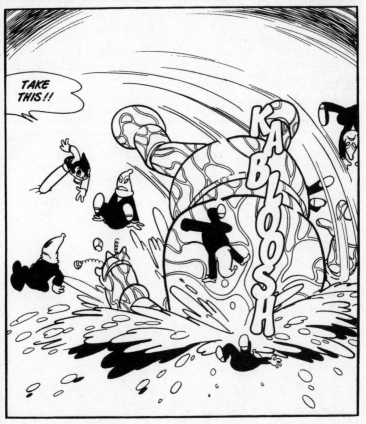

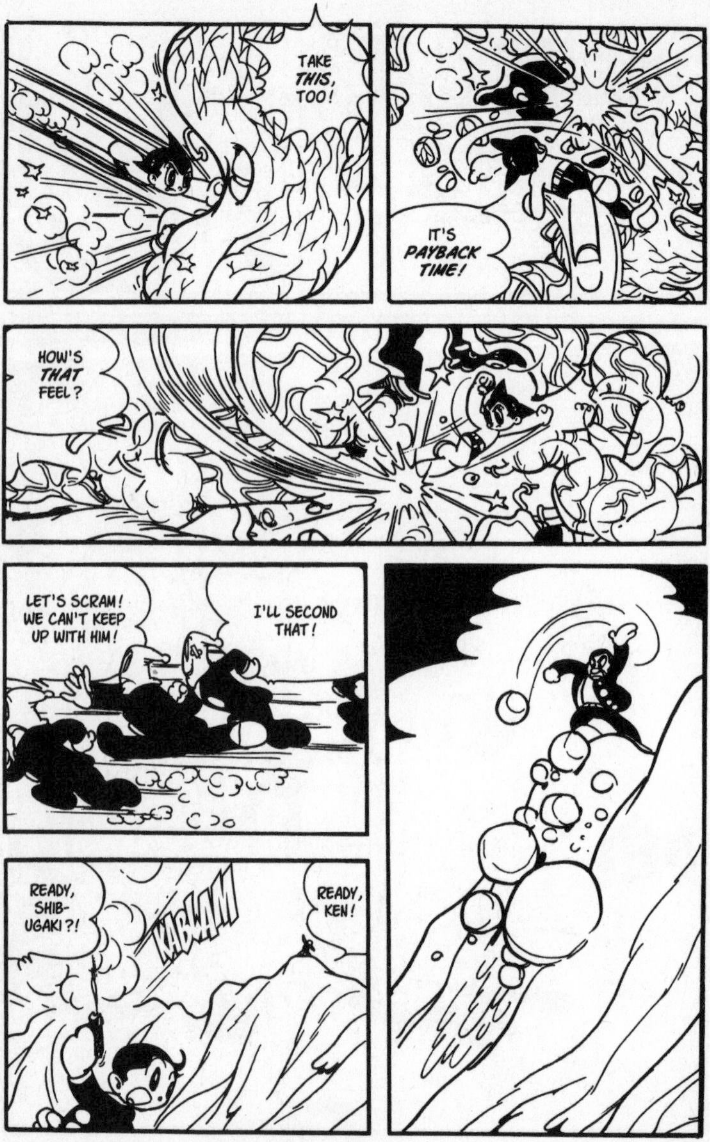
TAKE THIS, TOO!
IT'S PAYBACK TIME!
HOW'S THAT FEEL?
LET'S SCRAM! WE CAN'T KEEP UP WITH HIM!
I'LL SECOND THAT!
READY, SHIB-UGAKI?!
KABLAM
READY, KEN!

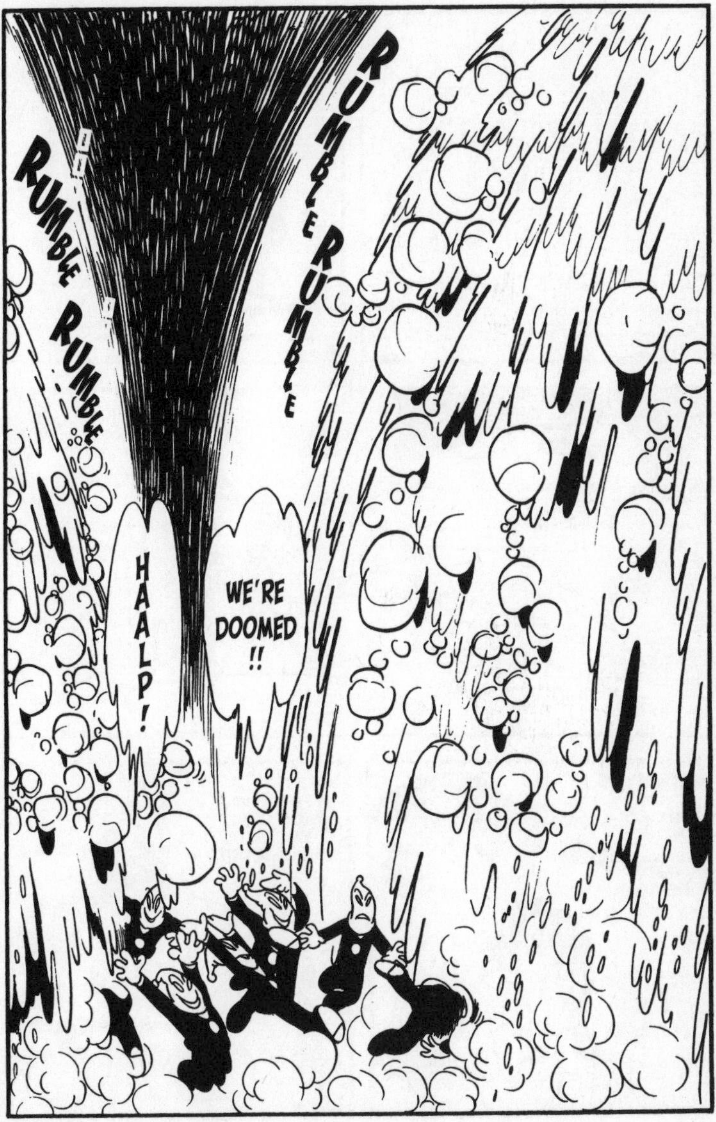
RUMBLE RUMBLE RUMBLE
RUMBLE RUMBLE RUMBLE
HAALP!
WE'RE DOOMED !!

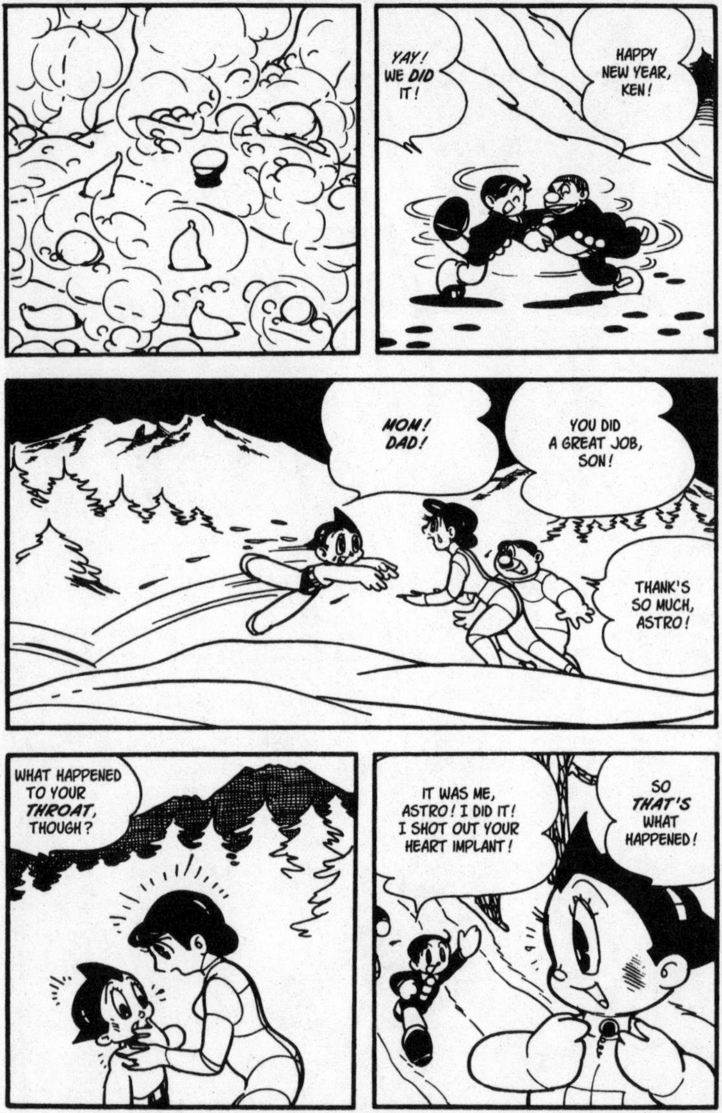
YAY! WE DID IT!
HAPPY NEW YEAR, KEN!
MOM! DAD!
YOU DID A GREAT JOB, SON!
THANK'S SO MUCH, ASTRO!
WHAT HAPPENED TO YOUR THROAT, THOUGH?
IT WAS ME, ASTRO! I DID IT! I SHOT OUT YOUR HEART IMPLANT!
SO THAT'S WHAT HAPPENED!

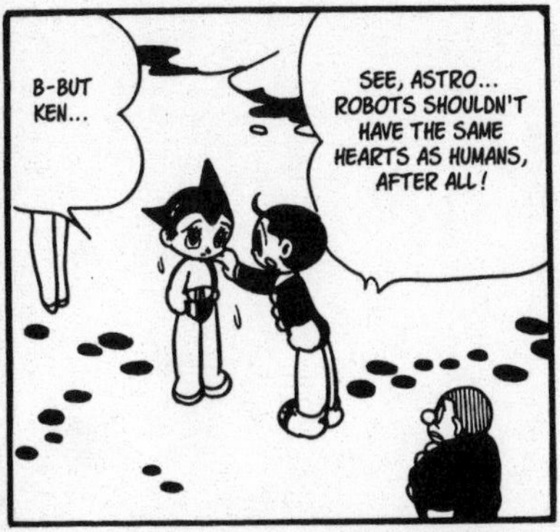
B-BUT KEN...
SEE, ASTRO... ROBOTS SHOULDN'T HAVE THE SAME HEARTS AS HUMANS, AFTER ALL!
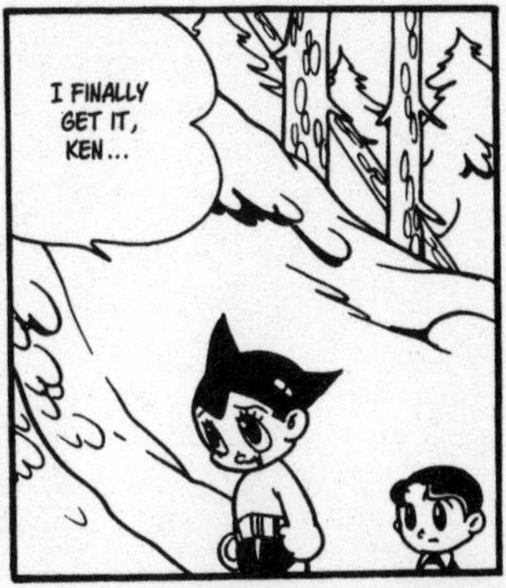
I FINALLY GET IT, KEN...
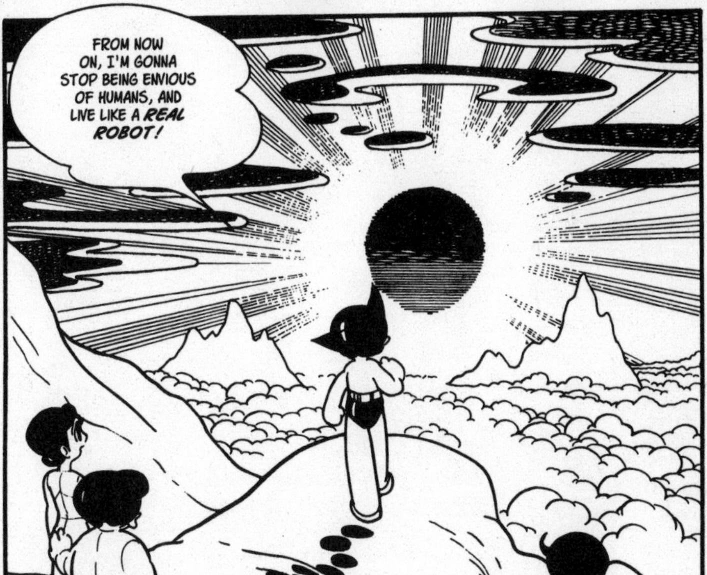
FROM NOW ON, I'M GONNA STOP BEING ENVIOUS OF HUMANS, AND LIVE LIKE A *REAL ROBOT!*

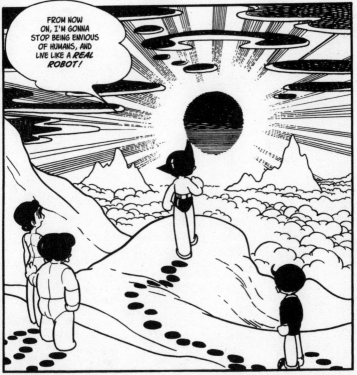

THE LYING
ROBOT

First appeared in the September 1964
edition of *Tetsuwan Atom Kurabu*.

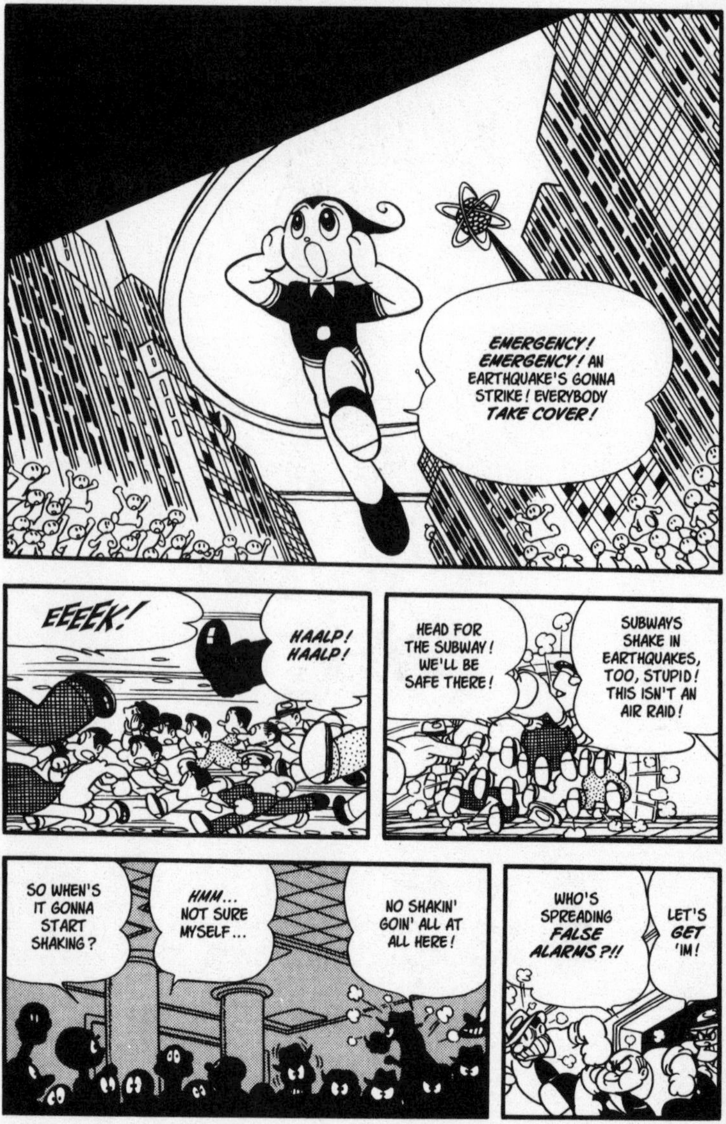
EMERGENCY! EMERGENCY! AN EARTHQUAKE'S GONNA STRIKE! EVERYBODY TAKE COVER!
EEEEK!
HAALP! HAALP!
HEAD FOR THE SUBWAY! WE'LL BE SAFE THERE!
SUBWAYS SHAKE IN EARTHQUAKES, TOO, STUPID! THIS ISN'T AN AIR RAID!
SO WHEN'S IT GONNA START SHAKING?
HMM... NOT SURE MYSELF...
NO SHAKIN' GOIN' ALL AT ALL HERE!
WHO'S SPREADING FALSE ALARMS?!!
LET'S GET 'IM!

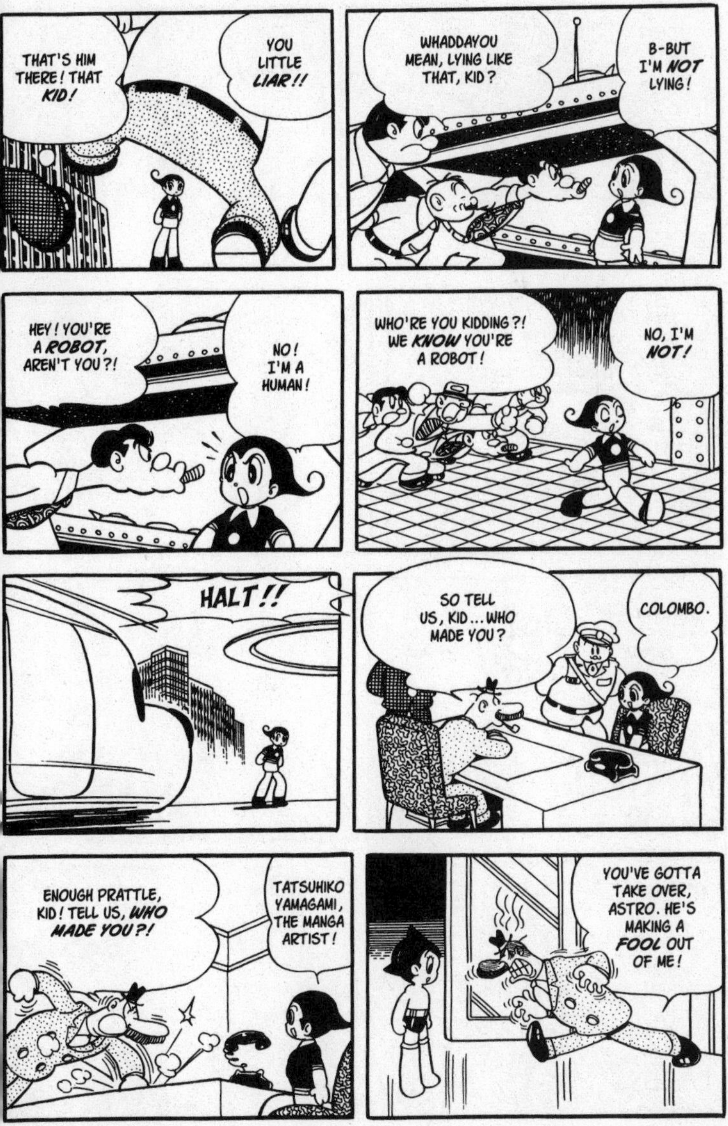
THAT'S HIM THERE! THAT KID!
YOU LITTLE LIAR!!
WHADDAYOU MEAN, LYING LIKE THAT, KID?
B-BUT I'M NOT LYING!
HEY! YOU'RE A ROBOT, AREN'T YOU?!
NO! I'M A HUMAN!
WHO'RE YOU KIDDING?! WE KNOW YOU'RE A ROBOT!
NO, I'M NOT!
HALT!!
SO TELL US, KID... WHO MADE YOU?
COLOMBO.
ENOUGH PRATTLE, KID! TELL US, WHO MADE YOU?!
TATSUHIKO YAMAGAMI, THE MANGA ARTIST!
YOU'VE GOTTA TAKE OVER, ASTRO. HE'S MAKING A FOOL OUT OF ME!

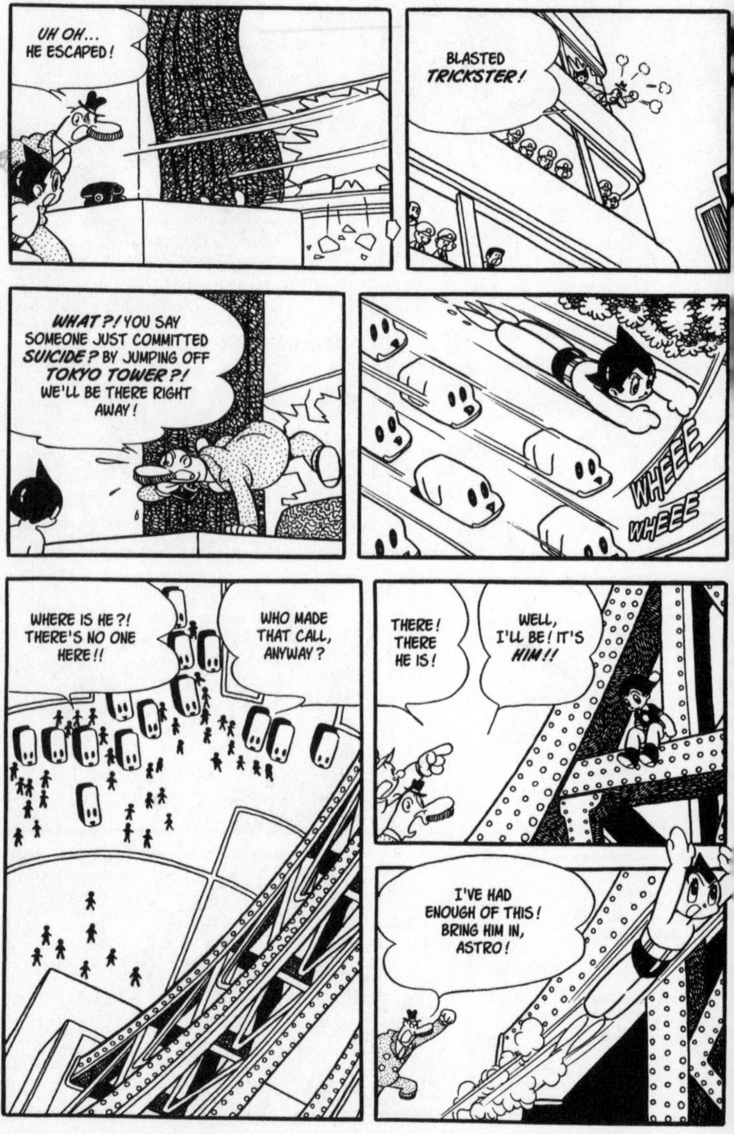
UH OH... HE ESCAPED!
BLASTED TRICKSTER!
WHAT?! YOU SAY SOMEONE JUST COMMITTED SUICIDE? BY JUMPING OFF TOKYO TOWER?! WE'LL BE THERE RIGHT AWAY!
WHEEE
WHEEE
WHERE IS HE?! THERE'S NO ONE HERE!!
WHO MADE THAT CALL, ANYWAY?
THERE! THERE HE IS!
WELL, I'LL BE! IT'S HIM!!
I'VE HAD ENOUGH OF THIS! BRING HIM IN, ASTRO!

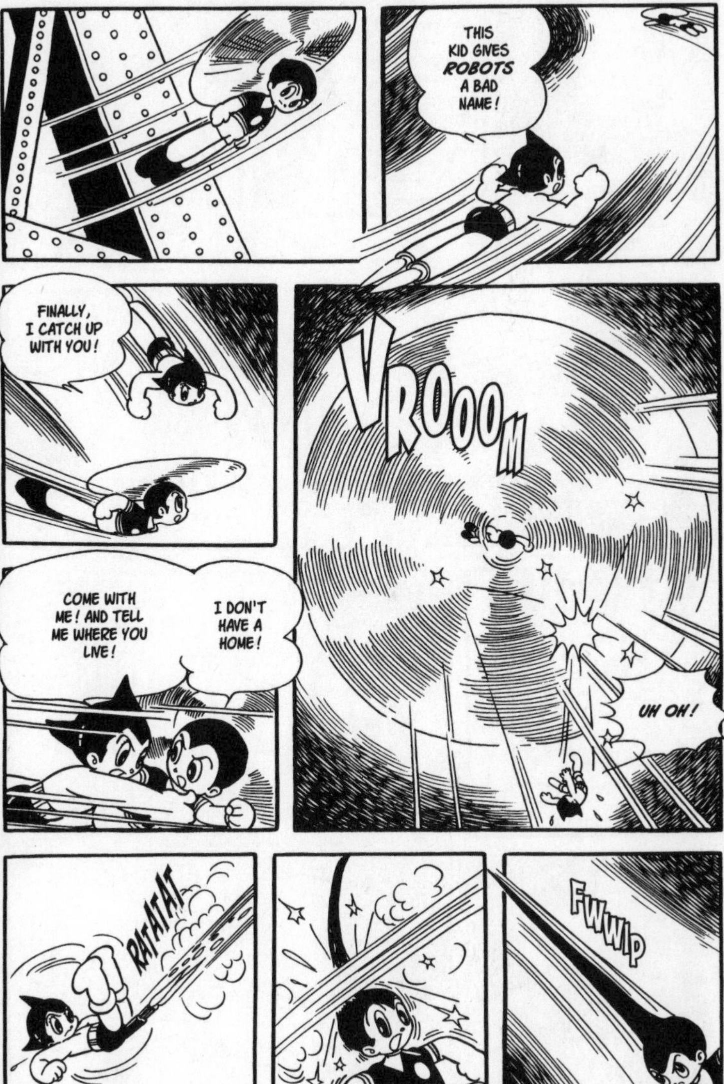
THIS KID GIVES ROBOTS A BAD NAME!
FINALLY, I CATCH UP WITH YOU!
COME WITH ME! AND TELL ME WHERE YOU LIVE!
I DON'T HAVE A HOME!
VROOOM
UH OH!
RATATAT
FWWIP

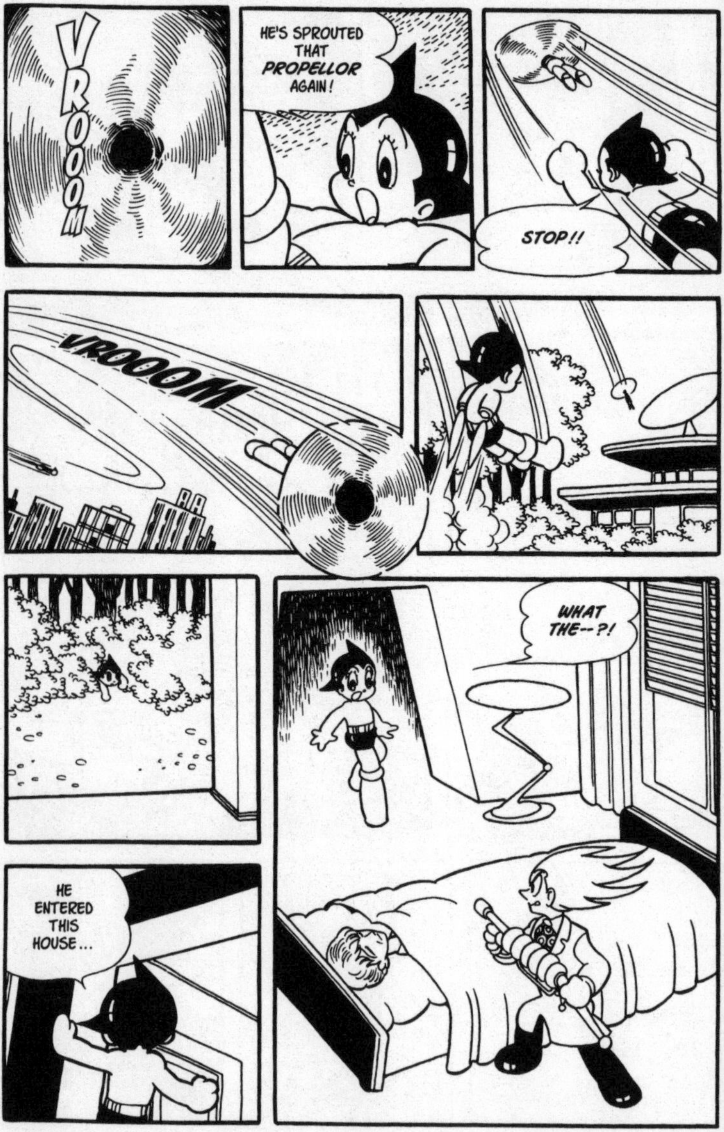
VROOOM
HE'S SPROUTED THAT PROPELLOR AGAIN!
STOP!!
VROOOOM
HE ENTERED THIS HOUSE...
WHAT THE--?!

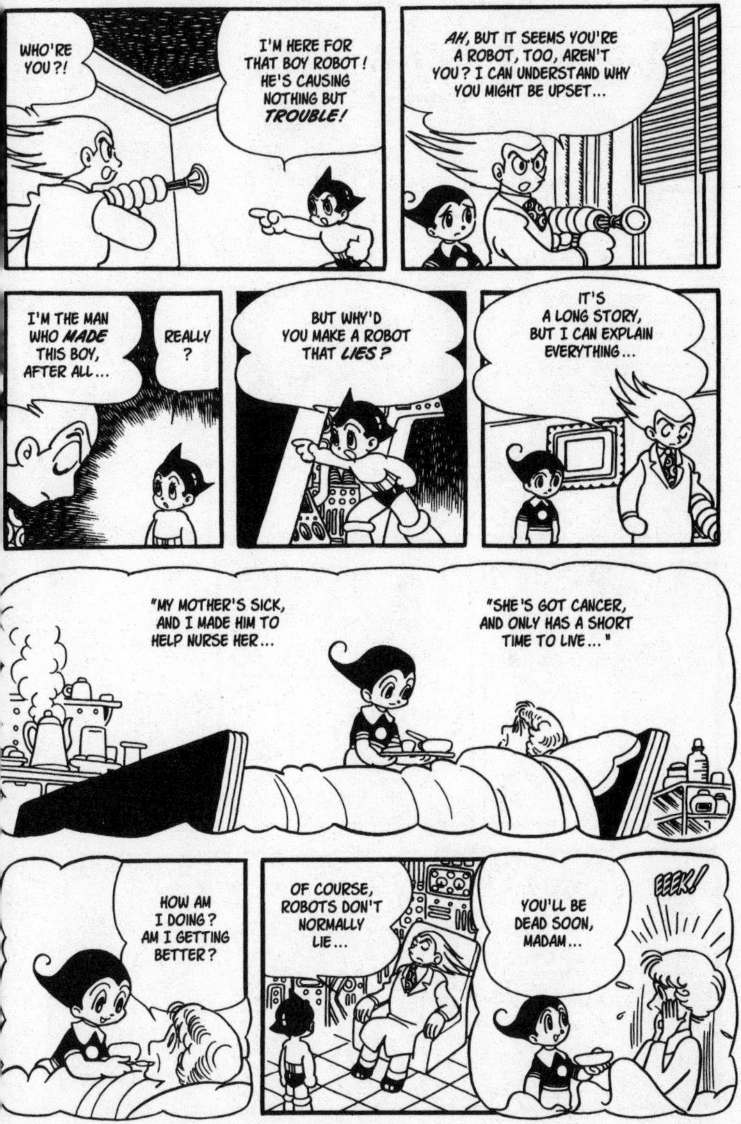

WHO'RE YOU?!
I'M HERE FOR THAT BOY ROBOT! HE'S CAUSING NOTHING BUT TROUBLE!
AH, BUT IT SEEMS YOU'RE A ROBOT, TOO, AREN'T YOU? I CAN UNDERSTAND WHY YOU MIGHT BE UPSET...
I'M THE MAN WHO MADE THIS BOY, AFTER ALL...
REALLY ?
BUT WHY'D YOU MAKE A ROBOT THAT LIES?
IT'S A LONG STORY, BUT I CAN EXPLAIN EVERYTHING...
"MY MOTHER'S SICK, AND I MADE HIM TO HELP NURSE HER...
"SHE'S GOT CANCER, AND ONLY HAS A SHORT TIME TO LIVE..."
HOW AM I DOING? AM I GETTING BETTER?
OF COURSE, ROBOTS DON'T NORMALLY LIE...
YOU'LL BE DEAD SOON, MADAM...
EEEK!

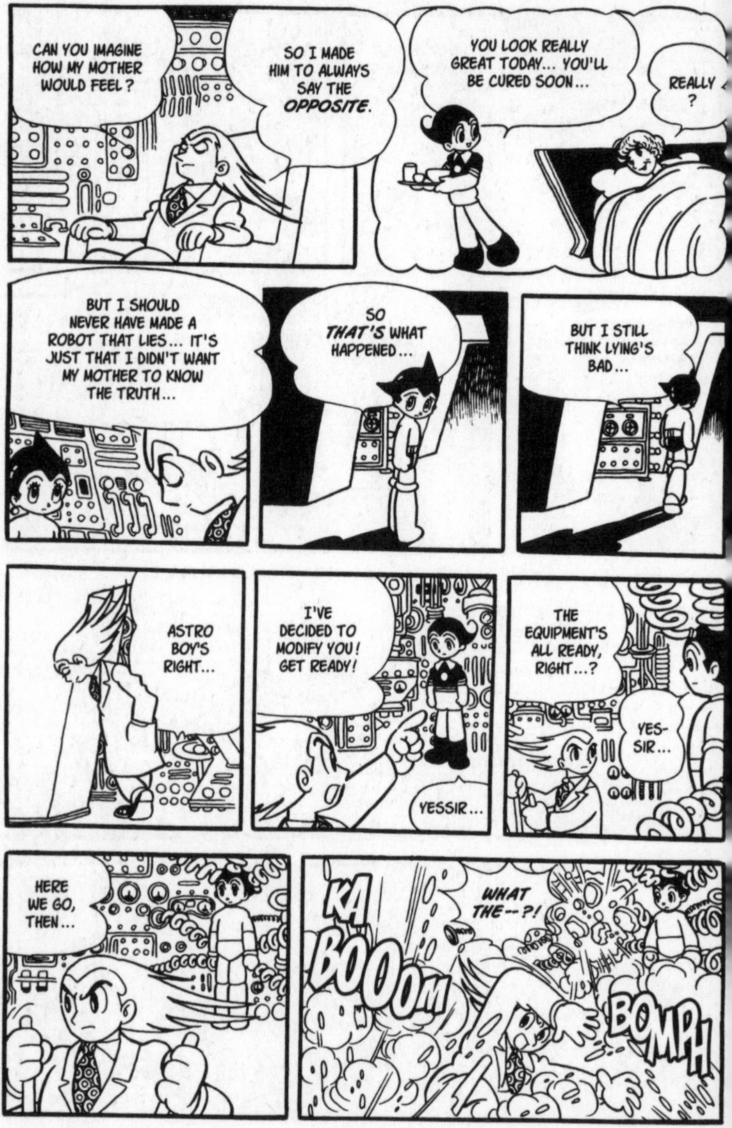
CAN YOU IMAGINE HOW MY MOTHER WOULD FEEL?
SO I MADE HIM TO ALWAYS SAY THE OPPOSITE.
YOU LOOK REALLY GREAT TODAY... YOU'LL BE CURED SOON...
REALLY ?
BUT I SHOULD NEVER HAVE MADE A ROBOT THAT LIES... IT'S JUST THAT I DIDN'T WANT MY MOTHER TO KNOW THE TRUTH...
SO THAT'S WHAT HAPPENED...
BUT I STILL THINK LYING'S BAD...
ASTRO BOY'S RIGHT...
I'VE DECIDED TO MODIFY YOU! GET READY!
YESSIR...
THE EQUIPMENT'S ALL READY, RIGHT...?
YES-SIR...
HERE WE GO, THEN...
KA BOOOOM
WHAT THE--?!
BOMPH

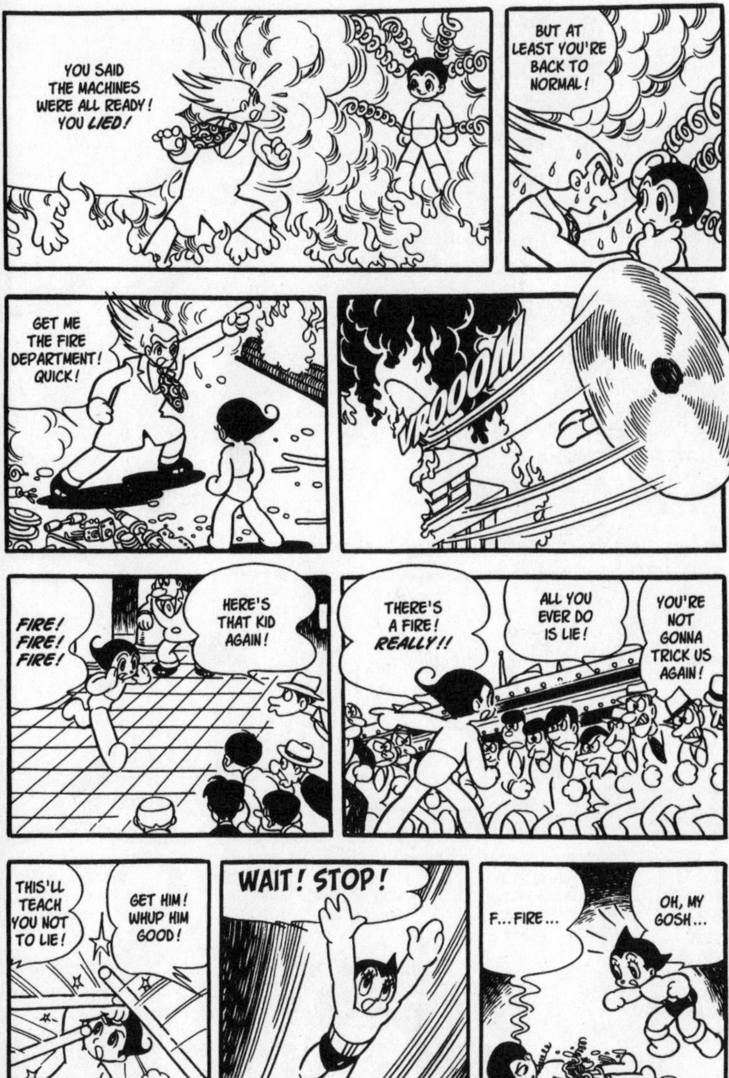
YOU SAID THE MACHINES WERE ALL READY! YOU *LIED!*
BUT AT LEAST YOU'RE BACK TO NORMAL!
GET ME THE FIRE DEPARTMENT! QUICK!
VROOOOM
FIRE! FIRE! FIRE!
HERE'S THAT KID AGAIN!
THERE'S A FIRE! *REALLY!!*
ALL YOU EVER DO IS LIE!
YOU'RE NOT GONNA TRICK US AGAIN!
THIS'LL TEACH YOU NOT TO LIE!
GET HIM! WHUP HIM GOOD!
WAIT! STOP!
F...FIRE...
OH, MY GOSH...

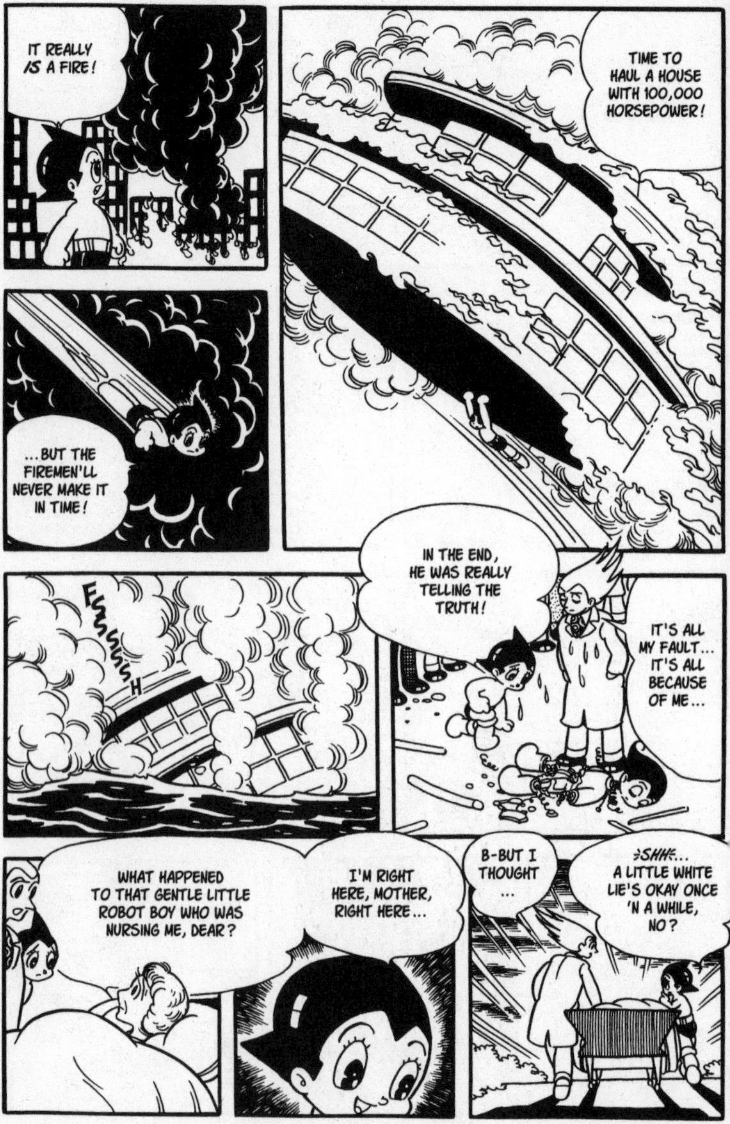
IT REALLY *IS* A FIRE!
...BUT THE FIREMEN'LL NEVER MAKE IT IN TIME!
TIME TO HAUL A HOUSE WITH 100,000 HORSEPOWER!
FSSSSSSH
IN THE END, HE WAS REALLY TELLING THE TRUTH!
IT'S ALL MY FAULT... IT'S ALL BECAUSE OF ME...
WHAT HAPPENED TO THAT GENTLE LITTLE ROBOT BOY WHO WAS NURSING ME, DEAR?
I'M RIGHT HERE, MOTHER, RIGHT HERE...
B-BUT I THOUGHT ...
SHH... A LITTLE WHITE LIE'S OKAY ONCE 'N A WHILE, NO?

ASTRO BOY'S ORIGINS AND HISTORY, PART 1

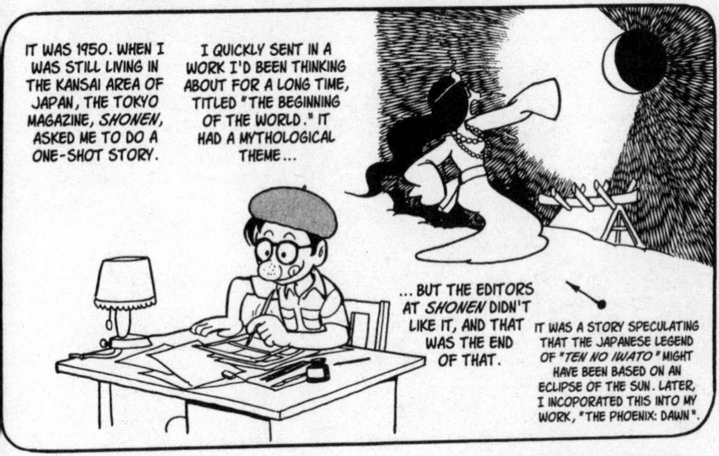
IT WAS 1950. WHEN I WAS STILL LIVING IN THE KANSAI AREA OF JAPAN, THE TOKYO MAGAZINE, *SHONEN*, ASKED ME TO DO A ONE-SHOT STORY.
I QUICKLY SENT IN A WORK I'D BEEN THINKING ABOUT FOR A LONG TIME, TITLED "THE BEGINNING OF THE WORLD." IT HAD A MYTHOLOGICAL THEME...
...BUT THE EDITORS AT *SHONEN* DIDN'T LIKE IT, AND THAT WAS THE END OF THAT.
IT WAS A STORY SPECULATING THAT THE JAPANESE LEGEND OF "*TEN NO IWATO*" MIGHT HAVE BEEN BASED ON AN ECLIPSE OF THE SUN. LATER, I INCOPORATED THIS INTO MY WORK, "THE PHOENIX: DAWN".

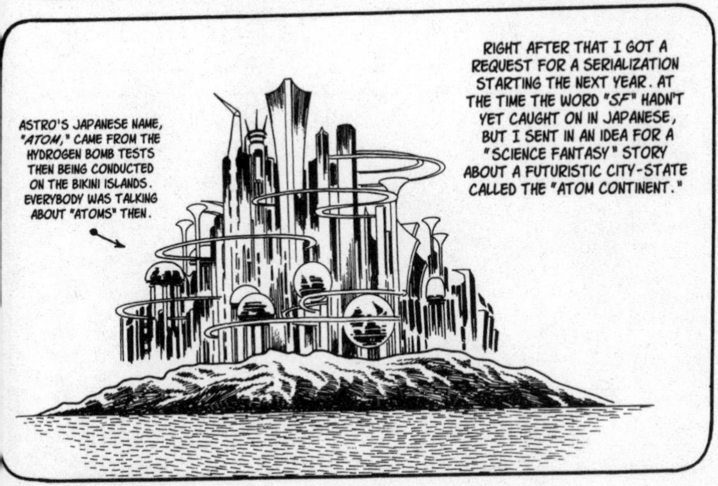
RIGHT AFTER THAT I GOT A REQUEST FOR A SERIALIZATION STARTING THE NEXT YEAR. AT THE TIME THE WORD "*SF*" HADN'T YET CAUGHT ON IN JAPANESE, BUT I SENT IN AN IDEA FOR A "SCIENCE FANTASY" STORY ABOUT A FUTURISTIC CITY-STATE CALLED THE "ATOM CONTINENT."
ASTRO'S JAPANESE NAME, "*ATOM*," CAME FROM THE HYDROGEN BOMB TESTS THEN BEING CONDUCTED ON THE BIKINI ISLANDS. EVERYBODY WAS TALKING ABOUT "ATOMS" THEN.

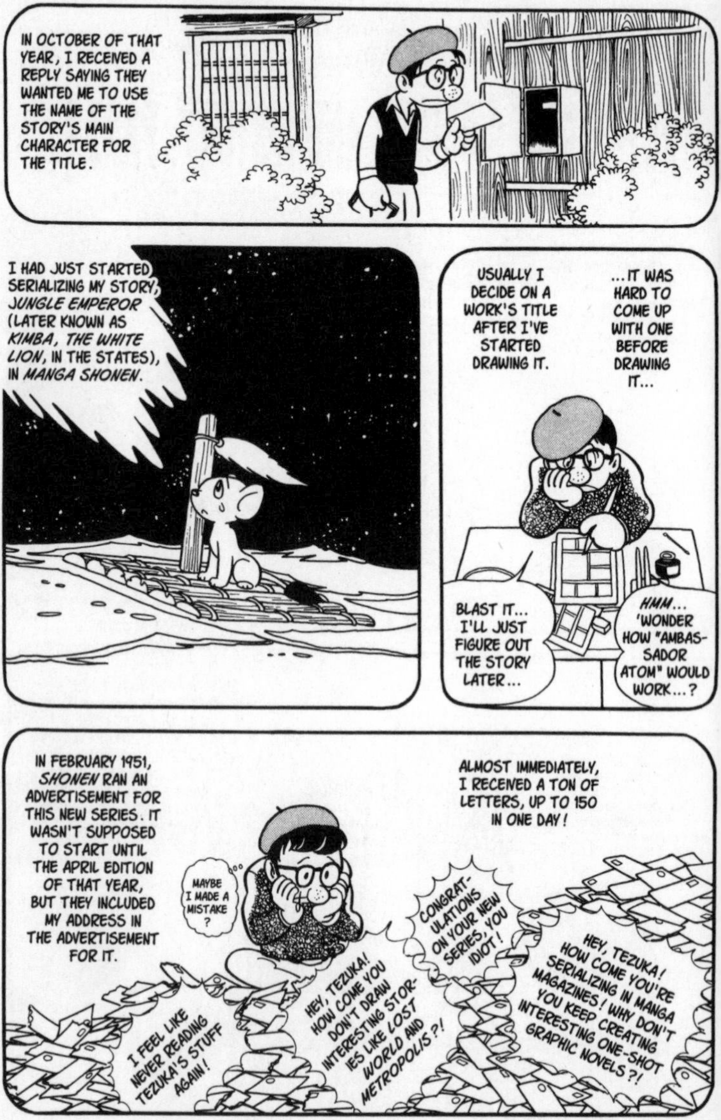
IN OCTOBER OF THAT YEAR, I RECEIVED A REPLY SAYING THEY WANTED ME TO USE THE NAME OF THE STORY'S MAIN CHARACTER FOR THE TITLE.
I HAD JUST STARTED SERIALIZING MY STORY, *JUNGLE EMPEROR* (LATER KNOWN AS *KIMBA, THE WHITE LION*, IN THE STATES), IN *MANGA SHONEN*.
USUALLY I DECIDE ON A WORK'S TITLE AFTER I'VE STARTED DRAWING IT.
...IT WAS HARD TO COME UP WITH ONE BEFORE DRAWING IT...
BLAST IT... I'LL JUST FIGURE OUT THE STORY LATER...
HMM... 'WONDER HOW "AMBASSADOR ATOM" WOULD WORK...?
IN FEBRUARY 1951, *SHONEN* RAN AN ADVERTISEMENT FOR THIS NEW SERIES. IT WASN'T SUPPOSED TO START UNTIL THE APRIL EDITION OF THAT YEAR, BUT THEY INCLUDED MY ADDRESS IN THE ADVERTISEMENT FOR IT.
ALMOST IMMEDIATELY, I RECEIVED A TON OF LETTERS, UP TO 150 IN ONE DAY!
MAYBE I MADE A MISTAKE?
CONGRATULATIONS ON YOUR NEW SERIES, YOU IDIOT!
I FEEL LIKE NEVER READING TEZUKA'S STUFF AGAIN!
HEY, TEZUKA! HOW COME YOU DON'T DRAW INTERESTING STORIES LIKE *LOST WORLD* AND *METROPOLIS*?!
HEY, TEZUKA! HOW COME YOU'RE SERIALIZING IN MANGA MAGAZINES! WHY DON'T YOU KEEP CREATING INTERESTING ONE-SHOT GRAPHIC NOVELS?!

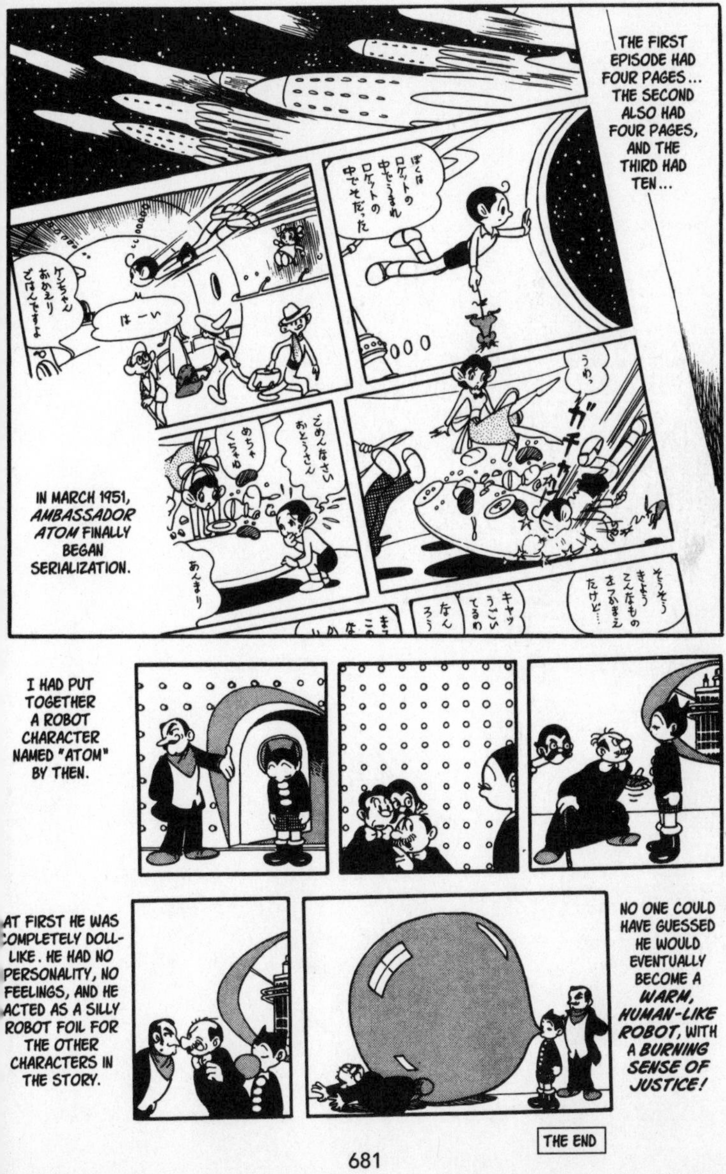

THE FIRST EPISODE HAD FOUR PAGES... THE SECOND ALSO HAD FOUR PAGES, AND THE THIRD HAD TEN...
ぼくはロケットの中でうまれロケットの中でそだった
ケンちゃんおかえりごはんですよ
はーい
うわっ
ガチャ
IN MARCH 1951, *AMBASSADOR ATOM* FINALLY BEGAN SERIALIZATION.
めちゃくちゃ
ごめんなさいおとうさん
あんまり
キャッうごいてるわ
なんだろう
そうそうきょうこんなものまでつかまえたけど…
I HAD PUT TOGETHER A ROBOT CHARACTER NAMED "ATOM" BY THEN.
AT FIRST HE WAS COMPLETELY DOLL-LIKE. HE HAD NO PERSONALITY, NO FEELINGS, AND HE ACTED AS A SILLY ROBOT FOIL FOR THE OTHER CHARACTERS IN THE STORY.
NO ONE COULD HAVE GUESSED HE WOULD EVENTUALLY BECOME A *WARM, HUMAN-LIKE ROBOT*, WITH A *BURNING SENSE OF JUSTICE!*
THE END

OSAMU TEZUKA

Osamu Tezuka (1928–1989) was born in the city of Toyonaka in Osaka, Japan, and raised in Takarazuka in Hyogo Prefecture. He graduated from the Medical Department of Osaka University and was later awarded a doctorate of medicine. Tezuka made his manga debut in 1946 with *Ma-chan's Diary* and had his first major hit in 1947 with *New Treasure Island*. Over his forty-year career, Tezuka produced over 150,000 pages of manga, including the creation of *Metropolis, Mighty Atom* (a.k.a. *Astro Boy*), *Jungle Emperor* (a.k.a. *Kimba the White Lion*), *Black Jack, Phoenix, Buddha*, and many more.

Tezuka's fascination with Disney cartoons led him to begin his own animation studio, creating the first serialized Japanese cartoon series, which was later exported to America as *Astro Boy* in 1963. Tezuka Productions went on to create animated versions of *Jungle Emperor* and *Phoenix*, among others.

Regarded as a national treasure, Tezuka received numerous awards and served in a variety of organizations. Tezuka became Japan's "comics ambassador," taking Japan's manga culture to the world. In 1980 he toured and lectured in America, including a speech at the United Nations.

Osamu Tezuka's work remains hugely popular in Japan and is translated throughout the world, where he is acclaimed as one of the giants of comics and animation. "Comics are an international language," Tezuka said. "They can cross boundaries and generations. Comics are a bridge between all cultures."

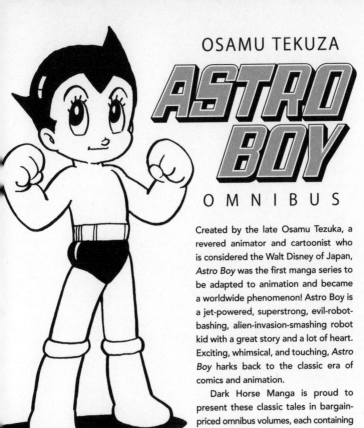

OSAMU TEKUZA

ASTRO BOY

OMNIBUS

Created by the late Osamu Tezuka, a revered animator and cartoonist who is considered the Walt Disney of Japan, *Astro Boy* was the first manga series to be adapted to animation and became a worldwide phenomenon! Astro Boy is a jet-powered, superstrong, evil-robot-bashing, alien-invasion-smashing robot kid with a great story and a lot of heart. Exciting, whimsical, and touching, *Astro Boy* harks back to the classic era of comics and animation.

Dark Horse Manga is proud to present these classic tales in bargain-priced omnibus volumes, each containing over 600 pages!

VOLUME 1
ISBN 978-1-61655-860-4
$19.99

VOLUME 2
ISBN 978-1-61655-861-1
$19.99

VOLUME 3
ISBN 978-1-61655-893-2
$19.99

AVAILABLE AT YOUR LOCAL COMICS SHOP OR BOOKSTORE
TO FIND A COMICS SHOP IN YOUR AREA, CALL 1-888-266-4226

For more information or to order direct:

- **On the web:** DarkHorse.com • **E-mail:** mailorder@darkhorse.com
- **Phone:** 1-800-862-0052 Mon.–Fri. 9 AM to 5 PM Pacific Time

DARK HORSE MANGA

DarkHorse.com

NEXTWORLD

OSAMU TEZUKA

From the creator of *Astro Boy* and *Metropolis* comes *Nextworld*, part of
Osamu Tezuka's cycle of original science-fiction graphic novels published
in the late 1940s and early 1950s. When nuclear testing creates mutated
animals with amazing supernatural abilities, the world's great nations are
drawn into political conflict that could light the fuse for World War III.

VOLUME 1
ISBN 978-1-56971-866-7

VOLUME 2
ISBN 978-1-56971-867-4

$13.99 each

7/16